THE
ASIAN
AMERICAN
ALMANAC

THE ASIAN AMERICAN ALMANAC

A Reference

Work on

Asians in

the United

States

Susan Gall,
Managing Editor

Irene Natividad,
Executive Editor

 Gale Research Inc. • DETROIT • WASHINGTON, D.C. • LONDON

Susan Gall, *Managing Editor*
Irene Natividad, *Executive Editor*

Gale Research Inc. Staff:

Neil R. Schlager,
Managing Editor, Multicultural Team
Joseph M. Palmisano, *Editor*
L. Mpho Mabunda,
Anna J. Sheets,
Joseph C. Tardiff, *Contributing Editors*
Ned Burels,
Melissa Ann Walsh, *Associate Editors*
Dawn R. Barry, *Assistant Editor*
Barbara A. Wallace,
Permissions Associate
Mary Beth Trimper,
Production Director
Mary Kelley, *Production Associate*

Cynthia Baldwin,
Production Design Manager
Barbara J. Yarrow,
Graphic Services Supervisor
Mary Kay Mencotti,
Creative Services Director
Mary Krzewinski, *Cover Designer*
Arthur Chartow, *Page Designer*
Pamela A. Hayes, *Photography Coordinator*
Willie F. Mathis, *Camera Operator*
Benita L. Spight, *Data Entry Supervisor*
Gwendolyn S. Tucker,
Data Entry Group Leader
Elizabeth Pilette, *Data Entry Associate*

Front cover photographs: Korean American girls, courtesy of Jamie Lew; Zubin Mehta, courtesy of Christian Steiner, Sony Classical.

∞™   This book is printed on acid-free paper that meets the minimum requirements of American National Standard for Information Sciences Permanent Paper for Printed Library Materials, ANSI Z39.48-1984.

♻   This book is printed on recycled paper that meets Environmental Protection Agency Standards.

Library of Congress Catalog Card Number 95-8520
A CIP record is available from the British Library

ISBN 0-8103-9193-7

Printed in the United States of America.
Library of Congress Cataloging-in-Publication Data
The Asian American Almanac: A Reference Work on Asians
in the United States / Susan Gall, Irene Natividad [editors].
    p. cm.
    Includes bibliographical refeerences and index.
    ISBN 0-8103-9193-7
    1. Asian Americans. I. Gall, Susan B. II. Natividad, Irene.
E184.06A824   1995
973'.0495--dc20   95-8520
                                                          CIP

I(T)P™ Gale Research Inc., an International Thomson Publishing company.
        ITP logo is a trademark under license.

10 9 8 7 6 5 4 3 2 1

Executive Editor

Irene Natividad

Contributing Editors

Le Xuan Khoa, Southeast Asian Resource Action Center (SEARAC)
Juanita Tamayo Lott, Tamayo Lott Associates
Helen Zia, Activist and writer

Advisors and Reviewers

Barbara Huie
Paul Igasaki, Asian Law Caucus
Daniel K. Inouye, United States Senator
Daphne Kwok, Organization of Chinese Americans
William Lee, Adland
Jeff Lin, International Examiner
Karen Narasaki, Japanese American Citizens League
Fred Peng, Assistant Secretary of the Navy
Canta Pian
Rick Quan, Television Sportscaster
Shazia Rafi, Parliamentarians for Global Action
Christine Takada, Office of the Governor, Illinois
Clarissa Tom, Asian and Pacific Islander Center for Census Information and Services (ACCIS)
Roslyn Tonai, National Japanese American Historical Society
Clifford Uyeda, National Japanese American Historical Society
K. Scott Wong, Williams College
Grace T. Yuan, Attorney
Melinda Yee, U.S. Department of Commerce
William J. Yoshino, Midwest Regional Director, Japanese American Citizens League
Jackie Young, State Legislature of Hawaii
Hoyt Zia, AMFAC/JMB Hawaii, Inc.

Contributors*

Susan Au Allen, Pan Asian American Chamber of Commerce
Carl Bankston III, Louisiana State University, Baton Rouge
Debra Baron, Writer
William Chong, Asian Americans for Equality
Beatriz C. Clewell, The Urban Institute
Shamita Das Dasgupta, Department of Psychology, Rutgers University, and founding member, Manavi
Jeane Detherage
Major General John Liu Fugh, Judge Advocate General, Army of the United States, retired
Margaret Fung, Asian American Legal Defense and Education Fund
Celia Genishi, Teachers College, Columbia University
Manjula Giri, Writer
A. Lin Goodwin, Teachers College, Columbia University
Jim Henry, Writer
Terry Hong, Journalist
Jayjia Hsia, Ph.D
Marina Hsieh, Boalt Hall, University of California, Berkeley
Lynne Iijima, Writer
Jung-Ah Kim, M.D.
Nan Kim, Journalist
Lillian Kimura, president, Japanese American Citizens League
Glenn Kitayama, Asian American Studies Center, University of California, Los Angeles
Ford Kuromoto, National Asian Pacific American Families Against Substance Abuse
Stewart Kwoh, Asian Pacific American Legal Center
Juanita Tamayo Lott
Jonathan Melegrito, Library of Congress
Kamla Motihar, Andrew. W. Mellon Foundation Library
Shirley L. Mow, Westchester Education Coalition, Inc.
Kim Moy, Journalist
Don Nakanishi, Asian American Studies Center, University of California, Los Angeles
Philip Tajitsu Nash, National Asian Pacific American Legal Consortium, writer and activist
Brian Niiya, Asian American Studies Center Reading Room, University of California, Los Angeles
Samuel Peng, National Center for Education Statistics
Tai A. Phan, National Center for Education Statistics
Natasha Rafi, Journalist
MieMie Sann, Akron Public Library
Alan R. Shoho, The University of Texas at San Antonio
John Stowe, College of Continuing Studies, New York University
Betty Lee Sung, Professor Emerita, Department of Asian Studies, City College of New York
Heny Suwardjono, Kent State University
Ltc. Ronald G. S. Tom, Army of the United States, retired
Clifford Uyeda, National Japanese American Historical Museum
Douglas Utter, Writer
Nguyen Van Hahn, Ph.D., California State University, Sacramento
Rosalie Wieder, Writer
Kent Wong, UCLA Labor Center
Nicole A. Wong, Editor, *Asian Law Journal,* University of California, Berkeley
Victoria Wong, Asian Americans for Equality, New York Immigration Coalition
Bruce Yamashita, U.S. Marine Corps Reserves
Sandra Yamate, Polychrome Publishing
Joanne Sanae Yamauchi, Ph.D., The American University
Connie Young Yu
Min Zhou, Louisiana State University, Baton Rouge
*Affiliations listed were accurate at the time of contribution.

Contents

Acknowledgments

Our sincere thanks to all the individuals in the Asian Pacific American community who have contributed their advice, support, and insights over the last three years as *The Asian American Almanac* grew from an idea to a book. Compiling a reference work of this magnitude covering the more than twenty nationalities and ethnicities comprising Asian America would not have been possible without the support of literally dozens of scholars, activists, and writers. Special recognition is given to those individuals who were interviewed, who loaned personal photos, or who otherwise assisted us in finding data on the Asian American community.

Also, we express our appreciation to the editors at Gale Research Inc. who supported us through this project, notably Christine Nasso, Amy Marcaccio, Larry Baker, Peg Bessette, Kelle Sisung, and Joe Palmisano.

To our Eastword Publications staff, we express our deep gratitude: to Deb Rutti, graphic artist and typesetter, whose patience and keen eye for detail are appreciated beyond expression; to Mary Jane Riddlebaugh, for preparing the comprehensive index to this volume; to Ruta Marino, proofreader; to Rosalie Wieder and Debby Baron for research and writing contributions; and to Brian Rajewski for consulting on various aspects of the project.

Finally, we wish to extend our deepest gratitude to the "godmother" of the *Almanac*—Managing Editor Susan Gall—whose patience, understanding and deep commitment to the development of this volume enabled it to happen. For her persistence in weathering the challenges she faced in realizing a complex project, we proudly name her an "Honorary Asian American."

Preface

So little is known about Asian Americans—their experiences, concerns, and contributions to American life—despite the fact that they are the fastest growing minority group in the United States. *The Asian American Almanac*, the first-ever reference book of this kind, sheds light on an ethnic/racial community that is still perceived as somewhat foreign despite their presence in this country dating back to the 18th century.

An outstanding group of scholars, writers, and practitioners have invested a great deal of time and energy to produce this volume in order to provide a detailed look inside the Asian American community. Their efforts will be welcomed by students, researchers, journalists, government officials, and the general public who are increasingly interested in finding more about this diverse and significant segment of the U.S. population.

The umbrella term "Asian American" covers over twenty individual and unique nationality and ethnic groups. The task of describing and documenting the experiences of each distinct community in the first edition of *The Asian American Almanac* was quite daunting. Our goal was to describe the Asian American experience in general, while preserving the distinct aspects of each group's journey from their native land to the United States. Common threads—such as exclusionary immigration policies, pervasive stereotypes, and an underlying current of anti-Asian sentiment—contribute to Asian Americans' need to work together as a community.

However, each of the more than twenty Asian American ethnic groups has experienced the United States—from immigration pattern to family life to employment—in its own way. We attempted to balance our coverage of the individual groups with that of Asian Americans as a single community.

We are proud to bring this information—never before available in a single volume—to individual Americans, schools, libraries, and organizations across the country. Not only will this work familiarize readers with a sometimes misunderstood community, but it will also provide Asian Americans with a source of pride regarding their identity as a community and their place in American history. For young Asian Americans, this volume allows them to learn more about the background of their specific ethnic group and to find role models among achievers across the ethnic spectrum that comprises the Asian community in the United States.

For me, helping to make this publication happen has been a very satisfying endeavor, for the book embodies the totality of the Asian American experience that had not been chronicled in a comprehensive manner before. It is also a major vehicle for gaining visibility for a community beyond the individual achievements of its academic, artistic, business, and political "stars."

Therefore, a minority group that, until now, was largely absent from library shelves now has something to fill that void—***The Asian American Almanac.***

—*Irene Natividad*
Executive Editor

About the Editor

Irene Natividad is a fixture on the global political scene, particularly in the arenas of women's issues and community empowerment. Working from a base in Washington, D.C., Natividad chairs the National Commission on Working Women, is a director of the Global Forum of Women, and heads the Philippine American Foundation. In addition, her company, Natividad and Associates, provides consulting services on political campaigning and constituency building. She was a founder and president of the Asian American Professional Women, founding director of the National Network of Asian American Women, and deputy vice chair of the Asian Pacific Caucus within the Democratic National Committee from 1982–84.

In 1985, when Natividad was elected to head the National Women's Political Caucus, she became the first Asian American ever to hold that post. Under her leadership, the Caucus established the Minority Women Candidates' Training Program. In addition, she commissioned polls and surveys on American voters' support of women candidates and pushed for women's appointments to state and federal government positions. In 1988, she spearheaded the Coalition for Women's Appointments that submitted names of possible women appointees to both Republican and Democratic presidential candidates. In 1994, she was named to the board of directors of Sallie Mae corporation—the $46 billion student loan financing company—by President Bill Clinton.

For her various activities on behalf of women and Asian Americans, Natividad has been named one of "100 Most Powerful Women in America" by *Ladies Home Journal* (1988); one of "74 Women Changing the Face of American Politics" by *Campaigns and Elections* magazine (1993); one of "25 Most Influential People in Asian America" by *A. Magazine* (1993–94); and one of "1000 Women for the Nineties" by *Mirabella* (1994). She has also been awarded two honorary doctorates; from Long Island University (1989) for her work on behalf of American women and from Marymount College (1994) for her activities on behalf of women internationally.

Born in the Philippines, Natividad moves easily around the globe, speaking six languages fluently and capably adapting to different cultures and customs. She lives in suburban Washington with her husband, Andrea Cortese, a satellite communcations executive. They have one son, Carlo Natividad-Cortese, who was born in 1984. (*See also* Prominent Asian Americans)

Introduction

The Asian American population segment has grown dramatically since 1970. According to the 1990 census in the United States, the number of persons of Asian and Pacific Islander descent doubled between 1980 and 1990, from 3.7 million to 7.2 million. Asian Pacific Americans, representing nearly 3 percent of the population, are the fastest growing population segment in the United States.

Contributors and Reviewers

Each of the chapters was prepared by a knowledgeable contributor—whose name appears at the end of his or her essay. Most contributors are of Asian descent, and many are leading experts in their field. A reference section appears at the end of the essays whenever appropriate. Essay drafts were reviewed by at least one knowledgeable person prior to inclusion in the *Almanac*.

Arrangement of Chapters

The **first fifteen chapters** of *The Asian American Almanac* describe the Asian Pacific Americans—in total, and by selected nationality/ethnicity.

Chapters 16 and 17 present the chronology of Asian America, and key documents in full or excerpted text. Included are laws and other documents of significance in Asian American history.

Chapters 19–21 deal with issues of population growth, including immigration, diversity and issues of interracial relations, and the refugee experience, notably for Southeast Asians.

Chapter 22–24 present issues of civil rights, voter participation and rights, and the U.S. legal system as it has impacted Asian Pacific Americans.

Chapter 25 provides an historical account of Asian Pacific American participation in the U.S. military, including a chronology of events and profiles of notable Asian Americans in various branches of the military.

Chapters 26 and 27 deal with Asian American families and women, with profiles and analysis of key characteristics.

Chapter 28 illustrates structure and history of selected Asian languages. Sample terms are illustrated with examples of the written language and pronunciation guides.

Chapter 29 presents Asian Americans in education from preschool through postgraduate school. Prepared by a panel of experts, this chapter deals with key issues impacting Asian Americans in the U.S. education system, and profiles five Asian Americans who have had an impact.

Chapters 30 and 31 deal with Asian Americans in the workplace; **Chapter 32** lists selected organizations of national significance.

Chapters 33–36 describe the cultural side of Asian America—from religion to literature to theatre to the media. **Chapters 37 and 38** profile notable Asian Americans in sports and describe the key martial arts.

Completing the volume, **Chapters 39–41** feature brief profiles of prominent Americans of Asian or Pacific Islander descent, concise descriptions of landmarks, and selected speeches by Asian Americans. Finally, **Chapter 42** is a selected bibliography for further research.

The comprehensive keyword index provides efficient access to the information in the *Almanac*.

More than 350 illustration—including photographs, drawings, tables, and figures—enhance the information provided by the essays.

This is the first edition of a new reference work covering a very complex and diverse community. Inevitably, there are gaps in coverage of some subjects, due to lack of reliable and accessible information. Many organizations and government agencies have just begun to add a category for Asian Americans—until recently, Asian Pacific Americans were typically categorized with "Other." For the *Almanac*, a great deal of effort went into recruiting knowledgeable, reputable contributors, and to ensure the accuracy of the data and interpretation they have presented in each chapter. Many contributors are recognized leaders in their respective fields; all are acknowledged to be competent researchers and capable writers. Research on many chapters is ongoing, and we welcome comments and suggestions.

Future editions of the *Asian American Almanac* will expand on the themes presented here. Please send comments to:

Editors
The Asian American Almanac
Gale Research Inc.
835 Penobscot Bldg.
Detroit, MI 48226

THE ASIAN AMERICAN ALMANAC

Who Are the Asian Pacific Americans?

◆ Asian and Pacific Islanders: A Diverse Population

◆ ASIAN AND PACIFIC ISLANDERS: A DIVERSE POPULATION

"Asian and Pacific Islanders" is the U.S. Census Bureau category describing over 30 diverse ethnic groups from South Asia (India), Southeast Asia (Vietnam), Central Asia (Peoples Republic of China), the Pacific Rim (Korea), and the Pacific Basin (Philippines). Included among the aforementioned groups are six island jurisdictions in the Pacific that are considered part of the United States.

These include American Samoa, Commonwealth of the Northern Mariana Islands, Federated States of Micronesia, Guam, the Republic of the Marshall Islands, and the Republic of Palau. Individuals born in Hawaii, American Samoa, and Guam have U.S. citizenship and can move freely throughout the Pacific Islands as well as the United States. The same is not true for other Pacific Island jurisdictions, however.

In 1980, the Asian and Pacific Islander population in the United States traced its ancestry to China (including Taiwan and Hong Kong), Philippines, Japan, India, Korea, and Vietnam. By 1989, immigrants from Vietnam had increased dramatically, making it the number one country of origin for immigrants in this category. The Philippines ranked second, followed by China, Korea, Laos, and India. Table 1.1 shows the countries from which Asian and Pacific Islanders immigrated between 1980 and 1989.

The March 1990 Current Population Survey by the U.S. Census Bureau categorizes Asians and Pacific Islanders from China, Mongolia, Pakistan, Sri Lanka, Maldives, India, Nepal, Bhutan, Bangladesh, Burma Laos, Thailand, Vietnam, Cambodia, North Korea, South Korea, Japan, Hong Kong, Macao, Taiwan, Philippines, Malaysia, and Polynesia.

The Asian and Pacific Islander populations are ethnically, culturally, and economically complex. In order to understand the many facets of this fast-growing population segment, it is important to examine demographic characteristics, the portrayal of Asian and Pacific Islanders in the media, gangs and crime, civil rights, and the myth of the "model minority."

Geographical Distribution

The states with the largest numbers of Asian and Pacific Islander populations according to U.S. Census Bureau figures are shown in Table 1.2.

The states with the largest percent increases in Asian and Pacific Island population from 1980 to 1989 were Rhode Island (245.6% increase), New Hampshire (219% increase), Georgia (208.6% increase), Wisconsin (195% increase), Minnesota (193.5% increase), Massachusetts (189.7% increase), and Florida (171.9% increase). In addition, many counties in southern California have experienced a dramatic shift in Asian and Pacific Island population patterns. In Los Angeles County, the largest populations are Chinese, Filipino, Korean, Japanese, and Vietnamese. In Orange County, the largest populations are Vietnamese, Chinese, Korean, and Japanese. In San Bernardino County, the largest populations are Filipino, Chinese, Vietnamese, Korean and Japanese. In Riverside County, the largest populations are Filipino, Chinese, Vietnamese, Japanese, and Korean. In San Diego County, the largest populations are Filipino, Vietnamese, Chinese, Japanese, and Korean.

Immigration Patterns

Between 1951 and 1960, Asian and Pacific Islanders accounted for only 6 percent of all immigrants entering the United States. In 1965, immigration policy was

Women in the Chinatown section of New York examine lingerie at a sidewalk vender's stand. About 150,000 people are jammed into Chinatown's 2 square miles, where people sometimes work for as little as $2 an hour for 10 or 12 hours a day, six or seven days a week. (AP/Wide World.)

changed, raising the quotas dramatically. The new immigration policy fostered family reunification and encouraged more skilled workers to immigrate to the United States.

Consequently, the 1980s witnessed a 75 percent increase in the number of Asian and Pacific Islanders entering the United States. During the 1990s, Asian and Pacific Islanders have had the highest rate of population growth of any group. In fact, the Census Bureau estimates that by the year 2050, Asian and Pacific Islanders will represent 10 percent of the total U.S. population, up from 3 percent in 1990.

Most Asians/Pacific Islander Americans live in western United States. In 1990, about 58 percent lived in the West, with an additional 300,000 or more living in the Pacific Islands.

Under the programs administered by the U.S. Office of Refugee Resettlement, refugees from Southeast Asia are systematically dispersed throughout the United States. However, many of them subsequently relocate to states in the West to reunite with relatives or join established communities of Asian/Pacific Islander

Americans. This phenomenon has been called "secondary migration."

Most Asian and Pacific Islanders move to large metropolitan areas; relatively few live in rural areas. Those who move to rural areas largely are experienced agricultural workers from Southeast Asia. The six metropolitan areas with the largest Asian and Pacific Islander populations in 1990 are shown in Table 1.3.

Income

In 1989, the median income of all Asian and Pacific Islanders was slightly higher than non-Hispanic whites. It is important to note, however, that income levels of Asian and Pacific Islanders may reflect their concentration in metropolitan areas where salaries and cost of living are relatively high. Also, the income statistic is based on family income; Asian and Pacific Islanders are more likely to live in extended family households and work in family businesses. According to the 1990 census, nearly 75 percent of the Asian and Pacific Islander population lived in married couple families as

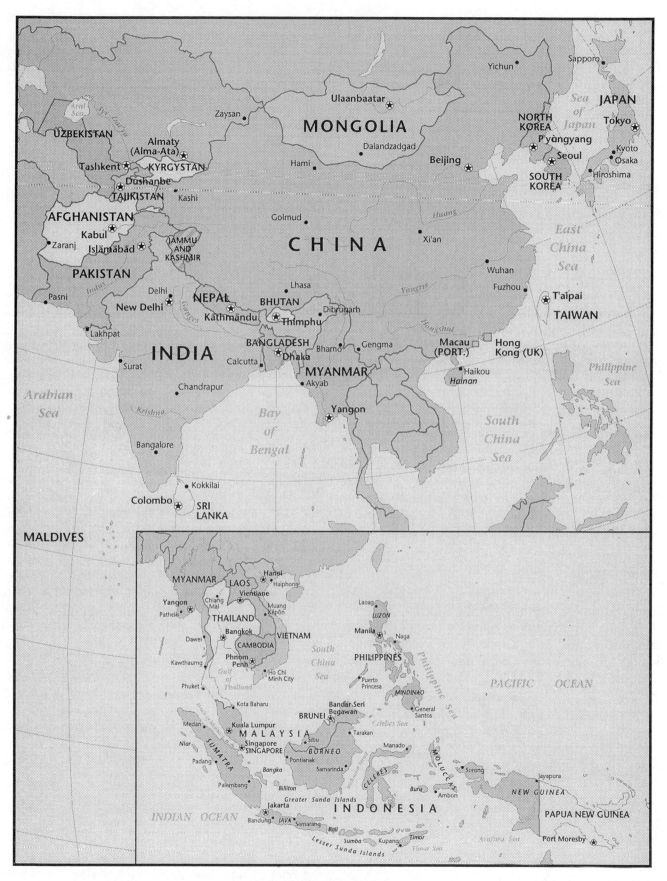

Map of Asia.

Table 1.1
Immigration by Asian Country of Origin, 1980-89

Country of Origin	Population 1980		Immigration, 1980 to 1989	
	Number	Percent	Number	Percent
China	812,178	22	433,031	15
Philippines	781,894	21	473,831	17
Japan	716,331	19	41,739	1
India	387,223	10	253,891	9
Korea	358,303	10	338,891	12
Vietnam	245,025	7	679,378	24
Samoa/Tonga/Guam	76,441	2	6,214	—
Laos (includes Hmong	52,887	1	256,727	9
Thailand	45,279	1	59638	2
Cambodia	16,044	—	210,724	7
Pakistan	15,792	—	55,900	2
Other	219,953	6	55,485	2
Total	3,276,440	100	2,865,339	100

Sources: *O'Hare, William P. and Judy C. Felt. Asian Americans: America's Fastest Growing Minority Group. Washington, D.C.: Population Reference Bureau, 1991; Bureau of the Census, Subject Reports. Asian and Pacific Islanders Population in the United States: 1980, PC80-2-1E. Washington, D.C.: U.S. Government Printing Office, 1980; and U.S. Immigration and Naturalization Service, 1989 Statistical Yearbook. Washington, D.C.: Government Printing Office, 1990. A dash indicates insufficient data.*

compared to 73 percent of non-Hispanic white households. In addition, Asian and Pacific Islander families tended to live in extended family households at twice the rate of non-Hispanic whites. Therefore, the average family levels may represent lower per person incomes for Asian and Pacific Islander families than for those of other ethnic groups.

Poverty Rates

At the same time, the poverty rate among Asian and Pacific Islanders increased. By the early 1990s, in fact, poverty rate had grown to be nearly twice that of non-Hispanic whites. This increase in poverty reflects a bimodal income pattern; some immigrants are skilled, educated, and able to develop careers in business, while others, such as Southeast Asian refugees, tend to lack the required education and skill level.

Statistics reveal that a majority of Asian and Pacific Islanders participate in government welfare programs. In 1990, for example, 59 percent of Asian/Pacific Islander Americans living in households before the poverty level participated in at least one welfare program. In fact, many Southeast Asian refugees begin their lives in the United States receiving welfare. These numbers contradict the stereotype that the Asian and Pacific Islanders do not receive or accept government welfare and that strong family and kinship support systems prevent Asian and Pacific Islanders from needing welfare assistance.

Poverty rates among new immigrants from Southeast Asia are the highest among Asian and Pacific Islander groups. Refugees and immigrants from Vietnam, Cambodia, and Laos comprise the largest proportion of these immigrants.

Table 1.2
Asian Pacific Islander Population by U.S. State, 1990

State	Population	Percent of State Total
California	2,845,659	9.6%
New York	693,760	3.9%
Hawaii	685,236	61.8%
Texas	319,459	1.9%
Illinois	285,311	2.5%

Source: *Asian Week, Asians in America, 1990 Census, Classification by States.*

Education

Asian and Pacific Islander cultures place an emphasis on education, hard work, and a striving for excellence. What is striking about the educational patterns among Asian and Pacific Islanders is that high school graduation rates are similar to non-Hispanic whites. However, 40 percent of Asian and Pacific Islanders continue into higher education, which is nearly twice the rate of non-Hispanic whites.

While some Asian and Pacific Islanders are well-educated in their own countries, there are also subgroups lacking similar education and skill levels. Twenty percent of Asian and Pacific Islanders in 1990 had less than a high school diploma. This figure is slightly higher than that of non-Hispanic whites and contradicts the stereotypical "Whiz Kids" image of Asian and Pacific Islanders.

Statistics show that even though the income of Asian and Pacific Islander families averaged slightly higher than that of non-Hispanic whites and more Asian and Pacific Islanders attended college, they earned less than non-Hispanic whites. In all age groups, non-Hispanic white males earned more money than Asian and Pacific Islander males with the same age and educational background. This indicates that employment discrimination may be keeping Asian and Pacific Islanders from benefiting appropriately from their education and work performance. The "glass ceiling" would seem to prevent many Asian and Pacific Islanders from advancing beyond a certain level in an organization.

Stereotype and Reality

The lead article in the August 1987 issue of Time, entitled "Those Asian American Whiz Kids," describes several Asian and Pacific Islanders that were very successful in school and related activities. The article drew the following conclusion, "The largely successful Asian American experience is a challenging counterpoint to the charges that U.S. schools are now producing less educated mainstream students and failing to help underclass Blacks and Hispanics."

Four months later, the Los Angeles Times published an article entitled "Lost in L.A." describing a teenager who was involved in a Chinatown robbery attempt. Sang Nam Chinh, a nineteen year-old refugee from Vietnam,

Table 1.3
Asian/Pacific Islander Population by U.S. Metropolitan Area

Metropolitan area	Total Asian	Ethnicity, In Percent of Total Asian Population						
		Chinese	Filipino	Japanese	Asian Indian	Korean	Vietnamese	Cambodian, Hmong, Lao
Los Angles-Long Beach, CA PMSA	925,561	26.5	23.7	14.0	4.7	15.7	6.8	3.4
New York, NY PMSA	553,443	44.6	8.9	4.8	19.2	13.5	1.6	0.6
Honolulu, HI MSA CA PMSA	413.349	15.3	29.0	47.2	0.2	5.5	1.3	0.4
San Francisco, CA PMSA	316,751	51.4	28.0	7.5	2.3	3.3	3.9	0.9
Oakland,CA PMSA	259.002	35.0	30.0	8.3	8.4	5.2	6.5	3.8
San Jose, CA PMSA	254,782	25.5	24.1	10.4	8.0	6.	21.3	2.2
Anaheim-Santa Ana, CA PMSA	240.703	17.2	12.6	12.3	6.3	15.0	30.0	3.1
Chicago, IL PMSA	227,742	17.7	23.9	7.6	23.6	14.7	3.2	2.0
Washington, DS-MD-VA MSA	200,113	19.5	13.4	4.9	17.8	19.9	11.7	3.2
San Diego, CA MSA	184,596	10.7	52.0	9.7	2.7	3.6	11.4	6.9
Seattle, WA PMSA	128,656	21.4	21.7	17.8	4.6	12.7	9.8	8.2
Houston, TX PMSA	125.529	23.4	10.7	3.0	20.5	5.6	25.3	3.0

Sources: *Asian/Pacific Islander Data Consortium. San Francisco: Asian and Pacific Islander Center for Census Information and Services, 1993, U.S. Census Bureau. Note: The U.S. Census Bureau designates PMSA as primary metropolitan area and MSA as metropolitan statistical area.*

was the lookout for a failed jewelry store robbery, in which one Los Angeles Police Department officer was killed and another wounded. Chinh was also wounded and later sent to prison.

These two articles illustrate vastly different accounts within the Asian and Pacific Islander community. In reality, members of the Asian and Pacific Islander population are both "successful" and "lost," and at all states in between on a continuum.

Media Portrayals

Although the print, electronic, and motion picture media are less direct in creating a culture of bigotry towards Asian and Pacific Islanders, they tend to act as a stimulus for stereotyping this group by either reflecting public attitudes or playing a role in shaping public opinion. The effects can be positive or negative. In the early 1990s, there were several motion pictures portraying Asian and Pacific Islanders as villains, criminals, and drug lords. For example, "The Year of the Dragon" portrays a gang of Chinese youth destroying a Chinatown restaurant in New York City, bribing the police and elected officials, challenging the Mafia's control over drug trafficking on the Lower Eastside, beheading a drug kingpin in Asia, gang raping a TV reporter, and murdering a police officer's wife. In the film "Showdown in Little Tokyo," a gang of Japanese American criminals begin a shooting spree in the Little Tokyo section of Los Angeles. The film adaptation of Michael Crichton's novel, "Rising Sun," shows Japanese nationals and Americans involved in an international organized crime syndicate. All these images perpetuate stereotypes that harm the image of Asian and Pacific Islanders. To be fair, though, not all movies and TV shows depict Asian and Pacific Islanders as wealthy criminals; however, even those that are more positive often foster ethnic stereotypes that have little to do with reality.

Television news has also contributed to the misunderstanding and negative attitudes towards Asian and Pacific Islanders. Since television reaches so many people vividly and quickly, it can have a tremendous impact on the way people perceive racial and ethnic groups. In April 1992, a jury acquitted the white police officers that were on trial for beating black motorist, Rodney King, in Los Angeles. During the civil disturbance and violence that followed the verdict, much of the television news coverage portrayed the looting and burning of Asian and Pacific Islander businesses (notably Korean-owned) as a result of strained relations between the African American population and Korean merchants. The television news coverage also showed Korean merchants firing guns at crowds of vandals. Based upon these reports, viewers may have drawn the assumption that Asians and Pacific Islanders were, in part, responsible for some of the violence after the Rodney King verdict, that Koreans and other Asian and Pacific Islanders were not responsible business operators, and that the African American and Asian and Pacific Islander populations were in violent conflict over racial issues.

In fact, not only were Korean businesses in South Central Los Angeles looted and burned, but many other businesses were destroyed as well, including many African American owned and operated businesses. Most of the damage to the Korean businesses took place in Koreatown, which is not located in South Central Los Angeles. The looting and burning in Koreatown was not done primarily by African Americans, but by immigrants and refugees from Central and South America living adjacent to Koreatown in the Pico Union area. The Korean merchants that were shown on television firing guns were actually protecting themselves and their property against armed looters, since the Los Angeles Police Department was unable to assist the merchants.

Distorted perceptions of Asian and Pacific Islander resulting from inaccurate media portrayals often leads to racism, and xenophobia. The result is the dehumanization of the total group, leading to violence as well as other forms of hate crimes, discrimination, and negative attitudes and policies directed against Asian and Pacific Islander immigrants and refugees.

The Myth of the "Model Minority"

Many people in mainstream United States view Asian and Pacific Islanders as a "model minority." This idea assumes that Asian and Pacific Islanders are a single, homogeneous group with a stable population. As a "model minority," the group is viewed as being exceedingly successful in schools, the workplace, and in socio-economic mobility. In addition, as a "model minority," the group is regarded as evidence that if people of color simply work hard enough, they will achieve the American dream.

This idea is dangerous for several reasons. First, it stereotypes Asian and Pacific Islanders as people successful on their own, with no problems. As a result, Asians and Pacific Islanders are given a low priority for public and private support in relation to social service programs, such as prevention and recovery from substance abuse. Second, it has the effect of blaming other people of color for their own problems and relieving society of a responsibility to assist these groups. Third, it often places unreasonable expectations on Asian and Pacific Islander children and their families by implying that everyone in the group must be successful. Finally, it establishes the erroneous implication that racism is no longer a salient socio-economic factor in America, since Asian and Pacific Islanders have achieved success through hard work and self-reliance.

In general perceiving Asian and Pacific Islanders as a "model minority" does not help in understanding or addressing Asian/Pacific American issues. The resulting confusion leads to conflicts among groups instead of seeking a greater understanding of Asian and Pacific Islander culture.

The Future

Clearly, Asian and Pacific Islanders will continue to grow as an important segment of the U.S. population. The rapid rate of growth will result in substantial clusters of Asian and Pacific Islander across most of the continental United States, Hawaii, Alaska, and the Pacific Islands. This diverse population will continue to reap both success and failure in its quest for an appropriate place in American life.

References

"Foot Soldiers Add Violent Twist to Asian Street Gangs." *Los Angeles Times*. August 15, 1993.

Kitano, H. and S. Sue. "The Model Minorities." *Journal of Social Issues*, vol. 29, No. 2, 1973: 1-9.

"Lost in L.A." *Los Angeles Times*, December 13, 1987.

O'Hare, W. and J. Felt. "Asian Americans: America's Fastest Growing Minority Group." *Population Reference Bureau*, No. 19: Washington D.C.: February 1991.

Suzuki, B. "Education and the Socialization of Asian Americans: A Revisionist Analysis of the 'Model Minority' Thesis." *Amerasia Journal*, vol. 4, no. 2, 1977: 23.

"Those Asian-American Whiz Kids." *Time*, August 31, 1987.

—Ford H. Kuramoto, D.S.W

Who Are the Asian Indian Americans?

♦ History of Immigration to the United States ♦ Educational Attainment
♦ Employment and Occupational Outlook ♦ Political Participation ♦ Affirmative Action
♦ Asian Indian Culture ♦ Arts ♦ Literature ♦ Festivals ♦ Notable Asian Indians

♦ HISTORY OF IMMIGRATION TO THE UNITED STATES

Throughout the nineteenth and twentieth centuries, Asian Indians have migrated in significant numbers to numerous Asian countries, including Myanmar, Sri Lanka, Malaysia, Indonesia, Japan, the Pacific Islands, the Caribbean Islands, and east and south Africa. More recently Asian Indians have immigrated to North America, Australia, New Zealand, and the Middle East. It is estimated that about 18 million Asian Indians have settled outside their homeland in different parts of the world.

The earliest account of an Asian Indian on American soil can be found in the diary of Rev. William Bentley of Salem, Massachusetts. Reverend Bentley wrote of "a tall, well-proportioned, dark complexioned man from Madras, with a soft countenance accompanying a British Sea Captain, plying a trading vessel between New England ports and coastal towns of Bombay, Calcutta, and Madras in 1790." Whether he stayed in Salem is not known; however, there is a further account of a half-dozen Asian Indians participating in Salem's Fourth of July parade in 1851.

The United States first established consular relations with India in 1838, and often managed them with the assistance of eminent local Parsis (members of a Zoro-astrian sect) as vice-consuls. These vice-consuls were chosen because they had visited the United States and were familiar with the conditions there. It was the Par-sis of Baroda in the 1870s who first expressed interest in migrating to the United States as a community, prob-ably emulating the example of citizens from Gujerat (known as Gujeratis) who had begun emigrating from

Bombay to such British colonies as Kenya, Uganda, Malawi, Rhodesia, and Zambia in quest of new homes and better opportunities. Many Gujeratis had success-fully established themselves as independent business-men, and had even entered British colonial administrations as civil servants. Despite efforts to dis-courage emigration by American Consuls in India, a few Indian merchants did immigrate to America.

Immigration records from 1871 through 1899 show a total of 491 Indian entrants. The Census of 1900 reported 2,050 Indians. The U.S. Immigration Commis-sion set up by Congress believes that prior to 1905, the majority of Asian Indians coming to the United States were professional men, merchants, and travelers, who settled largely in New York or elsewhere in the eastern United States. There were also a few Asian religious leaders who visited or migrated to the United States, including Swami Vivekananda, who came to speak at the First World Parliament of Religions held in Chicago in 1893. Since the early nineteenth century, Americans like Ralph Waldo Emerson and Henry David Thoreau had been enthralled with Indian religions and philoso-phy. Because of this, the term Boston Brahmin came into vogue among Boston's intellectual elite. Brahman is the highest, or priestly, caste among the Hindus in India. The term is sometimes used today disparagingly to connote a snobbish or aloof intellectual.

Among the Indians who came to the United States in the early 1900s were college students, initially studying at eastern universities like Cornell. By World War I, however, there was a significant cluster of Indian students in California, particularly at the Uni-versity of California at Berkeley. Another group of

Indian immigrants consisted of political refugees who considered the United States an ideal base for their revolutionary activities, which were designed to oust the English from India.

After crushing the 1857 revolt, British authorities tightened internal security in India. They did however, allow for the 1885 formation of the Indian National Congress, a moderate organization, to which the British made vague promises of economic reform and self-government.

As the nineteenth century ended, British imperial policies grew more rigid, and many Indian radicals grew impatient and began seeking more activist means of achieving independence. It was the activists who, on immigrating to America, formed a core group in an effort to launch the Indian revolution from their base in the United States.

A handful of Indians led by Har Dayal later organized the Ghadr ("revolution") Party, headquartered in San Francisco, in 1913. The party published a newspaper called *Ghadr* to carry its revolutionary message to India. It sought support for its movement in Germany as well, and the German Consul was its special guest at a rally in Sacramento in December 1913.

Contract Laborers Arrive

The character of Indian emigration changed after 1905, when the first wave of Indians, mainly agricultural workers from the northwest Indian province of Punjab began appearing in Canada. The majority of these workers were Sikhs, members of a religious sect in India. They came to Canada in response to promises of wonderful economic opportunities made by Canadian companies seeking contract labor. Though initially a trickle, between 1906 and 1908 nearly 5,000 Indians arrived in Canada, leading to stories of invasion by "hordes of hungry Hindus," a misnomer used for all immigrants from India. In reality only a small fraction of them were Hindus; one-third were Muslims, and an overwhelming majority were Sikhs.

The government of Canada quickly responded by passing regulations that prevented Indian emigrants from entering Canada if they arrived in a way other than by continuous journey from India. In addition, Indian immigrants to Canada were required to have at least $200 before entering the country. Some of the several thousand Indian emigrants turned away from Canada were drawn south of the border to Washington and Oregon.

Though mainly from an agricultural caste, Indian immigrants to the United States found employment in the railroad industry and lumber mills. Due to economic conditions, as well as the fact that many Indians lacked families (since initial immigrants were almost exclusively male), they worked long hours and for much lower wages than would have been paid to either whites or Chinese and Japanese workers. Consequently Indian laborers were soon viewed by many whites as a threat, even as Chinese and Japanese had once been perceived.

Many Indians migrated south into California and found employment in agriculture. Working 12 to 14 hours a day, they moved from place to place and farm to farm, following the rhythm of the crops. When their employment became jeopardized by white agricultural workers who began to intimidate them, they formed tenancy partnerships among themselves. Using money they had saved, they even bought some land. By 1919, they had leased 86,315 acres and owned 2,077 acres in California, producing mainly rice, cotton, nuts, fruits, and potatoes.

The Rise of Anti-Asian Sentiment

The Asiatic Exclusion League worked actively to tighten immigration restrictions against this new Indian "menace." In response, the United States denied entry to some 3,453 Asian Indians between 1908 and 1920. Indians sought to redress their grievances by legal means through petitions, memoranda, and the pleas of sympathetic lawmakers.

When these efforts failed to achieve results, Indians began seeking radical counsel by joining hands with Har Dayal and his Ghadr party. Har Dayal led an Indian protest delegation at the congressional hearings of a bill intended to exclude all Asian immigrants. He was arrested, and deportation proceedings were started against him. Har Dayal then surfaced in Germany, where an Indian Committee of National Independence had been formed. Some 400 other Indians also left the United States on Ghadr-organized missions. These, however, failed as a consequence of poor planning and effective British surveillance. By 1917, the Ghadr movement had more or less collapsed in America.

After the passage of the Immigration Act of 1917 and the Alien Land Law of 1920 (preventing those of Asian ancestry from owning land), some Indian immigrants were forced to become laborers again, while others continued to hold land in the names of their American friends, lawyers, and bankers. An increasing number of Indians began to marry Mexican women and transferred ownership of land to their wives and to their American-born children.

Between 1913 and 1946, 47 percent of the Indian men living in northern California were married to Mexican women, 76 percent in central California, and 92 percent in southern California. Over 50 percent of Mexican spouses were themselves immigrants from an agricultural working-class background. They had a network of Mexican family and friends. Therefore, when a Mexican woman married an Indian farmer, her sisters and friends were introduced to his friends, often leading to more marriages. In most cases, both husband and wife followed their own religions, though there were some conversions. Children were largely brought up in their mother's religion. Some of these marriages ended in divorce, and both men and women filed for divorce in equal number.

The 1920s saw a decline in the Asian Indian population in the United States. This continued until World War II, by which time their numbers had dwindled to 2,405. Of these, only 4 percent were professionals while 65 percent were in agriculture, with 15 percent being farmers and the remaining 50 percent laborers. Median years of schooling completed by Asian Indians at this time was only 3.7 years. Several factors accounted for this low figure, not the least of which were the restrictive immigration policies and attempts at deportation, although a large number left of their own volition. It was not until after the end of World War II that relations between India and the United States stabilized. At that time, Asian Indians were allowed to immigrate, to become citizens, to own property, and to marry Americans, which they had not been able to do legally prior to this period due to antimiscegenation laws. This started a second wave of immigration from India to the United States, which though initially a trickle (around 6,000 were admitted between 1947 and 1965), gathered momentum as the years progressed until their numbers reached 387,223 in 1980 and 786,694 in 1990.

Immigration Legislation Affecting Asian Indians

Issues, conditions, and circumstances that affected immigration and living conditions for Asian Indians in this country are inseparable from those that affected other Asians. From the Declaration of Independence in 1776 until 1882, the U.S. government neither controlled nor restricted immigration. There were no federal laws prohibiting immigration. The laws that were passed were expressly for the purpose of assisting immigrants. A few states—New York, New Jersey, Pennsylvania, and California—had their own immigration laws. However, in 1875 the U.S. Supreme Court declared some of them illegal infringements on Congress's exclusive power over foreign commerce.

The first American law concerning the movement of Asians into the United States was the Burlingame Treaty of 1868, negotiated with China to enable Americans to reside in and trade with China, and reciprocally recognizing the right of Chinese to do the same. Chinese were the first Asians to enter the United States in significant numbers, and were even officially welcomed

as a source of cheap labor for the development of the western frontier. However, the Chinese soon encountered fierce racial animosity, exacerbated by fear of competition from aliens, which promptly led to calls for restrictive federal immigration laws.

The Chinese Exclusion Act of 1882

The Chinese Exclusion Act of 1882, which debarred Chinese immigrant labor for ten years and prevented Chinese aliens from obtaining United States citizenship, marked the beginning of restrictive American immigration policy, and set the stage for discrimination against all Asians for some eighty-odd years. Successive administrators confided to authorities in India that they could not permit Indians to become regular immigrants to the United States without also lifting a similar ban on Chinese immigrants.

Asian Indian immigration to the United States did not begin in earnest until after 1905. The predominantly agricultural labor class that started to immigrate thereafter, though initially welcomed as railroad and lumbermill workers, soon encountered the same racial discrimination that plagued the Chinese and Japanese before them. Once again the Asiatic Exclusion League called for expulsion of this new "menace" from India, which they called "the tide of turbans."

A Joint Commission on Immigration was created, consisting of three members from each house of Congress and three outside members. Their 42-volume report led to The Immigration Act of 1917. This act, in addition to the exclusionary provisions already in existence, imposed further immigration restrictions by creating a Pacific barred zone, natives of which were inadmissible to the United States. This zone included China, Japan, India, Myanmar, Thailand, Malasia, the Asian portion of Russia, most of the Arabian Peninsula, Afghanistan, the Polynesian islands, and the East Indies (Indonesia). By this time there were about 8,000 Indians in the country.

The Alien Land Law (1920) and the Thind Case (1923)

Between 1905 and 1923, some 67 Indian nationals who had entered the country legally acquired citizenship through court procedures in no fewer than 32 courts in 17 states. Citizenship was granted to them under the 1790 Naturalization Law on the assumption that Indians were the "Mediterranean branch of the Caucasian family," unlike Chinese and Japanese who were denied that privilege. In 1922, Justice George Sutherland of the U.S. Supreme Court, in denying citizenship to Takao Ozawa of Japan, declared, "the words 'white person' are synonymous with the words

'Caucasian race'." This simplified the problem of eligibility for citizenship. Judge Charles E. Wolverton of the Oregon District Court decided in favor of citizenship for Bhagat Singh Thind in 1920 on the same grounds. The Immigration and Naturalization Service, however, disagreed with the Thind decision and appealed in 1923. Justice Sutherland, this time in delivering the court's decision, declared that "Thind, and consequently all India's nationals, were ineligible for U.S. citizenship, since the words of the statute of the 1790 act are to be interpreted in accordance with the understanding of the common man, as to what constitutes 'white', and common man is unfamiliar with the concept of 'Caucasian Race'." While the test in the Ozawa case had been race, not color, the test in the Thind case was color, not race. This made the California "Alien Land Law," which prohibited the ownership of land by people ineligible for citizenship, applicable to Indian nationals.

There was an attempt by the Immigration and Naturalization Service to apply the 1917 act retroactively by instituting proceedings against those who had already been granted citizenship. This was, of course, contested in the courts, and some did succeed in winning their case. However, this period saw a great decline in the Indian population in the United States.

The Immigration Act of 1924

The Immigration Act of 1924, or Quota Act of 1924, established limits on immigration for the first time. Quotas allocated for countries in the Pacific barred zone were intended for people born in those countries, who, by virtue of their color and race, were otherwise eligible for citizenship in the United States. This excluded Indians.

The Immigration Act of 1946

It was not until July 2, 1946, with the passage of Public Law 483, that Indians were officially included in the Immigration Act. It authorized "the admission into the United States of persons of races indigenous to India, [making] them racially eligible for naturalization and other purposes." The quota for immigrants from India was 100, and applied to all persons from India regardless of the country of their birth. This was the slender beginning of yet another wave of Indian immigration; during the first year of the law, only 18 Indians were admitted.

The Immigration and Nationality Act of 1952

The Immigration and Nationality Act of 1952 (known as the McCarran-Walter Act) codified all amendments to immigration law since World War II, and brought together for the first time all the legislation affecting immigration. It continued the 1924 quota system, but extended a small quota for each of the barred-zone Asian countries, with the proviso that nationals of other countries would be charged to the quota of an Asian country if so much as 50 percent of their ancestry was Asian.

The Immigration Act of 1965

The Immigration Act of 1965 instituted major reforms in immigration policy and resolved the racist features of earlier immigration laws. The national-origins quota system was abolished and the Pacific-barred zone provisions were repealed. A ceiling of 170,000 immigrant visas was established for Eastern Hemisphere nations and 120,000 visas were allotted for natives of independent Western Hemisphere countries. This did not include parents, spouses, or children of U.S. citizens. Each country had an annual limit of 29,000 immigrant visas. Seven selective preference categories were established, four of which provided for the reunion of families of U.S. citizens and resident aliens, two for professional, skilled, and unskilled workers needed in the U.S., and one for refugees, including those displaced by natural calamities.

After years of unsuccessful efforts by Truman and Eisenhower, President Kennedy's vision of a system governed not by the race of the immigrants but by their skills became reality. Little attention, however, seems to have been paid to the impact of the act on immigration trends from Asia and elsewhere.

Neither President Johnson nor Attorney General Robert Kennedy expected the ethnic mix of the country to be dramatically affected by the act. Between 1966 and 1970, immigration from India increased by 730 percent, from Hong Kong by 565 percent, and from Portugal by 338 percent. Though the 1965 amendments were intended to advance European immigration, by the 1990s Asians comprised 48 percent of legal immigrants while Europeans made up only 12 percent.

Japanese nationals comprised the largest Asian American immigrant group in 1965, followed by Chinese. By the 1990s, Chinese nationals had become the largest Asian American group, followed by Filipinos. Today, Koreans and Asian Indians have as large a community in the United States as the Japanese, and Vietnamese immigrants are likely to outnumber them by the year 2000.

The nature of immigration has also changed since 1965. Initially, a much higher proportion of immigrants came under the professional category than under the family category. Within a few years, however, naturalized citizens were able to take advantage of the family-reunification provisions, and a much larger proportion of Asian Americans were able to enter the United States this way. In 1969, only 27 percent of the total number of Indians entering the country came under the family category, whereas in 1990, 90 percent used this method.

1986 Amendments to the Immigration Act

In 1986, the Immigration Act was amended to prevent abuse and fraud. Prior to 1986 Indian men immigrated to the United States first, then sponsored their spouses to join them. The new amendments stipulated that the spouse is to be given conditional residency status for the first two years, which is to be changed to permanent residency status on joint petition by both parties three months prior to expiration of the two-year period.

1990 Amendments to the Immigration Act

The 1990 amendments to U.S. immigration law introduced radical changes to the qualifications for permanent residency in the United States based on the realization that the quality of life in modern society is determined not by the manual skills of its workforce but by its technological skills. First preference is now given to immigrants with extraordinary ability in the sciences, arts, education, business, or athletics. Several outstanding professors, researchers, and executives of multinational corporations have therefore obtained permanent status without much difficulty. Second preference is given to those members of professions who have advanced degrees or exceptional ability. Third preference is reserved for skilled workers. Fourth preference is given to special immigrants. Fifth preference is reserved for investors who can create at least ten jobs.

In the family category for permanent residency, the admittance for immediate relatives (spouses, unmarried children, and parents) of U.S. citizens continues to be unlimited. However, there are restrictions for the married children of U.S. citizens and the siblings of U.S. citizens.

There is a worldwide numerical limitation, and an annual limitation per country of not more than 7 percent of the worldwide quota.

Population Profile of Asian Indians

It was not until 1980 that the U.S. Bureau of the Census agreed to count Asian Indians as a separate population category. The census estimated the Asian Indian population to be 387,223, a mere 0.17 percent of the total U.S. population, and 10.4 percent of the total Asian/Pacific American population. By the end of the decade, from 1980 to 1990, the Indian population had increased by 125.6 percent to 786,694, which was still only 0.33 percent of the total U.S. population, and 11.6 percent of the total Asian/Pacific American population.

The total U.S. population had increased by 9.1 percent in the decade; the Asian/Pacific American population had grown by 95.2 percent.

The potential pool of Asian Indian immigrants has also increased as large numbers of students enter the country. In the 1980s, one-third of the students from India adjusted their status to that of immigrant. In the 1992-93 academic year, there were 35,946 students from India, a 10.5 percent increase over 1991-92.

By the year 2000, Asian Indians, now the fourth-largest immigrant group among Asian/Pacific Americans may well emerge as the third largest group. Although in 1980, 70.4 percent of the Asian Indian population was foreign born, by 1990 that number had risen to 75.4 percent, 47.7 percent of which had become naturalized citizens. Of these naturalized citizens, 75.7 percent had entered the country before 1980, and 24.3 percent had arrived between 1980 and 1990.

As seen in Table 2.1, only 612 Asian Indians immigrated between 1850 and 1900. From 1901 to 1930, there was an increase to 8,681 immigrants, after which immigration dropped to 496 persons between 1931-1940. After the 1946 Immigration Act, there was an increase again, and 3,734 Indians immigrated between 1941-1960. Thereafter, immigration rates were 27,189 between 1961-1970, with the most significant gains following the repeal of the national-origins quotas in 1964. They jumped to 164,134 between 1971-1980, and reached 261,841 between 1981-1990. Of the Asian Indian immigrants who arrived in 1991, 46 percent were subject to numerical limitation, and 53.6 percent were exempt.

Table 2.1
Asian Indian Immigration throughout History

Period in Years	Number of Immigrants Entering the U.S. from India
1850 to 1900	612
1901-1930	8,681
1931-1940	496
1941-1960	3,734
1961-1970	27,189
1971-1980	164,132
1981-1990	261,841

Source: Gall, Susan B. Statistical Record of Asian Americans. Detroit: Gale Research Inc., 1993; 411. Primary source: For 1851-1980, U.S. Commission on Civil Rights, The Economic Status of Americans of Asian Descent: An Exploratory Investigation. Washington, DC: U.S. Commission on Civil Rights Clearinghouse Publication 95, October 1988; 21. For 1981-1990, selected from U.S. Immigration and Naturalization Service (INS), Statistical Yearbook of the Immigration and Naturalization Service, 1991. Washington, DC: U.S. Government Printing Office, 1992; 32.

Table 2.2 illustrates that the settlement pattern of Indian immigrants in 1991 is in keeping with an earlier pattern. States that attracted new immigrants from India in 1991 were California (23 percent), New York (20 percent), New Jersey (11 percent), Illinois (8 percent), and Texas (5.7 percent). In Table 2.3, the metropolitan areas that most attracted 1991 Indian immigrants are listed. These were New York City (16.3 percent), Chicago (7.5 percent), Los Angeles/Long Beach (5.6 percent), San Jose (3.9 percent), Washington, DC (3.6 percent), Middlesex/Somerset/Hunterson, New Jersey (3.1 percent), Boston (3 percent), and Philadelphia (2.5 percent).

The ratio of Asian Indian men to Asian Indian women in the United States in 1990 was 54 percent male with a median age of 30.1, 46 percent female with a median age of 28.6, and an overall median age of 29.4. In 1980, the sex ratio was one to one with an overall median age of 29.6.

Only 2.6 percent of the Asian Indian population in the U.S. is 65 and older; over 72.1 percent is between the ages of 15 and 64, and 25.3 percent is 14 years and under. Thus, only a small proportion of the Indian population is in the older age group, compared to 12.9 percent whites, and 7.3 percent Asian/Pacific Americans. A large proportion of Asian Indians in the U.S. belong to an age group that typically makes contributions to society by paying taxes.

Among Asian Indians over 15 years of age in 1990, 65 percent of the males and 70 percent of the females were married, 31.3 percent of the males and 22 percent of the females had never married, 0.9 percent of the males and 1 percent of the females were separated, and 2 percent of the males and 2.1 percent of the females were divorced, while 0.8 percent of the males and 4.9 percent of the females were widowed.

Ninety-eight percent of Asian Indians live in household units, as compared to 73 percent of whites and 76 percent of Asian/Pacific Americans. Out of the 98 percent in household units, 8.8 percent live in extended family households with other relatives, and 9 percent live in non-family households. Only 0.3 percent live in unmarried partnership households.

Of the total number of Asian Indian households in the United States, 21.6 percent consist of five persons or more, 27.9 percent have four persons in the United States, 19.8 percent contain three persons, 18.6 percent have two persons, and 12.1 percent have one person.

Even though almost 78 percent of Asian Indians speak a language other than English at home, 70.3 percent speak English proficiently, 20.6 percent speak English well, 7.2 percent speak some English, and only 1.9 percent speak no English.

Table 2.2
Top Ten States of Intended Residence, 1991

State	Number	Percent
California	10,291	22.8%
New York	9,133	20.3%
New Jersey	4,939	11.0%
Illinois	3,827	8.5%
Texas	2,601	5.8%
Pennsylvania	1,361	3.0%
Florida	1,224	2.7%
Virginia	1,194	2.7%
Georgia	1,175	2.6%
Michigan	1,064	2.6^
Total, other states	8,251	18.3%
Total, all states	45,060	100.0%

Source: Statistical Yearbook of the Immigration and Naturalization Service, 1991.

Table 2.3
Immigration by Top Metropolitan Areas of Intended Resident, 1991

Metropolitan Area	Number	Percent
New York (NY)	7,368	16.4%
Chicago (IL)	3,409	7.6%
Los Angeles (CA)	2,565	5.7%
San Jose (CA)	1,774	3.9%
Washington (DC)	1,653	3.7%
Middlesex-Somerset-Hunterdon (NJ)	1,397	3.1%
Boston (MA)	1,352	3.0%
Philadelphia (PA)	1,127	

Source: Statistical Yearbook of the Immigration and Naturalization Service, 1991.

◆ EDUCATIONAL ATTAINMENT

A high rate of Asian Indians 25 years and over are college graduates (58 percent); 6 percent hold doctorates; 8 percent hold professional degrees; 19 percent have masters degrees, and 25 percent have bachelor's degrees. Only 15.3 percent have less than 12 grades of education; 11.6 percent of Asian Indians have a high-school education; 5.4 percent have an associates degrees; and 9.7 percent have had some college education, but no degree.

Academically, Asian Indians are generally high achievers. A 1984 study by Stanley Sue and Jennifer Abe, that compared predictors of academic achievement among Asian American and white students found that the mean high school grade-point average (HSGPA) was 3.69 for Asian Americans and 3.59 for whites.

Within the Asian American group, Asian Indians had the highest mean HSGPA of 3.80. Asian Americans also achieved higher-average SAT mathematical scores (584 versus 577 for whites), but lower SAT verbal scores (456 versus 512 for whites). Within the Asian American group, Asian Indians had the highest SAT verbal score of 520, though Chinese scored highest in the SAT mathematics section.

A large proportion of Asian Indian students, because of their top scores, are eligible for admission to elite universities; in fact, Asian students form a sizeable proportion of the student population at some schools. In 1991, California State University at San Francisco reported that 33 percent of their 14,672 undergraduate students were Asian Americans. Harvard, Yale, and Stanford had freshman classes in which 20 percent, 15 percent, and 24 percent of their students were Asian American, respectively, in 1990, and the top liberal arts colleges enrolled anywhere between 7 and 17 percent Asian American students.

Even though no data has been collected on the national origins of Asian Americans in higher education, an informal survey of Ivy League universities showed that Chinese Americans, South Asian Americans, Japanese Americans, and Korean Americans are well represented at the undergraduate level, while Chinese Americans and South Asian Americans (Asian Indians, Pakistanis, Bangladeshis, Sri Lankans) are best represented at the graduate level. This overrepresentation of Asian Americans in higher education has led to a curious phenomenon, a quota system by which less qualified white and black students gain admission over better-qualified Asians. Allegations of discrimination led several universities to examine their admissions procedures and prompted the involvement of government agencies in the 1980s, with mixed findings. These studies, however, did lead to some changes in admission policies with significant increases in Asian American enrollments as evidenced in 1990 figures.

There have been several efforts by the Asian Indian community to create chairs for Indian studies in selected universities. Columbia University created such a chair in the early 1990s. There is also a Chair for South Asian Studies at the University of California at Berkeley.

♦ EMPLOYMENT AND OCCUPATIONAL OUTLOOK

In 1990, 43.6 percent of Asian Indians were in professional and managerial positions, 33.2 percent had technical and administrative support occupations, 8 percent were in the service sector, 0.6 percent were in farming, 5.2 percent were in production and repair, and 9.4 percent had other occupations. Although most Indians

Table 2.4
Profile of Asian Indian Population in the United States, 1990

Characteristic	Number	Percent
Total Asian Indian Population	815,447	100%
Men		
Median age 30.1 yrs.	440,341	54%
Women		
Media age 28.6	375,106	46%
Age groups		
65 and over	21,202	2.6%
15 to 64 years	587,937	72.1%
Under 14 years	206,308	25.3%
Marital status, persons age 15 and over		
Married, men		65%
Married, women		70%
Never married, men		31.3%
Never married, women		22%
Separated, men		0.9%
Separated, women		1%
Divorced, men		2%
Divorced, women		2.1%
Widowed, men		0.8%
Widowed, women		4.9%
Households (98% of total)		
5 persons or more		21.6%
4 persons		27.9%
3 persons		19.8%
2 persons		18.6%
one person		12.1%

who came to United States in the 1960s and 1970s were professionals, later arrivals were not as well educated. In 1980, 48.5 percent of all Asian Indians living in the United States held managerial and professional positions; by 1990, their proportion had dropped to 43.6 percent. Many new Indian immigrants, who qualified for entry under the family-sponsorship category, came from small towns or the countryside. They represent a vast spectrum of economic and professional backgrounds, and work in a variety of jobs. They have also developed their own specialized niches, virtually monopolizing certain businesses or professions and slowly changing the commercial, political, and cultural profiles of the cities they live in.

The forces that draw immigrant groups to certain occupations and businesses are complex and varied. Their occupational choices are based on factors like skills and values learned in the old country, the paths followed by immigrants who preceded them, or merely the existence or lack of certain economic and employment options. However, once a niche is found, it creates a snowball effect, gathering labor from that ethnic group and expanding exponentially.

The common thread linking all immigrant work niches is the insider's edge on the profession. Recruiting through the ethnic network is the most efficient way for an employer to get workers. Ethnic labor, in particular family labor, is cheap and easily exploited and there is no linguistic, cultural, or discriminatory barrier.

For example, in New York City, where the Asian Indian population is 140,985, they have a virtual monopoly on newsstands. Since the mid-1980s, Indians have also been investing in gas stations, which are mainly owned by Punjabi Sikhs. Likewise, the growing presence in the jewelry trade of Asian Indians has made them the second-largest ethnic group after Hasidic Jews in the Diamond District. Most of the jewelers are Gujerati Jains, renowned as traders and merchants throughout India. Moreover, by 1987, 28 percent of all the independent motels in the U.S. were Indian owned. Interestingly, almost all the Indians involved in the motel business (which is completely built around the extended family network), carry the last name Patel, a subcaste from the Gujerat region that is known for its entrepreneurial expertise.

Business Ownership

Between 1982 and 1987, Asian Indian business ownership increased by 120 percent and receipts increased by 304 percent. In 1987, there were a total of 43,162 Asian Indian individual proprietorships and 3,935 Asian Indian partnerships. Receipts increased from $1.66 billion in 1982 to $6.715 billion in 1987.

Metropolitan areas with the highest number of Asian Indian owned businesses are New York, Los Angeles/Long Beach, and Chicago. Asian Indian companies are distributed in various sectors as follows: the service industry, 29,787 firms; retail trade, 9,314; finance, insurance, and real estate, 3,537; transportation and public utilities, 2,812; wholesale trade, 1,634; construction, 1,199; manufacturing, 878; agriculture and forestry, 358; and mining, 112.

Affluence and Poverty

Asian Americans are more likely to be affluent than any other ethnic group, including whites. While 35 percent of Asian American households have an income of $50,000 or more (versus 26 percent of white households), among Asian Indian households 44 percent have an income of $50,000 or more. Among native-born Indians, 27 percent have an income of $50,000 or more, while 44.5 percent of foreign-born Indians have an income of $50,000 or more.

The most affluent Asian Americans live in New York, New Jersey, or Connecticut. In Nassau County, New York, nearly two-thirds of all Asian households are affluent. Just 2 percent of Nassau County's households is Asian American, a share equal to the national average. Nationwide, Chinese make up the largest share of Asians and Pacific Islanders (32 percent), followed by Filipinos (19 percent), Japanese (12 percent), Asian Indians and Koreans (11 percent each), and Vietnamese (8 percent). But in Nassau County, Asian Indians and Chinese represent about 30 percent of all Asians in the county.

In 1989, 7.2 percent of Asian Indian families was below the poverty level, compared to 13.1 percent of all Asian Americans, and 7.8 percent of whites. Among native-born Asian Indians, 12 percent lived below the poverty level in 1989, as did 7.1 percent of foreign-born Asian Indians.

◆ POLITICAL PARTICIPATION

Some recent studies on political participation by people of Asian descent suggest that Asians are generally apolitical. Carole Uhlaner, Bruce Cain, and Rodney Kiewiet, in their 1980 study entitled "Political Participation of Ethnic Minorities in the 1980s," found that Asian Americans and Hispanics lagged noticeably behind both blacks and non-Hispanic whites in registration and voting. Studies in San Francisco in 1984 and in Los Angeles in 1986 found that while the voter-registration rate for the general California population was 73 percent, Indians had a voter registration rate of only 16.7 percent, Japanese had 43 percent, Chinese maintained 35.5 percent, and Filipinos had 27 percent.

These studies probably ignored the citizenship status of Asians, since groups with the lowest registered voters also have the highest percentage of foreign-born members. Given the shorter duration of their stay in the United States and their lesser degree of assimilation and westernization, this group is clearly more likely to lack a sense of political efficacy. Another factor to consider is the long history of disenfranchisement of ethnic minorities in the United States. It has also been suggested that since Asian Indians are such a highly educated, prosperous, and successful community, they are perhaps too content with the status quo, and lack motivation for more active involvement.

Asian Indian participation may have been limited in the past, but political participation in its broadest terms, encompasses a range of less high-profile activities—lobbying officials and their representatives, identifying issues worth fighting for, and determining institutional arenas for them. In this, Asian Indians have demonstrated their ability to operate within the political system. This can be seen in their successful movement to be counted as a separate population category, and their lobbying related to the new immigration bill, and their lobbying against military aid to Pakistan.

Nor are Asian Indians strangers to politicking, when one considers their early struggle for independence, through the Ghadr movement. One of the major reasons for Indian's politicization has been their experience with discrimination. To fight this bigotry, Indians formed such organizations as the India League of America, the Indian Association for American Citizenship, the Indian National Congress Association of America, and the Indian Welfare League.

With the growth of the Indian community, there has been increasing awareness of the need to participate in conventional electoral politics, to have representatives in Congress who can express their views on the issues that matter most to them. Demographically speaking, if 160,000 Indian Californians joined another Asian community to form an Asian voting bloc, they could begin to wield real political power.

Asian Indians in Politics

In the 1950s, Dalip Singh Saund of California became the first Asian Indian to be elected to Congress. By the mid-1990s, there were four Asian Indians who had declared their candidacy: Neil Dhillon of Maryland, Peter Mathews of California, John Abraham of New Jersey, and Ram Y. Uppuluri of Tennessee. Kumar Barve was the first Indian American to be elected to the Maryland State Legislature in 1990.

Three Asian Indians have won election's as mayors: Bala K. Srinivas in Holliwood Park, Texas; David Dhillon as City Manager in El Centro, California; and John Abraham, who lost his 1993 reelection bid for mayor of Teaneck, New Jersey.

There have also been some appointments to administrative positions; Dr. Arati Prabhakar served as research director of the National Institute of Standards and Technology, Department of Commerce, and T.R. Lakshmanan was head of the Bureau of Statistics in the Transportation Department. President Reagan appointed Dr. Joy Cherian to the Equal Employment Opportunity Commission. President Bush continued the effort by appointing Bharat Bhargava the assistant director of Minority Business Development Authority, Dr. Sambhu Banik the executive director for the Presidential Commission on Mental Retardation, and Dr. Gopal S. Pal a member of the board of regents, Uniformed Services University of the Health Sciences under the U.S. Defense Department.

With regard to party affiliation, a 1986 Los Angeles study found that, among Asian Indians, 59.1 percent were Democrats and 23.6 percent were Republicans. However, they are often inclined to cross party lines depending on the issues being addressed. Since 1982,

Dalip Singh Saund, Asian Indian politician, greets his brother, Karnail Singh (right) in Calcutta, India (AP/Wide World.)

the Asian Indian community has actively participated in presidential and congressional elections. In 1992, several Indian Americans actively campaigned for Bill Clinton as did several others for George Bush. Two community activists—Prakash Shah of Basking Ridge, New Jersey, and Ramesh Kapoor of Boston—served as trustees of the National Democratic Party. Dr. Zach Zachariah of Florida, who was Bush's 1992 finance committee chairman in that state, had the distinction of raising the most funds of any one person in that campaign.

In Minnesota, Gopal Khanna served as chairperson of the Asian Indian American Republican Affiliate (AIARA), which aims to increase Asian Indian participation in the affairs of Minnesota's Republican Party. Given the salience of ethnic politics in America, both the Democratic and the Republican parties stand to gain from the support of this hitherto politically uncommitted, growing, affluent community.

♦ AFFIRMATIVE ACTION

Affirmative action is a program designed to remedy the effects of past discrimination and to end such discrimination. It includes special efforts to hire and promote members of minority groups (including women) and people with disabilities. The term *affirmative action* was first used by President Lyndon B. Johnson in 1965. Colleges and universities use it when setting guidelines for admitting students of different ethnic and racial backgrounds.

In the nearly 30 years since affirmative action was born, massive Hispanic and Asian immigration has transformed the United States from a nation in which nearly three-quarters of the minority population was black to one in which less than half of that population is black. Between 1970 and 1990, the black population grew by 33 percent while the Hispanic and Asian American segments grew by 144 percent and 380 percent, respectively. As soon as new immigrants set foot in the United States, they have the same claim to consideration as minorities under affirmative-action programs as native-born blacks.

This has generated a philosophical debate: is affirmative action a policy designed for historical redress of past victimization or simply a tool to allow everybody the opportunity to participate? In this context, Hispanics claim past victimization resulting from conquest. Asians suffered from longstanding U.S. immigration policy that denied them citizenship and the right to own land or bring their families into the country.

On the other hand, Asian Americans, 62 percent of whom were born abroad have a median household income higher than that of whites and nearly twice that of blacks. Young Asian Americans are 40 percent more likely to graduate from college than whites, and three times as likely as blacks.

Affirmative Action and Government Contracts

Because of these factors, some people feel that Asian Americans should not participate in affirmative-action programs. The federal government (and some states) considers an Asian Indian businessman a minority businessman, qualified for government contracts reserved for such businesses. In Ohio, Asian Americans were included in the 1991 program that set aside 5 percent of all construction contracts and 15 percent of all goods and services contracts for certified minority companies. However, in 1992, the administration began removing Asian Indians from the program on the premise that Indian-owned businesses are not "disadvantaged business enterprises." This change is being contested by several Asian Indian companies. They contend that the fact that some Indians are affluent should not disqualify others from participating in such a program. They further maintain that they are historically disadvantaged; and that the poverty level

Sunil Gulat, Indian American executive with the World Cup Soccer. (G. Asha.)

among native-born Asian Indians is higher than that of the general population.

San Francisco's Board of Supervisors voted nine to one in June 1991 to categorize Asian Indians under the minority-owned business enterprise-law, which gives a 10 percent preference to minority-owned businesses bidding on city contracts. Asian Indians, once included in the program, were temporarily excluded in 1989.

African American opinion on this issue is equally divided. Some see the expansion of affirmative-action programs to include Hispanics and Asians as a threat, leading to interminority conflicts. However, there have been instances of public support for Asians and Hispanics by blacks, as in the decision by the National Association for the Advancement of Colored People (NAACP) to picket the Fairfax County Government Center in support of Dr. G.V.V. Rao, an Indian Public Works Department engineer who had been denied promotion on 23 occasions.

Programs like affirmative action generate an awareness among Asian American communities that they must work together to be heard on the issues that affect them most.

Affirmative Action in the Workplace

When discussing opportunities for Asian Americans to advance in the workplace, reference is often made to a "glass ceiling," or "bamboo curtain." These two terms describe a discriminatory barrier that prevents Americans of Asian descent from advancing beyond a certain level.

Discrimination has been documented in academia and elsewhere. There are over 5,000 faculty members of Indian origin teaching in various universities, many of whom have reached the level of department chair. However, some faculty members have been denied tenure even though they were as qualified or better qualified than others who were granted tenure. A few of these cases have been contested in the courts, and several others were referred to the Equal Employment Opportunity Commission (EEOC), a federal agency charged with ensuring fair employment practices.

In a survey of 325 white-collar Asian American professionals in California, 80 percent perceived that Asian Americans were underrepresented in upper-level management and believed that they earned $8,000 to $35,000 less than their white counterparts. According to Dr. Marilyn Fernandez, an Asian Indian professor of anthropology and sociology and one of the authors of the study, 58 percent of the respondents knew at least one Asian American who felt he or she had been denied promotion because of race.

The survey also found that the glass ceiling generally covers all employment sectors—government, nonprofit, and corporate. In the corporate sector, 66 percent of Asian Americans felt that chances for promotion were limited due to race. In the survey, discontent regarding promotion also seemed to increase with age.

♦ ASIAN INDIAN CULTURE

Religion

India's religious contribution to the United States can be dated to the early nineteenth century, when several religious reform movements like Brahmo Samaj and Theosophy sprung up. Theosophy, which had its origin in the United States in 1875, followed Buddhist and Brahmanic theories, especially pantheistic evolution and reincarnation. Pantheism equates God with the forces and laws of the universe, and tolerates the worship of all gods of different creeds and cultures.

Swami Vivekananda visited the United States from India for the first time in 1893 to attend the Parliament of World Religions. He toured America, and found that while scientific, industrial, and technological revolutions flourished, in his view there was a sort of spiritual emptiness in the United States.

Asian Indian Americans are often found in academic settings. (Rakesh Jain.)

Vivekananda established the Ramakrishna Mission in India to help revitalize Hindu society. In the United States he launched the Vedanta Society, whose goal was to bring Hindu teachers to the United States to teach the wisdom of the Vedas (the four collections of hymns, prayers, and liturgical formulas that comprise the earliest Hindu sacred writings), and to offer the spiritual nurturing that Vivekananda felt was badly needed. He came to be known as "the missionary from India to America."

From then on, religious figures from India visited the U.S. and established centers that combined spiritual guidance, meditation, teaching of the Vedas and scriptures, as well as a holistic way of living and healing. Some of these centers have expanded to promote other aspects of Indian art and culture.

Examples of such centers are: Self-Realization Fellowship, originating in California; the Ramakrishna Missions; Swami Muktananda's Ashram in South Fallsburg, Pennsylvania; the Himalayan Institute of Sri Rama in the Poconos, New York; various Arya Samaj centers; and Sri Satya Sai Baba Centers, numbering in the hundreds. In addition, there are hundreds of Hindu temples in the United States devoted to various Hindu

The author wearing a patola saree and musicians in native costumes. (Courtesy of Kamla Motihar.)

deities. With the influx of large numbers of Indian immigrants, these religious centers have become focal points for the preservation of Asian Indian religious, spiritual, and community activities.

In 1991, Bochasanwasi Swaminarayan Sanstha (BSS), based in Ahmadabad, India, organized a month-long festival in Edison, New Jersey, "to bring together all the Indians and Hindus to discuss aspects of Indian culture and religion that bring harmony." Models of traditional temples and historic and religious tableaus were constructed for the event. Staffing the festival were 2,600 volunteers who presented programs in music, arts, food, and religious teachings. BSS has either temples or community centers in New York, Houston, Atlanta, Chicago, Dallas, and Toronto.

Traditional Dress

With the infinite variety of regional cultures in India, there is a corresponding variety of traditional clothing. Predominant dress for Asian Indian women is the *saree* or *sari*, six yards of fabric, either silk, cotton, georgette, or chiffon, draped and pleated around the waist over a long petticoat, with the end gathered on one shoulder. A snug-fitting matching blouse, called a *choli*, is worn underneath silk, cotton, georgette, or chiffon. Styles of draping the saree vary from region to region; the fabric may be printed by various methods, or it may be painted by hand, embroidered, or woven in a variety of colors and designs.

For women from Punjab, the predominant dress is a long chemise called a *kurta*, worn over either baggy trousers, called *salwar*, or tight-fitting trousers gathered into pleats at the ankles, called *churidar*. A matching scarf, a *dopatta*, is draped around the shoulders. This type of dress, commonly called *salwar kameez*, or *Punjabi dress*, has been adopted all over India. It is especially favored by younger people, because of the degree of comfort that it provides.

In Rajasthan, women wear full-length flared skirts popularly known as *ghaghra*, with a *choli* top and a long scarf. The whole outfit is usually heavily embroidered, with an edging of silver or gold piping or tassels.

Traditional Indian dress for men is a long robe called a *sherwani* which is worn over either tight-fitting *churidars*, or a looser, straighter style of pants. Variations on this mode of dressing include a loose *kurta* worn over straight pants with a vest, or alternatively, a *kurta* worn over a *dhoti*, which is several yards of fabric draped into trousers around the legs. Most Asian Indian

Punjabi dress with kurta (chemise) over salwar (trousers) with dopatta scarf. (Courtesy of Kamla Motihar.)

Rajasthani dress with ghaghra (flared skirt) and choli (top). (Courtesy of Kamla Motihar.)

men in the United States and most men in India have adopted western dress, with traditional national dress reserved for ceremonial occasions.

Men in the Sikh community also wear the *khurta* and *churidar*, but add a *turban* to wear around their heads. Sikh religion requires them to wear a steel bangle around their wrist, a comb in their hair (which may never be cut), a little dagger known as a *kirpan*, and a pair of shorts. The Sikh women typically wear Punjabi dress.

Folk Dance

There are four major styles of dancing in India: *Bharat Natyam*, and *Kathakali* in the south and *Kathak ali* and *Manipuri* inthe north. Kathakali dancers wear elaborate costumes and makeup, which take over six hours to apply.

♦ ARTS

Organizations and museums like the Asia Society, New York's Metropolitan Museum of Art, the American Museum of Natural History, Bharatiya Vidya Bhawan, and the World Music Institute have sponsored

Indian arts, both visual and performing. Many Asian Indians themselves are dedicated in their personal pursuit of art.

Traditional Music

There are two main styles of music in India, namely *Hindustani*, which is prevalent in the north, and *Karnatak*, prevalent in the south. Both vocal and instrumental music may be rendered in either of these styles. Hindustani music has several variations, or substyles called *gharanas*, which are usually named after their region of origin, such as *Benarasi*, *Jaipuri*, etc. Musicians usually specialize in and are identified with a particular regional style.

The most popular musical instruments in India are the *sitar* in the north, and the *veena* in the south, both of which are instruments similar to a guitar. The *sitar* usually has one gourd, and a long neck with frets and strings. It is played with a steel plucker called a *mazrab* worn on the right index finger. The left index finger slides over the frets. The *veena* has two gourds at either end with strings and frets like the *sitar*.

Other popular instruments are violin, *sarod, shahnai, santoor, flute, dilruba,* harmonium, and special drums called *tabla, ghatam,* and *mridangam.*

To focus on the music of India, specialized organizations, such as the Indian Academy of Performing Arts, are devoted to Indian classical music and sponsor notable musicians from India for concert tours in the United States.

Several Indian musicians have established schools in the United States to keep Indian culture alive among young Asian Indians and interested Americans. A notable example is the institute established on the West Coast by Ali Akbar, master of the *sarod,* a traditional lute of northern India.

There have been some attempts to fuse Indian and Western music, notably by Ravi Shankar, a world-renowned sitarist, and by violinist Yehudi Menuhin. They worked together in the 1960s to produce collaborative recordings. Jazz musicians, like the late Miles Davis have used Indian musicians, especially percussionists, in their bands, and have performed Indian music.

Theater

Regional theater groups have developed across the United States, especially through local Asian Indian organizations. These organizations also sponsor regional arts as part of their local festivals.

Film

The internationally known film producer Ismail Merchant hails from Bombay. His partnership with James Ivory has produced such hits as *Heat and Dust* (1983), *Bostonians* (1984), *A Room with a View* (1986), *Howard's End* (1990), and *The Remains of the Day* (1993).

Mira Nair, a film director, has produced *Mississippi Masala,* starring Denzel Washington, and *Salaam, Bombay.* Both deal with the adjustments Asian Indians must make to live in the U.S. (*See also* Prominent Asian Americans.)

In addition, Deepa Mehta, an Indian Canadian, has contributed the film *Camilla* to the list of works by Asian Indians. *Camilla* stars Jessica Tandy and Bridget Fonda.

♦ LITERATURE

There are a number of successful Asian Indian American writers of both fiction and nonfiction. Some have been driven by their desire to preserve historical, religious, cultural, and social traditions for younger generations. Others have sought to articulate their own

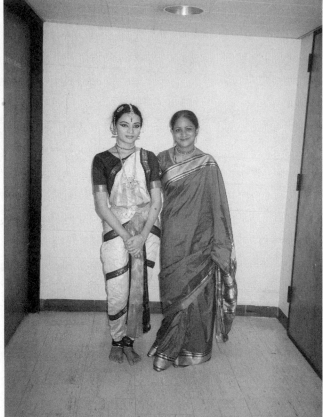

Bharat Natyam costume (left); one of the four major classical dance styles. (Courtesy of Kamla Motihar.)

experiences of biculturalism, of their Indian roots and heritage in survival against the onslaught of foreign influences. Yet others have remolded their thinking in an attempt to synthesize the best in both cultures.

Nonfiction Writers

Among notable nonfiction writers of Asian Indian descent are three whose works have achieved best-seller status. Dinesh D'Souza's works include a biography of evangelist Jerry Falwell entitled *Falwell, Before the Millenium: A Critical Biography* (1984); *The Catholic Classics* (1986); *My Dear Alex: Letters from the KGB* (1987); and his best-seller *Illiberal Education: The Politics of Race and Sex on Campus* (1991).

Ravi Batra's economic series includes the best-selling *The Great Depression of 1990* and *Surviving the Great Depression of 1990.*

Deepak Chopra, an endocrinologist turned ayurvedic practitioner, has published a series of highly successful books, including *Ageless Body, Timeless Mind: The Quantum Alternative to Growing Old* (1993); *Creating Affluence: Wealth Consciousness in the Field of All Opportunities* (1993); *Creating Health:*

Group of Kathakali dancers, one of the four major dance styles in India. (Courtesy of Kamla Motihar.)

How to Wake Up the Body's Intelligence (1991); *Perfect Health* (1991); *Unconditional Life* (1991); *Magical Mind, Magical Body* (1990); *The New Physics of Healing* (1990); *Quantum Healing: Exploring the Frontiers* (1989); *Return of the Rishi: A Doctor's Search* (1988); and *Creating Health: Beyond Prevention toward Perfection* (1987).

Ved Mehta, a journalist and biographer, is a staff writer for *The New Yorker*. In addition to the essays he publishes there, his works include: *Up at Oxford* (1993), *The Stolen Light* (1989), *Daddyji* (1988), *Sound Shadows of the New World* (1985), *The Ledge Between the Streams* (1984), *Fly and the Fly-Bottle: Encounters with British Intellectuals* (1983), *Vedi* (1982), *A Family Affair: India under Three Prime Ministers* (1982), *The Photographs of Chachaji: the Making of a Documentary Film* (1980), *Mamaji* (1979), *The New India* (1977), *Mahatma Gandhi and His Apostles* (1977), *John is Easy to Please: Encounters with the Written and Spoken Work* (1971), *Portrait of India* (1970), *Delinquent Chacha* (1966), *Walking the Indian Streets* (1960), and *Face to Face* (1957).

V. S. Naipaul, the journalist and novelist, has published *India—Million Mutinies Now* (1991); *A Turn in the South* (1989); *The Enigma of Arrival: A Novel* (1987); *A House for Mr. Biswas* (1983); *The Return of Eva Peron* (1980); and *A Bend in the River* (1979).

Fiction

Asian Indian fiction writers include such well-known figures as Bharati Mukherjee, National Book Critics Circle Award winner for *The Middleman and Other Stories* (1988). Her other works include *The Holder of the World* (1993); *Jasmine* (1989), *The Tiger's Daughter* (1972); *Wife* (1975); and *Darkness*.

Other Asian Indian fiction writers are: Gita Mehta, author of *A River Sutra* (1993), *Raj: A Novel* (1989), and *Karma Cola: Marketing the Mystic East* (1979); Vikram Seth, whose *A Suitable Boy* (1993) has been compared to the monumental works of Austen and Tolstoy, and whose other works include *All of You Who Sleep Tonight: Poems* (1990), *The Golden Gate: A Novel in Verse* (1986), and *From Heaven Lake* (1985); Shashi Tharoor wrote *The Five-Dollar Smile and Other Stories* (1993), *Show Business* (1992), *The Great Indian Novel* (1989), and *Reasons of State* (1982); Anita Desai, who published *Baumgartner's Bombay* (1989), *In Custody* (1985), which was made into a film in 1994, *Clear Light of Day* (1982), *Games at Twilight*

(1978), and *Fire on the Mountain* (1977); Kirin Narayan, writer of *Love, Stars, and All That* (1994).

Dhan Gopal Mukerji was the one of the first Asian Americans to write for children. His works include both animal fantasies like *The Chief of the Herd* (1929) and *Kari the Elephant* (1922) and novels—*Gay Neck: The Story of a Pigeon*, which won the Newberry Medal in 1927; *The Master Monkey* (1932); *Visit India with Me* (1929); *Ghond, the Hunter* (1929); *Hindu Fables for Little Children* (1929); and *Hari, the Jungle Lad* (1924). His works are replete with themes centering on the human spirit and its search for spirituality.

In the 1960s and 1970s, educational and political agendas prompted Rama Mehta to write such works as *A Story of India* (1966) and *The Life of Keshav* (1969). Inspired by nostalgia for India were Mehlli Gobhai, who wrote *Ramu and the Kite* (1968), Sharat Shetty, author of *A Hindu Boyhood* (1970), and Madhur Jaffrey, whose collection of folktales is titled *Seasons of Splendour* (1985).

♦ FESTIVALS

The variety of festivals in India is commensurate with the diversity of its people, languages, literature, regions, and religions. There are religious festivals like Dussehra, Diwali, Janmashtami, Id-Uz-Zuha, and Muharram. There are secular festivals, such as Independence Day and Republic Day. Then there are seasonal festivals like Pongal, Onam, and Basant Panchmi, which herald the end or the start of a season or celebration of harvest, though most seasonal festivals also have religious connotations. There are festivals to celebrate the births of religious figures like Buddha, Mahavir, Guru, Nanak, and others, and of historical and political figures like Mahatma Gandhi and Jawaharlal Nehru.

Major festivals and celebrations observed by Asian Indian Americans are highlighted in the following section.

Baisakhi

Baisakhi is the Hindu solar new year day, when people bathe in rivers and go to temples to offer worship. It is of special significance to the Sikhs, for on this day in 1699, Guru Gobind Singh organized them into *Khalsa*, the brotherhood of man. In Punjab, farmers begin the harvest on this day with great fanfare and dancing.

Buddha Purnima

Buddha Purnima marks the birth and enlightenment of Gautam Buddha.

Dussehra and Durga Puja

Dussehra and *Durga Puja*, representing the triumph of good over evil, are among the most popular of all festivals. They are celebrated in various ways throughout India. In the north, *Ram Lila*, a folk-theatre performance, recalls the life of the legendary hero Ram and his triumph over Ravana, the demon king whom Ram killed on this day. This act is commemorated by the burning of Ravana's firecracker-stuffed effigy. In Kulu, against the backdrop of snow-covered mountains, villagers dressed in their colorful best carry a procession of their deities, accompanied by music. In the south, Dussehra is celebrated with great pomp and sonorous ringing of the temple bells. In Bengal it is celebrated as *Durga Puja*, with four-day worship of the image of the goddess Durga, at the end of which the image is taken in a ceremonial procession and immersed in the river.

Deepavali (Diwali)

Twenty days after Dussehra, the festival of lights known as *Deepavali*, or *Diwali*, is observed. During this celebration every home in India is decorated with rows of small earthenware lamps filled with oil and a cotton wick. The festival is preceded by a thorough spring cleaning of home and hearth; this is done to welcome *Lakshmi*, the goddess of wealth. On the festival day, decked in new clothes, all the members of the family worship the goddess with gold, silver, sweets, and scented water. They also exchange gifts and partake of the family feast. Shops in the bazaars are also gaily decorated with lights and buntings. For businesses, this holiday ends the financial year, and shopkeepers mark the ceremonial beginning of a new one with new account books. *Deepavali* also celebrates of the homecoming and coronation of Ram after fourteen years of exile, during which he vanquished several evil kings and demons.

Gandhi Jayanti

Gandhi Jayanti is celebrated on October 2, the birthday of Mahatma Gandhi, the father of the India. This holiday is celebrated all over the country with special prayers.

Holi

Holi is the most boisterous of all Hindu festivals observed in the north. It heralds the end of cold weather and the onset of spring. Men, women, and children revel in throwing colored powder and squirting colored water at each other. This is one day in India when the traditional reserve between the two sexes is forsaken, and men and women frolic and play with each other without fear of inviting social wrath, even as Lord Krishna is supposed to have done with the *Gopis*. Bonfires are lit at night, and there is revelry and dancing around the fire.

The religious significance of Holi is illustrated by baking bread with a thread tied around it. The thread, which does not burn, represents Prahlad, a saintly child. He was taken into the fire by his aunt Holika in an attempt to destroy him, knowing that she was indestructible by fire. However, it was Holika and not Prahlad who was consumed by the flames.

Id'Ul'Fitr

Id'Ul'Fitr celebrates the end of Ramzan, the Muslim month of fasting. It is an occasion of feasting and rejoicing with family and friends, and the faithful gather in mosques to pray.

Id-Uz-Zuha

Id-Uz-Zaha commemorates the sacrifice of Abraham, when Muslims offer prayers all over the country.

Independence Day

This holiday, celebrated on August 15, commemorates the day in 1947 when India won its independence from Britain. In America, it is observed with a procession of colorful floats representing various facets of Asian Indian life in this country.

Janmashtami

Janmashtami, the birthday of Lord Krishna, the author of the *Bhagavad Gita*, is celebrated with nightlong prayers and singing of religious hymns in the temples. Scenes are enacted from Lord Krishna's early life, and with the rocking of a cradle that holds an image of the baby Krishna.

Mahavir Jayanti

Mahavir Jayanti marks the anniversary of the birth of Vardhamana Mahavira, the twenty-fourth Tirthankara, in the sixth century B.C.

Muharram

Muharram commemorates the martyrdom of Imam Hussain, the grandson of the holy Prophet Mohammed. It is observed by Shiite Muslims, who make processions of gaily decorated *tazias*, which are replicas of the martyr's tomb at Karbala in Iraq.

Onam

Onam is Kerala's most popular festival, a celebration of the harvest. The most exciting part of this festival in India is the snake-boat races which are held at palm-fringed lagoons.

Pongal or Sankranti

Pongal is a three-day harvest festival, and one of the most joyful events in the south of India. In Tamil Nadu, (formerly Madras), the newly harvested rice is ceremonially cooked. In some other parts of India, the festival is called *Sankranti*. Cows and bullocks are gaily decorated and fed on *pongal*, a sweetened rice and, in the evening, the cattle are led in a procession to the beat of drums.

Republic Day

January 26 marks the anniversary of the adoption of India's constitution in 1950. It is India's national day, celebrated in all the state capitals, but specially in Delhi with a magnificent parade with bedecked elephants, three divisions of the armed forces, and civilians.

◆ NOTABLE ASIAN INDIANS

Har Gobind Khorana

Har Gobind Khorana, Nobel laureate for medicine/physiology in 1968, was born in the small Indian village of Raipur, Punjab, in 1922. Khorana received his earliest education under a tree, where the local teacher held classes. He received his bachelor of arts degree from the University of Punjab in Lahore in 1943 and his master of science degree two years later. With a scholarship from the Indian government, he pursued further studies at the University of Liverpool, where he received his doctorate in organic chemistry in 1948. He was a Nuffield fellow at Cambridge University from 1940 to 1952, after which he went to the University of British Columbia. He moved to the University of Wisconsin in 1960, became a U.S. citizen in 1966, and in 1970 moved again with most of his research team to the Massachusetts Institute of Technology (MIT) as professor of biology and chemistry. His work on the genetic code, which defines the structure of gene—the basic unit of heredity, won him the Nobel Prize.

Subrahmanyan Chandrasekhar

Dr. S. Chandrasekhar, winner of the 1983 Nobel Prize in physics, was born in Lahore, India, in 1910. After studies at Presidency College in Madras, he went

Zubin Mehta.

Sitarist Ravi Shankar. (AP/Wide World.)

to Cambridge University, where he earned his doctorate in physics and was awarded a fellowship. In 1936 he moved to the U.S., where he has since worked at the University of Chicago and at Yerkes Observatory, Williams Bay, Wisconsin. He became a United States citizen in 1953. He is the nephew of Sir Chandrasekhar Venkataraman, who won the Nobel Prize in Physics in 1930 for his studies of the way light scatters.

Dr. S. Chandrasekhar won the Nobel Prize for his studies of the structure of white dwarfs, the bodies left after the collapse of a star. The research that led to his discovery of white dwarfs had been done while he was on a steamer from India to England. Philip Morrison, a professor of physics at the Massachusetts Institute of Technology said that Dr. Chandrasekhar's "mathematical insight and its elegance has been responsible for most of what we know about stars." Fortune magazine called him "the outstanding pure theorist of modern astronomy." He has been a recipient of number of awards, including the Royal Astronomical Society's Gold Medal in 1953, the Draper Award of the U.S. National Academy of Sciences in 1968, and the Padma Vibushan from the government of India. (*See also* Prominent Asian Americans.)

Dalip Singh Saund

Dalip Singh Saund was the first Asian Indian to be elected to Congress. Born in Punjab in 1899, he came to the United States in 1920 and became a successful farmer. Benefiting from the 1946 immigration law, he became a citizen in 1949 and was elected to the House of Representatives from the district covering California's Imperial and Riverside counties in 1957. He served on the House Committee on Foreign Relations and was reelected in 1960. A massive stroke in 1962 effectively terminated his political career; he died in 1973. (*See also* Prominent Asian Americans.)

Zubin Mehta

Zubin Mehta, former conductor and director of both the New York and the Los Angeles Philharmonic Orchestras, was born in Bombay in 1936, and came to United States in 1961. He studied music in Vienna, Canada, and the United States. He made his Metropolitan Opera debut on December 29, 1965, with a highly acclaimed performance of *Aida*. He won first prize in the Liverpool Conductors Competition in 1958, and was awarded the Padma Bhushan award by the government of India in 1976 for his contribution to the world of music, and for doing more to build bridges of understanding between East and West than almost any of his generation in India.

Ravi Shankar

Ravi Shankar, the Indian sitarist, is renowned for bringing Indian music to Western audiences. He was among the first musicians to study and compare eastern and Western classical music, and, in cooperation with Maestro Yehudi Menuhin, fuse the two. In 1966, he was invited to play at England's famous Bath Festival, where he was noticed by George Harrison, a member of the Beatles. Harrison was so entranced by Shankar's music that he became his disciple.

Ravi Shankar was born in India in 1920, and obtained his musical training from Ustad Allauddin Khan. He established Kinnara School of Music first in Bombay in 1962, and then in Los Angeles in 1967. He made several worldwide concert tours and won a number of awards, including the Silver Bear of Berlin (1962), Padma Bhushan(1967), International Music Council UNESCO Award (1975), and the Padma Vibhushan (1981).

Vijay Prabhakar

Dr. Vijay Prabhakar, now a consultant in Illinois, is an alumnus of Madras Medical College. He received his certificate in public health from California State University, Long Beach, in 1983. He then went to work for the Indian Health Service, a branch of the U.S. Department of Health and Human Services, which provides health care to Native American tribes. As Tribal Health Commissioner of the Wisconsin Winnebagos, Dr. Prabhakar developed innovative methods, procedures, and health-care delivery systems. He was also praised for his heroism during a time of political unrest in the Winnebago Nation in 1991, which saved lives, health, and property.

In addition to the highest Public Health Service Award, Prabhakar has several honors to his credit, including the University of Illinois Chancellor's Student Service Award (1986), The United Life Foundation Award for outstanding community health (1987), State of Wisconsin's Governor's Commendation (1989), Wisconsin State Senate Citation (1989), Traditional Winnebago Chief Honors with Indian Name and Eagle Feather (1990), National Honor Delta Omega Society Induction (1991), IHS Savings Award (1992), and American Indian Training Institute's National Health Administrator of the Year Award (1992).

References

Abraham, T. *Indian American Community: A Perspective*, 1993.

Asian Americans and Pacific Islanders in Philanthropy. *Invisible and In Need: Philanthropic Giving to Asian Americans and Pacific Islanders*. San Francisco: AAPIP, 1992.

Asiatic Exclusion League. "The Hindoo Question in California." In *Proceedings*, 1908.

Bachu, A. "Socioeconomic, Demographic, and Linguistic Characteristics of Asian Indian Migrants in the United States." Paper presented at the annual meeting of the Mid-Atlantic Region of the Association for Asian Studies. Philadelphia: University of Pennsylvania, (October 28-31, 1983).

Cain, B. E., D. R. Kiewiet, and C. Uhlaner. "The Political Impact of California's Minorities." Paper prepared for the Western Political Science Association. Eugene, Oregon, March 22, 1986.

Chandrasekhar, S. *From India to America*. La Jolla: Population Review Publications, 1982.

Chua-Eoan, H. G. "Strangers in Paradise." *Time*, April 9, 1990.

Daniels, R. *History of Indian Immigration to the United States*. New York: The Asia Society, 1989.

Fisher, M. P. *The Indians of New York City*. New Delhi: Heritage Publishers, 1980.

Fornaro, R. J. "Asian-Indians in America: Acculturation and Minority Status." *Migration Today* 12, no. 3 (1984): 29-32.

Gall, S. B., and T. L. Gall, eds. *A Statistical Record of Asian-Americans*. Detroit: Gale Research Inc., 1993.

Hess, G. "The Asian Indian Immigrants in the U.S.: the Early Phase, 1900-1965." *From India to America*, edited by S. Chandrasekhar. La Jolla: Population Review Books, 1976.

Hing, B. O. *Making and Remaking Asian America through Immigration Policy, 1850-1990*. Stanford: Stanford University Press, 1993.

Institute of International Education. *Open Doors 1992-1993: Report on International Educational Exchange*. New York: IIE, 1993.

Jensen, J. M. *Passage from India: Asian Indian Immigrants in North America*. New Haven: Yale University Press, 1993.

Karnow, S. N. Yoshihara. *Asian Americans in Transition*. New York: The Asia Society, 1992.

Khorana, M. G. "Break Your Silence." *Library Trends* 41, no. 3 (January 1993): 393.

La Chung. "SF Includes Asian Indians in Minority Law." *San Francisco Chronicle* (June 25, 1991): A14.

Lane, M. B. "Group Gets Heave-Ho as a Minority." *Plain Dealer* (December 22, 1993): 7B.

La Noune, G. R. "Immigration Undermines Support for Affirmative Action." *Oakland Post* 30, no. 47 (November 10, 1993): 4.

Lee, E. "Silicon Valley Study Finds Asian Americans Hitting the Glass Ceiling." *Asia Week* (October 8, 1993): 21.

Leonard, K. "Punjabi Farmers and California's Alien Land Law." *Agricultural History* 59, no. 4 (October 1985): 549-562.

Lim, G. "Asian Indians Recognized as Legitimate Minority in Ohio." *Asia Week* 14, no. 22 (1993): 3.

Lorch, D. "An Ethnic Road to Riches: The Immigrant Job Specialty." *New York Times* (January 12, 1992): 1.

Mahajan, R. "Self-serving and Redundant: A Student's Perspective of Indian Studies in the U.S." *India Currents* 7, no. 3 (1993): 7.

Mazumdar, S. "South Asians in the United States with a Focus on Asian Indians." In *UCLA Asian American Studies Center: The State of Asian Pacific America*, 1993; 283-301.

Nakanishi, D. "The UCLA Asian Pacific American Voter Registration Study." Report sponsored by the Asian/Pacific American Legal Center of Los Angeles, UCLA Graduate School of Education, 1986.

Ranganathan, M. "NAACP to Protest Discrimination Against Engineer." *News India* (November 12, 1993): 3.

Riche, M. F. "We're All Minorities Now." *American Demographics* (October 1991): 26.

Rothenberg, S. and W. McGurn. "The Invisible Success Story: Asian Americans and Politics." *National Review* (September 15, 1989): 43.

Saran, P. *The Asian Indian Experience in the United States.* Cambridge: Schenkman, 1985.

———. "Asian Indians in the United States." *Dictionary of Asian American History,* edited by H. Kim. Westport, Connecticut: Greenwood Press, 1986.

Saran, P. and E. Eames. *The New Ethnics: Asian Indians in the United States.* New York: Praeger, 1980.

Singh, G. "East Indians in the United States." *Sociology and Social Research* 30 (January-February, 1946): 208-216.

Sue, S. and J. Abe. *Predictors of Academic Achievement among Asian American and White Students.* New York: College Entrance Examination Board, 1988.

Takaki, R. *Strangers from a Different Shore.* Boston: Little, Brownand Company, 1989.

Tilove, J. "Immigration is Undoing Blacks' Job Gains." *Plain Dealer* (December 19, 1993): 25A.

Uhlaner, C., B. E. Cain, and D. R. Kiewiet. "Political Participation of Ethnic Minorities in the 1980s." *Political Behavior* 11, no.3 (September 1989): 195-231.

U.S. Commission on Civil Rights. *Civil Rights Issues Facing Asian Americans in the 1990's* (February).

U.S. Department of Commerce. Bureau of the Census. *Asian and Pacific Islander Population in the United States: 1980.* PC80-2-1E. Washington, D.C., 1988.

U.S. Department of Commerce. Bureau of the Census. *Asians and Pacific Islanders in the United States: 1990 Census of Population.* 1990CP-3-5. Washington, D.C., 1993.

U.S. Department of Commerce. Bureau of the Census. *The Asian and Pacific Islander Population in the United States: March 1991 and 1990.* by C. E. Bennett. Washington, D.C., 1992.

University of California. Asian American Studies Center. "The State of Asian Pacific America: A Public Policy Report." Los Angeles: Asian Pacific American Public Policy Institute, 1993.

Waldrop, J. and L. Jacobsen. "American Affluence." *American Demographics* (December 1992): 29.

Wherry, E. M. "Hindu Immigrants in America." *Missionary Review of the World* (December 1907): 918-919.

—*Kamla Motihar*
Director
Andrew W. Mellon Foundation Library

3

Who Are the Cambodian Americans?

◆ Overview ◆ History ◆ Assimilation and Acculturation ◆ Language
◆ Family and Community Dynamics ◆ Religion ◆ Employment and Economic Traditions
◆ Politics and Government ◆ Health and Mental Health Issues ◆ Notable Cambodian Americans
◆ Media ◆ Organizations and Associations

◆ OVERVIEW

Cambodia is a country of about 10,000,000 people, slightly smaller in size than the state of Oklahoma, located in Southeast Asia. It is bordered on the west and northwest by Thailand, on the north by Laos, on the east by the southern part of Vietnam, and on the south by the Gulf of Thailand. The climate is tropical, with monsoon rains from May to October and a dry season from December to March. There is little variation in temperature, which is hot most of the year. There are mountains in the southwest and north, but most of the country consists of low, flat plains. Three-quarters of the land are covered with forests and woodland, and much of the land is cultivated with rice paddies. Cambodia has few roads and bridges, and many of the existing roads and bridges are in poor condition due to years of war and political upheaval. Aside from rice, the main crop, Cambodia also produces rubber and corn.

The Cambodian people and their language are also known as "Khmer," a term that is much closer to their own word for themselves. About 90 percent of the people in Cambodia are ethnic Cambodians, or Khmer, 5 percent are Vietnamese, 1 percent are Chinese, and 4 percent belong to a variety of other ethnic groups. Most Cambodians are wet-rice farmers in their ancestral land. Ninety percent of them live in the countryside and live by subsistence farming. It is estimated that about 48 percent of Cambodian men and about 22 percent of Cambodian women can read and write. Cambodia is an overwhelmingly Buddhist country: 95 percent

of the population practice Theravada Buddhism, the type of Buddhism found in many of the countries in southern Asia. Other faiths include Mahayana Buddhism, the type of Buddhism found most often in northern parts of Asia, and tribal animistic religions. In recent years there have been a few converts to Christianity. The flag of Cambodia is blue with a white map of the country in the center.

◆ HISTORY

Before 1975, there were almost no people of Cambodian ancestry in the United States. They have settled in the U.S. as a result of the tragic events in their native country that followed the war in Indochina (the Vietnam War) in which the United States was deeply involved. Because Cambodian Americans are such a new part of this country, their history is especially important to them, and it is especially helpful to know something of Cambodian history in order to appreciate Cambodian culture and the unique situation of this ethnic group.

Origins

Cambodia is an ancient country with a long history that has been a source of pride and pain to the Cambodian people. The Cambodians probably lived originally in western China, but they migrated down the Mekong River valley into Indochina sometime before the common era. In Indochina, they came into contact with highly developed civilizations that had been heavily influenced by the culture of ancient India. From these civilizations, they took the religions of Hinduism and Buddhism and the idea of divine kingship. These religious and political ideas became the basis of the early Cambodian state. They also developed a sophisticated system of reservoirs and canals for irrigation, which relied on the power of the god-king to organize large numbers of people to build massive public works.

The greatest period in Cambodian history is known as the Angkorean period, after the huge complex of temples in northwestern Cambodia known as Angkor Wat, which literally means "city-temple." Most scholars place the Angkorean period as having lasted from about 802 to about 1431 A.D. During much of this time, Cambodia, or "Kambuja-Desa," as it is called in old inscriptions, was the most powerful kingdom in Southeast Asia, governing great expanses of territory that are now part of Thailand and southern Vietnam, as well as the land that remains a part of Cambodia today.

By the end of the Angkorean era, the kingdom of Kambuja-Desa came under increased pressure from the Siamese (Thai) on the west and the Vietnamese on the east. The ability of the royal bureaucracy to manage the complex irrigation system may also have weakened. Gradually, the capital and center of the kingdom shifted from Angkor Wat to Phnom Penh, which remains the capital today. Trade had become more important for the Cambodians, and Phnom Penh was located where the Mekong River and the Tonle Sap come together, an easier location from which to control trade from Laos and China.

From the 1400s on, the Cambodians lost territory to both the Siamese and the Vietnamese. By the 1800s, Cambodia had fallen almost entirely under the control of Vietnam and Siam, and Cambodia was sealed off from the outside influences that were beginning to affect other Southeast Asian countries. Vietnam, however, suffered from troubles of its own, since it had been split into northern and southern halves by rival ruling families. In 1788, the leader of a peasant rebellion managed to reunify Vietnam. One of the Vietnamese contenders for the throne, from the southern Nguyen family, sought help from the French, who, having entered Indochina, gradually established a colonial empire that became known as "French Indochina." In 1859, French Emperor Napoleon III sent troops to Vietnam. After four years, Cambodia became a French protectorate.

Cambodia Under the French

King Norodom, the King of Cambodia at the time the French established control, appears to have seen French protection as a way of keeping his neighbors at bay and perhaps also as a help in defeating the numerous revolts against him by his own subjects. However,

France gradually tightened its control over Cambodian political life. In 1904, Norodom died and the French made his half-brother Sisowath king. Sisowath and the two kings who followed him were all hand-picked and placed in office by French officials.

While there was a steady growth of Cambodian nationalism, the country remained at peace through the early part of the twentieth century. When World War II broke out and France was occupied by Germany, the French remained in control in Indochina, with the agreement of Germany's allies in Asia, the Japanese. In 1941, Monivong, the king who had followed Sisowath, died, and the French made Monivong's grandson, Norodom Sihanouk, king. Sihanouk was only 19 years of age at the time. Although he was highly intelligent, artistically talented, and apparently sincere in wanting to be a good ruler, Sihanouk had had no training for the throne and relied heavily on his French advisors in the early years of his rule.

Sihanouk was to dominate Cambodian history for most of the half-century following his coronation. He also developed from a client of the French into a determined, if cautious, adherent to the cause of Cambodian independence. The victory of Japanese troops over the allies provided many Asian colonies with evidence that the European colonists could be defeated. Anti-French feelings intensified in Cambodia when the French attempted, in the 1940s, to replace the traditional writing system with a system based on the letters used by Europeans. In 1945, Japanese troops disarmed the French forces in Cambodia. Sihanouk, in the first of many changes in alliance, promised cooperation with the Japanese, changed the name of the country to "Kampuchea," and declared independence from France.

The French reestablished themselves in Cambodia after the defeat of Japan, but their power had been seriously weakened. Nationalist feelings continued to grow stronger in Cambodia. In France, some young Cambodian students, influenced by the French Communist Party, began to formulate ideas that combined extreme nationalism with Communist ideology. One of these students was Saloth Sar, who later became known as Pol Pot, the leader of the Khmer Rouge. All nationalists looked back to the time of Angkor Wat as a symbol and ideal of Cambodian greatness.

By 1953, the war in neighboring Vietnam was becoming a problem for the French, and it was unpopular in France. Sihanouk's resistance to colonial rule and the prospect of fighting another full-scale war in Cambodia led France to grant Cambodia independence in 1953, but France retained much control over the Cambodian economy. In 1954, after the French had failed to reimpose their rule on Vietnam, delegates to the Geneva Conference agreed that elections would be held in all three of the countries of Indochina. In order to participate in the elections, Sihanouk abdicated his throne and was elected to the highest office in the country.

Sihanouk managed to keep his country neutral during many of the long years of war that raged in Vietnam and Laos. He was also, however, intolerant of Cambodian leftists, whom he labeled the "Khmer Rouge," or "Red Khmer," and many of these leftists fled into the countryside.

Cambodia, the Vietnam War, and the United States

The United States became involved in Southeast Asia to preserve a non-Communist regime in South Vietnam. In Laos, Cambodia's northern neighbor, there was something of an extension of the Vietnam war in the 1960s, in the form of a war between Lao guerilla forces allied with North Vietnam and the Royal government of Laos, which was pro-United States. The policies of Prince Sihanouk were primarily aimed at keeping Cambodia out of these wars and, until about 1970, he was largely successful. His constant attempts to play the different sides in the Vietnam conflict against each other, though, resulted in hostility toward him by the pro-United States governments of Thailand and South Vietnam and in a suspicious attitude toward him on the part of the United States. By 1966, Sihanouk had forged a secret alliance with North Vietnam because he felt certain that the Vietnamese Communists would win the war and because the North Vietnamese agreed, under the treaty, to respect the borders of Cambodia, to leave Cambodian civilians alone, and to avoid conflicts with the Cambodian army.

War in the surrounding countries undermined the economy of Cambodia and threatened to spill across the border. In the secret treaty, Sihanouk agreed to allow the North Vietnamese to station troops inside of Cambodia and to receive weapons brought from China and North Vietnam through the port of Sihanoukville. South Vietnam and the United States, although they did not know about the secret treaty, were aware of the North Vietnamese troops.

In 1970, apparently with U.S. support, the Cambodian general Lon Nol staged a coup while Sihanouk was in China. This was after the United States had already begun the secret aerial bombing of North Vietnamese military sites in Cambodia, with devastating results. When the United States welcomed a more cooperative regime, the Vietnam War had finally overtaken Cambodia. In May, 1970, U.S. and South Vietnamese forces invaded eastern Cambodia, driving the North Vietnamese forces further into the country.

Sihanouk, now out of power, joined forces with the Khmer Rouge guerrillas. Having the prince on their side gave the Khmer Rouge an enormous advantage in drawing support from the peasants, many of whom still regarded Sihanouk as an almost divine figure. At the same time, U.S. aerial bombing in the Cambodian countryside, directed against both the North Vietnamese and the Khmer Rouge, caused enormous disruption of the traditional society. In the first half of 1973, before the U.S. Congress prohibited further bombing in Cambodia, U.S. planes dropped over one hundred thousand tons of bombs on the country.

It is difficult to say to what extent the extreme radicalism of the Khmer Rouge was due to the bombing, or to far-left Maoist ideas developed by Khmer Rouge leaders as students in France, or to the carrying out of these ideas by generally very young and uneducated peasant soldiers. However, the Khmer Rouge appears to have already been uncompromising and brutal in the areas it controlled even before it took control of the whole country. In April, 1975, with the U.S. having pulled its troops out of Vietnam and Saigon about to fall to the Vietnamese Communists, the Khmer Rouge marched into Phnom Penh.

Revolution and War

Democratic Kampuchea, as Cambodia was now called, became a bizarre experiment in revolutionary social change. In order to create a completely new society in which everyone would be equal, the Khmer Rouge, under the leadership of Pol Pot, ordered everyone, including the elderly and sick, out of the cities and towns of Cambodia and into the countryside. Family life, all traces of individualism, and all attachments to old institutions, including religion, were abolished. A new calendar for a new era was invented, with 1975 renamed "Year Zero." All Cambodians were put to work at agricultural labor in order to build up the agricultural surplus of the nation to finance rapid industrialization. In effect, these uncompromising ideals turned the entire country into a collection of forced labor camps, with young soldiers whose lives had consisted mainly of bitter warfare as guards.

Estimates of the number of people who died under Pol Pot's Democratic Kampuchean regime vary from one million to over four million. It is not clear how many people were actually executed by the Khmer Rouge and how many people died of starvation and poor living conditions, some of which may have been the after-effects of war and U.S. bombing. Still, the period from 1975 to 1979 was traumatic for all Cambodians. Cambodians in the United States and elsewhere tell of seeing close friends and family members being killed by the Khmer Rouge and of enduring great suffering.

Democratic Kampuchea, in addition to espousing an extreme form of socialism, was also committed to

extreme nationalism. The Khmer Rouge wanted to rec-
reate the greatness of Cambodia in the Angkorean
period, which meant retaking the areas that had
become parts of Vietnam and Thailand. Border skir-
mishes between Cambodian and Vietnamese forces led
Vietnam to invade Cambodia on Christmas Day in 1978,
and by early January the Vietnamese held Phnom Penh.
In the chaos of war, the rice crop went untended and
thousands of Cambodians, starving and freed from the
Khmer Rouge labor camps, began crossing the border
into Thailand. Television cameras brought the images
of these refugees into the homes of the U.S. public and
other Westerners, and immigration from Cambodia to
the United States began as a response to the "Cambodian refugee crisis."

Under pressure from the United States and other
nations, the Vietnamese pulled their troops out of Cambodia in 1989, leaving the Cambodian government they
had created in power. The United Nations sought to
create a coalition government, including this Vietnam-
ese-backed government, forces loyal to Sihanouk (who
had broken with the Khmer Rouge almost immediately
after they took power), and other factions. By 1993, a
government had been elected under Sihanouk as constitutional monarch and head of state. The Khmer
Rouge refused to take part in this election and continued to oppose the new government.

Immigration

Large numbers of immigrants from Cambodia have
come to the United States only since 1979, when the
U.S. refugee program began accepting Cambodians in
refugee camps in Thailand. Most of these arrived in the
early 1980s. Of the 118,823 foreign-born Cambodians
identified by the 1990 Census in the United States, only
16,880 (or about 14 percent) had arrived before 1980.
As thousands of refugees from Vietnam, Laos, and Cambodia began to come into the U.S. each year, the United
States developed organizational procedures for resettlement. Voluntary agencies (or VOLAGS), many of
which were affiliated with U.S. churches, had been set
up by 1975 to assist the first wave of Vietnamese refugees. These agencies had the task of finding sponsors,
individuals, or groups who would assume financial and
personal responsibility for refugee families for up to
two years. By the early 1980s, refugee camps had been
set up in various countries throughout Southeast Asia.
Most Cambodians stayed in refugee camps in Thailand,
but many who were being prepared for resettlement in
the United States were sent to camps in the Philippines
or elsewhere. Agencies under contract to the U.S.
Department of State organized classes to teach English
to familiarize refugees with language and culture of the
United States. In 1980 and 1981, 34,107 Cambodians

entered the United States. From 1982 to 1984, the influx
continued, with 36,082 Cambodians entering the U.S.
After that time, the numbers began to grow smaller. In
1985 and 1986, 19,921 Cambodians reached U.S. soil,
and from 1987 to 1990, only 11,843 Cambodians were
admitted. By the early 1990s, prospects of a political
settlement in Cambodia removed much of the perceived urgency of accepting Cambodian refugees, and
immigration from Cambodia to the United States
decreased to very small numbers.

Settlement

The 1990 U.S. Census found almost 150,000 Cambodian Americans in the United States, although those
active in working with Cambodian immigrants warn
that the Census may have undercounted this group,
since the Cambodians are so new to U.S. society and
many may not have responded to the Census. The largest concentration of Cambodian Americans is in California, where close to 70,000, or nearly half of the
people of Cambodian ethnicity, appear to have settled.
The largest Cambodian community was Long Beach,
California, where over 17,000, according to Census,
made their home. Again, however, Cambodian American spokespersons maintain that these estimates are
dramatically low and that the actual number of Cambodian Americans was probably closer to twice that
many. Nearby Los Angeles also had a significant population of Cambodians of at least 4,250. Stockton, California, had the second largest Cambodian community,
numbering at least 10,000. Outside of California, the
greatest number of Cambodian Americans were found
in Massachusetts, where over 14,000 lived. About half
of the Massachusetts Cambodians lived in the city of
Lowell. Other states with large Cambodian populations
include Texas (at least 6,000), Pennsylvania (at least
5,500, located mostly in Philadelphia),Virginia (at least
4,000), New York (at least 4,000, over two-thirds of
whom lived in New York City), Minnesota (at least
4,000), and Illinois (over 3,000). Despite their large
numbers, Cambodian Americans remained very much
newcomers and often strangers in their adopted country. Only about one in every five foreign-born Cambodians in the United States had become a naturalized U.S.
citizen by the early 1990s.

♦ ASSIMILATION AND ACCULTURATION

Cambodian Americans are members of one of the
youngest ethnic groups in U.S. society. According to
the 1990 Census, the median age of people of Cambodian ancestry in the U.S. was only 19.4, compared to
34.1 for other U.S. residents. Almost half of the Cambodian Americans counted in that Census year were

under 18 years of age. About 42 percent of these Cambodian Americans below the age of 18 were born in the United States; most of the others arrived between 1980 and 1986.

Cambodian Americans also live in larger families than other U.S residents. The average number of people in their families was 5.03, compared to an average of 3.06 in white U.S. families and 3.48 in African American families. Both the youth of Cambodian Americans and their large families indicate that, small though their numbers are, they will continue to grow as a proportion of U.S. society.

Adjusting to U.S. society has been difficult for most Cambodians, who come from rural areas and have few relevant job skills and little familiarity with mainstream U.S. culture. One of the difficulties has been the problem of differences between generations, between older people who see themselves as Cambodians and sometimes speak little, if any English, and younger people who have either been born in the United States or have no memory of Cambodia and consider themselves entirely American. According to Cambodian American scholar and activist Dr. Sam-Ang Sam, many Cambodian young people are plagued by identity problems, leading them to discard their Cambodian first names in favor of English first names, and they must often deal with racism from classmates and with being teased about their "foreignness." To help maintain a sense of ethnic identity, many Cambodian American Buddhist monks have set up classes in their native language for young people, and Cambodian language classes are offered by many Cambodian community organizations.

Cambodian Americans won the sympathy of many U.S. citizens in 1979 and in the early 1980s, when the plight of Cambodian refugees in Thailand became world news. Since their arrival in the U.S., though, some unfortunate stereotypes of Cambodians have developed. Because Cambodian culture places a high value on courtesy and indirectness, other U.S. citizens sometimes stereotype them as passive. Among older Cambodian Americans some of this appearance of passivity results from their unfamiliarity with the larger U.S. society. Employers who give Cambodian Americans a chance, however, usually find that they are extremely hard-working, conscientious,and eager to adapt and make their way under any circumstances.

Wedding Ceremonies

Traditional Cambodian wedding ceremonies are still held by Cambodian Americans, and even members of other ethnic groups who have married Cambodians have celebrated these ceremonies. Although in Cambodia marriages are often arranged, it is becoming common for Cambodian American young people to choose their own partners. The bride in a Cambodian wedding wears a *kben*, an ornate brocade dress. She also wears many bracelets, anklets, and necklaces. Grooms sometimes wear the traditional baggy pantaloons and jacket, but western-style suits are becoming common.

A procession will bring gifts of food and drink to the bride's home. At the beginning of the wedding, the couple sits at a table covered with flowers, fruit, candles, and sometimes with a sword to chase evil spirits away. Friends and relatives take turns standing up in front of the crowd to talk about the new couple. A Buddhist monk cuts a lock of hair from the bride and the groom and mixes the two locks together in a bowl to symbolize the sharing of their lives. Gifts, frequently in the form of envelopes with money in them, are offered to the couple by the guests. At the end of the wedding, the couple goes through the ritual known as *ptem*, in which knots are tied in a white string bracelet to represent the elders' blessing.

Cambodian Proverbs

Linguist Karen Fisher-Nguyen has observed that proverbs in Cambodia before 1975 were so important a means of educating the young that they could be found in almost all of the teaching materials of the public schools, and that studying proverbs was actually a part of the school curriculum. Many Cambodian Americans continue to treasure their proverbs as expressions of the traditional wisdom of their people. The sayings below reflect many of their values and ideals:

> The new rice stalk stands erect; the old stalk, full of grain, leans over.
>
> Travel on a river by following its bends, live in a country by following its customs.
>
> The small boat should not try to be a big boat.
>
> Don't let an angry man wash your dishes; don't let a hungry man guard your rice.
>
> Drop by drop, the vessel will fill; pour it, and everything will spill.
>
> Men have words; elephants have tusks.
>
> If you don't take your wife's advice, you'll have no rice seed next year.
>
> Don't rush to dump your rain water when you hear the sound of thunder.
>
> Losing money is better than wasting words.

♦ LANGUAGE

Cambodian, or Khmer, is classified by linguists as an Austro-Asiatic language, related to Vietnamese, Mon (a language spoken in Burma and western Thailand), and various tribal languages of Southeast Asia. Although many major Asian languages, including Vietnamese, are tonal languages, Cambodian is not tonal: As in the European languages, tones of voice may indicate emotion, but they do not change the meanings of words. The Cambodian alphabet, which has 47 letters, is derived from the alphabet of ancient India, and it is similar to the Thai and Laotian alphabets, as the Thai and Lao people borrowed their systems of writing from the Cambodians.

Cambodian Greetings and Phrases

Cambodian has many sounds that are quite different from those of English, and these are represented by the letters of the Cambodian alphabet. Linguists usually use a phonetic alphabet to write these sounds in the characters used by English and other European languages, but the phrases below are written in a fashion that should provide nonspecialist speakers of American English with a fairly close approximation to their actual pronunciation: *Jum-ree-up soouh*—Good Day or Greetings; *Loak sohk suh-bye jeeuh tay?*—Are you well, sir?; *Loak-srey sohk suh-bye jeeuh tay?*—Are you well, madame?; *Baht, knyom sohk suh-bye jeeuh tay*—I'm fine (from a man); *Jah, knyom sohk suh-bye jeeuh tay*—I'm fine (from a woman); *Aw-khoon juhrun*—Thank you very much; *Sohm toh*—Excuse me, or I'm sorry; *Meun uh-wye tay*—Don't mention it, or you're welcome; *Teuh nah?*—Where are you going?; *Niyeh piesah anglay bahn tay?*—Can you speak English?; *Sdap bahn tay*—Do you understand?; *Sdap bahn*—I understand; *Sdap meun bahn*—I don't understand; *Sohm lee-uh haee*—Good-bye.

Literature

Much of the early literature of Cambodia is written in Sanscrit and known by modern scholars primarily from inscriptions on temples and other public buildings. Classical Cambodian literature is based on Indian models, and the *Reamker*, a Cambodian version of the Indian poem the *Ramayana*, is probably the most important piece of classical Cambodian literature. The *Reamker* is still known by Cambodians today. In the years before 1975, episodes from this poem were often acted out by dancers in the royal court or by villagers in village festivals. A collection of aphorisms, known as the *Chbab* (or "laws"), exists in both written and oral literature. Until recently, children were required to memorize the *Chbab* in school.Similar to the *Chbab* are the *Kotilok* (or "Art of Good Conduct"), which are fables designed to teach moral lessons.

European literary forms, such as novels, had taken root in Cambodia by the 1970s, but almost no literature was produced under the Khmer Rouge, and many intellectuals were killed during the Khmer Rouge regime. Since 1979, suffering under the Khmer Rouge has been a major theme in Cambodian literature, both in Cambodia and abroad. Among Cambodian Americans, also, the urge to bear witness to the horrors of the years from 1975 to 1979 has inspired most writing, and as a result, the autobiography is the most commonly employed literary form. Many of these Cambodian American authors have taken coauthors, but some, such as Someth May (see *Sources for Additional Study*), have mastered English sufficiently to write solely authored works.

♦ FAMILY AND COMMUNITY DYNAMICS

The family is extremely important to Cambodian Americans, in part because so many of them lost family members in their previous countries. They tend to have very large families. Children—especially young children—are treasured, and parents treat them with a great deal of affection. Despite the importance of family for Cambodian Americans, they have relatively high numbers of households headed by a single, female parent: In 1990 about 20 percent of Cambodian American households were headed by women, a factor that contributes to their poverty. This high proportion of female-headed households does not appear to be primarily the result of divorce, but rather of the fact that women outnumber men in the Cambodian population, due to years of war.

In Cambodia, men are generally more highly valued than women, although there is a much greater equality of men and women than in many other traditional societies, and the advice and opinions of women are highly regarded. Only men can occupy the prestigious status of the Buddhist monk. Insofar as education is made available to people in the Asian homeland, it is education primarily for men. The ideal woman is someone who is obedient to her husband, shows practical intelligence for taking care of household business and advising her husband in making decisions, and knows how to cook, wash clothes, and care for babies. In the refugee camps many Cambodian women had their first taste of formal education. In the U.S., young Cambodian American women are pursuing their educations in large numbers, and they have often become important as breadwinners for their families.

Interaction with Other Ethnic Minorities

Because Cambodian Americans have settled most often in urban areas, they have frequent contacts with disadvantaged members of other minority groups. Often these contacts are troubled by cultural misunderstandings and by the social problems frequently found in poor communities. In some areas where there are large Cambodian communities, Cambodian youth gangs have developed, in part as a matter of self-protection. Older Cambodians often see that they have much in common with their poor Asian, black, and Hispanic neighbors and will frequently distinguish these areas of "poor people" from the comfortable middle-class neighborhoods of the "Americans." Most Cambodian Americans are fairly dark-skinned and they are acutely aware of prejudice in America. They sometimes internalize this prejudice and express feelings of inadequacy because of it.

It has been noted that Cambodian Americans in Texas have frequent contacts with Mexicans or Mexican Americans, and that the members of the two ethnic groups accommodate one another easily. Cambodians may frequently be found as participants in Mexican American weekend markets, and many Cambodians in Texas have learned Spanish and follow Mexican customs in interacting with their Spanish-speaking peers.

Cambodian Music and Dance

Music is important to traditional Cambodian culture, and Cambodian Americans put a great deal of effort into maintaining this link with their heritage. Traditional music ensembles perform in almost all large Cambodian communities in the United States. There are six types of music ensembles, but the type known as *areak ka* is considered the most traditional and is used for popular religious ceremonies and wedding ceremonies. The instruments used in the *areak ka* ensemble are a three-stringed fiddle, a type of monochord, a long-necked lute, and goblet-drums. Other instruments that may be found in Cambodian ensembles include a quadruple-reed oboe, several types of gongs, a large barrel drum, a flute, a two-stringed fiddle, a three-stringed zither, hammered dulcimers, cymbals, and the xylophone. Although Cambodian music may sound somewhat strange at first to those who are unfamiliar with Asian music, most people of other ethnic backgrounds find, after a little exposure, that they can appreciate and enjoy this ancient yet vibrant art.

The best known Cambodian dance is called the "masked dance," because the dancers wear the masks of the characters they portray. The masked dance always tells the story of the *Ramayana*, an epic that the Cambodians took from ancient India. All parts in the masked dance, even those of women, are played by men. Cambodian classical ballet, or "court dance," on the other hand, has traditionally been danced by women, although men have been entering classical ballet since the 1950s. There are a number of Cambodian dancers in the United States, and the art of dance is also beginning to revive in Cambodia. Bringing this

part of the culture back to life, however, is difficult, since an estimated 90 percent of all trained dancers died during the Khmer Rouge regime.

Holidays Celebrated by Cambodian Americans

The most important Cambodian holiday, and the one celebrated most often in Cambodian America communities is the New Year, or *Chaul Chnam*. The New Year's celebration is usually held in mid-April and it lasts for three days. Many parties and dances are held during these three days, and traditional Cambodian music is usually heard at these events, although U.S. popular music has also become part of these celebrations. One New Year's tradition that many Cambodian Americans still observe is that of the game of *bos chhoung*. In this game, young men and women stand facing each other, about five feet apart. A young man takes a scarf rolled into a ball and throws it at a young woman in whom he is interested. She must catch the scarf, and if she misses it, she must sing and dance for him. If she catches the scarf, she will throw it back to him. If he misses it, he must do the singing and dancing. For Buddhist Cambodians, the New Year Festival is an important time to visit the temple to pray, meditate, and plan for the coming year.

♦ RELIGION

Buddhism is the traditional religion of Cambodia. Before 1975, the ruler of the country was the official protector of the religion and the monks were organized into a hierarchy overseen by the government. Monasteries and temples were found in all villages, and monks played an important role in the education of children and in passing on Cambodian culture. The people also supported their local monasteries, through gifts and by giving food to monks. Monks were forbidden to handle money and had to show humility by begging for their food. Every morning, the monks would go from house to house, with their eyes downcast, holding out their begging bowls into which the lay people would spoon rice. Although the religion was attacked by the radical Khmer Rouge during their regime and many monks were killed, the vast majority of Cambodians remain Buddhists and the faith remains an important part of the national culture.

Buddhism is divided into two schools of thought. The "Northern School," known as Mahayana Buddhism, is found most often in China, Japan, Tibet, Korea, and Vietnam. The "Southern School," called Theravada Buddhism, predominates in Laos, Thailand, Cambodia, Burma, and Sri Lanka. Theravada Buddhists stress the importance of becoming a monk and achieving Nirvana, a state in which there is no self or rebirth, through one's own efforts. Mahayana Buddhists lay more emphasis on help from Bodhisattvas, enlightened beings who have delayed achieving Nirvana in order to help others become enlightened.

The essence of the Buddhist faith is the belief that all worldly things are changing and impermanent. Those who are not aware of the impermanent nature of the world become attached to worldly things, and this leads to suffering. The suffering will continue as the soul goes through a cycle of rebirths, continually drawn back to worldly desires. Meditation and a moral, disciplined life can enable a believer to overcome desires. The soul that successfully overcomes all desires may reach Nirvana.

The law of Karma ("*Kam*" in the Cambodian language) controls life and rebirth. This law may be seen as a kind of spiritual accounting: good deeds, or "merit," help the soul to be reborn inbetter circumstances and to earn rewards in the present life; bad deeds cause the soul to be reborn in worse circumstances and can bring about bad luck. For these reasons, "making merit" is a central part of religion for Cambodians. Cambodian Buddhists see making merit as more than simply piling up spiritual credits by performing good works. Correct behavior and merit-making activities such as attending religious ceremonies or donating money to temples and food to monks are seen as upholding the order of the universe. These beliefs have often led Cambodians to wonder if the sufferings of their people might be due to some collective fault of the nation.

Some Cambodian Americans have converted to Christianity, either in the refugee camps, or after arriving in the United States. Often these conversions have been the result of spiritual crises brought about by the tragedies of recent Cambodian history. In many cases, people felt that Buddhism had somehow failed because of the death and destruction that had occurred in their country. In other cases, Christianity has seemed attractive because it is the religion of the majority of U.S. citizens, and conversion has seemed a good way to conform to U.S. society and to express gratitude to the religious organizations that played an important part in resettling refugees in the United States.

The majority of Cambodian Americans, however, continue the practice of their traditional religion. As more of them have settled in this country, and as they have established their own communities, observing their religious rituals has become easier. In 1979, there were only three Cambodian temples in the United States. By the early 1990s, more than 50 of these temples had been established in Cambodian communities throughout the U.S. Even in those communities in which no temples exist, living around other Cambodian Americans has made it possible for Buddhists to observe their rites in private homes or in community halls and other meeting places. Monasteries, or places where Buddhist monks live, are usually attached to the temples, or places of worship, and the monks are in charge of the temples and the religious rituals held in them. Most U.S. Buddhist temples are in houses or apartments, but there are some more traditionally styled temples, such as the large temple-monastery complex in Maryland.

♦ EMPLOYMENT AND ECONOMIC TRADITIONS

Adapting to the U.S. economy has been difficult for many people of Cambodian ancestry in the United States. Most of them were farmers in their previous country, and in the U.S. they have generally been settled in cities. They have high rates of unemployment and the jobs found by first-generation Cambodian Americans are most often low-paying jobs in service and manual labor occupations.

Cambodian Americans are, for the most part, a poor group. According to the 1990 U.S. Census, 42 percent of the families of Cambodian ethnicity were living below the poverty level and 51 percent of all Cambodian households rely on public assistance income. The median household income of Cambodian Americans in 1990 was only $18,837, compared to $30,056 for U.S. citizens in general. Cambodian Americans have a high rate of unemployment: About 10 percent of those in the labor force in 1990 were unemployed. This high rate of unemployment is largely a result of having arrived in this country so recently. If rates of unemployment are examined by years of arrival, it is clear that the longer Cambodian Americans have been in the United States, the higher the probability they will be employed. Nearly 17 percent of Cambodians in the labor force who arrived in the U.S between 1987 and 1990 were unemployed in 1990. Among those who arrived in 1985 or 1986, though, only about 12 percent were unemployed. Among Cambodians who arrived between 1982 and 1984, the percentage of unemployed in the labor force dropped to 11 percent. Only about 9 percent of those who arrived in 1980 and 1981 and only about 7 percent of those who arrived before 1980 were unemployed. These figures provide evidence for a trait noticed by many familiar with Cambodians in the U.S.: their eagerness to find work, even low-paying work, as soon as they have acquired sufficient language skills and familiarity with U.S. society.

Lack of formal education is a serious handicap for Cambodian Americans. Census statistics show that about 53 percent of Cambodian American men have a sixth grade education or less and 90 percent have less than 12 years of schooling. Women are faced with even more serious difficulties, since 66 percent of them have sixth grade educations or less and 95 percent have completed less than 12 years of schooling. Even when Cambodian Americans are from highly educated backgrounds, however, they often find that their educations are not relevant to the U.S. workplace, and they are handicapped by their language skills. The author Someth May, for example, worked before the publication of his book as a janitor, despite his elite background in his home country. Despite the limited educations of their parents, however, Cambodian American young people often do quite well in school and show themselves dedicated to acquiring more education. Only about 6 percent of Cambodian Americans between the ages of 16 and 19 are high-school dropouts, compared to about 10 percent of white Americans and about 14 percent of African Americans in the same age group.

♦ POLITICS AND GOVERNMENT

Most Cambodian Americans are concerned with questions of survival in the new country and are not actively involved in U.S. politics. They remain keenly interested in the reconstruction of their native country, and some Cambodian American organizations, such as the Cambodian Network Council (see below) are contributing to the rebuilding of Cambodia by sending trained Cambodian Americans and people of other ethnicities to Cambodia as volunteers.

♦ HEALTH AND MENTAL HEALTH ISSUES

In addition to the health problems faced by other poor groups in the United States, Cambodian Americans face special mental and physical health problems resulting from their tragic recent history. Almost all lived under the extreme brutality of the Khmer Rouge regime that ruled the country from 1975 to 1979, and their native country was in a state of war both before and since. Almost all, also, spent time living in refugee camps in Thailand or other Southeast Asian countries. Health professionals and others who work with Cambodian Americans often note that these experiences have left Cambodians with a sense of powerlessness that affects many even in America. Physical ailments often result from the emotional anguish they have suffered and continue to suffer. Among those who have been resettled in all Western countries there has appeared a strange malady often referred to as the "Pol Pot syndrome," after the leader of the Khmer Rouge. The "Pol Pot syndrome" includes insomnia, difficulty in breathing, loss of appetite, and pains in various parts of the body.

The stress that has led to such illnesses often tends to create a low general level of health for Cambodian Americans. In the entry on "Khmer" in *Refugees in the United States: A Reference Handbook*, May M. Ebihara reports that 84 percent of Cambodian households in California have reported that at least one household member was under the care of a medical doctor, compared to 45 percent of Vietnamese households and 24 percent of Hmong and Lao households. The syndrome known as "post traumatic stress disorder," a type of delayed reaction to extreme emotional stress that has been found to affect many Vietnam veterans, is also common among Cambodian refugees in the United States and other countries.

Traditional Cambodian healers, known as *krou Khmer*, may be found in many Cambodian American communities. Some of the techniques used by these healers are massages, "coining," and treatment with herbal medicines. "Coining," or *koh khchal*, is a method of using a coin dipped in kerosene to apply pressure to strategic points of the body. Many Western doctors believe that this actually can be an effective means of pain relief. Coining does leave bruise marks, however, and these can alarm medical personnel and others not familiar with this practice.

♦ NOTABLE CAMBODIAN AMERICANS

Cambodian Americans are beginning to make their marks in American society. Some notable examples follow:

Activism

Maha Ghosananda is a Buddhist monk who lives in Rhode Island, but frequently travels to Cambodia. Founder and Director of the Khmer Society of New England, he is one of the world's most prominent peace activists and has organized two marches for peace in Cambodia. He has also been nominated for the Nobel Peace Prize.

Vora Kanthoul is an authority on contemporary Cambodian issues and an influential figure in the Cambodian American community. He is Executive Director of the United Cambodian Community and teaches comparative world cultures at Long Beach City College. He studied in France, Russia, and Taiwan, and earned a Cambodian law degree in Phnom Penh and a Master's degree in political science from Southern Illinois University at Carbondale. From 1973 to 1975 he served in the Cambodian Foreign Service. In 1983 he served as Minister and Counselor of Cambodia's permanent mission to the United Nations.

Film

Haing Ngor is among the most famous Cambodian Americans. He is best known for his portrayal of the Cambodian interpreter and journalist Dith Pran in the film, *The Killing Fields*, for which Ngor won an Academy Award. Born in rural Cambodia, he worked his way through medical school and became an obstetrician and surgeon in Phnom Penh. After the Khmer Rouge takeover in 1975, his family was killed by Khmer Rouge execution squads. He escaped to Thailand in 1979 and came in to the U.S. in 1980.

See also Prominent Asian Americans

Journalism

Dith Pran, the subject of the film *The Killing Fields*, now works as a photographer in New York. Before 1975 in Cambodia, he worked as assistant and interpreter for *New York Times* correspondent Sydney Schanberg. When Pran's family escaped from Cambodia on the eve of the Khmer Rouge takeover, Pran stayed behind to help Schanberg, saving Schanberg and other journalists from execution. However, while Western journalists were able to leave, Pran himself was trapped in Cambodia under the Khmer Rouge from 1975 to 1979, when he escaped to Thailand, where he and Sydney Schanberg were reunited.

See also Prominent Asian Americans

Academia

Im Proum is a prominent linguist who currently lives in Fairfax, Virginia. He formerly taught at Cornell University, in New York State, where he coauthored several of the standard texts on the Cambodian language with Dr. Franklin Huffmann.

Sam Ang-Sam is a scholar, musician, and activist. He studied music at the University of Fine Arts in Phnom Penh and afterward continued his studies in the United States, where he received a Ph.D. in ethnomusicology from Wesleyan University. He later served on the faculty at the University of Washington in Seattle. He is currently director of the Cambodian Network Council in Washington, D.C., and travels around the world performing and teaching about Cambodian music.

Chinary Ung is a scholar and musician who lives in Tempe, Arizona, and teaches about Cambodian culture at Arizona State University. As a musician, Dr. Ung specializes in playing the Cambodian xylophone.

◆ MEDIA

Print

Because Cambodian Americans are still establishing themselves in this country, and because many Cambodian Americans still have limited levels of formal education, national Cambodian publications have not yet appeared on the U.S. scene. Educational materials, such as bilingual texts for Cambodian Americans, are available from the Folsom Cordova School District, 2460 Cordova Lane, Rancho Cordova, California 95670. Telephone: (916) 635-6815. Contact: Ms. Judy Lewis.

◆ ORGANIZATIONS AND ASSOCIATIONS

Cambodian Americans have formed a wide variety of organizations during the short time they have been a part of U.S. society. Most of these exist to help newly arrived Cambodians adjust to U.S. society, but they also provide information about Cambodian American culture, business, and other aspects of Cambodian life in this country.

Art of Apsara

2338 E. Anaheim, Ste. 105
Long Beach, CA 90804
(310) 438-3932
Mon Duch, director

Encourages the development and exhibition of contemporary Cambodian art. Runs a gallery in Long Beach, open to the general public.

Cambodian Network Council (CNC)

713 D St.
Washington, DC
(202) 546-9144
Dr. Sam-Ang Sam, contact

The primary national organization of Cambodians in the United States, this is an umbrella organization that seeks to facilitate communication among local Cambodian organizations, to help set up new local organizations, and to build coalitions. The CNC hosts an annual convention of Cambodian American associations. It also maintains a data bank of Cambodian American professionals and runs an international program sending volunteers to Cambodia to help in rebuilding the country.

United Cambodian Council (UCC)

2338 E. Anaheim, Ste. 200
Long Beach, CA 90804
(310) 433-2490

The largest Cambodian agency in the United States, the United Cambodian Council is located in Long Beach, the site of America's largest Cambodian community. Organized in 1977 by a group of Cambodian intellectuals to serve the needs of the Cambodians in Long Beach, the agency now helps anyone who needs its services. Although most of its clients are Southeast Asians, it assists low-income U.S. residents of all ethnicities. In addition to theemployment and language training generally offered by Cambodian service organizations, the UCC is a partner with St. Mary's Church in the Long Beach Southeast Asian Health Project, which provides a wide variety of health services and information. Mr. Vora Kanthoul, executive director.

Cambodian Family

1111 E. Wakeham Ave., Ste. D
Santa Ana, CA 92705
(714) 542-2907
Rivka Hirsch, director

Serves Cambodian Americans in the Santa Ana area. Offers English language training to Cambodian refugees, provides help in finding employment, gives classes in health education and parenting skills. Also offers programs for Cambodian American youth, including a gang prevention program, after-school classes, and Cambodian language classes.

Cambodian Association

5412 N. 5th St.
Philadelphia, PA 19121
(215) 324-4070
Walter Chin, director

Serves Cambodian Americans in the Philadelphia area. Helps newly arrived Cambodians with problems in education and housing, assists in preserving Cambodian culture, acts as an advocate for the interests of Cambodian Americans.

—Carl L. Bankston III

Who Are the Chinese Americans?

♦ Crossing the Oceans to the United States ♦ Nineteenth-Century China ♦ Early Immigrants
♦ Early Problems of Discrimination ♦ Early Contributions ♦ Labor Movement and Yellow Peril
♦ Exclusion Act ♦ Immigration Law ♦ Chinese Traditions and Customs ♦ Political and Social Ideas
♦ Early Heroes ♦ Transition: The Post War Period ♦ Professional Achievements
♦ Achieving Visibility ♦ New Challenges

♦ CROSSING THE OCEANS TO THE UNITED STATES

The relationship between the United States and China dates from even before the American Revolution. American ships brought tea, furnishings, porcelain, and silk from China; the Chinese imported ginseng from the American colonies. During this period, contact between the colonies and China was limited almost exclusively to trade.

The earliest Chinese arrivals to the United States may have landed in 1785, when a U.S. cargo ship, the *Pallas*, stranded three of its Chinese crewman in Baltimore when returning to China. Through a local merchant, they petitioned the Continental Congress for assistance until they could sail home.

The first true Chinese immigrant, as recorded by the Immigration Commission, did not arrive until 1820. For the next thirty years Chinese settlers were few and confined largely to the West Coast.

When gold was discovered at Sutter's Mill in 1848, there were already over 50 Chinese in California. Most were merchants and traders who had established businesses before the gold rush. By 1850, news of the wealth to be had from gold mining reached villages near Canton, luring 450 Chinese to the United States that year, and 2,716 the next. The high-water mark was in 1852, with an astonishing 20,000 Chinese arrivals. Immigration rates leveled off afterwards, averaging about 4,000 per year.

In December 1851, the newspaper *Alta California* reported a meeting of 300 Chinese in San Francisco, in which the group designated Selim E. Woodworth to "act in the capacity of arbitrator and advisor" for them. Other early newspaper accounts discuss the Chinese without prejudice, offering straightforward reports of their activities:

> About 200 Chinamen have come over who have formed an encampment on a vacant lot at the head of Clay Street. They have put up about 30 tents which look clean and white, and around and in which are scattered the various articles of Chinese wares and tools which they have brought over. They look cheerful and happy and will no doubt make good citizens and voters in a few years (August 22, 1851).

On the east coast, five Chinese students attended the Foreign Mission School at Cornwall, Connecticut. Among them was a young man named Yung Wing, who would become the first Chinese to graduate from a U.S. college—Yale, class of 1854. A naturalized U.S. citizen, Yung Wing returned to China and asked the Imperial Court to establish an education mission in the United States. He recruited 120 boys, most of them from the Canton region, to study in Connecticut and Massachusetts. Several years later, to the bitter disappointment of Yung Wing and the eager students, the mission was ordered withdrawn because the Imperial Court was alarmed at its subjects' exposure to Western influences, which the court deemed demoralizing and harmful.

♦ NINETEENTH-CENTURY CHINA

The idea of pursuing one's education or livelihood outside the Middle Kingdom, as the Chinese called their native country, was revolutionary. Imperial decree forbade emigration on pain of death. China's rulers considered themselves monarchs of the center of the world; with four thousand years of recorded history behind

Yung Wing, Yale College, 1854. (Courtesy Yale University Library.)

them, they were convinced that they alone embodied civilization. Other peoples, particularly Westerners, were viewed as uncultured and barbaric.

Emperor Shih Huang Ti of the Ch'in dynasty unified China in 221 B.C. and built a fortified line of defense along the northern border known as the Great Wall. Succeeding emperors continued this tradition of isolationist self-sufficiency. China's dynasty, the Manchus, ruled from 1644 to 1911, and was similarly indifferent to the rest of the world. In 1757, however, Emperor Chi'en Lung opened the port of Canton to international commerce. China's vast market potential attracted many Western nations, and England became the country's dominant trading partner. British ships brought the nineteenth century to a still-medieval China, and with it came opium, a drug that would ruin countless lives.

The imperial court objected to the illegal importation of the narcotic, but England continued its nefarious trade. As tension mounted, Emperor Tao Kuang sent Commissioner Lin Tse-hsu to Canton, where the commissioner ordered a ship loaded with opium burned in the harbor. England retaliated with force, easily defeating China in the First Opium War (1839-42).

The treaties imposed after the war forced China to open five ports to foreign trade (Amoy, Canton, Foochow, Ningpo, and Shanghai) and ceded the island of Hong Kong completely to British authority, which was further subdivided into French and U.S. areas. Belgium, France, Germany, Russia, and Sweden soon acquired their own territorial concessions of parcels of land over which they had special rights and privileges.

Western exploitation undermined the imperial government, which became incapable of dealing with encroaching foreign powers, internal disorder, and economic disaster. As a result, the angry population rose up in the violent T'ai P'ing Rebellion of 1851. Originating in the southern province of Kwangsi, the revolt was a devastating, widespread conflict. With Western aid, the Manchu government finally crushed the revolt in 1864, but the uprising took 30 million lives and devastated large farming districts.

Villages in southern China were left to fend for themselves in the aftermath. Small land owners were often forced to sell their holdings, and land was controlled by fewer and fewer people. Many farmers became peasants, tending land for large property owners. Famine was widespread and inflation, caused in part by the opium trade, made money nearly worthless. It was not uncommon for a destitute father to sell one of his children as a slave in order for the rest of the family to survive. For many, emigration became their only hope.

◆ EARLY IMMIGRANTS

They fled to sea ports, seeking passage as sailors or workers. These desperate peasants often found themselves trapped as coolies, slave laborers who were shipped to South America, Southeast Asia, or the West Indies. U.S. shippers dealt in this profitable trade, and accounts of the mistreatment of Chinese aboard such vessels are as horrifying as the descriptions of the eighteenth-century slave ships from Africa.

By the 1850s, the Chinese immigrants' most sought-after destination was *Gum San*, "the gold mountain," as they called the United States. News of rich diggings and good wages in Gum San fired the imagination of young men who were unable even to find the next meal in their homeland. Most arrived on a credit system, agreeing to pay off debts from future wages to brokers who advanced passage funds. Others borrowed from relatives, promising to send money back from abroad.

The eight-week passage from Canton to California was hazardous, and conditions on board were usually deplorable. Passengers suffered from seasickness, malnutrition, and other ailments, because companies frequently maximized their profits by exceeding the capacity of vessels. Regularly 400 to

500 passengers would be "packed into the hold of ships as thick as herrings in a box," reported the *Alta California*. Furthermore:

> Although generally very clean in their habits, it is not possible for them, under the circumstances, to preserve health, and living as they do upon light food, as just the subjects which scurvy would be apt to attack. One vessel. . .brought no less than 500. How can they be expected to escape without sickness under such circumstances? Captains of vessels ought not to pack them in like so much pork in a barrel (September 18, 1851).

Sails gave way to steam in 1867 when the Pacific Mail Steam Navigation Company began service from San Francisco to China. The journey was shorter and less perilous than by clipper ship, but passengers were still crowded and often seasick for five weeks.

Most Chinese immigrants known as Cantonese, were from the Pearl River Delta region of Kwangtung Providence in southern China. They were peasants who came from three major districts: Sam Yup, Sze Yup (mostly from Toisan), and Heungsan (later known as Chungsan), each with its distinct Cantonese dialect.

A worker in Gum San earning a dollar a day could help an entire clan by sending part of his wages back to his village. In desperate situations, husbands would leave their wives and children in the care of relatives to find work abroad; parents would send sons as young as ten, hoping that they would send money home to feed their kin.

Early arrivals were almost all men, since a respectable woman could not leave her parents' or in-laws' house. Chinese society was patriarchal, and only male children's names were recorded on the family tree; daughters' births were a disappointment. A woman did not even carry her family name, and when she married, she went to live with her husband and his parents. If he left for United States, she was ruled by her mother-in-law.

Not surprisingly, early Chinese American communities were bachelor societies governed by district associations. Typically, upon arrival in San Francisco newcomers were met by members of their district, people from their region who spoke the same dialect. They were housed at district headquarters and worked where their kinsmen had employment contracts or connections. This often meant a trek into hinterlands working at sites designated by their agents. Chinatowns of various sizes sprang up all along the West Coast, each with a cluster of stores, often with gambling rooms; district headquarters that also served as lodging houses; a temple; and, in the larger Chinatowns, a theater for operas performed by traveling troupes.

Although some Cantonese brought their wives to the United States, by 1880 men outnumbered women by 21 to one with 100,886 males and 4,779 women. When the Exclusion Act of 1882 curbed immigration, the ratio became even more desperate. In 1890, there were 28 men for every woman. Prostitution and gambling, hallmarks of frontier society, were predictable elements of the Chinese community as well. A few of the fraternal organizations called tongs met this demand by importing and selling slave girls. Rival groups often clashed in "tong wars," which made sensational news. Less well-known were the Chinese district association leaders who quietly sought to maintain peace and order.

In their new world the Chinese adapted as well as they could, honoring ancient traditions and observing the lunar calendar's many feast days. Their society was an insular one, its people purposeful and enterprising. B. E. Lloyd, an early historian, commented in 1876:

> . . . the progress of the city of San Francisco, and the State of California in these three decades is almost equal to the advance of other cities and countries during the years of a century! What has done this?—Labor. True, the foundations of this greatness were firmly implanted in the soil, and in the granite mountains, but it was not a spontaneous development. Hard, earnest work, by human hands, had to be and has been performed. And there has been no class of people among the inhabitants more busily employed than the Chinese population.

♦ EARLY PROBLEMS OF DISCRIMINATION

During the second half of the nineteenth century, immigrants from all over the world poured into California. Although resentment and strife were prevalent, the Chinese were not singled out for discrimination early on. In 1850, in fact, groups of Chinese were invited to march in President Zachery Taylor's funeral procession, and helped celebrate California's admission to the union later that year.

A wave of official intolerance spearheaded by oppressive taxes made life difficult for the Chinese, however. The foreign Miners Tax, levied in the 1850s, made Chinese the targets of both real and bogus tax collectors and drove many from the mines. The monthly Alien Poll Tax charged each Chinese $2.50 until it was declared unconstitutional in 1862.

The greatest discriminatory act to the Chinese was implemented in 1854, when the state of California barred any Chinese from testifying in court. In the case of *Hall v. People*, a white man had been convicted of murder by the testimony of Chinese witnesses. Judge Charles J. Murray reversed the verdict, citing the Criminal Act of 1850, which provided that "No Black, or Mulato person, or Indian, shall be allowed to give

In the 1870s, Chinese immigrants were often harassed and attacked upon arrival in San Francisco. (Courtesy, Bancroft Library, University of California, Berkeley.)

evidence in favor of, or against a White man." Murray declared Chinese equally ineligible, concluding: "The same rule which would admit them to testify would admit them to all equal rights of citizenship, and we might soon see them at the pools, in the jury box, upon the bench and in our legislative halls."

During the 18 years that the act was in effect, crimes against the Chinese in California were committed with virtual impunity. They were attacked on city streets while authorities looked the other way; in the mining districts they were beaten and often murdered. Even the *Shasta Republican* expressed outrage, claiming:

> Hundreds of Chinamen have been slaughtered in cold blood during the last five years by desperadoes that infest our state. The murder of Chinamen was almost of daily occurrence, yet in all this time we have heard of but two or three instances where the guilty parties have been brought to justice and punished according to law (December 18, 1956).

By 1855, the Chinese began to organize in protest. Twenty-seven merchants signed an open letter to the people of California, claiming:

> . . . instead of the equality and protection which seemed to be promised by the laws of a great nation . . . we find only inequality and oppression. Oppression by the law, which subjects us to exorbitant taxes imposed upon us exclusively—oppression without the pale of the law, which refuses us its protection and leaves us prey to vexations and humiliations which it seems to invoke upon our heads by placing us in an exceptional position.

This merchant group, which began as a chamber of commerce community advocate, later became the Chinese Consolidated Benevolent Association, more commonly known as the Chinese Six Companies. It acted as sovereign, settling internal disputes within the Chinese community, negotiating between Chinese and the government, and hiring attorneys to challenge unjust laws in the courts.

Despite such efforts the Chinese remained on the fringes of their appearance, language, and customs, and were denied citizenship by a 1790 law that made naturalization available only to "any alien being a free white person." After the Civil War, when citizenship was extended to those of African descent, Chinese

Three Chinese girls in San Franciso, circa 1890s. (Photo by Floyd Lumbard, courtesy of Lee and Barbara Lumbard.)

petitioners in western states were refused because they were neither black nor white.

Discrimination existed on other fronts as well. In 1859, the California Superintendent of Education asked that state funds be withheld from schools that enrolled Chinese students. The California legislature declared that "Negroes, Mongolians [Chinese], and Indians shall not be admitted into public schools" and mandated separate schools for them. In 1866, the state finally permitted Chinese to attend public schools, if the parents of white children did not object. In many areas, such as the Sacramento Delta region, Chinese attended "Oriental" schools until World War II. In some areas of the South there were separate schools for African American, Asian, and Caucasian children.

The Chinese were also refused housing in many areas, and this forced them into the crowded buildings and squalid enclaves of Chinatowns. In San Francisco in 1873, authorities further harassed the Chinese by enacting an ordinance that required 500 cubic feet of space for each boarding-house occupant. In one Chinatown raid the police arrested 51 lodgers in a basement on Jackson Street.

On the advice of lawyers hired by the Six Companies, the Chinese refused to pay the fine and were summarily jailed. To force them to pay, the San Francisco Board of Supervisors ruled that male prisoners' hair would be cut to one inch, a ruling aimed directly at the Chinese and their long braids or queues. Still other edicts affected Chinese burial customs and levied heavy license fees on Chinese-style laundries. Refusing to comply with the rulings, the Chinese raised funds to challenge them. Lawyers succeeded in rendering anti-Chinese laws unconstitutional in court. In 1879, for example Ho Ah How, who had been forced to accept lodging in quarters much smaller than 500 cubic feet, was arrested and fined ten dollars. He refused to pay and was imprisoned for five days, during which time the sheriff cut off his queue. How sued, and won. In the case of *Ho Ah Kow v. Sheriff Matthew Nunan*, Judge Steven J. Field declared that the hair-cutting law was a violation of the Civil Rights Act of 1870, the Fourteenth Amendment, and the Burlingame Treaty. The judge noted that "the ordinance is known in the community as the 'Queue Ordinance' being so designated from its purpose to reach the queues of the Chinese, and it is not enforced against other persons." He further warned that "hostile and spiteful" legislation could not be used to discourage immigration.

Nevertheless, "spiteful" legislation did indeed discourage immigration and intimidate and segregate Chinese Americans further. Laws specifically aimed at them were continually drafted in California and throughout the West. In addition to the poll tax, laundry license fees, the lodging house law, and other encumbrances, new sanctions banned Chinese from certain parts of town; others prohibited intermarriage with whites. This instilled in the Chinese a deep-seated distrust of U.S. law, which was repeatedly altered to be used against them.

◆ EARLY CONTRIBUTIONS

In 1862, the Joint Select Committee Relative to the Chinese Population of the state of California found that the Chinese contributed $14,000,000 to the state's economy in taxes, license fees, shipping fares, and purchases. In its report, the committee declared:

> "They work for us, they help build up our State by contributing largely to our taxes, to our shopping, farming and mechanical interests, without to any extent entering these departments as competitors; they are denied privileges equal with other foreigners; they cannot vote or testify in courts of justice, nor have they a voice in making our laws, nor mingle with us in social life. Certainly we have nothing to fear from a race so condemned and restricted. . . ."

Chinese laborers employed by the Central Pacific in the Sierra Nevada had to fight winter snow drifts to get the railroad built. (Association of American Railroads.)

Agriculture and Industry

Chinese workers were in fact the major labor force behind the development of the West. In cities they toiled in factories and sweat shops, making cigars, shoes, clothing, and gunpowder. They labored in coal and quicksilver mines, built roads, levees, and dams in the hinterlands. They reclaimed land, planted crops, and harvested them.

By the 1870s, the Chinese dominated the strawberry-growing industry in California, leasing acreage from white farmers and splitting the proceeds with them. The Chinese pioneered new methods of horticulture as well. In 1875, when Seth Lewelling developed a new type of cherry with his employee Ah Bing's help, he named the fine sweet fruit the Bing cherry. In 1888, Florida farmer Lue Gin Gong produced the Lue orange, which was awarded the Wilder medal by the Department of Agriculture.

Transcontinental Railroad

The most dramatic example of Chinese labor and skill, however, was the construction of the Central Pacific, the western portion of the great Transcontinental Railroad, from 1865 to 1869. Hired because there was a labor shortage, the first 50 Chinese proved their worth in handling pickaxes and moving boulders. Impressed, the railroad began to contract for more workers from China.

Ultimately, between ten and 12 thousand Chinese carved tunnels and laid track across the Sierra Nevadas. An estimated 1,200 of them were killed in the process, buried in avalanches during the severe winters or blown apart while handling explosives. The work required both skill and daring. Nowhere was this more apparent than in the men's extraordinary ability to carve ledges from cliffs while hanging in baskets. Their speed was also remarkable; when racing to meet the Union Pacific coming from the East, Chinese workers laid ten miles of track in one day.

Despite these accomplishments, doubts about their ability remained. When masonry work was required, the project's superintendent, James Strobridge, protested that the slightly built Chinese were not fit for the job. Construction chief Charles Crocker answered, "Didn't they build the Chinese wall, the biggest piece of masonry in the world?"

Chinese fisherman, circa 1895, Monterey, California. (Photo by Floyd Lumbard, courtesy Lee and Barbara Lumbard.)

Angry mobs attacked boarding houses in Chinatown, circa 1880. (Courtesy Bancroft Library.)

Testifying before a congressional hearing on Chinese immigration years later, Crocker recalled the courage and integrity of the Chinese railroad worker, declaring, "Without Chinese labor we would be thrown back in all branches of industry, farming, mining, reclaiming lands, and everything else."

Regardless of their contributions to the railroad, in 1872, Chinese were forbidden to have business licenses or to own land. They were forced to accept work whites did not want, becoming washermen, domestics, cooks, and peddlers. In the Northwest they worked in lumber camps and the fishing and canning industries. They manned yet another construction project in 1873 when 200 Chinese arrived in Augusta, Georgia, to build a canal that would generate power for new industry.

Riding the rails they once laid, Chinese drifted to cities and towns across the United States. They opened restaurants and laundries, often with gambling rooms in the rear. A Chinese recalling those days has commented, "We have but three businesses: the laundry business, the restaurant business, and the gambling business."

◆ LABOR MOVEMENT AND YELLOW PERIL

Anti-Chinese workers' groups had existed since the mid-1850s, and as labor troubles developed they grew in size and number. Their appeal stemmed from antipathy to people of color and from the fear that cheap Chinese labor would drive down wages, a bigoted combination of beliefs which came to be known as Yellow Peril. By 1870, groups such as the Anti-Coolie Association and the Supreme Order of the Caucasians launched boycotts of Chinese labor throughout the country. As tension grew, bloody riots erupted and Chinatowns from Denver to Los Angeles were attacked by violent mobs. Chinese fled to other Chinatowns for safety, especially San Francisco's, the largest and most established among them. By 1876, this community, with an area of only nine city blocks, housed over 30,000 people.

Eastward Migration

With the growing power of the labor movement, West Coast legislators were pressured to stop the influx of Chinese and end their "unfair" labor practices.

The East Coast on the other hand viewed the controversy as a West Coast problem, and as long as Chinese stayed west of the Rockies, easterners were generally unconcerned. In 1870, however, 75 Chinese workers were hired at a shoe factory in North Adams, Massachusetts, and labor groups throughout the East predicted a "coolie slavery" invasion. Chinese laundries soon sprang up in eastern cities, and small Chinatowns appeared in New York, Philadelphia, and Boston.

Newspapers capitalized on the public's fear and loathing, running inflammatory stories that detailed "heathen" Chinese practices, and gave fearsome descriptions of their living quarters, their corrupting influence on the morals of U.S. youth, and their threat to genteel womenfolk. Prominent citizens like Horace Greeley considered the Chinese unassimilable and unacceptable as permanent residents, because they were neither white nor Christian: "The Chinese are uncivilized, unclean, and filthy beyond all conception without any of the higher domestic or social relations; lustful and sensual in their dispositions; every female is a prostitute of the basest order." Naturally, such declarations only spread further prejudice and misconceptions.

The issue of Chinese labor was controversial in the South as well. The emancipation of the slaves left a need for labor in the cotton industry. In 1869, at a convention in Memphis, manufacturers and planters considered replacing slaves with Chinese workers. The Tennessee legislature, however, refused to allow imported labor into the state.

In the 1870s a widespread economic depression occurred, marked by bank and industry failures along with rising unemployment. The Panic of 1873 was caused partly by overcapitalizing railroad companies, and white citizens soon identified scapegoats: the railroads, big business, and the Chinese.

By 1876, intense anti-Chinese sentiment spurred a congressional investigation into Chinese immigration. During the hearings, which were held in San Francisco, the committee heard 1,200 pages of testimony. Some was from industrialists like Leland Stanford and Charles Crocker, who testified that the Chinese were industrious and dependable, and that without them the Transcontinental Railroad would not have been built. Farmers defended the Chinese as well, praising them for their agricultural skill. Several public officials, however, called the Chinese heathens who lived in filthy quarters. Labor leaders voiced their oppositions, too, arguing that the Chinese drove decent white men out of work, forcing their wives and children to starve.

Workingman's Party

Even congressional involvement failed to satisfy the discontented populace. Public resentment of big business, land monopolies, and widespread unemployment drew thousands of workers to anti-Chinese rallies, where the Chinese labor force became a convenient whipping post for all working-class ills. Several of these xenophobic groups coalesced into the Workingman's Party, led by Denis Kearney, an Irish immigrant.

The party's aims were clearly defined in its pamphlets, one of which stated, "The White freeman with his wife and children cannot live in the same atmosphere as the Coolie slave. One or the other must leave the State, and it must be the Chinaman." The party's rallying cry, "The Chinese Must Go," soon became a popular slogan. The group held labor rallies that frequently erupted into riots in which Chinese quarters were attacked. Particularly violent demonstrations occurred in San Francisco in the summer of 1877.

In this hostile atmosphere, state and local governments were increasingly pressured to stop Chinese immigration. Although they tried to do so, their attempts to drive the Chinese out with harassment and discriminatory laws were ultimately thwarted by the courts.

At the federal level, Democrats aligned with the labor movement voiced support for legislation that would suppress Chinese immigration almost completely. Republicans tended to side with the industrialists and landowners that employed Chinese workers, but they, too, heard their constituents clamor for a ban. The result was the Passenger Bill, which would have allowed only fifteen Chinese per incoming vessel. It was vetoed by President Hayes, and anti-Chinese groups demonstrated in protest.

The power of the Workingman's Party and rising influence of the West Coast began to prevail in 1880, when President Hayes renegotiated the Burlingame Treaty with China, securing the right of the United States to regulate, limit, or suspend (but not prohibit) Chinese immigration. In the same year, white mobs destroyed all Chinese homes and businesses in Denver, an ominous and sadly accurate portent.

♦ EXCLUSION ACT

Two years later, President Chester Arthur signed the Chinese Exclusion Act, which barred Chinese laborers from entering the United States for ten years; merchants, teachers, students, and travelers would be admitted under extremely strict regulations. Resident Chinese were required a permit to reenter if they left the country. Worst of all, the act guaranteed permanent alien status for all Chinese, stating that "hereafter no State court or court of the United States shall admit Chinese to citizenship; and all laws in conflict with this act are hereby repealed."

The September 1885 outbreak of anti-Chinese violence in Rock Springs, Wyoming. (Harper's Weekly, September 26, 1885.)

Even with the severity of this legislation, anti-Chinese violence continued. In 1885, several Chinese hop pickers in Washington's Issaquah Valley were murdered in their sleep by white gunmen. Later that year, Tacoma citizens attacked a Chinese settlement, driving hundreds out into a storm. A Seattle mob forced Chinese to board a steamship bound for San Francisco, prompting President Grover Cleveland to summon the National Guard to restore order. In Alaska, where Chinese were employed in the fishing and canning industries, a riot broke out at the mines on Douglas Island, and a hundred Chinese were forced aboard a boat and set adrift. The most violent disturbance of all was in Rock Springs, Wyoming, in September 1885. White coal miners attacked a local Chinese community, killing over forty people and driving another 500 into the desert. This time the president called out the army.

The issue of Chinese immigration remained troublesome, however. At an 1886 conference on the Chinese question in San Jose, California, elected officials urged a boycott of Chinese-made goods and all businesses that employed Chinese. Delegates eventually organized themselves into the Asiatic Exclusion League. This group initially comprised of 67 labor organizations, but which gradually expanded to more than 200 lobbied for harsh legal restrictions on Asian immigrants and participated in numerous violent confrontations with Asians.

Not content with the restrictions in the Exclusion Act, legislators passed new laws, making the legal noose around Chinese necks even tighter. The Scott Act of 1888 barred the return of Chinese laborers, even if they had reentry permits, and the Geary Act, which proposed extending the exclusion law was submitted to Congress. The Chinese Six Companies organized to oppose the bill, asking all Chinese to donate one dollar—a day's wages—to fund the legal challenge of *Fong Yue Ting v. the United States*.

The Companies' lawyers prepared a strong case, but lost in the Supreme Court. The Geary Act passed in 1892, excluding Chinese laborers for another decade and requiring every Chinese resident to carry an eligibility certificate at all times. In 1902, the Exclusion Law was extended indefinitely. Exclusion not only curtailed immigration, but reduced the Chinese population, as those disgusted by discriminatory laws went home. The 1890 census reported 107,488 Chinese in the United States. Ten years later there were 89,863, and in 1910, 71,531.

Barracks at Angel Island Immigration Station, 1935. (Photo by Hope Cahill, courtesy of Connie Young Yu.)

The Chinese government was angered by the ill treatment its nationals received in the United States, but it was virtually powerless to act. In 1905, China boycotted U.S. goods, but abandoned the policy a year later when it proved ineffective. As Japanese immigrants arrived, western states renewed their alarm over the Yellow Peril. Politicians and labor leaders pressed for legislation oppressive to all Asians. In 1906, California, Oregon, and Washington passed alien land acts forbidding those ineligible for citizenship from owning land. These laws were aimed directly at Japanese and Chinese immigrants.

Legacy of Angel Island Exclusion

In 1910, the Angel Island Immigration Station in San Francisco Bay became the point of entry for Asian immigrants. The site held hundreds of people at a time, many of them women and children, for two years or more while they proved their eligibility for residence. To circumvent exclusion laws and enter the country, many young immigrants procured false papers, claiming to be related to resident Chinese. To trap these "paper sons and daughters," new arrivals were asked hundreds of questions before an inquiry panel. Witnesses were called to corroborate their testimony, and each side's answers had to be identical. Anyone who failed the interrogation was held for deportation.

One child of 11 was asked 83 pages of questions before the panel ruled him ineligible. Like others denied entry, the boy appealed the decision in court. After a lengthy and tedious hearing the judge ruled in the boy's favor, remarking that anyone could make a few mistakes after days of questioning. The long detentions of those awaiting deportation often led to despair and sometimes even suicide. Others confined to the barracks carved poems that remain to this day, attesting to the detainees' fear and frustration.

In 1924, a smuggling ring was exposed on Angel Island. Immigration authorities were charged with taking bribes from immigrants and allowing them to enter the country illegally.

In 1978, Victor "Trader Vic" Bergerson, an internationally famous restaurateur and artist who has employed a great many Asians (some of whom underwent the Angel Island experience), conceived and donated to Angel Island a magnificent, eight-foot, 6,000-pound black granite monument. The inscription on the monument was written by Ngoot P. Chin of San Francisco, and was chosen from among many entries in a San Francisco Chinese community competition sponsored by the *Chinese Times* newspaper. For his efforts, Chin received a $1,000 cash award donated by Trader Vic. The Angel Island Immigration Station Historical Advisory Committee (ALLSHAC) chose the winning couplet. Translated, it reads:

> Leaving their homes and villages, they crossed the ocean Only to endure confinement in these barracks
>
> Conquering frontiers and barriers, they pioneered
>
> A new life by the Golden Gate.

The commemorative ceremony of April 28, 1979, honored not only the Asian immigrants who were detained on Angel Island, which remained in operation until 1940, but also memorialized those who suffered and died in their quest for a better life in the United States.

◆ IMMIGRATION LAW

The immigration law of 1924 was the final, most effective act against Chinese immigration. Previously, both U.S.-born and immigrant Chinese were allowed to bring their wives and families to the United States. This law, however, intended to phase Chinese out of the United States by preventing them from having families. It stipulated that aliens ineligible for citizenship would be prohibited from entering the country. The law was challenged in the Supreme Court in *Chang Chan et al. v. John D. Nagle*, but the court ruled that Chinese wives of U.S. citizens were not entitled to residence. As a result, the Chinese population continued to have disproportionate number of men to women until the early 1960s.

By the 1920s, Chinese were barred from owning land, from performing certain occupations, and from entering all but the fringes of U.S. society. They were perpetual aliens, the result of unfair immigration laws. Suspicious of government and far from the mainstream, they were regarded as stubbornly clannish outsiders locked into Chinatowns.

These discriminatory attitudes and laws exacted a terrible toll on those they affected. "Chinese didn't

Wedding photo of Mr. and Mrs. Lee Yoke Suey, circa 1900. Lee Yoke Suey, the son of transcontinental railroad worker Lee Wong Sang, was born in San Francisco, but his wife was detained on Angel Island for 16 months when she immigrated to the United States from China. (Courtesy of Connie Young Yu.)

become laundrymen by choice," said Wing Yee, a cafe owner in a small California railroad town whose story is typical of many. He explained that choices of profession and lifestyle were limited for the Chinese. His grandfather came to the United States, worked hard, saved his money, went back to China to get married, and was prevented by the exclusion laws from bringing his wife back with him. His father suffered the same experience and also left a wife in China. Wing Yee came to the United States to earn his living when he was 12. He, too, returned to China in 1935 to get married. A year later he came back to work in the cafe while his wife, who was pregnant, remained in China. Because of the exclusion laws, the family was cruelly separated, and Wing Yee did not see his oldest daughter until she was 13, when the laws were liberalized and the Yees were reunited.

With the beginning of World War II, the U.S. government viewed the Chinese in a more favorable light, as China, fighting Japanese invaders, became a staunch

ally. A new treaty abolished the one-sided privileges previously enjoyed by the United States and on December 17, 1943, Congress repealed the Exclusion Acts. While this was a great victory for the Chinese American Citizens Alliance, immigration was limited to 105 Chinese per year.

Winds of Change

Things improved somewhat in 1952, when the McCarran-Walter Act made all races eligible for naturalization and eliminated race as a bar to immigration. Subsequent laws, such as the Refugee Relief Act of 1953 and the Refugee Escape Act of 1957, also benefitted Chinese immigrants. By 1960, there were 237,292 Chinese in the United States, 135,549 male, 101,743 female; about 60 percent were native born. More than half lived in four cities: Honolulu, San Francisco, Oakland, and New York.

In 1962, President John F. Kennedy signed a presidential directive which allowed more than 15,000 refugees from communist China to enter the United States over a period of three years. The president stressed that U.S. immigration policy most be both fair and generous. In his special message to Congress on immigration, Kennedy stated, "It is time to correct the mistakes of the past and work toward a better future for all humanity."

Fulfilling Kennedy's vision, President Lyndon B. Johnson abolished the national origins quota system, replacing it with an annual allowance of 20,000 immigrants from each country. For the first time the Chinese saw immigration laws no longer as barriers or devices to separate families, but as a means to unite them. The era of discriminatory exclusion in immigration policy was over.

The monument to Chinese immigrants installed at Angel Island Immigration Station, at its unveiling in 1979. (Courtesy of Connie Young Yu.)

President Lyndon Johnson signing the repeal of the McCarran-Walter Act, replacing national origins quotas with an annual allowance of 20,000 immigrants from each country. (Photo by Yoichi R. Okamoto, courtesy of the LBJ Library Collection.)

♦ CHINESE TRADITIONS AND CUSTOMS

Nineteenth-century Cantonese immigrants brought with them a wealth of traditions. Struggling in their new environment, they clung to the beliefs and practices of their ancestors, which they handed down, often unaltered, to their children and grandchildren. Twentieth-century arrivals often found U.S.-born Chinese old-fashioned by comparison.

First-generation Chinese were influenced by U.S ways, however, and they incorporated these new customs into their lives while honoring the old ones. Chinese children celebrated U.S. holidays at school and observed traditional feast days at home. Christian converts often worshipped in church and paid their respects at the community temple with no conflict of conscience.

Religion

Traditional religion in China is an eclectic mix of Buddhism, Confucianism, and Taoism, and these beliefs were imported with early immigrants.

Buddhism teaches that all human life is bound by Samsara, an endless succession of rebirth and suffering. The cycle can be broken and nirvana attained by following the Eightfold Path, a life of contemplation and discipline.

Taoism is based on the writings of sixth-century philosopher Lao-tze, whose precepts espouse a simple life of harmony with nature. Taoists worship many deities, and their temples are ornate buildings with symbols orginating from Buddhism and Confucianism, both of which influenced Taoist thought.

The teachings of Confucius (551-478 B.C.), one of China's greatest philosophers, were incorporated into Chinese religious practices. Confucius stressed self-improvement, good deeds, the necessity of harmony in the home, and a deep respect for elders. Education is also highly valued. Many temples were housed in the top of a two-story building, with a Chinese language school located in the bottom.

Every early Chinese American community had a temple or an altar where worshippers made offerings and paid their respects to deities. Most of the temples were Taoist and built like those in China. Such temples remain in the California towns of Hanford, Weaverville, Marysville, Oroville, and San Francisco. In 1991, San Jose's Chinese community raised funds to replicate the

Vivian and Thomas Jew celebrating Chinese New Year, 1922, in Palo Alto, California. (Courtesy Thomas Jew.)

incense from the caretaker, make an offering, and ask for help from the gods, bowing respectfully before the altar. If the prayer is answered, the beneficiary may return and give the gods a gift of a plaque or an embroidered hanging for the temple.

Many early Chinatown stores also housed altars, where incense and offerings could be placed before favorite gods. Homes usually contained an image of the kitchen god. Even modern Chinese restaurants frequently have small altars. Lightbulbs have replaced candles in illuminating a god believed to bring good fortune to the establishment.

Most popular among the gods is Kwan Gung, a legendary general from the period of the Three Kingdoms (220–265), who represents justice and divine protection. Tien Ho is the queen of heaven and ruler of the seas. Wah Tau is the god of medicine. Kwan Yin, the goddess of mercy, was originally a Buddhist deity. In Marysville, California, a town that flourished during the Gold Rush, the Chinese built a temple to Bok Kai, the god of the waters. Visitors still attend the town's annual "Bomb Day" festivities during the second lunar month when the Bok Kai Parade with its splendid golden dragon weaves through the town as in the 1880s.

Christianity also has its adherents in the Chinese community. Many Chinatowns boast churches of various denominations whose services are in Chinese.

Ng Shing Gung, the Taoist Temple of the Five Deities that once was the pride of its Chinatown.

Chinese religion is a practical matter, with little debate over doctrines or dogma. There are no set services; worshippers can visit the temple any time, buy

Holidays

Nearly 5,000 years ago, imperial astrologers developed the lunar calendar to guide farmers in planting and harvesting. Each of the 12 years of the cycle is ruled by an animal deity: dragon, ram, monkey, rooster, dog, boar, rat, ox, tiger, rabbit, snake, and

The lunar calendar, 1900–2031.

Rat	Ox	Tiger	Hare (Rabbit)	Dragon	Snake	Horse	Sheep (Goat)	Monkey	Rooster	Dog	Pig
1900	1901	1902	1903	1904	1905	1906	1907	1908	1909	1910	1911
1912	1913	1914	1915	1916	1917	1918	1919	1920	1921	1922	1923
1924	1925	1926	1927	1928	1929	1930	1931	1932	1933	1934	1935
1936	1937	1938	1939	1940	1941	1942	1943	1944	1945	1946	1947
1948	1949	1950	1951	1952	1953	1954	1955	1956	1957	1958	1959
1960	1961	1962	1963	1964	1965	1966	1967	1968	1969	1970	1971
1972	1973	1974	1975	1976	1977	1978	1979	1980	1981	1982	1983
1984	1985	1986	1987	1988	1989	1990	1991	1992	1993	1994	1995
1996	1997	1998	1999	2000	2001	2002	2003	2004	2005	2006	2007
2008	2009	2010	2011	2012	2013	2014	2015	2016	2017	2018	2019
2020	2021	2022	2023	2024	2025	2026	2027	2028	2029	2030	2031

To calculate the year in the Chinese era, add 2,637 to the year shown. For example, 1996 is 4633 in the Chinese era.

horse. Each has its attributes and weaknesses, and is believed to confer its characteristics on those born during that year.

Although most Chinese, especially the young, have adopted U.S. customs, those of the lunar year are still observed and enjoyed in Chinese communities. Among these traditional holidays are the Moon Festival in the fall, Ching Ming (ritual visits) to ancestors' graves during the spring, and, most notably, Chinese New Year. This celebration not only begins the year, but its many omens signify how happy and prosperous the coming months will be. Flowers, for example, represent growth, and a blossom that opens on New Year's Day is believed to bring prosperity and good fortune.

Moon Festival

The Moon Festival, a celebration of longevity and fertility, occurs each autumn on the fifteenth day of the eighth lunar month. According to Chinese tradition, this is when the moon is farthest from the earth, perfectly round, and luminous. The festival falls between the summer and autumn harvests, a time to relax and enjoy the fruit of one's labors.

According to Chinese cosmology, the moon symbolizes the female principle of *yin*, which is believed to steer nature toward autumn coolness and winter darkness. Because of this, the women of the family offer sacrifices of fruit and special cakes to the moon from early evening until midnight.

In the formal Moon Festival ceremony five plates are filled with fruit: peaches, thought to bestow longevity, and apples and grapes, which represent fertility. These plates are laid upon the altar in honor of the moon.

The holiday dates from the Han Dynasty (202 B.C.-220 A.D.), when Emperor We Di held "viewing the moon" evenings and banquets. Subsequent dynasties continued the tradition, adding rituals such as lantern lighting and the music of gongs and drums.

An integral part of the celebration is the moon cake. These originated in the Yuan Dynasty (1260-1368) when China was ruled by the Mongolians, who were regarded as barbarians. Rebellious Chinese put papers with revolutionary messages inside the cakes. Although they were once made in intricate shapes like pagodas, horses, and riders, fish, and animals, the contemporary version is a simple brownish cake about four inches in round diameter symbolizing both the moon and the unity of the family. The five basic filling are: sweetened black been (*dou-sah*), lotus seed (*lin yung*), fruit with meat and nuts, (*gum tu*), yellow bean, (*dou yung*), and winter melon (*doogn-yung*). These fillings are often combined with coconut, pickled meat, ham, nuts, fruits, and in wealthier homes, salted duck-egg yolks. On the eve of the Moon Festival,

families and friends gather to eat the little round cakes and sip tea and wine.

Some families practice symbolic rituals. For example, women may fold paper to resemble gold bars and stack them onto a paper boat. The paper bars and the boat are then burned as a gift to the moon lady, Change E. According to legend, the fire will transform the paper into a real boat and gold. If the moon goddess is pleased with the offering, she will use it to travel to the moon, where she will meet her husband, Hou Yi, master archer of the skies. The more paper gold bars burned, the luckier the household, because she will have more money to give to Hou Yi.

Some Chinese celebrate as long as two weeks, observing all the proper rituals, such as bringing bright spring blossoms into the home, preparing special New Year foods and visiting friends and relatives. Public celebrations still use the traditional noisy strings of firecrackers to scare away evil spirits. This holiday has become popular with the U.S. public, and in many cities its parades and festivities have become major tourist attractions.

Celebrations of the Life Cycle

Whenever the Chinese celebrate, the color red predominates, because it symbolizes good luck and happiness. red is prominent in New Year celebrations. Eggs are dyed red to celebrate a birth, and a "red eggs and ginger" party is given for friends and family when the infant is between a month and a year old. Red envelopes filled with money are given to children on special occasions. Chinese brides traditionally wore red; contemporary brides may wear white for a church ceremony, and later change to a red *cheongsan* or an embroidered red jacket and skirt. Some simply wear a beautiful red heirloom jacket over a white gown.

The elderly are revered in Chinese tradition, and longevity banquets are frequently given in honor of those who have reached 70 or 80 years of age. A rice bowl and a pair of chopsticks are given to each guest upon leaving to wish the recipient long life and sustenance.

Funerals, too, are observed with much ritual and tradition. Nineteenth-century Chinese immigrants were usually returned to China for burial, because they feared that the deceased's spirit could not rest otherwise. The custom ended by the turn of the century.

A Chinese funeral, particularly that of a prominent person, usually began with a procession through town, accompanied by a band. Feasting at the gravesite followed, and special dishes with symbolic ingredients were served. Candy and a coin wrapped in white paper, the color of mourning, were given to each guest, to take away the bitterness of the event. This grand style of mourning is still practiced occasionally.

Food

Food is of major importance to Chinese, an attitude that reflects a hard pressed peasant society in which people greet one another with, "Have you eaten yet?" Rice is a staple and in traditional homes is served at each meal. Culinary customs, such as presenting a whole fish or an entire chicken chopped into serving pieces, are symbolic and reflect longstanding traditions. Cooking is a link between the generations, native-born and immigrant alike.

In 1849, there were three Chinese restaurants in San Francisco. Today they are as common in suburbs as in cities nationwide. Cantonese cooking, which was the first to become established in the United States, has been joined by the regional styles of Szechuan, Chu Chau, and Shanghai. Chinese cuisine has become one of the most popular ethnic foods in the United States, and eating with chopsticks is common among many non-Asian Americans. The Public Broadcasting Service even features "Yan Can Cook" starring chef Martin Yan, who teaches viewers how to prepare Chinese menus.

Medicine

In nineteenth-century San Francisco, Chinese were not allowed into \public hospitals and had to build their own facilities. Even after segregation ended, however, Western hospitals were greatly feared. To the Chinese, going to the hospital meant certain death. Traditional medicines bought at herb stores were preferred.

Today, there is widespread acceptance of Western medicine, but herbs and medicinal soups are still used for minor ailments by both immigrants and Asian Americans Acupuncture, an ancient Chinese medical practice using needles on special points of the body, is used by trained specialists in the United States to treat a variety of ailments.

♦ POLITICAL AND SOCIAL IDEAS

At the turn of the century, China's ruling Manchu dynasty was weak to the point of crumbling. The country had been defeated in its war with Japan (1894-1895) and the simmering resentment felt by many Chinese against government oppression began to erupt as revolutionary fervor.

Dr. Sun Yat-Sen, who would become China's first modern leader, called for a democratic revolution that would oust the corrupt imperial government. Forced into exile in Japan for his radical views, he also found a following among the Chinese American community. Sun made six visits to the United States between 1896 and 1911 to raise funds and support for his cause. He quickly became a hero, and Chinese from cities to agricultural work camps made generous donations. While

he was in Denver in 1911, the Manchus were finally overthrown, and Sun became the provisional president of the Republic of China. With the birth of the new republic, the Chinese cut off their queues, a hairstyle that had been imposed on them by the Manchus. The cruel tradition of binding a girl's feet to keep them unnaturally small was also abandoned.

Chinese immigrants kept abreast of these and other events by reading locally published Chinese newspapers. *The Chinese World*, founded in 1891, was the first bilingual daily. In 1900, the *Chung Sai Yat Bo*—the *Chinese American Daily News*—was published by Ng Poon Chew, who had arrived in 1881 as a boy of 13. A progressive journalist, he was also an ordained Presbyterian minister, who led his church in speaking out against the exclusion laws and in bridging the gap between Chinese Americans and non-Chinese Americans. Sun Yat-Sen and his followers also published a newspaper in San Francisco called *The Young China*.

The earliest Asian civil rights group was Native Sons of the Golden West, incorporated in 1895 to fight for justice, citizenship, and suffrage for Chinese immigrants. In 1911, the group lobbied successfully against a proposed constitutional amendment that would have denied the vote to anyone whose father was ineligible. As chapters expanded across the country, the Native Sons became the Chinese American Citizens Alliance. Through the years, it fought against attempts to disenfranchise citizens of Chinese ancestry, to segregate Chinese children in public schools, and to apply discriminatory regulations to Chinese businesses. It also challenged anti-Asian immigration policies, working tirelessly to repeal the exclusion laws.

♦ EARLY HEROES

Sun Yat-sen (1866-1925) was the symbol and leader of the Chinese nationalist revolution and the first president of the republic that succeeded the Manchu, or Qing (Ch'ing), dynasty in 1911. He is one of modern China's most revered political figures. In 1907, he issued a manifesto containing an early version of his famous Three Principles of the People (Sanmin Chui or San-min-chu-i)—roughly translatable as "nationalism, democracy, and the people's livelihood." Sun continued to publicize his revolutionary theories and to raise money from overseas supporters. When revolution finally erupted in 1911, Sun was named provisional president of the new Republic of China.

Another celebrated figure was Fung Joe Guey, a young Chinese inventor and aviator. In 1910, he built a biplane that he kept aloft over Piedmont, California, for twenty minutes. The picture book by Laurence Yep, *Dragonwings*, celebrates the achievement of this pioneer aviator. Thom Gunn was also an early Chinese

Sgt. Sing Kee and his parents were honored in a parade through San Jose, California in 1919. Sgt. Sing Kee had earned the Distinguished Service Cross in World War I for extraordinary bravery. (San Jose Historical Museum Archives.)

aviator who made the news. These men were exceptions, though. Many brave Chinese, particularly those who helped develop the West, remain nameless and ignored.

Because of the rampant anti-Chinese feeling in the country prior to World War II few Chinese American achievements were noted. Some heroes did emerge, however. When Sergeant Lou Sing Kee returned home from duty in France in 1919 wearing the Distinguished Service Cross for extraordinary bravery in action, the whole Chinese community of San Jose turned out to meet him at the railroad station. A parade escorted him to the fenced-in Chinatown, which was decorated with U.S. flags and banners. Children stared up at him worshipfully and the elders of the district associations embraced him. He was their ideal, a native born who exemplified the valor and loyalty of the Chinese American.

♦ TRANSITION: THE POST WAR PERIOD

During the period of exclusion the Chinese were "quiet Americans"—immigrants who didn't make waves.

In 1943, the exclusion laws were repealed, and Chinese were allowed naturalization, but fears of disenfranchisement and deportation still loomed. During the 1950s, communist paranoia bred fears of Chinese "Reds" infiltrating U.S. society. In response, Chinese Americans sought to show their patriotism and loyalty, remembering the incarceration of 110,000 Japanese Americans after Pearl Harbor.

To this end, Chinatown's chamber of commerce hosted civic activities and festivals. To offset unsavory stereotypes of Chinese quarters, those in San Francisco and New York organized public activities such as parades, beauty pageants, and cultural programs. Chinese Americans became more active in politics, and civic officials and candidates rode in the lunar New Year parades.

Naturally, large Chinese American communities retained their network of family and district associations. In 1962, San Francisco's Chinatown had 47 family associations and seven major district associations; the organization of Chinese Six Companies was the official representation of the Chinese associations. Through the years, the Six Companies became less political and more social, particularly in community activities.

Chang-Lin Tien was appointed chancellor of the University of California at Berkeley in 1990. (Photo by John Blaustein, courtesy of Chang-Lin Tien.)

♦ PROFESSIONAL ACHIEVEMENTS

Once it was almost impossible for a Chinese to be hired as a teacher, police officer, mechanic, accountant, or engineer. Union jobs were closed to them as well. All that changed in the 1960s, when Chinese entered all of these occupations and more.

If the old Chinese stereotype was that of a laundryman or servant, the new one seems to be the Chinese engineer or doctor; law study has also attracted many young Chinese American graduates. Chinese Americans have also entered many other areas, from firefighting and law enforcement to television newscasting and movie directing.

Science and Engineering

There was great pride in the Chinese community when the 1957 Nobel Prize for physics was won by two young Chinese Americans, Chen Ning Yang, who was thirty-four at the time, and Tsung Dao Lee, thirty. (See "Prominent Asian Americans" for profiles of both.) Their work was hailed by Columbia University's Physics Department as "the most important development in physics in the past ten years. Their achievement in disputing the accepted principle of the conservation of parity paved the way for a better understanding of the forces that govern our universe, and very likely to their better utilization for the benefit of mankind." Yang and Lee's Nobel Prize-winning work was verified by Dr. Chien Shing Wu (see Prominent Asian Americans), a fellow professor and experimental physicist at Columbia. Named by *Life* magazine as one of the most important women of the century in the United States. In 1958, Dr. Wu also received from Princeton the first honorary doctorate in science ever given to a woman.

Like Yang, Lee and Wu, Dr. Choh Hao Li won the prestigious 1962 Albert Lasker Medical Research Award in 1962. He is a leading authority on the pituitary gland, and came to the United States from China as a student.

Paul C. W. Chu is a University of Houston physicist who is working to develop superconductors. The October 18, 1993, issue of *Time* magazine called Chu "science's version of a champion pole vaulter".

Immigrant entrepreneurs have also become enormously successful, especially in Silicon Valley. Notable among them are computer-industry pioneers Dr. David Lam, David Lee, and Albert Yu, who all came to study at U.S. colleges in the 1960s and eventually founded their own companies.

Education

In 1926, Alice Fong Yu became the first Chinese American teacher at a public school. Her accomplishment was remarkable since she had at first been refused admission to a teacher's college because of her race. Until the 1940s, overt discrimination discouraged Chinese from pursuing careers in education; now they can be found at all levels of education, from grade school teachers to law school deans. In 1990, Chang-Lin Tien was appointed chancellor of the University of California in Berkeley, one of the largest universities in the United States. Rose Tang is chancellor of the West Valley Mission Community College District in California.

The number of Asians on campuses have grown to 10 percent or more of the student bodies of top colleges and universities. Newspapers and magazines have featured the "model minority," documenting the success of Asian college students. Among the native-born, however, the young often feel that their parents pressure them into the science professions. This has reinforced the stereotype of the Chinese American student as a "nerd" and math and science whiz, and many chafe at its restrictions.

Chinese language schools are also thriving. While in previous years they taught the Cantonese dialect, the influx of immigrants from mainland China and Taiwan now make Mandarin predominant. The Palo Alto, California, Chinese school, which enrolled 100 students in 1975 had four times that number in 1993.

Sports

In the 1850s, Yung Wing made a remarkable touchdown playing football at Yale, and a fellow Cantonese student was a coxswain on the rowing team, but in the following 100 years a Chinese American athlete was practically unheard of. Busy laboring for wages, early immigrants had little time to play.

Succeeding generations, however, have become increasingly involved in sports, demonstrating that given the opportunity, the Chinese, although often small in stature compared to many of European descent, could become top athletes. Many successful Chinese Americans encourage their children to pursue music, hobbies, and recreation, activities in which they themselves could not participate. It is a sign of their success that their offspring can enjoy leisure activities and not concentrate solely on making a living. Tennis, gymnastics, and track and field are among the sports that appeal to many Chinese Americans.

A growing number of Chinese American athletes have reached the top of their chosen sports. In the 1970s, Maureen Louie of San Francisco won numerous amateur and professional tennis titles. Michael Chang, another tennis player, was the youngest person to win the French Open. Tiffany Chin, a junior ice-skating champion, placed fourth in the 1984 Olympic women's figure skating competition. Figure skater Michelle Kwan won the silver medal in the 1994 Goodwill Games and was an alternate to the 1994 Winter Olympics. Jennifer Yu, Stanford all-American fencer and alternate to the 1988 Olympic team, was the 1990 national women's foil champion. At age 15 windsurfer Ted Huang was the youngest member of the 1985 U.S. sailboard team. He won regattas throughout the world while still a student at Stanford. Al J. Young has been the victor in scores of national drag races. (See also Asian Americans in Sports.)

Politics

Chinese Americans are more active politically than ever before, joining civic and service groups, boards of education, and volunteer committees. No longer fearful and suspicious of government, they welcome the opportunity to participate. They are more visible and more influential on the national scene as well, although to date only Hawaii has sent a Chinese American to Congress.

Hiriam Fong became that state's first senator in 1959. The son of an immigrant sugar-plantation worker and a tireless advocate of Hawaiian statehood, his landslide victory was a great source of great pride for the Chinese community.

In San Francisco, home of the nation's oldest Chinatown, Tom Hsieh became the first Chinese elected to the board of supervisors, winning a seat in 1986; he later ran unsuccessfully for mayor. Other notable Chinese Americans in politics are: Julia Chang Bloch, appointed by President Bush as ambassador to Nepal; Elaine Chao, director of the Peace Corps; Lily Lee Chen, a 1955 immigrant from Taiwan and member of the city council of Monterey Park, California, and in 1983 the first Chinese American woman mayor in the United States; Roger Chinn, mayor of Foster City, California; Roger Eng, former mayor of Los Altos, California; Art Wang, a member of Washington's state legislature; March Fong Eu, who was California's secretary of state for over a decade and was appointed in 1994 by President Bill Clinton as ambassador in Micronesia; and S. B. Woo, Delaware's lieutenant governor, who was defeated in his bids for House and Senate.

The campaign of Michael Woo, a 41 year-old Democrat running for mayor of Los Angeles in 1993 drew national attention. Woo, endorsed by President Clinton, was popular among young African- and Asian American voters. Ironically his father, an immigrant, was once forbidden to buy a house in a white section of Los Angeles. Woo condemned police brutality in the beating of African American Rodney King and called for racial harmony in the aftermath of the riots. Although he lost to Republican Richard Riordan, Woo inspired people of all races by focusing on the issues of justice and civil rights.

The judicial branch of the government has accepted Chinese Americans also, such as Thomas Tang of Arizona, who was appointed to the Ninth Circuit Court of Appeals in 1977. Other prominent judges include: Superior Court Judge Harry Low of San Francisco, Municipal Court Judge Lillian Sing of San Francisco, and James Chang of the Municipal Court of Santa Clara County.

Arts and Entertainment

Stage and Screen

Although they traveled far from home, Chinese immigrants never relinquished their cultural roots. Bringing their ancient and elaborate operas to the new world, they built theaters in which to perform them; San Francisco's Chinatown once had several. Traveling Chinese opera troupes still find enthusiastic audiences among Chinese American communities. Classics like *Dream of the Red Chamber*, *Lady White Snake*, and stories from the *Romance of the Three Kingdoms* are as popular today as they were a hundred years ago.

Lalu Nathoy, played by Rosalind Chao, was known as China Polly by the gold miners in the boarding house that she managed. She is displeased with the boarder's reaction to her cooking in this scene from "A Thousand Pieces of Gold," the film adaptation of Ruthanne Lum McCunn's story. (Courtesy of *American Playhouse*.)

Modern Chinese films are also enjoyed, including action-packed Hong Kong gangster movies, historical dramas like *Raise the Red Lantern*, and *The Wedding Banquet* a comedy from Taiwan.

Chinese have also struggled for a place in the U.S. entertainment industry. Anna May Wong was the first and for many years the only Chinese to succeed in Hollywood, starring in silent films in the 1920s. Beulah Quo, the first Asian woman to win an Emmy, produced a 1974 documentary on the great cinematographer James Wong Howe, whose credits include 120 films. Two of them, *The Rose Tattoo* and *Hud* won Academy Awards.

In the 1970s, young Asian Americans began to protest demeaning media stereotypes: such as the Charlie Chan and Fu Manchu caricatures, and the Suzy Wongs and sinister dragon ladies. Particularly offensive, however, were Asian characters portrayed by white actors.

Even Bruce Lee, the famous San Francisco-born actor and martial artist, lost a kung-fu role to a Caucasian. To find success he went to Hong Kong; there he made movies that became enormously popular all over the world. *Dragon*, his 1993 film biography, starred Hawaiian-Chinese actor, Jason Scott Lee, who also won the lead in another movie released that year, *Map of the Human Heart*.

The 1980s and 1990s gave Chinese Americans more opportunities in this medium, some in films written and directed by Asians. Director Wayne Wang made films on Chinese that were seen by a mainstream audience: *Dim Sum, Chan is Missing*, and *Eat a Bowl of Tea*. Peter Wang produced an amusing, true-to-life film about a Chinese American family visiting relatives in China, *The Great Wall*. The film version of *A Thousand Pieces of Gold*, Ruthanne Lum McCunn's story of a pioneer Chinese woman in Idaho whose father sold her into slavery, was warmly received, and starred the talented Rosalind Chao. Amy Tan's best seller, *The Joy Luck Club*, was made into a critically acclaimed film (directed by Wayne Wang) with an all-Asian cast.

On stage David Henry Hwang's Tony Award-winning *M. Butterfly* starred San Francisco-born actor B. D. Wong, who also had roles in the blockbuster *Jurassic Park* and the television sitcom about a Korean American family, "All American Girl" which debuted in 1994.

Many Chinese Americans also work in radio and television, from sportscasting to producing. Best known, perhaps is CBS's news anchor Connie Chung.

Literature

In the past two decades, the phenomenal success of several best-sellers with Chinese themes has done much to focus attention on the Chinese American experience and thought. Maxine Hong Kingston rose to national prominence with *Woman Warrior* in 1976; her subsequent works, *China Men* and *Tripmaster Monkey* have achieved critical acclaim as well. Betty Bao Lord's novel *Spring Moon* was also a large success. At the top of the charts for many weeks was *The Joy Luck Club* by Amy Tan, an intricate weaving of the tales of several immigrant women. Received just as enthusiastically was her second book, *The Kitchen God's Wife*, the heartrending tale of a woman who survived World War II in China and settled in the United States. Gus Lee's *China Boy*, a semi-autobiographical tale about growing up as a Chinese American, was also a bestseller. *Typical American* by Gish Jen tells the story of the immigrant Chang family and its pursuit of the American dream. David Wong Louie's collection of short stories with contrasting Asian American viewpoints, *Pangs of Love*, enchanted its audience.

With the new focus on multiculturalism in the United States, the sudden interest in Chinese American culture is startling, considering the difficulty many ethnic writers had in getting their works published before the 1970s. Until then, only C. Y. Lee's *The Flower Drum Song* a light, whimsical tale of Chinatown romances during the 1950s that was made into a musical and a film had achieved any mainstream success.

The Chinese American angry young man of the 1960s, Frank Chin, produced several controversial plays with themes on Chinese American consciousness and U.S. racism such as *Chickencoop Chinaman* and *Year of the Dragon*. The founder of the Asian American Theater workshop, author of fiction and essays, and editor of several anthologies, he never achieved widespread public recognition, but is viewed as a pioneer of Asian American literature.

The new writers, whose intriguing, innovative voices enliven haunting characters and circumstances, have caught the public's imagination. Amy Tan's stories are based on the oral histories of Chinese immigrant women, while Gus Lee tells of growing up in a predominantly black neighborhood. Publishers have discovered that there is a market for Chinese American stories, and that the general audience can empathize with an immigrant's struggle.

Smaller presses have produced some excellent collections of poetry, among them *Dreams in Harrison Park* by Nellie Wong and *Songs for Jadina* by Alan Chong Lau. Historical and academic writings by Chinese Americans are also emerging such as *Bittersweet Soil* by Suchen Chan, which discusses Chinese in agriculture, and *Making and Remaking Asian America through Immigration Policy* by Bill Ong Hing.

Art

As in the other professions, Chinese American artists, were once rare. Yun Gee (1906-1963) was an immigrant from Canton who joined the modernist art scene in the 1920s. He suffered the stigma of being a refugee from Chinatown in a white world. Married to a white woman, he was physically attacked several times while walking down the street with her. His dramatic surreal painting, *Where Is My Mother*, portrays an immigrant's loneliness in its artist's tearful face and in the background is the ship that brought him to the United States. His works were shown in many prominent museums and galleries, but in 1945 he suffered a mental breakdown that ended his brilliant career.

In contrast, Dong Kingman, born in Oakland in 1911, is a watercolorist and illustrator who has enjoyed much success. His delightful pictures of Chinatown, San Francisco, and other areas of California have become his trademark. He was the first Chinese American to have his work acquired by the Metropolitan Museum; his paintings are also displayed in other well-known prominent collections.

Today there are many young Chinese American artists, craftspeople, sculptors, illustrators, and painters. Some of their work appears in shows that focus on Asian Americans. One such artist, Flo Wong, works in several media. Her themes are distinctly Chinese American, and include drawings of her working-class family and childhood in a Chinese restaurant in Oakland. She is a director of the Asian Heritage Council, which has organized exhibits showcasing modern Asian American artists. Among those featured in the "Completing the Circle" exhibit was painter Bernice Bing, who noted, "Once upon a time it was rare to find any Asians in prestigious art schools."

Music

The most famous cellist in the United States is Yo Yo Ma, the son of immigrant musicians. Yo Yo attended Harvard before choosing a performance career; he has since been awarded a number of honorary degrees.

Jazz promoter Herb Wong, a San Francisco disc jockey for over 30 years, is also the president of the Association of Jazz Educators. He enjoys counseling young Asian musicians, encouraging them to be creative and to improvise, both in music and in life, because, as he says "I am an antagonist to stereotypes."

When told "You speak great American" and asked "Where do you come from?" Wong replies "I come from Here."

Fashion

While Chinese were traditionally relegated to the garment industry's sweatshops in the past, members of a new generation now work in showrooms, creating innovative designs for fashions from ready-to-wear to *haute couture*. Among them are Vera Wang, noted designer of bridal gowns, and Anna Sui, a Michigan designer who won the 1992 Perry Ellis Award for new fashion talent.

Architecture

The two most famous Asian American architects, I. M. Pei and Maya Lin, come from and reflect the thought of different generations.

Ieoh Ming Pei, born in China in 1917, designed the John F. Kennedy Memorial Library in Boston as well as an addition to the Louvre in Paris, and has directed redevelopment projects throughout the United States. He studied at the University of Pennsylvania and Massachusetts Institute of Technology and taught at Harvard before setting up his architectural firm in New York City. He has designed structures as diverse as an airport control tower and Syracuse University's School of Journalism.

Maya Lin, born in Ohio of immigrant parents, was a 21 year-old Yale senior when her entry (No. 1,026) was chosen as the winning design in the Vietnam Veterans Memorial competition in 1982. Her design was a strikingly simple yet imposing wall, engraved with the names of all the approximately 58,000 U.S. military personnel killed in the conflict. In 1988, she was chosen to design the Civil Rights Memorial in Montgomery, Alabama. Struck by a line from Martin Luther King, Jr.'s, "I Have A Dream" speech ("We will not be satisfied until justice rolls down like waters and righteousness like a mighty stream."), she designed a plaza whose dramatic fountain symbolized peace and healing. In her statement accompanying the drawing, Lin concluded, "The memorial plaza will be a contemplative area—a place to remember the civil rights movement, to honor those killed during the struggle, to appreciate how far the country has come in its quest for equality, and to consider how far it has to go." A documentary on Maya Lin's life, produced and directed by Chinese American Freida Lee Mock titled *Maya Lin. A Strong, Clear Vision*, was nominated in 1995 for an Academy Award.

◆ ACHIEVING VISIBILITY

Although Chinese Americans are regarded as the "model minority," Asian leaders point out the fallacy of such a stereotype, since struggling immigrants are often exploited by employers. Garment workers, for example, most of them women, often toil in substandard conditions for below-minimum wage. Even professionals can be confronted with "glass ceilings" in many companies. And despite much progress, the old fear of physical harm still looms.

In 1982, a young Chinese American named Vincent Chin was brutally murdered in Detroit by two white auto workers who called him a "Jap" and blamed him for their unemployment. They were convicted only of manslaughter, sentenced to three years probation, and fined a mere $3,780 each. Later, one of the men was convicted on federal grounds for civil rights violations, but was released upon appeal.

This crime and the perceived lack of justice fueled the anger of Chinese Americans and drew them even more tightly together, spawning both community coalitions and nationwide alliances. Unlike early organizations formed for protection and self-help, these new groups strive for civil rights and advocacy. Some have old roots, like the Chinese American Citizens Alliance, but many others are more contemporary.

The Chinese Historical Society of America, founded in 1965, is dedicated to preserving the little-known history of Chinese in the United States. A dynamic civil rights organization, Chinese for Affirmative Action, was established in San Francisco during the same decade by a group of activists led by Henry Der.

The Organization of Chinese Americans, headquartered in Washington, D.C., with branches throughout the nation, is an advocacy group that promotes Asian American involvement in government, and education, seeking equal justice and opportunity for Asian Americans. Some Chinese have branched off to form pan-Asian groups, the most prominent being Asian Americans for Community Involvement in Santa Clara County, California. Founded in 1973 by Chinese American psychiatrist, Dr. Allan Seid, this once-small advocacy group has grown into a large organization that provides a variety of services for its large constituency, which includes many immigrants.

◆ NEW CHALLENGES

The Vietnam War sent nearly a hundred thousand refugees, many of them ethnic Chinese, from Southeast Asia to the United States. In 1989, the collapse of the democracy movement in China prompted several thousand Chinese students already in the United States to stay and seek political asylum. Recently, stories of illegal immigrants smuggled in boats have made headlines. These and other events have once again raised public attention on immigration.

In difficult economic times, many U.S. citizens support immigration restriction, demanding that aliens and refugees seeking asylum from repressive policies be returned. With the nineteenth century cry "The Chinese Must Go" still echoing in their minds, fifth and sixth generation Chinese Americans have found that they do have something in common with new arrivals from Hong Kong, Taiwan, and mainland China. "We are looked upon as the same," they say, and feel that all Asians are affected by racial prejudice and need to join together to combat it.

Although attitudes in the United States are changing, race relations remains a prominent issue. Despite the challenges of economic hardship and prejudice, the Chinese are no longer powerless victims to be excluded or ignored. After nearly a century and a half in the United States, they are moving towards ever-greater participation in U.S. society and are in a position to help determine its direction in a positive way.

—Connie Young Yu

5

Who Are the Filipino Americans?

◆ Population ◆ Demographics ◆ Education ◆ The Family ◆ Languages
◆ Labor Force Participation ◆ Income ◆ Poverty ◆ Religion ◆ National Holidays
◆ History of Immigration ◆ Literature

Population of the Asian/Pacific Islander Population by Ethnicity in Percent of Asian Total, 1990

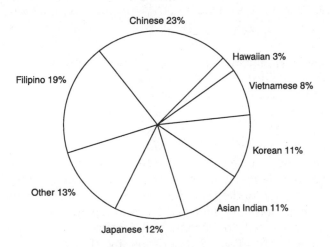

Source: Statistical Record of Asian Americans.

Filipino Americans are persons of Filipino ancestry who are citizens of the United States either by birth or naturalization. They are also Philippine nationals who have become permanent residents of the United States by virtue of being a registered alien or immigrant.

Filipino Americans are often mistaken for Hispanics, due to their Spanish surnames and also because many speak Spanish. This is not surprising since Filipinos adopted the language and customs of Spain as a result of a long history of Spanish rule, thereby sharing in a heritage similar to Hispanic groups.

Filipino Americans are sometimes referred to as "Pinoys," a slang term coined by the early Filipino immigrants themselves to signify ethnic pride and solidarity. Pinoys are a diverse people. They include "old-timers," or Philippine-born first-generation immigrants

that have been U.S. permanent residents since the 1920s, and "new-timers," whose ranks have burgeoned since the 1965 Immigration Reform Act. Pinoys also include American-born Filipino Americans of mixed Caucasian, East Indian, Hispanic, African, and Asian and Pacific Islander parentage.

Within Filipino American communities are found a diverse range of people representing a broad spectrum of social, cultural, and economic groups. Individual Filipinos have distinguished themselves in many areas, contributing many innovative ideas to American society such as the design of the Lunar Rover, the Boeing 747 pilot seat, and color photography airbrush retouching. A few Filipino words have been accepted into common English usage as well; among them are *yo-yo* and *boondocks*.

◆ POPULATION

The Filipino population in the United States has grown rapidly since the 1910 Census, the first year the Census Bureau began counting Filipinos as an individual group. In the years since, the number of Filipinos in the United States has grown from fewer than 3,000 to 1,406,770.

In 1990, Filipinos accounted for 19 percent of all Asians in the United States, forming the second-largest group among all Asian/Pacific Americans. This rapid growth is due to the increasing number of Filipinos who migrate to the United States every year. According to the 1990 Census, 64 percent of the Filipino population was born outside the United States. Moreover, the Philippines led all Asian nations in total immigration from 1980 through 1990, numbering 495,271. Korea followed with over 333,800 during the same period.

The disproportionately large Filipino population can be attributed to the exemption granted from the 1924 U.S. Immigration Act, which barred the entry of Asians

Table 5.1
Population of the United States by Asian Ethnicity by Decade, 1900 to 1990
U.S. population by Asian ethnic group by census year, 1900 to 1990.

Year	Total, U.S.	Total Asian (b)	Chinese	Filipino (a)	Asian Indian	Japanese	Korean	Vietnamese
1900	76,212,168	204,462	118,746	—	—	85,716	—	—
1910	92,228,531	249,926	94,414	2,767	—	152,745	5,008	—
1920	106,021,568	332,432	85,202	26,634	—	220,596	6,181	—
1930	123,202,660	489,326	102,159	108,424	—	278,743	8,332	—
1940	132,165,129	489,984	106,334	98,535	—	285,115	8,568	—
1950	151,325,798	599,091	150,005	122,707	—	326,379	7,030 (c)	—
1960	179,323,175	877,934	237,292	176,310	—	464,332	—	—
1970	203,211,926	1,429,562	436,062	343,060	—	591,290	69,150 (d)	—
1980	226,545,805	3,466,421	812,178	781,894	387,223	716,331	357,393	245,025
1990	248,709,873	7,273,662 (e)	1,645,472	1,406,770	815,447	847,562	798,849	614,547

Notes:
(a) Included with "other race" for the United States in 1900 and for Alaska in 1920 and 1950.
(b) Total only of Asian groups listed for the specific year. In 1980, includes 166,377 Asian Americans not listed in the table, as follows: Cambodian, 16,044; Hmong, 5,204; Laotian, 47,682; Thai, 45, 279; Hawaiian, 172,346; Guamanian, 39,520; Samoan, 30,695; Other A/PI, 69,625.
(c) Data for Hawaii only.
(d) Excludes Koreans in Alaska.
(e) Includes 1,145,015 Asians not listed in the table, as follows: Cambodian, 147,411; Hmong, 90,082; Laotian, 149,014; Thai, 91,275; Hawaiian, 211,014; Guamanian, 62,964; Samoan, 49,345; and Other A/PI, 343,910.

Source: *Statistical Record of Asian Americans.*

Filipino Population Distribution by Region of the United States, in Percent

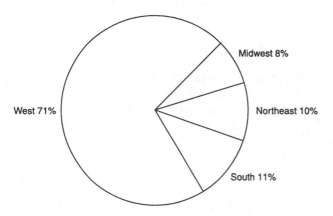

Midwest 8%
West 71%
Northeast 10%
South 11%

Source: *U.S Census Bureau.*

into the United States. The Philippines, a U.S. colony at the time, was primarily exempt because it the principal supplier of cheap farm labor to Guam, Hawaii, and the West Coast. Later, Filipino migration increased dramatically with the passage of the 1965 Immigration Act, which eased quota restrictions on Filipinos long after the Philippines became an independent nation.

The Philippines has been second only to Mexico in the total number of immigrants entering the United States annually since 1965, with the exception of those years immediately following the fall of South Vietnam, when a large number of Southeast Asian refugees immigrated to the United States. Because of the heavy immigration of Filipinos each year, Filipino Americans are projected to become the largest ethnic group among Asian/Pacific Americans by the year 2000. Moreover, Filipino Americans have one of the highest birth rates among all the minority groups, second only to Mexican Americans. This notably high birth rate is largely due to cultural and religious (predominantly Roman Catholic) norms.

According to the 1990 Census, the majority of the Filipino population, 71 percent, lived in the West, with the remainder distributed almost equally in the Northeast (10 percent), Midwest (8 percent), and South (11 percent). Fifty-two percent are concentrated in California (731,685) and Hawaii (168,682), where early Filipino immigrants settled due to the need for cheap labor on Hawaiian sugar plantations and California farms.

The commonwealth status of the Philippines in the 1920s also allowed for the recruitment of a substantial number of Filipinos into the U.S. Armed Forces. This accounts for the presence of large Filipino communities in the San Diego and Los Angeles areas, where there are large military installations.

Table 5.2
Immigrants Admitted to the United States by Selected Asian Ethnic Group by Decade, 1850-1990

Decade	Chinese	Japanese	Asian Indian	Korean	Filipino	Vietnamese
1850-1860	41,397	—	43	—	—	—
1861-1870	64,301	186	69	—	—	—
1871-1880	123,201	149	163	—	—	—
1881-1890	61,711	2,270	269	—	—	—
1891-1900	14,799	25,942	68	—	—	—
1901-1910	20,605	129,797	4,713	7,697	—	—
1911-1920	21,278	83,837	2,082	1,049	869	—
1921-1930	29,907	33,462	1,886	598	54,747	—
1931-1940	4,928	1,948	496	60	6,159	—
1941-1950	16,709	1,555	1,761	—	4,691	—
1951-1960	9,657 (a)	46,250	1,973	6,231	19,307	—
1961-1970	34,764	39,98	27,189	34,526	98,376	3,788
1971-1980	12,326	49,775	164,134	271,956	360,216	179,681
1981-1990	366,622 (b)	43.248	261,841	338,824	495,271	401,419

Notes:
(a) Beginning in 1957, Chinese total includes immigration from Taiwan.
(b) Beginning in 1982, Taiwan was no longer included in the Chinese total. Immigration from Taiwan to the United States from 1982 to 1990 was 118,105. These immigrants are not included in the total for Chinese which appears in the table.

Source: Statistical Record of Asian Americans.

Other states with large Filipino populations include Illinois (64,224), New York (62,259), New Jersey (53,146), and Washington (43,799). A warm climate and job opportunities also drew Filipino Americans to the South. Florida, where 31,945 Filipinos live, more than doubled its population in the decades after World War II. Other southern states with large concentrations of Filipinos include Virginia (35,067) and Texas (34,350). The smallest Filipino American communities are in Vermont (253) and Wyoming (408). In the nation's capital, there are 2,082 Filipino residents.

Traditionally, many Filipinos settled in the rural and urban areas of the western states, as well as in large urban areas such as Los Angeles, New York, and Chicago. There are over 150,000 in the city of Los Angeles alone. The growth in job opportunities in regional centers such as Houston resulted in mushrooming Filipino populations. More recently, they have located in metropolitan areas such as Hampton Roads, Philadelphia, Baltimore, Phoenix, and Boise.

Changing immigration patterns after World War II brought many new immigrants to the suburbs. Census figures show that in the 1980s many Filipinos settled in suburban areas rather than in central cities. Seeking better housing and schools, this wave of immigrants were better educated, more economically prosperous, and often lived among other ethnic Americans, rather than in Filipino or Asian communities, as has often been the pattern of previous immigrants. Today, the presence of Filipinos in U.S. communities is not resented as much as in the past; like other Asian Americans, they are generally perceived by their neighbors as a stabilizing influence.

♦ DEMOGRAPHICS

There are more Filipino women today than men, a contrast to the 1920s and 1930s when the Filipino American population was predominantly male. Even by 1940, the male-female ratio in the Filipino-American community was 456.7 to 100. This imbalance was due to the predominance of young single men who migrated to the United States before World War II. By 1960, however, this male/female ratio had changed to 175.4 to 100. By 1970, the ratio was 93.5 Filipino males per 100 Filipino females. In 1990, there were 86 males per 100 females.

The average age of the Filipino population jumped from 28.5 years in 1980 to 31.1 years in 1990, slightly older than the overall Asian American median age of 30 years, but younger than the U.S. median of 33 years. The largest number of Filipinos (73 percent) are 18 years and older.

♦ EDUCATION

Originally, many Filipinos came to the United States to attend high school or college, although later

Table 5.3
Filipino Population by Significant U.S. Metropolitan Areas
Filipino population in numbers, percent of the total area population, and percent of Asian/Pacific Islander area population, ranked by metropolitan area (a), 1990.

Metropolitan area (b)	Total population	Total A/PI population	Filipino		
			Number	Percent of total	Percent of A/PI
Los Angeles–Long Beach, CA PMSA	8,863,164	925,561	219,653	2.5%	24%
Honolulu, HI MSA	836,231	413,349	120,029	14.4%	29%
San Diego, CA MSA	2,498,016	184,596	95,945	3.8%	52%
San Francisco, CA PMSA	1,603,678	316,751	88,560	5.5%	28%
Oakland, CA PMSA	2,082,914	259,002	77,198	3.7%	30%
San Jose, CA PMSA	1,497,577	254,786	61,518	4.1%	24%
Chicago, IL PMSA	6,069,974	227,742	54,411	0.9%	24%
New York, NY PMSA	8,546,846	553,443	49,156	0.6%	9%
Anaheim–Santa Ana, CA PMSA	2,410,556	240,703	30,356	1.3%	13%
Vallejo–Fairfield–Napa, CA PMSA	451,186	43,289	29,760	6.6%	69%
Riverside–San Bernardino, CA PMSA	2,588,793	93,473	28,919	1.1%	31%
Seattle, WA PMSA	1,972,961	128,656	27,900	1.4%	22%
Washington, DC–MD–VA MSA	3,923,574	200,113	26,793	0.7%	13%
Sacramento, CA MSA	1,481,102	109,242	20,359	1.4%	19%
Norfolk–Virginia Beach–Newport News, VA MSA	1,396,107	34,004	19,858	1.4%	58%
Stockton, CA MSA	480,628	58,374	16,570	3.5%	28%
Houston, TX PMSA	3,301,937	125,529	13,404	0.4%	11%
Jersey City, NJ PMSA	553,099	36,564	13,222	2.4%	36%
Oxnard–Ventura, CA PMSA	669,016	32,699	12,690	1.9%	39%
Philadelphia, PA–NJ PMSA	4,856,881	103,537	12,233	0.3%	12%
Salinas–Seaside–Monterey, CA MSA	355,660	25,369	11,421	3.2%	45%
Newark, NJ PMSA	1,824,321	52,539	10,907	0.6%	21%
Bergen–Passaic, NJ PMSA	1,278,440	66,540	10,027	0.8%	15%

Notes:
(a) Includes metropolitan areas with Filipino population greater than 10,000.
(b) The U.S. Census Bureau designates the following: PMSA=primary metropolitan statistical area; MSA=metropolitan statistical area. See *Appendix* for detailed definitions.

Source: *Statistical Record of Asian Americans.*

immigration contained a much smaller number of students. As a group, Filipinos have shown a marked desire to educate themselves. Most of the very first arrivals were young men working their way through college. Many became frustrated, however, due the effects of discrimination and because they had to work to earn living and educational expenses.

It was during the 1920s that the number of Filipino students in the United States was at its peak. Between 1929 and 1930, there were 896 Filipino students attending college, 30 of whom were women. These students attended 124 different colleges throughout the United States. In 49 of these 124 colleges, there was only one Filipino student, and rarely were there more than five or six among the other institutions.

In 1990, 82.8 percent of all Filipinos age 25 and over were high school graduates, up from 74 percent in 1980. This figure was larger than the Asian American graduation rate of 78 percent. The corresponding figure for the total U.S. population was 75 percent. However, the percentage of Filipino high school graduates was considerably lower than that of the Japanese (87 percent) and East Indians (84.2 percent). Overall, Filipino men graduated from high school at a higher rate than Filipino women, 84.2 percent to 81.4 percent. This is a shift from 10 years ago when Filipinos were the only Asian/Pacific American group in which women outperformed men in the rate of high school graduation.

At the college level, 38.9 percent of all Filipinos age 25 and over were college graduates, compared to the

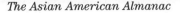

Filipino Population Distribution by State

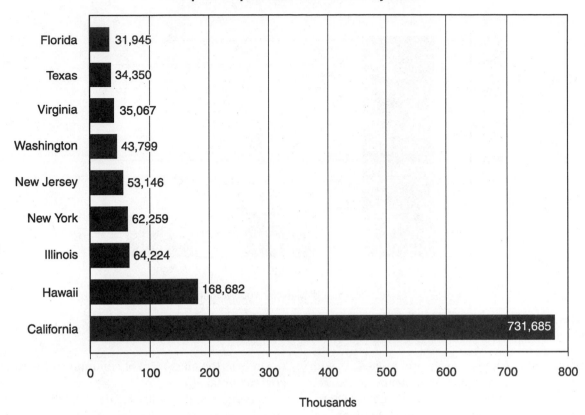

State	Population
Florida	31,945
Texas	34,350
Virginia	35,067
Washington	43,799
New Jersey	53,146
New York	62,259
Illinois	64,224
Hawaii	168,682
California	731,685

Thousands

Source: U.S Census Bureau.

38 percent of all Asian Americans in the same age bracket and 20 percent of the total U.S. population. More Filipino women held degrees than Filipino men, 41.6 percent to 36.2; no other Asian American group has this distinction. The corresponding figures for the total U.S. population were 32.7 percent and 43.2 percent, women to men. Among Asian groups, only Pakistanis and East Indians claimed higherpercentages of bachelor's degree recipients, 58 percent and 52 percent, respectively.

The Filipino community, like other major post-1965 immigrant groups from Asia, includes large numbers of graduates from institutions of higher education outside the United States. Yet, in spite of their higher education levels, Filipino immigrants that obtained their undergraduate or graduate degrees in the Philippines often find it difficult to get jobs in the United States commensurate with their academic credentials. Due to rigorous licensing requirements in the United States for certain professions—such as physicians, dentists, pharmacists, and lawyers—many immigrants that were professionals in their native country are unable to take up their professions in the United States and are often forced to accept lesser jobs on the socio-economic ladder.

Many Filipinos have difficulty with English proficiency. Over 70 dialects are spoken in the Philippines and 40 percent of foreign-born Filipino American students speak one of these dialects at home as their primary language. Even when students are functionally fluent in English, they often speak or write differently from standard English. Like other Asian/Pacific American groups, Filipino students may often be shy in class and reticent about asking for help. Standardized tests are another area of difficulty for Filipino students.

♦ THE FAMILY

Most Filipino families are headed by married couples (78 percent), while 15 percent are headed by women and only 6 percent by men. In this way, they are similar to the general U.S. population. Also, the average Filipino family had 4.0 persons in 1990, larger than the average of 3.8 persons for all Asian American families and the average of 3.2 persons for all U.S. families.

In the Philippines, individuals have the support and help of an extended family. In the United States, Filipinos do not regularly have such large family groups to depend upon. They have to learn to seek assistance

Trend in Ratio of Filipino Men per 100 Women in the United States, 1940 to 1990

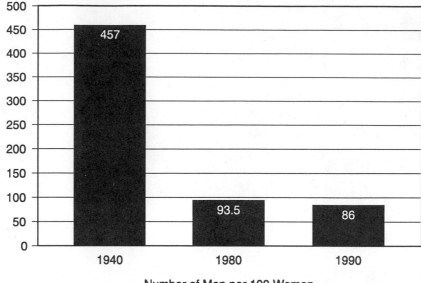

Number of Men per 100 Women

Source: *U.S Census Bureau.*

from government agencies and their churches. As with other immigrant groups, their American-born children often go to U.S. public schools and, consequently, become somewhat alienated from their heritage and culture. Filipino American families are constantly faced with the challenge of promoting Filipino culture and values among their children, while attempting to adapt to their new surroundings.

◆ LANGUAGES

Filipinos speak more than 70 dialects, although most of them can be classified under eight major language groups. The most common are Tagalog, Visayan, and Ilocano. A large majority of Filipinos in the United States, 66 percent, speak one of these languages, but the largest number still speak Tagalog. According to the 1990 U.S. Census, Tagalog is the sixth most-spoken foreign language and the second most-spoken Asian language in the United States. In California, where most Filipinos reside, Tagalog is ranked as the third most-spoken foreign language (464,644), after Chinese dialects (542,888) and Spanish (5.4 million).

Unlike other Asian groups, however, many Filipinos are familiar with English as soon as they arrive in the United States. This is due to the introduction of U.S. public education in the Philippines in the early 20th century. English was the medium of instruction in the schools, starting from first grade. It was also a unifying language, given the many different languages and dialects spoken in the country. It has, as well, served until

recently as the main form of communication in Filipino governmental affairs.

According to the 1990 Census, only 37 percent of Filipinos 5 years old or over do not speak English "very well" and 13 percent are "linguistically isolated," the lowest rate among all the Asian American groups. (The census defines linguistic isolation as "persons in households in which no one 14 years old or over speaks only English, and no one who speaks a language other than English speaks English 'very well.'")

◆ LABOR FORCE PARTICIPATION

Early Filipino immigrants were often farm and cannery workers. Most were migrant workers who harvested crops on California farms and in Hawaiian sugar cane fields. Thousands of Filipinos also took jobs in Alaskan salmon canneries during the summer months, working in factories 12 to 18 hours a day cleaning and packing salmon. During the off-season, they would go to Seattle and San Francisco to take service jobs. Since that time, though, Filipino American labor force participation has drastically been altered.

The civilian labor force participation rate among Filipino Americans age 16 years and over increased from 68 percent in 1970 to over 75 percent in 1990. Filipinos had the highest participation rate among all Asian Americans (67 percent) as well as all U.S. citizens (65 percent). Both Filipino men and women have higher labor force participation rates when compared to the general population. For example, in 1980, 68 percent of

Likelihood of Entering Management, Asian Men

American-born Chinese, Filipino, Japanese, and white men with a colege degree and twenty years experience who became managers, in percent.(a)

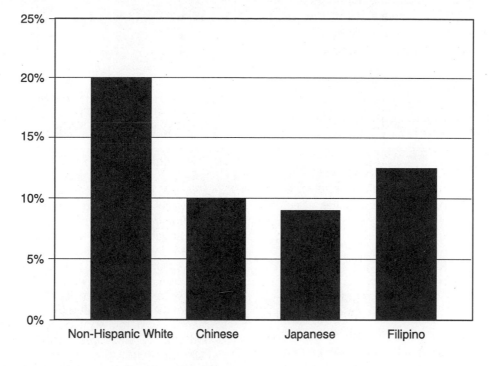

Notes:
(a) Data is adjusted for education, experience, industry, and other relevant factors.

Source: Statistical Record of Asian Americans.

Filipino women were in the labor force compared to 50 percent of all women in the United States. Moreover, Filipinos had the highest proportion among all Asian American families with three or more workers (30 percent) compared with the Asian American proportion of 20 percent and the national proportion of 13 percent.

According to the 1990 U.S. Census, over 55 percent of Filipino Americans hold white-collar jobs, including professional, technical, sales, and administrative positions. A breakdown of these figures reveals that 37 percent of gainfully employed Filipinos were in "technical, sales, and administrative" occupations, compared to the 33 percent of all Asian Americans and 32 percent of all U.S. citizens. Another 27 percent held "managerial and professional specialty" positions, compared to 26.4 percent for the nation and 31.2 percent for the Asian American population.

The ease with which Filipino Americans get these jobs is due to their language facility and the skills they learned in the Philippines. Consequently, while Filipinos may find employment in American firms more easily, other Asians surpass them in entrepreneurship. Unlike the Chinese, East Indians, and Koreans who often operate their own businesses, Filipinos have a very low levelof small-business ownership.

Of the remaining employed Filipino Americans, 16.8 percent were in service occupations; 11 percent were operators, fabricators, and laborers; 7.4 percent were in precision production, craft, and repair occupations; and 1.5 percent were in farming, forestry, and fishing occupations.

Filipino American physicians and nurses have made important contributions to medicine in the United States. During the 1980s, many U.S. hospitals experienced a shortage of medical professionals and thousands of trained Filipinos were available to fill the void. In the 1950s and 1960s, the U.S. government implemented a foreign-exchange program designed to train physicians and nurses in advanced medicine with an agreement that they return to their homeland to apply their skills there. Nearly 90 percent of those that signed up were Filipino. Many of them, however, did not go back home when their training ended.

In 1974, there were 7,000 Filipino American physicians in the United States. About 1,000 of them settled in New York City, which at the time had a Filipino American population of 45,000. Today, Filipino American physicians are on the staff of nearly every hospital in New York and New Jersey. In the 1970s, one-fifth of all nurses who graduated from nursing schools in the

Philippines came to the United States; only about one-third of those returned.

Also noteworthy, is the high representation of Filipinos in government jobs—a unique distinction among Asian/Pacific Americans. Filipinos have been serving in the U.S. Navy since the early 1900s, mostly as mess attendants or stewards. It may be that many are able to demonstrate skills acquired through their work experience with the U.S. Navy, helping them to gain civil service jobs. Furthermore, joining the Navy has always been a common means of U.S. immigration for Filipinos. In 1990, the U.S. Navy had a total of 18,889 Filipinos, including 18,232 enlisted personnel and 657 officers. Like other military retirees, many Filipinos settle in towns and cities near naval bases after they leave the service.

♦ INCOME

The median family income of Filipino Americans grew between 1980 and 1990. In 1990, the median income for all Filipino families was $46,698, compared to $41,583 for the total Asian American population. Only Japanese Americans and East Indians had a higher median family income, $51,550 and $49,309, respectively. The median family income of Filipino Americans was relatively high because it included a large segment of highly skilled and well-paid professionals and because 30 percent of Filipino families included three or more workers. This last figure was much higher than the corresponding figures of 20 percent for the Asian American population and 13 percent for the total U.S. population.

In terms of per capita income, Filipinos lagged slightly behind the U.S. population, with a 1990 per capita income in 1990 of $13,616, compared to $13,806 for all Asian Americans and $14,143 for the nation. Despite their high levels of education and high percentage of participation in the U.S. work force, Filipino Americans again had a disappointing per capita income in comparison to the 1980s.

Among Filipino Americans, those born in the United States had lower incomes than those born in the Philippines. The 1990 Census noted that native-born Filipino Americans had an average annual family income of $21,190, compared to a foreign-born Filipino income of $29,400. One logical conclusion is that Filipinos that immigrated to the United States were mostly professionals and were in a better position to earn higher incomes than Filipino Americans who were born and raised in the United States.

Lillian Gonzalez-Pardo, M.D.

Clinical Professor and Director, Division of Neurology Department of Pediatrics, The University of Kansas Medical Center.

Dr. Gonzalez-Pardo was the first Asian American to serve as president of the American Women's Medical Association (1992). She, like many other Filipino Americans, received part of her training in the Philippines and completed her advanced training in neurology in the United States. Although she returned to the Philippines to teach from 1969-71, the bulk of her medical career has been in pediatric neurology at The University of Kansas Medical Center. She is dedicated to increased biomedical research for women, reproductive rights, and sharing resources with other countries to improve the health care of women and children worldwide. She also developed Asian American Women Physicians Project, in cooperation with the Archives and Special Collection on Women in Medicine of the Medical College of Pennsylvania. The goal of the project was to develop educational materials about Asian American women physicians, from both the past and the present.

♦ POVERTY

The poverty rate among Filipino families declined from 7 percent in 1980 to 5 percent in 1990. In addition, Filipino Americans had the second lowest poverty rate among Asian Americans. This extremely low percentage may be attributable to the large numbers of post-1965 immigrants that were well-educated and employable, even though they may not have always found employment appropriate to their academic training and professional experience.

♦ RELIGION

Here in the United States, religion has continued to be an important part of Filipino life. Like most Americans, the majority of Filipinos in the United States are Christian; most, in fact, are Roman Catholic. The tradition of Christianity is largely due to 350 years of Spanish colonial rule when Spanish friars converted

Table 5.4
Filipino American service in the U.S. Navy by rank as of June 1992

Rank	Title	Filipino	Total Asian	Total, all active duty
E1	Seaman Recruit	499	675	22,974
E2	Seaman Apprentice	699	982	39,067
E3	Seaman	1,505	2,110	69,112
E4	Petty Officer 3rd Class	2,644	3,372	101,044
E5	Petty Officer 2nd Class	3,986	4,486	102,649
E6	Petty Officer 1st Class	4,715	4,991	84,281
E7	Chief Petty Officer	2,726	2,852	34,128
E8	Senior Chief Petty Officer	1,055	1,102	10,219
E9	Master Chief Petty Officer	403	423	4,842
W1	Warrant Officer 1	0	0	53
W2	Warrant Officer 2	43	46	1,534
W3	Warrant Officer 3	34	34	813
W4	Warrant Officer 4	17	18	533
O1	Ensign	101	243	7,753
02	Lieutenant Junior Grade	100	250	9,870
03	Lieutenant	213	474	24,382
04	Lieutenant Commander	89	193	13,368
05	Commander	46	95	7,847
06	Captain	14	36	3,612
07	Rear Admiral Lower Half	0	1	124
08	Rear Admiral Upper Half	0	0	80
09	Vice Admiral	0	1	29
010	Admiral	0	0	9
Total		18,889	22,384	538,323

Source: *Defense Manpower Data Center, unpublished data.*

Filipinos to Christianity. Some Filipino Americans are Muslim, however, and a few are Protestant.

For many Filipinos, the rituals of the Catholic Church are also centered around important family occasions and traditions. The christening of a new baby calls for a religious ceremony as well as a social celebration. Christian holidays like Christmas and Easter are observed with masses and church processions.

♦ NATIONAL HOLIDAYS

In the Philippines, the people frequently hold celebrations and festivals. In the United States, these festivals are continued as a way for Filipino Americans to remember and celebrate their culture and heritage. On June 12, for example, Filipino Americans all over the United States celebrate Philippine Independence Day. This cultural festival features parades, folk dances, food and craft fairs, music, and other various forms of cultural performances. Filipino Americans also observe Rizal Day on December 30 to commemorate the martyrdom of their national hero, Jose Rizal, as well as Philippine-American Friendship Day on July 4.

♦ HISTORY OF IMMIGRATION

It is often thought that Filipinos first came to the United States in the early 1900s. However, the presence of Filipinos in this country goes back much further.

The landing of the Spanish galleon, *Nuestra Senora de Esperanza* (Our Lady of Hope) in California on October 18, 1587, was the first recorded arrival of Filipinos in America. The Filipino members of the crew served as scouts for the landing party thatexplored the California coast. Hundreds of years later, close to two million Filipinos would arrive on the same shores and settle in what is now the United States.

The First Wave

In her book *Filipinos of Louisiana*, Marina Estrella Espina, a Filipino librarian at the University of New

They ventured off to America in the early 1900's—young, eager, minds filled with visions of gold-paved streets. They sought the 'land of opportunity' about which their American teachers had glowingly lectured. (Courtesy of Gene Viernes.)

Orleans, has documented what she describes as "the rich tapestry of Filipino life of eighteenth-century Louisiana." In this study, she has established a number of historical facts.

Filipinos were the earliest Asians to cross the Pacific Ocean for the North American continent by way of the Manila Galleon Trade that flourished between Mexico and the Philippines from 1565 to 1815. Hundreds of Spanish-speaking Filipino sailors were frequently conscripted to operate the ships. These seamen, then called "Manilamen," were harshly treated by their Spanish officers. To escape this brutality, many jumped ship as they landed in New Orleans around 1765, more than a decade before the American Revolution. Therefore, contrary to the general perception that Filipinos first came to the United States in the early 1900s to work in the fruit orchards and fish canneries of the Pacific Northwest, Filipinos had actually settled in early colonial times.

The first settlement of Filipino seafarers was located along the Mississippi Delta in the 19th century. Although the galleon trade ceased in 1815, historians presume that Filipinos continued to arrive on vessels sailing directly into New Orleans, where they eventually deserted their posts. What is certain is that by 1833, they had gathered in the fishing village of St. Malo at the mouth of the Mississippi. Most were hired for seasonal positions as fishers or hunters, but maintained a permanent residence in New Orleans with their families. After St. Malo was completely destroyed by a strong hurricane in 1893, the survivors established Manila Village, 40 miles south of New Orleans. By 1933, the village had a Filipino population of 1,500. The transplanted Filipinos of St. Malo and Manila Village became fishers in their new surroundings. They are credited with having introduced the process of sun-drying Louisiana shrimp for marketing outside the state.

According to Fred Cordova in his book *Filipinos: Forgotten Asian Americans*, these seafaring exiles and working sojourners comprise the first real wave of Filipino immigrants to the United States. This era extended from 1763 to 1906 and included other arrivals, such as stowaways, ship employees, and domestic workers. These Filipino immigrants eventually moved onto what became the states of California, Texas, and New Mexico.

In the early 1920's, Filipinos were recruited to work in the plantations of Hawaii, the farms of California and in the fishing and canning industries of the Northwest. Here are two Filipino immigrants embarking from a ship that brought them to Hawaii. (Courtesy of the Hawaii State Archives.)

The Second Wave

The first sizable group of Filipinos to enter the United States legally came in 1903, after the United States, having defeated Spain in the Spanish-American War of 1898, annexed the Philippines—which had been a Spanish colony for almost 400 years—and defeated the Philippine resistance movement. An estimated one million Filipinos lost their lives in this war of independence against American occupation forces.

Filipinos are the only Asian people colonized by the United States. For more than a generation, they experienced many U.S. influences: educational text in their public schools, motion pictures made in Hollywood, an English-language newspaper press, and U.S. professional sports. The emigrating Filipinos already knew much about the language and the institutions of the United States and expected to partake in the democratic privileges afforded U.S. citizens. In this regard, they resembled the Puerto Ricans who migrated to New York City and the East Coast. Unfortunately,

though, the high hopes of Filipinos were dashed by the economic realities that they faced in the United States.

Between 1903 and 1910, hundreds of bright Filipino students also came to the United States to further their studies. The first U.S. civil governor of the Philippines, William Howard Taft, inspired a plan whereby the colonial government sent young men to attend college in the United States. The government provided scholarships or "pensions" to the students. Thus, the students were called *pensionados*.

The arrival of these students marked the continued second wave of Filipino immigration to the United States, which stretched from 1906 to 1934. While education was their goal, there were other forces motivating them to come to the United States: desire for adventure, lack of employment in the Philippines, encouragement by teachers, and misleading advertising by predatory employers and steamship companies promising a better life in the United States.

After graduation, the pensionados were expected to return to the Philippines to spread the ideals of democracy to their people. And indeed, many pensionados did return to become political and business leaders. Their success, in turn, encouraged other students to

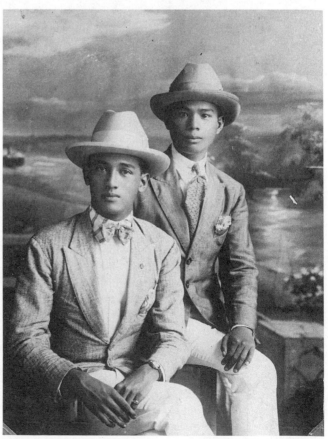

Filipino "pensionados" who came to the U.S. in the 1920's to study. (Courtesy of the Washington State Archives.)

Two young Filipino men. (Courtesy of the Pioneer Museum and Haggin Galleries.)

follow in their path. However, most of the thousands of subsequent Filipino students that arrived without government sponsorship had to discontinue their education for lack of funds and become laborers.

Although the great majority of Filipino students, pensionados or not, later engaged in the same type of menial labor out of necessity, the students were often different in socioeconomic and linguistic background from the bona fide immigrant laborers who came to Hawaii and California for the specific purpose of supplying much needed agricultural labor.

Like many Asian immigrants, Filipinos were drawn to the United States in the latter part of the 19th century by the demand for cheap labor to build the industrial and agricultural infrastructure of the West Coast. The importation of Filipino laborers started in 1906, shortly after the United States acquired the Philippines from Spain. Among the hundreds of laborers, most were male, single, and between the ages of 16 and 22 with little more than an eighth-grade education. A very small minority were married. Most left their families in the Philippines. Those who were more fortunate brought their families with them, despite expected hardships in an alien land.

Because most were unmarried and adventurous, seasonal labor did not immediately present the kinds of hardship normal to family-centered heads of households. However, the seasonal jobs frequently entrapped them in the economic cycle that kept them on the move and unable to establish an economic foothold inthe U.S. economy. Like Italian Americans on the East Coast, they found themselves in a contract system of labor not unlike the *padrone*-centered culture; five- to fifteen-man crews would hire out to a contractor who provided room, board, and a small wage. The small stature of the Filipinos made them prime candidates for stoop labor, and they often accepted jobs that others would not. Perhaps because of their knowledge of U.S. traditions and their familiarity with English, they were less docile than the Chinese who had preceded them. They frequently spoke up for their rights and fostered unionization, however, few rose above the ranks of common laborer. Outside of farming, only the salmon canning industry opened its doors to them in any significant way. Many sought employment later in the Merchant Marines and the U.S. Navy.

Meanwhile, due to an impending labor shortage, the Hawaiian Sugar Planters' Association (HSPA) began importing farm workers from Asia. Under the provisions of the Gentlemen's Agreement between Tokyo and Washington, the Japanese government voluntarily restricted the departure of male immigrant laborers to Hawaii and the U.S. mainland by refusing to issue them passports. Because the Japanese were the largest immigrant group working on the Hawaiian sugar plantations, the cessation of Japanese immigration threatened to cripple the thriving sugar industry. To ensure a steady supply of laborers, the HSPA recruited Philippine nationals. As foreign nationals of the United States, immigration was unrestricted.

Of the imported laborers, most signed up for three years and returned to their barrios with their savings; others stayed longer and wrote home of their successes, sending money along as evidence. Those who remained overseas sent dollars that could be used for purchasing land, paying taxes, financing family education, or fulfilling other obligations to the family. These obligations may well have been one reason why so many Filipinos stayed long beyond their original contract period. Some, in fact, never returned at all.

Conscious of the nationalities of their laborers, the employers resorted to divide-and-control tactics to prevent different ethnic groups from joining together in strikes. The Filipinos were imported, therefore, to keep other Asian laborers from demanding higher wages. This sometimes resulted in inter-ethnic tensions, including fistfights and riots in the labor camps. However, Filipino and Japanese workers eventually decided to unite and join forces against their employers. In

December 1919, the Japanese Federation of Labor and the Filipino Federation of Labor called for solidarity. Three thousand Filipino workers, joined by the Japanese, went on strike after the planters rejected their demand for higher wages. Altogether, 8,000 Filipino and Japanese strikers, 77 percent of the entire plantation workforce, brought production to a sudden stop, inflicting a $12-million loss on the sugar industry. They were later joined by Spanish, Portuguese, and Chinese in the first major inter-ethnic working-class struggle in Hawaii. Although the strikers gave up in July, the planters discreetly increased wages by 50 percent three months later. The two immigrant groups' coalition helped pave the way for the emergence of strong trade unionism in the territory of Hawaii in the 1940s.

Hawaii imported 71,594 Filipino laborers from 1907 to 1929. About 15,000 of these later moved to the West Coast in search of better economic opportunities. As of 1920, there were 13,061 Filipinos employed in the sugar industry, accounting for 30 percent of all plantation workers. Within ten years, the number of Filipino residents increased to 63,869, comprising 18 percent of the Hawaiian Islands' total population.

Large-scale Filipino immigration to the West Coast began in the 1920s. The Immigration Act of 1917 barred all immigrants from Asian countries except Japan and the Philippines. Like previous Asians, Filipino laborers were sought to fill demand for stoop agricultural work and other low-wage jobs. Furthermore, by 1924 Congress excluded Japanese from immigration, making Filipinos the only Asians admissible as immigrants. After 1924, there was a decreased need for Filipino labor in Hawaii. This marked the beginning of another exodus—this time to the U.S. mainland. The increased need for stoop laborers in California coincided with the decreased need for plantation workers in Hawaii. During the 1920 to 1929 period, the mainland received 51,875 Filipino laborers, 14,195 of whom had traveled from Hawaii.

In addition to providing seasonal farm labor, Filipino immigrants also worked in Alaskan salmon canneries. By 1924, the Filipinos were the largest immigrant group employed in the Alaskan canning industry, which had in the past primarily employed European American and native Alaskan workers.

By 1930, as a result of a relatively brief migratory movement, the number of Filipinos on the U.S. mainland swelled to 45,200. But, as in the cases of the Chinese and Japanese, opposition to Filipino immigration resulted in the exclusion of this group by the Tydings-McDuffie Act of 1934. This act, which created the Commonwealth of the Philippines, promised independence for the Philippine Islands after a ten-year trial period. In spite of the fact that the Philippine Islands did not become independent until 1946, the act

Filipino boy in cowboy or farm worker's outfit. (Courtesy of the Pioneer Museum and Haggin Galleries.)

limited immigration by considering the Commonwealth "as a separate country" with an annual quota of 50 immigrants.

This harsh treatment of Filipinos intensified during the Great Depression when many Americans lost their jobs. Because they were categorized as aliens, Filipino nationals were ineligible for federal aid in the United States. In addition to employment discrimination, housing was also a difficult problem. Many men during the winter months frequently shared one-room dwellings.

These unpleasant conditions were in part caused and certainly aggravated by the prejudice that the Filipinos experienced in the United States. The fact that they were dark-skinned "foreigners" was sufficient reason to expose them to discrimination. The competition that they presented, particularly to unskilled European Americans, further exacerbated the antagonism directed toward Filipinos.

Generally speaking, unlike the Chinese who usually remained in their urban enclaves and the family-centered Japanese, Filipino men—who tended to be socially inclined and outgoing in their attitudes toward the culture at large—were unattached and unaffected

Sixteen Filipino farm workers, Fabian Track, Belvedere Asparagus Ranch, San Joaquin Delta, California, May, 1950. (Courtesy of the Pioneer Museum and Haggin Galleries.)

by taboos concerning the crossing of racial lines. They frequently sought the company of European American women, particularly since as late as 1940 Filipino men outnumbered Filipino women by as much as 15 to 1. Many were often outraged at the Filipinos' forwardness, resulting in many brutal beatings and, occasionally, even riots. Indeed, the first Filipino men in the United States not only often lacked the basic organizational unit of the family, but were also deprived of Filipino women, as well as legally barred from marrying European American women.

The Third Wave

When World War II broke out, immigration to the United States stopped completely. But the aftermath of war brought a new wave of Filipinos to the United States. These post-war arrivals included U.S. resident aliens as well as military personnel and their dependents, students, and exchange workers. This era marked the third wave of Filipino immigration to the United States, which lasted from 1945 to 1965. In the meantime, Philippine-born Filipinos became eligible for U.S. citizenship.

Among the first to leave the Philippines in 1945 were children and grandchildren of Spanish-American War veterans. These were the Filipino descendants of white soldiers, sailors, and civil servants who had chosen to live in the Philippines after the Filipino-American War. Other new immigrants were war brides and children of Filipino soldiers who, having served in the U.S. armed forces, had become U.S. citizens, many of them seeing combat in the Pacific theatre and participating in the mopping-up operations of the Philippine liberation movement. Predominantly female, these were U.S. citizens or military dependents and did not fall under the quota system. Other military personnel included members of the U.S. Army's Philippine Scouts, who brought their families to the United States. Once travel restrictions were lifted and the annual quota raised to one hundred, others soon followed, among them many students and professionals.

The Fourth Wave

The passage of the 1965 Immigration Reform Act set into motion the fourth wave of Filipino immigration. Once the discriminatory quota system unfavorable to

Asians was abolished, Filipino immigration surged tremendously, more than quadrupling the Filipino American population from 176,130 in 1960 to 781,894 by 1980. Between 1965 and 1985, a total of 668,870 Filipino immigrants arrived in the United States. In addition, 120,000 Filipinos were admitted each year as non-residents: students, tourists, temporary workers, trainees, etc. The entry of immigrants through the family-reunification provisions of this Act added constantly to the burgeoning Filipino community.

Post-1965 Filipino immigrants included many Tagalog-speaking college-educated professionals, wives of U.S. military personnel, and Ilocano-speaking people from the rural areas of northern Luzon. The number of immigrant professionals from the Philippines grew from just over 1,900 to more than 17,000 after enactment of the Act. This emigration of highly skilled and technically trained workers from the Philippines became known as "the brain drain."

♦ LITERATURE

There is a rich body of literature by Filipino Americans that has developed within a historical and cultural framework, yet most of it is virtually unknown to students of literature. It addresses many subjects, including Filipino heritage, tradition, creativity, relationships, and identity, in a variety of genres ranging from poetry to personal narratives, from essays to fictional writing. These works reflect the anxiety felt by Filipino Americans in U.S. society. Among younger Filipino American writers, there has been a discovery that their own ethnic and cultural experiences should be explored. Among the notable Filipino Americans profiled in the next section are several writers of note.

Prominent Filipino Americans

Maniya Barredo (1951-)

Maniya Barredo was born in Manila, the Philippines. At the age of 18, she traveled to the United States to pursue a career in dance, and eventually became a prima ballerina with Atlanta Ballet. *See also* Prominent Asian Americans.

Carlos Bulosan (1913-1956)

Bulosan, a Filipino American poet and writer, is recognized as one of the most prolific writers in the United States. His autobiography, *America Is in the Heart*, published in 1946, was hailed as one of the fifty most important American books ever published. Capturing the Filipino American experience during the 1930s and 1940s, Bulosan told of his search for the ideal United States that he had learned about in school

Carlos Bulosan. (Courtesy of the Filipino American National Historical Society Collection.)

and the sometimes harsh realities that he had experienced when he came to the United States.

Born in the Luzon province of Pangasinan, Bulosan came to the United States in 1930 at the beginning of the Great Depression. As a 17 year old, he worked as a fish cannery laborer, houseboy, dishwasher, and field hand. He experienced much of the racism and violence that many Filipinos suffered during this period. At one point, a mob tarred and feathered him and chased him out of town.

Bulosan felt the need to write about his experiences and those of other Filipinos in the United States. He started relating his experiences by writing for a labor newspaper. In his posthumously published autobiography, Bulosan wrote about his seasonal employment at a salmon cannery in 1930.

Bulosan considered himself, above all, a poet and built his literary reputation on his poetry. He published two thin volumes of poetry, *A Letter from America* and *Chorus for America*. In 1934, he published the historically significant long poem, "The Voice of Bataan," written in memory of all the fighting men who died in Bataan. That same year, he published *The New Tide*, a bimonthly radical literary magazine. In 1944, another book, *The Laughter of My Father*, was published. An instant success, it was translated into several languages and read worldwide over wartime radio.

At other times in his life, Bulosan was involved with strictly more political news efforts. He worked on the *Philippine Commonwealth Times* and at least two other newspapers in the Stockton-Salinas areas that focused on the problems of Filipino workers.

In her preface to *Carlos Bulosan and His Poetry: A Biography and Anthology*, Susan Evangelista notes that the United States has seen in the last ten years growth in Filipino American consciousness, a searching for roots, and a reevaluation of the socio-historical experiences of Filipinos in the United States. In this reconstruction of the past, she adds, Filipino Americans wereled quite naturally back to Bulosan, especially to *America Is in the Heart*. Today, his poetry is again widely read and again serves a socio-political function in the creation of a certain type of ethnic consciousness among Filipino Americans.

The growth of interest in Bulosan's writings has led to the publication of two Bulosan collections: *The Philippines Is in the Heart* (New Day, 1978) and *Carlos Bulosan: An Introduction with Selections* (National Bookstore, 1983). *See also* Prominent Asian Americans.

Tia Carrere (1969-)

An acress of primarily Filipino descent, in 1992 Carrere scored major roles in two Hollywood productions: *Wayne's World*, where she played Cassandra, a heavy-metal rock and roll musician and girlfriend of the title character; and *Rising Sun*, a thriller based on the best-selling novel by Michael Crichton. Born in Hawaii, Carrere's birth name was Althea Janairo, but she has always used her childhood nickname, Tia. *See also* Prominent Asian Americans.

Maryles V. Casto

Maryles V. Casto is founder, owner, and manager of Casto Travel, the largest privately owned corporate travel agency in northern California. *See also* Prominent Asian Americans.

Benjamin J. Cayetano (1939-)

The highest elected Filipino American in the United States, Benjamin Cayetano was elected governor of Hawaii in November 1994. Prior to his election, he served as Hawaii's lieutenant governor from 1986 to 1994. He is widely recognized as one of Hawaii's most effective legislators. The son of a Filipino immigrant who worked as a waiter, Cayetano has risen from modest beginnings to the highest post in his state's government. *See also* Prominent Asian Americans.

Lilia C. Clemente (1941-)

Lilia C. Clemente is chairperson, chief executive officer, and founder of Clement Capital, Inc. (CCI), a Wall Street investment company. The firm manages the First Philippine Fund and Clemente Global Growth Fund, both listed on the New York Stock Exchange. The Clemente Korea Emerging Growth Fund is listed on the London Stock Exchange. *See also* Prominent Asian Americans.

Nester V. M. Gonzales (1915-)

Nestor V. M. Gonzales has won all the major Philippine literary awards: the Commonwealth Literary Award (1941), the Republic Award of Merit (1954), the Republic Cultural Heritage Award (1960), and the Rizal Pro Partia Award (1961). These honors do not seem lavish, though, when one considers the quantity of his writing: *The Winds of April* (1941), *Seven Hills Away* (1947), *Children of the Ash-Covered Loam* (1954), *A Season of Grace* (1956), *The Bamboo Dancers* (1959), *Look, Stranger, on This Island Now* (1963), and others.

The best of his stories present the rhythm and pulsation of the Filipinos' lives, particularly of those in the villages and frontiers freshly wrested from wild nature. The indomitable, stoic spirit of a pioneer farmer, the indestructible desire of an uneducated maidservant for her share of life and happiness, the tearless sorrow of a young mother who has just lost her infant, the feeling of loss and awe of a rustic settler suddenly plunged into an urban center. . . all are persuasively portrayed without any frills or fanfare of rhetoric.

The son of a teacher in Romblon province, Gonzales studied law and journalism before turning to creative writing. He has received several Rockefeller grants to travel and write on three continents. He was on the faculty of the University of the Philippines and divides his time between fiction writing and magazine editing.

Jessica Tarahata Hagedorn (1949-)

Born in the Philippines, Hagedorn's work has appeared in *Four Young Women* (1973), *Third World Women* (1973), *Time to Greez* (1975), *The Third Women* (1980), and *Yardbird Reader*, among other publications. She has also published *Dangerous Music* (1975) and *Dogeaters* (1990). She is hailed as one of a handful of minority women in the United States today that have not only created and pursued a literary tradition of their own, but have created works that represent some of the most exciting and creative innovations in contemporary literature. Like other minority women writers, her ethnicity influences her angle of vision with observations that revitalize Filipino American concepts of tradition and folklore, language and imagination.

She says, "I see my writing going further and further out in the direction of music and theatre, stand-up comedy, and the movies. . . . I hope to continue my work with my band, the Gangster Choir, in achieving these ends." *See also* Theatre.

Roman Gabriel (1940-)

Roman Gabriel was the quarterback for the Los Angeles Rams football team from 1962 to 1973. In his eleven seasons, he was chosen their most valuable player three times, was named to the All-Pro team four times, and was named the National Football League's Most Valuable Player in 1969. His father was a Filipino immigrant who supported the family as a cook for the Atlantic Coast Line Railroad. *See also* Sports and Athletics.

Emil Guillermo (1955-)

Emil Guillermo is a radio, television, and print journalist who came to national prminence as the weekend anchor of National Public Radio's news program "All Things Considered" which he hosted from 1989 to 1991. After a brief stint as press secretary to Congressman Norman Mineta, Guillermo returned to journalism in 1994. *See also* Prominent Asian Americans. l

Maria Luisa Mabilangan Haley (1940-)

IMaria Haley is the highest ranking Filipino American in the administration of President Bill Clinton. Born in Manila, Philippines, she came to the United States in the early 1970s. In 1979, she joined the transition team of the newly elected governor of Arkansas, Bill Clinton, and she has been a part of his organization ever since. *See also* Prominent Asian Americans.

Irene Natividad (1948-)

Born in Manila, the Philippines, Irene Natividad has lived and worked with people from around the world. She was the first Asian American to head the National Women's Political Caucus, and her work on behalf of women and Asian Americans has earned her many awards and honors: "100 Most Powerful Women in America" by *Ladies Home Journal* (1988); "74 Women Changing the Face of American Politics" by *Campaigns and Elections* magazine (1993); "25 Most Influential People in Asian America" by *A. Magazine* (1993 and 1994); and "1000 Women for the Nineties" by *Mirabella* (1994).

Natividad is the Executive Editor of the first edition of *The Asian American Almanac. See also* Prominent Asian Americans.

Josie Natori (1947-)

Born Josefina Cruz in Manila, the Philippines, Josie Natori presides over a multimillion dollar empire spread over many segments of the fashion industry. Specializing in fashions which feature the delicate embellishments—beadwork and embroidery—she manufactures her clothing and lingeried lines at a 900-employee factory in the Philippines. *See also* Prominent Asian Americans.

Bienvenido N. Santos (1911-)

During World War II, Santos lived and studied in the United States and traveled under U.S. government sponsorship to lecture on Philippine culture and to interact directly with Filipino Americans. Those years saw a great change in him: initially a popular storyteller describing charming, unaffected, simple folk in his tales, he returned to the Philippines more matured as a writer, but disheartened and full of stories about Filipinos in the United States. Among his works are a collection of his stories in *You Lovely People* (1956), *What the Hell for You Left Your Heart in San Francisco* (1987), *The Man Who (Thought He) Looked Like Robert Taylor* (1983), *The Volcano* (1986), *Villa Magdalena, The Praying Man,* and *The Wounded Stag and Other Poems* (1956). His latest book is a personal history entitled *Memory's Fiction* (1993).

For years, Santos served as president of the Legaspi Colleges before devoting his time to writing full-time. In 1965, he was honored with the Philippine Republic Cultural Heritage Award.

David Valderrama (1933-)

David M. Valderrama is the first probate judge in the United States of Filipino ancestry. As a delegate to the Assembly of Maryland, he is also the highest-ranking Filipino American elected official on the mainland United States. (Benjamin Cayetano, governor of Hawaii, is the highest ranking Filipino American in the United States.)

Born in Manila, the Philippines, Valderrama was 27 when he came to the United States to study law. His first political appointment came in 1985 when he served an unexpired term as judge.

Jose Garcia Villa (1914-)

Villa's book of poetry, *Have Come, Am Here,* appeared in 1942 and was immediately greeted with glowing praise by U.S. critics. He has also edited many magazines, won several literary prizes, and has a long list of publications, including *Footnote to Youth* (1933), *Many Voices* (1939), *Poems* (1941), *Volume II* (1949), *Selected Stories* (1962), and *The Essential Villa* (1965).

References

Alba, Richard D. *Ethnicity and Race in the U.S.A.: Toward the Twenty-First Century.* New York: Routledge, 1988.

Alegado, Dean."How the Exodus Began: The Third Wave, 1965-." *Katipunan Newsmagazine,* December 1987.

Almirol, Edwin B. *Ethnic Identity and Social Negotiation: A Study of a Filipino Community in California.* New York: AMS Press, 1985.

Anderson, Robert N. *Filipinos in Rural Hawaii.* Honolulu: University of Hawaii Press, 1984.

Blauner, Robert. *Racial Opression in America.* New York: Harper & Row, Publishers, 1972.

Bogardus, Emory S."Filipino Americans." In *Our Racial and National Minorities: Their History, Contributions, and Present Problems.* Edited by Francis J. Brown. New York: Prentice Hall, Inc., 1945.

Burma, John. *Spanish-Speaking Groups in the United States.* Durham, N.C.: Duke University Press, 1954.

Catapusan, B.T. *The Filipino Social Adjustment in the United States: A Dissertation.* Los Angeles: University of Southern California, 1940.

Chin, Frank, ed. *Aiieeeee! An Anthology of Asian-American Writers.* Washington, D.C.: Howard University Press, 1974.

Cordova, Fred. *Filipinos: Forgotten Asian Americans, A Pictoral Essay/1763-circa-1963.* Demonstration Project for Asian Americans, 1983.

Daniels, Roger. *Coming to America: A History of Immigration and Ethnicity in American Life.* New York: Harper Collins Publishers, 1990.

Dinnerstein, Leonard and David M. Reimers. *Ethnic Americans: A History of Immigration,* third ed. New York: Harper & Row Publishers, 1988.

Dinnerstein, Leonard, Roger L. Nichols, and David M. Reimers. *Natives and Strangers: Ethnic Groups and the Building of America.* New York: Oxford University Press, 1979.

The Emerging Minorities in America: A Resource Guide for Teachers. Santa Barbara: Clio Press, 1972.

Evangelista, Susan. *Carlos Bulosan and His Poetry: A Biography and Anthology.* Seattle and London: University of Washington Press, 1985.

Fuchs, Lawrence H. *The American Kaleidoscope: Race, Ethnicity and the Civic Culture.* Hanover: Wesleyan University Press, 1990.

Hagedorn, Jessica, ed. *Charlie Chan Is Dead: An Anthology of Contemporary Asian American Fiction.* New York: Penguin Books, 1993.

Handlin, Oscar. *A Pictoral History of Immigration.* New York: Crown Publishers, Inc., 1972.

Hecker, Melvin. "The Filipinos in America," *Ethnic America 1970-1977.* New York: Oceana Publications, 1979.

Hing, Bill Ong. *Making and Remaking Asian America through Immigration Policy 1850-1990.* Stanford: Stanford University Press, 1993.

Hsu, Kai-Yu and Helen Palubinskas. *Asian-American Authors.* New York: Houghton Mifflin Co., 1972.

Kim, Elaine H. *Asian American Literature: An Introduction to the Writings and Their Social Context.* Philadelphia: Temple University Press, 1982.

Kim, Hyung-chan and Cynthia C. Mejia. *The Filipinos in America 1898-1974, A Chronology and Fact Book.* New York: Oceana Publications, Inc., 1976.

Lasker, Bruno. *Filipino Immigration to Continental United States and to Hawaii.* Chicago: University of Chicago Press, 1931.

Lott, Juanita Tamayo. "Migration of a Mentality: The Filipino Community," *Asian-Americans: Social and Psychological Perspectives,* vol. 2. Palo Alto: Science and Behavior Books, 1980.

Mangiafico, Luciano. *Contemporary American Immigrants: Patterns of Filipino, Korean, and Chinese Settlement in the United States.* New York: Praeger, 1988.

Mariano, Honorante. "The Filipino Immigrants in the U.S. : A Thesis." University of Oregon, September 1933.

Mayberry, Jodine. *Recent American Immigrants: Filipinos.* New York: Franklin Watts, 1990.

Melendy, H. Brett. *Asians in America: Filipinos, Koreans, and East Indians.* Boston: Twayne Publishers, 1977.

Menez, Herminia Quimpo. *Folklore Communication among Filipinos in California.* New York: Arno Press, 1980.

Pido, Antonio J. A. "New Structures, New Immigrants: The Case of the Filipinos," *Sourcebook on the New Immigration.* Edited by Roy Simon Bryce-LaPorte. New Jersey: Transaction Books, 1980.

————. *The Filipinos in America: Macro/Micro Dimensions of Immigration and Integration.* New York: Center for Migration Studies, 1986.

Reimers, David M. *Still the Golden Door: The Third World Comes to America.* New York: Columbia University Press, 1985.

Rose, Peter. *They and We: Racial and Ethnic Relations in the United States.* New York: Random House.

Schrieke, Bertram. *Alien Americans: A Study of Race Relations.* New York: The Viking Press, 1936.

Solberg, S.E. and Sid White. *Peoples of Washington Perspectives on Cultural Diversity.* Pullman: Washington State University Press, 1989.

Sowell, Thomas, ed. *Essays and Data on American Ethnic Groups.* The Urban Institute, 1978.

Stegner, Wallace Earle, ed. *One Nation.* Boston: Houghton Mifflin Company, 1945.

Takaki, Ronald. *Strangers from a Different Shore.* Boston: Little, Brown, 1989.

Teodoro, Luis V, ed. *Out of This Struggle: The Filipinos in Hawaii.* Honolulu: University of Hawaii, 1981.

Tsuchida, John Nobuya. *A Guide on Asian & Pacific Islander American Students.* Washington, D.C.: National Education Association of the United States, 1991.

Virina, Czar. "In Search of Promised Lands." *Special Edition Press.* Vol. 1, no. 2, Spring, 1993.

—*Jonathan Melegrito*

Who are the Hmong Americans?

♦ Overview ♦ History ♦ Immigration ♦ Geographic Distribution ♦ Acculturation and Assimilation
♦ Language ♦ Myths, Legends, and Folktales ♦ Family and Community Dynamics ♦ Holidays
♦ Religion ♦ Employment and Economic Traditions ♦ Politics and Government
♦ Health and Mental Health Issues ♦ Notable Hmong Americans ♦ Media
♦ Organizations and Associations

♦ OVERVIEW

Social scientists estimate that there are between six and seven million Hmong in the world. Until recently, almost all of these people lived in the mountains of southern China, Laos, Thailand, and northern Vietnam. Chinese oppression during the nineteenth century and the rise of communism in Vietnam following World War II pushed many Hmong into Laos, where about 300,000 Hmong lived peacefully during the 1960s. After the royal Laotian government was overthrown by Communist forces in 1975, about one-third of the Laotian Hmong were killed, another third fled to Thailand, and the remaining third stayed in Laos. Many of those who took refuge in Thailand found homes in France or the United States. Overall, about 95,000 Hmong have settled in the United States as a result of American involvement in Southeast Asia. The Hmong are sometimes referred to by outsiders as the "Meo" (also spelled "Miao"), meaning savage, a name that the Hmong consider insulting.

The Hmong are divided into five major tribes: the White Hmong, the Black Hmong, the Flowery Hmong, the Red Hmong, and the Blue (also known as Green) Hmong. Most Hmong in the United States are from the White or Blue tribes. According to Hmong legend, these tribes were developed by ancient Chinese conquerors who forced the Hmong to divide into different groups and to identify themselves by wearing distinctive colors of clothing. However, clans, or large extended family groups, are more important to the Hmong than tribal membership. In Laos, there are about 20 of these clans, all identified by family names. While marriages between different clans are acceptable, marriage between individuals who share the same family name is considered incestuous and is strictly forbidden.

In Southeast Asia, the Hmong live in villages with an economy based on raising livestock and crops. They practice *swidden* (slash and burn) agriculture, meaning that the Hmong clear fields by burning, thereby fertilizing the ground with ashes. Since this kind of agriculture exhausts soil rapidly, Hmong villages must constantly be on the move. Their principal crops are corn and opium poppies, which they use for medicines and spiritual ceremonies, and sell to foreigners.

♦ HISTORY

Chinese historical sources indicate that the Hmong have lived in China since 2000 B.C. Many scholars believe that the Hmong may have lived in Siberia prior to this date because blond hair and blue eyes are occasionally found among the Hmong.

For centuries, the Hmong, who lived in the mountainous regions of southern China, struggled against the Chinese government to maintain their distinctive ethnic identity. In the 1700s, Chinese generals convinced Sonom, the last Hmong king, to surrender, promising him that he would be treated well and that his surrender would bring an honorable peace to the mountains. Instead, Sonom was taken to Beijing where he, his officers, and his officers and advisors were tortured to death in the presence of the Chinese Emperor.

After joining the Chinese Empire, the Hmong lost their original writing system and any Hmong caught using the Hmong alphabet was punished with death. Women of the tribes tried to keep the alphabet alive by sewing the letters into the patterns of their traditional clothes. Portions of this alphabet can be found on Hmong clothing today, but few people are capable of reading these carefully preserved designs.

After China was defeated by the British in 1842 during the first Opium War, the imperial Chinese government was forced to pay indemnities to the victors. To raise money, the government of China levied heavy taxes on its subjects, thus increasing tension between the Chinese authorities and the Hmong minority. Between 1850 and 1880, the Hmong waged a series of wars against the Chinese. Unsuccessful in their rebellion the Hmong fled southward; the majority of these emigrants settled in Laos, although many Hmong also migrated to Vietnam and Thailand.

The Hmong in Laos

In Laos, the Hmong met new oppressors—the French—who had claimed Vietnam, Laos, and Cambodia as part of their vast Indochinese Empire. French taxation led to two major revolts against the French by the Hmong, one in 1896 and one in the 1920s. The second revolt was initiated by Pa Chay, who called for the establishment of an independent Hmong kingdom and remains a hero to many Hmong today.

In an effort to pacify the Hmong, the French established an autonomous Hmong district that was allowed to partake in self-government. However, this created competition between the heads of the two major clans in the district, the Lo clan and the Ly clan. In 1922, a feud broke out between the two clans over who would become head of the district. To diffuse the perilous situation in 1938, the French organized a democratic election for chief of the district and two cousins, one a member of the Lo clan and the other a member of the Ly clan, ran for the office. Touby Lyfong of the Ly clan won the election, defeating Faydang Lobliayao of the Lo clan. The rivalry between these two men and their clans led to the permanent political separation of the Hmong in Laos. Touby Lyfong made common cause with the French and later allied himself with the Americans in their fight against the North Vietnamese Communists and their Laotian supporters. Faydang Lobliayao, on the other hand, joined forces with the Lao nationalists who favored total independence from France and later became an important leader of the Lao Communist forces.

United States Involvement in Southeast Asia

The United States became involved in Southeast Asia to preserve a non-Communist regime in South Vietnam. Because the *Pathet Lao*, the communist guerrillas of Laos, were allied with the North Vietnam's *Viet Minh* (later known as the *Viet Cong*), the United States provided economic and tactical support to the royal Lao government to fight the guerrillas, as well as the North Vietnamese troops. Many of the individuals recruited by the U.S. government were Hmong tribesmen led by Vang Pao, an anti-Communist Hmong military leader who had earlier assisted the French. According to many sources, the C.I.A. (Central Intelligence Agency) officials who organized the Hmong army promised the soldiers, who numbered 40,000 by 1969, that the United States would resettle the Hmong if they were defeated.

After American troops were withdrawn from Indochina in 1973, the Lao government was forced to negotiate with its enemies and to bring the pro-North Vietnamese leftists into a coalition government. Following the fall of South Vietnam in April 1975, the leftists in Laos consolidated their political power, the royal government crumbled, the king abdicated, and the Lao People's Democratic Republic proclaimed. Despite General Vang Pao's insistence that the United States had promised to resettle all of the Hmong soldiers, the U.S. government evacuated only about 1,000 Hmong in the first year.

The new Laotian government sent many Hmong to harsh reeducation camps. Others continued to fight against the new government and there are reports that the Lao People's Democratic Republic has used biological and chemical poisons in attempts to exterminate the Hmong rebels. Still other Hmong made their way across the border into Thailand, where they stayed in refugee camps for months or, in some cases, years.

♦ IMMIGRATION

In December 1975, the United States agreed to begin resettling Hmong and the U.S. Congress admitted 3,466. In 1976, 10,200 refugees from Laos (who had fled across the border into Thailand) were admitted to the United States; some of these immigrants were Hmong, although there is no official record of them. The number of Laotian immigrants then dipped to only 400 in 1977, but climbed to 8,000 in 1978. By the early 1980s, about 50,000 Hmong were living in the United States. By the time of the 1990 U.S. Census the number of Hmong in the United States had doubled to almost 100,000. Of the foreign-born Hmong in the United States in 1990, 75 percent had arrived during the 1980s, the majority of which had arrived in the first half of the decade.

♦ GEOGRAPHIC DISTRIBUTION

In 1990, the majority of Hmong Americans lived in California (43,000), Minnesota (17,000), and Wisconsin (16,000). When the Hmong began arriving in the United

States in the mid- to late-1970s, American refugee resettlement agencies dispersed the 12 traditional clans all over the country, placing small groups in 53 different cities and 25 different states, where voluntary agencies such as churches could be found to sponsor the refugees. Between 1981 and 1985, however, the Hmong reassembled through massive secondary migration, making their way across the country in small family groups. Drawn by the lure of reforming their clan-based society and by the moderate climate of the Pacific Coast, they congregated in farming towns and small cities in California. During this time, the Hmong migrated to the California cities of Fresno (18,000), Merced (7,500), Sacramento (5,000), Stockton (5,000), and Chico, Modesto, and Visalia (6,000).

◆ ACCULTURATION AND ASSIMILATION

Hmong Americans generally have a very positive view of their new country and younger generation tend to understand both cultures quite well. There is a general ignorance of the Hmong on the part of most Americans, however. Many Americans find it difficult to distinguish them from the Vietnamese or other Asian groups. Insofar as stereotypes have arisen, the Hmong are often seen as hard-working, but also extremely foreign. Many Americans are also perplexed by the colorful rituals of the Hmong and by the music that often accompanies them. Hmong Americans, however, tend to be friendly to members of other groups and welcome attempts on the part of outsiders to learn more about their culture. The Hmong themselves are rapidly becoming an American minority, rather than an alien group in American society. As of 1990, about one-third of the Hmong in the United States were born in this country. Since Hmong Americans tend to be very young, the proportion of Hmong who have personal memories of Laos is decreasing rapidly.

Many Hmong customs are not practiced in the United States, especially by those who have converted to Christianity. As might be expected in a group that has experienced such rapid social change, Hmong Americans are still trying to sort out what traditions may be retained in the new land, and what traditions must be left behind.

Birth Customs

It is the traditional Hmong belief that when a man dies he will be reborn as a woman and that when a woman dies she will be reborn as a man. Thus, every child born is seen as a reincarnated soul. The child is believed to join human society three days after he or she is born. Therefore, if a child dies within three days,

no funeral ceremonies are held since the child did not yet have a soul. After three days of life, a shaman evokes a soul to be reincarnated in the baby's body. The family's ancestors are called upon to join the living family members in blessing the incarnation and in protecting the baby. The baby is then given a silver necklace that is supposed to keep the newly reincarnated soul from wandering.

Marriage Customs

Hmong marriage customs, as well as popular attitudes toward marriage, have undergone rapid change as a result of the move to America. In Laos, members of the same clan, those who have the same family name, are not allowed to marry. However, men and women with different family names may engage in marriage, even if they are first cousins or otherwise closely related. Most often, young people met potential mates at the New Year's Festival, which brought together people from different villages. At the Festival, young women wore their most colorful skirts and showed off their sewing and embroidery skills, while young men displayed their horse-riding and other skills, and sometimes played musical instruments to serenade the young women. Men generally married at any age between 18 and 30 years, while women often married between 14 and 18 years.

Traditional Hmong marriages required the prospective groom to secure a go-between, most often a relative, who bargained with the young woman's family for a bridal price, usually paid in silver bars. Marriages were made public by a two-day feast, featuring a roasted pig. This feast symbolically joined the clans of the bride and groom, as well as the bride and groom themselves.

When a suitor could not reach an agreement on bridal price with the woman's family, the couple sometimes eloped, especially during the last 40 years when the social disruptions of war loosened parental control. Following the elopement, outside arbitrators helped to find an acceptable bridal price to pay in settlement. If the young woman did not want to elope, the suitor would sometimes kidnap her with the help of his friends and, following payment to her family, she would be recognized as his wife.

Although most Hmong men had one wife, polygyny, or marriage with several women, was an accepted practice. During the war, polygyny became common due to the custom that required Hmong men to marry the widows of their dead brothers in order to provide a means of support for the brothers' families. Wealthy men often had several wives as symbols of affluence. Moreover, clan leaders sometimes married several times to establish political alliances.

American culture and law has made it necessary for the Hmong to change many of their attitudes and practices with regard to family. On occasions, those who have failed to drop older practices have found themselves in conflict with the American legal system. There have been a few instances of young Hmong American men kidnapping and sexually assaulting young females. While they may have seen this as a culturally acceptable way to enter into marriage, American law defines this kind of activity as illicit abduction and rape. Some of the young women who have been abducted have perceived the events from the mainstream American perspective and have pressed charges.

The use of negotiators to arrange a marriage remains fairly common among Hmong Americans. However, many young women wait until their late teens or early 20s to marry. Surveys of Hmong Americans indicate that the majority believe that it is best for women to put off marriage until they are at least 18 years of age. Polygyny is rarely found among Hmong Americans.

Funerals

Before the Hmong came to America, the death of a family member was announced by firing three shots into the air. This action was thought to frighten away evil spirits. Today, this tradition is rarely followed by Hmong in the United States because of laws regulating the use of guns in populated areas.

The deceased is washed, dressed in new clothes, and left to lie in state. Mourners bearing gifts visit the home of the deceased, where they are fed by the family of the departed. A shaman makes an offering of a cup of alcohol to the dead person and tells the soul that the body has died. Colorful bits of paper, representing money for use in the spirit world, are burned and the shaman tells the soul the route it must follow to get to the ancestors and how to avoid dangers during the journey.

◆ LANGUAGE

Two tribal dialects of the Hmong language are spoken by Hmong in the United States: Blue Hmong and White Hmong. Hmong is monosyllabic and tonal, meaning that it consists mainly of one-syllable words, and words spoken with different tones take on different meanings. Hmong uses more tones than the major Asian tonal languages. White and Blue Hmong use eight different tones.

Until the mid-twentieth century, those Hmong who could write their language usually did so with Chinese characters. In the 1950s, American and French missionaries in Laos developed the Romanized Popular Alphabet (RPA), a means of writing Hmong with a version of the alphabet used by English and other western European languages. Because the Hmong language is substantially different from European languages, however, some characteristics of the RPA are not familiar to English speakers.

Each of the eight tones is indicated by a consonant written at the end of the word. When the letter "b," for example, is written at the end of a word, it is not pronounced. It serves merely to indicate that this word is spoken with a high tone. The letter "j" at the end of a word indicates a high falling tone, a bit like the sound of "day-o" in the old popular Caribbean song. A word ending in "v" is to be spoken with a mid rising tone, similar to the intonation at the end of a question in English. Moreover, "s" indicates a mid-low tone, "g" indicates a mid-low breathy tone, and "m" at the end of a word is spoken with a low glottalized tone, a tensing of the throat. Words ending in "d" have a low rising tone.

Most of the vowels and the consonants that do not occur at the ends of words have pronunciations similar to those of western European languages, but there are some differences. The consonant "x" is pronounced like the English "s," while "s" is pronounced like the English "sh." Likewise, "z" in the RPA has the sound of the "s" in "leisure." The Hmong "r" has no equivalent in English, but is closer to the English "t" or "d" than to the English sound "r." The consonant "c" in this writing system has a sound similar to the sound that "t" and "y" would make if we pronounced the words "quit you" very rapidly. The consonant "q" is like the English "k" or "g" but is pronounced further back in the throat. Finally, "w" has a sound that linguists call the "schwa," the vowel sound in the word "but," and "aw" is a longer version of this sound, somewhat like the vowel sound in "mud."

Greetings and Other Popular Expressions

The White Hmong phrases given here are written in the Romanized Popular Alphabet described above. Therefore, in words that end in consonants the final consonant is not pronounced. It indicates the tone with which the word should be spoken.

Common greetings include: *Koj tuaj los?* (literally, "You've come?"); *Kuv tuaj* ("I've come"); and *Mus ho tuaj* ("Come again"). It is not usually regarded as polite to ask a stranger's name; however, a Hmong may turn to someone else and ask *Tus no yog leej twg tub?* ("Whose son is this?"), *Tus no yog leej tus ntxhais?* ("Whose daughter is this?"), *Tus no yog leej tus pojniam?* ("Whose wife is this?"), or *Tus no yog leej tus txiv?* ("Whose husband is this?"). It is both polite and common to ask where someone lives: *Koj nyob qhov twg?* ("Where do you live?"). If a visitor starts to leave, a Hmong host may say *Nyob. Wb tham mentsis tso maj* ("Stay, and we'll chat a little first"), since it is considered polite to try and keep visitors from leaving. A useful phrase for anyone wanting to learn a little Hmong is *Lub no lus Hmoob hu li cas?* ("What is this called in Hmong?").

♦ MYTHS, LEGENDS, AND FOLKTALES

Hmong folktales and legends have traditionally been passed orally from generation to generation. In recent years, efforts have been made to record and preserve these ancient stories as younger members of the ethnic group are drawn into the mass media-based American culture. One of the most comprehensive collections is the large, bilingual volume *Myths, Legends, and Folktales from the Hmong of Laos* (Macalester College, St. Paul, Minn., 1985), edited by Charles Johnson.

The stories told by the Hmong date back to before they became part of the Chinese Empire. Magic, supernatural events, and spirits occupy a prominent place in these stories and, as in the folktales of other nations, animals can often talk. People occasionally transformed into animals, or animals into people. Reincarnation is common and characters may reappear after their deaths. Many Hmong stories convey moral lessons, relaying happy outcomes for honest, hard-working, and virtuous individuals, and unfortunate outcomes for the evil, lazy, or selfish.

Hmong literature in the United States is largely preserved by older Hmong. Young Hmong Americans, like young Americans of many ethnic groups, are frequently more familiar with the lore of pop culture than with the lore of their ancestors. The Hmong and those familiar with them, however, recognize the oral literature as a unique repository of spiritual values and hope that some of it may be saved.

♦ FAMILY AND COMMUNITY DYNAMICS

Adjusting to life in a highly industrialized society has not been easy for the Hmong. In 1990, almost two-thirds of Hmong Americans (63.6 percent) lived below the poverty level, compared to 7 percent of white Americans, and just over 23 percent of black Americans. The median household income of $14,276 was one of the lowest of any ethnic or racial group in the United States. As a result of these high levels of economic hardship, about three out of every four Hmong families (74.1 percent) were receiving public assistance in 1990.

Many of the difficulties faced by Hmong Americans result from inadequate educational preparation. Coming from a society based on agriculture and hunting, formal education was not a part of the traditional Hmong upbringing. Most adults, therefore, have very few educational credentials. Nearly 55 percent of Hmong over the age of 25 in the United States have less than a fifth grade education, and nearly 70 percent are not high school graduates. Despite these handicaps, however, young Hmong (those born or raised in the United States) have shown surprisingly high rates of college attendance. Almost 32 percent of Hmong aged 18 to 24 were in college in 1990, a rate of college attendance that is slightly below that of white Americans (39.5 percent) and slightly above that of black Americans (28.1 percent).

According to the 1990 U.S. Census, the average Hmong family held 6.38 individuals, compared to 3.73 individuals for the average Asian American family, 3.06 for the average white American family, and 3.48 for the average African American family. Over 60 percent of Hmong Americans were below the age of 18 in 1990, with the median age of Hmong Americans 12.7, compared to 30.4 for other Asian Americans and 34.1 for Americans in general. The size of Hmong families, therefore, contributes to the economic difficulties of the group, since adults must use their incomes to support more children than are found in most American households. However, while the extreme youth of Hmong Americans may complicate family economic situations at present, this youth, combined with the educational achievement of young Hmong, is also a source of great potential for future upward mobility.

Cultural differences between young Hmong and their parents create problems. Hmong parents expect to exercise a high degree of control over their children, which is frequently inconsistent with American beliefs about personal freedom. Moreover, young Hmong sometimes have difficulty in seeing the relevance of cultural values that are important to their parents. As a result of this generation gap, some social workers and people who work with agencies serving the Hmong say that teen-aged runaways have become a major problem among Hmong and of other Southeast Asian refugee groups.

Hmong Americans generally regard the husband as the chief decision-maker and head of the family. Nevertheless, women often wield a great deal of power in the family, since they are seen as having primary responsibility for the household. This is due to the fact that Hmong homes are viewed as "child-centered" places, where small children are regarded as treasures. As chief care-givers for children, Hmong American women can be extremely influential in their communities.

While the extended family is the basic unit of social organization for the Hmong in Asia, those in the United States often find difficulty in maintaining the tradition of the extended family. It is not possible for large numbers of people to live together under one roof in the new country due to landlord and government regulations on fire and housing codes. Hmong Americans, therefore, have had to break up into nuclear-style families.

The larger clan has also become less important to Hmong Americans. Clan elders previously took their functions from the rituals they performed in traditional ceremonies. Since the conversion of some Hmong to Christianity, however, these traditional ceremonies have become less important and less common. Also, many of the ceremonies require the sacrifice of animals, which is often illegal and typically frowned upon by other Americans. Many clan elders are gradually being replaced by newer and younger leaders who are well-educated and fluent in English and are, therefore, better able to help their families and other Hmong with the complexities of modern American society. However, clan leaders are still held in high regard and receive deference from the young. Newer leaders rely on the moral authority and blessings of the elders.

Interactions With Other Minorities

Hmong Americans interact most closely with ethnic Laotian Americans, with whom they work in a number of Southeast Asian refugee assistance organizations. Most Hmong speak Laotian, facilitating interaction. The Hmong also maintain friendly relations with members of most other groups, but intermarriage is still relatively rare because of the continued importance of clan and family.

♦ HOLIDAYS

The New Year Festival (*noj peb caug*) is the most important holiday of Hmong Americans. In Laos, this holiday begins with the crowing of the first rooster on the first day of the new moon in the twelfth month, or harvest time, and lasts four to seven days. The scheduling is somewhat more flexible in the United States and does not usually last as long, but it always takes place around the time of the new moon in December. The New Year festival is the only holiday shared by the entire Hmong community and is an important occasion for bringing different Hmong families together.

The purpose of the New Year ceremonies is to get rid of the evil influences of the old year and to invoke good fortune for the new. One of the central rituals of the New Year ceremonies is the "world renewal ritual." This involves a small tree traditionally brought in from the forest (although Hmong Americans may use a green stick, or other symbolic tree), which is placed in the ground at the celebration site. One end of a rope is tied to the top of the tree and the other end is held by one of the participants or tied to a rock. An elder stands near the tree holding a live chicken. The elder chants while the people circle the tree three times clockwise and four times counter-clockwise. The chanting during the clockwise movement is intended

to remove the accumulated bad fortune of the previous year and the chanting during the counter-clockwise movement is intended to call out good fortune. The evil fortune, in the traditional perspective, is believed to accumulate in the blood of the chicken. After the participants have finished circling the tree, the elder is supposed to take the chicken to a remote place in the forest and cut its throat to take away the evil influences, but this practice is frequently not carried out in the United States.

Other rituals associated with the New Year ceremonies involve calling home the ancestral spirits to enjoy the festivities with the living and offering sacrifices to the guardian spirits of each house. For American Hmong, the New Year serves as an opportunity to reaffirm their culture and to teach their children about their traditions. For this reason, New Year celebrations in the United States usually involve displays of traditional cultural practices, such as dances, intended to educate Hmong children born in the United States. Aspects of western culture, such as performances by rock bands, have been integrated into the ceremonies. Many New Year exhibitions and practices show a merging of custom with newly acquired cultural practices, as when young Hmong women participate in beauty pageants wearing their elaborate traditional dresses.

Because the New Year holiday brings together people from different clans, it is considered an important occasion for young couples to meet one another. Ball games, in which long lines of young unmarried men and women toss a ball back and forth with their favorites, are a colorful tradition brought to the United States that may be seen at each New Year celebration.

♦ RELIGION

The cult of spirits, shamanism, and ancestor worship compose the three major parts of traditional Hmong religion. It is a pantheistic religion, teaching that there are spirits residing in all things. According to Hmong religious beliefs, the world consists of two worlds, the invisible world of *yeeb ceeb*, which holds the spirits, and the visible world of *yaj ceeb*, which holds human beings, material objects, and nature.

The shaman is important because he can make contact with the world of the spirits. Each shaman has a set of spirits that serve as his allies in intervening with the unseen world on behalf of others. Some spirits, particularly those of ancestors, also make themselves accessible to people who are not shamans. Every householder, for example, feeds the spirits of the ancestors at feasts by placing a spoonful of rice and a spoonful of pork in the center of the table and inviting the ancestors to share in the feast. Because women are most often in charge of medicinal herbs, they are responsible for propitiating the spirits of medicine on special altars.

Some Hmong Americans adhere to the *Chao Fa* (in Lao, literally, "Lord of the Sky") religion. This religion is said to have begun in Laos in the 1960s when a Hmong prophet, Yang Chong Leu (sometimes written as Shang Lue Yang), announced that the Hmong would be sent a king who would lead them to salvation from their enemies provided the Hmong rejected lowland Laotian and western ways, and returned to the ways of their ancestors. Yang Chong Leu also taught an original system of writing known as *Pahawh Hmong*, which is still used by adherents to *Chao Fa* today. The prophet was killed in 1971, but his followers continued to grow in numbers and were active in the fight against the new Laotian government after 1975.

Missionaries from a wide variety of Christian denominations converted many Hmong in Laos. Even more Hmong converted to Christianity after their arrival to the United States. The Baptists, the Presbyterians, the Church of Christ, the Mormons, and the Jehovah's Witnesses have all been energetic in seeking converts among the Hmong in America. Since religion is regarded as the foundation of life among the Hmong, conversion has been among the most drastic social changes. In many cases, conversion to Christianity has split families, with some members taking up the new faith and some members adhering to traditional beliefs. Marriage practices, in particular, have been affected by religious conversion since many traditional Hmong practices, such as the bridal price, arranged marriage, bride kidnapping, and the marriage of girls, are strongly discouraged by Christian churches.

♦ EMPLOYMENT AND ECONOMIC TRADITIONS

Since most Hmong in Asia practice agriculture, early arrivals had few transferable skills, considering America's vast industrial economy. Hence, of the 40,649 Hmong Americans who were over the age of 16 in 1990, only 11,923 were included in the American labor force, and 18.3 percent of this Hmong American labor force was unemployed. Almost 80 percent of the Hmong Americans who do have jobs are in blue-collar occupations.

Employers who hire Hmong Americans generally hold high opinions of them. Most employers and managers who have experience with members of this group praise them for their hard work and honesty. Some supervisors have remarked that the Hmong have a more flexible concept of time than the American majority, and that this can sometimes lead to minor difficulties in the workplace. Most of the problems faced

by Hmong Americans, though, appear to result from an inadequate command of the English language.

One of the most interesting aspects of Hmong adaptation to the American economy has been their discovery of a demand for traditional handicrafts in the American market. For centuries, Hmong women have practiced an elaborate needlecraft known as *paj ntaub* (also frequently spelled *pa ndau*). This art combines the techniques of embroidery and applique to produce colorful, abstract, geometric designs. The needlecraft is done entirely by hand, without the use of instruments for measurement.

During the 1980s, a cottage industry of *paj ntaub* has emerged in large Hmong communities, especially in California. Responding to the American marketplace, Hmong artisans have begun to produce bedspreads, pillow cases, wall hangings, and other items appealing to buyers. This emerging industry confirms Hmong cultural value, while demonstrating the economic importance of women to their families and communities.

♦ POLITICS AND GOVERNMENT

Adaptation to American society is a matter of overriding concern to Hmong organizations, most of which are geared toward helping Hmong Americans with housing, employment, language issues, and other immediate problems. The Hmong National Development is one of the largest organizations of this kind and, as such, functions as an advocate in obtaining funding for local Hmong organizations.

Hmong Americans are also passionately concerned with political events in their native land, where the Communist party that overthrew the Laotian government remains in power today. Although the government of Laos appears to have moderated its position toward political opponents in recent years, most Hmong remain strongly opposed to the regime. In fact, some American Hmong communities provide economic aid for small groups of Hmong in Laos who are still fighting the government. It has been suggested that Hmong Americans have been coerced into making contributions to anti-Communist forces in their homelands by groups operating in the United States, but this has not been definitely established.

♦ HEALTH AND MENTAL HEALTH ISSUE

Traditional Hmong methods for healing are based on shamanism, which includes the use of herbal medicines, and massage. Shamanistic health practices stem from the belief that illness is essentially spiritual in nature. For this reason, some western students of Hmong shamanism have characterized it as a form of psychotherapy.

The shamanistic view of the world views reality as composed of two parts: the visible and the invisible. The visible part of the world is the material reality that we see around us. The invisible part of the world is the realm of spirits, including the souls of the living, the spirits of the dead, care-taker spirits, malevolent spirits, and others. The shaman is a person capable of making contact with the spirit-world and dealing with it on the behalf of others.

The Hmong recognize that illness can result from many causes, including natural causes, but they consider the chief cause of illness the loss of one's spirit or soul. The soul may become disconnected from the body and wander away from it, so that an individual may become alienated from his or her spiritual essence. Fear, loneliness, separation from loved ones, and other emotional stresses can rip the soul away from the body. This leads to a variety of physical symptoms, such as loss of weight and appetite, that usually lead to more serious diseases.

The "soul-caller" is one of the most important roles of traditional Hmong health care experts. There are many methods of calling a wandering soul back to its body. In less serious illnesses, parents or other family members may be able to perform the rituals needed. If a baby cries during the night, for example, an adult family member may go to the door and swing a burning stick back and forth to light the way for the baby's soul to return. In more serious illnesses, a shaman will be needed to perform rituals that typically include animal sacrifices.

Lost souls may also be found by someone who has a *neng*, a healing spirit in his own body. The *neng* and the healing skills that accompany it must be inherited from a clan member. A healer who has a *neng* can not only find lost souls, but he can also cure illnesses caused by evil spirits, frequently by engaging in battle with the evil spirit that has brought the sickness.

The Hmong have a great knowledge of curative herbs and most Hmong households in the United States have small herbal gardens. Women are almost always the experts in herbal medicines. Herbs and massages are often combined to treat ailments such as stomach aches.

While the Hmong are, generally speaking, a healthy people, during the late 1970s and 1980s, Hmong Americans attracted nationwide attention as victims of Sudden Unexpected Nocturnal Deaths Syndrome. Similar to Sudden Infant Death Syndrome, the illness strikes during sleep. The mysterious fatalities occurred almost exclusively among men, most of whom showed no prior signs of illness. Physicians have connected the disease to breathing difficulties, but many Hmong ascribe it to an evil spirit that sits on the chests of victims during slumber.

Western-style health care professionals often have difficulty winning the confidence of Hmong patients because the concepts of illness are so different. Those who have written on the subject feel that doctors, nurses, and other health-care providers who work with the Hmong must try to understand the Hmong approach. Some have also pointed out that the Hmong, with their intimate knowledge of herbal medicines, have much to teach American doctors.

◆ NOTABLE HMONG AMERICANS

Dr. Bruce (Thow Pao) Bliatout

Working as the Director of the International Health Center in Portland, Oregon, Dr. Bliatout first came to the United States in 1966, as a young exchange student. He returned to Laos, where he worked for the Laotian government until 1975. He then returned to the United States and earned a Ph.D. in public health. Dr. Bliatout is an authority on Sudden Death Syndrome (SUDS), and has written widely on the subject.

Vang Pao

Vang Pao was the leader of the Hmong army in Laos and is still widely respected, especially among older Hmong Americans. Today, he resides in Santa Ana, California.

Dr. Xoua Thao

Arriving in the United States in 1976 at the tender age of 14, Dr. Thao's mother is a traditional herbalist and his father is a shaman. As a result of his family background in healing, Dr. Thao developed an interest in medicine and attended medical school at Brown University, where he received his medical degree in 1989. He is currently president of Hmong National Development and is studying for a law degree.

Dr. Dao Yang

Dr. Yang became the first Hmong to receive a Ph.D. when he received a doctorate in social economics in France. He was one of the co-founders of Hmong National Development and remains active in social issues, such as the prevention of teen-age pregnancy. He currently resides in St. Paul, Minnesota.

◆ MEDIA

The *California Hmong Times* is the chief Hmong publication in the United States. It publishes news and general interest articles, with a focus on the American Hmong community. Subscriptions are available at: 1362 North Fresno Street, Fresno, California 93703.

♦ ORGANIZATIONS AND ASSOCIATIONS

Hmong Council

4753 E. Olive Ave., Ste. 102
Fresno, California 93702
(209) 456-1220
Houa Yang, President

Community organization serving America's largest Hmong population. Helps with housing problems, translations, health and social services, and conflict resolution.

Hmong National Development

PO Box 44350
Washington, D.C. 20036
(202) 586-7318
Dr. Xoua Thao, President
Lor Mong Lo, Executive Director

National, non-profit organization that promotes the interests of Hmong Americans throughout the United States. The HND helps to facilitate communication among local Hmong organizations and to advocate for increased resources to Hmong organizations and communities.

Lao Coalition of Washington State

4713 Rainier Ave.
Seattle, WA 98118
(206) 723-8440
Mr. Udong Sayasana, President

Coordinates the activities of 10 Laotian organizations, including Hmong organizations and organizations of other minority groups from Laos. The Coalition provides such social services as transitional counseling, transportation, and tutoring.

Lao Family Community, Inc.

807 N. Joaquin
Stockton, CA 95202
(209) 466-0721
Mr. Pheng Lo

Provides English training and vocational education, a variety of youth programs, and a gang prevention program to Hmong, Laotians, and other minorities from Southeast Asia.

Lao Hmong Association

214 E. Wisconsin Ave.
Appleton, WI 54911
(414) 739-7244
Mr. Lo Lee

Provides educational and social services to the Wisconsin Hmong community.

References

Chan, Sucheng, editor. *Hmong Means Free: Life in Laos and America*. Philadelphia, PA: Temple University Press, 1994.

Quincey, Keith. *Hmong: History of a People*. Cheney: Eastern Washington University Press.

Sherman, Spencer. "The Hmong in America: Laotian Refugees in the 'Land of the Giants'." *National Geographic Magazine*, October 1988, pp. 586-610.

Tal, Kali, editor. *Southeast Asian-American Communities*. Woodbridge, CT: Viet Nam Generation, 1992.

Vang, Pao. *Against All Odds: the Laotian Freedom Fighters*. Washington, D.C.: Heritage Foundation, 1987.

—Carl L. Bankston III

Who Are the Indonesian Americans?

♦ Overview ♦ Acculturation and Assimilation ♦ Language ♦ Family Life and Community Dynamics
♦ Religions ♦ Employment and Economic Traditions ♦ Politics and Government
♦ Health and Mental Health Issues ♦ Media ♦ Organizations and Associations

♦ OVERVIEW

The Republic of Indonesia is located in Southeast Asia, on an archipelago of more than 17,508 islands near the equator. The total land area is 782,665 square miles, and the sea area covers 1,222,466 square miles; altogether, it approximately matches the size of Mexico. The name Indonesia is coined from Greek: *indos*, India and *nesos*, islands.

Indonesia consists of an array of island stepping-stones scattered in the sea between the Malay Peninsula and Australia, astride the equator and spanning about an eighth of the world's circumference. By comparison, the continental United States, on the other side of the globe from Indonesia, stretches across about a sixth of the world's circumference. The islands and island groups consist of a Pacific set and an Indian Ocean set. The Indian Ocean islands are Sumatra, Java, Bali, and the Lesser Sundas, or, in Indonesian, *Sumatera*, *Djawa*, *Bali*, and *Nusa Tenggara*. The Pacific Ocean Islands are Borneo, Celebes, and the Moluccas, or *Kalimantan*, *Sulawesi*, and *Malukus*.

Indonesia's climate may be described as tropical, though land temperatures and rainfall vary considerably according to altitude and relative exposure to winds sweeping in from the ocean. On the whole, temperatures vary little at any one place, and rainfall is generally heavy.

Indonesia is a rich resource of oil, liquefied natural gas, rubber, palm oil, and tin. Its major export markets are the United States, Japan, Singapore, Netherlands, and Germany. The major supplier countries are the United States and Japan.

History

By the fifteenth century, when the Renaissance was just pulling Europe from the Middle Ages, the islands of Java and Sumatra already had a thousand-year heritage of advanced civilization spanning two major empires. From the seventh to the fourteenth century, the Buddhist kingdom of Srivijaya flourished on Sumatra. At its peak, the Srivijaya Empire reached as far as west Java and the Malay Peninsula. By the fourteenth century, the Hindu kingdom of Majapahit had risen in eastern Java. Gadjah Mada, the chief minister who ruled the empire from 1331 to 1364, succeeded in gaining allegiance from most of what is now known as modern Indonesia and much of the Malay archipelago as well.

Islam arrived in Indonesia in the twelfth century and had almost wholly supplanted Hinduism as the dominant religion in Java and Sumatra by the end of the sixteenth century. Bali, however retains its Hindu heritage to this day. In the eastern archipelago, both Christian and Islamic proselytizing took place in the sixteenth and seventeenth centuries, and currently there are large communities of both religions on these islands.

Beginning in the early seventeenth century, the Dutch exploited the weakness of the fragmented small kingdoms that were the heirs of Majapahit and slowly established themselves as rulers of almost all the islands of present-day Indonesia. The eastern half of the island of Timor was occupied by the Portuguese until 1975. During the three-hundred-year Dutch rule, the region then known as Netherlands East Indies became one of the world's richest colonial territories.

Modern Era

Much of Indonesia's history in the modern era revolves around Sukarno (born Kusnasosro; 1901-1979). The Indonesian independence movement began during the first decade of the twentieth century and expanded rapidly between the two World Wars. The Japanese occupied Indonesia for three years during World War II. On August 17, 1945, after Japan had agreed to surrender to the Allies, Sukarno and other nationalists declared national independence and established the Republic of Indonesia. From 1945 to 1949, the Dutch tried and failed to recapture the territory lost to Japan. The victory over the Dutch strengthened Indonesia's sense of national identity and its citizens' belief in nationalism. In 1950, Indonesia became a member of the United Nations.

During the following decade, Sukarno gained power by revising the 1945 Constitution, and he became the President for Life. The Sukarno government badly mismanaged Indonesia's economy. The government seized foreign-owned plantations but did not train people to operate them, and consequently, economic conditions worsened.

The Communist Party began to grow during the early 1960s, with Sukarno's encouragement. In 1965, a group of Indonesian army officers seized power by killing six generals and other officers. This event precipitated more bloodshed. The Indonesian army and civilian mobs killed between two and three hundred thousand people throughout Indonesia. Some of those killed were not Communists, but foreigners who had once controlled a great portion of the Indonesian economy. During the anti-Communism movement, Lieutenant General Suharto rose to power, outlawed the Communist Party, and reorganized the government. In 1968 Suharto was elected president and has been the head of the state ever since.

People

The population of the Republic of Indonesia, according to the 1990 census, is 180 million, which makes it the fourth most populous country in the world. The national motto is *Bhinneka Tunggal Ika*, which means "Unity in Diversity," a phrase that captures the people's strong national allegiance despite the variety of ethnicities and cultures.

The physical, cultural, and linguistic diversity of the Indonesian people reflects their country's past history and prehistory. At first, groups of people from the Asian mainland moved southeastward to the islands. Later groups, culturally more advanced than their predecessors, arrived to absorb the earlier immigrants or displace them, pushing them to remoter islands or less favorable habitats. By the early 1990s, Indonesia's society was divided into numerous ethnic groups and minorities. The largest group was the Javanese, at 45 percent of the total population. Sundanese made up 14 percent, followed by Madurese, 7.5 percent, and coastal Malays, 7.5 percent.

Most of those who choose to leave their country for other countries, including the United States, are from larger urban cities on Java. An ethnic group noted for their diverse cultural and religious backgrounds and geographical origins, Indonesians who live in the United States split their affection and loyalty between their new-found country and whatever part of their homeland they or their ancestors once inhabited.

One Indonesian American has summed up the feelings of this group with a poem:

Putjuk pauh delima batu

anak sembilang ditapak tangan.

Sunggoh djauh negeri satu

Hilang dimata dihati djangan.

Translated in English the poem reads:

A sprout of wild mango, a ruby,

a baby catfish cupped in the hand.

From far away the native land is all one:

Lost from view, not to be lost from the heart.

Art

The Indonesians' sense of art is closely related to their mystic sense of identity with nature and with God. Humanity, nature, and art constitute an unbroken continuity. According to the beliefs of Indonesians, nowhere else are art and beauty more a normal expression of daily living than in Bali, though Java is not far behind. Artistic expression in Indonesian art can be found in their dress, which is more than mere folk handicraft. Batik, a creative design on fabrics, can be achieved by two techniques. The older method is called *tjanting* because a crucible of that name is used to draw the design directly on the cotton, by means of hot wax. When cooled, the wax resists the dye into which the cloth is immersed, so that all of the cloth except the area bearing the design accepts the dye. The wax is then removed, and the dyeing process is repeated. The second technique is regarded by some as inferior because the batik it produces is perceived to be machine-made. Actually, the design is made by a *tjap*, a printing stamp that is applied by hand to the cloth.

Other distinctive arts of the Indonesian people are the dance dramas of Bali and the Mataram court tradition. Both are essentially religious in character, though some Balinese dance is frivolous, flirtatious, or playful. Puppet dramas, or *wajang*, have been popular for a long time. The most popular puppets are flat and made of leather, but wooden puppets are also used. The puppeteer sits in back of a white screen and moves the puppets to act out stories. A palm-oil lamp throws the shadows of the puppets onto the screen. The puppeteer also tells the story and speaks the part of each puppet. The plots usually involve a virtuous hero who triumphs over evil by means of supernatural powers and his own self-conquest. In the decorative arts, beautiful stone sculptures decorate Indonesia's ancient Hindu and Buddhist temples.

Indonesians also practice Western arts, from oil painting to metal sculpture, the subjects of which are often inspired by Indonesian life and traditions. The literary arts are also popular. Early Indonesian literature consisted largely of local folk tales and traditional religious stories. The works of classical Indonesian authors, such as Prapantja, are still read today, though modern literature in the Indonesian language began in the 1920s.

◆ ACCULTURATION AND ASSIMILATION

Like other immigrants to the United States, many Indonesian Americans reside in such large cities as Los Angeles, San Francisco, Houston, New York, and Chicago, in order to seek employment opportunities and maintain social ties with others of the same heritage.

Because of the relatively smaller size of the Indonesian community in the United States, as compared with communities of other Asians, e.g., Chinese, Japanese, and Philippine, there is less of a clearly defined Indonesian American establishment. There is no evidence of an "Indonesiatown" anywhere in the United States, though this may also be due to the fact that Indonesia has one of the most ethnically diverse populations in the world, with more than three hundred distinct groups.

The diversity in social classes, language, religion, ethnic and cultural backgrounds, and geographic locations may minimize the possibility of forming a community of common traditions. However, there are numerous kinds and sizes of organizations, clubs, and religious groups in cities where there is a relatively large concentration of Indonesians.

Indonesians in the United States meet the challenges of assimilation in many ways. When asked if she has had difficulty assimilating into U.S. society, one 56-year-old female Javanese Indonesian American responded in the affirmative. After living in the United States for five years, her attachment to the Indonesian culture has become stronger. She finds it easier to relate to older U.S. citizens than to the younger generation, probably due to both cultural and generational differences. She claims that the assimilation is continuing, with little

success. She cherishes such hallmarks of Indonesian culture as batik, the traditional puppet drama theater, *kain-kebaja* (a woman's long-sleeved garment on flowered or otherwise printed cotton), *gamelan* (percussion-ensemble music accompanied by a soloist's *suling* [flute] or voice), *nasi goreng* (fried rice), and *rijstafel*, an Indonesian meal that combines rice with meat, fish, vegetable, relish, and fritter side dishes.

When asked about her religious background, this woman's answer reflects her culture's acceptance of religions: She reads both Bible and Koran. During her lifetime, she has been trained in Kebatinan, Buddhism, and Islam teachings. In 1964, she became a baptized Southern Baptist in Indonesia. As a single mother of four and a grandmother of one, she participates in both U.S.-affiliated organizations and Indonesian social clubs such as Dharma Wanita, Ikatan Keluarga Indonesia di AS, and Washington Court Gamelan Ensemble Association.

Another Indonesian American female stated that the first four years of her life in the United States were difficult. She felt lonely, even though she was married to a U.S. citizen. After spending close to twenty years in the United States, however, she "feels more comfortable with Americans, because . . . Americans do not impose or expect a person to do a lot of things for them." She is a Protestant and goes to church often. She is not very active in the Indonesian-organized clubs. She says, "I rarely come to their meetings or events. I don't know why, I just don't feel comfortable."

◆ LANGUAGE

With over three hundred regional languages and dialects, there is a considerable diversity in the languages used in Indonesia. The major family of Indonesian language is the Austronesian. Bahasa Indonesian, a modified form of Malay, was named by Indonesian nationalists in 1928 as the official language. The majority of educated Indonesians in urban areas speak at least two languages.

Spoken Indonesian varies depending on the rank or status of the speaking partner. Respected elders are usually addressed in a kinship term—*bapak* (father or elder) or *ibu* (mother). Indirect references are usually preferred in conversation.

Most Indonesian names have two parts, although some Indonesians, including President Suharto, use only one name. In most cases it is appropriate to use the last part of the name before the indicator as a second reference. If no such filial indicator appears, use the last part of the name as a second reference. Names including "Abu" or "Abdul" should use that word plus the word immediately following as a second reference. Some Muslim names include a place name. The part of the name preceding the place name should be used on second reference, for example, Abdullah Udjong Buloh, Mr. Abdullah.

◆ FAMILY LIFE AND COMMUNITY DYNAMICS

Intermarriage is not uncommon between Indonesians and non-Indonesians in the United States, especially for the younger generation, though the elder-generation Indonesians prefer that their offspring marry others of Indonesian heritage. According to the *1990 Census of Population, Asians, and Pacific Islanders in the United States*, more than fifty percent of adult Indonesians are members of families with two parents. Seventy-eight percent of Indonesian families are married-couple families.

Cuisine and Dietary Aspects

Rice is a basic food among Indonesians. Indonesians boil or fry rice in various ways and serve it with a great variety of other foods. Food are usually cooked in coconut milk and oil and sometimes wrapped in banana or coconut leaves. Fish, chicken, and beef are cooked with spices and served with rice. Indonesians eat little pork, since most of them are Muslims, and Islam forbids it. Tea and coffee are favorite beverages.

At ceremonial occasions, including modern weddings, funerals, or state functions, foods such as *sate* (small pieces of meat roasted on a skewer), *krupuk* (fried shrimp- or fish-flavored chips made with rice flour), and highly spiced curries of chicken and goat are commonly served. These foods are often served buffet style and at room temperature. Food is eaten with fingertips or with a spoon and fork. Water is generally drunk only after the meal. These dietary customs are usually observed by Indonesian Americans during holidays and special events in the United States. For everyday meals, some Indonesians adapt readily to U.S. food, while others prefer Indonesian or Chinese cuisine.

Indonesian Students in the United States

Like many other immigrants, many Indonesians came to the United States to pursue education and U.S. university degrees. In recent years, many Indonesians have come as college or graduate school students. After they gain a U.S. education some of them choose to apply for permanent residency or for citizenship. Presently, approximately 26 percent of the Indonesians residing in the United State are between the ages of 25 and 34. The same percentage of Indonesians have bachelor's degrees.

The beginning of cooperation between the United States and Indonesia in the field of education began in the mid-1950s, when Indonesian students were sent to study at universities and colleges in the United States. In 1953, the ICA (now USAID) started providing scholarships for a number of medical faculty members of the University of Indonesia to study at the University of California at Berkeley. In 1956, the ICA provided scholarships for the teaching staff of Bandung Institute of Technology to study at the University of Kentucky.

The attitudes of Indonesian graduate students at selected universities in the United States were reported in Dr. Rustam Amir Effendi's doctoral dissertation of 1983. Students were polled about their success in academic adjustment and their academic satisfaction associated with their U.S. educational experiences. The seven universities in the United States that were selected were University of Illinois at Urbana-Champaign, University of Michigan, Michigan State University, University of Minnesota, Ohio University, Ohio State University, and University of Wisconsin. The questionnaires were used to collect such biographical information as age, gender, occupation in Indonesia, and university of origin in Indonesia. The other topics included in the questionnaire were students' adjustment to the general system of U.S. higher education, the English-language learning environment, the U.S. style of learning, and the efficient use of the library.

The study disclosed that approximately 80 percent of Indonesian students are male and that 50 percent of them are between the ages of 31 and 35. Slightly more than 50 percent of them had worked as professionals for several years after they acquired their undergraduate degrees in Indonesia and before coming to the United States. Most of them are university faculty or government officials. The popular areas of study subjects are engineering and social sciences. As expected, a high percentage of the students originated from the five top ranking universities in Indonesia: University of Indonesia, Gadjah Mada University, Erlangga University, Bandung Institute of Technology, and Bogor Institute of Agriculture. All these universities are located on the island of Java.

The data analysis of the academic adjustment indicates that Indonesian students find that, among the aspects of university life included in the survey, rules and regulations are the easiest thing for them to adjust to. They are most comfortable with those elements relating to general administrative procedures. At the other end of the continuum, Indonesian students rated "U.S. classroom environment" and "methods of teaching" the most difficult aspects for them to adjust to. The English-language learning environment caused difficulty for many. It is easier for them to read text materials than to adjust to the oral component of the learning process. In the area of efficient use of library, Indonesian students find it more difficult to use newer library technologies than the traditional card catalogs, due to the scarcity of new technologies and tools in university libraries in Indonesia.

The number of Indonesian students in the United States has grown steadily since 1983. The successful personal adjustment and academic achievement of these students are decided by mainly two factors: language efficiency and the ability to adjust to U.S. society. While some of them return to Indonesia, many choose to remain in the United States to continue their professional pursuits.

Immigration to the United States

The number of Indonesian immigrants or naturalized U.S. citizens is small when compared to those of Chinese, Japanese, and Philippine Americans. According to the 1990 Population Census, of 6,876,394 Asians, 30,085, or 0.4%, claimed to be Indonesian Americans or Indonesians residing in the United States.

In the midst of the power shift and government reorganization in the 1960s, many Indonesians left for other countries. Even though most Indonesians agreed that the Suharto government has brought peace to Indonesia—a remarkable accomplishment in this land of conflict, revolt, and coup—not all ethnic or political groups are cooperating with each other. In 1960s a large group of Indonesian Chinese left Indonesia. Since then, due to a quota imposed by the United States Immigration and Naturalization Office, a restricted number of Indonesians have been allowed to enter the United States.

Cultural Events and Holidays

Indonesians in the United States of different religious, cultural, and geographical background observe special events and holidays differently. However, there are three major events that a majority of them do observe.

The major holiday, *Idul Fitri* in Arabic, or *Hari Raja* or *Lebaran* in Indonesian, marks the end to the Muslims' obligatory fast during the 30-day fast of Ramadan. Many Indonesians enjoy a traditional Muslim feast. The date of this holiday is determined by the lunar calendar; therefore, the date varies from year to year. Other important holidays observed are Christmas and Easter, which are also national holidays in Indonesia. Independence Day is August 17. On this day, according to officials in the Indonesian Embassy and Consulate Generals, Indonesians in the United States are invited to celebrate along with Indonesian officials in a flag-raising ceremony and reception.

On these special occasions, some Indonesian men and women parade in their sarongs, traditional Indonesian garments with batik designs. Men wear batik shirts without ties and outside the trousers on many formal national occasions. The customary hat worn is a black felt cap, or *peci*, an item once associated with Muslims or Malays but having acquired a more secular, national meaning in the post-independence period. Indonesian men generally wear sarongs only in the home or on informal occasions. Women wear sarongs on formal occasions, along with the *kebaya*, a tight, low-cut, long-sleeved blouse. Women often tie their hair into a bun or attach a hairpiece.

The popular entertainment during these events likely includes the popular Balinese dance. Another favorite entertainment is the *wajang kulit*. Though the origins of *wajang kulit* are lost in antiquity, many scholars believe that it is indigenous to Indonesia and that other shadow-drama arts around the world derive from it. This shadow drama is so popular that those who grew up in Indonesia can recognize all the stylized puppets and the episodes of the dramatized epics.

◆ RELIGIONS

The religions in Indonesia are as numerous as the languages. Nearly ninety percent of Indonesians observe Islam, with significantly smaller populations observing Protestantism (six percent), Catholicism (three percent), Hinduism (two percent), and Buddhism (one percent). Many Chinese-Indonesians follow Buddhist teachings. All five play significant roles in Indonesian communities in and outside the United States

The high percentage of Muslims makes Indonesia the largest Islamic country in the world. Introduced to Indonesia by traders from India between the twelfth and fifteenth centuries, Islam, or *sharia* in Indonesian, is a strictly monotheistic religion in which God, Allah, is a pervasive, if somewhat distant, figure. The prophet Muhammad is not deified but is regarded as a human who was selected by God to spread the word to others through the Koran, Islam's holiest book. There are signification variations in the practice and interpretation of Islam in various parts of Indonesia. Overall, a less strict interpretation of Islam is practiced than in the Middle East.

There has been constant interaction between the Muslims and the Hindu-Buddhist population in Java Island ever since the initial introduction of Islam, and over time they have blended to form a loosely organized belief system called Javanism, or *agama Jawa*, which was officially recognized in the 1945 constitution.

The most rapidly growing religions in Indonesia are the Christian faiths, Roman Catholicism and Protestantism. The number of Christians in Indonesia is very small compared with the number of Muslims, but Christianity has a long history in Indonesia. It was introduced by Portuguese Jesuits and Dominicans in the sixteenth century. When the Dutch defeated Portugal in 1605, the Calvinist Dutch Reformed Church expelled Catholic missionaries and became the only Christian influence in the islands for three hundred years. Because Calvinism was a strict, austere, and intellectually uncompromising variety of Christianity that demanded a thorough understanding of scripture, Christianity gained few converts in Indonesia until the nineteenth century, when German Lutherans introduced evangelical freedom and Jesuits established successful missions, schools, and hospitals on some of the islands, including Timor and Flores.

Membership in Christian churches surged after the 1965 coup attempt, when all nonreligious persons were labeled atheists and were suspected to be Communists. By the 1990s, the majority of Christians in Indonesia were Protestants of one affiliation or another. Catholic congregations grew less rapidly, due to the Church's heavy reliance on Europeans in positions of leadership.

Hinduism is perceived to enforce a rigid caste structure, dividing people into classes: priests, ruler-warriors, and commoners-servants. However, the caste system has never been rigidly applied in Indonesia. The majority of the Hindus are in Bali, and they express their beliefs through art and ritual instead of scripture and law. Ceremonies at puberty, marriage, and, most notably, death are closely associated with the Balinese version of Hinduism.

Chinese Indonesians brought Buddhism to Indonesia, along with Taoism and Confucianism. This unique version of Buddhism was introduced by the founder of Perbuddhi, Bhikku Ashin Jinarakkhita. He claimed that there is a single supreme deity, Sang Hyand Adi Buddha. In the wake of the failed coup in 1965, many Indonesians registered as Buddhists—some simply to avoid being suspected as Communist sympathizers and others sincere enough to construct monasteries.

Although there are various schools of thought and practice among Indonesian Buddhists, they each acknowledge the Four Noble Truths and the Eightfold Path. The Four Noble Truths concern the suffering of all living beings, resulting from the craving for worldly belongings. The Eightfold Path leads to enlightenment, teaching purified views, speech, conduct, and mind. In Indonesia, Buddhism is highly individualistic, with each person held accountable for his or her own self. Anyone can meditate alone, anywhere. Temples and pagodas exist only to inspire the proper frame of mind for believers' devotion and self-awareness.

In Dr. Fredy Lowell Macarewa's doctoral dissertation (1988), he chronicles the efforts by the Seventh-Day Adventists, who practice an evangelical Christian faith, to reach Indonesian Americans. These efforts have not been entirely successful, however, because of the failure to comprehend the belief system unique to Indonesians, which grew out of the long transition from Dutch-Indonesian rule to Indonesian independence. Macarewa also recognizes that evangelizing Muslims is a difficult task, because of prejudice and antagonism between the followers of Christianity and Islamic Indonesia during the past fourteen centuries.

Besides Seventh-Day Adventism, there are other religious establishments for the Indonesian residing in the United States, as there are for Korean Americans and other Asian Americans. These churches or religious groups serve not only as sites for worship but also as centers for social and cultural activities.

♦ EMPLOYMENT AND ECONOMIC TRADITIONS

According to the 1990 census, one-third of employed Indonesian adults in the United States are managers; one-third are professionals; and one-third are in technical, sales, and administrative-support occupations. There is a growing number of Indonesians who make their living in the importing and exporting business. Trade between Indonesia and United States has been robust. In the early 1990s, U.S. imports from Indonesia, consisting mostly of oil, rubber, coffee, tin, spices, tea, plywood, and textiles, amounted to nearly $4 billion. Exports to Indonesia totaled $2.5 billion and included agricultural products, resins, aircraft and parts, and earth-moving equipment. To facilitate trade there are commercial trade organizations such as the American-ASEAN (Association of Southeast Nations) Trade Council, the American-Indonesian Chamber of Commerce, the Central Indonesian Trading Company, the Indonesian Investment Promotion Office, and the Indonesian Trade Promotion Center, all located in New York City. However, recently there have been organization branches established in other cities, including Los Angeles and Houston.

♦ POLITICS AND GOVERNMENT

The immigration bill passed by the Indonesian parliament March 4, 1993, is having an impact on the influx of Indonesians to the United States or other countries at the end of the twentieth century and beyond. The bill bars certain individuals from re-entering or leaving Indonesia if doing so could disrupt development, cause disunity among the Indonesian population, or threaten the individual's life or his or her family's life. Further, a time limit of between six months and two-and-a-half years was set on travel in and out of Indonesia, for those affected. There are no public records showing how many Indonesians are barred from leaving the country.

In November 1994, President Bill Clinton of the United States attended the Asian Pacific Economic Summit meeting in Jakarta. The discussion came around to minimizing restrictions for export and import between United States and Indonesia. It is expected that the increased trade between these two countries will bring more Indonesians to the United States.

♦ HEALTH AND MENTAL HEALTH ISSUES

There are no documented health problems or medical conditions that are specific to Indonesian Americans. Their views of the health care establishments in the United States are mixed. Indonesians in the United States are pleased by the accessibility and availability of such services, which are far superior to what is offered in Indonesia. Like most United States citizens, Indonesian business owners and professionals in private practice are insured at their own expense, while employees benefit from their employers' health plans when available. However, they all share concerns about the high cost of medical care and health insurance.

♦ MEDIA

Television can be found almost everywhere in Indonesia. Programs such as *Kojak* and *Dynasty* are popular. The prevalence of television helps the assimilation and acculturation of Indonesians when they first come to the United States. These programs, however, may skew their views and expectations of U.S. society.

Indonesian communities in the United States are linked by a publication titled *Indonesian Journal*, the first such commercial magazine in the United States, published since 1988. According to Mr. Mailangkay, editor and publisher, 7,000 copies of the monthly, Indonesian-language *Journal* are regularly distributed, free of charge, to the larger Indonesian communities in the country: New York, Chicago, Houston, San Francisco, and Los Angeles. Free copies are also distributed at Indonesian restaurants, churches, and other social organizations throughout the United States. Advertising revenues are its sole means of support. With the exception of some of the advertisements, the text of the publication is in Bahasa Indonesian. With reports on and announcements of cultural, social, and even political events in the United States as well as in Indonesia, this publication serves as an important vehicle of communication for Indonesians who reside in the United States.

Mr. Mailangkay is also responsible for another publication, *Indonesian Business Directory U.S.A.* Published

annually in English, it promotes trade between Indonesian Americans, U.S. citizens in Indonesia, and Indonesians in Indonesia. The latest directory lists over 350 Indonesian enterprises, Indonesian executives and entrepreneurs, and U.S. firms according to their businesses' characteristics.

The Indonesia Letter enjoys the largest distribution among publications of this variety. It has been published monthly by The Asia Letter, Ltd., in Los Angeles, since 1969. This publication provides commentary and analysis on the subject of Indonesia and news of its economic, political, and social development.

♦ ORGANIZATIONS AND ASSOCIATIONS

American Indonesian Chamber of Commerce

711 3rd Ave., 17th Fl.
New York, NY 10017
(212) 687-4505
Wayne Forrest, Executive Director

This unofficial and nonpolitical organization was incorporated in the United States in 1949, before Indonesia received full independence, a fact that signified the willingness of U.S. firms to trade directly with the emerging Republic of Indonesia. Since then, its mission has been to foster and promote trade and investment between United States and Indonesia. Currently, the American Indonesian Chamber of Commerce has over 150 members, including banks; energy companies; shipping lines; engineering firms; exporters; manufacturers; legal, public relations, and financial-service firms; and consulting and trading companies. The Chamber works closely with both Indonesians and U.S. citizens who are interested in doing export and import business from the United States or from Indonesia. Fax: (212) 867-9882.

American-ASEAN Trade Council

40 East 49th Street
New York, NY 10017

The Council membership consists of members of the American Indonesian Chamber of Commerce and the Philippine American Chamber of Commerce and ASEAN (Association of Southeast Asian Nations).

East Timor Project

PO Box 2197
Washington, DC 20013
Arnold S. Kohen, Coordinator

This organization seeks to draw public attention to the situations of political prisoners in Indonesia, and to conditions in East Timor. It was formerly named the Emergency Committee for Human Rights in Indonesia and Self-Determination on East Timor.

Indonesian American Society

c/o Major Hal Maynard
8725 Piccadilly
Springfield, VA 22151
(703) 425-5080

Indonesian Community Association

c/o Embassy of Indonesia
2020 Massachusetts Ave., NW
Washington, DC 20036
(202) 775-5200
Mr. Muchamad Sukarna, Chair

This association serves as the central point of networking among Indonesians residing in the United States. The chair serves as leader and coordinator for the Indonesian American community. Considered the official representation of Indonesia in the United States the association was formed to support such activities as family-oriented events, lectures, sports, and religious holidays. The association publication, *Warta IKI*, is published quarterly and distributed among Indonesian organizations in the United States.

Indonesian Students Association

c/o Embassy of Indonesia
2121 Massachusetts Ave., NW
Washington, DC 20036
(202) 293-1745

Founded to serve the needs of Indonesian students at colleges and universities in the United States. Branches of the organization are also in San Francisco, Los Angeles and other major cities.

References

Aznam, Suhaini. "Passport control; new immigration law can render citizens stateless," *Far Eastern Economic Review*, (March 26, 1992): 18-19.

Cordasco, Francesco. *Dictionary of American Immigration History*. Metuchen: Scarecrow Press, Inc., 1990.

De Leeuw, Ad'ele. *Indonesian Legends & Folk Tales*. New York: Nelson, 1961.

Effendi, Rustam Amir, "*A Study of Academic Adjustment and Academic Satisfaction as Perceived by Indonesian Graduate Students at Selected Universities in the United States*," (Ph.D. diss., Ohio University, 1983).

Multiculturalism in the United States; a Comparative Guide to Acculturation and Ethnicity. Westport: Greenwood Press, 1992.

Neill, Wilfred T. *Twentieth-century Indonesia*. New York: Columbia University Press, 1973.

1990 Census of Population, Asian and Pacific Islanders in the United States. United States Department of Commerce, Economics and Statistics Administration, Bureau of Census, 1993.

Notodiharjo, H. "International Cooperation in the Field of Education," *Prisma*, 4 (April, 1977): 24.

—*Eveline Yang*

Who Are the Japanese Americans?

♦ Japanese in the United States: Pre-1885 ♦ Japanese in the United States: 1885-1941
♦ Japanese Americans in World War II ♦ Japanese Americans: 1966-1988
♦ Japanese Americans in the Aftermath of Redress (1988-Present)
♦ Japanese Americans and Sports

Unlike many ethnic groups who came to the United States as immigrants or refugees, many of the first Asians in the United States—Chinese, Japanese, and Filipino—came as sojourners. In the case of the early Japanese immigrants, some sought to escape being drafted into the Japanese Army. Others were laborers and farmers who, for the most part, had every intention of eventually returning to Japan. In any event, unlike those immigrants who would and could embrace life in a new country and quickly discard many aspects of their culture and heritage, or refugees who might welcome asylum but still identify with their old country and steadfastly cling to its culture and traditions, the earliest Japanese in the United States did neither. In fact, U.S. legislative and social restrictions imposed upon them prohibited it. In order to understand and appreciate this, the history of the Japanese American community and its many guises need to be addressed.

♦ JAPANESE IN THE UNITED STATES: PRE-1885

From approximately the beginning of the 17th century until 1868, Japan was ruled by the Tokugawa Shogunate. Under the Tokugawas, the Japanese imperial government, having witnessed foreign domination in other Asian countries where missionaries were soon followed by military forces, expressly forbade travel to or from Japan and instilled in its people a sense of fear and suspicion of all that was foreign. The penalty for violating this policy of isolationism was death.

The Tokugawas maintained an isolationist stance for almost 230 years. Perhaps this period may have been longer had it not been for an ocean current called the Kuroshio, or the Black Current. The Kuroshio sweeps northward across the Pacific Ocean from Japan toward Alaska. The powerful current dragged a number of Japanese fishing ships away from familiar shores, and some were tragically shipwrecked. Survivors of shipwrecks were the first Japanese to arrive in the United States.

Although his shipwreck was unrelated to the pull of the Black Current, the best known of these shipwrecked fishermen was Manjiro Nakahama, who was also known as John Mung. After being rescued at sea by a U.S. ship, he was brought first to Hawaii, around 1841. He eventually acquired a U.S. education at Fairhaven, Massachusetts. Risking his own life, he later returned to Japan, where he joined with other Japanese to urge the lifting of the isolation policy.

In 1850, Hamada Hikozo, who became known as Joseph Heco, also was rescued at sea by a U.S. ship. He studied in Baltimore, Maryland, and in 1858, became the first Japanese naturalized as a U.S. citizen.

By 1853, with Commodore Matthew G. Perry and the U.S. fleet poised in Tokyo Bay, and a growing number of Japanese, such as Manjiro Nakahama, urging an end to isolationism, the end of Japanese isolationism was inevitable. In 1860, the first Japanese diplomatic delegation visited the United States with Nakahama serving as official interpreter. By 1868, the political shift from isolationist Tokugawas to the westward-looking Meiji clan was complete.

The Meiji government pursued a policy of increasing Western influence in Japan and forcing Japan into the 19th century world as rapidly as possible. In 1868, although emigration from Japan was still illegal and would remain so until 1884, the first contract laborers from Japan sneaked to Hawaii to work on the sugar plantations. As this was the first year of the Meiji Era, this group was called Gannen Mono, Gannen referring to the first year of the Meiji Era and Mono referring to people. Intended as an experiment for future temporary labor importation, it failed quickly.

The laborers, about 150 in number, were a group of artisans, criminals, former soldiers, intellectuals, farmers, and women who had been recruited off the streets of Yokohama. Many were unaccustomed to field work and unwilling to take orders from the plantation bosses. Certainly the treatment they received was poor and many of them headed for Honolulu, refusing to continue their work on the plantations.

Eventually, word reached Japan that these individuals were being mistreated, and they were told to return home. Approximately one-third of them did just that, but approximately 100 remained in Hawaii, many of the men eventually marrying Hawaiian women. As a consequence of this failed experiment, another two decades passed before the Japanese government in 1884 would allow its citizens to leave Japan as temporary laborers in Hawaii.

Ironically, the first effort at Japanese immigration to the continental United States took place in 1869 by a group of Japanese exiles seeking to escape the fall of the isolationist Tokugawa government and the return of imperial rule. They established the Wakamatsu Tea and Silk Colony at Gold Hill (Coloma), California, not far from Sacramento. The ill-fated colony managed to survive a few years, but eventually, the venture foundered. Today, the grave of Okei Ito, one of the members of the colony, is all that remains to mark the site.

Although Hamada Hikozo (Joseph Heco) became a naturalized U.S. citizen, he was the exception rather than the rule at the time. Several Japanese were able to become naturalized citizens of the Kingdom of Hawaii, but when Hawaii was annexed as a U.S. territory in 1898, the territorial government refused to recognize former Hawaiian citizens as U.S. citizens. The issue of Asian immigration and naturalization coupled with growing anti-Asian sentiment in the United States resulted in the Chinese Exclusion Act of 1882. The Chinese Exclusion Act barred Chinese from entering the United States and prevented those already residing in the country from being eligible for naturalization. Although specifically aimed at the Chinese, it would eventually be extended to apply to other Asians as well, including the Japanese, by means of the decision handed down in 1922 by the Supreme Court in Ozawa v. United States.

Nevertheless, in 1885, after the Japanese government permitted Hawaiian plantation owners to recruit contract Japanese laborers, the first group of laborers and their families arrived in Hawaii. For a short period of time thereafter, Japanese emigration to Hawaii and the United States progressed steadily. As seen in Table 8.1, the 1880 U.S. Census reported that 148 Japanese resided in the continental United States. Twenty years later, the 1900 Census figures counted 27,440 Japanese, approximately 1,000 of whom were women. The 1910 Census reported a Japanese population of 72,257 Japanese, including 4,502 U.S.-born children. By the 1920 Census, the Japanese population was reported to be 110,010, including 29,672 U.S.-born children.

Table 8.1
Japanese Population in the Continental United States, 1880-1920

Census year	Population, total Women	Children (U.S. born)
1880	148	—
1900	27,440	1,000
1910	72,257	4,502
1920	110,010	29,672

In 1924, the Asian Exclusion Act prohibited any further immigration from Japan. However, in less than forty years, the beginnings of a community took root.

♦ JAPANESE IN THE UNITED STATES: 1885-1941

With the restoration of imperial rule in 1868, the Meiji government of Japan began an aggressive pursuit of modernization and Westernization. This manifested itself most clearly in increased emphasis upon industrialization and militarization, the latter in reaction to fears of European and U.S. imperialism. In order to finance these efforts, taxes were imposed. Government attempts to decrease inflation resulted in an economic depression. Farmers were losing their lands due to an inability to pay taxes and the future looked bleak.

Consequently, in 1885, when the Japanese government announced openings for 600 emigrants for the first shipment of labor to Hawaii, it received 28,000 applications.

Most of these emigrants considered themselves *dekaseginin*, or laborers who would work temporarily in a foreign country. They were not seeking new homes or lives. Indeed, most had every intention of returning to Japan. Their goal was to work hard, make as much money as possible, and return to Japan "in glory," using their savings to discharge and erase family debts and regain lost property or purchase new land. Some hoped to use their savings to allow them to marry into a family of a higher social class, while others intended to live a life of luxury. Some sought to avoid conscription by the Japanese Army. Few dreamed that they might never return.

The Japanese government also believed these emigrants would eventually return to Japan. Fueled by a rising sense of nationalism, they tended to view these emigrants as representatives of Japan. It was important, therefore, that the emigrants maintain Japan's honor. Toward that end, there was concern that the Japanese bachelor communities would be prone to the problems of gambling, prostitution, and alcoholism. The Japanese government, therefore, encouraged the emigration of women, and Japanese emigrant men required little encouragement to bring wives to the United States. While in practice the theory failed to prevent gambling, prostitution, or alcoholism, it did result in the development of the picture bride system of marriage.

Picture Brides

The picture bride system, which reached its peak between 1910 and 1920, derived from the established Japanese custom of arranged marriage. The couple would exchange photographs and letters until the woman joined her husband in the United States. This system was not too different from the typical arranged marriages common in Japan at the time. Nevertheless, some Americans insisted the system was proof of the immorality of the Japanese and until 1918, the U.S. government refused to recognize the validity of such marriages, requiring mass weddings to take place on the shipyard docks where the picture brides disembarked.

Around the same time (early 1860s), Asa Mercer, the first president of the territorial university in Seattle, developed an enterprise to provide wives to the bachelor societies on the West Coast. He arranged for shiploads of Caucasian women, known as "Mercer Girls," to be brought from Boston and New York to Seattle, to become wives of the eligible and enthusiastic men of the area. Some so-called Mercer Girls were sold off at the dock to the highest bidder. During the same period, groups of young Caucasian women from Australia were arriving in Vancouver, British Columbia.

Yamato Colonies

There were some emigrants planning a more long-term, if not permanent, stay in the United States. Despite the failure of the earlier Wakamatsu Colony,

George Sukeji Morikami, c. 1965, last surviving member of the Yamato colony near Boca Raton, Florida. (Courtesy of the Morikami Museum.)

other farming colonies, each called Yamato Colony, were established in the San Joaquin Valley of California, near Boca Raton, Florida, and near Brownsville, Texas.

The Yamato Colony in Florida was established in 1904. Its founder was an U.S.-educated Japanese man named Jo Sakai. The colony struggled at first until 1906 when a successful pineapple crop seemed to signal the beginning of a bright future. The colony experienced steady growth and was eventually incorporated. In 1908, however, a blight struck the pineapple fields and crippled the colony's economy. Cuban competition in pineapples coupled with growing anti-Japanese sentiment in the area eventually brought an end to the colony. By the 1930s, only about 30 of the Japanese settlers remained. The last survivor, George Morikami, became wealthy in the post-World War II real estate market and donated money to build a park and a museum of Japanese culture. The Morikami Museum and Japanese Gardens remain today as reminders of this early Japanese colony.

The Yamato Colony in California was founded in 1906 by Kyutaro Abiko, a labor contractor and newspaper publisher. He began two subsequent colonies nearby, Cressy in 1918 and Cortez in 1919. Despite periods of financial difficulty and World War II, Abiko's colonies remain, to some degree, in operation today.

The Yamato Colony in Texas was started around 1917 as a sugar plantation. Although its sugar cane crop was successful, the venture was unprofitable as a result of a post-World War I economic depression. The colony disbanded around 1921, but many of the original colonists remained in Texas.

Regardless of their intention to settle permanently in the United States or return to Japan, the emigration of Japanese women resulted in the development of a family life that tended to encourage permanent settlement. The emigrant parents designated themselves as *issei* or "first generation" as in the first generation to live in the United States. The children born to these emigrants were *nisei* or the second generation to live in the United States, the first generation of Japanese to be born there. Some of the nisei, known as *kibei* or *kibei nisei*, were sent by their parents to Japan for their education, later returning to the United States. The majority of nisei grew up identifying themselves as Americans.

Exclusionist Policies

By the turn of the century, there was a growing nisei population. In 1906, the San Francisco School Board, attempted to segregate the Japanese children into schools with Chinese and Korean children. The Japanese government protested the decision, claiming that it violated a treaty provision which guaranteed that Japanese children in the United States would have equal education opportunities. Japan at this time had just defeated Russia in a territorial war and President Theodore Roosevelt was anxious for the United States to maintain a good relationship with Japan. He intervened in the school board's decision and in 1907, forced the segregation order to be rescinded. In return, in 1908, the Japanese government agreed to stop further Japanese immigration by ceasing to issue passports to laborers, except for "former residents, parents, wives or children of residents." Thus, the Japanese government was placated at the expense of further Japanese immigration to the United States. This later came to be known as the "Gentlemen's Agreement" of 1908.

Anti-Asian sentiment, particularly on the West Coast, was a growing problem. Anti-Japanese campaigns promoting fear of a "Yellow Peril" were being waged throughout the Western United States. Starting with California in 1913, a number of states, including Washington, Oregon, Idaho, Montana, Arizona, New Mexico, Nebraska, Texas, Kansas, Louisiana, Missouri, and Minnesota, enacted alien land laws which prohibited aliens ineligible for citizenship, such as Asians, from owning land. Since nisei children, having been born in the United States, were U.S. citizens, some Japanese families circumvented the alien land laws by purchasing land in their U.S.-born children's names and then serving as guardians of the property. Eventually, the alien land laws were revised to preclude this as well.

Meanwhile, in Hawaii, life for the issei was not much better. Beginning with the Organic Act of 1900, which prevented the importation of any additional laborers, labor disputes were becoming increasingly common. In 1909, the Waipahu Plantation Strike saw over 7,000 Japanese plantation workers strike for some three months. The basis for the strike was a protest of wage differences based upon ethnicity. Portuguese laborers were being paid more than their Japanese counterparts for the same work. The strike also marked a turning point in the attitudes of the Japanese in Hawaii. Whereas they had previously viewed their lives in Hawaii as temporary, the Waipahu Plantation strike reflected a budding transformation in self-identity from emigrant to immigrant, from Japanese to Japanese American. Japanese plantation workers were determined that their destiny and the destinies of their children were going to be linked with that of Hawaii.

The Waipahu Plantation strike was ultimately broken when the plantation owners brought in Koreans, Hawaiians, Chinese, Portuguese, and record numbers of Filipinos to replace the striking laborers. Still, three months after the strike started, the wage differences between the various ethnicities were eliminated.

Eleven years later, however, the working conditions of the sugar plantation laborers had not improved in any significant way. In 1920, 8,700 Japanese and Filipinos staged a six-month strike in which they were joined by Spanish, Portuguese, and Chinese laborers. The planters eventually broke the strike by importing Korean labor since Koreans were expected to be hostile to the Japanese. Nevertheless, the aftermath of the strike saw a new level of interethnic unity: the Japanese Federation of Labor and the Filipino Federation of Labor agreed to consolidate into one interracial union called the Hawaii Laborers' Association.

The enactment of the alien land laws did little to stem the rising tide of anti-Asian sentiment in the United States. Their effectiveness relied upon the ineligibility of Asian immigrants to become naturalized citizens. Underlying the issue of naturalization was the more menacing question of whether Japanese immigrants could be assimilated into U.S. society or was the culture they came from too different.

In 1921, the increased immigration issue was resolved through the Ladies' Agreement in which Japan agreed to bar the emigration of picture brides and virtually ended further Japanese emigration to the United States.

The U.S. Supreme Court decided the naturalization issue in 1922 in Ozawa v. United States. Takao Ozawa had arrived in the United States as a student in 1894. He graduated from high school in California and attended the University of California for three years. Moving to Hawaii, he worked for a U.S. company and settled down to raise his family. He married a woman who was U.S.-educated. He and his family belonged to a U.S. church and his children attended a U.S. school. English was the only language spoken in his home. He did not drink, smoke, or gamble. He was scrupulously careful not to maintain or establish any ties to the Japanese government or any Japanese churches, schools, community, or civic organizations. The U.S. District Court for the Territory of Hawaii declared that he was "in every way eminently qualified under the statutes to become an American citizen" except for one: he was not white. The Supreme Court upheld the decision because he was "not Caucasian."

Under the terms of the Gentlemen's Agreement, any female U.S. citizen that married someone ineligible for citizenship would automatically lose her citizenship. If the marriage were terminated by death or divorce, a Caucasian woman could regain her citizenship while a nisei woman could not since she belonged to a race ineligible for citizenship.

In 1924, Congress passed the Asian Exclusion Act which prohibited the immigration of aliens ineligible for citizenship. Although the Japanese were not named specifically, the law was nevertheless directed against them; the Chinese and Asian Indians were already excluded by other legislation. The cessation of Japanese immigration at this time would result in clearly defined generations of Japanese Americans: issei, nisei, sansei (third generation Americans of Japanese ancestry), yonsei (fourth generation), and gosei (fifth generation). Each encompasses a distinct age group with common cultural traits and societal norms.

Japanese American Citizens League (JACL)

The Japanese American Citizens League (JACL) was established in 1929, primarily in response to the growing anti-Japanese sentiment in the United States and the need to fight against discriminatory legislation. JACL continues to function today as the largest Asian American civil rights organization. Founded primarily by nisei, it also seeks to foster a Japanese American identity for all Japanese Americans.

Hawaii: Case Studies

In Hawaii, labor relations were not the only difficulty facing Japanese Americans. Many were also affected by racism and classism. Two separate incidents that resulted in well-publicized trials illustrate some of these problems.

On September 18, 1928, a nisei teenager named Myles Fukunaga dressed as a hospital orderly and picked up ten-year-old Gill Jamieson from school, ostensibly to take him to the hospital where his mother was being treated for injuries she received in a traffic accident. Fukunaga subsequently strangled the boy and left his body in a clearing located near the Ala Wai canal.

A few hours later, Frederick Jamieson, Gill's father and the vice president of the Hawaiian Trust Company, received a ransom note asking for $10,000. Following instructions in the note, Jamieson brought the ransom money to the designated place. He turned over $4,000 and then demanded to see his son. The kidnapper agreed but disappeared and did not return.

When news of the crime became public, vigilante groups scoured the Japanese sections of Oahu looking for suspects. Several young Japanese American men were arrested on little or no evidence. Two days later, on September 20th, the local newspaper received a note from the kidnapper that was verified with a bill from the ransom money. According to the note, the boy was dead. The writer would plead guilty and accept the death penalty. The boy's body was recovered later that day. Three days later, Fukunaga was arrested when he attempted to spend part of the ransom money. He immediately confessed. In the process he told his life story.

Myles Fukunaga was the eldest of six children born to a former plantation worker. He had graduated from school at the top of his class and loved Shakespeare and American movies; he embraced white American culture and despised the Japanese culture of his parents. He realized that his race and his family's poverty made his dreams unattainable. He was forced to postpone further education in order to help support his family. He worked 12-hour days at a hospital, giving $35 of his $40-a-month wages to his family. After two years, he asked for a $5 raise. He was denied any raise and quit. He found subsequent employment at a hotel where he worked 80 hours a week in the pantry. He attempted suicide and immersed himself in the worlds opened to him in books. Then he suffered appendicitis and while recovering was unable to work. Without his meager income, his family was unable to pay the rent on the small house they occupied. The Hawaiian Trust Company demanded immediate payment of $20 that the family did not have and threatened to evict them. Fukunaga felt responsible for his family's plight and motivated by a desire for revenge against a company that could not wait for a mere $20, developed the scheme to kidnap Jamieson's son. His plan was to use the ransom money to send his parents back to Japan, to confess to the murder and to be put to death. Although some segments of the Japanese American community protested that Fukunaga was obviously insane and that European American perpetrators of similar crimes received different treatment, Fukunaga was hanged on November 19, 1929.

The alleged rape of an European American woman and the subsequent trial for the act of five young Asian/Pacific American men—Horace Ida, David Takai, Ben Akakuelo, Joseph Kahahawai and Henry Chang—was a case in contrast.

On September 12, 1931, Thalia Fortescue Massie, the wife of U.S. Navy Lieutenant Thomas Massie, angrily left the Ala Wai Inn, a Honolulu nightclub, following an argument. Tipsy, she went for a walk around midnight. Approximately an hour later she flagged down a passing car, asking the driver if he was white. Bruised and suffering from a broken jaw, she claimed to have been abducted and beaten by five or six "Hawaiian" boys. She had not gotten a clear look at the assailants or their car's license plates. When she arrived home, her husband called the police. Up until this point the word "rape" had not been mentioned.

The five boys had been at a dance and involved in a traffic dispute. Matching the most general description of Massie's assailants, they were picked up and brought before her. Despite earlier statements that it had been too dark for her to see her assailants, she positively identified three of the five young men. Three of the young men had previous criminal record; two for attempted rape.

At trial, the emergency room doctor who had treated Massie testified that there was no physical evidence of rape. Massie's own doctor testified that she suffered from a condition that diminished the acuity of her vision and that she had been under the influence of opiates at the time she made the identification of her alleged assailants. The defendants produced numerous witnesses who testified as to their whereabouts at the time of the alleged attack. After deliberating for four days, the jury failed to reach a decision and a mistrial was declared. The defendants were released on bail.

Six days later, a group of vigilantes abducted Ida and beat him unconscious. On January 8, 1932, Massie's mother, Grace H.B. Fortescue, and Thomas Massie kidnapped Kahahawai and had him killed. The murderers were caught as they were trying to dispose of the body.

Renowned trial attorney Clarence Darrow was hired to defend the murderers. Despite his efforts to convince the jury that Mrs. Fortescue and Lt. Massie were temporarily insane at the time they had Kahahawai murdered, they were found guilty of manslaughter and sentenced to ten years of hard labor. Under pressure from military and business leaders, Governor Lawrence Judd commuted their sentences to one hour to be served in his office. The convicted murderers met with the governor and had cocktails during their one hour sentence and then left free. Efforts to retry the remaining young men accused of Massie's rape were eventually dropped. Nevertheless, the outcome of the case represented the embodiment of the fears of many in Hawaii's Japanese American and other ethnic communities regarding the degree to which justice was available.

Through the 1930s the relationship between the United States and Japan continued to deteriorate. By 1937 the United States had broken off commercial relations with Japan and, in 1940, President Franklin Delano Roosevelt declared an embargo on most goods to Japan. In July 1941, the United States led Britain and the Netherlands in an embargo on petroleum products to Japan, totally cutting off Japan's oil supply. In October 1941, the Japanese civilian government was replaced by a military cabinet headed by General Hideki Tojo.

In the meantime, the Japanese American community continued to grow and prosper. The 1940 Census found 126,947 Japanese in the United States, 79,642 of whom were U.S.-born. Indeed, in November 1941, after investigation on the West Coast and in Hawaii, Curtis B. Munson, a State Department special representative, prepared a 25-page report that was presented to President Roosevelt and the Secretary of State certifying that Japanese Americans were possessed of an extraordinary degree of loyalty to the United States and that the immigrant Japanese were of no danger to the United States. The report, which came to be known as the Munson Report, was corroborated by years of secret surveillance of the Japanese American community by both the FBI and Naval Intelligence. Nevertheless, the lives of many issei and nisei and the future of the Japanese American community were thrown into upheaval and disarray when, on December 7, 1941, Japan attacked the United States at Pearl Harbor.

◆ JAPANESE AMERICANS IN WORLD WAR II

Immediately after the attack on Pearl Harbor, over a thousand issei in Hawaii and on the West Coast who were prominent members of the Japanese American community (priests, teachers, civic leaders, etc.) were removed from their homes and imprisoned by the United States government. Neither they nor their families had any idea as to where they were being taken or what would happen to them.

Fueled by Secretary of the Navy Frank Knox's irresponsible and completely false attribution of the success of the Japanese attack on Pearl Harbor to fifth column Japanese Americans, the War Department suggested to General Delos C. Emmons, the Commander of the Army in Hawaii, that all Japanese Americans in Hawaii be interned. Emmons rejected the proposal; such a program would have been dangerous and impractical in that it would require badly needed construction materials and tie up valuable troop resources needed to guard the islands. Furthermore, a mass evacuation of the Japanese Americans would have resulted in severe disruptions of both the local economy and defense operations for the islands. Since Japanese Americans represented the majority of carpenters, transportation workers, and agricultural laborers, they were essential and, indeed, indispensable to the rebuilding of defenses at Pearl Harbor.

On the mainland, the Western Defense Command, headed by General John L. DeWitt, assumed Japanese disloyalty. DeWitt's aide, Karl R. Bendetsen, staunchly insisted that a substantial majority of the nisei bore allegiance to Japan and would engage in organized sabotage. Ignoring reports and evidence to the contrary, DeWitt was quick to embrace rumor and innuendo. Bendetsen would become one of the prime architects of the internment.

Popular opinion on the West Coast wanted the Japanese Americans out. After years of anti-Asian sentiment, the aftermath of Pearl Harbor saw a widespread and even more vociferous desire to rid the West Coast of Japanese Americans. The media continued to articulate anti-Japanese sentiments and advocate mass removal. Farming interests, such as the Western Growers Protective Association and the Grower-Shipper Vegetable Association, recognized a prime opportunity to rid themselves of competition from Japanese American farmers. State and local politicians began to jump on the bandwagon calling for Japanese American removal.

This type of racism and greed permeated some of the highest levels of the federal government, too. Assistant Secretary of War John J. McCloy was, perhaps, the government official most responsible for the internment of the Japanese Americans. Indeed, it was McCloy, an attorney, who revised DeWitt's military assessments regarding the need for incarceration of the Japanese Americans so as to support the excuse of military necessity. McCloy's revisions eventually would lead to the Supreme Court's upholding of the wartime convictions of Minoru Yasui, Gordon Hirabayashi, and Fred Korematsu.

On February 19, 1942, President Roosevelt signed Executive Order 9066, setting the stage for the evacuation and detention of Japanese Americans on the West Coast. Under General DeWitt's command, orders for the forced removal of the Japanese Americans on the West Coast were posted. The orders applied to "all persons of Japanese ancestry," including U.S.-born children.

Although Executive Order 9066 was ostensibly justified as a means of securing the United States from threats of espionage or sabotage, no case of espionage or sabotage was ever proven. However, not everyone obeyed.

Challenging the Internment Order

In Oregon, on March 28, 1942, Minoru Yasui, a nisei attorney, decided to challenge a related curfew order requiring all persons of Japanese ancestry to be indoors between 8:00 p.m. and 6:00 a.m.

In Washington, beginning on May 5, 1942, Gordon Hirabayashi, a student at the University of Washington, refused to obey the curfew order and to report for internment. Accompanied by his attorney, he went to the local FBI office with a written statement spelling out the bases for his challenging of the removal and curfew orders.

In California, Fred Korematsu was hoping to earn enough money to marry his Italian American fiancee and to move east. When his family reported for detention, he did not accompany them. On May 30, 1942, he was arrested for violating the internment order. All three men were convicted and imprisoned. They appealed their cases to the Supreme Court. The Court upheld their convictions, ruling that the evacuation was based upon military necessity.

A Japanese American woman, Endo, also challenged the internment order, and her challenge was denied in court as well.

Internment

The Japanese American internees were only allowed to bring with them what they could carry. Consequently, they were forced to sell or give away most of their possessions, including houses, furniture, refrigerators, pianos, cars, and pets. They were given little time to accomplish this, and it was not uncommon for them to receive only the most nominal amounts from buyers who knew that they had little recourse but to accept whatever was offered. Internees were forced to abandon businesses and jobs, with little hope of ever reclaiming them.

By June 1942, the Japanese Americans residing on the West Coast had been moved into temporary detention camps that were euphemistically called assembly centers. These so-called assembly centers were nothing more than the most makeshift of camps, housing people in what had previously been fairgrounds, stockyards, and race tracks. Filthy and smelly, these were places that had never been intended for human habitation. Nevertheless, Japanese American families found themselves living in stalls that had formerly housed cows and horses and being treated not much better. At Tanforan, a horse track that had been converted into an assembly center, the local county health officials had condemned the former horse stalls as being unfit to live in, yet Japanese American internees were forced to live there for almost six months.

Gradually, by November, 1942, the Japanese Americans were moved from the Assembly Centers to internment camps. There were ten such camps: Amache in Colorado, Topaz in Utah, Heart Mountain in Wyoming, Poston and Gila River in Arizona, Jerome and Rohwer in Arkansas, Minidoka in Idaho, and Manzanar and Tule Lake in California. Most of these were located in remote, desolate desert areas. Surrounded by dust, sand, and barbed wire fences with armed guard towers, the internees had no idea what was to become of them.

The internment camps were filled with wooden, tar paper barracks, with each barrack divided into smaller cubicles. A family could be housed in a single 20 foot by 20 foot cubicle with a pot bellied stove, a single electric light, and an army cot for each family member. Latrines and common bath facilities ensured a lack of privacy. Waiting in line was a common pastime: there were lines for every meal in the mess halls, for use of the laundry facilities, for use of the showers, for use of the latrines, for use of the camp sewing machines and for clinic service.

Makeshift schools were set up. Caucasian teachers from nearby towns and young Japanese American women struggled to provide some form of education to the thousands of school-age interned children.

In 1942, the U.S. government had classified all young Japanese American men as enemy aliens. By early 1943, however, the War Department, in response to intense lobbying efforts of the JACL, announced plans to form an all—Japanese American combat team. In Hawaii, General Emmons issued a call for 1,500 nisei army volunteers. In response, almost 10,000 nisei men volunteered. The 100th Infantry Battalion, comprised of 1,400 nisei from Hawaii, along with a few mainland volunteers, underwent training at Fort McCoy in Wisconsin and Camp Shelby in Mississippi before being shipped to North Africa and then to Italy. They fought in Italy until March, 1944. Three hundred of them were killed and 650 were wounded, giving them the name, "The Purple Heart Battalion."

In February 1943, all of the interned Japanese Americans, male and female, over the age of 17 were administered a loyalty questionnaire by the U.S. government. The purpose of the questionnaire was two-fold: 1) to assist authorities in the processing of individuals for work furloughs and possible resettlement outside of the West Coast; and 2) to register nisei men to be drafted for military service. During World War II, no other ethnic group had their loyalty challenged in this way; no group other than the Japanese Americans had to answer such a questionnaire.

Poorly drafted, questions 27 and 28 proved especially troublesome for many nisei. Question 27 (directed at draft-age males) asked: "Are you willing to serve in the armed forces of the United States on combat duty, wherever ordered?" Question 28 (directed at all internees) asked: "Will you swear unqualified allegiance to the United States of America and faithfully defend the United States from any or all attack by foreign or domestic sources, and forswear any form of allegiance or obedience to the Japanese emperor, or any other foreign government, power or organization?"

Together, these two questions asked Japanese Americans to make choices that by right they should never have been asked to make. U.S.-born nisei were asked to incriminate themselves, "forswearing" an allegiance to Japan that they never had. Issei, denied the right to seek naturalization, were asked to declare themselves stateless by renouncing the only citizenship they were allowed to possess. Furthermore, mixed answers (yes-no or no-yes) were unacceptable; only an unqualified yes-yes was acceptable to the government.

Of the approximately 21,000 nisei men eligible for the draft, some 4,600 answered "no" (or no response) to questions 27 and 28. Called the "No-No Boys," these men made the difficult decision to assert the violation of their constitutional rights and the denial of their civil liberties. Ordered from their homes and interned against their will for no crime other than their ancestry, these men felt it would be hypocritical to answer questions 27 and 28 in the affirmative. In fact, they felt it was hypocritical to provide any response to such questions.

Most nisei, however, made the equally difficult decision to answer questions 27 and 28 affirmatively. Few (around 1,200), however, volunteered for military service. Consequently, a draft was instituted. At Heart Mountain, a group called the Fair Play Committee was organized to resist the draft based upon the denial of constitutionally guaranteed civil rights to Japanese Americans. Some 315 nisei resisted the draft and were imprisoned at Leavenworth Federal Penitentiary in Kansas, McNeil Island Federal Penitentiary in Washington, or the federal prison at Tucson, Arizona.

The majority of nisei, however, believed that active participation in the defense of the United States was the best way of proving their loyalty to their country. They would serve in the military in spite of the unlawful denial of their own and their families' constitutional rights.

The loyalty oath required by questions 27 and 28 created a huge controversy among and caused bitter divisions within the Japanese American community, in some cases even resulting in violence. The wounds caused by this division of opinion would still be felt by Japanese Americans more than 50 years later. The argument over loyalty has masked the true issue, specifically the unlawful imprisonment of the Japanese Americans.

In May 1943, the all-Japanese American 442nd Regimental Combat Team began training and, by June 1944, it arrived in Italy to unite with the 100th Infantry Battalion. After fierce fighting in Italy, where casualties totaled over a quarter of the regiment, the nisei soldiers were sent to France where, fighting house to house, they seized the town of Bruyeres from German troops. Their motto was "Go for broke!" an expression which meant to "go all out."

In October 1944, the 100/442nd was ordered to rescue the Texas "Lost Battalion," which was surrounded and under fire from German troops in the Vosges Mountains. The battle raged for almost a week. At the end, however, the nisei soldiers accomplished their objective. They successfully rescued the 211 Texans. In doing so, they suffered over 800 casualties, including 184 dead.

The nisei soldiers continued to fight throughout the duration of the war in Europe, including the breaking of the supposedly impregnable "Gothic Line" in April 1945. The 522nd Artillery Battalion (of the 442nd RCT) was among the first U.S. troops to liberate the Dachau concentration camp. In May 1945, when the war in Europe came to an end, the 442nd had suffered almost 9,500 casualties, including 600 dead. They became the most decorated unit in U.S. military history for its size and length of service, earning 18,143 individual decorations, including a Congressional Medal of Honor, 47 Distinguished Service Crosses, 350 Silver Stars, 810 Bronze Stars, and over 3,600 Purple Hearts. They gave their lives and limbs to prove their loyalty.

Nisei and kibei (nisei who were sent to Japan for their education and later returned to the United States) soldiers served the United States in the Pacific as well as in Europe. Several thousand of them were recruited and trained for the Military Intelligence Service (MIS), where they acted as translators and interpreters. Nicknamed "Yankee Samurai," they were possessed of Japanese language skills, making them an invaluable asset. They undertook dangerous assignments that could include eavesdropping on Japanese officers, tapping communication lines, and communicating with the local people.

With the end of the war, the nisei soldiers returned to uncertain futures. The mainland nisei soldiers were returning, ironically, to barbed wire-enclosed internment camps. Although the evacuation order had been rescinded and some of the internees had been allowed to leave to resettle away from the West Coast (so long as they were scattered and dispersed) before the war's end, it remained to be seen whether Japanese Americans could ever return to the West Coast. In December 1944, the Supreme Court ruled in Ex parte Endo that loyal citizens could not be detained against their will any longer, opening the way for Japanese Americans to return to the West Coast.

Japanese Americans returning to the West Coast found a wide range of reaction. Some returned to find local people already prepared to help them resettle, while others were met by signs proclaiming "No Japs Allowed" and "No Japs Welcome." Many who returned to prewar homes found damaged houses, ruined fields, and little prospect to ever recover what they had lost. Others went to Denver, Salt Lake City, Chicago, and Cleveland, and from there to other cities and towns all the way to the Eastern seaboard.

In retrospect, some have tried to rationalize the internment, saying that it broke up the enclaves of Japanese on the West Coast and allowed for faster Japanese assimilation into mainstream United States society. Others insist that it destroyed the Japanese American community, paving the way for its gradual, but eventual disappearance. In either case, it was done without the consent of those affected and has proven to be a major focal point of the Japanese American experience.

♦ JAPANESE AMERICANS: 1966-1988

In the 1960s and 1970s, as the United States found itself immersed in the civil rights movement which was actively and vociferously condemning racism, the sansei or third generation Japanese Americans were beginning to come of age. Although some of the oldest sansei had been interned along with their parents and grandparents (some were born in internment camps), many sansei knew little about the internment of their families. Little information about the internment was available in books or textbooks. (Even as recently as the late 1960s the Justice Department was denying the existence of the internment camps.) Many issei and nisei, feeling a sense of shame and humiliation about the internment, were reluctant to speak about it. Nevertheless, in the atmosphere of the Civil Rights Movement, many sansei were becoming curious about and interested in their own families' histories while many nisei were re-examining their own thoughts and feelings about the internment.

In 1968, the Asian American Political Alliance (AAPA) was formed at the University of California at Berkeley and San Francisco State University. Rejecting the world view connoted by the term "Oriental," the Alliance began to promote the use of the term "Asian" in its place, thus signaling the start of the Asian American Movement.

The AAPA, along with an ad hoc JACL committee led by Raymond Okamura and Mary Anne Takagi, joined in a campaign to repeal the Emergency Detention Act of 1950, which authorized the incarceration of anyone of whom it was believed "probably will engage in, or probably will conspire with others to engage in, acts of espionage or sabotage." In light of the growing civil rights and anti-Vietnam War movements, there was concern that protesters could be interned just as the Japanese Americans had been during World War II. Support for the repeal gathered momentum until 1971 when the Emergency Detention Act was repealed.

Asian American Studies

Meanwhile, in 1969, the first Asian American studies programs were established at a few colleges and universities. This marked the first time that Asian American and Japanese American history was being taught in American institutions of higher education. Organized pilgrimages by Japanese Americans to the sites of internment camps, beginning with Manzanar and Tule Lake, were undertaken in 1969.

Redress Movement

It was in this setting that the demand for redress—compensation for the Japanese Americans who had been interned—began to gain momentum. As a concept, redress was not a new idea. It had its roots in the earliest protests against the internment: the Fair Play Committee at Heart Mountain; the limitations of the Evacuation Claims Act of 1948; and the determination of community leaders who, if they did not always agree upon the methods employed or the procedures followed, were nevertheless committed to the remedy of an injustice.

Ultimately, three lines of strategy were followed:

1) seeking the judicial overturn of the wartime convictions of Fred Korematsu, Minoru Yasui, and Gordon Hirabayashi which became known as the coram nobis cases;

2) legislative initiative; and

3) judicial remedy in the form of a class action lawsuit.

In 1970, the Japanese American Citizens League (JACL) held its biennial convention in Chicago. There, Edison Uno presented a resolution calling for JACL to seek legislation to compensate those Japanese Americans who had been interned. The resolution passed but little was done to act upon it. Redress resolutions were again introduced in 1972 and 1974, when it became the JACL's priority issue.

Precisely how, or if, that priority should be implemented was a subject of controversy that made it difficult to move forward. Not all Japanese Americans, or JACL members, were in agreement that redress should be pursued; there were some who felt the past was best left alone. After all, in 1974, for the first time, a Japanese American had been elected governor of a state when George R. Ariyoshi was elected governor of Hawaii. That same year, Norman Y. Mineta of California became the first mainland Japanese American elected to Congress.

To some, accomplishments such as these were clear evidence of the wisdom of putting aside the past. Others felt that nothing could compensate them for their suffering; there was concern expressed that many of the issei, who perhaps had suffered the most, had already died or were too elderly to want or need to undertake such a quest. Still others felt it was a form of welfare. For many, discussion of redress reopened old wounds.

Even among those who advocated redress, there was disagreement as to whether it should include individual monetary compensation. Furthermore, there was no clear consensus as to the best method by which to seek redress, much less any expectation for its success at anytime in the near future.

Nevertheless, by 1975, groups such as "E.O. 9066" in Los Angeles and the Seattle "JACL Redress Committee" had begun to activate a campaign for redress. As a preliminary step, in 1976, on February 19th, the 34th anniversary of the signing of Executive Order 9066 by President Roosevelt, President Gerald Ford issued "An American Promise," a presidential proclamation whereby Executive Order 9066 was rescinded.

At its 1976 convention, the JACL again adopted redress as its priority issue but with a significant difference from past resolutions: as a part of the priority resolution, monetary compensation became an essential element to any effort to achieve redress. The JACL proceeded to appoint a National Committee for Redress, chaired by Edison Uno.

In 1976, S.I. Hayakawa of California, an immigrant of Japanese ancestry from Canada, was elected to Congress. Hayakawa became the most well-known Japanese American opponent to redress. Ironically, Hayakawa himself had never suffered internment; he had spent the war in Chicago.

In 1978, the JACL held its biennial convention in Salt Lake City. Uno had died in 1977, and the National Committee for Redress was being chaired in the interim by Dr. Clifford Uyeda. There, Uyeda presented the committee's recommendation that $25,000 be sought for each individual (or his or her heirs) who had been interned and that a trust fund be established from which the demolished Japanese American communities could be rebuilt. The proposal was adopted unanimously, and Uyeda was elected national president of JACL. That same year saw the first "Day of Remembrance" to recall the Japanese American internment and to raise the level of public consciousness about it.

John Tateishi, a sansei, was appointed to replace Uyeda as chair of the National Committee for Redress.

In March 1979, he convened the committee to determine what approach to redress JACL would take. A lawsuit was not rejected outright, but the group pragmatically felt that an award sought through a judicial process would take much longer to accomplish. In discussions over the course of two days, the committee voted to seek the creation of a federal fact-finding commission, as suggested by Senator Daniel K. Inouye of Hawaii. Senator Inouye's reasoning was that a fact-finding commission would hold hearings across the U.S., thereby generating media coverage which would serve to educate U.S. citizens at large, and members of Congress as well. The commission would determine the consequences of the presidential internment order (Executive Order 9066) and make its findings and recommendations (if any) to Congress.

It was a controversial decision. The Committee argued that its decision was grounded in political reality; neither Congress nor the public were convinced any injustice had occurred and the myth of military necessity was still prevalent. Others, however, were disappointed by the Committee's decision and felt it stemmed from political cowardice.

One group born in reaction to the Committee's decision was the National Council for Japanese American Redress (NCJAR), led by William Hohri. Organized in Seattle in 1979, the NCJAR began a lobbying effort in Washington, D.C., and initiated efforts to seek support for redress from a variety of civil rights organizations, such as the American Civil Liberties Union, the American Friends Service Committee, the National Association for the Advancement of Colored People, and the Urban League. It undertook significant amounts of research concerning the internment at the National Archives and other sources.

The National Coalition for Redress Reparations (NCRR) was another group that objected to the formation of a government commission. Organized on July 12, 1980, its membership was initially comprised of a number of smaller Japanese American community organizations. The NCRR emphasized the importance of a grass roots voice from the Japanese American community. Although suspicious of the government commission, the NCRR would eventually organize community testimony for the commission hearings and ensure that the demand for monetary reparations remain a major aspect of redress.

On July 31, 1980, President Jimmy Carter signed a bill creating the "Commission on Wartime Relocation and Internment of Civilians" ("CWRIC") to study the impact of Executive Order 9066 upon Japanese Americans and to recommend appropriate remedies. In all, ten hearings with a total of over 750 witnesses were held between July and December, 1981. The Commission's report, titled *Personal Justice Denied*, was released on June 23,

1983. Its conclusion was unequivocal: the internment of Japanese Americans was not the result of military conditions but rather "race prejudice, war hysteria and a failure of political leadership." The internment had no justifiable cause that would warrant the denial of constitutionally guaranteed civil rights and liberties. Among the Commission's recommendations was that Congress pass a joint resolution that would be signed by the President and recognize the injustice that had been done, apologize, and grant each surviving victim of the internment $20,000 in redress. JACL endorsed the recommendations of the Commission.

In the meantime, the coram nobis cases were under way. In 1981, legal historian Peter Irons was doing research for a book he planned to write about the lawyers in the Yasui, Hirabayashi, Korematsu, and Endo cases. During his examination of archival documents, he found complaints from government lawyers that had been written in 1943 and 1944 which claimed that their superiors had suppressed evidence and, indeed, had lied to the Supreme Court in the cases of Yasui, Hirabayashi and Korematsu. These charges had been ignored then but with this newfound evidence, Irons believed that the three men had a chance to overturn their convictions by means of an obscure legal procedure: seeking a writ of error coram nobis.

A writ of error coram nobis comes from the Latin meaning "error before us." It can be invoked only after a defendant has been convicted and released from custody and then only to raise those errors of fact that had been deliberately withheld or concealed by the prosecution from the defense and the judge.

On January 19, 1983, Fred Korematsu's legal team, headed by sansei attorney Dale Minami, filed a petition for a Writ of Error Coram Nobis, wherein he challenged the validity of his earlier conviction. Korematsu's petition was based in part upon the evidence discovered by Irons that officials of the War Department and the Justice Department had knowingly altered, suppressed, and destroyed evidence contrary to its position. Later that month, identical petitions were filed in Seattle on behalf of Gordon Hirabayashi by his legal team, headed by Katherine Bannai, and in Portland on behalf of Minoru Yasui by his attorneys, led by Peggy Nagae Lum. And, on March 16, 1983, in Washington, D.C., NCJAR filed a class action lawsuit on behalf of all the internees.

Later, during that same year, on October 4th, in response to his petition for a writ of error coram nobis, Fred Korematsu's original conviction was vacated. The Court ruled that the government had no justification for the issuance of the internment orders and, indeed, based the internment upon "unsubstantiated facts, distortions and representations of at least one military commander, whose views were seriously tainted by racism." The judge, Marilyn Hall Patel, went on to say, "the potential for espionage or sabotage that had occurred or could occur in the future, was essentially non-existent or was controverted by evidence that was in the possession of the Navy, the Justice Department, the Federal Communications Commission and the Federal Bureau of Investigation."

Minoru Yasui's conviction was vacated in 1985 but unlike Judge Patel in the Korematsu case, Judge Robert C. Belloni declined to make a finding of government misconduct. Yasui appealed but died before his appeal could be heard, rendering it moot.

Gordon Hirabayashi's conviction for failure to report for internment was vacated in 1986 but Judge Donald Voorhees refused to vacate the curfew order conviction. The case was appealed to the Ninth Circuit Court of Appeals where, on September 24, 1987, Judge Schroeder ruled that "racial bias was the cornerstone of the internment orders," while the government's sole argument rested upon military necessity. Judge Voorhees ruling on the curfew order conviction was reversed and the case was remanded to him with instructions to vacate both of Hirabayashi's convictions. The curfew order conviction was vacated in 1988. Neither Korematsu's nor Hirabayashi's cases were appealed by the government to the Supreme Court, thus denying the Supreme Court an opportunity to rehear either case.

Two days after the Korematsu decision, redress bill HR 4110 was introduced in the House of Representatives by House Majority Leader Jim Wright with 72 cosponsors. A month later on November 6th, Senator Spark Matsunaga introduced redress bill S2216 in the Senate with 13 co-sponsors. Both bills sought implementation of the recommendations of the CWRIC. Although there was a clear majority in both houses of Congress committed to support redress, the bills failed. The strenuous objections raised by the administration of President Ronald Reagan to the issue of monetary redress appeared to be the major stumbling block to passage of any kind of monetary redress legislation.

Meanwhile, on March 16, 1983, the NCJAR filed a class action lawsuit against the government seeking $24 billion in damages. The NCJAR's class action suit was later dismissed in 1983 for untimely filing. This was reversed by an appeals court. Here, the Reagan administration did appeal to the Supreme Court, which, in 1987, ruled without opinion that the suit was barred by sovereign immunity, statute of limitations, and also, that it had been filed before the wrong court. The case was sent to the U.S. Court of Appeals for the Federal Circuit which dismissed the suit again, and eventually, in October, 1988, after President Reagan had signed the Civil Rights Act of 1988 granting redress (see below), the Supreme Court denied its last writ of

certiorari. Interestingly, the redress bill, which was making its way through Congress during this same period of time, included a clause calling for the "extinguishment of claims." Under this clause, anyone who accepted redress payments through legislation was barred from pursuing a lawsuit against the government for the same claim. Although it did not mention the class action by the NCJAR by name, there is ample evidence to suggest that the presence of this suit in the courts, a suit having the potential for costing the government a huge amount of money, made many in Congress much more amenable to the passage of redress legislation that would award $20,000 to internment survivors only, than they might normally have been.

In any event, in January, 1987, the House redress bill, HR 442, was introduced by House Majority Leader Tom Foley, with the eventual co-sponsorship of 140 other members of Congress. The Reagan administration continued its opposition. Nevertheless, on September 17, 1987, the bill passed by a vote of 243 to 141. On April 20, 1988, the Senate passed its version of the bill by a vote of 69 to 27. There were minor differences between the House and Senate versions. A revised version was approved by the Senate on July 27, 1988, and by the House on August 4, 1988.

On August 10, 1988, the bill, known as the Civil Liberties Act of 1988 was signed by President Reagan. Those who died before the bill was signed into law were entitled to nothing. The heirs of those who died after the bill became law were entitled to the full $20,000 redress.

The bill's passage, however, was not the end of the redress struggle. The authorization created by the Civil Liberties Act of 1988 had no bearing upon the appropriation of funds to finance redress. No payments were authorized in 1988 and no funds for payment were appropriated in 1989.

Senator Daniel K. Inouye proposed the addition of a provision to the 1990 appropriations bill for the Commerce, State, and Justice Departments which would make the already authorized redress payments an entitlement program beginning in fiscal year 1991 and thus not subject to sequestration or the deficit control restrictions. Senator Inouye's proposal passed. The amendment was accepted by the House of Representatives and the appropriations bill signed by President George Bush on November 21, 1989.

On October 9, 1990, the first letters of apology and redress payments were made, beginning with the oldest survivors. Regrettably, some half of the victims of the internment did not live to see redress achieved. Still, it was a monumental victory for the Japanese American community. Certainly redress was the culmination of many individuals' years of dedication and commitment to justice as an ideal.

♦ JAPANESE AMERICANS IN THE AFTERMATH OF REDRESS (1988-PRESENT)

People are shaped by their history and few examples more graphically illustrate that point than Japanese Americans. From their earliest history as undesired (and even forbidden) immigrants through the restrictions placed upon their ownership of land, their eligibility for citizenship, and the occupations open to them through the internment, including current concerns about the consequences of "Japan-bashing" in the media and race-motivated crimes and violence, Japanese Americans have been subjected to a steady stream of messages devaluing (and even disparaging) their Japanese heritage and encouraging European American acculturation.

Compounding the situation is the lack of substantial numbers of new immigrants. While other racial and ethnic groups have been subjected to the pressure to acculturate, most have also seen their cultural community reinforced in its identity by new immigrants. In the case of the Japanese Americans, immigration was closed by 1924; it was not reinstated until the 1952 McCarran-Walter Act and then in very minimal numbers. Those Japanese who did immigrate after 1952 did not necessarily identify with the Japanese American community. Pre-World War II Japanese American immigrants often recalled Meiji-era Japan, in custom, language, and viewpoint. Post-World War II immigrants were limited in number and had lived through the U.S. occupation and the resultant Westernization of Japan. For many of these later immigrants, the original issei and their Japanese culture were an anachronism.

Consequently, the upbringing of many sansei (third generation) and yonsei (fourth generation) has encouraged them to adopt European American behavior, values, and attitudes. Few speak Japanese or display knowledge of Japanese history, politics, art, or culture comparable to their familiarity with that of Western Europe. Until the redress movement was underway, many had little or no knowledge of their family history or wartime experience. Growing up, many had only minimal contacts with any organized Japanese American community.

Outmarriage

In addition, by the late 1960s there were increasing numbers of Japanese Americans attending colleges and universities around the country and, thereby, meeting people other than fellow Japanese Americans. This has resulted in an exceptionally high rate of outmarriage (marriage outside one's own racial or ethnic group) among sansei and yonsei. Some demographers predict that, given the predilection among children of biracial marriages to identify themselves as European American or African American rather than Japanese or Asian American, by the time the gosei (the fifth generation Japanese Americans) reach adulthood, the Japanese American community, as we know it, will very likely have disappeared.

Furthermore, while redress served to attract and interest many younger Japanese Americans in learning more about Japanese American and their own family history, culture, and heritage and encouraged their involvement and participation in community organizations, its accomplishment has also removed an issue that served as a rallying point to stimulate a sense of a Japanese American identity. The attainment of redress, coupled with the high degree of European American assimilation and acculturation by sansei and yonsei and the growing number of bicultural or multicultural Japanese Americans, has left many Japanese Americans questioning the need for and the reasons behind maintaining a sense of community and identity.

To some degree, some of the energy and efforts that previously might have been channeled into Japanese American issues such as redress have been refocused into a more pan-Asian American interest, involvement, and identity. Japanese Americans have been among the leaders in forging ties and providing direction and support among the diverse ethnicities and factions that comprise Asian America. Indeed, if the Japanese American community as we now know it is fated for eventual extinction, then within that evolutionary process Japanese Americans also appear to be among those in the forefront of a burgeoning Asian American community and identity.

So, just who are the Japanese Americans? They are Americans of Japanese ancestry and they are among the first pan-Asian Americans.

—Sandra Yamate

♦ JAPANESE AMERICANS AND SPORTS

Sports has played an undeniably important, if complex and sometimes contradictory role in the Japanese American community. Long stereotyped as unathletic, Japanese Americans have had for decades an elaborate league system in sports such as basketball and baseball for both girls and boys and men and women. Though they are often viewed as vehicles for assimilation for the U.S.-born generations, the segregated nature of these leagues and their intergenerational popularity actually served to bring the Japanese American community closer together. The widespread participation in these leagues has led to many Japanese Americans becoming outstanding athletes in these sports at the

Redress Program Regulations

The Civil Liberties Act of 1988 authorized compensation of $20,000 to eligible persons of Japanese Ancestry who were evacuated, relocated, or interned during World War II. The Act became law on August 10, 1988, and was assigned to the Department of Justice for implementation. The Office of Redress Administration (ORA) was created as a new organization within the Civil Rights Division of the Department, specifically to carry out the redress provisions of the Act.

The federal regulations were established by the Department of Justice to fulfill its responsibilities under the Act. They describe the Department's interpretation of the law's original language, and provide details about how the program operated. The regulations were signed by the Attorney General at the time, Dick Thornburgh, on August 10, 1989, and published in the Federal Register on August 18, 1989.

Eligibility of Redress

Individuals eligible for redress were required to be of Japanese ancestry, must have been U.S. citizens or permanent resident aliens during the internment period (from December 7, 1941 to June 30, 1946) and must have been living on August 10, 1988.

Most eligible individuals fell into one or more of the following categories:

- Those who were interned in Relocation Centers.
- Those who were held in Assembly Centers whether or not they later went to Relocation Centers.
- Those who were interned by the Department of Justice in any of the Immigration and Naturalization Service (INS) Camps.
- Those who filed Change of Residence Cards.
- Those who moved from prohibited zones on or after March 29, 1942.
- Those who were ordered to leave Bainbridge Island or Terminal Island.
- Those who were in the U.S. Military and were prohibited by government regulations from visiting their interned families or were subject to undue restrictions prior to visits.
- Those who were born in Assembly Centers, Relocation Centers, or Internment Camps, including those born to parents from Latin America who were interned in the United States.
- Those who were forcibly brought to the United States from Latin America for internment, and later acquired a change in immigration status to permanent resident, retroactive to the internment period.
- Those who spent the internment in institutions, such as sanitariums, under the administrative authority of the War Relocation Authority.

The Office of Redress Administration acknowledged that some eligible people did not fit any of these categories, and that historical records were missing even for some of those who do fit the categories described above. The regulations permitted "case-by-case" determinations under either set of circumstances. ORA asked persons who fit into this special case category to submit affidavits or other documentation to help ORA make an eligibility determination.

Redress Ineligibility

The Act excluded some people affected during the internment period from redress. These persons fell into the following general categories:

- Those who are not of Japanese ancestry, including spouses, who were evacuated, relocated, or interned.
- Those who were not U.S. citizens or permanent resident aliens, and did not have their status adjusted retroactively to the internment period.
- Those who relocated to an enemy country between December 7, 1941 and September 2, 1945. This includes children who relocated with their parents.
- Those who moved from the West Coast prior to March 29, 1942, for their own personal reasons, not in response to government action, and did not file Change of Residence Cards.
- Those who were born after their parents were no longer interned.
- Those who were born after their parents had moved from a prohibited zone.
- Those who remained in the U.S. Military, but lost no property as a result of government action, or were allowed to visit their interned families without undue restrictions.
- Those who were outside the boundaries of the United States, and did not or were unable to return during the internment period, even if their families were evacuated, interned, or relocated.

Verification of Eligibility

ORA established an information system that contained all the data that had been collected since the Office was established. These data include:

Historical Information: ORA obtained historical records created during the internment period from several sources, primarily the National Archives. From these records, ORA determined who was interned, who filed a Change of Residence Card, and other information critical in establishing redress eligibility.

Current Information: ORA collected current information from federal and state agencies (such as the Social Security Administration and state vital statistics bureaus), and from potential recipients, their friends, or families.

During the preliminary verification process, ORA compared current and historical information for each person.

When ORA reached a preliminary eligibility determination, the individual was contacted by letter. The law states that payment must be made in the order of birth, beginning with the oldest individuals eligible. Therefore, ORA contacted those eligible beginning with the oldest living on the date of the enactment of the law on August 10, 1988 (or his or her statutory heirs: spouse, children or parents) who have been located by the Administrator at that time.

The letter requested that individuals complete a Declaration of Eligibility and also submit certain documents to establish identity.

The Office of Redress Administration was responsible for determining eligibility. All individuals eligible for redress were required to return a completed Declaration and were asked to send other documents. For example, ORA may have requested one or more of the following:

- An original or a photocopy of a recent document with current legal name and address.
- Proof of date of birth.
- Proof of guardianship (if applicable).
- Proof of name change (if applicable).

And every heir was required to send:

- Proof of death of the eligible person (siblings may send one record per family).
- Proof of his/her relationship to the deceased person.

All photocopied documents were required to be notarized or to contain an authenticity clause signed under penalty of perjury. Wording for the authenticity clause was provided by ORA in the letter requesting the documentation. (ORA did not return any documents.)

Redress Payments

Payments began in October 1990. Although the Civil Liberties Act became law on August 10, 1988, ORA could not make payments until Congress and the President made funds available. A law signed by President George Bush on November 21, 1989, made Redress an entitlement, and established a three-year schedule for payments.

Under the 1989 law, enough money was set aside to make 25,000 redress payments in the first, year 25,000 payments in the second year, and 12,500 payments in the third year. Additional payments will be made in descending order, beginning with eligible people in the oldest age group (or their heirs) whom ORA has located at that time.

youth and high school levels. Very few Japanese Americans rise to the highest levels in these sports. Furthermore, sports in which Japanese Americans have become successful at the highest level are not the ones which draw the largest number of participants among Japanese American youth.

Both "Japanese" sports—with historical roots in Japan—and "American" sports—with historical roots in the Americas—played an important role in the lives of the earliest Japanese immigrants. The two most important sports to the issei (first-generation Japanese Americans) were clearly sumo and baseball. Sumo, a wrestling-like sport which has 2,000-year-old roots in Japan and is considered something of a national sport there, was brought over by the issei and continued to

play a major role in the Japanese American community through the Second World War. The sport involves two participants who face each other and try to force each other down or outside of the ring. The very first official immigrants from Japan arriving in Hawaii in February 1885 celebrated with a sumo match in front of an impressed Hawaiian King, David Kalakaua. As Japanese immigrants arrived in large numbers in the next two decades to work on Hawaiian sugar plantations, sumo's popularity as a recreational sport and as symbolic celebration grew. Sumo tournaments held to determine the best sumotori of each plantation camp evolved into inter-camp and inter-island tournaments, culminating in the first Hawaii Grand Sumo Tournament held in Honolulu on June 25, 1896.

Sumo

Sumo seemed to serve as a symbolic link to the Japanese culture and nation, as sumo tournaments were held in Hawaii in celebration of Japanese victories in the 1895 Sino-Japanese War and the 1906 Russo-Japanese War. In addition, the sport served to celebrate the arrival of visiting Japanese Navy ships during the early twentieth century and to raise spirits and solidarity during the bitter 1909 plantation strike of Japanese laborers and the World War II era mass incarceration of all West Coast Japanese Americans. Sumo was practiced by church groups, young and old men, and even by women. During the peak years of sumo popularity in the 1910s and 1920s, many prominent sumotori from Japan toured the immigrant communities and at least one *nisei* (second-generation Japanese Americans) ventured to Japan to try for a career in sumo. A slightly different variation of sumo flourished among Okinawan immigrants in the 1920s and 1930s.

Though sumo's popularity was already fading by the 1930s with the rise of the nisei generation and the intergenerational preoccupation with baseball, the coming of World War II was its death knell. In an atmosphere where all things Japanese were considered suspect, sumo was virtually stamped out in Hawaii, though it was practiced in some of the mainland internment camps. Though the sport still has its followers among Japanese Americans today—especially in Hawaii where a number of Hawaiian-born (but not Japanese American), Japan-trained sumotori rose to the top of the sport in recent decades—few Japanese Americans participate in the sport any more.

Athletic Leagues and Clubs

If sumo represented a link to Japan, baseball, at least on the surface, represented the acceptance and assimilation by issei to American culture. The first Japanese American baseball team, called "JBS," was formed in 1901 by Reverend Takie Okumura and was made up of students from his boarding school. Baseball soon became a favorite pastime among issei and nisei from both Hawaii and the mainland. In Hawaii, baseball was encouraged by the sugar plantations as healthy recreation which would occupy the workers and keep them out of trouble. Rivalries soon developed between different plantation teams. Similarly, Japanese American communities on the mainland formed teams that played one another.

With the birth and coming of age of the nisei in the 1910s and 1920s in Hawaii and about a decade later on the mainland, baseball and other sports began to be viewed as important elements in both their Americanization and in keeping them out of trouble. In Los Angeles,

home of the largest Japanese American community since the 1910s, the roots of nisei athletics can be traced to a Caucasian school teacher named Nellie Grace Oliver, who formed the Japanese Boys Club and the Japanese Girls Club on November 21, 1917, after observing nisei youngsters playing on the streets of Little Tokyo. The club and its many successors became known as the Olivers, the first of the nisei social clubs. The Olivers stressed sports and emphasized good citizenship and education.

As the Japanese American community in Los Angeles continued to grow in the 1920s, similar youth clubs formed in outlying areas. As early as 1926, a YMCA basketball league was operating in Los Angeles. Soon these groups were challenging each other in various sports. Contests took place in a haphazard and unregulated manner. In an attempt to regulate the proceedings, the Japanese Athletic Union (JAU) was formed in June, 1932. The similar Japanese Amateur Athletic Union (JAAU) had formed in the San Francisco Bay area around 1929. By 1934, a basketball championship game was taking place between the Southern California JAU champion and the Northern California JAAU champion. In the next few years, participation boomed among nisei Americans. According to Isami Waugh, there were over 400 nisei clubs in Southern California by 1938.

Though the scale was different, nisei sports seemed to develop along more or less similar models elsewhere on the mainland. Samuel Regalado described an eight-team Central Japanese (Baseball) League, which formed in Central California from 1934 to 1941 and noted the particularly bitter rivalry between the Livingston Dodgers and the Cortez Wildcats, for instance. In his study of baseball in the World War II internment camps, Jay Feldman notes that by the 1930s, "every community had a nisei team, ardently supported by issei immigrants." In his seminal study of the Japanese American community, Harry H. L. Kitano notes the presence of "the ambitious all-Japanese athletic leagues."

Though most of the teams and leagues in the United States were segregated in the multi-ethnic society of Hawaii, teams of various ethnic groups played against each other. The most famous Japanese American team was the Asahis formed as a sandlot team in 1905. The team became dominant in the multi-ethnic Oahu Junior League, winning titles from 1911 to 1914. The Asahis became a founding member of the Hawaii Baseball League in 1925, which was made up of segregated teams of various ethnic groups. In addition to the Asahis, the Japanese team, there were also the Braves, Portuguese; the All-Chinese: the Wanderers, Haole; the All-Hawaiian; and others. There was also the case of the Wapato Nippons, a nisei team competing in the mostly white leagues of eastern Washington whose success made them the pride of the Japanese American community there.

Like the role it played in other ethnic communities, sports served as a "middle ground," as Peter Levine described sports in a study of the Jewish community. Sports activity was a vehicle for assimilation in U.S. society: "The Nisei," Kitano asserts, "were free to develop in the American pattern. The play, the rules, the goals and values were all American; only the players were Japanese." However, the segregation of the leagues and the intergenerational support they received served to increase ethnic identification and solidarity. Given the difference in experiences and ideas between issei and nisei, sports was a means of finding common ground between the generations and cultures. For the nisei, sports was a form of recreation and a chance to be a star. For the issei, the segregated leagues insured that nisei would associate with other nisei, increasing ties among Japanese American communities, and serving as a convenient forum for betting and spectatorship. Successful teams became focal points of great pride for their communities. "A championship year," according to sansei (third-generation Japanese American) writer David Mas Masumoto, "would be remembered by a team and solidified a sense of community."

The mass removal and incarceration of West Coast Japanese Americans during World War II brought an end to the nisei sports leagues. In Hawaii, the Asahis became the Athletics and added non-Japanese players. Sports, however, still played an important role in the concentration camps that housed the uprooted Japanese Americans, and baseball continued to be the most popular sport among issei and nisei alike. At some camps, as many as 100 teams existed, with leagues for various age groups. In other camps where the populations of existing communities remained intact, teams were able to remain together and compete as before. Teams were also organized by block, or in the case of Tule Lake, by former camp. Nisei also competed in basketball, girls' volleyball and softball, and touch football, while issei busied themselves with *go*, cards, or baseball. As the title of a recent children's book on baseball in internment camps states, "baseball saved us."

The postwar era saw the rebuilding of Japanese American athletic leagues along the same lines as before the war, with basketball replacing baseball as the most popular sport. In 1946, the Nisei Athletic Union was formed in both southern and northern California, and play began in January 1947. The "resettlement" strategy of the War Relocation Authority led to the formation of postwar Japanese American communities in many places outside the West Coast where there had been no such communities before. It was not long before similar leagues emerged in places such as Chicago, where the Chicago Nisei Athletic Association was formed along a similar, but smaller, scale. The coming of age of the sansei in the 1950s and 1960s led to increasing popularity for these leagues, with participation probably peaking in the 1970s. The still segregated leagues continue to this day, though participation is falling with the declining population of young Japanese Americans.

Athletic Achievement by Japanese Americans

There have been successful Japanese American athletes in just about every sport. The most famous is probably 1992 Olympic gold medal-winning figure skater Kristi Yamaguchi. During the 1960s, gymnast Makoto Sakamoto was one of America's best, making the 1964 and 1972 Olympic teams. Boxer Paul Fujii was the junior-welterweight champion in 1967-68. Golfer Lenore Muraoka Rittenhouse is an LPGA regular, while David Ishii won the 1990 Hawaiian Open PGA event. Jockey George Taniguchi was a 1950s favorite, while Corey Nakatani is one of today's best. Standing at 5'8", Rick Noji holds a career best high jump of 7'7" and is a former Pac-10 high jump champion and a member of the 1991 American World Track and Field Championship team. Tennis players Ann Kiyomura and Tina Mochizuki played professionally in the 1970s and 1980s. The Sato family is one of America's first families of volleyball: Gary has been assistant coach of the U.S. men's national team in the 1988 and 1992 Olympics, while brother Eric has been a player on both teams; the '88 team won the gold medal. Sister Liane was on the women's Olympic volleyball team in 1988 and 1992. Hockey player Paul Kariya, who has been called the "Wayne Gretzky of college hockey," played for Canada in the 1994 Winter Olympics and was drafted by the Mighty Ducks in the NHL. In football, Pete Domoto was a guard and co-captain of the California Bears in the 1959 Rose Bowl, while Joe Nagata started at quarterback for Louisiana State in the 1944 Orange Bowl. University of Southern California wide receiver Johnny Morton is one of the best in school history and is currently a promising member of the Detroit Lions of the NFL. In basketball, Wataru "Wat" Misaka played in the 1944 NCAA champion and 1947 NIT champion Utah teams, playing every minute of every game of the NIT tournament. The 5'8" Misaka tried out for the New York Knicks and turned down an offer to play with the Harlem Globetrotters. Rex Walters was a first round NBA draft choice in 1993 and currently plays for the New Jersey Nets. Baseball player Lenny Sakata played eleven years in the majors and was a member of the 1983 World Series champion Orioles. Many Japanese American players played in the Japanese major leagues. Two of them—Bozo Wakabayashi and Wally

Yonamine—are in the Japanese Baseball Hall of Fame. Yonemine also had a brief stint as a pro football player for the San Francisco 49ers in 1947.

Japanese Americans have also been prominent as coaches, promoters, or officials in sports. Among the most notable, Les Murakami has been University of Hawaii baseball coach since 1971 and took his team to the NCAA College World Series in 1980. UH women's volleyball coach Dave Shoji oversees one of the nation's perennial powerhouses in that sport. Bill Kajikawa was head coach for the Arizona State University baseball and basketball teams in the 1950s. Dave Yanai is the longtime basketball coach at California State University, Dominguez Hills. Marcia Murota recently took the head women's basketball coaching job at California State University, Los Angeles. Among the prominent high school coaches are Harvey Kitani, basketball coach at Fairfax High, Los Angeles; Wendell Yoshida, girls basketball coach at Peninsula High, Palos Verdes, California; and legendary Waianae High football coach Larry Ginoza. Additionally, a great many Japanese Americans teach the martial arts.

Japanese American athletes have been most successful at the international level in three other sports. In nearly all the cases listed above (with exception of baseball), the athlete was a single outstanding performer who did not rise out of a tradition of great Japanese American performers. In each of these three sports, by contrast, a particular coach or promoter encouraged the participation of Japanese Americans. They are weightlifting in the 1940s and 1950s, swimming in the same two decades, and judo from the 1960s to the present.

The key figures in weightlifting are Hawaii-based, Korean American physician and coach Richard You and U.S. weightlifting promoter Bob Hoffman. Harold Sakata, native to Kona, Hawaii, whose story of a skinny kid turned muscle man by lifting homemade weights made of broomsticks, ketchup cans, and cement became a local legend, was the first to rise to international prominence, winning a silver medal at the 1948 London Olympics. Among his teammates on the 1948 team were Emerick Ishikawa, a five-time U.S. National Champion who finished fourth; Richard Tomita; Henry Kishikawa; and bronze medalist Richard Tom, a Chinese American. Hoffman, owner of York Barbell Company and *Strength and Health* magazine, was largely responsible for the rise in U.S. fortunes in weightlifting at the international level. He recruited outstanding prospects of all ethnicities for his York Barbell Club and gave them jobs at the company. The York Club's dominance in weightlifting was temporarily stopped in 1952, when a Hawaiian team coached by You won the national title. The team included '48 Olympians Kishikawa, Tomita, and Tom, along with Johnny Odo, Ed

Bailey, and Jojo Suzuki. Among those impressed with You's training of the group was a young lifter named Tommy Kono who subsequently went to train with You.

By any measure of achievement, Tommy Kono is probably the greatest of Japanese American athletes. Winner of Olympic gold medals in 1952 and 1956 and a silver in 1960, each time in a different weight class, he broke 26 world records and won six world championships. He also won four Mr. World and Mr. Universe bodybuilding titles between 1954 and 1961. In a 1984 International Weightlifting Federation poll, he was voted the greatest lifter of all time. After retiring from the sport, Kono coached the West German weightlifting team from 1969-72, the Mexican team from 1966-68, and the U.S. team in the 1976 Olympics. Though a resident of Hawaii since 1952, Kono was actually born in Sacramento, California, and is said to have taken up weightlifting while at Tule Lake.

Various factors in the world of weightlifting led to its decline by the late 1950s and the end of Japanese American prominence in the sport as well. However, inspired by the example of Kono, Hawaii native Brian Miyamoto won the U.S. title in the 132 1/4 pound division in 1983, while Chad Ikei, coached by Kono, won two U.S. Olympic Festival gold medals in the 1990s.

A key figure in bringing Japanese Americans into competitive swimming was a science teacher from Puunene, Maui: Soichi Sakamoto. Seeing his students frolicking in the omnipresent plantation irrigation canals only to be chased out by plantation police, he volunteered to supervise the students if they could be allowed to swim. To make the group goal-driven, he announced the formation of "The Three Year Swim Club (3YSC)," so named because the group's goal was to make the Olympic swimming team for the 1940 Olympics, three years in the future. Having had no formal training in swimming, Sakamoto devised his own training techniques, and the 100-member group soon became notable in the world swimming scene.

Sakamoto's first star was 16-year-old Kiyoshi "Keo" Nakama, who defeated 1936 Olympian Ralph Gilman in the 400-meter freestyle during the latter's visit to Hawaii in the summer of 1937. In 1938, Sakamoto took his team to the U.S. Outdoor Championships for the first time; Nakama took second in three different events. In April 1939, the 3YSC won its first national team title at the national meet in Detroit, Michigan, and Nakama won his first national title winning the 200-meter freestyle. The 3YSC repeated as national champion for the next two years; in the 1941 national meet at St. Louis, 3YSC members won eight out of the ten national titles. In addition to Nakama, freestyle sprinter Takashi "Halo" Hirose, Bunmei "Bunny" Nakama (Keo's brother), Bill Smith, Jr., and Jose Balmores were among 3YSC members who won national titles during this period. Had the

1940 Olympics not been canceled, 3YSC members would have probably dominated the team.

Keo Nakama went on to attend Ohio State University, winning 27 National Collegiate Athletic Association (NCAA), Big Ten, and AAU titles and setting a world record in the mile competition at the 1942 National AAU meet. He also captained the baseball team to a Big Ten title as a middle infielder. Sakamoto went on to coach the U.S. Olympic and the University of Hawaii swim teams. When the Olympics were reinstated in 1948, Bill Smith, Jr. won two gold medals. Hawaii swimmers Yoshinobu Oyakawa and Ford Konno followed Nakama to Ohio State. In the 1952 Olympics in Helsinki, Finland, Hilo native Oyakawa won the gold medal in the 100-meter backstroke. Honolulu native Konno won golds in the 1,500-meter freestyle and 800-meter freestyle relay and just missed winning a third in the 400-meter freestyle. Evelyn Kawamoto, another Sakamoto-trained swimmer, won two bronze medals in the 400-meter freestyle and 4 x 100-meter freestyle relay. In 1956, Oyakawa and Konno co-captained the U.S. Olympic swimming team.

It is believed that judo, a modern Japanese martial art developed from jujitsu, came over with the first issei to arrive in Hawaii. Its roots as an Olympic sport, however, can be traced to nisei Yosh Uchida of San Jose State University. In 1953, his efforts led to the recognition of judo as a sport by the AAU; San Jose State sponsored the first AAU championships that year. In 1962, Uchida organized the first national collegiate judo championship. San Jose State won the first national title and an incredible 28 of the next 31 subsequent college titles. In 1964, judo became an Olympic sport for the first time and Uchida was the coach of the U.S. team. Two of the four athletes on that team were from San Jose State. One was lightweight Paul Maruyama, who later coached the 1980 and 1984 Olympic teams. The other was Native American Ben Nighthorse Campbell, now a United States Senator from Colorado. Among the other Japanese American standouts to have passed through San Jose State are Keith Nakasone, 1978 Pan American games gold medalist and 1980 Olympic team member, Tony Okada and Sandy Atsuko Bacher, both of whom competed in the 1992 Olympics. Other Japanese American judo Olympians include Patrick Misugi Burris (1976), Steven Seck (1980), and Craig Agena (1984). The closest a U.S. olympian came to winning a gold medal in judo was in 1988, when Hawaii native and San Jose State athlete Kevin Asano won the silver medal at the Seoul Games.

The involvement of Japanese Americans in sports today is larger than ever with the rise of prominent athletes like figure skater Kristi Yamaguchi. Increasingly more Japanese Americans, especially women, are participating in high school and college sports teams. Japanese Americans are also increasingly contributing in coaching, especially in Hawaii. At the same time, interest in the segregated Japanese American basketball and baseball leagues is on the decline. Although recent generations of Japanese Americans are more likely to participate in sports with the general American public, it is likely that sports will continue to play an important role in the lives of Japanese Americans in the future.

—Brian Niiya

9

Who Are the Korean Americans?

♦ History of Immigration ♦ Community Organizations ♦ Churches
♦ Occupations and Small Businesses ♦ Customs and Traditions ♦ Language

Korean Americans comprise one of the fastest growing ethnic groups in the United States today. Although the 1990 U.S. Census estimated the Korean American population at 750,000, many believe the actual figure now exceeds one million. As seen in Table 9.1, Americans of Korean descent live in communities throughout the country, settling in great numbers in cities such as Chicago, Los Angeles, New York, Washington, D.C., and Anaheim, California.

Korean Americans possess a history in the United States that dates back to the turn of the century. Some are descendants of the initial group of Korean immigrant laborers that arrived in Hawaii to work on sugar plantations. Others came during and after the Korean War (1950-53) as students, war orphans, and wives of American servicemen. It was only after Congress enacted immigration policy reforms in 1965 that Koreans began coming to the United States in large numbers. Over the past three decades, the Korean American population has grown more than tenfold. Therefore, the vast majority of Korean communities are made up of relatively recent immigrants and their children. Many came to reunite with relatives and to flee the authoritarian political and social order in North and South Korea during the 1970s and 1980s. They arrived seeking a new life for themselves and for their children, hoping to find greater economic opportunities and personal freedom.

Philip Jaisohn. (Courtesy of H. W. Pak.)

♦ HISTORY OF IMMIGRATION

Early Immigration

The pioneers of the Korean community in the United States were a small group of exiles and immigrant laborers that arrived at the turn of the century. Between January 1903 and July 1907, a total of 7,226 Korean immigrants arrived in Hawaii and California.

The exiles consisted of political and social reformers that left Korea after a failed coup d'état in 1884. Among them was So Chae-pil (1866-1951), who founded the Independence Club, the leading organization of an ultimately unsuccessful reform movement in Korea during the late 1890s, and who later adopted the American name Philip Jaisohn. Jaisohn eventually

Table 9.1
Korean Population by Significant U.S. Metropolitan Areas

Korean population in numbers, percent of the total area population, and percent of Asian/Pacific Islander area population, ranked by metropolitan area (a), 1990.

Metropolitan area (b)	Total population	Total A/PI population	Number	Korean Percent of total	Percent of A/PI
Los Angeles–Long Beach, CA PMSA	8,863,164	925,561	145,431	1.6%	16%
New York, NY PMSA	8,546,846	553,443	74,632	0.9%	13%
Washington, DC–MD–VA MSA	3,923,574	200,113	39,850	1.0%	20%
Anaheim–Santa Ana, CA PMSA	2,410,556	240,703	35,919	1.5%	15%
Chicago, IL PMSA	6,069,974	227,742	33,465	0.6%	15%
Honolulu, HI MSA	836,231	413,349	22,646	2.7%	5%
Philadelphia, PA–NJ PMSA	4,856,881	103,537	22,028	0.5%	21%
Bergen–Passaic, NJ PMSA	1,278,440	66,540	17,018	1.3%	26%
Seattle, WA PMSA	1,972,961	128,656	16,311	0.8%	13%
San Jose, CA PMSA	1,497,577	254,786	15,565	1.0%	6%
Oakland, CA PMSA	2,082,914	259,002	13,478	0.7%	5%
Baltimore, MD MSA	2,382,172	42,017	12,967	0.5%	31%
San Francisco, CA PMSA	1,603,678	316,751	10,416	0.7%	3%
Riverside–San Bernardino, CA PMSA	2,588,793	93,473	10,166	0.4%	11%
Atlanta, GA MSA	2,833,511	50,872	10,120	0.4%	20%

Notes:
(a) Includes metropolitan areas with Korean population greater than 10,000.
(b) The U.S. Census Bureau designates the following: PMSA=primary metropolitan statistical area; MSA=metropolitan statistical area. See Appendix for detailed definitions.

Source: Asian/Pacific Islander Data Consortium. Primary source: U.S. Census Bureau, Summary Tape Files 1 and 3.

acquired U.S. citizenship and became the first Korean American medical doctor.

Several other reform movement leaders including Ahn Chang-ho (1878-1938), Park Yong-man (1881-1928), and Syngman Rhee (1875-1965) came to pursue advanced degrees at U.S. universities. As the number of Korean immigrants grew in Hawaii and California, these four individuals emerged as prominent community leaders. Along with other early immigrants, they helped to set up community organizations, churches, and schools. They also launched an active Korean national independence movement in the United States.

However, the majority of these early immigrants were male workers, who were recruited to work in the sugar cane fields. Though some Koreans found the decision to leave their homeland for an uncertain future a particularly difficult one, the harsh living conditions and political upheaval in Korea during this period forced many to emigrate in an effort to improve their lives.

These early Korean immigrants were hired under contract as plantation laborers to alleviate a labor shortage brought about when the Chinese Exclusion Acts, passed by the U.S. Congress, became applicable to Hawaii in 1898. However, many were ill-suited for plantation work and soon left the fields to start small businesses. About 2,000 of these immigrants moved to the U.S. mainland, where they operated small farms or opened retail stores.

After this first wave, which also included over 1,200 women and children, Korean immigration to the United States was largely suspended in 1905. During that year, Japan unofficially occupied Korea and assumed jurisdiction over its relations with foreign nations. Not wanting Korean immigrants to compete with Japanese workers already in Hawaii and needing to retain a sizeable pool of Korean labor to execute their expansionist programs on the Korean peninsula, the Japanese government halted immigration to the United States with one exception: Korean women.

Between 1910 and 1924, approximately 1,100 "picture brides" arrived in Hawaii to marry Korean workers. These women, who had been introduced to their prospective husbands through letters and photographs, were often better educated than their male counterparts. They brought a new energy and stability to the fledgling Korean American community.

The early Korean immigrants faced opposition and open discrimination from all corners of American society, including political camps, labor unions, and intellectual circles. While immigration laws separated the early immigrants from their families, they were also forced to endure overtly anti-Asian laws, including California's Anti-Miscegenation Law (1901), which barred Asian intermarriage with whites, and its Alien Land Law (1913), which prohibited Asians from owning land. At the time, Koreans were lumped together with the Chinese and Japanese who were similarly barred from desirable residential neighborhoods, quality schools, government jobs, and even teaching positions. Despite widespread discrimination, these early Korean immigrants focused their energies on homeland politics and their common dream of achieving Korean national independence.

Japan officially annexed the peninsula in 1910, and disturbing news of the suppression of Korean culture and extremely harsh treatment at the hands of Japanese colonizers further fueled the independence movement. In fact, many Korean immigrants, who otherwise remained uninvolved in politics, contributed significantly to the movement. Korean Americans played a key role in supporting their homeland's provisional government in Shanghai by fundraising and lobbying through diplomatic channels. Yet community leaders were divided on their strategies for pursuing Korean independence. One group led by Park Yong-man pushed for militant action, including military training of Koreans in the United States. Others, including So Chae-pil and Syngman Rhee, advocated educational and diplomatic activities.

The Korean independence movement in the United States peaked in response to the March 1919 uprising, when Japanese military power brutally suppressed a peaceful demonstration in Seoul. In the wake of the atrocities, the Western powers' indifference toward the events frustrated and discouraged those working towards Korean independence. Despite a depletion of energy and funds, activities related to the independence effort continued through 1945, when Korea achieved liberation from Japan.

Along with other Korean patriots who had been living in the United States, Syngman Rhee returned to a newly independent Korea to participate in the postwar reconstruction. Despite concerns in the U.S. State Department about his hardline conservative views, Rhee received the backing of American military authorities, who favored him particularly for his militant anti-Communist stance. In 1948, Rhee was elected president of the Republic of Korea (South Korea). However, he was keenly aware of the potential influence his detractors could wield by encouraging American criticism against him. Therefore, Rhee remained closely interested in the activities and opinions expressed in Korean American communities. His supporters and agents monitored anti-Rhee criticism in the

United States among Korean students and Korean Americans, refusing to grant or renew visas for outspoken declarations. President Rhee continued to rule Korea under an authoritarian regime until he was ousted by a student revolution in 1960.

Post-World War II Immigration

American involvement in the Korean War in the early 1950s brought about a second wave of Korean immigration, which included wives of American servicemen and war orphans adopted by American families. Between 1951 and 1964, approximately 6,500 brides and 6,300 adopted children came to the United States.

Beginning in the early 1950s, an increasing number of Korean students also came to study at U.S. colleges and universities, and a contingent of Korean doctors arrived to further their medical training at U.S. hospitals. Many of these students and doctors eventually returned to Korea where they made important contributions in policymaking and research as well as in university teaching. Those who stayed in the United States were welcomed as a fresh resource for the Korean American community, which previously only focused most of its attention on the cause of Korean independence.

Post-1965 Immigration

The latest and largest growth period of the Korean American community occurred after the passage of the Immigration and Naturalization Act of 1965. Since then, the ethnic Korean population in the United States has increased phenomenally and almost entirely as the result of immigration. Following the civil rights movement of the 1950s and 1960s, changes in U.S. immigration laws gave Asians an equal chance to emigrate. For the first time, entire families could move to the United States, not just individuals. Korean students and professionals were also able to apply for permanent residency and subsequently citizenship. These new citizens, along with the Korean wives of American servicemen, applied for permanent residency on behalf of siblings, parents, or spouses. Close relatives of citizens or permanent residents have constituted the majority of Korean immigrants since 1970.

Given the demographic pattern of family immigration, the post-1965 population of Korean Americans is usually identified along generational lines: *il-se* (the "first" generation) of adult immigrants; their children, often called *il-jom-o-se* (the "one-point-five" generation); and *i-se* (the "second" generation), or those born in the United States.

The ability of Koreans to emigrate as family groups sets this ethnic population apart from early Chinese,

**Table 9.2
Korean Immigration to the United States,
1946-1990**

Time period	Immigrants
1946-50	107
1951-55	581
1956-60	6,182
1961-65	10,179
1966-70	25,618
1971-75	112,493
1976-80	159,463
1981-85	166,021
1986-90	172,851

Source: U.S. Immigration and Naturalization Service.

Japanese, and Filipino immigrants, who came largely as individuals. But living as a nuclear family did not necessarily mean all members of a given Korean American household would become acculturated at a similar rate. In many cases, parents and children would operate in entirely different social spheres—one attuned to Korean values and language, the other following American mores and using English—except when the entire family gathered at home. Korean Americans therefore have had to confront intergenerational differences related to identity, language, and culture with an immediacy that was not as acute for some of the other older Asian American populations.

♦ COMMUNITY ORGANIZATIONS

A relatively recent immigration history had other effects on the growing Korean American community. For example, the post-1965 immigrants generally did not have to face the same kind of housing discrimination

**Table 9.3
Persons of Korean descent by state, 1990**

State	Population of Korean Descent
California	259,941
Illinois	41,506
Maryland	30,320
New Jersey	38,540
New York	95,648
Texas	31,775
Virginia	30,164
Washington	29,697

Source: Asian/Pacific Islander Date Consortium.

that older Asian American groups experienced. Although "Koreatowns" took root and grew in Los Angeles and other cities, Korean Americans were not forced to settle in ethnic enclaves but instead tended to scatter over wide areas. In fact, Korean Americans have one of the most widely dispersed settlement patterns among Asian Americans, second only to those of East Indian descent.

According to the 1990 Census, Korean Americans have their largest concentration in the West, where 44 percent live, while 23 percent reside in the Northeast, 19 percent in the South, and 14 percent in the Midwest.

One should bear in mind, however, that language difficulties and other obstacles to obtaining accurate demographic information resulted in U.S. Census figures that community leaders widely regard as underestimated. Because sustained emigration from Korea has also continued since 1990, the real numbers representing the Korean American community are even higher still.

Without a territorial base, Korean American communities are generally based on associations. Over time, Koreans in the United States have developed a complex network of churches, recreational clubs, business and professional associations, alumni organizations, and civic groups, all linked or publicized by the Korean-language news media. These organizations provide diverse services particularly for socially insular il-se Korean American communities, with many catering to the needs of recent immigrants. Korean associations, or Haninhoe, have also been established in all major metropolitan areas that have a large Korean population. Although the association president is elected through a community election, the degree to which a Korean association truly responds to the needs and concerns of its members varies greatly, depending on the city or region. On a national level, there are a handful of il-se groups, including the Korean Association of the United States as well as national business guilds such as the Korean American Grocers Organization (KAGRO) and the Korean Dry Cleaning and Laundry Association.

Because of language and cultural differences between the older and younger populations, few Korean American organizations have memberships that bridge these generations. However a growing number of younger Korean Americans are founding their own associations, which range in nature from social clubs to grassroots social-service organizations. Among college students, several hundred participate in the annual Korean American Students Conference (KASCON), held at a different university campus each year.

Churches serve a pivotal role in the Korean American community. (Jamie Lew.)

♦ CHURCHES

Frequently, churches in the United States have become the foundation for Korean American communities. Beyond their religious functions, churches have assumed multiple secular roles, providing direct services to both established residents and newer arrivals. At church, parishioners exchange employment and housing information, participate in language classes, and gather for social events. A church can also serve as a clearinghouse of information to ease the interaction of community members with the bureaucratic institutions of the larger society. It may offer counseling on various aspects of life, including immigration and naturalization, income taxes, health care, social security, and education. As Korean American communities have grown in the past quarter century, so have the roles of such churches and their ministers.

The historical and political significance of Christian churches, particularly Protestant denominations, in the Korean American community dates back to the earliest days of Korean immigration. Of the 7000 early immigrants, less than 500 were professed Christians, but that number grew rapidly in the two decades that followed. The church provided not only a community for

Korean immigrants but also a haven from the outside world, where they were subjected to isolation and racial discrimination. Eventually, the leadership of the early Korean American churches arose from the cadres of young intellectual patriots and political exiles fighting for Korean national independence from the Japanese. The most well-known community leaders of the time were also Christians, and churches became the local headquarters for the national independence movement, where strategies were debated and protest meetings held.

Today, while Christians are a minority in the mainly Buddhist country of South Korea, about 75 percent of Korean American families in the United States affiliate with a church, and 65 percent attend church regularly. Among the post-1965 group of Korean immigrants, Christian churches have emerged as basic grass-roots organizations in lieu of a territorial center for many Korean American communities. Serving a variety of social, spiritual, and psychological needs, the church is often expected to provide a "family atmosphere" that acts as a surrogate for the traditional Korean extended family. Such an environment also enables immigrants to regain the social status lost during the transition from their native land to a vastly different society. The

Yung Kim, a Korean American businessman in Baltimore, stands between a revolving plexiglass window and the wire-grated door to his store. (AP/Wide World.)

desire among immigrants for a familial closeness within the congregation has led to an increase in the number of small churches, although some very large metropolitan-area churches are flourishing with memberships numbering over 1,000.

Outside the home, churches are where Korean cultural values and nationalism are reaffirmed. In addition to Sunday Bible studies, churches may also run Saturday schools to teach the younger American-born generation the Korean language, as well as Korean history and culture. Meanwhile, it is not uncommon for a church to have multiple congregations, one for the older generation and recent immigrants with services in Korean, and another for students and young adults with services in English. In addition to churches, there are a handful of Buddhist temples that also serve these communities.

◆ OCCUPATIONS AND SMALL BUSINESSES

Korean Americans can be found in all walks of life. From high-school teachers to salespeople to medical doctors to farmers, they have moved into a wide range of occupations. But a considerable number of those who arrived in the country after 1965 earn their living by running small businesses, such as retail stores. Studies completed in Los Angeles, New York, Atlanta, and other cities show that about one-third of Korean immigrant breadwinners own their own businesses; about one-fifth are professionals; and the rest have other salaried jobs. Some Korean American immigrants began import/export businesses that transact with manufacturers in Korea. Many of those immigrants made their fortunes by capitalizing on the wig fad of the United States in the 1960s.

Others opened neighborhood groceries, liquor stores, dry cleaners, fast-food establishments, or clothing shops. Entrepreneurial activity flourished among these communities, with the number of businesses owned by Korean Americans quadrupling between 1977 and 1982. By the end of the 1980s, according to the U.S. Census Bureau, Korean Americans had achieved the highest business-ownership rate among all racial and ethnic groups in the nation.

Korean Americans opt to run their own businesses for various reasons. Although many are college-educated and held white-collar jobs in Korea, it is difficult

Table 9.4
Korean-Owned Businesses: Top Metropolitan Areas

Top twenty-five metropolitan statistical areas ranked by number of businesses whose owners are of Korean descent, 1987.

Rank	Metropolitan area	Korean-owned firms
1	Los Angeles-Long Beach, CA PMSA (a)	17,165
2	New York, NY PMSA	6,160
3	Washington, DC-MD-VA MSA (b)	4,416
4	Anaheim-Santa Ana, CA PMSA	3,925
5	Chicago, IL PMSA	3,878
6	Philadelphia, PA-NJ PMSA	2,069
7	Honolulu, HI MSA	1,968
8	Dallas, TX PMSA	1,887
9	San Jose, CA PMSA	1,449
10	San Francisco, CA PMSA	1,304
11	Atlanta, GA MSA	1,266
12	Baltimore, MD MSA	1,223
13	Seattle, WA PMSA	1,178
14	Houston, TX PMSA	1,115
15	Oakland, CA PMSA	1,082
16	Riverside-San Bernardino, CA PMSA	902
17	Bergen-Passaic, NJ PMSA	768
18	Denver, CO PMSA	731
19	Nassau-Suffolk, NY PMSA	688
20	Portland, OR PMSA	561
21	Detroit, MI PMSA	539
22	San Diego, CA MSA	525
23	Newark, NJ PMSA	518

Notes:
(a) Primary Metropolitan Statistical Area.
(b) Metropolitan Statistical Area.

Source: *Bureau of the Census, U.S. Department of Commerce.*

for Korean immigrants to obtain work commensurate with their experience. Language difficulties, restricted access to corporate America, and unfamiliarity with American culture are all contributing factors. But Korean Americans are also attracted to entrepreneurship, because, despite the long hours it demands, the business owner has autonomy and a degree of control over his or her environment. Of course, entrepreneurship can also be quite profitable, providing a source of income larger than what would otherwise be available to immigrants in non-professional occupations.

During the 1970s and 1980s in several American cities and suburbs, more and more established Jewish, Italian, and Irish American business owners began retiring or selling their stores, especially in inner-city areas. With few other avenues open to them, many

Korean Americans took advantage of these opportunities to own businesses.

However, those working in inner cities often found themselves caught up in the tensions of crime, poverty, and a race-class hierarchy that predated their arrival. These difficulties have sometimes been exacerbated by the fact that outside of business transactions, many Korean American merchants maintain little contact with their non-Korean customers from the neighborhoods in which they do business.

Truly the most devastating event for Korean American merchants and the community as a whole began on April 29, 1992, when riots erupted in Los Angeles after the verdict came down from the first Rodney King trial. The announcement of the police officers' acquittal triggered rioting and looting in South Central Los Angeles, eventually spreading to Koreatown and other areas. The violence was so intense that more than 50 persons were killed, and over 14,000 were arrested; property losses were estimated to be $1 billion. A summary of losses suffered by store type and ethnicity of the store owner appear in Table 9.5.

When the uprising subsided four days later, about 2,300 Korean-owned businesses had been looted or burned, and Korean American businesses suffered roughly half of the estimated $1 billion loss in Los Angeles County as a result of the riots. In Table 9.6, the losses suffered by business owners of Korean descent are summarized. Known among Koreans as Sa-I-Gu, literally "April 29th," the riots shattered the faith of Korean Americans who had slowly built their dreams in search of a better life. By February 1993, only 28 percent of businesses damaged or destroyed in the riots had reopened, according to a survey completed by the Korean American Inter-Agency Council.

Tensions existing between these Korean American business owners and their community customers have since prompted civic leaders to encourage and initiate greater contact and communication between business owners and the neighborhoods they serve.

♦ CUSTOMS AND TRADITIONS

South Korea has changed drastically from the country that many adult Korean immigrants recall from their childhood. From a war-torn country with an agricultural economy, South Korea has developed into a technologically advanced modern society. Yet South Korea remains one of the most Confucian of all Asian countries, and filial piety is regarded as an elemental factor in shaping and developing one's personality. Deference to elders and superiors is expected, and parents are to be accorded strict obedience and respect. While these values are also changing as Korean society modernizes, traditional beliefs still lie at the heart of its culture.

Regardless of religious affiliation, many Korean Americans remain influenced by the centuries-old Confucian ideology. In various ways the influence of Confucianism, as reflected in the beliefs, attitudes, and practices of Korean immigrants, had a wide-ranging impact on their activities and the way they formed communities. For example, a principle in Confucianism is the value placed on hierarchies of responsibility and authority, values which are reflected in the structures of most il-se community organizations and businesses. Korean Confucianism also calls for responsibility to and reliance upon one's family. The family, including the extended kin group, is the basic social unit among Koreans and Korean immigrants to the United States. For the post-1965 immigrants, family groups (and pseudo-extended kin comprised of friends' families) provide not only financial assistance, but also a central resource for information, employment, and emotional support.

The Rotating-Credit System of Kye

Korean Confucianism also places a high value on upward economic mobility. This is evidenced by a rotating-credit system called *kye*, which was prevalent in Korea during the seventeenth century and is still part of Korean American culture today. *Kyes* have

Table 9.5
Stores Damaged in the 1992 Los Angeles Civil Unrest by Ethnicity of Owner

Store type	Owner's surname category			
	Korean surname	Other Asian surname	Spanish surname	All other surnames
Total, all stores	674	22	35	197
Auto	20	2	2	6
Retail	238	8	9	56
Liquor	57	1	1	1
Market	95	2	2	18
Gas	24	2	1	8
Jewelry	12	1	1	8
Swapmeet	72	1	0	3
Cleaner	19	0	1	9
Food	14	0	0	7
Office	2	0	1	5
Other	87	6	11	62
Total	1314	45	64	380

Source: *Adapted from State (California) Insurance Commission list.*

provided funds for many Korean Americans to open up small businesses and to help pay for weddings, funerals, or college tuition.

A *kye* is made up of 12-20 individuals who meet socially once a month at a member's home or restaurant. Each member contributes an agreed-upon amount—ranging from less than $100 to several thousand—to a pool every month. At the meeting, one member receives the collective pot, but if a member has a particularly pressing need, he or she may be allowed to take the first turn. After each has had a turn, the *kye* disbands.

A *kye* could be described as an informal, scaled-down credit union that provides loans without the interest or hassle of a formal bank arrangement. Since many recent Korean immigrants are unfamiliar with American banking practices and lack extensive credit histories, they generally have considerable difficulty obtaining sizable loans from banks. *Kyes*, though operated informally among friends and acquaintances, can generate pools as small as a few thousand dollars or as large as a million dollars. Some people attribute the growth of entrepreneurship among Korean Americans to *kyes*, which have enabled enterprising immigrant families to open the doors of their first businesses. It has also been an effective way for families or individuals to overcome unexpected financial crises or burdens.

Obviously, trust is a crucial ingredient in a *kye*. The group must be confident that members will continue to pay into the pool even after they have had their turn. And, indeed, it is rare that a member does not follow through on his or her commitment, especially because *kyes* are often made up of family members, close friends, or fellow church parishioners. Most importantly, a *kye* gives Korean Americans an opportunity not only to participate in an economic network, but also to partake in a group that shares mutual emotional support and friendship.

♦ LANGUAGE

The Korean language is a unique characteristic of Korean culture which many immigrants have maintained in their families and communities. In both North and South Korea, people speak, write, and understand a common language, though accents vary distinctly from region to region on the peninsula. The language belongs to the Ural-Altaic group, which relates Korean to an assortment of languages in countries around the world, including Mongolian, Turkish, and Finnish.

Hangul, the Korean alphabet, was invented in the fifteenth century during the reign of King Sejong (1397-1450). Until then, Koreans used Chinese characters for writing, but only scholars and the wealthy could afford to master the manifold complexities of these ideographs. In 1446, a royal commission of scholars, after many years of study, developed a Korean phonetic alphabet composed of ten vowels and 14 consonants. Created as a written representation of spoken Korean, the new alphabet was designed to make literacy widespread among Koreans. To promote acceptance and use of the script, King Sejong had several texts immediately translated into *hangul*, including many Korean literary classics as well as agricultural manuals and military handbooks.

Table 9.6
Korean Stores Damaged in the Los Angeles Civil Unrest, 1992

	Total, all areas	Koreatown	South Central L.A.	All other areas
Number of stores	2,073	460	761	852
Value damage (1992 dollars)	$359 million	$73 million	$158 million	$128 million
Median value damage per store	$70,000	$60,000	$85,000	$60,000
Damage type, in percent				
Fire	38%	37%	48%	29%
Looted/partially looted	52%	56%	43%	58%
Unknown	10%	7%	9%	14%
Amount of damage, in percent				
Less than $10,000	5%	9%	1%	7%
$10,000–<$50,000	27%	29%	21%	31%
$50,000–<$100,000	27%	24%	31%	25%
$100,000–<$250,000	24%	25%	25%	22%
$250,000–<$1 million	14%	9%	19%	12%
$1 million +	3%	3%	3%	3%

Source: Summarized from Korea Central Daily list.

Signs in Koreatown, New York.

Thanks in part to the simplicity of *hangul*, over 95 percent of all Koreans can read and write, resulting in one of the world's highest literacy rates. While facility with Chinese characters is still equated with scholarly and literary prestige, all Koreans have great pride in their alphabet and commemorate its creation with a national holiday, *Hangul* Day, celebrated on October 9. Internationally, linguistic scholars praise the ingeniousness of the Korean alphabet, one of the most phonetically concise, and efficient means of writing among the world's languages.

Examining a modern South Korean newspaper article, one might observe that Korean script and Chinese characters are often intermingled within a single sentence, and sometimes in what appears to be a single word. That is because many Korean words have been borrowed or derived from Chinese, and South Koreans often use Chinese characters in written material to distinguish homonyms or to clarify words which have multiple meanings. North Korea, on the other hand, has eliminated Chinese characters from written Korean altogether.

Today, there are more than 68 million Korean speakers, ranking the language fifteenth among the world's most spoken languages. Korean speakers mainly live in North and South Korea. Elsewhere, the largest populations of persons of Korean descent are found in North America and Japan. Given the greater awareness of Korea's economic and geopolitical importance, an increasing number of non-Koreans have also begun studying the language.

Korean Names

Korean names usually consist of three syllables. One represents the family name. In Korea, just as in China and Japan, the surname always comes first. Another syllable stands for the generation name, which indicates a person's place within the total family. In other words, all the siblings and cousins of the same generation would share that syllable in their names, so that two sisters may be named *Young* Mi and *Young* Hee. The other syllable is the personal name, which does not necessarily come last. In some names, the personal precedes the generation name.

In choosing names for their children, parents may select those that are either purely Korean or have corresponding Chinese characters that represent the Korean name. Actually, according to Korean tradition, the paternal grandfather is usually given the honor of naming the newborn.

When the first child in a generation is born, the generation name is determined according to a 12-year cycle on the father's side. In this process, Koreans may refer to the extensive family trees, which are recorded in detailed genealogies that are still extant and maintained in many families.

According to one estimate, there are over one thousand clans in Korea, but only 326 surnames. The most common family name is Kim, and 20 to 25 percent of all Koreans bear that name. Over half of the population has one of the five major surnames, which besides Kim include: Lee (Rhee, Yi); Park (Pak, Bak); Choi (Choe, Chae); and Chung (Jung). Other common family names include Ahn, Cho, Han, Kang, Lim, and Yoo. Because surnames come last in the United States, Korean family names and given names are often inadvertently confused. Even when Korean Americans put their surnames at the end, family names like "Kim" and "Lee" are commonly mistaken for given names.

References

Barringer, Herbert R. and Sung-Nam Cho. *Koreans in the United States: A Fact Book.* Honolulu: Center for Korean Studies, University of Hawaii, 1989.

Chang, Edward T., ed. "Los Angeles-Struggles toward Multiethnic Community." *Amerasia Journal*, Vol. 19, No. 2, 1993.

Choy, Bong-Youn. *Koreans in America.* Chicago: Nelson-Hall, 1979.

Kim, Ilsoo. *New Urban Immigrants: The Korean Community in New York.* Princeton: Princeton University, 1981.

Kwon, Ho-Youn and Shin Kim, eds. *The Emerging Generation of Korean-Americans.* Seoul: Kyung-Hee University Press, 1993.

Lee, Joann Faung Jean. *Asian Americans: Oral Histories of First to Fourth Generation Americans from China, the Philippines, Japan, India, the Pacific Islands, Vietnam and Cambodia.* New York: The New Press, 1991.

Lee, Mary Paik. *Quiet Odyssey: A Pioneer Korean Woman in America.* Seattle: University of Washington, 1990.

Melendy, H. Brett. *Asians in America: Filipinos, Koreans, and East Indians.* Boston: Twayne, 1977.

Patterson, Wayne. *The Korean Frontier in America: Immigration to Hawaii, 1896-1910.* Honolulu: University of Hawaii, 1988.

Ong, Paul and Suzanne Hee. *Losses in the Los Angeles Civil Unrest April 29-May 1, 1992: Lists of the Damaged Properties, Korean Merchants and the L.A. Riot/Rebellion.* Los Angeles: UCLA Center for Pacific Rim Studies, University of California-Los Angeles, 1993.

Solberg, S.E. "The Literature of Korean America." *The Seattle Review,* Vol. XI, No. 1, Spring/Summer 1988.

Yu, Eui-Young. "The Korean American Community." *Korea Briefing.* Boulder: Westview, 1993.

———. "Korean Communities in America: Past, Present, and Future." *Amerasia Journal,* Vol. 10, No. 2, 1983.

———, Earl H. Phillips, and Eun Sik Yang. *Koreans in Los Angeles: Prospects and Promises.* Los Angeles: Center for Korean-American and Korean Studies, California State University, 1982.

—Nan Kim

10

Who Are the Laotian Americans?

◆ Overview ◆ History ◆ Acculturation and Assimilation ◆ Language
◆ Family and Community Dynamics ◆ Religion ◆ Employment and Economic Traditions
◆ Politics and Government ◆ Health and Mental Health Issues ◆ Notable Laotian Americans
◆ Associations and Organizations

◆ OVERVIEW

Located in Southeast Asia, Laos measures approximately 91,400 square miles (236,800 sq. km.), making it slightly larger than the state of Utah. The country shares its borders with Thailand in the southwest, Cambodia in the south, Burma in the west, China in the north, and Vietnam in the east. Laos has a tropical climate, with a rainy season that lasts from May to November and a dry season that lasts from December to April.

Laos has about 4,400,000 residents and an estimated population growth rate of 2.2 percent each year. Minority groups in this small, mountainous country include the Mon-Khmer, the Yao, and the Hmong. Approximately 85 to 90 percent of employed persons in Laos work in subsistence agriculture. Rice is the country's principal crop; other significant agricultural products include corn, tobacco, and tea. The majority of Laotians practice Theravada Buddhism, a form of Buddhism popular in Cambodia, Thailand, Burma, and Sri Lanka. In Laos, however, Buddhism is heavily influenced by the cult of *phi*, or "spirits," and Hinduism.

The Laotian flag has three horizonal bands, with red stripes at the top and bottom and a blue stripe in the middle. A large white disk is centered in the blue band. Many Laotian Americans identify more with the pre-1975 flag of the Kingdom of Laos than with the present-day flag of the country. This flag was red, with a three-headed white elephant situated on a five-step pedestal, under a white parasol with seven-layers. The elephant was symbolic of the ancient kingdom of Laos, known as "The Land of a Million Elephants." The parasol represented the monarchy and the five steps of the pedestal symbolized the five main precepts of Buddhism.

◆ HISTORY

Laotians trace their ancestry to the T'ai people, a tribe that migrated south from China beginning in the sixth century. Originally part of the Khmer (Cambodian) Empire, Laos achieved independence in 1353 when Fa Ngum, a prince from the city of Luang Prabang, claimed a large territory from the declining Empire and declared himself king, calling the newly established state Lan Xang, or "the Kingdom of a Million Elephants." Luang Prabang was the nation's capital for 200 years until, in 1563, a later king moved the capital to Vientiane, which serves as the capital of Laos today.

The Lao kingdom reached its height in the late 1600s, under King Souligna Vongsa. After his death in 1694, three claimants to the throne broke the kingdom into three distinct principalities, the kingdoms of Vientiane, Luang Prabang, and Champassak. Each kingdom struggled for power, causing the weakened Lao states to become vulnerable to the more powerful nations of Siam (Thailand) and Vietnam. While the Siamese took Vientiane, the Vietnamese took other parts of the Laos. By the mid 1800s, almost all of northern Laos was controlled by Vietnam, and almost all the southern and central parts of the country were controlled by Thailand. Only the area around Luang Prabang remained independent.

Modern Era

Vietnam suffered from its own internal problems in the late 1700s and early 1800s, and in 1859 was invaded by the French Emperor Napoleon III. By 1862, the Emperor of Vietnam was forced to recognize French possession of the southern provinces, and by the 1880s, France controlled all of Vietnam.

In 1893, when the Siamese, already holding southern Laos, attacked northern Laos, the French became a protectorate of the kingdom. Four years later, King Oun-Kham of Luang Prabang was forced to seek the help of France against invaders from China and, consequently, Luang Prabang also fell to France's growing Indochinese empire. By 1899, the French had unified all the old Laotian territories.

Although there were some local rebellions against French rule, mainly by the tribes of the hills and mountains, widespread Laotian resistance to the French did not begin until after World War II when Japan, which had assumed control over Indochina during the war years, was defeated. After France regained power in Indochina, the Laotian prime minister, Prince Phetsarath, declared Laos an independent kingdom and formed a group known as the Lao Issara, or "Free Lao." Some Laotians supported the French, feeling that their country was not ready for immediate independence. The Lao Issara, however, were strongly opposed to French control and became allies of the anti-French movement in neighboring Vietnam, the Viet Minh, led by Ho Chi Minh.

The Viet Minh defeated French troops at Dien Bien Phu in 1954. Afterward, an international conference held in Geneva separated Vietnam at the 17th parallel to prevent Ho Chi Minh's communist government from assuming control over the entire nation. Many Laotians supported the Viet Minh and, when North Vietnam invaded South Vietnam in 1959, Laos was drawn into the war.

The United States also became involved in the war to deter the spread of Communism in Southeast Asia. In Laos, U.S. forces provided tactical and economic support to the royal government but were unsuccessful in their efforts. U.S. troops withdrew from the area in 1973 and South Vietnam fell to its northern enemy in April 1975. Later that same year, Communist forces overthrew the Laotian government, renaming the country the Lao People's Democratic Republic.

Significant Immigration Waves

While there was some migration from Laos to the United States prior to 1975, the immigrants were so few that there is no official record of them. Available records do suggest, however, that they were highly professional and technically proficient. After 1975, thousands of Laotian people fled their homeland for the United States; the passage of the Indochina Migration and Refugee Assistance Act of 1975 by Congress aided them in this effort. Early Laotian immigrants included former government administrators, soldiers from the royal army, and shopkeepers. More recent immigrants from Laos included farmers and villagers who were not as educated as their predecessors.

While large numbers of Vietnamese and Cambodians began to settle in the United States almost immediately after socialist governments came to power in the Spring of 1975, Laotian refugees did not begin to arrive in America in great numbers until the following year. In contrast to the 126,000 Vietnamese and 4,600 Cambodians who arrived in 1975, only 800 refugees from Laos were admitted into the United States. This is partially due to the fact that the new Laotian government obtained power in a relatively peaceful manner, despite fighting between the Hmong and the Lao Issara (now known as the Pathet Lao, or "Lao Nation"). Moreover, the U.S. government was reluctant to accept refugees who had fled Laos for bordering Thailand, many of whom U.S. officials viewed as economic migrants, rather than refugees from political oppression.

In 1976, 10,200 refugees from Laos, who had fled across the border into Thailand, were admitted to the United States. The number of Laotian refugees dipped to only 400 in 1977, and then climbed to 8,000 in 1978. In the years between 1979 and 1981, the number of Laotians entering the United States increased dramatically, due to international attention given to the plight of Indochinese refugees in the late 1970s. During these three years, about 105,000 people from Laos resettled in America: 30,200 in 1979, 55,500 in 1980, and 19,300 in 1981. Although migration from Laos to America never again achieved the stature of this period, the resettlement of Laotians in the United States continued throughout the late 1980s and early 1990s.

Geographic Distribution of Laotian Americans

According to the U.S. Census, in 1990 there were about 150,000 Laotian Americans living in the United States. (This figure does not include the Hmong and other minority groups from Laos.) The majority of Laotian Americans (58,058) lived in California, primarily in Fresno (7,750), San Diego (6,261), Sacramento (4,885), and Stockton (4,045). Texas held the second largest number of Laotian Americans (9,332), with the majority living in Amarillo (1,188) and Denton (1,512). Minnesota and Washington State had the third and fourth largest Laotian American populations, with 6,831 and 6,191 residents, respectively. Thirty-four percent (2,325) of Minnesota's Laotian American population lived in Minneapolis and 46 percent (2,819) of Washington's Laotian American community lived in Seattle.

♦ ACCULTURATION AND ASSIMILATION

While few Laotian residents live in cities, Laotian Americans are an overwhelmingly urban people, with most living in large metropolitan centers. Of the 171,577 people in America born in Laos (this figure includes both ethnic Laotians and Hmong and excludes members of both groups born in America), 164,892 people (96 percent) lived in urban areas in 1990. The remaining 4 percent lived in rural communities. This is largely due to the fact that the vast majority of Laotians who immigrated to the United States were unaccustomed to an industrial society and spoke either very little or no English; they migrated to urban areas where they could find work that did not require many skills or language proficiency.

As a group, Laotian Americans are substantially younger than the national average. In 1990, the median age for Laotian Americans was 20.4 years while the median age for other U.S. citizens was 34.1 years. Moreover, Laotian Americans have larger families than other U.S. citizens. In 1990, the average number of people in each Laotian American family was 5.01 members, compared to an average of 3.06 members in white U.S. families and 3.48 members in African American families. These figures demonstrate that Laotian Americans are a dynamic, rapidly growing community.

Because Laotian Americans are relatively new members of U.S. society, it is difficult to predict to what extent they will assimilate. Few U.S. citizens have much knowledge of Laos and, as a result, there are few stereotypes, positive or negative, regarding Laotian Americans in particular.

Laotian American Values

Many Laotian Americans have retained the values they brought with them from their homeland. Most significant among these values is the practice of Buddhism, which pervades every aspect of Laotian American life. While individual Laotian Americans may not follow all Buddhist teachings, its philosophy serves as a guide for behavior.

Also characteristic of Laotian Americans is the familiar way in which they treat one another. Laotian American communities are closely knit and everyone is current on what everyone else is doing. Individuals often refer to one another by their first names. For example, "Khamsang Phoumvihane" would be respectfully addressed as "Mr. Khamsang," rather than "Mr. Phoumvihane."

Finally, the family is exceedingly important to Laotian Americans. In Laos, where the majority of people work in agriculture, families often work together to produce the goods necessary for their livelihood. In the United States, this practice has been altered somewhat since the majority of Laotian Americans work outside the home in urban communities. Nonetheless, Laotian Americans often live in close proximity to their extended family and such family values as respect for

one's parents have remained constant. Laotian American children are expected to respect and care for their parents throughout their adult life.

♦ LANGUAGE

Lao is a tonal language; therefore, the meaning of a word is determined by the tone or pitch at which it is spoken. Although the tones vary somewhat from one part of the country to another, the dialect of the capital, Vientiane, is considered standard Lao. In Vientiane there are six tones: low, mid, high, rising, high falling, and low falling. Changing the tone of a word makes it a different word. The sound "kow," pronounced much like the English "cow," spoken with a high tone means "an occasion, a time." "Kow" spoken with a rising tone means "white." Spoken with a mid tone, this word means "news." These tones give the Lao language a musical quality, so that its speakers often sound like they are singing or reciting melodic poetry.

The Lao alphabet is phonetic, meaning that each Lao letter stands for a sound. Lao writing has 27 consonant symbols that are used for 21 consonant sounds. There are more symbols than sounds because different consonants are used to begin words of different tones. Thus, the tones of Lao words are indicated by four tone marks written above the consonant of syllables and by spelling. The Lao alphabet also has 38 vowel symbols, representing 24 vowel sounds. These 24 sounds are made up of nine simple vowels and three diphthongs (vowels made up of two vowel sounds), each of which has a short form and a long form. The sounds are written with more than 24 symbols because some of them are written differently at the end of a word and in the middle of a word. All Lao words end in a vowel or in a consonant sound similar to the English "k," "p," "t," "m," "n," or "ng." This is why some Laotian Americans, who learned English as a second language, may occasionally pronounce "fish" as "fit" or "stiff" as "stip."

The graceful, curving letters of the Laotian alphabet are based on the Khmer (Cambodian) alphabet which, in turn, was developed from an ancient writing system in India. Although the Lao writing system is not the same as the Thai writing system, the two are very similar, and anyone who can read one language can read the other with only a little instruction.

Greetings and Other Popular Expressions

Common Laotian American greetings and expressions include: *Sabai dee baw*—how are you? (literally, are you well?); *Koy sabai dee*—I'm well; *Jao day*—and how are you? (used when responding to *Sabai dee*); *Pai sai*—where are you going? (used as a greeting); *Kawp jai*—thank you; *Kaw toht*—excuse me; *Baw pen nyang*—

you're welcome, never mind (literally, it's nothing); *Ma gin khao*—come eat! (literally, come eat rice); *Sab baw*—is the food good?; *Sab eelee*—it's delicious.

Laotian American Literature

Most Laotian literature consists of oral tales and religious texts. Laotian oral literature often takes the form of poetry, and is sung or chanted to the accompaniment of a hand-held bamboo pipe organ called the *khene* (pronounced like the word "can" in American English). Such poetry is most often used in theater, or opera, known as *maw lam*. The *maw lam leuang*, or "story *maw lam*," is similar to European opera; a cast of actors in costume sing and act out a story, often drawn from historical or religious legend. *Maw lam khoo*, or "*maw lam* of couples," involves a young man and a young woman. The man flirts with the woman through inventive methods and she refuses him with witty verse responses. *Maw lam chote*, or "*maw lam* competition," is a competition in verse sung between two people of the same gender, in which each challenges the other by asking questions or beginning a story that the other must finish. In *maw lam dio*, or "*maw lam* alone," a single narrator sings about almost any topic.

Among the many legends and folktales told by Laotians and Laotian Americans, the stories about the character Xieng Mieng are among the most popular. Xieng Mieng is a trickster figure who plays pranks on people of various social classes. Other popular tales involve legends taken from Buddhist writings, especially the *Sip Sat*, stories about the last 10 lives of the Buddha before he was reborn and achieved enlightenment. All Laotian religious literature is made up of the same Buddhist texts used by other Theravada Buddhists. These include the *Jataka*, the five *Vinaya*, the *Dighanikaya*, and the *Abhidamma*, all of which are scriptures written in Pali, an ancient language from India still used for religious purposes in countries practicing Theravada Buddhism. Verses in Pali known as the *parittam* are also important to Laotian Buddhists, and are chanted by monks to protect people from a variety of dangers.

In the United States, Laotian monks have successfully retained Laotian religious literature. In addition, secular legends and stories, told through the medium of *maw lam*, may be heard at gatherings in cities with large Laotian American communities.

♦ FAMILY AND COMMUNITY DYNAMICS

In Laos, men represent their family in village affairs, while women are responsible for running the household and controlling the financial affairs of the family. Among Laotian Americans, however, female employment is an important source of family income and it is common for Laotian American women to work outside the home. Fifty percent of Laotian American women and 58 percent of Laotian American men participate in the U.S. labor force. Because of the relative equality between men and women in Laotian American society, many Laotian American men share responsibility for completing household tasks. While Laotian American men almost always hold the official positions of leadership in community organizations, women are also quite active in their communities and are often important (though usually unacknowledged) decision makers.

The most common family arrangement in Laos is that of a nuclear family that lives in close proximity to their extended family. In the United States, extended families have, in many cases, become even more important to Laotian Americans for social and financial support. This interdependence may account for the low divorce rate among Laotian Americans. In 1990, only about 4 percent of Laotian Americans over the age of 15 who had been married were divorced, while nearly 12 percent of the U.S. population over 15 years of age who had been married were divorced.

The practice of dating is also new to Laotian American immigrants as it simply was not done in their homeland. In Laos couples usually come to know one another in the course of village life. In the United States, however, many young people date, although this custom is not always embraced by their parents.

Education

Since Laotian Americans are such a young group, their prospects for continuing adaptation are good, especially considering the scholastic successes of Laotian American children. In an influential book on the academic achievement of young Indochinese Americans, Nathan Caplan, John K. Whitmore, and Marcella H. Choy asserted that refugee children, including the Laotians, "spoke almost no English when they came, and they attend predominantly inner-city schools whose reputations for good education are poor. Yet by 1982, we find that the Indochinese had already begun to move ahead of other minorities on a national basis, and, two years later, their children are already doing very well on national tests" (Nathan Caplan, John K. Whitmore, and Marcella H. Choy, *The Boat People and Achievement in America: A Study of Family Life and Cultural Values* [Ann Arbor, University of Michigan Press, 1989], p. 75).

Despite these accomplishments, few Laotian American young people attend college; this may be attributed to the economic disadvantages of their families. Only 26.3 percent of Laotian Americans (not counting the Hmong) between the ages of 18 and 24 attended college in 1990 (compared to 39.5 percent of white Americans and 28.1 percent of African Americans). Laotian American young people also had relatively high drop-out rates; 12.2 percent of Laotian Americans between the ages of 16 and 19 were neither high school graduates nor enrolled in school in 1990 (compared to 9.8 percent of white U.S. citizens and 13.7 percent of African Americans).

Important Rituals

Many Laotian Americans retain the ritual practices of their culture. The most common of all Laotian rituals is the *baci* (pronounced "bah-see") or *sookhwan*, which is performed at important occasions. The word *sookhwan* may be interpreted as "the invitation of the *khwan*" or "the calling of the *khwan*." The *khwan* are 32 spirits that are believed to watch over the 32 bodily organs of the human body. Together, the *khwan* are thought to constitute the spiritual essence of a person. The *baci*, or *sookhwan*, is a ritual binding of the spirits to their possessor. Even Laotians who do not believe in the existence of the *khwan* will usually participate in the *baci* as a means of expressing goodwill and good luck to others.

In the *baci* ceremony, a respected person, usually an older man who has been a monk, performs the ceremony, invoking the *khwan* in a loud, song-like voice. He calls on the spirits of all present to cease wandering and to return to the bodies of those present. He then asks the *khwan* to bring well-being and happiness with them and to share in the feast that will follow. After the invocation to the *khwan* is finished, the celebrants take pieces of cotton thread from silver platters covered with food, and tie them around each other's wrists to bind the *khwan* in place. While tying the thread, they will wish one another health and prosperity. Often an egg is placed in the palm of someone whose wrist is being bound, as a symbol of fertility. Some of the threads must be left on for three days, and when they are removed they must be broken or untied, not cut. Non-Laotians are not only welcomed to this ceremony, they are frequently treated as guests of honor.

The *khwan* is also significant to traditional Laotian wedding ceremonies. When a couple adheres to Laotian traditions strictly, the groom goes to the bride's house the day before the wedding feast, where monks await with bowls of water. The couple's wrists are tied together with a long cotton thread, which is looped around the bowls of water and then tied to the wrists of the monks. The next morning, friends and relatives of the couple sprinkle them with the water, and then hold a *baci* ceremony. Afterward, the couple is seated together in front of all the guests and the monks chant prayers to bless the marriage.

Festivals

Most Laotian holidays and festivals have religious origins. The Lao word for "festival," *boon*, literally means "merit" or "good deed." Scheduled according to the lunar calendar, festivals usually take place at Buddhist temples, making it difficult for Laotian Americans to participate due to the limited availability of monks and temples in the United States. Two of the most important festivals are the *Pha Vet*, which commemorates the life of the Buddha in the fourth lunar month, and the *Boon Bang Fay*, or "rocket festival." Held in the sixth month to celebrate the Buddha, it includes setting off fireworks.

Cuisine

Laotian cuisine is spicy. Most meals contain either rice (*khao*) or rice noodles (*khao poon*). The rice may be glutinous (*khao nyao*) or nonglutinous (*khao chao*), but glutinous or "sticky" rice is the food most often associated with Laotian cuisine. The rice is accompanied by meat, fish, and vegetables. Meats are often chopped, pounded, and spiced to make a dish known as *lap* and fish is usually eaten with a special sauce called *nam ba*. The sticky rice is usually taken in the thumb and first three fingers and used to scoop up other foods. A papaya salad spiced with hot peppers, which is known as *tam mak hoong* to Laotians and *som tam* to Thais, is a popular snack food.

Many Laotian Americans still eat Lao-style foods at home. These dishes are also available at most Thai restaurants, since the cooking of Northeastern Thailand is almost identical to that of Laos. Sticky rice and other ingredients for Lao foods are likewise available at most stores that specialize in Asian foods. In areas that have large Laotian American communities, there are also a number of Lao Markets where these ingredients may be purchased.

Traditional Dress

On special occasions marked by the *sookhwan* ceremony, some Laotian American women wear traditional costumes. The staple of their attire is the *sinh*, a skirt made from a piece of brocade about two yards long that is wrapped around the waist. It is often held in place by a belt made of shiny metal buckles or rings. Accompanying the *sinh* is a shawl, or a strip of material, which is draped over the left shoulder and under the right arm. Laotian American men rarely wear an ethnic costume, except on stage during a *maw lam* performance, when actors sometimes don the *sampot*, or baggy trousers worn in Laos before French occupation.

Laotian Proverbs

Laotian proverbs often express an earthy and practical sort of folk wisdom that is rooted in the experiences of generations of hard-working farmers. The Lao have brought countless proverbs to America with them including the following examples:

If you're shy with your teacher, you'll have no knowledge; if you're shy with your lover, you'll have no bedmate.

Don't teach a crocodile how to swim.

Keep your ears to the fields and your eyes on the farm.

If you have money, you can talk; if you have wood, you can build your house.

Water a stump and you get nothing.

Speech is silver, silence is gold.

Follow the old people to avoid the bite of a dog.

It's easy to find friends who'll eat with you, but hard to find one who'll die with you.

It's easy to bend a young twig, but hard to bend an old tree.

◆ RELIGION

In Laos, almost all ethnic Laotians are Buddhists, and the temple, or *wat*, is the center of village life. Most Laotian Americans are Buddhists as well, although many have converted to Protestant Christianity, especially in areas where there are no large Laotian concentrations to sustain traditional religious practices. Laotian American Buddhist temples are frequently established in converted garages, private homes, and other makeshift religious centers.

Buddhism is divided into two schools of thought. The "Northern School," known as Mahayana Buddhism, is a school of Buddhism most often found in China, Japan, Tibet, Korea, and Vietnam. The "Southern School," or Theravada Buddhism, is predominant in Laos, Thailand, Cambodia, Burma, and Sri Lanka. Theravada Buddhists stress the importance of becoming a monk and achieving *Nirvana*, an ideal state in which an individual transcends suffering. Mahayana Buddhists rely more on *Bodhisattvas*, enlightened beings who delay achieving *Nirvana* in order to help others become enlightened.

Essential to the Buddhist faith is the belief that all worldly things are impermanent. Those who are not aware of this concept become attached to worldly things, and this leads to suffering. Their suffering continues as the soul goes through a cycle of rebirths, and they are continually drawn back to worldly desires. An individual may break this cycle by overcoming desire through meditation and a moral, disciplined life. The soul that successfully overcomes all worldly desires reaches *Nirvana*.

Also significant to Buddhism is *Karma*, which is a form of spiritual accounting: good deeds performed in this life enable the soul to be reborn in better circumstances; bad deeds cause the soul to be reborn in worse circumstances. Accordingly, performing good deeds, or "making merit" is important to all Laotians and Laotian Americans as well. One can make merit through acts of kindness. However, becoming a monk or supporting monks or a temple are considered the best methods for making merit. All Laotian men are expected to become monks, usually in early manhood, before marriage. It is also common for older men, especially widowers, to become monks. Laotian women may become nuns, although nuns are not as respected as monks. In Laos, some men are not able to fulfill their religious duty of entering the temple for a time. This is even more difficult for Laotian American men, because of demands in the workplace and the scarcity of temples in the United States. Laotian American monks sometimes share temples with Thai American or Cambodian American monks, since the latter also adhere to Theravada Buddhism.

A belief in spirits, or *phi* (pronounced like the English word "pea") dates back to the time before the Lao were introduced to Buddhism. Since then, the spirit cult has become a part of popular Buddhist practices in Laos. Some of these spirits are the spirits of human beings following death, or "ghosts." Other *phi* are benevolent guardians of people and places, or malevolent beings who cause harm and suffering.

◆ EMPLOYMENT AND ECONOMIC TRADITIONS

Although Laotian Americans have earned a reputation as hard-working people, many find themselves among the most disadvantaged in their new country. In 1990, while one out of every ten Americans lived below the poverty line, about one out of every three Laotian Americans lived below the poverty line. The median household income of Laotian Americans in that year was only $23,019, compared to $30,056 for other Americans. Unemployment among Laotian Americans is high (9.3 percent in 1990) and those with jobs tend to be concentrated in manual labor. Fully 44 percent of employed Laotian Americans held jobs classified as "operators, fabricators, and laborers" in 1990.

Many of the economic hardships of people in this ethnic group are due to their newness in America, and to the difficulties in making the change from a predominantly agricultural country to a highly industrialized country. Nearly 34 percent of Laotian Americans over the age of 25 had not completed fifth grade in 1990, compared to 2.7 percent of other U.S. citizens. While 75.2 percent of all adult U.S. citizens had completed high school, only 40 percent of adult Laotian Americans had finished high school. With regard to higher education, over 20 percent of Americans over 25 had finished college, while only about 5 percent of adult Laotian Americans were college graduates.

Learning English, also, has hindered the economic adjustment of Laotian Americans. Over two-thirds (68 percent) of Laotians over five years of age reported that they did not speak English very well in 1990. While adult education programs and classes in English as a second language in community colleges and other institutions have helped, the transition has not been easy.

Despite their economic difficulties, Laotian Americans generally have positive views of life in the United States, probably because they tend to contrast life in America with their experiences in war-ravaged Laos.

◆ POLITICS AND GOVERNMENT

Laotian Americans have not yet become very active in U.S. politics. In general, they tend to have a positive view of U.S. society and government, as might be expected of recent political refugees.

◆ HEALTH AND MENTAL HEALTH ISSUES

Traditional Laotian medicine involves massages and herbal cures. Practitioners of traditional medicine may be laypeople or monks. Since sickness is often seen as a problem of spiritual essence, the *khwan*, chants, and healing rituals are often used to cure illnesses. Although some traditional Lao medicine may be found in the United States, particularly in places that have large Laotian American communities, the practice of traditional medicine in America appears to be much less common than recourse to mainstream western medicine.

Laotian Americans are much more likely to visit a community clinic than any other type of medical establishment. As new arrivals, their mental health generally follows a pattern common to refugees. The first year in the United States tends to be a period of euphoria at having reached their destination. The second year tends to be a time of psychological shock and feelings of helplessness, as the strangeness of the new environment becomes apparent. New Laotian Americans usually begin to adjust during the third or fourth year.

◆ NOTABLE LAOTIAN AMERICANS

Although Laotian Americans are relatively new to the United States, many professional individuals have made significant contributions to the Laotian American community and U.S. society in general, specifically in professions requiring strong communication skills. Many Laotian American professionals are multilingual and serve as interpreters, negotiators, counselors, organization executives, and educators. For example, Banlang Phommasouvanh (1946-), a respected Laotian American educator, is the founder and executive director of the Lao Parent and Teacher Association. As such, she assists in promoting Lao culture, language, and arts through classes and support services. In 1990, Phommasouvanh received the Minnesota Governor's Commendation, Assisting the Pacific Minnesotans, State Council of Asia. In 1988, Lee Pao Xiong (1966-) served as an intern in the U.S. Senate. Also in 1988, he was one of 25 people chosen in a nationwide competition to attend the International Peace and Justice Seminar. From 1991-1993, Xiong was executive director of the Hmong Youth Association of Minnesota. Currently, he is executive director of the Hmong American Partnership in St. Paul, Minnesota. William Joua Xiong (1963-), who is proficient in Lao, Hmong, Thai, English, and French, served as an interpreter and translator at the U.S. Embassy in Bangkok in 1979. Presently a guidance counselor, he is also co-author of the *English-Hmong Dictionary* (1983).

◆ ASSOCIATIONS AND ORGANIZATIONS

Most Laotian organizations in the United States were established to help Laotian Americans adapt to life in a new country. Therefore, these organizations concentrate heavily on providing English language tutoring, job counseling, psychological counseling, and other social services. Because Laotian Americans are still establishing themselves in the United States, there are very few Laotian publications. Worthy of mention is the monthly, multilingual publication *New Life*, which has attained a wide readership among Laotian Americans. Published by the federal government, it provides international news and articles covering U.S. culture and institutions. *New Life* circulates 35,000 copies in Vietnamese, 10,000 in Lao, and 5,000 in Cambodian.

Lao Assistance Center of Minneapolis

1015 Olson Memorial Hwy.
Minneapolis, MN 55405
(612) 374-4967
Manivah Foun, executive director

Provides social services to the Laotian American community in Minneapolis.

Lao Coalition

4713 Rainier Ave.
Seattle, WA 98118
(206) 723-8440
Mr. Udong Sayasana, president

Located in Washington State, this organization coordinates the activities of 10 Laotian organizations (including Hmong organizations and organizations of other minority groups from Laos). The Coalition also provides social services, including transitional counseling, transportation, and tutoring. This is probably the best source for information on the Laotian American community of Washington.

Lao Family Community, Inc.

807 N. Joaquin
Stockton, CA 95202
(209) 466-0721
Mr. Pheng Lo

Provides training in English as a second language, vocational education, a variety of youth programs, and a gang prevention program for people from Laos and other countries in Southeast Asia.

Lao Lane Xang

5150 Cloverdale
Seattle, WA 98118
(206) 723-8440
Mr. Khamsang Thaviseth, president

A Lao cultural and social service organization with chapters in most areas that have large Laotian communities. It hosts annual meetings that gather Laotian American community leaders from various parts of the United States.

Migration and Refugee Services

1408 Carmel Ave.
Lafayette, LA 70501
(318) 261-5535
Mr. Khamla Luangsouphom, Diocese of Lafayette contact

Provides social services such as English language training and help in finding employment to the Laotian community in western Louisiana.

—*Carl L. Bankston III*

11

Who Are the Nepali Americans?

♦ Religion ♦ Education ♦ Labor and Employment ♦ Sports and Recreation
♦ Traditional Clothing ♦ Social Structure ♦ Colonization ♦ Political History
♦ Women ♦ The Nepalis in America ♦ Ritual Celebrations

Nepal borders China on the north and India on the south, east, and west. The total area of Nepal is 147,181 km2. (56,827 square miles), of which about two-thirds is covered by hills and mountains. It is a landlocked country in the Himalayas with three distinct geographical regions: the fertile, tropical plains of Terai; the central plateaus, covered with rainforest; and the Himalayan mountains. Eleven of the highest mountains in the world are in Nepal, including Mt. Everest.

The population has grown from 11 million in 1972 to 18.46 million in 1990. The literacy rate has gone from 7 percent in 1972 to 35 percent in 1992.

In 1991, 7.8, 45.6, and 46.6 percent of the population were found in the mountain, hill, and terai (flat land), respectively. Nepal is a Hindu state that is both multiracial and multilingual.

♦ RELIGION

Constitutionally, Nepal is a Hindu Kingdom, but other religions are tolerated. According to most recently available records, 89.5 percent of the population is Hindu; while Buddhists comprise about 5.3 percent, and Moslems 2.7 percent, with a small number of Christians and followers of various other religions. The Hindu festival *Durga Pooja* is the national holiday. Durga is the mother goddess of Hindu mythology. Buddhist holidays are also observed.

Nepali, derived from ancient sanskrit, is the official language of the country and is spoken by 70 percent of the population. Twenty other languages—including Maithali, Bhojpuri, Tharu, Tamang, and Newari—which are subdivided into many dialects, are also spoken.

♦ EDUCATION

It is estimated that 35 percent of the population is literate. For women, however, the rate is much lower,

about 19 percent. Persons enrolled in school, from vocational and technical schools to general higher education, numbered 1,003,810 in 1990.

♦ LABOR AND EMPLOYMENT

About 65.1 percent of the total working-age population was economically active in 1981, with 90 percent engaged in agricultural and allied activities. Until 1950, Nepal was sealed to outsiders. When it was opened, it welcomed business people, diplomats, and foreigners.

Katmandu became a modern city, complete with British education, modern hospitals, communications, and transportation. The city has become industrialized with manufacturing sectors whose products range from shoe production to cement.

♦ SPORTS AND RECREATION

Soccer, cricket, volleyball, badminton, and tennis are popular sports in the areas heavily influenced by the West, but in other parts of the country traditional Nepali sports such as *kabbadi* (run and catch) and *dandi biyo* (played with sticks) are popular. Folk music and dances are very popular as well.

♦ TRADITIONAL CLOTHING

Nepal comprises different ethnic groups and clothing varies from place to place among them.

For example, in the mountains, the traditional clothing is a full-sleeve blouse with long woolen tunics. In mid-hill regions, women wear saris—six-yard-long brightly decorated robes that are tucked around the body—and men wear half-tunics and trousers with a jacket and cap. In the plains, jackets and caps are used only during the winter.

Rice is the staple food of Nepal, but corn is also used extensively in the mountain regions. Rice is generally mixed with different kinds of beans and vegetables combined together in a dish called *dal*. Various kinds of pickles are a very popular delicacy.

♦ SOCIAL STRUCTURE

Nepalese society is structured in a hierarchy called a caste system, where people are divided into classes— or castes—that define their social and economic roles. Traditionally, the *Brahmans* and *Chetris Kshatriyas* in India engage in certain prescribed, exclusive activities as status groups. For the Brahman, the sacrifice, study of Vedas (Hindu sacred texts), and asceticism are assigned; whereas for the Chetris (Kshatriyas) political rule is assigned. The Vaisyas were permitted to farm and trade. Inferior to all are *Sudras* who are considered untouchable in the caste hierarchy. The King comes from the Chetris caste, and the ruling family of Rana is Chetris as well.

The caste system has dominated Nepal since the seventh century, when it is believed that the ruling caste from India fled a Muslim invasion to Nepal. These high-caste, well-educated Hindus gradually supplanted the local power structure and became rulers of the Nepalis, who were Tibeto/Burmese by ethnicity. In addition to taking political power, these Hindus became landowners, while the indigenous peoples became a subordinate class of peasants who worked the land and paid the landowners half the produce of the land they worked. With the 1950 revolution, deep seated resentment toward the higher castes, Brahmins and Chetris, surfaced among the other castes and sub-castes as well as among ethnic groups.

♦ COLONIZATION

Nepal was never colonized. During the British rule in India, Nepal fought a war with the British from 1814-1816. Afterwards, it was forced to give up some of its territories, a few of which returned in 1816. After the war, both countries signed a treaty, in which the British reserved the right to recruit the Nepalese into the British army.

♦ POLITICAL HISTORY

King Prithbi Narayan Shah, who is the ancestor of the present king, unified Nepal in 1769. In 1856, Jang Bahadur Rana, a confidante of the King, who at the time had been weakened politically by infighting among the royal family, persuaded the king to grant him absolute power. Once he had been named prime minister, Mr. Rana ruled Nepal dictatorially. His descendants continued to rule after him until the 1950 revolution. In this period, called the *Rana Regime*, the king became a figure head under the captivity of Ranas.

Beginning in the 1940s, Nepalis who were studying in India wanted to change the repressive political structure of Nepal. These expatriates formed the Nepali Congress (NC), based on the principles of the Democratic Socialist and the Nepal Communist parties. The Nepali Congress played a key role in bringing democracy, however briefly, to Nepal. The Nepal Communist party did not significantly participate in the 1950 revolution.

The changes Nepal went through in the 1950s greatly affected the social and economic structure of the entire country. The autocratic Rana family regime that had controlled the government for over 100 years was overthrown. Civil liberties were introduced, the country was opened up to the outside, and a new middle class came into being. Between 1950 and 1959, Nepal exercised something like a trial democracy. But then in 1960, political parties were again banned by King Mahendra, who imprisoned most of the political leaders. The first ever freely elected multiparty parliament was dissolved. King Mahendra introduced a *Panchayat* system in 1961. The Panchayat system was a national assembly made up entirely of the King's personal appointees; its members represented no political parties and were headed by the King, who retained all power, making him an absolute monarch.

Political party workers were exiled to India in the 1960s and 1970s. They continued their fight against the King but were not successful. In 1979, following an uprising of students and peasants, King Birendra granted political amnesty to all Nepali dissidents living in India. A referendum was held in 1980 to choose either a multiparty system or the ruling Panchayat system with "suitable reforms." The Panchayat system won by a 4-percent margin, but many believed that this victory had been rigged by the government. Political parties were once again banned; but they resumed their work underground. The tension between the King and party workers eased a bit after the referendum, but there were frequent protests and arrests.

1990 Democratic Movement

Nepal went through a 50-daylong pro-democracy movement in the spring of 1990 to eliminate the authoritarian Panchayat system. The movement began in March of 1989, when India refused to renew trade and transit treaties with Nepal, closing down all but two of its 15 trade routes. India was disturbed at Nepal's increasingly friendly relations with China, its neighbor to the north. Nepal, located between China and India, is heavily dependent on India for its trade and transit, since the Himalayas bar feasible transit through China.

India claimed that having friendlier relations with China was a violation of the 1950 treaty between Nepal and India. The contents of this treaty, which has never been published despite repeated demands, are unknown to most Nepalis.

Within a year of the embargo, the inflation rate rose to almost 300 percent, hitting both lower- and middle-class Nepalis. People were afraid to talk freely about their government's stand. If they did, they were imprisoned. The young generation was particularly restless about the ineptness of the Panchayat government to handle the trade embargo. Panchayat leaders and officials had been living luxurious lives, creating even more resentment. A coalition of various banned parties formed a united front, comprised of the centrist and leftist parties, launching the Movement for the Restoration of Democracy (MRD) in January of 1990. Women played an important role in this movement. The protests lasted until April 6, 1990. On that day, the King surrendered to this populist movement after a massacre of unarmed people who were demonstrating in front of his palace in Katmandu.

There has still not been a definitive or official accounting of the number of people killed, but about 200,000 people from Katmandu and neighboring areas demonstrated that day and were attacked by the military who opened fire on them. Witnesses reported that military trucks were loaded with bodies which were taken away and buried.

A general election was held on May 12, 1991. The Nepali Congress party (NC) won a majority of seats in the House of Representatives and formed a government headed by Prime Minister Girija Prasad Koirala. Out of 205 members, five women were elected from the NC and two from the United Communist Party (UML).

Today, an organization called the Alliance for Democracy and Human Rights in Nepal (ADHRAN) monitors human rights and democratic progress. The organization has approximately 120 members in the United States, works exclusively as a monitor, and does not involve itself in partisan Nepalese politics. Rajiv Dahal, an engineer and Nepali American, is president.

◆ WOMEN

Nepali women still work harder and produce more than men. A rural women's total work burden was at an average of 10.81 hours per day compared to 7.51 for men. Women not only contribute more time but also generate more income than men and children to the total household: 50 to 44 and 6 percent, respectively, according to 1981 figures, In addition, women's unpaid work (domestic labor, which can be quite onerous), particularly in rural areas, goes unaccounted in these statistics.

◆ THE NEPALIS IN AMERICA

According to the president of the Association of Nepalese Americans (ANA), there are about 6,000 Nepalis living in the United States, 40 percent of whom are professionals. The remaining 60 percent are shop owners, small-business owners and students. This number has been growing steadily since the mid-1980s.

There are approximately 15 Nepali social, cultural, and political, organizations in the United States. There are also newsletters published for Nepali Americans such as *Samachar-Bichar*, *Viewpoints*, and *Yeti View*.

◆ RITUAL CELEBRATIONS

Following the customs in Nepal, *Durga Pooja*, a celebration of the mother goddess of Hindu mythology, is widely celebrated among the Nepali community in the United States. It is known as *Dashain* among Nepalis, and falls in the month of October.

Nepali New Year, which falls in the month of April, is also celebrated in America. According to the Nepali calendar called *bikram sambat* it is now the year 2051.

Many Nepali Americans continue to practice the religions and customs of their homeland. Because their numbers are small, they have been able retain their traditions in America. The traditional Nepali wedding ceremony is an example.

In the Nepali wedding ceremony, men and women wear distinctively different wedding clothes. Men wear white and different light shades of plain trousers and tunics with a jacket or blazer and a traditional cap. Women wear mainly a red sari, a blouse, and a shawl with different kinds of jewels sewn into them. Green, purple, ruby, and other colors are permitted, but black and white are avoided by the bride.

Rituals of birth and death are also celebrated according to Hindu custom among most Nepali Americans. The Hindu priest is called on for both occasions. The birth ceremony, called *Nwaran*, which means name-giving ceremony, usually occurs on the seventh or the eleventh day after the birth of a child.

Another ceremony, the *Annaprasan* (rice-feeding ceremony) is generally celebrated when a child is six months old. The death ritual begins on the day of a person's death and lasts for 13 days afterward. It is called *kriya* in Nepali.

References

Acharya, Meena and Lynn Bennett. *The Rural Women of Nepal: An Aggregate Analysis and Summary of Eight Village Studies*, Washington D.C.: AID/PPC/WID, 1982.

Asia Watch, February, 1990.

Asmita, (a vernacular bimonthly, published in Katmandu for women), Summer 1990.

Bajracharya, Man Bajra. *Mythological History of the Nepal Valley from Swayambhu Purana and Naga and Serpent Symbolism,* Edited and translated by Warren W. Smith. New Delhi: Avalok Publishers, January 1978.

Bennett, Lynn. *Dangerous Wives and Sacred Sisters: Social and Symbolic Roles of High Caste Women of Nepal.* Columbia University, New York, 1983.

———. *Tradition and Change in the Legal Status of Nepalese Women,* Center for Economic Development and Administration, Tribhuwan University, Nepal, 1970.

Caplan, Lionel. *Land and Social Change in East Nepal: A Study of Hindu Tribal Relations,* Berkeley: University of California Press, 1970.

Dharamdasani, M.D. ed. *Democratic Nepal,* Salimar Publishing House.

Gandhi, M.K. *Caste Must Go and the Sin of Untouchability,* New Delhi: Na Jivan Trust.

Hamendorf, Furer. *Caste and Kin in Nepal, India and Ceylon,* New Delhi: Sterling Publishers Private Limited.

National Planning Commission, His Majesty's Government, Nepal.

Parajuli, Pramod. "Political Culture and the Future of Democracy in Nepal: Towards a Grassroots Democratic Strategy." Paper presented at the Nineteenth Annual Conference on South Asia, University of Wisconsin.

Pradhan, Beena. *Institutions Concerning Women in Nepal,* Katmandu: U.S. Aid Publications.

Regmi, M.C. *Thatched Huts and Stucco Palaces: Peasants and Landlords in Nineteenth Century in Nepal,* New Delhi: Vikas Publishing.

Rose, Leo and Margaret W. Fisher. *The Politics of Nepal: Persistence and Change in an Asian Monarchy.* New York: Cornell University Press, 1970.

Schular, Sydney. *The Other Side of Polyandry.* Westview Press.

Upreti, Prem. *Political Awakening in Nepal.* New Delhi: Vikas Publishing, 1992.

Weber, Max. *The Religion of India.* Translated and edited by H. Gerth and Don Martindale. New York: Free Press, 1967.

—Manjula Giri

Who Are the Pacific Islanders?

History ◆ Fijians ◆ Guamanians ◆ Native Hawaiians ◆ Northern Marianas Islanders
◆ Palauans ◆ American and Western Samoans ◆ Tongans

The designation Pacific Islander is used by demographers and U.S. government agencies to describe people of island groups in the Pacific Ocean. These are Fiji, Guam, Native Hawaiians, Commonwealth of the Northern Mariana Islands, Republic of Palau, American and Western Samoa, and Tonga. Individuals who were born in American Samoa and Guam have U.S. citizenship. Individuals born in Hawaii prior to its achieving statehood (that is, prior to August 21, 1959) similarly were entitled to U.S. citizenship. (Of course, all persons born in Hawaii since it became the fiftieth state are U.S. citizens.)

Pacific Islanders are usually divided into three main ethnic groups: Polynesians, Micronesians, and Melanesians. Originally intended to identify common physical and linguistic characteristics among certain groups of islanders, the geographical references to groups of islands are as follows:

Polynesia refers to the "many islands" that lie within the triangle formed by Hawaii, New Zealand, and Easter Island. The people within this area share a common basic language and social system.

Micronesia refers to the "small islands" stretching westward from the borders of Polynesia, north of the equator, and includes the islands north of new Guinea to the borders of Oceania (the name for the vast region of the Pacific containing Australia and many smaller islands). The people of this area have diverse languages and cultures.

Melanesia ("black islands") includes the islands south of the equator and west of Polynesia, New Guinea among them. Although the people of this area have darker skins than those of the other two groups, Melanesians have little in common with one another. A small group of Melanesian languages has been identified, but they form only a fraction of all the languages spoken in the area.

In the last 30 years, the number of Pacific Islander groups identified separately by the United States Census has grown from one in the 1970 census (Native Hawaiian) to eight groups in the 1990 census. These include Native Hawaiians, Samoans, Tongans, Guamanians, Tahitians, Northern Mariana Islanders, Palauans, and Fijians.

◆ HISTORY

There are many theories about the origin of the Pacific Islanders. Since the Norwegian Thor Heyerdahl tried to prove the migrations came from the east by making his celebrated voyage in the Kon-Tiki, scientists have shifted their theories to reflect the widely held view that the first people came into the area from the Southeast Asian peninsula at the time when New Guinea and Australia were still linked. These nomadic

Table 12.1
Pacific Islanders enumerated in the decennial census in the United States.

1970 Census Pacific Islanders	1980 Census Pacific Islanders	1990 Census Pacific Islanders
Native Hawaiian	Native Hawaiian	Native Hawaiian
	Samoan	Samoan
	Tongan	Tongan
	Micronesian	
	Guamanian	Guamanian
	Melanesian	
		Tahitian
		Northern Mariana Islander
		Palauan
		Fijian

143

hunter-gatherers found their way onto the Australian mainland. After the melting of the ice cap, some of the peoples who had a knowledge of farming and other sedentary skills moved into New Guinea and on to the other islands of Melanesia.

Much later, other people with more highly developed cultures came from Southeast Asia through what is now called Indonesia into Micronesia. Other Asian groups followed, including groups from the Philippines. After a time, the descendants of these people moved out of Micronesia into Polynesia.

According to one of many theories, the Polynesians first moved into the Tonga-Samoa area in about A.D. 300, eventually branching out to surrounding islands. Probably about A.D.1000, the Tahiti area to the east was settled. From there, people moved to Hawaii in the north, Easter Island in the east, and New Zealand in the south.

◆ FIJIANS

The people of the Fiji Islands are descended from seamen of mainland Asia who reached the islands approximately 3,500 years ago. Today, the population includes a large group of descendants of Indian laborers who were brought to work on sugar and pineapple plantations in the 1800s. Other ethnic groups include small numbers of Europeans, Chinese, and other Pacific Islanders.

The Fiji Islands lie in the belt of islands known as Melanesia in the Southwest Pacific Ocean. More than 800 islands form the group. The two main islands are Viti Levu and Vanua Levu, with more than half the total population residing on Viti Levu. The climate is tropical, with some areas receiving extensive rainfall, especially in April and November.

History

The early settlers developed a kind of pottery (Lapita) that has been used to date their society. For centuries, Fijians fought battles for control of the various islands, ruled by an array of chiefs. Excellent navigators and sailors, the Fijians established trade with other islands, eventually leading to settlements in Samoa, Tonga, and elsewhere in the region. Europeans came and began their influence in the islands after Dutch discovery of the islands in 1643. The British, French, and other Europeans encouraged the traditional infighting over control of the islands until 1850, when Ratu (Chief) Cakobau gained authority over all the islands. He enlisted the help of the British and in 1874 they adopted Fiji as a crown colony.

Vast epidemics killed nearly half the native Fijians, and foreign workers from India and China were imported, Indians surpassing Fijians in number after World War II.

In 1970, Fiji became an independent nation within the British Commonwealth, headed by the British monarch. After years of Fijian dominance, Indians gained majority in the cabinet in 1987, only to be overthrown by a military coup. Fiji became a republic in 1990. The population in 1992 was estimated at 758,275.

Culture

The basic unit of Fijian society is a patrilineal extended family, directed by a senior male. Several of these related families form a clan, which is led by a hereditary chief. Several clans with common ancestry form a tribe. These social organizations are still important within the Fijian community, although the influence of other cultures in the population has lessened their power. Men still dominate the Fijian family, doing the farming and fishing, while women tend the home.

Early Fijians were proud to be warriors, and rumors of cannibalism were common and lasted well into the 1800s, especially among European settlers who were victims.

Missionaries brought Christianity in the 1800s, which soon eclipsed the native religion, but Fijians retained some of their old beliefs and combined them with their new Christian teachings. Today, Hinduism, Islam and Chinese Confucian philosophy are also part of the religious makeup of Fiji.

Western influence is found in clothing, the prominence of radio and television, and in the development of light industries.

English is the official language, but Fijian is widely used. The literacy rate was was over 80% in 1985. A tradition of oral history in chant, song and dance preserves the old legends, myths and even stories of tribal warfare.

◆ GUAMANIANS

The 1990 U.S. Decennial Census listed 62,964 Guamanians, compared to 39,520 reported in 1980.

Today's Guamanians are almost 50% Chamorro, descendants of the original Chamorro, who migrated from the Malay Peninsula to the Pacific around 1500 B.C. Other settlers were from Spain and the Philippines Filipino, with later arrivals from the United States, Great Britain, Korea, China, and Japan. This diversity of explorers and settlers made Guam the multicultural society it is today.

Guam is the largest of the Mariana Islands in the Western Pacific Ocean. The island is volcanic in origin, with a tropical climate, and lies in the typhoon belt of the Western Pacific, often suffering widespread damage from the storms. The 1992 population was estimated at 142,271, excluding United States military personnel and their families. Guam is one of the most important U.S. military bases in the Pacific.

History

The original settlers on Guam were the Chamorro. When Ferdinand Magellan arrived in 1521, a 200-year decline in population began. Most of the approximately 100,000 original Chamorro had fled the island or perished in wars with the Spanish by 1741, leaving only about 5,000 inhabitants. Guam remained under Spanish rule until 1898, when it was ceded to the United States under the Treaty of Paris at the end of World War I. During World War II, Guam was occupied by Japanese forces but was recaptured by the United States after less than two months.

In 1950, the island was established as an unincorporated territory of the United States under the Organic Act of Guam. Guam, like American Samoa, sends a delegate to the U.S. Congress.

Culture

Before World War II, most Guamanians earned a living in farming. However, after 1947, most adults were employed by the U.S. armed forces. The island's economy has profited by the huge sums of money spent by the U.S. defense establishment. Tourism has become a major industry, also causing a boom in construction.

English is the official language, but Chamorro is taught in primary schools. Most Guamanians are Roman Catholics.

◆ NATIVE HAWAIIANS

The 1990 U.S. Decennial Census listed 211,014 Americans of Hawaiian descent, compared to 172,346 in 1980.

The people of the Hawaiian Islands are the descendants of both the original Polynesian inhabitants and more recent immigrants and their descendants. The Hawaiian Islands are made up principally of eight islands stretching for 390 miles in the Pacific Ocean about 2,100 miles southwest of San Francisco, California. These eight islands are Niihau, Kauai, Oahu, Molokai, Lanai, Maui, Kahoolawe, and Hawaii. Hawaii, the largest, contains two-thirds of the total land mass, and nearly all of the islands' population is concentrated on the four largest islands: Kauai, Oahu, Maui and Hawaii.

All are relatively young land masses formed by volcanic action only about 70 million years ago. The main islands contain volcanic mountains, although most are inactive. On the youngest, the island of Hawaii, active volcanoes still expel lava from time to time.

Hawaii's celebrated even, temperate climate is moderated by the trade winds from the northeast, and even though the latitude is tropical, the humidity remains low and temperatures remain at 70-80 degrees Fahrenheit year-round. Rainfall occurs mostly from October to April, but heavy rains can occur at any time.

History

About 1100 B.C., seafaring peoples began settling the South Pacific islands, later called Polynesia by Europeans. Probably between A.D. 300 and 500, the Polynesians settled the remote northern islands we now call Hawaii. They named the largest one *Havaiki*. They brought with them the plants, animals, and other elements of their former culture important to their way of life, especially the foods of their traditional diet: the staple taro (a tuber), coconuts, bananas, breadfruit, yams, and sugar cane.

In 1778, Captain James Cook, a British navigator and explorer, brought white men to the islands in his "discovery." At the same time, they introduced European technology and, unfortunately, European diseases to which the native population had no immunity. Within forty years, the population had declined substantially.

The new technology made a strong impression on a young and ambitious Hawaiian chief named Kamehameha. He quickly mastered the use of firearms and combined them with new sailing methods. With the support of the European in Hawaii at the time, he had conquered seven islands by 1810. Never before had a single Hawaiian chief wielded so much power, triumphing over all other chiefs and eventually becoming Hawaii's first king. Kamehameha died in 1819.

During Kamehameha's rule, Hawaii's role as a trade stopover grew among British and American whaling fleets, among other traders. Missionaries also arrived during this period. These invasions by outsiders disrupted and changed the Hawaiian culture irrevocably. In the 1850s and 1860s, the arrival of the sugar industry from America caused a major change in the islands' economy, and eventually even altered their ethnicity. By 1910, more than fifty sugar plantations employed over 50,000 workers, many of them contract laborers hired from Asian and European countries, followed by Chinese, Japanese, and Filipinos. Many of these people returned home at the end of their contracts, but many stayed, making Hawaii the diverse ethnic society it is today.

The Hawaiian Islands first became an American territory in 1893 when Queen Liliuokalani was overthrown by white American businessmen with military backing. They replaced Queen Liliuokalani with a provisional government. The United States government annexed the islands and created the Territory of Hawaii. (*See* Significant Documents) For the next nearly five decades, Hawaii became the center of expanding American military power in the Pacific. In 1941, the Japanese attacked Pearl Harbor on the island of Oahu, resulting in the United States entering World War II.

Hawaii became the fiftieth state of the United States in 1959, precipitating the growth of the tourist industry, which overtook both the military and sugar industries as the primary revenue source of the islands. Over thirty years later, activists in Hawaii are working to raise awareness of the negative impact tourism has on the environment and the rich Native Hawaiian culture.

Demographics

Today, Hawaii may be one of the most racially mixed societies in the world. The population has elements of white, Japanese, mixed and pure Hawaiian, Filipino, Chinese, black, and Korean peoples. Almost half of all Hawaiian marriages now occur between people of different races.

The Japanese came to Hawaii in the largest numbers and have only recently been outnumbered by the *haole* (the Hawaiian word for whites). Japanese Americans continue to dominate local politics, and their many religious shrines and temples, native foods and the Japanese-language media all contribute to a strong Japanese flavor in Hawaii.

Native Hawaiians suffered many setbacks in numbers and culture. Due to the introduction of European diseases, population decreased, and the efforts of the missionaries to eradicate Hawaiian ways tainted and diluted their cultural traditions. Their descendants are now making a strong comeback, determined to fight for Hawaiians' rights and preserve the old traditions.

Language

Most native-born Hawaiians speak a dialect of English called *pidgin*, which incorporates elements of the native Polynesian-based Hawaiian, English, and other Asian and Pacific languages. The indigenous Hawaiian language is dying as a spoken language—it is estimated that by the year 2020, it will survive only in isolated phrases and place names. Many Hawaiian words have found their way into mainstream American English, such as *aloha* (love, goodbye) and *lanai* (porch).

Family and Community Dynamics

The traditional Hawaiian family of the past relied on grandparents to raise the children—boys by the father's parents and girls by the mother's. Even though this practice is mostly discontinued today, children retain a special closeness with grandparents.

An integral part of Hawaiian Polynesian society were *kapu*, or prohibitions against certain types of behavior. Examples of kapu include men and women eating together, or letting one's shadow fall on any part of a king's body. Breaking a kapu (which later evolved into the word *taboo* in English) was usually punished by death.

The music and dance of Hawaii has influenced a worldwide audience. The traditional sounds of the Hawaiian guitar technique and the ukelele have become universally familiar. Traditional stories, poems, myths and histories have been chanted for centuries in the unwritten Hawaiian language. The traditional Hawaiian *hula* dance has become a part of world culture. Activists for Hawaiian culture protest the watering-down of cultural traditions for the amusement of tourists, and work to preserve the original forms of these traditions.

Modern Hawaiians have adopted Western-style dress, but elements of some traditions still exist. Women still wear the *muumuu*, a loose-fitting dress originally designed by the missionaries to preserve modesty.

In addition to celebrating all U. S. holidays, Hawaiians observe "Aloha Friday" each week, marked by a sense of fun and the wearing of bright colors, and (for women) a flower tucked behind the ear and a *lei*, a necklace of fresh flowers, around the neck.

Religion

The ancient Hawaiian religion incorporated hundreds of deities and included magical and animist beliefs; however, it disappeared in the early 1800s with the arrival of the missionaries. Ruins of the open-air temples, or *heiau*, are still common sights on all the islands. The old religion declined and Hawaii has as diverse a religious population as any other state in the United States.

Employment and Economy

By the late 1800s, sugar and, to a lesser degree, pineapple dominated the Hawaiian economy. They remain the principal export crops, although food and food products account for only about one-third of the total exports. Other important products of the islands are Macadamia nuts, papaya, and coffee from the Kona district of the island of Hawaii.

Tourism remains the major revenue source and employs many islanders in its various facets. Millions of visitors are lured to the islands every year by the pleasant climate and scenic beauty. Hawaii offers many diversions, from scuba diving, snorkeling, and fishing to the nightlife in the larger cities.

The civilian labor force is now firmly unionized after years of slow development. After World War II, the sugar and pineapple industries became organized. The Teamsters Union is also well established. The unemployment rate was 4.5% in 1992.

Notable Native Hawaiians

See Prominent Asian Americans

◆ NORTHERN MARIANA ISLANDERS

Northern Mariana Islanders are mainly descendants of the original Micronesian inhabitants known as the Chamorro. In addition, there are descendants of migrants from the Caroline Islands, Filipinos, Koreans and Americans.

The Northern Marianas are a U. S. commonwealth in the western Pacific Ocean, comprising all the Mariana Islands except Guam. Most of the people live on the three largest of the group of 16 volcanic islands. The climate is tropical, and the inhabited islands of Rota, Saipan, and Tinian are lush with tropical vegetation.

History

There is evidence on the island of Saipan of human habitation around 1500 B.C. The Marianas are believed to have been settled by migrants from the Philippines and Indonesia.

Ferdinand Magellan was the first European to reach the Marianas in 1521. The Spanish ruled until they were defeated by the United States in the Spanish-American War, ending in 1898. The islands were then sold to Germany. During World War I, the Japanese took over many German-held islands in the Western Pacific, including the Northern Marianas, which later served as an important Japanese military base in World War II. As United States forces occupied the islands during World War II, they imposed U.S. authority. In 1947, the Northern Mariana Islands became a United Nations trust territory under U.S. administration, and then in 1986, became a self-governing U.S. commonwealth of American citizens.

Culture

The traditional agricultural society was partly destroyed by land damage during World War II and never regained a foothold. Today, the people work mainly for the government or in tourism. Small industries, such as handicrafts, are nevertheless important to the tourist industry.

The population is mainly (90%) Roman Catholic. Literacy is high, with education compulsory until age 14.

◆ PALAUANS

Most Palauans are Micronesian descendants with some Melanesian genetic influence. Filipinos, Chinese, and Europeans have also migrated to Palau and assimilated. The population in 1990 was 15,122.

Palau is one of the Palau group of islands in the western Caroline Islands of the far western Pacific Ocean. The country consists of more than 200 islands near the equator, with a maritime tropical climate of high humidity and abundant rainfall, including typhoons and tropical storms.

History

The Carolinian archipelago was first sighted by European navigators in the sixteenth century. In 1686, a Spanish explorer named Yap Island, now part of the Federated States of Micronesia, "La Carolina," after King Charles II of Spain. The name later became the general name of all the islands. The Carolines were ruled by Spain until the end of the Spanish-American War, when they were sold to Germany. They were taken over by the Japanese at the onset of World War I, and then later occupied by United States forces during World War II.

In 1947, Palau became part of the United Nations Trust Territory of the Pacific Islands, administered by the U.S. Palau became a self-governing republic in 1980.

Culture

Palauan society is based on the maternal clan, with villages usually consisting of ten clans. The leader of the highest ranking clan becomes the village chief. Today's communities are plagued with a range of social problems due to rapid socioeconomic change. However, several youth, women's and community organizations provide economic and social assistance and leadership training

Due to limited natural resources, the Palauan economy has a narrow production base. Most people outside of the larger cities are farmers and raise livestock such as pigs, chickens, cattle, and goats. Commercial fishing is a major activity within the encircling barrier reef, and Palau has some of the best diving, snorkeling, and sport fishing areas in the world.

The most commonly spoken language is Palauan, related to Indonesian. It is the official language in addition to English. Most Palauans are Roman Catholics, but some Palauans still adhere to the traditional religious beliefs.

◆ AMERICAN AND WESTERN SAMOANS

The 1990 U.S. Decennial Census of the Population reported that 49,345 respondents indicated they were of Samoan descent, compared to 30,695 in 1980.

Samoans are Polynesians of the islands that make up American Samoa and Western Samoa, a cluster of islands in the Pacific Ocean, 2,300 miles southwest of Hawaii. Polynesia is a term that refers to a group of islands lying in a triangular area of the east-central Pacific Ocean from the Hawaiian Islands in the north to New Zealand in the west and Easter Island in the east. Samoa is contained in the area known as Western Polynesia, along with Tonga and adjacent groups. The native peoples of the islands are related by common linguistic, genetic, and cultural heritage known today as Polynesian.

Most Samoans live on the islands of Western Samoa, which is now an independent nation, with a total of 1,090 square miles. By comparison, American Samoa has only 76 square miles. Although Western Samoa became an independent nation in 1962, American Samoa, the far southeastern island, remains under U.S. control. American Samoa sends a delegate to the U.S. Congress (Guam is the only other Pacific Island with a delegate to Congress.)

The islands are volcanic in origin, with rugged terrain, heavy precipitation and lush vegetation. The majority of plants and animals on the islands today were brought by the Polynesians who settled there originally.

History

The native Samoans originated from the Malay Peninsula of Southeast Asia, whose people migrated throughout the islands of the South Pacific over 2,000 years. The wide expanses between the various islands probably contributed to the distinct cultures that grew up on them.

According to one archeological theory, the Polynesian migrants who came to Samoa could be the descendants of Mongoloids from the east Asian mainland who expanded into southeast Asia and to the Malay Peninsula, and traveled to the various islands across the Pacific in the Paleolithic or Old Stone Age. They intermarried with people of the Australoid strain, leading to their unique physical characteristics.

From A.D. 1200-1800, powerful chiefs and priests ruled Samoa. In the Western islands, two royal families dominated, whereas in the smaller eastern islands, independent chieftancies flourished.

Europeans first visited the islands in 1722, but not until 1830 did an English missionary first settle there. Soon, British, German, and American trade bases had been established in the islands. The "foreigners" took an interest in local politics and eventually set up a neutral government under a Samoan king to help the Samoans overcome centuries of tribal conflict and warfare. Western Samoa has been independent since 1962, after years of rule by Germany, New Zealand, and the United Nations. The far southeastern island remained under United States control, and today is known as American Samoa. The population of Western Samoa in 1991 was 159,862. The population of American Samoa in 1992 was 51,115. A substantial number of Samoans migrate to the United States, but they form less than 1% of the U.S. population.

Culture

Samoa is a multicultural society composed of descendants of Polynesians and the Europeans, Asians, and American who settled there. Family life is based on a closely knit extended family of two or three generations living together. Groups of related families are bound together under a chief chosen by his or her people. These lesser chiefs are in turn ruled by higher chiefs in wider-ranging areas, such as village chiefs. Each village also has a princess. The chief or *matai* wields a fair amount of power and often rises to the national level of politics.

The economy is primarily agricultural, with fishing also of importance. Tourism in Western Samoa has grown steadily. Samoans have adopted Western dress, but still wear traditional Samoan clothing for special occasions or cultural festivities. English is the official language, but Samoan, a Polynesian-based language is widely spoken. Ninety-nine percent of the population is literate.

Most Samoans are Christians, but their form of Christianity is infused with characteristics from the traditional Samoan religion. Samoans have a rich oral tradition of mythology, legends and facts about their history which provides them with a link to their past and a continuing sense of their culture today.

Notable Samoans

See Prominent Asian Americans *and* Sports and Athletics

◆ TONGANS

Most Tongans are Polynesians, descendants from one of the oldest kingdoms in the Pacific. The spiritual kings of Tonga, or *tu'i tongas*, can be traced back to the tenth century. The Tonga archipelago of volcanic islands, also known as the Friendly Islands, is located east of Fiji in the South Pacific Ocean. Of 172 islands, only 45 are inhabited. The climate is subtropical, with lush vegetation and abundant tropical flowers.

History

In 1643, Dutch explorers first discovered Tonga, followed by English and Spanish seamen. It was British Captain James Cook who gave the islands the name the Friendly Islands, having been impressed by the hospitality of the natives. The famous mutiny on the *H.M.S. Bounty* took place in Tongan waters. Christian missionaries arrived for the third time in the early 1830s and were successful in establishing an alliance with one of the chiefs, who eventually became the ruler of all Tonga as King George Tupou I in 1845.

The Kingdom of Tonga became a fully independent nation in 1970 after 70 years as a British protected state. Today, Tonga is an independent kingdom of about 100,000 people.

Culture

The majority of Tongans are Christian (98%) of various denominations, most belonging to the Free Wesleyan Church of Tonga. Both Tongan and English are spoken, with English taught as a second language in the schools. Adult literacy is over 90%. Family life centers around Polynesian traditions and the strong influence of the Christian faith, with kinship ties being an important part of village life.

The Tongan economy is largely agricultural, with principal exports of copra and coconut products and bananas. Fishing is growing in importance. The lush beauty of the islands has brought an increasing number of tourists, but still, unemployment is a steady problem.

The Tongan family is generally dependent on the land for its livelihood, with every Tongan male receiving 8-1/4 acres of land for cultivation when he reaches the age of 16.

References

Moss, Joyce and George Wilson. *Peoples of the World: Asians and Pacific Islanders.* Detroit [Washington, D.C.]: Gale Research, 1993.

Worldmark Encyclopedia of the Nations, Vol. 4. Asia & Oceania. Detroit [Washington, D.C.]:Gale Research, 1995.

—Debra Baron

Who Are the Pakistani Americans?

◆ Country of Origin ◆ Cultural Heritage ◆ Religion ◆ Political History of Pakistan
◆ Population in the United States and Demographics ◆ History of Immigration
◆ Income ◆ Social Structure

◆ COUNTRY OF ORIGIN

The name "Pakistan" means, "land of the pure." It was coined in 1933 by a young Indian Muslim student at Cambridge University in England. The word was meant to express the identity of the Muslims as a separate group from other religious sects in the Indian subcontinent. Pakistan came into being in August 1947, with the partition of British India into two separate states. Up until 1971, what is now Bangladesh was part of the Muslim majority area that seceded to Pakistan. Present day Pakistan borders India on the east, Afghanistan and Iran on the west, China and the central Asian republics on the north, and the Arabian Sea on the south. The total area of the country is 310,402 square miles excluding the disputed areas of Jammu and Kashmir presently administered by Pakistan. Pakistan has three distinct geographical regions, stretching through four provinces: the North West Frontier Province (NWFP), with the Himalayan mountains in the north, the fertile plains of the Punjab, and the desert areas of Sindh and Balochistan.

The population has grown from 84,253,644 in 1981 to 122,786,000 in 1993. The most densely populated region is the Punjab, followed by Sindh. Balochistan, which is mainly a desert, is very sparsely populated and the NWFP is largely a tribal area. Agriculture is the main occupation of a majority of the population, the principal crops being cotton, wheat, barley, millet, sugar cane, rice, maize, and fodder.

◆ CULTURAL HERITAGE

Pakistanis are greatly aware of their rich heritage dating back to the Indus valley civilization that existed at the same time as Mesopotamia. In 327 B.C., Alexander's army succeeded in conquering the northern areas and played a significant role in the ancient Ghandhara civilization. The local Buddhist culture at the time combined with Greek influence and nurtured many artists, intellectuals, and religious philosophers in the region. The Greeks along with the Arabs, Turks, Persians, Mongols, Afghans, Dravidians, the Huns, and the Kushans have contributed to Pakistan's historical experience and culture.

The conquest of Sindh by the Arabs in 711 A.D. started the phase of Muslim rule in India. These new rulers came from central Asia and Afghanistan and brought with them the Arabic, Persian, and Turkish languages. Contact with the regional languages of India resulted in the emergence of a new language, Urdu, which is now the national language of Pakistan. Although Urdu is the national language, English is widely spoken in business and government circles. The dominant local language, however, is Punjabi, spoken by 65 percent of the people, followed by Sindhi (11 percent) and Urdu (9 percent). The remaining 15 percent speak Pushto, Gujarati, and Baluchi. Less than 30 percent of the population is literate.

◆ RELIGION

Islam is the state religion and is professed by over 98 percent of the population. Eighty-five percent of the Muslims are Sunnis, and the rest are Shia. Hindus constitute a small minority, followed by Christians and Buddhists.

◆ POLITICAL HISTORY OF PAKISTAN

Although the idea was first conceived in the 1930s, the major Muslim political party of India, known as the All-India Muslim League, endorsed the concept of a separate country for Indian Muslims in 1940. The League swept the 1946-47 elections, and the British accepted partition. The Indian Independence Act was passed incorporating the principle of a separate Pakistan. The new state which came into being on August 14, 1947, included parts of Bengal and Assam as the eastern wing of Pakistan.

At the time of partition, the Hindu Maharaja of the predominantly Muslim state of Jammu and Kashmir acceded to India. Since division was based on population figures, Pakistan challenged the accession by sending troops into the area. The fight was halted by a UN cease-fire in 1949, leaving Pakistan in control of Azad Kashmir. The Kashmir issue, along with communal rioting at the time of partition, resulted in strained relations between India and Pakistan and have been the cause of two additional wars fought in 1965 and 1971, when Pakistan's eastern wing became the nation of Bangladesh.

Within the first year of Pakistan's inception, Mohammed Ali Jinnah, the president of the All-India Muslim League and Pakistan's first governor-general, died. In 1951, the country's first prime minister was assassinated. Both deaths were a serious blow to Pakistan's political development. In 1958, martial law was declared under Field-Marshal Ayub Khan. A series of unstable quasi-military regimes followed until the nation's first direct election on the basis of universal suffrage was conducted in 1970. The East Pakistani Awami League led the polls with the Pakistan's People's Party a close second. The Awami League was banned by the government on March 3, 1971. Tensions between the West Pakistanis and the East Pakistanis had been rising, largely over the issue of Urdu versus Bengali as the national language. Before issues could be resolved, war broke out between India and Pakistan. Following the surrender of 90,000 troops, Pakistan agreed to a cease-fire. Zulfiqar Ali Bhutto, a young lawyer from a feudal Sindhi family who had been educated at the University of California-Berkeley and Oxford University in England became prime minister of Pakistan. In July 1973, Pakistan officially recognized Bangladesh, and in August a new constitution was adopted.

A general election in 1977 resulted in an overwhelming victory for Bhutto's Pakistan's People's Party. However, the opposition denounced the returns as fraudulent. Before negotiations could be completed, the army took over and arrested many politicians, including Bhutto. General Mohammed Zia-ul-Haq, the army chief of staff, promised elections in 90 days, but elections never materialized. On February 6, 1979, the supreme court refused to overturn a death sentence imposed on Bhutto for conspiring to murder a political rival, and on April 4, despite appeals from all over the world, the former prime minister was hanged. A period of extreme unrest followed; the president banned all forms of party activity and imposed strict censorship on the media. General Zia concentrated on trying to create a government "in conformity with Islam," while the Movement for the Restoration of Democracy started gaining ground. Its Pakistani's People's Party section was headed by Bhutto's daughter, Benazir. On August 17, 1988, a crash of a C-130 plane in Punjab killed all on board including General Zia, Pakistan's top army leaders, and the U.S. ambassador to Pakistan. In November, exactly 90 days after General Zia's death, elections were held and Benazir Bhutto became the prime minister. Two years later, her government was dismissed under charges of corruption and nepotism. An interim government was followed by elections, and Mian Nawaz Sharif was sworn in as Pakistan's first Punjabi prime minister.

However, the Nawaz government was also later dismissed on charges of corruption; however, it was later surprisingly reinstated by the supreme court. The army chief of staff intervened at this point and both the prime minister and the president stepped down to hold elections. The 1993 elections brought the Pakistani People's Party back in power with Benazir Bhutto as the prime minister.

◆ POPULATION IN THE UNITED STATES AND DEMOGRAPHICS

There are approximately 500,000 to 750,000 Pakistanis in the United States. The largest concentration is in New York, California, Texas, and the Chicago metropolitan area. Pakistani immigrants, like their Indian counterparts, tend to settle near major urban centers. Cities like New York, Houston, Chicago, Detroit, and Los Angeles have large Pakistani American communities scattered throughout the suburbs. Pakistani Americans tend to prefer the Northeast and have generally avoided the South with the exception of Texas, Florida, and Georgia. Very few Pakistanis are found in South Carolina, Alabama, Mississippi, Arkansas, Kentucky, Tennessee, or West Virginia. This is mainly due to the industrial opportunities available in the Northeast as compared to more limited opportunities available in the agrarian South.

◆ HISTORY OF IMMIGRATION

The history of Pakistani immigration is closely linked to the overall South Asian immigration to the United States, since Pakistan came into being as late as 1947. Some of the first South Asians to visit the United States were religious scholars in the 1890s. At the turn of the century, the first group of East Indian immigrants arrived on the West Coast. These were mostly Sikhs from the Punjab who settled in British Columbia. In 1908, they numbered about 5,000 and were known as Hindus. These pioneer immigrants encountered racism and hostility from the local people, and in response they formed the Ghadr movement, led by an East Indian lecturer at Stanford University. The Ghadr Party in the United States provided a base for the Indian Nationalist movement in its struggle to gain independence from the British.

In the early years of the 20th century, most of the Indian immigrants were poor farmers. The Immigration Act of 1917 so curtailed the arrival of newcomers that in 1940, there were only 2,400 East Indians in the United States. Pakistanis started arriving in the United States in the 1950s. The most significant wave of Pakistani immigrants came after the Immigration Act of 1965 and continues today. This act, approved by U.S. President Lyndon B. Johnson, abolished the earlier individual country quotas and raised the total number of possible immigrants. Coinciding with political instability in Pakistan, this development in U.S. immigration policy led to a substantial increase in Pakistani immigration to the United States. Pakistan's role as an ally of the United States since the mid-1950s and during the Afghanistan war also helped foster closer relations between the two countries.

Pakistani students had traditionally gone to the United Kingdom for higher education, because Pakistan was a commonwealth member state. However, during the 1950s and 1960s, students started coming to the United States since the chances of employment were promising. Also, given the rise in racist hostilities towards South Asians in Britain, the prospect of moving to the United Kingdom was no longer appealing.

The migration of educated youth out of Pakistan has resulted in the "brain drain" problem faced by most developing countries. The most educated and talented citizens in the nation are lured away to foreign lands by career opportunities. This is particularly true for doctors. The difference between the average salary of medical doctors in the United States compared to those in Pakistan is phenomenal. Given that Pakistan has some of the best medical schools in the world, it is no wonder that there are so many Pakistani American doctors in the United States. Even other native Pakistani students majoring in science and technology abroad and intending to return home often find that they are over-qualified for jobs in Pakistan.

Language

A vast majority of Pakistani immigrants speak Punjabi. However, since English is also widely spoken in Pakistan, Pakistani Americans find it easy to adjust linguistically in their new home. English-language programs from the United States are broadcast on Pakistani television and U.S. products are easily available in stores. Hence, many in Pakistan are somewhat familiar with the language, idioms, and culture of the United States.

Education and Employment

A significant number of Pakistani Americans are highly educated. Many immigrated at a time when there was high demand for engineers, doctors, scientists, and teachers in the United States. In the 1960s, U.S. industry was rapidly expanding, and Pakistani immigrants helped fill the need for skilled professionals. As immigrants, their high levels of education and income prevented them from being "ghettoized" in inner city areas or in low-paying jobs. Since they were not competing for blue-collar jobs, there was virtually no conflict with the U.S. working class.

In general, there was little overt prejudice towards Pakistanis in searching for housing, since there is barely any historic basis for it. The prejudice Pakistanis face most often relates to their being Muslims, and hence, they may experience discrimination and resentment directed towards them whenever anti-Muslim sentiment is aroused.

Immigration in the 1990s

In the 1990s, Pakistani immigrants usually arrive in the United States as students and later find employment predominantly in the fields of medicine, engineering, and banking. However, immigration trends in the 1990s also depict the arrival of members of the Pakistani lower middle-class, which are not as educated and often find jobs as taxi drivers and small business owners. It is difficult to determine the exact numbers of the newcomers, since many arrive on tourist visas and stay illegally in the United States. During the late 1980s, there was a dramatic increase in Pakistani taxi drivers in major U.S. cities. Gas stations and newsstands, particularly in New York City, are favored businesses among the new wave of immigrants.

A Pakistani American family in traditional dress.

♦ INCOME

Pakistani Americans are among the highest salaried workers in the United States. They generally do very well in school, and their aspirations closely match the "American dream." Most are homeowners in suburban localities. There is little tendency to group together in a particular area. Hence, there are generally no significant ethnic neighborhoods where a Pakastani majority resides. The widespread availability of home mortgages combined with small down payment requirements encourages Pakistani immigrants to buy homes, since the status of home ownership is coveted. Property ownership in Pakistan is a symbol of respect and prosperity.

♦ SOCIAL STRUCTURE

Family

Pakistanis have strong extended family networks. It is common to find entire clans that have immigrated to the United States through one family member. Since children, particularly sons, are responsible for aging parents, it is common to have live-in grandparents.

Since the daughter or son-in-law is a potential caregiver, a lot of thought and consensus goes into arranging marriages. A union between cousins is generally considered to be ideal, since it ensures stability in the household, and the extended family's fortunes remain secure.

The greatest social crisis that Pakistanis face in the United States is how to bring up their children in the traditional way. This would exclude dating, late night parties, and the independence that is a normal way of life for U.S. teenagers. The fear of losing their children, particularly their daughters, to the Western way of life makes many immigrants contemplate returning to Pakistan or sending their children to study there. Many communities have established mosque schools for Islamic training to ensure that the children do not stray from their culture. Sometimes these efforts can be confusing for children, particularly if parents themselves do not follow the dictates of the religion very strictly.

The ultimate test for Pakistani Americans is marriage. It is considered very fortunate if a Pakistani American marries within the community or someone from the homeland. Since this culture is patrilineal, it is easier for a man to marry outside the Pakistani community, but it is extremely difficult for a woman to do so.

Women

According to official estimates, Pakistani women form only 12.1 percent of the salaried labor force in Pakistan. Other sources have attributed over 50 percent of agricultural work to rural women, with two-thirds of urban women and half of rural women also engaged in home-based or cottage industry. There are no known official figures on the number of professional Pakistani American women. In general, medicine is a popular career for Pakistani women, as is teaching and working in family-owned businesses.

Most Pakistani women come to the United States as brides, mothers, or sisters of immigrants. For many the culture shock is immense, and it takes a while for them to get used to the independence and the responsibilities of their new lives. Depending upon the socio-economic backgrounds of their families, the experience can be liberating or isolating. Traditionally, Pakistani women are used to being taken care of by their male relatives. For those accustomed to large extended family systems and spending leisure time with numerous friends and cousins, the loneliness of a single family home in the suburban United States can be a drastic change. Others coming from less privileged backgrounds find the conveniences of the West a welcome relief from the material hardships they left behind. Their status is elevated in relation to that of their kin in Pakistan.

A small, though increasing, number of Pakistani women are now arriving as students and seeking employment thereafter, just as their male counterparts have done. After experiencing an intellectual awakening and personal independence at U.S. university campuses, many of them find it hard to return and live under the watchful eyes of their parents.

Sports and Recreation

One of the most popular sports for Pakistanis is cricket, followed by squash, hockey, and polo. Many Pakistani Americans get together on weekends to play cricket. Musical evenings are another favored form of entertainment for Pakistanis and Pakistani Americans. Famous singers and musicians frequently perform in the United States, and proceeds are donated to charity. Pakistani television serials are very popular in the entire South Asian community and are broadcast on cable in the United States.

Traditional Clothing

Pakistan is comprised of different ethnic groups and, therefore, clothes vary according to regions, but generally speaking, both men and women wear the *shalwar kameez* (baggy trousers and long tunic). The men's outfits are in solid somber colors, while the women's clothes can be extremely colorful using yards of material draped in different ways. Cotton and linen are the preferred materials for daily wear, and silk is preferred for formal wear.

The most elaborate outfits are worn at weddings. Fabrics like brocade, velvet, silks, andsatins in jewel-like colors are embroidered with gold and silver threads. The traditional wedding dress for a woman is a red *gharara*—elaborate culottes with a short shirt and long veil that is draped over the head, sometimes covering the face. Men wear a raw silk *sherwani* (long coat) and turban. Pakistani weddings are colorful affairs with lots of dancing and singing, and the celebrations can go on for days.

Since Pakistani men also wear Western clothes, male immigrants to the United States find it easier than female immigrants to adapt to Western clothes. Pakistani clothes are generally ill-equipped to protect against North American winters, and immigrants have had to adapt to a different wardrobe.

Food

Pakistani food is similar to North Indian food. The curries are spicy and eaten with leavened bread called *chapatis* or *nan*. Rice is a staple, and so are lentils cooked with meat and spices. Rich, sticky sweets are a favorite particularly at weddings and festivals. The long, hot summers feature different varieties of mangos eaten ice cold or in the form of milk shakes and sherbets or pickled as condiments. Tea is preferred to coffee. Pakistanis are generally very hospitable; a visitor is commonly offered tea and snacks, not once but several times during a visit.

Pakistani American News Media

There are a number of Pakistani American newspapers that cater to local residents. Some of the more well-known ones are *Millat* and *Pakistan Calling*, both published in New York. In addition to these, Pakistanis often subscribe to their favorite magazine from Pakistan. Some of the most widely circulated magazines include *Newsline* and *Herald*. They help to inform Pakistani Americans of current affairs in Pakistan. Also, most major university campuses have Pakistani students associations that are very active in conjunction with other Pakistanis in the area, assisting in organizing social, religious, and political events.

Ritual Celebrations and National Holidays

All Islamic holidays are observed by Muslim Pakistani Americans. The faithful gather at local mosques on Eid-ul-Fitr and Eid-ul-Azha. The concentrated Pakistani American population in the New York area celebrates with a Pakistan Day Independence parade held around August 14. Colorful floats line Madison Avenue extending to Greenwich Village. The presence of local politicians at the parade is evidence of the increasing numbers and influence of the Pakistani American population.

References

Singh, Jane. *South Asians in North America: An Annotated and Selected Bibliography*. Berkeley, California: Center for South and Southeast Asia Studies, University of California, Berkeley, 1988.

Clarke, Colin, Ceri Peach, and Steven Vertovic, eds. *South Asians Overseas: Migration and ethnicity*. New York: Cambridge University Press, 1990.

Malik, Iftikhar Haider, *Pakistanis in Michigan: A Study of Third Culture and Acculturation*. New York: AMS Press, Inc., 1989.

Political Handbook, 1993. Pakistan Consulate, New York City, 1994.

—Natasha Rafi

14

Who Are the Thai Americans?

◆ Overview ◆ Acculturation and Assimilation ◆ Language ◆ Family and Community Dynamics
◆ Religion ◆ Employment and Economic Traditions ◆ Health and Mental Health Issues
◆ Individual and Group Contributions ◆ Media ◆ Organizations and Associations
◆ Museums and Research Centers

◆ OVERVIEW

The Kingdom of Thailand was known as Siam until 1939. The Thai name is *Prathet Thai* or *Muang Thai* ("Land of the Free"). It is somewhat smaller than Texas and located in Southeast Asia. In shape, Thailand resembles an elephant head. The country covers an area of 198,456 square miles (514,000 square kilometers) and shares a northern border with Burma and Laos; an eastern boundary with Laos, Kampuchea, and the Gulf of Thailand; and a southern border with Malaysia. Burma and the Andaman Sea lie on its western edge.

Thailand has a population of just over 58 million people. Ninety percent of the Thai people are Mongoloid, with lighter complexions than their Burmese, Kampuchean, and Malay neighbors. The largest minority group, about 10 percent of the population, is Chinese, followed by the Malay and various tribal groups, including the Lisu, Luwa, Shan, and Karen. Sixty to seventy thousand Vietnamese also live in Thailand. Nearly all people in the country follow the teachings of Buddhism. The 1932 constitution required that the king be a Buddhist, but it also called for freedom of worship, designating the monarch as "Defender of the Faith." The present king, Bhumibol Adulyadei, thus protects and improves the welfare of the small groups of Muslims, Christians, and Hindus who also worship in Thailand. The Western name of the capital city is Bangkok; in Thai, it is *Krung Thep* ("City of Angels") or *Pra Nakhorn* ("Heavenly Capital"). It is the seat of the royal house, government, and parliament. Thai is the official language of the country, with English the most widely spoken second language; Chinese and Malay are also spoken. Thailand's flag consists of a broad blue horizontal band at the center, with narrower bands of stripes above and below it; the inner ones are white, the outer ones red.

History

The Thais have an ancient and complex history. Early Thai people migrated south from China in the early centuries A.D. Despite the Thai's ethnic similarities with the South Chinese, they had not adopted many religious, educational, or governmental systems of Chinese culture. By the sixth century A.D., an important network of agricultural communities had spread as far south as Pattani, close to the modern border with Malaysia, and to the northeastern area of the country. The Thai nation became known as "Syam," from the Sanskrit *syam* meaning "dark" because of their relatively darker skin color. Eventually, this name became synonymous with the Thai kingdom and the name by which it was known for many years. In the thirteenth and fourteenth centuries, several Thai principalities in the Mekong valley united and sought to break from their Khmer (early Cambodian) rulers. Sukothai, which the Thai consider the first independent Siamese state, declared its independence in 1238 (1219, according to some records). The new kingdom expanded into Khmer and other territory on the Malay peninsula. Sri Indradit, the Thai leader of a Khmer garrison, was the first ruler; he was succeeded by his son, Ram Khamheng, who is still idolized as a hero of Siamese history. He organized a writing system (the basis for modern Thai) and codified the Thai form of Theravada Buddhism. This period is often viewed by modern-day Thais as a golden age of Siamese religion, politics, and culture. It was also one of great expansion: under Ram

Khamheng, the monarchy extended to Nakhon Si Thammarat in the south, to Vientiane and Luang Prabang in Laos, and to Pegu in southern Burma.

Ayutthaya, the capital city, was established after Ram Khamheng's death in 1317. The Thai kings of Ayutthaya became quite powerful in the fourteenth and fifteenth centuries, adopting Khmer court customs and language and gaining more absolute authority. During this period, Europeans—primarily the Dutch—began to pay visits to Siam, establishing diplomatic links with the powerful new kingdom. Early accounts note that the city and port of Ayutthaya astonished its European guests, who noted that London was nothing more than a village in comparison. On the whole, however, the Thai kingdom distrusted foreigners and maintained its distance from the European powers for several centuries.

In 1765, Ayutthaya suffered a devastating invasion from the Burmese, with whom the Thais had suffered hostile relations for at least 200 years. After several years of savage battle, the capital fell and the Burmese set about destroying anything the Thais held sacred, including temples, religious sculpture, and manuscripts. But the Burmese could not maintain a solid base of control, and they were ousted by Phraya Taksin, a Thai general who declared himself king in 1769 and ruled from a new capital, Thonburi, across the river from Bangkok. The Thais regained control of their country, but Taksin's megalomaniacal belief that he was the next Buddha led to his deposition and execution.

Chao Phraya Chakri, another general, was crowned in 1782 under the title Rama I. He moved the capital across the river to Bangkok. In 1809, Rama II, Chakri's son, assumed the throne and reigned until 1824. Rama III, also known as Phraya Nang Klao, ruled from 1824 through 1851; like his predecessor, he worked hard to restore the Thai culture that had been nearly completely destroyed in the Burmese invasion. Not until the reign of Rama IV, or King Mongkut, which began in 1851, did the Thai strengthen relations with Europeans. Rama IV worked with the British to establish trade treaties and modernize the government, and the country managed to avoid colonialization. During the monarchy of his son, Rama V (King Chulalongkorn), who ruled from 1868 to 1910, Siam lost some territory to French Laos and to British Burma. The short rule of Rama VI (1910-1925) saw the introduction of compulsory education and other educational reforms.

Modern Era

In the late 1920s and early 1930s, a group of Thai students living in Paris embraced democratic ideology to such a great extent that they were able to effect a successful—and bloodless—coup d'etat against the absolute monarchy in Siam. This occurred during the reign of Rama VII, between 1925 and 1935. In its stead, the Thai developed a constitutional monarchy using the British model, with a combined military-civilian group in charge of governing the country. The country's name was officially changed to Thailand in 1939 under the influence of Phibul Songkhram's government (he had been a key military figure in the 1932 coup), which lasted from 1932 to the end of World War II.

Japan occupied Thailand during World War II and Phibul declared war on the United States and Great Britain, but the Thai ambassador in Washington refused to make the declaration, eventually leading to Phibul's resignation in 1944. After a short stint of democratic civilian control, Phibul reappeared and took control in 1948, only to have much of his power taken away by General Sarit Thanarat, a military dictator. By 1958, Thanarat had abolished the constitution, dissolved the parliament, and outlawed all political parties. He maintained power until his death in 1963.

Army officers ruled the country from 1964 to 1973, during which time the United States was given permission to establish army bases on Thai soil to support the troops fighting in Vietnam. The generals who ran the country during the 1970s closely aligned Thailand with the United States during the war. Civilian participation in government has been allowed intermittently. In 1983 the constitution was amended to allow for a more democratically elected National Assembly, and the monarch has tended to exert a moderating influence on the military and on civilian politicians.

The success of a promilitary coalition in the March, 1992 elections touched off a series of disturbances in which 50 citizens died. The military suppressed a "prodemocracy" movement on the streets of Bangkok in May, 1992. Following the intervention of the king, another round of elections was held in September of that year, when the current prime minister, Chuan Leekphai, the leader of the Democrat Party, was elected.

Thai in the United States

Immigration by Thais to the United States was nearly nonexistent before 1960, when U.S. armed forces began arriving in Thailand during the Vietnam War. Interacting with U.S. citizens, Thais became more aware of the possibility for immigration to the United States. One of the main avenues of Thai immigration was via marriage to a U.S. citizen; by the 1970s, some 5,000 Thais had emigrated to this country, at a ratio of three women to every man. For the most part, these new immigrants were wives of men in the Air Force who had either been stationed in Thailand or had spent their vacations there while on active duty in Southeast Asia. By 1980, concentrations of Thai people had formed near military installations, especially Air Force bases, in certain U.S. counties. Groups of people of Thai ancestry were reported in the census in many such counties, ranging from Aroostook County (Loring Air Force Base) in Maine to Bossier Parish (Barksdale Air Force Base) in Louisiana and New Mexico's Curry County (Cannon Air Force Base). A few counties with a larger military presence such as Sarpy County in Nebraska, where the Strategic Air Command has been headquartered, and Solano County, California, where Travis Air Force Base is located, became home to larger groups. Fairly large concentrations of Thai were also found in Davis County, Indiana, the location of Hill Air Force Base; Eglin Air Force Base in Okaloosa County, Florida; and Wayne County, North Carolina, where Seymour Johnson Air Force Base is located.

The connection between servicemen who served on operations in Southeast Asia and concentrations of Thais extends also to those military installations that served as training centers during the war. The Army's Fort Bragg center, in Cumberland County, North Carolina, and the Army's intelligence school at Fort Huachuca in Cochise County, Arizona, both list people of Thai ancestry among their populations.

The Thai Dam, an ethnic group from the mountain valleys of northern Vietnam and Laos were also counted as emigrants of Thai ancestry by the U.S. Census Bureau, though they are actually refugees from other countries. They are centered in Iowa, with Des Moines their major settlement. Like other residents of this area, they have coped with problems of housing, crime, social isolation, and depression. Most of them are employed, but in low-paying menial jobs that offer little in the way of advancement.

During the 1980s, Thais emigrated to the United States at an average rate of 6,500 per year. Student or temporary visitor visas were a frequent venue to the United States. The main attraction of the United States is the wide array of opportunities and the higher wages. However, unlike other countries in Indochina, no people whose original homes were in Thailand have been forced to come to the United States as refugees.

In general, Thai communities are tightly knit and mimic the social networks of their native land. As of 1990, there were approximately 91,275 people of Thai ancestry living in the United States. The greatest number of Thais are in California, some 32,064. Most of these people are clustered in the Los Angeles area, some 19,016. There are also high numbers of people whose temporary visas have expired who are believed to be in this area, suggesting that this estimation is low. The homes and business of Thai immigrants are dispersed throughout the city, but there is a high concentration in Hollywood, between Hollywood and Olympic Boulevards and near Western Avenue. Thais own banks, gas stations, beauty parlors, travel agencies, grocery stores, and especially, Thai restaurants. Further exposure to the English language and U.S. culture has caused the population to disperse somewhat. New York, with a population of 6,230 (most in New York City) and Texas (primarily Houston and Dallas), with 5,816, have the second and third largest Thai populations, respectively.

♦ ACCULTURATION AND ASSIMILATION

In interviews, Thai Americans have noted that they adapt very well to U.S. society. Although they maintain their culture and ethnic traditions, they are willing to accept the norms as practiced in this society. This flexibility and adaptability has a profound effect on second generation, U.S.-born Thais who tend to be fully assimilated or Americanized. According to members of the community, the young people's acceptance of U.S. cultural ways has made these new changes more acceptable to their parents, facilitating relations between "established" U.S. citizens and newcomers. With the high concentration of Thais in California and recent efforts to define who is and is not "native," members of the Thai community have expressed fears that there may be problems in the future.

Traditions, Customs, and Beliefs

Thais do not shake hands when they meet. Instead, they keep their elbows at their sides and press their palms together at about chest height in a prayerlike gesture called *wai*. The head is bent in this greeting; the lower the head, the more respect one shows. Children may *wai* adults but they receive a smile in return.

Girls are affectionately called *muu* (pig) because not only is *muu* a favorite food, but it is rounded and rosy. One who asks a girl for sweet smelling roots (*kor horm*) can expect a kiss on the cheek in return. The feet are considered the lowest part of the body, both spiritually and physically. When visiting any religious edifice, feet must be pointed away from any Buddha images, which are always kept in high places and shown great respect. Thais consider pointing at something with one's feet to be the epitome of bad manners. The head is regarded as the highest part of the body; therefore Thais do not touch each other's hair, nor do they pat each other on the head.

A favorite Thai proverb is: Do good and receive good; do evil and receive evil. Fun is an essential ingredient of life for Thais; they try to include as much of it as possible. One surprising difference for Westerners is that Thais consider bats perfectly charming playthings and will laugh to see a Westerner recoil in the animal's presence.

Birth

Pregnant women are not given any gifts before a baby is born so as to keep her from being scared by evil spirits. These evil spirits are thought to be the spirits of women who died childless and unmarried. For a minimum of three days to a month after birth, the baby is still considered a spirit child. It is customary to refer to a newborn as frog, dog, toad, or other animal terms that are seen as helpful in escaping the attention of evil spirits. Parents often ask a monk or an elder to select an appropriate name for their child, usually of two or more syllables, which is used for legal and official purposes. Nearly all Thais have a one-syllable nickname, which usually translates as frog, rat, pig, fatty, or many versions of tiny. Like the formal name, a nickname is intended to keep the evil spirits away.

Spirit Houses

In Thailand, every house or building must have an accompanying spirit house, a place for the spirits (*Phra phum*) of that area to live in. Thais believe that families living in a home without a spirit house cause spirits to live with the family, which invites trouble. Spirit houses, which are about the same size as a birdhouse, are mounted on a pedestal and resemble Thai temples. In Thailand, large buildings such as hotels may have a spirit house as large as an average family dwelling. The spirit house is given the best location on the property and is shaded by the main house. Its position is planned at the time of the building's construction; then it is ceremonially erected. Corresponding improvements, including additions, are also made to the spirit house whenever modifications are made to the main house.

Weddings

Wedding ceremonies can be ornate affairs, or not occur at all. If a couple lives together for a while and has children together, they are recognized as "gradually married;" it is just as simple to gradually divorce. Most Thais do have a ceremony, however, and the wealthier members of the community consider this essential. The two families agree on the expenses of the ceremony and the "bride price." The couple begins their wedding day by feeding the monks in the early morning and receiving their blessings.

During the ceremony, the couple kneels side by side. An astrologer or a monk chooses a favorable time for the couple's heads to be linked with joined loops of *sai monkon* (white thread) by a senior elder. He pours sacred water over their hands, which they allow to drip into bowls of flowers. Guests bless the couple by pouring water in the same way. Despite the presence of monks, it is essentially a nonreligious ceremony and Thais do not make any vows to one another. The two linked but independent circles of the white thread serve to emphasize that the man and woman have each retained their individual identities at the same time that they have joined their destinies.

One tradition, practiced primarily in the countryside, is to have "sympathetic magic" performed by an older, successfully married couple. This duo lies in the marriage bed before the newlyweds, where they say many auspicious things about the bed and its superiority as a place for conception. They then get off the bed and strew it with symbols of fertility, such as a tomcat, bags of rice, sesame seeds and coins, a stone pestle, or a bowl of rainwater. The newlyweds are supposed to keep these objects (except the tomcat) in their bed for three days.

Even in cases in which the marriage has been sealed by a ceremony, divorce is a simple matter: If both parties consent, they sign a mutual statement to this effect at the district office. If only one party wants the divorce, he or she must show proof of the other's desertion or lack of maintenance for one year. The divorce rate among Thais, both officially and unofficially, is high, but the remarriage rate is high as well.

Funerals

For Thais, *ngarn sop* (the cremation ceremony) is the most important of all the rites. It is a family occasion and the presence of Buddhist monks is necessary. One baht coin is placed in the mouth of the corpse (to enable the dead person to buy his or her way into purgatory), and the hands are arranged into a *wai* and tied with white thread. A banknote, two flowers, and two candles are placed between the hands. White thread is used to tie the ankles as well, and the mouth and eyes are sealed with wax. The corpse is placed in a coffin with the feet facing west, the direction of the setting sun and of death.

Dressed in mourning black or white, the relatives gather around the body to hear the sutras of the monks sitting in a row on raised padded seats or on a platform. On the day that the body is cremated, which for persons of high rank can be as long as a year after the funeral ceremony, the coffin is carried out of the house feet first. In order to appease the spirits who are drawn to the funeral activities, rice is scattered on the ground. All the mourners are given small straw stars. These are thrown together on the funeral pyre, which has been piled up with wood under an ornate paste pagoda. The most exalted guest then lights this structure. The actual cremation is attended by the next of kin only and is usually held only a few yards from the funeral pyre. The occasion is generally followed by a funeral feast. On that evening and the two following, monks come to the house to chant blessings for the departed soul and for the protection of the living. According to Thai tradition, the departed family member is advancing along the cycle of death and rebirth towards the state of perfect peace; thus sadness has no place at this rite.

Although many of these traditional beliefs are retained by Thai Americans, according to interviews, Thais often try to adjust their beliefs in order to live in the United States comfortably. The cliché assumption about them is that Thais "bend with the wind," but assimilated Thai Americans are considered quite changed by their relatives back home. Thais are often perceived as too adaptable and lacking in innovation. A common expression, *mai pen rai*, meaning "never mind" or "it doesn't matter," has been seen by some U.S. citizens as an indication of the Thai's unwillingness to expand or develop ideas.

Because of their appearance, Thais are often mistaken for Chinese or Indochinese; one interviewee said he has often heard it said that "that they all look alike." Ignorance such as this has led to many misunderstandings, and can offend Thais, particularly since Thai culture is bound up with Buddhism and Indian culture far more than Chinese culture. In addition, Thais are often assumed to be refugees rather than perceived as the immigrants of choice that they are. Thai Americans are anxious that their presence be seen as a benefit, not a burden, to U.S. society.

♦ LANGUAGE

A member of the Sino-Tibetan family of languages, Thai is one of the oldest languages in East or Southeast Asia. Some anthropologists have hypothesized that it may even predate Chinese. The two languages share certain similarities since they are monosyllabic tonal languages; that is, since there are only 420 phonetically different words in Thai, a single syllable can have multiple meanings. Meanings are determined by five different tones (in Thai): a high or low tone; a level tone; and a falling or rising tone. For example, depending on the inflection, the syllable *mai* can mean "widow," "silk," "burn," "wood," "new," "not?" or "not." In addition to the similarities with Chinese, Thai has also borrowed from Pali and Sanskrit, notably the phonetic alphabet conceived by King Kham Heng in 1283 and still in use today. The signs of the alphabet take their pattern from Sanskrit; there are also supplemental signs for tones, which are like vowels and can stand beside, before, next to, or above the consonant to which they belong. This alphabet was adopted by the neighboring countries of Burma, Laos, and Kampuchea. Although the literacy rate is only 15 percent, most Thais who can read are also able to read ancient tablets because the alphabet has changed so little over the seven centuries since it was established.

Greetings and Popular Expressions

Common Thai greetings are: *Sa was dee*—Good morning, afternoon, or evening, as well as good-bye (by the host); *Lah kon*—Good-bye (by the guest); *Krab*—sir or madam, if one is male; *Ka*—sir or madam, if one is female; *Kob kun*—Thank you; *Prode*—Please; *Kor hi choke dee*—Good luck; *Farang*—foreigner. Aside from these words, there are also polite expressions and phrases that indicate to Thais that one knows something about their culture. One example is: *Chern krab* (if the speaker is male), *Chern kra* (if the speaker is female)—Please, you are welcome, it's all right, go ahead, you first (depending on the circumstances).

♦ FAMILY AND COMMUNITY DYNAMICS

Traditional Thai families form close-knit clans, often incorporating even servants and employees. Togetherness is a hallmark of the family structure: People never sleep alone, even in houses with ample room, unless they ask to do so. Virtually no one is left to live alone in an apartment or house. As a consequence, Thais make few complaints about academic dormitories or the dormitories provided by factories.

The family is highly structured, and each member has his or her specific place based on age, gender, and rank within the family. They can expect help and security as long as they remain within the confines of this order. Relationships are very strictly defined and named with terms so precise that they reveal the relation (parental, sibling, uncle, aunt, cousin), the relative age (younger, older), and side of the family (maternal or paternal). These terms are used more often in conversation than the person's given name. The biggest change that settlement in the United States has brought has been the diminishing of extended families. These are prevalent in Thailand, but the lifestyle and mobility of U.S. society has made the extended Thai family hard to maintain here. Virtually no families of Thai ancestry receive public assistance.

Arrival in the United States has brought an increase in self-determined marriages. Unlike other Asian countries, Thailand has been far more permissive towards marriages of personal choice, though parents generally have some say in the matter. Marriages tend to take place between families of equal social and economic status. There are no ethnic or religious restrictions, and intermarriage in Thailand is quite common, especially between Thai women and *farang* men.

Education has traditionally been of paramount importance to Thais. Educational accomplishment is considered a status-enhancing achievement. Until the late nineteenth century, the responsibility for educating the young lay entirely with the monks in the temple. Since the beginning of this century, however, overseas study and degrees have been actively sought and highly prized. Originally, this sort of education was open only to royalty, but, according to Immigration and Naturalization Services information, some 835 Thai students came to study in the U.S. in 1991.

Cuisine

Thai cooking is light, pungent, and flavorful, and contrary to popular belief, not particularly spicy. The mainstay of Thai cooking, like the rest of Southeast Asia's, is rice. In fact, the Thai words for "rice" and "food" are synonymous. Meals often include one spicy dish, such as a curry, with blander side dishes. Thai food is eaten with a spoon, using a fork to load it. Inviting someone to eat is a normal greeting, to which the polite response is that one has already eaten.

Presentation of food for the Thai is a work of art, especially if the meal marks a special occasion. Thais are renowned for their ability to carve fruit; melons, mandarins, and pomelos, to name just a few, are carved in the shapes of intricate flowers, classic designs, or birds. Staples of Thai cuisine include coriander roots, peppercorns and garlic (which are often ground together), lemon grass, *nam pla* (fish sauce), and *kapi* (shrimp paste). The meal generally begins with a soup, two or more *kaengs* (dishes that include thin, clear, souplike gravy; though Thais describe these sauces as "curry," it is not what most Westerners know as curry), and as many *krueng kieng* (side dishes) as possible. Among these, there might be a *phad* (stir fried) dish, something with *phrik* (hot chili peppers) in it, or a *thawd* (deep fried) dish. Thai cooks use very few recipes, preferring to taste and adjust seasonings as they cook.

Thai Traditional Costumes

Thai women wear a *prasin*, or wrap-around skirt (sarong), which they combine with a fitted, long-sleeved jacket. Among the most beautiful costumes are those worn by dancers of classical Thai ballet. Women wear a tight-fitting under jacket and a *panung*, or skirt, which is made of silk, silver, or gold brocade. The *panung* is pleated in front, and a belt holds it in place. A pailletted and jeweled velvet cape fastens to the front of the belt and drapes down behind to nearly the hem of the *panung*. A wide jewelled collar, armlets, necklace, and bracelets make up the rest of the costume, which is capped with a *tchedah*, the temple-style headdress. Dancers are sewn into their costumes before a performance. The jewels and metal thread can make the costume weigh nearly 40 pounds. Men's costumes feature tight-fitting silver thread brocade jackets with epaulettes and an ornately embroidered collar. Embroidered panels hang from his belt, and his calf-length pants are made of silk. His jewelled headdress has a tassel on the right, while the woman's is on the left. The costumes have no shoes, but many Thais choose to wear a sandal or Western-style footwear. Shoes are always removed when entering a house. Thai Americans wear ordinary Western clothes for everyday occasions.

Holidays Celebrated by Thai Americans

Thais are well known for enjoying festivities and holidays, even if they are not part of their culture; Bangkok residents were known to take part in the Christmas and even Bastille Day celebrations of the resident foreign communities. Thai holidays include New Year's Day (January 1); Chinese New Year (February 15); Magha Puja, which occurs on the full moon of the third lunar month (February) and commemorates the day when 1,250 disciples heard the Buddha speak; Chakri Day (April 6), which marks the enthronement of King Rama I; Songkran (mid-April), the Thai New Year, an occasion when caged birds and fish are set free and water is thrown by everyone on everyone else; Coronation Day (May 5); Visakha Puja (May, on the full moon of the sixth lunar month), is the holiest of Buddhist days: Lord Buddha's birth, enlightenment, and death; Queen's Birthday, August 12; King's Birthday, December 5.

♦ RELIGION

Ninety-five percent of all Thais identify themselves as Theravada Buddhists. Theravada Buddhism originated in India and stresses three principal aspects of existence: *dukkha* (suffering, dissatisfaction, disease), *annicaa* (impermanence, transiency of all things), and *anatta* (non-substantiality of reality; no permanence of the soul). These principles, which were articulated by Siddhartha Gautama in the sixth century, contrasted with the Hindu belief in an eternal, blissful Self. Buddhism, therefore, was originally a heresy against India's Brahman religion.

Gautama was given the title Buddha, or "enlightened one." He advocated the "eight-fold path" (*atthangika-magga*) which comprises high ethical standards for earning merit by conquering desire. The concept of reincarnation is nearly universally accepted. By feeding monks, making regular donations to temples and worshipping regularly at the *wat* (temple), Thais try to improve their situation—acquire enough merit (*bun*)—to lessen the number of rebirths, or subsequent reincarnations, a person must undergo before reaching

Nirvana. In addition, the accumulation of merit helps determine the quality of the individual's station in future lives. *Tham bun,* or merit making, is an important social and religious activity for Thais. Because the Buddhist teachings emphasize philanthropic donations as part of achieving merit, Thais tend to be supportive of a wide range of charities. The emphasis, however, is on charities that assist the indigent in Thailand.

Ordination into the Buddhist order of monks often serves to mark the entry into the adult world. (Ordination is for men only, though women can become nuns by shaving their heads, wearing white robes, and obtaining permission to reside in the nun's quarters on grounds within the temple. They do not officiate at any rituals.) Most Thai men *Buat Phra* (enter the monkhood) at some point in their lives, often just prior to their marriage. Many only stay for a short period, sometimes as little as a few days, but in general they remain for at least one *phansa,* the three-month Buddhist Lent that coincides with the rainy season. Among the prerequisites for ordination is four years' education. Most ordinations occur in July, just before Lent.

The *sukhwan nak* ceremony protects the candidate for ordination from the evil spirits. During this time, he is called a *nak,* which means dragon, referring to a Buddhist myth about a dragon who wanted to be a monk. In the ceremony, the *nak*'s head and eyebrows are shaved to symbolize his rejection of vanity and of sexuality. For three to four hours, a professional master of ceremonies sings of the mother's pain in giving birth to the child and emphasizes the many filial obligations of the young man. The ceremony concludes with all relatives and friends gathered in a circle holding a white thread and then passing three lighted candles in a clockwise direction. Guests generally give gifts of money.

The following morning, the *nak,* dressed in white, is carried on the shoulders of his friends under tall umbrellas in a colorful procession. He bows before his father, who hands him the saffron robes he will wear as a monk. He leads his son to the abbot and the four or more other monks who are seated on a raised platform before the main Buddha image. The *nak* asks permission for ordination after prostrating himself three times to the abbot. The abbot reads a scripture and drapes a yellow sash on the *nak*'s body to symbolize acceptance for ordination. He is then taken out of view and dressed in the saffron robes by the two monks who will oversee his instruction. He then requests the ten basic vows of a novice monk and repeats each as it is recited to him.

The father presents the alms bowls and other gifts to the abbot. Facing the Buddha, the candidate then answers questions to show that he has met the conditions for entry into the monkhood. The ceremony concludes with all the monks chanting and the new monk pouring water from a silver container into a bowl to symbolize the transference of all merit he has acquired from being a monk to his parents. They in turn perform the same ritual to transfer some of their new merit to other relatives. The ritual's emphasis is on his identity as a Buddhist and his newfound adult maturity. At the same time the rite reinforces the link between generations and the importance of family and community.

Thai Americans have accommodated themselves to the environment here by adapting their religious practices when necessary. One of the most far-reaching of these changes was the switch from lunar calendar days to the conventional Saturday or Sunday services that are offered here.

◆ EMPLOYMENT AND ECONOMIC TRADITIONS

Thai men tend to aspire to military or civil service jobs. Women have been traditionally engaged in running businesses, with real estate a popular choice for educated middle-class women. In the United States, most Thais are in small businesses or work as skilled laborers. Many women have opted for nursing careers. There are no Thai-only labor unions, nor do Thais particularly dominate one profession.

Involvement in Issues at Home

In interviews, Thai Americans have noted that they are not active in community politics in this country, but more concerned with issues in Thailand. This reflects the general insulation of the community, where there are specific delineations between northern and southern Thais and where intercommunity outreach with other groups has been almost nonexistent. Thai Americans are quite active in Thai politics and they keep an active watch on economic, political and social movements there. One interviewee noted that any mention of the homeland in the U.S. press or broadcast media is quickly spread throughout the community.

◆ HEALTH AND MENTAL HEALTH ISSUES

With the prevalence of prostitution in Bangkok, AIDS is a huge problem for Thailand. The Thai American community does not have any significant health problems.

◆ INDIVIDUAL AND GROUP CONTRIBUTIONS

Perhaps the greatest contribution from the small Thai American community has been their cuisine. Thai restaurants remain a popular choice in large cities, and the Thai style of cooking has even begun to appear in frozen dinners. Many Thai Americans work in the health-care industry as well. Because their community is so small, Thai Americans' statistics are generally tabulated with those of other Asian Americans; presumably this will change as the community grows.

◆ MEDIA

Television

THAI TV USA offers programming in Thai in the Los Angeles area. Contact: Paul Khongwittaya. Address: 1123 North Vine Street, Los Angeles, California 90038. Telephone: 213-962-6696. Fax: 213-464-2312.

◆ ORGANIZATIONS AND ASSOCIATIONS

The Thai Society of Southern California
2002 S. Atlantic Blvd.
Monterey Park, CA 91754
(213) 720-1596
K. Jongsatityoo, public relations officer
Fax: (213) 726-2666

—Megan Ratner

Who Are the Vietnamese Americans?

♦ First-Wave Immigrants ♦ The Boat People ♦ Immigration Since 1982 ♦ Culture Clash
♦ "A Drop of Blood" ♦ Religion ♦ Tet ♦ Organizations and Media ♦ Employment
♦ Secondary Immigration ♦ Controversies and Tensions ♦ Closing the Circle

Within a brief span of twenty years, Vietnamese immigrants to the United States have made remarkable progress building new lives in their adopted country. Numbering an estimated 850,000 in 1991, Vietnamese Americans are the nation's third largest Asian American population, following the Chinese and Filipinos. They are a diverse group that includes ethnic Chinese, tribal peoples such as the Hmong and Montagnards, and Amerasians, as well as the nearly 250,000 Vietnamese Americans born here since 1975. Even among Asian Americans, the Vietnamese are notable for their resilience in overcoming cultural and linguistic barriers and transcending the trauma of their troubled history.

That history and the United States's role in it have been crucial factors in shaping the Vietnamese experience in the United States. Located south of China on the Indochina peninsula, Vietnam, with a primarily agricultural economy, is one of the world's poorest countries. The annual per capita income of its nearly 65 million inhabitants is an estimated $500. It has been nicknamed "the lesser dragon" due in part to its curling S-like shape, but mainly because of the strong Chinese influence on Vietnam during its 1,000-year occupation of the country (111 B.C.-A.D. 939), which was followed by 900 contentious years of independence under eight different dynasties (A.D. 939-1883), and some seventy years of French colonial rule (1883-1945).

After World War II, Vietnam experienced thirty years of almost continuous warfare. From 1946 to 1954, the nationalist Vietminh, under the leadership of Ho Chi Minh, fought to wrest control of the newly declared Democratic Republic of Vietnam from the French, who withdrew militarily from the conflict following the 1954

Geneva Accords partitioning of the country along the 17th parallel. However, the communist North Vietnamese began almost immediately to wage a guerrilla war against the anti-communist South to reunify the country.

Prompted by fears that a North Vietnamese victory would lead to further communist takeovers throughout Southeast Asia, the United States made its fateful entry into the war. It had 12,000 military advisers in Vietnam by 1962 and sent in combat troops in 1965. In 1973, the United States's divisive military involvement in Vietnam came to an end with the withdrawal of its troops following the signing of the Paris Peace Treaty. However, the war was far from over for the Vietnamese. With the South Vietnamese army weakened by U.S. troop withdrawals and cuts in aid, North Vietnam continued its drive to take over the South, and Saigon fell to communist forces on April 30, 1975. The same day, 65,000 South Vietnamese fled the country. The first wave of Vietnamese immigration to the United States had begun.

♦ FIRST-WAVE IMMIGRANTS

The approximately 130,000 Vietnamese who came to the United States in 1975 following the fall of Saigon differed from latter groups of refugees in significant ways. They were generally better educated and wealthier, had a better command of English, and, in many cases, had military, political, or corporate ties to U.S. citizens. Many were high-ranking military officers and officials of the South Vietnamese government. An unusually high percentage were Roman Catholics. Because of their linguistic and professional skills, these refugees were readily integrated into U.S. society. By 1985, they had achieved economic parity with the general U.S. population. The 1965 Immigration and Nationality Act, which had opened the doors to non-European immigrants, made it easier for Vietnamese to enter the United States. Also, given the U.S. role in the Vietnam War, its government felt morally obligated to help them once Saigon fell to the North. Congress allocated $405 million in resettlement aid for the refugees and passed the 1975 Indochina Refugee Act, which allowed up to 200,000 Southeast Asians to enter the United States under special "parole" status that exempted them from the normal immigration process.

From the island of Guam, the refugees were moved to resettlement camps at four military bases in the United States: Camp Pendleton (California), Fort Chaffee (Arkansas), Eglin Air Force Base (Florida), and Fort Indiantown Gap (Pennsylvania). Here, their papers were processed, and they were offered English classes and assigned to private voluntary organizations (VOLAGs) that would match them with sponsors throughout the country. The goal was to have them spread out rather than concentrated in certain areas to minimize their economic impact on any one community. By the end of 1975, the first refugees were all resettled. Although they mostly held low-paying jobs and increasing numbers were being forced to go on welfare, the government planned to phase out its aid program by 1977 and assumed that its responsibility for Vietnamese refugees was nearing an end. However, events were soon to overtake this assumption in a dramatic fashion.

◆ THE BOAT PEOPLE

As the first wave of Vietnamese immigrants to the United States struggled to begin a new life, their compatriots at home faced increasingly harsh conditions under the communist regime. Many were sent to reeducation camps where they were forced to perform hard labor and undergo intensive indoctrination. Four million urban dwellers were evacuated to "new economic zones" in the countryside and put to work as farmers to alleviate the nation's food shortages. In addition, the government nationalized some 30,000 private businesses and began a new military draft after invading Cambodia in December 1978. Especially hard hit were Vietnam's ethnic Chinese. The long-standing Vietnamese resentment against this group turned to outright persecution when China became Vietnam's adversary in its hostilities with Cambodia. Chinese businesses were seized; Chinese schools were closed; and the Chinese themselves were subjected to restrictive curfews.

Between 1978 and 1979, thousands of ethnic Chinese fled overland to China. In late 1978, 85,000 Vietnamese—Chinese and others—took to the sea, having secured berths in rickety, overcrowded boats, for which they paid up to $2,000 apiece in gold. As they were turned away by countries of first asylum, such as Indonesia, Malaysia, and the Philippines, the plight of these refugees drew international attention. They ran out of food, fuel, and water. Many boats sank from overcrowding. Pirates overtook them in the South China Sea and the Gulf of Thailand, often raping and murdering their helpless victims. When this perilous form of exodus from Vietnam continued into 1979, the United States was forced to act. Rescue ships were sent to the area, and President Jimmy Carter acted to admit greater numbers of refugees into the country on humanitarian grounds. The Refugee Act of 1980 was passed, reducing entry restrictions for Vietnamese refugees. The second wave of Vietnamese immigration to the United States peaked with 95,000 new arrivals in 1980 and 86,000 in 1981. Altogether, 280,500 Vietnamese refugees entered the country between 1978 and 1982.

The new immigrants had a harder time adapting to life in the United States than their predecessors. Most first-wave Vietnamese had been urban dwellers. One-third held professional or white collar positions in Vietnam and more than a quarter of the heads of households had college degrees. In contrast, most of the new wave of immigrants had been fishermen or peasant farmers and had few transferable skills (although many ethnic Chinese had run small family businesses, an experience that would eventually prove useful for those who could scrape together the resources to start new businesses in the United States).

◆ IMMIGRATION SINCE 1982

Since 1982, the United States has accepted fewer refugees. To stem the continuing tide of boat people, the regime in Vietnam agreed to allow direct legal emigration to the United States, resulting in the institution of the Orderly Departure Program. In spite of the long waiting periods involved, 66,000 immigrants arrived in the United States between 1983 and 1991 under this program. Although Amerasians were included in the program, they benefited little from it because the Vietnamese government severely curtailed their emigration to pressure the United States for recognition and aid. In 1987, a mere 213 departures were approved. In the same year, however, the Amerasian Homecoming Act created special provisions for the immigration of 46,000 Amerasian teenagers and their families.

Refugees continued to leave Vietnam, but found the doors to other nations closing on them. Hong Kong, Malaysia, and Thailand considered the waves of boat people "economic migrants" rather than refugees. After the peak immigration years of the early 1980s, the United States admitted between 20,000 and 25,000 refugees—well below the legal maximums—each year for the remainder of the decade. By 1987, government funding of the Office of Refugee Resettlement had been cut to $340 million from a high of $902 million in 1981. With government support waning, Vietnamese Americans have created their own organizations to support the refugees and raise awareness of their situation, such as the Coalition for the Protection of Vietnamese Boat Refugees, and the Indochina Resource Action Center, a lobbying group in Washington, D.C. In addition, Vietnamese American families have played a prominent role in sponsoring new refugees and immigrants to the United States.

The refugee status accorded most Vietnamese who have come to the United States has played a key role both in the immigration process itself and in the resettlement experience of Vietnamese Americans. Although in reality the two categories often overlap in complex ways, for legal purposes "refugee" and "immigrant" are defined differently. An immigrant is one who chooses to leave; a refugee is forced to leave to avoid political, religious, or other types of persecution. Refugees are allowed into a country without regard to ordinary immigration quotas. Thus, unusually large numbers of Vietnamese have been admitted to the United States in a short time period. (Prior to 1970, Vietnamese immigration to the United States totaled only 3,788.) Also, refugees, unlike immigrants, receive various types of government aid. They are eligible for welfare programs (Aid to Families with Dependent Children, Supplemental Security Income, Medicaid, and food stamps) on the same means-tested basis as citizens. In addition, there are special federal programs, such as for refugees who do not meet AFDC or Medicaid criteria.

♦ CULTURE CLASH

Having survived the traumas and losses of war, the brutalities of reeducation camps, and terrors on the seas, the new immigrants faced the challenge of building a new life in an alien culture. The most immediate obstacle was language. Vietnamese and English are strikingly different. In English, one of the main ways of distinguishing meanings is inflection: different word forms for plural nouns and verb tense and agreement. Vietnamese, in contrast, is uninflected, and number and tense are distinguished lexically—that is, by other words in the clause. However, Vietnamese is primarily a tonal language, which means that tones have the same significance as letters in an alphabet. It is mainly by tonal variation (breathy, rising, falling, etc.) that Vietnamese speakers distinguish between otherwise identical words. Thus, the word *ma* may mean "ghost,"

"check," "but," "tomb," "horse," or "rice plant," depending solely on the speaker's tone of voice. There are three basic dialects, and most Vietnamese understand all three. The language was originally written using characters similar to those of Chinese, but this method was gradually replaced between the seventeenth and twentieth centuries by Quoc Ngu, a system of writing Vietnamese using the Roman alphabet devised by European missionaries. Vietnamese names also differ from English ones. As is generally the case with Asian names, the family name comes first and the personal name last. Also, all personal names have a specific meaning. For example, *Tuan Anh* means "famous person;" *Tuyen Thanh* means "gentle river;" and *Loan* (a popular female name) means "great beauty." There are only about thirty Vietnamese family names altogether. *Nguyen* (pronounced "win"), the most common one, is used by almost half the population.

New Vietnamese immigrants have had to adjust to cultural contrasts as dramatic as the difference in languages: contrasts that could make a harrowing experience out of even a routine trip to the supermarket. In Vietnam, product labels show only pictures of the product or its source, unlike the range of images U.S. citizens have come to expect from creative packaging. A Vietnamese mother visiting a Safeway in Oklahoma was horrified to discover pictures of babies on jars of Gerber's baby food and had to be reassured that U.S. citizens do not practice cannibalism. On the other hand, the traditional Vietnamese treatment of fevers and certain other ailments—rubbing tiger balm ointment into the skin with the rough edge of a coin leaving red marks on the skin—has been misinterpreted by some Americans as child abuse. The value placed by the Vietnamese on the Taoist principle of harmony, which often prevents them from openly voicing disagreement, has been another source of cross-cultural misunderstanding. For example, in many cases, refugee sponsors were led to believe that Vietnamese were interested in converting to the sponsor's religion when they were merely showing their appreciation for the sponsor's help by responding positively to inquiries about conversion and were not seriously considering it at all. What was meant as courtesy and tact was misinterpreted as dishonesty.

The strength of Vietnamese culture is attested to by the fact that even under one thousand years of Chinese rule, the people of Vietnam retained their own language and ethnic identity, rejecting Chinese social customs and institutions. Ultimately, the Vietnamese have adapted to life in the United States by a complex combination of both adjusting to and resisting American ways, while retaining their own values.

Southeast Asian refugees at Ft. Indiantown Gap, Pennsylvania, learn how to speak English as part of their resettlement training to help ease them into American society. (AP/Wide World.)

♦ "A DROP OF BLOOD"

Foremost among Vietnamese values is the importance of the family, expressed in the proverb "a drop of blood is better than an ocean of water." Among the Vietnamese, family loyalty is paramount, and aid from blood relatives is unquestioned. Often two to four generations of Vietnamese live under one roof. In 1985, there were 4.4 persons in the average Vietnamese American household. Extended families accounted for 55% of Vietnamese American households, while nuclear families made up 38%, and 7% consisted of family members living with non-relatives. Traditional Vietnamese custom distinguishes between the immediate family (*nha*), consisting of the nuclear family, the husband's parents, and the sons' spouses and offspring, and the *ho*, or extended family, made up of the *nha*, plus all other family members with the same name, and other relatives living in close proximity.

In addition to living relatives, the Vietnamese honor those who have passed away. Ancestor worship is a prominent feature of Vietnamese culture. In the home, altars dedicated to deceased relatives display the relative's picture together with candles, incense, religious objects, and flowers or other offerings, such as the relative's favorite food and beverage. Vietnamese Americans, especially the elderly, travel great distances to be with their families on the anniversary of an ancestor's death, or *ngay gio*, which is commemorated by a festive meal sometimes attended by as many as 100 relatives. The first day of *Tet*, the Vietnamese New Year, is dedicated to ancestors, as well as the holidays of *Thanh-Minh*, a day for visiting the graves of relatives with food, flowers, and incense, and *Trung Nguyen*, or Wandering Souls' Day. Another aspect of Vietnamese family loyalty is their intense concern for relatives still in Vietnam, to whom they send money (on average $100 per month per household) and goods hard to obtain there, such as medicine, vitamins, fabric, and cosmetics. Whenever possible, they sponsor their relatives to join them in the United States. Entire communities pool their resources to sponsor relatives in refugee camps overseas, raising funds at celebrations, religious services, and through special fund drives.

◆ RELIGION

Aside from family, the major source of cultural continuity and stability for Vietnamese Americans has been religion. An estimated 29-40% of Vietnamese Americans are Roman Catholics, a percentage disproportionate to the 10% Catholic minority in Vietnam itself, and one that reflects the high rate of Catholics in the first wave of immigration in 1975. Religious participation by Vietnamese Catholics was facilitated by the "personal parish" provision of the 1983 Code of Canon Law, which helped them establish their own parishes with Vietnamese priests. Today, there are 415 Vietnamese American priests and 400 "religious women" in the country. As of 1991, there were an estimated 100 Vietnamese Catholic communities in the United States and 22 official parishes. The largest, with 10,000 parishioners, was in New Orleans, followed by those in Port Arthur-Beaumont and Houston, Texas. There are also nine Catholic Vietnamese women's congregations in the country.

However, most Vietnamese Americans practice the major religion of their homeland—Buddhism. Introduced into Vietnam by the Chinese, the primary form to take root was Mahayana Buddhism, or the Greater Vehicle, rather than the Theravada, or Lesser Vehicle, a form of Buddhism that is predominant in India. Buddhism among the Vietnamese has been less readily understood and accepted by their U.S. neighbors than Catholicism. However, increased contact with and outreach

Vietnamese refugee Lo Huyhn spends a few playful moments with his daughter Hanh in San Diego, where they now reside. Huyhn, a former paratrooper in the South Vietnamese army, faces an uncertain future because of a disabling back injury that has left him unemployed. (AP/Wide World.)

by the Buddhist community has resulted in greater tolerance. In 1981, the Vietnamese Buddhist Temple in Los Angeles issued a book titled, *The Presence of Vietnamese Buddhists in America*, to commemorate the Buddha's 2,525th birthday. Copies were distributed to Vietnamese temples throughout the country to help promote cultural and religious interchange with U.S. citizens in their areas. In 1987, the Vietnamese Buddhist community in Port Arthur, Texas, completed the renovation of a Baptist church it had purchased to create a Buddhist temple. A number of native Texans participated in the dedication ceremonies, including Mayor Malcolm Clark. As of 1991, there were 80 Vietnamese Buddhist temples across the United States.

While most Vietnamese Americans are either Buddhist or Catholic, other religions are also represented among their numbers, including Confucianism (which some, however, regard as a spiritual philosophy rather than a religion), Taoism, Cao-Dai, which combines several Eastern belief systems, and Hoa-Hao, a meditative sect that originated in the Mekong Delta in 1939. There are also small Muslim and Protestant minorities among Vietnamese Americans.

♦ TET

Many customs have helped the Vietnamese Americans maintain cohesion and preserve their cultural identity, but none is more important than Tet, the Vietnamese New Year. This holiday—a New Year's celebration, spring festival, family reunion, and national holiday—would be the equivalent of Thanksgiving, Memorial Day, New Year's Day, and a birthday rolled into one. It is a time of rebirth and renewal. Members of the community try to settle old scores, pay their debts and forgive past mistakes, and vow to correct their own faults. It is widely believed that the first visitor received during the Tet holiday will affect a family's luck throughout the year. This visit is often "rigged" to ensure that the guest of choice is the first one to arrive. All Vietnamese are considered to have two birthdays: their own and Tet. Marking the first day of the lunar year, Tet usually occurs sometime between January 19th and February 20th. The full holiday lasts for up to seven days, but most people celebrate only the first three. Houses are cheerfully decorated, brightly colored clothing is worn, and special foods are prepared. (In Vietnam, families saved money all year for the Tet celebration.) The first day of Tet is reserved for honoring one's ancestors, who are invited to the festivities the night before at a special ceremony with firecrackers set off at midnight. Traditionally, the second day was set aside for honoring teachers (a sign of the value that Vietnamese place on education), and the third day was for visiting with friends. In the United States, Tet has taken on a special significance as a celebration of the refugees' new beginnings in their adopted country, as well as a time for remembrance—a bridge between the old and the new.

After Tet, the second largest festival is Trung Nguyen, or Wandering Souls' Day, on the 15th day of the 8th month, when the souls of the departed fly back to their relatives for food and shelter, and the wandering souls who have no families are fed as well. Another popular Vietnamese holiday is Trung Thu, also known as Children's Day or Mid-Autumn Festival, celebrated at the harvest moon by children carrying lighted lanterns in an evening procession to the accompaniment of drums and cymbals.

♦ ORGANIZATIONS AND MEDIA

There are several hundred Vietnamese American organizations throughout the country, including community centers, religious organizations, professional associations, political and lobbying groups, and even Vietnamese Lions clubs and scout troops. Increasingly, community organizations are taking the place of government and private sponsor support, offering counseling, legal help, youth and employment services, and senior citizens' programs. Many offer language and history courses and sponsor celebrations of non-Buddhist traditional holidays.

One particular type of organization, the Mutual Assistance Association (MAA), is especially visible in the form of a network of groups across the country. MAAs are private, nonprofit organizations managed and operated by refugees themselves. They perform a variety of functions within the community: assisting refugees in finding employment; offering adjustment skills training, such as learning to drive; and providing family reunification assistance through their nationwide network. Increasingly, MAAs are becoming politically active in lobbying members of Congress on refugee issues and forming political action and advocacy groups.

Vietnamese American media outlets are flourishing. There are over 20 Vietnamese newspapers in the Little Saigon community of Westminster, California alone. Elsewhere, popular publications include *Bau Nguyet Sau Thoi Dam* (New Forum), a bimonthly magazine (circulation over 4,000) published in Dallas by Hiep Thai Dang; *Viet Bao*, originally designed by Dr. David Vu of Oklahoma City solely for Vietnamese readers, but now expanding to serve English language users also; and *Asian Business and Community News*, a monthly newsletter published in Minnesota by Nghi Huynh. Most recently, journalists Tran Da Tu and Son Dieu Nguyen Viet Khanh co-founded *Viet and World Magazine*, an international monthly publication aimed at uniting the two million Vietnamese expatriates in 57 countries all over the world. Tu also publishes the *Vietnam Economic News*, which is distributed on the West Coast. Khanh and Tu have also formed United Media Corporation, a multimedia venture involving book, magazine, and video production.

♦ EMPLOYMENT

The phrase *tran can cu*, which denotes a combination of hard work, patience, tenacity, and a relentless drive to survive and succeed, is often used by the Vietnamese to describe themselves. Their employment history in the United States shows it to be an apt characterization. For most Vietnamese, employment in the United States initially meant a decline in status, often from white collar to blue collar occupations; former army generals worked in greenhouses, and bank managers in restaurant kitchens. Many were drawn to the "informal economy," working for Chinese

Former South Vietnam Premier Nguyen Cao Ky poses in the fishing village of Dulac, Louisiana. Ky now runs a shrimp processing plant in Dulac. (AP/Wide World.)

or Korean Americans, often in the garment or food preparation industries, under substandard health and safety conditions without having their income reported for tax or welfare purposes. In time, most first-wave immigrants worked their way up to better jobs, often by retraining in a new field or passing licensing requirements in their former profession. Second-wave and subsequent immigrants, who generally have fewer job skills, less education, and a poorer command of English, often have remained in blue collar or service sector jobs. A 1984 study of Chinese Vietnamese (many of whom were second-wave immigrants) found half in low-paying jobs with family income below the poverty level. While the incomes of first-wave immigrants equaled or exceeded the national average by 1985, Vietnamese who arrived in the United States between 1976 and 1979 were still earning an average of $14,000 per year in 1987, $3,000 under the U.S. median income.

While the previous occupations of many Vietnamese immigrants, such as farming, trading, or the military, were difficult to translate into positions in the United States, one group of workers was able to transfer its work experience more directly than most. Many fishermen settled in Texas and Louisiana, working around

the clock until they had saved enough money to buy their own boats. However, the intensive fishing practices that were the norm in Vietnam, such as using oversize nets, violated U.S. shrimp and crab fishing industry standards and caused resentment and even violence in some Gulf Coast towns.

Probably the most dramatic employment success for Vietnamese Americans has been in the area of small business. Usually family-run and often catering to Vietnamese customers, typical businesses include restaurants, specialty grocery stores, convenience stores, tailor shops, laundries, beauty salons, boutiques, real estate offices, and garages. The 1986 *Vietnamese Business Directory for Los Angeles and Orange Counties* lists over one thousand businesses, including computer stores, dancing schools, and photography studios. According to the U.S. Census Bureau, there were 25,671 Vietnamese-owned businesses (with receipts totaling $1.36 billion) in the United States in 1987, up from 4,989 in 1982—a staggering 414% increase in five years. The top sectors for Vietnamese businesses in that year were as follows: Services, 10,461; Retail, 6,646; Fishing, 2,230; Manufacturing, 1,947; and Finance, insurance, and real estate, 1,132. Reflecting overall demographic trends in

Moi Nguyen works in a garden in Versaille, Louisiana, a village near New Orleans. He says he emigrated from North Vietnam to South Vietnam in 1954, and then came to Louisiana in 1975. Around 70 percent of Versaille's 4,000 residents are refugees from South Vietnam. (AP/Wide World.)

Vietnamese refugee resettlement, over one third of all Vietnamese businesses are located in California. Business receipts in California's Little Saigon alone totaled $300 million in 1985.

The Vietnamese Chamber of Commerce promotes entrepreneurship through branches around the country, offering training workshops and a variety of publications for those considering opening their own businesses.

♦ SECONDARY IMMIGRATION

Besides the major waves of Vietnamese immigration described earlier, there has been an additional and very significant pattern of refugee movement—a wave of remigration, or secondary immigration, *within* the United States beginning shortly after 1975. Initially refugees moved to wherever they found a sponsor. These sponsors were often found in areas near the original resettlement camps in Arkansas, California, Florida, and Pennsylvania as well as in the five additional states—Iowa, Maine, New Mexico, Oklahoma, and Washington—whose governments sponsored first-wave

refugees. The largest group (27,199) settled in California, with an additional 9,130 in Texas and 3,500 to 7,000 each in Pennsylvania, Florida, Washington, Illinois, New York, and Louisiana. Government policy was to resettle no more than 3,000 refugees in any one area in order to restrict their economic impact on individual communities. However, this system fragmented kinship networks, the refugees' main source of support, and placed many immigrants in small, isolated communities, some with harsh, unfamiliar northern climates. As soon as they could, Vietnamese refugees throughout the country began a secondary migration to urban areas for proximity to relatives, better jobs and welfare benefits, warmer climates, and more comprehensive community services. This left nearly half of all Vietnamese Americans in California and Texas, a proportion that has remained stable throughout subsequent waves of refugee arrivals.

Other metropolitan areas with significant Vietnamese immigration in 1991 included: Anaheim-Santa Ana, 5,366; Los Angeles, 5,156; Houston, 2,518; Boston, 1,458; Atlanta, 1,275; Seattle, 1,255; and Dallas, 1,177. The largest Vietnamese communities are all in

California: Orange County (140,000), Los Angeles County (100,000), and Santa Clara (75,000). Westminster's Little Saigon, south of Los Angeles in Orange County, California, is the Vietnamese American "capital," with thousands of Vietnamese businesses, services, and organizations, and a 1991 population of 400,000.

♦ CONTROVERSIES AND TENSIONS

Despite their resilience and achievements, Vietnamese Americans face tensions and conflicts, some created by the refugee experience itself, others by Vietnam's history of war and political repression.

Life in the United States has upset the Vietnamese family's traditional balance of power between the generations. Parents see their authority declining as children become assimilated to U.S. culture, wearing trendy clothes, dating, and adopting an increasingly individualistic outlook in place of the traditional cooperative and communal one. One controversial challenge to parental authority is the conflict over corporal punishment, an accepted mode of discipline in Vietnam. Vietnamese American children and teenagers learn that what is considered proper discipline in the home is called child abuse outside it. Increasingly, children either threaten to call the police or actually do so when facing a beating. Parents see this as U.S. society undermining their authority within their families. This authority has also been weakened as children become more economically independent than they would have been in Vietnam through jobs, government college aid, and other resources. In many cases, parents are forced to rely on their children's command of English to help them carry out a variety of adult responsibilities. This places the young people in the role of family ambassador to institutions outside the Vietnamese community, further shifting the traditional familial balance of power. Parents worry that the loosening of traditionally strong generational ties will subvert their goal of attaining middle-class status through their children, as well as threatening the survival of Vietnamese identity and culture in this country.

The weakening of generational ties is related to the well-publicized problem of gang violence among Vietnamese American youth. One of the most sensational incidents occurred in 1991, when four Vietnamese gang members—three of them brothers—held 40 hostages at gunpoint for eight and a half hours in a Sacramento electronics store. The siege ended with a shootout which left three gunmen and three of the hostages dead. In Garden Grove, California, police have identified six different Vietnamese gangs. Unlike the Sacramento episode, most gang violence is directed at other Vietnamese, and takes place primarily in their homes, where they often keep their savings and valuables. These crimes often go unreported because victims do not trust police, fear reprisals, or do not want to give their community a bad reputation. There have also been reports of Houston gang members demanding protection money from area merchants. Although some gang members lead conventional lives at home and at school as those in the Sacramento shootout appear to have done, many are youths who came to the United States without families, do not attend or do poorly in school, and speak little English. Some communities have started to respond to gang activity by educating their members about the importance of reporting crimes and other aspects of law.

Another issue Vietnamese American communities must address is emotional health. Many refugees suffer from post-traumatic stress disorder after years of war and loss, but their culture traditionally uses no resources outside the family to cope with emotional distress. Religious and mental health professionals need extra sensitivity to help Vietnamese Americans while also respecting their culture. Reportedly, there is also tension between first- and second wave immigrants. The better educated, more successful first-wave Vietnamese criticize the more recent arrivals as lazy and overly dependent on welfare, while the second wave resents the privilege and perceived snobbery of the more established immigrants.

Relations between the United States and the Socialist Republic of Vietnam have been a highly divisive issue for Vietnamese Americans, many of whom spent years in reeducation camps after the fall of Saigon. The Vietnamese community's staunchly anti-communist majority—some of whom have even sent funds to an insurgent group in Vietnam—have clashed, sometimes explosively, with those advocating closer ties between the two nations. There have been firebombings and other types of attacks, and those traveling to Vietnam on business missions have faced death threats. In 1989, writer Doan Van Toai was shot and critically wounded over this issue.

♦ CLOSING THE CIRCLE

As U.S.-Vietnam relations continue to improve, many Vietnamese Americans are starting to revisit the homeland they left up to twenty years ago. Since the American trade embargo was lifted in February 1994, up to 10,000 Vietnamese a month make the trip. Many are second-generation immigrants who left their homeland as children. Some go solely to see relatives and satisfy curiosity about their homeland. Others, seeing opportunity in the land of devastation they remember, also go to do business, often as representatives of their U.S. employers. And a small but growing contingent is returning there to live. Called *Viet Kieu*, the returnees, often successful young professionals, want to return to their roots and recapture the simpler life their parents and grandparents lived. They can often benefit professionally from family connections, and, with the reciprocity characteristic of the Vietnamese family, some bring along money to help their families establish small businesses of their own. But even as they complete with optimism and pride the circle begun a generation ago in desperation, the Viet Kieu, like their thousands of peers on this side of the Pacific, remain indelibly changed by their experience in the United States and by the challenge of creating harmony—a traditional Vietnamese virtue—out of their discordant history and the melding of two very different cultures.

References

Auerbach, Susan. *Vietnamese Americans*. American Voices. Vero Beach: Rourke Corp., 1991.

Burkett, Tom. "Spreading the News: A New U.S.-based Magazine Bids to Unite 2 Million Vietnamese into a Global Village." *Transpacific*, June 1994.

Buttinger, Joseph. *Vietnam: A Political History*. New York: Frederick Praeger, 1966.

Freeman, James M. Freeman. *Hearts of Sorrow: Vietnamese-American Lives*. Stanford: Stanford UP, 1989.

"Home to America, if Not to Daddy." *The Economist*, May 19, 1990.

Karnow, Stanley. "Little Saigon, Where Vietnam Meets America." *Smithsonian*, Vol.23, No.5, August 1992.

Kibria, Nazli. *Family Tightrope: The Changing Lives of Vietnamese Americans*. Princeton: Princeton UP, 1993.

Mydans, Seth. "Former Refugees See Opportunity in Vietnam." *The New York Times*. Dec. 5, 1994.

Rutledge, Paul J. *The Vietnamese Experience in America*. Bloomington: Indiana University Press, 1992.

Stanek, Muriel. *We Came from Vietnam*. Niles: Albert Whitman, 1985.

Statistical Record of Asian Americans. Ed. Susan and Timothy Gall. Detroit: Gale Research, 1993.

"Their Bonnie Lies Over the Ocean." *The Economist*. April 27, 1991.

Vida, Nina. *Goodbye, Saigon*. New York: Crown Publishers, 1994.

Vidulich, Dorothy. "Religion Central for Vietnamese in U.S." *National Catholic Reporter*, Vol.30, No.44, Oct. 14, 1994.

Worldmark Encyclopedia of the Nations. Third Edition. Ed. Timothy Gall. Detroit: Gale Research, 1995.

—Rosalie Wieder

Chronology

499

Chinese priest named Hui Shen reportedly travels to the North American continent in the year Yung Yang during the Chin dynasty.

1763

Filipinos impressed into the Manila Galleon Trade (1565-1815) between Mexico and the Philippines settle in Louisiana after jumping ship. They build their villages on stilts and fish for their livelihood.

1781

One of the 46 founders of Pueblo de Nuestra Se_ora Reina del los Angeles, now the city of Los Angeles, was Antonio Miranda, of Philippine ancestry.

1784

The Empress of China, first clipper ship to reach China, is anchored at Canton.

1785

Three Chinese crewmen—Asing, Achyun, and Accun—are stranded in Baltimore for almost a year. They lived on public funds in care of Levi Hollingsworth, a merchant.

1787

September 17. The U.S. Constitution is signed at the Pennsylvania State House in Philadelphia, the present Independence Hall.

1788

June 21. The required nine states ratify the Constitution and it becomes the law of the land.

1790

The first U.S. Naturalization Act allows only "free white persons" to become American citizens.

1791

December 15. The Bill of Rights is ratified and becomes part of the Constitution.

1806

Eight shipwrecked Japanese sailors are picked up by an American ship and brought to Honolulu. They become the first Japanese to arrive in the kingdom of Hawaii.

1815

Filipino settlers in Louisiana fight with Jean Laffitte against the British during the Battle of New Orleans.

1830

First U.S. census notation of Chinese in America—the count is three. In 1840, Chinese counted by the census number eight; by 1850, the figure 758. These early census figures probably neglected some of the Asians and Pacific Islanders in the United States.

1843

May 7. The first Japanese arrive in the United States. The best known of these is Manjiro Nakahama, also known as John Mung. He was rescued at sea by an American whaling ship and subsequently educated at Fairhaven, Massachusetts.

1846

Two men from Manila apply for Hawaiian citizenship in Honolulu during the reign of King Kalakana.

Sketch by A. R. Ward of "European and Asiatic" workers completing the last mile of the Pacific Railroad. (Library of Congress.)

1848

Chinese begin to arrive, some as indentured servants, during the California Gold Rush. The bulk of these immigrants later became a source of cheap labor for railroads, mines, fisheries, farms, orchards, canneries, garment and cigar factories, bootmakers, etc.

1850

A Japanese, Hikozo Hamada, also known as Joseph Heco, is rescued at sea by an American sailing ship. He studies in Baltimore, Maryland, and becomes the first Japanese naturalized as an American citizen.

1854

U.S. signs treaty with Japan.

The Chinese Six Companies organizes to protect and regulate Chinese communities.

1856

Foreign miners are harshly taxed to prevent Chinese from panning for gold. Chinese labor soon becomes a sore point with unemployed whites who felt Chinese stole jobs because they were willing to work for low wages.

1859

Chinese are excluded from public schools in San Francisco.

1860

First official Japanese delegation visits the United States; Manjiro Nakahama (see 1843) serves as the official interpreter.

1862

Congress enacts a law that allows "any alien" honorably discharged from U.S. military service to apply for naturalization.

1863

Recruiting begins for Chinese laborers for the Central Pacific Railroad.

1868

About 149 Japanese contract workers arrive in Hawaii to work the sugar plantations.

A meeting of the Workingmen's Party in California. (Library of Congress.)

The United States ratifies the Burlingame Treaty with China, recognizing the right of Chinese to immigrate for "purpose of curiosity, trade, or permanent residence," but expressly restricts the right of naturalization.

1869

May 10. The Transcontinental Railroad is completed by driving a golden spike to join the two ends. Ninety percent of the laborers who built the railroad were Chinese immigrants.

Wakamatsu Tea and Silk Colony is established at Gold Hill (Coloma), California. The grave of "Okei," one of the members of the colony, commemorates the site.

1870

"Naturalization Act" excludes Chinese from citizenship and prohibits entry of wives of laborers (1910). Asian population exceeded 105,000.

Nationwide recession causes West Coast labor problems. "Cheap Chinese labor" becomes the scapegoat. Mobs destroy Chinese communities in many areas of California and other states.

1871

Japan and Hawaii sign a friendship treaty.

1873

Zun Zow Matzmulla becomes the first Japanese midshipman at the U.S. Naval Academy, graduating in 1873.

1876

U.S./Hawaii Reciprocity Treaty allows Hawaiian-grown sugar to enter the United States duty-free.

With economic collapse in the United States, Chinese laborers become scapegoats in some communities. Riots and bloodshed directed at Chinese break out in San Francisco and elsewhere.

1880

Census reports 148 Japanese in the continental United States.

Treaty between U.S. and China gives the United States the right to limit Chinese immigration.

1882

Chinese Exclusion Act prohibits entrance of Chinese laborers, and prohibits courts from issuing citizenship. It was intended to last for only ten years, but was later extended to 1902. The law was passed at the insistence of California.

Knights of Labor and Workingmen's Party (Dennis Kearny) cry "The Chinese Must Go!"

Chinese merchants, particularly launderers and miners, are excessively taxed and certain occupations are restricted: medicine, teaching, dentistry, mining, railroading, and manufacturing.

U.S. and Korea enter into their first treaty.

1883

The Japanese replace the Chinese as a source of cheap labor after the Exclusion Act.

1885

First 859 legal contract laborers, with their families, arrive in the kingdom of Hawaii. King Kalakaua is at the dock to welcome them. Japan had legalized emigration in 1884.

A small group of Korean officials—expelled following an unsuccessful coup attempt—arrive as exiles in San Francisco.

1889

In *Chae Chan Ping v. U.S.*, the Supreme Court decides that despite the Sino-American treaty of 1868 the United States may freely exclude Chinese under the Chinese Exclusion Act.

1890

Significant Japanese immigration begins, mostly male laborers from Hawaii.

Jujiro Wada ("Wadaju") receives honorary U.S. citizenship from the governor of the territory of Alaska for his daring rescue of an ice bound ship by making a long solo journey over ice to Nome for help. The famous Klondike and Fairbanks goldstrikes are both attributed to him.

August 24. Duke Kahanamoku, Native Hawaiian and Olympic swimmer is born in the palace of Princess Ruth in Honolulu, Hawaii.

1892

First Japanese language newspaper in kingdom of Hawaii started in Honolulu.

Geary Act, an extension of the 1882 Exclusion Act, prohibits Chinese immigration for another ten years and denies bail and writ of habeas corpus.

1896

In *Yick Wo v. Hopkins*, an important civil rights case, the Supreme Court rules that a San Francisco safety ordinance that is racially neutral but enforced exclusively against Chinese is unconstitutional and a violation of the Fourteenth Amendment.

The first Japanese-language school in the kingdom of Hawaii is started by Rev. Takie Okumura at Makiki Christian Church in Honolulu.

1898

Seven crewmen of Japanese ancestry die in the sinking of *U.S.S. Maine* in Havana Harbor. This incident begins the Spanish-American War. Other persons of Japanese ancestry serve in the U.S. Navy in the Battle of Manila Bay.

August 12. Increasingly controlled by American business interests, Hawaii is annexed to the United States.

December 10. The Treaty of Paris, which negotiates the end of the Spanish-American War, cedes the Philippines to the United States.

First Japanese language newspaper on the mainland is founded by Kyutaro Abiko in San Francisco. He later establishes the Yamato (farming) colony near Livingston, California.

Manjiro Nakahama (John Mung) dies in Japan.

1899

Buddhist Churches of America established in San Francisco.

1900

Japanese Association of America is founded in San Francisco to counter racial discrimination.

Japanese immigrants begin converting California's barren interior into rich vineyards and truck-farming areas.

Executive Order 589, commonly referred to as the "Gentlemen's Agreement" is issued by President Theodore Roosevelt. Japanese government refuses to issue passports for laborers emigrating to the American mainland, but through agreement allows departure for Hawaii.

Several Japanese become naturalized subjects of the kingdom of Hawaii, but the U.S. territorial government refuses to recognize them.

April 29. Congress passes "an act making appropriations for sundry civil expenses of the government for the fiscal year ending June 13, 1901, and for other purposes." This act empowers the Immigration

Commissioner to take charge of the administration of the Chinese Exclusion Law.

April 30. The Organic Act is signed into law by President William McKinley, establishing U.S. territorial government in Hawaii. Under this act, Chinese in Hawaii are required to apply for certificates of residence.

Some 60,000 Japanese immigrants reside in the Hawaiian Islands, comprising nearly 40 percent of the total population. On the mainland, there are only 24,000 Japanese immigrants.

June 3. The members of the Taft Commission arrive in Manila.

June 14. Hawaii is incorporated as a territory of the United States.

1901

January 9. The first Korean immigrant, Peter Ryu, arrives in Hawaii on a Japanese ship, Kongkong Maru.

Dr. Jokichi Takamine isolates pure epinephrine (adrenaline) at John Hopkins University. A long time resident of the United States, Dr. Takamine declines honorary citizenship until all immigrants of Japanese ancestry are allowed the right to become citizens.

March 3. Congress passes "An act supplementary to an act entitled an act to prohibit the coming of Chinese persons into the United States, approved May 5, 1892." This is an extension to what is commonly referred to as the "Chinese Exclusion Act."

July 4. William Taft becomes the first civil governor of the Philippines.

California's anti-miscegenation law is amended to bar marriages between whites and "Mongolians." This law remains in effect until November 1948.

1902

April 29. Congress passes "an act to prohibit the coming into and to regulate the residence within the United States, its territories and all territory under its jurisdiction, and the District of Columbia, of Chinese and persons of Chinese descent."

White miners drive out Japanese immigrants employed at the Yukon Mining Company at Atkin, Alaska.

Two hundred and thirty-four Chinese are illegally imprisoned in Boston.

July 1. The Philippine Organic Act passes the Senate. This law is the basis for the Philippine policy of the United States during the Taft era (1901-1913).

The Hawaiian Sugar Planters' Association employs David Deshler in Korea to recruit Korean laborers.

December 22. The first group of Korean emigrants aboard the S.S. Gaelic leaves Korea for Hawaii.

Congress indefinitely extends the prohibition against Chinese immigration and the denial of naturalization.

1903

January 13. One hundred Koreans arrive in Hawaii on the S.S. Gaelic and are inspected aboard the ship. Later, they are divided into small groups and are sent to plantations.

About 2,000 Japanese and Mexican sugar beet workers go on strike in Oxnard, California, and form the first successful farmworkers union. The American Federation of Labor, however, refuses to recognize a non-white union.

Seito Saibara, a former member of the Japanese Diet (parliament), settles near Houston to begin a rice-growing industry.

August 26. The pensionado program is authorized, providing aid to Filipinos who wish to study in the United States.

November 3. A group of 100 young Filipinos arrive in California. This is the beginning of the pensionado program, which by 1912 will educate 209 Filipinos and Filipinas in the United States. It costs the U.S. government $479,940.

Korean contract laborers arrive in Hawaii. They subsequently move to the mainland, often to work as railroad laborers.

1904

September 23. Executive Order 38 is issued by the government of the Philippine Islands, applying U.S. government regulations concerning Chinese to the Philippines.

November 29. Syngman Rhee (1875-1965), former politician and president of Korea, arrives in Hawaii aboard the Siberia and begins to organize Korean immigrants for the Korean national liberation movement.

Isamu Noguchi, Japanese American sculptor and architect, is born in Los Angeles to an American mother and a Japanese father.

Asian Indians begin to emigrate to the United States, and by 1923 number approximately 7,000; most of them live on the West Coast.

1905

February 10. The Korean Episcopal Church in Honolulu is founded.

May 14. The Asiatic Exclusion League, a group made up of representatives of 67 labor organizations, is established in San Francisco. Eventually, more than 200 labor unions joined the league to restric Asian immigration through the courts, through propoganda, and through violence.

China launches a nationwide boycott against U.S. goods to protest U.S. discrimination and prejudice against Chinese.

The Korean Evangelical Society is organized in San Francisco.

The Mutual Cooperation Federation is established among Koreans in San Francisco.

1906

March 16. A branch office of the Mutual Cooperation Federation is established in Los Angeles.

Hawaiian sugarcane companies begin recruiting indentured workers from the Philippines.

The San Francisco earthquake destroys the old Chinatown.

Anti-Japanese sentiment intensifies as a result of the quake and difficult economic conditions.

July 18. Future Senator Samuel I. Hayakawa is born in Vancouver, British Columbia, Canada.

The San Francisco School Board creates an international incident when it orders children of Chinese, Japanese and Korean residents to attend the segregated Oriental Public School. Asian American parents protest the decision.

October 26. Secretary Victor Metcalf (1884-1936) is sent to San Francisco by President Theodore Roosevelt to confer with city officials on the question of school segregation.

November. San Francisco School Board removes children of Japanese ancestry from regular school and places them in a segregated school. There were 93 such children, 25 of whom were American citizens.

Lajpat Rai (1865-1928), founder of the India Home Rule League of America, comes to the United States.

December. Negotiations to restrict Japanese immigration begin. They are carried out successfully, and a Gentlemen's Agreement is reached between the United States and Japan in 1908.

A group of fifteen Filipino workers arrive in Hawaii to work for the Hawaiian Sugar Planters' Association.

1907

January 17. U.S. Attorney Devlin files a brief on behalf of Aoki Keikichi against Principal Deane of Redding School to test the constitutionality of the segregation order issued by the San Francisco School Board.

The case of *Aoki v. Deane* is dismissed after President Roosevelt intervenes and forces the San Francisco School Board to rescind its segregation order.

February 20. President Roosevelt signs a bill that further restricts Japanese immigration.

February 26. "The Regulation Governing the Admission of Chinese" outlines procedures for interrogating Chinese entering the United States.

March 14. On the basis of the February 20 immigration law, President Roosevelt issues an Executive Order that bars Japanese from entering the mainland via Hawaii, Mexico, or Canada. In exchange for Roosevelt's intervention in the San Francisco school segregation case, Japan does not protest.

September 2. Representatives from 24 Korean organizations meet in Honolulu and decide to create the United Federation.

October 22. The United Federation publishes its newspaper, United Korean News.

"Gentlemen's Agreement" between the United States and Japan restricts immigration of Japanese laborers. This is a prelude to the passage of a Japanese exclusion act by Congress.

Recruitment intensifies for single Filipino men to work in Alaskan fisheries and the growing agribusiness of Hawaii and California.

American-educated Jo Kamosu Sakai petitions the state of Florida to incorporated the Yamato Colony Association, a settlement of Japanese farmers in southern Florida he founded to grow pineapples.

1908

March 9. The Gentlemen's Agreement between the United States and Japan is officially concluded.

March 23. Chang In-hwan (1875-1930), a Korean patriot, shoots to death an American, Durham Stevens, who supports Japanese takeover of Korea as a protectorate.

May 23. The Korean Women's Association is established in San Francisco.

Buntaro Kumagai, honorably discharged from the U.S. Army, is denied naturalization on the grounds that the words "any alien" means those who are "free white persons or those of African descent."

1909

February 1. The Mutual Cooperation Federation and the United Federation merge into one organization to work together for Korea's independence. The new organization is called the Korean National Association, and it begins publishing a newspaper, *The New Korea*.

August 5. The Payne-Aldrich Tarriff Act goes into effect. The Philippine Tarriff Act also becomes effective on this day. On October 3, 1913, the Payne-Aldrich Act is replaced by the Underwood-Simmons Act which establishes free trade between the Philippines and the United States.

Yung Wing publishes his autobiography, *My Life in China and America.*

Eight thousand Japanese sugar plantation workers go on a strike in Hawaii led by Fred Kinzaburo Makino, an Amerasian of Japanese and German heritage. This is the first major strike by Japanese workers in Hawaii.

1910

Twenty-seven anti-Japanese proposals are introduced by the California legislature. Governor Hiram Johnson, persuaded by President William Howard Taft, discourages the legislature from approving these proposals.

Japanese picture brides arrive in the United States.
Japan declares Korea its colony.

October 10. Syngman Rhee returns to Korea after receiving a Ph.D. degree from Princeton University. He is the first Korean to receive such a degree from an American institution of higher learning.

November 28. Sara Choe, married to Yi Nae-su, arrives in Hawaii. She is the first of 951 picture brides from Korea.

Angel Island was set up as a detention center for nonlaboring Asian immigrants. There are long waiting periods under inhumane conditions, and some commit suicide.

The Supreme Court broadened the 1870 Naturalization Act to include other Asians as well as the Chinese, whom the law originally targeted.

Arthur K. Ozawa, Hawaiian-born graduate of the University of Michigan Law School, is admitted to the bar in Michigan and Hawaii. He is believed to be the first Japanese American lawyer.

Namyo Bessho, honorably discharged after five years in the U.S. Navy, has his application for naturalization rejected.

Japan annexes Korea.

1911

February. Har Dayal (1884-1939), an Asian-Indian political leader, arrives in the United States and later works toward India's independence.

Yi Bom-jin, Korean Minister to Russia, commits suicide to protest Japanese seizure of Korea. He wills $3,000 to the Korean National Association to be used for its political work.

When 11 Korean apricot workers are driven out of Hemet, California, the Japanese consul general offers to assist them. In an indignant remonstrance to the California secretary of state, Korean associations in California assert their separate identity, refuse Japanese assistance, and win de facto recognition of the Korean community in Washington.

August. At an Amateur Athletic Union (AAU) swim meet held in Hawaii, Native Hawaiian Duke Kahanamoku breaks the world record for the 100-yard free-style by 4.6 seconds. Mainland officials question the results, so Hawaiian locals raise the funds to send Kahanamoku to the mainland, where he swims for the first time in a pool in Chicago. At the Olympic trials in Philadelphia, Kahanamoku wins a spot on the Olympic team.

1912

January 1. The Republic of China is founded by Dr. Sun Yat-sen (1866-1925), who becomes its first president.

January 29. The North American Business, Inc., is established by Ahn Chang-ho. The company makes investments in agriculture and business.

Summer. At the Olympic games in Stockholm, Sweden, Kahanamoku ties the world record in a qualifying heat for the 100-meter freestyle, and went on to win the Gold Medal.

September 16. The Korean Youth Corps, established in Hastings, Nebraska, under the leadership of Pak Yong-man (1881-1928), graduates its first class of 13 students.

1913

May 13. The Corps for the Advancement of Individuals is organized among Koreans in America. Ahn Chang-ho serves as chairman of the board of directors.

May 19. The California legislature passes the Alien Land Act, and it is signed into law. According to the statute, a person ineligible for U.S. citizenship is forbidden to purchase land for agricultural purposes, and may lease property for no more than three years. Similar laws are adopted in Washington, Oregon, Idaho, Montana, Arizona, New Mexico, Nebraska, Texas, Kansas, Louisiana, Missouri, and Minnesota.

The Korean Boarding School changes its name to the Central Institute, and Syngman Rhee becomes its principal.

November 1. The Hindu Association is established under the leadership of Har Dayal.

Olympian Duke Kahanamoku is greeted by President Calvin Coolidge. (International Swimming Hall of Fame.)

1914

June 10. The Korean Military Corps is organized by Pak Yong-man who believes that Korea's independence will come only if Japan is defeated militarily.

1915

Duke Kahanamoku, Gold Medalist in the 100-meter freestyle in 1912, causes a sensation when he visited Australia for a surfing exhibition.

Hearst newspapers report "Japan Plans to Invade and Conquer the U.S.," a florid and sensational story that launches an anti-Japanese campaign.

March 11. *The New Korea* is printed on an Intertype machine, invented by Yi Dae-wi.

October 15. Mike Masaoka, future national secretary for the Japanese American Citizens League, is born.

1916

The Wah Chang Trading Company is established in New York by Li K.C.

October 8. Future Senator Spark M. Matsunaga is born in Kauai, Hawaii.

1917

February 5. President Woodrow Wilson vetoes a bill passed by Congress on December 14, 1916, but Congress overrides his veto and it becomes effective on this day. The Asiatic Barred Zone Act precludes immigration from all of Asia and India.

March 6. Chandra K. Chakravarty, founder of the Pan Asiatic League, is arrested in connection with the Hindu Conspiracy case; Ram Chandra, who worked with Har Dayal for India's independence, is also tried in the case. He is shot to death in the courtroom on April 23, 1918.

June. Twenty-nine thousand *issei*, and some *nisei*, register for Selective Service in the Territory of Hawaii during World War I. (*Issei* refers to first immigrant generation; *nisei* refers to the first American-born generation.)

1918

July 29. The New Church, led by Syngman Rhee, is established among Koreans in Hawaii.

1919

March 1. Koreans in Korea protest Japanese colonial rule with a nonviolent nationwide demonstration. Many Koreans are killed by Japanese police. News of this protest, which begins the Korean Independence Movement, reaches Koreans in Hawaii and the mainland United States on March 9. The Korean National Association launches a fund-raising campaign for independence funds and collects $10,000.

April 14-16. One hundred fifty Koreans attend the first Korean Liberty Congress in Philadelphia, which is designed to draw the world's attention to the plight of Koreans in Korea.

September. Valentine Stuart McClatchy (1857-1938) forms the California Joint Immigration Committee and uses it to drum up support for his anti-Japanese activities.

The American Loyalty Club is organized in San Francisco by a small group of nisei.

The Korean Independence Movement and Declaration (3/1/1919) and the news of its brutal suppression by Japan energizes Korean American churches and study groups to redouble aid.

1920

January 19. California 1913 Alien Land Act is amended to close loopholes in the original law. The revised edict prohibits Asian immigrant parents from serving as guardians of property for their minor citizen children, and also prohibits any leasing of land to aliens.

Led by the Filipino Federation of Labor, plantation workers of Japanese and Filipino ancestry strike for six months in Hawaii demanding higher wages and better working conditions.

Duke Kahanamoku breaks his own world record for the 100-meter freestyle at the Olympic games in Antwerp, Belgium, just in time for his 30th birthday.

Women win the constitutional right to vote.

February 20. The School of Aviation is founded in Willows, California, when Kim Chong-nim donates three airplanes. Future pilots are to be trained to fight against the Japanese Empire.

Charles Ho Kim and Kim Hyong-sun establish the Kim Brothers Company in Reedley, California.

A special act directed against Chinese women denies them automatic citizenship if they marry an American citizen.

1921

January 22. The Caballeros de Dimas-Alang is established in San Francisco as a fraternal organization.

The Philippine Independent News, the first Filipino newspaper in the mainland United States, is published in Salinas, California.

Picture bride immigration stops after the United States convinces the Japanese government to cease issuing passports to prospective brides.

Fifty-eight Japanese immigrant laborers in Turlock, California, are forcibly removed and warned never to return.

There are about 1,000 immigrant Japanese mining coal in central Utah.

March 21. The Korean Resident Association is created in Hawaii.

May 19. President Warren Harding signs the nation's first quota immigration act into law. It eventually leads to the 1924 National Origins Act.

The Seattle Progressive Citizens League is established by nisei Americans to fight against racial discrimination.

July 7. The Comrade Society is organized, led by Syngman Rhee.

1922

September 22. Congress passes the Cable Act, which revokes the American citizenship of any citizen woman marrying an alien ineligible for U.S. citizenship.

November 13. In Ozawa *Takao v. United States* the Supreme Court upholds the Naturalization Law, which means that aliens (specifically Japanese and other Asian immigrants) are ineligible for citizenship and cannot be naturalized.

1923

February 19. In the case of *United States v. Bhagat Singh Thind*, the Supreme Court declares Asian Indians ineligible for U.S. citizenship.

March 5. The American Loyalty Club of Fresno is organized, and Thomas Yatabe is chosen president of the organization. This is the beginning of the Japanese American Citizens League.

The certificate of naturalization obtained in 1921 for Tokutaro Nishimura Slocum is revoked. Slocum was a sergeant major with the 82nd Division in France during World War I and was severely wounded.

1924

February 2. The Legionarios del Trabajo is organized in San Francisco.

May 26. President Calvin Coolidge signs into law the Immigration Act of 1924, also known as the Quota Immigration or National Origins Act. It excludes the immigration of all Asian laborers, except for Filipinos who were already U.S. nationals.

Duke Kahanamoku suffers his first defeat at the Olympic games in Paris, France, when he is beaten by 19-year-old Johnny Weissmuller, who went on to play Tarzan in several Hollywood movies. Kahanamoku won the Silver Medal, and his brother, Sam, won the Bronze.

Congress passes the American Indian Citizenship Act, allowing Native Americans to become citizens in their homeland.

Japan changes its nationality law so that children of Japanese parents born in the United States are not Japanese nationals, unless parents specifically register the child at a Japanese consulate within 14 days after birth. The law also allows children born prior to 1924 to renounce their Japanese nationality. The United States follows the same principle of conferring American citizenship upon children born of American parents in foreign countries.

September 7. Future Senator Daniel Inouye is born in Honolulu, Hawaii.

1925

May 25. The Supreme Court rules on the case of *Chang Chan et al. v. John D. Nagle*, declaring that Chinese wives of United States citizens are not allowed to come to the United States in accordance with the ImmigrationAct of 1924.

Legislative act makes Filipinos ineligible for U.S. citizenship unless they serve three years in the U.S. Navy.

A district court in Massachusetts approves naturalization for Hidemitsu Toyota, who served in the U.S. Coast Guard from (1913 to 1923). The Court of Appeals, however, cancels his certificate of citizenship, and the U.S. Supreme Court upholds the cancellation, ruling that he is ineligible for citizenship because he is neither white nor black.

1926

The China Institute in America, Inc., is founded to promote cultural understanding between China and the United States.

1927

The Supreme Court upholds the ruling of the Circuit Court of Appeals on the case of *Weedin v. Chin Bow* and declares that a person born abroad of U.S. parent(s) who has never lived in the United States cannot be a citizen of the United States.

The Great Depression increases anti-Asian attacks and riots, especially against Filipinos who were concentrated in agricultural stoop labor.

James Sakamoto (1903-1955), who later becomes an important figure in the development of the Japanese American Citizens League, becomes the first nisei to fight professionally at Madison Square Garden.

During the American Federation of Labor's annual convention, delegates resolve to encourage Congress to prohibit Filipino immigration.

1928

January 1. The *Japanese American Courier* is published by James Sakamoto in Seattle, Washington.

May 18. House Bill 13,900 is introduced by Congressman Richard J. Welch and Senator Hiram Johnson of California. The bill is designed to exclude Filipinos from the United States.

June 29. *The Samil Sinbo*, or *The Samil News*, is published by a group of Korean students in New York. Among them are Chang Dok-su, Yun Ch'i-yong, and Ho Chung, all of whom play major roles in South Korean politics after the end of World War II.

Dhan Gopal Mukerji publishes *Gay-Neck, The Story of a Pigeon*, which wins the Newbery Award. The book was also named by the American Institute of Graphic Arts as one of the fifty best books of the year.

1929

February 28. Philippine Labor Commissioner Cayetano Ligot recommends to the Hawaiian legislature that Filipinos be prevented from coming to Hawaii unless they have guaranteed jobs or sufficient funds with which to return home.

April. Kido Saburo, Thomas Yatabe, and Clarence Arai propose the establishment of the Japanese American Citizens League (JACL).

1930

January 22. Fermin Tober is killed during an anti-Filipino riot in Watsonville, California.

Kang Younghill (1903-1972) publishes *The Grass Roof*, which is well received by the U.S. public.

February 26. Los Angeles Superior Court judge J.K. Smith rules that Filipinos are members of the "Mongolian" race. This opens the way for invalidating more than 100 interracial marriages performed since 1921.

August 29. The Japanese American Citizens League, formed to focus on educational issues and civil rights, holds its first national convention in Seattle.

The U.S. Census counts 45,208 Filipinos and Filipino Americans in the 48 mainland states. The actual figure is probably higher.

1931

The Cable Act is amended, allowing U.S. women to retain their citizenship after marriage to aliens ineligible for U.S. citizenship.

The India Society of America is founded by Hari G. Govil in New York.

Bruno Lasker is commissioned to study Filipino immigration to Hawaii and the United States.

March 1. Koreans in Kauai establish the United Society.

September 18. Japan invades Manchuria, a region in northeastern China.

1932

In response to the Japanese occupation of Manchuria, Secretary of State Henry Stimson declares that the United States will not recognize territorial claims prompted by means of force. Chinese in the United States support U.S. policy and render financial support.

December 20. Congress passes the Hare-Hawes-Cutting Act, which bars Filipino immigration to the United States because they have been ruled ineligible for U.S. citizenship.

In the Cable Act, U.S.-born American women marrying foreign-born Asians automatically lose their citizenship, although they can regain it through the naturalization process.

Chinese tong wars erupt. Tongs were ostensibly mutual aid societies, but they often developed into organized crime syndicates that settled turf disputes with violence.

1933

Adolph Hitler named Chancellor of the Third Reich (Nazi Germany).

Japan withdraws from the League of Nations.

November 30. The Filipino Labor Union is founded; by the end of the year, it has established a number of branch offices in central California.

1934

March 24. President Franklin D. Roosevelt signs the Tydings-McDuffie Act, which prohibits Filipino immigration. The Act declares the Philippines a commonwealth, although true independence will not be granted until 10 years after the passage of the bill. All foreign-born Filipinos are now aliens, not nationals, and their immigration is restricted to 50 a year. This results in the separation of many families.

August 27. The Salinas Lettuce Strike, led by the Filipino Labor Union, is called against the Central California Vegetable Growers and Shippers' Association.

October 8. Syngman Rhee marries an Austrian woman, Francesca Donner, and draws a great deal of criticism from the Hawaiian-Korean community because she is white.

1935

July 10. The Filipino Repatriation Act is signed into law, allowing Filipinos in the United States to go back to the Philippine Islands at government expense. Once there, however, they can only return as part of the annual quota.

Italy's army invades the kingdom of Abyssinia (Ethiopia).

After years of campaigning for the restoration of his naturalized U.S. citizenship, Slocum finally succeeds. The congressional bill that restores his U.S. citizenship

also grants citizenship to approximately 500 Asians who served honorably with the U.S. armed forces during World War I.

August 17. The Philippine Commonwealth is organized and M. D. Guervarra elected president.

Lin Yutang (1895-1976) publishes *My Country and My People*.

1936

Abiko Kyutaro (1865-1936), founder of the *Nichi Bei Times*, dies.

In a bloody rebellion, Japanese Army officers try to take over the Japanese government. The rebels surrender only when Emperor Hirohito himself appeals to them to put down their arms.

Cable Act of 1922 repealed.

After the Sian Incident, during which Chiang Kai-shek was imprisoned by his generals, Chinese in the United States send cables to the rebels urging them to release Chiang. Chiang is released on December 25.

Ahn Ik-t'ae (1906-1965), a Korean composer in Philadelphia, completes his composition of the Korean national anthem.

November. Japan joins Germany and Italy in an Anti-Comintern Pact against the Soviet Union.

The Congress of Industrial Organization (CIO) admits workers of Japanese ancestry and other non-whites into mainstream organized labor.

1937

One of the first sociological studies on Koreans in Hawaii is completed by Bernice B.H. Kim at the University of Hawaii.

July 7. Full-scale war between Japan and China begins. Many concerned Chinese in the United States send their financial contributions to help China repel aggression.

United States breaks off commercial relations with Japan.

October 21. Haan Kil-soo, a Korean resident in Hawaii, testifies before the Congressional State Committee that the Japanese government is attempting to unite Asians in Hawaii against the whites.

1938

March 24-26. The first Filipino National Conference is held in Sacramento, California.

Hiram Fong (1907-) is elected to the legislature of the Territory of Hawaii.

V.S. McClatchy (1857-1938), leader of the anti-Japanese movement, dies.

1939

June 30. *The Filipino Journal* is published by the Filipino Agricultural Workers Union.

Korean Americans picket in Los Angeles against U.S. scrap iron and airplane fuel shipments to Japan. This is the first public demonstration in the United States against Japan's invasion of China.

September 1. German troops invade Poland. Britain and France declare war on Germany.

The Intermountain District Council of the Japanese American Citizens League is organized by Mike Masaoka.

1940

President Franklin Roosevelt declares an embargo on most goods to Japan.

The Metropolitan Museum of Art in New York acquires a painting by Chinese American watercolorist Dong Kingman. This purchase was the first acquisition by that museum of any work by an Asian American artist.

March 9. Leaders of the Japanese American Citizens League meet with the Los Angeles City Council and assure members of their loyalty.

March 21. Leaders of the Japanese American Citizens League meet with officials of the Army and Navy Intelligence Service and pledge their loyalty and cooperation.

July 14. German troops occupy Paris. Italy enters the war on Germany's side.

September. Germany, Japan, and Italy sign the Tripartite Pact, committing each of them to wage war against any nation that attacks any of the signatories.

Franklin D. Roosevelt is re-elected as president to an unprecedented third term.

September 7. Haan Kil-soo urges Koreans registering as aliens in Hawaii, as required by the Alien Registration Act of 1940, to do so as Koreans and not as Japanese subjects.

1941

Haan Kil-soo charges that Japan plans to attack the United States and that the Japanese in Hawaii are ready to assist Japan in case of war with the United States.

February 2. Upon his arrival in the United States, Japanese Ambassador Admiral Kichisaburo Nomura tells all Japanese Americans to be loyal and true to the United States.

May 9. The Japanese American Creed by Mike Masaoka is published in the Congressional Record.

June 22. Germany invades the Soviet Union.

July. President Roosevelt places an embargo on the shipment of petroleum products to Japan. To impede Japan's war effort, the British and Dutch impose similar sanctions, cutting off Japan's oil supply.

Japanese troops occupy Indonesia.

July 26. The United States abrogates its treaty of commerce and friendship with Japan and freezes the assets of Japanese nationals in the United States.

October 16. In Japan, the civilian government under Prince Fumimaro Konoye falls and is replaced by a military cabinet headed by General Hideki Tojo.

November. A report prepared by Curtis B. Munson and submitted to the president and secretary of state certifies that Japanese Americans possess an extraordinary degree of loyalty to the United States, and that immigrant Japanese are of no danger to the United States. Years of secret surveillance by the FBI and office of Naval Intelligence corroborate the report.

November 25. Japan's naval fleet sails for Hawaii.

December 7. Japan makes a surprise attack on Pearl Harbor.

Hawaii's governor places the islands under martial law. Restrictions apply to everyone.

December 8. The United States declares war on Japan.

December 9. One hundred sixty Hawaiian issei community leaders are sent to the Sand Island (Honolulu) detention camp.

December 11. Germany and Italy declare war on the United States.

In response, the United States declares war on Germany and Italy.

December 15. Secretary of the Navy Frank Knox states that "the most effective fifth-column work of the entire war was done in Hawaii," implicating Japanese Americans as saboteurs. The statement, later found to be based largely on rumors, was completely misleading and false.

December 18. General Delos C. Emmons is named new commander of the Army and Admiral Chester Nimitz becomes commander of the Navy. General Walter C. Short and Admiral Husband E. Kimmel, who previously occupied the positions were each cited for "error of judgment" because they failed to foresee the Japanese attack and were forced to retire.

December 19. General Emmons rejects a suggestion made by the Joint Chiefs of Staff in Washington to intern all persons of Japanese ancestry residing in Hawaii at either the former leper colony site on Molokai or in mainland detention camps.

December 24. General John L. DeWitt, head of the Western Defense Command, rejects the idea of interning Japanese Americans by stating, "An American citizen, after all, is an American citizen." He changed his mind later.

Massive voluntary enlistment of Asian Americans into U.S. armed forces begins. Nisei volunteers come from Hawaii and internment camps.

Kido Saburo (1902-1977), president of the Japanese American Citizens League, sends a telegram to President Franklin Roosevelt pledging the loyalty and cooperation of the nisei.

1942

January 5. War Department classifies Japanese American men of draft age as 4C, enemy aliens. This designation is not changed until January 1943.

January 25. The Roberts Commission issues its investigation report on the attack on Pearl Harbor. Based on rumors and innuendo, the report heightens the fear of possible sabotage on the West Coast.

January 26. Hearst newspapers on the West Coast engage in a vilifying attack on Japanese Americans and begin the public outcry for a mass exclusion policy.

February 9. General Emmons rejects a War Department order directing him to fire all Japanese American civilians employed by the Army in Hawaii.

February 19. President Roosevelt signs Executive Order 9066 authorizing the Secretary of War or his designated military commander to establish military areas and to evacuate civilians from these areas. This action is responsible for removing and relocating more than 110,000 persons of Japanese ancestry from the West Coast.

February 20. The first boatload of 172 issei internees depart Honolulu for mainland internment camps. By the end of 1943, a total of 1,037 Japanese will be sent from Hawaii to mainland internment camps.

February 21. The Tolan Committee holds its first meeting in San Francisco.

A Caucasian is convicted of spying for Japan. Between 1942 and 1944, 18 Caucasians were charged with spying for Japan; at least ten were convicted. In contrast, no person of Japanese ancestry was ever charged with espionage.

February 25. Residents of Japanese ancestry on Terminal Island in Los Angeles harbor are given 48 hours to leave the island.

March 1. General DeWitt establishes the Wartime Civilian Control Administration (WCAA) to handle forced removal and interim detention. Col. Karl R. Bendetsen is put in charge.

March 2. General DeWitt, Western Defense commander, issues Proclamation No. 1 ordering the removal of persons of Japanese ancestry from Bainbridge Island, WA. This is the first of a series of 108 military proclamations which result in the detention of over 120,000 Japanese Americans from the West Coast.

March 18. President Roosevelt signs Executive Order 9102 establishing the War Relocation Authority.

March 21. Congress passes Public Law 77-503, making any violation of the military orders under Executive Order 9066 a crime.

March 28. Minoru Yasui turns himself in for arrest at the Portland Oregon, police station to test the discriminatory curfew regulations issued by General DeWitt.

April 2. California fires all Japanese Americans in the state's civil service.

April 20. At the request of the U.S. government, 141 South American civilians of Japanese ancestry arrive in San Francisco aboard a U.S. vessel. By the end of 1943, 2,100 persons of Japanese ancestry, most from Peru, have been taken as hostage for future prisoner exchanges.

April 22. The War Department completes the formation of the First Filipino Infantry Battalion.

May 5. Gordon Hirabayashi of Seattle refuses to follow curfew and exclusion orders to test the constitutionality of the military orders.

May 12. Kanesaburo Oshima is shot and killed by a guard at the Fort Sills, Oklahoma, Internment Camp.

Fred Korematsu is arrested in Oakland, California, for violating orders to report for detention.

May. Of those sent into detention camps, the average age for issei males is 54 years; for issei females it is 47 years.

Captain Joseph J. Rocheford breaks the Japanese naval code that helps the United States win the Battle of Midway.

May 26. An all-nisei infantry battalion is formed in Hawaii.

June 1. The Army Intelligence School which teaches Japanese to soldiers, moves from San Francisco's

Presidio to Camp Savage, Minnesota, and is reorganized as the Military Intelligence Service (MIS) Language School.

June 4-6. The Battle of Midway, considered the turning point of the war in the Pacific. U.S. Naval Intelligence reports that the Japanese naval fleet is virtually destroyed.

The threat of a West Coast invasion, the premise for interning Japanese Americans, no longer exists. At this time only 17,000 Japanese are in detention camps; 120,000 will eventually be held.

June 5. Japanese are removed from Military Area No. 1, which includes the western half of Washington, Oregon, and California and southern Arizona.

Under DeWitt's order, all persons of Japanese ancestry in the Pacific Coast region are now in temporary detention camps called "assembly centers."

The all-nisei battalion from Hawaii is sent for training at Camp McCoy, Wisconsin, and on June 12 becomes the 100th Infantry Battalion.

June 17. Milton Eisenhower resigns as director of the War Relocation Authority (WRA), the governmental body that provided for the relocation, maintenance, and supervision of Japanese Americans whose removal seemed necessary for national security. Eisenhower had stated he was "sick of the job" and often had trouble sleeping at night. He is succeeded by Dillon S. Myer.

June 26. Native Sons of the Golden West, a Chinese civil rights group, files suit in San Francisco to strip Japanese Americans of their citizenship.

July 27. Hirota Isomura and Toshio Obata are shot and killed by guards at the Lordsburg, New Mexico, internment camp. Both victims were invalids, Obata a hospital patient.

October 30. The Army completes its transfer of all inmates from 15 temporary assembly centers to 10 permanent WRA detention camps, called Relocation Centers.

November 18. The Poston strike occurs at the Poston War Relocation Center.

December 6. Mass demonstrations erupt at the Manzanar, California, detention camp to protest the arrest without charge of Harry Ueno. James Ito and James Kanagawa are killed when military police fire into a crowd.

1943

February. 100th Infantry Battalion at Camp McCoy, Wisconsin, is ordered to Camp Shelby, Mississippi, to complete training.

February 5. The Wyoming state legislature denies U.S. citizens at its Heart Mountain detention camp the right to vote. Similar laws are passed by other detention-camp states.

February 8. A loyalty questionnaire is administered at all ten detention camps to men and women over age 17.

February 14. Congress of American Citizens is formed at Heart Mountain to protest the loyalty questionnaire under the circumstance of imprisonment without due process.

March 20. WRA is authorized to issue conditional leave permits for those cleared by Washington. Leaves were issued with restrictions.

April. War Department insists on revising DeWitt's Final Report to conceal evidence that would be damaging to the government in the pending Hirabayashi and Yasui cases.

April 9. Nationals of the United States and citizens of the Philippines are allowed to hold real property in California, according to Robert W. Kenny, Attorney General of California.

April 11. James Hatsuaki Wakasa, age 63, is shot and killed by a camp guard at the Topaz detention camp in Utah for wandering too close to the fence.

April 13. DeWitt testifies before the House Naval Affairs Subcommittee in San Francisco: "A Jap's a Jap. You can't change him by giving him a piece of paper."

April 17. U.S. Attorney General Francis Biddle in his memo to the President states: "I shall not institute criminal proceedings [against Italian and German aliens] on exclusion orders which seem to me unconstitutional . . . It [Executive Order 9066] was never intended to apply to Italians and Germans."

May. The all-Japanese American 442nd Regimental Combat Team (RCT) assembles for training at Camp Shelby, Mississippi.

June 21. The Supreme Court rules on *Hirabayashi v. United States*, declaring that the curfew law imposed on all persons of Japanese ancestry is constitutional.

June 29. Galley proof of DeWitt's original Final Report is destroyed and all records on the matter placed in a confidential file.

July 15. WRA designates Tule Lake, California, as a segregation center for those detainees who would not sign the loyalty oath.

September 2. The 100th Infantry Battalion, which had left Camp Shelby (Mississippi) on August 11th, lands at Oran, North Africa. On September 26, the 100th secures a beachhead landing at Salerno, Italy.

November 4. A mass demonstration takes place at Tule Lake to protest the death of a farm worker. The Army takes over the camp with tanks and continues to occupy it until January 14, 1944.

Chinese immigrants are granted the right to naturalization as a gesture of goodwill toward an ally.

December 1. Elmer Kira is shot and wounded by a guard at the Gila River, Arizona, detention camp. He is transferred to Arizona State Hospital.

December 4. Military Order No. 4, which exempts Koreans in the United States from enemy alien status, is issued.

December 9. The Senate passes Joint Resolution 93, granting Philippine independence by presidential proclamation once the Japanese have been defeated and normal conditions have been restored in the islands.

The all-nisei 100th Battalion is incorporated into the 442nd Regimental Combat Team.

December 17. Congress passes the so-called Magnuson Act, "to repeal the Chinese Exclusion Act, to establish quotas, and for other purposes." This law allows Chinese to become naturalized citizens and gives China a quota of 105 immigrants per year.

1944

January. DeWitt's Final Report, containing false claims, is released by the War Department.

January 20. War Department reinstates the draft for nisei in detention camps.

February 16. WRA is transferred to Department of Interior.

March 1. The Heart Mountain Fair Play Committee holds a mass meeting. Four hundred nisei vote unanimously to resist the draft until their constitutional rights are restored.

March 24. One hundred six nisei soldiers at Fort McClellan, Alabama, refuse to undergo combat training in protest of their families continued incarceration. Twenty-one are court-martialed and sentenced to prison. Others are assigned to the 1800th General Service Battalion.

May 24. James Okamoto is shot and killed by a guard at Tule Lake.

June 2. The 442nd Regimental Combat Team, which later includes the all nisei 100th Battalion, lands in Italy. It suffers 314 percent casualties in unit strength and becomes the most decorated unit for its size and length of service during World War II.

June 10. The 100th Infantry Battalion and 442nd RCT are united. By then the 100th have over 900 casualties and is known as the "Purple Heart Battalion."

June 26. Sixty-three young nisei men at Heart Mountain are convicted of refusing to report for induction. Two hundred sixty-seven from all detention camps are eventually convicted of draft resistance.

July 1. President Roosevelt signs Public Law No. 405, allowing U.S. citizens to renounce their citizenship in time of war.

August 1. Manuel Quezon (1878-1944) dies in New York.

The War Relocation Authority announces that all relocation centers will be closed by the end of 1945.

The Philippine Cultural Society is established in San Francisco.

The Indian Society of Yuba and Sutter counties is organized by a group of East Indians living along the Feather River and in Yuba City, California.

August 30. Koreans in the mainland United States organize the Post-War Assistance Society and begin to send relief goods to Korea. Another society with an identical name is established in Hawaii on March 10 and begins to collect relief goods to be sent to Korea after the war.

September 7. The Western Defense Command issues Public Proclamation No. 24 revoking exclusion orders and military restrictions against persons of Japanese ancestry.

October 19. Martial law is terminated in Hawaii.

October 30. The 100th/442nd rescues the Texas "Lost Battalion" after five days of continuous battle. The unit suffers over 800 casualties, including 184 dead, to rescue 211 Texans.

November 2. Seven leaders of the Heart Mountain Fair Play Committee are convicted of counseling others to resist the draft.

December 17. Anticipating the Supreme Court's decision on the following day, the War Department revokes the West Coast exclusion order against Japanese Americans, effective January 2, 1945.

December 18. The Supreme Court rules on the cases of *Korematsu v. United States* and *Endo, Ex parte*. In *Korematsu*, the Court rules the evacuation order (Executive Order 9066) constitutional. In *Endo*, the same Court declares contradictorily that the government cannot hold a loyal, law-abiding citizen in detention against his or her will.

December 28. President Harry S. Truman signs into law the War Brides Act of 1945, allowing 722 Chinese and 2,042 Japanese to come to the United States between 1946 and 1953.

1945

January 2. Japanese Americans forcibly interned are allowed to return to the West Coast as of this date.

April 5. The supposedly impregnable Gothic Line is broken by the 100th/442nd Regimental Combat Team in the Po Valley (Italy) Campaign.

April 29. The 522nd Artillery Battalion (of the 442nd RCT, temporarily assigned to another unit) is among the first U.S. troops to liberate the Dachau concentration camp in Germany.

May 7. Germany surrenders.

June. Japan wants to end the war and seeks mediation from the Soviet Union.

August 6. The first atomic bomb is dropped on Hiroshima, Japan.

August 8. The Soviet Union enters the war against Japan and invades Manchuria.

August 9. The second atomic bomb is dropped on Nagasaki, Japan.

August 14. Japanese Emperor Hirohito broadcasts Japan's decision to surrender.

September 2. Japan's surrender is formalized aboard the *USS Missouri* in Tokyo Bay.

December 14. The 10th District Court of Appeals overturns the convictions of the seven Heart Mountain Fair Play Committee leaders.

1946

January 9. The first Congressional Medal of Honor awarded to a Japanese American is given posthumously to Pfc. Sadao S. Munemori, who was killed in action on April 5, 1945 in Italy. This honor is bestowed after an investigation by the chairman of the Military Affairs Committee found that no nisei had been granted the Medal of Honor despite the fact that a substantial number had been recommended.

February 23 . A group of 432 persons of Japanese ancestry are repatriated to Japan. They are known as disloyal citizens.

March 20. The last of the detention camps, Tule Lake, closes.

June 14. President Harry S Truman signs the Filipino Naturalization Act into law.

June 29. Congress approves G.I. Fiancées Act, which enables fiancées (or fiancés) of U.S. military personnel to immigrate to the United States. Immigrants from Japan are allowed for the first time since 1924.

June 30. The War Relocation Authority program is officially finished.

July 2. The Luce-Celler Bill is signed into law, allowing Asian Indians to become U.S. citizens and establishing a quota of 100 immigrants from India to the United States per year.

July 4. The Philippines gain independence from the United States. This had been promised in 1934 when the Tydings-McDuffie Act was passed.

July 15. The all-Japanese military unit, the 100th/442nd, parades down Constitution Avenue in Washington and receives a Presidential Unit Citation (their 7th) from President Truman.

Filipino and Indian immigrants gain naturalization privileges in recognition of their support and contribution during World War II.

1947

Chinese in the United States send $70 million to their families, relatives, and organizations in China between 1938 and 1947.

December 12. President Harry S Truman grants full pardon to all 267 Japanese American draft resisters.

1948

January 19. In *The People v. Oyama*, the Supreme Court rules California's escheat action—in which the state had attempted to seize lands belonging to Japanese Americans—unconstitutional.

At the London Olympics, Filipina American Vicki Manalo Draves becomes the first woman in Olympic history to win both the high (platform) and low (springboard) diving gold medals. Another diver, Korean American Major Sammy Lee, wins the gold medal in the men's diving division; he will later win another gold medal at the 1952 Helsinki Games.

May 3. In *Shelley v. Kraemer*, the Supreme Court rules that race-restrictive housing covenants are unenforceable.

June 7. The Supreme Court invalidates racial restrictions for commercial fishing licenses in *Takahashi v. California Fish and Game Commission*

Olympic divers, Korean American Sammy Lee (second from left) and Filipina American Victoria Manalo-Draves, both capture gold medals at the 1948 Olympics. (International Swimming Hall of Fame.)

declaring Section 990 of the Fish and Game Code of California unconstitutional.

June 25. President Harry S Truman signs into law the Displaced Persons Act of 1948, allowing as many as 15,000 Chinese in the United States to adjust their legal status.

July 2. President Truman signs into law the Japanese American Evacuation Claims Act, enabling former detainees to file claims against the government for their financial losses. Unfortunately, claimants receive less than ten cents on the dollar for lost property. Many could not even file a claim because required documentation had been lost or destroyed during the incarceration.

October 6. The Supreme Court declares California's ban on interracial marriage unconstitutional.

1949

October 7. Iva Toguri D'Aquino (1916-), also known as Tokyo Rose, is sentenced to a 10-year prison term in San Francisco. She is released on January 28, 1956.

1950

June 25. The Korean War begins. The conflict brings Korean war brides to the United States; many U.S. citizens adopt Korean war orphans.

September 23. The McCurran Internal Security Act is passed. Its Title II provision, citing the incarceration of Japanese Americans as a precedent, authorizes the President to incarcerate any person on mere suspicion without evidence. Six sites for detention camps in the United States are designated, one of which is Tule Lake.

1951

Chinese in the United States are prevented from sending money to their families and relatives in mainland China.

April 11. General MacArthur is relieved of his command by President Truman when they disagree over how to conductthe war.

September. Japan signs a peace treaty with the United States and 47 other nations by which Japan regains her independence. On the same day, Japan signs a security treaty with the United States that continues U.S. military bases in Japan and commits the United States to defend Japan.

The MGM movie, *Go For Broke*, based on the 100th/442nd Regimental Combat Team is released.

So Jae-p'ill (1866-1951), also known as Philip Jaisohn, dies. He was the first Korean to become a naturalized citizen.

1952

April. The U.S.-Japan peace treaty, signed in September 1951, formally ending war between the two nations, goes into effect.

April 17. In its ruling on *Fujii v. California*, the California Supreme Court rules that alien land laws violate the Fourteenth Amendment by being racially discriminatory.

At the Summer Olympics in Helsinki, Japanese Americans Ford Konno and Yoshinbu Oyakawa win Olympic gold medals in swimming for the first time; Japanese American Tommy Kono wins the gold for weight-lifting; and Korean American Sammy Lee sets new records when he wins his second gold medal for diving. Lee's achievement came on August 1, 1952, his 32nd birthday.

The McCarran-Walter Immigration and Nationality Act goes into effect, repealing the National Origins Act of 1924 and allowing immigration quotas to Japan and other Asian countries. McCarran-Walter Act (Immigration and Nationality Act of 1952) confers the rights of naturalization and eventual citizenship for Asians not born in the United States and sets a quota of 105 immigrants per year for each Asian country.

1953

The Refugee Relief Act, expiring at the end of 1956, allows Chinese political refugees to come to the United States.

May 2. The day is declared Korean Day in the United States, and U.S. citizens are encouraged to make donations in money and materials to assist Koreans.

July 23. The armistice ending the Korean War is signed.

September 25. California Governor Earl Warren appoints John F. Aiso of Los Angeles the first judge of nisei origin on the mainland.

1954

Chinese in the United States with technical knowledge are allowed to leave for mainland China.

South Americans of Japanese ancestry held as hostages in U.S. detention camps are allowed to apply for permanent residence status in the United States after Peru refuses them reentry. Attorney Wayne M. Collins of San Francisco is instrumental in this effort.

1955

James Wong Howe (1898-1975) wins an Oscar for cinematography on *The Rose Tattoo*, which helps to revive his career with the major studios.

Although Filipino Americans are the second fastest growing ethnic group in the United States, their average income is very low.

1956

Dalip Singh Saund, Asian Indian American, wins election to the U.S. House of Representatives from the 29th district in California, becoming the first member of the U.S. House of Representatives of Asian descent.

The Filipino United Community Organization is established in San Jose, California.

Harry Holt, a resident of Creswell, Oregon, returns from Korea with eight Korean orphans, whom he adopts. Later he establishes the Holt Adoption Agency, which brings thousands of Korean orphans to the United States.

California alien land laws are repealed by a two to one majority by the voters of California.

1957

Chen-Ning Yang (1922-) and Tsung-dao Lee (1926-) share the Nobel Prize for physics.

Chin-Yang (C.Y.) Lee publishes the best-selling *Flower Drum Song*, which would provide the basis for the highly successfuly Rodgers and Hammerstein musical on Broadway.

Sessue Hayakawa (1889-1973) stars in *Bridge on the River Kwai*.

May 1. The Korean Foundation is organized with Kim Ho as its president to promote higher education among Koreans in the United States.

1959

August 21. Hawaii becomes the fiftieth state of the Union.

Hiram Fong becomes the first Chinese American elected to the Senate, and Daniel Inouye is the first Japanese American to be elected to the House of Representatives. Senator Fong and Congressman Inouye are from Hawaii.

President Lyndon Johnson chose the Statue of Liberty as the site for the signing of the immigration law repealing quotas by national origin. The photographer, Japanese American Yoichi R. Okamoto, served as official White House photographer from 1964–68. (LBJ Library Collection.)

The Immigration and Naturalization Service establishes a procedure to monitor the status of illegal Chinese immigrants, resulting in 8,000 confessions.

Wilfred C. Tsukiyama becomes the first Chief Justice of Hawaii's Supreme Court.

1962

Daniel Inouye is elected U.S. senator from Hawaii.

"Spark" Masayaki Matsunaga is elected to the U.S. House of Representatives from Hawaii, where he would serve seven terms before being elected to the U.S. Senate.

Seiji Horiuchi of Brighton, Colorado, becomes the first Japanese American elected to a mainland state legislature.

Zubin Mehta, at age 26, becomes the music director of the Los Angeles Philharmonic. He is the youngest conductor of a major American Orchestra.

1964

Patsy Takemoto Mink is elected to Congress.

Yoichi R. Okamoto, a Japanese American, becomes head of the White House photo office for President Lyndon Johnson. He will remain in that post until 1968.

Chinese American author Bette Bao Lord publishes *Eighth Moon: The True Story of a Young Girl's Life in Communist China*, recounting the experiences of her sister, Sansan.

August 7. In the Tonkin Gulf Resolution, Congress formally authorizes President Lyndon B. Johnson to take military action against North Vietnam.

1965

January. Patsy Takemoto Mink takes the oath of office for the first of six consecutive terms as Hawaii's representative to the U.S. Congress. She is the first woman to represent Hawaii, and the first Asian American woman elected to Congress.

October 3. The president signs a new immigration law that not only repeals the National Origins Act of 1924, but also establishes a new immigration policy to enable large numbers of Asian immigrants to come to the United States.

Rapid population growth, urbanization, and the increasingly authoritarian character of the Korean government fuels Korean immigration to the United States. By 1976, Korean immigration exceeded 30,000, leading to the emergence of "Koreatowns" in Los Angeles and Chicago.

The Filipino American Political Association is established in San Francisco.

1966

Chinese American Gerald Tsai starts the Manhattan Fund, riding the the tide of the "go-go" years on Wall Street.

March Fong Eu is elected to the California Legislature, becoming the first Asian American assemblywoman in California history.

Mako, the Japanese American actor, earns an Oscar nomination for Best Supporting Actor in *The Sand Pebbles*. He wins a Golden Globe Award for the performance as well.

1967

June. Anti-miscegenation laws are ruled unconstitutional by the U.S. Supreme Court. (*Loving v. Virginia.*)

1968

Har Gobind Khorana (1922-) is awarded the Nobel Prize for physiology.

The Whitney Museum stages a retrospective of the work of Isamu Noguchi, sculptor and architect.

Student protests begin at San Francisco State College, spilling over to the University of California at Berkeley in 1969.

Duke Kahanamoku, Native Hawaiian Olympic swimmer and world-class surfer, dies at the age of 77.

1969

Filipino American Roman Gabriel, professional football player with the Los Angeles Rams, wins the Jim Thorpe Trophy, the National Football League's Most Valuable Player award given by the Associated Press. Quarterback Gabriel completes 196 of 371 passes that year for 2,779 yards, and sets a Rams record with 25 touchdown passes.

As a result of the student protests, Asian American studies programs are established at colleges. Japanese American history is taught as an academic subject for the first time.

Sociologist and professor Harry Kitano publishes *Japanese Americans*, the first coherent account of the experiences of Japanese Americans after World War II.

Florence Makita Hongo brings together a dozen Japanese American educators in California to establish what will become the Japanese American Curriculum Project (JACP), the nations' largest nonprofit clearinghouse for Asian American books and educational materials. In 1994, the group will change its name to Asian American Curriculum Project.

The first pilgrimages to the former mass-detention campsites of Tule Lake and Manzanar begin. Other sites are visited in later years. The annual Manzanar pilgrimage is the most consistent.

Yoko Ono married musician and ex-Beatle, John Lennon.

1970

The Japanese American Citizens League (JACL) national convention held in Chicago passes the first of numerous resolutions seeking redress for World War II internment of Japanese Americans.

Japanese American employees of the state of California receive retirement credit for time spent in detention camps. Eventually, similar credits were allowed for federal employees and those receiving Social Security.

Seiji Ozawa is made artistic director of the Tanglewood Music Festival in Massachusetts, the summer home of the Boston Symphony Orchestra.

1971

Norman Mineta is elected mayor of San Jose, California, becoming the first Japanese American mayor of a major city.

Robert Matsui wins his first political campaign when he is elected to Sacramento, California City Council where he would serve until his successful run for U.S. Congress in 1978.

Title II of the McCurran Internal Security Act, which would have legalized detention camps during times of national emergency, is repealed.

The court awards $10,000 per individual to 1200 Vietnam war protesters who were arrested on the Capitol steps and detained without being charged for up to 72 hours.

President Richard Nixon appoints judge Herbert Choy, Korean American to the U.S. Court of Appeals for the Ninth Circuit. Choy becomes the first Asian American to be named to a federal court.

Diver Greg Louganis scores a perfect ten in the Amateur Athletic Union (AAU) Junior Olympics.

1972

Ken Kawaichi and Dale Minami cofound the Asian Law Caucus (ALC), a legal advocacy organization dedicated to helping Asian Americans in the areas of civil

Greg Louganis displays his score, a perfect ten. (International Swimming Hall of Fame.)

rights, employment and housing discrimination, and immigration. Minami becomes ALC's first attorney.

Martial law in the Philippines increases political activism among Filipino Americans.

May 10. The Ryukyu Islands, including Okinawa, are restored to Japan, ending the United States' 27-year occupation.

1973

Seiji Ozawa becomes music director of the Boston Symphony Orchestra.

Major General Dewey K. K. Lowe, USAF, becomes the first Asian American promoted to flag rank in the U.S. Armed Forces.

The Manzanar detention camp is designated a California state historical landmark, with a bronze plaque installed to commemorate the site. In subsequent years, many other detention campsites are given similar designations and plaques.

Japanese American writer Jeanne Wakatsuki Houston, with her husband James Houston, publishes *Farewell to Manzanar*, a recollection of the Wakatsuki

family's memories of three-and-a-half years of internment during World War II.

George Morikami donates 35 acreas to the Palm Beach County (Florida) for the establishment of a park. Morikami Park was dedicated the following year.

Chinese Americans organize under the leadership of K.L. Wang to educate the public on cultural and civil rights issues concerning Chinese Americans. Their inaugural ball was held in June in Washington, D.C.

July 20. Chinese American actor and martial artist Bruce Lee, dies mysteriously at the age of 32.

1974

March Fong Eu is elected Secretary of State in California with a record-setting three million votes. Eu would be relected four times; in 1994, while serving her fifth term, she was appointed ambassador to Micronesia.

In *Lau v. Nichols*, the Supreme Court rules that failure to provide adequate education for non-English-speaking students violates the Equal Protection Clause of the Constitution.

Norman Y. Mineta of California becomes the first mainland Japanese American elected to Congress.

George R. Ariyoshi of Hawaii becomes the first Japanese American elected governor of a state.

1975

April 15. The Interagency Task Force iscreated to coordinate all U.S. government activities in evacuating U.S. citizens as well as certain Vietnamese citizens from Vietnam.

Shahir Kadir, an Indonesian entrepreneur, successfully challenges a discriminatory District of Columbia law limiting business ownership to U.S. citizens.

The fall of Vietnam and Cambodia begins large-scale immigration of Vietnamese, Laotian, and Cambodian refugees to the United States. Repression within Vietnam and Laos results in many boat people escaping and seeking immigration to the United States.

May 24. The Indochina Migration and Refugee Assistance Act is passed to provide funds for refugee resettlement programs.

Ann Kiyomura, a Japanese American, and Kazuko Sawamatsu of Japan win the Wimbledon women's doubles tennis title.

E.O. 9066, Inc. in Los Angeles and the Seattle JACL Redress Committee become the first groups to activate a redress campaign.

Emperor Hirohito of Japan makes his first post-World War II visit to the United States.

1976

September 10. The Indochinese Refugee Children Assistance Act provides funds for the education of refugee children from Vietnam, Cambodia, and Laos.

"Spark" Masayuki Matsunaga is elected to the U.S. Senate from Hawaii after serving seven consecutive terms in the U.S. House of Representatives.

Chinese American author Maxine Hong Kingston publishes *The Woman Warrior*, portraying the conflicting messages sent to her as she forged her own identity as a Chinese American woman.

Alfred Wong is the first Asian/Pacific American appointed Marshal of the U.S. Supreme Court. He was also the first to serve as special agent in the White House Secret Service.

Eduardo Manlapit becomes the first Filipino American county executive in the United States, serving as mayor of Kauai.

Samuel Ting (1936-) shares the Nobel Prize for physics with Burton Richter.

Executive Order 9066, responsible for the evacuation, removal, and detention of persons of Japanese ancestry during World War II, is officially rescinded.

S.I. Hayakawa is elected to U.S. Senate, becoming the first immigrant (Canadian-born) of Japanese ancestry elected to Congress.

1977

January 19. Iva Toguri D'Aquino (Tokyo Rose) is pardoned by President Gerald Ford.

Morikami Park, Museum of Japanese Culture, and Japanese Gardens is opened to the public on land given to Palm Beach County, Florida, by Japanese American George Morikami.

The Honorable Patsy T. Mink is appointed assistant secretary of state in the Oceans and International Environment and Scientific Affairs (OES) by President Carter.

1978

Robert Matsui is elected to the U.S. Congress as the representative from California's fifth district, the Sacramento area.

Asian Indian American Zubin Mehta becomes the music director of the New York Philharmonic.

The East Wing of the National Gallery of Art in Washington, D.C., designed by Chinese American architect I.M. Pei, is dedicated.

The Walker Art Center in Minneapolis stages a retrospective of the work of Japanese American sculptor, Isamu Noguchi.

House Joint Resolution 10007 officially recognizes Asian/Pacific American Heritage Week.

Japanese American Citizens League (JACL) national convention held in Salt Lake City resolves to seek $25,000 for each detainee and launches a national redress campaign.

November 25. The first Day of Remembrance pilgrimage and program are held at the former temporary detention camp site in Puyallup, Washington.

1979

John Ta-Chuan Fang establishes *Asian Week*, a national weekly English-language newspaper covering Asian American news.

Ruthann Lum McCunn publishes *An Illustrated History of the Chinese in America*.

The John F. Kennedy Library, designed by Chinese American architect I.M. Pei, is dedicated in Cambridge, Massachusetts.

A national Asian/Pacific American movement to unify all Asian Americans begins under the leadership of Mary and Mark Au. Their Asian American Heritage Council, Inc. is intended to educate communities about cultural and civil rights issues. The first festival is held on the Washington Monument grounds in Washington, D.C.

February 19. On the anniversary of the signing of E.O. 9066, the cities of San Francisco and San Bruno, California, proclaim a day of remembrance and mark the occasion with a pilgrimage to the Tanforan camp in San Bruno. Other cities, counties, and states also proclaim this a day of remembrance.

The National Council for Japanese American Redress is formed in Seattle. Its goal is to effect a judicial remedy for wartime detention.

1980

The Refugee Act of 1980 is signed into law by President Jimmy Carter, enabling more refugees to enter the United States.

Asian/Pacific Americans, according to the U.S. Census Bureau, number 3.5 million, or 1.5% of the total U.S. population which is double the 1970 figure.

July 31. The Commission on Wartime Relocation and Internment of Civilians (CWRIC) begins gathering facts to determine if any wrong was committed against U.S. citizens affected by Executive Order 9066.

The National Coalition for Redress/Reparations is formed in Los Angeles and San Francisco. It provides an activist workforce for the redress campaign. Bay Area Attorneys for Redress begin meeting in the San Francisco area. Three years later, the group is restructured as the Committee to Reverse the Japanese

Jan Scruggs, left, founder and president of the Vietnam Veterans Memorial Fund and Maya Lin, the designer of the memorial.. (AP/World Wide.)

American Wartime Cases to handle the *coram nobis* petitions for Fred Korematsu, Gordon Hirabayashi, and Minoru Yasui. Attorneys in the Pacific Northwest join the group.

Pakistani American Safi Qureshey, with Thomas Yuen and Albert Wong, pool $2,000 in resources to found AST Research. By 1992, Qureshey was the only remaining partner, and AST Research was well established on the Fortune 500 list of leading U.S. companies, and was the fourth largest producer of personal computers behind IBM, Apple, and Compaq.

The 1980 census reports that there arc 3,726,440 Asians and Pacific Islanders in the United States.

1981

Chinese American architect and sculptor Maya Lin submits the winning design for the Vietnam Veterans Memorial in Washington. The design features two highly polished walls of black granite, set in a "V" and inscribed with the names of the almost 58,000 dead or missing veterans of the Vietnam Way. Lin's design was chosen from 1,420 entries.

Rear Admiral Ming Chang, is the first Asian/Pacific American promoted to flag rank, after having held major command positions in the U.S. Navy.

Bette Bao Lord publishes *Spring Moon*, a bestseller and National Book Award Nominee which offered a fictional account of her return to China.

The U.S. Immigration and Naturalization Service grants Taiwan a separate immigration quota to facilitate family reunifications.

The Ku Klux Klan of Texas burns boats symbolizing their opposition to Vietnamese immigration and resettlement programs.

July 14. The first of ten public hearings commences in Washington, D.C. The committee hears over 750 witnesses.

1982

June 22. Vincènt Chin, a 27-year-old Chinese American in Detroit, is bludgeoned to death with a baseball bat by two unemployed autoworkers who blame layoffs in the auto industry on the Japanesc. The two assailants mistake Chin for being Japanese.

Chol Soo Lee is acquitted by a San Francisco jury. This Korean immigrant spent nine years in prison for a killing that he did not commit.

A proposed immigration reform and control bill is defeated in the House. It would have had an adverse effect on the Asian American community, because it imposed employer sanctions and changed the preference system that fosters family reunification.

Dishonorable discharges of the Fort McClellan protesters and members of the 1800th General Services Battalion are changed to honorable and their prison records erased.

The California legislature agrees to pay $5,000 restitution to 314 Japanese American state employees who were forced to leave their jobs in 1942. In subsequent years, similar restitutions are granted by other cities, counties, and states on the West Coast.

1983

Subrahmanyan Chandrashekhar (1910-) is awarded the Nobel Prize for physics.

In Fort Dodge, Iowa, a Laotian immigrant named Thong Soukaseume, is assaulted by a man yelling, "Remember Pearl Harbor," and "Go back to Japan, you Kamikaze pilot."

A congressional committee issues a report criticizing the government's incarceration of 110,000 Japanese Americans during World War II.

In an expression of humanitarian concern for abandoned Amerasian children of U.S. servicemen, Congress authorizes the admission of Amerasian children from Korea, Vietnam, and Thailand.

Asian American communities across the country are outraged by the probation sentence given to the two men who beat Chinese American Vincent Chin to death in Detroit. A federal grand jury later indicts the two men on federal civil rights charges. Trial on federal charges held in June 1984.

June 23. Report of the Commission of Wartime Relocation and Internment of Civilians (CWRIC), *Personal Justice Denied*, is released. The commission concluded that exclusion, expulsion, and incarceration were not justified by military necessity, and that the decision was based on race prejudice, war hysteria, and a failure of political leadership. The authors recommend that Congress pass a joint resolution, to be signed by the President, recognizing the grave injustice done to Japanese Americans with the nation's apologies and that it offer a one-time per capita compensatory payment of $20,000 to each of the approximately 60,000 surviving persons excluded from their places of residence by E.O. 9066.

October 4. In response to a petition for a writ of error coram nobis by Fred Korematsu, the Federal District Court of San Francisco reverses Korematsu's original conviction and rules that the government had no justification for issuing the internment orders.

October 6. Redress bill HR 4110 is introduced in the House of Representatives by Majority Leader Jim Wright of Texas and 72 cosponsors to implement the Commission of Wartime Relocation and Internment of Civilians (CWRIC) recommendations.

November 6. Senator Spark Matsunaga introduces redress Senate bill 2216 with 13 cosponsors.

1984

October 18. The assassination of Henry Liu by agents of the government of Taiwan touches off an international incident. As a result, the U.S. government changes its policy toward the Taiwanese government.

In Davis, California, Thong Hy Huynh is stabbed to death on the Davis High School grounds in a fight with two white students, who had been taunting Huynh and three other Vietnamese students with racial epithets for weeks.

Chinese American skater, Tiffany Chin, places fourth in figure skating at the Winter Olympics.

Greg Louganis, Samoan American diver, wins the Gold Medal in platform diving at the Olympics in Los Angeles. He became the first diver in history to break the 700-point mark, with his score of 710.91. He also won the Gold Medal in springboard diving, becoming the first man in 56 years to win both diving titles at the same Olympics.

Chinese American Bette Bao Lord publishes her first children's book, *In the Year of the Boar and Jackie Robinson*, a fictionalized account of her first year in America.

Roland Ebans is found guilty of violating Vincent Chin's civil rights on June 28, 1984, and was sentenced to 25 years in prison.

S. B. Woo is elected Lieutenant Governor in Delaware, the highest state office attained by an Asian American.

Cathy-Lynn Song wins the Yale Series of Younger Poets Award for her volume of poetry, *Picture Bride*.

California state legislature proclaims "that February 19, 1984, and February 19th of each year thereafter be recognized as 'A Day of Remembrance,' a time set aside so that Californians might reflect upon their shared responsibility to uphold the Constitution and moral rights of all individuals at all times."

1985

Asian Week reports that there are 4.8 million Asians in the United States and that this population will reach 6.5 million by 1990.

A Vietnamese Chinese restaurant owner in Boston, Massachusetts, is beaten by two white youths. The words "Gook sucks" are scratched in the restaurant window.

Greg Louganis, diver, wins the Sullivan Award presented by the Amateur Athletic Union (AAU) to the outstanding amateur athlete of the year.

Irene Natividad, Filipina American, is the first Asian American to be elected to head the National Women's Political Caucus.

Beulah Quo, Chinese American actress, joins the cast of the daytime soap opera, *General Hospital*, as Olin, a hip housekeeper. Quo is the only Asian American actor whose story line recurred on a soap opera over several years, lasting until 1991.

January 24. Lt. Col. Ellison Onizuka flies as a missions specialist on STS 51-c, the first space shuttle mission, thus becoming the first Asian American in space.

March 25. Dr. Haing S. Ngor wins an Oscar as best supporting actor at the Fifty-seventh Annual Academy Awards on for his first acting role in *Killing Fields*. He became the first Asian American ever to receive an Oscar for acting.

May 1. Dr. Taylor Wang, a Chinese American physicist, becomes the second Asian American in space when he flies aboard the *Challenger*.

October. A federal district court in Portland, Oregon, overturns Minoru Yasui's conviction of violating a curfew order during World War II.

1986

January 29. Lt. Col. Ellison Onizuka, the first Asian American astronaut, perishes along with six other crew members when the space shuttle Challenger explodes immediately after takeoff.

July 4. Chinese American architect I.M. Pei is one of 12 foreign-born Americans to receive the Medal of Liberty from President Roanld Reagan at the centennial of the Statue of Liberty.

July. Fourteen-year-old violinist Midori, performing at the Tanglewood Music Festival in Massachusetts, performed Leonard Bernstein's "Serenade." When her E-string broke, she picked up the concertmaster's violin and continued, but the E-string broke again. She continued with the assistant concertmaster's instruments and finished her performance flawlessly.

Dr. Yuan T. Lee, professor at the University of California, Berkeley campus, is awarded the Nobel Prize in chemistry.

Ismail Merchant, with James Ivory, produce a film adaptation of E.M. Forster's *A Room with a View*.

A federal district court in Seattle, invalidates Gordon Hirabayashi's 1942 conviction for violating wartime internment orders.

1987

HR442, the Civil Liberties Act of 1987 is submitted to the House of Representatives on January 6, 1987; and S1009, "A bill to accept the findings and implement recommendations of the Commission of Wartime Relocation and Internment of Civilians," is submitted to the Senate on April 10, 1987.

Patricia Saiki is the first Republican to represent Hawaii in the U.S. House of Representatives. She will serve until 1991.

Ajai Singh "Sonny" Mehta becomes head of Alfred A. Knopf, a division of Random House publishing. Alfred A. Knopf writers have won more Nobel Prizes than those of any other publisher.

A group of youths attack and kill Navroze Mody, an Indian man in Jersey City, New Jersey. The youths are allegedly affiliated with the "Dotbusters," referring to the decorative "dot" worn on theforehead of many Indian women.

A Filipino American family is taunted and harassed after moving into a mostly white neighborhood in Queens, New York. White youths hurl objects at family members and shout gibberish attempting to imitate the speakers of Tagalog, a Filipino language.

Ronald Ebans, after a trial in Cincinnati, Ohio, is acquitted of the murder of Vincent Chin in April 1987, after having not spent a single day in jail for the 1992 murder.

President Ronald Reagan appoints Asian Indian American Joy Cherian to the U.S. Equal Employment Opportunity Commission (EEOC).

May 4. Senator Daniel Inouye, chairman of the Senate Select Committee investigating the Iran-Contra affair, convenes joint House and Senate investigative hearings. Inouye also has served as a member of the Senate Select Committee on Watergate.

June 1. The Supreme Court, in an 8-0 vote sends the lawsuit stemming from Japanese American detention back to lower court. No ruling was made. The Court states that the case was improperly heard by the District of Columbia Court of Appeals rather than the Federal Circuit Court of Appeal.

October 1. The Japanese American Exhibit opens at the Smithsonian's National Museum of American History, in Washington, D.C.

The Immigration Reform and Control Act of 1985 was passed by the House of Representatives on October 15, 1987, passed by the Senate on October 17, 1987, and signed by the President on November 6, 1987.

President Bush prepares to sign a proclamation declaring May as Asian Pacific American Heritage Month during ceremonies in Washington. Attending the ceremony are, from left, Taylor Wang, Virginia Cha, I.M. Pei, Samuel Lee, Nancy Kwan, and T.D. Lee. (AP/Wide World.)

Unlike PL No. 99-603, which raised the Hong Kong quota from 600 to 5,000 a year, this act allows aliens who can prove that they were in the United States prior to January 1, 1982 to apply for temporary status and become U.S. citizens after seven years from the time of application. There are no changes in the preference system that allows for family reunification.

1988

Greg Louganis wins Gold Medals for both platform and springboard diving at the Olympic Games in Seoul, Korea. He becomes the first athlete to win two diving medals in successive Olympics. He wins the Olympic Spirit Award, designating him the most inspiring athlete among the 9,600 competing in Seoul.

David Henry Hwang's play, *M. Butterfly*, wins the Tony Award. The play, which grossed $35 million, also won the Drama Desk, Outer Critics Circle, and John Gassner awards.

Sichan Siv is appointed deputy assistant to President Reagan.

Ladies Home Journal names California Secretary of State March Fong Eu one of America's "100 Most Important Women."

In Berkeley, California, racist graffiti proclaiming "Japs and Chinks Only!" is found on a door of the Ethnic Studies Department of the University of California.

July 27. Senate passes revised redress bill HR 4110.

August 4. House of Representatives passes revised redress bill HR 4110.

August 10. The Civil Liberties Act of 1988 (Redress bill HR 4110 for Japanese Americans) is signed by President Reagan.

1989

The Coalition of Asian Pacific Americans, the first Asian Pacific political action committee, is founded.

The Honorable Elaine L. Chao is appointed as deputy secretary of the Department of Transportation in President Bush's cabinet.

The Boy of the Three-Year Nap by Dianne Snyder with illustrations by Japanese American artist Allen Say, wins the Caldecott Honor award for picture books.

Attorney General Dick Thonburgh presents $20,000 checks to three elderly Japanese Americans interned during World War II, during a ceremony at the Justice Department. Accepting the checks are, from left, Kisa Iseri, Hau Dairiki, and Mamoru Eto. They were also prosented with a signed apology from President Bush for their wrongful detention. (AP/Wide World.)

Patrick Purdy fires 105 rounds with an assault rifle at children at an elementary schoolyard in Stockton, California, killing five Southeast Asian children and then himself. Purdy blames all minorities for his failings targeting Southeast Asians for his homicidal plans.

Two white men kill 24-year-old Ming Hai "Jim" Loo, a Chinese American man, outside a pool hall in Raleigh, North Carolina, after shouting "We shouldn't put up with Vietnamese in our country."

Julia Chang Bloch is the first Asian American to serve as an U.S. Ambassador to Nepal.

Manny Crisostomo, a native of Guam, won a Pulitzer Prize for feature photography in the *Detroit Free Press*.

Michael Chang won the French Open, the youngest male and the first U.S. winner since 1955.

September 21. A bill to make redress funding an entitlement program is signed by President Bush.

1990

Representative Frank Horton introduced HR 3802 and Senator Spark Matsunaga introduced Senate Bill 2111 for an Asian/Pacific American Heritage Month, which was not acted upon.

Republican Cheryl Lau, a Native Hawaiian, is elected Secretary of State of Nevada, becoming the first Asian American to be elected to statewide office.

Two white men beat up Xan Than Ly, a Laotian American restaurant employee in Yuba City, California, after watching him drive his truck with two white female coworkers who asked for a ride. Using a hammer, they attack Ly and the women, breaking the windows of Ly's truck.

President Bush extends the celebration of Asian/Pacific American heritage to a month in his proclamation designating May 1990 as Asian/Pacific American Heritage Month.

Hawaii commemorates the 100th anniversary of the birth of Native Hawaiian Olympic swimmer Duke Kahanamoku by dedicating a nine-foot bronze statue on Waikiki Beach, "The Bronze Duke of Waikiki." The statue stands with its back to the ocean, with a 12-foot surfboard at its side.

October 9. The first redress checks and government apologies are presented by U.S. Attorney General Richard Thornburgh to recipients at ceremony in Washington, D.C.

1991

Major General John Liu Fugh earns the position of judge advocate general of the army, a post he will hold until his retirement in 1993. Major Fugh is the first Chinese American to attain general officer status in the military.

The Academy Award for Best Documentary Short Subject is awarded to Steven Okazaki for *Days of Waiting*, the story of artist Estelle Ishigo, a Caucasian woman who chose internment over separation from her Japanese American husband.

Japanese American photojournalist Paul Kuroda is named Newpaper Photographer of the Year by the National Press Photographers Association and the University of Missouri School of Journalism.

Chinese American Gus Lee publishes the semi-autobiographical novel *China Boy*, introducing the American-born son of Chinese parents, Kai Ting. It was a Literary Guild selection and one of the *New York Times'* "Best 100 for 1991."

H.J. Res. 173, introduced by Congressman Frank Horton, is passed by the House of Representatives on April 24, 1991, by the Senate on April 25, 1991, and approved by President Bush on May 6, 1991, designating May 1991 and May 1992 as Asian Pacific American heritage months.

Patricia Saiki, former representative to Congress from Hawaii, is appointed to head the U.S. Small Business Administration by President George Bush.

The Census Bureau reports that the Asian Pacific Islander population in the United States increased from 3,500,439 in 1980 to 7,273,662 in 1990, underwent a growth of 107.8 percent in ten years.

The JACL Pacific Southwest Regional office in Los Angeles, California, receives 15 hate letters in six months. Phrases like "You birds should move back to Tokyo instead of lobbying constantly for Jap ideas in America" fill the postcards.

President George Bush appoints Chinese American Elaine Chao to head the Peach Corps.

1992

An economic downturn in the United States causes a wave of Japan bashing.

Norman Mineta, representative to U.S. Congress from San Jose, California since 1974, is elected chair of the House Public Works and Transpotation Committee.

Korean American Eugene Chung joins the New England Patriots professional football team, becoming the third Asian American, and second Korean American, to play professional football in the United States.

Kristi Yamaguchi becomes the first Asian American to win the gold medal for women' figure skating in the 1992 Winter Olympics. Her career began in 1986 in the Junior Ladies Competition.

Korean American businessman Jay Kim is elected to Congress from the newly created 41st District of California, becoming the first Korean American member of Congress.

Lillian Kimura is elected the first woman president of the Japanese American Citizens League (JACL)>

Lillian Gonzalez-Pardo, a Filipina American physician, becomes the first Asian American to be elected national president of the American Medical Women's Association.

Oncologist Reginald C.S. Ho becomes the first Native Hawaiian to head the American Cancer Society.

Clayton Fong appointed Deputy Assistant to President Bush in May.

Chinese American Elaine Chao is selected to head the United Way.

Ismail Merchant, with collaborator James Ivory, produces a successful film adaptation of E. M. Forster's *Howards End*.

1993

Chinese American Connie Chung joins Dan Rather as co-anchor of the *CBS Evening News*, and is named anchor of a prime-time news magazine, *Eye to Eye with Connie Chung*.

Maya Lin, Chinese American scultor and architect, installs *The Women's Table* at Yale University, her alma mater. The granite sculpture and water table is dedicated to women, past and present, at Yale.

The Poetry Society of America awards its prestigious Shelley Memorial Award to Cathy-Lynn Song. Song also won the Hawaii Award for Literature the same year.

Fashion designer Anna Sui wins the Perry Ellis Award for New Fashion Talent.

Arati Prabhakar, Asian Indian American scientist, is appointed to head the National Institute of Standards and Technology (NIST) by President Bill Clinton. She is the first Asian American to hold the post.

March 30. Eiko Ishioka wins the Academy Award for Best Costume Design for *Bram Stoker's Dracula*.

April 3. Brandon Lee is accidentally shot to death by a prop gin during the last stages of filming *The Crow*. Lee is the son of Chinese American actor Bruce Lee.

1994

Korean American comedian Margaret Cho is the first Asian American to star in her own television show, *All-American Girl*, a sitcom about a Korean American family.

Gus Lee publishes *Honor and Duty*, the second installment in his semiautobiographical tale of the life of Kai Ting. In *Honor and Duty*, Lee recounts Kai Ting's experiences at West Point.

Grandfather's Journey by Allen Say, published in 1993, tells the story of Say's grandfather in Japan and America. It wins the 1994 Caldecott Medal for most distinguished children's American picture book.

Los Angeles Superior Court Judge, Japanese American Lance Ito, is assigned to hear the high-profile double-murder case of O.J. Simpson, Hall of Fame football player and television celebrity.

President Bill Clinton appoints March Fong Eu, then-Secretary of State of California, to become ambassador to Micronesia.

Lieutenant Colonel Richard Sakakida, a Japanese American who worked as a counterintelligence agent in the Philippines during World War II, receives the Legion of Honor from the government of the Philippines in recognition of his meritorious service to the Filipino American Freedom Fighters. He was also awarded the Bronze Star Medal from the U.S. Air Force for his distingguished service to the American military.

February. Pioneer Asian American actor and director Mako is honored with a star on the Hollywood Walk of Fame.

Asian Indian American Prema Mathai-Davis bacame the first foreign-born woman to lead the Young Woman's Christian Association (YWCA).

July. Chinese American astronaut Leroy Chiao flies on the space shuttle Columbia, conducting life and material science experiments.

References

Hatamiya, Leslie. *Walk with Pride: Taking steps to Address Anti- Asian Violence* San Francisco: Japanese American Citizens League, 1992, p. 7.

Au, Mark and Mary. Asian Pacific American Heritage Month, National Leadership Conference, May 1—3, 1992, Asian Pacific American Heritage Council, Inc.

Americans of Japanese Ancestry and the United States Constitution, 1787-1987.

—Prepared with the assistance of Roslyn Tonai and Clifford Uyeda of the National Japanese American National Museum and Mark and Mary Au, Asian Pacific American Heritage Council.

Significant Documents

♦ Treaty Between the United States and China, 1880
♦ Chinese Exclusion Act, 1882 ♦ Geary Law, 1892
♦ Joint Resolution to Provide for Annexing the Hawaiian Islands to the United States, 1898
♦ Organic Act, 1900 ♦ Executive Order known as the "Gentlemen's Agreement," 1907
♦ Immigration Act, 1917 ♦ Cable Act, 1922 ♦ Immigration Act, 1924
♦ Tydings-McDuffie Act, 1934 ♦ Presidential Proclamation, 1938
♦ Public Proclamation No. 1, 1942 ♦ Executive Order 9066, 1942 ♦ Public Law 503, 1942
♦ Repeal of Chinese Exclusion Acts, 1943 ♦ War Brides Act, 1945
♦ Presidential Proclamation, 1947
♦ Immigration and Naturalization Act, 1952 ♦ Immigration and Nationality Act Amendments, 1965
♦ Directive No. 15 ♦ Refugee Act, 1980
♦ Commission on Wartime Relocation and Internment of Civilians Act, 1980
♦ The Civil Liberties Act, 1988 ♦ Hate Crimes Statistics Act, 1990 ♦ Civil Rights Act, 1991
♦ Asian /Pacific American Heritage Month, 1991 and 1992
♦ Voting Rights Language Assistance Act, 1992
♦ 100th Anniversary of the Overthrow of the Hawaiian Kingdom, 1993

♦ TREATY BETWEEN THE UNITED STATES AND CHINA, 1880

This treaty gave the United States the right to limit the number of Chinese immigrants entering the United States.

Whereas a Treaty between the United States of America and China, for the modification of the existing treaties between the two countries, by providing for the future regulation of Chinese immigration into the United States, was concluded and signed at Peking in the English and Chinese languages, on the seventeenth day of November in the year of our Lord one thousand eight hundred and eighty, the original of the English text of which Treaty is word for word as follows:

Whereas, in the eighth year of Hsien Feng, Anno Domini 1858, a treaty of peace and friendship was concluded between the United States of America and China, and to which were added, in the seventh year of Tung Chih, Anno Domini 1868, certain supplementary

articles to the advantage of both parties, which supplementary articles were to be perpetually observed and obeyed: —and

Whereas the Government of the United States, because of the constantly increasing immigration of Chinese laborers to the territory of the United States, and the embarrassments consequent upon such immigration, now desires to negotiate a modification of the existing Treaties which shall not be in direct contravention of their spirit: —

Now, therefore, the President of the United States of America has appointed James B. Angell, of Michigan, John F. Swift, of California, and William Henry Trescot, of South Carolina as his Commissioners Plenipotentiary; and His Imperial Majesty, the Emperor of China, has appointed Pao Chun, a member of His Imperial Majesty's Privy Council, and Superintendent of the Board of Civil Office; and Li Hungtsao, a member of His Imperial Majesty's Privy Council, as his Commissioners Plenipotentiary; and the said Commissioners Plenipotentiary, having conjointly examined their full powers, and having discussed the points of possible modification in existing Treaties, have agreed upon the following articles in modification.

ARTICLE I

Whereas in the opinion of the Government of the United States, the coming of Chinese laborers to the United States, or their residence therein, affects or threatens to affect the interests of their country, or to endanger the good order of the said country of or any locality within the territory thereof, the Government of China agrees that the Government of the United States may regulate, limit, or suspend such coming or residence, but may not absolutely prohibit it. The limitation or suspension shall be reasonable and shall apply only to Chinese who may go to the United States as laborers, other classes not being included in the limitations. Legislation taken in regard to Chinese laborers will be of such a character only as is necessary to enforce the regulation, limitation, or suspension of immigration, and immigrants shall not be subject to personal inaltreatment or abuse.

ARTICLE II

Chinese subjects, whether proceeding to the United States as teachers, students, merchants or from curiosity, together with their body and household servants, and Chinese laborers who are now in the United States shall be allowed to go and come of their own free will and accord, and shall be accorded all the rights, privileges, immunities, and exemptions which are accorded to the citizens and subjects of the most favored nation.

ARTICLE III

If Chinese laborers, or Chinese of any other class, now either permanently or temporarily residing in the territory of the United States, meet with ill treatment at the hands of any other persons, the Government of the United States will exert all its power to devise measures for their protection and to secure to them the same rights, privileges, immunities, and exemptions as may be enjoyed by the citizens or subjects of the most favored nation, and to which they are entitled by treaty.

ARTICLE IV

The high contracting Powers having agreed upon the foregoing articles, whenever the Government of the United States shall adopt legislative measures in accordance therewith, such measures will be communicated to the Government of China. If the measures as enacted are found to work hardship upon the subjects of China, the Chinese Minister at Washington may bring the matter to the notice of the United States Minister at Peking and consider the subject with him, to the end that mutual and unqualified benefit may result.

In faith whereof the respective Plenipotentiaries have signed and sealed the foregoing at Peking, in English and Chinese being three originals of each text of even tenor and date, the ratifications of which shall be exchanged at Peking within one year from date of its execution.

Done at Peking, this seventeenth day of November, in the year of our Lord, 1880. Kuanghsu, sixth year, tenth moon, fifteenth day.

James B. Angell.

John F. Swift.

Wm. Henry Trescot.

Pao Chun.

Li Hungtsao.

And whereas the said Treaty has been duly ratified on both parts and the respective ratifications were exchanged at Peking on the 19th day of July 1881:

Now, therefore, be it known that I, Chester A. Arthur, President of the United States of America, have caused the said Treaty to be made public to the end that the same and every article and clause thereof may be observed and fulfilled with good faith by the United States and the citizens thereof.

In witness whereof, I have hereunto set my hand and caused the seal of the United States to be affixed.

Done in Washington this fifth day of October in the year of our Lord one thousand eight hundred and eighty-one, and of the Independence of the United States the one hundred and sixth.

Chester A. Arthur

By the President:

James G. Blaine

Secretary of State.

November 17, 1880

A supplemental treaty prohibited Chinese subjects from importing opium into the United States, limited fees charged on goods transported to and from the other country, and provided a procedure for resolving disputes in China between United States citizens and Chinese subjects.

◆ CHINESE EXCLUSION ACT, 1882

This act suspended the immigration of Chinese laborers to the United States for ten years.

Whereas, in the opinion of the Government of the United States the coming of Chinese laborers to this country endangers the good order of certain localities within the territory thereof: Therefore,

Be it enacted by the Senate and House of Representatives of the United States of America in Congress assembled, That from and after the expiration of ninety days next after the passage of this act, and until the expiration of ten years next after the passage of this act, the coming of Chinese laborers to the United States be, and the same is hereby, suspended; and during such suspension it shall not be lawful for any Chinese laborer to come, or, having so come after the expiration of said ninety days, to remain within the United States.

Section 2

That the master of any vessel who shall knowingly bring within the United States on such vessel, and land or permit to be landed, any Chinese laborer, from any foreign port or place, shall be deemed guilty of a misdemeanor, and on conviction thereof shall be punished by a fine of not more than five hundred dollars for each and every such Chinese laborer so brought, and may be also imprisoned for a term not exceeding one year.

Section 3

That the two foregoing sections shall not apply to Chinese laborers who were in the United States on the seventeenth day of November, eighteen hundred and eighty of ninety days next after the passage of this act, and who shall produce to such master before going on board such vessel, and shall produce to the collector of the port of the United States at which such vessel shall arrive, the evidence hereinafter in this act required of his being one of the laborers in this section mentioned; nor shall the two foregoing sections apply to the case of any master whose vessel, being bound to a port not within the United States, shall come within the jurisdiction of the United States by reason of being in distress or in stress of weather, or touching at any port of the United States on its voyage to any foreign port or place: Provided, That all Chinese laborers brought on such vessel shall depart with the vessel on leaving port.

Section 4

That for the purpose of properly identifying Chinese laborers who were in the United States on the seventeenth day of November, eighteen hundred and eighty, or who shall have come into the same before the expiration of ninety days next after the passage of this act, and in order to furnish them with the proper evidence of their right to go from and come to the United States of their free will and accord, as provided by the treaty between the United States and China dated November seventeenth, eighteen hundred and eighty, the collector of customs of the district from which any such Chinese laborer shall depart from the United States shall, in

person or by deputy, go on board each vessel having on board any such Chinese laborer and cleared or about to sail from his district for a foreign port, and on such vessel make a list of all such Chinese laborers, which shall be entered in registry-books to be kept for that purpose, in which shall be stated the name, age, occupation, last place of residence, physical marks or peculiarities, and all facts necessary for the identification of each of such Chinese laborers, which books shall be safely kept in the custom-house; and every such Chinese laborer so departing from the United States shall be entitled to, and shall receive, free of any charge or cost upon application therefore, from the collector or his deputy, at the time such list is taken, a certificate, signed by the collector or his deputy and attested by his seal of office, in such form as the Secretary of the Treasury shall prescribe, which certificate shall contain a statement of the name, age, occupation, last place of residence, personal description, and facts of identification of the Chinese laborer to whom the certificate is issued, corresponding with the said list and registry in all particulars. In case any Chinese laborer after having received such certificate shall leave such vessel before her departure he shall deliver his certificate to the master of the vessel, and if such Chinese laborer shall fail to return to such vessel before her departure from port the certificate shall be delivered by the master to the collector of customs for cancellation. The certificate herein provided for shall entitle the Chinese laborer to whom the same is issued to return to and re-enter the United States upon producing and delivering the same to the collector of customs of the district at which such Chinese laborer shall seek to re-enter; and upon delivery of such certificate by such Chinese laborer to the collector of customs at the time of re-entry in the United States, said collector shall cause the same to be filed in the custom-house and duly canceled.

Section 5

That any Chinese laborer mentioned in section four of this act being in the United States, and desiring to depart from the United States by land, shall have the right to demand and receive, free of charge or cost, a certificate of identification similar to that provided for in section four of this act to be issued to such Chinese laborers as may desire to leave the United States by water; and it is hereby made the duty of the collector of customs of the district next adjoining the foreign country to which said Chinese laborer desires to go to issue such certificate, free of charge or cost, upon application by such Chinese laborer, and to enter the same upon registry-books to be kept by him for the purpose, as provided for in section four of this act.

Section 6

That in order to the faithful execution of articles one and two of the treaty in this act before mentioned, every Chinese person other than a laborer who may be entitled by said treaty and this act to come within the United States, and who shall be about to come to the United States, shall be identified as so entitled by the Chinese Government in each case, such identity to be evidenced by a certificate issued under the authority of said government, which certificate shall be in the English language or (if not in the English language) accompanied by a translation into English, stating such right to come, and which certificate shall state the name, title, or official rank, if any, the age, height, and all physical peculiarities, former and present occupation or profession, and place of residence in China of the person to whom the certificate is issued and that such person is entitled conformably to the treaty in this act mentioned to come within the United States. Such certificate shall be prima-facie evidence of the fact set forth therein, and shall be produced to the collector of customs, or his deputy, of the port in the district in the United States at which the person named therein shall arrive.

Section 7

That any person who shall knowingly and falsely alter or substitute any name for the name written in such certificate or forge any such certificate, or knowingly utter any forged or fraudulent certificate, or falsely impersonate any person named in any such certificate, shall be deemed guilty of a misdemeanor; and upon conviction thereof shall be fined in a sum not exceeding one thousand dollars, and imprisoned in a penitentiary for a term of not more than five years.

Section 8

That the master of any vessel arriving in the United States from any foreign port or place shall, at the same time he delivers a manifest of the cargo, and if there be no cargo, then at the time of making a report of the entry of the vessel pursuant to law, in addition to the other matter required to be reported, and before landing, or permitting to land, any Chinese passengers, deliver and report to the collector of customs of the district in which such vessels shall have arrived a separate list of all Chinese passengers taken on board his vessel at any foreign port or place, and all such passengers on board the vessel at that time. Such list shall show the names of such passengers (and if accredited officers of the Chinese Government traveling on the business of that government, or their servants, with a note of such facts), and the names and other particulars, as shown by their respective certificates; and such list shall be sworn to by the master in the manner required by law in relation to the manifest of the cargo. Any willful refusal or neglect of any such master to comply with the provisions of this section shall incur the same penalties and forfeiture as are provided for a refusal or neglect to report and deliver a manifest of the cargo.

Section 9

That before any Chinese passengers are landed from any such vessel, the collector, or his deputy, shall proceed to examine such passengers, comparing the certificates with the list and with the passengers; and no passenger shall be allowed to land in the United States from such vessel in violation of law.

Section 10

That every vessel whose master shall knowingly violate any of the provisions of this act shall be deemed forfeited to the United States, and shall be liable to seizure and condemnation in any district of the United States into which such vessel may enter or in which she may be found.

Section 11

That any person who shall knowingly bring into or cause to be brought into the United States by land, or who shall knowingly aid or abet the same, or aid or abet the landing in the United States from any vessel of any Chinese person not lawfully entitled to enter the United States, shall be deemed guilty of a misdemeanor, and shall, on conviction thereof, be fined in a sum not exceeding one thousand dollars, and imprisoned for a term not exceeding one year.

Section 12

That no Chinese person shall be permitted to enter the United States by land without producing to the proper officer of customs the certificate in this act required of Chinese persons seeking to land from a vessel. And any Chinese person found unlawfully within the United States shall be caused to be removed therefrom to the country from whence he came, by direction of the President of the United States, and at the cost of the United States, after being brought before some justice, judge, or commissioner of a court of the United States and found to be one not lawfully entitled to be or remain in the United States.

Section 13

That this act shall apply to diplomatic and other officers of the Chinese Government traveling upon the business of that government, whose credentials shall be taken as equivalent to the certificate in this act mentioned, and shall exempt them and their body and household servants from the provisions of this act as to other Chinese persons.

Section 14

That hereafter no State court or court of the United States shall admit Chinese to citizenship; and all laws in conflict with this act are hereby repealed.

Section 15

That the words "Chinese laborers", wherever used in this act, shall be construed to mean both skilled and unskilled laborers and Chinese employed in mining.

Approved, May 6, 1882.

◆ IRWIN CONVENTION, 1885

This act made it illegal to help aliens hired as laborers immigrate to the United States or its territories. Its intention was to stop the flow of Japanese contract laborers to Hawaii.

Be it enacted by the Senate and House of Representatives of the United States of America in Congress assembled, That from and after the passage of this act it shall be unlawful for any person, company, partnership, or corporation, in any manner whatsoever, to repay the transportation, or in any way assist or encourage the importation or migration of any alien or aliens, any foreigner or foreigners, into the United States, its Territories, or the District of Columbia, under contract or agreement, parol or special, express or implied, made previous to the importation or migration of such alien or aliens, foreigner or foreigners, to perform labor or service of any kind in the United States, its Territories, or the District of Columbia.

Section 2

That all contracts or agreements, express or implied, parol, or special, which may hereafter be made by and between any personal company, partnership, or corporation, and any foreigner or foreigners, alien or aliens, to perform labor or service or having reference to the performance of labor or service by any person in the United States, its Territories, or the District of Columbia previous to the migration or importation of the person or persons whose labor or service is contracted for into the United States, shall be utterly void and of no effect.

Section 3

That for every violation of any of the provisions of section one of this act the person, partnership, company, or corporation violating the same, by knowingly assisting, encouraging or soliciting the migration or importation of any alien or aliens, foreigner or foreigners, into the United States, its Territories, or the District of Columbia, to perform labor or service of any kind under contract or agreement, express or implied, parol or special, with such alien or aliens, foreigner or foreigners, previous to becoming residents or citizens of the United States, shall forfeit and pay for every such offense the sum of one thousand dollars, which may be used for and recovered by the United States or by any person who shall first bring his action therefore including any such alien or foreigner who may be a party to any such contract or agreement, as debts of like amount are now recovered in the circuit courts of the United States; and separate suits may be brought for each alien or foreigner being a party to such contract or agreement aforesaid. And it shall be the duty of the district attorney of the proper district to prosecute every such suit at the expense of the United States.

Section 4

That the master of any vessel who shall knowingly bring within the United States on any such vessel, and land, or permit to be landed, from any foreign port or place, any alien laborer, mechanic, or artisan who, previous to embarkation on such vessel, had entered into contract or agreement, parol or special, express or implied, to perform labor or service in the United States, shall be deemed guilty of a misdemeanor, and on conviction thereof, shall be punished by a fine of not more than five hundred dollars for each and every such alien laborer, mechanic or artisan so brought as aforesaid, and may also be imprisoned for a term not exceeding six months.

Section 5

That nothing in this act shall be so construed as to prevent any citizen or subject of any foreign country temporarily residing in the United States, either in private or official capacity, from engaging, under contract or otherwise, persons not residents or citizens of the United States to act as private secretaries, servants, or domestics for such foreigner temporarily residing in the United States as aforesaid; nor shall this act be so construed as to prevent any person, or persons, partnership, or corporation from engaging, under contract or agreement, skilled workman in foreign countries to perform labor in the United States in or upon any new industry not at present established in the United States:

Provided, That skilled labor for that purpose cannot be otherwise obtained; nor shall the provisions of this act apply to professional actors, artists, lecturers, or singers, nor to persons employed strictly as personal or domestic servants: Provided, That nothing in this act shall be construed as prohibiting any individual from assisting any member of his family or any relative or personal friend, to migrate from any foreign country to the United States, for the purpose of settlement here.

Section 6

That all laws or parts of laws conflicting herewith be, and the same are hereby, repealed.

◆ GEARY LAW, 1892

This law renewed the 1882 Chinese Exclusion Act, prohibiting immigration of Chinese laborers for another ten years.

◆ JOINT RESOLUTION TO PROVIDE FOR ANNEXING THE HAWAIIAN ISLANDS TO THE UNITED STATES, JULY 7, 1898

Whereas the Government of the Republic of Hawaii having, in due form, signified its consent, in the manner provided by its constitution, to cede absolutely and without reserve to the United States of America all rights of sovereignty of whatsoever kind in and over the Hawaiian Islands and their dependencies, and also to cede and transfer to the United States the absolute fee and ownership of all public, Government, or Crown lands, public buildings or edifices, ports, harbors, military equipment, and all other public property of every kind and description belonging to the Government of the Hawaiian Islands, together with every right and appurtenance thereunto appertaining: Therefore,

Resolved by the Senate and House of Representatives of the United States of America in Congress assembled, That said cession is accepted, ratified, and confirmed, and that the said Hawaiian Islands and their dependencies by, and they are hereby, annexed as a part of the territory of the United States and are subject to the sovereign dominion thereof, and that all and singular the property and rights hereinbefore mentioned are vested in the United States of America.

The existing laws of the United States relative to public lands shall not apply to such lands in the Hawaiian Islands; but the Congress of the United States shall enact special laws for their management and disposition : Provided, That all revenue from or proceeds of the same, except as regards such part there of as may be used or occupied for the civil, military, or naval purposes of the United States, or may be assigned for the use of the local government, shall be used solely for the benefit of the inhabitants of the Hawaiian Islands for educational and other public purposes.

Until Congress shall provide for the government of such islands all the civil, judicial, and military powers exercised by the officers of the existing government in said islands shall be vested in such person or persons and shall be exercised in such manner as the President of the United States shall direct: and the President shall have power to remove said officers and fill the vacancies so occasioned.

The existing treaties of the Hawaiian Islands with foreign nations shall forthwith cease and determine, being replaced by such treaties as may exist, or as may be hereafter concluded, between the United States and such foreign nations. The municipal legislation of the Hawaiian Islands, not enacted for the fulfillment of the treaties so extinguished, and not inconsistent with this joint resolution nor contrary to the Constitution of the United States nor to any existing treaty of the United States, shall remain in force until the Congress of the United States shall otherwise determine.

Until legislation shall be enacted extending the United States customs laws and regulations to the Hawaiian Islands the existing customs relations of the Hawaiian Islands with the United States and other countries shall remain unchanged.

The public debt of the Republic of Hawaii, lawfully existing at the date of the passage of this joint resolution, including the amounts due to depositors in the Hawaiian Postal Savings Bank, is hereby assumed by the Government of the United States; but the liability of the United States in this regard shall in no case exceed four million dollars. So long, however, as the existing Government and the present commercial relations of the Hawaiian Islands are continued as hereinbefore provided said Government shall continue to pay the interest on said debt.

There shall be no further immigration of Chinese into the Hawaiian Islands, except upon such conditions as are now or may hereafter be allowed by the laws of the United States; and no Chinese, by reason of anything herein contained, shall be allowed to enter the United States from the Hawaiian Islands.

The President shall appoint five commissioners, at least two of whom shall be residents of the Hawaiian Islands, who shall, as soon as reasonably practicable, recommend to Congress such legislation concerning the Hawaiian Islands as they shall deem necessary or proper.

SECTION 2

That the commissioners hereinbefore provided for shall be appointed by the President, by and with the advice and consent of the Senate.

SECTION 3

That the sum of one hundred thousand dollars, or so much thereof as may be necessary, is hereby appropriated, out of any money in the Treasury not otherwise appropriated, and to be immediately available, to be expended at the discretion of the President of the United States of America, for the purpose of carrying this joint resolution into effect.

Approved, July 7, 1898.

♦ ORGANIC ACT, 1900

This lengthy act outlined a government for the new Territory of Hawaii.

Section 1

That the phrase "the laws of Hawaii," as used in this Act without qualifying words, shall mean the constitution and laws of the Republic of Hawaii, in force on the twelfth day of August, eighteen hundred and ninety-eight, at the time of the transfer of the sovereignty of the Hawaiian Islands to the United States of America.

The constitution and statute laws of the Republic of Hawaii then in force, set forth in a compilation made by Sidney M. Ballou under the authority of the legislature, and published in two volumes entitled "Civil Laws" and "Penal Laws," respectively, and in the Session Laws of the Legislature for the session of eighteen hundred and ninety-eight, are referred to in this Act as "Civil Laws," "Penal Laws," and "Session Laws."

Section 2

Territory of Hawaii

That the islands acquired by the United States of America under an Act of Congress entitled "Joint resolution to provide for annexing the Hawaiian Islands to the United States," approved July seventh, eighteen hundred and ninety-eight, shall be known as the Territory of Hawaii.

Section 3

Government of the Territory of Hawaii

That a Territorial government is hereby established over the said Territory, with its capital at Honolulu, on the island of Oahu.

Section 4

Citizenship

That all persons who were citizens of the Republic of Hawaii on August twelfth, eighteen hundred and ninety-eight, are hereby declared to be citizens of the United States and citizens of the Territory of Hawaii.

And all citizens of the United States resident in the Hawaiian Islands who were resident there on or since August twelfth, eighteen hundred and ninety-eight, and all the citizens of the United States who shall hereafter reside in the Territory of Hawaii for one year shall be citizens of the Territory of Hawaii.

Section 5

Application of the Laws of the United States

That the Constitution, and, except as herein otherwise provided, all the laws of the United States which are not locally inapplicable, shall have the same force and effect within the said Territory as elsewhere in the United States:

Provided, That sections eighteen hundred and fifty and eighteen hundred and ninety of the Revised Statutes of the United States shall not apply to the Territory of Hawaii.

Section 6

Government of the Territory of Hawaii

That the laws of Hawaii not inconsistent with the Constitution or laws of the United States or the provisions of this Act shall continue in force, subject to repeal or amendment by the legislature of Hawaii or the Congress of the United States.

Section 7

That the constitution of the Republic of Hawaii and the laws of Hawaii, as set forth in the following acts, chapters, and sections of the civil laws, penal laws, and session laws, and relating to the following subjects, are hereby repealed . . . *The remainder of Section 7 specifies the civil, penal, and session laws that are repealed.*

Section 8

Certain Offices Abolished

That the offices of President, minister of foreign affairs, minister of the interior, minister of finance, minister of public instruction, auditor-general, deputy auditor-general, surveyor-general, marshal, and deputy marshal of the Republic of Hawaii are hereby abolished.

Section 9

Amendment of Official Titles

That wherever the words "President of the Republic of Hawaii," or "Republic of Hawaii," or "Government of the Republic of Hawaii," or their equivalents, occur in the laws of Hawaii not repealed by this Act, they are hereby amended to read "Governor of the Territory of

Hawaii," or "Territory of Hawaii," or "Government of the Territory of Hawaii," or their equivalents, as the context requires.

Section 10

Construction of Existing Statutes

That all rights of action, suits at law and in equity, prosecutions, and judgments existing prior to the taking effect of this Act shall continue to be as effectual as if this Act had not been passed; and those in favor of or against the Republic of Hawaii, and not assumed by or transferred to the United States, shall be equally valid in favor of or against the government of the Territory of Hawaii. All offenses which by statute then in force were punishable as offenses against the Republic of Hawaii shall be punishable as offenses against the government of the Territory of Hawaii, unless such statute is inconsistent with this Act, or shall be repealed or changed by law. No person shall be subject to imprisonment for nonpayment of taxes nor for debt. All criminal and penal proceedings then pending in the courts of the Republic of Hawaii shall be prosecuted to final judgment and execution in the name of the Territory of Hawaii; all such proceedings, all actions at law, suits in equity, and other proceedings then pending in the courts of the Republic of Hawaii shall be carried on to final judgment and execution in the corresponding courts of the Territory of Hawaii; and all process issued and sentences imposed before this Act takes effect shall be as valid as if issued or imposed in the name of the Territory of Hawaii:

Provided, That no suit or proceedings shall be maintained for the specific performance of any contract heretofore or hereafter entered into for personal labor or service, nor shall any remedy exist or be enforced for breach of any such contract, except in a civil suit or proceeding instituted solely to recover damages for such breach:

Provided further, That the provisions of this section shall not modify or change the laws of the United States applicable to merchant seaman.

That all contracts made since August twelfth, eighteen hundred and ninety-eight, by which persons are held for service for a definite term, are hereby declared null and void and terminated, and no law shall be passed to enforce said contracts in any way; and it shall be the duty of the United States marshal to at once notify such persons so held of the termination of their contracts.

That the Act approved February twenty-sixth, eighteen hundred and eighty-five, "To prohibit the importation and migration of foreigners and aliens under contract or agreement to perform labor in the United States, its Territories, and the District of Columbia,"

and the Acts amendatory thereof and supplemental thereto, be, and the same are hereby extended to and made applicable to the Territory of Hawaii.

Section 11

Style of Process

That the style of all process in the Territorial courts shall hereafter run in the name of "The Territory of Hawaii," and all prosecutions shall be carried on in the name and by the authority of the Territory of Hawaii.

Chapter 2—The Legislature
Section 12

The Legislative Power

That the legislature of the Territory of Hawaii shall consist of two houses, styled, respectively, the senate and house of representatives, which shall organize and sit separately, except as otherwise herein provided.

The two houses shall be styled "The legislature of the Territory of Hawaii."

Section 13

That no person shall sit as a senator or representative in the legislature unless elected under and in conformity with this Act.

Section 14

General Elections

That a general election shall be held on the Tuesday next after the first Monday in November, nineteen hundred, and every second year thereafter:

Provided, however, That the governor may, in his discretion, on thirty days' notice, order a special election before the first general election, if, in his opinion, the public interests shall require a special session of the legislature.

Section 15

Each House Judge of Qualifications of Members

That each house shall be the judge of the elections, returns, and qualifications of its own members.

Section 16

Disqualifications of Legislators

That no member of the legislature shall, during the term for which he is elected, be appointed or elected to any office of the Territory of Hawaii.

Section 17

Disqualifications of Government Officers and Employees

That no person holding office in or under or by authority of the Government of the United States or of the Territory of Hawaii shall be eligible to election to the legislature, or to hold the position of a member of the same while holding said office.

Section 18

No idiot or insane person, and no person who shall be expelled from the legislature for giving or receiving bribes or being accessory thereto, and no person who, in due course of law, shall have been convicted of any criminal offense punishable by imprisonment, whether with or without hard labor, for a term exceeding one year, whether with or without fine, shall register to vote or shall vote or hold any office in, or under, or by authority of, the government, unless the person so convicted shall have been pardoned and restored to his civil rights.

Section 19

Oath of Office

That every member of the legislature, and all officers of the government of the Territory of Hawaii, shall take the following oath or affirmation:

I solemnly swear (or affirm), in the presence of Almighty God, that I will faithfully support the Constitution and laws of the United States, and conscientiously and impartially discharge my duties as a member of the legislature, or as an officer of the government of the Territory of Hawaii (as the case may be).

Section 20

Officers and Rules

That the senate and house of representatives shall each choose its own officers, determine the rules of its own proceedings, not inconsistent with this Act, and keep a journal.

Section 21

Ayes and Noes

That the ayes and noes of the members of any question shall, at the desire of one-fifth of the members present, be entered on the journal.

Section 22

Quorum

That a majority of the number of members to which each house is entitled shall constitute a quorum of such house for the conduct of ordinary business, of which quorum a majority vote shall suffice: but the final passage of a law in each house shall require the vote of a majority of all the members to which such house is entitled.

Section 23

That a smaller number than a quorum may adjourn from day to day, and compel the attendance of absent members, in such manner and under such penalties as each house may provide.

Section 24

That, for the purpose of ascertaining whether there is a quorum present, the chairman shall count the number of members present.

Section 25

That each house may punish by fine, or by imprisonment not exceeding thirty days, any person not a member of either house who shall be guilty of disrespect of such house by any disorderly or contemptuous behavior in its presence or that of any committee thereof; or who shall, on account of the exercise of any legislative function, threaten harm to the body or estate of any of the members of such house; or who shall assault, arrest, or detain any witness or other person ordered to attend such house, on his way going to or returning therefrom; or who shall rescue any person arrested by order of such house.

But the person charged with the offense shall be informed, in writing, of the charge made against him, and have an opportunity to present evidence and be heard in his own defense.

Section 26

Compensation of Members

That the members of the legislature shall receive for their services, in addition to mileage at the rate of ten cents a mile each way, the sum of four hundred dollars for each regular session of the legislature, payable in three equal installments on and after the first, thirtieth, and fiftieth days of the session, and the sum of two hundred dollars for each extra session of the legislature.

Section 27

Punishment of Members

That each house may punish its own members for disorderly behavior or neglect of duty, by censure, or by a two-thirds vote suspend or expel a member.

Section 28

Exemption from Liability

That no member of the legislature shall be held to answer before any other tribunal for any words uttered in the exercise of his legislative functions in either house.

Section 29

Exemption from Arrest

That the members of the legislature shall, in all cases except treason, felony, or breach of the peace, be privileged from arrest during their attendance at the sessions of the respective houses, and in going to and returning from the same:

Provided, That such privilege as going to and returning shall not cover a period of over ten days each way.

Section 30

The Senate

Sections 30 through 34 discuss the make-up of the state senate, senatorial districts and eligibility for serving.

Section 35

The House of Representatives

Sections 35 through 40 detail the makeup of the state house of representatives, representative districts and eligibility for serving.

Section 41

Legislation

Sections 41 through 54 discuss legislative procedures and appropriations. It is specified that all proceedings must be conducted in English.

Section 55

Legislative Power

That the legislative power of the Territory shall extend to all rightful subjects of legislation not inconsistent with the Constitution and laws of the United States locally applicable. The legislature, at its first regular session after the census enumeration shall be ascertained, and from time to time thereafter, shall reapportion the membership in the senate and house of representatives among the senatorial and representative districts on the basis of the population in each of said districts who are citizens of the Territory; but the legislature shall not grant to any corporation, association, or individual any special or exclusive privilege, immunity, or franchise without the approval of Congress; nor shall it grant private charters, but it may by general act permit persons to associate themselves together as bodies corporate for manufacturing, agricultural, and other industrial pursuits, and for conducting the business of insurance, savings banks, banks of discount and deposit (but not of issue), loan, trust, and guaranty associations, for the establishment and conduct of cemeteries, and for the construction and operation of railroads, wagon roads, vessels, and irrigating ditches, and the colonization and improvement of lands in connection therewith, or for colleges, seminaries, churches, libraries, or any other benevolent, charitable or scientific association:

Provided, That no corporation, domestic or foreign, shall acquire and hold real estate in Hawaii in excess of one thousand acres; and all real estate acquired or held by such corporation or association contrary hereto shall be forfeited and escheat to the United States, but existing vested rights in real estate shall not be impaired. No divorce shall be granted by the legislature, nor shall any divorce be granted by the courts of the Territory unless the applicant therefor shall have resided in the Territory for two years next preceding the application, but this provision shall not affect any action pending when this Act takes effect; nor shall any lottery or sale of lottery tickets be allowed; nor shall spirituous or intoxicating liquors be sold except under such regulations and restrictions as the Territorial legislature shall provide; nor shall any public money be appropriated for the support or benefit of any sectarian, denominational, or private school, or any school not under the exclusive control of the government; nor shall the government of the Territory of Hawaii, or any political or municipal corporation or subdivision of the Territory, make any subscription to the capital stock of any incorporated company, or in any manner lend its credit for the use thereof; nor shall any debt be authorized to be contracted by or on behalf of the Territory, or any political or municipal corporation or subdivision thereof, except to pay the interest upon the existing indebtedness, to suppress insurrection, or to provide for the common defense, except that in addition to any indebtedness created for such purposes the legislature may authorize loans by the Territory, or any such subdivision thereof, for the erection of penal, charitable, and educational institutions, and for public buildings, wharves, roads, and harbor and other public improvements, but the total of such indebtedness incurred in any one year by the Territory or any subdivision shall not exceed one per centum upon the assessed value of taxable property of the Territory or subdivision thereof, as the case may be, as shown by the last general assessment for taxation, and the total indebtedness for the Territory shall not at any time be extended beyond seven per centum of such assessed value, and the total indebtedness for the Territory shall not at any time be extended beyond seven per centum of such assessed value, and the total indebtedness of any subdivision shall not at any time be extended beyond three per centum of such assessed value, but nothing in this provision shall prevent the refunding of any existing indebtedness at any time; nor shall any such loan be made upon the credit of the public domain or any part thereof, nor shall any bond or other instrument of any such indebtedness be issued unless made redeemable in not more than five years and payable in not more than fifteen years from the date of the issue thereof; nor shall any such bond or indebtedness be incurred until approved by the President of the United States.

Section 56

Town, City, and County Government

That the legislature may create counties and town and city municipalities within the Territory of Hawaii and provide for the government thereof.

Section 57

Elections

Election procedures and voter qualifications are described in Sections 57 through 65.

Chapter 3—The Executive
Section 66

The Executive Power

That the executive power of the government of the Territory of Hawaii shall be vested in a governor, who shall be appointed by the President, by and with the advice and consent of the Senate of the United States, and shall hold office for four years and until his successor shall be appointed and qualified, unless sooner removed by the President. He shall be not less than thirty-five years of age; shall be a citizen of the Territory of Hawaii; shall be commander in chief of the militia thereof; may grant pardons or reprieves for offenses against the laws of the said Territory and reprieves for offenses against the laws of the United States until the decision of the President is made known thereon.

Section 6

Enforcement of Law

That the governor shall be responsible for the faithful execution of the laws of the United States and of the Territory of Hawaii within the said Territory, and whenever it becomes necessary he may call upon the commanders of the military and naval forces of the United States in the Territory of Hawaii, or summon the *posse comitatus*, or call out the militia of the Territory to prevent or suppress lawless violence, invasion, insurrection, or rebellion in said Territory, and he may, in case of rebellion or invasion, or imminent danger thereof, when the public safety requires it, suspend the privilege of the writ of habeas corpus, or place the Territory, or any part thereof, under martial law until communication can be had with the President and his decision thereon made known.

Section 68

General Powers of the Governor

That all the powers and duties which, by the laws of Hawaii, are conferred upon or required of the President or any minister of the Republic of Hawaii (acting alone or in connection with any other officer or person or body) or the cabinet or executive council, and not inconsistent with the Constitution or laws of the United States, are conferred upon and required of the governor of the Territory of Hawaii, unless otherwise provided.

Section 69

Sections 69 through 80 name and describe other government positions, including attorney-general, treasurers, superintendent of public instruction and commissioner of public lands.

Chapter 4—The Judiciary
Section 81

Sections 81 through 84 discuss the courts.

Chapter 5—United States Officers
Section 85

Delegate to Congress

That a Delegate to the House of Representatives of the United States, to serve during each Congress, shall be elected by the voters qualified to vote for members of the house of representatives of the legislature; such Delegate shall possess the qualifications necessary for membership of the senate of the legislature of Hawaii. The times, places, and manner of holding elections shall be as fixed by law. The person having the greatest number of votes shall be declared by the governor duly elected, and a certificate shall be given accordingly. Every such Delegate shall have a seat in the House of Representatives, with the right of debate, but not of voting.

Section 86

Federal Court

That there shall be established in said Territory a district court to consist of one judge, who shall reside therein and be called the district judge. The President of the United States, by and with the advice and consent of the Senate of the United States, shall appoint a district judge, a district attorney, and a marshal of the United States for the said district, and said judge, attorney, and marshal shall hold office for six years unless sooner removed by the President. Said court shall have, in addition to the ordinary jurisdiction of district courts of the United States, jurisdiction of all cases cognizable in a circuit court of the United States, and shall proceed therein in the same manner as a circuit court; and said judge, district attorney, and marshal shall have and exercise in the Territory of Hawaii all the powers conferred by the laws of the United States upon the judges, district attorneys, and marshals of district and circuit courts of the United States. . . .

Section 87

Internal-Revenue District

That the Territory of Hawaii shall constitute a district for the collection of the internal revenue of the United States, with a collector, whose office shall be at Honolulu, and deputy collectors at such other places in the several islands as the Secretary of the Treasury shall direct.

Section 88

Customs District

That the Territory of Hawaii shall comprise a customs district of the United States, with ports of entry and delivery at Honolulu, Hilo, Mahukona, and Kahului.

Chapter 6—Miscellaneous
Section 89

Revenues from Wharves

That until further provision is made by Congress the wharves and landings constructed or controlled by the Republic of Hawaii on any seacoast, bay, roadstead, or harbor shall remain under the control of the government of the Territory of Hawaii, which shall receive and enjoy all revenues derived therefrom, on condition that said property shall be kept in good condition for the use and convenience of commerce, but no tolls or charges shall be made by the government of the Territory of Hawaii for the use of any such property by the United States, or by any vessel of war, tug, revenue cutter, or other boat or transport in the service of the United States.

Section 90

That Hawaiian postage stamps, postal cards, and stamped envelopes at the post-offices of the Hawaiian Islands when this Act takes effect shall not be sold, but, together with those that shall thereafter be received at such offices as herein provided, shall be canceled under the direction of the Postmaster-General of the United States; those previously sold and uncanceled shall, if presented at such offices within six months after this Act takes effect, be received at their face value in exchange for postage stamps, postal cards, and stamped envelopes of the United States of the same aggregate face value and, so far as may be, ofsuch denominations as desired.

Section 91

That the public property ceded and transferred to the United States by the Republic of Hawaii under the joint resolution of annexation, approved July seventh, eighteen hundred and ninety-eight, shall be and remain in the possession, use, and control of the government of the Territory of Hawaii, and shall be maintained, managed, and cared for by it, at its own expense, until otherwise provided for by Congress, or taken for the uses and purposes of the United States by direction of the President or of the governor of Hawaii. And all moneys in the Hawaiian treasury, and all the revenues and other property acquired by the Republic of Hawaii since said cession shall be and remain the property of the Territory of Hawaii.

Section 92

That the following officers shall receive the following annual salaries, to be paid by the United States: The governor, five thousand dollars; the secretary of the Territory, three thousand dollars; the chief justice of the supreme court of the Territory, five thousand five hundred dollars, and the associate justices of the supreme court, five thousand dollars each. The salaries of the said chief justice and the associate justices of the supreme court, and the judges of the circuit courts as above provided shall be paid by the United States; the United States district judge, five thousand dollars; the United States marshal, two thousand five hundred dollars; the United States district attorney, three thousand dollars. And the governor shall receive annually, in addition to his salary, the sum of five hundred dollars for stationery, postage, and incidentals; also his traveling expenses while absent from the capital on official business, and the sum of two thousand dollars annually for his private secretary.

Section 93

Imports from Hawaii into the United States

That imports from any of the Hawaiian Islands, into any State or any other Territory of the United States, of any dutiable articles not the growth, production, or manufacture of said islands, and imported into them from any foreign country after July seventh, eighteen hundred and ninety-eight, and before this Act takes effect, shall pay the same duties that are imposed on the same articles when imported into the United States from any foreign country.

Section 94

Investigation of Fisheries

That the Commissioner of Fish and Fisheries of the United States is empowered and required to examine into the entire subject of fisheries and the laws relating to the fishing rights in the Territory of Hawaii, and report to the President touching the same, and to recommend such changes in said laws as he shall see fit.

Section 95

Repeal of Laws Conferring Exclusive Fishing Rights

That all laws of the Republic of Hawaii which confer exclusive fishing rights upon any person or persons are hereby repealed, and all fisheries in the sea waters of the Territory of Hawaii not included in any fish pond or artificial inclosure shall be free to all citizens of the United States, subject, however, to vested rights; but no such vested right shall be valid after three years from the taking effect of this Act unless established as hereinafter provided.

Section 96

Proceedings for Opening Fisheries to Citizens

That any person who claims a private right to any such fishery shall, within two years after the taking effect of this Act, file his petition in a circuit court of the Territory of Hawaii, setting forth his claim to such fishing right, service of which petition shall be made upon the attorney-general, who shall conduct the case for the Territory, and such case shall be conducted as an ordinary action at law.

That if such fishing right be established, the attorney-general of the Territory of Hawaii may proceed, in such manner as may be provided by law for the condemnation of property for public use, to condemn such private right of fishing to the use of the citizens of the United States upon making just compensation, which compensation, when lawfully ascertained, shall be paid out of any money in the treasury of the Territory of Hawaii not otherwise appropriated.

Section 97

Quarantine

That quarantine stations shall be established at such places in the Territory of Hawaii as the Supervising Surgeon-General of the Marine-Hospital Service of the United States shall direct, and the quarantine regulations for said islands relating to the importation of diseases from other countries shall be under the control of the Government of the United States. . . .

The health laws of the government of Hawaii relating to the harbor of Honolulu and other harbors and inlets from the sea and to the internal control of the health of the islands shall remain in the jurisdiction of the government of the Territory of Hawaii, subject to the quarantine laws and regulations of the United States.

Section 98

That all vessels carrying Hawaiian registers on the twelfth day of August, eighteen hundred and ninety-eight, and which were owned bona fide by citizens of the United States, or the citizens of Hawaii, together with the following-named vessels claiming Hawaii register, Star of France, Euterpe, Star of Russia, Falls of Clyde, and Wilscott, shall be entitled to be registered as American vessels, with the benefits and privileges appertaining thereto, and the coasting trade between the islands aforesaid and any other portion of the United States, shall be regulated in accordance with the provisions of law applicable to such trade between any two great coasting districts.

Section 99

That the portion of the public domain heretofore known as Crown land is hereby declared to have been, on the twelfth day of August, eighteen hundred and ninety-eight, and prior thereto, the property of the Hawaiian government, and to be free and clear from any trust of or concerning the same, and from all claim of any nature whatsoever, upon the rents, issues, and profits thereof. It shall be subject to alienation and other uses as may be provided by law.

Section 100

That for the purposes of naturalization under the laws of the United States residence in the Hawaiian Islands prior to the taking effect of this Act shall be deemed equivalent to residence in the United States and in the Territory of Hawaii, and the requirement of a previous declaration of intention to become a citizen of the United States and to renounce former allegiance shall not apply to persons who have resided in said islands at least five years prior to the taking effect of this Act; but all other provisions of the laws of the United States relating to naturalization shall, so far as applicable, apply to persons in the said islands.

Section 101

That Chinese in the Hawaiian Islands when this Act takes effect may within one year thereafter obtain certificates of residence as required by "An Act to prohibit the coming of Chinese persons into the United States," approved May fifth, eighteen hundred and ninety-two, as amended by an Act approved November third, eighteen hundred and ninety-three, entitled "An Act to amend an Act entitled 'An Act to prohibit the coming of Chinese persons into the United States,' approved May fifth, eighteen hundred and ninety-two," and until the expiration of said year shall not be deemed to be unlawfully in the United States if found therein without such certificates:

Provided, however, That no Chinese laborer, whether he shall hold such certificate or not, shall be allowed to enter any Sate, Territory, or District of the United States from the Hawaiian Islands.

Section 102

That the laws of Hawaii relating to the establishment and conduct of any postal savings bank or institution are hereby abolished. . . .

Section 103

That any money of the Hawaiian Postal Savings Bank that shall remain unpaid to the persons entitled thereto on the first day of July, nineteen hundred and one, and any assets of said bank shall be turned over by the government of Hawaii to the Treasurer of the United States, and the Secretary of the Treasury shall cause an account to be stated, as of said date, between such government of Hawaii and the United States in respect to said Hawaiian Postal Savings Bank.

Section 104

This Act shall take effect forty-five days from and after the date of the approval thereof, excepting only as to section fifty-two, relating to appropriations, which shall take effect upon such approval.

◆ EXECUTIVE ORDER KNOWN AS THE "GENTLEMEN'S AGREEMENT," 1907

Whereas, by the act entitled "An Act to regulate the immigration of aliens into the United States," approved February 20, 1907, whenever the President is satisfied

that passports issued by any foreign government to its citizens to go to any country other than the United States or to any insular possession of the United States or to the Canal Zone, are being used for the purpose of enabling the holders to come to the continental territory of the United States to the detriment of labor conditions therein, it is made the duty of the President to refuse to permit such citizens of the country issuing such passports to enter the continental territory of the United States from such country or from such insular possession or from the Canal Zone;

And Whereas, upon sufficient evidence produced before me by the Department of Commerce and Labor, I am satisfied that passports issued by the Government of Japan to citizens of that country or Korea and who are laborers, skilled or unskilled, to go to Mexico, to Canada and to Hawaii, are being used for the purpose of enabling the holders thereof to come to the continental territory of the United States to the detriment of labor conditions therein;

I hereby order that such citizens of Japan or Korea, to-wit: Japanese or Korean laborers, skilled and unskilled, who have received passports to go to Mexico, Canada or Hawaii, and come therefrom, be refused permission to enter the continental territory of the United States.

It is further ordered that the Secretary of Commerce and Labor be, and he hereby is, directed to take, thru Bureau and Immigration and Naturalization, such measures and to make and enforce such rules and regulations as may be necessary to carry this order into effect.

Theodore Roosevelt
The White House,
March 14, 1907
No. 589

◆ IMMIGRATION ACT, 1917

In effect, this act created "barred zones" from which immigrants were prohibited. "Barred zones" included parts of China, all of India, Burma, Siam, Asiatic Russia, Polynesian Islands and part of Afghanistan.

Section 1

Be it enacted by the Senate and House of Representatives of the United States of America in Congress assembled, That the word "alien" wherever used in this Act shall include any person not a native-born or naturalized citizen of the United States; but this definition shall not be held to include Indians of the United States not taxed or citizens of the islands under the jurisdiction of the United States. That the term "United States" as used in the title as well as in the various sections of this Act shall be construed to mean the United States, and any waters, territory, or other place subject to the jurisdiction thereof, except the Isthmian Canal Zone; but if any alien shall leave the Canal Zone or any insular possession of the United States and attempt to enter any other place under the jurisdiction of the United States, nothing contained in this Act shall be construed as permitting him to enter under any other conditions than those applicable to all aliens. That the term "seaman" as used in this Act shall include every person signed on the ship's articles and employed in any capacity on board any vessel arriving in the United States from any foreign port or place.

That this Act shall be enforced in the Philippine Islands by officers of the general government thereof, unless and until it is superseded by an act passed by the Philippine Legislature and approved by the President of the United States to regulate immigration in the Philippine Islands as authorized in the Act entitled "An Act to declare the purpose of the people of the United States as to the future political status of the people of the Philippine Islands, and to provide a more autonomous government for those islands," approved August twenty-ninth, nineteen hundred and sixteen.

Section 2

That there shall be levied, collected, and paid a tax of $8 for every alien, including alien seamen regularly admitted as provided in this Act, entering the United States:

Provided, That children under sixteen years of age who accompany their father or their mother shall not be subject to said tax. The said tax shall be paid to the collector of customs of the port or customs district to which said alien shall come, or, if there be no collector at such port or district, then to the collector nearest thereto, by the master, agent, owner, or consignee of the vessel, transportation line, or other conveyance, or vehicle bringing such alien to the United States is impracticable. The tax imposed by this section shall be a lien upon the vessel or other vehicle of carriage or transportation bringing such aliens to the United States, and shall be a debt in favor of the United States against the owner or owners of such vessel or other vehicle, and the payment of such tax may be enforced by any legal or equitable remedy. That the said tax shall not be levied on account of aliens who enter the United States after an uninterrupted residence of at least one year immediately precedingsuch entrance in the Dominion of Canada, Newfoundland, the Republic of Cuba, or the Republic of Mexico, for a temporary stay, nor on account of otherwise admissible residents or citizens of any possession of the United States, nor on account of aliens in transit through the United States,

nor upon aliens who have been lawfully admitted to the United States and who later shall go in transit from one part of the United States to another through foreign contiguous territory, and the Commissioner General of Immigration with the approval of the Secretary of Labor shall issue rules and regulations and prescribe the conditions necessary to prevent abuse of these exceptions:

Provided, That the Commissioner General of Immigration, under the direction or with the approval of the Secretary of Labor, by agreement with transportation lines, as provided in section twenty-three of this Act, may arrange in some other manner for the payment of the tax imposed by this section upon any or all aliens seeking admission from foreign contiguous territory:

Provided further, That said tax, when levied upon aliens entering the Philippine Islands, shall be paid into the treasury of said islands, to be expended for the benefit of such islands:

Provided further, That in the case of aliens applying for admission from foreign contiguous territory and rejected, the head tax collected shall upon application, upon a blank which shall be furnished and explained to him, be refunded to the alien.

Section 3

That the following classes of aliens shall be excluded from admission into the United States: All idiots, imbeciles, feeble-minded persons, epileptics, insane persons; persons who have had one or more attacks of insanity at any time previously; persons of constitutional psychopathic inferiority; persons with chronic alcoholism; paupers; professional beggars; vagrants; persons afflicted with tuberculosis in any form or with a loathsome or dangerous contagious disease; persons not comprehended within any of the foregoing excluded classes who are found to be and are certified by the examining surgeon as being mentally or physically defective, such physical defect being of a nature which may affect the ability of such alien to earn a living; persons who have been convicted of or admit having committed a felony or other crime or misdemeanor involving moral turpitude; polygamists, or persons who practice polygamy or believe in or advocate the practice of polygamy; anarchists, or persons who believe in or advocate the overthrow by force or violence of the Government of the United States, or of all forms of law, or who disbelieve in or are opposed to organized government, or who advocate the assassination of public officials, or who advocate or teach the unlawful destruction of property; persons who are members of or affiliated with any organization entertaining and teaching disbelief in or opposition to organized government, or who advocate or teach the duty, necessity, or propriety of the unlawful assaulting or killing of any officer or officers, either of specific individuals or of officers generally, of the Government of the United States or of any other organized government, because of his or their official character, or who advocate or teach the unlawful destruction of property; prostitutes, or persons coming into the United States for the purpose of prostitution or for any other immoral purpose; persons who directly or indirectly procure or attempt to procure or import prostitutes of persons for the purpose of prostitution or for any other immoral purpose; persons who are supported by or receive in whole or in part the proceeds of prostitution; persons hereinafter called contract laborers, who have been induced, assisted, encouraged, or solicited to migrate to this country by offers or promises of employment, . . .; persons whose tickets or passage is paid for with the money of another, or who are assisted by others to come, unless it is affirmatively and satisfactorily shown that such persons do not belong to one of the foregoing excluded classes; persons whose ticket or passage is paid for by any corporation, association, society, municipality, or foreign Government, either directly or indirectly; stowaways, except that any such stowaway, if otherwise admissible, may be admitted in the discretion of the Secretary of Labor; all children under sixteen years of age, unaccompanied by or not coming to one or both of their parents, except that any such children may, in the discretion of the Secretary of Labor, be admitted if in his opinion they are not likely to become a public charge and are otherwise eligible; unless otherwise provided for by existing treaties, persons who are natives of islands not possessed by the United States adjacent to the Continent of Asia, situate south of the twentieth parallel latitude north, west of the one hundred and sixtieth meridian of longitude east from Greenwich, and north of the tenth parallel of latitude south, or who are natives of any country, province, or dependency situate of the Continent of Asia west of the one hundred and tenth meridian of longitude east from Greenwich and east of the fiftieth meridian of longitude east from Greenwich and south of the fiftieth parallel of latitude north, except that portion of said territory situate between the fiftieth and the sixty-fourth meridians of longitude east from Greenwich and the twenty-fourth meridians of longitude east from Greenwich and the twenty-fourth and thirty-eighth parallels of latitude north, and no alien now in any way excluded from, or prevented from entering, the United States shall be admitted to the United States. The provision next foregoing, however, shall not apply to persons of the following status or occupations: Government officers, ministers or religious teachers, missionaries, lawyers, physicians, chemists, civil engineers, teachers, students, authors, artists, merchants, and travelers for curiosity or pleasure, nor to their legal wives or their children under sixteen years of age who shall accompany them or who subsequently may apply for admission to the United States, but such persons or their legal wives or foreign-born children who fail to maintain in the United States a status or occupation placing them within the excepted classes shall be deemed to be in the United States contrary to law, and shall be subject to deportation as provided in section nineteen of this Act.

That after three months from the passage of this Act, in addition to the aliens who are by law now excluded from admission into the United States, the following persons shall also be excluded from admission thereto, to wit:

All aliens over sixteen years of age, physically capable of reading, who can not read the English language, or some other language or dialect, including Hebrew or Yiddish:

Provided, That any admissible alien, or any alien heretofore or hereafter legally admitted, or any citizen of the United States, may bring in or send for his father or grandfather over fifty-five years of age, his wife, his mother, his grandmother, or his unmarried or widowed daughter, if otherwise admissible, whether such relative can read or not; and such relative shall be permitted to enter. . . That the following classes of persons shall be exempt from the operation of the illiteracy test, to wit: All aliens who shall prove to the satisfaction of the proper immigration officer or to the Secretary of Labor that they are seeking admission to the United States to avoid religious persecution in the country of their last permanent residence, whether such persecution be evidenced by overt acts or by laws or governmental regulations that discriminate against the alien or the race to which he belongs because of his religious faith; all aliens who have been lawfully admitted to the United States and who have resided therein continuously for five years, and who return to the United States within six months from the date of their departure therefrom; all aliens in transit through the United States; all aliens who have been lawfully admitted to the United States and who later shall go in transit from one part of the United States to another through foreign contiguous territory:

Provided, That nothing in this Act shall exclude, if otherwise admissible, persons convicted, or who admit the commission, or who teach or advocate the commission, of an offense purely political:

Provided further, That the provisions of this Act, relating to the payments for tickets or passage by any corporation, association, society, municipality, or foreign Government shall not apply to the tickets or passage of aliens in immediate and continuous transit through the United States to foreign contiguous territory:

Provided further, That skilled labor, if otherwise admissible, may be imported if labor of like kind unemployed can not be found in this country, and the question of the necessity of importing such skilled labor in any particular instance may be determined by the Secretary of Labor upon the application of any person interested, such application to be made before such importation, and such determination by the Secretary of Labor to be reached after a full hearing and an investigation into the facts of the case:

Provided further, That the provisions of this law applicable to contract labor shall not be held to exclude professional actors, artists, lecturers, singers, nurses, ministers of any religious denomination, professors for colleges or seminaries, persons belonging to any recognized learned profession, or persons employed as domestic servants:

Provided further, There whenever the President shall be satisfied that passports issued by any foreign Government to its citizens or subjects to go to any country other than the United States, or to any insular possession of the United States or to the Canal Zone, are being used for the purpose of enabling the holder to come to the continental territory of the United States to the detriment of labor conditions therein, the President shall refuse to permit such citizens or subjects of the country issuing such passports to enter the continental territory of the United States from such other country or from such insular possession or from the Canal Zone:

Provided further, That aliens returning after a temporary absence to an unrelinquished United States domicile of seven consecutive years may be admitted in the discretion of the Secretary of Labor, and under such conditions as he may prescribe:

Provided further, That nothing in the contract-labor or reading-test provisions of this Act shall be construed to prevent, hinder, or restrict any alien exhibitor, or holder of concession or privilege for any fair or exposition authorized by Act of Congress, from bringing into the United States, under contract, such otherwise admissible alien mechanics, artisans, agents, or other employees, natives of his country as may be necessary for installing or conducting his exhibit or for preparing for installing or conducting any business authorized or permitted under any concession or privilege which may have been or may be granted by any such fair or exposition in connection therewith, under such rules and regulations as the Commissioner General of Immigration, with the approval of the Secretary of Labor, may prescribe both as to the admission and return of such persons:

Provided further, That the Commissioner General of Immigration with the approval of the Secretary of Labor shall issue rules and prescribe conditions, including exaction of such bonds as may be necessary, to control and regulate the admission and return of otherwise inadmissible aliens applying for temporary admission:

Provided further, That nothing in this Act shall be construed to apply to accredited officials of foreign Governments, nor to their suites, families, or guests.

Section 4

That the importation into the United States of any alien for the purpose of prostitution, or for any other immoral purpose, is hereby forbidden. . . *The remainder of Section 4 sets forth punishments for offenders.*

Section 5

That it shall be unlawful for any person, company, partnership, or corporation, in any manner whatsoever, to prepay the transportation or in any way to induce, assist, encourage, or solicit, or attempt to induce, assist, encourage, or solicit the importation or migration of any contract laborer or contract laborers into the United States, unless such contract laborer or contract laborers are exempted under the fifth proviso of section three of this Act, or have been imported with the permission of the Secretary of Labor in accordance with the fourth proviso of said section. . . *The remainder of Section 5 establishes punishments for violators.*

Section 6

That it shall be unlawful and be deemed a violation of section five of this Act to induce, assist, encourage, or solicit or attempt to induce, assist, encourage, or solicit any alien to come into the United States by promise of employment through advertisements printed, published, or distributed in any foreign country, whether such promise is true or false, and either the civil or criminal penalty or both imposed by said section shall be applicable to such a case.

Section 7

That it shall be unlawful for any person, association, society, company, partnership, corporation, or others engaged in the business of transporting aliens to or within the United States, including owners, masters, officers, and agents of vessels, directly or indirectly, by writing, printing, oral representation, payment of any commissions to an alien coming into the United States, allowance of any rebates to an alien coming into the United States, or otherwise to solicit, invite, or encourage or attempt to solicit, invite, or encourage any alien to come into the United States, and anyone violating any provision hereof shall be subject to either the civil or the criminal prosecution, or both, prescribed by section five of this Act. . . Fines and sanctions are set in the rest of Section 7.

Section 8

That any person, including the master, agent, owner, or consignee of any vessel, who shall bring into or land in the United States, by vessel or otherwise, or shall attempt, by himself or through another, to bring into or land in the United States, by vessel or otherwise, or shall conceal or harbor, or attempt to conceal or harbor, or assist or abet another to conceal or harbor in any place, including any building, vessel, railway car, conveyance, or vehicle, any alien not duly admitted by an immigrant inspector or not lawfully entitled to enter or to reside within the United States under the terms of this Act, shall be deemed guilty of a misdemeanor, and upon conviction thereof shall be punished by a fine not exceeding $2,000 and by imprisonment for a term not exceeding five years, for each and every alien so landed or brought in or attempted to be landed or brought in.

Section 9

That it shall be unlawful for any person, including any transportation company other than railway lines entering the United States from foreign contiguous territory, or the owner, master, agent, or consignee of any vessel to bring to the United States either from a foreign country or any insular possession of the United States any alien afflicted with idiocy, insanity, imbecility, feeble-mindedness, epilepsy, constitutional psychopathic inferiority, chronic alcoholism, tuberculosis in any form, or a loathsome or dangerous contagious disease. . . *The remainder of Section 9 states that transportation companies are responsible for knowing the legal and health status of aliens they are transporting, and sets penalties for violators.*

Section 10

That it shall be the duty of every person, including owners, officers, and agents of vessels or transportation lines, or international bridges or toll roads, other than railway lines which may enter into a contract as provided in section twenty-three of this Act, bringing an alien to, or providing a means for an alien to come to, any seaport or land border port of the United States, to prevent the landing of such alien in the United States at any time or place other than as designated by the immigration officers, and the failure of any such person,

owner, officer, or agent to comply with the foregoing requirements shall be deemed a misdemeanor and on conviction thereof shall be punished by a fine in each case of not less than $200 nor more than $1,000, or by imprisonment for a term not exceeding one year, or by both such fine and imprisonment; or, if in the opinion of the Secretary of Labor it is impracticable or inconvenient to prosecute the person, owner, master, officer, or agent of any such vessel, a penalty of $1,000 shall be a lien upon the vessel whose owner, master, officer, or agent violates the provisions of this section, and such vessel shall be libeled therefore in the appropriate United States court.

Section 11

That for the purpose of determining whether aliens arriving at ports of the United States belong to any of the classes excluded by this Act, either by reason of being afflicted with any of the diseases or mental or physical defects or disabilities mentioned in section three hereof, or otherwise, or whenever the Secretary of Labor has received information showing that any aliens are coming from a country or have embarked at a place where any of said diseases are prevalent or epidemic, the Commissioner General of Immigration, with the approval of the Secretary of Labor, may direct that such aliens shall be detained on board the vessel bringing them, or in a United States immigration station at the expense of such vessel, as circumstances may require or justify, a sufficient time to enable the immigration officers and medical officers stationed at such ports to subject such aliens to an observation and examination sufficient to determine whether or not they belong to the said excluded classes by reason of being afflicted in the manner indicated. . . .

Section 11a

That the Secretary of Labor is hereby authorized and directed to enter into negotiations through the Department of State, with countries vessels of which bring aliens to the United States, with a view to detailing inspectors and matrons of the United States Immigration Service for duty on vessels carrying immigrant or emigrant passengers between foreign ports and ports of the United States. When such inspectors and matrons are detailed for said duty they shall remain in that part of the vessel where immigrant passengers are carried; and it shall be their duty to observe such passengers during the voyage and report to the immigration authorities in charge at the port of landing any information of value in determining the admissibility of such passengers that may have become known to them during the voyage.

Section 12

Section 12 requires vessel commanders or owners to provide detailed information about alien passengers to United States government representatives.

Section 13

That all aliens arriving by water at the ports of the United States shall be listed in convenient groups, the names of those coming from the same locality to be assembled so far as practicable, and no one list or manifest shall contain more than thirty names. . . The remainder of Sections 13 and 14 details procedures to be followed with alien passenger lists.

Section 15

That upon the arrival at a port of the United States of any vessel bringing aliens it shall be the duty of the proper immigration officials to go or to send competent assistants to the vessel and there inspect all such aliens or said immigration officials may order a temporary removal of such aliens for examination at a designated time and place, but such temporary removal shall not be considered a landing, nor shall it relieve vessels, the transportation lines, masters, agents, owners, or consignees of the vessel upon which said aliens are brought to any port of the United States from any of the obligations which, in case such aliens remain on board, would under the provisions of this Act bind the said vessels, transportation lines, masters, agents, owners, or consignees:

Provided, That where removal is made to premises owned or controlled by the United States, said vessels, transportation lines, masters, agents, owners, or consignees, and each of them, shall, so long as detention there lasts, be relieved of responsibility for the safekeeping of such aliens. Whenever a temporary removal of aliens is made the vessels or transportation lines which brought them and the masters, owners, agents, and consignees of the vessel upon which they arrive shall pay all expenses of such removal and all expenses arising during subsequent detention, pending decision on the aliens' eligibility to enter the United States and until they are either allowed to land or returned to the care of the lines or to the vessel which brought them, such expenses to include those of maintenance, medical treatment in hospital or elsewhere, burial in the event of death, and transfer to the vessel in the event of deportation, excepting only where they arise under the terms of any of the provisos of section eighteen hereof. Any refusal or failure to comply with the provisions hereof shall be punished in the manner specified in section eighteen of this Act.

Section 16

That the physical and mental examination of all arriving aliens shall be made by medical officers of the United States Public Health Service who shall have had at least two years' experience in the practice of their profession since receiving the degree of doctor of medicine, and who shall conduct all medical examinations and shall certify, for the information of the immigration officers and the boards of special inquiry hereinafter provided for, any and all physical and mental defects or diseases observed by said medical officers in any such alien: or, should medical officers of the United States Public Health Service be not available, civil surgeons of not less than four years' professional experience may be employed in such emergency for such service upon such terms as may be prescribed by the Commissioner General of Immigration, under the direction or with the approval of the Secretary of Labor. . . That the inspection, other than the physical and mental examination, of aliens, including those seeking admission or readmission to or the privilege of passing through or residing in the United States, and the examination of aliens arrested within the United States under this Act, shall be conducted by immigrant inspectors, except as hereinafter provided in regard to boards of special inquiry. All aliens arriving at ports of the United States shall be examined by at least two immigrant inspectors at the discretion of the Secretary of Labor and under such regulations as he may prescribe. Immigrant inspectors are hereby authorized and empowered to board and search for aliens any vessel, railway car, or any other conveyance, or vehicle in which they believe aliens are being brought into the United States. Said inspectors shall have power to administer oaths and to take and consider evidence touching the right of any alien to enter, reenter, pass through, or reside in the United States, and, where such action may be necessary, to make a written record of such evidence; and any person to whom such an oath has been administered, under the provisions of this Act, who shall knowingly or willfully give false evidence or swear to any false statement in any way affecting or in relation to the right of any alien to admission, or readmission to, or to pass through, or to reside in the United States shall be deemed guilty of perjury and be punished as provided by section one hundred and twenty-five of the Act approved March fourth, nineteen hundred and nine, entitled "An Act to codify, revise, and amend the penal laws of the United States." All aliens coming to the United States shall be required to state under oath the purposes for which they come, the length of time they intend to remain in the United States, whether or not they intend to abide in the United States permanently and become citizens thereof, and such other items of information regarding themselves as will aid the immigration officials in determining whether they belong to any of the excluded classes enumerated in section three hereof. Any commissioner of immigration or inspector in charge shall also have power to require by subpoena the attendance and testimony of witnesses before said inspectors and the production of books, papers, and documents touching the right of any alien to enter, reenter, reside in, or pass through the United States, and to that end may invoke the aid of any court of the United States; and any district court within the jurisdiction of which investigations are being conducted by an immigrant inspector may, in the event of neglect or refusal to respond to a subpoena issued by any commissioner of immigration or inspector in charge or refusal to testify before said immigrant inspector, issue an order requiring such person to appear before said immigrant inspector, produce books, papers, and documents if demanded, and testify; and any failure to obey such order of the court may be punished by the court as a contempt thereof. That any person, including employees, officials, or agents of transportation companies, who shall assault, resist, prevent, impede, or interfere with any immigration official or employee in the performance of his duty under this Act shall be deemed guilty of a misdemeanor, and on conviction thereof shall be punished by imprisonment for a term of not more than one year, or by a fine of not more than $2,000 or both; and any person who shall use any deadly or dangerous weapon in resisting any immigration official or employee in the performance of his duty shall be deemed guilty of a felony and shall, on conviction thereof, be punished by imprisonment for not more than ten years. Every alien who may not appear to the examining immigrant inspector at the port of arrival to be clearly and beyond a doubt entitled to land shall be detained for examination in relation thereto by a board of special inquiry. In the event of rejection by the board of special inquiry, in all cases where an appeal of the Secretary of Labor is permitted by this Act, the alien shall be so informed and shall have the right to be represented by counsel or other adviser on such appeal. The decision of an immigrant inspector, if favorable to the admission of any alien, shall be subject to challenge by any other immigrant inspector, and such challenge shall operate to take the alien whose right to land is so challenged before a board of special inquiry for its investigation.

Section 17

That board of special inquiry shall be appointed by the commissioner of immigration or inspector in charge at the various ports of arrival as may be necessary for the prompt determination of all cases of immigrants detained at such ports under the provisions of the law. Each board shall consist of three members, who shall be selected from such of the immigrant officials in the service as the Commissioner General of Immigration, with the approval of the Secretary of Labor, shall from time to time designate as qualified to serve on such boards. When in the opinion of the Secretary of Labor the maintenance of a permanent board of special inquiry for service at any sea or land border port is not warranted, regularly constituted boards may be detailed from other stations for temporary service at such port, or, if that be impracticable, the Secretary of Labor shall authorize the creation of boards of special inquiry by the immigration officials in charge at such ports, and shall determine what Government officials or other persons shall be eligible for service on such boards. Such boards shall have authority to determine whether an alien who has been duly held shall be allowed to land or shall be deported. All hearings before such boards shall be separate and apart from the public, but the immigrant may have one friend or relative present under such regulations as may be prescribed by the Secretary of Labor. Such boards shall keep a complete permanent record of their proceedings and of all such testimony as may be produced before them; and the decisions of any two members of the board shall prevail, but either the alien or any dissenting member of the said board may appeal through the commissioner of immigration at the port of arrival and the Commissioner General of Immigration to the Secretary of Labor, and the taking of such appeal shall operate to stay any action in regard to the final disposal of any alien whose case is so appealed until the receipt by the commissioner of immigration at the port of arrival of such decision which shall be rendered solely upon the evidence adduced before the board of special inquiry. In every case where an alien is excluded from admission into the United States, under any law or treaty now existing or hereafter made, the decision of a board of special inquiry adverse to the admission of such alien shall be final, unless reversed on appeal to the Secretary of Labor:

Provided, That the decision of a board of special inquiry shall be based upon the certificate of the examining medical officer and, except as provided in section twenty-one hereof, shall be final as to the rejection of aliens affected with tuberculosis in any form or with a loathsome or dangerous contagious disease, or with any mental or physical disability which would bring such aliens within any of the classes excluded from admission to the United States under section three of this Act.

Section 18

That all aliens brought to this country in violation of law shall be immediately sent back, in accommodations of the same class in which they arrived, to the country whence they respectively came, on the vessels bringing them, unless in the opinion of the Secretary of Labor immediate deportation is not practicable or proper. . . *The remainder of Section 18 details penalties for violations and discusses exceptions to be made for medical or safety reasons.*

Section 19

That at any time within five years after entry, any alien who at the time of entry was a member of one or more of the classes excluded by law; any alien who shall have entered or who shall be found in the United States in violation of this Act, or in violation of any other law of the United States; any alien who at any time after entry shall be found advocating or teaching the unlawful destruction of property, or advocating or teaching anarchy, or the overthrow by force or violence of the Government of the United States or of all forms of law or the assassination of public officials; any alien who within five years after entry becomes a public charge from causes not affirmatively shown to have arisen subsequent to landing; except as hereinafter provided, any alien who is hereafter sentenced to imprisonment for a term of one year or more because of conviction in this country of a crime involving moral turpitude, committed within five years after the entry of the alien to the United States, or who is hereafter sentenced more than once to such a term of imprisonment because of conviction in this country of any crime involving moral turpitude, committed at any time after entry. . . any alien who was convicted, or who admits the commission, prior to entry, of a felony or other crime or misdemeanor involving moral turpitude; at any time within three years after entry, any alien who shall have entered the United States by water at any time or place other than as designated by immigration officials, or by land at any place other than one designated as a port of entry for aliens by the Commissioner General of Immigration, or at any time not designated by immigration officials, or who enters without inspection, shall, upon the warrant of the Secretary of Labor, be taken into custody and deported:

Provided, That the marriage to an American citizen of a female of the sexually immoral classes the exclusion or deportation of which is prescribed by this Act shall not invest such female with United States citizenship if the marriage of such alien female shall be solemnized after her arrest or after the commission of acts which make her liable to deportation under this Act:

Provided further, That the provision of this section respecting the deportation of aliens convicted of a crime involving moral turpitude shall not apply to one who has been pardoned, nor shall such deportation be made or directed if the court, or judge thereof, sentencing such alien for such crime shall, at the time of imposing judgment or passing sentence or within thirty days thereafter, due notice having first been given to representatives of the State, make a recommendation to the Secretary of Labor that such alien shall not be deported in pursuance of this Act; nor shall any alien convicted as aforesaid be deported until after the termination of his imprisonment:

Provided further, That the provisions of this section, with the exceptions hereinbefore noted, shall be applicable to the classes of aliens therein mentioned irrespective of the time of their entry into the United States:

Provided further, That the provisions of this section shall also apply to the cases of aliens who come to the mainland of the United States from the insular possessions thereof:

Provided further, That any person who shall be arrested under the provisions of this section, on the ground that he has entered or been found in the United States in violation of any other law thereof which imposes on such person the burden of proving his right to enter or remain, and who shall fail to establish the existence of the right claimed, shall be deported to the place specified in such other law. In every case where any person is ordered deported from the United States under the provisions of this Act, or of any law or treaty, the decision of the Secretary of Labor shall be final.

Section 20

That the deportation of aliens provided for in this Act shall, at the option of the Secretary of Labor, be to the country whence they came or to the foreign port at which such aliens embarked for the United States; or, if such embarkation was for foreign contiguous territory, to the foreign port at which they embarked for such territory; or, if such aliens entered foreign contiguous territory from the United States and later entered the United States, or if such aliens are held by the country from which they entered the United States not to be subjects or citizens of such country, and such country refuses to permit their reentry, or imposes any condition upon permitting reentry, then to the country of which such aliens are subjects or citizens, or to the country in which they resided prior to entering the country from which they entered the United States. If deportation proceedings are instituted at any time within five years after the entry of the alien, such deportation, including one-half of the entire cost of removal to the port of deportation, shall be at the expense of the contractor, procurer, or other person by whom the alien was unlawfully induced to enter the United States, or, if that can not be done, then the cost of removal to the port of deportation shall be at the expense of the appropriation for the enforcement of this Act, and the deportation from such port shall be at the expense of the owner, or owners of such vessels or transportation line by which such aliens respectively came, or, if that is not practicable, at the expense of the appropriation for the enforcement of this Act. If deportation proceedings are instituted later than five years after the entry of the alien, or, if the deportation is made by reason of causes arising subsequent to entry, the cost thereof shall be payable from the appropriation for the enforcement of this Act. A failure or refusal on the part of the masters, agents, owners, or consignees of vessels to comply with the order of the Secretary of Labor to take on board, guard safely, and transport to the designation specified any alien ordered to be deported under the provisions of this Act shall be punished by the imposition of the penalties prescribed in section eighteen of this Act:

Provided, That when in the opinion of the Secretary of Labor the mental or physical condition of such alien is such as to require personal care and attendance, the said Secretary shall when necessary employ a suitable person for that purpose, who shall accompany such alien to his or her final destination, and the expense incident to such service shall be defrayed in the same manner as the expense of deporting the accompanied alien is defrayed. Pending the final disposal of the case of any alien so taken into custody, he may be released under a bond in the penalty of not less than $500 with security approved by the Secretary of Labor, conditioned that such alien shall be produced when required for a hearing or hearings in regard to the charge upon which he has been taken into custody, and for deportation if he shall be found to be unlawfully within the United States.

Section 21

That any alien liable to be excluded because likely to become a public charge or because of physical disability other than tuberculosis in any form or a loathsome or dangerous contagious disease may, if otherwise admissible, nevertheless be admitted in the discretion of the Secretary of Labor upon the giving of a suitable and proper bond or undertaking, approved by said Secretary, in such amount and containing such conditions as he may prescribe, to the United States and to all States, Territories, countries, towns, municipalities, and districts thereof, holding the United States and all States, Territories, counties, towns, municipalities, and districts thereof harmless against such alien becoming a public charge. In lieu of such bond, such alien may deposit in cash with the Secretary of Labor such amount as the Secretary of Labor may require, which amount shall be deposited by said Secretary in the United States Postal Savings Bank, a receipt therefore to be given the person furnishing said sum, showing the fact and object of its receipt and such other information as said Secretary may deem advisable. All accruing interest on said deposit during the same time shall be held in the United States Postal Savings Bank shall be paid to the person furnishing the sum for deposit. In the event of such alien becoming a public charge, the Secretary of Labor shall dispose of said deposit in the same manner as if same had been collected under a bond as provided in this section. In the event of the permanent departure from the United States, the naturalization, or the death of such alien, the said sum shall be returned to the person by whom furnished, or to his legal representatives. The admission of such alien shall be a consideration for the giving of such bond, undertaking, or cash deposit. Suit may be brought thereon in the name and by the proper law officers either of the United States Government or of any State, Territory, District, county, town, or municipality in which such alien becomes a public charge.

Section 22

That whenever an alien shall have been naturalized or shall have taken up his permanent residence in this country, and thereafter shall send for his wife or minor children to join him, and said wife or any of said minor children shall be found to be affected with any contagious disorder, such wife or minor children shall be held, under such regulations as the Secretary of Labor shall prescribe, until it shall be determined whether the disorder will be easily curable or whether they can be permitted to land without danger to other persons; and they shall not be either admitted or deported until such facts have been ascertained; and if it shall be determined that the disorder is easily curable and the husband or father or other responsible person is willing to bear the expense of the treatment, they may be accorded treatment in hospital until cured and then be admitted, or if it shall be determined that they can be permitted to land without danger to other persons, they may, if otherwise admissible, thereupon be admitted:

Provided, That if the person sending for wife or minor children is naturalized, a wife to whom married or a minor child born subsequent to such husband or father's naturalization shall be admitted without detention for treatment in hospital, and with respect to a wife to whom married or a minor child born prior to such husband or father's naturalization the provisions of this section shall be observed, even though such person is unable to pay the expense of treatment, in which case the expense shall be paid from the appropriation for the enforcement of this Act.

Section 23

Sections 23 through 27 discuss the duties of the Commissions General of Immigration and other administrative matters.

Section 28

That any person who knowingly aids or assists any anarchist or any person who believes in or advocates the overthrow by force or violence of the Government of the United States, or who disbelieves in or is opposed to organized government, or all forms of law, or who advocates the assassination of public officials, or who is a member of or affiliated with any organization entertaining or teaching disbelief in or opposition to organized government, or who advocates or teaches the duty, necessity, or propriety of the unlawful assaulting or killing of any officer or officers, either of specific individuals or of officers generally, of the Government of the United States or of any other organized government, because of his or their official character, to enter the United States, or who connives or conspires with any person or persons to allow, procure, or permit any such anarchist or person aforesaid to enter therein, shall be deemed guilty of a felony, and on conviction thereof shall be punished by a fine of not more than $5,000 or by imprisonment for not more than five years, or both.

Any person who knowingly aids or assists any alien who advocates or teaches the unlawful destruction of property to enter the United States shall be deemed guilty of a misdemeanor and on conviction thereof shall be punished by a fine of not more than $1,000, or by imprisonment for not more than six months, or by both such fine and imprisonment.

Section 29

That the President of the United States is authorized, in the name of the Government of the United States, to call, in his discretion, an international conference, to assemble at such point as may be agreed upon, or to send special commissioners to any foreign country, for the purpose of regulating by international agreement, subject to the advice and consent of the Senate of the United States, the immigration of aliens to the United States; of providing for the mental, moral, and physical examination of such aliens by American consuls or other officers of the United States Government at the ports of embarkation, or elsewhere; of securing the assistance of foreign Governments in their own territories to present the evasion of the laws of the United States governing immigration to the United States; of entering into such international agreements as may be proper to prevent the immigration of aliens who, under the laws of the United States, are or may be excluded from entering the United States, and of regulating any matters pertaining to such immigration.

Section 30

That there shall be maintained a division of information in the Bureau of Immigration; and the Secretary of Labor shall provide such clerical and other assistance as may be necessary. It shall be the duty of said division to promote a beneficial distribution of aliens admitted into the United States among the several States and Territories desiring immigration. Correspondence shall be had with the proper officials of the States and Territories, and said division shall gather from all available sources useful information regarding the resources, products, and physical characteristics of each State and Territory, and shall publish such information in different languages and distribute the publications among all admitted aliens at the immigrant stations of the United States and to such other persons as may desire the same. When any State or Territory appoints and maintains an agent or agents to represent it at any of the immigrant stations of the United States, such agents shall, under regulations prescribed by the Commissioner General of Immigration, subject to the approval of the Secretary of Labor, have access to aliens who have been admitted to the United States for the purpose of presenting, either orally or in writing, the special inducements offered by such State or Territory to aliens to settle therein. While on duty at any immigrant station such agents shall be subject to all the regulations prescribed by the Commissioner General of Immigration, who, with the approval of the Secretary of Labor, may, for violation of any such regulations, deny to the agent guilty of such violation any of the privileges herein granted.

Section 31

That any person, including the owner, agent, consignee, or master of any vessel arriving in the United States from any foreign port or place, who shall knowingly sign on the ship's articles or bring to the United States as one of the crew of such vessel, any alien, with intent to permit such alien to land in the United States in violation of the laws and treaties of the United States regulating the immigration of aliens, or who shall falsely and knowingly represent to the immigration authorities at the port of arrival that any such alien is a bona fide member of the crew, shall be liable to a penalty not exceeding $5,000, for which sum the said vessel shall be liable and may be seized and proceeded against by way of libel in any district court of the United States having jurisdiction of the offense.

Section 32

That no alien excluded from admission into the United States by any law, convention, or treaty of the United States regulating the immigration of aliens, and employed on board any vessel arriving in the United States from any foreign port or place, shall be permitted to land in the United States, except temporarily for medical treatment. . . .

Section 33

That it shall be unlawful and be deemed a violation of the preceding section to pay off or discharge any alien employed on board any vessel arriving in the United States from any foreign port or place, unless duly admitted pursuant to the laws and treaties of the United States regulating the immigration of aliens. . . .

Section 34

That any alien seaman who shall land in a port of the United States contrary to the provisions of this Act shall be deemed to be unlawfully in the United States, and shall, at any time within three years thereafter, upon the warrant of the Secretary of Labor, be taken into custody and brought before a board of special inquiry for examination as to his qualifications for admission to the United States, and if not admitted said alien seaman shall be deported at the expense of the appropriation for this Act as provided in section twenty of this Act.

Section 35

That it shall be unlawful for any vessel carrying passengers between a port of the United States and a port of a foreign country, upon arrival in the United States, to have on board employed thereon any alien afflicted with idiocy, imbecility, insanity, epilepsy, tuberculosis in any form, or a loathsome or dangerous contagious disease. . .

Section 36

Instructs those responsible for arriving vessels to deliver lists of aliens employed on the vessels to immigration officials, and informs them of their responsibilities for keeping track of those employers.

Section 37

That the word "person" as used in this Act shall be construed to import both plural and the singular, as the case may be, and shall include corporations, companies, and associations. When construing and enforcing the provisions of this Act, the act, omission, or failure of any director, officer, agent, or employee of any corporation, company, or association acting within the scope of his employment or office shall in every case be deemed to be the act, omission, or failure of such corporation, company, or association, as well as that of the person acting for or in behalf of such corporation, company, or association.

Section 38

Provided, That this Act shall not be construed to repeal, alter, or amend existing laws relating to the immigration or exclusion of Chinese persons or persons of Chinese descent, except as provided in section nineteen hereof, nor to repeal, alter, or amend section six, chapter four hundred and fifty-three, third session Fifty-eighth Congress, approved February sixth, nineteen hundred and five, nor to repeal, alter, or amend the Act approved August second, eighteen hundred and eighty-two, entitled "An Act to regulate the carriage of passengers by sea," and amendments thereto, except as provided in section eleven hereof:

Provided further, That nothing contained in this Act shall be construed to affect any prosecution, suit, action, or proceedings brought, or any act, thing, or matter, civil or criminal, done or existing at the time of the taking effect of this Act, except as mentioned in the third proviso of section nineteen hereof; but as to all such prosecutions, suits, actions, proceedings, acts, things, or matters, the laws or parts of laws repealed or amended by this Act are hereby continued in force and effect.

◆ CABLE ACT, 1922

After this act was approved, female citizens of the United States who married men ineligible for citizenship lost her own citizenship.

Be it enacted by the Senate and House of Representatives of the United States of America in Congress assembled, That the right of any woman to become a naturalized citizen of the United States shall not be denied or abridged because of her sex or because she is a married woman.

Section 2

That any woman who marries a citizen of the United States after the passage of this Act, or any woman whose husband is naturalized after the passage of this Act, shall not become a citizen of the United States by reason of such marriage or naturalization; but, if eligible to citizenship, she may be naturalized upon full and complete compliance with all requirements of the naturalization laws, with the following exceptions:

(a) No declaration of intention shall be required;

(b) In lieu of the five-year period of residence within the State or Territory where the naturalization court is held, she shall have resided continuously in the United States, Hawaii, Alaska, or Puerto Rico for at least one year immediately preceding the filing of the petition.

Section 3

That a woman citizen of the United States shall not cease to be a citizen of the United States by reason of her marriage after the passage of this Act, unless she makes a formal renunciation of her citizenship before a court having jurisdiction over naturalization of aliens: Provided, That any woman citizen who marries an alien ineligible to citizenship shall cease to be a citizen of the United States. If at the termination of the marital status she is a citizen of the United States she shall retain her citizenship regardless of her residence. If during the continuance of the marital status she resides continuously for two years in a foreign State of which her husband is a citizen or subject, or for five years continuously outside the United States, she shall thereafter be subject to the same presumption as is a naturalized citizen of the United States under the second paragraph of section 2 of the Act entitled "An Act in reference to the expatriation of citizens and their protection abroad," approved March 2, 1907. Nothing herein shall be construed to repeal or amend the provisions of Revised Statutes 1999 or of section 2 of the Expatriation Act of 1907 with reference to expatriation.

Section 4

That a woman who, before the passage of this Act, has lost her United States citizenship by reason of her marriage to an alien eligible for citizenship, may be naturalized as provided by section 2 of this Act: Provided, That no certificate of arrival shall be required to be filed with her petition if during the continuance of the marital status she shall have resided within the United States. After her naturalization she shall have the same citizenship status as if her marriage had taken place after the passage of this Act.

Section 5

That no woman whose husband is not eligible to citizenship shall be naturalized during the continuance of the marital status.

Section 6

That section 1994 of the Revised Statutes and section 4 of the Expatriation Act of 1907 are repealed. Such repeal shall not terminate citizenship acquired or retained under either of such sections nor restore citizenship lost under section 4 of the Expatriation Act of 1907.

Section 7

That section 3 of the Expatriation Act of 1907 is repealed. Such repeal shall not restore citizenship lost under such section nor terminate citizenship resumed under such section. A woman who has resumed under such section citizenship lost by marriage shall, upon the passage of this Act, have for all purposes the same citizenship status as immediately preceding her marriage.

Approved, September 22, 1922.

♦ IMMIGRATION ACT, 1924

This Act, with its specifications about "quota" and "non-quota" immigrants, denied immigration to virtually all Asians.

Section 2

(a) A consular officer upon the application of any immigrant (as defined in section 3) may (under the conditions hereinafter prescribed and subject to the limitations prescribed in this Act or regulations made thereunder as to the number of immigration visas which may be issued by such officer) issue to such immigrant an immigration visa which shall consist of one copy of the application provided for in section 7, visaed by such consular officer. Such visa shall specify (1) the nationality of the immigrant; (2) whether he is a quota immigrant (as defined in section 5) or a non-quota immigrant (as defined in section 4); (3) the date on which the validity of the immigration visa shall expire; and (4) such additional information necessary to the proper enforcement of the immigration laws and the naturalization laws as may be by regulations prescribed.

(b) The immigrant shall furnish two copies of his photograph to the consular officer. One copy shall be permanently attached by the consular officer to the immigration visa and the other copy shall be disposed of as may be by regulations prescribed.

(c) The validity of an immigration visa shall expire at the end of such period, specified in the immigration visa, not exceeding four months, as shall be by regulations prescribed. In the case of an immigrant arriving in the United States by water, or arriving by water in foreign contiguous territory on a continuous voyage to the United States, if the vessel, before the expiration of the validity of his immigration visa, departed from the last port outside the United States and outside foreign contiguous territory at which the immigrant embarked, and if the immigrant proceeds on a continuous voyage to the United States, then, regardless of the time of his arrival in the United States, the validity of his immigration visa shall not be considered to have expired.

(d) If an immigrant is required by any law, or regulations or orders made pursuant to law, to secure the visa of his passport by a consular officer before being permitted to enter the United States, such immigrant shall not be required to secure any other visa of his passport than the immigration visa issued under this Act, but a record of the number and date of his immigration visa shall be noted on his passport without charge therefor. This subdivision shall not apply to an immigrant who is relieved, under subdivision (b) of section 13, from obtaining an immigration visa.

(e) The manifest or list of passengers required by the immigration laws shall contain a place for entering thereon the date, place of issuance, and number of the immigration visa of each immigrant. The immigrant shall surrender his immigration visa to the immigration officer at the port of inspection, who shall at the time of inspection indorse on the immigration visa the date, the port of entry, and the name of the vessel, if any, on which the immigrant arrived. The immigration visa shall be transmitted forthwith by the immigration officer in charge at the port of inspection to the Department of Labor under regulations prescribed by the Secretary of Labor.

(f) No immigration visa shall be issued to an immigrant if it appears to the consular officer, from statements in the application, or in the papers submitted therewith, that the immigrant is inadmissible to the United States under the immigration laws, nor shall such immigration visa be issued if the application fails to comply with the provisions of this Act, nor shall such immigration visa be issued if the consular officer knows or has reason to believe that the immigrant is inadmissible to the United States under the immigration laws.

(g) Nothing in this Act shall be construed to entitle an immigrant, to whom an immigration visa has been issued, to enter the United States, if, upon arrival in the United States, he is found to be inadmissible to the United States under the immigration laws. The substance of this subdivision shall be printed conspicuously upon every immigration visa.

(h) A fee of $9 shall be charged for the issuance of each immigration visa, which shall be covered into the Treasury as miscellaneous receipts.

Section 3

Definition of "Immigrant"

When used in this Act the term "immigrant" means any alien departing from any place outside the United States destined for the United States, except (1) a government official, his family, attendants, servants, and employees, (2) an alien visiting the United States temporarily as a tourist or temporarily for business or pleasure, (3) an alien in continuous transit through the United States, (4) an alien lawfully admitted to the United States who later goes in transit from one part of the United States to another through foreign contiguous territory, (5) a bona fide alien seaman serving as such on a vessel arriving at a port of the United States and seeking to enter temporarily the United States solely in the pursuit of his calling as a seaman, and (6) an alien entitled to enter the United States solely to carry on trade under and in pursuance of the provisions of a present existing treaty of commerce and navigation.

Section 4

Non-Quota Immigrants

When used in this Act the term "non-quota immigrant" means—

(a) An immigrant who is the unmarried child under 18 years of age, or the wife, of a citizen of the United States who resides therein at the time of the filing of a petition under section 9;

(b) An immigrant previously lawfully admitted to the United States, who is returning from a temporary visit abroad;

(c) An immigrant who was born in the Dominion of Canada, Newfoundland, the Republic of Mexico, the Republic of Cuba, the Republic of Haiti, the Dominican Republic, the Canal Zone, or an independent country of Central or South America, and his wife, and his unmarried children under 18 years of age, if accompanying or following to join him;

(d) An immigrant who continuously for at least two years immediately preceding the time of his application for admission to the United States has been, and who seeks to enter the United States solely for the purpose of, carrying on the vocation of minister of any religious denomination, or professor of a college, academy, seminary, or university; and his wife, and his unmarried children under 18 years of age, if accompanying or following to join him; or

(e) An immigrant who is a bona fide student at least 15 years of age and who seeks to enter the United States solely for the purpose of study at an accredited school, college, academy, seminary, or university, particularly designated by him and approved by the Secretary of

Labor, which shall have agreed to report to the Secretary of Labor the termination of attendance of each immigrant student, and if any such institution of learning fails to make such reports promptly the approval shall be withdrawn.

Section 5

Quota Immigrants

When used in this Act the term "quota immigrant" means any immigrant who is not a non-quota immigrant. An alien who is not particularly specified in this Act as a non-quota immigrant or a non-immigrant shall not be admitted as a non-quota immigrant or a non-immigrant by reason of relationship to any individual who is so specified or by reason of being excepted from the operation of any other law regulating or forbidding immigration.

Section 6

Preferences within Quotas

(a) In the issuance of immigration visas to quota immigrants preference shall be given—

(1) To a quota immigrant who is the unmarried child under 21 years of age, the father, the mother, the husband, or the wife, of a citizen of the United States who is 21 years of age or over; and

(2) To a quota immigrant who is skilled in agriculture, and his wife, and his dependent children under the age of 16 years, if accompanying or following to join him. The preference provided in this paragraph shall not apply to immigrants of any nationality the annual quota for which is less than 300.

(3) The preference provided in subdivision (a) shall not in the case of quota immigrants of any nationality exceed 50 per

Section 7

Application for Immigration Visa

(a) Every immigrant applying for an immigration visa shall make application therefor in duplicate in such form as shall be by regulations prescribed.

(b) In the application the immigrant shall state (1) the immigrant's full and true name; age, sex, and race; the date and place of birth; places of residence for the five years immediately preceding his application; whether married or single, and the names and places of residence of wife or husband and minor children, if any; calling or occupation; personal description (including height, complexion, color of hair and eyes, and marks of identification); ability to speak, read, and write; names and addresses of parents, and if nei-

ther parent living, then the name and address of his nearest relative in the country from which he comes; port of entry into the United States; final destination, if any, beyond the port of entry; whether he has a ticket through to such final destination; whether going to join a relative or friend, and, if so, what relative or friend and his name and complete address; the purpose for which he is going to the United States; the length of time he intends to remain in the United States; whether or not he intends to abide in the United States permanently; whether ever in prison or almshouse; whether he or either of his parents has ever been in an institution or hospital for the care and treatment of the insane; (2) if he claims to be a non-quota immigrant, the facts on which he bases such claim; and (3) such additional information necessary to the proper enforcement of the immigration laws and the naturalization laws, as may be by regulations prescribed.

(c) The immigrant shall furnish, if available, to the consular officer, with his application, two copies of his "dossier" and prison record and military record, two certified copies of his birth certificate, and two copies of all other available public records concerning him kept by the Government to which he owes allegiance. One copy of the documents so furnished shall be permanently attached to each copy of the application and become a part thereof. An immigrant having an unexpired permit issued under the provisions of section 10 shall not be subject to this subdivision. In the case of an application made before September 1, 1924, if it appears to the satisfaction of the consular officer that the immigrant has obtained a visa of his passport before the enactment of this Act, and is unable to obtain the documents referred to in this subdivision without undue expense and delay, owing to absence from the country from which such documents should be obtained, the consular officer may relieve such immigrant from the requirements of this subdivision.

(d) In the application the immigrant shall also state (to such extent as shall be by regulations prescribed) whether or not he is a member of each class of individuals excluded from admission to the United States under the immigration laws, and such classes shall be stated on the blank in such form as shall be by regulations prescribed, and the immigrant shall answer separately as to each class.

(e) If the immigrant is unable to state that he does not come within any of the excluded classes, but claims to be for any legal reason exempt from exclusion, he shall state fully in the application the grounds for such alleged exemption.

(f) Each copy of the application shall be signed by the immigrant in the presence of the consular officer and verified by the oath of the immigrant administered by the consular officer. One copy of the application, when visaed by the consular officer, shall become the immigration visa, and the other copy shall be disposed of as may be by regulations prescribed.

(g) In the case of an immigrant under eighteen years of age the application may be made and verified by such individual as shall be by regulations prescribed.

(h) A fee of $1 shall be charged for the furnishing and verification of each application, which shall include the furnishing and verification of the duplicate, and shall be covered into the Treasury as miscellaneous receipts.

Section 8

Non-Quota Immigration Visas

A consular officer may, subject to the limitations provided in sections 2 and 9, issue an immigration visa to a non-quota immigrant as such upon satisfactory proof, under regulations prescribed under this Act, that the applicant is entitled to be regarded as a non-quota immigrant.

Section 9

Issuance of Immigration Visa to Relatives

(a) In case of any immigrant claiming in his application for an immigration visa to be a non-quota immigrant by reason of relationship under the provisions of subdivision (a) of section 4, or to be entitled to preference by reason of relationship to a citizen of the United States under the provisions of section 6, the consular officer shall not issue such immigration visa or grant such preference until he has been authorized to do so as hereinafter in this section provided.

(b) Any citizen of the United States claiming that any immigrant is his relative, and that such immigrant is properly admissible to the United States as a non-quota immigrant under the provisions of subdivision (a) of section 4 or is entitled to preference as a relative under section 6, may file with the Commissioner General a petition in such form as may be by regulations prescribed, stating (1) the petitioner's name and address; (2) if a citizen by birth, the date and place of his birth; (3) if a naturalized citizen, the date and place of his admission to citizenship and the number of his certificate, if any; (4) the name and address of his employer or the address of his place of business or occupation if he is not an employee; (5) the degree of the relationship of the immigrant for whom such petition is made, and the names of all the places where such immigrant has resided prior to and at the time when the petition is filed; (6) that the petitioner is able to and will support the immigrant if necessary to prevent such immigrant

from becoming a public charge; and (7) such additional information necessary to the proper enforcement of the immigration laws and the naturalization laws as may be by regulations prescribed.

(c) The petition shall be made under oath administered by any individual having power to administer oaths, if executed in the United States, but, if executed outside the United States, administered by a consular officer. The petition shall be supported by any documentary evidence required by regulations prescribed under this Act. Application may be made in the same petition for admission of more than one individual.

(d) The petition shall be accompanied by the statements of two or more responsible citizens of the United States, to whom the petitioner has been personally known for at least one year, that to the best of their knowledge and belief the statements made in the petition are true and that the petitioner is a responsible individual able to support the immigrant or immigrants for whose admission application is made. These statements shall be attested in the same way as the petition.

(e) If the Commissioner General finds the facts stated in the petition to be true, and that the immigrant in respect of whom the petition is made is entitled to be admitted to the United States as a non-quota immigrant under subdivision (a) of section 4 or is entitled to preference as a relative under section 6, he shall, with the approval of the Secretary of Labor, inform the Secretary of State of his decision, and the Secretary of State shall then authorize the consular officer with whom the application for the immigration visa has been filed to issue the immigration visa or grant the preference.

(f) Nothing in this section shall be construed to entitle an immigrant, in respect of whom a petition under this section is granted, to enter the United States as a non-quota immigrant, if, upon arrival in the United States, he is found not be a non-quota immigrant.

Section 10

Section 10 establishes procedures for aliens who wish to leave the country temporarily after having been admitted.

Section 11

(a) The annual quota of any nationality shall be 2 per centum of the number of foreign-born individuals of such nationality resident in continental United States as determined by the United States census of 1890, but the minimum quota of any nationality shall be 100.

(b) The annual quota of any nationality for the fiscal year beginning July 1, 1927, and for each fiscal year thereafter, shall be a number which bears the same ratio to 150,000 as the number of inhabitants in continental United States in 1920 having that national origin (ascertained as hereinafter provided in this section) bears to the number of inhabitants in continental United States in 1920, but the minimum quota of any nationality shall be 100.

(c) For the purpose of subdivision (b) national origin shall be ascertained by determining as nearly as may be, in respect of each geographical area which under section 12 is to be treated as a separate country (except the geographical areas specified in subdivision (c) of section 4) the number of inhabitants in continental United States in 1920 whose origin by birth or ancestry is attributable to such geographical area. Such determination shall not be made by tracing the ancestors or descendants of particular individuals, but shall be based upon statistics of immigration and emigration, together with rates of increase of population as shown by successive decennial United States censuses, and such other data as may be found to be reliable.

(d) For the purpose of subdivisions (b) and (c) the term "inhabitants in continental United States in 1920" does not include (1) immigrants from the geographical areas specified in subdivision (c) of section 4 or their descendants, (2) aliens ineligible to citizenship or their descendants, (3) the descendants of slave immigrants, or (4) the descendants of American aborigines.

(e) The determination provided for in subdivision (c) of this section shall be made by the Secretary of State, the Secretary of Commerce, and the Secretary of Labor, jointly. In making such determination such officials may call for information and expert assistance from the Bureau of the Census. Such officials shall, jointly, report to the President the quota of each nationality, determined as provided in subdivision (b), and the President shall proclaim and make known the quotas so reported. Such proclamation shall be made on or before April 1, 1927. . . .

(f) There shall be issued to quota immigrants of any nationality (1) no more immigration visas in any fiscal year than the quota for such nationality, and (2) in any calendar month of any fiscal year no more immigration visas than 10 per centum of the quota for such nationality, except that if such quota is less than 300 the number to be issued in any calendar month shall be prescribed by the Commissioner General, with the approval of the Secretary of Labor, but the total number to be issued during the fiscal year shall not be in excess of the quota for such nationality.

(g) Nothing in this Act shall prevent the issuance (without increasing the total number of immigration visas which may be issued) of an immigration visa to an immigrant as a quota immigrant even though he is a non-quota immigrant.

Section 12

Nationality

(a) For the purposes of this Act nationality shall be determined by country of birth, treating as separate countries the colonies, dependencies, or self-governing dominions, for which separate enumeration was made in the United States census of 1890; except that (1) the nationality of a child under twenty-one years of age not born in the United States, accompanied by its alien parent not born in the United States, shall be determined by the country of birth of such parent if such parent is entitled to an immigration visa, and the nationality of a child under twenty-one years of age not born in the United States, accompanied by both alien parents not born in the United States, shall be determined by the country of birth of the father if the father is entitled to an immigration visa; and (2) if a wife is of a different nationality from her alien husband and the entire number of immigration visas which may be issued to quota immigrants of her nationality for the calendar month has already been issued, her nationality may be determined by the country of birth of her husband if she is accompanying him and he is entitled to an immigration visa, unless the total number of immigration visas which may be issued to quota immigrants of the nationality of the husband for the calendar month has already been issued. An immigrant born in the United States who has lost his United States citizenship shall be considered as having been born in the country of which he is a citizen or subject, or if he is not a citizen or subject of any country, then in the country from which he comes.

(b) The Secretary of State, the Secretary of Commerce, and the Secretary of Labor, jointly, shall, as soon as feasible after the enactment of this Act, prepare a statement showing the number of individuals of the various nationalities resident in continental United States as determined by the United States census of 1890, which statement shall be the population basis for the purposes of subdivision (a) of section 11. . . *The remainder of Section 12 details further how quotas are determined and reported.*

Section 13

(a) No immigrant shall be admitted to the United States unless he (1) has an unexpired immigration visa or was born subsequent to the issuance of the immigration visa of the accompanying parent, (2) is of the nationality specified in the immigration visa, (3) is a non-quota immigrant if specified in the visa in the immigration visa as such, and (4) is otherwise admissible under the immigration laws.

(b) In such classes of cases and under such conditions as may be by regulations prescribed immigrants who have been legally admitted to the United States and who depart therefrom temporarily may be admitted to the United States without being required to obtain an immigration visa.

(c) No alien ineligible to citizenship shall be admitted to the United States unless such alien (1) is admissible as a non-quota immigrant under the provisions of subdivisions (b), (d), or (e) of section 4, or (2) is the wife, or the unmarried child under 18 years of age, of an immigrant admissible under such subdivision (d), and is accompanying or following to join him, or (3) is not an immigrant as defined in section 3.

(d) The Secretary of Labor may admit to the United States any otherwise admissible immigrant not admissible under clause (2) or (3) of subdivision (a) of this section, if satisfied that such inadmissibility was not known to, and could not have been ascertained by the exercise of reasonable diligence by, such immigrant prior to the departure of the vessel from the last port outside the United States and outside foreign contiguous territory, or, in the case of an immigrant coming from foreign contiguous territory, prior to the application of the immigrant for admission.

(e) No quota immigrant shall be admitted under subdivision (d) if the entire number of immigration visas which may be issued to quota immigrants of the same nationality for the fiscal year has already been issued. If such entire number of immigration visas has not been issued, then the Secretary of State, upon the admission of a quota immigrant under subdivision (d), shall reduce by one the number of immigration visas which may be issued to quota immigrants of the same nationality during the fiscal year in which such immigrant is admitted; but if the Secretary of State finds that it will not be practicable to make such reduction before the end of such fiscal year, then such immigrant shall not be admitted. . . .

Section 14

Deportation

Any alien who at any time after entering the United States is found to have been at the time of entry not entitled under this Act to enter the United States, or to have remained therein for a longer time than permitted under this Act or regulations made thereunder, shall be taken into custody and deported in the same manner as provided for in sections 19 and 20 of the Immigration Act of 1917:

Provided, That the Secretary of Labor may, under such conditions and restrictions as to support and care as he may deem necessary, permit permanently to remain in the United States, any alien child who, when under sixteen years of age was heretofore temporarily admitted to the United States and who is now within

the United States and either of whose parents is a citizen of the United States.

Section 15

Maintenance of Exempt Status

The admission to the United States of an alien excepted from the class of immigrants by clause (2), (3), (4), (5), or (6) of section 3, or declared to be a non-quota immigrant by subdivision (e) of section 4, shall be for such time as may be by regulations prescribed, and under such conditions as may be by regulations prescribed (including, when deemed necessary for the classes mentioned in clauses (2), (3), (4), or (6) of section 3, the giving of bond with sufficient surety, in such sum and containing such conditions as may be by regulations prescribed) to insure that, at the expiration of such time or upon failure to maintain the status under which admitted, he will depart from the United States.

Section 16

Penalty for Illegal Transportation

(a) It shall be unlawful for any person, including any transportation company, or the owner, master, agent, charterer, or consignee of any vessel, to bring to the United States by water from any place outside thereof (other than foreign contiguous territory) (1) any immigrant who does not have an unexpired immigration visa, or (2) any quota immigrant having an immigration visa the visa in which specifies him as a non-quota immigrant. . . *The remainder of Section 16 establishes penalties for violations.*

Section 17

Entry from Foreign Contiguous Territory

The Commissioner General, with the approval of the Secretary of Labor, shall have power to enter into contracts with transportation lines for the entry and inspection of aliens coming to the United States from or through foreign contiguous territory. In prescribing rules and regulations and making contracts for the entry and inspection of aliens applying for admission from or through foreign contiguous territory due care shall be exercised to avoid any discriminatory action in favor of transportation companies transporting to such territory aliens destined to the United States, and all such transportation companies shall be required, as a condition precedent to the inspection or examination under such rules and contracts at the ports of such contiguous territory of aliens brought thereto by them, to submit to and comply with all the requirements of this Act which would apply were they bringing such aliens directly to ports of the United States. After this section takes effect no alien applying for admission from or through foreign contiguous territory (except an alien previously lawfully admitted to the United States who is returning from a temporary visit to such territory) shall be permitted to enter the United States unless upon proving that he was brought to such territory by a transportation company which had submitted to and complied with all the requirements of this Act, or that he entered, or has resided in, such territory more than two years prior to the time of his application for admission to the United States.

Section 18

Unused Immigration Visas

If a quota immigrant of any nationality having an immigration visa is excluded from admission to the United States under the immigration laws and deported, or does not apply for admission to the United States before the expiration of the validity of the immigration visa, or if an alien of any nationality having an immigration visa issued to him as a quota immigrant is found not be a quota immigrant, no additional immigration visa shall be issued in lieu thereof to any other immigrant.

Section 19

Section 19 and 20 discusses alien seamen and their rights and responsibilities.

Section 21

(a) Permits issued under section 10 shall be printed on distinctive safety paper and shall be prepared and issued under regulations prescribed under this Act.

(b) The Public Printer is authorized to print for sale to the public by the Superintendent of Public Documents, upon prepayment, additional copies of blank forms of manifests and crew lists to be prescribed by the Secretary of Labor pursuant to the provisions of sections 12, 13, 14, and 36 of the Immigration Act of 1917.

Section 22

Offenses in Connection with Documents

(a) Any person who knowingly (1) forges, counterfeits, alters, or falsely makes any immigration visa or permit, or (2) utters, uses, attempts to use, possesses, obtains, accepts, or receives any immigration visa or permit, knowing it to be forged, counterfeited, altered, or falsely made, or to have been procured by means of any false claim or statement, or to have been otherwise procured by fraud or unlawfully obtained; or who, except under direction of the Secretary of Labor or other proper officer, knowingly (3) possesses any blank permit, (4) engraves, sells, brings into the United States, or has in his control or possession any plate in the likeness of a plate designed for the printing of permits, (5) makes any print, photograph, or impression in the likeness of any immigration visa or permit, or (6) has in his possession a distinctive paper which has been adopted by the Secretary of Labor for the printing of immigration visas or permits, shall, upon conviction thereof, be fined not more than $10,000, or imprisoned for not more than five years, or both.

(b) Any individual who (1) when applying for an immigration visa or permit, or for admission to the United States, personate another, or falsely appears in the name of a deceased individual, or evades or attempts to evade the immigration laws by appearing under an assumed or fictitious name, or (2) sells or otherwise disposes of, or offers to sell or otherwise dispose of, or utters, an immigration visa or permit, to any person not authorized by law to receive such document shall, upon conviction thereof, be fined not more than $10,000 or imprisoned for not more than five years, or both.

(c) Whoever knowingly makes under oath any false statement in any application, affidavit, or other document required by the immigration laws or regulations prescribed thereunder, shall, upon conviction thereof, be fined not more than $10,000, or imprisoned for not more than five years, or both.

Section 23

Burden of Proof

Whenever any alien attempts to enter the United States the burden of proof shall be upon such alien to establish that he is not subject to exclusion under any provision of the immigration laws; and in any deportation proceeding against any alien the burden of proof shall be upon such alien to show that he entered the United States lawfully, and the time, place, and manner of such entry into the United States; but in presenting such proof he shall be entitled to the production of his immigration visa, if any, or of other documents concerning such entry, in the custody of the Department of Labor.

Section 24

Rules and Regulations

The Commissioner General, with the approval of the Secretary of Labor, shall prescribe rules and regulations for the enforcement of the provisions of this Act; but all such rules and regulations, in so far as they relate to the administration of this Act by consular officers, shall be prescribed by the Secretary of State on the recommendation of the Secretary of Labor.

Section 25

Act To Be in Addition to Immigration Laws

The provisions of this Act are in addition to and not in substitution for the provisions of the immigration laws, and shall be enforced as a part of such laws, and all the penal or other provisions of such laws, not inapplicable, shall apply to and be enforced in connection with the provisions of this Act. An alien, although admissible under the provisions of this Act, shall not be admitted to the United States if he is excluded by any provision of the immigration laws other than this Act, and an alien, although admissible under the provisions of the immigration laws other than this Act, shall not be admitted to the United States if he is excluded by any provision of this Act.

Section 26

Steamship Fines under 1917 Act

Section 26 amends Section 9 of the Immigration Act of 1917, which discusses fines levied against vessel operators who violate rules regarding alien passengers.

Section 27

Section 27 amends Section 10 of the Immigration Act of 1917, which restricts alien landings to designated entry locations.

Section 28

The remainder of the Act, Sections 28-32, defines terms and states effective dates for provisions described in it.

♦ TYDINGS-MCDUFFIES ACT, 1934

This Act limited immigration from the Philippines to 50 persons per year.

♦ PRESIDENTIAL PROCLAMATION, APRIL 28, 1938

On April 28, 1938 Franklin D. Roosevelt,President of the United States of America, made a proclamation establishing immigration quotas by country.

[52 Stat. No. 2283]

A Proclamation

WHEREAS the Acting Secretary of State, the Secretary of Commerce, and the Secretary of Labor have reported to the President that pursuant to the duty imposed and the authority conferred upon them in and by sections 11 and 12 of the Immigration Act approved May 26, 1924 (43 Stat. 161), they jointly have made the revision provided for in section 12 of the said act and have fixed the quota of each respective nationality in accordance therewith to be as hereinafter set forth:

NOW, THEREFORE, I, FRANKLIN D. ROOSEVELT, President of the United States of America, acting under and by virtue of the power in me vested by the aforesaid act of Congress, do hereby proclaim and make known that the annual quota of each nationality effective for the remainder of the fiscal year ending June 30, 1938, and for each fiscal year thereafter, has been determined in accordance with the law to be, and shall be, as follows:

National Origin Immigration Quotas

Country or Area	Quota
Afghanistan	100
Albania	1000
Andorra	100
Arabian peninsula (except Muscat, Aden Settlement and Protectorate, and Saudi Arabia)	100
Australia (including Tasmania, Papua, and all islands appertaining to Australia)	100
Belgium	1,304
Bhutan	100
Bulgaria	100
Cameroons (British mandate)	100
Cameroun (French mandate)	100
China	100
Czechoslovakia	2,874
Danzig, Free City of	100
Denmark	1,181
Egypt	100
Estonia	116
Ethiopia (Abyssinia)	100
Finland	569
France	3,086
Germany	27,370
Great Britain and Northern Ireland	65,721
Greece	307
Hungary	869
Iceland	100
India	100
Iran	100
Iraq	100
Ireland (Eire)	17,853
Italy	5,802
Japan	100
Latvia	236
Liberia	100
Liechtenstein	100
Lithuania	386
Luxemburg	100

Country or Area	Quota
Monaco	100
Morocco (French and Spanish zones and Tangier)	100
Muscat (Oman)	100
Nauru (British mandate)	100
Nepal	100
Netherlands	3,153
New Guinea, Territory of (including appertaining islands) (Australian mandate)	100
New Zealand	100
Norway	2,377
Palestine (with Trans-Jordan) (British mandate)	100
Poland	6,524
Portugal	440
Ruanda and Urundi (Belgian mandate)	100
Rumania	377
Samoa, Western (mandate of New Zealand)	100
San Marino	100
Saudi Arabia	100
Siam	100
South Africa, Union of	100
South-West Africa (mandate of the Union of South Africa)	100
Spain	252
Sweden	3,314
Switzerland	1,707
Syria and the Lebanon (French mandate)	123
Tanganyika Territory (British mandate)	100
Togoland (British mandate)	100
Togoland (French mandate)	100
Turkey	226
Union of Soviet Socialist Republics	2,712
Yap and other Pacific islands under Japanese mandate	100
Yugoslavia	845

The immigration quotas assigned to the various countries and quote areas are designed solely for purposes of compliance with the pertinent provisions of the Immigration Act of 1924 and are not to be regarded as having any significance extraneous to this object.

This proclamation shall take effect immediately, and shall supersede Proclamation No. 2048 of June 16, 1933.

IN WITNESS WHEREOF, I have hereunto set my hand and caused the seal of the United States to be affixed.

DONE at the City of Washington this 28th day of April, in the year of our Lord nineteen hundred and thirty-eight and of the Independence of the United States of America the one hundred and sixty-second.

Franklin D. Roosevelt

♦ PUBLIC PROCLAMATION NO. 1, MARCH 2, 1942

Headquarters Western Defense Command and Fourth Army, Presidio of San Franciso, California

TO: The people within the States of Arizona, California, Oregon, and Washington, and the Public Generally

WHEREAS, By virtue of orders issued by the War Department on December 11, 1941, that portion of the United States lying within the States of Washington, Oregon, California, Montana, Idaho, Nevada, Utah and Arizona and the Territory of Alaska has been established as the Western Defense Command and designated as a Theatre of Operations under my command; and

WHEREAS, By Executive Order No. 9066, dated February 19, 1942, the President of the United States authorized and directed the Secretary of War and the Military Commanders whom he may from time to time designate, whenever he or any such designated commander deems such action necessary or desirable, to prescribe military areas in such places and of such extent as he or the appropriate Military Commander may determine, from which any or all persons may be excluded, and with respect to which the right of any person to enter, remain in, or leave shall be subject to whatever restrictions the Secretary of War or the appropriate Military Commander may impose in his discretion; and

WHEREAS, The Secretary of War on February 20, 1942, designated the undersigned as the Military Commander to carry out the duties and responsibilities imposed by said Executive Order for that portion of the United States embraced in the Western Defense Command; and

WHEREAS, The Western Defense Command embraces the entire Pacific Coast of the United States which by its geographical location is particularly subject to attack, to attempted invasion by the armed forces of nations with which the United States is now at war, and, in connection therewith, is subject to espionage and acts of sabotage, thereby requiring the adoption of military measures necessary to establish safeguards against such enemy operations:

NOW THEREFORE, I, J. L. DeWitt, Lieutenant General, U. S. Army, by virtue of the authority vested in me be the President of the United States and by the Secretary of War and my powers and prerogatives as Commanding General of the Western Defense Command, do hereby declare that:

1. The present situation requires as a matter of military necessity the establishment in the territory embraced by the Western Defense Command of Military Areas and Zones thereof as defined in Exhibit 1, hereto attached, and as generally shown on the map attached hereto and marked Exhibit 2.

2. Military Areas No. 1 and 2, as particularly described and generally shown hereinafter and in Exhibits 1 and 2 hereto, are hereby designated and established.

3. Within Military Areas Nos. 1 and 2 there are established Zone A-1, lying wholly within Military Area No. 1; Zones A-2 to A-99, inclusive, some of which are in Military Area No. 1, and the other in Military Area No. 2; and Zone B, comprising all that part of Military Area No. 1 not included within Zones A-1 to A-99, inclusive; all as more particularly described and defined and generally shown hereinafter and in Exhibits 1 and 2.

Military Area No. 2 comprises all that part of the States of Washington, Oregon, California and Arizona which is not included within Military Area NO. 1, and is shown on the map (Exhibit 2) as an unshaded area.

4. Such persons or classes of persons as the situation may require will be subsequent proclamation be excluded from all of Military Area No. 1 and also from such of those zones herein described as Zones A-2 to A-99, inclusive, as are within Military Area No. 2.

Certain persons or classes of persons who are by subsequent proclamation excluded from the zones last above mentioned may be permitted, under certain regulations and restrictions to be hereafter prescribed, to enter upon or remain within Zone B.

The designation of Military Area No. 2 as such does not contemplate any prohibition or regulation or restriction except with respect to the zones established therein.

5. Any Japanese, German or Italian alien, or any person of Japanese Ancestry now resident in Military Area No. 1 who changes his place of habitual residence is hereby required to obtain and execute a "Change of Residence Notice" at any United States Post Office within the States of Washington, Oregon, California and Arizona. Such notice must be executed at any such Post Office not more than five nor less than one day prior to any such change of residence. Nothing contained herein shall be construed to affect the existing regulations of the U. S. Attorney General which require aliens of enemy nationalities to obtain travel permits from U. S. Attorneys and to notify the Federal Bureau of Investigation and the Commissioner of Immigration of any change in permanent address.

6. The designation of prohibited and restricted areas within the Western Defense Command by the Attorney General of the United States under the Proclamations of December 7 and 8, 1941, and the instructions, rules and regulations prescribed by him with respect to such prohibited and restricted areas, are hereby adopted and continued in full force and effect.

The duty and responsibility of the Federal Bureau of Investigation with respect to the investigation of alleged acts of espionage and sabotage are not altered by this proclamation.

J. L. DeWitt
Lieutenant General, U. S. Army
Commanding.

The remaining pages (3-30) describe in detail the zones covered by this proclamation. The map accompanying this section illustrates the areas of the states of Washington, Oregon, and California which were designated "Military Areas". Zones A2-A99 represent bridges, power plants, and other locations considered to be important to the Western Defense Command Effort.

EXHIBIT No. 1

Description of Military Area No. 1

Beginning at the point in the State of Washington where the westerly line of U. S. Highway #97 intersects the International Boundary Line between Canada and the United States; thence in a southerly direction along the westerly line of U. S. Highway #97 to the point where the same intersects the westerly line, projected, of U. S. Highway #10-A near the junction of the Columbia River with the Wenatchee River; thence southerly along the westerly and southerly line of U. W. Highway #10-A to the bridge across the Columbia River connecting Wenatchee and East Wenatchee, Washington; thence southerly along the westerly bank of the Columbia River to the westerly side of the ferry landing approximately 2 miles south of Maryhill, Washington; thence southerly across the Columbia River to the point where the southerly line of U. S. Highway #30 intersects the westerly line of U. S. Highway #97; thence southerly along the westerly line of U. S. Highway #97 through the State of Oregon and into the State of California to the point where the same, projected, intersects the westerly line of U. S. Highway #99; thence southerly along the said westerly line of U. S. Highway #99 to the point where the same intersects the westerly line.

♦ EXECUTIVE ORDER 9066, 1942

President Franklin Roosevelt's order led to the establishment of internment camps and the forced evacuation of people of Japanese ancestry.

Authorizing the Secretary of War to prescribe Military Areas.

WHEREAS the successful prosecution of the war requires every possible protection against espionage and against sabotage to national-defense material, national-defense premises, and national-defense utilities as defined in Section 4, Act of April 20, 1918, 40

Stat. 533, as amended by the Act of November 30, 1940, 54 Stat. 1220, and the Act of August 21, 1941, 55 Stat. 655 (U.S.C., Title 50, Sec 104):

NOW, THEREFORE, by virtue of the authority vested in me as President of the United States, and Commander in Chief of the Army and Navy, I hereby authorize and direct the Secretary of War, and the Military Commanders whom he may from time to time designate, whenever he or any designated Commander deems such action necessary or desirable, to prescribe military areas in such places and of such extent as he or the appropriate Military Commander may determine, from which any or all persons may be excluded, and with respect to which, the right of any person to enter, remain in, or leave shall be subject to whatever restrictions the Secretary of War or the appropriate Military Commander may determine, from which any or all persons may be excluded, and with respect to which, the right of any person to enter, remaining, or leave shall be subject to whatever restrictions the Secretary of War or the appropriate Military Commander may impose in his discretion. The Secretary of War is hereby authorized to provide for residents of any such area who are excluded therefrom, such transportation, food, shelter, and other accommodations as may be necessary, in the judgment of the Secretary of War or the said Military Commander, and until other arrangements are made, to accomplish the purpose of this order. The designation of military areas in any region or locality shall supersede designations of prohibited and restricted areas by the Attorney General under the Proclamations of December 7 and 8, 1941, and shall supersede the responsibility and authority of the Attorney General under the said Proclamations in respect of such prohibited and restricted areas.

I hereby further authorize and direct the Secretary of War and said Military Commanders to take such other Commander to take such other steps as he or the appropriate Military Commander may deem advisable to enforce compliance with the restrictions applicable to each Military area hereinabove authorized to be designated, including the use of Federal troops and other Federal Agencies, with authority to accept assistance of state and local agencies.

I hereby further authorize and direct all Executive Departments, independent establishments and other Federal Agencies, to assist the Secretary of War or the said Military Commanders in carrying out this Executive Order, including the furnishing of medical aid, hospitalization, food, clothing, transportation, use of land, shelter, and other supplies, equipment, utilities, facilities, and services.

This order shall not be construed as modifying or limiting in any way the authority heretofore granted under Executive Order No. 8972, dated December 12, 1941, nor shall it be construed as limiting or modifying the duty and responsibility of the Federal Bureau of Investigation, with respect to the investigation of alleged acts of sabotage or the duty and responsibility of the Attorney General and the Department of Justice under the Proclamations of December 7 and 8, 1941, prescribing regulations for the conduct and control of alien enemies, except as such duty and responsibility is superseded by the designation of military areas hereunder.

Franklin D. Roosevelt
The White House, February 19, 1942.

◆ PUBLIC LAW 503, 1942

Provided penal sanctions for those who disobeyed Executive Order 9066.

Be it enacted by the Senate and House of Representatives of the United States of America in Congress assembled, That whoever shall enter, remain in, leave, or commit any act in any military area or military zone prescribed, under the authority of an Executive order of the President, by the Secretary of War, or by any military commander designated by the Secretary of War, contrary to the restrictions applicable to any such area or zone or contrary to the order of the Secretary of War or any such military commander, shall, if it appears that he knew or should have known of the existence and extent of the restrictions or order and that his act was in violation thereof, be guilty of a misdemeanor and upon conviction shall be liable to a fine of not to exceed $5,000 or to imprisonment for not more than one year, or both, for each offense.

Approved, March 21, 1942.

◆ REPEAL OF CHINESE EXCLUSION ACTS, 1943

Besides repealing the Chinese Exclusion Law of 1882 and its amendments, this act granted naturalization rights and a small immigration quota to the Chinese.

Be it enacted by the Senate and House of Representatives of the United States of America in Congress assembled, That the following Acts or parts of Acts relating to the exclusion or deportation of persons of the Chinese race are hereby repealed: May 6, 1882 (22 Stat. L. 58); July 5, 1884 (23 Stat. L. 115); September 13, 1888 (25 Stat. L. 476); October 1, 1888 (25 Stat. L. 504); May 5, 1892 (27 Stat. L. 25); November 3, 1893 (28 Stat. L. 7); that portion of section 1 of the Act of July 7, 1898 (30 Stat. L. 750, 751), which reads as follows: "There shall be no further immigration of Chinese into the Hawaiian Islands except upon such conditions as are now or may hereafter be allowed by the laws of the

United States; and no Chinese, by reason of anything herein contained, shall be allowed to enter the United States from the Hawaiian Islands."; section 101 of the Act of April 30, 1900 (31 Stat. L. 141, 161); those portions of section 1 of the Act of June 6, 1900 (31 Stat. L. 588, 611), which read as follows: "And nothing in section four of the Act of August fifth, eighteen hundred and eighty-two (Twenty-second Statutes at Large, page two hundred and twenty-five), shall be construed to prevent the Secretary of the Treasury from hereafter detailing one officer employed in the enforcement of the Chinese Exclusion Acts for duty at the Treasury Department at Washington. *** and hereafter the Commissioner-General of Immigration, in addition to his other duties, shall have charge of the administration of the Chinese exclusion law ***, under the supervision and direction of the Secretary of the Treasury."; March 3, 1901 (31 Stat. L. 1093); April 29, 1902 (32 Stat. L. 176); April 27, 1904 (33 Stat. L. 428); section 25 of the Act of March 3, 1911 (36 Stat. L. 1087, 1094); that portion of the Act of August 24, 1912 (37 Stat. L. 417, 476), which reads as follows: "Provided, That all charges for maintenance or return of Chinese persons applying for admission to the United States shall hereafter be paid or reimbursed to the United States by the person, company, partnership, or corporation, bringing such Chinese to a port of the United States as applicants for admission."; that portion of the Act of June 23, 1913 (38 Stat. L. 4. 65), which reads as follows: "Provided, That from and after July first, nineteen hundred and thirteen, all Chinese persons ordered deported under judicial writs shall be delivered by the marshal of the district or his deputy into the custody of any officer designated for that purpose by the Secretary of Commerce and Labor, for conveyance to the frontier or seaboard for deportation in the same manner as aliens deported under the immigration laws."

SECTION 2

With the exception of those coming under subsections (b), (d), (e), and (f) section 4, Immigration Act of 1924 (43 Stat. 155; 44 Stat. 812; 45 Stat. 1009; 46 Stat. 854; 47 Stat. 656; 8 U.S.C. 204), all Chinese persons entering the United States annually as immigrants shall be allocated to the quota for the Chinese computed under the provisions of section 11 of the said Act. A preference up to 75 per centum of the quota shall be given to Chinese born and resident in China.

SECTION 3

Section 303 of the Nationality Act of 1940, as amended (54 Stat. 1140; 8 U.S.C. 703), is hereby amended by striking out the word "and" before the word "descendants", changing the colon after the word "Hemisphere" to a comma, and adding the following: "and Chinese persons or persons of Chinese descent:".

Approved December 17, 1943.

♦ WAR BRIDES ACT, 1945

[59 Stat. L. 271]

This act allowed United States armed forces personnel to bring alien spouses and minor children to the United States.

Be it enacted by the Senate and House of Representatives of the United States of America in Congress assembled, That notwithstanding any of the several clauses of section 3 of the Act of February 5, 1917, excluding physically and mentally defective aliens, and notwithstanding the documentary requirements of any of the immigration laws or regulations, Executive orders, or Presidential proclamations issued thereunder, alien spouses or alien children of United States citizens serving in, or having an honorable discharge certificates from the armed forces of the United States during the Second World War shall, if otherwise admissible under the immigration laws and if application for admission is made within three years of the effective date of this Act, be admitted to the United States: Provided, That every alien of the foregoing description shall be medically examined at the time of arrival in accordance with the provisions of section 16 of the Act of February 5, 1917, and if found suffering from any disability which would be the basis for a ground of exclusion except for the provision of this Act, the Immigration and Naturalization Service shall forthwith notify the appropriate public medical officer of the local community to which the alien is destined: Provided further,

Section 2

That the provisions of this Act shall not affect the duties of the United States Public Health Service so far as they relate to quarantinable diseases.

Regardless of section 9 of the Immigration Act of 1924, any alien admitted under section 1 of this Act shall be deemed to be a nonquota immigrant as defined in section 4 (a) of the Immigration Act of 1924.

Section 3

Any alien admitted under section 1 of this Act who at any time returns to the United States after a temporary absence abroad shall not be excluded because of the disability or disabilities that existed at the time of that admissions.

Section 4

No fine or penalty shall be imposed under the Act of February 5, 1917, except those arising under section 14, because of the transportation to the United States of any alien admitted under this Act.

Section 5

For the purpose of this Act, the Second World War shall be deemed to have commenced on December 7, 1941, and to have ceased upon the termination of hostilities as declared by the President or by a joint resolution of Congress.

Approved December 28, 1945.

◆ PRESIDENTIAL PROCLAMATION DECEMBER 23, 1947

[62 Stat. No. 2762]

Granting pardon to certain persons convicted of violating the Selective Training and Service Act of 1940 as amended by the President of the United States of America.

A Proclamation

WHEREAS by Executive Order No. 9814 of December 23, 1946, there was established the President's Amnesty Board, the functions and duties of which were set out in paragraph 2 of the said Executive order as follows:

"The Board, under such regulations as it may prescribe, shall examine and consider the cases of all persons convicted of violation of the Selective Training and Service Act of 1940, as amended (50 U.S.C. App. 301 ff.), or of any rule or regulation prescribed under or pursuant to that Act, or convicted of a conspiracy to violate that Act or any rule or regulation prescribed under or pursuant thereto. In any case in which it deems it desirable to do so, the Board shall make a report to the Attorney General which shall include its findings and its recommendations as to whether Executive clemency should be granted or denied, and, in any case in which it recommends that Executive clemency be granted, its recommendations with respect to the form that such clemency should take. The Attorney General shall report the findings and recommendations of the Board to the President, with such further recommendations as he may desire to make." and

WHEREAS the Board, after considering all cases coming within the scope of paragraph 2 of the said Executive order, has made a report to the Attorney General, which includes the findings of the Board and its recommendation that Executive clemency be granted in certain of such cases; and

WHEREAS the Attorney General has submitted such report to me with his approval of the recommendation made by the Board with respect to Executive clemency; and

WHEREAS upon consideration of the report and recommendation of the Board and the recommendation of the Attorney General, it appears that certain persons convicted of violating the Selective Training and Service Act of 1940 as amended ought to have restored to them the political, civil, and other rights of which they were deprived by reason of such conviction and which may not be restored to them unless they are pardoned:

NOW, THEREFORE, I, HARRY S. TRUMAN, President of the United States of America, under and by virtue of the authority vested in me by Article II of the Constitution of the United States, do hereby grant a full pardon to those persons convicted of violating the Selective Training and Service Act of 1940 as amended whose names are included in the list of names attached hereto and hereby made a part of this proclamation.

IN WITNESS WHEREOF, I have hereunto set my hand and caused the seal of the United States of America to be affixed.

DONE at the City of Washington this 23rd day of December in the year of our Lord nineteen hundred and forty-seven and of the Independence of the United States of America the one hundred and seventy-second.

HARRY S. TRUMAN

A list of 1,523 names of those pardoned followed, including approximately 270 Japanese-Americans.

◆ IMMIGRATION AND NATURALIZATION ACT, 1952

[66 Stat. L. 414]

This extensive act regulating immigration and naturalization, grants the right of naturalization to all immigrants and establishes quotas by country of origin for immigrants. It is also known as the "McCarran-Walter Act."

Title I

Provides definitions of immigrant terminology and defines the powers and duties of the Attorney General, Commissioner, Secretary of State, and Bureau of Security and Consular Affairs.

Title II
Chapter 1—Quota system

This chapter establishes numerical limitations and annual quotas based upon national origin.

Sec. 201. (a) The annual quota of any quota area shall be one-sixth of 1 per centum of the number of inhabitants in the continental United States in 1920, which number, except for the purpose of computing quotas for quota areas with the Asia-Pacific triangle, shall be the same number heretofore determined under the provision of Section 11 of the Immigration Act of 1924, attributable by national origin to such quota area: *Provided,* That the quota existing for Chinese persons prior to the date of enactment of this Act shall be continued, and, except as otherwise provided in section 202 (e), the minimum quota for any quota area shall be one hundred.

The remainder of Sec. 201 specifies rules for issuing visas relative to quotas. Parts (a) through (d) of Sec. 202 defines the country of origin for the purposes of charging immigrants against the applicable quotas.

Sec. 202 (e)

, but any increase in the number of minimum quota areas above twenty within the Asia-Pacific triangle shall result in a proportionate decrease in each minimum quota of such area in order that the sum total of all minimum quotas within the Asia-Pacific triangle shall not exceed two thousand.

Sec. 203 deals with allocation of immigrant visas within quotas. (a) sets out allotment procedures for each fiscal year.

(b) With reference to determination of the quota to which shall be chargeable an immigrant who is attributable by as much as one-half of his ancestry to a people or peoples indigenous to the Asia-Pacific triangle comprising all quota areas and all colonies and other dependent areas situate wholly east of meridian sixty degrees east of Greenwich, wholly west of the meridian one hundred and sixty-five degrees west, and wholly north of the parallel twenty-five degrees south latitude—

(1) there is hereby established, in addition to quotas for separate quota areas comprising independent countries, self-governing dominions, and territories under the international trusteeship system of the United Nations situate wholly within said Asia-Pacific triangle, an Asia-Pacific quota of one hundred annually,_

(2) such immigrant born within a separate quota area situate wholly within such Asia-Pacific triangle shall not be chargeable to the Asia-Pacific quota, but shall be chargeable to the quota for the separate quota area in which he was born;

(3) such immigrant born within a colony or other dependent area situate wholly within said Asia-Pacific triangle, shall be chargeable to the quota of that quota area;

(4) such immigrant born outside the Asia-Pacific triangle who is attributable by as much as one-half of his ancestry to a people or peoples indigenous to not more than one separate quota area, situate wholly within the Asia-Pacific triangle, shall be chargeable to the quota of that quota area;

(5) such immigrant born outside the Asia-Pacific triangle who is attributable by as much as one-half of his ancestry to people or peoples indigenous to one or more colonies or other dependent areas situate wholly within the Asia-Pacific triangle, shall be chargeable to the Asia-Pacific quota;

(6) such immigrant born outside the Asia-Pacific triangle who is attributable by as much as one-half of his ancestry to peoples indigenous to two or more separate quota areas situate wholly within the Asia-Pacific triangle, or to a quota area or areas and one or more colonies and other dependent areas situate wholly therein, shall be chargeable to the Asia-Pacific quota.

The remainder of this act sets qualifications and procedures for admission of aliens, including regulations for exclusion and deportation.

◆ IMMIGRATION AND NATIONALITY ACT AMENDMENTS, 1965

Asian countries gained equal footing with other countries through this act, which abolished "national origins" as a basis for allocation of immigration quotas.

An Act

To amend the Immigration and Nationality Act, and for other purposes.

Be it enacted by the Senate and House of Representatives of the United States of America in Congress assembled, That section 201 of the Immigration and Nationality Act (66 Stat. 175; 8 U.S.C. 1151) be amended to read as follows:

"Sec. 201. (a) Exclusive of special immigrants defined in section 101(a)(27), and of the immediate relatives of United States citizens specified in subsections (b) of this section, the number of aliens who may be issued immigrant visas or who may otherwise acquire the status of an alien lawfully admitted to the United States for permanent residence, or who may, pursuant to section 203(a)(7) enter conditionally, (i) shall not in any of the first three quarters of any fiscal year exceed a total of 45,000 and (ii) shall not in any fiscal year exceed a total of 170,000."

"(b) The "immediate relatives" referred to in subsection (a) of this section shall mean the children, spouses, and parents of a citizen of the United States:

Provided, That in the case of parents, such citizen must be at least twenty-one years of age. The immediate relatives specified in this subsection who are otherwise qualified for admission as immigrants shall be admitted as such, without regard to the numerical limitations in this Act."

"(c) During the period from July 1, 1965, through June 30, 1968, the annual quota of any quota area shall be the same as that which existed for that area on June 30, 1965. The Secretary of State shall, not later than on the sixtieth day immediately following the date of enactment of this subsection and again on or before September 1, 1966, and September 1, 1967, determine and proclaim the amount of quota numbers which remain unused at the end of the fiscal year ending on June 30, 1965, June 30, 1966, and June 30, 1967, respectively, and are available for distribution pursuant to subsection (d) of this section."

"(d) Quota numbers not issued or otherwise used during the previous fiscal year, as determined in accordance with subsection (c) hereof, shall be transferred to an immigration pool. Allocation of numbers from the pool and from national quotas shall not together exceed in any fiscal year the numerical limitations in subsection (a) of this section. The immigration pool shall be made available to immigrants otherwise admissible under the provisions of this Act who are unable to obtain prompt issuance of a preference visa due to oversubscription of their quotas, or subquotas as determined by the Secretary of State. Visas and conditional entries shall be allocated from the immigration pool within the percentage limitations and in the order of priority specified in section 203 without regard to the quota to which the alien is chargeable."

"(e) The immigration pool and the quotas of quota areas shall terminate June 30, 1968. Thereafter immigrants admissible under the provisions of this Act who are subject to the numerical limitations of subsection (a) of this section shall be admitted in accordance with the percentage limitations and in the order of priority specified in section 203."

Section 2

Section 202 of the Immigration and Nationality Act (66 Stat. 175; 8 U.S.C. 1152) is amended to read as follows:

"(a) No person shall receive any preference or priority or be discriminated against in the issuance of an immigrant visa because of his race, sex, nationality, place of birth, or place of residence, except as specifically provided in section 101(a)(27), section 201(b), and section 203:

Provided, That the total number of immigrant visas and the number of conditional entries made available to natives of any single foreign state under paragraphs (1) through (8) of section 203(a) shall not exceed 20,000 in any fiscal year

Provided Further, That the foregoing proviso shall not operate to reduce the number of immigrants who may be admitted under the quota of any quota area before June 30, 1968.

"(b) Each independent country, self-governing dominion, mandated territory, and territory under the international trusteeship system of the United Nations, other than the United States and its outlying possessions shall be treated as a separate foreign state for the purposes of the numerical limitation set forth in the proviso to subsection (a) of this section when approved by the Secretary of State. All other inhabited lands shall be attributed to a foreign state specified by the Secretary of State. For the purposes of this Act the foreign state to which an immigrant is chargeable shall be determined by birth within such foreign state except that (1) an alien child when accompanied by his alien parent or parents, may be charged to the same foreign state as the accompanying parent or of either accompanying parent if such parent has received or would be qualified for an immigrant visa, if necessary to prevent the separation of the child from the accompanying parent or parents, and if the foreign state to which such parent has been or would be chargeable has not exceeded the numerical limitation set forth in the proviso to subsection (a) of this section for that fiscal year; (2) if an alien is chargeable to a different foreign state from that of his accompanying spouse, the foreign state to which such alien is chargeable may, if necessary to prevent the separation of husband and wife, be determined by the foreign state of the accompanying spouse, if such spouse has received or would be qualified for an immigrant visa and if the foreign state to which such spouse has been or would be chargeable has not exceeded the numerical limitation set forth in the proviso to subsection (a) of this section for that fiscal year; (3) an alien born in the United States shall be considered as having been born in the country of which he is a citizen or subject, or if he is not a citizen or subject of any country then in the last foreign country in which he had his residence as determined by the consular officer; (4) an alien born within any foreign state in which neither of his parents was born and in which neither of his parents had a residence at the time of such aliens birth may be charged to the foreign state of either parent.

"(c) Any immigrant born in a colony or other component or dependent area of a foreign state unless a special immigrant as provided in section 101(a)(27) or an immediate relative of a United States citizen as specified in section 201(b), shall be chargeable, for the purpose of limitation set forth in section 202(a), to the foreign state, except that the number of persons born in any such colony or other component or dependent area overseas from the foreign state chargeable to the foreign state in any one fiscal year shall not exceed 1 per centum of the maximum number of immigrant visas available to such foreign state.

"(d) In the case of any change in the territorial limits of foreign states, the Secretary of State shall, upon recognition of such change, issue appropriate instructions to all diplomatic and consular offices.

Section 3

Section 203 of the Immigration and Nationality Act (66 Stat. 175; 8 U.S.C. 1153) is amended to read as follows:

"Section 203, (a) Aliens who are subject to the numerical limitations specified in section 201(a) shall be allotted visas or their conditional entry authorized, as the case may be, as follows:

"(1) Visas shall be first made available, in a number not to exceed 20 per centum of the number specified in section 201(a)(ii), to qualified immigrants who are the unmarried sons or daughters of citizens of the United States.

"(2) Visas shall next be made available, in a number not to exceed 20 per centum of the number specified in section 201(a)(ii), plus any visas not required for the classes specified in paragraph (1), to qualified immigrants who are the spouses, unmarried sons or unmarried daughters of an alien lawfully admitted for permanent residence.

"(3) Visas shall next be made available, in a number not to exceed 10 per centum of the number specified in section 201(a)(ii), to qualified immigrants who are members of the professions, or who because of their exceptional ability in the sciences or the arts will substantially benefit prospectively the national economy, cultural interests, or welfare of the United States.

"(4) Visas shall next be made available, in a number not to exceed 10 per centum of the number specified in section 201(a)(ii), plus any visas not required for the classes specified in paragraphs (1) through (3), to qualified immigrants who are the married sons or the married daughters of citizens of the United States.

"(5) Visas shall next be made available, in a number not to exceed 24 per centum of the number specified in section 201(a)(ii), plus any visas not required for the classes specified in paragraphs (1) through (4), to qualified immigrants who are the brothers or sisters of citizens of the United States.

"(6) Visas shall next be made available, in a number not to exceed 10 per centum of the number specified in section 201(a)(ii), to qualified immigrants who are capable of performing specified skilled or unskilled labor, not of a temporary or seasonal nature, for which a shortage of employable and willing persons exists in the United States.

"(7) Conditional entries shall next be made available by the Attorney General, pursuant to such regulations as he may prescribe and in a number not to exceed 6 per centum of the number specified in section 201(a)(ii), to aliens who satisfy an Immigration and Naturalization Service officer at an examination in any non-Communist or non-Communist-dominated country, (A) that (i) because of persecution or fear of persecution on account of race, religion, or political opinion they have fled (i) from any Communist or Communist-dominated country or area, or (ii) from any country within the general area of the Middle East, and (ii) are unable or unwilling to return to such country or area on account of race, religion, or political opinion, and (iii) are not nationals of the countries or areas in which their application for conditional entry is made; or (B) that they are persons uprooted by catastrophic national calamity as defined by the President who are unable to return to their usual place of abode. For the purpose of the foregoing the term 'general area of the Middle East' means the area between and including (1) Libya on the west, (2) Turkey on the north, (3) Pakistan on the east, and (4) Saudi Arabia and Ethiopia on the south:

Provided, That immigrant visas in a number not exceeding one-half the number specified in this paragraph may be made available, in lieu of conditional entries of a like number, to such aliens who have been continuously physically present in the United States for a period of at least two years prior to application for adjustment of status.

"(8) Visas authorized in any fiscal year, less those required for issuance to the classes specified in paragraphs (1) through (6) and less the number of conditional entries and visas made available pursuant to paragraph (7), shall be made available to other qualified immigrants strictly in the chronological order in which they qualify. Waiting lists of applicants shall be maintained in accordance with regulations prescribed by the Secretary of State. No immigrant visa shall be issued to a nonpreference immigrant under this paragraph, or to an immigrant with a preference under paragraph (3) or (6) of this subsection, until the consular officer is in receipt of a determination made by the Secretary of Labor pursuant to the provisions of section 212(a)(14).

"(9) A spouse or child as defined in section 101(b)(1)(A), (B), (C), (D), or (E) shall if not otherwise entitled to an immigrant status and the immediate issuance of a visa or to conditional entry under paragraphs (1) through (8), be entitled to the same status, and the same order of consideration provided in subsection (b), if accompanying, or following to join, his spouse or parent.

"(b) In considering applications for immigrant visas under subsection (a) consideration shall be given to applicants in the order in which the classes of which they are members are listed in subsection (a).

"(c) Immigrant visas issued pursuant to paragraphs (1) through (6) of subsection (a) shall be issued to eligible immigrants in the order in which a petition in behalf of each such immigrant is filed with the Attorney General as provided in section 204.

"(d) Every immigrant shall be presumed to be a non-preference immigrant until he establishes to the satisfaction of the consular officer and the immigration officer that he is entitled to a preference status under paragraphs (1) through (7) of subsection (a), or to a special immigrant status under section 101(a)(27), or that he is an immediate relative of a United States citizen as specified in section 201(b). In the case of any alien claiming in his application for an immigrant visa to be an immediate relative of a United States citizen as specified in section 201(b) or to be entitled to preference immigrant status under paragraphs (1) through (6) of subsection (a), the consular officer shall not grant such status until he has been authorized to do so as provided by section 204.

"(e) For the purposes of carrying out his responsibilities in the orderly administration of this section, the Secretary of State is authorized to make reasonable estimates of the anticipated numbers of visas to be issued during any quarter of any fiscal year within each of the categories of subsection (a) and to rely upon such estimates in authorizing the issuance of such visas. The Secretary of State, in his discretion, may terminate the registration on a waiting list of any alien who fails to evidence his continued intention to apply for a visa in such manner as may be by regulation prescribed.

"(f) The Attorney General shall submit to the Congress a report containing complete and detailed statement of facts in the case of each alien who conditionally entered the United States pursuant to subsection (a)(7) of this section. Such reports shall be submitted on or before January 15 and June 15 of each year.

"(g) Any alien who conditionally entered the United States as a refugee, pursuant to subsection (a)(7) of this section, whose conditional entry has not been terminated by the Attorney General pursuant to such regulations as he may prescribe, who has been in the United States for at least two years, and who has not acquired permanent residence, shall forthwith return or be returned to the custody of the Immigration and Naturalization Service and shall thereupon be inspected and examined for admission into the United States and his case dealt with in accordance with the provisions of sections 235, 236, and 237 of this Act.

"(h) Any alien who pursuant to subsection (g) of this section, is found, upon inspection by the immigration officer or after hearing before a special inquiry officer, to be admissible as an immigrant under this Act at the time of his inspection and examination, except for the fact that he was not and is not in possession of the documents required by section 212(a)(20), shall be regarded as lawfully admitted to the United States for permanent residence as of the date of his arrival."

Section 4

Section 204 of the Immigration and Nationality Act (66 Stat. 176; 8 U.S.C. 1154) is amended to read as follows:

"Sec. 204 (a) Any citizen of the United States claiming that an alien is entitled to a preference status by reason of the relationships described in paragraphs (1), (4), or (5) of section 203(a), or to an immediate relative status under section 201(b), or any alien lawfully admitted for permanent residence claiming that an alien is entitled to a preference status by reason of the relationship described in section 203(a)(2), or any alien desiring to be classified as a preference immigrant under section 203(a)(3) (or any person on behalf of such an alien), or any person desiring and intending to employ within the United States an alien entitled to classification as a preference immigrant under section 203(a)(6), may file a petition with the Attorney General for such classification."

"(b) After an investigation of the facts in each case, and after consultation with the Secretary of Labor with respect to petitions to accord a status under section 203(a)(3) or (6), the Attorney General shall, if he determines that the facts stated in the petition are true and that the alien in behalf of whom the petition is made is an immediate relative specified in section 201(b) or is eligible for a preference status under section 203(a), approve the petition and forward one copy thereof to the Department of State. The Secretary of State shall then authorize the consular officer concerned to grant the preference status.

"(c) Notwithstanding the provisions of subsection (b) no more than two petitions may be approved for one petitioner in behalf of a child as defined in section 101(b)(1)(E) or (F) unless necessary to prevent the separation of brothers and sisters and no petition shall be approved if the alien has previously been accorded a nonquota or preference status as a spouse of a citizen of the United States or the spouse of an alien lawfully admitted for permanent residence, by reason of a marriage determined by the Attorney General to have been entered into for the purpose of evading the immigration laws."

Section 5

Section 205 of the Immigration and Nationality Act (66 Stat. 176; 8 U.S.C. 1155) is amended to read as follows:

"Section 205. The Attorney General may, at any time, for what he deems to be good and sufficient cause, revoke the approval of any petition approved by him under section 204. Such revocation shall be effective as of the date of approval of any such petition. In no case, however, shall such revocation have effect unless there is mailed to the petitioner's last known address a notice of the revocation and unless notice of the revocation is communicated through the Secretary of State to the beneficiary of the petition before such beneficiary commences his journey to the United States. If notice of revocation is not so given, and the beneficiary applies for admission to the United States, his admissibility shall be determined in the manner provided for by sections 235 and 236."

Section 6

Section 206 of the Immigration and Nationality Act (66 Stat. 181; 8 U.S.C. 1156) is amended to read as follows:

"Section 206. If an immigrant having an immigrant visa is excluded from admission to the United States and deported, or does not apply for admission before the expiration of the validity of his visa, or if an alien having an immigrant visa issued to him as a preference immigrant is found not to be a preference immigrant, an immigrant visa or a preference immigrant visa, as the case may be, may be issued in lieu thereof to another qualified alien."

Section 7

Section 207 of the Immigration and Nationality Act (66 Stat. 181; 8 U.S.C. 1157) is stricken).

Section 8

Section 101 of the Immigration and Nationality Act (66 Stat. 166; 8 U.S.C. 1101) is amended as follows:

(a) Paragraph (27) of subsection (a) is amended to read as follows:

"(27) The term 'special immigrant' means—

"(A) an immigrant who was born in any independent foreign country of the Western Hemisphere or in the Canal Zone and the spouse and children of any such immigrant, if accompanying, or following to join him:

Provided, That no immigrant visa shall be issued pursuant to this clause until the consular officer is in receipt of a determination made by the Secretary of Labor pursuant to the provisions of section 212(a)(14);

"(B) an immigrant, lawfully admitted for permanent residence, who is returning from a temporary visit abroad;

"(C) an immigrant who was a citizen of the United States and may, under section 324(a) or 327 of title III, apply for reacquisition of citizenship;

"(D)(i) an immigrant who continuously for at least two years immediately preceding the time of his application for admission to the United States has been, and who seeks to enter the United States solely for the purpose of carrying on the vocation of minister of a religious denomination, and whose services are needed by such religious denomination having a bona fide organization in the United States; and (ii) the spouse or the child of any such immigrant, if accompanying or following to join him; or

"(E) an immigrant who is an employee, or an honorably retired former employee, of the United States Government abroad, and who has performed faithful service for a total of fifteen years, or more, and his accompanying spouse and children:

Provided, That the principal officer of a Foreign Service establishment, in his discretion, shall have recommended the granting of special immigrant status to such alien in exceptional circumstances and the Secretary of State approves such recommendation and finds that it is in the national interest to grant such status."

(b) Paragraph (32) of subsection (a) is amended to read as follows:

"(32) The term 'profession' shall include but not be limited to architects, engineers, lawyers, physicians, surgeons, and teachers in elementary or secondary schools, colleges, academies, or seminaries."

(c) Subparagraph (1)(F) of subsection (b) is amended to read as follows:

"(F) a child, under the age of fourteen at the time a petition is filed in his behalf to accord a classification as an immediate relative under section 201(b), who is an orphan because of the death or disappearance of, abandonment or desertion by, or separation or loss from, both parents, or for whom the sole or surviving parent is incapable of providing the proper care which will be provided the child if admitted to the United States and who has in writing irrevocably released the child for emigration and adoption; who has been adopted abroad by a United States citizen and his spouse who personally saw and observed the child prior to or during the adoption proceedings; or who is coming to the United States for adoption by a United States citizen and spouse who have complied with the preadoption requirements, if any, of the child's proposed residence:

Provided, That no natural parent or prior adoptive parent of any such child shall thereafter, by virtue of such parentage, be accorded any right, privilege, or status under this Act."

Section 9

Section 211 of the Immigration and Nationality Act (66 Stat. 181; 8 U.S.C. 1181) is amended to read as follows:

"Section 211. (a) Except as provided in subsection (b) no immigrant shall be admitted into the United States unless at the time of application for admission he (1) has a valid unexpired immigrant visa or was born subsequent to the issuance of such visa of the accompanying parent, and (2) presents a valid unexpired passport or other suitable travel document, or document of identity and nationality, if such document is required under the regulations issued by the Attorney General. With respect to immigrants to be admitted under quotas of quota areas prior to June 30, 1968, no immigrant visa shall be deemed valid unless the immigrant is properly chargeable to the quota area under the quota of which the visa is issued.

"(b) Notwithstanding the provisions of section 212(a)(20) of this Act in such cases or in such classes of cases and under such conditions as may be by regulations prescribed, returning resident immigrants, defined in section 101(a)(27)(B), who are otherwise admissible may be readmitted to the United States by the Attorney General in his discretion without being required to obtain a passport, immigrant visa, reentry permit or other documentation."

Section 10

Section 212(a) of the Immigration and Nationality Act (66 Stat. 182; 8 U.S.C. 1182) is amended as follows:

(a) Paragraph (14) is amended to read as follows:

"Aliens seeking to enter the United States, for the purpose of performing skilled or unskilled labor, unless the Secretary of Labor has determined and certified to the Secretary of State and to the Attorney General that (A) there are not sufficient workers in the United States who are able, willing, qualified, and available at the time of application for a visa and admission to the United States and at the place to which the alien is destined to perform such skilled or unskilled labor, and (B) the employment of such aliens will not adversely affect the wages and working conditions of the workers in the United States similarly employed. The exclusion of aliens under this paragraph shall apply to special immigrants defined in section 101(a)(27)(A) (other than the parents, spouses, or children of United States citizens or of aliens lawfully admitted to the United States for permanent residence), to preference immigrant aliens described in section 203(a)(3) and (6), and to nonpreference immigrant aliens described in section 203(a)(8);".

(b) Paragraph (20) is amended by deleting the letter "(e)" and substituting therefor the letter "(a)."

(c) Paragraph (21) is amended by deleting the word "quota."

(d) Paragraph (24) is amended by deleting the language within the parentheses and substituting therefor the following: "other than aliens described in section 101(a)(27)(A) and (B)."

Section 11

The Immigration and Nationality Act (66 Stat. 175; 8 U.S.C. 1151) is amended as follows:

(a) Section 221(a) is amended by deleting the words "the particular nonquota category in which the immigrant is classified, if a nonquota immigrant," and substituting in lieu thereof the words "the preference, nonpreference, immediate relative, or special immigration classification to which the alien is charged."

(b) The fourth sentence of subsection 221(c) is amended by deleting the word "quota" preceding the word "number;" the word "quota" preceding the word "year;" and the words "a quota" preceding the word "immigrant," and substituting in lieu thereof the word "an."

(c) Section 222(a) is amended by deleting the words "preference quota or a nonquota immigrant" and substituting in lieu thereof the words "an immediate relative within the meaning of section 201(b) or a preference or special immigrant."

(d) Section 224 is amended to read as follows: "A consular officer may, subject to the limitations provided in section 221, issue an immigrant visa to a special immigrant or immediate relative as such upon satisfactory proof, under regulations prescribed under this Act, that the applicant is entitled to special immigrant or immediate relative status."

(e) Section 241(a)(10) is amended by substituting for the words "Section 101(a)(27)(C)" the words "Section 101(a)(27)(A)."

(f) Section 243(h) is amended by striking out "physical persecution" and inserting in lieu thereof "persecution on account of race, religion, or political opinion."

Section 12

Sections 12 through 20 detail further amendments and state the laws effective date.

Section 21

(a) There is hereby established a Select Commission on Western Hemisphere Immigration (hereinafter referred to as the "Commission") to be composed of fifteen members. The President shall appoint the Chairman of the Commission and four other members thereof. The President of the Senate, with the approval of the majority and minority leaders of the Senate, shall appoint five members from the membership of the Senate. The Speaker of the House of Representatives, with the approval of the majority and minority leaders of the House, shall appoint five members from the membership of the House. Not more than three members appointed by the President of the Senate and the Speaker of the House of Representatives, respectively, shall be members of the same political party. A vacancy in the membership of the Commission shall be filled in the same manner as the original designation and appointment.

(b) The Commission shall study the following matters;

(1) Prevailing and projected demographic, technological, and economic trends, particularly as they pertain to Western Hemisphere nations;

(2) Present and projected unemployment in the United States, by occupations, industries, geographic areas and other factors, in relation to immigration from the Western Hemisphere;

(3) The interrelationships between immigration, present and future, and existing and contemplated national and international programs and projects of Western Hemisphere nations, including programs and projects for economic and social development;

(4) The operation of the immigration laws of the United States as they pertain to Western Hemisphere nations, including the adjustment of status for Cuban refugees, with emphasis on the adequacy of such laws from the standpoint of fairness and from the standpoint of the impact of such laws on employment and working conditions within the United States;

(5) The implications of the foregoing with respect to the security and international relations of Western Hemisphere nations; and

(6) Any other matters which the Commission believes to be germane to the purposes for which it was established.

(c) On or before July 1, 1967, the Commission shall make a first report to the President and the Congress, and on or before January 15, 1968, the Commission shall make a final report to the President and the Congress. Such reports shall include the recommendations of the Commission as to what changes, if any, are needed in the immigration laws in the light of its study. The Commission's recommendations shall include, but shall not be limited to, recommendations as to whether, and if so how, numerical limitations should be imposed upon immigration to the United States from the nations of the Western Hemisphere. In formulating its recommendations on the latter subject, the Commission shall give particular attention to the impact of such immigration on employment and working conditions within the United States to the necessity of preserving the special relationship of the United States with its sister Republics of the Western Hemisphere. . . .

◆ DIRECTIVE NO. 15

This Directive supersedes section 7(h) and Exhibit F of AMB Circular A-46 dated May 3, 1974 and as revised May 12, 1977.

Race and Ethnic Standards for Federal Statistics and Administrative Reporting

Issued by U.S. Office of Federal Statistical Policy and Standards, U.S. Department of Commerce, May 1978.

This Directive provides standard classifications for recordkeeping, collection, and presentation of data on race and ethnicity in Federal program administrative reporting and statistical activities. These classifications should not be interpreted as being scientific or anthropological in nature, nor should they be viewed as determinants of eligibility for participation in any Federal program. They have been developed in response to needs expressed by both the executive branch and the Congress to provide for the collection and use of compatible, nonduplicated, exchangeable racial and ethnic data by Federal agencies.

Definitions

The basic racial and ethnic categories for Federal statistics and program administrative reporting are defined as follows:

a. *American Indian or Alaskan Native.* A person having origins in any of the original peoples of North America, and who maintains cultural identification through tribal affiliation or community recognition.

b. *Asian or Pacific Islander.* A person having origins in any of the original peoples of the Far East, Southeast Asia, the Indian subcontinent, or the Pacific Islands. This area includes, for example, China, India, Japan, Korea, the Philippine Islands, and Samoa.

c. *Black.* A person having origins in any of the black racial groups of Africa.

d. *Hispanic.* A person of Mexican, Puerto Rican, Cuban, Central or South American or other Spanish culture or origin, regardless of race.

e. *White.* A person having origins in any of the original peoples of Europe, North Africa, or the Middle East.

2. Utilization for Recordkeeping and Reporting

To provide flexibility, it is preferable to collect data on race and ethnicity separately. If separate race and ethnic categories are used, the minimum designations are:

a. *Race:*
— American Indian or Alaskan Native
— Asian or Pacific Islander
— Black
— White
b. *Ethnicity:*
— Hispanic origin
— Not of Hispanic origin

When race and ethnicity are collected separately, the number of White and Black persons who are Hispanic must be identifiable, and capable of being reported in that category.

If a combined format is used to collect racial and ethnic data, the minimum acceptable categories are:

American Indian or Alaskan Native
Asian or Pacific Islander
Black, not of Hispanic origin
White, not of Hispanic origin.

The category which most closely reflects the individual's recognition in his community should be used for purposes of reporting on persons who are of mixed racial and/or ethnic origins.

In no case should the provisions of this Directive be construed to limit the collection of data to the categories described above. However, any reporting required which uses more additional categories can be aggregated into these basic racial/ethnic categories.

The minimum standard collection categories shall be utilized for reporting as follows:

a. *Civil rights compliance reporting.* The categories specified above will be used by all agencies in either the separate or combined format for civil rights compliance reportings and equal employment reporting for both the public and private sectors and for all levels of government. Any variation requiring less detailed data or data which cannot be aggregated into the basic categories will have to be specifically approved by the Office of Federal Statistical Policy and Standards for executive agencies. More detailed reporting which can be aggregated to the basic categories may be used at the agencies' discretion.

b. *General program administrative and grant reporting.* Whenever an agency subject to this Directive issues new or revised administrative reporting or recordkeeping requirements which include racial or ethnic data, the agency will use the race/ethnic categories described above. A variance can be specifically requested from the Office of Federal Statistical Policy and Standards, but such a variance will be granted only if the agency can demonstrate that it is not reasonable for the primary reporter to determine the racial or ethnic background in terms of the specified categories, and that such determination is not critical to the administration of the program in question, or if the specific program is directed to only one or a limited number of race/ethnic groups, e.g., Indian tribal activities.

c. *Statistical reporting.* The categories described in this Directive will be used as a minimum for federally sponsored statistical data collection where race and/or ethnicity is required, except when: the collection involves a sample of such size that the data on the smaller categories would be unreliable, or when the collection effort focuses on a specific racial or ethnic group. A repetitive survey shall be deemed to have an adequate sample size if the racial and ethnic data can be reliably aggregated on a biennial basis. Any other variation will have to be specifically authorized by OMB through the reports clearance process (see OMB Circular No. A-40). In those cases where the data collection is not subject to the reports [??] should be made to the OFSPS.

3. Effective Date

The provisions of this Directive are effective immediately for all *new* and *revised* recordkeeping or reporting requirements containing racial and/or ethnic information. All *existing* recordkeeping or reporting requirements shall be made consistent with this Directive at the time they are submitted for extension, or not later than January 1, 1980.

4. Presentation of Race/Ethnic Data

Displays of racial and ethnic compliance and statistical data will use the category designations listed above. The designation "nonwhite" is not acceptable for use in the presentation of Federal Government data. It is not to be used in any publication or compliance or statistical data or in the text of any compliance or statistical report.

In cases where the above designations are considered inappropriate for presentation of statistical data on particular programs or for particular regional areas, the sponsoring agency may use:

(1) The designations "Black and Other Races" or "All Other Races," as collective descriptions of minority races when the most summary distinction between the majority and minority races is appropriate;

(2) The designations "White," "Black," and "All Other Races" when the distinction among the majority race, the principal minority race and other races is appropriate; or

(3) The designation of a particular minority race or races, and the inclusion of "Whites" with "All Other Races," if such a collective description is appropriate.

In displaying detailed information which represents a combination of race and ethnicity, the description of the data being displayed must clearly indicate that both bases of classification are being used.

When the primary focus of a statistical report is on two or more specific identifiable groups in the population, one or more of which is racial or ethnic, it is acceptable to display data for each of the particular groups separately and to describe data relating to the remainder of the population by an appropriate collective description.

U.S. DEPARTMENT OF COMMERCE
Juanita M. Kreps, Secretary
Courtenay M. Slater, Chief Economist
Office of Federal Statistical Policy and Standards
Joseph W. Duncan, Director
Issued: May 1978

♦ REFUGEE ACT, 1980

This act systematized admission of refugees to the United States. An "Orderly Departure Program" was established to enable Vietnamese people to emigrate legally.

Title I—Purpose

Section 101. (a) The Congress declares that it is the historic policy of the United States to respond to the urgent needs of persons subject to persecution in their homelands, including, where appropriate, humanitarian assistance for their care and maintenance in asylum areas, efforts to promote opportunities for resettlement or voluntary repatriation, aid for necessary transportation and processing, admission to this country of refugees of special humanitarian concern to the United States, and transitional assistance to refugees in the United States. The Congress further declares that it is the policy of the United States to encourage all nations to provide assistance and resettlement opportunities to refugees to the fullest extent possible.

(b) The objectives of this Act are to provide a permanent and systematic procedure for the admission to this country of refugees of special humanitarian concern to the United States, and to provide comprehensive and uniform provisions for the effective resettlement and absorption of those refugees who are admitted.

Title II—Admission of Refugees

Section 201. (a) Section 101(a) of the Immigration and Nationality Act (8 U.S.C. 1101(a)) is amended by adding after paragraph (41) the following new paragraph:

"(42) The term 'refugee' means (A) any person who is outside any country of such person's nationality or, in the case of a person having no nationality, is outside any country in which such person last habitually resided, and who is unable or unwilling to return to, and is unable or unwilling to avail himself or herself of the protection of, that country because of persecution or a well-founded fear of persecution on account of race, religion, nationality, membership in a particular social group, or political opinion, or (B) in such special circumstances as the President after appropriate consultation (as defined in section 207(e) of this Act) may specify, any person who is within the country of such person's nationality or, in the case of a person having no nationality, within the country in which such person is habitually residing, and who is persecuted or who has a well-founded fear of persecution on account of race, religion, nationality, membership in a particular social group, or political opinion. The term 'refugee' does not include any person who ordered, incited, assisted, or otherwise participated in the persecution of any person on account of race, religion, nationality, membership in a particular social group, or political opinion."

(b) Chapter 1 of title II of such Act is amended by adding after section 206(8 U.S.C. 1156) the following new sections:

Annual Admission of Refugees and Admission of Emergency Situation Refugees

Section 207. (a)(1) Except as provided in subsection (b), the number of refugees who may be admitted under this section in fiscal year 1980, 1981, or 1982, may not exceed fifty thousand unless the President determines, before the beginning of the fiscal year and after appropriate consultation (as defined in subsection (e)), that admission of a specific number of refugees in excess of such number is justified by humanitarian concerns or is otherwise in the national interest.

"(2) Except as provided in subsection (b), the number of refugees who may be admitted under this section in any fiscal year after fiscal year 1982 shall be such number as the President determines, before the beginning of the fiscal year and after appropriate consultation, is justified by humanitarian concerns or is otherwise in the national interest.

"(3) Admissions under this subsection shall be allocated among refugees of special humanitarian concern to the United States in accordance with a determination made by the President after appropriate consultation.

"(b) If the President determines, after appropriate consultation, that (1) an unforeseen emergency refugee situation exists, (2) the admission of certain refugees in response to the emergency refugee situation is justified by grave humanitarian concerns or is otherwise in the national interest, and (3) the admission to the United States of these refugees cannot be accomplished under subsection (a), the President may fix a number of refugees to be admitted to the United States during the succeeding period (not to exceed twelve months) in response to the emergency refugee situation and such admissions shall be allocated among refugees of special humanitarian concern to the United States in accordance with a determination made by the President after the appropriate consultation provided under this subsection.

"(c)(1) Subject to the numerical limitations established pursuant to subsections (a) and (b), the Attorney General may, in the Attorney General's discretion and pursuant to such regulations as the Attorney General may prescribe, admit any refugee who is not firmly resettled in any foreign country, is determined to be of special humanitarian concern to the United States, and is admissible (except as otherwise provided under paragraph (3)) as an immigrant under this Act.

"(2) A spouse or child (as defined in section 101(b)(1)(A), (B), (C), (D), or (E)) of any refugee who qualifies for admission under paragraph (1) shall, if not otherwise entitled to admission under paragraph (1) and if not a person described in the second sentence of section 101(a)(42), be entitled to the same admission status as such refugee if accompanying, or following to join, such refugee and if the spouse or child is admissible (except as otherwise provided under paragraph (3)) as an immigrant under this Act. Upon the spouse's or child's admission to the United States, such admission shall be charged against the numerical limitation established in accordance with the appropriate subsection under which the refugee's admission is charged.

"(3) The provisions of paragraphs (14), (15), (20), (21), (25), and (32) of section 212(a) shall not be applicable to any alien seeking admission to the United States under this subsection, and the Attorney General may waive any other provision of such section (other than paragraph (27), (29), or (33) and other than so much of paragraph (23) as relates to trafficking in narcotics) with respect to such an alien for humanitarian purposes, to assure family unity, or when it is otherwise in the public interest. Any such waiver by the Attorney General shall be in writing and shall be granted only on an individual basis following an investigation. The Attorney General shall provide for the annual reporting to Congress of the number of waivers granted under this paragraph in the previous fiscal year and a summary of the reasons for granting such waivers.

"(4) The refugee status of any alien (and of the spouse or child of the alien) may be terminated by the Attorney General pursuant to such regulations as the Attorney General may prescribe if the Attorney General determines that the alien was not in fact a refugee within the meaning of section 1019(a)(42) at the time of the alien's admission.

"(d)(1) Before the start of each fiscal year the President shall report to the Committees on the Judiciary of the House of Representatives and of the Senate regarding the foreseeable number of refugees who will be in need of resettlement during the fiscal year and the anticipated allocation of refugee admissions during the fiscal year. The President shall provide for periodic discussions between designated representatives of the President and members of such committees regarding changes in the worldwide refugee situation, the progress of refugee admissions among refugees.

"(2) As soon as possible after representatives of the President initiate appropriate consultation with respect to the number of refugee admissions under subsection (a) or with respect to the admission of refugees in response to an emergency refugee situation under subsection (b), the Committees on the Judiciary of the House of Representatives and of the Senate shall cause to have printed in the Congressional Record the substance of such consultation.

"(3)(A) After the President initiates appropriate consultation prior to making a determination under subsection (a), a hearing to review the proposed determination shall be held unless public disclosure of the details of the proposal would jeopardize the lives or safety of individuals.

"(B) After the President initiates appropriate consultation prior to making a determination, under subsection (b), that the number of refugee admissions should be increased because of an unforeseen emergency refugee situation, to the extent that time and the nature of the emergency refugee situation permit, a hearing to review the proposal to increase refugee admissions shall be held unless public disclosure of the details of the proposal would jeopardize the lives or safety of individuals.

"(e) For purposes of this section, the term 'appropriate consultation' means, with respect to the admission of refugees and allocation of refugee admissions, discussions in person by designated Cabinet-level representatives of the President with members of the Committees on the Judiciary of the Senate and of the House of Representatives to review the refugee situation or emergency refugee situation, to project the extent of possible participation of the United States therein, to discuss the reasons for believing that the proposed admission of refugees is justified by humanitarian concerns or grave humanitarian concerns or is otherwise in the national interest, and to provide such members with the following information:

"(1) A description of the nature of the refugee situation.

"(2) A description of the number and allocation for the refugees to be admitted and an analysis of conditions within the countries from which they came.

"(3) A description of the proposed plans for their movement and resettlement and the estimated cost of their movement and resettlement.

"(4) An analysis of the anticipated social, economic, and demographic impact of their admission to the United States.

"(5) A description of the extent to which other countries will admit and assist in the resettlement of such refugees.

"(6) An analysis of the impact of the participation of the United States in the resettlement of such refugees on the foreign policy interests of the United States.

"(7) Such additional information as may be appropriate or requested by such members.

To the extent possible, information described in this subsection shall be provided at least two weeks in advance of discussions in person by designated representatives of the President with such members.

Asylum Procedure

Section 208. (a) The Attorney General shall establish a procedure for an alien physically present in the United States or at a land border or port of entry, irrespective of such alien's status, to apply for asylum, and the alien may be granted asylum in the discretion of the Attorney General. . . .

Adjustment of Status of Refugees

Section 209. (a)(1) Any alien who has been admitted to the United States under section 207—

"(A) whose admission has not been terminated by the Attorney General pursuant to such regulations as the Attorney General may prescribe,

"(B) who has been physically present in the United States for at least one year, and

"(C) who has not acquired permanent resident status, shall, at the end of such year period, return or be returned to the custody of the Service for inspection and examination for admission to the United States as an immigrant in accordance with the provisions of sections 235, 236, and 237.

"(2) Any alien who is found upon inspection and examination by an immigration officer pursuant to paragraph (1) or after a hearing before a special inquiry officer to be admissible (except as otherwise provided under subsection (c)) as an immigrant under this Act at the time of the alien's inspection and examination shall, notwithstanding any numerical limitation specified in this Act, be regarded as lawfully admitted to the United States for permanent residence as of the date of such alien's arrival into the United States.

"(b) Not more than five thousand of the refugee admissions authorized under section 207(a) in any fiscal year may be made available by the Attorney General, in the Attorney General's discretion and under such regulations as the Attorney General may prescribe, to adjust to the status of an alien lawfully admitted for permanent residence the status of any alien granted asylum who—

"(1) applies for such adjustment,

"(2) has been physically present in the United States for at least one year after being granted asylum,

"(3) continues to be a refugee within the meaning of section 101(a)(42)(A) or a spouse or child of such a refugee,

"(4) is not firmly resettled in any foreign country, and

"(5) is admissible (except as otherwise provided under subsection (c)) as an immigrant under this Act at the time of examination for adjustment of such alien. . . .

Section 202. Section 211 of the Immigration and Nationality Act (8 U.S.C. 1181) is amended—. . . .

Section 203. (a) Subsection (a) of section 201 of the Immigration and Nationality Act (8 U.S.C. 1151) is amended to read as follows:

"(a) Exclusive of special immigrants defined in section 101(a)(27), immediate relatives specified in subsection (b) of this section, and aliens who are admitted or granted asylum under section 207 or 208, the number of aliens born in any foreign state or dependent area who may be issued immigrant visas or who may otherwise acquire the status of an alien lawfully admitted to the United States for permanent residence, shall not in any of the first three quarters of any fiscal year exceed a total of seventy-two thousand and shall not in any fiscal year exceed two hundred and seventy thousand."

"(b) Section 202 of such Act (8 U.S.C. 1152) is amended—. . . .

(e) Subsection (h) of section 243 of such Act (8 U.S.C. 1253) is amended to read as follows:

"(h)(1) The Attorney General shall not deport or return any alien (other than an alien described in section 241(a)(19)) to a country if the Attorney General determines that such alien's life or freedom would be threatened in such country on account of race, religion, nationality, membership in a particular social group, or political opinion.

"(2) Paragraph (1) shall not apply to any alien if the Attorney General determines that—

"(A) the alien ordered, incited, assisted, or otherwise participated in the persecution of any person on account of race, religion, nationality, membership in a particular social group, or political opinion;

"(B) the alien, having been convicted by a final judgment of a particularly serious crime, constitutes a danger to the community of the United States;

"(C) there are serious reasons for considering that the alien has committed a serious nonpolitical crime outside the United States prior to the arrival of the alien to the United States; or

"(D) there are reasonable grounds for regarding the alien as a danger to the security of the United States.

Title III—United States Coordinator for Refugee Affairs and Assistance for Effective Resettlement of Refugees in the United States

Part A—United States Coordinator for Refugee Affairs

Section 301. (a) The President shall appoint, by and with the advice and consent of the Senate, a United States Coordinator for Refugee Affairs (hereinafter in this part referred to as the "Coordinator"). The Coordinator shall have the rank of Ambassador-at-Large.

(b) The Coordinator shall be responsible to the President for —

(1) the development of overall United States refugee admission and resettlement policy;

(2) the coordination of all United States domestic and international refugee admission and resettlement programs in a manner that assures that policy objectives are met in a timely fashion;

(3) the design of an overall budget strategy to provide individual agencies with policy guidance on refugee matters in the preparation of their budget requests, and to provide the Office of Management and Budget with an overview of all refugee-related budget requests;

(4) the presentation to the Congress of the Administration's overall refugee policy and the relationship of individual agency refugee budgets to that overall policy;

(5) advising the President, Secretary of State, Attorney General, and the Secretary of Health and Human Services on the relationship of overall United States refugee policy to the admission of refugees to, and the resettlement of refugees in, the United States;

(6) under the direction of the Secretary of State, representation and negotiation on behalf of the United States with foreign governments and international organizations in discussions on refugee matters and, when appropriate, submitting refugee issues for inclusion in other international negotiations;

(7) development of an effective and responsive liaison between the Federal Government and voluntary organizations, Governors and mayors, and others involved in refugee relief and resettlement work to reflect overall United States Government policy;

(8) making recommendations to the President and to the Congress with respect to policies for, objectives of, and establishment of priorities for, Federal functions relating to refugee admission and resettlement in the United States; and

(9) reviewing the regulations, guidelines, requirements, criteria, and procedures of Federal departments and agencies applicable to the performance of functions relating to refugee admission and resettlement in the United States.

(c)(1) In the conduct of the Coordinator's duties, the Coordinator shall consult regularly with States, localities, and private nonprofit voluntary agencies concerning the sponsorship process and the intended distribution of refugees.

(2) The Secretary of Labor and the Secretary of Education shall provide the Coordinator with regular reports describing the efforts of their respective departments to increase refugee access to programs within their jurisdiction, and the Coordinator shall include information on such programs in reports submitted under section 413(a)(1) of the Immigration and Nationality Act.

Part B—Assistance for Effective Resettlement of Refugees in the United States

Section 311. (a) Title IV of the Immigration and Nationality Act is amended—

(1) by striking out the title heading and inserting in lieu thereof the following:

Title IV—Miscellaneous and Refugee Assistance

Chapter 1—Miscellaneous; and (2) by adding at the end thereof the following new chapter:

Chapter 2—Refugee Assistance Office of Refugee Resettlement

Section 411. (a) There is established, within the Department of Health and Human Services, an office to be known as the Office of Refugee Resettlement (hereinafter in this chapter referred to as the 'Office'). The head of the Office shall be a Director (hereinafter in this chapter referred to as the 'Director'), to be appointed by the Secretary of Health and Human Services (hereinafter in this chapter referred to as the 'Secretary').

"(b) The function of the Office and its Director is to fund and administer (directly or through arrangements with other Federal agencies), in consultation with and under the general policy guidance of the United States Coordinator for Refugee Affairs (hereinafter in this chapter referred to as the 'Coordinator'), programs of the Federal Government under this chapter.

Authorization for Programs for Domestic Resettlement of and Assistance to Refugees

Section 412. (a) Conditions and Considerations.—(1) In providing assistance under this section, the Director shall, to the extent of available appropriations, (A) make available sufficient resources for employment training and placement in order to achieve economic self-sufficiency among refugees as quickly as possible, (B) provide refugees with the opportunity to acquire sufficient English language training to enable them to become effectively resettled as quickly as possible, (C) insure that cash assistance is made available to refugees in such a manner as not to discourage their economic self-sufficiency, in accordance with subsection (e)(2), and (D) insure that women have the same opportunities as men to participate in training and instruction.

"(2) The Director, together with the Coordinator, shall consult regularly with State and local governments and private nonprofit voluntary agencies concerning the sponsorship process and the intended distribution of refugees among the States and localities.

"(3) In the provisions of domestic assistance under this section, the Director shall make a periodic assessment, based on refugee population and other relevant factors, of the relative needs of refugees for assistance and services under this chapter and the resources available to meet such needs. In allocating resources, the Director shall avoid duplication of services and provide for maximum coordination between agencies providing related services.

"(4) No grant or contract may be awarded under this section unless an appropriate proposal and application (including a description of the agency's ability to perform the services specified in the proposal) are submitted to, and approved by, the appropriate administering official. Grants and contracts under this section shall be made to those agencies which the appropriate administering official determines can best perform the services. Payments may be made for activities authorized under this chapter in advance or by way of reimbursement. In carrying out this section, the Director, the Secretary of State, and any such other appropriate administering official are authorized—

"(A) to make loans, and

"(B) to accept and use money, funds, property, and services of any kind made available by gift, devise, bequest, grant, or otherwise for the purpose of carrying out this section.

"(5) Assistance and services funded under this section shall be provided to refugees without regard to race, religion, nationality, sex, or political opinion.

"(6) As a condition for receiving assistance under this section, a State must—

"(A) submit to the Director a plan which provides—

"(i) a description of how the State intends to encourage effective refugee resettlement and to promote economic self-sufficiency as quickly as possible,

"(ii) a description of how the State will insure that language training and employment services are made available to refugees receiving cash assistance,

"(iii) for the designation of an individual, employed by the State, who will be responsible for insuring coordination of public and private resources in refugee resettlement,

"(iv) for the care and supervision of and legal responsibility for unaccompanied refugee children in the State, and

"(v) for the identification of refugees who at the time of resettlement in the State are determined to have medical conditions requiring, or medical histories indicating a need for, treatment or observation and such monitoring of such treatment or observation as may be necessary;

"(B) meet standards, goals, and priorities, developed by the Director, which assure the effective resettlement of refugees and which promote their economic self-sufficiency as quickly as possible and the efficient provision of services; and

"(C) submit to the Director, within a reasonable period of time after the end of each fiscal year, a report on the uses of funds provided under this chapter which the State is responsible for administering.

"(7) The Secretary, together with the Secretary of State with respect to assistance provided by the Secretary of State under subsection (b), shall develop a system of monitoring the assistance provided under this section. . .

"(b) Program of Initial Resettlement.—(1)(A) For—

"(i) fiscal years 1980 and 1981, the Secretary of State is authorized, and

"(ii) fiscal year 1982 and succeeding fiscal years, the Director (except as provided in subparagraph (B)) is authorized, to make grants to, and contracts with, public or private nonprofit agencies for initial resettlement (including initial reception and placement with sponsors) of refugees in the United States. Grants to, or contracts with, private nonprofit voluntary agencies under this paragraph shall be made consistent with the objectives of this chapter, taking into account the different resettlement approaches and practices of such agencies. Resettlement assistance under this paragraph shall be provided in coordination with the Director's provision of other assistance under this chapter. The Secretary of State and the Director shall jointly monitor the assistance provided during fiscal years 1980 and 1981 under this paragraph.

"(B) The President shall provide for a study of which agency is best able to administer the program under this paragraph and shall report, not later than March 1, 1981, to the Congress on such study. . .

"(2) The Director is authorized to develop programs for such orientation, instruction in English, and job training for refugees, and such other education and training of refugees, as facilitates their resettlement in the United States. The Director is authorized to implement such programs, in accordance with the provisions of this section, with respect to refugees in the United States. The Secretary of State is authorized to implement such programs with respect to refugees awaiting entry into the United States.

"(3) The Secretary is authorized, in consultation with the Coordinator, to make arrangements (including cooperative arrangements with other Federal agencies) for the temporary care of refugees in the United States in emergency circumstances. . .

"(c) Project Grants and Contracts for Services for Refugees.—The Director is authorized to make grants to, and enter into contracts with, public or private nonprofit agencies for projects specifically designed—

"(1) to assist refugees in obtaining the skills which are necessary for economic self-sufficiency, including projects for job training, employment services, day care, professional refresher training, and other recertification services;

"(2) to provide training in English where necessary (regardless of whether the refugees are employed or receiving cash or other assistance); and

"(3) to provide where specific needs have been shown and recognized by the Director, health (including mental health) services, social services, educational and other services.

"(d) Assistance for Refugee Children.—(1) The Director is authorized to make grants, and enter into contracts, for payments for projects to provide special educational services (including English language training) to refugee children in elementary and secondary schools where a demonstrated need has been shown.

"(2)(A) The Director is authorized to provide assistance, reimbursement to states, and grants to and contracts with public and private nonprofit agencies, for the provision of child welfare services, including foster care maintenance payments and services and health care, furnished to any refugee child (except as provided in subparagraph (B)) during the thirty-six month-period beginning with the first month in which such refugee child is in the United States.

"(B)(i) In the case of a refugee child who is unaccompanied by a parent or other close adult relative (as defined by the Director) the services described in subparagraph (A) may be furnished until the month after the child attains eighteen years of age (or such higher age as the State's child welfare services plan under part B of title IV of the Social Security Act prescribes for the availability of such services to any other child in that State.)

"(ii) The Director shall attempt to arrange for the placement under the laws of the States of such unaccompanied refugee children, who have been accepted for admission to the United States, before (or as soon as possible after) their arrival in the United States. During any interim period while such a child is in the United States or in transit to the United States but before the child is so placed, the Director shall assume legal responsibility (including financial responsibility) for the child, if necessary, and is authorized to make necessary decisions to provide for the child's immediate care.

"(iii) In carrying out the Director's responsibilities under clause (ii), the Director is authorized to enter into contracts with appropriate public or private nonprofit agencies under such conditions as the Director determines to be appropriate.

"(iv) The Director shall prepare and maintain a list of (I) all such unaccompanied children who have entered the United States after April 1, 1975, (II) the names and last known residences of their parents (if living) at the time of arrival, and (III) the children's location, status, and progress.

"(e) Cash Assistance and Medical Assistance to Refugees.—(1) The Director is authorized to provide assistance, reimbursement to States, and grants to, and contracts with, public or private nonprofit agencies for up to 100 per centum of the cash assistance and medical assistance provided to any refugee during the thirty-six month period beginning with the first month in which such refugee has entered the United States and for the identifiable and reasonable administrative costs of providing this assistance.

"(2) Cash assistance provided under this subsection to an employable refugee is conditioned, except for good cause shown—

"(A) on the refugee's registration with an appropriate agency providing employment services described in subsection (c)(1), or, if there is no such agency available, with an appropriate State or local employment service; and

"(B) on the refugee's acceptance of appropriate offers of employment; except that subparagraph (A) does not apply during the first sixty days after the date of the refugee's entry.

"(3) The director shall develop plans to provide English training and other appropriate services and training to refugees receiving cash assistance.

"(4) If a refugee is eligible for aid or assistance under a State plan approved under part A of title IV or under title XIX of the Social Security Act, or for supplemental security income benefits (including State supplementary payments) under the program established under title XVI of that Act, funds authorized under this subsection shall only be used for the non-Federal share of such aid or assistance, or for such supplementary payments, with respect to cash and medical assistance provided with respect to such refugee under this paragraph.

"(5) The Director is authorized to allow for the provision of medical assistance under paragraph (1) to any refugee, during the one-year period after entry, who does not qualify for assistance under a State plan approved under title XIX of the Social Security Act on account of any resources or income requirements of such plan, but only if the Director determines that—

"(A) this will (I) encourage economic self-sufficiency, or (ii) avoid a significant burden on State and local governments; and

"(B) the refugee meets such alternative financial resources and income requirements as the Director shall establish.

Congressional Reports

Section 413. (a)(1) The Secretary, in consultation with the Coordinator, shall submit a report on activities under this chapter to the Committees on the Judiciary of the House of Representatives and of the Senate not later than the January 31 following the end of each fiscal year, beginning with fiscal year 1980.

"(2) Each such report shall contain—

"(A) an updated profile of the employment and labor force statistics for refugees who have entered under this act since May 1975, as well as a description of the extent to which refugees received the forms of assistance or services under this chapter during that period;

"(B) a description of the geographic location of refugees;

"(C) a summary of the results of the monitoring and evaluation conducted under section 412(a)(7) during the period for which the report is submitted;

"(D) a description of (i) the activities, expenditures, and policies of the Office under this chapter and of the activities of States, voluntary agencies, and sponsors, and (ii) the Director's plans for improvement of refugee resettlement;

"(E) evaluations of the extent to which (i) the services provided under this chapter are assisting refugees in achieving economic self-sufficiency, achieving ability in English, and achieving employment commensurate with their skills and abilities, and (ii) any fraud, abuse, or mismanagement has been reported in the provisions of services or assistance;

"(F) a description of any assistance provided by the Director pursuant to section 412(e)(5);

"(G) a summary of the location and status of unaccompanied refugee children admitted to the United States; and

"(H) a summary of the information compiled and evaluation made under section 412(a)(8).

"(b) The Secretary, in consultation with the Coordinator, shall conduct and report to Congress, not later than one year after the date of the enactment of this chapter, an analysis of—

"(1) resettlement systems used by other countries and the applicability of such systems to the United States;

"(2) the desirability of using a system other than the current welfare system for the provision of cash assistance, medical assistance, or both, to refugees; and

"(3) alternative resettlement strategies.

Authorization of Appropriations

Section 414. (a)(1) There are hereby authorized to be appropriated for fiscal year 1980 and for each of the two succeeding fiscal years, such sums as may be necessary for the purpose of providing initial resettlement assistance, cash and medical assistance, and child welfare services under subsections (b)(1), (b)(3), (b)(4), (d)(2), and (e) of section 412.

"(2) There are hereby authorized to be appropriated for fiscal year 1980 and for each of the two succeeding fiscal years $200,000,000, for the purpose of carrying out the provisions (other than those described in paragraph (1)) of this chapter.

"(b) The authority to enter into contracts under this chapter shall be effective for any fiscal year only to such extent or in such amounts as are provided in advance in appropriation Acts.". . .

Title IV—Social Services for Certain Applicants for Asylum

Section 401. (a) The Director of the Office of Refugee Resettlement is authorized to use funds appropriated under paragraphs (1) and (2) of section 414(a) of the Immigration and Nationality Act to reimburse State and local public agencies for expenses which those agencies incurred, at any time, in providing aliens described in subsection (c) of this section with social services of the types for which reimbursements were made with respect to refugees under paragraphs (3) through (6) of section 2(b) of the Migration and Refugee Assistance Act of 1962 (as in effect prior to the enactment of this Act) or under any other Federal law.

(b) The Attorney General is authorized to grant to an alien described in subsection (c) of this section permission to engage in employment in the United States and to provide to that alien an "employment authorized" endorsement or other appropriate work permit.

(c) This section applies with respect to any alien in the United States (1) who has applied before November 1, 1979, for asylum in the United States, (2) who has not been granted asylum, and (3) with respect to whom a final, nonappealable, and legally enforceable order of deportation or exclusion has not been entered.

Approved March 17, 1980.

◆ COMMISSION ON WARTIME RELOCATION AND INTERNMENT OF CIVILIANS ACT, 1980

[94 Stat. L. 96-317]

The commission established by this act was to conduct hearings about civilians, most of them of Japanese descent, who were detained in internment camps during World War II.

This act may be cited as the "Commission on Wartime Relocation and Internment of Civilians Act".

Section 2

Findings and Purpose

(a) The Congress finds that—

(1) approximately one hundred and twenty thousand civilians were relocated and detained in internment camps pursuant to Executive Order Numbered 9066, issued February 19, 1942, and other associated actions of the Federal Government;

(2) approximately one thousand Aleut civilian American citizens were relocated and, in some cases, detained in internment camps pursuant to directives of United States military forces during World War II and other associated actions of the Federal Government; and

(3) no sufficient inquiry has been made into the matters described in paragraphs (1) and (2).

(b) It is the purpose of this Act to establish a commission to—

(1) review the facts and circumstances surrounding Executive Order Numbered 9066, issued February 19, 1942, and the impact of such Executive order on American citizens and permanent resident aliens;

(2) review directives of United States military forces requiring the relocation and, in some cases, detention in internment camps of American citizens, including Aleut civilians, and permanent resident aliens of the Aleutian and Probilof Islands; and

(3) recommend appropriate remedies.

Section 3

Establishment of Commission

(a) There is established the Commission on Wartime Relocation and Internment of Civilians (hereinafter referred to as the "Commission").

(b) The Commission shall be composed of seven members, who shall be appointed within ninety days after the date of enactment of this Act as follows:

(1) Three members shall be appointed by the President.

(2) Two members shall be appointed by the Speaker of the House of Representatives.

(3) Two members shall be appointed by the President pro tempore of the Senate.

(c) The term of office for members shall be for the life of the Commission. A vacancy in the Commission shall not affect its powers, and shall be filled in the same manner in which the original appointment was made.

(d) The first meeting of the Commission shall be called by the President within one hundred and twenty days after the date of enactment of this Act, or within thirty days after the date on which legislation is enacted making appropriations to carry out this Act, whichever date is later.

(e) Four members of the Commission shall constitute a quorum, but a lesser number may hold hearings.

(f) The Commission shall elect a Chairman and Vice Chairman from among its members. The term of office of each shall be for the life of the Commission.

(g) Each member of the Commission who is not otherwise employed by the United States Government shall receive compensation at a rate equal to the daily rate prescribed for GS-18 under the General Schedule contained in section 5332 of title 5, United States Code, for each day, including traveltime, he or she is engaged in the actual performance of his or her duties as a member of the Commission. A member of the Commission who is an officer or employee of the United States Commission who is an officer or employee of the United States Government shall serve without additional compensation. All members of the Commission shall be reimbursed for travel, subsistence, and other necessary expenses incurred by them in the performance of their duties.

Section 4

Duties of the Commission

(a) It shall be the duty of the Commission to—

(1) review the facts and circumstances surrounding Executive Order Numbered 9066, issued February 19, 1942 and the impact of such Executive order on American citizens and permanent resident aliens;

(2) review directives of United States military forces requiring the relocation and, in some cases, detention in internment camps of American citizens, including Aleut civilians, and permanent resident aliens of the Aleutian and Pribilof Islands; and

(3) recommend appropriate remedies.

(b) The Commission shall hold public hearings in such cities of the United States that it finds appropriate.

(c) The Commission shall submit a written report of its findings and recommendations to Congress not later than the date which is one year after the date of the first meeting called pursuant to section 3(d) of this Act.

Section 5

Powers of the Commission

(a) The Commission or, on the authorization of the Commission, any subcommittee or member thereof, may for the purpose of carrying out the provisions of this Act, hold such hearings and sit and act at such times and places, and request the attendance and testimony of such witnesses and the production of such books, records, correspondence, memorandum, papers, and documents as the Commission or such subcommittee or member may deem advisable. The Commission may request the Attorney General to invoke the aid of an appropriate United States district court to require, by subpoena or otherwise, such attendance, testimony, or production.

(b) The Commission may acquire directly from the head of any department, agency, independent instrumentality, or other authority of the executive branch of the Government, available information which the Commission considers useful in the discharge of its duties. All departments, agencies, and independent instrumentalities, or other authorities of the Commission and furnish all information requested by the Commission to the extent permitted by law.

Section 6

The Commission is authorized to—

(1) appoint and fix the compensation of such personnel as may be necessary, without regard to the provisions of title 5, United States Code, governing appointments in the competitive service, and without regard to the provisions of chapter 51 and subchapter III of chapter 53 of such title relating to classification and General Schedule pay rates, except that the compensation of any employee of the Commission may not exceed a rate equivalent to the rate payable under GS-18 of the General Schedule under section 5332 of such title;

(2) obtain the services of experts and consultants in accordance with the provisions of section 3109 of such title;

(3) enter into agreements with the Administrator of General Services for procurement of necessary financial and administrative services, for which payment shall be made by reimbursement from funds of the Commission in such amounts as may be agreed upon by the Chairman of the Commission and the Administrator;

(4) procure supplies, services, and property by contract in accordance with applicable laws and regulations and to the extent or in such amounts as are provided in appropriation Acts; and

(5) enter into contracts with Federal or State agencies, private firms, institutions, and agencies for the conduct of research or surveys, the preparation of reports, and other activities necessary to the discharge of the duties of the Commission, to the extent or in such amounts as are provided in appropriation Acts.

Section 7

The Commission shall terminate ninety days after the date on which the report of the Commission is submitted to Congress pursuant to section 4(c) of this Act.

Section 8

To carry out the provisions of this Act, there are authorized to be appropriated $1,500,000.

Approved July 31, 1980.

◆ THE CIVIL LIBERTIES ACT, 1988 PUBLIC LAW 100-383

[102 Stat. 903 L. 100-383]

An Act

To implement recommendations of the Commission on Wartime Relocation and Internment of Civilians.

Be it enacted by the Senate and House of Representatives of the United States of America in Congress assembled,

Section 1

Purposes.

The purposes of this Act are to—

(1) acknowledge the fundamental injustice of the evacuation, relocation, and internment of United States citizens and permanent resident aliens of Japanese ancestry during World War II;

(2) apologize on behalf of the people of the United States for the evacuation, relocation, and internment of such citizens and permanent resident aliens;

(3) provide for a public education fund to finance efforts to inform the public about the internment of such individuals so as to prevent the recurrence of any similar event;

(4) make restitution to those individuals of Japanese ancestry who were interned;

(5) make restitution to Aleut residents of the Pribilof Islands and the Aleutian Islands west of Unimak Island, in settlement of United States obligations in equity and at law, for—

(A) injustices suffered and unreasonable hardships endured while those Aleut residents were under United States control during World War II;

(B) personal property taken or destroyed by United States forces during World War II;

(C) community property, including community church property, taken or destroyed by United States forces during World War II; and

(D) traditional village lands on Attu Island not rehabilitated after World War II for Aleut occupation or other productive use;

(6) discourage the occurrence of similar injustices and violations of civil liberties in the future; and

(7) make more credible and sincere any declaration of concern by the United States over violations of human rights committed by other nations.

Section 2

Statement of The Congress.

(a) With Regard To Individuals Of Japanese Ancestry.—The Congress recognizes that, as described by the Commission on Wartime Relocation and Internment of Civilians, a grave injustice was done to both citizens and permanent resident aliens of Japanese ancestry by the evacuation, relocation, and internment of civilians during World War II. As the Commission documents, these actions were carried out without adequate security reasons and without any acts of espionage or sabotage documented by the Commission, and were motivated largely by racial prejudice, wartime hysteria, and a failure of political leadership. The excluded individuals of Japanese ancestry suffered enormous damages, both material and intangible, and there were incalculable losses in education and job training, all of which resulted in significant human suffering for which appropriate compensation has not been made. For these fundamental violations of the basic civil liberties and constitutional rights of these individuals of Japanese ancestry, the Congress apologizes on behalf of the Nation.

(b) With Respect To The Aleuts.—The Congress recognizes that, as described by the Commission on Wartime Relocation and Internment of Civilians, the Aleut civilian residents of the Pribilof Islands and the Aleutian Islands west of Unimak Island were relocated during World War II to temporary camps in isolated regions of southeast Alaska where they remained, under United States control and in the care of the United States, until long after any potential danger to their home villages had passed. The United States failed to provide reasonable care for the Aleuts, and this resulted in widespread illness, disease, and death among the residents of the camps; and the United States further failed to protect Aleut personal and community property while such property wasin its possession or under its control. The United States has not compensated the Aleuts adequately for the conversion or destruction of personal property, and the conversion or destruction of community property caused by the United States military occupation of Aleut villages during World War II. There is no remedy for injustices suffered by the Aleuts during World War II except an Act of Congress providing appropriate compensation for those losses which are attributable to the conduct of United States forces and other officials and employees of the United States.

♦ HATE CRIMES STATISTICS ACT, 1990

[104 Stat. 140L. 101-275]

An act to provide for the acquisition and publication of data about crimes that manifest prejudice based on certain group characteristics.

Be it enacted by the Senate and House of Representatives of the United States of America in Congress assembled, That

(1) this Act may be cited as the "Hate Crime Statistics Act".

(b)(1) Under the authority of section 534 of title 28, United States Code, the Attorney General shall acquire data, for the calendar year 1990 and each of the succeeding 4 calendar years, about crimes that manifest evidence of prejudice based on race, religion, sexual orientation, or ethnicity, including where appropriate the crimes of murder, non-negligent manslaughter, forcible rape, aggravated assault, simple assault, intimidation, arson; and destruction, damage or vandalism of property.

(2) The Attorney General shall establish guidelines for the collection of such data including the necessary evidence and criteria that must be present for a finding of manifest prejudice and procedures for carrying out the purposes of this section.

(3) Nothing in this section creates a cause of action or a right to bring an action, including an action based on discrimination due to sexual orientation. As used in this section, the term "sexual orientation" means consensual homosexuality or heterosexuality. This subsection does not limit any existing cause of action or right to bring an action, including any action under the Administrative Procedure Act or the All Writs Act.

(4) Data acquired under this section shall be used only for research or statistical purposes and may not contain any information that may reveal the identity of an individual victim of a crime.

(5) The Attorney General shall publish an annual summary of the data acquired under this section.

(c) There are authorized to be appropriated such sums as may be necessary to carry out the provisions of this section through fiscal year 1994.

Sec. 2.(a) Congress finds that

(1) the American family life is the foundation of American Society,

(2) Federal policy should encourage the well-being, financial security, and health of the American family,

(3) schools should not de-emphasize the critical value of American family life.

(b) Nothing in this Act shall be construed, nor shall any funds appropriated to carry out the purpose of the Act be used, to promote or encourage homosexuality.

Approved April 23, 1990.

♦ CIVIL RIGHTS ACT, 1991

[105 Stat.1071.L.102-166]

An act to amend the Civil Rights Act of 1964 to strengthen and improve Federal civil rights laws, to provide for damages in cases on intentional employment discrimination, to clarify provisions regarding disparate impact actions, and for other purposes.

(Editor's note: Wards Cove Packing Co. workers are exempted from this law.)

Be it enacted by the Senate and House of Representatives of the United States of American in Congress assembled,

Section 1

Short Title.

This Act may be cited as the "Civil Rights Act of 1991.

Section 2

Findings.

The Congress finds that —

(1) additional remedies under Federal law are needed to deter unlawful harassment and intentional discrimination in the workplace;

(2) the decision of the Supreme Court in Wards Cove Packing Co. v. Atonio, 490 U.S. 642 (1989) has weakened the scope and effectiveness of Federal civil rights protections; and

(3) legislation is necessary to provide additional protections against unlawful discrimination in employment.

Section 3

Purposes.

The purposes of this Act are —

(1) to provide appropriate remedies for intentional discrimination and unlawful harassment in the workplace;

(2) to codify the concepts of "business necessity" and "job related" enunciated by the Supreme Court in Griggs v. Duke Power Co., 401 U.S. 424 (1971), and in the other Supreme Court decisions prior to Wards Cove Packing Co. v. Atonia, 490 U.S. 642 (1989);

(3) to confirm statutory authority and provide statutory guidelines for the adjudication of disparate impact suits under title VII of the Civil Rights Act of 1964 (42 U.S.C. 2000e et seq.); and

(4) to respond to recent divisions of the Supreme Court by expanding the scope of relevant civil rights statutes in order to provide adequate protection to victims of discrimination.

The text of the law defines procedures for taking legal action against discrimination in the workplace.

♦ ASIAN /PACIFIC AMERICAN HERITAGE MONTH, 1991 AND 1992

By the President of the United States of America
A Proclamation

With characteristic clarity and force, Walt Whitman wrote: "The United States themselves are essentially the greatest poem. . . . Here is not merely a nation but a teeming nation of nations." Those immortal words eloquently describe America's ethnic diversity —a diversity we celebrate with pride during Asian/Pacific American Heritage Month.

The Asian/Pacific American heritage is marked by its richness and depth. The world marvels at the wealth of ancient art and philosophy, the fine craftsmanship, and the colorful literature and folklore that have sprung from Asia and the Pacific Islands. Whether they trace their roots to places like Cambodia, Vietnam, Korea, the Philippines, and the Marshall Islands or cherish their identities as natives of Hawaii and Guam, all Asian and Pacific Americans can take pride in this celebration of their heritage.

By preserving the time-honored customs and traditions of their ancestral homelands, Americans of Asian and Pacific descent have greatly enriched our Nation's culture. They have also made many outstanding contributions to American history. Indeed, this country's westward expansion and economic development were greatly influenced by thousands of Chinese and other Asians who immigrated during the 19th century. Today recent immigrants from South Asia are giving our Nation new appreciation for that region of the world.

Over the years—and often in the face of great obstacles—Asian and Pacific Americans have worked hard to reap the rewards of freedom and opportunity. Many have arrived in the United States after long and arduous journeys, escaping tyranny and oppression with little more than the clothes on their backs. Yet, believing in

America's promise of liberty and justice for all and imbued with a strong sense of self-discipline, sacrifice, courage, and honor, they have steadily advanced, earning the respect and admiration of their fellow citizens. Today we give special and long-overdue recognition to the nisei who fought for our country in Europe during World War II. During one of America's darker hours, they affirmed the patriotism and loyalty of Japanese Americans and, in so doing, taught us an important lesson about tolerance and justice.

Time and again throughout our Nation's history, Asian and Pacific Americans have proved their devotion to the ideals of freedom and democratic government. Those ideals animate and guide our policies toward Asia and the Pacific today. The economic dynamism of the Pacific Rim is a crucial source of growth for the global economy, and the United States will continue working to promote economic cooperation and the expansion of free markets throughout the region. The United States also remains committed to the security of our allies and to the advancement of human rights throughout Asia and the Pacific.

The political and economic ties that exist between the United States and countries in Asia and the Pacific are fortified by strong bonds of kinship and culture. All Americans are enriched by those ties, and thus we proudly unite in observing Asian/Pacific American Heritage Month.

The Congress, by House Joint Resolution 173, has designated May 1991 and May 1992 as "Asian/Pacific American Heritage Month" and has authorized and requested the President to issue a proclamation in observance of these occasions.

Now, therefore, I George Bush, President of the United States of America, do hereby proclaim the months of May 1991 and May 1992 as Asian/Pacific American Heritage Month, I call upon the people of the United States to observe these occasions with appropriate programs, ceremonies, and activities.

In witness whereof, I have hereunto set my hand this sixth day of May, in the year of our Lord nineteen hundred and ninety-one, and of the Independence of the United States of America the two hundred and fifteenth.

♦ VOTING RIGHTS LANGUAGE ASSISTANCE ACT, 1992

[106 Stat.921 L.102-344]

An Act

To Amend the Voting Rights Act of 1965 with respect to bilingual election requirements.

Be it enacted by the Senate and House of Representatives of the United States of America in Congress assembled,

Section 1

Short Title

This Act may be cited as the "Voting Rights Language Assistance Act of 1991".

Section 2

Extension of Language Minority Provisions

Subsection (b) of section 203 of the Voting Rights Act of 1965 (42 U.S.C. 1973aa-1a(b) is amended to read as follows:

"(b) BILINGUAL VOTING MATERIALS REQUIREMENT.—

"(1) GENERALLY.—Before August 6, 2007, no covered State or political subdivision shall provide voting materials only in the English language.

"(2) COVERED STATES AND POLITICAL SUBDIVISIONS.—

"(A) GENERALLY.—A State or political subdivision is a covered State or political subdivision for the purposes of this subsection if the Director of the Census determines, based on census data, that—

"(i)(I) more than 5 percent of the citizens of voting age of such State or political subdivision are members of a single language minority and are limited-English proficient;

"(II) more than 10,000 of the citizens of voting age of such political subdivision are members of a single language minority and are limited-English proficient; or

"(III) in the case of a political subdivision that contains all or any part of an Indian reservation, more than 5 percent of the American Indian or Alaska Native citizens of voting age within the Indian reservation are members of a single language minority and are limited-English proficient; and

"(ii) the illiteracy rate of the citizens in the language minority as a group is higher than the national illiteracy rate.

"(B) EXCEPTION.—The prohibitions of this subsection do not apply in any political subdivision that has less than 5 percent voting age limited-English proficient citizens of each language minority which comprises over 5 percent of the statewide limited-English proficient population of voting age citizens, unless the political subdivision is a covered political subdivision independently from its State.

"(3) DEFINITIONS.—As used in this section—

"(A) the term 'voting materials' means registration or voting notices, forms, instructions, assistance, or other materials or information relating to the electoral process, including ballots;

"(B) the term 'limited-English proficient' means unable to speak or understand English adequately enough to participate in the electoral process;

"(C) the term 'Indian reservation' means any area that is an American Indian or Alaska Native area, as defined by the Census Bureau for the purposes of the 1990 decennial census;

"(D) the term 'citizens' means citizens of the United States; and

"(E) the term 'illiteracy' means the failure to complete the 5th primary grade.

"(4) SPECIAL RULE.—The determinations of the Director of the Census under this subsection shall be effective upon publication in the Federal Register and shall not be subject to review in any court."

Approved August 26, 1992.

♦ 100TH ANNIVERSARY OF THE OVERTHROW OF THE HAWAIIAN KINGDOM PUBLIC LAW 103-150—NOV. 23, 1993, 103RD CONGRESS JOINT RESOLUTION

To acknowledge the 100th anniversary of the January 17, 1893 overthrow of the Kingdom of Hawaii, and to offer an apology to Native Hawaiians on behalf of the United States for the overthrow of the Kingdom of Hawaii.

Whereas, prior to the arrival of the first Europeans in 1778, the Native Hawaiian people lived in a highly organized, self-sufficient, subsistent social system based on communal land tenure with a sophisticated language, culture, and religion;

Whereas a unified monarchical government of the Hawaiian Islands was established in 1810 under Kamehameha I, the first King of Hawaii;

Whereas, from 1826 until 1893, the United States recognized the independence of the Kingdom of Hawaii, extended full and complete diplomatic recognition to the Hawaiian Government, and entered into treaties and conventions with the Hawaiian monarchs to govern commerce and navigation in 1826, 1842, 1849, 1875, and 1887;

Whereas the Congregational Church (now known as the United Church of Christ), through its American Board of Commissioners for Foreign Missions, sponsored and sent more than 100 missionaries to the Kingdom of Hawaii between 1820 and 1850;

Whereas, on January 14, 1893, John L. Stevens (hereafter referred to in this Resolution as the –United States Minister+), the United States Minister assigned to the sovereign and independent Kingdom of Hawaii conspired with a small group of non-Hawaiian residents of the Kingdom of Hawaii, including citizens of the United States, to overthrow the indigenous and lawful Government of Hawaii;

Whereas, in pursuance of the conspiracy to overthrow the Government of Hawaii, the United States Minister and the naval representatives of the United States caused armed naval forces of the United States to invade the sovereign Hawaiian nation on January 16, 1893, and to position themselves near the Hawaiian Government buildings and the Iolani Palace to intimidate Queen Liliuokalani and her Government;

Whereas, on the afternoon of January 17, 1893, a Committee of Safety that represented the American and European sugar planters, descendants of missionaries, and financiers deposed the Hawaiian monarchy and proclaimed the establishment of a Provisional Government;

Whereas the United States Minister thereupon extended diplomatic recognition to the Provisional Government that was formed by the conspirators without the consent of the Native Hawaiian people or the lawful Government of Hawaii and in violation of treaties between the two nations and of international law;

Whereas, soon thereafter, when informed of the risk of bloodshed with resistance, Queen Liliuokalani issued the following statement yielding her authority to the United States Government rather than to the Provisional Government;

—I Liliuokalani, by the Grace of God and under the Constitution of the Hawaiian Kingdom, Queen, do hereby solemnly protest against any and all acts done against myself and the Constitutional Government of the Hawaiian Kingdom by certain persons claiming to have established a Provisional Government of and for this Kingdom.+

—That I yield to the superior force of the United States of America whose Minister Plenipotentiary, His Excellency John L. Stevens, has caused United States troops to be landed at Honolulu and declared that he would support the Provisional Government.+

—Now to avoid any collision of armed forces, and perhaps the loss of life, I do this under protest and impelled by said force yield my authority until such time as the Government of the United States shall, upon facts being presented to it, undo the action of its representatives and reinstate me in the authority which I claim as the Constitutional Sovereign of the Hawaiian Islands.+

Done at Honolulu this 17th day of January, A.D. 1893;

Whereas, without the active support and intervention by the United States diplomatic and military representatives, the insurrection against the Government of Queen Liliuokalani would have failed for lack of popular support and insufficient arms;

Whereas, on February 1, 1893, the United States Minister raised the American flag and proclaimed Hawaii to be a protectorate of the United States;

Whereas the report of a Presidentially established investigation conducted by former Congressman James Blount into the events surrounding the insurrection and overthrow of January 17, 1893, concluded that the United States diplomatic and military representatives had abused their authority and were responsible for the change in government;

Whereas, as a result of this investigation, the United States Minister to Hawaii was recalled from his diplomatic post and the military commander of the United States armed forces stationed in Hawaii was disciplined and forced to resign his commission;

Whereas, in a message to Congress on December 18, 1893, President Grover Cleveland reported fully and accurately on the illegal acts of the conspirators, described such acts as an –act of war, committed with the participation of a diplomatic representative of the United States and without authority of Congress,+ and acknowledged that by such acts the government of a peaceful and friendly people was overthrown;

Whereas President Cleveland further concluded that a –substantial wrong has thus been done which a due regard for our national character as well as the rights of the injured people requires we should endeavor to repair+ and called for the restoration of the Hawaiian monarchy;

Whereas the Provisional Government protested President Cleveland+s call for the restoration of the monarchy and continued to hold state power and pursue annexation to the United States;

Whereas the Provisional Government successfully lobbied the Committee on Foreign Relations of the Senate (hereafter referred to in this Resolution as the – Committee+) to conduct a new investigation into the events surrounding the overthrow of the monarchy;

Whereas the Committee and its chairman, Senator John Morgan, conducted hearings in Washington, D.C., from December 27, 1893, through February 26, 1894, in which members of the Provisional Government justified and condoned the actions of the United States Minister and recommended annexation of Hawaii;

Whereas, although the Provisional Government was able to obscure the role of the United States in the illegal overthrow of the Hawaiian monarchy, it was unable to rally the support from two-thirds of the Senate needed to ratify a treaty of annexation;

Whereas, on July 4, 1894, the Provisional Government declared itself to be the Republic of Hawaii;

Whereas on January 24, 1895, while imprisoned in Iolani Palace, Queen Liliuokalani was forced by representatives of the Republic of Hawaii to officially abdicate her throne;

Whereas, in the 1896 United States Presidential election, William McKinley replaced Grover Cleveland;

Whereas, on July 7, 1898, as a consequence of the Spanish-American War, President McKinley signed the Newlands Joint Resolution that provided for the annexation of Hawaii;

Whereas, through the Newlands Resolution, the self-declared Republic of Hawaii ceded sovereignty over the Hawaiian Islands to the United States.

Whereas the Republic of Hawaii also ceded 1,800,000 acres of crown, government and public lands of the Kingdom of Hawaii, without the consent of or compensation to the Native Hawaiian people of Hawaii or their sovereign government;

Whereas the Congress, through the Newlands Resolution, ratified the cession, annexed Hawaii as part of the United States, and vested title to the lands in Hawaii in the United States;

Whereas the Newlands Resolution also specified that treaties existing between Hawaii and foreign nations were to immediately cease and be replaced by United States treaties with such nations;

Whereas the Newlands Resolution effected the transaction between the Republic of Hawaii and the United States Government;

Whereas the indigenous Hawaiian people never directly relinquished their claims to their inherent sovereignty as a people or over their national lands to the United States, either through their monarchy or through a plebiscite or referendum;

Whereas, on April 30, 1900, President McKinley signed the Organic Act that provided a government for the territory of Hawaii and defined the political structure and powers of the newly established Territorial Government and its relationship to the United States;

Whereas, on August 21, 1959, Hawaii became the 50th State of the United States;

Whereas the health and well-being of the Native Hawaiian people is intrinsically tied to their deep feelings and attachment to the land;

Whereas the long-range economic and social changes in Hawaii over the nineteenth and early twentieth centuries have been devastating to the population and to the health and well-being of the Hawaiian people;

Whereas the Native Hawaiian people are determined to preserve, develop and transmit to future generations their ancestral territory, and their cultural identity in accordance with their own spiritual and traditional beliefs, customs, practices, language, and social institutions;

Whereas, in order to promote racial harmony and cultural understanding, the Legislature of the State of Hawaii has determined that the year 1993 should serve Hawaii as a year of special reflection on the rights and dignities of the Native Hawaiians in the Hawaiian and the American societies;

Whereas the Eighteenth General Synod of the United Church of Christ in recognition of the denomination's historical complicity in the illegal overthrow of the Kingdom of Hawaii in 1893 directed the Office of the President of the United Church of Christ to offer a public apology to the native Hawaiian people and to initiate the process of reconciliation between the United Church of Christ and the Native Hawaiians; and

Whereas it is proper and timely for the Congress on the occasion of the impending one hundredth anniversary of the event, to acknowledge the historic significance of the illegal overthrow of the Kingdom of Hawaii, to express its deep regret to the Native Hawaiian people, and to support the reconciliation efforts of the State of Hawaii and the United Church of Christ with Native Hawaiians: Now, therefore, be it.

Resolved by the Senate and House of Representatives of the United States of America in Congress assembled,

Section 1

Acknowledgment and Apology

The Congress —

(1) on the occasion of the 100th anniversary of the illegal overthrow of the Kingdom of Hawaii on January 17, 1893, acknowledges the historical significance of this event which resulted in the suppression of the inherent sovereignty of the Native Hawaiian people;

(2) recognizes and commends efforts of reconciliation initiated by the State of Hawaii and the United Church of Christ with Native Hawaiians;

(3) apologizes to Native Hawaiians on behalf of the people of the United States for the overthrow of the Kingdom of Hawaii on January 17, 1893 with the participation of agents and citizens of the United States, and the deprivation of the rights of Native Hawaiians to self-determination;

(4) expresses its commitment to acknowledge the ramifications of the overthrow of the Kingdom of Hawaii, in order to provide a proper foundation for reconciliation between the United States and the Native Hawaiian people; and

(5) urges the President of the United States to also acknowledge the ramifications of the overthrow of the Kingdom of Hawaii and to support reconciliation efforts between the United States and the Native Hawaiian people.

Section 2

Definitions

As used in this Joint Resolution, the term, –Native Hawaiian+ means any individual who is a descendent of the aboriginal people who, prior to 1778, occupied and exercised sovereignty in the area that now constitutes the State of Hawai.

Section 3

Disclaimer

Nothing in this Joint Resolution is intended to serve as a settlement of any claims against the United States.

Approved November 23, 1993.

Immigration

♦ Beginnings: 1850 to 1920 ♦ Between the Wars: The Triumph of Exclusionism
♦ After Vietnam: Refugees from Southeast Asia

Asian immigration to the United States in significant numbers began in the 1850s and reached its first major peak shortly after 1900. (*See* Chart 18.1, and Tables 18.1 and 18.2.) While the experience of each nationality group was unique, there were certain elements common to all. Chinese, Japanese, and, later, Koreans, Asian Indians, and Filipinos all sought to escape lives of poverty by responding to growing demands for cheap agricultural and industrial labor. While commercial recruiters courted them eagerly, once the new immigrants arrived they faced a growing tide of bigotry fueled by white workers' fears of economic competition and culminating in a series of restrictive policies that virtually sealed off the country to further Asian immigration by the 1920s.

♦ BEGINNINGS: 1850 TO 1920

From China

It was the California gold rush that first drew large numbers of Chinese to the United States. As the immigrants sent word back home of riches to be had on *Gam Saan* (or "Gold Mountain"), new arrivals joined them at a rate that grew rapidly from 450 in 1850, to 2,716 the following year, to 20,000 in 1852, the peak year. At first, most Chinese earned their living providing services to white miners, working as cooks, dishwashers, and laundrymen, or becoming merchants. However, when they sought the wealth of the gold fields for themselves, whites retaliated with harassment, discriminatory policies, and violence, all of which drove total immigration down to 4,000 by 1853.

In the 1860s, however, the United States once again beckoned to the Chinese, this time with work on the transcontinental railway, and, once again, thousands came. At the height of construction, nine out of ten workers on the Central Pacific Railroad were Chinese.

Even after the Central Pacific was finally connected to the Union Pacific in 1869—an event made possible largely by Chinese labor—there were still new rail lines to build as well as agricultural work on farms and orchards. The Burlingame Treaty of 1868 between the United States and China mandated the "inalienable right" of all people to travel freely from one country to another and provided for reciprocity of travel privileges between the two countries.

By the 1870s, California's Chinese male population totaled nearly 59,000 or roughly 14 percent of the state's work force. Chinese were active in the shoe, rope, and cigar industries. However, once the financial panic of 1873 and the ensuing depression drove thousands of easterners to California looking for jobs—and competing with Chinese workers for those jobs—anti-Asian sentiment flared again. California passed a series of anti-Chinese state laws, all of which were eventually found unconstitutional.

Finally, in 1882, the western states, in league with the South, pushed through federal legislation.to respond to the perceived Chinese threat. The Chinese Exclusion Act banned immigration by Chinese workers and denied future citizenship to all Chinese already in the country. This act was broadened in a number of ways by the turn of the century and renewed indefinitely in 1902, and the size of the United States's Chinese population decreased rapidly.

From Japan

Japanese immigration to the United States was also set in motion in the 1850s. In 1853 Commodore Matthew Perry opened Japan to diplomatic and economic relations with the West after 400 years of isolation. During the decade, some 1,500 mostly upper-class Japanese came to the United States to learn its language and customs. However, large-scale Japanese immigration to the

U.S. really had its roots in the development of sugar and pineapple plantations in Hawaii and the recruitment of Japanese to work on them beginning in 1868. By the 1880s thousands had emigrated to the island. When the United States annexed Hawaii in 1900, its Japanese residents gained the right to enter the U.S. without passports. Thousands of *issei*, or immigrants, moved to the West Coast, taking up farming and other occupations. There were 25,000 Japanese in the country by the end of the century and 70,000 by 1910. Meanwhile, as the Chinese left, discouraged by restrictive immigration policies, anti-Asian feeling started to focus on the Japanese. The coalition of western labor interests and southern segregationists that had promoted anti-Chinese legislation pressured President Roosevelt into signing the 1907-8 Gentlemen's Agreement, by which the Japanese government agreed to severely limit the number of passports issued for emigration to the U.S. California's 1913 Alien Land Act denying land ownership to aliens ineligible for citizenship was also aimed primarily at the Japanese. (It was found constitutional by a federal court in 1923 and subsequently copied in other states.)

From Korea

The plantations of Hawaii also attracted large numbers of Koreans fleeing drought and the hardships imposed on them by Japanese rule of their homeland. Many Koreans, who had been converted to Christianity,were recruited to go overseas by missionaries (40 percent of all Korean immigrants to the U.S. were Christians). Between 1903 and 1907, 7,226 Koreans emigrated to Hawaii, and many subsequently traveled to the mainland. However, Korean immigration to the U.S. was abruptly curtailed in 1905 when Japan, having declared Korea a protectorate, prohibited Korean emigration to Hawaii to curb competition against Japanese workers on the island and reduce participation by Koreans abroad in movements to liberate their homeland. In addition, a 1907 executive order by the U.S. prohibited further remigration by Koreans from Hawaii to the mainland. Altogether, some 8,000 Koreans emigrated to the United States between 1903 and 1920, including "picture brides" who emigrated to marry Korean laborers overseas.

From India

Asian Indian immigration to the U.S. had an important element in common with Korean immigration. Both were closely linked to subjugation of one's homeland by a foreign power—Korea by the Japanese and India by the British. Asian Indians began emigrating to the United States in around 1870. By 1900, the Indian community in the U.S. numbered 2,050, mostly of the professional and merchant classes. Some were anti-British insurgents seeking a base of operations following British crackdowns on anti-imperialist activities. Unlike other groups of Asians, these initial Indian immigrants settled mostly in New York and other parts of the East. However, the greater part of immigration by Asian Indians occurred after 1905, when small farmers, mostly Sikhs forced into debt by colonial policies, began emigrating to different countries. Between 1906 and 1908 nearly 5,000 Indian contract laborers, mostly from the Punjab region, immigrated to Canada. When that country began turning thousands of them away, some migrated southward to Washington and Oregon, where many worked on the railroad or in lumber mills. Others found agricultural employment in California. Although 3,453 Asian Indians were denied entry into the U.S. between 1908 and 1920 due to exclusionist policies, 6,400 had been admitted by 1920.

♦ BETWEEN THE WARS: THE TRIUMPH OF EXCLUSIONISM

By the beginning of the twentieth century, most U.S. policies restricting immigration were aimed at Asians, but many in the country were becoming alarmed at the number of new immigrants from southern and eastern Europe. In 1910 the congressionally appointed Dillingham commission issued a report on immigration, complete with "scientific" findings proving the inferiority of recent immigrants compared to the original settlers from northern and western Europe.

Immigration Acts of 1917 and 1924

The Immigration Act of 1917, based on the findings of this commission, required immigrants over the age of 16 to take a literacy test and prohibited all immigration by laborers from the "Asiatic Barred Zone," which included India, Indochina, Afghanistan, Arabia, the East Indies, and other, smaller Asian countries. (China and Japan, already covered by previous measures, were not included in this one.) However, neither this act nor the subsequent Quota Act of 1921 limited immigration sufficiently to satisfy the restrictionists, and the nation's exclusionary zeal finally culminated in the Immigration Act of 1924. In addition to reducing total annual immigration levels and setting quotas that favored northern and western Europeans, the Immigration Act barred entry completely to "aliens ineligible for citizenship," reaffirming Chinese exclusion and effectively ending all further Japanese immigration. In combination with the 1917 Act, with its Asiatic Barred Zone, the 1924 Immigration Act essentially ended Asian immigration to the United States for twenty years.

Filipinos—American Nationals

As the 1920s advanced, however, rising immigration levels for one particular group made it apparent that these exclusionary policies hadn't quite accomplished their mission—there was one group of Asians who remained untouched by them. Filipinos, who had begun arriving in the United States around 1910, were not subject to immigration laws because they were not, technically, foreigners: the Philippines was a U.S. territory, acquired at the end of the Spanish-American War and its inhabitants, while not U.S. citizens, were considered "American nationals." After annexation of the islands by the United States in 1898, rural Filipinos were forced to turn over a large share of their income to distant landlords. Driven into debt, many emigrated to Hawaii in the early 1900s and, starting in 1910, to the U.S. mainland, where most worked as migrant farmers. A rapid influx of immigrants in the 1920s brought a dramatic rise in the total U.S. Filipino population from 5,603 in 1920 to 45,208 by the end of the decade. Like other Asian immigrants before them, Filipinos found themselves subjected to white working-class backlash and racist attitudes. Anti-Filipino violence erupted in California in the late 1920s, ignited by competition for jobs and by the association of some Filipinos with white women, which was seen as a threat to "racial purity." With the 1924 Immigration Act not applicable to Filipinos, it was finally determined that the only way to exclude them as immigrants was to turn them into foreigners by granting independence to their country. The 1934 Tydings-McDuffie Act established the Philippines as a commonwealth and provided for its independence in ten years. Filipinos were reclassified as aliens with an annual quota of only 50 (although more could enter Hawaii when their labor was needed on plantations). At this point, immigration by Filipinos had already declined dramatically—from 11,360 to 1,302 between 1929 and 1932—due to the continuing hostility they faced.

◆ POST-WORLD WAR II LIBERALIZATION

World War II bolstered Asian immigration to the United States in several ways. After China became a U.S. ally in its war with Japan, Congress finally repealed the Chinese Exclusion Act on December 17, 1943 and opened up U.S. citizenship to foreign-born Chinese. However, the Chinese received only a token quota of 105, and were the sole exception to the exclusion of Asian immigrants from the country. Eventually, though, the struggle against the Nazis weakened popular tolerance for discrimination based on notions of racial superiority.

Luce-Celler Bill and War Brides Act

In 1946 the Luce-Celler Bill granted small immigration quotas and naturalization rights to Asian Indians and Filipinos. The following year, the War Brides Act of 1946 was amended to allow entry to Chinese war brides of Chinese American soldiers. By 1953, over 7,000 Chinese women had immigrated as war brides.

McCarran-Walter Act

The Immigration and Nationality Act of 1952 (the McCarran-Walter Act) systematized U.S. immigration policy. While it officially ended the total exclusion policies that had been directed at Asians in the past, the act remained discriminatory, according immigrants from northern and western Europe 85 percent of the total annual quota. Japan was given a quota of 185; China's quota remained at 105, and countries in the area designated as the Asia-Pacific Triangle received quotas of 100 each. The act did, however, remove all bans on the naturalization of foreign-born Asians. It also created special-preference categories for immigrants with special technical or other skills and increased the number of nonquota immigrants, including immediate relatives of citizens and permanent residents.

Immigration Act of 1965 (Hart-Celler Act)

By the late fifties and early sixties, U.S. immigration policy as articulated by the McCarran-Walter Act was becoming increasingly incompatible with changing attitudes toward race at home, as well as with the country's Cold War positioning as "leader of the free world." Urged by Presidents Kennedy and Johnson, Congress enacted a wide-ranging immigration policy reform. Known as the Hart-Celler Act of 1965, it abolished the national origins quota system and the designation of the Asia-Pacific Triangle, finally terminating discrimination against Asian immigrants. The total annual immigration ceiling was raised to 290,000, with 170,000 visas available altogether for countries in the Eastern hemisphere and no limit for any one country. Applicants were to be approved on a first-come first-served basis, with special preferences for family reunification and vocational skills.

The 1965 Immigration Act drastically changed the nature of immigration to the United States. (*See* Chart 18.1) Between 1920 and 1960, 60 percent of all immigrants to the U.S. came from Europe, 35 percent from Central and South America, and only 3 percent from Asia. By 1975 Europe accounted for 19 percent of all immigration, while the totals for Asia and the Americas had risen, respectively, to 34 and 43 percent. Chinese immigration rose from 1,000 quota and nonquota immigrants per year in the decade preceding 1965 to 9,000 in 1975. Immigration by Asian Indians rose from 300 in

1965 to 14,000 in 1975. Over the next three decades, Korean immigration grew more than tenfold, as families were reunited and many fled authoritarian regimes in both the North and South. The Immigration Act of 1965 also set the stage for a new and unanticipated wave of immigration from Southeast Asia that began ten years later and dramatically altered the composition of the Asian American community itself. Tables 18.3 through 18.13 provide information on immigration from Asian countries to the top ten states in the United States in 1991.

♦ AFTER VIETNAM: REFUGEES FROM SOUTHEAST ASIA

On April 30, 1975—the day Saigon fell to the North Vietnamese—65,000 South Vietnamese fled the country, beginning the first wave of Vietnamese immigration to the United States. By the end of the year, the U.S. had accepted a total of 130,000 refugees from the war-torn country. Many in this first wave of Vietnamese refugees were well-educated urban dwellers with corporate, military, or political ties to the U.S., making their resettlement process a relatively smooth one (by 1985 they had achieved economic parity with the general U.S. population). While the 1965 Immigration Act insured that they would not be turned away on racial grounds, special legislation was necessary to admit such a large group of immigrants at one time.

Indochina Refugee Act

Congress passed the 1975 Indochina Refugee Act, allowing up to 200,000 Vietnamese and other Southeast Asians to enter the U.S. exempt from the normal immigration process and restrictions. From Guam, the refugees were moved to four resettlement camps at military bases and matched with sponsor families in different parts of the country to lessen their economic impact on any one area. By the end of 1975, most had been resettled. However, continuing repression in Vietnam—including reeducation camps, forcible resettlement, and privatization of businesses—led to a new wave of emigration in the late 1970s. Vietnam's ethnic Chinese, in particular, were harshly persecuted, as China had become Vietnam's adversary in its war with Cambodia. In late 1978, 85,000 Vietnamese took to the sea in rickety, overcrowded boats. After they had been turned away by neighboring countries, the United States was forced to act, and ships were sent to rescue the imperiled "boat people."

Refugee Act of 1980 and Amerasian Homecoming Act

The Refugee Act of 1980 once again reduced entry restrictions for Vietnamese refugees and the Orderly Departure Program was established allowing specified numbers of Vietnamese to emigrate legally to the U.S. The second wave of Vietnamese immigration peaked with 95,000 new arrivals in 1980 and 86,000 in 1981. While 66,000 immigrants were admitted to the U.S. between 1983 and 1991 under the Orderly Departure Program, Amerasians benefited very little from it, for the Vietnamese government sharply curtailed their emigration to pressure the U.S. for recognition and aid. Because of this, the U.S. Congress passed the Amerasian Homecoming Act creating special provisions for immigration by Amerasian teenagers and their families.

Parallel waves of refugees have been admitted to the United States from other Southeast Asian countries since 1975, which was also the year that the Pathet Lao seized power in Laos, and the Khmer Rouge in Cambodia. When Vietnam invaded Cambodia in 1979, hundreds of thousands of Cambodians fled to refugee camps in Thailand. Over 100,000 were resettled in the United States by the end of the decade, as well as a comparable number of Laotian refugees.

The refugee status of many Southeast Asians has played a key role in their immigration and resettlement. For legal purposes, "immigrant" and "refugee" are defined differently. An immigrant chooses to leave; a refugee is forced to leave by political, religious, or other forms of persecution. Because refugees are allowed into a country without regard to ordinary immigration quotas, unusually large numbers of Southeast Asians have been admitted to the United States within a relatively short time.

Those who are officially refugees rather than immigrants also receive various types of government assistance. They are eligible for welfare programs (Aid to Families with Dependent Children, Supplemental Security Income, Medicaid, and food stamps) on the same means-tested basis as citizens and also served by special federal programs for those who do not meet AFDC or Medicaid criteria.

—Rosalie Wieder

Chart 18.1
Immigration Trends by Race and Decade, 1820-1980

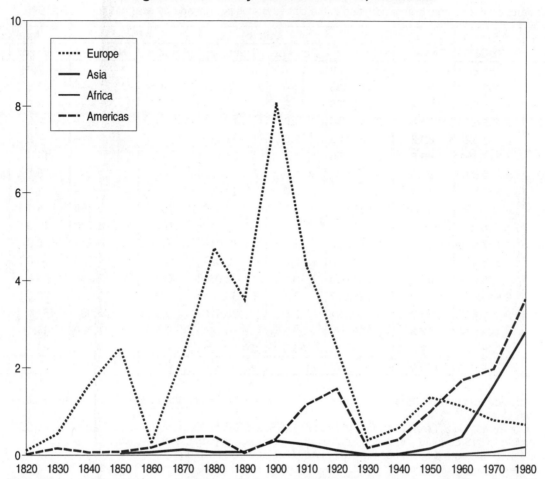

Source: *Data for 1981 to 1990 are from U.S. Immigration and Naturalization Service (INS), Statistical Yearbook of the Immigration and Naturalization Service, 1991 (Washington, DC: U.S. Government Printing Office, 1992), table 3, p. 32. Data for 1820 to 1980 were adapted from Leon F. Bouvier and Robert W. Gardner, "Immigration to the U.S.: The Unfinished Story," Population Bulletin 41, no. 4 (November 1986): table 1, p. 8. Primary source: INS, Statistical Yearbook (Washington, DC: U.S. Government Printing Office, 1986), table IMM 1.2.*

Table 18.1
Immigration by Region of Last Residence, 1820-1990

Number and percent of total immigrants admitted to the United States per decade by world region, 1820-1990.

Intercensal decade	Total	Europe (a) Percent	Europe (a) Number	Asia (b) Percent	Asia (b) Number	Africa Percent	Africa Number	Americas (c) Percent	Americas (c) Number
1821-1830	151,824	70.1	106,429	—	—	—	—	7.9	11,994
1831-1840	599,125	81.7	489,485	—	—	—	—	25.6	153,376
1841-1850	1,713,251	93.2	1,596,750	—	—	—	—	3.6	61,680
1851-1860	2,598,214	94.4	2,452,714	1.6	4,1571	—	—	2.9	75,348
1861-1870	2,314,824	89.2	2,064,823	2.8	64,815	—	—	7.2	166,667
1871-1880	2,812,191	80.8	2,272,250	4.4	123,736	—	—	14.4	404,956
1881-1890	5,246,613	90.3	4,737,691	1.3	68,206	—	—	8.1	424,976
1891-1900	3,687,564	96.4	3,554,811	2.0	73,751	—	—	1.1	40,563
1901-1910	8,795,386	91.6	8,056,573	3.7	325,430	0.1	8,795	4.1	360,610
1911-1920	5,735,811	75.3	4,319,066	4.3	246,640	0.1	5,736	19.9	1,141,426
1921-1930	4,107,209	60.0	2,464,325	2.7	110,895	0.2	8,214	36.9	1,515,560
1931-1940	528,431	65.8	347,708	3.0	15,853	0.3	1,585	30.3	160,114
1941-1950	1,035,039	60.0	621,023	3.1	32,086	0.7	7,245	34.3	355,019
1951-1960	2,515,479	52.7	1,325,657	6.1	153,444	0.6	15,093	39.6	996,130
1961-1970	3,321,677	33.8	1,122,727	12.9	428,496	0.9	29,895	51.7	1,717,307
1971-1980	4,493,314	17.8	799,810	35.3	1,586,140	1.8	80,880	44.1	1,981,551
1981-1990	7,338,062	9.6	705,630	38.3	2,817,391	2.6	192,212	48.7	3,580,928
Totals	56,994,014	65.0	37,037,472	11.7	6,088,454	0.6	349,655	23.0	13,148,205

Notes:

A dash (—) indicates less than 0.05 percent. Numbers may not add to totals due to rounding and the exclusion of data for immigrants from Oceania.

(a) Includes all of former USSR except 1931-1950 when USSR is divided into European USSR and Asian USSR.

(b) Asia, according to INS definition, includes Southwest Asia, e.g., Iraq, Israel, Syria, Turkey.

(c) Includes Canada, Mexico, the Caribbean, Central America, and South America.

Source: *Data for 1981 to 1990 are from U.S. Immigration and Naturalization Service (INS), Statistical Yearbook of the Immigration and Naturalization Service, 1991 (Washington, DC: U.S. Government Printing Office, 1992), table 3, p. 32. Data for 1820 to 1980 were adapted from Leon F. Bouvier and Robert W. Gardner, "Immigration to the U.S.: The Unfinished Story," Population Bulletin 41, no. 4 (November 1986): table 1, p. 8. Primary source: INS, Statistical Yearbook (Washington, DC: U.S. Government Printing Office, 1986), table IMM 1.2.*

Table 18.2
Immigration by Country of Origin, 1850-1990

Immigrants admitted to the United States by selected Asian ethnic group by decade, 1850-1990.

Decade	Chinese	Japanese	Asian Indian	Korean	Filipino	Vietnamese
1850-1860	41,397	—	43	—	—	—
1861-1870	64,301	186	69	—	—	—
1871-1880	123,201	149	163	—	—	—
1881-1890	61,711	2,270	269	—	—	—
1891-1900	14,799	25,942	68	—	—	—
1901-1910	20,605	129,797	4,713	7,697	—	—
1911-1920	21,278	83,837	2,082	1,049	869	—
1921-1930	29,907	33,462	1,886	598	54,747	—
1931-1940	4,928	1,948	496	60	6,159	—
1941-1950	16,709	1,555	1,761	—	4,691	—
1951-1960	9,657 (a)	46,250	1,973	6,231	19,307	—
1961-1970	34,764	39,98	27,189	34,526	98,376	3,788
1971-1980	12,326	49,775	164,134	271,956	360,216	179,681
1981-1990	366,622 (b)	43,248	261,841	338,824	495,271	401,419

Notes:
A dash (–) represents less than 0.5 percent.
(a) Beginning in 1957, Chinese total includes immigration from Taiwan.
(b) Beginning in 1982, Taiwan was no longer included in the Chinese total. Immigration from Taiwan to the United States from 1982 to 1990 was 118,105. These immigrants are not included in the total for Chinese which appears in the table.

Sources: For 1851-1980, U.S. Commission on Civil Rights, The Economic Status of Americans of Asian Descent: An Exploratory Investigation (Washington, DC: U.S. Commission on Civil Rights Clearinghouse Publication 95, October 1988), table 2.2, p. 21. For 1981-1990, selected from U.S. Immigration and Naturalization Service (INS), Statistical Yearbook of the Immigration and Naturalization Service, 1991 (Washington, DC: U.S. Government Printing Office, 1992), table 3, p. 32. Primary source: For 1851-1980, INS, Statistical Yearbook of the Immigration and Naturalization Service, various years. Data on Filipino migration to mainland United States for the decades 1911-1940 were derived from the INS Report of the Commissioner General of Immigration.

Table 18.3
Immigration to California by
Country of Birth, 1991

Numbers of immigrants to California, total to the United States and percent to California by selected Asian country of birth, 1991.

Country	Total to California	Total to the U.S.	Percent to California
Bangladesh	1,064	10,676	10.0%
China (a)	12,265	33,025	37.1%
Hong Kong	4,468	10,427	42.9%
India	10,291	45,064	22.8%
Korea	7,301	26,518	27.5%
Pakistan	3,084	20,355	15.2%
Philippines	32,698	63,596	51.4%
Taiwan	5,840	13,274	44.0%
Vietnam	21,542	55,307	39.0%

Note:
(a) The INS uses the designation "China, Mainland" for immigrants from areas under the control of the government in Beijing.

Source: *CompilMed from data in Statistical Yearbook of the Immigration and Naturalization Service, 1991 (Washington, DC: U.S. Government Printing Office, 1992), table 16, p. 58.*

Table 18.5
Immigration to Illinois by
Country of Birth, 1991

Numbers of immigrants to Illinois, total to U.S. and percent to Illinois by selected Asian country of birth, 1991.

Country	Total to Illinois	Total to the U.S.	Percent to Illinois
Bangladesh	118	10,676	1.1%
China (a)	1,164	33,025	3.5%
Hong Kong	293	10,427	2.8%
India	3,827	45,064	8.5%
Korea	1,162	26,518	4.4%
Pakistan	1,464	20,355	7.2%
Philippines	2,924	63,596	4.6%
Taiwan	368	13,274	2.8%
Vietnam	967	55,307	1.8%

Note:
(a) The INS uses the designation "China, Mainland" for immigrants from areas under the control of the government in Beijing.

Source: *Compiled from data in Statistical Yearbook of the Immigration and Naturalization Service, 1991 (Washington, DC: U.S. Government Printing Office, 1992), table 16, p. 58.*

Table 18.4
Immigration to Florida by
Country of Birth, 1991

Numbers of immigrants to Florida, total to U.S. and percent to Florida by selected Asian country of birth, 1991.

Country	Total to Florida	Total to the U.S.	Percent to Florida
Bangladesh	371	10,676	3.5%
China (a)	495	33,025	1.5%
Hong Kong	217	10,427	2.1%
India	1,224	45,064	2.7%
Korea	424	26,518	1.6%
Pakistan	855	20,355	4.2%
Philippines	1,501	63,596	2.4%
Taiwan	191	13,274	1.4%
Vietnam	1,623	55,307	3.0%

Note:
(a) The INS uses the designation "China, Mainland" for immigrants from areas under the control of the government in Beijing.

Source: *Compiled from data in Statistical Yearbook of the Immigration and Naturalization Service, 1991 (Washington, DC: U.S. Government Printing Office, 1992), table 16, p. 58.*

Table 18.6
Immigration to Maryland by
Country of Birth, 1991

Numbers of immigrants to Maryland, total to U.S. and percent to Maryland by selected Asian country of birth, 1991.

Country	Total to Maryland	Total to the U.S.	Percent to Maryland
Bangladesh	125	10,676	1.2%
China (a)	499	33,025	1.5%
Hong Kong	124	10,427	1.2%
India	984	45,064	2.2%
Korea	1,048	26,518	4.0%
Pakistan	377	20,355	1.9%
Philippines	791	63,596	1.2%
Taiwan	272	13,274	2.1%
Vietnam	697	55,307	1.3%

Note:
(a) The INS uses the designation "China, Mainland" for immigrants from areas under the control of the government in Beijing.

Source: *Compiled from data in Statistical Yearbook of the Immigration and Naturalization Service, 1991 (Washington, DC: U.S. Government Printing Office, 1992), table 16, p. 58.*

Table 18.7
Immigration to Massachusetts by Country of Birth, 1991

Numbers of immigrants to Massachusetts, total to U.S. and percent to Masschusetts by selected Asian country of birth, 1991.

Country	Total to Massachusetts	Total to the U.S.	Percent to Massachusetts
Bangladesh	126	10,676	1.2%
China (a)	1,150	33,025	3.5%
Hong Kong	451	10,427	4.3%
India	1,061	45,064	2.4%
Korea	232	26,518	0.9%
Pakistan	249	20,355	1.2%
Philippines	411	63,596	0.7%
Taiwan	264	13,274	2.0%
Vietnam	1,961	55,307	3.6%

Note:
(a) The INS uses the designation "China, Mainland" for immigrants from areas under the control of the government in Beijing.

Source: *Compiled from data in Statistical Yearbook of the Immigration and Naturalization Service, 1991 (Washington, DC: U.S. Government Printing Office, 1992), table 16, p. 58.*

Table 18.9
Immigration to New Jersey by Country of Birth, 1991

Numbers of immigrants to New Jersey, total to U.S. and percent to New Jersey by selected Asian country of birth, 1991.

Country	Total to New Jersey	Total to the U.S.	Percent to New Jersey
Bangladesh	560	10,676	5.3%
China (a)	1,020	33,025	3.1%
Hong Kong	291	10,427	2.8%
India	4,939	45,064	11.0%
Korea	1,434	26,518	5.4%
Pakistan	1,296	20,355	6.4%
Philippines	2,885	63,596	4.5%
Taiwan	86.3	13,274	6.5%
Vietnam	886	55,307	1.6%

Note:
(a) The INS uses the designation "China, Mainland" for immigrants from areas under the control of the government in Beijing.

Source: *Compiled from data in Statistical Yearbook of the Immigration and Naturalization Service, 1991 (Washington, DC: U.S. Government Printing Office, 1992), table 16, p. 58.*

Table 18.8
Immigration to Michigan by Country of Birth, 1991

Numbers of immigrants to Michigan, total to U.S. and percent to Michigan by selected Asian country of birth, 1991.

Country	Total to Michigan	Total to the U.S.	Percent to Michigan
Bangladesh	136	10,676	1.3%
China (a)	326	33,025	1.0%
Hong Kong	96	10,427	0.9%
India	1,064	45,064	2.4%
Korea	482	26,518	1.8%
Pakistan	304	20,355	1.5%
Philippines	659	63,596	1.0%
Taiwan	229	13,274	1.7%
Vietnam	685	55,307	1.2%

Note:
(a) The INS uses the designation "China, Mainland" for immigrants from areas under the control of the government in Beijing.

Source: *Compiled from data in Statistical Yearbook of the Immigration and Naturalization Service, 1991 (Washington, DC: U.S. Government Printing Office, 1992), table 16, p. 58.*

Table 18.10
Immigration to New York by Country of Birth, 1991

Numbers of immigrants to New York, total to U.S. and percent to New York by selected Asian country of birth, 1991.

Country	Total to New York	Total to the U.S.	Percent to New York
Bangladesh	6,854	10,676	64.2%
China (a)	9,667	33,025	29.3%
Hong Kong	2,311	10,427	22.2%
India	9,133	45,064	20.3%
Korea	5,209	26,518	19.6%
Pakistan	7,504	20,355	36.9%
Philippines	4,045	63,596	6.4%
Taiwan	1,581	13,274	11.9%
Vietnam	2,235	55,307	4.0%

Note:
(a) The INS uses the designation "China, Mainland" for immigrants from areas under the control of the government in Beijing.

Source: *Compiled from data in Statistical Yearbook of the Immigration and Naturalization Service, 1991 (Washington, DC: U.S. Government Printing Office, 1992), table 16, p. 58.*

Table 18.11
Immigration to Pennsylvania by Country of Birth, 1991

Numbers of immigrants to Pennsylvania, total to U.S. and percent to Pennsylvania by selected Asian country of birth, 1991.

Country	Total to Pennsylvania	Total to the U.S.	Percent to Pennsylvania
Bangladesh	78	10,676	0.7%
China (a)	542	33,025	1.6%
Hong Kong	163	10,427	1.6%
India	1,361	45,064	3.0%
Korea	983	26,518	3.7%
Pakistan	251	20,355	1.2%
Philippines	555	63,596	0.9%
Taiwan	264	13,274	2.0%
Vietnam	1,619	55,307	2.9%

Note:
(a) The INS uses the designation "China, Mainland" for immigrants from areas under the control of the government in Beijing.

Source: *Compiled from data in Statistical Yearbook of the Immigration and Naturalization Service, 1991 (Washington, DC: U.S. Government Printing Office, 1992), table 16, p. 58.*

Table 18.13
Immigration to Washington by Country of Birth, 1991

Numbers of immigrants to Washington, total to U.S. and percent to Washington by selected Asian country of birth, 1991.

Country	Total to Washington	Total to the U.S.	Percent to Washington
Bangladesh	27	10,676	0.3%
China (a)	55	33,025	0.2%
Hong Kong	291	10,427	2.8%
India	386	45,064	0.9%
Korea	811	26,518	3.1%
Pakistan	94	20,355	0.5%
Philippines	1,563	63,596	2.5%
Taiwan	266	13,274	2.0%
Vietnam	1,889	55,307	3.4%

Note:
(a) The INS uses the designation "China, Mainland" for immigrants from areas under the control of the government in Beijing.

Source: *Compiled from data in Statistical Yearbook of the Immigration and Naturalization Service, 1991 (Washington, DC: U.S. Government Printing Office, 1992), table 16, p. 58.*

Table 18.12
Immigration to Texas by Country of Birth, 1991

Numbers of immigrants to Texas, total to U.S. and percent to Texas by selected Asian country of birth, 1991.

Country	Total to Texas	Total to the U.S.	Percent to Texas
Bangladesh	340	10,676	3.2%
China (a)	790	33,025	2.4%
Hong Kong	307	10,427	2.9%
India	2,601	45,064	5.8%
Korea	1,104	26,518	4.2%
Pakistan	1,806	20,355	8.9%
Philippines	1,775	63,596	2.8%
Taiwan	875	13,274	6.6%
Vietnam	5,257	55,307	9.5%

Note:
(a) The INS uses the designation "China, Mainland" for immigrants from areas under the control of the government in Beijing.

Source: *Compiled from data in Statistical Yearbook of the Immigration and Naturalization Service, 1991 (Washington, DC: U.S. Government Printing Office, 1992), table 16, p. 58.*

Population Growth and Distribution

♦ Pacific Islanders and Southeast Asians ♦ Early Growth and Migration
♦ Population in the First Centennial: 1790 to 1890
♦ The Industrial Period through the Post-World War II Era, 1900-1960
♦ The 1970 Census: Less than 1 Percent of the American Population
♦ The 1980 Census: The Watershed of Decennial Censuses
♦ The 1990 Census: A More Diverse and Dynamic Population ♦ Future Growth and Distribution

The growth and distribution of the Asian and Pacific Islander population in the United States has been dependent upon U.S. policies directed to peoples from Asia and Pacific Islands. Immigration policies of exclusion and inclusion were established for peoples from this region as early as the nineteenth century. Additionally, policies of trade and national security coupled with colonial relationships have contributed to the differential growth and distribution of particular ethnic groups.

The first wave of Asian and Pacific Islander immigrants to the United States were Chinese and Japanese who were recruited to serve as labor in the agricultural and industrial sectors of the developing West Coast and Hawaii between the mid-nineteenth and early twentieth centuries. Korean, Filipino, and Asian Indian laborers followed in smaller numbers at the turn of the century.

A second wave of Asians and Pacific Islanders immigrated to the United States as a result of various wars and U.S. foreign policy. The Spanish-American War in 1898 resulted in the U.S. acquisition of the Philippines, Hawaii, and Guam as territories. World War II brought Chinese, Filipino, and Japanese brides of U.S. servicemen as well as intellectuals and professionals from war-torn and poor Asian countries. After the Korean War, many Korean war brides immigrated to the United States as well. The war in Southeast Asia resulted in the immigration not only of Vietnamese, Cambodian, and other Southeast Asian brides but Amerasian families, immigrants, and refugees.

With the passage of the Immigration Act of 1965, many professional, entrepreneurial, and service-labor immigrants from more-established groups of Chinese and Filipinos as well as newer groups from Korea, the Indian subcontinent, and Southeast Asia immigrated to the United States. Together with American-born Asian and Pacific Islander communities, they contributed to a post-industrial U.S. economy.

♦ PACIFIC ISLANDERS AND SOUTHEAST ASIANS

The growth and distribution of two specific populations warrant special attention. The first are the Pacific Islander groups who are indigenous peoples of the Americas. For the most part, they are not immigrants to this nation but preceded the founding settlers of the United States. Hawaiians and Guamanians are U.S. citizens; American Samoans are nationals. A distinct minority are immigrants such as Western Samoans. Like other original peoples of the Americas, their primary concern is maintaining their identity, curtailing declines in their numbers, and discouraging geographical dispersal of their communities. The second are Southeast Asians who are not immigrants per se. The migration of peoples from Vietnam, Laos, and Cambodia was largely caused by political persecution and colonial-superpower client wars. Specific war-refugee resettlement policies were developed in the 1970s and 1980s for these populations that differentiate their demographic characteristics, geographical distribution, and socioeconomic status from the general Asian and Pacific Islander population.

Much of the following presentation is based on census data that have been collected since 1860. General findings are made with caution given this populations's great heterogeneity and current flux of continued demographic changes.

♦ EARLY GROWTH AND MIGRATION

Population Trends

The 1990 Census indicated that the Asian and Pacific Islander population was the fastest growing in the United States. It more than doubled between 1970 and 1980 and doubled again between 1980 and 1990. In this twenty-year span, the Asian and Pacific Islander population more than quadrupled from 1.5 million to 7.2 million.

The dramatic growth and diversity of the Asian and Pacific Islander population in the United States in the last two decades are due primarily to: the elimination of exclusionary immigration policies directed at Asian immigrants that greatly curtailed their entry between 1882 and 1964, refugee resettlement policies for Southeast Asians since 1975, natural increases in individual communities with the establishment of permanent American residence, and federal initiatives to provide a complete count of this population since the 1970 Census.

This twenty-year growth, however, is in direct contrast to the prior 110 years of an Asian and Pacific Islander presence in the United States. Between 1860 and 1970, the Asian and Pacific Islander population constituted less than 1 percent of the total American population and was concentrated in the western states.

Even in the recent period of rapid growth, 1970 to 1990, its proportion of the national population remained relatively modest, increasing from less than 1 percent to just under 3 percent.

In 1990, the Asian and Pacific Islander population was the second-smallest racial/ethnic group in the United States, after the American Indian/Alaskan Native population.

Projections for the year 2050 indicate that the Asian and Pacific Islander population will continue to be the fastest-growing group in the United States, increasing to 40 million or 11 percent of the total population. This will still be smaller than the projected Hispanic and black populations. The Hispanic population, projected to be 81 million in 2050, is expected to constitute 21 percent of the total population. The black population is expected to rise to 62 million or 16 percent of the total U.S. population. The non-Hispanic white population is expected to number 202 million and still constitute a majority of the population at 53 percent. The indigenous population of American Indians/Alaskan Natives is expected to double by 2050, remaining the smallest group.

A second notable area of growth for the Asian and Pacific Islander population between 1970 and 1990 was in the increase of specific Asian and Pacific American ethnic groups. As recently as 1970, census data were available only for four Asian groups—Japanese, Chinese, Filipino, and Korean—and one Pacific Islander group—Hawaiian. By 1980, detailed data were available for 12 Asian groups—Chinese, Filipino, Japanese, Asian Indian, Korean, Vietnamese, Laotian, Thai, Cambodian, Pakistani, Indonesian, and Hmong—and six Pacific Islander groups—Hawaiian, Samoan, Tongan, Micronesian, Guamanian, and Melanesian. By 1990, detailed data were available for 17 Asian groups—Chinese, Filipino, Japanese, Asian Indian, Korean, Vietnamese,

Table 19.1
Asian and Pacific Islander Population, 1900 to 1990

Year	Total U.S. population	Total U.S. Asian Pacific Islander population	Asian Pacific Islander, percent of total
1900	76,212,168	204,462	—
1910	92,228,531	249,926	—
1920	106,021,568	332,432	—
1930	123,202,660	489,326	—
1940	132,165,129	489,984	—
1950	151,325,798	599,091	
1960	179,323,175	877,934	—
1970	203,211,926	1,429,562	0.7%
1980	226,545,805	3,466,421	1.5%
1990	248,709,873	7,273,662	2.9%

Source: U.S. Bureau of Census, Decennial Censuses of Population. A dash (—) indicates that the percentage is less that 0.5.

Laotian, Cambodian, Thai, Hmong, Pakistani, Indonesian, Malayan, Bangladeshi, Sri Lankan, Burmese, and Okinawan—and eight Pacific Islander groups—Hawaiian, Samoan, Guamanian, Tongan, Tahitian, Northern Mariana Islander, Palauan, and Fijian.

With respect to distribution, the Asian and Pacific Islander population is much more concentrated than the total population. This has been the historical pattern for most racial and ethnic minorities, including Asians and Pacific Islanders. Racial minorities are regionally concentrated in the Pacific Rim, sunbelt states, and the South. In 1990 over one out of two (56 percent) Asian and Pacific Islanders lived in the West compared to one out of five (21 percent) residents nationally. The majority of the black population was found in its historical areas of residence—the South and mid-Atlantic. This is consistent with the legacy of the African slave trade. Hispanics remain concentrated in the Southwest in lands that were once under Spanish rule and ceded from Mexico to the United States under the Treaty of Guadalupe-Hidalgo.

As recently as 1940, almost 100 percent of Asian and Pacific Islanders lived on the West coast. By 1990, concentration in the West continued but dispersal to other regions was clearly established. New York replaced Hawaii as the state with the second-largest number of Asian and Pacific Islanders. In 1990 the majority of this population lived in only three states—California, New York, and Hawaii.

Of all racial and ethnic groups, the Asian and Pacific Islander population was the most highly urbanized in 1990 with 95 percent living in urban areas. By comparison, 75 percent of the total U.S. population lived in urban areas. Ninety-six percent of Asian groups resided in urban areas compared to 89 percent of Pacific Islanders. Over half (54 percent) lived in only five metropolitan areas: Los Angeles/Anaheim/Riverside; San Francisco/Oakland/San Jose; New York/northern New Jersey/Long Island; Honolulu; and Chicago/Gary/Lake County.

Migration from Asian and Pacific Lands

The first migration from Asia occurred some 20,000 to 40,000 years ago when natives of present-day Siberia crossed the Bering Strait to North America. Their descendants are today's American Indians and Alaska Natives. Several scholars date the settlement of Asian and Pacific Islanders in the colonial United States from 1763. The galleon trade that flourished between Manila and Acapulco, from 1565 to 1815, brought Chinese and Filipino sailors to North America. To escape harsh working conditions, several jumped ship and settled in Mexico and along the Gulf of Mexico. Historical records indicate that as early as 1763, Filipinos or

Table 19.2
Asian and Pacific Islander Population by Region of the United States

Region	Total population	Asian Pacific Islander population
Total (thousands)	248,886	7,023
Northwest, in percent	20.4%	17.3%
Midwest	24.1%	10.3%
South	34.2%	13.8%
West	21.2%	58.5%

Source: *U.S. Bureau of Census, The Asian and Pacific Islander Population in the United States: March 1991 and 1990.*

"Manilamen" settled in Louisiana. Their descendants include present-day tenth-generation Louisianans.

The second but more sizable presence of Asians began with the discovery of gold in California in 1848. Immigration statistics, collected since 1820, reported 13,100 Chinese admitted to the United States in 1853. In prior years, only 198 Asians had been recorded as immigrants.

Most Pacific Islanders are not considered immigrants to the United States. Hawaii was an independent monarchy before becoming a United States territory in 1898 and the fiftieth state in 1959. Guam was colonized by Spain in 1561 and ceded to the United States after the Spanish-American War in 1898. It became a U.S. territory in 1950 and American citizenship was conferred on the Guamanian population. By contrast, the Samoan island chain consists of American Samoa, a U.S. territory, and Western Samoa, an independent nation since 1962.

Historical Statistical Record

As with immigration statistics, census data historically have recorded selected nationalities or ethnic groups of Asian and Pacific Islanders rather than the total group. This enumeration was determined by which groups were immigrating to the United States at various times. This is in contrast to whites, blacks, and American Indians for whom census data have been collected as a homogeneous group. In a very few selected censuses, blacks have been delineated as mulattos, quadroons, and octoroons. American Indians have been classified as reservation or non-reservation Indians and by tribe. Hispanics historically have been classified as white, except in the 1930 Census when Mexicans were a separate racial category. In the 1970 Census, with the federal government's objective for a more accurate and comprehensive enumeration of the American population, particularly undercounted minorities, data were collected on selected Latino ethnic groups, as well as the total Hispanic population. For Asian and Pacific Islanders, however, a count of the total population was not available until the 1980 Census and this was on a sample basis only. It was not until the most recent census, 1990, that a total Asian and Pacific Islander population count was available.

◆ POPULATION IN THE FIRST CENTENNIAL: 1790 TO 1890

Since 1790, the United States has conducted a constitutionally mandated census of the American people for apportionment, redistricting, and other federal objectives. Census data on Asians, however, was unavailable until the mid- nineteenth century, and was limited to Chinese and Japanese, the only Asian groups to immigrate during this period. Data have been collected on the Chinese population since the 1860 Census, and on the Japanese since 1870. No census data were available for Pacific Islanders until Pacific territories were acquired by the United States after the Spanish-American War of 1898.

Rapid growth of the Chinese American population occurred during the first three decades since the 1860 census and was concentrated in the West. Between 1860 and 1870, it grew from 35,000 to 63,000. Between 1870 and 1880, it increased from 63,000 to 105,000. With the passage of the 1882 Chinese Exclusion Act, however, growth was curtailed. The 1890 Census recorded 108,000 Chinese. Not until after World War II did this population renew its growth.

Early censuses also documented a low proportion of Asian American females. The ratio was quite drastic, reflecting the need for cheap manual labor in railroads, mining, agriculture, and manufacturing and later in personal services such as laundering and cooking. In 1860, the ratio was 33 Chinese males to one Chinese female; in 1870, 29 to two; and, in both 1880 and 1890, 25 to one. The disproportionately low number of Chinese females was reinforced by an 1884 federal court ruling that excluded the wives of Chinese laborers from immigrating to the United States. This decision kept the Chinese population in the United States overwhelmingly male through the end of the century.

The Japanese depicted a growth pattern similar to the Chinese in the nineteenth century but with much lower numbers. A total of 55 Japanese were counted in 1870 of whom eight were women. In 1880, there were 134 males to 14 Japanese females. Between 1880 and 1890, however, the Japanese population grew from 148 to 2,039, and was also concentrated in the West. This surge coincided with the diminished growth of the Chinese population. Japanese males outnumbered Japanese females until 1960. At the end of the century, the Asian American population was roughly 0.05 percent of the total U.S. population. There was no recorded count of the Pacific Islander population.

◆ THE INDUSTRIAL PERIOD THROUGH THE POST-WORLD WAR II ERA, 1900-1960

Growth

At the dawn of the twentieth century, the Asian and Pacific Islander population was about 0.03 percent of the total population. The 1900 Census included the territory of Hawaii for the first time. Overall, the Asian American population grew numerically, but proportionally remained less than 1 percent of the total population. Specific exclusion laws directed at the Chinese were followed by the 1907 Gentlemen's Agreement between Japan and the United States restricting future Japanese immigration. These laws were followed by the Immigration Act of 1917, which prohibited immigration from a broad zone that included parts of China, all of India, Myanmar, Thailand, Asiatic Russia, the Polynesian Islands, and part of Afghanistan. These acts together stifled the growth of the Asian and Pacific Islander population through World War II.

After the war, several laws removed immigration restrictions for Asian and Pacific Islanders. These included the 1946 War Brides Act, the Displaced Persons Act (1948-1954), and the 1952 Immigration and Naturalization Act, commonly known as the McCarran-Walter Act. Immigration quotas were still quite low at 100 persons each for countries of the Asia-Pacific Triangle. Preferential categories were given to skilled immigrants and non-quota exemptions were given to immediate relatives of American citizens. The sum of such a modest immigration allocation was sufficient to raise the 1960 Census count of Asian and Pacific Islander population to 878,000, a 75-percent increase from the 1940 Census count of 500,000.

Within specific Asian and Pacific Islander groups, Chinese population growth stagnated until the end of World War II. In part this was due to the orientation of each group and its relations with the United States. A prevailing Chinese orientation was that their stay in this country was temporary. One came to Gold Mountain (as the United States was known), a land of economic opportunity, to earn one's fortune and eventually return to China. American exclusionary policies on immigration (beginning with the 1882 Chinese Exclusion Act), property ownership (Chinese were ineligible to own property), and citizenship (all aliens became ineligible for citizenship) reinforced the temporary-resident status of Chinese.

Between 1900 and 1940, growth in the Chinese population was limited virtually to natural increases. During World War II, however, China was an ally of the United States and Chinese Americans joined the armed forces. Given this situation, exclusionary immigration laws began to be repealed and special acts (mentioned above) to increase immigration were implemented. By 1950, growth was on the rise due to immigration; that year's census showed an increase of 46,000 persons over 1940 with an overall count of 150,005 Chinese. By 1960, Chinese Americans numbered 237,292.

The Japanese population, by contrast, increased consistently in all decades and was the largest of all enumerated Asian American groups in this period. Interestingly, the Japanese population continued to grow, despite Executive Order 589 (commonly known as the Gentlemen's Agreement), which curtailed immigration of Japanese laborers. Between 1900 and 1910, the Japanese population grew from 86,000 to 153,000. While this community was disproportionately male, it was not as extreme a disparity as that in the Chinese and Filipino populations. While female immigration was minimal in the nineteenth century, more cordial relations between the Japanese and United States governments encouraged immigration of wives and "picture brides," or brides who came to the United States in arranged marriages accomplished through the exchange of pictures. This increased the number of Japanese women in the first two decades of the twentieth century.

By 1920, there were 38,303 females out of a total Japanese population of 111,010. By 1920, there were roughly two males for each female, a ratio not attained until 1950 for the Chinese and 1960 for Filipinos. Sizable numbers of Japanese immigrant women helped establish the Japanese American family in significant numbers in its second generation. The Japanese were the first Asian and Pacific Islander group to shift from a society of single male sojourners to a permanent resident population of family units. By 1960, the Japanese population had grown to 464,332 and maintained the majority of the Asian American population at 53 percent.

In the 1910 Census, the Filipino population was enumerated for the first time. Unlike the Japanese and Chinese who were subject to exclusionary immigration laws, Filipinos were American nationals, since the Philippines had been ceded to the United States following the Spanish-American War of 1898.

They were encouraged to go to Hawaii and California as replacement and supplemental labor for their Chinese and Japanese predecessors. Similar to the Chinese during their first three decades in the United States, Filipinos increased dramatically as a cheap, primarily male, labor supply on Hawaiian plantations and in California agriculture. Their numbers increased almost tenfold between 1910 and 1920, from 2,800 to 27,000. Between 1920 and 1930, they quadrupled to 108,000. The ratio of Filipino males to females in 1930 was 11 to two. Alarmed by the growing numbers of a mainly single male population, the U.S. government initiated a repatriation movement to the Philippines. In 1940, the Filipino population of 99,000 reflected a decrease of 9 percent from the 1930 count of 108,000. However, Filipino and American cooperation during World War II and the establishment of the Republic of the Philippines were followed by relaxed immigration restrictions. By 1950, the Filipino population had increased to 123,000 and in 1960 stood at 176,310.

The 1910 Census also obtained separate figures for Koreans and Asian Indians. However, these groups have

Table 19.3
Asian Pacific Islander Immigration by Country of Origin, 1850–1960

Decade	Chinese	Japanese	Asian Indian	Korean	Filipino	Vietamese
1850–1860	41,397	—	43	—	—	—
1861–1870	64,301	186	69	—	—	—
1871–1880	123,201	149	163	—	—	—
1881–1890	61,711	2,270	269	—	—	—
1891–1900	14,799	25,942	68	—	—	—
1901–1910	20,605	129,797	4,713	7,697	—	—
1911–1920	21,278	83,837	2,082	1,049	869	—
1921–1930	29,907	33,462	1,886	598	54,747	—
1931–1940	4,928	1,948	496	60	6,159	—
1941–1950	16,709	1,555	1,761	—	4,691	—
1951–1960	9,657	46,250	1,973	6,231	19,307	—

Source: U.S. Commission on Civil Rights, *The Economic Status of Americans of Asian Descent: An Exploratory Investigation,* 1988.

President Lyndon Johnson chose Liberty Island as the site for the ceremonial signing of the 1965 Immigration Act. (Yoichi R. Okamoto, courtesy of LBJ Library.)

Chinese held the majority of the Asian/Pacific American population at 58 percent; Japanese had the remaining 42 percent. By the 1960 Census, three groups comprised the enumerated Asian American population. Japanese were a majority at 53 percent. Chinese accounted for 27 percent, and Filipinos 20 percent.

At a total of 877,934, Asian/Pacific Americans represented about 0.5 percent of the total U.S. population.

The growth of Asian American populations consisted of both immigrant and American-born generations. Family formation in the early decades was established within the Japanese population as picture brides were allowed to join their husbands in Hawaii and California.

The Chinese and Filipino populations, being disproportionately male due to restrictions on female immigration, were primarily bachelor societies. However, they also produced families since many Chinese returned to China to father children, and more Filipinos entered interracial unions.

The immigration of Asian wives—Chinese, Filipino, Japanese, and Korean—after World War II and the Korean War produced a sex ratio approaching the norm, increased American-born Asian children, and established permanent families and communities.

Distribution

Throughout the latter portion of the nineteenth century and the first half of the twentieth century, the Asian and Pacific Islander population continued to be concentrated in the West. Earlier decades found the overwhelming majority of the Chinese population in the West. In 1880, 97 percent were clustered in the Pacific and mountain regions which comprise the West. Eighty-three percent resided in the Pacific region alone. In contrast to other Asian and Pacific Islander groups, however, this concentration diminished over time so that by 1950 only three out of five Chinese lived in the Pacific and mountain regions.

A somewhat different residential pattern was established by the Japanese. In 1880, with a total population of 148, about three out of five Japanese lived in the Pacific and mountain regions. By 1950, their concentration in the Pacific and mountain regions had increased to four out of five.

From 1900 to 1960, the Chinese were predominantly an urban population. In 1910, three out of four Chinese resided in urban areas, and by 1950, this had increased to more than nine out of ten. The Japanese, with their traditional farming background, were almost equally divided between urban and rural residences in 1910. By 1950, however, seven out of ten were found in urban areas. This is partly due to the government's relocation of 112,000 Japanese from the Pacific Coast during

been included in subsequent censuses on an intermittent basis. Such inclusion reflects a selective classification and enumeration process based on immigration.

Between 1900 and 1960, the sizes of the Korean and Asian Indian populations were small, no more than 9,000 for Koreans in a given decade and fewer than 3,000 for Asian Indians.

In the 1900 Census, only two Asian American groups and no Pacific Islander groups were enumerated.

World War II. Many were forced to sell their property or lost their farms. At the end of the war, few resumed farm work upon their return.

Filipinos also worked on farms in Hawaii and California but provided personal services and manual labor in urban areas as well. In 1960, over one-fourth lived in rural areas.

The Impact of Post-1965 Immigration and Refugee Resettlement

If Asian and Pacific Islander population projections had been based on its pre-1965 growth, they would be described as a small and invisible population. In 1949, sociologist Rose Hum Lee had already written about the decline of Chinatown in the United States. Japanese American citizens and permanent residents, incarcerated during World War II as security risks on the basis of their Japanese ancestry, were dispersed to areas away from their West Coast homes. In 1960, with such low numbers, Koreans and Asian Indians were not even separately enumerated. Asian Indians were subsumed under the white category in 1950, 1960, and even 1970.

The passage and subsequent implementation of the 1965 Immigration Act brought tremendous growth and diversity to the Asian and Pacific Islander population.

Earlier Filipinos and Chinese settlers were joined by new arrivals from the Philippines, mainland China, Hong Kong, and Taiwan whose annual numbers ranged between 45,000 to 65,000. In comparison, Japanese immigration was limited to an annual average of 4,000.

Korean immigrants averaged over 30,000 a year and Asian Indians over 25,000. While earlier immigrants were primarily from working-class backgrounds with a core of highly skilled professionals, new immigrants were affluent entrepreneurs, working-class relatives of earlier immigrants, highly educated middle-class professionals, and illiterate war refugees with no material possessions.

Refugee policies further affected the growth and diversity of the Asian and Pacific Islander population.

The end of the war in southeast Asia in 1975 was followed by resettlement of refugees, which added new groups to the Asian and Pacific Islander population in the United States. Most dramatically, between 1977 and 1978, the number of Vietnamese immigrants increased from 4,600 to 89,000. Cambodian and Lao immigrants also began to increase in 1977, ranging from 10,000 to 20,000 per year.

This shaped the growth and distribution of the Asian and Pacific Islander population in the United States from 1970 through 1990.

♦ THE 1970 CENSUS: LESS THAN ONE PERCENT OF THE AMERICAN POPULATION

Growth

Although the Asian and Pacific Islander population was still less than 1 percent of the total U.S. population in 1970, shifting growth trends could already be observed. The 1970 Census provided detailed data for selected Asian and Pacific Islander groups. Demographic and socioeconomic data were available for four Asian American groups: Chinese, Filipino, Japanese, and Korean. The only Pacific Islander group with detailed data was Hawaiian.

In 1970, Japanese, Chinese, and Filipinos in the United States numbered 1,369,000, an increase of 56 percent over 1960. By comparison, the total population increased only 13 percent during this period. Japanese were the largest group at 591,000, Chinese numbered 435,000 persons, and Filipinos had a population of 343,000. Two-thirds of the increase in the Japanese population was due to natural increase but Chinese and Filipinos could credit two-thirds of their growth to immigration. Hawaiians, a native population composed of both full and mixed Hawaiians, numbered almost 100,000. Enumerated as a separate ethnic group, Koreans totaled 70,000. This represented a tenfold increase from their 1950 total of 7,000. These five groups

Table 19.4
Asian Pacific Islander Immigration by Country of Origin, 1960–1990

Decade	Chinese	Japanese	Asian Indian	Korean	Filipino	Vietnamese
1961–1970	34,764	39,980	27,198	34,526	98,376	3,788
1971–1980	124,326	49,775	164,134	271,956	360,216	179,681
1981–1990	366,622	43,248	261,841	338,824	295,271	201,419

Notes:
Beginning in 1982, Taiwan was no longer included in the Chinese total. Immigration from Taiwan to the United States from 1982 to 1990 was 118,105. These immigrants are not included in the total for Chinese that appears in the table.

Source: Statistical Yearbook of the Immigration and Naturalization Service, various years.

together comprised less than 1 percent of the U.S. population.

In terms of nativity, the Asian and Pacific Islander groups of the United States were primarily an American-born population in 1970. Exclusionary immigration laws limited most growth to natural increase for several decades. Almost four out of five Japanese were American-born as were roughly half the Chinese (47 percent), Filipino (53 percent), and Korean (46 percent) populations. Hawaiians were almost 100 percent American-born.

Distribution

Seventy-two percent of all Japanese, Chinese, Filipinos, and Hawaiians living in the United States were settled in the West in 1970. Over one-third of all Japanese, Chinese, and Filipinos lived in California and over one-fourth lived in Hawaii. Almost three-fourths of all Hawaiians resided in Hawaii; another 14 percent settled in California. The Chinese were the only Asian group in 1970 that had a substantial proportion residing outside the West coast. Over one-fourth (27 percent) lived in the Northeast, with almost 20 percent of all Chinese living in the state of New York.

Relative to 1960, however, Asian concentration in the West diminished in 1970. This modest but distinct shift was captured in U.S. Immigration and Naturalization Service records for 1965 to 1973, which indicated that recent Asian immigrants were less likely to reside in the West. Koreans, the newest Asian settlers, were the least concentrated group with less than one-third of Korean immigrants residing in the West. Almost four out of five American-born Asians lived in the West compared to three out of five foreign-born Asians. This dispersal increased the number of Asians outside the West. While the Asian population increased by 69 percent in the West, growth outside that area was over 100 percent. Asians in the South increased by 106 percent, 124 percent in the Northeast, and a high of 143 percent in the North Central region of the United States between 1960 and 1970.

In 1970, 90 percent of Asians living in the United States were urban residents compared to 73 percent of the total population. However, this varied by individual groups. The Chinese population had the highest level at 97 percent—similar to 1960. Japanese and Filipino rural residents decreased as their participation in agriculture declined drastically.

In 1960, over one-fourth of Filipinos lived in rural areas but this proportion sank to 14 percent by 1970. This decrease was due to the death of first-generation single males, many of whom were rural workers, just as the numbers of new, primarily cosmopolitan and professional immigrants began to grow. These Filipinos settled in metropolitan areas. Additionally, the younger, second- and third-generation Filipino Americans, like the total population, moved to urban areas for education and employment opportunities.

Japanese also moved from rural to urban areas as second- and third-generation Japanese Americans migrated to metropolitan areas. While 18 percent of the Japanese population resided in rural areas in 1960, this proportion was down to 11 percent by 1970.

Rural and urban distribution varied by state among Filipinos and Japanese. A greater proportion of Japanese and Filipinos in Hawaii lived in rural areas than in California. Nearly a third of Filipinos and 14 percent of Japanese in Hawaii lived in rural areas compared to 6 percent of Japanese and 7 percent of Filipinos in California.

The national move from rural to urban areas was accompanied by a move from large cities to suburbs. By 1970 more Americans resided in surrounding suburbs than central cities. Nationally, 31 percent of the total population lived in central cities of 50,000 or more with a greater proportion (37 percent) residing in surrounding suburbs. For the Asian and Pacific Islander population, however, the proportion living in central cities in 1970 was greater than the proportion in the suburbs. Almost one out of two (48 percent) Japanese and Filipinos lived in central cities. Their proportion in the suburbs was similar to the total population. Among the Chinese, over two out of three (68 percent) lived in central cities while one-fourth lived in the suburbs.

◆ THE 1980 CENSUS: THE WATERSHED OF DECENNIAL CENSUSES

The enumeration of the Asian and Pacific Islander population in the 1980 Census is noteworthy in two ways. It was the first census to identify and provide data on the total Asian and Pacific Islander populations and their subgroups in all states, although on a sample basis. Prior to the 1980 Census, individual Asian and Pacific Islander groups were enumerated but there was no total count for Asian and Pacific Islander populations. Secondly, the 1980 Census was the first to capture the group's dramatic increase and diversity. Between 1970 and 1980, Chinese and Filipino immigrants were joined by new arrivals from the Indian subcontinent and Korea. Additionally, with the end of the war in Southeast Asia, 400,000 refugees from Vietnam, Cambodia, and Laos came to the United States between 1975 and 1980.

While natural increase and immigration accounted for much of this growth, changes in federal statistical policy and census definitions of race also helped identify more groups. The civil rights movement of the 1950s and 1960s made all Americans acutely aware that

Table 19.5
Population in the United States
by Race/Ethnicity, 1980.

Race/ethnicity	Total, 1980
Total U.S. Population	226,545,805
Asian/Pacific Islander	3,726,440
Chinese	812,178
Filipino	781,894
Japanese	716,331
Asian Indian	387,223
Korean	357,393
Vietnamese	245,025
Cambodian	16,044
Hmong	5,204
Laotian	47,683
Thai	45,279
Hawaiian	172,346
Guamanian	39,520
Samoan	30,695
Other Asian or Pacific Islander	69,625

Source: Asian and Pacific Islander Center for Census Information and Services (ACCIS), 1990.

racial and ethnic minorities were excluded from full participation as citizens and permanent residents. To remedy this situation, the federal government adopted policies and programs intended to foster full and equal participation. Statistical policies were directed to more comprehensive and accurate counts of racial and ethnic minorities to determine their needs for and access to federal services. Between 1970 and 1980, several initiatives were taken. The Office of Management and Budget issued Directive 15 to federal agencies to collect racial and ethnic data by five major categories, including Asian and Pacific Islander. The other categories were: white, black, American Indian/Alaskan Native, and Hispanic. The Bureau of the Census, in concert with governmental agencies and Asian and Pacific Islander community organizations, began planning for a more detailed count of this population, comparable to work initiated for the black and Hispanic populations in the 1970 Census. Additionally, the Department of Commerce formally established an Asian and Pacific Islander Advisory Committee to the 1980 Census. Comparable committees were also established for the black, American Indian/Alaskan Native, and Hispanic populations. Finally, congressional legislation was enacted to enumerate the Asian and Pacific Islander population more accurately and inclusively.

Several findings surfaced in the 1980 Census that were reaffirmed in 1990. These include: tremendous numerical and proportional growth; more diverse groups within this umbrella; the increase of the foreign-born population over American-born; continued growth outside the West Coast; the variation of residence by ethnicity and time of immigration; the predominance of six Asian groups: Chinese, Filipino, Japanese, Asian Indian, Korean, and Vietnamese; the predominance of Hawaiians among Pacific Islander groups; the much smaller proportion of Pacific Islanders than Asian Americans; and the relative lack of Japanese immigration compared to other groups, accompanied by a declining proportion of the Japanese American population relative to the Chinese and Filipino populations and the total Asian and Pacific Islander population.

National Population Statistics and Identification of Specific Groups

The Asian and Pacific Islander population numbered more than 3.7 million in 1980, more than double its 1970 count of 1.5 million. Its proportion of the total population also doubled in this ten-year period from 0.8 percent to 1.6 percent. The Asian American population numbered 3,466,874, and the Pacific Islander population numbered 259,566. Twelve Asian groups were enumerated and identified by detailed socioeconomic characteristics. Ranked from largest to smallest they were: Chinese, Filipino, Japanese, Korean, Vietnamese, Asian Indian, Thai, Laotian, Cambodian, Pakistani, Indonesian, and Hmong, followed by all other Asians. Similarly, detailed data were available for five Pacific Islander groups—Hawaiian, Samoan, Guamanian, Tongan, Melanesian, and all other Pacific Islanders.

In summary, over 20 Asian and Pacific Islander groups were identified in the 1980 Census compared with only five in 1970.

While the Asian and Pacific Islander population is described as quite heterogeneous, given the many ethnic groups in this category, the 1980 Census found that 90 percent of all Asian Americans were found in only six groups—Chinese, Filipino, Japanese, Asian Indian, Korean, and Vietnamese. Fully two-thirds of all Asian Americans were either Chinese, Filipino, or Japanese.

Pacific Islanders constituted only 7 percent of the total Asian and Pacific Islander population in the United States in 1980. Two-thirds were Hawaiian. In terms of specific island groups, 85 percent were Polynesian, 14 percent Micronesian and 1 percent Melanesian. Of the approximately 170,000 Pacific Islanders living in the United States, Polynesians, Hawaiians, Samoans, and Tongans were the largest groups. Among Samoans, a greater proportion were born in Western Samoa (134,000) than American Samoa (9,000). Among some 36,000 Micronesians, over 80 percent were Guamanian. The largest Melanesian group were Fijians at fewer than 3,000.

The Changing Makeup of the Pan Asian Population, 1970-1980

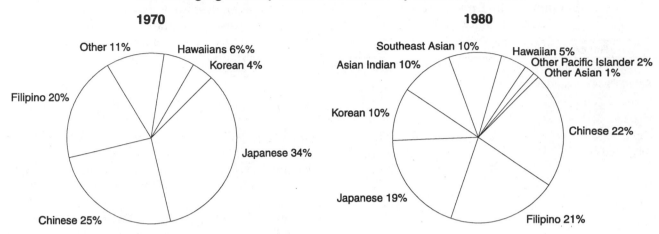

1970

Other 11%
Hawaiians 6%%
Korean 4%
Filipino 20%
Japanese 34%
Chinese 25%

1980

Southeast Asian 10%
Asian Indian 10%
Hawaiian 5%
Other Pacific Islander 2%
Other Asian 1%
Korean 10%
Chinese 22%
Japanese 19%
Filipino 21%

Source: *U.S. Bureau of the Census, We, the Asian Americans (Washington, D.C.: GPO, 1973) p. 2; and U.S. Bureau of the Census, We, the Asian and Pacific Isalander Americans (Washington, D.C.: GPO, 1988) p. 2.*

In contrast to 1970, when most Asian and Pacific Islanders were native-born, the 1980 population was predominantly foreign-born (59 percent). This was almost ten times the proportion of foreign-born residents for the total U.S. population (6 percent). Variation by group ranged from a high of 90.5 percent for Vietnamese to a low of 1.6 percent for Hawaiians. About 65 percent of Asians were foreign-born; only 12 percent of Pacific Islander's were foreign-born.

This population shift was due to massive immigration and the fertility of immigrant women. In 1980, immigrant Asian American women had a fertility rate one-third higher than native-born Asian American women. Fertility levels for Pacific Islander women in 1980 were higher than those for Asian women and for the total population of American women.

Between 1971 and 1980 over 1.4 million Asian immigrants, including Southeast Asian refugees, came to the United States. This exceeded the 1970 Census count of the entire Asian and Pacific Islander population.

Distribution

By 1980, the shift of Asian and Pacific Islanders from the West Coast to other regions was noticeable. While the majority—almost three out of five (58 percent)—of this population still lived in the West, this was less than the almost three out of four persons (72 percent) from 1970. By comparison, 19 percent of the total U.S. population lives in the West. The concentration of the Asian and Pacific Islander population was also evident in the few states in which it resides. Seventy percent lived in just five states: California, Hawaii, New York, Illinois, and Texas.

In terms of nativity, the pattern discerned from the 1980 Census, which had also been observed in 1970 was

that greater proportions of foreign-born Asian Americans, primarily newer immigrants, resided outside the West Coast. The West contained almost equal proportions of American-born (42.2 percent) and foreign-born Asian Americans (51.8 percent), but had the lowest proportion of foreign-born Asian Americans. The Northeast had the highest proportion of foreign-born Asian Americans, with 74.3 percent of all Asian Americans in this region being foreign-born, followed by the South at 73.1 percent, and the Midwest with 71.3 percent.

At the subnational level and by ethnic group, however, the distribution and residence of Asian and Pacific Islanders varied considerably, depending on period of immigration and occupation of immigrant. Native Hawaiians, Guamanians, and Samoans were concentrated in California and Hawaii. California was the place of residence for over one-third (35.2 percent) of all Asians and Pacific Islanders. The largest groups were also concentrated in this state, except Asian Indians whose largest American population was in New York. Approximately 18 percent each of Asian Indians and Chinese lived in the state of New York. One-third (34 percent) of Asian Indians and over one-fourth of the Chinese population resided in the Northeast.

In summary, as in 1970, 90 percent of the Asian and Pacific Islander population lived in urban areas and were about equally divided between central cities and suburbs. Over 45 percent resided in just five metropolitan areas: Los Angeles/Long Beach, San Francisco/Oakland, New York, Chicago, and Honolulu.

Refugee Resettlement

Growth and settlement patterns of Vietnamese, Cambodians, and Laotians since the mid-1970s are directly attributable to the end of the war in Southeast

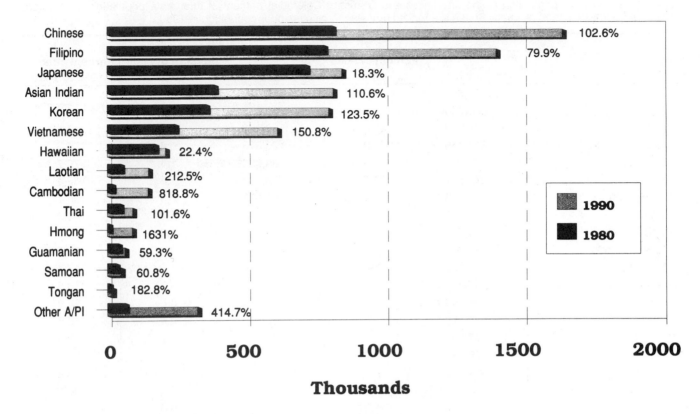

Percent Increase by Ethnicity of Asian and Pacific Islander Populations in the United States: 1980 to 1990

Chinese — 102.6%
Filipino — 79.9%
Japanese — 18.3%
Asian Indian — 110.6%
Korean — 123.5%
Vietnamese — 150.8%
Hawaiian — 22.4%
Laotian — 212.5%
Cambodian — 818.8%
Thai — 101.6%
Hmong — 1631%
Guamanian — 59.3%
Samoan — 60.8%
Tongan — 182.8%
Other A/PI — 414.7%

1990
1980

0   500   1000   1500   2000

Thousands

Source: U.S Bureau of the Census, 1993, Asian/Pacific Islander Data Consortium.

Asia. The Vietnamese were the first wave of immigrants to arrive in large numbers. Initial government policy was to disperse them across the country to minimize their impact on local resources. However, secondary migration occurred almost immediately as Vietnamese moved to warmer climates and Asian American population centers in metropolitan areas of the West and the South. Thus, despite government resettlement policies, these new Asian populations became concentrated in the West, but to a lesser extent than the earlier Chinese, Japanese, and Filipino immigrants. Over one-third of the Vietnamese population (34.8 percent) resided in California in 1980. Nearly half (46 percent) of all Vietnamese and Laotians lived in the West as did over half (56 percent) of all Cambodians.

◆ THE 1990 CENSUS: A MORE DIVERSE AND DYNAMIC POPULATION

Data from the 1990 Census expand upon the findings and trends discerned from the 1980 Census. The 1990 data of Asian and Pacific Islander populations have received greater attention than in the 1980 Census

for two reasons. One is that the 1990 Census data were released much earlier and with greater levels of detail for all racial and ethnic groups than the 1980 Census. By 1991, the Bureau of the Census was able to release counts of all racial and ethnic groups by geographic area. In contrast, the subject report for Asian and Pacific Islander populations in the 1980 Census was not released until 1988. Second, the 1990 Census reinforced the 1980 Census trend of greater growth of minority groups. It captured dramatically the tremendous growth rate of all racial and ethnic minorities, especially newer groups, relative to a non-Hispanic white majority.

While growth rates were impressive for all groups, the Asian and Pacific Islander population had almost quadrupled in 20 years, growing from less than 1 percent to 3 percent of the American population. Between 1960 and 1990, this group had the sharpest rate of increase for all racial and ethnic groups. Between 1980 and 1990, the total American population grew at a lower rate (9.8 percent) than between 1960 and 1970 (13.3 percent). Both the white and black populations showed greater increases between 1960 and 1970 than between 1980 and 1990. For American Indians and

Table 19.6
Asian/Pacific Islander Population, Ranked by State, 1980 and 1990

Asian/Pacific Islander population of the fifty states and District of Columbia, percent of total state population, and percent change from 1980 to 1990 by state. States are ranked by Asian/Pacific Islander population in 1990.

State	1990 Population	1990 Percent of state total	1980 Population (a)	1980 Percent of state total	Percent change, 1980 to 1990
California	2,845,659	9.6	1,253,818	5.3	127.0
New York	693,760	3.9	310,526	1.8	123.4
Hawaii	685,236	61.8	583,252	60.5	17.5
Texas	319,459	1.9	120,313	0.8	165.5
Illinois	285,311	2.5	159,653	1.4	78.7
New Jersey	272,521	3.5	103,848	1.4	162.4
Washington	210,958	4.3	102,537	2.5	105.7
Virginia	159,053	2.6	66,209	1.2	140.2
Florida	154,302	1.2	56,740	0.6	171.9
Massachusetts	143,392	2.4	49,501	0.9	189.7
Maryland	139,719	2.9	64,278	1.5	117.4
Pennsylvania	137,438	1.2	64,379	0.5	113.5
Michigan	104,983	1.1	56,790	0.6	84.9
Ohio	91,179	0.8	47,820	0.4	90.7
Minnesota	77,886	1.8	26,536	0.7	193.5
Georgia	75,781	1.2	24,457	0.4	208.6
Oregon	69,269	2.4	34,775	1.3	99.2
Colorado	59,862	1.8	29,916	1.0	100.1
Arizona	55,206	1.5	22,032	0.8	150.6
Wisconsin	53,583	1.1	18,164	0.4	195.0
North Carolina	52,166	0.8	21,176	0.4	146.3
Connecticut	50,698	1.5	18,970	0.6	167.3
Missouri	41,277	0.8	23,096	0.5	78.7
Louisiana	41,099	1.0	23,779	0.6	72.8
Nevada	38,127	3.2	14,164	1.8	169.2
Indiana	37,617	0.7	20,557	0.4	83.0
Oklahoma	33,563	1.1	17,275	0.6	94.3
Utah	33,371	1.9	15,076	1.0	121.4
Tennessee	31,839	0.7	13,963	0.3	128.0
Kansas	31,750	1.3	15,078	0.6	110.6
Iowa	25,476	0.9	11,577	0.4	120.1
South Carolina	22,382	0.6	11,834	0.4	89.1
Alabama	21,797	0.5	9,734	0.2	123.9
Alaska	19,728	3.6	8.054	2.0	144.9
Rhode Island	18,325	1.8	5,303	0.6	245.6
Kentucky	17,812	0.5	9,970	0.3	78.7
New Mexico	14,124	0.9	6,825	0.5	106.9
Mississippi	13,016	0.5	7,412	0.3	75.6
Arkansas	12,530	0.5	6,740	0.3	85.9
Nebraska	12,422	0.8	7,002	0.4	77.4
District of Columbia	11,214	1.8	6,636	1.0	120.3
Idaho	9,365	0.9	5,948	0.6	57.4
New Hampshire	9,343	0.8	2,929	0.3	219.0
Delaware	9,057	1.4	4,112	0.7	120.3

Table 19.6
Asian/Pacific Islander Population, Ranked by State, 1980 and 1990 (Continued)

Asian/Pacific Islander population of the fifty states and District of Columbia, percent of total state population, and percent change from 1980 to 1990 by state. States are ranked by Asian/Pacific Islander population in 1990.

State	1990		1980		Percent change, 1980 to 1990
	Population	Percent of state total	Population (a)	Percent of state total	
West Virginia	7,459	0.4	5,194	0.3	43.6
Maine	6,683	0.5	2,947	0.3	126.8
Montana	4,259	0.5	2,503	0.3	70.2
North Dakota	3,462	0.5	1,979	0.3	74.9
Vermont	3,215	0.6	1,355	0.3	137.3
South Dakota	3,123	0.4	1,738	0.3	79.7
Wyoming	2,806	0.6	1,969	0.4	42.5

Notes:
(a) The 1980 numbers for Asian/Pacific Islanders shown in this table are not entirely comparable with the 1990 counts. The 1980 count of 3,500,439 Asian/Pacific Islanders based on 100 percent tabulations includes only the nine specific Asian/Pacific Islander groups listed separately in the 1980 race item on the Decennial Census survey. The 1980 total Asian/Pacific Islander population of 3,726,440 from sample tabulations is comparable to the 1990 count; these figures include groups not listed separately in the race item on the 1980 census form.

Source: Asian Week, Asians in America, 1990 Census, Classification by States, (San Francisco, CA: Asian Week, 1993), p. 4. Primary source: U.S. Census Bureau.

Asian and Pacific Islanders, the greatest percentage increase occurred between 1970 and 1980 (71.7 and 127.5 percent, respectively). While the growth rate for Asian and Pacific Islanders between 1980 and 1990 was less than the previous decade, it was a 107.8 percent increase, greater than any other group.

National Population Statistics and Identification of Specific Groups

The Asian and Pacific Islander population in the United States doubled between 1980 and 1990. It numbered 7.3 million in 1990 constituting almost 3 percent of the total population. The six largest groups—Chinese, Filipino, Japanese, Korean, Asian Indian, and Vietnamese—accounted for 84 percent of this diverse population, down from 90 percent in 1980. Among 6,908,638 Asians, Chinese were the largest group at 24 percent. Among the 365,024 Pacific Islanders, Hawaiians continued to be the majority at 58 percent. In 1990, detailed data were available for 17 Asian groups—Chinese, Filipino, Japanese, Asian Indian, Korean, Vietnamese, Laotian, Cambodian, Thai, Hmong, Pakistani, Indonesian, Malayan, Bangladeshi, Sri Lankan, Burmese, and Okinawan—and eight Pacific Islander groups—Hawaiian, Samoan, Guamanian, Tongan, Tahitian, Northern Mariana Islander, Palauan, and Fijian.

Specific Asian groups enumerated were Chinese, Filipino, Japanese, Korean, Vietnamese, Asian Indian,

Thai, and Laotian; Pacific Islanders were Hawaiian, Samoan, Guamanian, Tongan, and Fijian.

As in the previous decade, this dramatic growth rate was primarily due to immigration, which accounted for three-fourths of the increase.

Between 1981 and 1990, almost 2 million immigrants arrived in the United States from Asian countries. This is over one-quarter (27 percent) of the Asian and Pacific Islander population in 1990.

Distribution

According to the 1990 Census, the Asian and Pacific Islander population continued to be concentrated in the West with over half (56 percent) living in this region in 1990. The West Coast, the most racially diverse of all U.S. regions, also had the greatest concentration of American Indians (47.6 percent) and Hispanics (45.2 percent). By contrast, it was the area of least concentration for blacks and whites.

The Asian and Pacific Islander population increased by at least 40 percent in all states except Hawaii, where it is a numerical majority. But even in Hawaii, the growth rate was 17 percent. According to U.S. Immigration and Naturalization Service records, approximately 36 percent of the 2 million Asian immigrants who entered the United States between 1982 and 1989, intended to reside in California. Another 11 percent

Table 19.7
Pacific Islander Population by Metropolitan Areas

Metropolitan Area	Total population	Percent Asian Pacific Islander
Los Angeles—Anaheim—Riverside, CA CMSA	14,531,529	9.2%
San Francisco—Oakland—San Jose,CA CMSA	6,253,311	14.8%
New York—Northern New Jersey—Long Island, NY—NJ—CT CMSA	18,087,251	4.8%
Honolulu, HI MSA	836,231	49%
Chicago—Gary—Lake County, IL—IN—WI CMSA	8,065,633	3.2%
Washington, DC—MD—VA MSA	3,923,574	5%

Source: Asian/Pacific Islander Data Consortium, 1993.

intended to reside in New York, and about 5 percent in either Texas or Illinois.

These intentions were borne out in the 1990 Census. A majority of the Asian and Pacific Islander population lived in just three states—California, New York, and Hawaii—compared to nine states for the total population. In California, the Asian and Pacific Islander population was 10 percent of the total population. In Hawaii, they comprised over half the state's population. Seventy percent of all Asians and Pacific Islanders lived in just five states—California, New York, Hawaii, Texas, and Illinois. Of note was the continued population increase outside the West Coast. More than two out of five Asians and Pacific Islanders, 44 percent, lived in the Northeast, Midwest, and South.

The largest increase during the 1980s was in California, where a substantial percentage of this population's growth occurred. California's Asian and Pacific Islander population rose 127 percent from 1,254,00 in 1980 to 2,846,000 in 1990, a population larger than the total population of 22 states. New York and Hawaii had Asian and Pacific Islander populations of 500,00 or more. Thirteen states had an Asian and Pacific Islander population of 100,000 or more in 1990, compared to only seven in 1980.

Within groups, several shifts occurred. By 1990, there were more Asian Indians in California (160,000) than in New York (141,000). Vietnamese had replaced Chinese as the largest Asian and Pacific Islander group in Texas. Filipinos were the largest group in California followed by Chinese and Japanese.

Almost half (44 percent) of Pacific Islanders in the United States in 1990 resided in Hawaii. Fewer than one-third (30 percent) lived in California, and 4 percent were in Washington state. Two out of three Hawaiians lived in Hawaii. About half of all Samoans and Guamanians and four out of five Fijians lived in California. Due to their relationship with Mormon missionaries, one out of four Tongans lived in Utah.

At the county level, Asian and Pacific Islanders, along with American Indians/Alaskan Natives, blacks, and Hispanics comprised over 50 percent of the population in 186 of America's 3,248 counties. In 46 counties, these four populations comprised 75 percent of the total population. Starr County, Texas, had the highest proportion of these groups at 98 percent. Los Angeles County had the largest number of Hispanics, blacks, and Asian/Pacific Americans.

Refugee Resettlement

The initial dispersal policy and the subsequent clustering caused by internal migration created a mixed distribution pattern for Southeast Asian refugees between 1980 and 1990. By the middle of 1981, over one-third (35 percent) of all Asian American refugees lived in California and were clustered in five counties: Los Angeles, Orange, San Diego, San Francisco, and Santa Clara. Sizable numbers also resettled in Houston, the Washington, D.C., metropolitan area, Seattle, New Orleans, and Minneapolis.

In 1990, Vietnamese and Laotians continued to reside in great numbers in California and Texas. The Washington, D.C., and Seattle metropolitan areas also showed sizable numbers of refugees. Cambodians resided primarily in California and Massachusetts with smaller numbers in the Philadelphia and Seattle metropolitan areas. The Hmong population was the largest Asian and Pacific Islander population in Minnesota (16,000) in 1990 followed by Koreans and Vietnamese. In Texas, Vietnamese were the largest among Asian and Pacific Islander groups (70,000) followed by Chinese and Japanese.

Urbanization

While most of the U.S. population, 75 percent, lived in urban areas in 1980, Asian Pacific Americans continued to be the most urban of all racial and ethnic groups at 94 percent. This was a greater proportion than their 90 percent urban residence in 1980. Chinese were the most urban at 97 percent.

The concentration of Asian and Pacific Islanders in urban communities is also evident by the very few metropolitan areas in which they are found. In 1990, over half (57 percent) lived in one of six metropolitan areas: Los Angeles/Anaheim/Riverside; San Francisco/Oakland-San Jose; New York/northern New Jersey/Long Island; Honolulu; Chicago; and Washington, D.C.

According to the March 1991 Current Population Survey, 94 percent of Asian and Pacific Islanders lived in metropolitan areas in 1991, the same percent as in 1990. The 1990 Census indicated that the distribution of Asians also varied by metropolitan area.

Ranked by metropolitan areas, the Los Angeles/Long Beach metropolitan area had the largest number of Asians, almost 1 million. Chinese, Filipinos, and Koreans were the largest groups in this area. Ranked second, the New York City metropolitan area had over half a million Asian Americans, of whom fewer than half (44 percent) were Chinese. Japanese were the largest group (47 percent) in the third-ranked Honolulu metropolitan area.

Table 19.8
Asian/Pacific Islander Population by U.S. Metropolitan Area and Ethnicity

Asian/Pacific Islander population in numbers and percent of A/PI population of U.S. Metropolitan Statistical Areas (MSAs), ranked by metropolitan area, 1990.

Metropolitan area (a)	Total Asian	Percent of total Asian population										
		Chinese	Filipino	Japa-nese	Asian Indian	Korean	Viet-namese	Cam-bodian	Hmong	Laotian	Thai	Other Asian
Los Angeles–Long Beach, CA PMSA	925,561	26.47	23.73	14.02	4.74	15.71	6.76	3.01	0.04	0.40	2.05	3.06
New York, NY PMSA	553,443	44.60	8.88	4.77	19.20	13.49	1.63	0.49	0.00	0.08	0.85	6.00
Honolulu, HI MSA	413,349	15.31	29.04	47.21	0.21	5.48	1.27	0.03	0.00	0.40	0.26	0.81
San Francisco, CA PMSA	316,751	51.35	27.96	7.48	2.69	3.29	3.93	0.52	0.00	0.35	0.44	1.99
Oakland, CA PMSA	259,002	35.02	29.81	8.29	8.35	5.20	6.46	1.46	0.01	2.30	0.46	2.63
San Jose, CA PMSA	254,786	25.52	24.14	10.41	7.91	6.11	21.28	1.55	0.02	0.64	0.35	2.07
Anaheim–Santa Ana, CA PMSA	240,703	17.20	12.61	12.34	6.32	14.92	29.84	1.65	0.24	1.20	0.93	2.75
Chicago, IL PMSA	227,742	17.65	23.89	7.60	23.58	14.69	3.21	1.08	0.09	0.78	1.74	5.69
Washington, DC–MD–VA MSA	200,113	19.51	13.39	4.90	17.76	19.91	11.70	1.94	0.00	1.30	2.19	7.41
San Diego, CA MSA	184,596	10.66	51.98	9.68	2.73	3.64	11.44	2.27	0.86	3.81	0.60	2.34
Seattle, WA PMSA	128,656	21.37	21.69	17.75	4.60	12.68	9.81	4.51	0.35	3.32	1.03	2.91
Houston, TX PMSA	125,529	23.38	10.68	2.94	20.49	5.63	26.32	1.83	0.00	1.16	1.02	6.56
Sacramento, CA MSA	109,242	27.06	18.64	15.62	6.68	5.01	9.57	0.83	5.19	7.20	0.75	3.45
Philadelphia, PA–NJ PMSA	103,537	21.55	11.82	4.16	19.95	21.28	10.06	4.47	0.07	1.22	0.77	4.66
Boston, MA PMSA	94,362	46.79	4.23	6.92	13.04	7.42	9.96	5.26	0.00	0.93	1.00	4.44
Riverside–San Bernardino, CA PMSA	93,473	14.09	30.94	9.59	8.01	10.88	12.11	2.61	0.63	2.09	2.65	6.40
Bergen–Passaic, NJ PMSA	66,540	15.62	15.07	15.75	22.69	25.58	0.69	0.02	0.00	0.11	0.71	3.77
Dallas, TX PMSA	66,250	20.45	8.32	4.56	19.93	13.53	17.39	3.34	0.14	4.04	2.15	6.15
Minneapolis–St. Paul, MN–WI MSA	64,484	11.59	5.05	4.37	11.24	13.52	12.13	4.12	25.49	7.81	0.62	4.06
Nassau–Suffolk, NY PMSA	62,050	29.42	11.85	6.51	28.24	14.54	2.01	0.09	0.00	0.17	1.14	6.01
Stockton, CA MSA	58,374	9.46	28.39	6.45	5.82	1.12	11.92	17.73	7.93	7.26	0.23	3.71
Detroit, MI PMSA	57,141	16.77	17.06	10.58	28.52	12.24	3.07	0.48	2.63	1.54	1.00	6.10
Middlesex–Somerset–Hunterdon, NJ PMSA	56,669	26.26	14.36	2.18	40.54	9.03	2.34	0.04	0.04	0.09	0.38	4.74
Fresno, CA MSA	56,517	8.48	7.63	11.89	9.23	1.74	3.55	6.74	32.42	14.46	0.68	3.16

Notes:
(a) The U.S. Bureau of Census designates the following: PMSA=primary metropolitan statistical area; MSA=metropolitan statistical area. See Appendix for detailed definitions.

Source: Asian/Pacific Islander Data Consortium (San Francisco, CA: Asian and Pacific Islander Center for Census Information and Services, 1993). Primary source: U.S. Census Bureau, Summary Tape Files 1 and 3.

Table 19.9
Asian Indian Population by Significant U.S. Metropolitan Areas

Asian Indian population in numbers, percent of the total area population, and percent of Asian/Pacific Islander area population, ranked by metropolitan area (a), 1990.

Metropolitan area (b)	Total population	Total A/PI population	Asian Indian		
			Number	Percent of total	Percent of A/PI
New York, NY PMSA	8,546,846	553,443	106,270	1.2%	19%
Chicago, IL PMSA	6,069,974	227,742	53,702	0.9%	24%
Los Angeles–Long Beach, CA PMSA	8,863,164	925,561	43,829	0.5%	5%
Washington, DC–MD–VA MSA	3,923,574	200,113	35,533	0.9%	18%
Houston, TX PMSA	3,301,937	125,529	25,720	0.8%	20%
Middlesex–Somerset–Hunterdon, NJ PMSA	1,019,835	56,669	22,972	2.3%	41%
Oakland, CA PMSA	2,082,914	259,002	21,633	1.0%	8%
Philadelphia, PA–NJ PMSA	4,856,881	103,537	20,657	0.4%	20%
San Jose, CA PMSA	1,497,577	254,786	20,164	1.4%	8%
Nassau–Suffolk, NY PMSA	2,609,212	62,050	17,523	0.7%	28%
Detroit, MI PMSA	4,382,299	57,141	16,298	0.4%	29%
Newark, NJ PMSA	1,824,321	52,539	15,842	0.9%	30%
Anaheim–Santa Ana, CA PMSA	2,410,556	240,703	15,212	0.6%	6%
Bergen–Passaic, NJ PMSA	1,278,440	66,540	15,095	1.2%	23%
Dallas, TX PMSA	2,553,362	66,250	13,201	0.5%	20%
Boston, MA PMSA	2,870,669	94,362	12,301	0.4%	13%
Jersey City, NJ PMSA	553,099	36,564	11,552	2.1%	32%

Notes:
(a) Includes metropolitan areas with Asian Indian population greater than 11,000.
(b) The U.S. Census Bureau designates the following: PMSA=primary metropolitan statistical area; MSA=metropolitan statistical area. See *Appendix* for detailed definitions.

Source: *Asian/Pacific Islander Data Consortium (San Francisco, CA: Asian and Pacific Islander Center for Census Information and Services, 1993). Primary source: U.S. Census Bureau, Summary Tape Files 1 and 3.*

Table 19.10
Cambodian Population by Significant U.S. Metropolitan Areas

Cambodian population in numbers, percent of the total area population, and percent of Asian/Pacific Islander area population, ranked by metropolitan area (a), 1990.

Metropolitan area (b)	Total population	Total A/PI population	Cambodian		
			Number	Percent of total	Percent of A/PI
Los Angeles–Long Beach, CA PMSA	8,863,164	925,561	27,819	0.3%	3%
Stockton, CA MSA	480,628	58,374	10,350	2.2%	18%
Lowell, MA–NH PMSA	273,067	14,205	6,516	2.4%	46%
Seattle, WA PMSA	1,972,961	128,656	5,800	0.3%	5%
Boston, MA PMSA	2,870,669	94,362	4,967	0.2%	5%
Philadelphia, PA–NJ PMSA	4,856,881	103,537	4,633	0.1%	4%
San Diego, CA MSA	2,498,016	184,596	4,185	0.2%	2%

Notes:
(a) Includes metropolitan areas with Cambodian population greater than 4,000.
(b) The U.S. Census Bureau designates the following: PMSA=primary metropolitan statistical area; MSA=metropolitan statistical area. See Appendix for detailed definitions.

Source: *Asian/Pacific Islander Data Consortium (San Francisco, CA: Asian and Pacific Islander Center for Census Information and Services, 1993). Primary source: U.S. Census Bureau, Summary Tape Files 1 and 3.*

By subgroup, the greatest number of Chinese were found in the New York City area. Filipinos, Cambodians, and Koreans were most populous in the Los Angeles/Long Beach area, as were the Japanese in Honolulu and Asian Indians in New York. The largest numbers of Vietnamese were in the Anaheim/Santa Ana area. The Lao population was highest in Fresno, where they continued their suburban migration observed in the 1970 Census.

In 1991, almost half of the Asian and Pacific Islander population (49 percent) lived in suburban areas and less than half (45 percent) lived in central cities. By 1991 only 6 percent of the Asian and Pacific Islander population was in nonmetropolitan residences.

By comparison, two-thirds of non-Hispanic whites lived in suburbs, and one-fourth resided in nonmetropolitan areas in 1991.

◆ FUTURE GROWTH AND DISTRIBUTION

The Asian and Pacific Islander population is expected to be the fastest-growing population segment with a predicted annual growth rate around 4 percent in the 1990s.

Between 1990 and 1992 alone it increased from 7.3 million to 9 million. Ironically, just as the Asian and Pacific Islander population is becoming a visible and regionally dispersed population in the United States, its continued growth beyond this decade may be questionable. The future growth of the Asian and Pacific Islander population depends upon both traditional and nontraditional factors.

Traditional growth factors include continued immigration and natural increase. Growth projections assume steady immigration throughout the 1990s,

Table 19.11
Chinese Population by Significant U.S. Metropolitan Areas

Chinese population in numbers, percent of the total area population, and percent of Asian/Pacific Islander area population, ranked by metropolitan area (a), 1990.

Metropolitan area (b)	Total population	Total A/PI population	Chinese		
			Number	Percent of total	Percent of A/PI
New York, NY PMSA	8,546,846	553,443	246,817	2.9%	45%
Los Angeles–Long Beach, CA PMSA	8,863,164	925,561	245,033	2.8%	26%
San Francisco, CA PMSA	1,603,678	316,751	162,636	10.1%	51%
Oakland, CA PMSA	2,082,914	259,002	90,691	4.4%	35%
San Jose, CA PMSA	1,497,577	254,786	65,027	4.3%	26%
Honolulu, HI MSA	836,231	413,349	63,265	7.6%	15%
Boston, MA PMSA	2,870,669	94,362	44,155	1.5%	47%
Anaheim–Santa Ana, CA PMSA	2,410,556	240,703	41,403	1.7%	17%
Chicago, IL PMSA	6,069,974	227,742	40,189	0.7%	18%
Washington, DC–MD–VA MSA	3,923,574	200,113	39,034	1.9%	20%
Sacramento, CA MSA	1,481,102	109,242	29,558	2.0%	27%
Houston, TX PMSA	3,301,937	125,529	29,345	0.9%	23%
Seattle, WA PMSA	1,972,961	128,656	27,490	1.4%	21%
Philadelphia, PA–NJ PMSA	4,856,881	103,537	22,311	0.5%	22%
San Diego, CA MSA	2,498,016	184,596	19,686	0.8%	11%
Nassau–Suffolk, NY PMSA	2,609,212	62,050	18,257	0.7%	29%
Middlesex–Somerset–Hunterdon, NJ PMSA	1,019,835	56,669	14,883	1.5%	26%
Newark, NJ PMSA	1,824,321	52,539	14,020	0.8%	27%
Dallas, TX PMSA	2,553,362	66,250	13,546	0.5%	20%
Riverside–San Bernardino, CA PMSA	2,588,793	93,473	13,166	0.5%	14%
Bergen–Passaic, NJ PMSA	1,278,440	66,540	10,391	0.8%	16%

Notes:
(a) Includes metropolitan areas with Chinese population greater than 10,000.
(b) The U.S. Census Bureau designates the following: PMSA=primary metropolitan statistical area; MSA=metropolitan statistical area. See *Appendix* for detailed definitions.

Source: *Asian/Pacific Islander Data Consortium (San Francisco, CA: Asian and Pacific Islander Center for Census Information and Services, 1993). Primary source: U.S. Census Bureau, Summary Tape Files 1 and 3.*

resulting in healthy increases for the foreseeable future but not the phenomenal growth of the 1980s. Natural increase is also expected, since the overall Asian and Pacific Islander population is young, still in its child-bearing years. Females constitute a majority of the population. In 1991, the median age of the Asian and Pacific Islander population was 30.4 compared to a median age of 33.9 for whites.

While the black and Hispanic populations are among the youngest nationally, some Asian and Pacific Islander groups are even younger. In 1980, the median ages of blacks and Hispanics were 26.1 and 23.8, respectively. Vietnamese, Guamanian, and Samoan median ages were 22.6, 21.5, and 19.2; these are faster-growing populations

because of their youth and higher fertility. Additionally, Asian and Pacific Islander families continue to grow. In 1991, they comprised about 2 percent of all American families, and had a higher proportion of large families.

In 1991, almost three out of four (73 percent) Asian and Pacific Islander families had three or more persons. In comparison, about three out of five (59 percent) of all American families consisted of this many persons. By the middle of the twenty-first century, the Asian and Pacific Islander population is projected to almost quadruple to 11 percent of the total population. Continuous immigration and the endurance of racial and ethnic residences and businesses may be sufficient to ensure this growth.

Table 19.12
Filipino Population by Significant U.S. Metropolitan Areas

Filipino population in numbers, percent of the total area population, and percent of Asian/Pacific Islander area population, ranked by metropolitan area (a), 1990.

Metropolitan area (b)	Total population	Total A/PI population	Filipino		
			Number	Percent of total	Percent of A/PI
Los Angeles–Long Beach, CA PMSA	8,863,164	925,561	219,653	2.5%	24%
Honolulu, HI MSA	836,231	413,349	120,029	14.4%	29%
San Diego, CA MSA	2,498,016	184,596	95,945	3.8%	52%
San Francisco, CA PMSA	1,603,678	316,751	88,560	5.5%	28%
Oakland, CA PMSA	2,082,914	259,002	77,198	3.7%	30%
San Jose, CA PMSA	1,497,577	254,786	61,518	4.1%	24%
Chicago, IL PMSA	6,069,974	227,742	54,411	0.9%	24%
New York, NY PMSA	8,546,846	553,443	49,156	0.6%	9%
Anaheim–Santa Ana, CA PMSA	2,410,556	240,703	30,356	1.3%	13%
Vallejo–Fairfield–Napa, CA PMSA	451,186	43,289	29,760	6.6%	69%
Riverside–San Bernardino, CA PMSA	2,588,793	93,473	28,919	1.1%	31%
Seattle, WA PMSA	1,972,961	128,656	27,900	1.4%	22%
Washington, DC–MD–VA MSA	3,923,574	200,113	26,793	0.7%	13%
Sacramento, CA MSA	1,481,102	109,242	20,359	1.4%	19%
Norfolk–Virginia Beach–Newport News, VA MSA	1,396,107	34,004	19,858	1.4%	58%
Stockton, CA MSA	480,628	58,374	16,570	3.5%	28%
Houston, TX PMSA	3,301,937	125,529	13,404	0.4%	11%
Jersey City, NJ PMSA	553,099	36,564	13,222	2.4%	36%
Oxnard–Ventura, CA PMSA	669,016	32,699	12,690	1.9%	39%
Philadelphia, PA–NJ PMSA	4,856,881	103,537	12,233	0.3%	12%
Salinas–Seaside–Monterey, CA MSA	355,660	25,369	11,421	3.2%	45%
Newark, NJ PMSA	1,824,321	52,539	10,907	0.6%	21%
Bergen–Passaic, NJ PMSA	1,278,440	66,540	10,027	0.8%	15%

Notes:
(a) Includes metropolitan areas with Filipino population greater than 10,000.
(b) The U.S. Census Bureau designates the following: PMSA=primary metropolitan statistical area; MSA=metropolitan statistical area. See *Appendix* for detailed definitions.

Source: *Asian/Pacific Islander Data Consortium (San Francisco, CA: Asian and Pacific Islander Center for Census Information and Services, 1993). Primary source: U.S. Census Bureau, Summary Tape Files 1 and 3.*

Nevertheless, there are two nontraditional factors to be considered. One is the increasingly interracial composition of this population.

While interracial unions accounted for only 2 percent of 53 million marriages in 1991, they varied by racial and ethnic group. Seven percent of marriages by blacks were to a non-black spouse. For married Hispanics and Asian and Pacific Islanders, one-quarter had spouses outside their race. Interracial unions in the Asian and Pacific Islander population existed even within a number of first-generation immigrants, notably brides of U.S. servicemen since World War II. Subsequent generations continued this pattern. In 1970, one-third of all married Japanese women and almost one-fourth of Filipino women were married to persons outside their ethnic group. This was more striking for younger women ages 16 to 24, with almost half of both Japanese and Filipino women married to spouses outside of their ethnic group. In 1980, for native-born Asian Americans, interracial unions continued at a sizeable rate. In California, 23 percent of Japanese

American women had married non-Japanese husbands and over half (58 percent) of Filipino American wives had non- Filipino husbands.

While interracial unions nationally have increased from 1 to 2 percent of all marriages over the last two decades, interracial births have increased from 1 to 3 percent of all births. According to the National Center for Health Statistics, the total births of mixed parentage to Asian and Pacific Islanders and whites almost doubled between 1978 and 1989. Among births to Japanese and white parents, the increase was so great that there were 39 percent more Japanese-white mixed births than births to parents who were both Japanese. This trend is also found among American Indians who have high interracial marital and birth rates.

A related nontraditional factor is potential changes in classification of this population. Although they are a small proportion of the total group population, there is discussion about moving Pacific Islanders out of this category. In 1993, Hawaiians, who are an indigenous people, requested federal designation as Native

Table 19.13
Hmong Population by Significant U.S. Metropolitan Areas

Hmong population in numbers, percent of the total area population, and percent of Asian/Pacific Islander area population, ranked by metropolitan area (a), 1990.

Metropolitan area (b)	Total population	Total A/PI population	Hmong		
			Number	Percent of total	Percent of A/PI
Fresno, CA MSA	667,490	56,517	18,321	2.7%	32%
Minneapolis–St. Paul, MN–WI MSA	2,464,124	64,484	16,435	0.7%	25%
Merced, CA MSA	178,403	14,759	6,458	3.6%	44%
Sacramento, CA MSA	1,481,102	109,242	5,673	0.4%	5%
Stockton, CA MSA	480,628	58,374	4,628	1.6%	8%
Milwaukee, WI PMSA	1,432,149	18,445	3,404	0.2%	18%
Yuba City, CA MSA	122,643	10,705	2,299	1.9%	21%
Appleton–Oshkosh–Neenah, WI MSA	315,121	3,772	2,157	0.7%	57%
Wausau, WI MSA	115,400	2,489	1,968	1.7%	79%
La Crosse, WI MSA	97,904	2,638	1,933	2.0%	73%
Visalia–Tulare–Porterville, CA MSA	311,921	13,013	1,874	0.6%	14%
Eau Claire, WI MSA	137,543	2,376	1,601	1.2%	67%
San Diego, CA MSA	2,498,016	184,596	1,585	0.1%	1%
Detroit, MI PMSA	4,382,299	57,141	1,503	0.0%	3%
Green Bay, WI MSA	194,594	2,490	1,410	0.7%	57%
Chico, CA MSA	182,120	4,927	1,294	0.7%	26%
Sheboygan, WI MSA	103,877	2,039	1,255	1.2%	62%

Notes:
(a) Includes metropolitan areas with Hmong population greater than 1,000.
(b) The U.S. Census Bureau designates the following: PMSA=primary metropolitan statistical area; MSA=metropolitan statistical area. See *Appendix* for detailed definitions.

Source: Asian/Pacific Islander Data Consortium (San Francisco, CA: Asian and Pacific Islander Center for Census Information and Services, 1993). Primary source: U.S. Census Bureau, Summary Tape Files 1 and 3.

Table 19.14
Japanese Population by Significant U.S. Metropolitan Areas

Japanese population in numbers, percent of the total area population, and percent of Asian/Pacific Islander area population, ranked by metropolitan area (a), 1990.

Metropolitan area (b)	Total population	Total A/PI population	Japanese		
			Number	Percent of total	Percent of A/PI
Honolulu, HI MSA	836,231	413,349	195,149	23.3%	47%
Los Angeles–Long Beach, CA PMSA	8,863,164	925,561	129,736	1.5%	14%
Anaheim–Santa Ana, CA PMSA	2,410,556	240,703	29,704	1.2%	12%
San Jose, CA PMSA	1,497,577	254,786	26,516	1.8%	10%
New York, NY PMSA	8,546,846	553,443	26,422	0.3%	5%
San Francisco, CA PMSA	1,603,678	316,751	23,682	1.5%	7%
Seattle, WA PMSA	1,972,961	128,656	22,835	1.2%	18%
Oakland, CA PMSA	2,082,914	259,002	21,477	1.0%	8%
San Diego, CA MSA	2,498,016	184,596	17,869	0.7%	16%
Chicago, IL PMSA	6,069,974	227,742	17,310	0.3%	8%
Sacramento, CA MSA	1,481,102	109,242	17,067	1.2%	16%
Bergen–Passaic, NJ PMSA	1,278,440	66,540	10,482	0.8%	16%

Notes:
(a) Includes metropolitan areas with Japanese population greater than 10,000.
(b) The U.S. Census Bureau designates the following: PMSA=primary metropolitan statistical area; MSA=metropolitan statistical area. See *Appendix* for detailed definitions.

Source: *Asian/Pacific Islander Data Consortium (San Francisco, CA: Asian and Pacific Islander Center for Census Information and Services, 1993). Primary source: U.S. Census Bureau, Summary Tape Files 1 and 3.*

Table 19.15
Korean Population by Significant U.S. Metropolitan Areas

Korean population in numbers, percent of the total area population, and percent of Asian/Pacific Islander area population, ranked by metropolitan area (a), 1990.

Metropolitan area (b)	Total population	Total A/PI population	Korean		
			Number	Percent of total	Percent of A/PI
Los Angeles–Long Beach, CA PMSA	8,863,164	925,561	145,431	1.6%	16%
New York, NY PMSA	8,546,846	553,443	74,632	0.9%	13%
Washington, DC–MD–VA MSA	3,923,574	200,113	39,850	1.0%	20%
Anaheim–Santa Ana, CA PMSA	2,410,556	240,703	35,919	1.5%	15%
Chicago, IL PMSA	6,069,974	227,742	33,465	0.6%	15%
Honolulu, HI MSA	836,231	413,349	22,646	2.7%	5%
Philadelphia, PA–NJ PMSA	4,856,881	103,537	22,028	0.5%	21%
Bergen–Passaic, NJ PMSA	1,278,440	66,540	17,018	1.3%	26%
Seattle, WA PMSA	1,972,961	128,656	16,311	0.8%	13%
San Jose, CA PMSA	1,497,577	254,786	15,565	1.0%	6%
Oakland, CA PMSA	2,082,914	259,002	13,478	0.7%	5%
Baltimore, MD MSA	2,382,172	42,017	12,967	0.5%	31%
San Francisco, CA PMSA	1,603,678	316,751	10,416	0.7%	3%
Riverside–San Bernardino, CA PMSA	2,588,793	93,473	10,166	0.4%	11%
Atlanta, GA MSA	2,833,511	50,872	10,120	0.4%	20%

Notes:
(a) Includes metropolitan areas with Korean population greater than 10,000.
(b) The U.S. Census Bureau designates the following: PMSA=primary metropolitan statistical area; MSA=metropolitan statistical area. See *Appendix* for detailed definitions.

Source: *Asian/Pacific Islander Data Consortium (San Francisco, CA: Asian and Pacific Islander Center for Census Information and Services, 1993). Primary source: U.S. Census Bureau, Summary Tape Files 1 and 3.*

Americans along with American Indians and Alaskan Natives. While such a change is numerically and proportionally small, it sets a precedent that specific groups may choose to be included or excluded from major racial and ethnic categories.

In summary, the multiracial trend suggests a new group whose interracial composition is masked by an Asian and Pacific Islander population label which may or may not be sufficient to describe it. The future addition or subtraction of Asian and Pacific Islanders of mixed origins will affect the increase or decrease of this population. Additionally, the continued inclusion of Hawaiians as Pacific Islanders is questionable; their deletion would affect the continued growth count of the Asian and Pacific Islander population. Finally, the continued dispersal of Asians and Pacific Islanders into suburban communities may erode the need for a distinct racial and ethnic identity and a pan-Asian category.

It remains to be seen whether members of this highly heterogeneous, interracial, increasingly dispersed, and economically mobile population, particularly among certain groups, will continue to classify themselves as Asians and Pacific Islanders.

References

Barringer, H., R. Gardner, and M. Levin. *Asians and Pacific Islanders in the United States*. New York: Russell Sage Foundation, 1993.

Esperitu, Yan Le. *Asian American Pan Ethnicity: Bridging Institutions and Identities*. Philadelphia: Temple University Press, 1992.

Gall, S., and T. Gall, eds. *Statistical Record of Asian Americans*. Detroit: Gale Research, Inc., 1993.

Knoll, T. *Becoming Americans: Asian Sojourners, Immigrants and Refugees in the Western United States*. Portland Coast to Coast Books, 1982.

Table 19.16
Laotian Population by Significant U.S. Metropolitan Areas

Laotian population in numbers, percent of the total area population, and percent of Asian/Pacific Islander area population, ranked by metropolitan area (a), 1990.

Metropolitan area (b)	Total population	Total A/PI population	Laotian Number	Laotian Percent of total	Laotian Percent of A/PI
Fresno, CA MSA	667,490	56,517	8,174	1.2%	14%
Sacramento, CA MSA	1,481,102	109,242	7,861	0.5%	7%
San Diego, CA MSA	2,498,016	184,596	7,025	0.3%	4%
Oakland, CA PMSA	2,082,914	259,002	5,964	0.3%	2%
Minneapolis–St. Paul, MN–WI MSA	2,464,124	64,484	5,039	0.2%	8%
Seattle, WA PMSA	1,972,961	128,656	4,270	0.2%	3%
Stockton, CA MSA	480,628	58,374	4,236	0.9%	7%
Los Angeles–Long Beach, CA PMSA	8,863,164	925,561	3,742	<0.1%	<1%
Visalia–Tulare–Porterville, CA MSA	311,921	13,013	3,033	1.7%	23%
Fort Worth–Arlington, TX PMSA	1,332,053	29,040	2,971	0.2%	10%
Portland, OR PMSA	1,239,842	43,768	2,901	0.2%	7%
Atlanta, GA MSA	2,833,511	50,872	2,898	0.1%	6%
Anaheim–Santa Ana, CA PMSA	2,410,556	240,703	2,893	0.1%	1%
Dallas, TX PMSA	2,553,362	66,250	2,678	0.1%	4%
Washington, DC–MD–VA MSA	3,923,574	200,113	2,603	0.1%	1%
Modesto, CA MSA	370,522	18,072	2,415	0.7%	13%
Nashville, TN MSA	985,026	9,843	2,337	0.2%	24%
Merced, CA MSA	178,403	14,759	2,052	1.2%	14%
Milwaukee, WI PMSA	1,432,149	18,445	2,033	0.1%	11%

Notes:
(a) Includes metropolitan areas with Laotian population greater than 2,000.
(b) The U.S. Census Bureau designates the following: PMSA=primary metropolitan statistical area; MSA=metropolitan statistical area. See *Appendix* for detailed definitions.

Source: Asian/Pacific Islander Data Consortium (San Francisco, CA: Asian and Pacific Islander Center for Census Information and Services, 1993). Primary source: U.S. Census Bureau, Summary Tape Files 1 and 3.

Table 19.17
Thai Population by Significant U.S. Metropolitan Areas

Thai population in numbers, percent of the total area population, and percent of Asian/Pacific Islander area population, ranked by metropolitan area (a), 1990.

Metropolitan area (b)	Total population	Total A/PI population	Thai Number	Thai Percent of total	Thai Percent of A/PI
Los Angeles–Long Beach, CA PMSA	8,863,164	925,561	19,016	0.2%	2.1%
New York, NY PMSA	8,546,846	553,443	4,684	0.1%	0.8%
Washington, DC–MD–VA MSA	3,923,574	200,113	4,381	0.1%	2.2%
Chicago, IL PMSA	6,069,974	227,742	3,955	0.1%	1.7%
Riverside–San Bernardino, CA PMSA	2,588,793	93,473	2,474	0.1%	2.6%
Anaheim–Santa Ana, CA PMSA	2,410,556	240,703	2,227	0.1%	0.9%
Las Vegas, NV MSA	741,459	24,296	1,533	0.2%	6.3%
Dallas, TX PMSA	2,553,362	66,250	1,424	0.1%	2.1%
San Francisco, CA PMSA	1,603,678	316,751	1,394	0.1%	0.4%
Seattle, WA PMSA	1,972,961	128,656	1,323	0.1%	1.0%
Houston, TX PMSA	3,301,937	125,529	1,281	0.0%	1.0%
Oakland, CA PMSA	2,082,914	259,002	1,183	0.1%	0.5%
San Diego, CA MSA	2,498,016	184,596	1,109	<0.1%	0.6%
Honolulu, HI MSA	836,231	413,349	1,065	0.1%	0.3%

Notes:
(a) Includes metropolitan areas with Thai population greater than 1,000.
(b) The U.S. Census Bureau designates the following: PMSA=primary metropolitan statistical area; MSA=metropolitan statistical area. See *Appendix* for detailed definitions.

Source: *Asian/Pacific Islander Data Consortium (San Francisco, CA: Asian and Pacific Islander Center for Census Information and Services, 1993). Primary source: U.S. Census Bureau, Summary Tape Files 1 and 3.*

Table 19.18
Vietnamese Population by Significant U.S. Metropolitan Areas

Vietnamese population in numbers, percent of the total area population, and percent of Asian/Pacific Islander area population, ranked by metropolitan area (a), 1990.

Metropolitan area (b)	Total population	Total A/PI population	Vietnamese Number	Vietnamese Percent of total	Vietnamese Percent of A/PI
Anaheim–Santa Ana, CA PMSA	2,410,556	240,703	71,822	3.0%	30%
Los Angeles–Long Beach, CA PMSA	8,863,164	925,561	62,594	0.7%	7%
San Jose, CA PMSA	1,497,577	254,786	54,212	3.6%	21%
Houston, TX PMSA	3,301,937	125,529	33,035	1.0%	26%
Washington, DC–MD–VA MSA	3,923,574	200,113	23,408	0.6%	12%
San Diego, CA MSA	2,498,016	184,596	21,118	0.9%	11%
Oakland, CA PMSA	2,082,914	259,002	16,732	0.8%	6%
Seattle, WA PMSA	1,972,961	128,656	12,617	0.6%	18%
San Francisco, CA PMSA	1,603,678	316,751	12,451	0.8%	4%
Dallas, TX PMSA	2,553,362	66,250	11,522	0.5%	17%
New Orleans, LA MSA	1,238,816	21,112	11,419	0.9%	54%
Riverside–San Bernardino, CA PMSA	2,588,793	93,473	11,315	0.4%	12%
Sacramento, CA MSA	1,481,102	109,242	10,454	0.7%	15%
Philadelphia, PA–NJ PMSA	4,856,881	103,537	10,418	0.2%	10%

Notes:
(a) Includes metropolitan areas with Asian Indian population greater than 10,000.
(b) The U.S. Census Bureau designates the following: PMSA=primary metropolitan statistical area; MSA=metropolitan statistical area. See *Appendix* for detailed definitions.

Source: *Asian/Pacific Islander Data Consortium (San Francisco, CA: Asian and Pacific Islander Center for Census Information and Services, 1993). Primary source: U.S. Census Bureau, Summary Tape Files 1 and 3.*

Table 19.19
Asian and Pacific Islander Population Projections in Percent, 1990 to 2050

Year	Asian and Pacific Islander in millions	Asian and Pacific Islander as a percent of total population
1990	7.3	2.8%
1995	9.6	3.7%
2000	11.9	4.5%
2010	14.2	5.9%
2030	16.3	8.4%
2050	18.4	10.1%

Source: Population Projectsion of the United States by Age, Sex, Race, and Hispanic Origin: 1992–2050.

Table 19.20
Asian Pacific Islander Population by Age

Age	Total Population in percent	Asian and Pacific Islander in percent
Under 5 years	7.8%	8.6%
5 to 9 years	7.4%	8.6%
10 to 14 years	7.1%	8.1%
15 to 19 years	6.8%	8.3%
20 to 24 years	7.2%	7.2%
25 to 29 years	8.3%	8.4%
30 to 34 years	8.9%	8.8%
35 to 44 years	15.5%	17.0%
45 to 54 years	10.3%	10.8$
55 to 64 years	8.6%	6.8%
65 to 74 years	7.3%	5.3%
75 years and over	4.8%	2.0%
16 years and over	76.4%	73.3%
18 years and over	73.8%	69.6%
21 years and over	69.6%	65.1%
65 years and over	12.1%	7.3%
Median age (years)	33.0	30.4

Table 19.21
Asian Pacific Islander Families by Size, 1991.

Size of family	Total population in percent	Asian and Pacific Islander in percent
Two persons	41.6%	25.5%
Three persons	23.1	21.4
Four persons	21.3	27.8
Five persons	9.0	12.9
Six persons	3.1	6.6
Seven or more persons	1.9	5.7

Source: The Asian and Pacific Islander Population in the United States: March 1991 and 1990.

Lott, J. "The Continuing Significance of Race and Ethnicity: A Reassessment of Statistical Policy Directive 15." Written testimony. House Subcommittee on Census, Statistics and Postal Personnel, U.S. Congress. Washington, D.C., April 14, 1993.

Lyman, Stanford M. *The Asian in North America.* Santa Barbara: American Bibliographic Center-Clio Press, 1977.

O'Hare, W. and J. Felt. *Asian Americans: America's Fastest Growing Minority Group.* Population Reference Bureau, Washington, D.C., February 1991.

O'Hare, W. "America's Minorities—The Demographics of Diversity." *Population Bulletin* 47, no. 4, December 1992.

U.S. Bureau of the Census. *Japanese, Chinese and Filipinos in the United States.* 1970 Census of Population Subject Reports, PC(2)-1G. Washington, D.C., July 1973.

———. *Asian and Pacific Islander Populations in the United States: 1980.* PC80-2-1E, Washington, D.C., January 1988.

———. *We, the Asian and Pacific Islander Americans.* Washington, D.C., September 1988.

———. *200 Years of U.S. Census Taking.* Washington, D.C., November 1989.

———. *Studies in American Fertility.* P-23, No. 176. Washington, D.C., October 1991.

———. *The Asian and Pacific Islander Population in the United States: March 1991 and 1990.* P20-459, Washington, D.C., August 1992.

———. *General Population Characteristics, United States: 1990 Census of Population.* 1990 CP-1-1. Washington, D.C., November 1992.

———. *Historical Statistics of the United States: Colonial Times to 1970.* White Plains, New York: Kraus International Publications, 1989.

U. S. Department of Health, Education and Welfare. Office of the Assistant Secretary for Planning and Evaluation. *A Study of Selected Socio-Economic Characteristics of Ethnic Minorities Based on the 1970 Census, Volume II: Asian Americans.* Washington, D.C., July 1974

—Juanita Tamayo Lott

Racial Diversity and Interracial Relations

◆ Racial Diversity in Asia, and the Americas ◆ American Citizenship
◆ Racial Diversity in Twentieth-Century United States ◆ Interracial Relations
◆ Multiracial Cooperation and Coalitions ◆ Interracial Antagonism, Conflict, and Violence
◆ Multiracial Children

◆ RACIAL DIVERSITY IN ASIA AND THE AMERICAS

Racial diversity and interracial relations, both cooperative and competitive, are not unique to the United States but exist in many parts of the world. What is unique to this nation is that the majority of issues involving race have been treated biracially, in terms of black and white, with whites representing the majority of the population and blacks maintaining a powerful minority status. Other populations have been relegated to a level of secondary importance. Federal statistical policy designates blacks as the principal minority. Other minority groups are defined not so much by race, per se, but by nonracial factors. In the case of peoples indigenous to the Americas, it is by tribal affiliation; for Hispanics, and Asian Americans, national origin is the defining feature.

The increasing numbers of these latter minority groups and heightened awareness of their historical and current disparities suggest that this nation can no longer be defined as a biracial society. The United States is a truly multiracial and multicultural society. In the twenty-first century one of every three Americans will be either American Indian/Alaskan Native, African American, Hispanic American, or Asian/Pacific American. Already, these groups have become more visible in terms of numbers, political representation, and geographical distribution.

Asia and the Pacific

An understanding of the racial dynamics of Asian/Pacific Americans begins with a discussion of the diversity of the Asian continent, the islands of the Pacific and their peoples.

Asia is the largest continent in the world both in terms of land mass and population. It covers almost one-third of the world's land area and contains about three-fifths of the global population. Its diverse terrain ranges from the snow-covered, frozen lands of Mongolia to the tropical islands of Southeast Asia. Its peoples are equally diverse, being multiethnic, multiracial, and multilingual. Asians residing at Middle Eastern and African borders, for example, possess features that are comparable to their neighbors. Similarly, those in Central Asia have features akin to Europeans. Within Asian countries, there are various ethnic, linguistic, and religious minority groups.

The racial diversity of Asia and the Pacific has further been expanded with the Asian diaspora. This is a term used to describe the migration and resettlement of groups of Asian peoples. For centuries, groups of Asians migrated to other lands. The Chinese and Indians, as entrepreneurs, settled in multiracial Southeast Asian countries such as Singapore, Malaysia, Indonesia, and the Philippines. They provided a critical business component in many of these countries. Beyond the continent, Asians dispersed as laborers across the Pacific, first to the Americas—including Peru, Cuba, Mexico, Canada, Hawaii, and California—and subsequently to Europe and Africa.

The islands of the Pacific were interim ports between Asia and the Americas, Europe, and Africa. Pacific Islanders were exposed to traders, sailors, colonizers, and missionaries from different cultures. Given this history, racial diversity was relatively common for

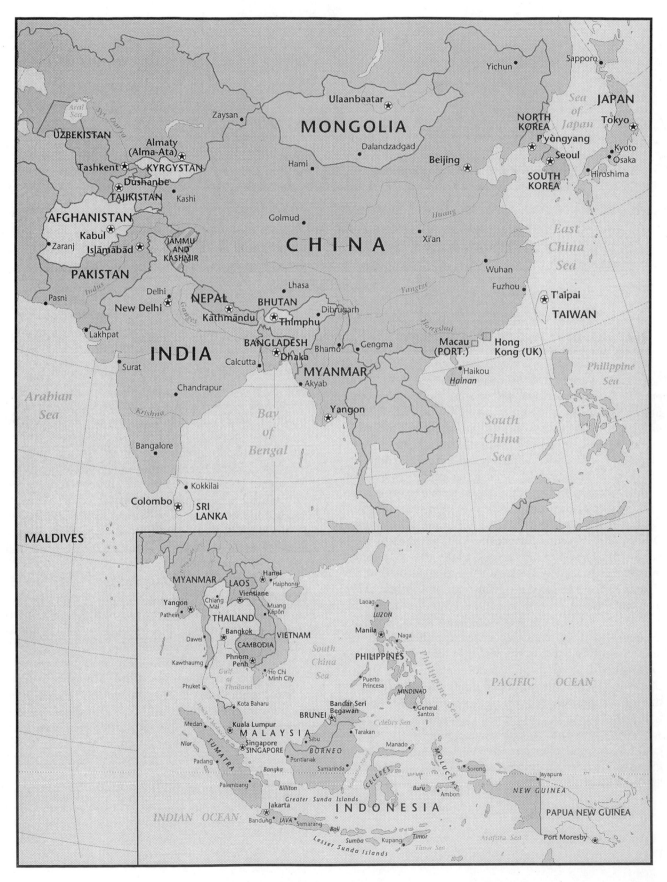

Map of Asia.

the peoples of Asia and the Pacific prior to their residence in the United States.

The Americas

Like Asia, the Americas were also populated by different racial and ethnic groups. Long before the founding of the United States, racial diversity existed in North America. Different indigenous groups included peoples such as the Aleuts, Eskimos, Hawaiians, and the ancestors of American Indians. They were joined in the post-Columbian period by peoples of African and Spanish ancestry who explored and settled in the Americas. The intermingling of indigenous peoples and colonizers produced a uniquely New World mixture of Indian, European, African, and, with the Manila Galleon Trade, Asian ancestries. Other European colonizers such as the French, Dutch, and British also added to this mixture, but to a lesser degree than the Spaniards.

The United States

In contrast to the multiracial and multiethnic societies of Asia and Spanish America, the early settlers of the United States were a homogeneous group, mainly immigrants from western European nations. According to the first census, taken in 1790, about four out of five whites living in the United States were of English or Welsh origin. The remainder, in descending order, consisted of Scottish, German, Dutch, Irish, and French immigrants.

♦ AMERICAN CITIZENSHIP

At the time of the first census, racial categorization was used to restrict and exclude selected racial populations from full participation in American society as citizens. The first census, taken in 1790, classified people by their race only and whether they were free or slave. Specifically, the 1790 Census enumerated: free white males, free white females, other free persons (including some American Indians and free blacks), and slaves. The first census distinguished Indians for purposes of taxation but not representation. People of African ancestry were classified as slaves and were counted for apportionment purposes as three-fifths of a white person. Blacks at this time comprised one-fifth of the American population.

In subsequent censuses, race and color gained more prominence. In particular, the black population was differentiated in greater detail by color, blood quantum, and free status.

Furthermore, attention was given to nationality- and ethnicity-related items which were used to inform immigration policies in the first half of the twentieth

Table 20.1
Diverse Early American Population,
1790, 1860, and 1890
U.S. Census Bureau racial categories selected censuses.

1790	1860	1890
White	White	White
	Colored	Black
		Mulatto
		Quadroon
		Indian
		Chinese
		Japanese

Source: Tamayo Lott Associates, Silver Spring, MD 20904, 1994.

century. These policies restricted, at various times, immigrants from southern Europe, Asia, Mexico, and Latin America.

♦ RACIAL DIVERSITY IN TWENTIETH-CENTURY UNITED STATES

The cumulative effect of restricted immigration and the abolition of slavery was an increase in the white population, primarily through high birth rates. Throughout the nineteenth century and the first half of the twentieth century, the term "American" became synonymous with "white." Regardless of national origin or nativity, persons of European ancestry were

Table 20.2
Diverse American Population, 1890 to 1970
U.S. Census Bureau racial categories, selected censuses 1890 to 1970.

1890	1930	1960	1970
White	White	White	White
Negro	Negro	Negro	Negro or Black
Indian	Indian	American Indian	American Indian
		Aleut	Aleut
		Eskimo	Eskimo
Chinese	Chinese	Chinese	Chinese
Japanese	Japanese	Japanese	Japanese
	Filipino	Filipino	Filipino
	Korean		Korean
			Hawaiian
			Part Hawaiian
	Mexican		
	Hindu		
	Other	(etc)	Other

Source: Tamayo Lott Associates, Silver Spring, MD 20904, 1994.

Table 20.3
Diverse American Population, 1860 to 1990

U.S. population distribution by race/ethnicity, selected censuses, in percent.

Distribution in Percent	1860	1930	1960	1990
White	85.6	88.7	88.6	80.3
Black/Negro	14.1	9.7	10.5	12.1
Hispanic	—	1.2	—	9.0
Indian/Alaskan Native	—	—	0.3	0.8
Asian/Pacific	—	0.3	0.4	2.9
Other	0.2	0.1	0.1	3.9

Source: Tamayo Lott Associates, Silver Spring, MD 20904, 1994.

combined into a generic and homogenous category commonly referred to as "the melting pot." As late as 1960, whites comprised close to 90 percent of the United States population. This rise was accompanied by decreases or stagnation in other racial and ethnic groups. The black population, for example, which had been one-fifth of the population in 1790 had decreased to one-tenth by 1960.

After 1960 however, this pattern was reversed. With the passage and full implementation of the 1965 immigration amendments, accompanied by higher minority fertility rates, the white proportion of the population began to decline as that of racial and ethnic minority groups increased.

1900 to 1960

Racial and ethnic minorities comprised a stable but small proportion of the American population during the first half of the twentieth century. They increased from 10 to 20 million during this period. Proportionally, blacks accounted for about 11 percent of the American population while whites maintained the remaining 89 percent. Other racial and ethnic minority groups in the United States did not comprise even 1 percent of the total population. Even in 1970, whites contributed to 87

Table 20.4
Diverse American Population, 1970 to 1990

U.S. population distribution by race/ethnicity, selected censuses, in percent.

Distribution in Percent	1970	1980	1990
White	87.0	83.1	80.3
Black/Negro	11.1	11.7	12.1
Hispanic	4.5	6.4	9.0
Indian/Alaskan Native	0.4	0.6	0.8
Asian/Pacific	1.0	1.5	2.9
Other	0.4	3.0	3.9

Source: Tamayo Lott Associates, Silver Spring, MD 20904, 1994.

percent of the population and blacks continued to be the only sizable minority at 11 percent. Together, blacks and whites composed 98 percent of the total American population. Because the Immigration and Naturalization Act was implemented in 1965, Asians and Pacific Islanders had increased to represent 1 percent of the population in 1970. The remaining 1 percent was divided between American Indians, Alaskan Natives, and others.

Minority Population Growth from 1960 to 1990

Racial and ethnic minorities in the United States experienced a tremendous growth from 1960 to 1990. Their numbers tripled from 20 million in 1960 to 60 million in 1990. This increase was due to both the relaxation of immigration restrictions and higher fertility rates in minority groups than the white population.

Native-born racial and ethnic minorities experiencing the greatest population growth during this period included African Americans, American Indians, Mexican Americans, Puerto Ricans, and Hawaiians. Also characteristic of these groups were younger median ages than the white population.

For racial and ethnic minorities with larger proportions of foreign-born than native-born members, such as Asian Americans and Hispanics population growth was due primarily to an increase in immigration. However, fertility rates and prime childbearing ages also contributed to growth. Within the Asian and Hispanic communities, immigrant women generally had a greater number of children than their American-born counterparts.

Between 1970 and 1990, racial and ethnic minorities increased from about one-eighth to one-fourth of the population. In 1990 blacks comprised 12 percent of the population, Hispanics 9 percent, American Indians/Alaskan Natives about 1 percent, and Asian/Pacific Americans about 3 percent. Census Bureau projections indicate that this proportion will likely increase to

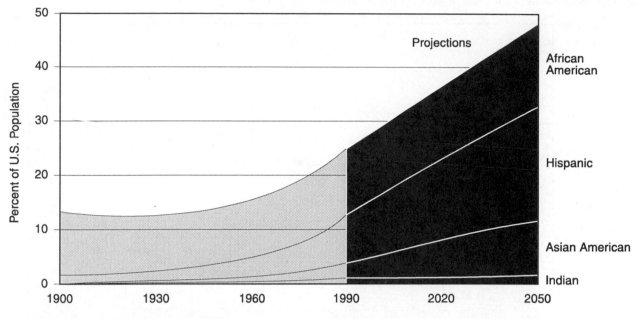

Minority Population Growth, 1960 to 1990

Source: Population Bulletin, December 1992.

almost half by the year 2050. In less than sixty years, racial/ethnic minorities will comprise about 47 percent of the American population while non-Hispanic whites will comprise 53 percent. The American Indian/Alaskan Native and black populations are projected to double between 1992 and 2050. The Hispanic population is projected to triple and the Asian/Pacific population will likely quadruple over this same period while growth in the non-Hispanic white population will be 5 percent.

Regional and Local Distribution by Race

Racial and ethnic minorities now constitute over half the population in many of the nation's largest cities. Among the ten largest cities in the United States,

Table 20.5
Population Projections by Race and Hispanic Origin, in Percent, 1990 to 2050

Population by race/ethnicity and Hispanic origin in 1990, in percent, and five-year projections in percent, for 1995 to 2050.

In percent	Total	Race				Hispanic origin	Not of Hispanic origin, by race			
		Asian (b)	White	Black	American Indian (a)	(c)	Asian (b)	White	Black	American Indian (a)
1990	100.0	3.0	83.9	12.3	0.8	9.0	2.8	75.7	11.8	0.7
Projections										
1995	100.0	3.7	82.8	12.6	0.9	10.1	3.5	73.6	12.1	0.7
2000	100.0	4.5	81.7	12.9	0.9	11.1	4.2	71.6	12.3	0.8
2005	100.0	5.2	80.7	13.2	0.9	12.2	4.9	69.6	12.6	0.8
2010	100.0	5.9	79.6	13.6	0.9	13.2	5.5	67.6	12.8	0.8
2020	100.0	7.2	77.7	14.2	1.0	15.2	6.8	63.9	13.3	0.9
2030	100.0	8.4	75.8	14.8	1.0	17.2	7.9	60.2	13.8	0.9
2040	100.0	9.6	73.8	15.5	1.1	19.2	9.1	56.4	14.4	1.0
2050	100.0	10.7	71.8	16.2	1.2	21.1	10.1	52.7	15.0	1.1

Notes:
(a) American Indian represents American Indian, Eskimo, and Aleut.
(b) Asian represents Asian and Pacific Islander.
(c) Persons of Hispanic origin may be of any race.

Source: U.S. Department of Commerce, Bureau of the Census.

Asian/Pacific Islander Population, 1900 to 2050

Historical and projected population of Asian/Pacific Americans.

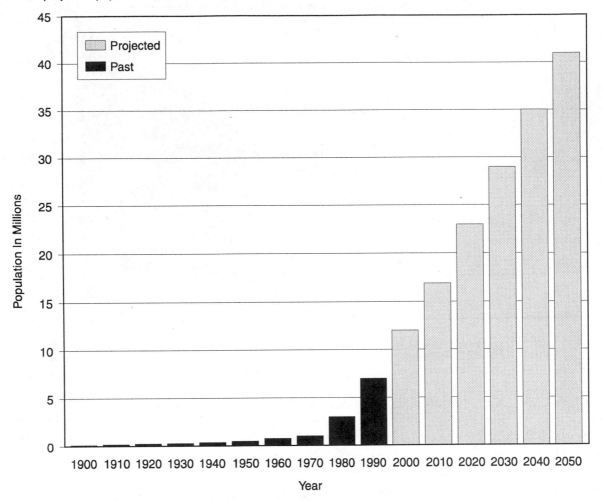

Source: U.S. Department of Commerce, Bureau of the Census.

only three—Philadelphia, Phoenix, and San Diego—had a non-Hispanic white majority. In 1990, among the twenty largest cities, African Americans were a majority in four—Detroit, Baltimore, Memphis, and Washington, D.C.—and Hispanics were a majority in one, San Antonio. Over half of the racial and ethnic minorities in the United States live in just five states—California, Texas, New York, Florida, and Illinois. Over half of Asian Americans and Pacific Islanders live in California, New York, and Hawaii.

Hispanics are highly concentrated in the Southwest but are also found in large numbers in New York and Florida. African Americans, while more dispersed than other minority groups, have a high proportion of residency in southern states. Of all persons in the United States 18 years and younger, over half are from racial and ethnic minority groups. Furthermore, in 1987 the majority of students in the ten largest school systems were racial and ethnic minorities.

Greater Diversity of Racial/Ethnic Groups by Ancestry

The diversity of racial and ethnic groups in the United States is further evidenced by ancestry. Some 600 different ancestry groups were identified in the 1990 Census. Ninety percent of the U.S. population reported at least one specific ethnic group while 10 percent did not report an ancestry. The largest ancestry groups—German, Irish, English, African American, Italian, unspecified American, Mexican, French, Polish, and American Indian—are derived from settlers who came to the United States in its first century (1776-1875).

Groups with one to two million persons—such as French Canadian, Puerto Rican, Chinese, Filipino, and Japanese—represent communities established in the second century (1876-1975). Ancestry groups with 75,000 to 100,000 persons—including Nigerian, Panamanian, Hmong, Turkish, Israeli, Egyptian, Trindidadian,

Table 20.6
Population of Twenty Largest U.S. Cities by Race/Ethnicity, 1990

			Percent of Population Non-Hispanic				
City	State	Population (1000s)	White	African American	Asian (includes Pacific Islanders)	American Indian (includes Eskimos and Aleuts)	Hispanic
New York	NY	7.323	43	25	7	—	24
Los Angeles	CA	3,485	37	39	4	—	40
Chicago	IL	2,784	38	39	4	—	20
Houston	TX	1,631	41	27	4	—	28
Philadelphia	PA	1,586	52	39	3	—	6
San Diego	CA	1,111	59	9	11	1	21
Detroit	MI	1,028	21	75	1	—	3
Dallas	TX	1,007	48	29	2	—	21
Phoenix	AZ	983	72	5	2	2	20
San Antonio	TX	936	36	7	1	—	56
San Jose	CA	782	50	4	19	1	27
Baltimore	MD	736	39	59	1	—	1
Indianapolis	IN	731	75	23	1	—	1
San Francisco	CA	724	47	11	28	—	14
Jacksonville	FL	635	70	25	2	—	3
Columbus	OH	633	74	22	2	—	1
Milwaukee	WI	628	61	30	2	1	6
Memphis	TN	610	44	55	1	—	1
Washington	DC	607	27	65	2	—	5
Boston	MA	574	59	24	5	—	11

Source: *1990 Census Summary Tape File 1C.*

and Tobagonian—are the most recent immigrants to the United States.

Several Asian and Pacific Island ancestries living in the United States ranked among the top 100 ancestry groups in the 1990 Census. Chinese and Filipino residents were ranked twenty-fifth and twenty-sixth, respectively. Other groups included Japanese, Korean, Asian Indian, Vietnamese, Taiwanese, Hawaiian, Laotian, Pakistani, Hmong, Samoan, and generic Asian.

Diversity by ancestry among Asian and Pacific Islanders was consistent with diversity by race. In the 1990 Census, 17 separate Asian groups were enumerated the according to their race.

These were Chinese, Filipino, Japanese, Asian Indian, Korean, Vietnamese, Cambodian, Hmong, Laotian, Thai, Bangladeshi, Burmese, Indonesian, Malayan, Okinawan, Pakistani, and Sri Lankan. Separate Pacific Islander groups included Hawaiian, Samoan, Guamanian, Tongan, Tahitian, Paluan, and Fijian.

Greater Diversity of Racial/Ethnic Groups by Nativity

Racial diversity is also related to nativity. A majority of racial and ethnic minorities—blacks, Mexican Americans, Hawaiians, and Japanese Americans—are primarily native born. The proportion of racial and ethnic minorities who are foreign born is directly related to the size of their immigrant population, including the refugee population. In the 1990 Census, about two-thirds of the foreign-born population classified by race were Hispanic and Asian. Twenty-five percent of the immigrant population were born in Asian countries, over 9 percent were born in the Caribbean, and over 31 percent were born in South America, Central America, or Mexico. Twenty-two percent of all immigrants were European born, while African-born immigrants continued to be the lowest proportion at less than 2 percent. Historically the foreign-born population has maintained a small percentage of the total United States population. In 1960, it represented about 5 percent and in 1990

Population in the United States, 1992 and 2050 (Projections)

Population by race/ethnicity, in millions.

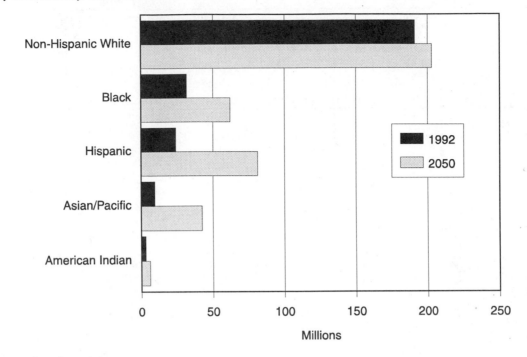

Source: Tamayo Lott Associates.

about 8 percent. This is an increase from less than 10 million to almost 20 million people during this time. Of the foreign-born population, 40 percent were naturalized citizens in 1990. The ten largest states—California, New York, Florida, Texas, New Jersey, Illinois, Massachusetts, Pennsylvania, Michigan, and Washington—contained almost 80 percent of the foreign-born population. Four of these states—California, New York, Texas, and Illinois, and Hawaii—contain 70 percent of the Asian/Pacific American population. The majority of

Table 20.7
Largest Ancestry Groups,1990

Ancestry of U.S. population in millions.

Ancestry	Population in Millions
German	58
Irish	39
English	33
African American	24
Italian	15
Unspecified American	12
Mexican	12
French	10
Polish	9
American Indian	9

Source: Tamayo Lott Associates, Silver Spring, MD 20904, 1994.

these immigrants settled in California, Florida, and Texas, quintupling the foreign-born population of these states. In 1960 New York had almost one-fourth of the foreign-born population, but was down to 14 percent in 1990. By comparison, California contained about 14 percent of the foreign-born population in 1960, but by 1990 had almost one-third of all non-U.S.-born persons.

While the foreign born represent only a small segment of both the total and Pacific Islander populations, immigrants comprised more than half of all Asian Americans in 1990.

This is due to the tremendous increase of immigrants and refugees from Asian lands in the 1980s. As late as 1970, the majority of Asian Americans were American born. By 1980, over half, 59 percent, were born in other countries. This was exceeded in 1990, when two-thirds of both the Asian and Pacific Islander populations were foreign born. In California, where two out of five Asian Americans and Pacific Islanders reside—totaling 10 percent of the state's population in 1990—two-thirds were foreign born.

Diversity by Time of Settlement and by Interracial Births

Foreign-born immigrant populations represent several distinct sociocultural groups that go beyond current government racial and ethnic classifications. One

Asian/Pacific Islander Population, 1990 and 2050 (Projections)

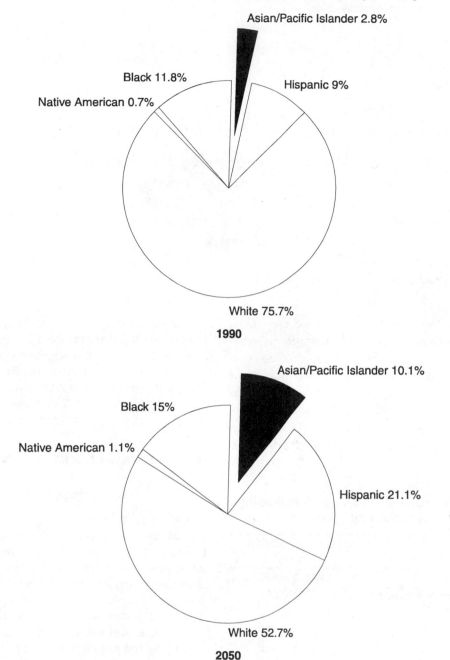

1990

Asian/Pacific Islander 2.8%

Hispanic 9%

Black 11.8%

Native American 0.7%

White 75.7%

2050

Asian/Pacific Islander 10.1%

Hispanic 21.1%

Black 15%

Native American 1.1%

White 52.7%

Source: *U.S. Department of Commerce, Bureau of the Census.*

way they can be further distinguished is by their length of settlement in the Americas.

The first people to live in the Americas were the indigenous or aboriginal inhabitants. These inhabitants were followed by the cultures of western Europe and Africa (1776 to 1875) and selected Latino and Asian groups, notably Mexican Americans, Chinese, Japanese, Filipinos, Puerto Ricans, and Cubans (1867 to 1975). More recently, since 1976, these earlier settlers were joined by immigrants from all over the globe,

many of whom may not have come directly from their country of origin to the United States, but from another country where they have resided for several generations. These groups include Vietnamese, Chinese, and Asian Ugandans. For these immigrants of the post-civil rights era, the concept of a biracial society limited to blacks and whites is foreign.

These three types of settlers are joined by a uniquely American group—multiracial children. While such children have existed since the birth of this nation,

Race and Ethnicity of U.S. Immigrants, 1960 to 1990

Immigrants to the U.S. by race/ethnicity, in percent.

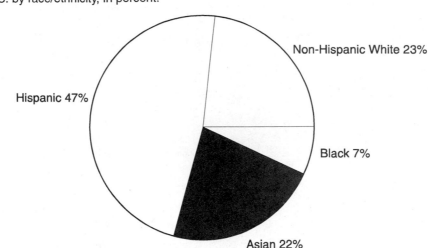

Source: Tamayo Lott Associates, Silver Spring, MD 20904, 1994.

antimiscegenation laws and the usage of race as a defining factor have either rendered this group invisible or labeled them as a minority. In the last two decades, this pattern has been amended as multiracial people have become more visible and articulate. In 1992 approximately 3 percent of all American births were classified as biracial or multiracial. While this is a small proportion nationally, it is noteworthy that the rate of increase of biracial births has tripled in the last twenty years. Furthermore, biracial persons are more likely to be found in younger age groups. In a national sample of 800 school districts only 13 percent did not have any biracial students. Given these figures the twenty-first century will see even greater multiracial and multicultural diversity in the United States.

♦ INTERRACIAL RELATIONS

Three Sets of Relations

Interracial relations in the United States have been characterized in three ways: an absence of relations, positive or cooperative relations, and negative or antagonistic relations. Given the evolution of racial diversity in this country, the historical focus of attention has been on relations between the white majority and the black minority. Even with the recognition of other racial and ethnic minorities, blacks have been viewed as the principal minority because of their historically greater numbers. Other racial and ethnic minorities in the United States, notably American Indians, Asian/Pacific Americans, and Hispanics have also been viewed in relation to a white majority. As these latter groups have increased, however, relations among racial and ethnic minorities are gaining prominence.

Absence of relations

In this category of relations (i.e., no interrelations) groups coexist but remain autonomous. At one extreme there is a mutual tolerance and social order so that groups living in proximity can conduct their daily lives and avoid potential conflicts. At the other

Table 20.8
Population in the United States by Asian/Pacific Islander Ethnicity, 1990

	U.S. population 1990
Total U.S. Population	248,709,873
Asian/Pacific Islander American	7,273,662
Chinese	1,645,472
Filipino	1,406,770
Japanese	847,562
Asian Indian	815,447
Korean	798,849
Vietnamese	614,547
Cambodian	147,411
Hmong	90,082
Laotian	149,014
Thai	91,275
Hawaiian	211,014
Guamanian	62,964
Samoan	49,345
Other Asian/Pacific Islander	343,910

Source: U.S. Census Bureau, summary Tape File 1A, 1992.

Ten States with Largest Foreign-Born Population, 1960 and 1990

Population that is foreign-born, 1960 and 1990, in millions.

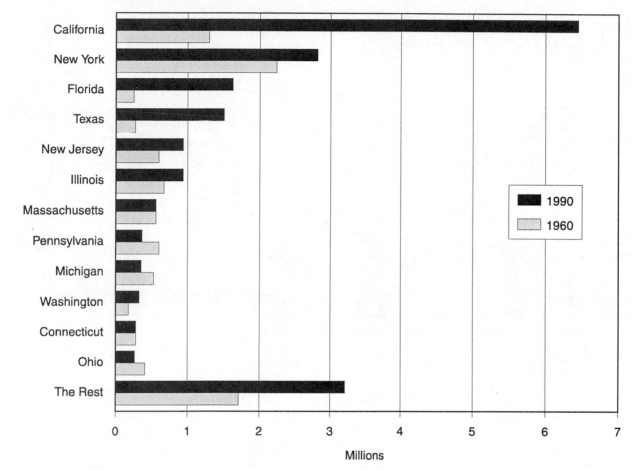

Source: *Tamayo Lott Associates, Silver Spring, MD 20904, 1994.*

extreme, there is a complete withdrawal from interaction with one another to concentrate on one's own community.

Cooperation

A second category of group relations is characterized by cooperation. Such relations exist for short, issue-specific coalitions, such as a national coalition for the passage of particular legislation (i.e. the Civil Rights Act of 1991).

Mutual relations can also be used for long-term or institutional commitments, such as human-relations commissions.

Antagonism

This third set of relations is characterized by competition, exploitation, and antagonism between a majority and minority group, with the former being dominant and more powerful.

Among minority groups, however, dominance and power are relative, varying with the situation. This set

of relations among Asian Americans and other minorities has attracted the greatest attention in recent years.

Relations with Other Racial and Ethnic Minorities

Historically, Asians and other racial and ethnic minorities have had limited interaction because of their selected geographical concentrations. Initial points of settlement for Asians and Pacific Islanders were the Pacific Islands, Hawaii, California, and, subsequently, New York. The majority of blacks settled in the South and mid-Atlantic region, and most Hispanics have moved to the Southwest and California. The initial settlement area for Puerto Ricans was in New York, while Cubans originally migrated to Florida. American Indians, driven from their lands by European settlers, were placed on reservation lands in the Southwest and in California. Alaskan Natives, like Pacific Islanders, have remained primarily in indigenous lands.

Foreign-Born Asian/Pacific Islander Population in Percent

The foreign-born Asian/Pacific Islander population in the United States, in percent, 1989.

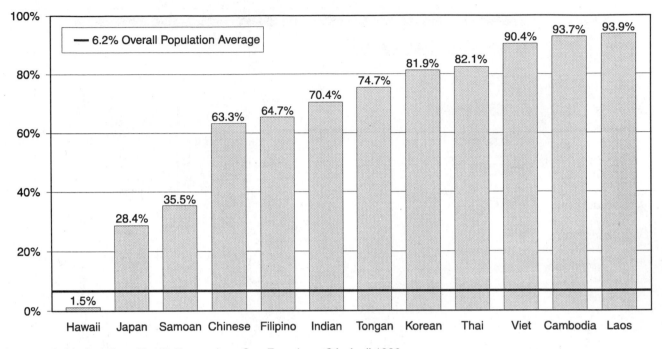

Source: *Asian American Health Forum, Inc., San Francisco, CA, April 1989.*

It is only in recent decades, with increased migration to metropolitan areas and the enactment of the 1965 Immigration Act, that diverse racial minorities have resided in the same cities, although not necessarily in the same neighborhoods.

It should be noted, however, that racial and ethnic minorities had some early contact due to residential segregation. Prior to the passage of Title VII of the Civil Rights Act of 1968, racial and ethnic minorities could be legally excluded from living in the same neighborhoods as whites. As a result, many minority communities were established. For example, in the 1950s and 1960s, the Japanese American population was concentrated in Japantown in San Francisco next to the Fillmore, a predominantly black neighborhood.

In addition, the International District in Seattle has traditionally been home to Asian Americans, blacks, and American Indians.

Today, racial and ethnic minorities are no longer geographically isolated and their dispersal has been uneven across the country. Over half of the racial and ethnic minorities live in just five states—California, Texas, New York, Florida, and Illinois. Twenty percent reside in California. As of 1990, racial and ethnic minority groups were a majority, in 11 of the 20 largest U.S. cities. In these cities their distribution varied. For example, the largest racial minority in Washington D.C. was African American; in San Francisco, Asian American; and in Los Angeles, Hispanic American. In Houston, African American and Hispanic Americans populations are about equal; in San Diego, Asian American and African American populations are of similar proportions. Additionally, upwardly mobile minorities are increasingly found in traditionally white suburbs, especially in the West. In 1990, over half of the minorities (52 percent) in western metropolitan areas lived in the suburbs. Suburbanization is primarily true of particular Asian American groups and to a lesser extent for Hispanics and blacks.

According to current U.S. Census Bureau estimates, the Hispanic population is projected to be larger than the black population by the year 2020. Coupled with their generally low socioeconomic status and young population, Hispanics challenge the notion of blacks as the principal minority. American Indians, Aleuts, and Eskimos, with their relatively smaller population and low socioeconomic status, continue to be the least visible minority. Asian Americans and Pacific Islanders, with their relatively low numbers and high socioeconomic status, have earned the label of "model minority." Like any stereotype, this label is inaccurate, and creates pressure on many Asian/Pacific Americans whose socioeconomic status does not match the "model."

Relations with the White Majority

Any formal and informal relationships between racial and ethnic minorities, nonetheless, have been overshadowed and shaped by each community's relationship to the larger society. The great proportion of interaction for each of the minority groups has been with the white majority. This interaction has been guided by their specific historical relationship to the majority society. For blacks, this relationship began with slavery. For American Indians, Aleuts, Eskimos, Hawaiians, and a large segment of the Hispanic population (mainly Mexican Americans and Puerto Ricans), this relationship originated as one of conquered peoples in their own lands. The relationship between Asian Americans and the majority began as the former found employment in the United States as immigrant workers, first in the agricultural and industrial eras of the United States and more recently in highly technological and electronic labor markets. A contemporary relationship between minority groups and the white majority that cuts across many nationalities is that of involuntary immigrants, or refugees who flee to the United States as a result of American foreign policy, political instability, or internal civil wars. In recent years, many refugees have come to the United States from Southeast Asia and Central America.

♦ MULTIRACIAL COOPERATION AND COALITIONS

Because the experiences of racial and ethnic minorities in the United States traditionally have been of restriction and exclusion, the story of these groups oftentimes has been limited to a history of racism. Nevertheless, throughout their history in the United States, Asian Americans have worked in cooperation with other minority groups as well as with the dominant society to achieve mutual objectives, especially at the local level.

Early Intergroup Relations

The first exclusionary policy of the United States was directed at Asians in the Chinese Exclusion Act of 1888. While this policy demonstrated strong national anti-Asian sentiment in terms of labor competition and immigration restrictions, it also aroused some support for the Chinese. During debate on the Exclusion Act in the 1870s and 1880s, black leaders, such as Frederick Douglass and the black press, condemned Chinese exclusion. While blacks viewed the Chinese as foreign economic competition, they also perceived that the Chinese Exclusion Act was based upon racial policies; while immigration from Asia was being curtailed, Europeans were encouraged to migrate in larger numbers. Subsequently, in 1915 the United States Congress introduced an amendment to a proposed immigration bill, excluding all members of the African race from admission to this nation. The amendment was defeated after intensive lobbying by the National Association for the Advancement of Colored People (NAACP).

The first documented examples of multiracial cooperation and coalition involving Asian Americans were in the labor movement of the early twentieth century. In 1903, some 2,000 Japanese and Mexican sugar beet workers organized a labor strike in Oxnard, California, to protest low pay and mistreatment.

This led to the formation the Sugar Beet and Farm Laborers Union. The California State Federation of the American Federation of Labor (AFL) supported the strikers and petitioned the AFL to invite all sugar beet workers as members of the California federation. In 1905, the Rocky Springs, Wyoming, chapter of the United Mine Workers of America invited over 500 Japanese mine workers to join the union. In both instances, however, Samuel Gompers, the national president of the AFL responded by barring nonwhite workers.

Multiracial Cooperation during the Civil Rights Era

During the civil rights movement of the 1950s and 1960s, several Asian Americans, such as Franklin Fung Chow of San Francisco and Andrea Kochiyama Homan of New York City, rode buses in the South as freedom riders.

Other Asian American civil rights leaders, exhibited at the Japanese American National Museum in Los Angeles, include Reverend Seichi Michael Yasutake and Yuri and Bill Kochiyman of Harlem.

Also from the civil rights movement was the historic Delano grape strike of 1965, which was initiated by Filipino farm workers.

The Filipino Agricultural Workers Organizing Committee and the Mexican National Farm Worker Association merged to form the United Farm Workers Union. Composed of Filipino and Mexican American farm laborers, this coalition produced a successful strike and a nationwide boycott against California grape growers. The strike and boycott resulted in contracts guaranteeing a minimum wage and safe working conditions for farm workers. While Mexican American Cesar Chavez is the recognized leader of this movement, Filipino Americans Larry Itliong and Philip Vera Cruz held strategic leadership positions as well. Vera Cruz served as the second vice-president of the union and was the union's highest-ranking Filipino officer.

Early alliances among different racial and ethnic groups were also found on college campuses in research centers and schools specializing in ethnic studies, including black studies, Chicano or Latino studies, Asian American studies, and Native American studies. Pioneering programs were developed at San Francisco

Board members of United Farmworkers Union (AFL/CIO) gather on stage at dedication of Filipino Retirement Vilage. From left to right are Eliseo Medina, Phillip Vera Cruz, Pete Velasco, Mak Lyons, Cesar Chavez, Richard Chavez, unidentified aide to Cesar Chavez, and Dolores Huerta. (AP/Wide World.)

State College, the University of California-Berkeley, and the University of California-Los Angeles in the late 1960s and early 1970s. Their curriculum was linked to community-based field work for majority and minority students in self-help projects such as tutorial programs for school-age children in minority communities.

The landmark Supreme Court case on civil rights for minority language rights was the 1974 case, Lau v. Nichols.

While the Hispanic population is most commonly associated with bilingual education and other language minority programs, Lau v. Nichols was filed on behalf of limited English-speaking Chinese students in the San Francisco school district. Support for this case and its subsequent implementation came from Latino and other bilingual communities.

Current and Emerging Coalitions

As Asian Americans increase in number and diversity, they join in coalition with other groups. These vary from region to region depending upon racial/ethnic composition and socioeconomic status. Some coalitions promote mutual understanding and involve intergroup programs, such as cross-cultural training, mutual-heritage celebrations, conflict mediation and resolution seminars, and development of personal relations. Some alliances are formed to address similar needs via direct service programs. Newer Asian Americans groups—including Vietnamese, Cambodians, Laotians, and Koreans—have joined with other groups—such as Hispanics—to promote bilingual education programs. Organizations such as the Coalition of Immigrant and Refugee Rights and Services, a network of over 85 San Francisco Bay area organizations, link groups with common issues, combining, for example, Asian and Hispanic immigrant and refugee women with mainstream women for the prevention of domestic violence.

Other coalitions are institutionally based. The Urban Strategies Council is a multiracial, multicultural policy group in Oakland, California, with focused initiatives aimed at reducing persistent urban poverty among African-, Hispanic-, and Asian American youth in the city. The Japanese American National Museum in Los Angeles, fosters a multicultural and multiracial perspective with trilingual materials and exhibits in English,

Japanese, and Spanish. Other types of institutionally based coalitions exist at several American universities where students of color demand more courses and programs directed to their needs as minorities.

Coalitions focused around specific policy issues secured the passage of the Civil Rights Act of 1991 and renewed the Voting Rights Act in 1992, reflecting the distribution and language diversity of Asian American and other new immigrant groups. While interracial cooperation, specifically through coalitions, has existed in the past and present, greater attention is usually given to the more dramatic results of interracial conflict and antagonism.

♦ INTERRACIAL ANTAGONISM, CONFLICT, AND VIOLENCE

Images of Asian Americans

In certain regions and periods of history, Asian and Pacific Americans have been singled out for hostile treatment. Notable events include the 1882 Chinese Exclusion Act, which abolished immigration from China for over eighty years, and Executive Order 9066, which permitted the internment of 110,000 Japanese Americans living on the West Coast during World War II. More recent hate crimes include the 1982 slaying of Vincent Chin, a Chinese American in Detroit, who was mistaken for a Japanese national responsible for the decline of the U.S. auto industry. Racial antagonism directed at Asian Americans is largely drawn from various racial images based on past relations between Asian nations and the United States. These images can be simultaneously positive and negative, resulting in such contradictory images as invisibility and high visibility as well as "model minority" and "foreign enemy."

Invisibility and Visibility

Formal documentation of Asians as a racial group began as early as 1860 when 33,149 Chinese were enumerated by the Census. In the 1870 Census, a total of 55 Japanese were counted. Filipinos and Koreans were first counted in 1910. At this time, the small number of Asian Americans, combined with their geographical concentration, rendered them invisible at the national level. Yet, to the United States government, Asians were a distinct enough group to track via the Census, even when they amounted to less than 0.01 percent of the population. This statistical image was in contrast to the media images of Asian Americans in the nineteenth and early twentieth centuries, which depicted them as "a flood tide" and "yellow hordes."

Asian Americans as Foreigners

Asian Americans have also been depicted as foreigners and were told to "go back to where they came from." Various anti-Asian legislation and policies in the nineteenth and early twentieth centuries exclusive immigration laws, antimiscegenation laws, and alien land laws—mandated their unique civil status as aliens not eligible for citizenship.

Asian Americans being perceived of as foreigners is perpetuated today in several ways. First, there are the "sojourners," i.e., Asian nationals, such as Japanese nationals, who live, work, or study in the United States for several years. Second are the recent immigrants and refugees who view themselves as expatriates. Third are the highly skilled and better-educated immigrants who are part of the Asian diaspora and view themselves as quite cosmopolitan. They may have been Asian British, Asian Canadian, or Asian Caribbean who migrated to the United States and became Asian American.

Asian Americans as the Enemy

During wars and times of economic depression, Asian Americans have been viewed as the enemy. Many of the wars fought by the United States in the last 100 years have been in Asian lands—the Spanish American War in the Philippines; World War II, fought partly in Japan, China, and the Philippines; the Korean War in Korea; and the Vietnam War in Vietnam, Cambodia, and Laos.

The most vivid example of this racial stereotype is the World War II evacuation and internment of 110,00 West Coast Japanese based on Executive Order 9066. Two-thirds were American citizens and the rest permanent residents. They were treated as prisoners of war even though no charges were brought against them and claims of a threat to national security were unsubstantiated. No comparable action was taken against German or Italian Americans despite the fact that Germany and Italy were also at war with the United States. [See Internment of Japanese Americans, covered in detail elsewhere in this volume.]

During the Great Depression of 1930, racial and ethnic minorities were viewed not only as competition for jobs but also as competition for social services. Filipinos were repatriated to the Philippines and Mexicans were deported to Mexico, although, like the interned Japanese Americans, they were not foreign born. Several Filipinos were nationals of the United States during this period and many Mexicans were born in the United States.

Asian Americans as the "Model Minority"

At the opposite extreme from their image as "the enemy," many contemporary Asian/Pacific Americans are viewed as a "model minority" in comparison with other racial and ethnic minorities. In the aggregate, their income and education levels are higher than other minorities. Some Asian American groups have higher income and education levels than even non-Hispanic whites. The model-minority image stresses compatibility with mainstream values and standards of success while emphasizing differences from blacks and Hispanics. This image sets them in a competitive relationship with other racial and ethnic minorities and provokes a resentful backlash against Asian and Pacific Americans.

Brown and Yellow Asian Americans

Racial stratification and tensions also occur within Asian and Pacific American communities. Many successful and prominent Asian Americans (known as the "yellow majority"), trace their ancestry to Asian countries such as Japan, China and the Indian subcontinent. Less successful and less visible Asian/Pacific Americans (known as the "brown minority") include persons from Southeast Asian countries such as Vietnam and the Philippines or Pacific Island territories such as Guam. In the state of Hawaii, for example, Japanese Americans tend to be in positions of power and many Filipino Americans, Samoans, and native Hawaiians are of lower socioeconomic status.

The Resurgence of Hate Violence

Nineteenth-century anti-Asian sentiment against labor immigration has a modern counterpart in hate violence against Asian and Pacific Islanders. The earlier racial antagonism resulted in the exclusionary immigration laws and segregation policies that were enforced throughout the first half of the twentieth century, culminating in the Japanese internment. Racism receded briefly in the post-World War II era when society was more receptive to equality for all Americans.

However, with passage of the Immigration Act of 1965 and the subsequent enactment of refugee policies in the 1980s, Asians once again were viewed as labor competition and a drain on resources. Dramatic increases in the Asian and Pacific Islander population occurred just as the American economy declined. Between 1980 and 1990, this group's population more than doubled at a time when United States manufacturing industries experienced major layoffs and corporations were downsizing. Furthermore, this minority population itself was becoming more diverse, expanding from four or five subgroups to over 20. Many of them, such as Cambodians and Vietnamese, were new settlers. Distinctions between native-born and foreign-born residents, earlier settlers and new arrivals, however, blurred in the face of racism.

In 1986 the U.S. Commission on Civil Rights documented an increase in occurrences of anti-Asian activity that included vandalism, harassment, intimidation, and violence. A major factor contributing to such activities was the increased visibility of Asian Americans due to a large influx of refugees and immigrants from Asia. Moreover, the continuing poor performance of the American economy, deepening economic competition among racial and ethnic groups, racial integration of neighborhoods (both in the inner cities and suburbs), insensitive or inadequate media coverage of minority groups, and inadequate police response to hate crimes further contributed to such crimes.

In 1990, the federal Hate Crimes Statistics Act was enacted to develop and implement a uniform system of data collection. Although statistics compiled from this act are limited, with fewer than 5,000 hate crimes reported nationwide in 1991, the data indicate a sizable number of hate violence against Asian and Pacific Americans. Of all reported hate crimes in 1990, 6 percent were against Asian and Pacific Americans. This is twice their percentage in the total population.

Prime examples of hate and violence against this segment of the population are the racially motivated murders of Asian Americans. The most prominent was the 1982 slaying of Vincent Chin on June 19, 1982, 100 years after the Chinese Exclusion Act. At a gathering with some friends in a Detroit bar to celebrate his upcoming wedding, the twenty-seven year old was accosted by Ronald Ebens and Michael Nitz, two white automobile factory workers. They reportedly called him a "Jap" and blamed him for the loss of jobs in the American automobile industry. The two men chased Chin out of the bar and Nitz held Chin while Ebens beat him "numerous times in the knee, the chest, and the head" with a baseball bat. Chin died of his injuries four days later. In 1983, the two men were charged with second-degree murder but were subsequently allowed to plead guilty to the lesser charge of manslaughter. They were sentenced to three years probation and fined $3,780 in the Wayne County Circuit Court. The U.S. Department of Justice subsequently brought a civil rights charge against the two men that, in 1984, acquitted Nitz and convicted Ebens, who was sentenced to twenty-five years in prison. The case was appealed and retried in the U.S. Appellate Court in Cincinnati, Ohio, which acquitted Ebens in 1987.

Another highly publicized murder was the January 17, 1988, massacre of schoolchildren at Cleveland Elementary School in Stockton, California. A white male, Patrick Edward Purdy, fired an AK-47 assault rifle into the school yard, killing five Southeast Asian children and wounding thirty others. The California attorney general's report on this crime concluded that: "It appears highly probable that Purdy deliberately chose

Cleveland Elementary School as the location for his murderous assault in substantial part because it was heavily populated by Southeast Asian children. His frequent comments about Southeast Asians indicate a particular animosity against them."

Racial antagonism is directed at both immigrant and American-born Asian and Pacific Americans by various ethnic groups and across a variety of regions. In New Jersey, hate groups such as the Dotbusters and Edison Boys have organized against Southeast Asians. Vietnamese and Cambodian refugees in Massachusetts and Chicago are fearful, as are Korean store owners in New York City and Philadelphia. Internationally, U.S. trade competition with Japan has resulted in "Japan bashing." This identifies all Asian and Pacific Americans, including several generations of American-born citizens, with Japanese nationals in negative and harmful ways.

The most publicized incidents of intergroup antagonism are not between majority and minority groups but among racial and ethnic minorities themselves. In particular, tensions between immigrant Korean business owners and their native-born African American clients in American cities are clearly visible. Over 3,000 Asian-owned businesses were targeted by rioters in the 1992 Los Angeles riots, which erupted following the first trial of the white police officers accused of beating black motorist Rodney King. The National Asian Pacific American Legal Consortium concluded in May 1993 that: "Throughout the country, tensions between communities of color are exacerbated by a lack of jobs and genuine economic development and inadequate education, health care, and housing. In many instances, the frustration within each community is so high that interethnic discussions are non-existent or fruitless."

♦ MULTIRACIAL CHILDREN

Asian Americans are becoming a more interracial population. For almost two centuries, the United States has not only restricted racial diversity but denied the existence of interracial children. For years children with one white and one nonwhite parent were officially defined as nonwhite by various means including blood quantum. Children with two racial and ethnic minority parents, were often not accepted by either group. For many years Amerasians, the offspring of Asian women and American soldiers in various wars, have been placed in this position.

When antimiscegenation laws were abolished in 1967, multiracial children began to be recognized. Associations for multiracial peoples are growing and becoming more vocal, even to the point of requesting their own census classification. While mixed-race marriages accounted for about 2 percent of the 53 million married couples in 1991, about one-fourth of Asian Americans were married to spouses outside of their race. This high intermarriage rate has led to a growing number of interracial children.

Nationally, mixed-race babies comprise about 3 percent of all births. Nearly one-third of Asian babies, however, had one parent who was not Asian. The most obvious example are the children of U.S. servicemen and Asian women. These relationships have existed and produced interracial children since the first American military intervention in Asia during the Filipino revolutionary war against Spain in 1898. The children of veterans of the Vietnam War became especially visible and their relationship to the United States was formalized in the Amerasian Homecoming Act of 1987. Also emerging are mestizos, Asians who are Hispanic. In the 1990 Census, over 4 percent of Asian/Pacific Americans were of Hispanic origin. By contrast, less than 3 percent of blacks claimed Hispanic origin.

References

Kalish, Susan. "Interracial Baby Boomlet in Progress?" *Population Today*, no. 12 (December 1992).

Lieberson, Stanley and Mary Waters. *From Many Strands: Ethnic and Racial Groups in Contemporary America*. New York: Russell Sage Foundation, 1988.

Lott, Juanita Tamayo. *The Role of Minorities in the 1992 U.S.Elections: Asian Pacific Americans and the Electoral Process*. Washington D.C.: background paper for the United States Information Agency, September 1992.

———. *Towards a Greater Understanding of Black and Hispanic Relations: Demographic, Historical and Policy Perspectives*. Washington, D.C.: paper commissioned by the U.S. Department of Justices, Community Relations Service, October 1990.

National Asian Pacific American Legal Consortium. *Understanding Violence against Asian Americans*. Washington, D.C., May 1993.

O'Hare, William P. "America's Minorities—The Demographics of Diversity." *Population Bulletin* 47, no. 4, (December 1992).

Tachiki, Amy et al. *Roots: An Asian American Reader*. University of California, Asian American Studies Center, 1971.

U.S. Bureau of the Census, *200 Years of U.S. Census Taking*. Washington, D.C., November 1989.

———. *United States Population Estimates by Age, Sex, Race and Hispanic Origin: 1980 to 1988*. P-25, no. 1045, Washington, D.C., January 1990.

———. *Population Projections of the United States by Age, Sex, Race and Hispanic Origin: 1992 to 2050*. P-25, no. 1092, Washington, D.C., November 1992.

U.S. Commission on Civil Rights. *Recent Activities against Citizens and Residents of Asian Descent*. Clearinghouse Publication, no. 88, Washington, D.C., September 1986.

——— *Civil Rights Issues Facing Asian Americans in the 1990s*. Washington, D.C., February 1992.

—Juanita Tamayo Lott

The Refugees of Southeast Asia

♦ Exodus from Southeast Asia ♦ Special Refugee Categories and Programs
♦ Refugee Assistance Programs ♦ The Southeast Asian Refugee Experience ♦ Conclusion

Migration and resettlement of immigrant groups to the United States have always been part of the country's heritage. This pattern continues even today with the migration of over one million Southeast Asian refugees into the United States. This resettlement both symbolizes the humanitarian response of American society to the plight of the Southeast Asian refugees and shows the determination of the newcomers to succeed in the land of freedom and opportunity. This chapter will examine the circumstances that dictated the mass refugee exodus from Southeast Asia, describe the various waves of Southeast Asian immigrants that arrived in this country, discuss U.S. resettlement efforts and refugee assistance programs, and report on the experiences of Southeast Asian refugees in the United States.

♦ EXODUS FROM SOUTHEAST ASIA

In the spring of 1975, the Vietnam War took a dramatic turn. Following fierce offensives, many cities and provinces in South Vietnam and Cambodia fell to the communist forces, causing panic amongst the population. The eventual surrender of the South Vietnamese government on April 30, 1975, forced many to escape the country through various means.

Hundreds of thousands of Southeast Asians fearing reprisal escaped on foot to Thailand through the jungles of Laos and Cambodia. Many Vietnamese took to the sea in small fishing or merchant boats in their quest for freedom and waited to be picked up by the U.S. Navy or foreign commercial vessels. A number of Vietnamese air force pilots flew planes or helicopters loaded with dependents to U.S. bases in Thailand or to U.S. aircraft carriers patrolling the international zone around South Vietnam. Under the supervision of the Special Interagency Task Force formed by President

Gerald Ford, the U.S. embassy evacuated all Americans and many Southeast Asians in South Vietnam during the last days of the fighting. Evacuees were transported on military airplanes to reception camps in Guam, where Southeast Asian refugees were processed for admission into the United States.

This mass exodus from Southeast Asia remained steady for almost two decades. In spite of significant dangers and the tight control of national boundaries by Southeast Asian governments, a large number of Southeast Asians continued to flee their native lands in search of freedom.

By early 1980, the number of refugees that reached the shores of Thailand, Singapore, Malaysia, Hong Kong, Guam, and the Philippines was estimated at 375,000. Food shortages, unsanitary conditions, lack of clothing and shelter, and extremely limited medical services all contributed to the subhuman living conditions facing the refugees in these camps. Still, more refugees arrived daily, fleeing persecution by communist regimes and clinging to the hope for a better life.

By mid-1989, over 1.5 million people had left Southeast Asia.

Even reports that boatloads of refugees were being turned back to sea did not dissuade others from taking flight. The map in Figure 21.1 summarizes both arrivals and departures of Vietnamese boat people to the camps from 1977 to 1988 and lists camp populations in 1989.

Although assistance poured into these overcrowded camps from all over the world, the magnitude and suddenness of the problem overwhelmed many countries, especially Thailand, Malaysia, and Hong Kong, which received the bulk of the boat people. Thailand alone had granted temporary asylum to 337,000 Laotians by 1989, including 267,915 that departed for resettlement in third countries, mostly to the United States.

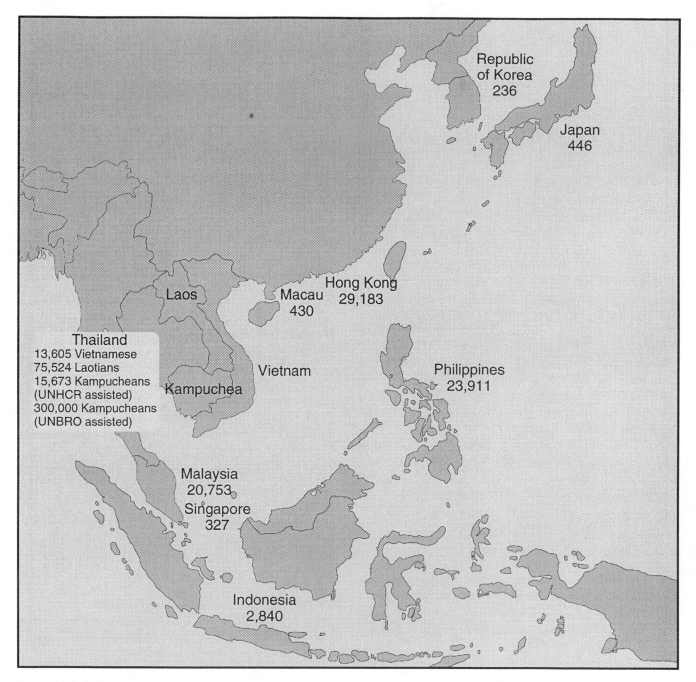

Figure 21.1. Refugees in camps in Southeast Asia, 1989.

Repatriation

In 1989, an international conference on refugees was held in Geneva to develop a comprehensive plan of action for screening political refugees. The conference established March 14, 1989, as the cut-off date for admission to various resettlement countries, including the United States. During the screening process, many of the refugees in the camps were evaluated as economic refugees and were forced to return to their homeland. This is called *forced repatriation*.

With repatriation viewed as the only viable solution to the refugee problem in Southeast Asia, international support began to swell for further assistance to the growing number of refugees repatriated to their homelands. However, voluntary repatriation began with 75 Vietnamese boat people from the Hong Kong camps on March 2, 1989, under the auspices of the United Nations High Commissioner for Refugees (UNHCR). Over 60,000 were returned to Vietnam under the United Nations-sponsored repatriation program. Under the comprehensive plan of action, between 80,000 and

Table 21.1
Southeast Asian Refugee and Amerasian Arrivals: 1975 through September 30, 1992

Time of Arrival	Total
Resettled under Special Parole Program (1975)	129,792
Resettled under Humanitarian Parole Program (1975)	602
Resettled under Special Lao Program (1976)	3,466
Resettled under Expanded Parole Program (1976)	11,000
Resettled under "Boat Cases" Program as of August 1, 1977	1,883
Resettled under Indochinese Parole Programs:	
August 1, 1977 — September 30, 1977	680
October 1, 1977 — September 30, 1978	20,397
October 1, 1978 — September 30, 1979	80,678
October 1, 1979 — September 30, 1980	166,727
Resettled under Refugee Act of 1980:	
October 1, 1980 — September 30, 1981	132,454
October 1, 1981 — September 30, 1982	72,155
October 1, 1982 — September 30, 1983	39,167
October 1, 1983 — September 30, 1984	52,000
October 1, 1984 — September 30, 1985	49,853
October 1, 1985 — September 30, 1986	45,391
October 1, 1986 — September 30, 1987	40,164
October 1, 1987 — September 30, 1988	35,083
October 1, 1988 — September 30, 1989	37,066
October 1, 1989 — September 30, 1990	38,758
October 1, 1990 — September 30, 1991	37,958
October 1, 1991 — September 30, 1992	34,298
Total, Indochinese Refugees	1,029,572
Resettled under Amerasian Homecoming Act of 1988:	
October 1, 1987 — September 30, 1988	366
October 1, 1988 — September 30, 1989	8,714
October 1, 1989 — September 30, 1990	13,359
October 1, 1990 — September 30, 1991	16,501
October 1, 1991 — September 30, 1992	17,100
Total, Amerasians (includes accompanying family members)	56,040
Total, Southeast Asian Refugees and Amerasians	1,085,612

Source: U.S. Department of Health and Human Services, Office of Refugee Resettlement, Refugee Resettlement Program, Report to the Congress, January 31, 1993, p. A.1.

85,000 Vietnamese asylum seekers were returned to Vietnam. Hundreds of thousands of Cambodians and Laotians were also repatriated. By the end of 1991, Thailand had 59,000 Laotian refugees, of which 7,500 were resettled in the United States in 1992, and 1,770 were repatriated; over 10,000 returned to Laos on their own. In an agreement signed with the UNHCR, all Laotians that were not planning to resettle in third countries would be forced to repatriate by the end of 1994.

Since 1992, arrivals of boat people in Southeast Asian camps have virtually come to an end. All refugee camps in Southeast Asia are scheduled to be closed by 1996.

Southeast Asian Refugees Reach the United States

The first wave of refugees from Southeast Asia, approximately 130,000 men, women, and children, arrived in the United States in 1975; the flow of refugees from Vietnam, Cambodia, and Laos has been fairly constant ever since. These early arrivals were temporarily

Table 21.2
Southeast Asian Refugee Arrivals by Nationality (1975-1991)

Fiscal Year (a)	Cambodia	Laos	Vietnam (c)	Total
1975	4,600	800	125,000	130,394
1976 (b)	1,100	10,200	3,200	14,466
1977	300	400	1,900	2,563
1978	1,300	8,000	11,100	20,397
1979	6,000	30,200	44,500	80,678
1980	16,000	55,500	95,200	166,727
1981	27,100	19,300	8,610	132,454
1982	20,100	9,400	42,600	72,155
1983	13,191	2,946	23,030	39,167
1984	19,849	7,224	24,927	52,000
1985	19,237	5,233	25,383	49,853
1986	10,054	12,894	22,443	45,391
1987	1,949	15,604	22,611	40,164
1988	2,900	14,589	17,958	35,447
1989	2,220	12,762	30,805	45,787
1990	2,325	8,712	41,021	52,065
1991	186	9,231	45,034	54,451

Notes:
(a) Figures for fiscal years 1975-1991 are estimates from Linda Gordon. Yearly totals correspond to official records maintained by the Department of Health and Human Services. Totals for nationality groups do not add to overall totals due to rounding.
(b) Includes transition quarter.
(c) Beginning with 1988, figures for Vietnam include Amerasians and their family members admitted on immigrant visas but eligible for refugee program services.

Source: Statistical Record of Asian Americans, Susan Gall, ed., 1993, Table 572, p. 451.

housed in refugee camps set up by the U.S. government. Several charity organizations, working closely with and supported by the federal government, immediately began resettlement efforts.

Table 21.3
Ten States with Largest Southeast Asian
Residential Concentrations, 1992

State	Number	Percent
California	409,800	39.8%
Texas	76,900	7.5
Washington	47,800	4.6
Minnesota	37,700	3.7
New York	36,000	3.5
Massachusetts	32,200	3.1
Pennsylvania	31,600	3.1
Illinois	31,000	3.0
Virginia	26,100	2.5
Oregon	22,200	2.2
Total	715,300	72.9%

Source: U.S. Department of Health and Human Services, Office of Refugee Resettlement, Refugee Resettlement Program, Report to the Congress, January 31, 1993, p. 50.

With the assistance of these private sponsors, the refugees were relocated to communities across the nation.

In July 1979, President Jimmy Carter expanded the admission quota for Southeast Asian refugees from 7,000 to 14,000 per month. This announcement brought large numbers of all three Southeast Asian nationality groups into the country. From 1975 through 1987, Southeast Asian refugees accounted for the majority of refugee admissions into the United States.

Most were admitted between 1975 and 1980 as "parolees" by a series of parole authorizations granted by the U.S. attorney general under the Immigration and Naturalization Act. Prior to the Refugee Act of 1980, six different parole programs were implemented.

Among the 130,000 who arrived in 1975, approximately 125,000 were Vietnamese. The 118,000 arrivals between 1976 and 1979 were ethnically more heterogeneous, with about 60,000 Vietnamese, 49,000 Laotian (including a substantial number of Hmong), and 9,000 Cambodians. In subsequent years, the ethnic composition of the refugee population has expanded to include other ethnic groups from Southeast Asia as well.

By the end of 1992, the Southeast Asian refugee population in the United States was composed primarily of the following ethnic groups: Vietnamese, including ethnic Chinese and Montagnards; Cambodians; and Laotians, including Hmong, lowland Laotians, and smaller tribal groups from the highlands of Laos, including the Iu-Mien, the Khmu, the Lahu, and the Lua' group. By the end of 1993, however, the number of refugees arriving in the United States had declined.

Migration Trends

The receiving communities that offered their hospitality to the newcomers through the sponsorship mechanism were scattered throughout many states. Gradually, the general trend in residence of the Southeast Asians began to reflect different rates of resettlement in various states. By 1980, Vietnamese and Cambodians displayed similar resettlement patterns, with clusters concentrated in the Southwest. In contrast, Laotians were more likely to resettle in the northern and midwestern states.

Interstate migration soon began to establish flows and counterflows, substantially increasing all three nationality groups in California, Texas, and eight other states. The tendency of refugees to concentrate in these states, especially in California, was reinforced by family reunification. Table 21.3 lists the ten states with the largest refugee populations.

Collectively, these ten states received over 715,000 Southeast Asians, or about 73 percent of the total. As the leading state, California has become the home of 409,800 refugees since 1975, almost 40 percent of the total Southeast Asian refugee population in the United States. This pattern of concentration remained noticeable during 1991, when close to 38 percent of arrivals from Southeast Asia settled in California, more than the number who settled in the next nine most populous states combined.

During 1992, displaying the same general residential pattern as in the previous year, 36 percent of the Southeast Asians and Amerasians resettled initially in California; 8 percent went to Texas. Each of the next six states with high refugee concentrations (Washington, Georgia, New York, Minnesota, Massachusetts, and Wisconsin) received 3 to 4 percent. The distribution of Vietnamese, the largest group among the Southeast Asians, mirrored the initial resettlement trend, with 41 percent going to California, 9 percent to Texas, and 3 to 5 percent each to Washington, Georgia, Massachusetts, and Virginia. Wisconsin and Minnesota, on the other hand, received large numbers of Laotians.

After being resettled initially in a community, a substantial number of refugees decided to move to another city or state. This secondary migration was often a response to several factors, such as warmer climate, availability of employment opportunities and better training programs, more generous welfare benefits, reunification with relatives, and the ambiance of a larger ethnic community. From 1975 to 1980, about 26 percent of the Southeast Asians in California had migrated from other states, indicating a rather strong attraction to the Golden State. However, secondary migration to California from 1983 to 1992 declined slowly. The state's severe economic recession during 1991 to 1993 might have influenced the rate of secondary migration in those years.

♦ SPECIAL REFUGEE CATEGORIES AND PROGRAMS

Unaccompanied Minors

Many children without parents or guardians, often referred to as "unaccompanied minors," found themselves among the refugees from Southeast Asia. From 1979 to 1992, a total of 10,638 unaccompanied minors were cared for in a federally funded program. This program, operated by volunteer agencies, private organizations, and state governments, cared for the children until they reached the age of emancipation. As of September 30, 1992, this program continued to care for 2,149 refugee children in projects throughout the United States.

With more of the youths reaching emancipation age and fewer unaccompanied minors being admitted into the United States in the 1990s, the number of children in the program dropped sharply. Many former program participants have "graduated" and are doing well as young adults in their new society.

Orderly Departure Program

During the late 1970s, the United States and the free world community became alarmed at the large number of refugees fleeing Vietnam in unseaworthy fishing boats. Many were preyed upon by pirates in the Gulf of Thailand. The potential for loss of life created by this situation called for international action. Therefore, the Orderly Departure Program (ODP) was established in May 1979 to provide a safe alternative to clandestine escape by sea. Refugees were allowed to leave Vietnam directly for resettlement in one of two dozen countries, including the United States.

Under the purview of the Refugee Act of 1980, ODP applicants were interviewed in Vietnam by officers who rotated on two-week duty assignments from the U.S. Immigration and Naturalization Service (INS) overseas district office in Bangkok, Thailand. The refugees were then admitted into the United States. They later became permanent residents, and many eventually became U.S. citizens. The Vietnamese admitted into the United States under the ODP program, mostly

Table 21.4
Southeast Asian Refugee and Amerasian Arrivals by State of Initial Resettlement (FY 1992)

State	Amerasian Immigrants (a)	Country of Citizenship			
		Cambodia	Laos	Vietnam	Total (b)
Alabama	202	4	0	61	267
Alaska	36	0	0	20	56
Arizona	473	0	0	399	872
Arkansas	10	0	0	46	56
California	3,488	92	4,115	10,885	18,580
Colorado	184	0	31	233	448
Connecticut	189	0	18	163	370
Delaware	0	0	0	12	12
Dist. Columbia	549	0	6	330	885
Florida	457	3	4	621	1,085
Georgia	908	1	27	1,027	1,963
Hawaii	156	0	1	165	322
Idaho	24	0	0	39	63
Illinois	339	5	29	373	746
Indiana	14	0	0	115	129
Iowa	384	0	15	269	668
Kansas	188	0	28	298	514
Kentucky	210	0	2	177	389
Louisiana	285	5	24	469	783
Maine	47	0	0	11	58
Maryland	327	0	0	42	769
Massachusetts	367	16	40	1,003	1,426
Michigan	294	0	230	446	970
Minnesota	247	11	985	445	1,688
Mississippi	16	0	0	28	44
Missouri	626	0	6	421	1,053
Montana	0	0	0	1	1
Nebraska	293	0	4	273	570
Nevada	2	0	7	84	93
New Hampshire	14	0	9	75	98
New Jersey	275	1	0	291	567
New Mexico	133	0	0	80	213
New York	1,153	22	42	712	1,929
North Carolina	397	0	37	250	684
North Dakota	116	0	0	13	129
Ohio	83	0	37	192	312
Oklahoma	137	0	8	180	325
Oregon	353	7	46	507	913
Pennsylvania	558	1	50	528	1,137
Rhode Island	7	8	21	8	44
South Carolina	10	0	2	68	80
South Dakota	69	0	0	6	75
Tennessee	274	0	12	262	548
Texas	1,614	0	18	2,488	4,120
Utah	208	0	5	191	404

Table 21.4
Southeast Asian Refugee and Amerasian Arrivals by State of Initial Resettlement (FY 1992) (Continued)

State	Amerasian Immigrants (a)	Country of Citizenship			
		Cambodia	Laos	Vietnam	Total (b)
Vermont	157	0	0	1	158
Virginia	318	1	1	860	1,180
Washington	852	8	79	1,218	2,157
West Virginia	41	0	0	5	46
Wisconsin	11	0	1,333	45	1,389
Wyoming	0	0	0	5	5
Other (b)	5	0	0	0	5
Total	17,100	185	7,272	26,841	51,508

Notes:
(a) This tabulation includes infants born in the Refugee Processing Center in the Philippines who had been granted Amerasian status retroactively by legislation signed November 5, 1990.
(b) National total includes refugees from other Southeast Asian nations not listed separately.

Source: *U.S. Department of Health and Human Services, Office of Refugee Resettlement, Refugee Resettlement Program, Report to the Congress, January 31, 1993, pp. A.8-A.9.*

for family reunification, accounted for 165,000 admissions by mid-1989, and continued to represent a significant portion of the arrivals in the early 1990s. During 1992, about 25,200 refugee applications were approved within this program.

Humanitarian Operation Program

In 1989, after many years of intense American diplomatic efforts, the Socialist Republic of Vietnam agreed to release its former reeducation camp detainees, or political prisoners, for emigration to the United States. Most of these were military or civilian officials of the former government of South Vietnam detained en masse since 1975. During their long incarceration, the detainees endured extreme shortages of food and clothing, unsanitary living conditions, and were subjected to severe physical and mental mistreatment. Their release from the camps pushed them into a precarious existence as outcasts in a socialist society. Their only hope was to leave Vietnam for the United States with their families. By the end of 1993, the Humanitarian Operation Program had brought 70,000 of these former political prisoners and members of their families to the United States.

Amerasian Program

Amerasians are those children born in Vietnam during the war to Vietnamese mothers and American fathers. These bi-racial children were ostracized in Vietnam as youngsters without education or employment potential. Over 56,000 Amerasian youths and their family members arrived in the United States

under the Amerasian Homecoming Act of 1988 (Public Law No. 100-202).

After 1975, Amerasians were admitted to the United States as immigrants, but were eligible for assistance benefits as refugees. Those not living with relatives in the United States were cared for in about 55 cluster resettlement projects throughout the country, under an agreement between the Office of Refugee Resettlement (ORR) and InterAction, Inc., a resettlement organization that assists Amerasians in cooperation with local affiliates of the national voluntary agencies.

Resettlement Organizations

In response to the need to coordinate refugee admission and resettlement efforts during the height of the "boat people" exodus from Vietnam, President Jimmy Carter established the Office of the U.S. Coordinator for Refugee Affairs in February 1979. This office developed overall refugee admission and resettlement policy and budget strategy. In addition, it coordinated policy on refugee admission and assistance activities among federal and state governments, resettlement organizations, and international communities. In recent years, the Office of the U.S. Coordinator held, with the U.S. Congress, a series of annual public hearings involving state agencies and private resettlement organizations that sought to establish the proposed annual admission level for the coming fiscal year.

In 1991, for the first time, Southeast Asian community leaders from across the nation were invited by the Office of Refugee Resettlement to meet with the Office of the U.S. Coordinator in this consultation process to testify during congressional hearings. Based on the

Table 21.5
Secondary Migration of Southeast Asians with less than Three Years of Residence, as of June 30, 1992 (a)

State	In-Migrants	Out-Migrants	Net Migration (b)
Alaska (d)	0	51	(51)
Arizona (c)	138	315	(177)
Arkansas (c)	131	25	106
California	952	1,578	(626)
Colorado (c)	189	183	6
Connecticut	30	113	(83)
Delaware	0	1	(1)
Dist. Columbia	4	377	(373)
Florida	274	344	(70)
Georgia (c)	201	280	(79)
Hawaii	2	40	(38)
Idaho (c)	31	103	(72)
Illinois	690	270	420
Indiana	4	85	(81)
Iowa (c)	254	115	139
Kansas	134	133	1
Kentucky (d)	0	129	(129)
Louisiana (c)	295	114	181
Maine	0	41	(41)
Maryland (c)	312	235	77
Massachusetts	74	326	(252)
Michigan (c)	133	159	(26)
Minnesota	50	280	(230)
Mississippi	20	14	6
Missouri	48	352	(304)
Montana	0	23	(23)
Nebraska	52	132	(80)
Nevada	8	37	(29)
New Hampshire	2	51	(49)
New Jersey	36	333	(297)
New Mexico	26	84	(58)
New York	308	851	(543)
North Carolina (c)	1,310	49	1,261
North Dakota	0	73	(73)
Ohio (c)	58	181	(123)
Oklahoma (c)	105	70	35
Oregon	108	325	(217)
Pennsylvania	130	390	(260)
Rhode Island (c)	39	96	(57)
South Carolina	4	36	(32)
South Dakota	86	31	55
Tennessee	0	242	(242)
Texas	721	770	(49)
Utah	4	89	(85)
Vermont	2	30	(28)

Table 21.5
Secondary Migration of Southeast Asians with less than Three Years of Residence, as of June 30, 1992 (a) (Continued)

State	In-Migrants	Out-Migrants	Net Migration (b)
Virginia (b)	160	268	(108)
Washington (c)	3,058	186	2,872
West Virginia	0	10	(10)
Wisconsin	20	146	(126)
Wyoming (c)	0	24	(24)
Other (d)	0	10	(10)

Notes:
(a) This table represents a compilation of unadjusted data reports by the State on Form ORR-11. The population base is refugees receiving State-administered services on 6/30/92. Secondary migration is defined as a change of residence across a State line at any time between initial arrival in the U.S. and the reporting date. With regard to any given State, out-migrants are persons initially placed there who were living elsewhere on the reporting date, while in-migrants are persons living there on the reporting date who were initially placed elsewhere.
(b) Numbers of brackets denote net out-migration.
(c) Reporting base includes refugees receiving social services without cash or medical assistance as well as those receiving such assistance.
(d) Not participating in the refugee program.

Source: U.S. Department of Health and Human Services, Office of Refugee Resettlement, Refugee Resettlement Program, Report to the Congress, January 31, 1993, pp. A.30 - A.31.

Office's recommendation, President George Bush established a ceiling of 142,000 refugee admissions for 1992 and 132,000 for 1993.

The U.S. Senate amended the Foreign Relations Authorization Act on January 28, 1994, eliminating the Office of the U.S. Coordinator for Refugee Affairs. Refugee programs are now coordinated by the Secretary of State, the Secretary of Health and Human Services, and the Attorney General.

Results of Resettlement

From the inception of its resettlement effort in 1975, the U.S. government wanted to disperse Southeast Asian refugees throughout the country, hoping to minimize the socioeconomic impact on any single community and to facilitate the refugees adaptation. For a variety of cultural and socioeconomic reasons, the policy produced mixed results.

Many refugees opted to live in a few selected states, with California leading the list. New arrivals joined their families in these states, significantly expanding the size of existing refugee communities. In addition, secondary migration occurred when refugees moved from the states where they were initially resettled. Many have moved to California or other states with large refugee concentrations. This secondary migration process, compounded by new arrivals, has strained the limited resources available to refugee assistance programs.

Voluntary Agencies

For many years, nonprofit resettlement organizations, called voluntary agencies, sponsored and resettled refugees arriving in the United States from troubled places around the world. Under cooperative agreements with the U.S. Department of State, which funded initial domestic resettlement and overseas assistance programs, 12 voluntary agencies assumed responsibility for the initial reception and resettlement of new arrivals in this country.

Established resettlement agencies included the American Council for Nationalities Service, Church World Service, Episcopal Migration Ministries, Ethiopian Community Development Council, Hebrew Immigrant Aid Society, International Rescue Committee, Lutheran Immigration and Refugee Service, Tolstoy Foundation, United States Catholic Conference, World Relief of the National Association of Evangelicals, and the Iowa Department of Human Services.

Refugee applicants were approved by the Immigration and Naturalization Service for admission into the United States from both Vietnam and refugee camps in Southeast Asia. These refugees were assisted in processing and establishing the required documentation by the joint voluntary agency representatives stationed in Southeast Asia. Agency representatives also helped arrange sponsorship for the refugees in the United States. Working in cooperation with other U.S. and international agencies, staff members handled all aspects of the refugee relocation process, such as

Table 21.6
Domestic Resettlement Appropriations FY 1991 and FY 1992

ORR Obligations: (Amounts in $000)	FY 1992	FY 1991
A. State-administered program:		
1. Cash, assistance, medical assistance, unaccompanied minors, and State administration (a)	$232,477	$230,724
2. Social Services (State formula allocation)	67,009	66,811
3. Targeted Assistance (State formula allocation)	43,916	43,915
4. Mutual Assistance Associations (MAA) Incentive Grants	3,467	3,485 (b)
Subtotal, State-administered program	$346,869	
B. Discretionary Allocations:		
5. Targeted Assistance (Ten Percent)	4,880	4,893
6. Social Services Allocations	12,476	12,457
Subtotal, Discretionary Allocations	$17,356	
C. Alternative Programs:		
7. Voluntary Agency Matching Grant program	39,036	339,035
8. Privately-administered Wilson/Fish projects	1,739	3,489
Subtotal, Alternative Programs	$40,775	$42,524
D. Preventive Health: Screening and Health Services	$5,631	$5,631
Total, Refugee Program Obligations	$410,630	$410,440

Notes:
(a) Includes cash and medical assistance provided under Oregon's State-administered Wilson/Fish
(b) MAA Incentive Grants were part of Discretionary Grants during FY 1991.

Sources: *U.S. Department of Health and Human Services, Office of Refugee Resettlement, Refugee Resettlement Program, Reports to the Congress, January 31, 1992, p. 13.*

arranging for transportation with the International Organization for Migration. The joint voluntary agency staff coordinated new arrival distribution with national resettlement agencies in New York. Voluntary agency affiliates in local communities made arrangements with the refugee's relatives already in the United States, or with church groups, private organizations, and individual families to sponsor new arrivals during their first three months in the United States.

♦ REFUGEE ASSISTANCE PROGRAMS

Refugees with adequate English language and occupational skills often quickly find employment, become economically self-reliant, and quietly fade into the multiethnic population of the host country. However, a substantial number of Southeast Asian refugees may lack these skills and need financial and medical assistance in rebuilding their lives. They often face formidable language and cultural barriers, lack marketable skills, and have a large family to support. They must usually rely either partially or entirely on government assistance programs for some time before becoming completely independent. These programs provide cash and medical assistance, English-language classes, employment

training, and social services, all aimed at helping the new arrivals gain employment as soon as possible. With this valuable assistance made available by the federal government and with contributions from local governments and the private sector, the refugees become more quickly acclimated to life in the United States.

Assistance Program Structure and Funding

The federal assistance program for all refugees admitted into the United States has been administered by the Office of Refugee Resettlement (ORR) of the U.S. Department of Health and Human Services. During the first month, initial reception and resettlement support is provided by the local affiliates of the national voluntary agencies and funded by the U.S. Department of State. After this period, refugees that need additional help can turn to several interrelated assistance programs in their communities.

Supported by ORR, state governments plan, administer, and coordinate the assistance programs, which are then implemented by state, county, and city offices, voluntary agency affiliates, and some nonprofit organizations in the receiving communities. In the process, the states also manage income and medical assistance, and social services for needy refugees. Care for unaccompanied children, as mandated by the Refugee Act of 1980 is also managed by the states.

Congressional appropriations for domestic refugee assistance programs amounted to $410 million annually from 1991 through 1993, with essentially the same expenditure categories. For 1994, $400 million was appropriated; for 1995, a budget request of $413.7 made by the Clinton administration for the domestic refugee resettlement and assistance programs.

Cash and medical assistance for all refugees administered by the states accounted for $232.5 million in 1992, the largest category of program obligations. Later in 1995, $278.1 million was proposed for transitional and medical services. Social services and targeted assistance given to refugees in communities also represent major components of the national resettlement activities.

For 1992, appropriations for domestic resettlement managed by the Office of Refugee Resettlement, however, do not reflect the $734 million obligated by the Bureau for Refugee Programs under the U.S. State Department. These funds support major international refugee relief programs, like those conducted by the Office of the United Nations High Commissioner for Refugees, the International Committee of the Red Cross, and other emergency assistance programs worldwide. Two major components of the bureau budget are the costs of refugee processing and documentation in Southeast Asia, and support for resettling of new arrivals during their first three months in the United States.

Cash Assistance

The most significant public assistance program available to needy refugees is cash assistance. Eligible refugees with children are provided with income by Aid to Families with Dependent Children (AFDC) on the same basis as U.S. citizens. Many refugee families have relied on this welfare program.

Supplemental Security Income (SSI) benefits are also available for aged, blind, and disabled refugees. New arrivals who do not meet AFDC or SSI eligibility criteria can, for a limited time, receive financial help through the Refugee Cash Assistance (RCA) program. Food stamps are also provided in some cases to those refugees in need.

Many refugees that arrived with limited resources found cash assistance and food stamps to be their primary source of income during their initial period of resettlement in the United States. Some general assistance programs funded by local governments have also benefited those refugees who need help, but who are not eligible for AFDC, SSI, or RCA.

Medical Assistance

Poor living standards in their country of origin and unsanitary conditions in refugee camps cause medical problems among refugees from Southeast Asia. Medical screening and treatment by U.S.-supported health programs takes place in Southeast Asian refugee processing centers, especially for tuberculosis and hepatitis-B. After arriving in the United States, further assessment, follow-up care, and treatment of those with health problems remains a high priority for refugee assistance programs.

To ensure that refugee medical problems do not become public health issues, health officials provide additional health screening, treatment, and prevention programs as the refugees resettle in communities throughout the nation. These federally-funded resettlement services are part of an interagency agreement between ORR and the Office of Refugee Health, which coordinates refugee health activities. Undertaken primarily by the National Centers for Disease Control, health-assessment, diagnosis, and treatment are conducted in cooperation with state governments, local hospitals, clinics, and county health centers.

Medicaid benefits also are available for refugees that meet eligibility criteria. Under certain time limitations, needy refugees not qualified for Medicaid may receive services from the Refugee Medical Assistance (RMA) program. In addition, General Medical Assistance (GMA) programs, funded by state or local governments, are a last resort.

Cash and medical assistance programs provide needy refugees with the opportunity and time they need to become familiar with their new society before finding employment. These programs also help them to become independent more quickly. Some refugees, however, have become dependent on these assistance programs. This creates negative publicity for refugee communities and lessens the chances of public assistance for future arrivals.

Local Social Services Programs

In their efforts to adjust to U.S. society, Southeast Asian refugees participate in a variety of social programs provided by public and private agencies. English classes, vocational training, employment counseling, and job-placement services are generally available as priority services in areas with high refugee concentrations. In addition, orientation, transportation, child care, translation, and social adjustment services are provided to new arrivals.

Counties with the largest refugee populations also offer social services. These programs have been offered through targeted assistance funding over the past decade.

Table 21.7
Planned Secondary Resettlement Program (PSR) Summary (1983 - 1991)

Outcomes for refugee families who have been assisted with resettlement to communities where they are more likely to achieve self-sufficiency in the United States, since 1983.

Number of PSR participants:

422 families (1,700 individuals) have relocated.

Employment:

All families found full-time employment. Almost 90% work in production jobs in factories.

Wages:

Men earn an average of $6.90 per hour; women, $5.81.

Family Income:

Average monthly income for all participants is $1,952. Monthly income ranged from $1,830 for 1991 participants to $2,300 for participants with several years of experience.

Welfare Dependency:

Welfare dependency decreased from 100% prior to relocation to zero after relocation, with the exception of elderly refugees on Supplemental Security Income (SSI).

Home Ownership:

103 PSR families have become homeowners.

Secondary Migration:

Approximately 95% of PSR participants have remained in their new communities.

Cost and Benefits:

Average cost per family of resettlement through PSR is $8,000.

Average welfare cost savings per family are estimated to be $987 per month. PSR families repay resettlement cost to government in approximately eight months.

Source: U.S. Department of Health and Human Services, Office of Refugee Resettlement, Refugee Resettlement Program, Report to the Congress, January 31, 1992), pp. 34-35. The Planned Secondary Resettlement (PSR) program provides an opportunity for unemployed refugees and their families to relocate from areas of high welfare dependency to communities offering favorable employment prospects. Eligibility is limited to refugees who have experienced continuing unemployment. Statistical Record of Asian Americans, Susan Gall (ed.), 1993, Table 567, p. 446.

Planned Secondary Resettlement

To gain access to better employment opportunities in some states, unemployed refugees living in highly welfare-dependent areas have participated in planned secondary resettlement. This program, operated by several refugee community-based organizations and voluntary agencies, has assisted refugees with relocation since 1983. By 1991, some 422 refugee families and 1,700 individuals had benefitted from this successful relocation program.

In addition, many Southeast Asian refugees have applied for Office of Refugee Resettlement (ORR) discretionary grants, which are awarded by public agencies and nonprofit organizations in response to the needs of new arrivals in their communities. Funded by $12.5 million from ORR in 1992, these projects served Amerasians and former political prisoners from Vietnam, and financed refugee microenterprise loans.

Employment Training

All refugee assistance programs are designed to encourage economic independence. Accordingly, much emphasis has been placed on job training and employment services. Refugees are made aware of these services through announcements and news articles in numerous Asian-language newspapers and magazines.

In addition, the ORR appropriation in 1992 supported the Key States Initiative, a program that sought to increase employment and reduce welfare dependency, and the Job Link Program, which introduced employable refugees to potential employers.

Over many years, refugees have also improved their employability through a network of interrelated service programs provided by nonprofit community organizations. Thousands of participants complete the training and join the work force, successfully becoming productive members of their new society.

Table 21.8
Current and Previous Occupational Status of Southeast Asian Refugees (1991-1992)

Occupation	1991		1992	
	In Country of Origin	In U.S.	In Country of Origin	In U.S.
Professional/Managerial	9.4%	1.4%	11.2%	0.9%
Sales/Clerical	26.2%	16.2%	30.4%	18.5%
Total, White Collar	35.6%	17.6%	41.6%	19.4%
Skilled	13.8%	24.4%	4.8%	19.4%
Semi-skilled	3.5%	35.4%	12.9%	30.5%
Laborers	0.0%	4.3%	1.0%	12.4%
Total, Blue Collar	17.3%	64.1%	18.7%	63.3%
Service workers	7.7%	17.7%	9.3%	17.7%
Farmers/fishers	39.4%	0.6%	36.8%	0.6%

Source: U.S. Department of Health and Human Services, Office of Refugee Resettlement, Refugee Resettlement Program, Reports to the Congress, January 31, 1993, p. 56; and January 31, 1992, p. 54.

♦ THE SOUTHEAST ASIAN REFUGEE EXPERIENCE

The Challenging Road to Self-Sufficiency

For Southeast Asian refugees, pursuit of the American dream often began soon after their arrival. Those with adequate English proficiency and marketable skills have found employment in a wide spectrum of professions, ranging from law enforcement and education to small business ownership.

The Vietnamese, due to their larger share of the refugee population and their educational background, have gained a higher representation in professional occupations when compared to the other Southeast Asian refugee groups. It is not uncommon to find Vietnamese on the faculty of major universities, among physicians in well-known medical establishments, or on the technical staff in various engineering firms. Many have also entered government service, while others thrive in business. The Laotians, Cambodians, and Chinese-Vietnamese have also found places among the American professional community, although at slower rates.

However, the occupational status of Southeast Asians in the United States is generally lower than that once

Table 21.9
Current Employment Status of Southeast Asian Refugees (a), 1992

Year of Entry	Labor Force Participation (%)					Unemployment Rate (%)				
	1988	1989	1990	1991	1992	1988	1989	1990	1991	1992
1992	—	—	—	—	33	—	—	—	—	32
1991	—	—	—	23	37	—	—	—	14	19
1990	—	—	21	35	34	—	—	31	28	14
1989	—	21	35	32	37	—	27	14	18	11
1988	20	30	33	36	35	21	24	5	12	14
1987	30	35	30	31	35	24	5	2	9	6
Total Sample (b)	37	37	36	36	37	8	11	8	14	16
U.S. Rates (c)	66	66	66	66	66	5	5	55	64	72

Notes:
(a) Household members 16 years of age and older.
(b) The figures for "total sample" include members of households whose sampled person arrived during the 5-year period preceding the survey.
(c) September unadjusted figures from the Bureau of Labor Statistics, Department of Labor.

Source: U.S. Department of Health and Human Services, Office of Refugee Resettlement, Refugee Resettlement Program, Reports to the Congress, January 31, 1993, p. 53.

held in their country of origin. For example, while only 19 percent of refugee workers held white-collar jobs in the United States in 1992, some 42 percent indicated they had held professional occupations in Southeast Asia.

In the endeavor to achieve economic self-sufficiency, the refugee experience suggests that success in finding work depends not only on employability, but also on the length of residence in the United States.

A 1992 survey of Southeast Asian refugees during their first five years in the United States found that the labor force participation rate for refugees aged 16 and older was 37 percent, while the unemployment rate was 16 percent. For the total U.S. population, the corresponding rates were 66 and 7.2 percent. In general, the survey revealed that the longer the refugees lived in the United States, the higher their labor force participation rate.

As more Southeast Asians have found and retained employment, their annual income has grown steadily, increasing their federal income tax contributions. Data from the Internal Revenue Service (IRS) in 1991 indicates that refugees who arrived between 1975 and 1979 doubled their cumulative annual income from $1.193 billion in 1982 to $2.231 billion in 1988. Due to their educational background, language proficiency, and longer acclimation period, refugees that arrived in 1975 earned substantially more than those that joined them in the United States during the following years.

Cultural Preservation and Community Development

Arts

While their cultures and traditions are rich and diverse, Southeast Asians share a common experience as refugees from the Vietnam War. For two decades, the images of their countries and national customs have remained the major source of inspiration for a considerable volume of art, literature, music, and other intellectual accomplishments by refugee artists and scholars.

Refugee writers, artists, and performers are strongly committed to preserving Southeast Asian cultures. They are supported by their growing communities in the United States, as well as the larger American society.

Education

Through the National Association for the Advancement of Education of Southeast Asians, and other cultural organizations, many Southeast Asian educators and scholars have promoted their native languages and cultures. Since about 1985, American academicians and educators have become interested and involved in refugee educational programs and cultural adaptation activities.

Community Activism

Community-based organizations, often referred to as Mutual Assistance Associations (MAAs), have become active in the Southeast Asian communities. These nonprofit groups provide orientation, training, social services, and cultural activities for the refugee communities from which they draw their membership and support. Since the early 1980s, over 1,000 have been formed nationwide.

Many of these associations offer valuable volunteer services to the community, especially to new arrivals. As incorporated nonprofit groups with former refugees comprising at least 51 percent of their boards of directors, over 150 MAAs have successfully become social services providers to promote refugee economic self-sufficiency, with annual funding from the Office of Refugee Resettlement (ORR) and other government agencies. Their financial support from the federal government is based on the proportion of the state's refugee population during the previous three years, as mandated by Section 6(a)(3) of the Refugee Assistance Extension Act of 1986.

MAA community development efforts and leadership training activities have been funded by ORR since the late 1980s, with allocations of about $3 million annually. In 1991, several regional and national leaders were invited by ORR to meet voluntary agency and state government representatives and discuss assistance program development at the national level.

About a half dozen MAAs have become major community organizations, with annual budgets over $1 million drawn from diverse funding sources. Among them are the United Cambodian Community in Long Beach and the Indochinese Mutual Assistance Association in San Diego. Most of the remaining small-to-medium community-based nonprofit organizations offer language training and social services for refugees, forming

Table 21.10
Income Reported (in $ Millions) by Southeast Asian Refugees (1982 - 1988)

Tax Year	All Cohorts	1975 Arrivals	1976-79 Arrivals
1982	$1,193	$963	$229
1983	$1,286	$1,024	$262
1984	$1,527	$1,202	$326
1985	$1,628	$1,267	$361
1986	$1,780	$1,376	$404
1987	$1,991	$1,527	$463
1988	$2,231	$1,699	$532

Source: U.S. Department of Health and Human Services, Office of Refugee Resettlement, Refugee Resettlement Program, Reports to the Congress, January 31, 1991, p. 99.

an initiative bridge between the growing refugee community and the larger society.

As the initiative becomes stronger, MAAs symbolize the emerging empowerment of refugee enclaves nationwide, especially in California and other states with high refugee concentrations. Among them are the Vietnamese Community of Orange County, the Los Angeles Unified Vietnamese Community Council, and the San Francisco Center for Southeast Asian Refugee Resettlement. Equally efficient are the Hmong Association of Brown County in Wisconsin, the Vietnamese Association of Illinois, the International Refugee Center of Oregon, the Cambodian Community of Massachusetts, the Vietnamese American Civic Association in Boston, and the Refugee Service Alliance in Houston. Efforts to establish regional and national MAA networks in recent years have shown modest success. It is hoped that by establishing a national network among community groups, the Southeast Asian refugee community will develop a mechanism for addressing its issues and concerns.

Business and Entrepreneurship

As refugee enclaves expanded in the early 1980s, small businesses emerged. Initial capital for most of these family businesses often came from both personal savings and loans from within the refugee community. This economic development effort may have originated from the entrepreneurial talent the refugees brought with them from Southeast Asia. In Orange County, Southern California, Vietnamese transformed a previously underdeveloped area into a thriving business community, appropriately named Little Saigon. These small businesses offer ethnic food, services, and merchandise not readily available elsewhere and employ many refugees.

Other communities with large Southeast Asian populations have witnessed a similar pattern of small-business development catering mainly to the refugee clientele. Grocery stores, restaurants, tailors, bookstores, hairdressers, health clinics, legal offices, and entertainment facilities can be found clustered in these growing small-business communities. The growth of these entrepreneurial ventures indicates that self-employment is the road of choice to economic success for many refugees in America. In 1988, the Immigration and Naturalization Service reported that more than 10,700 refugees who arrived between 1975 and 1979 received income from self-employment. This reflects the potential for significant economic contribution from Southeast Asian refugees.

While refugee-owned enterprises appear to be flourishing, they also have problems with ownership stability, financing, and management capability. As more refugee households join business communities, contact with the mainstream society grows allowing these businesses to expand. With proper financial management and marketing, the outlook for economic growth is positive. A small number of Southeast Asian entrepreneurs with ability and vision have successfully penetrated the mainstream American market, becoming role models and even idols for thousands of aspiring refugee workers and business owners alike.

Crime and Gang Activity

As is true with other ethnic groups, Southeast Asian communities have their share of problems. Preying on helpless victims of their own ethnic background, criminal activity by Southeast Asian gangs began to rise in the early 1990s. A correlation can be made between the growing number of these youth gangs and the increase in high school dropout rates among Southeast Asians. Also, the strength and cohesiveness of the traditional Southeast Asian family unit has been noticeably eroded by the demands of daily life in a new society. Therefore, parents struggling to adapt find less and less time to spend with their children, who oftentimes turn to gang activity in their search for identity and belonging.

Recognizing these deeply rooted and complex problems, several community-based projects are supported by the Office of Refugee Resettlement (ORR) to mitigate refugee crime victimization and improve the links between Southeast Asian communities and law-enforcement agencies.

Political Empowerment

Many Southeast Asians have been attracted to work in refugee-assistance programs at the local, state, and national levels. In communities across the country, they have become leaders, managing the day-to-day operations of resettlement and training projects to assist their fellow countrymen. In the early 1980s, in fact, Arizona, California, Minnesota, and Washington began to recruit former refugees to coordinate state and county programs. These prominent positions in the public sector, as well as advancements made in the private sector, have heightened the refugees' involvement in the political process.

Concurrent with socioeconomic progress and community development, political activities began to solidify in cities and states where a large number of Southeast Asian residents had become naturalized citizens. Refugees admitted under the Refugee Act of 1980 were allowed to adjust their immigration status to permanent resident after one year in the United States and were eligible to apply for naturalization five years after gaining permanent resident status. About 254,000 former Southeast Asian refugees became naturalized citizens between 1980 and 1991. In addition, children born to naturalized parents and persons married to U.S. citizens also became citizens under existing law.

As the number of Southeast Asians becoming naturalized citizens increased, and as they became more familiar with the American political structure, a power base of Southeast Asian voters began to grow. Political activities often began with a limited number of well-connected community activists. However, they soon attracted the attention of politicians from both the Democratic and the Republican parties seeking the support of the growing Southeast Asian population.

In the late 1980s, recognizing the growing participation of Southeast Asian refugees in mainstream politics, governors from several states appointed Vietnamese Americans to positions of high visibility. These state government posts were designed to promote sociocultural relations and enhance service delivery to the multiethnic population in their respective states.

At the national level, several Southeast Asians were appointed to various positions in the federal government during the Reagan and Bush administrations. A few of these political appointees have participated in policy and program issues directly impacting the Southeast Asian refugee communities. Notable among these appointees was Sichan Siv, a Cambodian American. Appointed deputy assistant to former President George Bush, he was responsible for public liaison at the White House. In recent years, a Vietnamese American was appointed to serve as deputy director of the Office of Bilingual Education and Minority Language Affairs (OBEMLA), Department of Education. In addition, other Southeast Asian Americans have also been invited to join federal advisory committees, gaining more exposure to the national political system.

In the early 1990s, American voters began to take Southeast Asians seriously as political candidates. In some areas with high refugee concentrations, Southeast Asians ran for city council seats and other local offices with promising chances of victory. In late 1992, Tony Lam became the first Vietnamese American to win a seat on the city council of Westminster, a southern California city with a flourishing Vietnamese American business community. In communities across the United States, former refugees have been chosen to represent the concerns of local citizens on school boards and other community organizations.

Although recent voter turnout among Southeast Asians has been quite low in comparison to the general population, these success stories signal the emerging Southeast Asian voter community as a potentially significant force in American politics. As ethnic population segments grow and band together, the Southeast Asian American community will become an even greater participant in the political system.

◆ CONCLUSION

Beginning in 1975 and continuing into the 1990s, over one million Southeast Asians fled their homelands in order to pursue the American dream in refugee communities across the nation. A growing number Southeast Asian refugees have made significant progress in their adaptation and contribution to American society. However, for those refugees dependent on long-term public assistance, the picture may not be as bright.

With public sentiment toward immigrants as a whole becoming less favorable and assistance from the federal government likely to be reduced in response to increased budgetary constraints, resourceful refugee communities and their leaders will need to discover alternative ways to succeed in mainstream society. One such way might be through political involvement at the local, regional, and national levels. This will likely accelerate as a result of further progress in socioeconomic adaptation of Southeast Asians. The desire of the younger generation to participate directly in the U.S. political process will contribute to political gains.

References

Gall, Susan B. Ed. *Statistical Record of Asian Americans*. Detroit: Gale Research Inc., 1993.

Lewis, Judy. *Selected Sources—People from Cambodia, Laos & Vietnam*. Southeast Asia Community Resource Center, Folsom Cordova Unified School District, 1993.

Nguyen, Van Hanh. "Indochinese Refugee Resettlement in the United States: A Socioeconomic Analysis." In *Public Service Review*. Davis: University of California, June 1982.

U.S. Committee for Refugees. *Refugee Reports*. 14, no. 5 (May 31, 1993): 9-10.

U.S. Department of Health, Education and Welfare. *Report to the Congress*, 1975.

U.S. Department of Health, Education and Welfare. *Report to the Congress*, 1977.

U.S. Department of Health and Human Services. Office of Refugee Resettlement. *Refugee Resettlement Program, Report to the Congress*, January 31, 1991.

U.S. Department of Health and Human Services. Office of Refugee Resettlement. *Refugee Resettlement Program, Report to the Congress*, January 31, 1992.

U.S. Department of Health and Human Services. Office of Refugee Resettlement. *Refugee Resettlement Program, Report to the Congress*, January 31, 1993.

U.S. Department of Health and Human Services. Office of Refugee Resettlement. *Update*, February 1994; 2.

—Nguyen Van Hanh, Ph.D.

Civil Rights

◆ Asian America in the Sixties ◆ Anti-Asian Violence: A National Problem
◆ Asian American Involvement in the Political Process: Case Study
◆ Asian American Labor Activism: Organizational Profile

◆ ASIAN AMERICA IN THE SIXTIES

1963 Civil Rights March on Washington

More than 200,000 demonstrators led by the Reverend Martin Luther King gathered on August 28, 1963, for a march on Washington, DC, to protest civil rights violations. It was a significant day for the United States. Earlier in the summer, nonviolent civil rights protests in the South (particularly the highly publicized King-led demonstration in Birmingham, Alabama) had been met with fire hoses, police beatings, and jail time. As the nation watched in horror, President John F. Kennedy was forced to confront the civil rights issue and face a new era of race relations.

On that eventful day in August, individuals and organizations from around the country, both black and white, joined this march for jobs and freedom. One of the groups participating was the Japanese American Citizens League (JACL). Formed in 1930 under the banner of loyalty, patriotism, and U.S. citizenship, the JACL was a nisei (second-generation Japanese American) civic organization dedicated to gaining acceptance for its people. Oftentimes, the group's conciliatory methods proved to be controversial among some Japanese Americans. JACL's cooperation with the government over the Japanese American internment, for example, was seen as a major failure by some other nisei. However, such methods proved successful in the legislative arena. Among the numerous bills they sponsored was the 1952 McCarran-Walter Act which relaxed immigration restrictions from Japan (and other countries), allowing issei (first-generation Japanese Americans) to become naturalized citizens. By the 1960s, JACL had firmly established itself as the leading representative for Japanese Americans.

In many ways, the August 1963 March on Washington was the United States presenting its best face—Americans joining together to demonstrate their yearning for peace and justice for all people. Two months earlier, however, the JACL found itself in a precarious position on the issue of demonstrations. As the lone Asian American organization on the National Leadership Conference on Civil Rights (a coalition of concerned groups from around the country), they were morally obligated to help expedite the realization of equal rights and treatment for all Americans. However, former JACL wartime president and influential leader Saburo Kido, for one, believed that "direct action" was inappropriate. In a June 1963 interview with Pacific Citizen, Kido stated: "We should reserve our freedom of action so that we need not become involved in any riotous demonstrations. We must help to preserve a lawful approach to the solution."

Patrick Okura, JACL president during this period, recalled the debates over the issue in Bill Hosokawa's JACL: In Quest of Justice:

There were a number of older nisei who were fairly well established in business and who were proud that we had pulled ourselves up by our bootstraps following the Evacuation. [Japanese Americans were forcibly interned in camps during World War II.] It was the feeling of the great majority of our [JACL] chapter leaders that what the blacks did was their business, their problem, and that they should improve their lot in the same way we had, and that we shouldn't get involved in the civil rights movement.

Okura, however, along with a number of other influential liberal leaders in the JACL, was able to convince the organization to participate in the March on Washington. Thirty-five people marched under the JACL banner on August 28, 1963, in the only known contingent representing Asian Americans. In September, *Pacific Citizen* reported on other Asians who had also participated independently or with groups such as the churches led by Reverend Alfred Akamatsu of New York and Mrs. Min Mochizuki of Kalamazoo, Michigan. It was a proud day for the JACL leaders. To their relief, they had made the correct decision to participate.

The events leading up to the march were significant because they raised more questions than answers about civil rights for Asian Americans. For example, why were so few groups and individuals involved in the civil rights movement? What did civil rights mean to Asian America? In a February 1994 interview, Los Angeles activist Jim Matsuoka offered his opinion:

> At that time [early 1960s], we [Japanese Americans] were still trying to economically and psychologically recover from the repression of the concentration camps. We weren't really involved in the civil rights movement as a group. Hell, we were still working on the basic questions like, 'What are we? . . . Orientals? . . . Asians?' There weren't a whole lot of us [Asian Americans] out there in those days.

In the following sections, some of the civil rights activities that engaged Asian Americans in the 1960s will be highlighted. We will examine the student movement, the farmworkers movement, and the immigration reform movement. While these were technically separate from the civil rights movement, they were similar in spirit. They helped fuel the rise of the Asian American movement of the late 1960s and early 1970s.

The Student Movement

In the 1960s, many Asian Americans felt that they had no political outlet for their activism and ended up joining other organizations. Yuri and Bill Kochiyama, a nisei couple from New York City, became activists when they moved to Harlem in 1960 and joined the predominantly African-American Harlem Parents Committee, an organization dedicated to the educational well-being of the area's children. Along with other parents, they enrolled their children in the alternative Harlem Freedom School and worked in other community campaigns for justice. In 1964, Yuri joined Malcolm X's Organization for Afro-American Unity (OAAU) and later organized a meeting between the leader and a group of atomic bomb survivors from Japan.

In 1965, Yuri Kochiyama witnessed the tragic assassination of Malcolm X, and was pictured in *Life* magazine cradling the head of the slain leader. Later in the decade, she joined Asian Americans for Action (AAA), which was formed by fellow nisei women Kazu Iijima and Min Matsuda. Through their political activities,

they asked every Asian American they encountered at demonstrations to join the group. Eventually, most of the AAA membership consisted of radical Asian American student activists from the New Left or Black Power Movement.

Alan Nishio, a future leader in the National Coalition for Redress/Reparations (NCRR) received his activist baptism by participating in the Free Speech Movement while a student at the University of California—Berkeley. The experience led him to join the Student Nonviolent Coordinating Committee (SNCC), which at the time was organizing students for voter-registration drives and Freedom Rides in the South.

Later, however, Nishio left the group because he was uncertain of his role in the predominantly black and white organization. Nishio was later instrumental in forming the Asian American Political Alliance at the University of Southern California in 1968 and has been extremely active in Asian American political activities ever since.

Evelyn Yoshimura was another student who grew up during the 1960s. When she was a teenager living in the Crenshaw district of Los Angeles, she remembered hearing about the assassination of Malcolm X and also recalled an encounter with a member of the Nation of Islam. In a 1989 *Amerasia Journal* article, Yoshimura wrote about this "meticulously dressed young black man—head shaven clean, wearing a bow tie—selling Muhammad Speaks." The experience clearly made an impression on her. It was the first time that anyone had ever referred to her as an "Asian sister."

When Yoshimura entered California State University at Long Beach in 1966, she wanted to join a group that shared her life experiences as an Asian American, but found nothing appealing. Yoshimura recalled that period:

> There were some students who were forming a group to protest the Vietnam War and racism on campus. I went to a few meetings, and some of them had been at [the University of California] Berkeley during the Free Speech Demonstrations. They had a lot of experiences to share, but I didn't like being lectured to about racism by middle-class white students, some of whom had never seen a person of color before coming to college.

San Francisco State Strike

In the meantime at San Francisco State College, students in the Third World Liberation Front (TWLF), a coalition of African-American, Latino, and Asian American student groups, began demanding reforms that addressed the concerns of students of color and the surrounding community. After more than a year of negotiating with the school and organizing students, they called a strike on November 6, 1968, that became the longest student strike in United States history. When it was finally settled in March 1969, many of the students' demands were met, including the establishment of a School of Ethnic Studies.

Intercollegiate Chinese for Social Action

One of the groups involved in the TWLF was the Intercollegiate Chinese for Social Action (ICSA). Formed in November 1967, ICSA obtained funding from the Associated Students to work with the local San Francisco Chinatown. They set up a youth center, initiated a tutorial project for teenagers, volunteered at the War on Poverty office, and also taught English to Chinese immigrants.

Philippine American Collegiate Endeavor (PACE)

Another group that was active in the TWLF was the Philippine-American Collegiate Endeavor (PACE). They were organized in the spring of 1968 to encourage Pilipino American students to fight for positive change in their community and on campus. ("Pilipino" is the term preferred by many who trace their ancestry to the Philippines.) They organized high school recruitment drives that encouraged Pilipino youth to apply to college through the Equal Opportunity Program, held tutorials and counseling programs to help retain students once they were admitted, and worked vigorously within Manilatown, where a large concentration of Pilipino Americans lived. The organization was incredibly successful in identifying the needs of Pilipino Americans; out of the estimated 125 Pilipino students on campus, close to 70 were PACE members.

Asian American Political Alliance (AAPA)

The Asian American Political Alliance (AAPA) was the third Asian American group to be involved with the TWLF. It was formed in the summer of 1968 by three Japanese American women as a chapter of the original group organized at the University of California—Berkeley. The political development of the San Francisco State College AAPA was heavily influenced by the University of California-Berkeley group. According to William Wei in *The Asian American Movement*, the Berkeley AAPA was formed by Asian American members of the radical Peace and Freedom Party (which included members of the Black Panther Party and anti-war activists), who wanted to organize around issues facing all Asian Americans and recognize their common history of struggle in the United States. The group's name is believed to be the first use of Asian instead of Oriental.

Some members organized political study groups and read the writings of Mao Zedong, Franz Fanon, and the Black Panthers. Others, including poet Janice Mirikitani, published *Aion*, one of the first Asian American journals.

The legacy left by the Asian American activists in the San Francisco State strike cannot be underestimated. Besides establishing ethnic studies, which soon spread to colleges on both coasts, the students helped inspire a wellspring of activism that created Asian American community centers, self-help clinics, and other institutions that are still in operation.

The Farmworkers Movement

"When my mother asked me how long I planned to stay away, I told her three years. Well, I've been here in the U.S. almost 50 years now and I haven't been back yet . . . I always just had enough money to send home but as far as having enough money for myself to return and lead my own life, it never happened. My life here was always just a matter of survival . . . That's the way it has been for most of us Pilipino old-timers." These were the words of activist Philip Vera Cruz, Pilipino labor activist.

Pilipino Americans, since their arrival in the United States in the 1920s, helped build the farmworkers movement through leadership and backbreaking labor. Philip Vera Cruz and Larry Itliong were two of the many Manongs (Pilipino American early immigrants) who participated in numerous strikes against growers for fair wages and working conditions. On September 8, 1965, Vera Cruz and Itliong, as part of the largely Pilipino American Agricultural Workers Organizing Committee (AWOC), voted to strike against the Delano, California, grape growers. In retrospect, it was arguably the most significant strike vote ever taken in the history of the farmworkers movement.

Before 1965, the farmworkers movement was organized along traditional trade union lines. The timing and the prolonged nature of the strike, however, called for different measures. With the assassination of Malcolm X in New York and with civil rights movement in full force in the South, AWOC found an important ally in the National Farm Workers Association (NFWA), a primarily Chicano labor union led by Cesar Chavez. As the strike progressed, AWOK and NFWA worked together to build support for their movement. According to Reverend Wayne C. Hartmire, Jr., an organizer of the strike, significant help came from students, including the Student Nonviolent Coordinating Committee (SNCC), the Congress of Racial Equality (CORE), churches, labor organizations, and other institutions.

In March 1966, six months after the strike began, NFWA raised the stakes by organizing a 200-mile march from Delano to the California state capitol in Sacramento. Larry Itliong, the highest-ranking Pilipino officer in AWOC, and several other Pilipino leaders in the union including Vera Cruz broke ranks with director Al Green, and joined the NFWA march under the AWOC banner. With camaraderie at a new high among the unions, the two merged in August of 1966 as the United Farm Workers Organizing Committee (UFWOC), which later shortened its name to the United Farm Workers (UFW). Chavez was named director of the new union while Itliong, Vera Cruz, and Andy Imutan from AWOK were among those named vice-presidents, essentially acting as part of a board of directors.

The UFW won concessions from the growers later in 1966, but faced many more battles during the decade. Eventually, on July 29, 1970, the Delano growers were forced to recognize the UFW and signed labor contracts with the union. In 1971, Vera Cruz became the highest-ranking Pilipino in the union when he was elected second vice-president in the UFW's first official election. As the years passed, however, Pilipino influence in the union gradually declined as the manongs retired and were replaced by younger Mexican American workers.

Immigration Act of 1965

The Immigration Act of 1965 was perhaps the most significant piece of legislation passed in the 1960s for Asian Americans. Inspired by President John F. Kennedy's New Frontiers and President Lyndon B. Johnson's Great Society programs, it was clearly intended to demonstrate that the United States, in the midst of the battle over civil rights, promoted freedom and equal treatment. It invalidated the 1924 Immigration Act, which restricted Asian immigration and favored immigrants from Western Europe, and attracted the brightest minds from around the world with no special preference given to countries.

Before 1965, the Asian American population was extremely small. Japanese Americans, for example, constituted the largest Asian American group with a 1960 population of only 464,332. Chinese Americans had the next largest population with 237,292, while Pilipino Americans had a population of 176,310 in 1960. The Korean American and Asian Indian American populations were only 11,000 and 12,296, respectively.

Since the 1965 Immigration Act took effect, however, Asian immigration has exploded. Overall, the Asian American population has soared from approximately 1.2 million in 1965 to almost 7.3 million in 1990—a 600 percent increase. Japanese Americans, whom some policy experts believed would benefit the most from the act, doubled their population to almost 850,000. Other groups, however, quickly surpassed them. Chinese Americans, the second largest Asian group in

1965, increased their population by about 450 percent to become the largest group in 1990. Pilipino Americans grew sevenfold to become the second largest.

However, the biggest changes were reserved for the Korean American and Asian Indian American populations. By 1990, they had grown 18 times and 16 times, respectively, rivaling the Japanese American population. Nobody, not even Asian Americans, could have foreseen the dramatic changes that have taken place since 1965.

With this population increase (including the dramatically expanding Southeast Asian American population) comes many benefits, including the cultural diversity that each group brings to the United States. In the long term, the growth of the different groups will eventually translate into increased political power and access to institutions. (In retrospect, it is amazing how much was accomplished by Asian American activists in the 1960s considering the minuscule population figures.)

With growth, however, also comes many challenges. If history is to be used as a barometer for future events, any population growth by a nonwhite group will result in racial tension and oftentimes violence. Asian American activists must be assertive and willing to apply lessons learned from the past.

—Glen Kitayama and Don Nakanishi

◆ ANTI-ASIAN VIOLENCE: A NATIONAL PROBLEM

The first national audit of violence against Asian/Pacific Americans (anti-Asian violence) was conducted in 1994 by the National Asian Pacific American Legal Consortium (NAPALC). This audit assessed the extent of anti-Asian violence in the United States, with the goal of motivating public and private leaders to address this widespread and serious problem. While acts of discriminatory violence occur throughout U.S. history, in the 1980s and 1990s, violent threats and acts committed because of race, national origin, religion, sexual orientation, or other characteristics emerged as a national problem.

Violence against a person because of membership in a certain group violates that individual's civil rights. It harms not only the victim, but also sends a menacing message to other members of vulnerable communities. Hate violence has a chilling effect on the targeted community and, by extension, on all Americans' lives.

Hate violence may be broadly defined as any verbal or physical act that intimidates, threatens, or injures a person or person's property because of membership in a targeted group. That membership can be based on actual or perceived race, ethnicity, national origin, religion, gender, sexual orientation, or age. Such acts may occur as spoken or written threats, harassment, graffiti, vandalism, property damage, and physical assaults, or attacks resulting in serious injury or death.

By contrast, hate crime is defined as a violation of a criminal or penal statute. Regardless of whether a hate crime has occurred, all hate violence should be reported and investigated, because many incidents that begin as name-calling sometimes escalate into violence and serious physical injury, even death. All circumstances of a particular crime must be examined to discover whether racial motivation is a factor. The crime should be investigated as a hate crime if the slightest suggestion exists that the act was racially motivated. Historically, hate crimes have been underreported, and direct evidence of racial bias often only emerges after a thorough investigation.

Hate Crime on the Rise

The number of hate crimes increased in the late 1980s and early 1990s. Of the 8,918 hate crimes reported in 1992, acts against Asian/Pacific Americans comprised 3.4 percent of the total, an amount higher than the 3 percent that they represent in the U.S. population.

The number of hate crimes may be even greater than reported, since the federal Hate-Crimes Statistics Act, enacted in 1990 to develop and implement a uniform system of data collection, does not make hate-crimes reporting mandatory for enforcement agencies. Only 27 percent of police departments around the nation reported bias-incident statistics in 1991, and in 1992 the figure had risen to only 53 percent. Even in California, where 40 percent of the total Asian/Pacific American population lives, and where 10 percent of the population is Asian/Pacific American, only 75 hate-crime incidents were reported for all ethnic groups, since only seven law enforcement agencies participated in the data collection process in 1992.

This article will briefly review the history of violence against Asian/Pacific Americans, recent cases being handled by the National Asian Pacific American Legal Consortium, and national trends on the subject. It then provides some policy recommendations to respond to the problem of anti-Asian violence.

Chronology of Anti-Asian Sentiment

Since their arrival in the United States over 140 years ago, Asian/Pacific Americans have been victims of legally sanctioned racism and economic injustices, including denial of access to the legal system, exclusionary immigration policies, and the internment of Japanese Americans during World War II. Although de jure (by law) discrimination is outlawed today, the legacy of racism continues in social outlets, such as entertainment. In best-selling novels and blockbuster movies, Asian/Pacific Americans continue to be cast as untrustworthy foreigners and devious economic competitors. Stereotypes and caricatures also scapegoat Asian/Pacific Americans by inaccurately linking the downturn in the U.S. economy with the doubling of the population since 1980. These stereotypical images may result in anti-Asian hate incidents.

Anti-Asian sentiment appears to occur in waves, reflecting changes in immigration and economic conditions. During the 1870s, as the United States suffered from an economic recession, growing numbers of unemployed white workers vented their resentment on underpaid Chinese Americans. This resulted in widespread public rhetoric excoriating Asian immigrants. Politicians exploited the public frustration, stirring up anti-Chinese sentiment. In the process, federal, state, and local legislatures passed blatantly discriminatory laws.

For example, the Sidewalk Ordinance of 1870 prohibited persons from walking on the streets while using poles to carry goods, a practice used only by Chinese Americans at the time. The federal Chinese Exclusion Act of 1882 effectively barred immigration from all Asian countries except the Philippines and remained in effect until 1943.

Despite the history of anti-Asian violence, the Asian/Pacific American community did not advance an organized response until the second half of the twentieth century.

1982. Vincent Chin, a young Chinese American engineer celebrating at his own bachelor party, was brutally beaten to death with a baseball bat by two white auto workers who thought he was Japanese and blamed him for the demise of the U.S. auto industry. This tragedy galvanized the Asian/Pacific American community to organize. Unfortunately, the Chin murder was not an isolated occurrence.

May 1983. A young Vietnamese American high school student, Thona Huynh, was stabbed to death in Davis, California, by a white student after racial taunting by a group of white students.

September 1987. A Cambodian American teenager was drowned by a youth shouting racial slurs in Lowell, Massachusetts.

1989. Patrick Purdy, who hated Southeast Asians because of the Vietnam War, killed five children and wounded more that 20 others by firing an assault rifle in a Stockton, California, schoolyard.

1989. Ming Hai "Jim" Loo, a Chinese American, was beaten to death in Raleigh, North Carolina, by white men who blamed him for the death of U.S. service personnel in Vietnam; the men told authorities that they attacked Loo "because they didn't like Vietnamese" and because "their brothers went over to Vietnam in the war, and they never came back."

June 1990. In Houston, a Vietnamese American youth pleaded for his life while two skinheads beat and kicked him to death.

Summer 1993. A south Sacramento, California, African American bookstore had racist graffiti marked on its windows and was vandalized.

August 1993. Sacramento-area Asian American was physically attacked by a white man who told him to "show your Kung Fu."

August 14, 1993. Sophy Soeung and Sam Nhang Nhem, two male Cambodian tenants of a Wattupa Heights apartment complex in Fall River, Massachusetts, were attacked after taking out the trash. Over a dozen white men kicked and punched the Cambodians for three or four minutes. Although Seng survived the severe beating, Nhem died shortly after the attack. On August 17, Harold Robert Latour, a 23-year-old Fall River resident, was arrested as one of the alleged attackers and was charged with first-degree murder, two counts of assault and battery using a dangerous weapon, and one count of intimidating an individual on the basis of race, color, or national origin.

In the week following the murder and beating, refugee-community representatives successfully pressured the Bristol County district attorney's office to label the incident a hate crime. The attack had initially been deemed "isolated" by the Fall River's police chief, but the Cambodian Community of Greater Fall River's Crisis Intervention Program believed the assailants were racially motivated because they used the word "gook" in reference to one of their victims.

The case was investigated by Asian American Legal Defense and Education Fund attorney Elizabeth Ou Yang as a National Asian Pacific American Legal Consortium member. Apparently, Latour and the other white men used racially offensive slurs during the Cambodians' family barbecue, which preceded the beating, according to OuYang, who also believed the beating to be a hate crime. The Consortium initiated a letter-writing campaign to the District Attorney's office, calling for a full investigation and prosecution of all responsible parties.

On November 30, 1993. Robert Latour was indicted by a grand jury for murder and the racially motivated crime of assault and battery. Two others were also charged for the beating of Sophy Soeng.

October 2, 1993. The Japanese American Citizens League (JACL) office in Sacramento, which had been particularly outspoken in its denunciation of racism and hate crimes, was firebombed at 2 a.m. when a Molotov cocktail was tossed through a window. The office sustained over $20,000 in damages. The Aryan Liberation Front, a white supremacist group, called a local television station, KLBR-TV, to claim responsibility for this and two other firebombings in 1993: the Jewish Temple B'nai Israel and the Sacramento NAACP office.

October 5, 1993. A firebombing occurred at the house of Jimmie Yee, a Sacramento councilman and vocal critic of recent Sacramento firebombings. Both Yee and his wife were at home when the firebombing occurred at 2 a.m., although neither were hurt. The bombing occurred on the scheduled date of a press conference featuring a speech by Yee on the October 2 JACL firebombing.

December 1993. A black man carrying notes detailing his racial hatred killed five people, including two Asian/Pacific Americans, on a Long Island railroad train.

Consortium Case Studies

Hate violence generates an enormous toll of human suffering and pain that reaches beyond cold hard statistics. Four case examples from the Asian Pacific American Legal Consortium's 1993 docket follow.

Luyen Phan Nguyen

Mr. Luyen Phan Nguyen, a 19-year-old Vietnamese American pre-med student, was beaten to death on August 15, 1992, in Coral Springs, Florida by a mob of white youths who called out "Chink," "Vietcong," "Sayonara," and other racist slurs. Fifteen youths chased, surrounded, and beat Nguyen so severely that he died two days later of a brain hemorrhage caused by a fractured neck.

After legal intervention by the Consortium and community organizations, seven people were arrested and charged with the Nguyen killing. Bradley Mills, the first of the seven to be tried, was convicted of second-degree murder and sentenced to 50 years in prison on December 9, 1992. The remaining six defendants are scheduled to be tried in early 1994.

Dr. Kaushal Sharan

Dr. Kaushal Sharan, an Asian Indian doctor in Jersey City, New Jersey, was walking home after visiting his brother in September 1987, when he was attacked in front of a firehouse and a local youth hangout. White youths hurled racial epithets at him as they beat him, leaving him unconscious and severely injured. At that time, many South Asians in Jersey City had been attacked during a wave of beatings and vandalism. These crimes were committed by racist gangs known as the Dotbusters (referring to the red bindi worn by East Indian women on their foreheads) and the Lost Boys.

After local police failed to make any arrests in the beating, Consortium staff and local South Asian leaders successfully urged the U.S. Justice Department to investigate Dotbuster activity. In September 1992, nearly five years after the attack, three men were indicted for federal criminal civil rights charges. One was the son of the local police lieutenant, and another had become a local county officer.

In January 1993, federal criminal trials were held in Camden, New Jersey, for three young men charged with the beating. The jury was unable to reach a unanimous verdict after a three-week trial. Under community pressure, the Justice Department retried the case against one defendant in May 1993. The second trial resulted in an acquittal. The Justice Department then declined to retry the other two defendants. According to the judge, the federal government's case was weakened significantly by the failure of local police to thoroughly investigate this case from the start.

Sam Nang Nhem

On August 14, 1993, Sam Nang Nhem, a 21 year-old Cambodian American father of a four-month old infant, was subjected to racial taunts and repeatedly kicked in the head by white youth in the Wattupa Heights Housing Development in Fall River, Massachusetts. With Nhem was Sophy Soeng, who was attacked but survived. Nhem died two days later from massive blood loss and severe brain damage.

The Consortium initiated a letter-writing campaign to the District Attorney's office calling for a full investigation and prosecution of all responsible parties. On November 30, 1993, Robert Latour was indicted by a grand jury for murder and the racially motivated crime of assault and battery. Two others were charged, in addition to Latour, for the beating of Sophy Soeng.

San Francisco Housing Authority

When Southeast Asian tenants moved into certain San Francisco Housing Authority (SFHA) housing projects, many were subjected to name-calling, physical and emotional intimidation, threats, assaults, and even beatings and killings. Children were harassed and assaulted on their way to and from school. Units were robbed and vandalized, with rocks and eggs thrown at windows. Tenants with limited English-speaking abilities, such as those from Southeast Asia, could not even report such incidents because there were no bilingual housing project staff. The residents felt alienated, isolated, and helpless, and many fled for their safety.

In 1993, a recognizable pattern in this harassment and hate violence developed. Consortium and Asian Law Caucus (ALC) attorneys realized the problem was more than a few racist individuals. The antagonism toward these tenants arose from larger institutional

dynamics, including economic and language issues, as well as from ignorance and prejudice. Individual prosecution of the perpetrators would not fully address the problem, but institutional change within the SFHA and the Federal Department of Housing and Urban Development (HUD) would.

After filing a lawsuit on behalf of the tenants against the SFHA and HUD, the Consortium, through the ALC, reached a tentative settlement. The agencies agreed to improve security, provide language assistance, institute staff training, provide support services for new tenants and community organizations, and change discriminatory assignment and transfer policies. This settlement offers a model for improving community relations and reducing racial hostility in other housing projects with similar problems.

National Issues and Trends

Despite the problem of severe underreporting and difficulties encountered in conducting their national audit of anti-Asian violence, NAPALC's report revealed several issues and trends: the deadly nature of the problem, law enforcement responses, anti-Asian sentiments, inter-ethnic conflicts, targeting of small Asian businesses, school conflicts, white supremacist groups, and constitutional challenges to anti-bias legislation.

Deadly Nature of the Problem

Physical assaults are the most common form of attack against Asian/Pacific Americans. More than 30 percent of hate crimes are personal assaults, and a victim of a hate crime is three times more likely to be personally assaulted than a victim of a nonhate crime. A study issued by the National Institute Against Prejudice and Violence found that physical assaults, 24.8 percent of reported incidents, are the most common form of hate crimes committed against Asian/Pacific Americans. In 1991, the Los Angeles County Commission on Human Relations also reported that physical assaults had overtaken graffiti as the most common form of hate crime.

Moreover, hate violence is "far more lethal than other kinds of attacks, resulting in the hospitalization of . . . victims four times more often than is true for other assaults . . . Half [of the bias incidents] involved assaults." The victims were injured in 74 percent of the cases; the national average for injury to an assault victim is 29 percent. At least one victim required hospitalization in 30 percent of the prejudiced-based assaults, while for other assaults the average national figure is 7 percent." Anti-Asian violence, like other forms of hate violence, is much more dangerous than similar acts not motivated by hate.

Local Law Enforcement Responses

The data indicate an extremely low level of local law enforcement response to hate-violence incidents. Several underlying factors may account for this:

• Limited or no outreach to local Asian/Pacific American communities;

• Insensitivity by police to the issue of hate violence;

• Inadequate training of law enforcement officers;

• Lack of bilingual and Asian/Pacific American police officers;

• Supervisory practices and policies within law enforcement offices that fail to hold police officers accountable for enforcing laws against perpetrators of hate violence.

Often, local law enforcement officers fail to identify and classify hate-crime incidents. For example, a Los Angeles Police Department officer responded to a call from a Japanese American woman whose car had been spray painted with graffiti such as "Go home nip." The officer refused to classify the case as a hate crime, stating that it was a case of simple vandalism. No correction or arrest was ever made. The failure of law enforcement officers to classify hate crimes creates a vicious circle: When a hate crime is reported, the investigating officer often does not correctly identify it. The story of this insensitivity then circulates among community members who then believe that local law enforcement officers do not care about them. The community members then decide to continue not reporting hate crimes, and the cycle continues.

Moreover, few police report forms include designations for bias-motivated incidents. Many police officers then do not think to investigate the incident or inquire whether it is bias-related. In addition, many forms do not indicate the victim's race or ethnicity, making it difficult to research anti-Asian bias.

In some regions of the United States, law enforcement officials recognize the severity of the problem of hate crimes and the need to address them. In San Francisco, for example both the police department (SFPD) and the district attorney's office have specialized hate crime units, with personnel trained to handle these cases. The hate crime unit supervisor also trains police officers at local stations, in the police academy, and in other police departments, and co-chairs the Bay Area Hate Crimes Investigator's Association.

As a result of the *Nguyen v. SFHA* case, the SFPD established a housing task force within the San Francisco Police Department to deal with the security problems in the San Francisco housing projects. Using a policy called community policing, specific officers are assigned to particular projects, enabling them to become familiar with neighborhood residents. This establishes a positive relationship before a crisis occurs, making tenants much more likely to contact the police in the event of an incident.

The Maryland State Police Department also collects and analyzes hate-crime data, a task for which it employs a full-time civilian analyst. As a result, Maryland reported a total of 939 racial hate crimes in 1992, with 51 Asian/Pacific American victims and five separately categorized Asian Indian victims. No other state had such comprehensive numbers for its size. Such efforts create new ways for law enforcement officers and community activists to work together to reduce hate violence.

Anti-Immigrant Sentiment

Historically, economic recessions have triggered a backlash against recent immigrants. Today, Asian/Pacific Americans are experiencing the same types of racial discrimination and violence that their ancestors did in the late 1800s. Greater numbers and increasing visibility in the last decade make Asian/Pacific Americans a favorite scapegoat of recession-weary public officials. Both Republican and Democratic politicians have used the recent influx of Chinese refugees as political cover to curtail political asylum and entitlements to benefits for immigrants in the United States. Governor Pete Wilson (R-CA), facing a tough reelection campaign, called for denying citizenship (which is now guaranteed by the Constitution) to the children of illegal immigrants.

Anti-immigrant fury often is triggered by current events that depict Asian/Pacific Americans in a negative light. Most notably, on June 6, 1993, the freighter *Golden Venture* ran aground in Queens, New York, carrying nearly 300 Chinese indentured servants into the United States. The incident ignited a wave of strong anti-immigrant sentiments and negative media stereotypes as national and local news reports focused on what was believed to be uncontrolled illegal immigrant smuggling by Asian gangs.

The backlash resulted in heightened efforts to restrict legal immigration and dismantle political asylum, in unwarranted detention of Asian/Pacific Americans at international airports, in searches of Asian/Pacific American homes for undocumented aliens, and in an onslaught of hate letters directed at all Asian/Pacific Americans.

A letter circulated in East Brunswick, New Jersey, in July 1993 was signed by the Ping Pong Exterminators. It stated:

> Enough is Enough. It is now time to send these illegals and slave traders to where they come from. We will get rid of Chinese from the Garden State beginning one month from July 4th. They are criminals hiding behind

their BMWs, Benz and use their laundry, restaurant and massage parlors to cheat this country. They are infiltrating into safe communities of the Garden State and bringing big city criminal gangs with them. Look what happened in Teaneck. We will start with Edison and East Brunswick, two of the safest communities these Chinese gangs have picked to infiltrate. If you think what is happening in Germany is violent, you ain't seen nothing yet. There will be Chinese blood and bones all over if they don't quit voluntarily by August 5th. God save and bless America. God bless the Ping Pong Exterminators.

Similar hate letters were circulated to Asian/Pacific American residents in East Vineland, New Jersey, and New York City.

Inter-Ethnic Conflicts

Many communities of color, particularly in low-income neighborhoods, are forced to work and live side by side and compete for scarce resources. With few publicized examples of intercommunity cooperation and many examples of problems being described in the media, the stage was set in the early 1990s for tensions to lead to inter-community violence.

Targeting Small Asian Businesses

Newly arrived immigrants, unable to find employment, often become entrepreneurs. By pooling their resources either through family or informal banking arrangements, they are able to open small businesses. To keep costs down, they often work long hours and require their children to help around the store. This exacerbates frictions with local residents, who see few new jobs going to the community.

Some problems also arise because of miscommunication caused by language and culture barriers. For example, when an Asian/Pacific American merchant does not place change in a customer's hand or refuses to participate in informal banter, the merchant's behavior is seen as rude by some African American customers. To many Korean American cashiers, however, personal modesty or lack of English language skills may prompt this behavior.

No matter what the source of the problems, when they are not defused by dialogue and problem solving, isolated incidents can flare into major confrontations. The killing in 1992 of Latasha Harlins, a black teenaged customer, by Sun Ja Du, a Korean American merchant in Los Angeles, sparked boycotts of Korean American stores by members of the African American community. Other boycotts, for both similar and different reasons, were held in Brooklyn, New York, and other cities.

The April 1992 uprisings in Los Angeles, ignited by not-guilty verdicts in the trial of white policemen accused of beating black motorist Rodney King, were another example of targeted anti-Asian merchant violence. The first stores to go up in flames were swapmeets, owned primarily by Korean and Chinese Americans. Specific buildings and stores owned by Asian/Pacific Americans were targeted by looters who would drive by establishments owned by Asian/Pacific Americans and return to firebomb them.

In Los Angeles in 1993, there were 43 killings of Asian/Pacific American merchants within three months. In Washington, DC, in 1993, there were nine killings of Asian/Pacific American merchants, four in September alone. In conversations with Asian/Pacific American shop owners throughout the country, many feel that they are targeted more than other merchants because of their race and because policymakers choose to make scapegoats the local merchants rather than address systemic issues related to local economic recessions. While the merchant associations acknowledge that they work in high-crime areas, they believe that they are assaulted or killed more often than other merchants during the commission of a burglary. They also believe that inter-ethnic tensions exacerbate or even cause much of the crime.

Although inter-ethnic tensions based on economic and racial differences continue to make dialogue on these issues difficult, coalitions of Asian/Pacific Americans, African Americans, and Hispanic Americans are being formed to create community banks, to foster economic development, and to convert liquor stores into other uses. These coalitions represent the first step toward the problem solving and resource sharing needed to make inner cities safe and livable for all Americans.

School Conflicts

Sparse data about anti-Asian violence on campuses and in elementary and secondary schools resulted in only five anti-Asian incidents recorded on college campuses and only three more recorded in K-12 classrooms nationwide in 1993. However, incidents of hate violence increasingly have been perpetrated against and by youth. Efforts to address the needs and concerns of Asian/Pacific American young people must be included in any strategy to deal with hate violence.

Asian/Pacific American students, particularly immigrant and limited-English speaking youth, have been targeted for harassment and other forms of violence in public schools. Asian American Legal Defense Fund (ALDEF) and APALC have intervened in a number of violent episodes by providing resources for mediation and conflict resolution. School workshops and sensitivity-training sessions are also included as a way to reduce tension and provide alternatives for violence.

In San Francisco, the Asian Law Caucus works through an umbrella organization known as the Intergroup Clearinghouse to implement model bias-free school plans in selected middle and high schools. Each school creates a committee of students, faculty, administrators, staff, parents, and community groups to promote dialogue between students and school personnel, give assistance to victims, provide orientation for new students, and encourage teacher training techniques such as cooperative learning.

College campuses are not immune from hate crimes either. Efforts to combat anti-Asian violence must be directed there as well. Schools from states as widely dispersed as Connecticut, Nevada, and Wisconsin have had widely publicized incidents of anti-Asian violence on campus in recent years. While more data is needed before conclusive analysis is possible, one factor seems to be the lack of a supportive local Asian American community. In Carbondale, Illinois, for example, an apartment building that housed Asian international students was torched on December 5, 1992. No arrests were made. At the University of Nevada at Las Vegas on July 22, 1993, an East Indian graduate student fled a building with his body on fire. Just prior to his death, he described two men who threw a liquid on him and said that there were too many of his kind on campus. Although no arrests were made and the death was ruled accidental, the FBI is investigating the matter.

White Supremacist Groups

Organized hate groups pose a special danger both because of their violent actions and because their presence sends a message to the public that intolerance is acceptable. This message then encourages others to act out their bigotry. Although violent, organized hate groups do not appear to be as visibly anti-Asian as in the past, their presence is still strong. In July 1993, for example, a series of firebombings began in Sacramento, California, with the destruction of a synagogue and an office of the National Association for the Advancement of Colored People (NAACP). On October 2, 1993, the office of the Sacramento chapter of the Japanese American Citizen League (JACL) went up in flames. On October 5, 1993, the home of a Sacramento City Council member of Chinese American ancestry, Jimmy Yee, was firebomed in the early morning.

A hate group called the Aryan Liberation Front claimed responsibility for all of the incidents after the latest firebombing. On November 6, 1993, after working with the community and offering a reward of over $55,000 (which was donated by individuals), law officers arrested and charged a suspect. Authorities believe that he acted alone.

Constitutional Challenges to Hate-Crimes Statutes

Despite the fact that legislators nationwide have responded to the rise in hate-violence incidents by enacting criminal and civil anti-bias laws and bias-crime reporting statutes, the constitutionality of these laws is being challenged on First Amendment grounds. In June 1992, the United States Supreme Court in *R.A.V. v. City of St. Paul, Minnesota* [112 S. Ct. 2538, 2549 (1992)] held that the city of St. Paul's hate-crime ordinance was unconstitutional because it limited free speech by limiting hateful expressions. This decision sparked constitutional challenges to a number of states' hate-crimes laws. For example, a challenge to California's hate-crimes laws on First Amendment grounds is scheduled to be heard in late 1994 by the California Supreme Court. This case, *People v. M.S.*, will be heard with a companion case, *People v. Aishman*, which challenges a related law.

However, Supreme Court decision, *Wisconsin v. Mitchell*, [113 S.Ct. 2194 (1993)], upheld the constitutionality of Wisconsin's hate-crime penalty statute. The Court held that the Wisconsin statute did not punish hateful thought, but criminal actions motivated by hate.

Asian Pacific American Legal Consortium Recommendations

To respond to the anti-Asian violence documented in its first annual audit, the Consortium proposed a multifaceted program that includes both trial- and appeals-court legal advocacy, legislative advocacy, data collection and analysis, and collaborative efforts with advocates for Asian/Pacific Americans and other communities affected by the national epidemic of hate violence. However, in order for anti-Asian violence to be addressed effectively, government, business, religious, education, and community leaders must both speak out and act in responsible ways. Some recommendations follow:

• Hate crimes should be swiftly and completely condemned by political, religious, business, community, and education leaders;

• All suspected hate crimes should be thoroughly investigated;

• All federal, state, and local agencies charged with the collection of hate-crime statistics under the Federal Hate Crimes Statistics Act and similar local laws should collect those statistics promptly and completely, with the threat of economic disincentives for noncomplying jurisdictions;

• More funding should be given to the U.S. Department of Justice's community relations service and its other efforts to bring communities together;

• Greater attention on all levels of government should be paid to increasing economic redevelopment in our impoverished inner cities;

• Federal Hate Crimes Statistics Act should be reauthorized and funded, and the Penalty Enhancement Act and Bias Crimes Compensation Act should be passed and funded;

• State statutes and regulations to address issues of data collection, civil rights protections, and penalty enhancement for bias crimes should be passed and enforced;

• Multicultural communication, collaboration, and dispute-resolution training for judges, lawyers, caseworkers, and others involved in the legal system should be implemented with dispatch in every court system;

• More Asian-language interpreters should be hired in courts and police stations located near Asian/Pacific American communities;

• Ethnically and linguistically diverse police officers at federal, state, and local levels should be recruited, screened, and given multicultural communication, collaboration, and dispute-resolution training;

• Independent prosecutors should be appointed when local prosecutors are not adequately addressing suspected anti-Asian animus;

• Specialized hate-crime units for prosecutor and law enforcement offices should be established where appropriate;

• Civilian review boards to oversee police misconduct cases should be created and given adequate funding; community policing should be encouraged and funded;

• Asian/Pacific American victims should be more vigilant about identifying and reporting hate crimes;

• Finally, and most importantly, education efforts among youth should be encouraged and funded, so that multicultural communication, collaboration, and dispute-resolution skills can be taught in schools and other appropriate settings.

Conclusion

Anti-Asian violence, like the violence directed against anyone because of race, religion, sexual orientation, or gender, is not simply a legal or criminal justice problem. Broader remedies must be explored to counter underlying bigotry and prejudice. These include education; a strong, principled, and timely response to hate violence; and economic justice. Hate violence is an issue that unites all of us, because we are all vulnerable to irrational hatred. Interethnic tensions are very complex, and economic and political empowerment issues must be explored and creative solutions implemented.

The audit was a first step in bringing national visibility to a problem that has not received adequate attention, by proving, despite difficulties in gathering statistics and undercounting, that this problem exists nationwide. The next step is up to each of us.

—National Asian Pacific American Legal Consortium
Philip Tajitsu Nash

♦ ASIAN AMERICAN INVOLVEMENT IN THE POLITICAL PROCESS: CASE STUDY

The Eighth Amendment to the United States Constitution guarantees the right to vote for every citizen. But if the Asian/Pacific American community does not exercise this right, is it being deprived of anything? Does it have the right to file lawsuits or otherwise complain when it seemingly shuns the voting booth? Or is apathy and lack of involvement a product of systemic discrimination?

In exploring these questions, this section will examine the Asian/Pacific American community's involvement in the California redistricting efforts of 1991. Questions were raised and coalitions formed or dissolved through the activism of legal and community groups during this process. As will been seen, many important issues must still be resolved before the Asian/Pacific American community can go forward.

Call for Action

The 1990 Census revealed that the Asian/Pacific American communities had increased by 127 percent in California and comprised 10 percent of the state's population. Across the United States, smaller refugee groups, like Hmongs and Laotians, grew by as much as 500 percent in some regions. Overall, the Asian/Pacific American community doubled in size from 1970 to 1980 and again from 1980 to 1990. U.S. Census Bureau projections predict that the Asian/Pacific American population segment will grow another 70 percent by the year 2000. Furthermore, the congressional redistricting efforts that followed the 1970 and 1980 censuses have since fragmented many Asian/Pacific American communities.

Given the region's dramatic population increase and results of past redistricting, a number of Asian/Pacific American community activists in Los Angeles decided that the California 1991 redistricting effort needed an Asian/Pacific American voice. To that end, they established the Coalition of Asian Pacific Americans for Fair Reapportionment (CAPAFR); a similar organization with the same name was formed in the San Francisco Bay Area.

The Legal Standard

CAPAFR wanted to keep Asian/Pacific American community together in one district to maximize their potential voting power. To do this, they needed to prove that the districts that they proposed contained geographically compact Asian/Pacific American community that could elect a candidate of choice. The geographic compactness requirement is necessary to draw districts for voting purposes. The ability to elect standard would prove to be the Asian/Pacific American community's biggest stumbling block. The term "candidate of choice" could mean electing an Asian/Pacific American candidate, but is not necessary to the definition.

Even without actual census numbers, CAPAFR knew that at least three areas of Los Angeles would need to be investigated: Central Los Angeles (Chinatown, Koreatown, Little Tokyo, and Pilipinotown), which had a higher concentration of Asian/Pacific Americans than any other area; San Gabriel Valley (the cities of Monterey Park, Alhambra, Rosemead, and Temple City), which had the fastest-growing Asian/Pacific American community; South Bay (the cities of Gardena, Torrance, Carson, and Long Beach), which had the most established community outside of Chinatown and Little Tokyo.

Central Los Angeles also had a large number of new Hispanics and a small but significant African American community. In the San Gabriel Valley, Hispanics are the predominant minority group. The Mexican American Legal Defense and Educational Fund (MALDEF) was already working on its proposed maps, as was the National Association for Advancement of Colored People (NAACP). Therefore, CAPAFR recognized that it would eventually need to build bridges with these other groups. But first, it needed census numbers to set specific goals.

Assessing Census Figures

Demographers are an important component of a voting-rights lawsuit. They know where people live, what languages they speak, whether or not they are U.S. citizens, and can supply other vital information which providing factual support for legal theories. CAPAFR found a demographer in Los Angeles who was affiliated with a major university and had the computer time and capability to download census tract figures and manipulate the numbers to develop proposed districts. This was fortunate because few demographers study the Asian/Pacific American community.

Although Central Los Angeles had one of the largest concentrations of Asian/Pacific Americans, this group consisted primarily of young people (under 18) and newer immigrants who were not yet eligible for citizenship. The area also had one of the lowest voter registration rates and an even lower voter turnout. When a region is considered for redistricting, the only people who count are those who are citizens over the age of 18. Asian/Pacific Americans who fit both criteria were few in number. CAPAFR took the position that the Asian/Pacific Americans in Central Los Angeles would become citizens within the next ten years; therefore, everyone, regardless of citizenship or age, should be counted toward the redistricting. Because this position runs counter to the legal standard, the Asian Pacific American Legal Center (APALC) and the Asian Law Caucus (ALC), attorneys for CAPAFR, decided to challenge the law and try to change the standard to "population totals" rather than "citizens of voting age."

At the same time, MALDEF and the NAACP were also drawing maps in Central Los Angeles to ensure that their community would be able to elect a candidate of choice. Although each group tried to demonstrate sensitivity to the other groups' interests, the three drew markedly different maps. The Hispanic-American community, which also had a young population that tended to lack citizenship, had the advantage of a higher overall number. To obtain a district with enough citizen voters, however, it needed to reach into large areas of the Asian/Pacific American community, cutting Koreatown and Pilipinotown in half.

Alternatively, African Americans tended to be citizens over the age of 18 and had a high voter-registration rate, but a low voter turnout. In order to create a district in which an African-American candidate of choice could win, they, too, needed to reach into Koreatown and cut it in half.

The stage was set for conflict. In order for Hispanic Americans or African Americans to protect their communities' interests, the Asian/Pacific American sphere was infringed upon. The districts the Asian/Pacific Americans wanted would cause the African-American community to be cut in half and keep the Hispanic-American community from creating a district with enough citizen voters.

All three groups, protected under the Voting Rights Act, are allowed to protect their communities' interests by creating districts that allow them the ability to elect candidates of choice. But if all three have the same rights, and these rights are in conflict, how can this be resolved? There is no legal remedy for this situation. Traditional voting rights analysis deals only with conflict between black and white communities. There is little precedent in the area of multiethnic voting rights.

Redistricting the San Gabriel Valley was different from Central Los Angeles in a number of ways. First, the Asian/Pacific American community was more geographically compact. Instead of being spread out among four different ethnic-specific "towns" as they are in Central Los Angeles, Asian/Pacific Americans are grouped in the cities of Monterey Park, Alhambra, Rosemead, and Temple City. In fact, according to census figures, Asian/Pacific Americans make up 58 percent of Monterey Park's population. Secondly, due to a number of socioeconomic and cultural factors, Asian/Pacific Americans in the San Gabriel Valley participated in the political process to a greater degree and were able to run successfully for office more consistently. Additionally, Hispanics were the only other major ethnic population group in this area, making negotiations easier. More importantly, both Hispanic Americans and Asian/Pacific Americans demonstrated a genuine willingness to cooperate and to listen to other groups' concerns. That high level of cooperation was based on the understanding that presenting a united front would give both groups the best chance of protecting their respective rights. Conflicts did arise, but the Hispanic Americans and Asian/Pacific Americans realized that a failure to compromise would result in a redistricting plan drawn by outsiders that would satisfy neither group.

In light of that realization, the San Gabriel Valley Latino Redistricting Committee and San Gabriel Valley-CAPAFR came to the negotiating table prepared to make some real sacrifices. These were made more easily since Asian/Pacific Americans and Hispanic Americans kept the long-term interests of both groups—such as the mutual desire to engage in joint community projects in the future—squarely in the negotiations' foreground. This commitment to preserve minority political rights for both parties enabled the two groups to present to the special masters the only proposed redrawn map that the panel adopted in its entirety.

Once the new Asian/Pacific American districts were drawn, it was essential to demonstrate the ability to elect a candidate of choice. This is the challenge that the attorneys faced in convincing the California Supreme Court to uphold the proposed redistricting.

Asian/Pacific American Elected Officials

As of 1994, there were a number of Asian/Pacific American elected officials in California—Secretary of State March Fong Eu (appointed in 1994 by President Bill Clinton to become Ambassador to Micronesia), as well as Congressmen Norman Mineta and Robert Matsui, to name a few. So why do Asian/Pacific Americans complain that they have no representation?

Their dissatisfaction stems from the fact that in 1994 only about 2 percent of California's congressional representatives and only one of the 120 state legislators were Asian American. These are troubling statistics given that Asian Americans comprise 10 percent of California's population. Furthermore, when there is an issue that is important to Asian/Pacific American community, the Asian/Pacific American elected officials find it difficult to aggressively advocate for it, because they often represent districts with significant non-Asian/Pacific American populations.

Legally, the fact that Asian/Pacific American politicians are able to win votes from other racial/ethnic groups presents another problem. In a lawsuit, in order to establish that Asian/Pacific American voting rights have been infringed upon, the plaintiff must prove that the white majority votes as a bloc against the Asian/Pacific American candidate of choice.

The fact that whites will vote for Asian/Pacific Americans, however, seems to undermine the legal argument. During the redistricting process, the APALC and the ALC decided to temporarily sidestep this issue. They focused instead on areas of the state like San Francisco and Los Angeles, which have large numbers of Asian/Pacific Americans, yet have rarely elected Asian/Pacific American candidates. Refocusing the debate means that government will need to address it at some later point. Until more data and documentation are collected from large communities of Asian/Pacific Americans that vote, but are thwarted by racial bloc voting, opponents will continue to point to the numbers of Asian/Pacific American elected officials as an indication that no discrimination exists.

Pan-Asian Voting Patterns

APALC and ALC attorneys argued to the California Supreme Court that all Asian/Pacific Americans vote cohesively. They think and vote alike and, therefore, should have their own district. The onus then fell on the Asian/Pacific American community and its demographers to prove this argument.

Initial examination of Asian/Pacific American voting patterns seemed to indicate that, in fact, Asian/Pacific Americans do not vote cohesively. This was not surprising, given that large segments of the Asian/Pacific American community are foreign born and that they divide themselves into ethnic enclaves with specific needs. This situation is further complicated by class divisions that not only split ethnic groups, but create barriers between immigrant and refugee communities.

Despite this, there were indications that regardless of ethnicity or class, Asian/Pacific Americans do have common interests and that the majority would support some of the same issues. This is important because voter cohesion is the biggest issue facing Asian/Pacific American communities today. Without a strong indication that Asian/Pacific Americans vote together, a voting rights challenge cannot be sustained.

An exit poll was conducted during Monterey Park's city council election in 1988. (An exit poll is a series of questions asked of a voter leaving the polling place. The questions are designed to gather demographic information, e.g., "What is your ethnicity?" and data on voting patterns, e.g., "Who did you vote for?") Done in the wake of virulent racism against the Chinese residents of Monterey Park, the exit poll showed that Asians (regardless of the ethnicity) voted for the Chinese candidate, while whites voted for the white candidate. This was important demographic data to bolster the legal elements of Asian/Pacific American voter cohesion and white bloc voting.

There was also anecdotal evidence that Asian/Pacific Americans that ran for office were able to register a large number of Asian/Pacific American voters, that Asian/Pacific American candidates were able to raise funds best in Asian/Pacific American communities, and that predominantly Asian/Pacific American precincts voted for Asian/Pacific American candidates. Statistically sound evidence is better than anecdotal narrative, but with limited data on voting patterns, the APALC and the ALC included both in the papers submitted to the California Supreme Court, arguing that voting pattern data from one city could be translated to other areas.

For example, assume City H is 40 percent Asian/Pacific American and 60 percent white. The Asian/Pacific Americans vote for the same candidates and vote the same on issues. The whites vote for their own candidates and the same on issues. Since the whites outnumber the Asian/Pacific Americans, white-supported candidates and issues will always win. If, however, City H were drawn into five city council districts, with each district electing its own city council representative, the Asian/Pacific Americans would be the majority population in two of the districts. Therefore, they could elect two candidates of choice; in the past, they were unable to elect even one.

Consider another example. Assume City K is 40 percent Asian/Pacific American and 60 percent white. The Asian/Pacific American population is made up of fifth-generation Chinese Americans, newer immigrants from Hong Kong, and Chinese and Vietnamese refugees. None of the groups substantially interact with each other or with the larger white community. A Chinese candidate ran in the last city council election, but was not elected. It seems that the refugee group did not vote at all, and those from Hong Kong vocally opposed the Chinese American candidate because of a prior run-in with the president of the Chinese Business Association.

City H is the ideal place to argue for redistricting, while City K is not. In City H, the Asian/Pacific American community has a clear agenda and candidates, but are denied a meaningful ability to participate in the political process because of white bloc voting. Transforming hypothetical City K into City H takes a multipronged approach, including promoting naturalization and voter registration, conducting exit polls, and gathering other demographic statistics.

Naturalization

As the California case identified clearly, the only people at that matter when redistricting is being considered are U.S. citizens who are 18 years and older. While there is very little any community can do to speed up the aging process, the naturalization process can be expedited. In 1994, APALC began a citizenship project that includes application processing, workshops, educational programs, and media.

Voter Registration

Low registration rates are endemic to any disenfranchised community. Members feel that their votes do not count; therefore, they do not vote, and, consequently, elected officials ignore their concerns. Real community concerns are not addressed, so members feel that their votes do not count, and, therefore, they do not vote.

One way to break this vicious cycle is to start or increase voter registration. Usually this is best done when there is an Asian/Pacific American running for office or when there is an issue that directly affects the Asian/Pacific American community.

Exit Polls

Statistics are imperative to prove that Asian/Pacific Americans vote together as a bloc. Exit polls are generally the best way to establish such a voting pattern; however, anecdotal evidence is helpful to bolster or to explain any deviation in the data. While exit polls should be conducted in a scientific manner with the assistance of an academician (demographer, urban planner, statistician, etc.), smaller, more focused exit polls can be conducted by community groups, yielding similar results.

Information about numbers of viable Asian/Pacific American candidates who did not win elections is also important. To demonstrate discrimination, economic data could show that Asian/Pacific Americans are the poorest in the city, with the fewest resources, and are unable to access the political system.

Conclusion

For the Asian/Pacific American community to acquire political clout by the year 2000, the following things need to happen:

• Establish new legal theories. There is no legal precedent to deal with multiethnic voting rights or the rights communities that do not comprise a majority of a city or a district;

• Gather data. Exit polls need to be conducted at each election. These can be done for school board elections, small city council elections, and primaries. Demographic data is also important in tracking levels of discrimination and identifying new issues;

• Provide bilingual ballots. Since 1992, Los Angeles, New York, and San Francisco have had Asian-language ballots. It is vital to enforce this new right and include more languages in this effort;

• Increase voter registration and naturalization;

• Build coalitions; since the legal standard recognizes only groups who are the majority in their city, Asian/Pacific Americans must build bridges with other groups of color to form a "minority majority";

• Field viable candidates, since courts look to the viability of a candidate to determine discrimination.

—*Stewart Kwoh*

♦ ASIAN AMERICAN LABOR ACTIVISM: ORGANIZATIONAL PROFILE

Asian Pacific American Labor Alliance (APALA)

At its annual convention in 1993, the Asian Pacific American Labor Alliance (APALA) passed resolutions in support of the Wards Cove workers, deploring the increase in hate crimes, encouraging Asian-immigrant worker unionization, opposing the North American Free Trade Agreement, and condemning anti-immigrant sentiment.

APALA also honored four pioneers in the crusade for Asian American civil rights. Among them Fred Korematsu, the civil rights proponent who called upon the U.S. Supreme Court to rule on the internment of Japanese Americans during World War II. The courts vindicated Korematsu in the mid-1980s. Another pioneer honored was Yuri Kochiyama, a peace and community activist from New York who is known throughout the United States. Kochiyama, who died in 1994, was pictured in *Life* magazine with Malcolm X. Also honored was David Trask, Jr., a noted Hawaiian labor leader, and Frank Atonio, who brought forward a complaint in the important labor discrimination case known as Wards Cove.

Origins

The APALA was founded on May 1, 1992, at a national convention in Washington, D.C. Although Asian Americans have been part of the United States

work force for nearly 150 years, the occasion marked the formation of the nation's first Asian American labor organization. APALA reflects the culmination of many years of Asian American labor activism, and signals a new era in the labor movement to organize Asian American workers, promote their participation within the ranks of the labor movement, and forge a new path in the larger fight for equality and justice.

At the founding convention, 500 Asian American unionists participated, representing 35 unions from 22 states and a wide range of Asian and Pacific Islander heritages. For the first time, Asian American unionists from all over the country had an opportunity to meet one another, address common interests, and plan for the future.

Agenda for Action

APALA's founding convention launched major national campaigns to tackle two issues: organizing and civil rights. The national organizing campaign aimed to build both national membership and chapters of APALA. Branches were established in New York, Washington, D.C., San Francisco, Oakland, Seattle, Olympia, San Diego, Los Angeles, and other cities as well as in Hawaii and Orange County, California. The affiliates played a crucial role in building bridges between labor unions and the Asian American community, and in promoting labor activism.

Organizing also involved building unions in Asian American communities. Asian-immigrant workers were frequently concentrated in low-wage, labor-intensive jobs that lacked health benefits, job security, and other protections that unions provide. While some unions reached out to Asian-immigrant workers before the establishment of APALA, there was no nationally coordinated effort to organize them.

To advance this campaign, APALA launched a joint national training program with the AFL-CIO Organizing Institute to recruit and train a new generation of Asian American labor organizers. Special efforts were made to attract Asian union members, community activists, and student leaders. Three separate training programs were held, and many graduates of this program have been successfully placed in organizing drives targeting Asian American workers from New York to California.

Today when unions allocate resources to organize Asian American workers, including hiring staff with language skills and knowledge of the community, they are met with success. APALA's national coordination and planning has systematically advanced an organizing agenda for Asian American workers across the country.

The other major campaign launched at APALA's founding convention was to advance a national civil rights agenda for Asian American workers that would support civil-rights and worker's-rights legislation, oppose anti-Asian violence, ensure fair representation for Asians within the political process, and promote Asian American political power.

APALA is one of a handful of national Asian American organizations headquartered in Washington, D.C. It continues to work in close cooperation with other Asian American civil rights organizations and with the national AFL-CIO civil rights department to advance a common agenda. The organizations lobby on Capitol Hill, issue joint statements, coordinate national media work, and forge a civil rights agenda for Asian Americans.

Wards Cove Case

One civil rights campaign that APALA has actively pursued involves the Wards Cove cannery workers of Alaska. The Asian/Pacific Islander workers of Wards Cove filed a discrimination suit in 1974 to protest the "plantation style" segregation at the cannery. All of the best jobs were reserved for whites, while Asian and Pacific Islander workers were relegated to inferior job assignments, as well as separate dining and living facilities. This case went all the way to the U.S. Supreme Court, where it was used to set a more difficult standard for proving employment discrimination. This was changed by Congress in the Civil Rights Act of 1991. However, due to an exemption proposed by Alaskan senators, the Wards Cove workers were excluded from protection by the very law that was enacted to correct the previous court ruling. The message from Congress was clear: the rights and interests of Asian and Pacific Island workers could be trampled upon with impunity.

APALA has lobbied Congress to overturn the Wards Cove exemption. At APALA's second national convention in 1993, Frank Atonio, the named plaintiff in the Wards Cove case, was honored in a poignant ceremony. In addition, a resolution was adopted at the convention to continue support for Wards Cove workers.

APALA supports a range of social issues critical to Asian/Pacific Americans, including access to education, health care, and voting rights, and also works with other labor and community organizations to counter the anti-immigrant sentiment in the United States.

Growing Asian American Work Force

Since racially restrictive immigration quotas were lifted in the 1960s, the Asian American community has grown exponentially. Asian Americans constitute the fastest-growing ethnic population in the United States today and are projected to reach over 10 million by the year 2000.

Although much attention has focused on the large number of businesses and highly paid professionals within the Asian American community, most Asian Americans are blue-collar workers. They are concentrated in urban areas, and many recent immigrants are exploited at work.

Model Minority: Myth vs. Reality

A bipolar situation exists within the Asian American community, in sharp contrast to the model minority myth promoted by certain political leaders and media reports. The image of Asian Americans attaining unprecedented educational and economic success obscures the harsh realities of daily life faced by many. A recent report by the UCLA Asian American Studies Center documented high levels of poverty within the Asian American community, even among those with jobs.

Many recent Asian immigrant workers are trapped in ethnic enclaves due to language and cultural barriers. Relationships between Asian bosses and Asian workers are frequently extensions of previous inequities that existed in native countries. Immigrants may feel indebted for the opportunity to work, and Asian bosses often foster company loyalty and undermine collective action among workers by giving bonuses for hard work and special gifts during holidays. In addition, the Asian American merchant class has historically dominated many community and social functions, maintaining extensive control over various aspects of workers' lives.

Contract labor is also a pervasive problem in Asian-American communities. It is especially prevalent in the garment industry, janitorial services and building maintenance, and construction. In this system, payment is made on a per-project basis. This creates an unstable work force with limited accountability of the bosses.

A campaign launched by Asian immigrant women in San Francisco drew national attention to the abuse of contract labor. The group was denied pay from a contractor who produced clothes for designer Jessica McClintock. After a lengthy and bitterly fought campaign, these workers won a significant victory when Jessica McClintock agreed to pay back wages owed to them retroactively.

For Asian immigrant workers, exploitation and abuse are a part of daily reality. Basic violations of minimum-wage laws, child-labor laws, and health and safety laws are common. Asian immigrant workers are often unaware of their rights, or fearful of retribution if they take action. Many lack health insurance, vacation or sick pay, or retirement plans.

To ensure greater power and control in the workplace, workers must organize and demand change. Unions offer an opportunity for collective bargaining for improved wages, benefits, and working conditions.

They also provide an opportunity for greater participation, decision making, and leadership development.

Asian Americans in the Labor Movement

The labor history of Asians in the United States varied and extensive. Asian Americans built the Transcontinental Railroad, worked in the mines, farmed the plantations of Hawaii and California's Central Valley, worked in the fish canning industries along to the Pacific coast, and labored in sweatshops, laundries, and restaurants from Honolulu to New York.

Although Asian American workers toiled for generations to build this country, the American labor movement historically opposed Asian immigration and union membership. The American Federation of Labor and the California Workingmen's Party forcefully demanded passage of the Chinese Exclusion Act of 1882, which curtailed immigration of Chinese workers and prohibited naturalization for Chinese in the United States.

Labor unions blamed Asians for unemployment and other social ills. Union leaders feared that Asian labor would be used to lower wages and break strikes. They opposed the inclusion of Asian workers into unions, believing that they could neither be assimilated nor organized.

In spite of the exclusion policies of labor unions Asian American workers organized themselves. As early as 1867, thousands of Chinese American railroad workers led a strike to demand higher wages. From the plantations of Hawaii to the fields of California, Asian American workers took collective action to demand better living and working conditions. Asian American workers were active in the 1934 West Coast general strike and participated in numerous labor-organizing activities in the 1930s. In the 1960s, Filipino workers launched the historic Delano grape strike in California's Central Valley. The United Farm Workers Union was established in 1965 as a merger between Filipino American and a Mexican American farmworkers organizations.

Since the 1960s, with the tremendous growth of the Asian American work force, the number of Asian/Pacific Americans in labor unions has also grown. Hundreds of thousands of Asian/Pacific Americans are union members, including New York garment workers in the International Ladies' Garment Workers Union, Seattle cannery workers in the International Longshoremen and Warehousemen Workers Union, Honolulu government workers in the American Federation of State County and Municipal Employees, San Francisco nurses in the Service Employees International Union, and Los Angeles supermarket workers in the United Food and Commercial Workers Union.

Asian/Pacific American Labor Pioneers

At the APALA founding convention in 1992, a special banquet was held to honor seven of the Asian/Pacific American Labor pioneers who reflect the rich legacy of Asian American labor activism: Sue Kunitomi Embrey, Morgan Jin, Ah Quon McElrath, Art Takei, Philip Vera Cruz, George Wong, and Karl Yoneda.

Sue Kunitomi Embrey

Sue Kunitomi Embrey has been a member of the United Teachers of Los Angeles/American Federation of Teachers and the National Education Association. She was a founding member and chairperson of the Manzanar Committee, which successfully lobbied to have the former World War II Japanese American internment camp site declared a national historic site. Her lifework continues to integrate union activism with community activism.

Morgan Jin

Morgan Jin is vice-chairman of the newspaper guild unit at the *New York Times*. He was one of four plaintiffs in an unprecedented discrimination case that resulted in an affirmative action program for hiring African-American, Hispanic-American, and Asian American employees at the *Times*. He has also been active on the Asian Labor Committee in New York.

Ah Quon McElrath

Ah Quon McElrath has worked with the International Longshoremen's and Warehousemen's Union Local 142 in Hawaii since the 1930s. She was involved with the ILWU during the historic Hilo Massacre of 1938, and has assisted in union-organizing campaigns for decades. She has written and taught extensively and has inspired many with her unswerving dedication to social justice.

Art Takei

Art Takei began his union career as a supermarket worker in 1954 and rose through the ranks of the United Food and Commercial Workers Union to become assistant to the president of local 770, one of the highest-ranking Asian American union officials in Southern California. He was a founder of the Alliance of Asian Pacific American Labor, the first Asian American labor committee in Los Angeles. Since retiring from the UFCW, he has dedicated countless hours to assisting the development of the Asian Pacific American Labor Alliance both locally and nationally.

Philip Vera Cruz

Philip Vera Cruz is a former vice-president of the United Farm Workers Union who embodies the history of the manong generation, the first wave of Filipino immigrants who came to the United States in the 1920s and 1930s. He worked for many years as a farm worker and was active with the Agricultural Workers Organizing Committee, which subsequently merged to form the United Farm Workers Union. Vera Cruz became the union's highest-ranking Filipino officer, and has inspired generations of Filipino and Asian American student and community activists throughout the years.

George Wong

George Wong was a staff member of the Graphic Communications Union and was instrumental in organizing the *Chinese Times* newspaper in San Francisco. He was founder and president of the Asian American Federation of Union Members in San Francisco. Wong has been a respected leader of the Chinese American community and labor community in San Francisco for decades.

Karl Yoneda

Karl Yoneda joined the International Longshoremen's and Warehousemen's Union in 1936, and was briefly imprisoned in the 1930s for his political activities. Over the years, he has organized unemployed workers, helped to build the Los Angeles Farm Workers Organizing Committee, and edited the *Rodo Shimbum (Labor News)*. Yoneda has been an outspoken labor and community activist for many decades and has written extensively in both Japanese and English.

These seven Asian/Pacific American labor pioneers represent the finest qualities of Asian American labor activists. They are unsung heroes of the Asian/Pacific American community and American labor movement, and have received little recognition. It was only fitting for them to be honored at the founding convention of APALA, for through their hard work and dedication they have paved the way for other Asian American labor activists to carry on.

Looking to the Future

The decades of the 1980s and 1990s have been difficult times for the American labor movement. The percentage of workers who are members of unions declined from about 35 percent in the 1960s to about 17 percent in the mid-1990s. The changing nature of work, the globalization of capital and labor, the shift from an industrial economy to a service economy, government policies, and labor laws have all contributed to this substantial decline in union strength. Some regard labor unions as outdated, old-fashioned, and out of touch with the contemporary needs of working people. Others predict the complete demise of the U.S. labor movement in both size and influence.

However, the leaders of APALA have a much more optimistic view of labor's future. From their perspective, even in the days of labor union glory, Asian American workers were largely excluded. In that sense, the formation of APALA reflects opportunities that may not have previously existed for Asian/Pacific Americans.

The U.S. work force is changing dramatically, and the percentage of Asian Americans in it will continue to grow into the next century. During this time women, people of color, and immigrants will become the new majority in the workplace. To ensure labor movement survival, unions must organize the emerging work force.

Unions remain the best way for Asian American workers to fight exploitation and discrimination at work. Their staffs, resources, and political clout empower communities and help to ensure social justice. They are important organizations that bring together workers of all colors around a common agenda, building multiracial unity.

For Asian/Pacific American workers, the time has come. A new generation of Asian American labor activists is emerging. There is new potential for organizing unions. By building alliances between unions and Asian American communities, defending civil and workers' rights, and embracing a vision of multiracial unity among workers of all colors, APALA will help to build a new labor movement that reflects the hopes and aspirations of all working people.

—Kent Wong
Director of the UCLA Center for Labor Research and
Education, Institute of Industrial Relations
Founder and National President
Asian Pacific American Labor Alliance

Voters and Voting Rights

♦ Barriers to Political Participation ♦ Redistricting: Objectives and Impact
♦ The Voting Rights Act: Difficult Questions, New Opportunities

In the period between 1980 to 1990, the Asian American population doubled to number 7.5 million. Based on census projections and current immigration patterns, it is estimated that there will be a total of almost 23 million Asian Americans by the year 2020. As Asian Americans register to vote in greater numbers, they will have a growing influence on elections at all levels.

Although many segments of the Asian American community have enjoyed economic success and a high level of educational achievement, the actual level of political participation among Asian Americans has lagged far behind the rate of population growth. The stereotype of Asian Americans as a model minority has obscured the continuing barriers that prevent Americans of Asian descent from effectively participating in politics as candidates or in elections as voters.

♦ BARRIERS TO POLITICAL PARTICIPATION

Throughout history in the United States, Asian Americans have been disenfranchised by discriminatory laws that denied citizenship to Asian immigrants and rendered them ineligible to vote. Asian Americans were effectively denied equal access to the ballot until 1943, when the Chinese were first permitted to become citizens. In 1946, Filipinos and East Indians were allowed to gain citizenship after service in the U.S. military. It was not until 1952 that persons of Japanese descent were able to become naturalized citizens of the United States.

Since the removal of these historical barriers to citizenship, naturalization rates among Asian immigrants have been among the highest of any immigrant group. In 1992, the Philippines, Vietnam, China, India, and Korea ranked among the top ten countries of persons naturalized, and between the years of 1982-1989,

these five countries were the source of 679,153 naturalized citizens.

While these higher rates of naturalization could result in a significant Asian American voting bloc in the future, the following factors continue to limit full Asian American participation in the political process.

Immigration Status

Many Asian American communities are still largely comprised of permanent residents and are not yet eligible to vote. Across the United States, 62 percent of all Asian Americans are foreign-born. The percentages are even higher among certain Asian groups and, in particular, urban areas. Given the predominantly immigrant character of most Asian American communities across the country, large numbers of Asian immigrants lack political representation and a meaningful voice in governmental decision making that affects their livelihood.

Limited English Proficiency

Because a large percentage of Asian Americans are foreign-born, they are less likely to be fully proficient in English. According to the 1990 Census, there were 512,719 Asian Americans in New York City of which 44 percent or 228,085 individuals did not speak English very well; 354,684 residents speak an Asian language at home. It is estimated that as many as 65 percent of Chinese Americans working in New York City's Chinatown do not speak English well or at all. In Los Angeles County, California, with its population of 954,485 Asian Americans, 378,921 do not speak English very well; 676,001 residents speak an Asian language at home.

While immigrants must demonstrate a basic understanding of English in order to become naturalized citizens, this proficiency does not approach the comprehension levels needed to understand complicated electoral

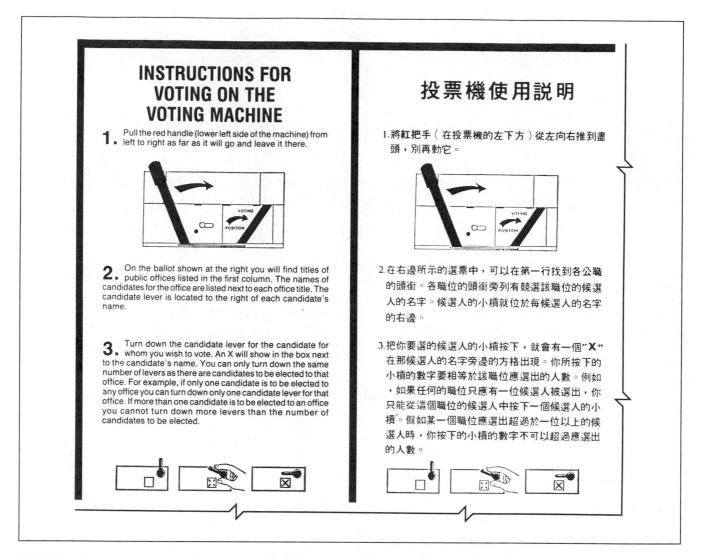

INSTRUCTIONS FOR VOTING ON THE VOTING MACHINE

1. Pull the red handle (lower left side of the machine) from left to right as far as it will go and leave it there.

2. On the ballot shown at the right you will find titles of public offices listed in the first column. The names of candidates for the office are listed next to each office title. The candidate lever is located to the right of each candidate's name.

3. Turn down the candidate lever for the candidate for whom you wish to vote. An X will show in the box next to the candidate's name. You can only turn down the same number of levers as there are candidates to be elected to that office. For example, if only one candidate is to be elected to any office you can turn down only one candidate lever for that office. If more than one candidate is to be elected to an office you cannot turn down more levers than the number of candidates to be elected.

投票機使用説明

1. 將紅把手（在投票機的左下方）從左向右推到盡頭，別再動它。

2. 在右邊所示的選票中，可以在第一行找到各公職的頭銜。各職位的頭銜旁列有競選該職位的候選人的名字。候選人的小槓就位於每候選人的名字的右邊。

3. 把你要選的候選人的小槓按下，就會有一個"**X**"在那候選人的名字旁邊的方格出現。你所按下的小槓的數字要相等於該職位應選出的人數。例如，如果任何的職位只應有一位候選人被選出，你只能從這個職位的候選人中按下一個候選人的小槓。假如某一個職位應選出超過於一位以上的候選人時，你按下的小槓的數字不可以超過應選出的人數。

Voting machine instructions in English and Chinese from bilingual ballots used for the first time in New York City in the November 1994 elections.

procedures or obscure ballot propositions and referenda. Limited educational opportunities, as well as the difficulties of learning to read and write a language that utilizes an unfamiliar romanized alphabet, create barriers for Asian Americans, even though they may be well-informed about political issues through the Asian-language media and other sources.

Low Voter Registration Rates

The number of registered Asian American voters continues to be relatively small across the nation. In New York City, Asians constitute 6 percent of the eligible voting population, but represent only 2 percent of the city's 3.4 million registered voters. An estimated 24 percent of all eligible Asian Americans, or 67,848 individuals, were registered to vote in 1992. As Table 1 illustrates, this rate is much lower than for any other group of voters in New York City.

Table 23.1
Voter Registration in New York City in Percent
Number of eligible voters who were registered in 1992 by ethnicity.

Ethnicity	Eligible Voters Who Registered To Vote In Percent
Asian American	24%
White	77%
Black	81%
Hispanic	54%

Nonetheless, this number of Asian American voters steadily increased by 17,000 from the previous year's total of 50,615 Asian American registered voters. Likewise in northern California, Asians comprise 30 percent of San Francisco's population but less than 5 percent of its registered voters. And in Daly City,

One section of the bilingual ballot used in New York City in November 1994, in English and Chinese.

California, Filipinos constitute 35 percent of the population, but only 11 percent (4,000 out of 35,000) of its registered voters.

◆ REDISTRICTING: OBJECTIVES AND IMPACT

In recent decades, reapportionment plans have diluted Asian American political power by fragmenting communities into several districts or failing to take into account their common interests with other voting blocs. The arbitrary drawing of district lines as a result of political deals or, in some instances, sheer ignorance has inhibited the Asian American community's ability to organize and develop strong political cohesiveness.

Despite rapid growth over the past decade, Asian Americans still comprise a relatively small part of the general population and are often not sufficiently concentrated geographically to form a majority within any district.

New York's Chinatown

In 1982, the Asian American Legal Defense and Education Fund (AALDEF) based in New York City submitted its objections to the Justice Department regarding the New York state legislative redistricting plan that divided Manhattan's Chinatown between two state assembly districts. Few community groups understood the significance of redistricting, and despite the fragmentation of New York City's largest Asian American community, the plan was approved.

By 1991, there was much greater Asian American involvement in the New York City Council redistricting process. Numerous groups sought to influence the decisions of the Districting Commission, which was charged with drawing lines for a newly expanded 51-member City Council. In Lower Manhattan's Chinatown, which has the city's largest concentration of Asian Americans, the vast majority of community groups argued for a multiracial Asian-Latino district on the Lower East Side, which would have linked together communities of color that shared common interests in fighting against gentrification and supporting bilingual education and immigrant services.

But after months of bitterly contentious public hearings, the Districting Commission ultimately created a Asian district linked to the predominantly affluent white populations of Battery Park City, Tribeca, and Soho. The principle of keeping Asian population clusters within a single district was preserved, but Asian

Americans were submerged within a much larger white population. In the four primary and general elections for City Council held since 1991, Asian American candidates were soundly defeated.

California Challenges

Asian American voting rights advocates in California faced similarly disappointing experiences in 1991. The Coalition for Asian Pacific Americans for Fair Reapportionment (CAPAFR), a broad-based coalition of groups around the state, was actively involved in the redistricting process and filed amicus briefs in the California Supreme Court in Wilson v. Eu. CAPAFR objected to the special master's redistricting plan because Asian American communities were split in the San Francisco Bay area and Central Los Angeles. These claims were ultimately rejected.

Lack of Asian American Representation

Hawaii has elected three Asian Americans to Congress: Senators Daniel K. Inouye and Daniel K. Akaka and Representative Patsy Mink. Outside of Hawaii, there are very few elected Asian American officials in the mainland United States. In 1994 in California, where Asian Americans comprise 10 percent of the state's population, there are only three Asian American congressional representatives: Norman Y. Mineta, Robert Matsui, and Jay Kim. Also serving in the U.S. Congress are Delegate Eni F. H. Faleomavaega, representing American Samoa and Delegate Robert Underwood representing Guam.

In California in 1994, out of 120 state legislators, none was Asian American. March Fong Eu, formerly California Secretary of State, was the only Asian American to win statewide election in California; in 1993, she was appointed by President Bill Clinton to serve as ambassador to Micronesia.

Michael Woo, formerly the only Asian American elected to the Los Angeles City Council, staged an unsuccessful run for mayor in 1993, and in June 1994, was defeated in the Democratic primary to become that party's candidate for secretary of state.

In 1994 in San Francisco, where Asian Americans account for 30 percent of the city's population, only one Asian American, Tom Hsieh, has served on the board of supervisors. In New York City, whereas of 1994 the Asian American population exceeded half a million, no Asian American has ever been elected to a legislative office in the past century.

It was only in 1988 that two Asian Americans were elected as civil court judges in New York County: Dorothy Chin Brandt and Peter Tom. Peter Tom went on to win election to the New York Supreme Court (a trial court). Tom is the first Asian American judge to be appointed to a bench by Governor Mario Cuomo. Cuomo selected Tom for the Appellate Division, First Department (New York's intermediate appeals court).

Other states with Asian Americans in elected posts are Washington, where Velma Veloria is a state representative from Seattle; Maryland, where Kumar Barve and David Valderrama both serve in the House of Delegates; Florida, where Mimi Kim McAndrews is a state representative; and Nevada, where Cheryl Lau is secretary of state and will be a 1994 candidate for governor.

Electoral success remains elusive for Asian Americans. But Asian American representation is still an important goal because it encourages greater minority participation in the electoral process and provides Asian American voters with a greater sense of inclusion in government.

◆ THE VOTING RIGHTS ACT: DIFFICULT QUESTIONS, NEW OPPORTUNITIES

The Voting Rights Act was designed to ensure that racial and language minorities that have been excluded from the political process—African Americans, Asian Americans, Latinos and Native Americans—are given an equal opportunity to elect candidates of their choice. The act provides a means for racial and language minorities to file private lawsuits in federal court to challenge practices that restrict access to the ballot, as well as discriminatory redistricting plans that dilute minority voting strength.

Under the 1986 Supreme Court case Thornburgh v. Gingles, Voting Rights Act plaintiffs must show that the minority population is large and geographically compact, politically cohesive, and unsuccessful in electing candidates, because such political campaigns are usually thwarted by racial bloc voting.

However, in analyzing voting rights, early research and thinking evolved from consideration of an African American minority and a white majority. For Asian Americans, this framework poses several troublesome questions especially in multiethnic settings. For example, Asian Americans who have had relative mobility in their residential choices often live in geographically dispersed communities, which could leave them without legal recourse if geographical compactness remains a primary focus in voting rights analysis. Moreover, despite their rapid population growth in the past decade, Asian Americans often lack sufficient numbers to constitute a majority within any single-member district. While Asian Americans might establish the ability to influence the outcome of certain elections for legal purposes, the case law on influence claims remains unclear. Finally, Asian Americans could successfully join with other politically cohesive minority groups to form a majority multiethnic district. But recent court decisions have often viewed multiple minority groups as having competing interests and an insufficient level of political cohesiveness.

As a newly enfranchised minority community, Asian Americans have not demonstrated clearly defined voting patterns, and the number of Asian American candidates remains small. There is little data to document political cohesiveness among various Asian ethnic groups or between Asian Americans and other communities of color. An expansion of voting rights analysis could provide support for the claims of all protected classes of voters.

Alternative Remedies in Redistricting Cases

Proportional Voting

Other alternatives exist to enhance access to political representation for Asian Americans and other minorities. One example is the design of proportional voting schemes that have led to a degree of electoral success in local New York City school board elections for Asian Americans. In these cases, voters (including noncitizen parents of school-age children) rank their candidates in order of preference. In the May 1993 New York City school board elections, four out of nine Asian American candidates won in Manhattan and Queens, the counties that have the largest concentrations of Asian American voters. Those who won their elections were all women: Louisa Chan, Pauline Chu, Po-ling Ng, and Mee Ling Eng. A fifth school board member, James Chin, was elected in Staten Island; however, this county is not covered under the Voting Rights Act.

Cumulative Voting

Similarly in New York City, cumulative voting could provide an effective way for Asian American communities that are geographically dispersed to elect an Asian American to New York City's governing body. For example, if New York's 51 city council members were elected in borough-wide, multi-member districts, there would have been ten council seats in Manhattan. In cumulative voting, Manhattan residents could give their ten votes to a single candidate or multiple votes to any number of candidates. Asian American voters in coalition with other residents sharing common interests could cast all ten of their votes for an Asian American candidate, thereby enhancing their voting strength and electing a minority candidate of their choice.

The exploration of alternative remedies for Asian Americans must not be used to undercut existing legal frameworks that have proven to be effective for other communities of color. Voting should be an exercise to foster inter-group cooperation and empowerment rather than conflict and competition. However, given the changing demographics that have led to increasingly multiethnic neighborhoods throughout our nation, it is imperative to seek new ways to protect the fundamental voting rights of all minority groups.

Language Minorities

The Voting Rights Language Assistance Act of 1992 (known as Section 203) expanded the minority language provisions of the Voting Rights Act. This section holds the greatest promise for enhancing the political empowerment of Asian Americans. Section 203 requires bilingual materials and voting assistance for any language minority group with over 10,000 voting age citizens in a single county.

Previously, bilingual voting assistance had been mandated only when language minorities comprised 5 percent of a subdivision's voting age population, a coverage formula that excluded large Asian American communities in New York City, Los Angeles, and San Francisco.

As a result of the 1992 amendments to Section 203, over 200,000 Asian Americans with limited English proficiency are eligible to receive bilingual ballots, registration materials, notices, interpreters, and other voting assistance in ten counties in New York, California, and Hawaii.

Section 203 has had major positive impacts in Asian American communities across the country. At the most fundamental level, the availability of bilingual forms in Asian languages has aided grassroots efforts to increase voter registration among eligible Asian Americans.

Nonpartisan groups, such as the Chinatown Voter Education Alliance and the Coalition of Korean American Voters in New York City, as well as Asian Americans engaged in partisan campaigns, can more effectively reach their constituents with bilingual voting materials.

Increased Voter Turnout

Bilingual ballots have encouraged greater participation and turnout among Asian American voters on election day. In an Asian American Legal Defense and Education Fund (AALDEF) exit poll of 2,297 Asian American voters in New York City, 30 percent of Chinese American voters used bilingual ballots in the 1992 presidential election. According to the New York City Board of Elections, 4,616 Chinese American voters received bilingual assistance in the 1993 mayoral elections. It can be assumed that those voters would have been less likely to vote in either election had bilingual materials not been available.

The voting rights section of the Justice Department's Civil Rights Division has vigorously enforced the rights of over 54,000 Chinese American voters in New York City who are entitled to bilingual assistance. Federal observers were sent to New York City to monitor four elections during the period from 1991 to 1993. A range of problems faced by Asian American voters was carefully documented: for example, harassment by election inspectors, haphazard distribution of sample bilingual ballots, inaccuracies in translated materials, and unqualified interpreters.

Under the Voting Rights Act, the Justice Department twice refused to approve certain aspects of the New York City Board of Elections Chinese-language assistance program. On May 13, 1994, the Justice Department ruled that machine ballots must be fully translated, including the candidates' names into Chinese.

The Justice Department's actions in New York City have generated great interest in Asian American communities across the country. This activity provides an excellent model for Section 203 enforcement efforts in other jurisdictions that are currently required to provide language assistance in Chinese, Japanese, Tagalog, and Vietnamese.

Voting Rights and Activism

Asian Americans have benefited from the pioneering work and enormous sacrifices made by thousands of civil rights activists of all racial and ethnic backgrounds who have given their time, energy, and sometimes even their lives to ensure the voting rights of all Americans.

In the final decade of the twentieth century, the Voting Rights Act is beginning to have real significance for a growing population of Asian Americans. There must be a commitment at all levels of government to vigorously enforce civil rights laws that will enable Asian Americans to overcome a legacy of institutional racism and participate fully in the democratic process.

References

Ancheta and Imahara. "Multi-Ethnic Voting Rights: Redefining Vote Dilution in Communities of Color." 27 *University of San Francisco Law Review* 815, 1993.

Ong. *The State of Asian Pacific America: Economic Diversity, Issues and Policies*, 1994.

New York City Voter Assistance Commission, *Annual Report*, January 1992-July 1993, August 1993.

Reed. "Of Boroughs, Boundaries and Bullwinkles: The Limitations of Single-Member Districts in a Multiracial Context," 19 *Fordham Urban Law Journal* 759 (1992).

U.S. Commission on Civil Rights. *Civil Rights Issues Facing Asian Americans in the 1990s*, February 1992.

—Margaret Fung

The Legal System
in the United States

♦ Laws against Asian/Pacific Americans
♦ Mobilization against Anti-Asian/Pacific Laws and Judicial Decisions ♦ Lawmakers and Lawyers
♦ The Criminal Justice System ♦ The Civil Justice System

♦ LAWS AGAINST ASIAN/PACIFIC AMERICANS

Early Anti-Asian Laws

Anti-Asian sentiment and legal exclusion have been dominant factors in Asian/Pacific American history. The influx of Chinese immigrants into California in the 1850s provoked an anti-Chinese backlash in California that was felt from union halls to the governor's office. In response to the immigration wave, the California legislature passed a number of laws that were either explicitly prejudicial or effectively discriminated against the Chinese.

In 1850, for example, the state legislature passed a $3.00 tax on any foreign miner not intending to become a citizen, when, in fact, Chinese were prohibited from becoming citizens under federal law. An estimated 5 million dollars, about half of the state's revenue, was collected from Chinese before the tax was voided twenty years later. In 1882, in an attempt to "protect Free White Labor against competition with Chinese Coolie Labor, and to Discourage the Immigration of the Chinese," California passed a head tax of $2.50 per month for most Chinese living in the state. At the end of the century, hard economic times inspired many more discriminatory laws affecting Asians in both the economic and social arenas. Ship captains faced fines and imprisonment for bringing Chinese to the Pacific coast; California schools were segregated to separate Chinese, Native American, and African American children from white children; the state legislature passed an anti-miscegenation law prohibiting the marriage of

whites to persons "negro, mulatto, or Mongolian." Also during this period, mobs attacked and killed Chinese and Filipinos in several western states.

Cries of "yellow peril" also reached the nation's capitol. In 1882, Congress overwhelmingly passed the Chinese Exclusion Act, barring all Chinese laborers from entering the United States and prohibiting naturalization of those already here. This act was the first immigration restriction to bar a specific nationality. Several Chinese immigrants challenged the constitutionality of the act, but the Supreme Court of the United States rebuffed their claims in a series of cases beginning in 1889. The Court deferred to the government's sovereign right to exclude or deport alien residents. It also recognized national security concerns as a justification for restricting the "scourge of yellow people" entering the labor market. In 1917, Congress created the "Asiatic barred zone," which excluded immigration from most Asian countries other than Japan. The Immigration Act of 1924 effectively barred all Asian/Pacific immigration by prohibiting admission of any "alien ineligible [for] citizenship."

Asians and Pacific Islanders mobilized and brought challenges to such laws in state and federal courts as early as the nineteenth century. Not surprisingly, court records do not tell the complete story, because most grievances were unreported and, if reported, were judged under laws and by courts that often allowed discrimination against Asian/Pacific persons. For example, in 1854, the California Supreme Court barred the testimony of Chinese witnesses in the trial of a white man charged with the murder of a Chinese man.

Although the relevant law prohibited the testimony of any "Black or Mulatto person, or Indian," the court in *People v. Hall* reasoned that the law also applied to Chinese as a non-white race. In the court's view, the Chinese were "a race of people whom nature has marked as inferior, and who are incapable of progress or intellectual development beyond a certain point."

Despite such setbacks, Asian/Pacific Americans continued to appeal to the courts for legal protection. In *Yick Wo v. Hopkins* in 1886, they won a major victory when Chinese laundry owners challenged a San Francisco ordinance that prohibited operating laundries in wooden buildings without the consent of county supervisors. The Supreme Court of the United States struck down the ordinance because it enabled local officials selectively to drive out Chinese businesses, even though the law did not literally target any racial class. *Yick Wo v. Hopkins* remains a landmark in constitutional law because it establishes that seemingly neutral laws may still be unconstitutional if they are applied in a discriminatory way. In addition, the case extended the constitutional protection of equal treatment under the laws to non-citizens.

Overall, however, anti-Asian legislation and legal defeats were common through the turn of the century. Alien land laws passed in Washington and California in the early 1900s prohibited persons ineligible for citizenship from purchasing land. These laws specifically targeted newly arriving Japanese farmers and, like earlier anti-Chinese laws, were used to discourage immigration, Notwithstanding the constitutional protection granted in the *Yick Wo* case, the Supreme Court of the United States turned a blind eye to the discriminatory effects of land laws on Japanese residents and upheld them in both states. Judicial tolerance of anti-Asian laws reached its most significant expression in World War II when detention and curfew laws against 120,000 Japanese American citizens withstood constitutional challenges.

Anti-Asian Laws Today

The legacy of exclusion and the specter of anti-Asian sentiment continues to appear in laws affecting Asian/Pacific Americans. Record immigration of Asians and Pacific Islanders to the United States, almost 3 million people in the 1980s, more than twice the number of the previous decade, will likely aggravate the current immigration controversy. Rumblings of resentment, especially from border states, herald another wave of xenophobic sentiment. The two issues discussed in this section illustrate some of the racial tensions that continue to challenge Asian/Pacific Americans.

Official English Movement

The 1980s witnessed the rise of the "Official English" movement, a campaign to establish English as the official language of all government business. Proponents of English as the only official language argue that multilingualism encourages racial and ethnic divisiveness and is contrary to the cherished notion of an American "melting pot." United States English, a national lobbying group claiming more than 500,000 members in 1993, has spearheaded most of the Official English campaigns. The organization lobbies for exclusive use of English in government, restriction of bilingual education, elimination of multilingual ballots, and an English language amendment to the United States Constitution. Opponents of the movement respond that conducting public business only in English effectively discriminates against and disenfranchises growing immigrant populations of limited or no English-speaking ability.

Some of the goals of United States English have become reality. In 1984, 70 percent of voting Californians passed an initiative to rescind bilingual ballots and voting materials. Two years later, they returned to the polls and approved an English Language Amendment to the State Constitution to "preserve, protect and strengthen . . . English." The amendment is largely symbolic since it does not require the elimination of any currently existing multilingual government services. It has, however, been used to justify "English only" rules in the workplace and to stop further creation of multilingual programs. Proponents of the initiative point to the voting results as a strong mandate approving English as the official language; seventy-three percent of the electorate voted for it, including a majority of Asian/Pacific American, and Hispanic voters. Similar amendments were passed in Colorado, Florida, and Arizona in 1988. In 1990, however, a federal court declared the Arizona amendment violated the First Amendment of the United States Constitution, thereby casting doubt on the legal status of other such measures.

Opponents of the Official English movement maintain that multilingualism will marginalize many non-English speaking Americans who cannot read or cast a ballot. The number of people with limited English proficiency is growing; immigration now outstrips new births as the leading source of Asian/Pacific American population growth. According to 1990 census figures, the five largest Asian ethnic groups in the United States, comprising three-fourths of all Asians in the country, are Chinese, Filipino, Japanese, East Indian, and Korean. Sixty-two to eighty-two percent of each of these groups, except the Japanese, are foreign-born, and 55 to 73 percent of each of the non-Japanese groups speaks a language other than English at home.

In response to this population growth, Congress passed the Federal Voting Rights Language Assistance Act of 1992, broadening the availability of bilingual ballots. The 1992 standard should allow at least sizable populations of Asian/Pacific language speakers to qualify for bilingual ballots.

Interethnic Conflict

A second illustration of a recent anti-Asian law arises from conflicts among minority groups. Tensions between Korean American and African-American communities fueled the recent response to the reissuing of liquor licenses in riot-ravaged South Central Los Angeles neighborhoods. The riots following the 1992 acquittal of four white police officers charged with the beating of African-American motorist Rodney King devastated the already economically depressed area of South Central Los Angeles. The fires and looting destroyed about 200 of the 500 Korean American-owned businesses across the city.

In the subsequent rebuilding, the Los Angeles City Council passed an ordinance to expedite permit procedures for those businesses damaged in the riots that were not "materially detrimental" to the neighborhood. However, swap meet concessions, auto repair shops, gun stores, second-hand stores, and businesses selling alcoholic beverages were required to apply for relicensing through a public hearing. This process slowed and even prevented the reopening of those businesses. Asian/Pacific American community leaders claimed that the hearing requirement was imposed on some categories of businesses operated disproportionately by Korean Americans. While the new city ordinance did not explicitly target them, many Korean Americans felt it was used to drive them out of business. African-American community members argued that Korean American businesses exacerbated conditions in a community that was overwhelmed by alcohol-related violence and was saturated with the city's highest concentration of liquor stores, about one for every 700 residents. Opponents of relicensing rallied at hearings to object to the liquor license applications of many Korean Americans. A coalition of African-American and Asian/Pacific American groups began constructive steps in 1993, announcing a $260,000 grant from the city to start a Liquor Store Conversion Program that would help former Korean American liquor storeowners start alternative businesses. By the end of 1993, however, 45 percent of the Korean American-owned businesses had not reopened, and only one storeowner had taken advantage of the program.

The Los Angeles ordinance raises memories of the laundry ordinance that was overturned in *Yick Wo*, and is a reminder that seemingly neutral laws, if misapplied,

might perpetuate racial discrimination. The Korean American/African-American conflict also illustrates the additional political, social, and economic complications that our modern multiethnic society poses. Interethnic conflict threatens to inhibit coalition-building among racial and ethnic groups and to further divide interests along racial lines.

◆ MOBILIZATION AGAINST ANTI-ASIAN/ PACIFIC LAWS AND JUDICIAL DECISIONS

Asian/Pacific Americans developed political power in the United States despite, or perhaps as a necessary response to, the prevalence of public and private discrimination. Over the years, Asian/Pacific American communities grew, consolidated, and organized in response to anti-Asian laws. Asian/Pacific Americans became increasingly efficacious in bringing their concerns not only to the judiciary, but also to the legislative and executive branches of government. This section examines three examples of national efforts for redress by Asian/Pacific Americans: first, the movement to repeal the Chinese Exclusion Act; second, the campaign for reparations for the wartime internment of Japanese Americans; and finally, the shaping of the Civil Rights Act of 1991.

Repeal of the Chinese Exclusion Act

An early victory for Asian/Pacific Americans in Congress was the repeal of the Chinese Exclusion Act of 1882, which was passed at the height of Chinese immigration and anti-Chinese sentiment in the nineteenth century and which responded to and further fostered the swell of nativism in the country. Although the first legal challenge to the Act had proven unsuccessful, Chinese Americans seized a new opportunity to overturn it 61 years after its passage.

The Japanese attack on Pearl Harbor transformed the relationship of white Americans with Chinese in the United States. China became an important ally of the United States. On December 22, 1941, a few weeks after Pearl Harbor, a *Time* magazine article described how to distinguish Chinese "friends" from Japanese "enemies." Sensing the shift of attitudes, Chinese American groups sought congressional repeal of the Chinese Exclusion Act. They received vital political support from the "China Lobby," a small group of Congressmembers and Chinese sympathizers. After many deals and international negotiations, Congress repealed the Chinese Exclusion Act in 1943. Although, it set a quota on Chinese immigration far below that of Europeans, repeal of the Act was nevertheless a substantial achievement.

Reparations for Wartime Internment Japanese Americans

While wartime improved the standing of Chinese Americans, the status of Japanese Americans deteriorated. The internment of 120,000 American citizens of Japanese descent was one of the greatest tragedies in Asian/Pacific American history. Ironically, this incident eventually brought Asian/Pacific Americans one of their greatest victories on Capitol Hill. Following the bombing of Pearl Harbor, President Franklin Delano Roosevelt authorized the evacuation of Japanese Americans living in certain areas to "relocation centers" in the central United States. With often less than a few days to evacuate their homes, Japanese American families were forced to give up their jobs and sell their properties at far below market value. One citizen, Fred Korematsu, disobeyed the evacuation order and was convicted in 1943. In the nation's highest court, he and two other Japanese Americans, also convicted under wartime curfews, argued that singling out Japanese American citizens for such harsh deprivations was unconstitutional.

In the 1944 decision, *Korematsu v. United States*, the Supreme Court upheld the convictions in all three cases based on government evidence of "wartime necessity." After the war, Congress granted token financial redress amounting to only 10 cents on every dollar lost to internees under the Evacuation Claims Act of 1948.

A generation later, the Japanese American Citizens League (JACL), the National Committee for Redress and Reparations (NCRR), and grassroots groups of former internees and academics renewed the call for redress and reparations. Although President Gerald Ford officially conceded that the internment had been "a mistake," Japanese Americans considered this proclamation insufficient and unacceptable. In 1984 Fred Korematsu himself, backed by a coalition of Asian/Pacific American attorneys and advocacy groups, returned to court with newly declassified evidence to challenge his conviction. The evidence established that the government had known Japanese Americans did not pose a threat to national security as it had claimed and that the government had mislead the Court in the earlier proceedings. The federal judge rehearing Korematsu's case overturned his conviction and the two curfew convictions. With the reversal of his conviction, Fred Korematsu obtained from the court an official repudiation of the factual basis of the original decision in *Korematsu v. United States*.

The campaign for redress appealed not only to the courts, but also to Congress. After the legal victory in *Korematsu II*, the JACL and NCRR returned to Capitol Hill to lobby for redress for all surviving internees.

The facts uncovered in the new court proceedings aided Congress in passing "House Resolution 442," which provided an official apology for the internment, set aside $20,000 for each surviving internee or internee's survivors, and made $12,000 payments to certain Aleuts and Pribiloff Islanders who suffered because of United States' actions in World War II. Over $1.5 billion has been paid to Japanese American claimants. The Act also created a $50 million trust fund for educating people about the internment. The effort to pass the Act helped consolidate a national Asian/Pacific American lobbying group and an Asian/Pacific American presence in Washington, D.C.

Wards Cove and the Civil Rights Act of 1991

Asian/Pacific Americans have continued to file legal challenges to change other discriminatory conditions. In the case of *Wards Cove Packing Co. v. Atonio*, for example, 2,000 Filipino and Native Alaskan cannery workers sued their employer for discriminatory employment practices that one Supreme Court Justice characterized as "a kind of overt and institutionalized racism we have not dealt with in years." The workers claimed that they were systematically steered away from higher paying jobs in favor of white workers, that they were segregated in on-site living quarters and dining areas, and that they were assigned badges according to race and sex. Even so, in 1989 a majority of the Supreme Court rejected the workers' claims, applying a new standard of proof that made it extraordinarily difficult for employees to prove illegal race discrimination. That decision prompted civil rights advocates to take their case to Congress. The Civil Rights Act of 1990 overturned the *Wards Cove* decision, but President George Bush vetoed the legislation. In the ensuing year of negotiations, exclusion of the *Wards Cove* plaintiffs from the benefits of new legislation became the price of the Alaskan delegation's vote. Consequently, the Civil Rights Act of 1991 corrected the damage done by the *Wards Cove* decision to anti-discrimination laws, but provided no relief to Wards Cove workers themselves. After passage of the 1991 Act, the National Asian Pacific American Bar Association (NAPABA) joined other national groups challenging parts of the new Act in court. Joined by a dozen other Asian/Pacific American groups, NAPABA submitted a supplemental brief to the Supreme Court presenting the argument that exclusion of the Wards Cove workers was a violation of the Equal Protection Clause. Although this legal challenge was unsuccessful, the *Wards Cove* case inspired new efforts in the unfolding history of Asian/Pacific Americans' challenges to discrimination.

Concurrent with their legal challenge to the Act's exclusion of Wards Cove workers, Asian/Pacific Americans sought attention and commitment from the executive branch. An increasing number of Asian/Pacific Americans have attained important positions in the Clinton Administration and in Congress, where they lobbied on the *Wards Cove* issue. Both President Bill Clinton and United States Attorney General Janet Reno publicly stated that they supported repeal of the section of the Civil Rights Act of 1991 that excludes Wards Cove workers. Although developments in employment law since 1991 reduced the practical significance of repeal, acknowledging the injustice to Wards Cove workers still has symbolic importance. The quick response to *Wards Cove*—months, rather than generations, after the injustice—also reflects the community's increased political organization.

◆ LAWMAKERS AND LAWYERS

The Executive and Legislative Branches

Assuring justice for Asian/Pacific Americans begins not with lawyers, but lawmakers. The noticeable absence of Asian/Pacific American local, state, and national government officials, even in highly populated areas such as California and New York, merits a closer examination. Asian/Pacific Americans have long been regarded as apolitical or unsuited for the aggressiveness of American politics; an assumption that analysts support by low voter registration and turnout from Asian/Pacific American communities. Recent scholarship has challenged these stereotypes of political passivity, studying structural impediments to participation in our democracy. Some analysts explain the lack of political involvement as the product of a large immigrant population that either cannot or does not know how to vote. Voting rights advocates point to the legacy of disenfranchisement, language barriers in the electoral process, and the dilution of Asian/Pacific Americans' voting power in at-large and general elections where their numbers may be too low to have an effect on the outcome.

Whatever the explanation, the proportion of Asian/Pacific American elected officials is lower than the presence of Asian/Pacific American persons in the general population. In California, where Asian/Pacific Americans account for more than 10 percent of the population, there were only 46 elected Asian representatives out of 2,861 statewide in 1990, less than 2 percent of elected officials. However, Californians have elected both U.S. and foreign-born Asian Americans to Congress, statewide offices, and local offices.

The low number of elected Asian/Pacific Americans does not necessarily mean political impotence for the community. Some political analysts suggest that Asian/Pacific American political power is wielded in ways that cannot be measured by voter registration or turnout. For example, politicians have long sought campaign contributions from Asian/Pacific Americans, although some contributors complain that politicians accept their support yet remain unresponsive to community concerns. Regional Asian/Pacific American community groups also have a significant presence in local politics. At the national level, several prominent groups consistently lobby on issues of importance to the community; the Federal Register lists at least one Asian/Pacific American organization among those recently contributing more than $20,000 to influence ethnic and immigration policy issues.

Finally, Asian/Pacific Americans have made significant gains at the appointive level. At the end of the Bush administration in 1992, Asian/Pacific Americans held 124 appointed federal government offices. By the beginning of 1995, they had obtained 150 substantial appointments in the Clinton Administration.

The Judiciary

The nation's judiciary also does not fully reflect the presence of Asian/Pacific Americans in the country. Among more than 27,000 federal and state judges in the United States in 1993, only 204, less than one percent, were Asian/Pacific Americans. Only 20 sat in federal courts. California had the largest number of Asian/Pacific American judges at 89. This figure is still far from reflecting the proportion of the group in the state. Hawaii had the second highest number of Asian/Pacific American judges, 58, followed by Washington, 14, and 8 each in New York and Pennsylvania. Thirty-three states had no Asian/Pacific American state or federal judges.

New York State's Judicial Commission on Minorities conducted a comprehensive study in 1991 of its judiciary. Its four-volume self-examination reported that three prominent minorities—African Americans, Hispanics and Asian Americans—were dramatically underrepresented on the bench in comparison to their numbers in the overall population. In 1989, Asian/Pacific Americans accounted for only 0.26 percent of New York's state judges, although 3.9 percent of New York residents are of Asian or Pacific Islander descent. The disparity between the proportion of minority judges and the proportion of minority lawyers, however, was "statistically insignificant," according to the report. Although the Commission did not find any support for the proposition that minority judges decide cases differently than their white colleagues, the perception that a racially diverse bench would be more fair was found among both minority judges and minority litigators. Twice as many Asian lawyers, and even more African American and Hispanic attorneys, compared to non-minority lawyers, asserted that race was a significant factor in courtrooms.

The New York Commission found that both the elective and appointive process of elevating judges to the bench had failed to achieve minority representation for a variety of reasons. Although more than twice as many minorities were appointed or elected to the New York state bench between 1983 and 1988 than during the previous nine-year period, the Commission concluded that there was still a pool of minority applicants who were not appointed, despite being rated as qualified. Minorities lag behind their white peers in forming professional ties and gaining access to the positions that are needed for entry into the judiciary. The Commission also found flaws in the process of appointment by judicial screening and nominating panels. Minorities were dramatically underrepresented on the selection panels themselves, and race was not considered an important factor in nominations.

Public hearings held in California in 1991 regarding racial and ethnic bias in the state court system echoed the New York study: sitting judges do not reflect the racial and ethnic diversity of the communities they serve. In testimony before the committee, two Asian/Pacific American attorneys described their discomfort at being excluded from the "old boy network" of the court and complained that they lacked the access to the bench that their white colleagues enjoyed. Other speakers described a perceived abuse of judicial power in a system in which judges tolerate racism among court staff and "side with White attorneys against minorities."

The final report of the California Judicial Council concluded that racial bias not only places Asian/Pacific American lawyers at a disadvantage but also litigants, defendants, and witnesses who are of Asian/Pacific descent. Asian/Pacific Americans have much less familiarity with the courts than any other racial or ethnic group and hold a significant distrust for the judicial system. Seventy-six percent of Asian/Pacific Americans surveyed believed that the courts treat people with a good understanding of English better than people who speak little or no English. All racial and ethnic groups surveyed agreed that the courts should guarantee adequate numbers of foreign-language interpreters. Although Congress has passed a Court Interpreters Act that mandates certified interpreters to translate courtroom testimony, certification is available only in Spanish. Asian-language interpreters are still requested on an ad hoc basis and accurate interpretation of testimony is not guaranteed.

The Legal Profession

The almost 10,000 Asian/Pacific American lawyers made up only 1.4 percent of lawyers nationwide in 1990. Although this is barely half the percentage of Asian/Pacific Americans in the general population, it is a significant increase over the 3,776 Asian/Pacific American lawyers identified ten years earlier. Despite a late entry into the profession, Asian/Pacific Americans are now the fastest growing ethnic group in the bar.

On the whole, Asian/Pacific Americans have done better in reaching parity in the legal profession than their minority colleagues. Minority attorneys have disproportionately entered public interest law or government, according to some observers, in part because discrimination in large law firms has forced minorities into less lucrative areas of practice. However, statistics on the graduating class of law students in 1993 show only a one percent gap between the rate that non-minority and Asian/Pacific American law graduates entered private practice; Asian/Pacific Americans entered private practice at higher rates than other minority groups. Indeed, the median starting salary of Asian/Pacific American lawyers in 1993 was $43,000, $7,000 higher than the median of all other ethnic groups, including whites. This disparity is in part because Asian/Pacific Americans are geographically concentrated on the East and West Coasts, where lawyers' starting salaries exceed other areas of the country. Asian/Pacific American lawyers tend to move into government positions more than their white colleagues, but less than African American and Hispanic lawyers.

The number of practicing lawyers lags behind these promising rates of entry for law graduates. Part of this is due to low numbers of Asian/Pacific American law graduates in the past; it is unclear if lower retention of Asian/Pacific Americans is also a factor. In 1989, Asian/Pacific American lawyers made up only 1.3 percent of lawyers in the 250 largest law firms nationwide. This figure represented a greater proportion of their presence in the total attorney population than other racial minorities in large firms.

A review of the academic backgrounds of the minorities recruited in these law firms may indicate higher requirements of achievement for minority candidates. Sixty percent of all minority lawyers in New York law firms graduated from one of only four of the nation's top-ranked law schools. In contrast, the same percentage of white attorneys in these firms graduated from ten different law schools, indicating a broader acceptance of white candidates' qualifications. Once employed, Asian/Pacific Americans continue to face glass ceilings in law firms. In 1989, only 0.5 percent of partners in large law firms were Asian/Pacific Americans.

A 1988 survey commissioned by the Bar Association of San Francisco startled many and confirmed the suspicions of some in the local legal community. The study found that racial and ethnic minorities faced both objective and subjective disadvantages in the city's law firms, a problem borne out by the low number of minority attorneys. The report concluded that minority attorneys were much more likely than whites to be asked inappropriate and offensive questions during hiring interviews, earned less than white attorneys at similar points in their careers, and were twice as likely to be passed over or denied promotion. Perhaps because of their greater ability to penetrate large law firms, however, Asian/Pacific Americans perceived less discrimination in the profession than African Americans and Hispanics who were surveyed.

Legal Education

The future of Asian/Pacific American representation in the legal profession will be shaped by the recent surge of applicants to law schools. Asian/Pacific American applicants to law schools increased steadily in the 1980s. By 1992, Asian/Pacific Americans submitted nearly 5.7 percent of the 86,500 total applications to accredited law schools. This may reflect the fact that Asian/Pacific Americans finish college at a higher rate than any other racial group, a success rate attributed in part to the selective immigration of educated Asians and Pacific Islanders. In addition, affirmative action programs aimed at increasing diversity in law school student bodies have increased recruitment and admission of Asian/Pacific Americans. Whether these policies will continue for Asian/Pacific Americans or any minority groups is an open question. In the past decade, however, these policies, along with an explosion in applications and a generally higher rate of admissions compared to other minorities, have resulted in a growth of Asian/Pacific Americans from 17 to 28 percent of all minority law students. In 1992-93, Asians and Pacific Islanders made up 4.5 percent of the total enrollment in the American Bar Association accredited law schools, up from 1.6 percent a decade earlier, and from 0.7 percent two decades ago.

Parallel to this growth, Asian/Pacific Americans were also the fastest-growing minority group among law school graduates. The number of Asian/Pacific graduates in 1993 was almost 300 percent more than the graduating class a decade ago. The total number of law degrees conferred annually grew by less than 10 percent in the same period. Asian/Pacific Americans are still a relatively small part of graduating classes in absolute numbers. In 1993, only 1,554 J.D. graduates from accredited law schools were Asian/Pacific American, compared to more than 34,000 non-minorities, 2,368 African

Americans, and 1,682 Mexican American, Puerto Rican, and other Hispanics. Asian/Pacific Americans and other minorities also appear to lag behind non-minorities in passing state bar examinations that are required for practice. In a study of 15 New York law schools, the pass rate of white applicants on the July bar exam in the last several years averaged 73 percent, more than Asian Americans at 62 percent, Hispanics at 41 percent, and African Americans at 31 percent.

The profile of legal educators has not mirrored the changing face of law school student bodies. American Bar Association records identify only 203 law faculty or administrators as Asian/Pacific American, 1.5 percent of the total roster. Only 66 of these Asian/Pacific Americans were in full-time positions. A comparison of the American Bar Association's 1993 data on all minority law faculty administrators and first-year students shows that the proportion of minority faculty trails behind minority law student representation. Asian/Pacific Americans show the biggest disparity, making up 5.5 percent of first-year students, but only 1.2 percent of the full-time faculty.

The contributions of Asian/Pacific Americans in law schools are just beginning to be felt. Although student-run law journals focusing on African American and Latino legal issues have been in existence since the 1970s, the nation's first Asian/Pacific American law journals were not published until 1993. *Asian Law Journal* at the University of California at Berkeley and *Asian American and Pacific Islander Law Journal* at the University of California at Los Angeles pioneered institutional recognition of Asian/Pacific American legal scholarship.

◆ THE CRIMINAL JUSTICE SYSTEM

The nation's criminal justice system affects Asian/Pacific Americans as both potential perpetrators and victims. On both sides of the equation, biases, lack of cultural sophistication, and low representation of Asian/Pacific Americans in the ranks of law enforcement limit government effectiveness. As if locked into stereotypes of old Asian gangster movies, police have focused on high profile gang-related crime to the neglect of less visible problems within Asian/Pacific American communities, such as hate crimes and domestic violence. Language barriers and community distrust of police further hinder law enforcement and raise a host of obstacles in the criminal courts.

Criminal Defendants

The U.S. Justice Department reports that Asian/Pacific Americans comprised less than 1 percent of the population in state and federal correctional facilities and prisons in 1990. The largest concentration of Asian/Pacific American prisoners, 3.5 percent of the inmate population, was in the western states, where more than half of the country's Asian/Pacific Americans live. According to the same report, there were 14 Asian/Pacific Americans on death row as of 1990, only 0.5 percent of the death row population nationwide.

The arrest rates for Asian/Pacific Americans are also lower than their presence in the population. In 1991, Asian/Pacific Americans accounted for 0.8 percent of all arrests of persons 18 years and over and 1.6 percent of arrests of persons under 18. The largest number of arrests of Asian/Pacific Americans were for property crimes and for driving under the influence. The highest rate of arrest by far was for illegal gambling. Asian/Pacific Americans accounted for 8.2 percent (1,024) of the total gambling arrests in 1991, reflecting what some critics believe is a police emphasis on this activity in Asian/Pacific American communities. The higher arrest rates of Asian/Pacific American juveniles also suggest a focus on youth gangs.

The apparent concentration of resources on organized crime and gang activity reflects an explicit law enforcement objective. A 1991 subcommittee report to the United States Senate found that Asian criminal gangs posed a "most immediate and serious threat" and that there had been a substantial increase in Asian-organized crime activity in the United States, particularly by Hong Kong Chinese, and Vietnamese gangs. The report said that organized crime activities, primarily illegal gambling and prostitution, had expanded into more serious and violent offenses. Federal agencies are increasingly concerned with overseas crime organizations known as "triads," as well as Asian American street gangs, that are involved in money laundering, business extortion, alien smuggling, home invasion robberies, computer chip theft, and narcotics trafficking. They expect this activity will increase as Hong Kong gang members emigrate to the United States before governance of the colony is turned over to the People's Republic of China in 1997.

Increased concern about Asian/Pacific American criminal activity is attributed to several factors. The growth of the Asian/Pacific American population in the United States has increased the number of crimes by this group and has drawn more attention to their activities. In addition, Asian/Pacific American criminals are more frequently committing crimes outside of primarily Asian/Pacific American neighborhoods and against non-Asian victims. Prior to 1965, most crime in Asian/Pacific American communities involved Chinese Americans and consisted of victimless crimes such as prostitution, gambling, and drunken and disorderly conduct. Delinquency rates among Chinese American adolescents were low, despite difficulties facing many Asian/

Pacific American youths living in crime-prone urban neighborhoods, often with little adult supervision. Liberalized immigration laws in the mid-1960s brought a dramatic increase in the number and diversity of Asian and Pacific Islander immigrants and taxed already overburdened social services. Tight community control within Chinatowns began to break down, opening the door to more frequent and serious criminal activity. Although few statistics are kept on crime rates in Asian/Pacific American communities, in 1985, 46 percent of Los Angeles County Sheriff stations surveyed reported an increase in crimes by Asians, and 40 percent were aware of organized crime or Asian/Pacific American gang activity in their jurisdiction.

The increasing national attention on gang activity in general has fueled additional concern about Asian criminal activity. Important distinctions exist, however, between Asian/Pacific American gangs and their African-American and Hispanic counterparts. Chinese American gangs tend to have a strict hierarchical organization and are often associated with "tongs," influential American descendants of secret societies originally organized in China to resist imperial rule. Younger immigrants from Hong Kong, Southeast Asia, and the Philippines, alienated by the language and culture of their new country, may join such groups for social support. Authorities cite the "traditional closed nature of Asian cultures" and law enforcement agencies' lack of Asian language capability as obstacles to penetrating and prosecuting Asian/Pacific American gangs. In order to respond to their unique operation, recruitment of more Asian/Pacific American officers has become a high priority in some jurisdictions.

Police efforts against Asian/Pacific American gangs have, in some cases, pushed Constitutional boundaries. Some law enforcement agencies use "known gang identifiers" to stop, question, and sometimes harass youths matching standardized profiles. For example, one California county sheriff's manual instructed its deputies to identify Asian/Pacific American gang members by "Fila Brand sports clothing; military fatigue shirts or black jackets; camouflage military clothing in combination with black or other dark clothing; baggy clothing; and business suits or other 'conventional clothing'." Descriptions such as these are so vague and broad that Asian/Pacific Americans with no connections to any gang will also fall under suspicion.

Zealous police efforts against gangs have also included the use of "jade books." These contain mugshots of Asian/Pacific Americans for use in criminal investigations. In 1989, the San Jose, California, police department began to use a mugbook containing 436 photographs of Asian/Pacific American men between the ages of 18 and 25, most of them Vietnamese Americans. The department admitted that at least 10 percent of the men had never been arrested, and some had never been charged with or convicted of any crime. One young Vietnamese American man, who previously had been questioned by the police but never charged, was placed in the mugbook and mistakenly identified in connection with a home invasion robbery. After spending more than $20,000 in attorney's fees, being imprisoned for more than three months, and losing business contracts, the young man was acquitted by a jury. In 1992, the San Jose Police Department revised its policy to include only photos of persons "legally detained" or identified as members of a gang by a reliable informant or by two independent sources of unknown reliability. Similar "jade books" have been used in other California cities and in Philadelphia, Pennsylvania, to identify possible gang members. The clumsiness of these efforts highlights the special difficulties faced by law enforcement authorities in addressing criminal activity in different cultures.

Victims of Crime

Like most Americans in the early 1990s, Asian/Pacific Americans ranked crime second only to jobs as the more important political issue of the day. But the justice system's current focus on overseas organized crime and on Asian gang activity diverts resources away from protecting Asian/Pacific Americans who are also targets of other types of crime. Many Asian/Pacific Americans suffer from higher crime rates that plague poor neighborhoods. These are the areas that bear greater stresses with fewer resources. Criminals both in and outside the community also target Asian/Pacific American immigrants, since they may be more susceptible to theft and fraud and less likely to report criminal activity. Crimes that have until recently been considered taboo in the larger public's discussions, such as hate crimes and domestic violence, have remained virtually invisible in Asian/Pacific American communities because of underreporting and ineffective police responses.

Hate Crimes

Hate crimes are illegal acts committed against a person because of the victim's characteristics, such as race, religion, or sexual orientation. They may take the form of vandalism, assault, intimidation, or murder. Asian/Pacific Americans, even those who have grown up in this country, are often still regarded as "foreigners" who "look different" and thus may draw the ire of nativists, xenophobes, and people angry with immigrants in the United States or with Asian countries.

The most well-known hate crime against an Asian/Pacific American is the fatal beating of Vincent Chin in 1982. Chin, a Chinese American, met some friends at a Detroit, Michigan, bar to celebrate his upcoming wedding. Two white men, Ronald Ebens and Michael Nitz, who had recently lost their jobs in the automotive industry confronted Chin in the bar. They reportedly called him a "Jap" and blamed him for the loss of their jobs. Ebens and Nitz chased Chin out of the bar, held him and repeatedly beat him in the head, chest, and knees with a baseball bat. Chin died of his injuries four days later. Ebens and Nitz pleaded guilty to manslaughter after the local district attorney agreed not to charge them with second-degree murder. They were each sentenced to three years probation and fined $3,780. The judge justified the unusually light sentence by finding that the defendants had no previous history of violence and were unlikely to violate probation. The U.S. Department of Justice brought federal civil rights charges against Ebens and Nitz, but the two were eventually acquitted and neither served any prison time.

Unfortunately, Vincent Chin is only one of many victims attacked because of his race. In 1987, a youth shouting racist epithets drowned a Cambodian American teenager in Lowell, Massachusetts. In 1989, two white brothers who said they "didn't like Vietnamese" beat to death Chinese American Ming Hai "Jim" Loo in Raleigh, North Carolina. In 1992, a mob of 15 white youths screamed "chink," "Vietcong," and "sayonara" as they attacked Luyen Phan Nguyen in Coral Springs, Florida. The 19-year-old pre-medical student died two days later of a brain hemorrhage caused by a fractured neck.

Hate violence has become an increasingly important issue for ethnic minorities, particularly with the rise of neo-Nazi groups in the United States. In 1990, the United States Congress passed the Hate Crimes Statistics Act to begin recording incidences of hate crimes nationwide. The U.S. Department of Justice reported that in 1991, bias against Asians/Pacific Americans inspired 6 percent of the 4,755 hate crimes reported by law enforcement agencies in 32 states. Asian/Pacific Americans make up only 2.9 percent of the national population. Still, the incidence of reported hate crimes against them is below the proportion of similar crimes against African Americans at 35.5 percent and Jews at 19.3 percent. The same report found that whites made up 36.8 percent of the offenders in hate crimes, while Asian/Pacific Americans accounted for 1 percent of the perpetrators. The race of offenders in 43.3 percent of the incidents was unknown. The National Asian Pacific American Legal Consortium has begun to track both hate crimes and hate violence, defined as any verbal or physical act that intimidates, threatens, or injures a person or person's property because of membership in a targeted group. In 1993, the Consortium documented 335 incidents against Asian/Pacific Americans. At least 30 Asian/Pacific Americans died in these incidents.

As demographics change, particularly in metropolitan areas, hate crimes between ethnic minority groups may rise. Conflicts between Asian/Pacific Americans and African Americans have received attention in New York City and Los Angeles. Korean American-owned stores in predominantly African American neighborhoods have been the center of controversy and are often targets of crime. Some African Americans accuse Korean American businesses of hostility to their customers and of price gouging in economically depressed neighborhoods. A fight between a Haitian American customer and a Korean American store employee in Flatbush, New York, sparked a year-long boycott of two Korean American owned stores in 1990. Two years later in Los Angeles, a Korean American store owner shot and killed a 15-year-old African-American girl who, the owner believed, was trying to shoplift a bottle of orange juice. The Korean American woman was convicted of voluntary manslaughter and sentenced to probation, a small fine, and community service. This unusually light sentence outraged the African-American community, exacerbating the tensions between Korean Americans and African Americans that fueled the explosive riots in South Central Los Angeles in 1992. Although classified as mere property crimes, much of the $500 million in property and business losses suffered by Korean Americans during the Los Angeles riots was caused by racially motivated hate crimes. A year later, tensions remained high. In 1993, Los Angeles businesses reported 46 gun-related incidents. A total of 19 Korean Americans were killed in these incidents, 30 of which occurred in South Central Los Angeles.

While civil rights groups have struggled, in some cases successfully, for legislation against hate violence, criminalizing hate speech raises more complex problems. Hate speech against Asian/Pacific Americans ranges from vicious epithets to more subtle forms of anti-Asian bias, such as the anti-Asian images perpetuated in the popular media or in rhetoric about the nation's economic competitiveness. Some legal scholars argue that racist epithets are the equivalent of racially motivated violence and should be criminalized. In a 1992 decision, however, the Supreme Court declared that regulation of speech solely because of its hostility or favoritism to groups was inconsistent with the guarantee of freedom of speech provided by the First Amendment of the U.S. Constitution.

Other Crimes

Crimes committed by Asian/Pacific Americans against people in their own communities are particularly resistant to prevention and enforcement by authorities. One example is the growing phenomenon of home invasion robberies, where Asian/Pacific American intruders, often gang members, break into homes of other Asian/Pacific Americans, tie them up, torture, and rob them. These intruders tend to target victims that speak their language, who are known or likely to have valuables stored in their homes, and who are unlikely to report even serious crimes to the police. The intruders often intimidate their victims by killing one person or by threatening to return if the victims go to the police. For similar reasons, Asian/Pacific American businesses are often the targets of extortion. Experts estimate that as many as 80 to 90 percent of Asian/Pacific American businesses are intimidated into paying protection money to one or more gangs. General anti-gang enforcement efforts may mitigate the incidence of these crimes by locking up some perpetrators, but they do not specifically address prevention of these types of crimes by likely victims or intervention on their behalf.

Domestic violence is another serious crime that plagues Asian/Pacific American communities, yet poses uniquely complicated barriers to prevention and prosecution. It is one of the most underreported crimes in the United States, the primary cause of injury to women, and linked to one in three homicides. In California, homicide is the second leading cause of death for young Asian/Pacific American women, compared to the third-ranked cause for young white women. While few statistics are kept on domestic violence, particularly in Asian/Pacific American communities, shelter workers report that batterers are both Asian/Pacific American and non-Asian/Pacific American men. For Asian/Pacific American women, the trauma of battery may be compounded by dependency on a spouse for immigration status, limited economic options, and isolation from her family and her community.

The Asian/Pacific American and non-Asian/Pacific American communities have, for the most part, turned their backs on domestic violence by denying its existence or accepting the problem as "traditional" parts of the culture. Asian/Pacific American women have few institutional resources for support. Language barriers and distrust of the police often deter women from seeking official intervention and fewer than half a dozen shelters for battered women in the United States are designed to aid Asian/Pacific Americans. Since 1988, the Asian Women's Shelter in San Francisco, California, has been home to more than 250 Chinese, Korean, Laotian, Indonesian, Filipino, Japanese, Vietnamese, Sri Lankan, and Cambodian American women and children. It provides services in 19 different languages and dialects to help the women find housing, legal assistance, health care, and job training. Responding to the unique problems of immigrant women, in 1994 Congress passed the Safe Homes for Women Act. The Act includes a provision for immigrant women who are battered by their spouses to petition for their own residency in the United States.

Law Enforcement

One of the primary ways to improve law enforcement efforts within Asian/Pacific American communities is to build trust and understanding between the communities' members and local law enforcement. In 1988, the California Attorney General estimated that only 40 to 50 percent of crimes against Asian/Pacific Americans were reported to the police. In addition to distrust of the authorities, many Asian/Pacific Americans, particularly recent immigrants, are reluctant to turn to the police for help because of language barriers. According to the attorney general, more than half of California's police departments reported they did not have a sufficient number of Asian language interpreters. Moreover, the report noted that communication barriers at the time of arrest commonly resulted in release of the perpetrator, and sometimes arrest of the victim.

Police in some areas may be not only ignorant of Asian and Pacific Islander cultures, but actually hostile to them. Incidents nationwide of police harassment and brutality against Asian/Pacific Americans and other minorities tend to discourage reliance on the police for protection and encourage avoidance of any contact with the police.

Meaningful law enforcement requires much more than national policies that target gangs of young men in Chinatowns. Much work remains to be done to create ties between local law enforcement and Asian/Pacific American communities. The strikingly different ethnic composition of police forces from the communities they serve has hindered effective law enforcement in residential areas for minorities. Affirmative action and recruitment by local law enforcement agencies has only begun to close this gap. New York City has the greatest number of Asian/Pacific Americans residents of any American metropolitan area, over one-half million in 1990. Although Asian/Pacific Americans are 7.0 percent of the total population of New York City, they make up only 0.7 percent of the city's full-time police force. Similarly, in Los Angeles, California, Asian/Pacific Americans make up 9.8 percent of the city's population, but only 2.1 and 2.8 percent of the full-time force of the Los Angeles Police Department and the Los Angeles County Sheriff's Department, respectively.

More Asian/Pacific American officers would improve cultural understanding and trust, and begin to overcome basic obstacles such as different languages. In Oakland, California, where the Asian/Pacific American community includes Cambodians, Laotians, Vietnamese, and Hmong among other

groups, Asian/Pacific Americans make up 15.8 percent of the population, but only 8 percent of the police force. However, Oakland's Asian Advisory Committee on Crime maintains an office in Chinatown which is staffed by full-time police officers, social workers, and community volunteers that provide language assistance, counseling, and other services. Some areas with growing Asian American populations such as Boston, Phoenix, Seattle, and many cities in California have also adopted community-based policing programs. In part an outgrowth of anti-gang units, these community policing programs encourage greater cooperation between police and residents in Asian/Pacific American neighborhoods.

The Criminal Courts

Distrust of state authority affects not only the relationship of Asian/Pacific Americans and the police, but also the interaction of Asian/Pacific Americans with the court system. The New York State Judicial Commission on Minorities found that Asian/Pacific Americans are generally distrustful of the judicial process. California's Committee on Racial and Ethnic Bias in the Courts also heard complaints from minorities maintaining that they "could not get a fair shake" from the system. Some attribute distrust to historical prejudice against Asian/Pacific Americans in the courtroom, recalling *People v. Hall*, for example, when the California Supreme Court barred Chinese Americans from giving testimony in court.

Today, structural barriers persist. Asian/Pacific Americans are often disadvantaged by lack of English-language skills, deterring many from using the court system because of difficulty in reporting crimes or in testifying. The situation is further exacerbated when foreign-language minorities are not provided with trained interpreters to help them talk to their lawyer and to the court. In criminal trials, Asian/Pacific Americans must contend with the same difficulties that other minority defendants, victims, witnesses, and personnel often face. These include racial overtones in the investigation and prosecution of a case and stereotyping in the selection and deliberation of a jury.

A tragic example of a clash of cultures occurred in 1992 when Yoshi Hattori, a 16-year old Japanese exchange student, and his white friend rang the wrong doorbell in a Louisiana suburb looking for a Halloween party. Hearing his wife's frightened call, Rodney Peairs came to the door with a .44-caliber Magnum and ordered Hattori to "freeze." Hattori apparently did not understand Peairs' command and came within five feet of the doorway where Peairs shot him. Peairs' trial for manslaughter opened with his lawyer's argument that Hattori was "not an American or Oriental or any other known being walking up to the front door," but a frightening and inexplicable figure. Peairs testified that "I had no choice. . . . I couldn't understand why this person wouldn't stop." The state jury acquitted Peairs in three hours. In a subsequent civil trial, a federal judge found "no justification whatsoever that a killing was necessary" and ordered Peairs to pay Hattori's parents $653,000 in damages and funeral costs.

Even when differences of culture are explicitly recognized, difficult and controversial issues remain. For example, some Asian/Pacific American defendants might assert a "cultural defense"; a claim that the defendant's behavior should be judged by the standards of his or her culture, not the norms of the larger society. For example, the mitigating circumstances of culture were accepted in the 1985 case of *People v. Moua* in which a Hmong American man was charged with rape and kidnapping for performing "marriage by capture." According to Hmong ritual, the "groom" takes the woman to his family's house and consummates the marriage over her protest. In *Moua*, the woman claimed she was not merely feigning protest, but truly objecting to the marriage. After his conviction, the court considered the defendant's cultural explanation of his acts and sentenced him to only 90 days in prison.

In the 1985 case of *People v. Kimura*, a Japanese American woman was charged with the murder of her two children after she tried to commit *oyakoshinju*, or parent-child suicide. Upon learning of her husband's infidelity, Kimura had attempted suicide to rid herself of shame and had felt she could not leave her children behind. About 4,000 members of the Japanese American community in Los Angeles filed a petition supporting Kimura and explaining to the court that *oyakoshinju* is an accepted practice in Japanese culture. The court rejected the cultural defense, but reduced the charge to voluntary manslaughter and sentenced Kimura to one year in prison and five years probation after finding that she suffered from temporary insanity.

Cultural defense cases raise serious legal and ethical issues for Asian/Pacific Americans. Cultural explanations are important circumstances necessary to consider in the administration of individualized justice. However, deference to culture may also result in unequal applications of the law and reinforce stereotypes and perceived unfairness. Furthermore, as hate crimes demonstrate, cultural motives are a double-edged sword for Asian/Pacific Americans who may be victims as well as defendants. The circumstances posed by these cases illustrate the gaps that still exist between Asian/Pacific American communities and the American legal system.

◆ THE CIVIL JUSTICE SYSTEM

The criminal side of the American legal system captures only a small fraction of the role of law in the everyday lives of Asian/Pacific Americans. Although little data exists on Asian/Pacific Americans' use of the civil courts, observers suggest that most private disputes in Asian/Pacific Americans communities are resolved outside the courts. Civil courts pose many of the same obstacles as do their criminal counterparts: insufficient translation services, racial and ethnic bias, and a disproportionately low presence of Asian/Pacific American personnel.

The history of Asian/Pacific Americans in this country reveals that despite obstacles from the earliest days they have mobilized against discriminatory laws both in and out of the courts. Although key legal challenges by Asian/Pacific Americans have not always met with success, these battles have helped clarify important aspects of constitutional law for all Americans, from the requirements of due process to the meaning of equality. Advocates for Asian/Pacific American rights have not only forged their own agenda, they have also built upon the civil rights movement of other minority groups in this century. Laws enacted in the 1960s, largely in response to the African American civil rights movement, have benefitted Asian/Pacific Americans in areas such as fair employment and housing, affirmative action, and school desegregation. For example, Asian/Pacific Americans have argued that laws forbidding discrimination by employers on the basis of race or nationality also prohibit "English only" workplace rules and discrimination based on language accents. Because Asian/Pacific Americans are often not the largest minority group in an area and because they have a high percentage of new immigrants with language needs, their concerns often overlap with those of Hispanic communities on issues such as immigration, multilingual services, and voting rights.

Many legal challenges are, of course, unique to the Asian/Pacific American community or to distinct ethnic subgroups within the community. Immigration concerns, for example, are closely tied to the United States' economic and diplomatic relations with different Asian and Pacific Island nations. In the area of voting rights, Asian/Pacific American voters often do not qualify for the benefits of the Voting Rights Act because of their small numbers, residential patterns, and language differences. Asian/Pacific Americans must also confront prejudices that accompany the stereotype of a "model minority." Images of success encourage the false assumption that Asian/Pacific Americans do not deserve legal protection and, paradoxically, fuel a backlash against all affirmative action programs. Because the many legal concerns of Asian/Pacific Americans are too varied to be addressed in a single chapter, other chapters in this book address civil rights, immigration, education, and other relevant issues.

More Asian/Pacific Americans are entering the system as law-makers, lawyers, police officers, and empowered members of their larger multi-ethnic communities. As they confront the many legal challenges that the future will bring, they will continue to transform our civil and criminal laws from swords of discrimination into sources of protection.

References

American Bar Association. *A Review of Legal Education in the United States*. Spring 1993.

Asian American Legal Defense and Education Fund. "Giuliani Captures Asian American Vote by 3-1." *Outlook* (spring 1994): 1, 4.

Bai, Su Sun. "Affirmative Pursuit of Political Equality for Asian Pacific Americans: Reclaiming the Voting Rights Act." 139 *University of Pennsylvania Law Review* 731, 1991.

The Bar Association of San Francisco. *1993 Interim Report: Goals and Timetables for Minority Hiring and Advancement*. December 1993.

Bennett, Claudette E., Economics and Statistics Administration, Bureau of the Census, U.S. Department of Commerce."The Asian and Pacific Islander Population in the United States: March 1991 and 1990." *Current Population Reports, Population Characteristics*. P 20-459. Washington, D.C.: U.S. Government Printing Office, 1992.

Bresler, Fenton. *The Chinese Mafia*. New York: 1980.

California Judicial Council. *Public Hearings on Racial and Ethnic Bias in the California State Court System*. 1991-1992.

California Judicial Council. *Fairness in the California State Courts: A Survey of the Public, Attorneys and Court Personnel*. 1994.

Chin, Ko-lin. *Chinese Subculture and Criminality: Non-traditional Crime Groups in America*. New York: 1990.

Comment. "One Person's Culture is Another's Crime." 9 *Loyola of Los Angeles International and Comparative Law Journal* 751, 1987.

Daniels, Roger. *The Politics of Prejudice*. Berkeley: 1962.

Gall, Susan & Timothy L. Gall, eds. *Statistical Record of Asian Americans*. Detroit: Gale Research Inc., 1993.

Hata, Jr., Don Teruo, and Nadine Ishitani Hata. "Run Out and Ripped Off," *Civil Rights Digest*, vol. 9, no. 1, Fall 1976.

Higham, John. *Strangers in the Land*. New York: 1975.

Hing, Bill Ong. *Making and Remaking Asian America Through Immigration Policy 1850-1990*. Stanford: 1993.

Hoexter, Corrine K. *From Canton to California: The Epic of Chinese Immigration*. New York: 1976.

Irons, Peter. *Justice At War: The Story of the Japanese American Internment Cases*. New York: 1983.

Jensen, Rita Henley. "Minorities Didn't Share in Firm Growth." *The National Journal*, vol. 12, no. 24, February 19, 1990.

Law School Admissions Service, Minority Databank. *Minority Participation in Legal Education and the Profession*. 1990.

McClain, Jr., Charles J. *In Search of Equality: The Chinese Struggles Against Discrimination in Nineteenth-Century America*. Berkeley: 1994.

Matsuda, Mari J. "Public Response to Racist Speech: Considering the Victim's Story." 87 *Michigan Law Review* 2320, 1989.

Muto, Sheila. "A Guarded Truth: Korean Merchants Return to South Central." *The Pacific*, vol. 4, no. 2, Spring 1994.

National Asian Pacific Legal Consortium. *Audit of Violence Against Asian Pacific Americans, 1993*. Washington, D.C.: 1994.

National Association for Law Placement. *Annual Employment Report and Salary Survey*. 1994.

New York State Commission on Minorities. *Final Report*. April 1991.

O'Hare, William and Judy C. Felt. "Asian Americans: America's Fastest Growing Minority Group." *Population Reference Bureau Bulletin*, no. 19, February 1991.

Riggs, Fred. *Pressures on Congress: A Study of the Repeal of Chinese Exclusion Act*. New York: 1950.

Russell, Margaret M. "Entering Great America: Reflections on Race and the Convergence of Progressive Legal Theory and Practice." 43 *Hastings Law Journal* 749, 1992.

Takaki, Ronald. *Strangers From a Different Shore: A History of Asian Americans*. New York: 1989.

Tamayo, William, Robin Toma, and Stewart Kwoh. *The Voting Rights of Asian Pacific Americans*. Public Policy Project, Asian American Studies Center, University of California. Los Angeles: UCLA, 1991.

U.S. Commission on Civil Rights. *The Tarnished Golden Door: Civil Rights Issues in Immigration*. September 1980.

U.S. Commission on Civil Rights. *Civil Rights Issues Facing Asian Americans in the 1990s*. February 1992.

U.S. Department of Justice, Federal Bureau of Investigation. *Crime in the United States 1991: Uniform Crime Reports*. August 30, 1992.

Zuckerman, Edward. *Almanac of Federal PACs, 1994-1995*. Arlington: 1994.

—Marina C. Hsieh and Nicole A. Wong

Asian Americans in the U.S. Military

♦ Spanish-American War (1898) ♦ Period before World War II ♦ World War II (1941-1945)
♦ Korean War (1950-1953) ♦ Vietnam War (1965-1973) ♦ Asian/Pacific American Servicemen
♦ Outstanding Asian/Pacific American Military Figures ♦ Asian Pacific Military Heroes
♦ Top-Ranking Asian/Pacific Americans ♦ Chronology ♦ Contemporary Issues
♦ Veterans Organizations

Central to the historical development of the United States military is the involvement of a multitude of immigrants from many continents. Although the service of Asian/Pacific Americans has been relatively recent in U.S. military history, their contributions to the nation's defense have been no less significant than those of immigrants from other ethnic groups.

Throughout the history of the United States, there have been influxes of immigrants of all nationalities, the majority pursuing a common desire for a better life for themselves and future generations. In contrast to many European cultures, early Asian/Pacific Americans suffered from extreme prejudice upon their arrival to the United States. Consequently, they were excluded from "free immigration" until 1965. Since that time, Asian/Pacific immigrants have flowed to America at a rate of 20,000 or more a month.

The Immigration and Naturalization Act of 1965 abolished the national-origins system that had granted almost exclusive immigration preference to Europeans since 1924. After 1965, chaotic political unrest in Southeast Asia and subsequent United States military involvement in that region led to a consistent wave of Asian immigration. These recent immigrants to the United States are as diverse as the cultures that comprise the American "melting pot" and represent all segments of the social and economic ladder.

Today, more than 4 million Americans can trace their ancestry to Asia or the Pacific Islands. In addition to a history of proud accomplishments and contributions in the arts, literature, science, technology, agriculture, industry, and commerce, Asian/Pacific Americans have fought in America's wars since the Spanish-American War of 1898. Despite nearly constant adversity and frequent violence against them, Asian/ Pacific Americans have served loyally and contributed significantly to the national security goals of the United States.

Table 25.1
Active Duty Personnel by Service Branch

Service	Chinese	Japanese	Korean	Filipino	Vietnamese	Other Asian	Total Asian	All Personnel
Army	362	451	1,198	3,046	425	1,412	6,894	571,619
Navy	440	685	672	18,096	669	1,028	21,590	503,886
Air Force	383	717	438	3,925	6	2,285	7,754	441,578
Marines	120	148	240	1,002	174	360	2,044	179,160
Total	1,305	2,001	2,548	26,069	1,274	5,085	38,382	1,696,243

Source: *Defense Manpower Data Center, Arlington, VA, December 1993.*

Chinese, Japanese, Koreans, Filipinos, Vietnamese, and, to a lesser degree, Pacific Islanders, all have significant representation in the Armed Forces of the United States, as seen in Table 25.1. The large numbers of Filipinos in the various branches are due to a number of factors, including America's colonial relationship with the Philippines, which allowed Filipinos access to military service—within restrictions—long before other ethnicities were allowed even to immigrate to the United States in large numbers.

Asian/Pacific Americans in military service can be found at most ranks, from enlisted personnel (ranks 0–9) to officers (ranks 10–30). Table 25.2 shows the numbers of Asian/ Pacific Americans who have achieved ranks 0 through 30. Table 25.3 provides an explanation of each rank by service branch. Despite the gains Asian/ Pacific Americans have made in the military, the number of Asians, as a percentage of the whole, decreases as rank increases. Asians are currently the fastest-growing segment of America's population and are expected to increase to a projected 10 million by the year 2000. The future will see an accompanying rise in the number of military recruits from this minority group.

Asian/Pacific Americans first served in the military when the USS Maine was sunk in Havana Harbor in 1898, an incident which led to the Spanish-American War. Despite their presence in the service, Asian/Pacific Americans became the victims of discrimination in the selective-service process during World War I and World War II. Besides African Americans, circumstances of nonselection, nonacceptance, and noninduction also affected, in order of magnitude, Japanese Americans, Chinese Americans, and Filipino Americans. Between 1940 and 1947, this problem was probably most severe for Japanese Americans, who had experienced a consistent history of civilian discrimination.

Table 25.2
Active Duty Personnel in All Service Branches by Rank

Rank	Chinese	Japanese	Korean	Filipino	Vietnamese	Other Asian	Total Asian	All Personnel
0	0	0	0	0	0	0	0	33
1	65	38	180	731	136	258	1,408	76,127
2	78	55	251	1,182	166	339	2,071	117,138
3	123	145	372	2,235	326	686	3,887	214,298
4	206	266	515	4,439	307	1,036	6,769	348,496
5	133	290	314	5,608	138	727	7,210	296,221
6	96	276	219	5,618	33	542	6,784	215,996
7	76	187	155	3,320	8	437	4,183	124,912
8	20	61	35	1,077	0	115	1,308	31,669
9	11	22	6	465	0	59	563	12,936
10	0	0	0	0	0	0	0	0
11	1	2	3	16	0	5	27	2,466
12	3	8	15	56	0	14	96	7,790
13	0	7	4	50	0	11	72	5,154
14	1	5	1	24	0	3	34	2,505
15	0	0	0	0	0	1	1	96
20	0	0	0	0	0	0	0	96
21	52	69	121	193	49	108	592	24,944
22	75	69	83	211	39	134	611	29,996
23	187	248	176	476	67	335	1,489	94,022
24	93	146	59	192	2	171	663	47,720
25	53	83	25	118	1	76	356	29,978
26	30	22	14	58	2	26	152	12,698
27	0	2	0	0	0	0	2	487
28	2	0	0	0	0	1	3	336
29	0	0	0	0	0	1	1	113
30	0	0	0	0	0	0	0	36
Total	1,305	2,001	2,548	26,069	1,274	5,085	38,282	1,696,243

Source: Defense Manpower Data Center, Arlington, VA, December 1993.

USS Maine in Havana Harbor, 1898. (Courtesy of U.S. Army Military History Institute.)

The attack on Pearl Harbor of December 7, 1941, served, on the one hand, to accentuate this discrimination even further, while also galvanizing Japanese Americans to join the service to prove their loyalty to the American people. Nisei (second-generation Japanese in the United States) soldiers more than proved their loyalty and acquitted themselves extremely well of unfair accusation of being disloyal to the United States. Much of the respect they garnered was earned with their combat prowess in a variety of campaigns in the European theater. The most famous of the all-Asian units was the Japanese American 100th Infantry Battalion, 442nd Regimental Combat Team.

Despite the military contributions of Asian/Pacific Americans, discrimination—while it did decrease—did not disappear completely. By the end of hostilities in World War II there was even some resurgence. However, by the time of the Vietnam War, official segregation of minorities was long a thing of the past. Asian/Pacific Americans were subject to the draft under the same rules as all other Americans and were integrated throughout the armed forces. As a result, in subsequent wars, from Korea to the Persian Gulf, Asian/Pacific American soldiers continued to distinguish themselves in service. Just as the Asian/Pacific immigrant has blended into American culture, the Asian/Pacific American has also mixed into the ranks of the United States Armed Forces.

The accomplishments of Asian/Pacific Americans in America's military service are well documented and have established a place for this minority group in the military history of the United States. Specifically, the

Table 25.3
U.S. Military Rank Titles by Service Branch

Rank	Air Force	Army	Navy	Marines
1	Airman Basic	Private	Seaman Recruit	Private
2	Airman	Private E2	Seaman apprentice	Private 1st Class
3	Airman 1st Class	Private 1st Class	Seaman	Lance Corporal
4	Senior Airman	Specialist	Petty Officer 3rd Class	Corporal
5	Staff Sergeant	Sergeant	Petty Officer 2nd Class	Sergeant
6	Technical Sergeant	Staff Sergeant	Petty Officer 1st Class	Staff Sergeant
7	Master Sergeant	Sergeant 1st Class	Chief Petty Officer	Gunnery Sergeant
8	Senior Master Sergeant	Master Sergeant or 1st Sergeant	Senior Chief Petty Officer	1st Sergeant or Master Sergeant
9	Chief Master Sergeant		Master Chief Petty Officer	Sergeant Major Gunnery or Sergeant Major
10				
11	2nd Lieutenant	2nd Lieutenant	Ensign	2nd Lieutenant
12	1st Lieutenant	1st Lieutenant	Lieutenant Junior Grade	1st Lieutenant
13	Captain	Captain	Lieutenant	Captain
14	Major	Major	Lieutenant Commander	Major
15	Lieutenant Colonel	Lieutenant Colonel	Commander	Lieutenant Colonel
20	Colonel	Colonel	Captain	Colonel
21	Brigadier General	Brigadier General	Rear Admiral Lower Half	Brigadier General
22	Major General	Major General	Rear Admiral Upper Half	Major General
23	Lieutenant General	Lieutenant General	Vice Admiral	Lieutenant General
24	General	General	Admiral	General

Source: *Defense Manpower Data Center, Arlington, VA, December 1993.*

Ellison Onizuka. (Courtesy of NASA.)

exploits of the 100th Infantry Battalion, 442nd Regimental Combat Team are unprecedented in the annals of American military combat. The unit was "the most decorated unit for its size and length of service in the history of the United States." (See "The History of the 100th Battalion" section of this chapter.) More recently, individual Asian/Pacific Americans have carried the torch of distinguished achievement in the service of the United States military.

Colonel Ellison S. Onizuka, United States Air Force, was the first Japanese American and the first citizen from Hawaii to become an astronaut. He was killed in the explosion of the Space Shuttle Challenger on January 28, 1986. Subsequently, the Air Force named a base in California in his honor.

In 1987, Hoang Nhu Tran, a Vietnamese refugee, graduated first in his class of 960 students from the United States Air Force Academy and was named a Rhodes scholar. He was also the recipient of the 1986 Time magazine College Achievement Award. Hoang Nhu Tran is only one of many Asian/Pacific Americans who are making headway in the military academies and have, in recent years, attended them in increasing numbers, as is shown in Tables 4, 5, and 6.

As the fastest-growing population segment in the United States, Asian/Pacific Americans will likely represent a larger percentage of recruits in the future.

♦ SPANISH-AMERICAN WAR (1898)

Early history of Asian/Pacific American participation in the United States Armed Forces is poorly recorded and generally referred to only incidentally. The initial participation of Asian/Pacific Americans in America's wars was during the Spanish-American War when seven Isei men, or first-generation Japanese, and one Chinese man were reported to have been among the crew members killed during the sinking of the USS

Table 25.4
United States Military Academy at West Point

Year	Asian Pacific American Graduates	Males	Females	Total Graduates, All Ethnicities
1986	26	22	4	1,006
1987	22	21	1	1,042
1989	33	29	4	981
1990	41	37	4	1,066
1991	31	30	1	931
1992	36	32	4	965
1993	55	47	8	943
Current enrollment				
1994	61	49	12	1,019
1995	81	66	15	1,080
1996	66	53	13	1,085
1997	37	33	4	1,067

Source: *Department of the Army, U.S. Military Academy Public Affairs Office, West Point, NY, August 1993.*

Maine in Havana Harbor in 1898. In addition, Filipino Army units fought side by side with the United States Navy against the Spanish in Manila. Ironically, those same soldiers would eventually fight against the United States Army in the Philippine struggle for independence from 1898 to 1902.

♦ PERIOD BEFORE WORLD WAR II

Following Spain's defeat and the quelling of the Philippine insurrection, the United States formed the Philippine Scouts within the United States Army. Filipinos were considered American nationals, and the Philippine Division was fully integrated into the United States Army. Filipino officers, however, could only be assigned to the Scouts and were limited to the rank of major. The Philippine Scouts remained in existence through World War II, and were an integral part of the United States Army in the Philippines. General Douglas MacArthur served with the Scouts on several occasions and was their division commander in the late 1920s. He also served as the court-martial officer for 200 rebellious scouts in 1924, sentencing them all to dishonorable discharges and five years of hard labor.

Table 25.5
United States Naval Academy

Year	Asian Pacific American Graduates	Males	Females	Total Graduates, All Ethnicities
1986	49	49	—	1,028
1987	37	37	—	1,036
1988	37	37	—	1,060
1989	50	50	—	1,082
1990	54	54	—	108
1991	44	44	—	955
1992	46	46	—	1,031
1993	63	49	14	1,051
Current enrollment				
1994	46	42	4	—
1995	46	39	7	—
1996	49	40	9	—
1997	41	32	9	—

Source: Department of the Navy, U.S. Naval Academy Public Affairs Office, Annapolis, MD, August 1993.

Table 25.6
United States Air Force Academy

Year	Asian Pacific American Graduates	Males	Females	Total Graduates, All Ethnicities
1986	25	25	—	961
1987	47	47	—	969
1988	32	32	—	1,074
1989	27	27	—	1,022
1990	27	27	—	993
1991	32	32	—	977
1992	34	34	—	na
1993	32	32	—	na
Current enrollment				
1994	36	36	—	—
1995	33	33	—	—
1996	33	33	—	—
1997	45	45	—	—

Source: Department of the Navy, U.S. Air Force Academy Public Affairs Office, Colorado Springs, CO, August 1993.

Philippine Scouts, around 1900. (Courtesy of U.S. Army Military History Institute.)

In 1903, the United States Navy listed nine Filipinos in its ranks. By 1905, the number was 178. Filipinos were restricted to the steward rating until the late 1970s, but were found throughout the navy on ships, at shore stations, and wherever senior navy officers were assigned. Between World Wars I and II, the number of Filipinos in the armed forces remained at roughly 4,000. Despite their restrictions, duty in the navy was far more desirable than remaining an impoverished civilian. A Filipino steward serving in the navy until retirement could combine his pension and savings, and live rather handsomely in his Philippine hometown.

Enlistment of native Filipinos in the navy during World War II was not allowed, but immigrant Filipinos in the United States were allowed to join both the navy and army. However, as before, Filipinos in the navy were limited to the steward rating. After the allied landing in the Philippines in 1944, native Filipinos were again recruited by the United States Navy, with 2000 enlistments by 1946.

♦ WORLD WAR II (1941-1945)

The attack on Pearl Harbor on the morning of December 7, 1941, had both positive and negative impact on Asian/Pacific Americans. It resulted, on the one hand, in the internment and economic deprivation of 110,000 Japanese Americans. Following President Franklin Roosevelt's signing of Executive Order 9066, Americans of Japanese ancestry were forcibly removed from their homes on the West Coast and were relocated to internment camps away from coastal regions. In the early 1990s Congress passed a bill compensating Japanese Americans with symbolic redress payments for the mistreatment they endured during the years of internment.

On the other hand, the infamous attack on Pearl Harbor and the rapid expansion of the war effort that followed opened the United States Armed Forces to immigrants who had previously been denied enlistment and provided many other job opportunities for those who did not serve in the military. Asian/Pacific American communities saw the war as a chance to prove their loyalty and value as Americans.

Korean Americans in World War II

On the evening of December 7, 1941, Korean residents of Los Angeles congregated at the headquarters of the Korean National Association and passed three resolutions:

First Filipino Infantry Battalion. (Courtesy of U.S. Army Military History Institute.)

• Koreans shall promote unity during the war and act harmoniously.

• Koreans shall work for the defense of the country where they reside and . . . should volunteer for National Guard duty, should purchase war bonds and . . . volunteer for appropriate duties.

• Koreans shall wear a badge identifying them as Koreans, for security purposes.

By December 29, 1941, fifty Koreans had registered for and begun training with the California National Guard. The formation of a Korean Guard unit soon followed. On December 4, 1943, Military Order Number 45 was issued, exempting Koreans from enemy alien status and granting them the right to enlist in any of the armed services.

♦ CHINESE AMERICANS IN WORLD WAR II

The Japanese attack on Pearl Harbor also initiated a series of profound changes for Chinese Americans, who already felt tremendous animosity toward the Japanese because of Japan's brutal invasion and occupation of China. America's entry into the war provided Chinese Americans the opportunity to take action.

They worked in defense industries, frequently in scientific and technical positions that commanded higher wages. The navy waived its alien restrictions and recruited 500 Chinese Americans as apprentice seamen immediately after Pearl Harbor. Chinese community leaders urged young Chinese to enlist as a demonstration of the loyalty of all Chinese Americans. This call was widely heeded; the New York Chinatown community, for instance, cheered enthusiastically when the first draft numbers included Chinese Americans. Of the eleven Chinese Americans of draft age in Butte, Montana, all had enlisted prior to being drafted. And, in battle, Chinese Americans fought side by side with white Americans, whose ancestors, ironically, had attempted to expel the Chinese from America.

During the war, over 20 percent of the 59,803 Chinese adult males in the United States in 1941, including citizens, residents, and students, enlisted or were drafted into the United States Army. Smaller numbers also served in the navy and air corps. The known Chinese American death total from the war numbered 214 servicemen. Although the number is small in comparison with the rest of the population, it nevertheless demonstrates the loyalty and patriotism of a people long discriminated against in the United States. World

War II unmistakably altered America's image of the Chinese, just as Chinese self-image also changed. Chinese Americans began to discard some traditional Chinese traits while adopting American ones, but they continued to maintain such Chinese values as reverence for family, respect for education and hard work, cultivation of propriety, and patience and restrictiveness in the upbringing of their offspring.

Filipino Americans in World War II

The Filipino American experience roughly paralleled that of the Koreans and Chinese. The Filipino community did not have the others' solidarity, but they were willing, if not eager, participants in the war against Japan. The Philippines had a long colonial history with the United States when it fell to Japan, and most Americans generally accepted that the Japanese had to be driven out. Thousands of Filipino Americans volunteered for military service immediately after Pearl Harbor, but were refused due to the United States citizenship requirement for enlistment. However, by December 20, 1941, Congress had passed resolutions allowing virtually unlimited enlistment and employment of Filipino Americans in the war effort.

On April 22, 1942, the First Filipino Infantry Battalion, United States Army, was activated at Camp San Luis Obispo, California, under the command of three Filipino officers and an American colonel. The Secretary of War issued a statement on February 19, 1942, inaugurating the battalion.

> This new unit is formed in recognition of the intense loyalty and patriotism of those Filipinos who are now residing in the U.S. It provides for them a means of serving in the Armed Forces of the United States, and the eventual opportunity of fighting on the soil of their homeland.

On August 2, 1942, the Third Battalion, Filipino Unit of the California State Militia of Salinas, received its colors. The First Filipino Regiment came home to San Francisco in 1946 with 555 men, mostly Filipinos. The unit closely resembled the famed 442nd Regimental Combat Team in prestige and combat distinction. But unlike the 442nd Regiment, the role of Filipinos in the war is not widely known or recorded. The regiment had been organized with one primary task in mind, pre-invasion intelligence operations. Six months before the Leyte Gulf landing in the Pacific Ocean on October 20, 1944, the First (Filipino) Reconnaissance Battalion was ashore gathering information. The remainder of the regiment participated in the campaign for Samar and Leyte.

The Filipino American units played a significant role in the eventual recapture of the Philippines. Their efforts and those of the Filipinos at home gained them greater recognition in Congress and led directly to the July 12, 1946, legislation that granted Filipinos the right to become citizens.

Pacific Islanders in World War II

Pacific Islanders also took an active role in the American victory over Japan. They developed a special relationship with United States Navy and Marine Corps units throughout the Pacific. Samoans, Fijians, Guamanians, and others enlisted in the navy and marine corps and served as infantrymen, guides, translators, coast-watchers (surveillance), and in numerous other capacities. These islanders shared with the United States a desire to defeat the Japanese and free their homelands from Japanese occupation.

Japanese Americans in World War II

The story of Japanese Americans during World War II is closely interwoven with the story of the vindication of a relatively large segment of the American immigrant population: the 300,000 Japanese Americans living in the United States and the Territory of Hawaii in 1942.

In the month preceding the attack on Pearl Harbor, the American public viewed Japanese Americans with great suspicion. Shortly after December 7, 1941, the Selective Service System automatically reclassified all Japanese Americans as 4-F (physically, mentally, or morally unfit) and later as 4-C (not acceptable for military service because of nationality or ancestry). However, because translators were considered critical to the war effort, the Selective Service relaxed its rules and qualified Japanese Americans for military enlistment.

The Fourth Army Intelligence School was created in San Francisco in November 1941. Japanese American instructors established within it a Japanese military language school to teach soldiers born of Japanese parents and raised in the United States a useful amount of their ancestral language before being sent to the Pacific. These soldiers used their skills to interrogate prisoners, analyze documents, and to familiarize others with Japanese geography and map reading. The need for translators was so great that the program was expanded and reorganized as the Military Intelligence Service Language School on June 1, 1942.

Japanese American translators were assigned to nearly every unit in all major engagements from Guadalcanal and Attu to the march into Tokyo. Their contributions were invaluable in achieving victory in the Pacific. In recognition of their accomplishments, Major General Charles A. Willoughby, General MacArthur's chief of intelligence, stated, "Never before in history did an army know so much concerning its enemy, prior to its actual engagement, as did the American Army during most of the Pacific campaigns." General Joseph Stilwell paid tribute to the Japanese American translators (and soldiers) under his command in the China, Burma, and India theater of operations by stating, "The Nisei bought an awful big hunk of America with their blood." The more than 6,000 Japanese Americans who were trained to serve in the Pacific became the eyes and ears of the Allied fighting forces and were credited with saving countless American and Allied lives.

Joe Rosenthal, Associated Press photojournalist, who won the Pulitzer Prize for his photo of the raising of the flag at the crater rim of Mount Suribachi, wrote of the special difficulties faced by Japanese American soldiers in the Pacific:

Usually they work with headquarters in serving as interpreters. Armed with hand grenades at the entrances to Japanese pillboxes or caves, they often convince the enemy to surrender where other officers, lacking the proper diction of the Japanese language, would fail. They work so close to the enemy on these missions that, with the danger of being killed by Japanese, they run the risk of being shot, unintentionally, by our own Marines. Their dungarees soon become ragged in rough country and the similarity of their physical appearance to that of the Japanese enemy makes their job much tougher. Many have paid with their lives, and many more have been wounded. They have done an outstanding job, and their heroism should be recognized. It has been recognized. It has been recognized by the Marine commanders where I saw them in action at Guam, Peleliu, and Iwo.

The following additional comments are excerpts from a variety of other sources regarding the performance of Japanese American translators during World War II in the Pacific.

The official reports of the American Division disclosed that the work of the Japanese language specialists was largely responsible for the Division Commander knowing well in advance where, approximately at what time and in what strength the enemy would attack the division along the Torokina River near Bougainville.

From Guadalcanal, an island in the Pacific, Lieutenant Colonel John A. Burden, then captain in the G-2 Section of the XIV Corps and one of the two white American graduates of the first class at the Presidio, wrote:

The use of Nisei in the combat area is essential to efficient work. There has been a great deal of prejudice and opposition to the use of Nisei in combat areas. The two arguments advanced are: Americans of Japanese ancestry are not to be trusted, and the lives of the Nisei would be endangered due to the strong sentiment against Japanese prevailing in the area. Both of these arguments have been thoroughly disproved by experiences on Guadalcanal, and I am glad to say that those who opposed the use of Nisei the most are now their most enthusiastic advocates. It has been proved that only the Nisei are capable of rapid translation of written orders and diaries, and their use is essential in obtaining the information contained in them.

Major General Ralph C. Smith, who commanded the Twenty-seventh Infantry Division added, "The language section attached to the Twenty-seventh Division was invaluable in the Makin operation."

Recognition also has been given to the work of these Japanese Americans in the field. At least fifty received direct commissions from the ranks as Second Lieutenants, and another twenty or thirty were commissioned through the various Officer Candidate Schools in Australia and in the United States. In addition to serving as translators, 3,700 Japanese Americans also participated in combat in the Pacific. They saw action in the battles of New Guinea, the Marianas, the Philippines, and Okinawa.

100th Infantry Battalion, 442nd Regimental Combat Team

In the European Theater of Operations, Japanese American accomplishments were also remarkable and are more well-known. The exploits of the 100th Infantry Battalion, 442nd Regimental Combat Team stand at the forefront of these achievements. The following time line presents a chronology of its service.

The History of the 100th Battalion, 442nd Regimental Combat Team in the European Theater

1942

A battalion is created from interned Japanese Americans in Hawaii. It is designated the 100th Infantry Battalion.

February. The 100th is transferred to Shelby, Mississippi for large unit training.

1943

February. The 100th's training record is so superb that the 442nd Regimental Combat Team is activated. Meanwhile, a call is sent out for additional Japanese to volunteer for service. Three thousand men from Hawaii and 1,500 from the mainland respond, many of whom have families held in internment camps.

August 11. The 100th is sent overseas.

September 19. The 100th is engaged in its first firefight. They are subsequently engaged in fierce fighting

"442 Combat Team at Leghorn," Painting by Dong Kingman. (Courtesy of U.S. Army Center of Military History.)

at three separate crossings of the Rapido River, as well as at Volturno, Cassino, and the Anzio beachhead. Over 100 Purple Hearts were awarded during this period, earning the 100th the name "Purple Heart Battalion."

1944

June. The superb combat record of the 100th, plus an excellent training record, leads to the decision to send the 442nd into action overseas, and on this date the two join forces north of Rome.

June 26. The 442nd engages the enemy in battle; it is the first of five major campaigns it will fight before the war's end.

October 18. The 442nd liberates the French town of Bruyeres after three days of intense fighting.

October 27. The 442nd, after a rest of only four days, receives orders to break the German ring surrounding the "Lost Battalion" of the 141st Regiment, Thirty-sixth Division, which had been isolated for almost a week and was low on food and ammunition. In the next four days, the 442nd engaged in fierce battles that left more than 200 men dead, with over 600 injured. Of 200

riflemen in Company K, there were only 17 left; Company I had only eight men left.

November 8. The 442nd is relieved and sent to southern France to guard the French-Italian border, where it is brought back to life with replacements of men and a fresh supply of materials.

1945

March. The 442nd is sent to Italy to create a diversionary action in the western anchor of the Gothic Line, an enemy sector that had defied Allied assault for more than five months.

April 5. A frontal assault on the enemy's guns, which held complete control of the area, was impossible, so the 442nd was sent to conduct a surprise attack by scaling an unguarded ridge to the enemy's rear. In 32 minutes, the men took two key mountaintop positions. This break in the enemy lines led to the total destruction of the Gothic Line.

The 442nd are the first Allied troops to reach Turin. They are in complete control of the western sector when, on May 2, the Third Reich surrenders.

In less than two years, the 100th Infantry Combat Battalion and the 442nd Regimental Combat Team successfully fought in seven major military campaigns: Naples, Foggio; Rome, Arno; Southern France (Operation Anvil); Rhineland; North Apennines; Central Europe; and the Po Valley. They suffered 9,486 casualties, including 650 soldiers who were killed in action. The total number of casualties was more than twice the assigned complement of men in the unit. Table 25.7 lists the awards and citations they received.

Table 25.7
Awards and Citations Earned by the 442nd Regimental Combat Team

1	Congressional Medal of Honor
52	Distinguished Service Crosses
1	Distinguished Service Medal
560	Silver Stars plus 28 Oak Leaf Clusters
22	Legions of Merit
15	Soldier's Medals
4,000	Bronze Stars with 1,200 Oak Leaf Clusters
9,486	Purple Hearts
18,143	Individual decorations for personal valor

One of the noteworthy figures of the 442nd Regimental Combat Team was future United States Senator Daniel Inouye, a Democrat from Hawaii. As a young First Lieutenant, he lost an arm in Europe. During his time with the "Go for Broke" unit, Lieutenant Inouye was awarded the Distinguished Service Cross and two Purple Hearts.

Overall, more than 33,000 Japanese Americans served in World War II. Besides translators and combat soldiers, some served as nurses, doctors, therapists, and pharmacists in unsegregated combat units in all theaters and in the Women's Army Corps. They demonstrated that a person of Japanese ancestry was basically no different from an American of European ancestry in fighting for the principles of the United States. Never again would Japanese American loyalty as a group be doubted—they had earned a place in American history. More importantly, Asian/Pacific Americans had made an indelible mark in the military history of the United States with their loyalty, patriotism, valor, and sacrifice.

◆ KOREAN WAR (1950-1953)

Following World War II, Asian/Pacific Americans were fully integrated into the armed forces. Segregated units were no longer formed, although some units, such as the 100th Battalion Hawaii National Guard, maintain a predominantly Asian Pacific/American-membership.

First Lieutenant Daniel K. Inouye, who lost his arm during his tour of duty with the 442nd Regimental Combat team, went on to become U.S. senator from Hawaii. (Courtesy, office of Senator Inoye.)

The outbreak of war in Korea found United States forces unprepared. Reserves and National Guard units were mobilized. The draft was expanded and few groups were exempted from service. The severe shortage of frontline combat soldiers led to the foundation of the Korean Augmentation to U.S. Army (KATUSA) Program. The original KATUSA program started casually during the Korean War, when stragglers from the Korean Army began joining U.S. Army units, primarily for rations and shelter. In August 1950, General Douglas MacArthur officially made plans for 20,000 to 30,000 Korean Army recruits to be assigned to U.S. units at the rate of about 100 per company or battery. This initial effort was somewhat less than successful, however, mostly due to the language barrier.

The KATUSA program still exists today and is managed by the U.S. Eighth Army, U.S. Forces Korea. Current participants are members of the Republic of Korea (ROK) Army who are recruited for three-year tours of duty with the U.S. Army. They are recruited, paid, promoted, and disciplined by the ROK Army but are under the operational command and control of the U.S.

Hiroshi H. Miyamura. (Courtesy of U.S. Army Military History Institute.)

Herbert K. Pililaau. (Courtesy of U.S. Army Military History Institute.)

Army. They are fully integrated into American units and are treated in exactly the same manner as U.S. soldiers. They are assigned a military specialty, but without any specific training in it. A KATUSA soldier will normally remain within the same company or battery for the duration of his or her tour of service. In addition to military specialty duties, they act as interpreters and are invaluable in helping Americans adapt to Korean customs. They directly enhance combat readiness and reduce support costs for American units in Korea. There are approximately 6,200 KATUSA soldiers assigned to the Eighth Army today.

Japanese Americans also served with distinction in the Korean War. When the war broke out in 1950, many Nisei, who had decided to make the military their career, were among the first American troops to be sent to the peninsula. The United States was short of Korean translators at the time, just as it had lacked Japanese translators in World War II. However, since almost all Korean adults were familiar with the Japanese language, Japanese Americans once again satisfied a military need and provided invaluable service to the United States. Nisei soldiers were immediately assigned to army units such as the First Cavalry,

Twenty-fifth Infantry Division, Fifth Army Regimental Combat Team, and Twenty-seventh Infantry in places like Taejon, Chonju, and Taegu.

One veteran of the 442nd Regimental Combat Team during World War II, Sergeant Hiroshi Miyamura, was recalled to active duty and received the Congressional Medal of Honor for action near Taejon-ni, Korea, on April 24-25, 1951, when he ordered and covered the withdrawal of his squad against a numerically superior enemy force. Despite depleting his ammunition and suffering severe wounds, he fought on but was finally overwhelmed and captured, and subsequently spent twenty-nine months in a North Korean prison camp. After repatriation, he received his Congressional Medal of Honor from President Dwight D. Eisenhower in 1954. Sergeant Leroy A. Mendonca and Private First Class Herbert K. Pililaau also won the Congressional Medal of Honor for valor, but at the cost of their lives.

◆ VIETNAM WAR (1965-1973)

By the time of the Vietnam War, official segregation of minorities in the United States Armed Forces was long a thing of the past. Asian/Pacific Americans were subject to the draft under the same rules as all other Americans and were integrated throughout the military where they continued to distinguish themselves in combat.

Despite wounds that disabled one arm and partial blindness caused by fragments from a white phosphorous grenade, Sergeant First Class Rodney J. T. Yano saved the lives of fellow crew members by dumping burning ammunition and supplies from an airborne helicopter. Corporal Terry T. Kawamura sacrificed his life to save several of his fellow soldiers from serious injury or death by throwing his body on an explosive charge. Both Japanese Americans from Hawaii were awarded the Congressional Medal of Honor posthumously.

♦ ASIAN/PACIFIC AMERICAN SERVICEMEN

The post-World War II period saw black service personnel take up the struggle against the remaining traces of segregation and discrimination in the United States Armed Forces. For the Asian/Pacific American, segregation and discrimination issues had virtually resolved themselves. The Asian/Pacific American group is not a homogenous one; each of the groups within it has its own distinct values. All, however, emphasize discipline, family, hard work, patience, and education and share a tendency to disdain the limelight. Asian/Pacific Americans fought for and achieved the rights of citizenship and the opportunity to serve and defend the United States.

Today, Asian/Pacific Americans comprise about 2 percent of the United States Armed Forces, including the service academies to each of the three services. The percentage of Asian/Pacific American general/flag officers roughly parallels its representation in the total force. Their representation in the armed forces is in approximate alignment with their portion of the United States population. In conclusion, it would be fair to say that Asian/Pacific Americans have come a long way in the United States Armed Forces in a relatively short period of time.

♦ OUTSTANDING ASIAN/PACIFIC AMERICAN MILITARY FIGURES

Hoang Nhu Tran (1965-)

On April 28, 1975, Hoang Nhu Tran was a frightened nine year-old Vietnamese boy on a leaky boat in the middle of the South China Sea, one of thousands of homeless "boat people" who fled invading North Vietnamese troops as Saigon fell.

After a Philippine freighter rescued Tran and his family from the landing barge and took them to Guam,

Hoang Nhu Tran graduating as valedictorian from the Air Force Academy.

the Hoangs were relocated to Fort Collins, Colorado, by the Lutheran Church after a six-week stay at Camp Pendleton, San Diego.

Although he struggled with English, spelling, and science, Tran mastered these subjects at Rocky Mountain High School in Fort Collins. His grades produced offers of college scholarships, but he favored the Air Force Academy. Tran won an appointment from Senator William L. Armstrong (Republican-Colorado) and entered the Air Force Academy in July 1983.

Four years later, Tran became the first Asian/Pacific American to be class valedictorian at the Air Force Academy. In addition, he went onto Oxford University for two years as an air force second lieutenant and the first Vietnamese Rhodes scholar. After completing his studies at Oxford, Tran enrolled at Harvard Medical School on a full scholarship and is currently training to be a surgeon.

Tran's goal after medical school is "to pay back what was given . . . by America . . . I want to serve the world, to help all mankind."

Rear Admiral Ming E. Chang (1932-)

Admiral Ming E. Chang rose to be the highest-ranking Chinese American in the U.S. Navy.

William Shao Chang Chen.

science degree in aeronautical and astronomical engineering, both from the University of Michigan. He also has a master of arts in business administration from Auburn University.

General Chen earned his commission through the ROTC (Reserve Officer Training Corps) program and served early in his career as the Tactical Officer Monitor, Thirty-fifth Artillery Brigade, Fort Meade Maryland. His later posts included: Chief, High-Altitude Missile Section, United States Army Combat Developments Command; Executive Officer, Defense Attaché Officer, Vientiane, Laos; and Commanding General, United States Army Missile Command.

Among his decorations are the Distinguished Service Medal, Legion of Merit, Bronze Star, Meritorious Service Medal (with five Oak Leaf Clusters), Joint Service Commendation Medal (with Oak Leaf Clusters), and the Army Commendation Medal.

Brigadier General David Earl Kaleokaika Cooper (1941-)

General Cooper has served nearly thirty years in the U.S. Army. He is currently Chief of Staff, First United States Army.

Born in Shanghai, China, Chang received a bachelor of science degree in physics from the College of William and Mary and a second bachelor of science degree in engineering electronics from the Naval Postgraduate School.

After being commissioned an ensign in the naval reserve and later augmented in the U.S. Navy, he served as commanding officer of several ships, including the USS Rathburne and USS Reeves. He also was the Commander, Carrier Group Three; Commander, Third Fleet; and Commander, Cruiser Destroyer Group Two. He culminated his distinguished naval career as the navy's Inspector General.

Major General William Shao Chang Chen (Ret.) (1939-)

Major General William Sheo Chang Chen served over thirty years in the U.S. Army. His last assignment was as Program Executive Officer, Global Protection Against Limited Strikes, in the office of the Assistant Secretary of the Army.

General Chen was born in Shanghai, China, on November 11, 1939. He earned a bachelor of science degree in engineering mathematics and a master of

David Earl Kaleokaika Cooper.

Cooper was born on August 12, 1941, in Honolulu, Hawaii. He earned a bachelor of arts degree in English from the University of Hawaii, a master of arts degree in English literature from the University of Missouri, and a master of science degree in psychology counseling from the University of Long Island.

In addition to the schooling mentioned above, General Cooper received training at the Infantry School, the Armor School, the Army Command and General Staff College, and the U.S. Army War College. Among his many major duty assignments are: Executive Officer, Company A, First Battalion, Seventh Infantry, U.S. Army Europe; Battalion S-3 Officer (Operations) Second Battalion (Airborne), U.S. Army Vietnam; Chief, Plans, Programs, and Management Division, Office of the Assistant Chief of Staff for Personnel; Director, Department of English, U.S. Military Academy, West Point, New York; and Chief of Staff, Fourth United States Army.

The General has been highly decorated. Among his commendations are: the Distinguished Service Medal, Silver Star (with Oak Leaf Clusters), Legion of Merit (with two Oak Leaf Clusters), Bronze Star Medal with "V" Device (with 5 Oak Leaf Clusters), and Purple Heart (with two Oak Leaf Clusters).

Major General John L. Fugh (1934-)

Born in Beijing, China, General John L. Fugh became the first Chinese American to attain general officer status in the United States Army.

At the age of 15, Fugh and his family left China for Hong Kong and eventually emigrated to the United States. He earned a bachelor of science degree in international relations from the Georgetown University School of Foreign Service and graduated from the George Washington University School of Law. Fugh then received a commission as an officer in the Judge Advocate General's (JAG) Corps.

Upon attaining the position of The Judge Advocate General (TJAG), the pinnacle of the JAG Corps, Fugh advanced the reputation of the JAG Corps by providing proactive legal support. Specifically, he accomplished the following:

• Emphasized the role of judge advocates in helping the army deal with increasingly important contract matters and environmental problems.

• Provided legal assistance to the families of soldiers who served in Operation Desert Storm, which took place from January to April 1991.

• Established a program for human-rights training in developing countries and published the War Crimes Report—the first American effort since World War II to systematically document enemy war crimes.

• Led the army successfully through critical litigation

John L. Fugh.

challenges to its promotion boards, homosexual-exclusion policy, and conscientious-objector policy.

His awards include the Distinguished Service Medal, Defense Superior Service Medal, Legion of Merit (with Oak Leaf Cluster), Meritorious Service Medal (with Oak Leaf Cluster), Air Medal, Joint Service Commendation Medal, and the Army Commendation Medal (with Oak Leaf Cluster).

Ensign Michael Hsu

Ensign Michael Hsu graduated from the Naval Academy in 1993 with a degree in systems engineering. He was selected for the Pownall Scholarship, a two-year program of graduate studies at Cambridge University. There, Hsu is studying astronautical engineering and management. He plans to enter the naval aviation program after completing his studies at Cambridge.

While at the academy, Hsu contributed to two design projects. First, he worked on the nuclear power system for the first lunar outpost at Los Alamos National Laboratory and presented a paper on the project at a conference of the American Institute of Aeronautics and Astronautics. Second, as a Trident Scholar, Hsu's project involved giving a robot the capability to visually track objects the way humans do.

Senator Daniel K. Inouye (1924-)

Senator Daniel K. Inouye was born on September 7, 1924, in Honolulu, Hawaii. He graduated from the University of Hawaii with a bachelor of arts degree and earned a J.D. (Doctor of Law) from George Washington University.

Inouye was 18 years old when he volunteered for military service in early 1943 along with 10,000 other Hawaiian Nisei (second-generation Americans of Japanese ancestry). He was barely 20 when he earned a battlefield commission (second lieutenant) in France.

Nine days before the end of World War II in Italy, Inouye led an assault against a German position on Mount Nebbione. Forty yards from the German bunkers, he stood up and threw a grenade into a machine-gun nest, cutting down the crew with his submachine gun. However, a bullet tore into his abdomen. Ignoring the wound, Inouye charged up the hill and lobbed two grenades into a second machine-gun emplacement. As he pulled the pin on his last grenade and attempted to throw it, a German fired a rifle grenade at him from a distance of ten yards. The rifle grenade smashed into his right elbow and exploded, all but tearing off Inouye's right arm. The arm dangled uselessly, but still clutched his live grenade. He pried it from the right fist with his left hand and tossed it toward the German, killing him.

Inouye then directed the final assault which took the ridge. But he suffered another bullet wound, this time to his right leg. It was the end of the war for Second Lieutenant Inouye. Inouye lost his right arm, ending his lifelong dream of becoming a doctor. He received the Distinguished Service Cross for his action. Earlier he had been awarded the Bronze Star.

Although his hopes of becoming a physician were shattered by the loss of his arm, Inouye turned to law and became the first United States Congressman from the State of Hawaii. He was elected to the United States Senate in 1962 and has served in that position for more than 30 years.

Lieutenant Colonel Gero Iwai (1905-1972)

Gero Iwai was the earliest and the most senior of any Japanese American known to have served in American military intelligence.

Born on November 5, 1905, Iwai received his military training from the University of Hawaii where he was among the first Japanese Americans to complete the ROTC (Reserve Officer Training Corps) course and earn a reserve army commission as a second lieutenant. Beginning August 19, 1931, when he enlisted in the army, Iwai pursued and fulfilled a military career in counterintelligence work that spanned 26 years. He served in Hawaii prior to and during World War II and later in occupied Japan.

Immediately after the Pearl Harbor attack on December 7, 1941, Iwai worked with the Office of Naval Intelligence and the FBI to interrogate the first Japanese prisoner of war of World War II, the captured commander of the Japanese midget submarine grounded at Waimanalo Beach. The drawing "Questioning a Prisoner" by Edward Laning depicts the interrogation of a Japanese prisoner of war by U.S. personnel. Documents found on the submarine were among the first direct sources of counterintelligence information recovered during World War II.

Iwai's counterintelligence investigations and reports prior to the outbreak of war were instrumental in disproving allegations of espionage and disloyalty by Japanese American residents in Hawaii. Iwai's performance from 1941 onward won him a promotion to major in 1945. From September 1945 through August 1949, he served as a counterintelligence officer during the occupation of Japan. He earned a promotion to lieutenant colonel in 1950. In 1951, Iwai supervised security for Japan's Prime Minister during peace treaty negotiations and ceremonies in San Francisco.

He retired from military service on June 30, 1957, and died on April 9, 1972, at 67 years of age.

Master Sergeant Roy H. Matsumoto

Master Sergeant Roy H. Matsumoto was born in Los Angeles, California. In the fall of 1942, Matsumoto and his family were incarcerated in internment camps along with many other Japanese American families.

After six months of confinement in Arkansas, Matsumoto volunteered for military service, serving as a Japanese translator. He was assigned to the 5307th Composite Unit (Provisional), better known as Merrill's Marauders, in the China-Burma-India theater of operations. His unit would trek the jungles of Burma, conducting operations behind enemy lines to sever Japanese communications and supply lines.

Matsumoto carried out many dangerous missions by infiltrating Japanese lines every night to listen and snipe. While on an intelligence-gathering mission during the siege at Nhpum Ga, he returned one night with news of an impending attack. The Marauders met the enemy with devastating fire. When the attack failed, Matsumoto stood and yelled in Japanese for the attack to continue. The next wave met the same fate as the first. The siege was finally lifted after ten days by an attack of the remaining Marauders. The Marauders continued to march and captured the all-weather airstrip at Myitkyina where Matsumoto was in the last group of 17 men to be evacuated after the mission.

Matsumoto then joined the 475th Infantry "Mars Task Force" where he was attached to the Chinese Nationalist Army guerrilla forces behind enemy lines to serve as an intelligence NCO near the French Indochina border.

Interrogation of Japanese prisoner of war, depicted by Edward Laning. (Courtesy of U.S. Army Center of Military History.)

On July 19, 1993, Matsumoto was inducted into the U.S. Army Ranger Hall of Fame for his extraordinary courage and service with Merrill's Marauders.

Major Ellison S. Onizuka (1946-1986)

Major Ellison S. Onizuka was born on June 24, 1946, in Kealakekua, Kona, Hawaii. He graduated from Konawaena High School in 1964 and received his bachelor and master of science degrees in aerospace engineering in June and December 1969, respectively, from the University of Colorado.

Onizuka began active duty with the United States Air Force (USAF) in January 1970, after receiving his commission as a distinguished military graduate of the University of Colorado four-year Reserve Officer Training Corps (ROTC) program. He was selected as an astronaut candidate by NASA in January 1978. In August 1979, Onizuka completed a one-year training and evaluation period, making him eligible for assignment as a mission specialist on future space shuttle flight crews.

Onizuka was a mission specialist on the first space shuttle Department of Defense mission, which was launched from Kennedy Space Center, Florida, on January 24, 1985. On January 28, 1986, Onizuka was one of

seven persons killed when the space shuttle Challenger exploded. The air force named a base in California in his honor.

Lieutenant General Allen K. Ono (1933-)

Lieutenant General Allen K. Ono rose to become the highest ranking Asian/Pacific American in the United States Military.

Born in Honolulu, Hawaii on December 31, 1933, Ono was educated in Hawaii. He attended the University of Hawaii and received a bachelor of arts degree in government. Ono received a master of science degree in communications from Shippensburg State College and a degree from Northwestern University's Executive Management Program.

After serving in the infantry for six years, he moved into the military administration field and served in various adjutant-general positions. Ono also worked in the army's recruiting program and eventually became the commanding general of the army's recruiting command.

Ono was promoted to lieutenant general in 1987 and closed out his career as deputy chief of staff for personnel, United States Army, Washington, DC. In this capacity, he directed the Army's military and civilian personnel operations, handling such contentious issues as recruitment, retention, pay and entitlements, and family support.

Commander Douglas T. Wada (1910-)

Described as the only Japanese American specifically recruited to serve in the U.S. Naval Intelligence Service before, during, and after World War II, Commander Douglas T. Wada's military career was an incredible, one-of-a-kind experience.

Born in Honolulu in 1910, Wada attended the University of Hawaii from 1933 to 1937, where he was recruited by a classmate in anticipation of the need for a language specialist in the event of war with Japan. Prior to the outbreak of World War II, Wada worked on highly classified assignments such as radio and wireless intercepts. Immediately after the Pearl Harbor attack, Wada helped translate the navigational chart taken from the Japanese midget submarine beached at Waimanalo and documents confiscated from the Japanese consulate by Honolulu police on the morning of the attack. Very few people knew of Wada's work and affiliation with Naval Intelligence.

Following the Japanese surrender in August 1945, Wada was assigned to the Prosecution Section, International Tribunal for the Far East, to assist in the prosecution of Class-A war criminals, including General Hideki Tojo and other high-ranking Japanese war leaders. He directed the Interpreters Section until his reassignment in 1946 to the 14th Naval District Intelligence Office. Wada's mission was to identify communists within the Pearl Harbor naval base. During this period, he wrote a report, entitled "Brief History of Communism in Hawaii," which was considered the authority on the subject by other investigative agencies.

Wada retired from the Navy in 1975 with the rank of Commander.

♦ ASIAN PACIFIC MILITARY HEROES

The exploits of the 100th Infantry Battalion/442nd Regimental Combat Team epitomize the loyalty and valor of Asian/Pacific Americans, particularly those who have paid the ultimate sacrifice of life, in service to the United States. Since the Spanish-American War, the United States has awarded the Congressional Medal of Honor (CMH) to the following nine Asian/Pacific Americans. (The men are listed in the order in which they received this award. An * indicates that the award was given posthumously.)

Private Jose B. Nisperos
34th Company, Philippine Scouts, U.S. Army

Born in San Fernandos Union, Philippine Islands, Nisperos was the first Asian/Pacific American to win the Congressional Medal of Honor. He was cited for valor on September 24, 1911, while fighting at Lapurap, Basilan, Philippine Islands. Despite being badly wounded (his left arm was broken and lacerated, and he had received several spear wounds in the body so that he could not stand), Nisperos continued to fire his rifle with one hand until the enemy was repulsed, thereby aiding materially in preventing the annihilation of his party and the mutilation of their bodies.

Fireman Second Class Telesforo Trinidad
U.S. Navy

Born in New Washington Capig, Philippine Islands, Telesforo Trinidad displayed extraordinary heroism when a boiler exploded aboard the USS San Diego, on January 21, 1915. Trinidad was driven out of fireroom no. 2 by the explosion, but immediately returned and rescued an injured shipmate. While bringing his shipmate out, he was caught in another explosion. After insuring the safety of the sailor and without regard for his own life, Trinidad assisted in rescuing another injured man. He suffered burns on the face by the blast from the second explosion.

Sergeant Jose Calugas
Battery B, 88th Field Artillery, Philippine Scouts, U.S. Army

Born in Barrio Tagsing, Leon, Iloilo, Philippine Islands, Jose Calugas was cited for bravery during hostilities that took place near Culis, Bataan Province, Philippine Islands, on January 16, 1942. While under heavy Japanese artillery attack, he ran 1,000 yards to a partially destroyed gun position whose cannoneers were either killed or wounded. Upon reaching the position, Calugas organized a volunteer squad that put the guns back in commission and fired effectively against the enemy.

Private First Class Sadao S. Munemori*
Company A, 100th Infantry Battalion, 442nd Regimental Combat Team, U.S. Army

Born in Los Angeles, Sadao S. Munemori fought with great gallantry near Seravezza, Italy, on April 5, 1945. When his unit was pinned down by fire from the enemy's strong mountain defense, command of the squad fell to him after its leader was wounded. Munemori singly made frontal assaults through direct fire and destroyed two machine guns. While withdrawing under heavy fire from other enemy emplacements, he had nearly reached a shell crater occupied by two of his men when an unexploded grenade rolled into the crater. Immediately, Munemori, exposing himself to withering fire, dove on the grenade and smothered

Jose Calugas. (Courtesy of U.S. Army Military History Institute.)

the blast with his body. By his supremely heroic action, Munemori saved two of his men at the cost of his own life.

Corporal Hiroshi H. Miyamura
Company H, 7th Infantry Regiment,
3rd Infantry Division, U.S. Army

Born in Gallup, New Mexico, Hiroshi H. Miyamura distinguished himself by conspicuous gallantry against the enemy near Taejon-ni, Korea, on April 24 and 25, 1951. On the night of April 24, the enemy attacked and threatened to overrun the defensive position occupied by Company H. Aware of the imminent danger to his men, Squad Leader Miyamura immediately engaged the enemy with a bayonet in hand-to-hand combat. He killed about ten of the enemy. Returning to his position, Miyamura administered first aid to the wounded and directed their evacuation. As the enemy attacked again, he provided machine gun fire until his ammunition was expended and then ordered the withdrawal of the squad while he stayed behind to render the gun inoperable. Next, Miyamura covered the withdrawal of a second gun position, killing more than 50 of the

enemy before running out of ammunition and being severely wounded. Despite his wounds, he continued to fight the enemy until the position was finally overrun and Miyamura was captured.

Private First Class Herbert K. Pililaau*
Company C, 23rd Infantry Regiment,
2nd Infantry Division, U.S. Army

Born in Waianae, Oahu, Territory of Hawaii, he was engaged in heavy combat near Pia-ri, Korea, on September 17, 1951. Pililaau's platoon held a key terrain feature on "Heartbreak Ridge" against wave after wave of enemy troops. The unit repulsed each attack until its ammunition was almost exhausted and it was ordered to withdraw. Pililaau volunteered to cover the withdrawal. He first engaged the enemy with automatic fire and grenades and then fought in hand-to-hand combat until being overcome and mortally wounded. When the position was subsequently retaken, more than 40 enemy dead were counted in the area Pililaau defended.

Sergeant Leroy A. Mendonca*
Company B, Seventh Infantry Regiment,
3rd Infantry Division, U.S. Army

Born in Honolulu, Leroy Mendonca was cited for conspicuous gallantry against the enemy near Chichon, Korea, on July 4, 1951. After his platoon had captured Hill 586, the enemy counterattacked during the night with a numerically superior force. When the unit was outflanked and under heavy pressure, it was ordered to withdraw to a secondary defensive position. Mendonca volunteered to cover its withdrawal. After using all of his ammunition and grenades, he fought on with his bayonet until he was mortally wounded. Mendonca was credited with an estimated 37 enemy casualties, and with enabling his unit to repel the enemy's attack and retain possession of the vital hilltop.

Sergeant First Class Rodney J. T. Yano*
Air Cavalry Troop, 11th Armored Cavalry
Regiment, U.S. Army

Born in Kealake Kua, Hawaii, Rodney Yano was a crew chief on the troop's command-and-control helicopter during action against enemy forces entrenched in the dense jungle of Bien Hao, Republic of Vietnam, on January 1, 1969. Exposed to intense small-arms and anti-aircraft fire, Yano delivered suppressive fire upon the enemy and marked their positions with smoke and white phosphorous grenades. A grenade exploded prematurely, covered him with burning phosphorous and left him mortally wounded. The flaming fragments also caused the supplies to burn and ammunition to

Paul Y. Chinen.

explode. Despite having the use of only one arm and being partially blinded by the initial explosion, Yano began hurling blazing ammunition from the helicopter. In doing so, he suffered additional wounds, but he persisted until the danger had past. His action, at the cost of his life, averted loss of life and additional injury to the rest of the crew.

Corporal Terry Teruo Kawamura*
173rd Engineer Company,
173rd Airborne Brigade, U.S. Army

Born in Wahiawa, Hawaii, Terry Kawamura was cited for risking his life above and beyond the call of duty at Camp Radcliff, Republic of Vietnam, on the evening of March 20, 1969. An enemy demolition team had infiltrated the unit quarter area and opened fire with automatic weapons. When an explosion tore a hole in the roof of a room full of American servicemen, Kawamura grabbed his gun and, while running to the door to return fire, saw another explosive charge being thrown through the hole in the roof. Disregarding his own safety, Kawamura unhesitatingly hurled himself on the charge, preventing the serious injury or death of several members of his unit.

♦ TOP-RANKING ASIAN/PACIFIC AMERICANS

Brigadier General Paul Y. Chinen
Commanding General, United States Army Engineer Division, North Atlantic
New York, New York

Paul Y. Chinen, born in Honolulu, was commissioned into the United States Army as a Second Lieutenant through the ROTC (Reserve Officer Training Corps).

He earned a bachelor of science degree in civil engineering from Seattle University and a master of science in structural engineering from Iowa State University of Science and Technology.

His assignments include commander, Company C, Seventieth Engineer Battalion, U.S. Army, Vietnam; assistant corps engineer, 18th Airborne Corps, Fort Bragg, North Carolina; commander, 27th Engineer Battalion, Fort Bragg, North Carolina; group commander, 36th Engineer Group, Fort Benning, Georgia; Assistant Commandant, U.S. Army Engineer School, Fort Belvoir, Virginia; commanding general, U.S. Army Engineer Division, Ohio River, Cincinnati, Ohio; and deputy chief of staff for base operations support, U.S. Army Training and Doctrine Command, Fort Monroe, Virginia.

His decorations include the Legion of Merit, Bronze Star (with four Oak Leaf Clusters), Meritorious Service Medal (with four Oak Leaf Clusters), and the Army Commendation Medal.

Major General (Dr.) Vernon Chong
Chief Surgeon, European Command

Born in Fresno, California, Vernon Chong earned a bachelor of arts degree in basic medical sciences from Stanford University and a doctor of medicine degree from Stanford University School of Medicine.

General Chong participated in the manned space program as a member of the launch site recovery forces for all of the Apollo, Skylab, and Apollo-Soyuz manned missions. He served as a member of the board of regents of the National Library of Medicine and as an adviser to the board of regents of the Uniformed Services University of the Health Sciences.

In addition, his assignments include deputy commander and director of hospital services, U.S. Air Force Regional Hospital, March Air Force Base, California; commander and Director of Hospital Services, David Grant U.S. Air Force Medical Center, Travis Air Force Base, California; commander, Malcolm Grow U.S. Air Force Medical Center, Andrews Air Force Base, Maryland; command surgeon, Military Airlift Command, Scott Air Force Base, Illinois;

Eugene S. Imai.

Dwight M. Kealoha.

and commander, Wilford Hall U.S. Air Force Medical Center, Lackland Air Force Base, Texas.

His awards and decorations include the Distinguished Service Medal, Legion of Merit (with Oak Leaf Cluster), Meritorious Service Medal, and the Air Force Commendation Medal.

Major General John R. D'Araujo, Jr.
Director, Army National Guard
National Guard Bureau, Washington, D.C.

Born in Hilo, Hawaii, John R. D'Araujo, Jr., was commissioned into the U. S. Army as a second lieutenant through the Officer Candidate School (OCS). He received a bachelor of science degree in liberal arts from the University of New York.

His assignments include platoon commander, First Battalion, 487th Artillery, U.S. Army, Vietnam; commander, Mobile Advisory Team III-42, U.S. Army, Vietnam; operations officer, 298th Artillery Group, Army National Guard, Hawaii; commander, Command and Control Headquarters, Army National Guard, Hawaii; property and fiscal officer, Army National Guard, Guam; chief, Mobilization and Readiness Division, National Guard Bureau, Washington, D.C.; chief,

Organization and Training Division, National Guard Bureau, Washington, D.C.; Commander, 29th Infantry Brigade, Army National Guard, Hawaii; and Deputy Director, Army National Guard, National Guard Bureau, Washington, D.C.

His decorations and badges include the Legion of Merit (with two Oak Leaf Clusters), Bronze Star Medal, Meritorious Service Medal (with two Oak Leaf Clusters), Army Achievement Medal, and the Combat Infantryman Badge.

Brigadier General Eugene S. Imai
Assistant Adjutant General, Army
Hawaii Army National Guard,
Fort Ruger, Hawaii

Born in Honolulu, Eugene S. Imai received his commission as a second lieutenant through the ROTC (Reserve Officer Training Corps) program. He earned his bachelor of arts degree in political science and master's degree in business administration from the University of Hawaii.

His assignments include commanding officer, 621st Personnel Service Company; commander, 621st Administrative Service Detachment; Adjutant General,

Robert K. U. Kihune.

Headquarters, IX Corps; Detachment commander, 1085th Training Exercise and Maneuver Group; chief of staff, Headquarters, IX Corps; and Chief Plans Officer, Headquarters, State Area Command, Hawaii Army National Guard.

His decorations include the Legion of Merit, Bronze Star Medal, Meritorious Service Medal, Army Commendation Medal, and the Army Reserve Components Achievement Medal (with four Oak Leaf Clusters).

Brigadier General Dwight M. Kealoha

Commander, 15th Air Base Wing
Hickam Air Force Base, Hawaii

Dwight M. Kealoha, born in Honolulu, received a bachelor's degree from the University of Hawaii and a master's in business administration from the University of Utah.

During his tour of duty on the Air Staff, Headquarters, U.S. Air Force, Washington, D.C., General Kealoha prepared the U.S. response to the North Atlantic Treaty Organization's defense planning questionnaire; led the basing action for the introduction of the TR-1, EF-111, ground-launched cruise missile, additional KC-135 aircraft and the F-16 fighter to U.S. Air Force in Europe;

and was one of five Air Force officers selected to serve on the Reagan transition team.

His other significant assignments include instructor pilot and standardization and evaluation flight examiner, 32nd Tactical Reconnaissance Squadron, Royal Air Force Station, Alconbury, England; commander, 509th Tactical Fighter Squadron, Royal Air Force Station, Bentwaters, England; commander, 48th Combat Support Group, Royal Air Force Station Lakenheath, England; commander, 513th Airborne Command and Control Wing, Royal Air Force Station, Mildenhall, England; assistant deputy for plans, Programs and Policy, U.S. Air Force, Europe, Ramstein Air Base, Germany; and commander, 375th Airlift Wing, Scott Air Force Base, Illinois.

His awards and decorations include the Defense Superior Service Medal, Legion of Merit, Distinguished Flying Cross (with Oak Leaf Cluster), Meritorious Service Medal (with Oak Leaf Cluster), Sir Medal (with nine Oak Leaf Clusters), and the Air Force Commendation Medal.

Vice Admiral Robert K. U. Kihune

Director, Naval Training and Doctrine (N7)
Chief of Naval Education and Training
Office of the Chief of Naval Operations
Washington, D.C.

Born in Lahaina, Hawaii, Robert K. U. Kihune attended the United States Naval Academy where he received a bachelor of science degree in naval science. He was commissioned ensign upon graduation in 1959. Admiral Kihune also received a bachelor of science degree in communications engineering from the Naval Postgraduate School, Monterey, California, in 1965.

His assignments include tours in various positions aboard the USS Pritchett, USS Farragut, and USS Davidson; commanding officer, USS Cochrane; commander, Destroyer Squadron 35; commander, Naval Surface Force, Pacific; Director, Command, Control and Communications Systems, U.S. European Command; commander, Cruiser Destroyer Group Five; commander, Naval Surface Force, U.S. Pacific Fleet; and assistant chief of naval operations, Surface Warfare (OP-03), Office of the Chief of Naval Operations.

Admiral Kihune's medals and awards include the Distinguished Service Medal, Defense Superior Service Medal, Legion of Merit (with two Gold Stars), Meritorious Service Medal, Navy Commendation Medal, Armed Forces Expeditionary Medal (with three Bronze Stars), and the Vietnam Service Medal (with three Bronze Stars).

Major General Edward V. Richardson

The Adjutant General, Hawaii Air National Guard

Edward V. Richardson, born in Puunene, Maui, Hawaii, graduated from the University of Hawaii. He began his military career by joining the Hawaii Air

Edward V. Richardson.

Ray R. Sareeram.

National Guard. General Richardson completed the U.S. Air Force Aviation Cadet Pilot Training Program and was commissioned a second lieutenant.

His assignments include instructor pilot and standardization and evaluation flight officer, 199th Fighter Interceptor Squadron; flying safety officer, 154th Fighter Group; commander, 199th Fighter Interceptor Squadron; and commander, Hawaii Air National Guard.

His military awards and decorations include the Meritorious Service Medal, Air Medal (with one Bronze Oak Leaf Cluster), Combat Readiness Medal (with four Bronze Oak Leaf Clusters), Hawaii National Guard Medal for Merit, and the Hawaii National Guard Commendation Medal.

Rear Admiral Ray R. Sareeram
Director, Supply Programs and Policy Division (N41), Office of the Chief of Naval Operations, Washington, DC

Born in Orangevale, California, Ray R. Sareeram earned an associate degree from Sacramento Junior College, a bachelor of arts in business administration from Sacramento State College, and a master's in business administration from the University of Michigan.

After enlisting in the Naval Reserve and being honorably discharged, Admiral Sareeram was commissioned as an ensign in the Naval Reserve. He was later inducted into the U.S. Navy. His assignments include assistant chief of staff for supply, Naval Surface Group, Western Pacific; deputy commander, Financial Management/Comptroller, Naval Supply Systems Command Headquarters; commander, Defense Depot, Ogden, Utah; commanding officer, Naval Supply Center, Oakland, California; and fleet supply officer, U.S. Pacific Fleet, Pearl Harbor, Hawaii.

His medals and awards include the Defense Superior Service Medal, Legion of Merit (with one Gold Star), Bronze Star Medal, and the Meritorious Service Medal (with three Gold Stars).

Brigadier General Eric K. Shinseki
Director of Training, Office of the Deputy Chief of Staff for Operations and Training, United States Army, Washington, D.C.

Eric K. Shinseki was born in Lihue, Kauai, Hawaii and attended the United States Military Academy. He graduated with a bachelor of science degree and was commissioned as a second lieutenant. General Shinseki also earned a master of arts degree in English from Duke University. His assignments include commander, A Troop, Third Squadron, Fifth Cavalry, Ninth Infantry Division, U.S. Army, Vietnam; instructor, Department of English, United States Military Academy, West Point, New York; commander, Third Squadron, Seventh Cavalry, Third Infantry Division, U.S. Army, Europe and Seventh Army; commander, Second Brigade, Third Infantry Division, U.S. Army, Europe and Seventh Army; assistant division commander, Third Infantry Division (Mechanized), U.S. Army, Europe and Seventh Army; and deputy chief of staff, Administration/Logistics, Allied Land Forces, Southern Europe.

His awards and decorations include the Legion of Merit (with Oak Leaf Clusters), Bronze Star Medal with "V" Device (with two Oak Leaf Clusters), Purple Heart (with Oak Leaf Cluster), Meritorious Service Medal (with three Oak Leaf Clusters), Air Medal, and the Army Commendation Medal (with Oak Leaf Cluster).

Brigadier General Frederick G. Wong
Director, Officer Personnel Management
Directorate, United States Total Army
Personnel Command, Alexandria, Virginia

Born in Hawaii, Frederick G. Wong received his commission as a second lieutenant from the ROTC (Reserve Officer Training Corps) program. He earned both a bachelor of arts degree in social science and a master of arts degree in guidance and counseling from Eastern Washington University.

His assignments include commander, Company B, Third Battalion, Fourth Combat Support Training Brigade, Fort Polk, Louisiana; commander, Company B, First Battalion, 27th Infantry Regiment, 25th Infantry Division, U.S. Army, Vietnam; deputy commander, Mohringen Community, VII Corps, U.S. Army, Europe and Seventh Army; executive officer, First Battalion, 28th Infantry Regiment, First Infantry Division, Fort Riley, Kansas; commander, Second Battalion, 19th Infantry Regiment, 24th Infantry Division (Mechanized), Fort Stewart, Georgia; commander, Second Brigade, 24th Infantry Division (Mechanized), Fort Stewart, Georgia; deputy director for plans, J-5, U.S. Pacific Command, Camp H. M. Smith, Hawaii; assistant division commander, Fifth Infantry Division (Mechanized), Fort Polk, Louisiana; and assistant division commander, Second Armored Division, Fort Hood, Texas.

His decorations include the Silver Star, Legion of Merit (with two Oak Leaf Clusters), Bronze Star Medal (with two "V" Devices), Bronze Star Medal (with Oak Leaf Cluster), Purple Heart (with Oak Leaf Cluster), Meritorious Service Medal (with three Oak Leaf Clusters), Air Medal, and the Army Commendation Medal (with two Oak Leaf Clusters).

Eric K. Shinseki.

◆ CHRONOLOGY

1848-1852

Chinese arrive as indentured servants during the California Gold Rush. The majority of Chinese immigrants come soon after as a cheap source of labor to work on the railroads, in mines, and in other industries.

1869

Zun Zow Matzmulla becomes the first Japanese midshipman at the U.S. Naval Academy. He graduated in 1873.

1870

The Naturalization Act excludes Chinese from citizenship and prohibits the entry of foreign-born wives of laborers into the United States.

1882

The Chinese Exclusion Act suspends immigration of Chinese laborers for ten years, separating the families of men who married before leaving for overseas.

Frederick G. Wong.

1883

Japanese replace the Chinese as a source of cheap labor after the Exclusion Act.

1892

The Geary Act prohibits Chinese immigration for another ten years and denies bail for writ of habeus corpus.

1898

February 15. Seven Japanese Americans and one Chinese American are killed when the USS Maine is blown up in Havana Harbor.

1898

May 1. Japanese Americans serve on U.S. warships in the Battle of Manila.

1902

Congress indefinitely extends the prohibition against Chinese immigration and the denial of naturalization.

1903

Korean contract laborers arrive in Hawaii and begin moving to the United States in 1904.

1905

Ying Shing Wen and Ting Chia Chen are the first Chinese Americans to attend the U.S. Military Academy at West Point. They graduate in 1909.

1907

The Gentlemen's Agreement restricts Japanese immigration of laborers. This is a prelude to the passage of a Japanese Exclusion Act by Congress. As a result, single Filipino men are recruited to work in Alaskan fisheries and the growing agribusiness of Hawaii and California.

1910

The United States Supreme Court extends the 1870 Naturalization Act prohibiting Chinese citizenship to include all Asians. This year also marks the start of large-scale immigration of Korean laborers, picture brides, and political-refugees to the United States.

1911

Jose Nisperos, a Filipino American sailor, becomes the first Asian/Pacific American to win the Congressional Medal of Honor, the nation's highest award for bravery.

1917

The Selective Service Act is enacted as a law without racial provisions, however discriminatory military practices persist.

1918

Edward Chapin Chew becomes the first Chinese American army officer commissioned as a second lieutenant by the United States Military Academy at West Point.

1924

The Exclusionary Immigration Act completely ends Asian immigration. Only Filipinos, who are subjects of the United States, are excepted from the law.

1925

The Legislative Act makes Filipinos ineligible for U.S. citizenship unless they serve three years in the navy.

Battle of Manila. (Courtesy of U.S. Army Military History Institute.)

1934

Tydings-McDuffie Act gives the Philippine Islands independence and sets an immigration quota of 50 Filipinos per year.

1940

The Selective Training and Service Act is enacted. It contains certain provisions to guarantee a program without racial restrictions.

March 21. Leaders of the Japanese American Citizens League meet with army and navy intelligence services officials and pledge their loyalty and cooperation.

1941

November 1. The Fourth Army Intelligence School opens in a converted hangar at Crissy Field, The Presidio, San Francisco. Japanese American instructors establish a Japanese military language program in the school.

December 7. After the Japanese attack on Pearl Harbor, Korean residents of Los Angeles pass three resolutions declaring their loyalty and full support to the United States. Kido Saburo, president of the Japanese American Citizens League, sends a telegram to President Franklin D. Roosevelt pledging the loyalty and cooperation of the Nisei (second generation Japanese Americans).

December 29. Fifty Koreans register for the California National Guard and begin training.

1942

February 19. President Roosevelt signs Executive Order 9066, authorizing the Secretary of War, or his designated military commander, to establish military areas and to evacuate civilians from these areas. From 1942 to 1945, Executive Order 9066 placed over 110,000 Japanese Americans (primarily citizens) in ten internment camps.

March 18. President Roosevelt signs Executive Order 9012, establishing the War Relocation Authority.

March 23. General John L. DeWitt, commander of the Western defense command, issues Civilian Expulsion Order No. 1, ordering the removal of persons of Japanese ancestry from Bainbridge Island, Washington.

April 22. War Department activates the First Filipino Infantry Battalion at Camp San Luis Obispo, California, with three Filipino officers and an American army colonel in command.

June. The U.S. Army organizes the first Japanese American unit in Hawaii and designates it the 100th Infantry Battalion.

June 5. Japanese are removed from Military Area No. 1, which includes the western half of Washington, Oregon, California, and southern Arizona.

August 2. The Third Battalion, Filipino Unit of the California State Militia of Salinas, receives its colors.

1943

First Lieutenant Masao Yamada becomes the first Japanese American army chaplain. Second Lieutenant Wilbur Carl Tze becomes the first Chinese American officer in the Marine Corps. The Magnuson Act finally repeals the Chinese Exclusion Act of 1882.

January 28. Secretary of War Henry Stimson decides to allow the formation of an all-Nisei combat unit.

February 1. The 442nd Regimental Combat Team is activated. It is comprised of the 442nd Infantry Regiment, the 522nd Field Artillery Battalion, the 232nd Engineer Combat Company, and later the 206th Army Ground Forces Band.

August 11. The 100th Infantry Battalion, 442nd Regimental Combat Team is sent to the European theater.

November 18. The War Department reclassifies American citizens of Japanese ancestry for military service, restoring their rights and duties of citizenship denied shortly after the attack on Pearl Harbor.

December 4. The United States issues Military Order Number 45, exempting Koreans from enemy alien status, thereby opening all of the Armed Services to Korean immigrants.

1944

September 7. The Western Defense Command issues Public Proclamation No. 24, revoking exclusion orders and military restrictions against persons of Japanese ancestry.

October 27. The 442nd Regimental Combat Team rescues the "Lost Battalion" of the 36th Division from certain annihilation by a superior German force. It takes the 442nd Regimental Combat Team only 32 minutes to smash the German stranglehold that had defied other Allied forces for five weeks.

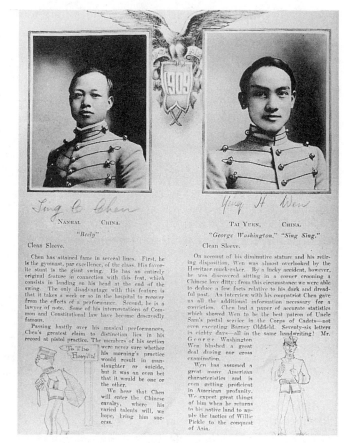

Page from the 1909 U.S. Military Academy yearbook, *Howitzer*, showing Ting C. Chen and Ying H. Wen.

December 18. The War Relocation Authority announces that all relocation centers will be closed by the end of 1945.

1945

August. Lieutenants George K. Kayano and Thomas T. Imada, Japanese Americans, are part of General Douglas MacArthur's official party during prearmistice negotiations with Japanese envoys to end World War II in the Pacific.

1946

March 7. Private First Class Sadao S. Munemori becomes the first Japanese American to be awarded the Congressional Medal of Honor.

June. The Fourth Army Intelligence School is deactivated after graduating about 6,000 students.

June 30. The War Relocation Authority program is officially ended.

July 15. The 442nd Regimental Combat Team comes to Washington, D.C., and parades down Constitution Avenue to the Ellipse where President Harry S. Truman awards the Presidential Distinguished Unit Citation to the unit.

1947

Article 27 of the U.S.-Republic of the Philippines Military Bases Agreement allows the U.S. government to enlist citizens of the Philippines into the Armed Forces of the United States.

1948

July 2. President Harry Truman signs into law the Japanese American Evacuation Claims Act, enabling former evacuees to file claims against the government for their financial losses during evacuation.

1950

The McCarran-Walter Act confers the right of naturalization and eventual citizenship for Asians not born in the United States and sets a quota of 105 immigrants per year for Asian countries.

1952

June 18. Private First Class Herbert K. Pililaau becomes the first American of Hawaiian ancestry to win the Congressional Medal of Honor for action in the Korean War.

1965

The National Origins Act raises Asian immigration to 20,000 per year, same as for Europeans.

1975

The fall of Saigon signals the arrival of large numbers of Vietnamese immigrants in the United States. Rising political unrest throughout Southeast Asia forces thousands of Cambodians, Laotians, and other Vietnamese to settle in the U.S. Over 700,000 of these refugees are estimated to have settled in the United States between 1975 and 1985.

April 15. The Interagency Task Force is created to coordinate all U.S. Government activities in evacuating U.S. citizens and certain Vietnamese citizens from Vietnam.

May 24. The Indochina Migration and Refugee Assistance Act is passed to provide funds for resettlement programs.

1976

September 10. Executive Order 9066, responsible for the evacuation, removal, and detention of persons of Japanese ancestry during World War II, is officially rescinded.

1980

July 31. The Commission on Wartime Relocation and Internment of Civilians is created to gather facts for determining if any wrong was committed against American citizens through Executive Order 9066.

1984

Filipino World War II veterans are denied U.S. citizenship and over 1,000 veterans face deportation.

August 1. John Fugh becomes the first Chinese American to be promoted to General Officer in the United States Army.

1985

Commander T. E. Bugarin becomes the first Filipino American to command a surface ship of the line when he assumes command of the USS Saginaw.

January 24. U.S. Air Force Major Ellison S. Onizuka, the first Asian/Pacific American astronaut, is a mission specialist on the first Department of Defense space shuttle mission.

1986

January 28. Major Onizuka is killed in the explosion of the space shuttle Challenger.

1987

May. Hoang Nhu Tran, a former Vietnamese boat person, graduates first in his class of 960 at the U.S. Air Force Academy.

1988

President Ronald Reagan signs into law the Civil Liberties Act, which apologizes and offers redress to thousands of Japanese Americans who were denied their civil rights by the U.S. government during World War II.

1993

July 19. Master Sergeant Roy H. Matsumoto, U.S. Army (retired), is inducted into the U.S. Army Ranger Hall of Fame for extraordinary courage and service with the 5307th Composite Unit known as Merrill's Marauders in the China-Burma-India theatre of operations during World War II.

◆ CONTEMPORARY MILITARY ISSUES

Equal Opportunity in the Military

Achieving increased status in the U.S. military is an ongoing challenge for minorities, including Asian/Pacific Americans. Minorities have succeeded in battling against some blatant forms of discrimination, such as the segregation of troops that existed through World War II. However, eliminating segregation has not and will not rid the military of the underlying problems of racism and inequality.

Asian/Pacific Americans are the fastest-growing minority group in the United States. Although they comprised only 2.9 percent of the total U.S. population in 1980, they increased by 95 percent by 1990. This is especially significant considering that they were less than 1 percent of the population in 1970. In the year 2020, the Asian/Pacific American population is projected to increase to 20 million, or about 8 percent of the total population. Most of this growth is expected to come from immigration.

Demographers predict that in 2020, 54 percent of Asian/Pacific Americans will be foreign born and that the number of children and young adults (age 0 to 24) in this group will increase from approximately 3 million in 1990 to 6.2 million. Historically, the children of immigrants have found jobs, education, and social status in the military, including scores of Asian/Pacific Americans.

The struggle for equal opportunity has not been and will not be easy. Some factors affect only Asian/Pacific Americans, and others are common to all minorities. The challenge is to build minority coalitions toward common goals, while recognizing the specific problems facing Asian/Pacific Americans.

Fighting the Stereotype

Asian/Pacific Americans must often resist being stereotyped as nonathletic nonassertive, followers. These stereotypes are particularly damaging in a military system where promotion, retention, and accessions are often based on strength, assertiveness, and leadership. Because wars in the 20th century have often pitted the U.S. against Asian nations, Asian/Pacific Americans have been unfairly questioned about their national loyalty.

The last three major U.S. wars were against Asian countries: World War II (Japan), the Korean War (North Korea and China), and the Vietnam War (North Vietnam). In recent years, negative attitudes toward Asians that developed from these military ventures have been exacerbated by the increasing economic strength of the Pacific Rim nations. This history, coupled with increased economic competition from Asian nations, has caused a backlash against Asian/Pacific Americans who proudly volunteer to serve their country.

Asian/Pacific Americans lack political and social clout. For this reason, they are often overlooked by government, academia, and the media, who still view race relations as a black/white paradigm. For example, a 1991 General Accounting Office (GAS) report on the distribution of minorities and women among major occupation groups in the military services did not even list Asian/Pacific Americans as a group, relegating them to the category of "other." How can Asian/Pacific Americans begin to address the problems that they face if the military does not recognize them?

In comparison to other minority groups, Asian/Pacific Americans are a small proportion of the armed forces. In addition, statistics show that in the Air Force, Navy, and Marine Corps, minority officers are not promoted in proportionate numbers. The problem becomes more acute the higher up the ladder of command as proportionally fewer minority candidates are promoted to the higher ranks of the officer corps.

Minority groups must build coalitions to pressure the military to improve systems and attitudes that negatively affect them. In the mid-1990s, articles appeared in military newspapers such as the *Navy Times* and *Air Force Times* with the titles such as "Bias and the Marine Corps," "Budget Cuts Blamed for Minority Hiring Woes," and "Minority Facing Promotion Discrimination." This situation led Congressman Ron Dellums, a Democrat from California who served as Chairman of the House Armed Service Committee, to hold congressional hearings to study the special problems facing minorities in the military.

Compliant Process Flawed

Fighting discrimination is difficult in the current system. An aggrieved serviceperson must complain to his or her commanding officer about discriminatory treatment, but the commanding officer is often part of the problem. The current military administrative review process may be interpreted as being inadequate. For example, the naval discharge review board and board for the correction of naval records have stated that they do not have jurisdiction over cases brought before them by candidates who attended Officer Candidate School. If this interpretation is upheld, then an entire class of service personnel in the military are being denied due process and basic constitutional protection.

Brave Asian/Pacific American soldiers, sailors, airmen, and marines have fought and died throughout the military history of the United States. They fought not only to win wars, but also for the ideals of democracy, freedom, and liberty. It is due, in part, to their sacrifices alongside their fellow Americans that discrimination has decreased in the armed forces. However, lingering discriminatory attitudes need to be eradicated. Succeeding generations of Asian/Pacific Americans must persevere and continue the struggle for fair and equal treatment in the U.S. military.

Case Study: Yamashita Discrimination Suit

In 1989, Bruce I. Yamashita, a graduate of Georgetown University Law Center and the School of Foreign Service, entered the U.S. Marine Corps Officer Candidate School (OCS) in Quantico, Virginia. Captain of his high school football team and student body president, he was a proud U.S. citizen expecting only to be given an equal opportunity to succeed or fail. However, he has described his experience in officer candidate school as "a nightmare." For nine weeks, he was racially harassed and physically abused. On the first day, a staff sergeant asked rhetorically, "You speak English?" and then screamed, "Well, we don't want your kind around here, go back to your own country!" A master sergeant spoke to him in broken Japanese for the entire course while he spoke to every other candidate in English. A staff sergeant told him, "During World War II, we whipped your Japanese ass!" Yet another sergeant regularly addressed him as Kawasaki, Yamaha, or some other Japanese product. He was called Kamikaze Man and was physically thrown to the ground. Another sergeant threw a rubbish can that barely missed his head. Two days before the graduation ceremony and after completing the entire nine-week course, Yamashita was disenrolled due to unsatisfactory leadership. Of the five candidates disenrolled from his platoon that day, four were minorities. Only one minority was allowed to graduate.

Yamashita's grandfather immigrated to Hawaii to work in the sugar plantations in 1892. His parents, both born and raised in Hawaii, helped build the 50th state. His father's youngest brother was a member of the legendary U.S. Army 442nd Regimental Combat Team, all of whose members were Japanese American, during World War II. Members of the 442nd had volunteered for military service, even while other Japanese Americans were being locked up in internment camps. They fought and died to free Europe, but also to prove, once and for all, that they were loyal U.S. citizens. For Yamashita to be told 50 years later "Go back to your own country!" was an outrage and attack on the very ideas behind the founding of the United States.

Yamashita returned to Hawaii, and decided to fight back. He wrote to the commandant of the Marine Corps, who ordered an investigation. The investigation concluded that nothing happened and implied that he was a liar. In October 1991, with the help of the Japanese American Citizen League-Honolulu Chapter, he began a five-year legal, political, and media battle with the U.S. Marine Corps. Two months later, the Marine Corps reopened the case.

A year-long investigation sustained the most egregious incidents of racial harassment and unfair treatment. The Marine Corps apologized and offered Yamashita the opportunity to return to OCS and compete for a commission. He refused, contending that, but for the discriminatory and unlawful conduct, he would have graduated with his OCS contemporaries.

Yamashita appeared before the naval discharge review board where he used Marine Corps statistics to show a pattern of discrimination against minorities form 1982 to 1990. A year later, in early 1993, the Marine Corps finally offered him a commission as a second lieutenant, the rank he would have received had he been commissioned in 1989. Yamashita refused to accept it. If the Marine Corps was committed to equal opportunity, then it would have to account for the years that had passed since his class—the 140th had graduated in 1989.

In December 1993, the Secretary of the Navy, John Dalton, intervened in the case. He ordered the Marine Corps to commission Yamashita to the rank of captain. On March 18, 1994, in the House Armed Services Committee Room of the U.S. House of Representatives, which was filled with family, friends, and supporters, Yamashita was commissioned a captain in the United States Marine Corps Reserve. It took five long years, but justice was finally won.

Reform in Marine Corps Policies and Procedures

In the nearly five years that Captain Yamashita pursued his case, a series of significant reforms were enacted to increase equal opportunity and reduce racial bias. The accomplishments are summarized below:

1. The Yamashita case revealed a pattern of discrimination against minorities at officer candidate school from 1982 to 1990 based on the Marine Corps' own statistics.

2. The Marine Corps established a special quality management board to look into the disparity of treatment between white and minority candidates at OCS. This panel concluded that the Marine Corps has a problem with regard to the procuring, promoting, and retaining of minority officers.

3. The Marine Corps revised its OCS standing operating procedures (OCS SOP) to prohibit the sort of racial harassment and unfair treatment that Captain Yamashita endured.

Bruce Yamashita being commissioned to the rank of captain.

4. This case provided the impetus for Congressional action requiring all branches of the armed forces to publish and enforce anti-discrimination policies at all military schools. This legislation cited Captain Yamashita's case as the rationale for such mandates.

—Bruce Yamashita

◆ VETERANS ORGANIZATIONS

Asian/Pacific American Heritage Council

P.O. Box 8135
Rockville, Maryland 20856

China-Burma-India Veterans Association

Mr. Dwight O. King
P.O. Box 2665
LaHabra, California 90631

Chosen Few Association

Colonel George A. Rasula, U.S.A., retired
500 Squire Circle
Clemson, South Carolina 29631

Civil Defense Council, United States

Mr. J. Herbert Stimpson
P.O. Box 370
Portsmouth, Virginia 22046

Combined National Veterans Association of America

Mr. George A. Lange, Jr.
6935 North 26th Street
Falls Church, Virginia 22046

Company C, Staff Battalion, Headquaters and Service Group

General HQ, Far East Command (Tokyo, Japan)
Mr. Harold E. Harlow
7103 West Meadows Lane
Greenfield, Indiana 46140

Congressional Medal of Honor Society

Mr. Gerald F. White
c/o USS Yorktown
40 Patriot Point Road
Mt. Pleasant, South Carolina 29464

Constabulatary Association, United States

Mr. Bud Groner
257 Georgetowne Boulevard
Daytona Beach, Florida 32119-8903

Council on America's Military Past (CAMP)

Colonel Edward L. Boyer, AUS, retired
P.O. Box 1151
Fort Myer, Virginia 22211-0151

Filipino War Veterans of America, Incorporated

Mr. Gregorio P. Chua
563 Sixth Avenue
San Francisco, California 94118

Guam Society of America, Incorporated

Box 180 (c/o NCSS)
Longworth House Office Building
Washington, D.C. 20515

IA DRANG Valley Alumni 1965

Mr. Bill Dreischer
1406 Devonshire Road
Hauppauge, New York 11788

Korean Military Assistance Group-Chejudo-1952

Mr. George C. Haffner
60 Delwood Road
Stratford, Connecticut 06497

**Korean Service Veterans Association
of Pennsylvania, Inc.**

Commander Francis J. Burskey
Box 418
Carrolltown, Pennsylvania 15722

Korean War Vets Association, Incorporated

Mr. Dick Adams
P.O. Box 127
Caruthers, California 93609

Legion of Valor of the U.S.A., Incorporated

CSM M. G. Worley, DSC, U.S.A., retired
92 Oak Leaf Lane
Chapel Hill, North Carolina 27516

Medal of Honor Historical Society

Mr. Edward F. Murphy
1317 East Hale Street
Mesa, Arizona 85203

Military Intelligence Service (MIS)

Japanese American Chapter
Mr. Fred Murakami
2511 Babcock Road
Vienna, Virginia 22181

National Association of Concerned Veterans

Mr. Ken Hubbs
P.O. Box 1803
Washington, D. C. 20013

Organization of Chinese Americans, Incorporated

P.O. Box 592
Merrifield, Virginia 20044

**Organization of Pan Asian American Women,
Incorporated**

915 15th Street, N.W.
Suite 600
Washington, D.C. 20005

**Progressive Alliance of Filipinos and Americans,
Incorporated**

8207 Barrett Road
Fort Washington, Maryland 20744

442nd Veterans Club

Mr. Robert Sasaki
933 Willi Willi Street
Honolulu, Hawaii 96826

*—Major General John Liu Fugh (ret.)
and Ltc. Ronald Tom (ret.)*

Family

♦ Confucianism ♦ China under Mao ♦ Japanese and Korean Societies
♦ Hindu and Muslim Societies ♦ Malayan Society ♦ Separated Families ♦ Filipino Immigration
♦ Japanese Immigration ♦ War Brides ♦ Recent Immigrant Families ♦ "Relay Immigration"
♦ American-Born Families ♦ Marriage ♦ Generation Gap ♦ The Elderly ♦ Intermarried Families
♦ Child-Rearing Practices ♦ Family Income ♦ Refugee Families ♦ Conclusion

The Asian American family cannot be described as one model but many. The Asian American population in the United States is not monolithic and can be divided by family type, period of immigration, socio-economic class, as well as ethnic identity. The main ethnic groups are the Chinese, Japanese, Korean, Filipino, Vietnamese, Asian Indians, Pakistani, and other Southeast Asians. Family type includes separated families, recent immigrant families, native-born, foreign-born families, war-bride families, intermarried families, and refugee families. All of these are influenced by when the family members immigrated and by the family's social and economic background or under what conditions the family immigrated. Table 26.1 illustrates typical family types for the six largest Asian American groups.

Obviously, an intact native-born family is quite different from a separated family, where some members are still in the homeland. Even when intact, families differ according to their culture. An Asian Indian family, for example, is quite different from a Filipino family. When one spouse is of another race or ethnicity, as with "war bride" marriages for example, this factor creates changed cultural climate in the family. There are similarities between many Asian cultures, but with so many groups and types, obviously no one Asian group can be looked upon as representative of the Asian American family.

Each Asian group carries its own national cultural background, belief system, geography, and economic history. Although Asian Americans have migrated to the United States, their family ideologies, molded by their cultural identity and experience, influence their family lives. It is best to first review briefly some of these traditional Asian belief systems.

Table 26.1
Family Types of Asian Americans

Family Type	Chinese	Japanese	Korean	Indian	Filipino	Vietnamese
Separated	X				X	
Recent Immigrant	X	(1)	X	X	X	X
Native-born	X	X	X	X	X	
War Bride		X	X		X	X
Intermarried	X	X	X		X	X
Refugee						X

Note:
Where no X is indicated, the incidence of such family type is small.
(1) With recent Japanese immigration, those who are admitted are usually families of businessmen.

♦ CONFUCIANISM

In China, Japan, Korea, and Vietnam, Confucianism, with its emphasis on parental authority and honor, social hierarchy, male dominance, duty, and obligation, laid the foundation for the family as the basic building block of society. Confucius set down the rules for a stable and orderly society. His teachings were based on a concept of the right and proper relationship of man to man. Each person had his/her place in relationship to everyone else in a social hierarchy. Relationships were clear-cut so everyone knew how to behave and how to deal with one another. For example, father's brothers and mother's brothers were not just called Uncle; they were addressed by different terms respective to the paternal or maternal side. Also, certain obligations were due to a father's brothers, but not a mother's brothers.

Under Confucianism, male dominance meant that women had to submit to the authority of men, otherwise known as a patriarchy. Patrilineage meant that kinship and inheritance was on the father's side; the mother's side of the family was of little importance. Daughters or wives did not inherit wealth. However, sons were obligated to take care of parents. Families were patrilocal, meaning a wife joined her husband's family and identified wholly on that side, often with minimal ties with the maternal family.

Confucius believed that with age comes wisdom, so he conferred upon elders a higher status and due respect. Children must honor and obey their parents, putting their parents' comfort, interest, and wishes above their own. This is the keystone to Confucian teachings regarding the family, and it is called filial piety. A man was judged by how filial he was to his parents; a woman to her parents-in-law.

Correct behavior entailed duty and obligation to the family. Always, this obligation took precedence over one's own interest. But family meant more than father, mother, and offspring. Vertically, the extended family could include three to four generations. Horizontally, it could include families of uncles on the father's side. Although this was the ideal, most families consisted of smaller units. Even when families did not "share the same rice pot," they were duty-bound to help one another. This help was given as a matter of course, because one was entitled to help in turn. The sense of family obligation was especially strong. It gave male immigrants the motivation to labor and toil to support relatives back in the home country. It also often produced the pool of resources that enabled the immigrant to go abroad in the first place.

♦ CHINA UNDER MAO

For centuries, Asian countries that followed Confucianism found security, stability, and nurturance in their families, but when China came under communist rule in 1949, Mao Zedong wanted to break the mold and recast Chinese society.

For one, he declared that "women hold up half the sky." Therefore, they should be equal to men. This was a radical break from the past. He promulgated a new marriage law that gave women the right to divorce and to inherit. Women were entitled to an education and brought into the work force outside of the home. Mao Zedong wanted to break the strong bonds of family loyalty and transfer that loyalty to the state. Property belonged to the state, so parental hold over inheritance to land and wealth was eliminated. Parental authority was undermined. Family size was controlled by the one-family-one-child decree. After Mao's death, the increasing movement of Chinese society from agrarian to industrialized reduced the extended family to a nuclear one. Families became more of a consuming unit than a productive unit, and family ties were loosened.

♦ JAPANESE AND KOREAN SOCIETIES

In Japan, the patriarchal mold of families was very similar to the Chinese system. In fact, it could be said the Japanese family was just as authoritarian and hierarchical, but female subordination was more acute. For example, in the Japanese language, separate forms of speech were assigned to women. At the end of World War II, the country lay in ruins, and under occupation, it quickly adopted a capitalist economic system. Within a short period of time, it vaulted to prominence as a highly industrialized country and a technological leader. But industrialization did not lead to much change within the family. The economy and the family were kept separate and apart. Women in the work force were kept in low-level jobs and encouraged to retain their traditional roles as wives and mothers. Japanese priority was on rearing and nurturing the younger generations.

Korean civilization closely followed the Chinese and Japanese models. For centuries, it was ruled first by China and then by Japan. It became independent after World War II, but shortly thereafter, split into North and South Korea; North Korea has a communist form of government. The Korean War, in which the United States fought with the South Koreans against North Korea, brought about drastic changes in Korean society.

◆ HINDU AND MUSLIM SOCIETIES

Female subordination was also a dominant feature of countries where many inhabitants have lived under Hinduism, such as India, as well as Muslim countries where many have lived according to the Koran, such as Pakistan. As set forth in the Hindi Laws of Manu:

> In childhood a female must be dependent on her father; in youth on her husband; her lord being dead, on her sons. A woman must never seek independence.

These words were exactly the same as those of Confucius. However, Manu went further: Hinduism viewed women as temptresses.

> It is the nature of women in this world to cause the seduction of men; for which reason the wise are never unguarded in the company of females.

Therefore women were kept apart from men. They lived in separate parts of the house and seldom left their dwellings.

In Muslim countries, women practiced "purdah." They never showed themselves to men other than their husbands. They were clothed head to foot in tent-like garments, and when they ventured outside of the home, they wore veils to cover their faces. Divorce was almost unheard of in Hindu families, but Muslim men could sever the marriage ties by saying, "I divorce thee" four times. Muslim men were entitled to have four wives.

◆ MALAYAN SOCIETY

Malayan culture is found in the countries of Indonesia, New Guinea, and the Philippines, to name a few. Here women were accorded higher status. Filipino society was not patrilineal, but bilateral. In other words, relatives on both the father's and the mother's side were considered family. Women were not put behind veils, cloaks, and doors. Women held the purse strings and often operated businesses. But Filipino culture was also greatly influenced by its 400 years of Spanish rule and half-century of U.S. rule. These brought Western and Catholic ideas of the family to the Philippine Islands.

In all Asian societies, polygamy, or having more than one wife at a time, was an accepted practice, and parents wielded almost absolute authority over their children. Large families were desired. Sons were preferred over daughters. Children were taught to emulate adults and assume family responsibility at an early age. Marriages were arranged by the parents, although nowadays, young people insist upon having some say in choosing their mates.

◆ SEPARATED FAMILIES

If it is assumed that a family consists of at least a husband and a wife, then for the earliest Asian group to come to the United States, the Chinese, family life was rare to the point of non-existence. The 1890 Census counted 27 Chinese males to every one Chinese female. Able-bodied males emigrated without women. Their initial intention was not to stay, and the journey was long and hazardous. Wives were left behind to care for the husband's parents, per Confucian teachings. Thus Chinese American communities were characterized as "bachelor societies," although most of the men were married with children. They had all the obligations of family men, but none of the comforts. They made occasional conjugal trips home, then returned to toil in the United States. Many children grew up hardly knowing their fathers. Wives saw their husbands only on those rare visits. These were families united by blood and bond, but physically separated. Social scientists have labeled such families "mutilated." A 19th-century southern Chinese folk song expresses the tremendous sadness and tragedy of these broken homes:

> Flowers shall be my headdress once again
> For my dear husband will soon return from a
> distant shore.
> Ten long years did I wait
> Trying hard to remember his face
> As I toiled at my spinning wheel each lonely night.

Another poem is still recited in the Guangdong countryside:

> If you have a daughter, don't marry her to a Gold
> Mountain guy.
> Out of ten years, he will not be in bed for one.
> The spider will spin webs on top of the bedposts,
> While dust fully covers one side of the bed
> (Tschen: 95).

If Chinese women did not immigrate to the United States earlier, they were unable to enter later. In 1882, Congress passed the Chinese Exclusion Act, which denied entry to all Chinese laborers. Wives of laborers were classified as laborers, although they would have been homemakers. Government officials, merchants, students, teachers, and tourists were exempt from the exclusion laws, but only merchants came in any number. They could bring their wives with them, so merchants' and their wives formed the majority of the few Chinese families on the American scene.

As women were absent, children and families were few. Intermarriage with local women was banned by miscegenation laws. Such unions were not recognized legally in most of the Western states, and the penalties for violation were severe: the marriages were null and void; the children were considered illegitimate; and some states levied a fine against the couple and the minister who performed the ceremony. In states such as Georgia, Mississippi, Missouri, and Virginia, a Chinese man could be jailed for marrying a white woman. The Cable Act of 1922 discouraged U.S. women from marrying Chinese men because marriage to an alien meant loss of their own citizenship. Chinese aliens were not allowed to apply for naturalization no matter how long they had lived here. Chinese exclusion was in force from 1882 until 1943. Even when the exclusionary laws were repealed, the laws only allowed 105 persons of Chinese ancestry to enter the United States per year. The Cable Act was repealed in 1931, but miscegenation laws were not declared unconstitutional until 1967.

Picture Brides

Exclusion limited the number of Chinese immigrants, but the ever-growing need for labor in the U.S. Western states plus a lack of legal barriers for non-Chinese Asians encouraged Japanese and Korean migration. Unlike the Chinese, both Japanese and Koreans were allowed to send for "picture brides" as soon as they managed to accumulate some savings. The men had to show they had at least $800. They chose a wife from photos sent by their families. This practice enabled Japanese and Korean men to form families in this country and to produce American-born children, laying the groundwork for successive generations of Japanese and Korean Americans. Anti-Asian feelings brought about a clamor for exclusion, but because the number of Koreans was small, the Gentlemen's Agreement of 1908 restricted only Japanese immigration. It was not until the 1924 Immigration Act that all Asians, except for Filipinos, were denied entry into the United States.

◆ FILIPINO IMMIGRATION

Filipino immigration boomed after the Japanese labor supply was cut off. The 1924 Immigration Act did not apply to them because the Philippine Islands was U.S. territory. But like the Chinese, most left their wives behind. As migratory farm laborers, Filipinos followed the crops. Employers preferred to hire able-bodied males without family encumbrance. In California, where large numbers settled, Filipinos had an affinity with Mexicans because of their common Hispanic heritage (The Philippines had a long history of Spanish rule). Many Filipinos took Mexican wives. Children of these unions were biracial, but most assumed a Hispanic identity. As with their Asian predecessors, Filipino immigration was cut off in 1935.

◆ JAPANESE IMMIGRATION

With more Asians barred from immigrating and a scarcity of Asian women already in the country, Asian American families in the first half of this century consisted of just a few American-born. These groups usually kept to their ethnic communities, and children were often sent back to the ancestral lands for upbringing and education. The Japanese were the only Asians with American-born children in any numbers. Generations were clearly delineated; first-generation Japanese were called *issei*, second-generation *nisei*, third-generation *sansei*, fourth-generation *yonsei*, and fifth-generation *gosei*.

With Japanese immigration cut off in 1924, no more issei came. Those who arrived earlier gave birth to the nisei generation, which by the 1940s outnumbered the issei two to one. This was about the same time as the Japanese attack on Pearl Harbor, when many nisei and their parents were put into internment camps as "enemy aliens."

Issei men who were suspected of loyalty to Japan were separated from their wives and children and sent to different camps. Authority and respect for elders was undermined by communal life in the internment camps. Nisei tried to disassociate themselves from Japan by becoming "super Americans." Instead of seeing themselves as victims, they wanted to hide the shame of being in camps and were even reluctant to tell their children, the sansei, about it. They were called the "silent generation." For many, camp incarceration lasted for three years, from 1942 to 1945. In 1990, the United States Congress acknowledged that the government had made a grievous mistake and made a formal apology to Japanese Americans. It also attempted to make some restitution in symbolic monetary compensation for the losses suffered by Japanese Americans during this period.

◆ WAR BRIDES

World War II was the catalyst for tremendous changes. China was allied with the United States, so Chinese exclusion from immigration was repealed. The War Brides Act of 1946 allowed men who had served in the armed forces to bring their wives and children to this country without adhering to the immigration quota of 105 Chinese persons a year. From 1948 to 1953, almost every Chinese immigrant who disembarked at an American port of entry was a young Chinese woman with or without young children in tow. For these six years, females averaged close to 90 percent of total Chinese migration. With these women came the makings of Chinese American families. Few Chinese women married non-Chinese military men.

For other Asians, the War Brides Act brought a different group of wives: Asian women married to U.S. servicemen. More than 2 million servicemen had been stationed in Japan as occupation troops from 1946 to 1952. An estimated 55,000 to 60,000 Japanese women married American soldiers. American troops fought in the Korean War (1950-1953) and were stationed in Korea until 1990. More than 40,000 GIs married Korean women and brought them to the United States. With a U.S. naval base in Manila, about the same number of Filipinas arrived as GI brides. After the Vietnam War, Vietnamese GI brides also arrived in the United States.

Once they entered the country, GI brides followed their husbands to their hometowns, and they are widely dispersed and little is known about them. They are hard to trace because these Asian women have taken their husbands' Anglicized names. These families are entirely different from any of those known before. Certainly they do not conform to the traditional Asian families, in which marriages were often arranged by the parents, and investigations were made of both the bride's and groom's families beforehand to match them up. Certainly, they were unlike most of the prevailing U.S. families because the circumstances under which they met and married were out of the ordinary. The Asian women had experienced war and upheaval in their homelands. Their own men had been drastically reduced in number by war casualties. The American soldiers, sailors, and marines—GIs as they were known—were fighting a war or stationed abroad under hostile conditions. They were lonely and far away from their loved ones at home. Local women filled the void for female companionship, even though these women came from totally different backgrounds and were of a different race. Many liaisons developed into marriage. When these GIs came home, they brought their Asian wives with them. Men who served in the European theaters of war underwent similar experiences, but their European brides were of the same racial and similar cultural background of the U.S. majority.

Japanese war brides started coming in the late 1940s and reached their peak in the 1950s and 1960s; Korean and Filipina war brides started coming in the 1950s. Some continue to arrive as U.S. Armed Forces installations are still in these countries. Vietnamese war brides began coming in the 1970s and continued into the 1980s.

Huge cultural differences may separate these couples. Many brides had already undergone tremendous conflict and psychological strain generated by their families and communities to the interracial marriages. One Japanese bride revealed: "I felt like a traitor. I knew my family was deeply hurt and ashamed that I was dating an American G.I." The grooms' families often were not accepting as well.

Many of these couples could communicate in only the simplest phrases in each other's language. Customs and traditions were different. Compelled to move to their husbands' hometowns, the brides often met with a hostile reception. Cut off from their family and ethnic communities, they often felt alienated and lonely. It is claimed that many Asian women who married black men experienced even greater problems of non-acceptance. Only a few studies have been done on the outcome of these GI marriages. Evelyn Nakano Glenn in her book, *Issei, Nisei, War Bride* (Glenn: 231) wrote:

> In contrast to the extreme durability of issei and nisei marriages, war-bride marriages were unstable and frequently disrupted by divorce. Among the twelve war brides in the interview group, only five were still married to and living with their first husbands. . . Even for those in long-term first or second marriages, marital conflicts and problems were much more conspicuous than among the issei and nisei.

Bok Lim Kim, who was among the first and the few to write about Asian war brides, supports the claim that these marriages undergo more stress. She wrote:

> . . . all of the studies indicate common areas of difficulties and stress which could contribute to marriage dissolution or family disorganization. In addition to strains on the marital relationship, Asian women undergo severe personal disorientation when adjustment cannot be facilitated (Kim, B.L.: 112).

The war-bride families were a discrete phenomenon, although their numbers were large in comparison to the few existing Asian American families. It was not until 1965, when changes in immigration laws were made that Asian American families appeared in any number. By 1990, the census counted one and a half million Asian American families.

♦ RECENT IMMIGRANT FAMILIES

The 1965 Immigration Act did away with national quotas and allowed any one country up to 20,000 admittees. Prior to passage of this act, China had a quota of 105; Japan had a quota of 185. All other Asian countries had the minimum quota of 100. The new law encouraged family reunification. Four of the six preferences, or classifications for immigration, or permanent residency were given to family members. Those who were citizens could send for immediate family members (spouses, minor children, and parents) outside the quotas. Unanticipated by lawmakers, Asian immigration shot up. Immigrants arrived not just from China, Japan, or Korea, but from all Asian countries and other continents as well.

Table 26.2
Immigration to the United States from Selected Asian Countries, by Five Year Periods, 1966 to 1990

Year	All Asia	China	Japan	Phil. Is.	Korea	India	Vietnam
1966-70	279,578	97,957	21,911	85,636	25,618	27,859	3,788
1971-75	534,401	108,119	25,989	153,254	112,493	72,912	15,250
1976-80	890,044	142,904	21,925	206,962	159,463	103,804	163,431
1981-85	1,212,724	206,395	20,020	221,166	166,021	119,701	234,875
1986-90	733,637	245,307	23,228	273,805	172,851	142,140	166,544

Note:
China includes Hong Kong and Taiwan.

Source: Barringer, et al. Asians and Pacific Islanders in the U.S., 25-26.

Individuals and families from all ages and different socioeconomic classes arrived. With political unrest in Asian countries, the American dream beckoned. Immigrant streams from Asian countries made up close to half of all those arriving to live in the United States during the 1980s. The following is a table showing the major Asian immigrant groups from 1970 to 1990.

Observe from Table 26.2 how rapidly Asian immigration increased. In every case, numbers exceeded the annual quotas, because once individuals became citizens, they could bring their immediate family members into the country without regard to the quotas. In addition, Taiwan and Hong Kong were granted separate quotas, 20,000 for Taiwan in 1980 and 10,000 for Hong Kong in 1990. Vietnamese and Southeast Asians entered under the Refugee Relief Act and immigration quotas.

♦ "RELAY IMMIGRATION"

Most Asian immigrants did not enter the United States as a family group. A distinctive feature was "relay immigration," one member of a family will arrive first, find employment and housing, and then send for other members. It used to be that the men came first, but often women are now preceding men from several places, such as the Philippines, Hong Kong, and Taiwan. A fairly common practice is to send the wife abroad with the children, while the husband stays in his position or with his business back home, and he comes to the United States for an occasional visit. Another practice is to send the children for schooling in the United States, while the parents remain in the home country until a child secures employment or by another means acquires permanent residency status and can apply for the parents to join him or her. For many other families, the pattern of separation permanently persists.

When the husband and wife are established in the United States, they may send for the parents, generally on the husband's side. Since spouses, minor children, and parents are not figured in the quota, there may not be a long wait for an entry visa to the United States. Many Asian countries require exit visas, but it is commonly easy to get the permission for the older nationals to emigrate. Parents are sent so that sons can fulfill their filial obligation of taking care of their parents. The mother-in-law may also be needed to care for the children, when both husband and wife find work.

About five years after individuals arrive as permanent residents, they can apply for U.S. citizenship. As permanent residents, or resident aliens, they may send for immediate family members by filing applications for them with the U.S. Immigration and Naturalization Service (INS). INS gives priority to parents sending for children or vice versa over brothers and sisters sending for siblings, which must wait for quota slots. Thus begins the lateral reunification of the family in this country. Of course, the process is long and drawn out, and years may pass before the extended family is finally resettled in the United States.

Because of the recency of immigration laws permitting Asians to enter, the Asian American population remains predominantly foreign-born. Table 26.3 shows the percentage of foreign-born of selected Asian groups in the United States. Close to 80 percent of the Vietnamese are foreign-born, as well as close to 70 percent of the Chinese and 75 percent of Indians. Only the Japanese show a preponderance of American-born. The numerical dominance of foreign-born may indicate that most Asian American families are recent immigrants and will cling more to their native culture.

♦ AMERICAN-BORN FAMILIES

The structure, lifestyle, and behavior patterns of this type of family depends upon several factors, the first among them being generation. The further removed from the immigrant generation, the more acculturated a person is to U.S. norms. Often by the third generation, U.S. customs prevail in issues of dating, choosing a mate, following wedding customs, role expectations, child rearing, and care of the elderly.

Another factor is place of residence. If the family resides in an ethnic community, the traditional customs of the homeland will have a heavy influence. If a family is isolated from members of its ethnic group, it is likely that it will follow U.S. practices more closely.

Social class is a third factor. The upper middle class may have the time and money to devote to a stable, close-knit unit adhering more to its cultural heritage. The poorer classes may be preoccupied with economic survival, in which the parents work long hard hours and the children have to assume more adult responsibilities. However, cultural roots tend to run deep and even American-born Asian American families retain a deep sense of family responsibility.

♦ MARRIAGE

In Asian countries, marriage is very important. It is the obligation of parents to find a mate for their sons and daughters. If the son is poor, he will get a less desirable wife. The same goes for a daughter. However, if she is pretty though poor, she may marry into a wealthy home as the concubine or second wife. Though currently outlawed in many Asian countries, polygamy was accepted in many of these countries for centuries.

Marriages are still arranged in many countries. Prime Minister of Pakistan Benazir Bhutto herself, a Harvard and Oxford graduate, accepted the man her family chose for her in marriage. Many young people are rejecting this practice, but there is no body of tradition of dating and courtship to help them find mates.

Table 26.3
Native-and Foreign-Born Asian Americans in the U.S. by Percent, 1990

	Native-born	Foreign-born
Asian	34.4	65.6
Chinese	30.7	69.3
Filipino	34.2	61.8
Indian	24.6	75.4
Japanese	67.6	32.4
Korean	27.3	72.7
Vietnamese	20.1	79.9

Source: U.S. Census Current Population Studies, 3-5, Table 1.

Their parents can offer little assistance because many never went through the courtship process themselves. This is a difficult period of transition, and new customs must be forged. Many Asians are still uncomfortable with the sexual mores of the West.

Marital Status

Table 26.4 shows marital status of Asian Americans in the United States, age 15 years and over. The first column is that of non-Asians shown for comparison. About a third of all Asians are single or have never been married, except for the Vietnamese. The reason for the large number of single Vietnamese is their refugee status. These figures are higher for Asians than for non-Asians. The answer may lie in the fact that Asian Americans between the ages of 15 to 22 may still be enrolled in school and postpone marriage until graduation. Another reason may be that they may

Table 26.4
Marital Status of Asians and Non-Asians in the U.S. by Percent, 1990

Marital Status	Non-Asian	Asian	Chinese	Filipino	Indian	Japanese	Korean	Vietnamese
Males 15+								
Never married	29.9	37.1	35.7	34.9	31.4	36.8	35.2	51.0
Married not sep	58.3	57.6	59.8	58.3	64.9	56.2	60.6	43.8
Separated	2.0	1.3	0.9	1.5	1.0	1.0	1.2	2.3
Widowed	2.5	1.2	1.4	1.6	0.8	1.7	0.7	0.9
Divorced	7.3	2.8	2.3	3.7	2.0	4.2	5.5	2.0
Females 15+								
Never married	23.0	26.6	28.0	26.9	21.9	23.6	23.8	35.0
Married not sep	52.8	60.1	59.9	58.8	70.0	59.9	62.1	52.6
Separated	2.6	1.7	1.2	2.1	1.0	1.2	1.6	2.8
Widowed	12.1	7.1	7.5	7.1	4.9	8.8	7.1	5.9
Divorced	9.5	2.6	3.3	5.1	2.1	6.5	5.4	3.8

Source: U.S. Census Current Population Studies, 3-5, Table 1.

Table 26.5
Family Characteristics of Asian American
Families in the U.S. 1990

	Female Head of Household No Husband Present	Unmarried Partner Households	Children Under 18 Living with Two Parents
Non Asian	16.1	4.9	72.7
Asian	11.5	2.9	84.6
Chinese	9.4	2.1	87.6
Filipino	15.1	3.9	80.9
Indian	4.5	1.3	91.8
Japanese	11.9	4.4	86.1
Korean	11.3	2.1	89.0
Vietnamese	15.9	3.0	76.6

Source: U.S. Census Current Population Studies, 3-5, Table 2.

have difficulty finding mates because of the sex ratio differential or lack of courtship experience.

The high value that Asians place upon family is reflected in the lower rates of separation and divorce and the higher number of children under 18 living with both parents. (See Table 26.5). The divorce rates are 2.8 for Asian males and 7.3 for non-Asian males. For Asian females, it is 2.6 and for non-Asian females, it is 9.5. Asian families appear to generally be more stable. Among Asians, the Japanese and Korean American families have higher rates of divorce. The reason may be due to the large number of war-bride families or the more acculturated sansei or yonsei Japanese American families. A large proportion of elderly females are widowed in all groups. Table 26.5 shows that the percentage of female-headed households among Asian American families fluctuates widely according to ethnicity and family type.

Working Wives

Transplanted from Asian to U.S. soil, Asians bring with them many of their practices, customs, and beliefs. However, with acculturation, they must adapt to doing many tasks differently, and conditions force them to live differently. The most important change is that the wife may need to seek a job outside of the home. The labor force participation rate of Asian women is generally slightly higher than that of non-Asian women.

Among non-Asian women, 56.7 percent work outside the home, versus 60 percent of Asian women. The rate for Asian women may actually be higher than 60 percent, because many Asians operate small family businesses such as restaurants, greengroceries, and

dry-cleaning establishments. Because this is unpaid labor, it is not counted as employment. The paying jobs open to them are often garment factory work, hotel cleaning, restaurant work, household jobs, or work that does not require high English proficiency. The jobs often pay little, have bad working conditions, and involve long hours. Still, newly in the United States, the women have little choice but to accept jobs which may be generally thought to be undesirable.

Because Filipina and Indian women speak English, they have an advantage in securing more desirable employment. The Philippines and India have histories of colonial rule, the Philippines as a United States territory and India as a British colony. English was a medium used in education and government. Filipinas migrate to the United States as nurses, many with job offers already secured. The sex ratio of Filipinos is so heavily weighted toward females that many Filipinas have to earn their own livelihood. Recent female Indian immigrants are usually highly educated. With their academic and professional skill and knowledge of English, they can often easily acquire clerical or professional positions.

Japanese wives of businessmen generally do not work. Their job is to make a home for their husbands and take care of the children.

Working wives contribute earnings to the family income. This means a substantial portion of it, since Asian women seem to get jobs quicker than Asian men. Oftentimes, the men are often unwilling at first to accept menial and lower-status jobs than those they had back home. Working outside the home leads to some measure of independence for the women, but it also reduces the time they have for domestic chores and time to look after the children. The quality of home life may therefore suffer.

In New York's Chinatown, where Chinese women work primarily as seamstresses in garment factories, one can see children sitting at their mothers' feet. Usually, however, the children go to daycare or after-school

Table 26.6
Labor Force Participation Rate of Females 16+
in the U.S. by Percent, 1990

Non-Asians	56.7%
Asians	60.0
Chinese	59.2
Filipino	72.3
Indian	58.6
Japanese	55.5
Korean	55.5
Vietnamese	55.8

Source: U.S. Census Current Population Studies, 3-5, Table 4.

Jayram Patel and his wife Nila and daughter Krupa greet a traveler at their motel along I-75 near Sparks, Georgia. The Patels are among a large number of Asian Indians who have bought motels since immigrating to the United States. (AP/Wide World.)

centers. At dinner time, if a rush job is to be completed, the mother cannot go home to cook the family meal. Instead, she hands the children a few dollars for dinner.

Working wives in Asian families may lead to a reversal of roles between husbands and wives or a modification of female subordination to more egalitarian relationships among husbands and wives. This may be difficult for Asian families to adapt to, which may lead to marital stress. Although they put in long hours working outside of the home, Asian women may find all their domestic chores waiting for them at home. Asian men and women find that they must make major adjustments to survive the new lifestyle.

Fertility

The birth rate drops when women work outside the home. The cost of bringing up children in the United States and the lack of relatives nearby to help in child rearing also deter couples from having large families. In most Asian countries, having large families was a blessing; in the United States, it is often viewed as a financial burden.

Table 26.7 shows the number of children born to women in the childbearing ages of 15-44 per 1,000 women. With the exception of Vietnamese, the fertility rate of non-Asian women is higher than that of Asian women. In fact, the Japanese and Chinese rates are extremely low, 822 and 875, respectively, or less than one child per woman. To maintain the population

Table 26.7
Children Born to Women Age 15-44, 1990

Children Born	
Women 15-44	**Per 1000 Women**
Non-Asian	1,228
Asian	1,080
Chinese	875
Filipino	1,079
Indian	1,163
Japanese	822
Korean	1,007
Vietnamese	1,304

Source: U.S. Census Current Population Studies, 3-5 Table 1.

Wives of Japanese businessmen take a painting course at the Honda of America Center in Dublin, Ohio. (AP/Wide World.)

without growth, women must give birth to 2.1 children. Below this number, the population will decline.

◆ GENERATION GAP

Immigrants who arrive as children will more quickly absorb U.S. ways of thought and behavior. They will also more easily acquire English at school and play. They observe the different customs and patterns that are not the same as those taught or modeled by their parents at home. Asian children begin to question their parents' ways.

Also, when the parents arrive in the United States, work schedules limit their time for English classes. When their English proficiency is low or lacking, they must rely upon their children to be intermediaries in their contact with the outside world. With the children leading and the parents following, a reversal of parent-child role ensues, and respect for the parents may decrease. Bicultural conflicts can create a wide gap between immigrant generation parents and their children. Whereas parents once commanded respect and obedience, they now experience dependence upon their children.

◆ THE ELDERLY

When there were few Asian American families in the United States, the elderly tended to go back to their native country. Today, the migration stream is reversed. Older Asians continue to arrive, even into their 60s and 70s. The first column in Table 26.8 shows the percentage of Asians 65 years old and over. The second and third columns give the gender breakdown of the elderly by percentage. More women survive into old age than men. For example 60.6 percent of non-Asians over 65 are female. Korean women make up 64.3 percent of Koreans over 65.

Unfortunately, it is more difficult for older people to adapt to new ways and to acquire a new language. If they live with their adult children, they are somewhat protected, but there are problems. One is the even wider gap between them and their grandchildren. Asian children growing up in the United States usually lose or never acquire fluency in their ethnic tongue, and often the grandparents cannot speak English, resulting in little communication between them. Asian American children may not have learned to respect the elderly as is practiced in Asian countries.

Chinese American Carol Hall and her daughter, Lanette, Locke, California. (AP/Wide World.)

If the family lives far away from an ethnic community, the elderly suffer loneliness. Even if living with their children, the elderly are often left home during the day as the family goes off to work or school. They cannot talk to the neighbors and are afraid to venture out, and they are isolated. Coming from Asian countries where people live closely packed together, this can be strange and alienating.

♦ INTERMARRIED FAMILIES

Families in which one spouse is Asian and the other non-Asian are increasing in number. Although marriage between Asians and whites was forbidden by law in many western and southern states until 1967, it did take place elsewhere, although it was not commonplace, since societal disapproval and sanctions deterred such unions.

Contemporary intermarried couples are somewhat different from the intermarried "war brides" arrangements of the past. According to Bok Lim Kim's study, "war bride" marriages have been more vulnerable to collapse. Intermarriages taking place in the United States are not the same. In today's more open and tolerant society, young persons of all races and ethnic groups often go to school, work, and socialize together, and may fall in love. Intermarried couples today are generally better educated, have better jobs, and higher incomes than in-married couples.

Nevertheless, unlike endogamous marriages where both spouses are of the same ethnic group, an

Table 26.8
Elderly Persons 65 Years and Over
by Sex and Percent, 1990

Persons 65+	Pct Total Population	Male	Female
Non-Asian	12.7	39.4	60.6
Asian	6.2	44.7	46.4
Chinese	8.0	46.4	53.6
Filipino	7.1	47.4	52.6
Indian	3.5	46.6	53.4
Japanese	12.3	43.5	56.5
Korean	4.3	35.7	64.3
Vietnamese	2.8	42.5	57.5

Source: U.S. Census Current Population Studies, 3-5 Table 1.

Helen and Yee Wan Lee, Chinese American children, New York. (AP/Wide World.)

intermarriage may face opposition from both families and society. Because the two come from different backgrounds, questions raised include: Will they be able to get along? Whose customs will they adopt? Whose religion will they practice? How will they bring up their children?

Considering the extra obstacles in an intermarriage, breakups are expected to occur at a higher rate. Most studies confirm an historically higher divorce rate. However, Betty Lee Sung, in her study of Chinese American intermarriage in New York City, found that the divorce rates for in-married and out-married Chinese were about the same during the 1980s. In her

book, she found that family disapproval was the major roadblock to intermarriage. However, attitudes are changing rapidly, and with increased acceptance, family pressures may lessen and make intermarried life easier.

Children of intermarried couples may have physical features completely different from their parents; since they are an amalgam of both. In the past, such children were derided as half-breeds belonging to neither group. This may be why intermarried couples have fewer children. Table 26.9 shows the number of children born to intermarried Chinese women. In families where both husband and wife are Chinese, 15 percent

Table 26.9
Fertility of Married Women Involving Chinese Spouse In and Outmarriage, by Percent, 1980

	Children Ever Born						
	0	1	2	3	4	4	6+
In-marriage	15%	16%	28%	19%	19%	5%	6%
Out-marriage:							
Non-Chinese Wife	49%	21%	16%	11%	3%	0%	0%
Chinese Wife	30%	26%	20%	11%	9%	3%	1%

Source: Betty Lee Sung, Chinese American Intermarriage, p. 101.

The Nguyen family in their coffee shop in Pittsburgh, still hipe to be reunited with the two daughters they left behind in Vietnam in 1975. (AP/Wide World.)

have no children. In families where the wife is Chinese, 30 percent have no children. Where the wife is non-Chinese, 49 percent have no children. In every instance, intermarried families have fewer children.

Problems faced by biracial children are often related to physical appearance, ethnic identity, cultural conflicts, and alienation. Children may not feel that they belong to any group. They may be caught in the crossfire of cultures, unless their parents are well assimilated. They may feel cut off and isolated in society and even among relatives. However, as the rate of intermarriage increases, these problems may decrease.

Some children of biracial unions have written about their experiences. George Kich, in his dissertation, "Eurasians: Ethnic/Racial Identity Development of Biracial Japanese/White Adults" (1982:118), wrote about a common feeling:

> Some people of mixed heritage background are trying to make a choice, rather than accept what they are. They're trying to make a choice and gain acceptance from that choice. But, you've got to be what you are regardless. . . . if you're half anything. You've got to decide that you are what you are and be comfortable

with it. The problem with most mixed bloods is they're not comfortable with what they are. . . When you try to be something else, people don't always let you be that.

Because many Asian Americans have recently immigrated, they hold a strong ethnic identity about them. Intermarriage rates among Asians are likely to remain low for sometime yet. However, patterns among other groups indicate that with subsequent generations, intermarriage will increase. Family structure, lifestyle, and customs will reflect the variety of admixture among couples.

◆ CHILD-REARING PRACTICES

The Asian American family is strict in child-rearing, demanding respect and obedience and practicing corporal punishment when it determines necessary. Parents try to pass on Asian values to their children, which are sometimes resisted. They often encourage dependency upon the family instead of independence, and sense of right and wrong is constantly stressed. Children are prodded to act responsibly early on.

Table 26.10
Family Income and Families Living Below Poverty Level in 1989

	Non-Asians and Asian Americans		
	Median Family Income	Mean Family Income	Pct Below Poverty Level
Non-Asians	$35,108	$43,622	9.9%
Asians	41,583	51,632	11.4
Chinese	41,316	51,931	11.1
Filipino	46,698	53,474	5.2
Indian	49,309	65,381	7.2
Japanese	51,550	60,305	3.4
Korean	33,909	45,760	14.7
Vietnamese	30,550	36,783	23.8

Source: U.S. Census Current Population Studies,3-5 Table 5.

Teachers, the media, and authorities are constantly praising Asian children for being well behaved, studious, and quiet: however, Asian American children may feel pulled in two directions if they observe their schoolmates and playmates living by different standards. Envying the freedom that some of their peers enjoy, they may become embittered, leading to a serious generation gap between them and their parents and grandparents.

◆ FAMILY INCOME

Considering that two-thirds of Asian Americans are foreign-born, the families do rather well financially. Their incomes are above the U.S. median and mean. Table 26.10 gives the median and mean family income as well as the percentage of families below poverty level.

◆ REFUGEE FAMILIES

Another type of Asian American family is the refugee family. Only Vietnamese families have been shown in the tables, but there are also Cambodian, Lao, Hmong, Thai, and some Chinese refugees resulting from the political turmoil surrounding the Vietnam War. These Southeast Asians came after 1975 when the United States pulled out of Vietnam in a hasty evacuation with little time to gather family members and belongings. Afterwards, a massive refugee resettlement program placed many refugees in the United States.

Under communist rule in Asian countries, refugees continued to flee from their countries. Most frequently, they ventured to sea in flimsy boats hoping to reach friendly shores. However, many were placed in impoverished refugee camps until countries agreed to accept them. A tide of these "boat people" reached Malaysia, Thailand, Hong Kong, and the Philippines in 1979. Many others drowned or were preyed upon by pirates. If they reached a refugee camp, they usually spent years there before being processed for migration to an accepting country. Family members were separated or perished in the ordeal. It is estimated that only four out of ten "boat people" survived. When refugees were accepted for resettlement, they were provided with transportation, clothing, and pocket money upon being sent to a destination. Literally, they had nothing but the shirts on their backs when arriving in the United States.

These people had known nothing but conflict and strife. Mostly men survived the ordeals. Therefore, the gender ratio for Vietnamese is 110.8. Fifty-one percent of Vietnamese men have never been married. Their family income is the lowest of all Asian American groups with 23.8 percent living below the poverty level. President Bill Clinton lifted sanctions against Vietnam in February 1994. It is hoped that the reestablishment of relations between the two countries will enable more women to emigrate abroad or refugees to return to their families in Southeast Asia.

◆ CONCLUSION

We end as we began, saying there is no umbrella that will cover Asian American families per se. In fact, we have seen aberrations from the norm in the separated, war-bride, interned, and refugee families. Asian American families have been buffeted on all sides by discriminatory laws, wars, social and economic changes, and uprooting. The biggest challenge may be how families can adapt and integrate their ethnic values with U.S. values.

References

Barringer, Herbert, Robert Gardner and Michael Levin. *Asians and Pacific Islanders in the United States*. New York: Russell Sage Foundation, 1993.

Chan, Sucheng. *Asian Americans: An Interpretive History*. Boston: Twayne Publishers, 1991.

Cheung, M. "Elderly Chinese Living in the U.S.: Assimilation or Adjustment." *Social Work* 34 (Sept. 1989) 457-461.

Chia, Rosina C. "Family Values of American versus Chinese American Parents." *Journal of Asian American Psychological Association 1*, 13:1 (1989) 8-11.

Chipp, Sylvia and Justin Green, eds. *Asian Women in Transition*. University Park, PA: Pennsylvania State U. Press, 1980.

Glenn, Evelyn Nakano. *Issei, Nisei, War Bride*. Philadelphia: Pennsylvania University Press, 1986.

JWK International Corp. "Conference on Pacific and Asian American Families and Health, Education,Welfare and Related Issues". National Institutes of Education, Dept. of HEW, March 9-12, 1978.

Kich, George Kitahara. "Eurasians: Ethnic/Racial Identity Development of Biracial Japanese/White Adults." Ph.D. dissertation. Berkeley: Wright Institute, 1982.

Kim, Bok Lim. "Asian Wives of U.S. Servicemen." *Amerasia Journal* 4:1 (1977:) 91-113.

Kim, Haeyun Juliana. "Voices from the Shadow: Lives of Korean War Brides." *Amerasia Journal* 17:1 (1991) 15-30.

Lin, Chin-Yau C. "A Comparison of Child Rearing Practices among Chinese, Chinese American and Non-Asian American Parents." Ph.D. Dissertation. Virginia Polytechnic Institute, 1988.

Mace, David and Vera. *Marriage East and West*. New York: Doubleday Dolphin Books, 1959.

Spickard, Paul R. *Mixed Blood: Intermarriage and Ethnic Identity in Twentieth Century America*. Madison: University of Wisconsin Press, 1989.

Sung, Betty Lee. *Adjustment Experience of Chinese Immigrant Children in New York*. Staten Island, New York: Center for Migration Studies, 1987.

———. *Chinese American Intermarriage*. Staten Island, New York: Center for Migration Studies, 1990.

———. *Mountain of Gold*. New York: Macmillan, 1967.

———. A Survey of Chinese American Manpower and Employment. New York: Praeger, 1976.

Tschen, John, ed. Genthe's Photographs of San Francisco's Chinatown, 1895-1906. New York: Dover Publications, 1984.

Williams, Teresa K. "Marriage Between Japanese Women and U.S. Servicemen since World War II." *Amerasia Journal* 17:1 (Spring 1991) 135-54.

—Betty Lee Sung
Professor Emerita and Former Chair
Department of Asian Studies
City College of New York

Women

♦ Early History ♦ Education and Work ♦ Marriage and the Family ♦ Leadership

Like the larger Asian-American population, Asian-American women reflect a variety of national origins and cultural backgrounds. Whatever their heritage, however, they share a common experience. They were frequently called upon to augment their family income by working, even after their children were born. This was difficult, because they lacked the extended family of the old country that provided both child care and home management support. Asian women were farmers, cooks, seamstresses, laundresses, and frequently, unpaid help in family businesses. The work perhaps the most physically demanding was that on the Hawaiian sugar plantations, where Asian wives and mothers toiled unceasingly both in the fields and at home.

The history of Asian-American women, beginning in the 19th century, differs from that of European women. During early Asian emigration to the United States, unlike European women, many Asian women were barred from travel by social or moral custom, leaving them behind to care for parents and children. U.S. immigration policy further limited their travel classifying them as aliens ineligible for admission. (All Asians were denied U.S. naturalization until the mid-1900s.)

The first approved legislation aimed at stalling Asian immigration was the Chinese Exclusion Act of 1882. Originally intended to last ten years, it was later extended indefinitely to exclude Chinese nationals from entering the United States. The National Origins Act of 1924 ceased Japanese, Korean, and Asian Indian immigration. The Tydings-McDuffie Act of 1934 restricted the entry of Filipinos to 50 persons a year.

These exclusionary laws had profound effects on the development of families in Asian-American communities. Not until 1965 were the Asian immigration quotas finally increased to encourage the reunification of families.

In a reversal of early immigration trends, recent patterns show more Asian women immigrating to the United States than Asian men. This trend is likely to continue as young, professional Asian women seek the educational and career opportunities that the United States offers.

♦ EARLY HISTORY

Among the five major Asian immigrant groups (Chinese, Japanese, Korean, Filipino, and Asian Indian), there have existed different patterns and attitudes toward the migration of women.

Chinese

Almost all of the early Chinese immigrants were men. Wives were expected to remain at home and attend to their families, including the husbands' aging parents; single women did not travel alone to distant places. By this arrangement, Chinese parents hoped to secure their sons' filial obligations (sending money home), insuring their eventual return, a motive known as the "hostage theory." "The mother wanted her son to come back," said one Chinese woman. "If wife go to America, then son no go back home and no send money."

In the United States, Chinese men were recruited to work in lumber mills, railroads, mines, and farms on the mainland. Employers wanted workers who were not encumbered by families so that they could be moved easily from one job to the next. This created an almost exclusively male immigrant society that by 1852 numbered nearly 12,000, only seven of whom were women. By 1870, the ratio had improved somewhat—at 14 to 1. In 1900, only 5 percent of the 89,863 Chinese in the United States were female. Of the small numbers of Chinese women in California, most were prostitutes who had been tricked into the profession or kidnapped and sold to brothel owners. The 1870 Census recorded over 2,100 Chinese prostitutes in California. Because so many Chinese women were forced to earn their living in this way, California enacted the Page Law in 1875, which barred most Chinese women from entering the United States, under the assumption that they were all prostitutes. This, unfortunately, also dashed the hopes of any Chinese wives who wished to immigrate.

Even very young Chinese girls were traded for money. Historian Ronald Takaki records the memories of Lilac Chen, who was sold into prostitution by her father when she was six: "And that worthless father, my own father, imagine . . . sold me on the ferry boat. Locked me in the cabin while he was negotiating my sale." Another young woman, Wong Ah So, was falsely promised marriage, only to find herself an enslaved prostitute: "I was nineteen when this man came to my mother and said that in America there was a great deal of gold . . . He was a laundryman, but said he earned plenty of money. He was very nice to me, and my mother liked him, so my mother was glad to have me go with him as his wife. I thought that I was his wife, and was very grateful that he was taking me to such a grand, free country, where everyone was rich and happy."

A woman's purchase price was just over $500. To reap the maximum profit from each prostitute, brothel owners fed them little, and worked them in tiny "cribs" that measured only 4 by 6 feet. Others were luckier, and found themselves in high-class bordellos. Most, however, were shipped out to mining and railroad camps, where they proved a good investment for their owners.

Getting out of prostitution meant working off a contract held by one's owner, but this often proved extremely difficult, if not impossible. Women, especially those who tried to escape, were frequently beaten and whipped, sometimes to death. Opium addiction was a tragic side effect, and suicide was common.

After enforcement of the Page Law in 1875, the number of Chinese prostitutes dwindled, and by 1880, an estimated 761 could be found in California. Some had managed to buy their freedom, and others had escaped to the Presbyterian Mission in San Francisco, a haven run by white women. Many of the women married Chinese laborers and worked in family businesses or in canneries and the garment industry. Before legal restrictions were passed, however, some Chinese men did manage to bring their wives with them, even if they had to arrange a marriage in absentia or go back to China to marry them first. One story reported in 1869 told of a wife who defied social custom, her parents, family, and even her husband to cross the ocean alone and come to the United States. Asserting that she was entitled to live with her husband, she came to California, where she found work as a seamstress.

Such success stories were the exception, however. Far more typical, especially after the exclusion laws were passed, were similar to the case of a man named Lee Chew, who moaned, "In all New York there are less than forty Chinese women, . . . and it is impossible to get a Chinese woman out here unless one goes to China and marries her there, and then he must collect affidavits to prove that she is really his wife. That is in the case of a merchant. A laundryman can't bring his wife here under any circumstances."

Japanese

Unlike the Chinese patrilineal system where all adult sons shared equally in the family property and in the care of their parents, the Japanese had an inheritance system where only one son, usually the eldest, inherited the property and kept the family line intact. With no prospects of earning a living at home, many Japanese migrants left to seek their fortunes in the new world.

The Japanese government regulated emigration tightly, allowing only the healthy and educated to leave. Although conscious of the need to alleviate population problems in their tiny, crowded country, the Japanese strived to maintain their national honor overseas as well. Because the government wanted to prevent the problems common in an all-male colony, such as drinking and prostitution, female emigration was also encouraged.

Given these circumstances, Japanese women came in far greater numbers than their Chinese counterparts. Between 1911 and 1920, 39 percent of Japanese immigrants were women. While Chinese women of the 1800s led a severely circumscribed existence in the United States, their Japanese contemporaries were working in shops and in the textile industry. They were less fearful of traveling great distances and, having been educated (as required by the Emperor), were more prone to venture to new places.

Many of these women came as "picture brides," a form of arranged marriage used by Japanese men in the United States. Using a go-between, potential mates exchanged photographs, and matches were made. This customary practice fostered the migration of women to the United States and worked to maintain the tradition of strong Japanese families.

In addition, the Japanese government was able to negotiate the 1908 Gentlemen's Agreement with the United States, an important political development that further influenced the number of Japanese women in the United States. Unlike the 1882 Chinese Exclusion Act, which prohibited the entry of laborers and their families, this contract allowed Japanese women to enter the United States as family members of Japanese men in the United States.

Female immigration was also determined by destination. During the latter years of the 19th century, Hawaiian planters required almost half of their immigrant laborers to be women. From 1894 to 1908 (that is, before the Gentlemen's Agreement), thousands of Japanese women came to Hawaii as contract workers, almost three-quarters as field laborers. Planters also promoted family emigration because it gave them better workers who were unlikely to return to their homeland.

Other Japanese women went to the mainland, where they worked with their husbands, usually without pay. Wives were a particular asset for farmers, whose jobs required almost continuous toil.

Korean

When Hawaiian planters attempted to balance the ethnic composition of their workforce (hoping to prevent laborers from organizing unions), they turned to Korean workers, many of whom were Christian and wanted to settle with their families in the United States for religious reasons. Others left with their wives and children because of the fear they would not be able to return to Korea, which had fallen under Japanese domination. Some women were picture brides—over 1,000 came by 1924.

In all, about 20 percent of Korean immigrants to Hawaii were women and children, with the group about equally split between the two. The proportion of Korean men to women in Hawaii at the beginning of the 20th century was 10 to 1; in 20 years it had declined to 3 to 1.

The Japanese government eventually curbed Korean immigration to Hawaii to prevent competition with Japanese laborers and to pacify the Korean-independence movement that had taken hold in the United States.

Filipino

When the Philippines became a territory of the United States in 1898, thousands of Filipinos, mostly single young men, began to migrate to Hawaii and the U.S. mainland. California alone recorded over 31,000 Filipino immigrants between 1920 and 1929; 84 percent were younger than 30. Like the other Asian immigrant groups in the United States, the gender ratio among Filipinos was severely skewed: 4 to 1 in Hawaii and 19 to 1 on the West Coast.

As with the Chinese, culture was an important factor in the migration of Filipino women—moral tradition restricted them from traveling without fathers or husbands. Even so, about 4,000 Filipino women had reached Hawaii by 1920. In ten years they numbered 10,000, 42 percent of them married.

Like the Japanese who preceded them, Filipino men were more likely to take their wives and families to Hawaii, where they could earn a steady living, than to the mainland, where they would be subject to transient agricultural work. In addition, realizing that family men made more reliable workers, plantation owners encouraged the immigration of Filipino women. In some cases, men sent for their wives after discovering they could not earn enough to return home as wealthy men.

Asian Indian

Between 1899 and 1920, 7,300 Asian Indian immigrants came to the West Coast of the United States, most of them male farm laborers who settled in California. Unfortunately, strong anti-Asian sentiment turned public opinion against the men, who were called "Hindus" regardless of their religious affiliation. As most of them were Sikhs, they were also given the derogatory label of "turban heads" or "rag heads." Churches took an active stand against their immigration, calling the newcomers "barbaric and superstitious." Indians were considered impossible to assimilate into U.S. society.

Asian Indian men often did not want to bring their wives to the United States where Western norms and values dominated. However, the men's preference for their own countrywomen further limited the establishment of new families in the United States, as did anti-miscegenation laws that forbade the marriage of Asians and whites. Eventually, many early Asian Indian-immigrants married into Mexican families and assimilated into that community. With the 1924 National Origins Act prohibition of nearly all Asian entrants, by 1940, 66 percent of Asian Indians in the United States were over 40, and 85 percent of them were blue-collar workers with little education. The population declined further through the 1950s, increasing significantly only after the Immigration and Naturalization Act of 1965.

The history of Asian Indian women in the United States before 1965 is short. Nearly 72 percent of those currently in the United States, therefore entered the country after 1970, usually as a sponsored spouse or relative of a U.S. permanent resident. Even during this short time Asian Indian women have proven largely to be high achievers. In 1990, half the women over 25 had earned a bachelor's degree or higher, while 55.2 percent of those aged 25 to 34 had achieved the same. Of 59 percent of working women over 16, 35 percent were managers or professionals; 42 percent held administrative support jobs. The median annual income of Asian Indian women in 1989 was $11,746.

Asian Indian society is organized hierarchically by age, sex, class, and caste. This means the eldest male in a family is given the most respect and highest status, while the youngest female is given the lowest. Interestingly, the culture abounds in contradictory images of women. On the one hand, they are considered

Korean American women in a neighborhood grocery store. (Jamie Lew.)

secondary and subservient to men. On the other, they are often regarded as powerful and the ultimate source of dynamism in the universe. Thus, it is not uncommon to find Asian Indian women who are assertive and autonomous or passive and dependent.

◆ EDUCATION AND WORK

Asians have always revered education as the path to success. However, Asian women were expected to fulfill traditional roles as wives and mothers, and often were not rendered opportunity to achieve higher education. If a family's income was limited, provisions were made for sons to go to college, a situation Jade Snow Wong described in her book *Fifth Chinese Daughter*. Young women of today must still juggle familial expectations with their own goals for a career.

It is argued that the advancement of Asian-American women at the workplace has been hampered by stereotypical attitudes regarding them as meek and unamibitious. Shirley Hune, associate dean of graduate programs at UCLA, once remarked, "[The] glass ceiling for Asian-American males is a cement floor for Asian-American women."

The 1990 Census reported that Asians and Pacific Islanders who arrived between 1980 and 1990 have a poverty rate three times that of those who entered before 1980. Women in this group are particularly handicapped, especially by their low proficiency in English. According to researcher Elaine Kim, without programs to promote language facility ". . . we can expect that Asian immigrant women will be forced to continue battling against low wages, poor benefits and working conditions, and [that they will] lack affordable health care, child care, and housing . . . The tradition of family-owned business remains attractive to many recent Asian immigrants, who view long hours and unpaid or low-paid family labor in independent enterprises as preferable to entrapment in dead-end low-wage menial labor working for someone else."

◆ MARRIAGE AND THE FAMILY

A characteristic among all Asian groups is the importance placed on the family. Parents expect daughters to marry, raise a family, and supervise their children's education. Acculturation to life in the United States has challenged this, and Asian-American women living with parents who are steeped in ethnic tradition are especially conflicted. Although unwilling to submit to tradition they are reluctant to reject it, equally torn between a desire to embrace the freedom of U.S. lifestyle and their obligation to their parents' culture.

Role reversal, loss of identity, and questioning of authority are other factors that can contribute to family and cultural breakdown. As women work outside the home, they become more independent and assertive, a direct assault on traditional Asian cultures. Ethnically oriented centers and shelters have been established to help women cope with cultural conflict or other problems in the family. Despite these pressures, though, the family unit remains a strong force in Asian communities.

Asian Indian Women: A Case Study

Indian parents make matches for their children through formal or informal networks and interviews. Since more emphasis is given to the family unit, it is assumed that a marriage is not just a union between two individuals, but an alliance between families. Thus, family members actively participate in the confirmation of a marriage, which is deemed sacred in the Hindu tradition, and its dissolution through divorce is not traditionally accepted.

The conduct and deportment of women are closely linked with family integrity and honor in Asian Indian culture, giving women the unduly heavy burden of maintaining their family's place in society. Since daughters are perceived as future keepers of hearth and home, their activity and appearance are monitored more strictly than that of young men.

Within the immigrant community, this produces discontent among second-generation women chafing at rigid old-world restrictions. Most Asian Indian immigrant parents, for example, do not allow their children, particularly daughters, to date. This leads to cultural stress for Asian Indian young women raised in the United States and can cause serious intergenerational conflicts.

In contrast, immigration has emancipated many first-generation women, offering them the opportunity to work and earn money. Away from the strictures of an extended family and a gender-stratified mainstream society, many of the older women have asserted their independence and authority.

Unhappily, these changes in women's traditional roles may have contributed to violent retaliation within the family. Asian Indian women's organizations report that domestic violence is the most significant problem faced by Asian Indian women in the United States. In response, several groups that provide culturally

specific support and assistance have been formed since the mid-1980s.

Interracial Marriages

A study of the increasing rate of interracial marriage among Asian Americans conducted by UCLA sociologist Dr. Harry H. L. Kitano led him to speculate that the Japanese-American community as it is known today will be gone by 2050. The rate of outmarriage by Asian women is greater than by Asian men, most profoundly among Japanese women. In 1989, Dr. Kitano's study found that outmarriages by Japanese, Chinese, and Korean women in Los Angeles County averaged about 60 percent. Nationwide, Chinese outmarriages peaked in 1977 at 49 percent, and fell to 33.9 percent in 1989.

Among all Asian Americans, about 15 percent are in interracial marriages. The rate of these unions is likely to be greater in regions where the Asian-American population is sparser than in Los Angeles, for example.

The downside of these cross-cultural unions is that Asian women who are involved in them may feel emotionally isolated. Because their traditional mores, norms, and behavior—from avoidance of confrontation to subtle and nonverbal forms of communication—differ from U.S. culture, Asian women married to non-Asian men may often feel alienated. Those who marry U.S. servicemen overseas also usually have a difficult time adjusting. They may sense being rejected by their husbands' families and also by their own.

A troubling issue in the 1990s is the possible exploitation of Asian women as mail-order brides. Women are recruited to appear in catalogs that are read by American men looking for Asian wives. Such unions are unpredictable, however, and some women have found themselves mistreated and abused once in the United States.

◆ LEADERSHIP

Traditional cultural values can work against Asian women that assume leadership positions. They may be taught not to be assertive and to defer to men. Mothers caution daughters against behavior that could make them "unmarriageable." To overcome these barriers, Asian women's groups have been formed to help address these issues. Increasing numbers of Asian-American women are also becoming active in the larger women's movement, striving for their gender and racial equality. Many of these are also heavily involved in community improvement programs.

This community activism was initially hampered by both the ethnic diversity among Asian Americans and the prohibition against their immigration or citizenship in the United States.

Asian women are beginning to make their presence felt in state and local government. On the national scene, Patsy Mink was elected to the House of Representatives. A number of Asian-American women acquired high positions in the Clinton administration, including Doris Matsui, Shirley Sagawa, Sharon Maeda, Ginger Lew, Melinda Yee, and Maria Luisa Haley.

While a large number of Asian Indian women are involved in service and clerical jobs, others have reached high positions in government, academia, research, and business. Many are involved in family ventures such as motels, ethnic shops, newspaper stands, or restaurants. Asian Indian women have produced and directed movies, gained fame as writers, and established themselves as models and fashion and jewelry designers. Others are active in social-change movements that, while feminist, remain distinct from mainstream groups by their emphasis on ethnic identity.

In spite of their impressive list of achievements, Asian women are still largely invisible as a group. Perhaps the increasing interest in Asia as a potential market for U.S. industries will bring attention and resources to both immigrant communities and women's issues. Certainly, there are many ways for Asian-American women of all ancestries to assume leadership positions and contribute to society.

References

Agarwal, P. *Passage from India: Post 1965 Indian Immigrants and Their Children—Conflicts, Concerns, and Solutions.* Palos Verdes, California: Yuvati Publications, 1991.

"Asian American Women Struggling to Move Past Cultural Expectations." *New York Times,* January 23, 1994.

Chan, Sucheng. *Asian Americans: An Interpretive History.* Boston: Twayne Publishers, 1991.

Chandrasekhar, S., ed. *From India to America: A Brief History of Immigration—Problems of Discrimination, Admission, and Assimilation.* La Jolla, California: A Population Review Book, 1982.

Dasgupta, S. D. "The Gift of Utter Daring: Cultural Continuity in Asian-Indian Communities." In *Women, Communities, and Cultures: South Asians in America,* S. Mazumdar and J. Vaid, eds.

"Diffusion of J. A. Community Seen by 2050." *Pacific Citizen,* June 18, 1993.

Helwig, A. W., and U. M. Helwig. *An Immigrant Success Story: Asian Indians in America* . Philadelphia: University of Pennsylvania Press, 1990.

Karnow, Stanley and Nancy Yoshihara. *Asian Americans in Transition.* New York: Asia Society, 1992.

Kim, Elaine H. *With Silk Wings: Asian American Women at Work.* Asian Women United of California, 1983.

Leonard, K. "Marriage and Family Life among Early Asian Indian Immigrants." In *From India to America: A Brief History of Immigration—Problems of Discrimination, Admission, and Assimilation,* edited by S. Chandrasekhar. La Jolla, California: A Population Review Book, 1982.

Roland, A. "Indians in America: Adaptation of the Bicultural Self." *Committee on South Asian Women Bulletin* 7, nos, 3-4, 23-28.

———. "Indian Women in Cross-Cultural Marriages: Reflection in the Mirror of the American Lifestyle." In *Proceedings of the Conference on Family,* 19-23. Bronx: National Federation of American Indian Associations, 1988.

Takaki, Ronald. *A Different Mirror: A History of Multicultural America.* Boston: Little, Brown and Company, 1993.

———. *Strangers from a Different Shore: A History of Asian Americans.* Boston: Little, Brown and Company, 1989.

U.S. Bureau of the Census. *1990 Census of Population: Social and Economic Characteristics, United States.* Washington, D.C.: Government Printing Office, 1993.

———. *Statistical Abstract of the U.S.: 1992.* Washington, D.C.: Government Printing Office, 1993.

—Lillian Kimura and Shamita Das Dasgupta

Languages

♦ Bengali ♦ Burmese Language ♦ The Chinese Language ♦ India: Its Languages
♦ Indonesian ♦ The Japanese Language ♦ The Korean Language ♦ The Pilipino Language
♦ Urdu, Hindi, and Bengali

♦ BENGALI

(*See also* sections on Hindi and Urdu)

Bengali (also known as Bangla) is the official language of Bangladesh, and is spoken by almost all Bangladeshis. In the 1950s, Bengali and Urdu were given equal status as official languages. Non-Bengali migrants from India speak Urdu, however, and it is widely understood in urban areas. Tribal groups such as the Chittagong, Noakhali, and Sylhet, speak distinct dialects. Bengali is the language of instruction in Bangladesh schools, but English is widely understood amont the educated population.

Development of the Bengali Language

Bengali is the language of well over 100 million people. A third of them live in the Indian provinces of West Bengal and Tripura; the remainder live in Bangladesh. Bengali is one of the 14 official languages of India and was one of two in undivided Pakistan. It is taught up to the postgraduate level in the humanities and through the junior college level in the sciences. It is used for religious purposes second only to Sanskrit for Hindus and Arabic for Muslims.

The Bengali language developed at approximately the same time as Punjabi and Hindustani; that is, following the exclusion of Sanskirt and the formation of the *Prakrits*, or regional languages. Linguistically, it is closest to Assamese, followed by Oriya, and then Hindi.

Bengali script is derived from the ancient Indian Brahami, slightly different from the Devanagari script. The writing goes from left to right, hanging from the line. It contains upstrokes as well as downstrokes and uses looped or arched angles. There are no capitals, and punctuation is used as in English. Clauses have a free word order, which means that the language is highly inflected. For example, the sentence "She had an old house" could also be, "She had of old things a house" or "An old house was what she had" or a number of other ways. Bengali syntax is head final, unlike English, which means that it has postpositions rather than prepositions.

The *Dacca* dialect of the Bengali language can be heard spoken mainly by the lower middle classes in and around the city of Dacca and in other concentrated areas of West Bengal. *Chalit* is usually spoken by the college-educated upper and middle classes. Older residents speak a mixture of pidgin Urdu and Bengali known as *Kutti Kutti*, which means "belonging to the fort." The Muslim spelling in this dialect differs slightly from the general standard. Another dialect, the *Chittagong*, is the least widely understood due to its obscure phonology or pronunciation.

Some Bengalis also speak Urdu, Hindi, and English, particularly in urban areas. Bengali has two standards known as *Chalit* and *Sandhu*, the latter being the dominant one. The major basis of the Chalit standard has been the speech of the villages of Hooghly and Krishnagore, located north of Calcutta.

Like the development of Urdu, verse was the first literary form of expression in Bengali. The earliest specimens date back to the Mahayana Buddhist Pala dynasty, which ruled from the eighth to the twelfth century. This influence was so profound that phrases and idioms in the language's modern form can be traced to these texts. Members of the Natha sect wrote their first verse narratives of romantic tales of queens and princes in the Bengali language.

The Islamic culture came to the Bengal region in 1200 when Turkish invaders overthrew the Sena kings. The next century was a bleak period for language and literature, since scholars—both Buddhist and Brahmin—were scattered all over the Indian countryside.

But in the fourteenth century, the Muslim kings started speaking Bengali and began to patronize the native literature. Muslim poets wrote in Bengali and the first Bengali translations of the Hindu religious texts *Ramayana* and *Mahabharata* were made at the behest of one Muslim ruler. In addition, Bengali was accepted as the chief official language at the Arakan court.

The Muslim writers, in turn, added Persian legends and Islamic fairy tales to Bengali literature, as well as Islamic history and religious beliefs. This mixture of Hindu, Muslim, and traditional legends produced a peculiar type of Sufism that can be seen in the poems of the period.

Bengali prose, which had been confined to legal documents until the eighteenth century, began to flourish when a printing press was set up by Christian missionaries in the region. Proverbs were the first example of non-verse literature to be written, of which more than a thousand are extant. These stories were followed by nursery rhymes and fairy tales. The British presence in India brought the strongest wave of European influence to the Bengali region. Calcutta, the capital of British India, became its cultural and political stronghold. As a result, Bengali was the first Indian language to be effected by European influence.

The nineteenth century saw the emergence of perhaps the most famous Bengali poet, Rabindranath Tagore. Born in 1861, Tagore began composing poems as a child and continued to do so till his death in 1941. He was awarded the Nobel prize in 1913, the first Asian writer to be so honored. Tagore's creativity inspired other Bengali writers to strive to make their literature among the richest in India. This endeavor continues to be a source of great pride for both Hindu and Muslim.

◆ BURMESE LANGUAGE

Burmese has been the official language of Myanmar, formerly the Socialist Republic of the Union of Burma, since the end of British rule in 1948. Burmese is spoken by about 50 million people around the world. Current estimates put the number of Burmese-speaking people in the United States at around 30,000, with communities of significant size existing in California, Illinois, Maryland, Massachusetts, New York, Ohio, Pennsylvania, and Texas.

Besides Burmese, over a hundred languages are in fact spoken in Myanmar, all of which belong to three basic groups. The majority of these, including Burmese itself, are classified as the Burmic branch of the Tibeto-Burmese group, a subcategory of the Sino-Tibetan languages. Moving west and south from China for many generations, Burmese reached its current locale around the ninth century A.D. Yi, a language still spoken in southern China, is closely related to Burmese. Halted in

its southward move by the Bay of Bengal and the Andaman Sea, Burmese encountered the Mon language. In the course of the next two centuries, this Mon-Kmer offshoot of the Austro-Asiatic linguistic group mixed with Burmese to some extent becoming the source of its writing system. The Pali scriptures of Buddhism completed the crystallization of classical Burmese during this period, adding ideological organization to the language.

Like other languages of the Sino-Tibetan group, Burmese is monosyllabic. Each root is a single syllable, uninflected. Most words remain monosyllabic, differing from European languages in that respect. There are, however, many polysyllabic word/phrase combinations, such as nya.ne.saun, "afternoon," compounding nya, "night," ne, "sun," and saun, "to lean."

Significant tonality is another feature of Burmese common to Asian languages of this group, of which Mandarin Chinese is a part. This means that a word may vary in meaning or grammatically according to whether it is pronounced in a high or low tone, or scales up or down between these tones. In Burmese there are three tonal types: the level, the heavy falling, and "creaky" tones. These cadences are not used merely to indicate differences in emphasis; tonal variation has lexical and even grammatical significance. For example, myin—the verb "to see" when spoken in the level tone, becomes the noun "horse" in the heavy falling accent.

These changes are represented in the written language by various diacritical marks. Four-syllable set phrases are common, produced by adding a rhyming word to the key word and then duplicating this double syllable, as in ke.pya.ke.ya, "hurriedly."

The Pali alphabet used for written Burmese is made up of eight vowels, three diphthongs, thirty-two consonants, and several tones. In graphic form, this beautiful script consists largely of circular marks variously arranged. It is said to have developed originally as a means of writing with a stylus on palm leaves, which would split if incised with a straight line.

—Douglas Utter and Mie Mie Sann, MLS

◆ THE CHINESE LANGUAGE

More than one billion people speak some form of Chinese, the most common form being Mandarin—called Pǔtōnghùa in China and Gúoyǔ in Taiwan. Mandarin is the official language of both China (The People's Republic of China) and Taiwan (The Republic of China), although in Taiwan about 75% of the population speak the Taiwanese Mín dialect at home. In Hong Kong—which will be returned to The People's Republic of China in 1997—Cantonese or Yùe is the Chinese dialect most people speak. The Cantonese and Taiwanese

BURMESE

Numbers	Pronunciation	Script	Expressions	Pronunciation	Script
1. one	ti'	တစ်	hello	byou.	မင်္ဂ
2. two	hni'	နှစ်	goodbye	thwa:ba-do.	သွား ပါ တော့
3. three	thoun:	သုံး	how are you?	nei kaun:ye.la:?	နေ ကောင်း လား
4. four	lei:	လေး	how do you do?	ma-ye.la:?	မာ ရဲ့ လား
5. five	nga:	ငါး	never mind	nei-bazei	နေ ပါ စေ
6. six	hcau'	ခြောက်	no	ma-hou'-phu:	မ ဟုတ် ဘူး
7. seven	hkun-ni'	ခုနှစ်	yes	hou'ke.	ဟုတ် ကဲ့
8. eight	hyi'	ရှစ်	please	tahsei'	တ ဆိ ပ
9. nine	kou:	ကိုး	thank you	cei:zu: tin-ba-de	ကျေး ဇူး တင် ပါ တယ်
10. ten	tahse	တစ် ဆယ်	excuse me	hkwin.pyu.ba	ခွင့် ပြု ပါ

dialects, like many other Chinese dialects, are not understood by Mandarin speakers. However, many speakers of Cantonese and Taiwanese do speak and understand Mandarin. In fact, Cantonese, Taiwanese, and Mandarin are the most commonly heard "Chinese languages" in the United States and Canada.

Most Westerners would call Cantonese and Taiwanese "Chinese languages," but Chinese language specialists would disagree. The Chinese consider Cantonese and Taiwanese as dialects and not languages, because all literate Chinese can communicate very well via the Chinese written characters. Therefore the Cantonese and Taiwanese dialects are all united through the 4,000 year-old Chinese characters.

Other major Chinese dialects include the Wu dialect in Shanghai (80,000,000 speakers); Xiang in Hunan (45,000,000 speakers); Hakka in both southern China and in Taiwan (35,000,000 speakers); and the Gan dialect in Jiangxi (22,000,000 speakers). There are also hundreds of minor dialects throughout China.

It should also be noted that in China there are truly "foreign" languages such as Mongolian, Tibetan, Korean, and Uighur to name a few.

The Chinese have been able to maintain unity and communicate effectively, due to the Chinese written language. Since the Chinese language does not have a phonetic alphabet, all people who learn Chinese must learn one character at a time. After six years of elementary school, most students can read and write about 3,000 characters—enough to read a newspaper and to be considered functionally literate. Most educated Chinese do not use more than 7,000 characters.

The Origin of the Characters

Chinese characters originate from two main sources: oracle bones and bronzes. In 1899, Liu E, a Chinese scholar, visited a pharmacy to get some medicine for a sick friend. The medicine consisted of "dragon" bones. These bones had to be ground into powder before they could be used. While waiting, he noticed that some of the bones had what appeared to be writing on them. The writing looked like Chinese characters. Weeks later, after his friend had recovered, Mr. Liu and friend, Wang Yirong, went in search of more of these dragon bones. They bought as many of

CHINESE

Numbers	Pronunciation	Script	Expressions	Pronunciation	Script
1. one	yi	一	hello	mi hǎo	你好
2. two	èr	二	good evening	wǎn ān	晚安
3. three	sān	三	how are you?	mi hǎo ma?	你好吗?
4. four	si	四	you're welcome	búkèqi	不客气
5. five	wǔ	五	no	búshì	不是
6. six	liù	六	yes	shì	是
7. seven	qi	七	please	qǐng	请
8. eight	bā	八	thank you	xie xie	谢谢
9. nine	jiǔ	九	pardon me	dùibu qí	对不起
10. ten	shí	十			

them as they could find in the pharmacies throughout Beijing.

Prior to this time, the only book that had been written about Chinese characters was a dictionary called Shǔowén Jiězì, published in A.D. 121. This dictionary gave in-depth explanations of about 9,000 Chinese characters.

Mr. Liu published his book on these dragon bone inscriptions in 1903. Tracing the bones back to the Shang dynasty (1523–1028 B.C.), he discovered that they had been used by the king of the Shang dynasty to contact the spirits of dead ancestors and to seek answers concerning hunting, harvests, dreams, birth, and death. His diviners would take the shoulder blade of an ox or a turtle shell and rub it smooth. Next they bore holes on it, as they shouted out the question to their ancestors, simultaneously placing a hot rod into one of the holes. The bones would crack in many different directions. It was then the diviners' duty to interpret the meanings of these cracks. Finally, signs would be written beside these cracks. These signs were the early Chinese characters that Liu E saw in the Beijing pharmacy in 1899.

Today, more than 175,000 oracle bones have been found, of which 50,000 have inscriptions. In *China: Empire of Living Symbols*, Cecilia Lindquist explains the history and etymology of Chinese characters in detail and in easy-to-read prose.

Linguists have also gone into detail concerning the second source of Chinese characters: the bronzes. From 1928 to 1937, excavations were conducted to the south of Beijing in Anyang, the capital city of the Shang dynasty. While looking for more oracle bones, archaeologists also discovered bronzes in various sizes and shapes, most of them with inscriptions. These bronzes were most likely used as part of sacrificial ceremonies, during which the king would make offerings on behalf of all his subjects. According to research conducted by Zhou Fagao, 5,000 bronzes with inscriptions on them had been unearthed by the 1970s. These bronzes date back to the end of the Zhou dynasty (1027–221 B.C.). During Confucius's time (551-479 B.C.), Chinese characters were becoming standardized. Yet it was not until the Qin dynasty (221–206 B.C.) that the Chinese written language was unified and officially standardized.

Pictographs (Pictures)		Ancient	Present
Examples:	sun	⊙	日
	moon	 ⅀	月

Ideographs (Symbols)		Ancient	Present
Examples:	up	⸳	上
	down	 ⸳	下

Ideographic Combinations

Examples:	tree	木	+ tree	木	= forest	林	
	small	小	+ big	大	= sharp	尖	

Ideograph/sound characters

Examples:	woman	女	+ *ma*	馬	= mother	媽	
	insect	虫	+ *ma*	馬	= ant	螞	

Transferable characters

Example:　*ba* 爸 comes from *fu* 父 father

Loan characters

Example:　Originally 西 meant "to perch."

Because birds usually return to perch on their nests at sunset and the sun sets in the west, the word for "to perch" was borrowed to mean "west" (西).

Six Categories of Chinese Characters

Chinese characters are divided into six different types: pictographs, ideographs, ideographic combinations, ideograph/sound characters, transferable characters, and loan characters. Many people think of Chinese characters as pictographic, although less than five percent of them actually are pictographic. The majority (95 percent) of Chinese characters are ideograph/sound characters.

Grammar

Some Chinese who have studied English will tell you that the Chinese language has no grammar. This is not accurate; there are rules for Chinese grammar. These rules are neither as complex nor as numerous as they are for English.

In general, Chinese follows the subject-verb-object order; the subject comes first, and is followed by a verb, and then an object. For example, *Wŏ xǐhuān ni* means "I (subject) like (verb) you (object)." However, the Chinese also use the subject-object-verb order. A sentence to illustrate this is *Tǎ bǎ shū mài le*:

He (*Tǎ* = subject)

bǎ = object marker (telling the listener that the word that follows it is an object)

book (*shū* - object)

sold (*mài le* - verb + past-tense indicator).

The object-subject-verb order is also used by the Chinese. For example:

1) *Gǒu, wǒ bù xǐhuān.* "Dog, I don't like."
   object - topic, subject, negative, verb

2) *Diànnǎu, wǒ xúehùi le.* "Computer, I learned."
   object - topic, subject, verb

In addition to word order, the verb is also important in Chinese grammar. Verbs in general have no inflection for past or future tenses. Thus, tense is indicated by the use of other words, such as time words—tomorrow, yesterday, five minutes ago. Examples of this are "I tomorrow go," (*Wǒ míngtiān qù*) and "Yesterday he come + le, a past tense indicator," (*Tā zúotiān lái le*).

Tones

Mandarin Chinese has four stressed tones, plus an unstressed one. (Cantonese has nine tones). The first tone is the high level tone, *mā* ("mother"). Next, is the second tone: middle level and rising, *má* ("hemp"). The third tone is the low level and rising, *mǎ* ("horse"). And the fourth tone is the high level and falling, *mà* (to scold). Beginning learners of Mandarin Chinese that converse in non-tone languages often have difficulty with tones. Although not lexically or grammatically significant, English speakers also use rising and falling tones. For example, if you tell your father that you just smashed up the car, what is he going to say? I am quite sure he is going to ask you one question: "You *what?*" Or if your teacher asks you a question in class concerning the homework assignment, the usual response is: "*Me?*" These are all rising intonations and we use them all the time. Americans even use the falling tone (the fourth tone) in English. For example, if you see a very young child about to touch a hot stove, what will you say to the child? "*No!*" This is the falling tone.

Romanization

When Chinese want to write a Chinese character in English, they cannot just write it as they do in Chinese. They need to use some form of phonetic notation, which is referred to as "romanization." Several forms are used in China: for example, *Hànyǔ Pinyin*. *Hànyǔ* means "Chinese language," and *Pinyin* means "spelling and sound." Thus, to write Chinese in English, the Chinese use the Mandarin Chinese pronunciation to spell out the sounds. Hànyǔ Pinyin is the official romanization system of the Chinese government, the United Nations, the Library of Congress, and the U.S. Postal Service.

However, not all teachers of Chinese in the United States use this system. For example, some teachers of Chinese from Taiwan may use the National Phonetic System. Others may use the Yale University Romanization system of writing Chinese. In fact, Far Eastern Publications at Yale University has one of the most extensive and systematic collection of materials for learning Chinese in the United States.

Finally, the Wade-Giles system has been used in books about Chinese history, politics, and literature for about 80 years, 40 years longer than the Hànyǔ Pinyin system. However, the Hànyǔ Pinyin system is used in China and worldwide with increasing frequency. Consequently, people communicating with the Chinese should be familiar with the Hànyǔ Pinyin writing system.

Let's look at the word for "thank you" in Chinese:

National Phonetic Alphabet

Yale Romanization system	*syè syè*
Wade–Giles system	*hsieh hsieh*
Hanyu Pinyin system	*xiè xiè*

Xiè rhymes with shave, without the "ve." Thus, *xiè xiè* sounds like shay shay.

Pronunciation

The official spelling system used for Chinese characters by the government of The People's Republic of China is the Hànyǔ Pinyin system. However, in this system there are some letters that puzzle many Americans. Some examples follow:

c is pronounced like *ts*, as in the word cats.

ao is pronounced like *ow*, as in the word cow.

Thus, *cǎo* ("grass") in Pinyin is pronounced like *tsow*.

zh is pronounced like *j* as in the word jello

Thus, *zhōngguó* ("China") in Pinyin is pronounced like *Jong gwo*.

q is pronounced like *ch*, as in the word chew.

i is pronounced like *e*, as in the word eat.

Thus, *qi* ("seven") is pronounced like *chee*, as in cheese.

x is pronounced similar to *sh* as in she.

Thus, *xigūa* ("watermelon") is pronounced like *shee gwa*.

Family Names

The Chinese say the last name first, then follow it with the first name, which is usually comprised of one or two characters. For example, Deng Xiaoping is not Mr. Ping, but rather Mr. Deng; Xiaoping is his first name. While some Chinese have two first names, others have only one. For instance, Li Bai (the famous poet of the Tang dynasty) is Mr. Li and his first name is Bai. However, there are also a few Chinese who have a double last name. The two characters of a double last name are always treated as one. Sima Qian (a Chinese historian) is an example of this.

Some common Chinese last names are Chen, Dai, Feng, Lu, Qian, Wang, and Zhang.

Simplified Characters

Chinese characters have gone through 4,000 years of change. During this time, their shapes have been altered to varying degrees. Yet, even today many Chinese can recognize many of the characters that were written on the bronzes and the oracle bones. The most recent stage of revision was the simplification of the Chinese characters. Even though many Chinese characters were simplified in the 1950s, they were not officially used until the late 1970s. In fact, the 1964 list contains some 2,238 simplified characters, about one third of the seven to eight thousand total characters required to write modern Chinese. In Taiwan, simplified characters are not officially allowed to be used in print. However, students do simplify the Chinese characters themselves while taking notes.

In general, simplified characters are used only in China (The Peoples Republic of China) and Singapore. Most Chinese newspapers published outside of China continue to use the traditional form of the Chinese characters. In fact, most natives of Taiwan would have a difficult time recognizing many of the simplified characters. In the United States, teachers of the Chinese language usually teach the traditional characters first, later introducing the simplified form. Since all Chinese books published before 1949 were in printed traditional form, it is often essential for anyone communicating in the Chinese language to know both forms. The traditional characters connect us to the Chinese culture of the past, and the simplified characters bring us into the reality of the modern-day China.

References

Chang, Raymond and Margaret S. Chang. *Speaking of Chinese.* New York: Norton, 1978.

DeFrancis, John. *The Chinese Language: Fact and Fantasy.* Honolulu: University of Hawaii Press, 1984.

Lindquist, Cecilia. *China: Empire of Living Symbols.* New York:Addison-Wesley, 1991.

Newman, Richard. *About Chinese.* New York: Penguin Books, 1971.

Ramsey, S. Robert. *The Languages of China.* Princeton, NJ: Princeton University Press, 1987.

—John E. Stowe, Ph.D.

♦ INDIA: ITS LANGUAGES

See also Bengali, Hindi, and Urdu.

The are nearly 2,000 languages and dialects in India. Hindi, English, and 14 regional languages are officially recognized by the constitution. Hindi is spoken by over 30 percent of the population.

♦ INDONESIAN

Bahasa Indonesia is the official language of Indonesia, but the use of some 250 local languages continues. For industry and commerce, English is widely used.

Names

In general, a person carries his/her own full name, which may consist of one to three word. One-word names are very common, especially in Java. If a name has more than one word, the last word does not necessarily represent a family name. Only in some areas of the country, names carry a family name.

There are no specific conventions of how people get their names but in many cases, a person's name reveals his or her region or ethnic group. Names also reveal whether a person comes from an urban or rural area—urban names tend to be wordy or to sound westernized, whereas rural names tend to be traditionally short and simple.

Reference

Echols, John M. and Hassan Shadily. *Kamus Inggris Indonesia, An English-Indonesian Dictionary.* Jakarta: PT Gramedia Puslaka Utama, 1990.

—Heny Suwardjono

♦ THE JAPANESE LANGUAGE

Origin

To this day the exact origin of the spoken and written Japanese language is still unclear. However, historical documentation can enlighten us to some facts related to its development. First, in Japan as we know it today, Japanese was spoken as early as the third century A.D. In the middle of the fourth century, the independent tribes were united under the Yamato clan, and

INDONESIAN

Numbers (Bilangan)	Pronunciation	Expressions (Ungkapan)	Pronunciation
1. one	satu	hello	halo
2. two	dua	good-bye	selamat tinggal
3. three	tiga	good evening	selamat malam
4. four	empat	how are you?	apa kabar?
5. five	lima	you're welcome	sama-sama
6. six	enam	no	tidak
7. seven	tujuh	yes	ya
8. eight	delapan	thank you	terima kasih
9. nine	sembilan	pardon me	maaf
10. ten	sepuluh		

the spoken language at that time was called Yamatoko-toba. Language in Japan was preliterate. Intermittent contacts between Korea and Japan introduced books written in Chinese to Japan. In the third century A.D., language in Korea was also preliterate, but Korean scholars began to use Chinese characters to express themselves in writing.

In A.D. 285, two Korean scholars, Want In (Wani in Japanese) and Ajikki of the Paekche (Korean) dynasty, went to Japan as teachers. They brought with them one

copy of *One Thousand Character Classic* and ten copies of *The Analects of Confucius*. Buddhist scriptures, written in Chinese characters, were introduced to Japan in A.D. 552. Since Japan did not have its own writing system, the aristocracy studied philosophical and religious books in Chinese using Chinese characters (*kanji*) to write ideas in Japanese.

Kanji was the first of the four writing forms the Japanese use today. The other three forms are *katakana*, *hiragana*, and *ramaji*. Kanji (Chinese characters)—phonetically equivalent to the sounds of Yamatokotoba—were called *Man'yogana*, and later developed into katakana and hiragana.

During the eighth century, Buddhist culture flourished. At this time, the Chinese Tang dynasty (A.D. 618–906) was at its peak. The Tang dynasty in China had a strong influence on Japan as well as on most of the countries in the Far East. However, it was not until the ninth century that kanbun (Chinese writing) became the leading form of literary expression in Japan. Around the tenth century, a uniquely Japanese syllabary derived from the Chinese written characters developed. In a syllabary, as opposed to an alphabet, each symbol represents a syllable rather than a letter. The invention of these symbols, called *kana*, allowed the Japanese to express themselves in their own form of writing for the first time in their history.

Kana

Kana takes two forms: katakana and hiragana. The katakana writing form appeared after the introduction of Chinese characters. Katakana characters are more

INDONESIAN ALPHABET

a	like a in argue	n	like en in end
b	like bay	o	like o in go
c	like che in cherry	p	like pay
d	like day	q	like key
e	like e in egg	r	like er in error
f	like ef in chef	s	like es in escalator
g	like gay	t	like tay in stay
h	like ha in harmony	u	like oo in food
i	like ee in see	v	like ve in velocity
j	like je in jelly	w	like way in subway
k	like ca in calculate	x	like ex in extreme
l	like el in elbow	y	like ye in yellow
m	like em in embody	z	like zet in zeta

JAPANESE

Numbers	Pronunciation	Script	Expressions	Pronunciation	Script
1. one	ichi	一	hello	konnichiwa	こんにちは
2. two	ni	二	good evening	kombanwa	こんばんは
3. three	san	三	how are you?	ogenki desu ka?	おげんきですか
4. four	shi (yon)	四	you're welcome	dō itashimashite	どういたしまして
5. five	go	五	no	iie	いいえ
6. six	roku	六	yes	hai	はい
7. seven	shichi (nana)	七	please	dōzo	どうぞ
8. eight	hachi	八	thank you	arigatō	ありがとう
9. nine	kyū	九	pardon me	sumimasen	すみません
10. ten	jū	十			

rigid or straight looking than other forms of Japanese writing. They originated by abbreviating or simplifying some part of the Chinese characters. Katakana is usually used for communicating foreign names, concepts, and inventions. Many words written in katakana may be recognized by anyone who knows English. *Jon-sumisu*, *ká-puru*, and *rajio* are three words in katakana that come from English. They are "John Smith," "car pool," and "radio," respectively.

The third form of Japanese writing is hiragana, which employs soft, cursive, flowing symbols. This form has been called "the soul of the Japanese." Many culturally important terms such as *wa* ("harmony") and *giri* ("duty or obligation") were originally written in hiragana. However, today, all three of these important Japanese concepts are written in kanji.

The Japanese Sentence

The Japanese sentence is written in a combination of different ranji and kana symbols. By looking at a simple sentence, some particular features of the Japanese language can be clearly noticed.

私はアメリカ人です。

Watashi   wa   amerika   jin   desu.

"I am American."

Watashi = "I" [Kanji]

wa = topic market [Hiragana]

amerika = "America" [Katakana]

jin = "person" [Kanji]

desu = equivalent to the verb "to be" [Hiragana]

Kanji, the characters adopted from the Chinese language, are used to represent basic ideas (e.g., nouns, verbs, adjectives) and Japanese names. Kana (hiragana and katakana) are the phonetic symbols which represent sounds; each symbol begins with a consonant and ends with a vowel. Altogether there are 46 sounds; this is the Japanese "alphabet."

Each kanji (Chinese character) has only one syllable; therefore, it was difficult to transcribe Japanese words (Yamatokotoba), because almost all of them have many syllables. Consequently, the Japanese of the ninth century began to use kanji as phonetic symbols. This system was cumbersome and inefficient, which encouraged the emergence of katakana and hiragana. The katakana symbols were written to the right of (along side) the kanji to help readers with the pronunciation of the kanji.

In addition, there were the hiragana symbols, which were used only by women. The hiragana writing system became one of the most important writing systems in Japan at this time because it allowed the Japanese to put spoken Japanese into written form without the use of any other language (i.e., Chinese). However, since China was a powerful country with a strong cultural, literary, and religious influence, kanji (Chinese characters) were still used by Japanese men as a sign of learnedness.

Today the Chinese influence on the Japanese language is still very strong, as a large percentage of Japanese vocabulary words are derived from Chinese. More and more English words are coming into the Japanese language, however. These are called *gairaigo* (words of foreign origin). Examples of gairaigo are *kóhí kappu*, *terebi*, and *kamera*—"coffee cup," "television," and "camera" in English.

Japanese is written either vertically from right to left or horizontally from left to right. Most books, newspapers, magazines, and formal letters are written vertically; word processing and informal writing is usually done horizontally.

Romanization

The fourth form of writing in Japanese is called *Romaji*. It is based on the Latin alphabet, hence its romanized characters (*roma*—Roman; *ji*—characters or words). Two systems of Romaji, the Kunreishiki system ("Official System") and the Hepburn system, are employed today in teaching Japanese to non-native speakers. Even though most Japanese–English dictionaries use the Hepburn system, a modified Hepburn system is the most popular because it is easier for English speakers to recognize and pronounce.

Grammar

The sentence structure in Japanese is different from the sentence structure of English. The sentence, in English, "John ran to school." is, in Japanese, "John to school ran." Word order in Japanese is subject-object-verb. Korean verbs are also always at the end of the sentence; however, in Chinese, the verbs are at the end of the sentence only sometimes.

Japanese nouns can be either singular or plural. For example, *Kippu o kaimashita* means, "I bought a/ some ticket/tickets." One discerns the meaning from the context or by the measure words, i.e., a pair of tickets. In this way, Japanese is similar to both Chinese and Korean.

Japanese verbs and adjectives are inflected—that is, they change—to communicate present and past tense, as well as affirmative and negative. For example:

kaimasu = "to buy," "am buying;"

kaimashita = "bought;"

atarashii = "new;"

atarashikunai = "not new."

In English, prepositions are used; in Japanese, postpositions are used and occur after nouns. For example, *Eigo de* (literally, "English in") means "in English."

Politeness

Many levels of politeness are used in Japanese. When speaking to someone older or to a supervisor, a polite, formal form of speech is used. In English this is similar to asking for a menu with the phrase, "May I have a menu, please" as opposed to the informal, "Ya gotta menu?" In Japanese, a humble or modest form of speech is also used. *Onegaishimasu* is an example of this, meaning, "Would you do this for me, please?"

Names

In Japanese, the last name is spoken before the first name. *San* is added to the last name to show respect. This is equivalent to Mr., Mrs., Miss, or Ms.

Some common last names are Kato, Sato, Nakamura, and Tanaka. Some common male given names are Hiroshi, Kiyoshi, Taro, and Yoshio. Typical female given names are Kazuko, Keiko, Michiki, and Yoko. Thus, Nakamura Yoshio would be Mr. Yoshio Nakamura in English and Nakamura-san in Japanese. Kato Michiko, would be Miss, Ms., or Mrs. Kato in English and Kato-san in Japanese.

Pronunciation

Most Japanese kanji have two or more pronunciations. One pronunciation comes from Chinese (*on* pronunciation) and the other from the native Japanese (*kun* pronunciation). The pronunciation is usually established by the context.

The pronunciation of the five vowel sounds (a, i, u, e, o), however, does not vary in Japanese. They are always pronounced:

A as in father,

I as in beet,

U as in who,

E as in bait,

O as in boat.

The basic Korean alphabet consists of 10 vowels and 14 consonants.

Basic Vowels: ㅏ ㅑ ㅓ ㅕ   ㅗ ㅛ ㅜ ㅠ ㅡ ㅣ

           a   ya   o`   yo`   o   yo   u   yu   u`   i

Basic Consonants:

	Name	Sound			Name	Sound
ㄱ	기역 kiyo`k	k,g		ㅇ	이응 iu`ng	(ng)
ㄴ	니은 niu`n	n		ㅈ	지읏 chiu`t'	ch,j(t)
ㄷ	디귿 tiku`t	t,d		ㅊ	치읓 ch'iu`t'	ch'(t)
ㄹ	리을 riu`l	r,l		ㅋ	키읔 k'iu`k'	k'
ㅁ	미음 miu`m	m		ㅌ	티읕 t'iu`t'	t'
ㅂ	비읍 piu`p	p,b		ㅍ	피읖 p'iu`p'	p'
ㅅ	시옷 siot'	s(t)		ㅎ	히읗 hiu`t	h(t)

( ) sound of final consonants

There are also 11 compound vowels and 5 compound consonants in the Korean alphabet.

Compound Vowels: ㅐ ㅒ ㅔ ㅖ ㅘ ㅙ

         ae   yae   e   ye   wa   wae

ㅚ ㅝ ㅞ ㅟ ㅢ

   oe   wo`   we   wi   ui

Compound Consonants: ㄲ ㄸ ㅃ ㅆ ㅉ

                            kk   tt   pp   ss   tch

Figure 28.1 The Korean alphabet.

References

Benedict, Ruth. *The Chrysanthemum and the Sword: Patterns of Japanese Culture*. Boston: Houghton Mifflin, 1977.

Christopher, Robert C. *The Japanese Mind*. New York: Fawcett Columbine, 1977.

Hadamitzky, Wolfgang and Mark Spahn. *Kanji and Kana*. Rutland, Vermont: Charles E. Tuttle Co., 1981.

Japan Travel Bureau. *Illustrated Japanese Characters*. Tokyo: Japan Travel Bureau, 1989.

Reischauer, Edwin O. *The Japanese Today: Change and Continuity*. Cambridge: Harvard University Press, 1988.

Vogel, Ezra F. *Japan As Number 1*. Cambridge: Harvard University Press, 1979.

—*John E. Stowe, Ph.D.*

♦ THE KOREAN LANGUAGE

Koreans have a strong national identity, in part because they all speak and write the same language. Although there are several Korean dialects, they are similar enough so that all Koreans can communicate with each other. A dialect from Seoul is used as the standard.

The Korean language belongs to the Ural-Altaic language group of Central Asia that also includes Turkish, Hungarian, Finnish, Mongolian, Tibetan, and Japanese. Both written and spoken Korean have been influenced by the Chinese language, due largely to China's immense political and cultural impact on Korea over the centuries. Korean also resembles Japanese in grammatical structure. Both Korean and

KOREAN

Numbers	Pronunciation	Script	Expressions	Pronunciation	Script
1. one	hana	하나	hello	annyo`ng-haseyo	안녕하세요
2. two	tul	둘	goodbye	annyo`nghi gaseyo	안녕히 가세요.
3. three	set'	셋	how are you?	o`tto`ke chinaeshimnika?	어떻게 지내십니까?
4. four	net'	넷	you're welcome	cho`nmaneyo	천만에요
5. five	taso`t'	다섯	no	anio	아니오
6. six	yo`so`t'	여섯	yes	ye	예
7. seven	ikop	일곱	please	chebal	제발
8. eight	yo`to`l	여덟	thank you	komapsu`mnida	고맙습니다.
9. nine	ahop	아홉	pardon me	choesong-hamnida	죄송합니다.
10. ten	yo`l	열			

Japanese have borrowed words and idioms from the Chinese language.

The Korean language is written with a largely phonetic alphabet called *Han'gul*, which was created in 1443 by a group of scholars. This Korean script, Han'gul, or "great letters," is considered to be one of the most linguistically efficient writing systems in the world. Before the invention of these simple phonetic symbols, Korean was written by means of Chinese characters, which represent lexical and semantic images rather than phonetics.

The Korean alphabet originally had ten vowels and 14 consonants. Since its inception, five consonants and 11 vowels have been added. These can be combined to form numerous syllabic groupings. Han'gul is simple, systematic, and comprehensive. It is also easy to learn, print, and apply to computer systems.

There are two systems for romanizing Korean: the McCune-Reischauer system developed in 1939 and now conventional in English, and an ROK (South Korea) Ministry of Education system developed in 1959. In 1984, the ROK system was modified to align with the McCune-Reischauer system.

Since 1949, the Democratic People's Republic of Korea (DPRK), or North Korea, has used only Han'gul (calling it *Choson Muntcha*) for writing. In 1964, Kim Il-Sung called for purification of Korean by replacing borrowed words from English and Japanese with native Korean or familiar Chinese terms. The Republic of Korea (ROK), or South Korea, has undertaken similar "language beautification" drives designed to eliminate borrowing from Japanese and other languages.

Names

Korean names almost invariably consist of three Chinese characters that are pronounced with three Korean syllables. The family names comes first and the remaining two characters form the given name. One of these often identifies the generation.

There are about 300 family names in Korea, but only a handful of these cover the vast majority of the population. Among the most common names are Kim, Lee or Yi, Park or Pak, An, Chang, Cho, Ch'oe, Cho'ng, Han or Hahn, Kang, Yu, and Yun.

Korean women do not change their names when married. Koreans do not refer to others by their given name except among peers and very close friends. Even among siblings, the younger ones are not supposed to address the elder ones by given names. A girl calls her older sister *o'nni* and her older brother *oppa*. A boy calls his older sister *nuna* and his older brother *hyo'ng*.

References

Facts About Korea. Seoul: Korean Overseas Information Service, 1991.

—*Jung-Ah Kim, M.D.*

◆ THE PILIPINO LANGUAGE

In the Philippines there are two official languages, Pilipino and English. The national language, Pilipino, is based on Tagalog and is mandatory in public and private schools. It was adopted as the national language in 1946, and is understood by the majority of Filipinos. The English language, which is widely used in schools, is also spoken and understood by the majority of Filipinos.

Although Spanish was an official language in the Philippines prior to 1973, it is now spoken by a small minority of the population. More than 80 indigenous languages and dialects (primarily of Malay-Indonesian origin) are spoken in the Philippines. Besides Tagalog, which is spoken around Manila, the principal languages include: Cebuano, spoken in the Visayas; Ilocano, spoken in Northern Luzon; and Panay-Hiligaynon.

—*Jeane Detherage*

◆ URDU, HINDI, AND BENGALI

Modern Urdu, Hindi, and Bengali respectively trace their ancestry back 3000 years to the earliest Vedic hymn. From the old Vedic evolved Sanskrit, used among the Brahmins, or priestly class, to preserve the sanctity of the hymns. During the Middle Ages, the influence of the Sanskrit language had declined to a point where, like Latin, it was used only in religious contexts and as a medium for literature. Natural language development produced a cultural language, *Sanskrit*, and a vernacular, *Prakrit*. Since the Hindu religion had adopted Sanskrit as its exclusive language and since Sanskrit was no longer effective in solely manifesting cultured expression, non-Hindus adopted other languages for their sacred and philosophic texts. The Buddhists, for example, used Pali in their teachings.

Through the gradual process of change in natural languages, Punjabi, Bengali, and numerous local languages and dialects emerged. Believed to be the forerunner of Urdu and Hindi, Khari Boli, was spoken in and around the city of Delhi, India. The Muslim rulers referred to it as Hindi or the Indian language. During Muslim rule in India, its connection to the Persian, Arabic, and Turkish languages influenced the development of what later came to be known as Urdu, the national language of Pakistan.

Hindi and Urdu are essentially two forms of the original Hindustani language. Although the speaker of one can usually understand a speaker of the other, their scripts are different. Hindus adopted the Sanskrit script and Muslims (Urdu speakers) used the Persian or Arabic script that the Moghuls brought to the subcontinent. The Bengali language developed as a distinct regional language in West Bengal, however, and out of it emerged a rich tradition in poetry and literature unparalleled on the Indian subcontinent.

Development of the Urdu Language

Urdu is the national language of Pakistan. Although native speakers account for only nine percent of the total population, it is now spoken and understood by over a hundred million people. Urdu traces its origins to the end of the twelfth century, when the Muslims, including Turks, Afghans, and Iranians, came to Delhi as new settlers. They brought with them at least four languages—Arabic, Persian, Turkish, and an early version of Punjabi.

When Delhi became the capital of Muslim sovereignty in India, a mixed, or *pidgin* (trade language) form of speech, known as *Rekta*, emerged. Based on *Khari Boli*, this new language, or Creole (a language that evolves out of a pidgin form), included many Arabic and Persian words as well. Since it developed in India, the Muslims called it Hindi or Hindavi, the language of India. Over the years this language assumed various names like *Zaban-e-Dehli*, *Zaban-e-Hindustan*, *Zaban-e-Urdu-e-Mualla*, *Zaban-e-Urdu*, and finally simply Urdu. Urdu is a word derived from the cantonment (military station) area of Mughal Delhi, known as *urdu-e-mualla* or "the exalted camp." While most educated Muslims of East Asia knew some Arabic, only those who joined the clergy or became maulvis were required to acquire a thorough knowledge of it; rather, it was the Persian language that became the accepted medium of Indo-Muslim education, government, and commerce.

Urdu was taken to different parts of the Indian subcontinent by travelers from the north. Due to the dominance of the Persian language among the educated Indians, however, Urdu was neglected as a literary language. It was the kingdoms of the Decca that developed the language to its fullest extent forming the basis of old Urdu.

Amir Khusrau (1253-1325) was the first eminent poet to use Urdu for literary expression. He called it *Zaban-e-Dehli*, or the language of Delhi. Sufi Muslims were also known to use old Urdu. It was not until the seventeenth century that Urdu literature in the form of poems and *marsias* (mourning poems) came into being. After the death of King Aurengzeb, there was greater contact between the north and the south, and the language developed into Northern Urdu.

The poet Wali inspired other writers to switch from Persian to Urdu, a language previously considered to belong to the lower classes. These writers refined the language by removing selected vernacular words and phrases and replacing them with those of Persian. By the eighteenth century, Urdu had developed into a language, with Persian, Arabic, and some Turkish words forming a major part of its vocabulary. It remained the language of poets, replacing Persian as the literary medium used by the ruling Muslim elite. The highest point of its stylistic quality may be found in the works of Ghalib (d.1869), the greatest of classical Urdu poets, who also wrote in Persian.

As with most languages, spoken Urdu is very different from written Urdu, which tends to be more colorful and flowery given its poetic nature. Urdu script is an adaptation of Persian and Arabic script. By 1800, the phonetic writing system or alphabet of the language had been fully developed.

Modern Urdu has fifty *phonemes*, or mutually exclusive sounds, including 38 consonants, 10 vowels, one nasal, and one phoneme of juncture, reflecting Indic, Persian, and Arabic influence. Urdu has two genders, masculine and feminine, which distinguish adjectives, pronouns, and participles. This feature in Urdu verbal participles is found neither in Sanskrit nor in Persian.

In 1800 the British established Fort William College in Calcutta to teach Indian languages to British personnel. This produced some of the first textbooks and grammar books of Urdu. The British called the language Hindustani and adopted it for administrative purposes, making it the official language across northern India and the Decca. This action fueled a linguistic rivalry between Urdu and Hindi speakers, which had begun in the late eighteenth century.

The Hindu middle class eventually forced the British to reduce Urdu's official recognition, although British personnel continued to use it, and the Hindi-Urdu debate persisted. After India gained its independence from Great Britian, Urdu survived as a state language only in Kashmir and Pakistan. From 1947 until the secession of Bangladesh in 1971, both Urdu and Bengali shared official status in an uncomfortable compromise.

In present-day Pakistan, Urdu remains the official state language. However, the Islamic regime of General Zia in the 1980s encouraged greater use of Persian and Arabic words, particularly in the news media, further widening the gap between spoken and written Urdu. Regional languages like Punjabi continue to be spoken widely, although Urdu is the *lingua franca* of business and culture throughout Pakistan and is a compulsory subject of study in school up to the college level. Modern writers have begun using colloquial Urdu without sacrificing the eloquent effect of the Persian influence.

Development of the Hindi Language

Hindi is the predominant and official language of modern India, and it is written in the Sanskrit, or Devanagari, script. It is most widely spoken by natives of north India from Rajhastan to Bihar; English is also widely used as a means of conversation and for administrative purposes. This medium is particularly important for south Indians, whose mother tongue language is Tamil. India also recognizes 14 regional languages (or *bhashas*) in addition to Hindi and English.

Medieval Rajhastani, a city in India, was known for its rich courtly, romantic, and martial literature, produced by poets in the Rajput courts. At the other end of the country in Avadh, the Avadhi dialect of Hindi was used by the poet Tulsidas for the Ramayan epic, which is regarded as the high point of Hindi literature.

From the late fifteenth century onward, literary Hindi was based on the Delhi-area dialect known as *Braj Bhasa*. The Braj area included the Mughal capital of Agra and southeast part of Delhi, which is associated with the childhood of Lord Krishna. Numerous sixteenth-century poems about Krishna established Braj for literary use all over north India. These poems were recognized for their religious significance and were awarded the patronage of Mughal royalty. Until the late 1800s it was Braj, not Khari Boli, that represented the Hindi language to the Hindu population of the area.

When British authorities encouraged Urdu to be used as an official language, with a Khari Boli-based Sanskrited Hindi written in Nagari script, the new linguistic style challenged the Braj tradition in literature. The British government's use of Urdu further reinforced the fact that there was no widely accepted style of Hindi that could be fully adopted by the population. The underprivileged Hindu majority began to oppose the use of standard Urdu. This became an important factor in the conflict leading to the eventual partition of India and Pakistan in 1947.

In the years before the partition, Mahatma Gandhi tried to find a compromise in the Hindi/Urdu debate but his ideas were not taken up by either faction. The Hindi movement coalesced in Benares and Allahabad, which were the bases of Hindu power in northern India. Many Hindi writers were located in these cities; their Urdu counterparts were based primarily in Delhi and Lucknow.

The central basis of their rivalry was which script to use. Because early literature had been an oral tradition, written expression was considered among many to be unimportant. However, mounting resistance to the influence of the English language and a renewed pride in India's heritage led Hindi writers to begin using Sanskritized style of prose based on nationalist themes. These new Hindi authors belonged to the literate classes, whose first attempts at creative writing were modeled after English or Bengali prose; but with the increasing identification with India's past among educated Hindi speakers, there emerged an interest to learn and use Sanskrit as well as Urdu, and eventually Urdu came to be associated only with Muslims.

The 1948 constitution made *Nagari* the standard script of Hindi, the national language. However, Arabic numerals continued to be used, and English remained an official language over the next 15 years. Despite concerted attempts to promote modern Sanskrited Hindi among the various regions of India, the language nevertheless is favored mainly by Hindu nationalists.

Although standard Hindi has become more widely used since the partition of India and Pakistan, it has not completely overtaken English or colloquial Hindustani, nor has the backlash from south India helped the development of Hindi. Real power seems to lie with the mass media, particularly the film industry, which uses a natural mixture of languages intelligible to Hindi and Urdu speakers alike.

Basic Hindi word order is subject-object-verb. Personal pronouns need not be explicitly stated because pronounial information is reflected by the speaker's inflection of the verb. Therefore, a verb can appear alone as a sentence.

Hindu men are usually addressed by their last name with a polite term *ji* added to it. For example, Mr. Sharma would be *Sharma ji*. Hindu women, however, are usually known by their first name. For example, Miss Sita would be called *Sita ji*. As in Urdu, Hindi has two genders, the masculine and the feminine.

At the national level, English continues to be the language of the elite; in fact, private schools, offer only an elementary form of Hindi. It is colloquial Hindustani that is widely spoken.

References

Beg, M. K. A. *Urdu Grammar: History and Structure*. New Delhi: Bahri Publications, 1988.

Maniruzzaman. *Studies in the Bangla Language*. Dhaka: Adiabad Sahitya Bhaban & Bhasha Tattva Kendra, 1991.

Narula, S. S. *Hindi Language—A Scientific History*. Delhi: Oriental Publishers and Distributors, 1976.

Ray, P. S., M.A. Hai, and L. Ray. *Bengali Language Handbook*. Center for Applied Linguistics, 1966.

Shackle, Christopher and Rupert Snell. *Hindi and Urdu Since 1800: A Common Reader*. New Delhi: Heritage Publishers, 1990.

Sharma, D. N. and James W. Stone. *Hindi: An Active Introduction*. Washington, D.C.: U.S Foreign Service Institute, 1970.

—Natasha Rafi

Education

♦ Pre-Kindergarten and Elementary Education ♦ Higher Education
♦ Access to Higher Education ♦ Financing College Education
♦ Teaching and Teacher Education ♦ Asian Americans in Science
♦ Notable Asian Americans in Education

As a result of liberalized immigration policies, Asian Americans have become the fastest-growing racial/ethnic group in the United States. Between 1961 and 1970, 445,300 Asians immigrated to the United States. This number more than tripled to 1,633,800 from 1971 to 1980, and swelled again to 2,817,400 from 1981 to 1990. As the Asian population in the United States has increased, so has its representation in schools, colleges, and universities.

Asian groups have attracted much attention due to their success in prestigious academic competitions, admission into highly selective colleges, and inclination to concentrate their studies in science and engineering. The media tends to overemphasize the academic achievements of Asian students, labeling them as the "model minority." The academic performance of Asian Americans often overshadows the difficulties faced by them. For example, Asian ethnic groups showed significantly different high school completion rates in the 1980 Census; only 22 percent of the Hmong population and 43 percent of Cambodians completed high school, compared with more than 80 percent of Asian Indians, Japanese, Indonesian, and Pakistani individuals. There are also differences in the educational needs of recent immigrants and American-born citizens, as well as between established immigrants and financially deprived newcomers.

Some issues that face young Asian Americans when they enter the U.S. educational system include cultural conflicts, linguistic challenges, access to institutions of higher learning, and financing college education. Asians fear that if they are considered "overrepresented" in college and universities and in certain professions, they will be awarded financial aid at lower rates than other racial/ethnic applicant groups, including whites. At the same time, they worry that their "underrepresentation" in some fields (e.g., education, humanities, public affairs) is being overlooked. College and university administrators must balance equality of educational opportunity and proportional representation, which may be problematic with Asian American applicants.

This chapter presents an overview of the educational progress made by Asian Americans. It contains seven sections and begins by examining pre-kindergarten and elementary schooling for Asian American children. Celia Genishi's analysis depicting the pattern of ability and family influence on achievement in Asian American children will be reviewed. Genishi also looks at cultural conflicts in schooling and discusses curriculum and instruction for Asian American children of diverse language groups. A mixed picture of the strengths and weaknesses of Asian American children emerges, as does a call to schools to provide more responsive instruction for Asian American students' needs.

The second section presents trends in the preparation, participation, and achievement of Asian Americans in higher education. Using SAT Student Descriptive Questionnaire data, college-bound Asian Americans and their preparation for college are profiled. Access to and enrollment of Asian Americans in higher education are reported, with a comparison of undergraduate, graduate, and professional school enrollments. Choice of majors and degrees earned at each level are also discussed.

Section 3 discusses Asian American access to higher education with regard to admission policies and practices of public and private institutions. In the early 1980s, the number of Asian American freshmen diminished with each entering class, despite steadily growing, well-qualified applicant pools. While attention focused on undergraduate admission at Brown, Stanford, Harvard, University of California-Berkeley, and University of California-Los Angeles (UCLA), other evidence indicated that in some fields, graduate and professional schools may have discriminatory policies against Asian applicants.

Section 4 summarizes information about how Asian Americans finance their college education. Samuel Peng and Tai A. Phan review the various sources of financial support (family, federal, state, and institutional aid) that Asian Americans generally receive. They compare average college costs with those of other racial/ethnic groups. On the whole, Asian Americans are less likely to benefit from aid programs than other minorities. As tuition costs rise, the reasons for lower aid rates, particularly for disadvantaged immigrant groups, are worth investigating.

In section 5 A. Lin Goodwin examines the profile of Asian teachers, including educational background, native language, family background, degree-level aspirations, area of specialty, and college experiences. She also attempts to ascertain why teaching ranks so low among Asian Americans as a career. For the teaching force to be truly diverse, Goodwin stresses that Asian Americans should be encouraged to enter the teaching profession.

Section 6 looks at the concentration of Asian Americans in science and engineering, and examines the reasons for their interest and success in these fields. Using National Assessment of Educational Progress (NAEP) data, Beatriz Chu Clewell discusses the achievement of Asian American students in the fourth, eighth, and twelfth grades and compares them to whites, African Americans, and Hispanic Americans. The data reveal many contradictions and puzzling results with regard to home environment, attitudes, and science proficiency in the early grades. Profiles of Asian American college-bound seniors with respect to high school preparation and achievement and the pattern of participation in science and engineering were consistent at the postsecondary level from entry into the freshman year to graduation from a doctoral program.

In section 7, Alan Shoho profiles five prominent Asian American scholars: Kathryn Hu-Pei Au, Kenji Hakuta, Samuel Ichiye Hayakawa, Ronald Takaki, and Lily Wong Fillmore. These are individuals who have improved learning for students from kindergarten to postsecondary education in a wide variety of fields, such as multicultural literacy, bilingual education, semantics, ethnic studies, and linguistics, including semantics and English as a Second Language (ESL).

Asian Americans have a checkered pattern of academic performance. The lack of data on the educational status of individual Asian ethnic subgroups is problematic. There is sufficient evidence suggesting that differences in educational achievement indeed exist, particularly among recent immigrant groups and indigent newcomers. An underlying theme throughout all sections of this chapter is the need for institutions and educational systems to understand and accommodate for the diversity of the Asian American population.

—*Shirley L. Mow*
Westchester Education Coalition, Inc.

◆ PRE-KINDERGARTEN AND ELEMENTARY EDUCATION

Despite the myth that Asian American students comprise a "model minority" and excel in school, their actual educational achievement is uneven and little understood. This section focuses on Asian American students in the earliest stages of formal education, pre-kindergarten and elementary school.

Demographics

The Asian and Asian American population was the fastest growing ethnic group in the United States during the decade from 1980 to 1990. During this time, the U.S. Census shows that it grew from 3,726,440 to 7,272,662, an increase of almost 100 percent. By the year 2000, it is estimated that Asian Americans will represent 4 percent of the U.S. population.

In New York City, the number of Asians and Pacific Islanders more than doubled between 1980 and 1990, increasing their share of the city's population from 3.3 percent to 6.7 percent. This growing population has generated a rapidly rising school-age cohort. Since 1975, there has been a steady annual increase of approximately 3,000 to 5,000 Asian American students in the New York City public school system. At current growth rates, Asian Americans will comprise 10 percent of the New York City public school student population by the year 2000. Across the United States in 1990, there were 130,203 children of Asian or Pacific Islander descent enrolled in pre-primary school and 1,427,074 in elementary or high school (See Table 29.1).

Although there is a tendency to emphasize the educational achievements of the Asian American population, it is, in fact, a highly diverse group with varied histories and cultures. The major categories of origin for Asian Americans are listed here (in alphabetical order): East Asian (including Chinese, Japanese, Korean, and Filipino); Pacific Islanders (including Fijian, Guamanian, Hawaiian, Marshall Islander, Melanesian, Palauan, Samoan, Tahitian, Tongan, Trukese, and Yapese); South Asians (including Bangladeshi, Bhutanese, Burmese, Indian, Nepali, Pakistani, Sri Lankan, and Sikimese); Southeast Asians (including

Table 29.1
Asian/Pacific Islander School Enrollment by State, Preprimary to College

Numbers of Asian/Pacific Islanders age three years and over enrolled in schools in the United States, 1990.

State	Enrolled in:							
	White				Asian or Pacific Islander			
	Preprimary school	Elementary or high school	College	Not enrolled in school	Preprimary school	Elementary or high school	College	Not enrolled in school
Alabama	42,241	480,429	192,902	2,146,889	341	4,708	4,236	11,494
Alaska	9,403	73,864	31,145	279,417	456	3,874	1,434	12,423
Arizona	47,833	460,329	246,642	2,088,322	996	10,110	9,535	30,662
Arkansas	25,537	322,453	99,598	1,422,066	89	3,068	1,436	7,012
California	360,684	3,119,767	1,738,288	14,442,767	46,538	572,418	379,093	1,713,658
Colorado	59,631	475,863	235,374	2,014,312	1,363	12,511	8,767	33,582
Connecticut	60,480	398,993	209,601	2,081,516	1,226	9,369	7,077	28,726
Delaware	9,943	79,552	41,275	382,497	194	1,534	1,451	5,206
Florida	170,393	1,385,232	666,176	8,155,240	2,512	30,252	19,470	92,291
Georgia	81,525	728,099	270,515	3,332,261	1,231	15,503	8,407	45,249
Hawaii	7,540	52,245	26,270	266,904	12,528	124,968	52,165	468,171
Idaho	17,667	196,194	62,928	630,979	137	1,975	1,462	5,121
Illinois	182,292	1,382,046	656,594	6,370,263	5,699	57,544	42,329	166,241
Indiana	86,658	855,850	322,997	3,548,623	814	6,560	8,364	19,021
Iowa	—	—	—	—	—	—	—	—
Kansas	44,648	376,922	164,880	1,552,028	580	7,271	6,362	15,255
Kentucky	46,060	590,792	191,175	2,432,143	416	3,601	2,941	9,478
Louisiana	52,720	496,850	181,998	1,990,471	671	9,478	5,660	22,020
Maine	23,549	202,566	71,536	861,273	162	1,844	867	3,662
Maryland	67,564	482,046	253,753	2,448,176	2,775	26,132	19,335	83,277
Massachusetts	105,990	742,717	465,580	3,887,330	2,873	27,715	27,865	75,205
Michigan	166,386	1,309,449	594,402	5,361,421	2,759	23,748	18,130	52,555
Minnesota	86,175	692,305	302,553	2,873,744	2,367	23,026	10,484	35,049
Mississippi	—	—	—	—	—	—	—	—
Missouri	—	—	—	—	—	—	—	—
Montana	13,000	135,822	45,793	516,871	99	811	717	2,366
Nebraska	—	—	—	—	—	—	—	—
Nevada	16,079	148,626	61,679	743,262	449	6,538	3,375	26,064
New Hampshire	21,648	173,013	74,316	769,307	257	1,813	1,427	5,020
New Jersey	123,900	864,349	400,518	4,507,590	6,462	54,227	27,807	168,331
New Mexico	17,282	210,445	85,846	784,847	283	2,882	2,029	8,447
New York	246,000	1,931,168	1,028,139	9,681,384	10,697	120,885	89,219	438,734
North Carolina	74,796	737,655	332,248	3,675,751	1,009	9,918	7,795	29,265
North Dakota	10,020	109,333	45,072	415,368	67	606	763	1,562
Ohio	173,677	1,589,567	619,467	6,752,519	1,996	18,107	16,507	48,694
Oklahoma	42,600	431,685	175,661	1,837,775	601	6,652	7,152	16,870
Oregon	48,282	427,003	177,928	1,878,090	1,404	13,434	12,662	36,780
Pennsylvania	185,912	1,568,308	672,314	7,699,031	2,908	28,740	22,669	74,108
Rhode Island	15,111	129,322	80,662	658,774	281	4,119	2,706	9,412
South Carolina	36,171	381,467	156,068	1,739,176	342	4,498	2,933	12,716
South Dakota	11,371	113,911	38,007	447,094	55	753	639	1,649
Tennessee	56,985	640,092	225,467	2,973,176	634	6,415	4,000	18,127

Table 29.1
Asian/Pacific Islander School Enrollment by State, Preprimary to College (Continued)

Numbers of Asian/Pacific Islanders age three years and over enrolled in schools in the United States, 1990.

State	Enrolled in:							
	White				Asian or Pacific Islander			
	Preprimary school	Elementary or high school	College	Not enrolled in school	Preprimary school	Elementary or high school	College	Not enrolled in school
Texas	231,125	2,281,927	906,990	8,797,600	5,813	67,122	48,035	178,888
Utah	41,156	393,353	136,470	952,788	715	7,868	5,539	16,675
Vermont	10,956	92,020	39,494	388,098	119	616	667	1,504
Virginia	88,369	714,414	342,954	3,452,598	2,414	32,546	20,169	96,644
Washington	89,301	689,235	288,014	3,062,836	4,715	44,889	26,778	124,899
West Virginia	20,482	303,566	91,659	1,251,294	172	1,579	1,476	3,980
Wisconsin	87,592	754,335	317,667	3,172,381	1,950	14,236	9,810	22,436
Wyoming	8,422	85,565	31,452	283,014	34	611	525	1,397

Notes:
— Data was unavailable at time of publication.

Source: U.S. Bureau of Census, summary Tape File 3A.

Hmong, Indonesian, Khmer, Lao, Malayan, Mien, Singaporean, Thai, and Vietnamese).

Within the Asian American and Pacific Islander population, 22.6 percent report Chinese ancestry, 19.3 percent Filipino, 11.7 percent Japanese, 11.2 percent Indian, 11 percent Korean, and 8.4 percent Vietnamese. Reporting other Asian or Pacific Islander ancestries were 15.8 percent.

Given their geographic and cultural diversity, it is impossible to categorize Asian Americans into a single group. Neither is there one Asian American educational experience. The rapid growth of some Asian American populations has led to the emergence of problematic issues that should attract concern. For example, the Asian American high school dropout rate was 7.4 percent in 1991; by 1992, the rate had risen to 14.5 percent. This means that the rate doubled in one year, while dropout rates for other major ethnic groups remained relatively unchanged.

Characteristics of Asian American Students

Documentation of the achievements of Asian students offers studies contrasting American and Asian educational systems. However, there has been little research on Asian American learners. This is particularly true at the preschool and elementary levels.

In the 1960s, researchers (Lesser, Fifer, and Clark in 1965, and Stodolsky and Lesser in 1967) studied patterns of ability among Chinese, Jewish, African American, and Puerto Rican children in Boston and New York City. They found that the Chinese children outperformed all others on reasoning and spatial scales, were about the same as the Jewish sample in number-related skills, and were below all other groups except for Puerto Rican children in verbal abilities. (Tasks were administered in children's home dialects so that lack of English proficiency was not a factor.)

Research from the 1970s showed Asian immigrant and Asian American elementary school students' intelligence test scores to be consistently higher than those of white students. Jayjia Hsia reported on this research in 1983 and also pointed out the general lack of research on cognitive and learning styles among Asian American students. Studies performed in the 1960s and 1970s on Asian American cooperativeness and math skills have contributed to the stereotype that all Asian students are docile, superior in math, and weak in comparison in language-related abilities. The generalizations documented are suspect because these studies were very few and because the increased number and diversity of Asian American groups in the United States make the findings invalid. Research into the behavior and achievement of cultural groups must be considered in conjunction with the subjects' socioeconomic circumstances for findings to be meaningful. More recent studies indicate that some Asian American students perform better in cooperative rather than competitive situations, and that they are influenced more by external than internal motivators.

Family Influence on Achievement

The degree to which family influence affects achievement is also difficult to generalize. Lee attempted to explain the academic success of sixth- and seventh-grade Japanese American, Chinese American, and Korean American students in Illinois. She found that Asian American parents had higher expectations for their children's educational achievement than white parents.

In a 1987 study involving high school students in the San Francisco Bay area, researchers (Dornbusch, Ritter, Leiderman, Roberts, and Fraleigh) found it difficult to fit Asian American parents into standard parenting classifications—known as "Baumrind's typology"—which categorized them as authoritarian (strict), permissive, or authoritative (influential). The researchers attempted to relate parenting styles to student grades. Of the parents in the sample, which included Asian American, African American, European American, and Mexican American, only the Asian American parents could not be readily classified according to the typology. Within the other groups, students with authoritative parents had higher grades; Asian American students, in contrast, had parents who were more authoritarian and less authoritative. Both of these studies of Asian American parents raise questions about their applicability to Asian Americans in general and suggest a need to examine the validity of instruments or typologies that may not have been developed with culturally diverse groups in mind.

Curriculum

Teaching about diverse cultural groups has traditionally been part of the social studies curriculum. Recently, educators from a range of fields and age/grade levels addressed controversies over a general multicultural curriculum from preschool and elementary years through higher education. It is argued that as the population and demographics of the United States changes, particularly in urban areas, there is a need to include the history and culture of multiple groups, including Asians and Asian Americans.

National clearinghouses such as Education Resources Information Center (ERIC) have disseminated programs and curricula related to Asians and Asian Americans since the 1980s. In the early 1990s, areas of focus included programs in bilingual math and science, multicultural arts, ethnic and women's studies, and English as a second language within Asian American studies. Not surprisingly, federal funded programs have been developed largely for Chinese and Filipino speakers, the two largest Asian American language groups. Unfortunately, they are often not available in a

Cover illustration by Laurence Yep for *Dragonwings*.

format that teachers can readily adapt. Further, the languages and dialects of Asian Americans are so numerous that curricula specific to many are unavailable.

The subject areas that affect the greatest number of students in and out of Asian American communities are literature and the language arts. There are growing numbers of books written for children and young adults focusing on Asian Americans' stories in the United States. Notable among them are *Children of the River* (1989), by Crew; *Screen of Frogs: An Old Tale* (1993), *The Terrible Eek: A Japanese Tale* (1991), and *The Journey: Japanese Americans, Racism, and Renewal* (1990), by Sheila Hamanaka; and the works of Allen Say, Yoshiko Uchida, and Lawrence Yep.

Guidelines for the selection and use of literature in curricula have been developed by numerous education scholars, notably Duff and Tongchinsub (1990), Harris (1991), Pang, and Colvin, Tran, and Barba (1992). Because literature is increasingly used as the primary material for reading instruction, it is likely to become the major curricular tool for broadening public knowledge about the history and contemporary experiences of Asian Americans.

Cover illustration for *Grandfather's Journey.*

Cover illustration for *The Boy of the Three-Year Nap.*

Linguistic Abilities and Challenges

In 1980, an estimated 34,637,000 people in the United States lived in families where a language other than English was spoken. The number is increasing, and for some groups of Asian Americans, this means that more children enter school without a knowledge of English.

In 1990 a total of 769,000 people lived in homes with Chinese speakers and 713,000 lived in homes with Filipino speakers. By the year 2000, it is predicted that 38,300 five- to fourteen-year-old Filipino speakers and 36,200 five- to fourteen-year-old Chinese speakers will be categorized as "limited English proficient."

English as a Second Language

The capacity to acquire and use a first language is universal. Given ordinary physical and emotional circumstances, everyone acquires the language of the surrounding environment. In the United States, most people believe that if one's mother tongue is not English, he or she must learn English as a second language since the ability to speak and write English is key to success in school. Research on how Asian American students learn English as a second language and how well they achieve in school is complex. Two researchers, Cummins and Hakuta, present evidence that a child's ability to speak two languages (the home or primary language and a second language) leads to superior cognitive abilities and academic achievement. A strong argument in favor of bilingual education, according to research, is that students learn all subject matter better if maintaining their home language (L1) while acquiring or learning a second language (L2).

Despite these findings, there is little public support for bilingual programs that foster maintenance of the L1. Many teachers and parents expect schools to take primary responsibility for teaching English as the foundation for academic learning and standard mode of communication. Indeed, researchers Duncan and DeAvila found that English proficiency is the most consistent predictor of achievement among language minority groups.

Other studies presented more specific findings: English proficiency, as measured by reading scores on the California Test of Basic Skills or CTBS, predicted grade-point average among Southeast Asian students. However, math proficiency, as measured by the CTBS, was an even better predictor of grade-point average for this group. Research findings suggest that bilingual children are likely to demonstrate higher cognitive ability.

Instructional Practices: One Language or Two?

There is a broad range of practices with contrasting instructional goals for children of diverse language groups:

• Maintenance program. This approach uses only L1, the home language, in all areas of instruction.

• Bilingual program. This approach uses both L1 and the second language, L2 (English), in instruction.

• Sheltered English program. This approach uses L2 with many contextual cues and visual props, but without a focus on grammar.

Table 29.2
Home Language by State, 1991

State	Only English	Chinese	Japanese	Korean	Tagalog	Vietnamese	Mon-Khmer	Greek	Italian
Alabama	3,651,936	3,728	2,480	3,232	1,019	2,231	435	1,937	2,853
Alaska	435,260	815	1,450	3,333	5,124	273	57	212	289
Arizona	2,674,519	9,536	3,362	4,829	4,188	4,186	769	2,202	8,892
Arkansas	2,125,884	1,387	1,083	1,112	894	1,701	75	565	1,279
California	18,764,213	575,447	147,451	215,845	464,644	233,074	59,622	32,889	111,133
Colorado	2,722,355	6,261	5,083	8,306	2,769	5,901	807	2,226	5,656
Connecticut	2,593,825	8,234	2,918	2,792	3026	3,378	1,116	10,554	71,309
Delaware	575,393	1,805	424	932	602	382	42	1,177	3,376
Florida	9,996,969	20,839	7,485	9,299	19,618	13,648	1,185	21,396	70,636
Georgia	5,699,642	11,181	6,270	13,433	3,503	6,483	1,659	3,399	4,686
Hawaii	771,485	26,366	69,587	14,636	55,341	4,620	81	177	949
Idaho	867,708	1,029	1,287	550	441	528	50	262	640
Illinois	9,086,726	41,807	13,174	33,973	46,453	7,572	2,565	42,976	66,903
Indiana	4,900,334	6,017	4,722	3,693	2,367	2,112	243	5,287	5,264
Iowa	—	—	—	—	—	—	—	—	—
Kansas	2,158,011	4,272	1,416	3,221	1,375	5,625	576	564	1,402
Kentucky	3,348,473	2,596	2,306	2,676	1,098	1,491	174	664	1,850
Louisiana	3,494,359	4,727	1,385	2,607	2,214	14,352	187	1,391	4,933
Maine	1,036,681	709	553	562	608	6,91	772	1,085	1,814
Maryland	4,030,234	24,508	5,090	23,563	11,329	7,181	1,773	13,146	15,980
Massachusetts	47,53,523	43,248	6,849	7,935	3,800	12,655	1,2178	33,006	81,987
Michigan	8,024,930	15,378	8,478	9,978	8,707	4,817	541	13,431	38,023
Minnesota	3,811,700	6,844	1871	3,368	2,414	8,314	2,699	1,351	2,870
Mississippi	—	—	—	—	—	—	—	—	—
Missouri	—	—	—	—	—	—	—	—	—
Montana	703,198	487	609	283	256	211	6	303	767
Nebraska	—	—	—	—	—	—	—	—	—
Nevada	964,298	5,204	2,322	3,324	8,007	1,739	215	1,313	5,335
New Hampshire	935,825	1,520	465	995	575	187	259	4,086	2,440
New Jersey	5,794,548	47,334	14,272	30,712	38,107	4,892	486	28,080	154,160
New Mexico	896,049	1,686	1,134	1,173	1,017	1,144	37	578	1,880
New York	12,834,328	247,334	29,845	80,394	46,276	11,531	3,169	87,608	400,218
North Carolina	5,931,435	7,252	4,949	6,053	3,019	4,111	1,420	5,354	4,801
North Dakota	543,942	425	171	387	331	212	14	49	106
Ohio	9,517,064	15,475	9,058	8,515	6,328	3,997	1,932	15,391	41,179
Oklahoma	2,775,957	5,052	2,003	3,471	1,462	5,998	303	662	2,022
Oregon	2,448,772	10,099	6,724	5,574	3,391	7,468	2,036	1,295	3,114
Pennsylvania	10,278,294	24,857	5,570	181,16	7,605	12,843	4,232	17,982	103,844
Rhode Island	776,931	2,640	407	716	1,069	570	3,285	1,853	2,0619
South Carolina	3,118,376	2,343	2,133	2,318	2,976	1,457	227	2,940	2,735
South Dakota	599,232	376	212	392	305	199	140	144	210
Tennessee	44,131,93	5,024	3,393	3,775	1,687	2,058	888	1,598	2,501
Texas	11,635,518	52,220	11,898	26,228	22,256	57,736	5,620	6,422	10,871

Table 29.2
Home Language by State, 1991 (Continued)

State	Only English	Chinese	Japanese	Korean	Tagalog	Vietnamese	Mon-Khmer	Greek	Italian
Utah	1,432,947	4,483	4,428	2,294	962	2,285	981	1,886	2,446
Vermont	491,112	453	289	144	187	137	12	421	1,289
Virginia	5,327,898	18,037	5,370	25,736	21,018	19,025	3,319	7,453	9,567
Washington	4,098,706	26,378	17,626	23,190	24,574	15,488	9,579	2,959	6,305
West Virginia	1,642,729	1,089	808	586	815	215	16	946	4,691
Wisconsin	4,267,496	5,762	1,884	2,788	1,830	1,899	344	2856	8,661
Wyoming	394,904	401	239	168	198	60	9	321	460
Total	187,346,912	1,302,665	420,533	617,207	835,785	496,677	126,135	382,397	1,292,945

Notes:
— Data unavailable at time of publication.

Source: Asian/Pacific Islander Data Consortium (San Francisco: Asian and Pacific Islander Center for Census Information and Services, 1993). Primary source: U.S. Census Bureau, Summary Tape Files 1 and 3.

• Natural approach, content-based instruction. This approach teaches L2, English, as a specific part of the curriculum.

• Immersion program. In this approach only L2 is used in all areas of instruction, without a focus on learning L2 consciously but acquiring it unconsciously.

Although each approach has specific characteristics that differentiate it from the others, in practice these programs overlap and are modified by individual schools and teachers. As noted earlier, programs that introduce children to English early in their schooling are the most common. This preference for early teaching of English reflects social and political realities. The United States is an English-speaking country. Thus, English is the primary tool for succeeding in school and securing employment.

Yet experts in bilingual education argue that schools do children and their families a disservice if they foster the loss of the home language, which can sever cultural roots and family connection, traditionally of great importance in Asian American families. The challenge to educators is to provide information about the entire range of language programs and to open and sustain dialogues with parents and other community members so that everyone becomes aware of bilingual education programs and of their advantages and disadvantages.

Cultural Conflicts in Schooling

Individuals of groups whose history and culture differ from that of mainstream United States probably experience some degree of difficulty in adjusting to U.S. schools. Asian Americans students observe classrooms and school values that contrast with their Asian values. At the same time, their efforts to adapt to the values and behavior of their U.S. peers may put them into conflict with their parents or family members.

Betty Lee Sung, noted Asian American academician, identified a number of conflicts that many Asian American students face, whether they are immigrants to or natives of the United States:

Asian children are raised to divert aggressive behavior, whereas a "macho," tough, masculine image is popular in U.S. culture. This is a particular problem for Asian male students.

Sexual appeal is subtle in Asian cultures, whereas in the United States sexual appeal is overt. Teenage Asian females are most affected by this issue.

Asian children are often quick to report wrongdoing to teachers; their U.S. peers view reporters as "tattlers."

Greater value is placed on scholastic achievement in Asian cultures than in U.S. culture.

Being thrifty is a valuable trait in many Asian cultures, whereas conspicuous consumption is practiced in many U.S. communities.

Immigrant Asian parents discourage their children from becoming independent and from socializing outside of the family until a later age than many U.S. parents.

Immigrant Asian children struggle with the fact that in the United States authority figures are not shown great respect by their inferiors. They find this to be especially noteworthy in the relationship between students and teachers.

Asians often view themselves in terms of their relationships with other people. Their success and happiness are dependent upon others, whereas much of American culture stresses individualism.

Table 29.3
English Proficiency by Age and U.S. State, 1990

State	5 to 17 years Speak English			18 to 64 years Speak English			65 over Speak English		
	Very well	Well	Not well or not at all	Very well	Well	Not well or not at all	Very well	Well	Not well or not at all
Alabama	1,682	607	466	6,018	4,377	2,091	222	167	212
Alaska	1,391	373	240	4,738	3,363	1900	114	206	365
Arizona	3,026	1178	564	12,058	8,380	4255	687	439	656
Arkansas	1,484	344	227	3,041	1,908	1,538	137	107	186
California	192,323	106,536	66,479	608,057	433,836	328,312	44,086	38,862	87,494
Colorado	3,848	1,691	1,207	11,181	8,709	5,971	761	541	1,258
Connecticut	2,677	1,184	796	10,507	6,362	4,098	395	161	567
Delaware	468	126	62	2,298	1,383	551	84	38	63
Florida	8,696	3,477	1,289	35,168	21,953	10,937	1,665	1,044	1,765
Georgia	5,768	2,579	1,636	16,293	13,916	9,529	444	206	884
Hawaii	1,5934	7,397	3,158	71,775	46,531	26,170	20,430	18,308	16,299
Idaho	558	118	96	2,042	1,179	691	172	118	85
Illinois	1,7276	6,481	3,807	65,849	39,577	22,375	3,223	2,523	5,662
Indiana	2,101	692	541	9,381	5,957	3,348	395	140	339
Iowa	—	—	—	—	—	—	—	—	—
Kansas	2,517	1,315	734	6,776	5,950	3,570	188	72	284
Kentucky	1,122	457	426	4,899	3,071	1,898	138	83	200
Louisiana	4,081	2,371	958	9,181	6,524	4,932	282	144	544
Maine	457	243	105	1,534	1,091	622	25	22	79
Maryland	9,041	2,976	1,733	31,725	20,693	13,099	1,387	1,056	2,450
Massachusetts	8,636	6,314	4,194	30,559	22,456	19,438	1,226	811	3,072
Michigan	6,687	2,777	1,724	23,572	13,873	8,073	938	586	1,196
Minnesota	5,869	4,849	3,890	11,461	10,967	8,954	283	166	1,337
Mississippi	—	—	—	—	—	—	—	—	—
Missouri	—	—	—	—	—	—	—	—	—
Montana	229	84	44	1,093	594	248	36	35	49
Nebraska	—	—	—	—	—	—	—	—	—
Nevada	2,497	897	400	9,786	6,630	3,298	507	347	708
New Hampshire	490	267	126	2,044	1,341	712	33	40	87
New Jersey	16,893	6,405	3726	61,154	37,838	19,189	2,234	2,001	4,231
New Mexico	822	411	136	3,192	2,013	1,035	183	81	77
New York	42,822	20,635	11,127	133,414	104,370	114,186	5,620	5,259	22,440
North Carolina	3,330	1,477	883	12,512	8,547	5,181	402	213	538
North Dakota	107	36	17	884	582	177	1	8	0
Ohio	5,010	2,522	1,593	21,689	13,650	7,631	888	456	1,156
Oklahoma	2,156	995	580	8,540	6,464	3,034	315	104	387
Oregon	4,750	1,988	825	14,116	10,747	7,051	1,134	610	1,249
Pennsylvania	9,364	4,059	2,958	29,234	20,032	14,800	1,178	865	2,295
Rhode Island	1,465	1141	929	3,888	2,113	2,679	221	68	252
South Carolina	1,250	551	170	5,967	3,510	1,681	345	104	171
South Dakota	177	51	55	923	567	257	16	5	3
Tennessee	2,590	809	633	8,194	5,281	3,263	365	197	304
Texas	25,808	9,701	5,655	71,530	54,959	30,944	2,224	1,409	4,803
Utah	2,928	1,118	434	8,652	5,013	2,996	492	273	440

Table 29.3
English Proficiency by Age and U.S. State, 1990 (Continued)

State	5 to 17 years Speak English			18 to 64 years Speak English			65 over Speak English		
	Very well	Well	Not well or not at all	Very well	Well	Not well or not at all	Very well	Well	Not well or not at all
Vermont	131	52	15	676	421	225	36	14	16
Virginia	11,109	4,137	2,127	39,826	25,966	15,402	1,307	984	2,573
Washington	14,976	6,956	4,060	44,665	30,603	22,333	3,051	2,521	4,651
West Virginia	464	95	81	2,025	1,096	413	115	27	54
Wisconsin	3,548	3,492	2,907	8,976	6,814	6,433	379	240	926
Wyoming	62	12	4	516	373	157	49	35	2

Notes:
— Data unavailable at time of publication.

Source: Asian/Pacific Islander Data Consortium (San Francisco: Asian and Pacific Islander Center for Census Information and Services, 1993). Primary source: U.S. Census Bureau, Summary Tape Files 1 and 3.

In addition to the contrasts that Sung highlights, there is a notable difference between U.S. and Asian classrooms in the value placed on verbal acuity. Being talkative at appropriate times is often a positive trait in U.S. classrooms. Asian American students, who come from cultures in which talking a lot is considered rude, find this problematic; it seems neither natural nor respectful for students to be verbally expressive. These conflicting cultural characteristics affect individual students differently, but because of the traditionally strong link between Asian American children and their families, disagreements may become intense and close relationships may become fragile the longer a child is exposed to U.S. classroom culture. However, very few descriptive accounts of how students are affected by these conflicts in and out of school are available.

Conclusions: A Mixed Picture

The increasing diversity within the Asian American population creates a mixed picture of the strengths and weaknesses of Asian American preschool and elementary students and raises questions about the schools' ability to address these students' needs. Learning English is clearly a prime consideration, but this also implies a possible weakening of ties to family members and their culturally defined habits and expectations.

Far more needs to be known about all aspects of this mixed picture: from demographic data to knowledge of how children learn—namely, how they learn to adapt to a full range of curricular content, to speak and write English, to adjust to the varied demands of schooling, and to reconcile the values of American culture with those of their families. Greater attention to the specific needs of each individual Asian American community is needed, along with resources for innovative programs and research on how educational practices affect young learners in these communities.

—Celia Genishi
Teachers College, Columbia University

◆ HIGHER EDUCATION

The fact that the number of Asian Americans in the United States doubled during the 1980s and continues to grow has enormous implications for higher education. As a group, Asian Americans are the most-educated ethnic population in the United States. The 1991 Census reported that 81.8 percent of Asian Americans over 25 had completed high school, compared with 79.9 percent of whites and 78.4 percent of the total U.S. population.

Asian Americans are also more likely to have completed four years of college than any other ethnic group including whites. In 1980, 33 percent of Asian Americans age 25 and over had at least four years of college. By 1990, the proportion rose to 40 percent, almost double the 23 percent for whites.

Asian American participation in higher education will most likely continue to grow because of the increasing number of Asian American students in elementary and secondary public schools. Enrollment is projected to reach 1.6 million in 1995 with more than 98,000 high school graduates in the same year.

As a group, Asian Americans appear to be slightly overrepresented at many levels of the educational

Table 29.4
Educational Attainment of Persons 25 Years Old and Over, by Sex, Region, and Race: March 1991
(Numbers in thousands)

Educational attainment	Total population			Asian and Pacific Islander		
	Both sexes	Male	Female	Both sexes	Male	Female
United States						
Total, 25 years old and over	158,694	75,487	83,207	4,158	1,931	2,227
Elementary:						
Total	10.6	11.0	10.3	12.4	10.2	14.3
0 to 4 years	2.4	2.7	2.1	5.3	4.3	6.2
5 to 7 years	3.8	3.9	3.7	4.4	3.2	5.4
8 years	4.4	4.5	4.4	2.7	2.7	2.7
High School:						
Total	49.6	46.5	52.4	34.4	32.4	36.1
1 to 3 years	11.0	10.4	11.4	5.8	6.0	5.7
4 years	38.6	36.0	41.0	28.5	26.4	30.3
College:						
Total	39.8	42.5	37.4	53.2	57.4	49.6
1 to 3 years	18.4	18.2	18.6	14.2	14.2	14.2
4 years	12.7	13.6	11.9	23.3	22.8	23.7
5 or more years	8.8	10.8	6.9	15.8	20.4	11.8
Percent 4 years of high school or more	78.4	78.5	78.3	81.8	83.8	80.0

Source: Claudette E. Bennett, Economics and Statistics Administration, Bureau of the Census, U.S. Department of Commerce, The Asian and Pacific Islander Population in the United States: March 1990 and 1991, Current Population Reports, Population Characteristics, P20-459 (Washington, DC: U.S. Government Printing Office, August 1992)

system, although some Asian American subgroups may be underrepresented. Because data on more than 30 different ethnic groups are lumped together into the Asian American category, it is not possible to examine the differences in participation and achievement of the individual Asian ethnic groups. This section will focus on the preparation, enrollment, and achievement of Asian Americans in higher education as a group.

College Preparation

What factors are related to the relatively high level of participation by Asian Americans in higher education? How do they progress through the educational pipeline? As indicated earlier, more Asians are college bound, as evidenced by the increasing numbers who take the Scholastic Assessment Test (SAT). In 1993, 83,096 Asians took the SAT, up from 68,824 in 1988, a 20.7 percent increase in five years. Asians accounted for 7.5 percent of all SAT takers and were overrepresented compared to their proportion of the general population. On the other hand, fewer and fewer white students are taking the SAT, declining by more than 112,000 students, or 13.8 percent, over the same period.

The Student Descriptive Questionnaire (SDQ) of the

SAT provides background data on college-bound Asian high school seniors including noncitizens and citizens.

SAT Scores

The Scholastic Assessment Test (SAT) consists of two parts—verbal and math. In 1993, the mean verbal test score for Asian students was 415 (of a possible 800), a seven point improvement over the mean of 408 in 1988. Similarly, Asian students' 1993 mean math score of 535 was higher than the mean of 522 in 1988. Compared with white SAT test takers, Asians scored lower on the verbal portion of the test but higher on the math section. Asian females were as likely as males to take the SAT, although they scored lower than males on both the verbal and math portions of the test. (Interestingly, this same scoring difference between males and females occurred among all ethnic groups).

High School Participation and Achievement

In preparation for college, most Asian students completed an aggregate of study in six academic subjects in high school. Many of them planned to get advanced-placement credit for these subjects in college. Table 29.5 shows that a majority (80 percent) of the students

Table 29.5
Years of Study by Subject, in Percent Asian College-Bound Seniors: 1993 SAT Profiles

Years	English	Art/Music	Social Science/ History	Foreign Lang/ Class Lang	Natural Sciences	Mathematics
More than 4 yrs	13	6	8	8	15	21
4 yrs	67	8	32	20	35	51
3 or 3.5 yrs	15	9	41	30	32	22
2 or 2.5 yrs	4	17	14	29	14	4
1 or 1.5 yrs	1	36	3	6	3	0
less than 1 yr	0	23	1	6	1	0

Notes:
Totals do not equal 100 percent because of "no responses."

Source: The College Board, College-Bound Seniors, Asian Report: 1993 Profile of SAT and Achievement Test Takers (New York: The College Board), unpublished data.

took at least four years of English, three years of social sciences and history (81 percent), and three years of foreign or classical languages (58 percent). In most instances, the foreign language taken was either French or Spanish, but a significant number of students (22 percent) also studied other languages less likely to be studied by other U.S. students.

Overall, Asian students were more likely than all test applicants to take science and math courses. Eighty-two percent of Asian test applicants completed at least three years of natural sciences and almost all (94 percent) took at least three years of mathematics. On the other hand, they were less likely to take art or music in high school. Asian female students were more inclined to study art, music, foreign and classical languages, but were less inclined to study math or natural sciences than their male counterparts.

Table 29.6 compares high school rank and grade point average (GPA) with mean SAT scores of Asian test applicants. More than a quarter of the students

Table 29.6
Asian College-Bound Seniors: 1993 SAT Profiles High School Rank and GPA

	Number of SAT Takers	Percent	% Male/Female	SAT-V Mean	SAT-M Mean
High School Rank					
Top Tenth	20,815	29	50/50	502	630
Second Tenth	17,526	25	50/50	418	553
Second Fifth	17,629	25	52/48	384	505
Third Fifth	12,508	18	50/50	351	447
Fourth Fifth	1,854	3	54/46	330	411
Fifth Fifth	517	1	53/47	313	387
No response	7,844	—	—	—	—
High School GPA					
A+ (97-100)	6,138	8	48/52	546	658
A (93-96)	13,992	18	45/55	476	607
A- (90-92)	13,703	18	47/53	439	571
B (80-89)	34,047	45	51/49	380	496
C (70-79)	8,195	11	59/41	337	437
D, E, or F (Below 70)	402	1	69/31	324	473
No response	2,216	—	—	—	—

Source: The College Board, College-Bound Seniors Asian Report: 1993 Profile of SAT and Achievement Test Takers (New York: The College Board), unpublished data.

Table 29.7
Asian College-Bound Seniors: 1993 SAT Profiles Intended College Major and Degree-Level Goal

	Number of SAT Takers	Percent	% Male/Female	SAT-V Mean	SAT-M Mean
Intended College Major					
Agriculture/Natural Resources	340	0	45/55	408	483
Architecture/Environ. Design	2,337	3	61/39	382	537
Arts: Visual & Performing	3,258	4	39/61	386	491
Biological Sciences	4,680	6	45/55	467	577
Business & Commerce	12,860	17	46/54	378	509
Communications	1,699	2	25/75	443	503
Computer/Information Sciences	2,994	4	71/29	381	541
Education	2,210	3	23/77	385	477
Engineering	11,703	15	82/18	421	590
Foreign/Classical Languages	400	1	24/76	397	536
General/Interdisciplinary	216	0	37/63	501	567
Health & Allied Services	19,456	25	41/59	428	532
Home Economics	136	0	23/77	346	449
Language & Literature	679	1	26/74	508	555
Library & Archival Sciences	23	0	48/52	394	499
Mathematics	462	1	53/47	410	625
Military Sciences	247	0	81/19	404	487
Philosophy/Religion/Theology	177	0	60/40	456	534
Physical Sciences	1107	1	62/38	472	619
Public Affairs & Services	917	1	50/50	372	452
Social Sciences & History	6,244	8	33/67	459	534
Technical & Vocational	486	1	70/30	308	421
Undecided	3,879	5	50/50	418	539
Degree Level Goal					
Certificate Program	1,152	2	54/46	318	463
Associate Degree	873	1	45/55	304	406
Bachelor's Degree	13,129	17	50/50	355	475
Master's Degree	21,611	29	52/48	410	538
Doctoral/Related Degree	25,822	34	50/50	473	588
Other	654	1	45/55	301	432
Undecided	12,358	16	47/53	400	520

*Source:*The College Board, *College-Bound Seniors Asian Report: 1993 Profile of SAT and Achievement Test Takers (New York: The College Board), unpublished data.*

ranked in the top tenth: twenty-five percent in both the second tenth and the second fifth of their class. The majority of Asian students achieved high school grade averages of B or better. Not surprisingly, those students who placed higher in school rank or who completed more years of study in academic subjects had higher GPAs and scored higher on the SAT in both the verbal and math sections than students with lower school rank, lower GPAs, or fewer years of study.

American College Testing (ACT) data also reported that students who prepare academically for college by taking core high school or college preparatory programs consistently score higher on the ACT Assessment than students who do not. This relationship generally holds true across ethnic groups, as well as across family income levels.

Type and Location of High School Attended

The overwhelming majority, 83 percent, of the Asian SAT applicants attended public schools. Relatively few, 11 percent, went to religious-affiliated high schools and a small percentage, 6 percent, attended independent

Table 29.8
Total Enrollment in Higher Education by Race/Ethnicity: Fall 1980 to 1991
(Numbers in Thousands)

	1980	1982	1984	1986	1988	1990	1991	Percent change 1980-90	Percent change 1990-91
All institutions	12,087	12,388	12,235	12,504	13,043	13,820	14,359	14.3	3.9
White (non-hispanic)	9,833	9,997	9,815	9,921	10,283	10,723	10,990	9.1	2.5
Total minority	1,949	2,059	2,085	2,238	2,400	2,706	2,953	38.8	9.1
African American (non-Hispanic)	1,107	1,101	1,076	1,082	1,130	1,247	1,335	12.6	7.1
Hispanic	472	519	535	618	680	783	867	65.9	10.7
Asian American (a)	286	351	390	448	497	573	637	100.0	11.2
American Indian (b)	84	88	84	90	93	103	114	22.6	10.7
Nonresident Alien	305	331	335	345	361	391	416	28.2	6.4

Notes:
Because of underreporting/nonreporting of racial/ethnic data, data prior to 1986 were estimated when possible. Also, due to rounding, detail may not add to totals. Data for fall 1990 have been revised from previously published figures. For fall of 1991, the response rate was 90.9 percent for institutions of higher education while in the fall of 1990, the response rate for institutions of higher education was 86.8 percent. Imputed enrollment data (for nonresponding institutions and cases with incomplete data) accounted for on average less than 3.5 percent of the enrollment data for four year institutions and are substantially higher (approximately 24 percent) for two-year institutions.
(a) Asian American includes Pacific Islanders.
(b) American Indian includes Alaskan Natives.

Source: *U.S. Department of Education, National Center for Education Statistics, Trends in Enrollment in Higher Education by Racial/Ethnic Category: Fall 1980 through Fall 1991. Washington, D.C.: U.S. Department of Education, January 1993. Deborah J. Carter and Reginald Wilson, Minorities in Higher Education: 1992 (Washington, D.C.: American Council on Education).*

schools. Those who attended independent schools had higher mean scores on both the verbal and math sections of the test than those who attended public or religious-affiliated institutions.

Student and Family Background

Recent Asian college-bound seniors are not likely to be the first in their family to go to college. Parents of almost a third of the students had baccalaureate degrees, 28 percent had graduate degrees, and 5 percent had associate's degrees. Only 11 percent of the parents had no high school diploma.

Asian SAT takers were also likely to be noncitizens. Only 57 percent of the Asian high school seniors who took the SAT were U.S. citizens, compared to 98 percent of whites and 92 percent of the national sample. Twenty-eight percent were permanent residents and fifteen percent had nonresident status. Interestingly, noncitizens scored significantly higher on the math section of the test than U.S. citizens. As expected, U.S. citizens scored higher on the verbal portion than noncitizens. English was the first language for only 30 percent of the Asian students, compared to 83 percent of all test applicants.

College Major And Degree Goal

The most popular intended undergraduate majors among college-bound Asian students were health and allied services (25 percent), business (17 percent), and engineering (15 percent). These fields were also common choices among all test applicants. Not surprisingly, Asians planning to major in math or physical sciences scored highest in the math portion of the SAT. Similarly, those intending to pursue undergraduate studies in language and literature achieved the highest scores in the verbal section of the test. While females were more likely to major in social science, history, business, and health and allied services, males had greater preference for engineering, computer science, and physical sciences. Overall, there appeared to be a slight shift among Asians away from business and engineering toward the health fields during the early 1990s.

Since 1988, degree aspirations of Asian high school seniors appear to have risen. The proportion of those indicating the baccalaureate as their degree goal dropped, with a corresponding rise in the proportion of those aspiring to the doctorate. Those intending to earn master's or doctoral degrees scored higher on both the verbal and math sections of the SAT than those pursuing associate's or bachelor's degrees.

Table 29.9
Asian American Total Enrollment in Higher Education by Type and Control of Institution,
Fall 1980 to 1991
(Numbers in Thousands)

Type	1980	1982	1984	1986	1988	1990	1991	% Change 90-91
4-yr Inst.	162	193	223	262	297	357	381	6.7
2-yr Inst.	124	158	167	186	199	215	256	19.1
Pub. Inst.	240	296	323	371	406	461	516	11.9
Indep. Inst.	47	55	67	77	91	112	121	8.0

Notes:
Because of underreporting/nonreporting or racial/ethnic data, data prior to 1986 were estimated when possible. Also, due to rounding, detail may not add to totals. Data for Fall 1990 have been revised from previously published figures. For Fall of 1991, the response rate was 90.9 percent for institutions of higher education while in the Fall of 1990, the response rate for institutions of higher education was 86.8 percent.

Source: Deborah J. Carter and Reginald Wilson, Minorities in Higher Education: 1992 (Washington, D.C.: American Council on Education). U.S. Department of Education. National Center for Education Statistics. Friends in Enrollment in Higher Education by Racial Ethnic Category: Fall 1980 through Fall 1991. Washington, D.C.: U.S. Department of Education, January 1993.

Higher Education Enrollment

Large-scale databases, such as those maintained by the National Center for Education Statistics (NCES), Higher Education Information System (HEGIS), the Integrated Postsecondary Education Data System (IPEDS), and the National Research Council's Survey of Earned Doctorates, collect useful data on college-enrollment trends, fields of study, and degrees conferred by ethnicity. Nonresident aliens are generally separated as a distinct category and are not included in the ethnic groupings in most of these data compilations.

In 1990, for every 100 students attending U.S. colleges and universities, four were Asian Americans. Table 29.8 shows that between 1980 and 1990, Asian Americans were the fastest-growing ethnic group in higher education. Their total number rose from 286,000 in 1980 to 573,000 in 1990, a 100-percent increase. By contrast, enrollment of African Americans increased by 12.6 percent, Hispanics by 65.9 percent, whites by 9.1 percent, and total enrollment by 14.3 percent during the same period.

Type and Control of Institution

Increases in Asian American participation in higher education continue to outpace other ethnic groups in the 1990s. From 1990 to 1991, total enrollment increased by 3.9 percent, while Asian American enrollment grew more than 11 percent, the largest increase among all ethnic groups. Much of the increase occurred at community colleges (19.1 percent). In 1991, however, Asian Americans were still more likely to attend four-year institutions (59.8 percent) than two-year colleges (40.2 percent).

Asian Americans were also four times more likely to attend public than private institutions of higher education, a trend that is likely to continue in the 1990s. Between 1990 and 1991, Asian American enrollment at public institutions increased 11.9 percent, compared to 8 percent at independent colleges. This may reflect rising tuition costs and the desire of new immigrant groups to attend community colleges closer to home.

State Enrollment Trends

In the 1980s, the Asian American population increased in every state and doubled in 31. Asian American enrollment in higher education during this time doubled in 36 states. Two-thirds of this population growth occurred in California, New York, Texas, and Illinois. In these states, Asian Americans were generally overrepresented in higher education compared to their proportion of the total population.

Table 29.10 compares Asian American enrollments at two- and four-year institutions in California, New York, Texas, and Illinois. In California, where Asian Americans represented 9.6 percent of the population in 1990, they accounted for 10.4 percent of all enrollments at two-year colleges and 16.5 percent at four-year institutions. Similarly, in Illinois, they represented 2.5 percent of the total population, but accounted for 3.8 percent of community college enrollment and 5.1 percent of four-year college enrollment. Asian Americans comprised 3.9 percent of New York's total population compared to 2.8 percent of all community college students and 5.7 percent of all four-year enrollees.

From 1980 to 1990, Texas reported the largest percentage increases in the number of Asian Americans

Table 29.10
Asian American Higher Education Enrollment by State and Type of Institution, 1980 and 1990

| STATES | Percent of State Population | | Percent Change | TWO-YEAR INSTITUTIONS | | | | | FOUR-YEAR INSTITUTIONS | | | | | ALL INSTITUTIONS | | |
| | | | | | Percent | | Percent | Percent Change | | Percent | | Percent | Percent Change | | | Percent Change |
	1980	1990	1980-90	1980	1980	1990	1990	1980-90	1980	1980	1990	1990	1980-90	1980	1990	1980-90
California	5.3	9.6	127.0	71,653	6.3	111,355	10.4	55.4	57,645	8.8	116,017	16.5	101.3	129,298	227,372	5.9
Illinois	1.4	2.5	78.7	5,640	1.8	13,636	3.8	141.8	8,060	2.4	18,717	5.1	132.2	13,700	32,353	136.2
New York	1.8	3.9	123.4	3,712	1.3	7,759	2.8	109.0	18,894	2.7	43,282	5.7	129.1	22,606	51,040	125.8
Texas	0.8	1.9	165.5	2,674	1.0	10,593	2.7	296.1	4,652	1.1	17,314	3.4	272.2	7,326	27,907	280.9

Notes:
Although the HEGIS and IPEDS data reported here are historically comparable in items of the reporting institutions, there are some differences in imputation procedures in the two surveys.

Source: Deborah J. Carter and Reginald Wilson, Minorities in Higher Education: 1992 (Washington, D.C.: American Council on Education)Bureau of the Census, 1990 Census. U.S. Department of Education, National Center for Education Statistics, 1980 Higher Education Information System (HEGIS) and 1990 Integrated Postsecondary Education Data System (IPIDS), Fall Enrollment Surveys.

enrolled at community colleges (296.1 percent) and four-year institutions (272.2 percent) among all states. Asian Americans made up 2.7 percent of the total enrollment at two-year institutions and 3.4 percent at four-year institutions—approximately equal to their representation in the total state population.

Undergraduate Enrollment

The number of Asian American undergraduates almost doubled (98 percent) in the 1980s. The increase for all minority undergraduates was 37.3 percent and 13.2 percent for total undergraduate enrollment. Of the 638,000 Asian Americans enrolled in colleges and universities in the United States in 1991, 88 percent were undergraduates.

From 1990 to 1991, Asian Americans, along with Native Americans, reported the largest increase, 11.6 percent in undergraduate enrollment among all ethnic groups. In comparison, African American undergraduate enrollment grew by 7.1 percent, Hispanic by 10.9 percent, and white by 2.5 percent. Total undergraduate enrollment increased by 4.0 percent.

In the academic year 1992-93, Asian Americans accounted for 3.7 percent of all college freshmen, a slight overrepresentation compared to their proportion of the total population. This perhaps is an indication that Asian American participation in higher education will continue to be strong in the 1990s.

Graduate Enrollment

Table 29.11 shows that there were 53,000 Asian Americans enrolled in graduate programs in 1990, which represents 9.2 percent of all Asian Americans in higher education. This number grew from 28,000 in 1980, an 89.3-percent increase over ten years. The increasing number of Asian Americans seeking graduate education appears to be continuing into the 1990s. From 1990 to 1991, except for Native Americans, Asian Americans reported the largest graduate enrollment increase, 9.4 percent, among all ethnic groups. By comparison, African American graduate enrollment increased by 6.0 percent, Hispanic by 8.5 percent, white by 2.4 percent, and total graduate enrollment by 3.3 percent. Asian Americans accounted for 3.5 percent of all graduate enrollment in 1991.

Profile of GRE Test Applicants

Who goes to graduate schools? The Graduate Record Examination (GRE) is a standardized, nationwide test, like the SAT, taken by students who plan to enroll in graduate programs. Descriptive data collected from the GRE are broken down by ethnicity and provide a profile of Asian American test applicants. Although nonresident alien students also take the test, the following information pertains only to U.S. citizens who cite their ethnicity as Asian American.

In 1990-91, 8,853 Asian Americans took the GRE General Test, accounting for 3 percent of all test applicants. This number represents a 13-percent increase in one year compared to a gain of 9 percent for whites and 11 percent for all test applicants. Asian Americans generally scored higher than all test applicants on the quantitative portion of the test, but lower on the verbal and analytical sections. Asian American females were as likely to take the GRE as males. Their average scores on the verbal section were slightly higher than those of their male counterparts. However, at 575 points on the quantitative and 537 points on the analytical sections of the test, females were 73 points and 10 points lower than males, respectively.

Table 29.11
Undergraduate, Graduate, and Professional School Enrollment
in Higher Education by Race/Ethnicity, Fall 1980 to 1991
(Numbers in Thousands)

	1980	1982	1984	1986	1988	1990	Percent Change 1980-90	1991	Percent Change 1990-91
Undergraduate Total	10,560	10,875	10,610	10,798	11,304	11,959	13.2	12,439	4.0
White (non-Hispanic)	8,556	8,749	8,484	8,558	8,907	9,273	8.3	9,508	3.5
Total Minority	1,797	1,907	1,911	2,036	2,192	2,468	37.3	2,698	9.3
African American (non-Hispanic)	1,028	1,028	995	996	1,039	1,147	11.6	1,229	7.1
Hispanic	438	485	495	563	631	725	65.5	804	10.9
Asian American (a)	253	313	343	393	437	501	98.0	559	11.6
American Indian (b)	79	82	78	83	86	95	20.3	106	11.6
Nonresident Alien	208	220	216	205	205	219	5.3	234	6.6
Graduate Total	1,250	1,235	1,344	1,435	1,472	1,586	26.9	1,639	3.3
White (non-Hispanic)	1,030	1,002	1,087	1,133	1,153	1,228	19.2	1,258	2.4
Total Minority	125	123	141	167	167	190	52.0	205	7.9
African American (non-Hispanic)	66	61	67	72	76	84	27.3	89	6.0
Hispanic	27	27	32	46	39	47	74.1	51	8.5
Asian American (a)	28	30	37	43	46	53	89.3	58	9.4
American Indian (b)	4	5	5	5	6	6	50.0	7	16.7
Nonresident Alien	94	108	115	136	151	167	77.7	177	6.0
Professional School Total	277	278	278	270	267	274	-1.1	281	2.6
White (non-Hispanic)	248	246	243	231	223	222	10.5	224	0.9
Total Minority	26	29	32	36	39	47	80.8	50	6.4
African American (non-Hispanic)	13	13	13	14	14	16	23.1	17	5.3
Hispanic	7	7	8	9	9	11	57.1	11	0.0
Asian American (a)	6	8	9	11	14	19	216.7	21	10.5
American Indian (b)	1	1	1	1	1	1	0.0	1	0.0
Nonresident Alien	3	3	3	4	5	5	40.0	6	20.0

Notes:
Because of underreporting/nonreporting or racial/ethnic data, data prior to 1986 were estimated when possible. Also, due to rounding, detail may not add to totals. Data for Fall 1990 have been revised from previously published figures. For Fall of 1991, the response rate was 90.9 percent for institutions of higher education while in the Fall of 1990, the response rate for institutions of higher education was 86.8 percent.
(a) Asian American includes Pacific Islanders.
(b) American Indian includes Alaskan Natives.

Source: *Deborah J. Carter and Reginald Wilson, Minorities in Higher Education: 1992 (Washington, D.C.: American Council on Education). U.S. Department of Education, National Center for Education Statistics. Trends in Enrollment in Higher Education by Racial Ethnic Category: Fall 1980 through Fall 1991. Washington, D.C.: U.S. Department of Education, January 1993.*

About 25 percent of the Asian American test applicants majored in engineering as undergraduates. Smaller percentages majored in humanities, arts, life sciences, or physical sciences; very few majored in business. A third more social science majors were bound for graduate school in 1991 than the year before. Among all GRE examinees, the largest group majored in social science, with the exception of Asian Americans, who more commonly majored in engineering.

Degree Objective and Planned Graduate Field

Generally, Asian Americans have the same graduate degree objectives as other ethnic groups. The majority of them, approximately 59 percent, planned to earn

Table 29.12
Asian American GRE General Test Examinees
by Broad Intended Graduate Major Field
1990 - 1991
(U.S. Citizens Only)

Field	Number	Percent	% of Total
Business	159	19	6
Education	555	65	1
Engineering	1,741	205	10
Humanities/Art	611	72	2
Life Sciences	1,390	164	3
Physical Sci.	939	111	6
Social Sci.	1,141	135	3
Other fields	767	90	3
Undecided	1,177	139	3
Total	8,480	1,000	3

Source: Graduate Record Examination Board, Examinee and Score Trends for the GRE General Test: 1989-90, 1990-91 (Princeton, NJ: Educational Testing Service) Unpublished Data

master's degrees. The rest viewed earning a doctorate or entering a postdoctorate program as their educational goals. This proportion has remained fairly constant over the years and may be influenced by the planned field of study. Asian Americans strongly favor engineering and the sciences, fields in which the acquisition of a doctorate is desirable.

For the past dozen years, engineering has consistently ranked at the top and education at the bottom as intended graduate fields of study among Asian American GRE examinees. They accounted for 10 percent of all applicants planned to pursue graduate studies in engineering, but comprised only 1 percent of those going into education.

Professional Schools

Although their overall numbers are still relatively small, more and more Asian Americans are opting to pursue professional degrees in law and medicine. In 1990, 19,000 Asian Americans were enrolled in professional schools, representing 6.9 percent of all professional school students. Table 29.11 shows that Asian American enrollment in professional schools increased 10.5 percent from 1990 to 1991 and tripled during the preceding decade.

Law School

Much of this increase was attributable to sharp increases in Asian American attendance at law and medical schools. For example, in 1991-92, 5,028 Asian Americans were enrolled in law school J.D. programs, a twofold increase in five years.

Asian American law school applicants also doubled from 1985 to 1989. Of the 2,949 Asian Americans applying to law school in 1988-89, 1,004, or 34 percent, were denied admission; 1,777, or 60.3 percent, were admitted; of those admitted, 1,445 registered. In comparison, 62 percent of white and 59.2 percent of all applicants were admitted. Asian American applicants who were admitted scored 8.1 points higher on the LSAT (the standard graduate exam for law school applicants) than those denied admission; average GPA was also

Table 29.13
Applicants to Law Schools: 1984-85 through 1988-89

Numbers of applicants to American Bar Association law schools, mean Law School Admissions Test (LSAT) score, and percent by race/ethnicity, 1984-85 through 1988-89.

Racial/ethnic group	1984-85		1985-86		1986-87		1987-88		1988-89		1989-89 Mean
	Count	%	Count	%	Count	%	Count	%	Count	%	LSAT
Totals	60,338	—	65,168	—	68,804	—	78,930	—	87,227	—	—
Asian/Pacific Islander	1,270	2.1	1,561	2.4	1,854	2.7	2,284	2.9	2,949	3.4	3,1.8
American Indian	359	0.6	356	0.5	377	0.5	380	0.5	412	0.5	2,8.0
Black/Afro American	4,406	7.3	4,889,	7.5	5079	7.4	5,758	7.3	6,158	7.1	2,3.2
Caucasian/White	50,241	83.3	53538	82.2	56,027	81.4	61,844	78.4	69,113	79.2	3,3.2
Chicano/Mexican American	739	1.2	839	1.3	843	1.2	783	1.0	906	1.0	2,7.8
Hispanic	1,200	2.0	1,382,	2.1	1,484	2.2	1,838	2.3	2,133	2.4	2,8.4
Puerto Rican	815	1.4	1002	1.5	1,012	1.5	1,034	1.3	1,138	1.3	1,9.6

Source: Law School Admission Services, Minority Databook, Minority Participation in Legal Education and the Profession (Newtown, PA: Law School Admission Services, Inc., 1990), table IV-3c, p. 34. Reprinted by permission. Primary source: Law School Admission Services, National Statistical Report 1984-85 through 1988-89.

Table 29.14
U.S. Medical School Applicants: 1986-1992

Numbers of U.S. medical school applicants and applicants accepted, total and Asian/Pacific Islander, 1986-1992.

Applicants	1986	1987	1988	1989	1990	1991	1992
Total Applicants	31,323	28,123	26,721	26,915	29,243	33,301	37,410
Total Accepted Applicants	17,092	17,027	17,108	16,975	17,206	17,436	17,464
Asian/Pacific Islander							
Applicants	2,988	3,198	3,349	3,661	4,345	5,487	6,225
Accepted Applicants	1,563	1,895	2,123	2,250	2,583	2,778	2,719

Source: Association of American Medical College, Facts: Applicants, Matriculants, and Graduates, 1986-1992 (Washington, DC: AAMC, October 20, 1992), p. 6-7. Also in source: data on white, underrepresented minorities, (including black, American Indian/Alaskan native, Mexican American/Chicano, Puerto Rican/mainland), and other minorities (including Commonwealth Puerto Rican, and other Hispanic). Asians or Pacific Islanders are not classified as "underrepresented." Data is also included on applicants by state and by Medical College Admissions Test (MCAT) MCAT score and grade point average.

higher. Compared to admitted white students, admitted Asian American students had slightly lower average LSAT scores and GPAs.

Medical School

Twice as many Asian Americans applied to medical school in 1991-92 as in 1985-86, accounting for 16.5 percent of total medical school applications. Of those who applied, 50.6 percent were accepted. The number of accepted Asian American applicants steadily increased in the 1970s and 1980s, peaking in 1988-89 at 63.4 percent. By 1994, the trend had reversed, with the proportion of admits declining almost 13 percent.

From the mid-1980s to the mid-1990s, Asian American enrollment in medical school rose steadily, while total medical school enrollments either declined or remained constant. For example, from 1991 to 1992,

Asian American enrollment grew 5.9 percent—although total enrollment increased less than 1 percent—making up 15.1 percent of total medical school enrollment. Females accounted for a large portion of the increase.

Degrees Earned

From the mid- to late 1980s, Asian Americans earned more degrees at all levels of the educational system—35.4 percent more associate's degrees, 53.8 percent more bachelor's degrees, 36.8 percent more master's degrees, and 83.7 percent more first professional degrees. These increases reflect a steady growth in participation and achievement of Asian Americans throughout all of higher education. However, a different picture emerged in the 1990s.

Table 29.15
Medical School Enrollments by Sex: 1986-1992

Total and Asian/Pacific Islander number enrolled in U.S. medical schools by sex, 1986-1992, and percent change, 1991 to 1992.

Enrollment	1986	1987	1988	1989	1990	1991	1992	% Change '91 to '92
Enrollment, total	66,125	65,735	65,300	65,016	65,163	65,602	66,142	0.8%
Asian or Pacific Islander, total	4,883	5,738	6,595	7,489	8,436	9,438	9,994	5.9%
Men, total	44,025	43,191	42,315	41,503	40,877	40,640	40,104	-1.3%
Asian/Pacific Islander, men	3,195	3,686	4,205	4,710	5,256	5,804	6,051	4.3%
Women, total	22,100	22,544	22,985	23,513	24,286	24,962	26,038	4.3%
Asian/Pacific Islander, women	1,688	2,052	2,390	2,779	3,180	3,634	3,943	8.5%

Source: Association of American Medical Colleges, Facts: Applicants, Matriculants, and Graduates, 1986-1992 (Washington, DC: AAMC, October 20, 1992), p. 10. Also in Source: data on white, underrepresented minorities , (including black, American Indian/Alaskan native, Mexican American/Chicano, Puerto Rican/mainland), and other minorities (including Commonwealth Puerto Rican, and other Hispanic). Asians or Pacific Islanders are not classified as "underrepresented." Data is also included on applicants by state and by MCAT score and grade point average.

Table 29.16
Asian American Degrees Earned by Sex for Selected Years

	1985		1987		1989		1990		Percent Change 1989-90
	Total	Percent	Total	Percent	Total	Percent	Total	Percent	
Associate's Degrees									
Total	429,815	100.0	436,299	100.0	432,144	100.0	448,997	100.0	3.9
Men (a)	190,409	44.3	190,832	43.7	183,963	42.6	188,160	41.9	2.3
Women (b)	239,406	55.7	245,467	56.3	248,181	57.4	260,834	58.1	5.1
White (non-Hispanic)	355,343	82.7	361,819	82.9	354,815	82.1	368,529	82.1	3.9
Men	157,278	82.6	158,126	82.9	150,950	82.1	154,301	82.0	2.2
Women	198,065	82.7	203,693	83.0	203,863	82.1	214,228	82.1	5.1
Asian American (c)	9,914	2.3	11,794	2.7	12,531	2.3	13,426	3.0	7.1
Men	5,492	2.9	6,172	3.2	6,375	3.5	6,470	3.4	1.5
Women	4,422	1.8	5,622	2.3	6,156	2.5	6,956	2.7	13.0
Bachelor's Degrees									
Total	968,311	100.0	991,260	100.0	1,016,350	100.0	1,046,930	100.0	3.0
Men (a)	476,148	49.2	480,780	48.5	481,946	47.4	490,101	46.8	1.7
Women (b)	492,163	50.8	510,480	51.5	534,404	52.6	556,829	53.2	4.2
White (non-Hispanic)	826,106	85.3	841,821	84.9	859,699	84.6	882,996	84.3	2.7
Men	405,085	85.1	406,751	84.6	407,142	84.5	413,469	84.4	1.6
Women	421,021	85.5	435,069	85.2	452,557	84.7	469,527	84.3	3.7
Asian American (c)	25,395	2.6	32,618	3.3	37,686	3.7	39,059	3.7	3.5
Men	13,554	2.8	17,249	3.6	19,271	4.0	19,617	4.0	1.8
Women	11,841	2.4	15,369	3.0	18,415	3.4	19,442	3.5	5.6
Master's Degrees									
Total	280,421	100.0	289,341	100.0	309,770	100.0	321,992	100.0	3.9
Men (a)	139,417	49.7	141,264	48.8	148,872	48.1	152,907	47.5	2.7
Women (b)	141,004	50.3	148,077	51.2	160,898	51.9	169,085	52.5	5.1
White (non-Hispanic)	223,628	79.7	228,870	79.1	241,607	78.0	251,518	78.1	4.1
Men	106,059	76.1	105,573	74.7	109,709	73.7	112,976	73.9	3.0
Women	117,569	83.4	123,297	83.3	133,047	82.7	138,542	81.9	4.1
Asian American (c)	7,782	2.8	8,558	3.0	10,336	3.3	10,646	3.3	3.0
Men	4,842	3.5	5,238	3.7	6,050	4.1	6,070	4.0	0.3
Women	2,940	2.1	3,320	2.2	4,286	2.7	4,576	2.7	6.6
First Professional Degrees									
Total	71,057	100.0	71,617	100.0	70,736	100.0	70,736	100.0	-0.2
Men (a)	47,501	66.8	46,522	65.0	45,046	63.6	43,819	61.9	-2.7
Women (b)	23,556	33.2	25,095	35.0	25,810	36.4	26,917	38.1	4.3
White (non-Hispanic)	63,219	89.0	62,688	87.5	61,214	86.4	60,291	85.2	-1.5
Men	42,630	89.7	41,149	88.5	39,399	87.5	37,909	86.5	-3.8
Women	20,589	87.4	21,539	85.8	21,815	84.5	22,382	83.2	2.5
Asian American (c)	1,816	2.6	2,270	3.2	2,976	4.2	3,336	4.7	12.1
Men	1,152	2.4	1,420	3.1	1,819	4.0	1,966	4.5	8.1
Women	664	2.8	850	3.4	1,157	4.5	1,370	5.1	18.4

Notes:
As of academic year 1989, degrees conferred by race/ethnicity were released annually instead of biannually. Data for academic year 1989 have been revised from previously published figures.

Source: *U.S. Department of Education, National Center for Education Statistics, Race/Ethnicity Trends in Degrees Conferred by Institutions of Higher Education: 1980-81 through 1990-91. Washington D.C. Office of Educational Research and Improvement, May 1992.*

Table 29.17
Bachelor's Degrees Earned by Asian Americans for Selected Fields by Sex, 1981, 1989, 1990

	1981 Total	1989 Total	1990 Total	Percent Change	
				1981-90	1989-90
Education					
Total	723	1,106	931	28.8	-15.8
Men	258	262	264	2.3	0.8
Women	465	844	667	43.4	-21.0
Business					
Total	3,943	7,973	8,326	111.2	4.4
Men	2,121	3,633	3,643	71.8	0.3
Women	1,822	4,340	4,683	157.0	7.9
Social Sciences					
Total	1,645	3,970	4,315	162.3	8.7
Men	860	1,947	2,143	149.2	10.1
Women	785	2,023	2,172	176.7	7.4
Health Professions					
Total	1,312	1,710	1,882	43.4	10.1
Men	299	400	403	34.8	0.8
Women	1,013	1,310	1,479	46.0	12.9
Biological/Life Sciences					
Total	1,489	2,954	3,322	123.1	12.5
Men	830	1,475	1,613	94.3	9.4
Women	659	1,479	1,709	159.3	15.6
Engineering					
Total	3,066	6,903	6,922	125.8	0.3
Men	2,699	5,676	5,647	109.2	-0.5
Women	367	1,227	1,275	247.4	3.9

Notes:
Some institutions did not report the racial/ethnic data for earned degrees. Data of some of these nonreporting institutions were imputed. Data for academic year 1989 have been revised from previously published numbers. Data represent programs, not organizational units within institutions. Because of rounding, details may not add to totals.

Source: *Carter & Wilson, Office of Minorities in Higher Education, Minorities in Higher Education: 1992: Eleventh annual Status Report, Washington, D.C.: American Council on Education, January 1993. U.S. Department of Education, National Center for Education Statistics, Race/Ethnicity Trends in Degrees Conferred by Institutions of Higher Education: 1980-81 through 1990-91. Washington D.C. Office of Educational Research and Improvement, May 1992.*

Associate's Degrees

In the 1990s, the number of associate's degrees awarded to Asian Americans continued to increase—by 7.1 percent from 12,531 in 1989 to 13,426 in 1990. Except for Hispanics, this was the largest increase among all ethnic groups including whites. Asian American women accounted for most of the increase. Moreover, Asian American females earned 57.3 percent more associate's degrees in 1990, triple the increase of 17.8 percent for males.

Bachelor's Degrees

Table 29.16 shows that at the baccalaureate level, 39,059 degrees were awarded to Asian Americans in

1990, a 3.6-percent increase over 1989. This was the smallest gain among all minority groups, indicating a leveling off of bachelor's degrees awarded to Asian Americans. As was the case with associate's degrees, women accounted for most of the growth in degrees earned.

Although the number of degrees awarded in business and engineering to Asian Americans increased by only 0.3 percent and 4.4 percent from 1989 to 1990, respectively, baccalaureates awarded to Asian Americans were predominantly in these fields. Baccalaureates earned in the biological/life sciences, health professions, and social science are increasing at greater rates, 12.5 percent, 10.1 percent, and 8.7 percent, respectively. Conversely, baccalaureates awarded to

Table 29.18
Master's Degrees Earned by Asian Americans for Selected Fields by Sex, 1981, 1989, 1990

				Percent Change	
	1981 Total	1989 Total	1990 Total	1981-90	1989-90
Education					
Total	973	961	1,023	5.1	6.5
Men	291	259	254	-12.7	-1.9
Women	682	702	769	12.8	9.5
Business					
Total	1,633	2,924	3,004	84.0	2.7
Men	1,161	1,850	1,902	63.8	2.8
Women	472	1,074	1,102	133.5	2.6
Social Sciences					
Total	233	319	372	59.7	16.6
Men	147	184	214	45.6	16.3
Women	86	135	158	83.7	17.0
Health Professions					
Total	448	551	633	41.3	14.9
Men	164	165	194	18.3	17.6
Women	284	386	439	54.6	13.7
Biological/Life Sciences					
Total	306	408	377	23.2	-7.6
Men	149	175	145	-2.7	-17.1
Women	157	233	232	47.8	0.4
Engineering					
Total	1,079	2,098	2,012	86.5	-4.1
Men	974	1,795	1,682	72.7	-6.3
Women	105	303	330	214.3	8.9

Notes:
Some institutions did not report the racial/ethnic data for earned degrees. Data of some of these nonreporting institutions were imputed. Data for academic year 1989 have been revised from previously published numbers. Data represent programs, not organizational units within institutions. Because of rounding, details may not add to totals.

Source: *Carter & Wilson, Office of Minorities in Higher Education, Minorities in Higher Education: 1992: Eleventh annual Status Report, Washington, D.C.: American Council on Education, January 1993. U.S. Department of Education, National Center for Education Statistics, Race/Ethnicity Trends in Degrees Conferred by Institutions of Higher Education: 1980-81 through 1990-91. Washington D.C. Office of Educational Research and Improvement, May 1992.*

Asian Americans in education declined almost 16 percent, including a 21-percent decline among Asian American women. In general, Asian Americans are more likely to earn their baccalaureates in engineering, business, and the sciences, and are less likely to attain degrees in education, humanities, and social science. These trends are not as pronounced for women.

Master's Degrees

Asian Americans earned 6.8 percent more master's degrees in 1989 than 1990. This increase trailed all ethnic groups except Native Americans. Again, Asian American women accounted for the largest share of this modest increase.

From 1989 to 1990, more Asian Americans were opting to earn master's degrees in social science and the health professions, perhaps reflecting the greater number of degrees awarded to women. On the other hand, master's degrees in public affairs were less popular, declining in the number awarded by 7.6 percent. While engineering remains highly favored by Asian Americans, the number of master's degrees earned in the field also fell off. Declines in the two fields were almost totally attributable to fewer degrees earned by males.

Table 29.18 shows that during a ten-year period, the number of master's degrees awarded to Asian Americans increased in all six subject fields reported. The largest increase occurred in engineering and business,

Table 29.19
First Professional Degrees Conferred: 1980-1990
Number and percent of total professional degrees conferred by race/ethnicity, 1980 to 1990(1982-83 excluded).

Race/ethnicity	1980-81 Number	1980-81 Percent	1984-85 Number	1984-85 Percent	1986-87 Number	1986-87 Percent	1988-89 Number	1988-89 Percent	1989-90 Number	1989-90 Percent
Total	71,340	100.0%	71,057	100.0%	71,617	100.0%	70,856	100.0%	70,736	100.0%
Asian/Pacific Islander	1,456	2.0%	1,816	2.6%	2,270	3.2%	2,976	4.2%	3,336	4.7%
White non-Hispanic	64,551	90.5%	63,219	89.0%	62,688	87.5%	61,214	86.4%	60,291	85.2%
Black non-Hispanic	2,931	4.1%	3,029	4.3%	3,420	4.8%	3,148	4.4%	3,389	4.8%
Hispanic	1,541	2.2%	1,884	2.7%	2,051	2.9%	2,269	3.2%	2,427	3.4%
American Native/ Alaskan Native	192	0.3%	248	0.3%	304	0.4%	264	0.4%	257	0.4%
Nonresident alien	669	0.9%	861	1.2%	884	1.2%	985	1.4%	1,036	1.5%

Source: *U.S. Department of Education, National Center for Education Statistics, Race/Ethnicity Trends in Degrees Conferred by Institutions of Higher Education: 1980-81 through 1989-90 (Washington, DC: U.S. Department of Education, 1992), table 2, p. 8. Primary sources: U.S. Department of Education, National Center for Education Statistics, Higher Education General Information Survey, "Degrees and Other Formal Awards Conferred in Institutions of Higher Education," various years; and Integrated Postsecondary Education Data Systems (IPEDS), "Completions" and "Consolidated" surveys, various years. Data for 1980-81 and 1984-85 do not include imputations for race/ethnicity. Data for 1988-89 have been revised from previously published figures.*

despite little growth or decline in recent years. More master's degrees were also earned in social science, with the increases occurring during the latter part of the decade. As for education, recent increases in degrees awarded reversed a previous net decrease for the decade.

First Professional Degrees

At the first professional degree level, Asian Americans reported a 12.1 percent increase in degrees earned from 1989 to 1990—the largest increase among the four minority groups. In comparison, Hispanics posted a gain of 7 percent, African Americans posted a gain of 7.7 percent, and Native Americans posted a loss of 2.7 percent. The increase for Asian American females was 10 percent higher than for males. Table 29.16 shows that while Asian American professional degree recipients almost doubled from 1985 to 1990, white degree recipients declined.

The increase in the number of Asian Americans graduating from medical school is particularly striking. In 1986, 909 Asian Americans graduated from medical school, accounting for 5.6 percent of all medical school graduates. By 1992, 1,920 Asian Americans graduated, raising their representation of the total to 12.5 percent. The rapid increase is not expected to continue because of the decline in the rate of Asian American applicants being admitted since 1988.

Doctoral Degrees

Data from the National Research Council indicate that among all ethnic groups, including whites, Asian

Americans recorded the largest increase (63.9 percent) in the number of doctorates earned over the last ten years. By contrast, the number of doctorates earned by whites and all U.S. citizens declined 0.6 percent and 1.4 percent, respectively. The biggest gains for Asian Americans occurred between 1982-1983 and 1987-1988. Gains made by females (95.3 percent) were twice that of males (48.9 percent). Interestingly, these increases coincided with the doubling of the number of doctorates earned by noncitizens.

Except for social science, increases in doctorates earned by Asian Americans were distributed across most fields—28.8 percent in physical sciences, 25.7 percent in humanities, 22.7 percent in education, 20.8 percent in life sciences, and 17.8 percent in engineering. Native Americans and African Americans reported greater increases, while whites and Hispanics had less growth in doctorates earned in most fields than Asian Americans.

U.S. universities awarded a record number (38,814) of doctorates in 1992, continuing, but at a more modest rate, the upward surge that began in the latter half of the 1980s. Most of the growth is attributable to the increasing number of Ph.D. degrees awarded to noncitizens, who earned 32 percent of the doctorates in 1992. Among U.S. citizens, Asian Americans earned 828 doctorates, or 3.3 percent, of the total awarded to U.S. citizens. Those earned by Asian Americans were concentrated in physical sciences and engineering (47 percent).

In summary, Asian Americans are participating in increasing numbers all along the educational pipeline.

Table 29.20
Doctoral Degrees by U.S. Citizenship by Race/Ethnicity and Sex, 1980 to 1991

	1981	1982	1983	1984	1985	1986	1987	1988	1989	1990	1991	Percent Change 1981-91	Percent Change 1990-91
Doctorates (a)													
Total	31,357	31,106	31,280	31,332	31,291	31,896	32,367	33,489	34,318	36,057	37,451	19.4	3.9
Men	21,465	21,013	20,747	29,633	20,547	20,590	20,941	21,677	21,811	22,955	23,686	10.3	3.2
Women	9,892	10,093	10,533	10,699	10,744	11,306	11426	11812	12,507	13,102	13,765	39.2	5.1
U.S. Citizens (b)													
All U.S. Citizens	25,061	24,388	24,358	24,026	23,363	23,081	22,991	23,288	23,400	24,886	24,721	-1.4	-0.7
Men	16,360	15,559	15,119	14,729	14,217	13,633	13,581	13,725	13,397	14,151	13,885	-15.1	-1.9
Women	8,701	8,829	9,239	9,297	9,146	9,448	9,410	9,563	10,003	10,735	10,836	24.5	0.9
White	21,980	21,677	21,699	21,349	20,757	20,626	20,470	20,782	20,893	22,156	21,859	-0.6	-4.3
Men	14,459	13,987	13,609	13,170	12,805	12,303	12,172	12,343	11,989	12,679	12,364	-14.5	-2.5
Women	7,521	7,690	8,090	8,179	7,952	8,323	8,298	8,439	8,904	9,477	9,495	26.2	0.2
African American	1,013	1,047	922	953	912	823	767	814	821	897	933	-7.9	4.0
Men	499	483	413	427	379	322	317	315	327	350	385	-22.8	10.0
Women	514	564	509	526	533	501	450	499	494	547	548	6.6	0.2
Hispanic	464	535	539	536	561	572	619	597	582	718	708	52.6	-1.4
Men	275	344	288	314	300	303	333	323	309	378	358	30.2	-5.3
Women	189	191	251	222	261	269	286	274	273	340	350	85.2	2.9
Asian American	465	452	492	512	516	531	542	614	626	640	762	63.9	19.1
Men	315	281	312	338	329	348	369	414	441	426	469	48.9	10.1
Women	150	171	180	174	187	183	173	200	185	214	293	95.3	36.9
American Indian (c)	85	77	81	74	95	99	115	94	94	96	128	50.6	33.3
Men	56	44	50	54	39	58	62	52	49	52	73	30.4	40.4
Women	29	33	31	20	56	41	53	42	45	44	55	89.7	25.0
Non-U.S. Citizens													
Total	5,221	5,432	5,774	6,054	6,553	6,707	7,187	7,817	8,273	9,769	10,666	104.3	9.2
Men	4,360	4,536	4,825	5,024	5,394	5,481	5,839	6,298	6,582	7,804	8,346	91.4	6.9
Women	861	896	949	1,030	1,159	1,226	1,348	1,219	1,691	1,965	2,320	169.5	18.1

Notes:
(a) Includes doctorates with unknown citizenship status and unknown race/ethnicity.
(b) Includes doctorates with unknown race/ethnicity.
(c) American Indian includes Alaskan Natives.

Source: *Carter & Wilson, Office of Minorities in Higher Education, Minorities in Higher Education: 1992: Eleventh Annual Status Report, Washington, D.C.: American Council on Education, January 1993. National Research Council, Doctorate Records File, various years.*

Growth in their numbers in high school, college, graduate, and professional schools in the 1980s were dramatic, but have become more modest since the beginning of the 1990s. Most of the gains in enrollment and degrees earned were attributable to significant increases made by Asian American women.

Generally, Asian Americans show a strong preference for studies in engineering, sciences, and business, as evidenced by their undergraduate and graduate majors and the fields in which they earn their degrees. With the increasing numbers of Asian American women entering higher education in varying fields, this trend may not be so pronounced in the future.

Data available on access, persistence, and achievement in higher education present an overall picture of Asian American students. As a group comprised of many separate nationalities, Asian Americans appear to be overrepresented at many levels of higher education, even though some individual groups are underrepresented. Unfortunately, the aggregation of more than 30 different Asian ethnic groups into a single category—Asian Americans—allows their overall educational achievement to mask individual group needs and problems.

—Shirley L. Mow
Westchester Education Coalition, Inc.

Table 29.21
Doctoral Degrees by Field, U.S. Citizenship and Race/Ethnicity, 1980, 1989, 1990 and 1991

	1980	1989	1990	1991	Percent Change 1990-91	1980	1989	1990	1991	Percent Change 1990-91
			TOTAL					**PHYSICAL SCIENCES**		
Total Doctorates (a)	31,020	34,319	36,027	37,451	4.0	4,111	5,457	5,872	6,276	6.9
American Indian	75	94	96	128	33.3	5	18	5	14	180.0
Asian	2,621	5,150	5,080	7,271	19.6	505	1,262	1,563	1,846	18.1
Black	1,445	1,229	1,255	1,355	8.0	50	68	53	90	69.8
Hispanic	821	1,041	1,192	1,280	7.4	91	150	166	192	15.7
White	23,805	23,112	24,246	24,671	1.8	3,013	3,374	3,516	3,707	5.4
U.S. Citizens (b)	25,222	23,400	24,886	24,721	-0.7	3,072	3,233	3,407	3,450	1.3
American Indian	75	94	96	128	33.3	5	18	5	14	180.0
Asian American	458	526	640	762	19.1	75	117	111	143	28.8
African American	1,032	821	897	933	4.0	25	35	27	40	48.1
Hispanic	412	582	718	708	-1.4	27	70	85	80	-5.9
White	21,994	20,893	22,156	21,859	-1.3	2,715	2,908	3,097	3,107	0.3
			ENGINEERING					**HUMANITIES**		
Total Doctorates (a)	2,479	4,530	4,900	5,212	6.4	3,871	3,569	3,819	4,094	7.2
American Indian	3	7	4	6	50.0	3	7	8	10	25.0
Asian	740	1,612	1,800	2,182	21.2	132	206	213	302	41.8
Black	57	57	74	77	4.1	127	95	87	122	40.2
Hispanic	77	116	124	127	2.4	118	131	177	188	6.2
White	1,428	2,196	2,352	2,310	-1.8	3,191	2,750	3,031	3,203	5.7
U.S. Citizens (b)	1,255	1,864	1,953	1,977	1.2	3,395	2,726	3,091	3,151	1.9
American Indian	3	7	4	6	50.0	3	7	8	10	25.0
Asian American	73	173	157	185	17.8	40	40	35	44	25.7
African American	11	24	28	43	53.6	97	72	72	91	26.4
Hispanic	18	34	39	47	20.5	79	84	111	110	-0.9
White	1,068	1,583	1,686	1,659	-1.6	3,021	2,464	2,820	2843	0.8
			LIFE SCIENCES					**SOCIAL SCIENCES**		
Total Doctorates (a)	5,461	6,349	6,629	6,928	4.5	5,856	5,972	6,089	6,127	0.6
American Indian	7	12	9	-19	111.1	13	18	23	21	-8.7
Asian	482	839	1,125	1,365	21.3	320	556	596	695	16.6
Black	161	177	166	192	15.7	249	247	269	280	4.1
Hispanic	173	222	241	263	9.1	150	196	234	259	10.7
White	4,258	4,484	4,558	4,665	2.3	4,691	4,091	4,364	4,357	-0.2
U.S. Citizens (b)	4,415	4,533	4,612	4,629	0.4	4,992	4,307	4,655	4,499	-3.4
American Indian	7	12	9	19	111.1	13	18	23	21	-8.7
Asian American	102	138	154	186	20.8	79	70	86	84	-2.3
African American	55	76	73	85	16.4	180	170	180	192	6.7
Hispanic	36	83	103	97	-5.8	93	130	169	176	4.1
White	3,958	4,142	4,206	4,174	-0.8	4,402	3,860	4,122	3,975	-3.6
			EDUCATION					**PROFESSIONAL-OTHER**		
Total Doctorates (a)	7,586	6,280	6,485	5,397	-1.4	656	2,196	2,270	2,417	6.5
American Indian	43	25	37	52	40.5	1	7	10	6	-40.0
Asian	242	330	353	412	16.7	100	340	426	469	10.1
Black	701	487	513	487	-5.1	100	98	94	107	13.8
Hispanic	83	188	201	207	3.0	29	38	49	44	-10.2
White	5,919	4,692	4,922	4,862	-1.2	1,305	1,479	1,503	1,567	4.3
U.S. Citizens (b)	6,749	5,243	5,629	5,424	-3.6	1,344	1,494	1,539	1,591	3.4
American Indian	43	25	37	52	40.5	1	7	10	6	-40.0
Asian American	65	57	66	31	22.7	24	31	31	39	25.8
African American	591	390	455	404	-11.2	63	54	62	78	25.8
Hispanic	144	156	160	170	-5.6	15	25	31	28	-9.7
White	5,652	4,574	4,837	1,680	-3.2	1,178	1,362	1,388	1,421	2.4

Notes:
(a) Total Doctorates number includes unknown citizenship status and unknown race.
(b) Total for other categories include unknown race.

Source: Carter & Wilson, *Minorities in Higher Education: 1992.* National Research Council, *Doctorate Records File, various years.*

♦ ACCESS TO HIGHER EDUCATION

On February 10, 1992, Martin Peretz described, in the *New Republic*, a telling game he played with friends near the Harvard Yard. The winner was to be the one whose estimate was nearest to the actual time it would take for 100 young Asians to pass before their eyes. The guesses ranged from 28 to 45 minutes. Peretz reported that in just 11 minutes, they had counted 101 Asians. Peretz used this story to laud Harvard for its diversity in terms of "telltale names and ethnic hue," to highlight the presence of substantial proportions of Asian students in selective institutions such as Harvard, Stanford, Yale, University of California at Los Angeles (UCLA), and the University of Michigan, and to rebuke other members of other (minority) groups who ". . . can't work or won't."

Myth of the "Model Minority"

In his article, Peretz voiced his beliefs and divisive opinions that could have contributed to public misconception of the status of Asian American students in higher education in the United States. Peretz considered Asian American youth to be "model minority" students, who would have encountered few problems getting into colleges and universities of their choice, and indeed, who already take up considerably more than their "fair share" of slots at the best schools.

Increasing Barriers to Higher Education

On the other hand, throughout the 1980s, growing numbers of Asian American students, their families, and communities were increasingly concerned with the rising barriers they faced in pursuit of quality higher education. Disadvantaged newly arrived immigrants from Asia, on the other hand, struggled to meet the minimal English language requirements for admission to affordable, two-year community colleges.

How readily can Asian Americans access higher education? The answer depends on which Asian Americans are being discussed, what kinds of institutions they are seeking to attend, and which areas of study within those institutions they hope to pursue. Unprecedented numbers of Asian Americans are going to two- and four-year colleges, graduate schools, and professional schools. At the same time, increasing numbers of well-qualified Asian Americans are being rejected by their first- and even second-choice institutions.

Admissions Policies and Practices

Private as well as public institutions of higher education publish their admissions policies in yearly catalogs. A careful reading can yield useful information about applicant qualities that are considered important to admission decisions at any particular department, faculty, or school.

Large public institutions with thousands of applicants each year process applications by computer and use unambiguous, quantifiable, often legislative-mandated standards. Selective private schools are more likely to require personal interviews and use flexible, subjective criteria in addition to objective data for admissions decisions. These qualitative factors may include interview ratings, evidence of extracurricular interests, and other prerogative requirements such as religious affiliation, family ties, or social/economic prestige.

Ethnic and gender diversity in the student body is a goal of most institutions. Yet, without taking into account drastic demographic changes of the Asian American population during the past two decades, some institutions have come to view Asian American applicants as a falsely homogeneous, "overrepresented" group that dilute rather than contribute to campus diversity.

Undergraduate Admissions

Institutional selectivity is defined in several ways. The most highly selective institutions—those of choice among growing numbers of academically capable, well-prepared Asian American applicants—number no more than 30 on most published lists. Perhaps another 50 would be named as highly selective. For many academically capable Asian American applicants, especially those from immigrant families with limited understanding of American society, that list of potential college choices may well be much shorter.

What does selectivity mean? One popular college guide describes selectivity as " . . . a comparative measure of the scholastic potential of the student body, an indication of the hurdles a student will face in applying for admission . . . ." Selectivity is also measured in terms of the number admitted versus the number of applicants. The most selective institutions can be defined as those that accept 30 percent or less of their applicants, more selective institutions accepted 31 to 80 percent of their applicants, less selective institutions accept 81 to 95 percent of applicants, and least selective accept more than 95 percent of applicants.

A 1985 survey of two- and four-year undergraduate institutions compared acceptance rates by ethnic group at 98 of the most selective public and private colleges. Asian American students were more likely than other groups to be accepted by the most selective public institutions, and less likely to be accepted by the most selective private institutions. Across all types of undergraduate institutions, Asian Americans were less likely than average to be accepted by both public and private schools, by about 6 percent in the case of public schools, and by 14 percent for private schools.

In addition to strict academic standards, the nation's most selective schools strive for balance in terms of demographics: ethnic, socioeconomic, region, rural, or inner-city residence. Some requirements might be waived for applicants who are star athletes, gifted artists, exceptional leaders, underrepresented minorities, alumni or faculty offspring (referred to as "legacies"), and poor or challenged by special handicaps.

Barriers to Access

Is there valid evidence that Asian American applicants encounter more barriers than all other qualified applicants? During the early 1980s, Asian American undergraduates at selective campuses on both coasts became alarmed by trends of steady or shrinking numbers of Asian American freshmen with each entering class, in spite of steadily growing, well-qualified, applicant pools that reflected Asian population increases. Asian American student publications voiced suspicion of hidden Asian quotas, and demanded clarification of admissions policies to ensure equality of access. Investigations of specific institutions and entire state higher-education systems were launched by the institutions and systems themselves, and by Asian American students, education-policy researchers, blue-ribbon community panels, state agencies, and the Office of Civil Rights (OCR) of the U.S. Department of Education. Most studies found that Asian American applicants to highly selective public and private institutions were academically as strong or stronger than average, based upon criteria such as total credits earned, quality of curricula, grade-point averages, standardized test scores, and scholastic honors. However, for a variety of reasons, Asian American acceptance rates remained lower than average, and those accepted apparently had to present exceptionally strong profiles.

Some private universities, including Brown in Rhode Island and Stanford in California, have clarified or changed their admissions policies and procedures to correct past biases identified through self-examination, with subsequent increases in admission rates of Asian American applicants approaching those of white applicants.

In 1990, Harvard was cleared by OCR in an investigation instigated by complaints of discriminatory practices in admissions. The complaints charged that Harvard violated Title VI of the 1964 Civil Rights Act, which bars discrimination on the basis of race, color, or national origin. The findings of the OCR investigation revealed that the lower acceptance rate of Asian Americans was related to factors such as fewer Asians among alumni legacies and recruited athletes.

At many selective public and private institutions with nationwide applicant pools, Asian American students accounted for 15 to 20 percent of entering freshmen classes. There are regional differences—selective institutions on East and West coasts were selected by growing numbers of qualified Asian Americans.

A large concentration of the Asian American population is in the western part of the United States. The 1990 Census reported one in ten Californians was Asian. For eligible Asian high school graduates from American-born and immigrant families, the prestigious University of California (UC) system has been a top choice. Relatively more Asian Americans are eligible to apply to the UC system than all other groups, and a higher proportion of those eligible actually apply for admission to UC, particularly to the Berkeley and Los Angeles campuses.

In 1985, an Asian American Task Force on University Admissions was appointed by the University of California at Berkeley. It was formed in response to concerns about declining Asian American admissions and the increasing number of Asian Americans being redirected to other UC campuses. The Task Force found that these changes were due to admissions procedures that targeted Asian immigrants with strong mathematical skills and limited proficiency in English. Vigorous protest by students and Asian American community groups changed admissions policy and increased Asian admissions.

A similar scene unfolded at University of California at Los Angeles (UCLA). By 1991, Asian Americans were 39 percent of entering freshmen and had surpassed whites as the largest group on campus. Yet Asian American students continued to voice their concern that they had a harder time than white or other minority students in winning acceptance to their top-choice faculties and campuses.

In addition to quantitative, objective admission criteria, the UC system had begun to use complex, supplementary selection criteria for more than half the admits. A 1987 report on admissions at UC Berkeley from 1981 to 1987 by the auditor general of California concluded that out of 49 paired comparisons between white and Asian applicant groups, white admission rates were higher than Asian rates in 37 instances. The most notable discrepancy was found for the chemistry department in 1987, where the white admit rate was almost a third higher than the Asian. Only in humanities departments with few Asian students were Asian American admit rates as high as the white applicants.

The trends of lower admit rates for Asian applicants in science and engineering departments were also observed at UCLA. In part, the phenomenon was related to high proportions of Asian American applicants who chose quantitative fields of study, with the result that they basically competed against each other. Other minority students were targets for affirmative action via Education Opportunity Programs (EOP), and white students were wooed to minimize white flight from urban campuses. Asian American students, faculty, and staff at California State University (CSU) and community college systems reported similar trends of too many Asian applicants to science and technology faculties and fewer with adequate qualifications or interest in the humanities. Proposed changes in admissions requirements, particularly in high school English credits required for CSU eligibility, would have impacted immigrant students, not only Asian, but Hispanic as well.

The California university system has not ignored Asian Americans' complaints. Institutional responses to community concerns have included: offering Asian language tests for immigrant students to fulfill foreign language requirements; recruiting Asian administrators; increasing course offerings in Asian American studies; keeping institutional databases by Asian ethnic groups to consider underserved groups for affirmative action programs available to other minorities such as the Education Opportunity Program; and giving consideration to immigrant and language status; and offering student services targeted to Asian Americans, particularly newcomers.

Graduate and Professional School Admissions

Undergraduate admissions has been the focus of Asian American pressure on higher education. However, there is accumulating evidence that, at least in some fields, graduate and professional schools also showed bias against Asian American applicants. In this context, bias is evidenced by the fact that significant numbers of accepted white applicants were not as academically qualified as some rejected Asians, using objective criteria such as course credits, test scores, and grade-point averages.

Asian American concerns about the disparity between white and Asian admissions were further reinforced in 1990 when the Office of Civil Rights (OCR) of the U.S. Department of Education announced that UCLA had given illegal preference to whites over Asians in admissions to its graduate mathematics department.

These issues are complex. In order to understand why some fields of study seem to have been particularly tough for capable Asian American applicants, factors of applicant abilities, achievement, and demand for admission with the limited supply of places in graduate and professional programs need to be taken into account.

In 1990, 4 out of 100 U.S. graduate school applicants were Asian American. Graduate faculties admit students and award teaching or research fellowships and assistantships on the basis of academic criteria, letters of recommendation, and promise of future scholarly and research productivity. Because most graduate students receive financial aid and support for their research, admission without some form of financial aid can be tantamount to rejection. Teaching assistantships are awarded to those who demonstrate the academic promise and communication skills needed to teach students in the classroom and laboratory. Asian American graduate students were reported more likely to receive university financial aid, but less likely to receive government or national fellowships than their peers.

Applicants to graduate schools take a standardized test called the Graduate Record Examination (GRE), which has a quantitative (math) section and a verbal section. Validity studies have found quantitative scores to be the best predictor of performance in quantitative fields. Compared with white GRE test applicants, Asian Americans typically performed better in tests of developed mathematical abilities, less well in verbal tasks. Yet, quantitative scores have generally underestimated non-native Asian test applicants' true mathematical ability, because they had trouble with story problems due to limited reading comprehension. That is, their scores would have been even higher had they understood the questions in narrative problems.

With the exception of three fields (biological sciences, mathematical sciences, and engineering), Asian American graduate-student enrollment has not exceeded population figures. Some graduate faculties, particularly in the humanities, have recruited low-income Asian Americans as members of underrepresented minority groups. In fields crowded with Asian nationals and Asian Americans, access can be exceptionally difficult. Those who seek graduate studies in the quantitative, scientific fields were more likely to encounter stiff competition from each other and from Asian nationals. By the mid-1990s, it was projected that the number of jobs in science and engineering would be declining in the United States. Due to changes in the international political scene, the disintegration of the former Soviet Union decreased U.S. spending on defense, weapons, and related technology, would reduce competition for related graduate studies overall.

In 1989, about 4 percent of first professional degrees were awarded to Asian Americans. Asian American law school enrollment has increased steadily in the past two decades. In 1989, four out of 100 law school applicants were Asian. Asian American applicants' typical LSAT scores were slightly lower than the white average and higher than other minority candidates, with differences among Asian American ethnic groups. Filipino

Americans, for cultural and historic reasons, have been more likely to pursue law than other Asian groups. Limited English proficiency deters recent immigrants from pursuing law as a career. For qualified Asian American applicants with demonstrable communications skills, however, access to ABA-approved law schools has been no more difficult than for their peers. Some law schools, such as the University of California-Berkeley law school, Boalt Hall, have even targeted affirmative action programs to recruit disadvantaged Asian and Pacific American students.

Graduate schools of management have also experienced growing numbers of Asian American applicants. In 1990-91, five out of every 100 management school applicants were Asian American. Their Graduate Management Aptitude Test (GMAT) total score average was 499, compared to the white average of 512. As of the mid-1990s, enrollment figures for Asian Americans in graduate management does not suggest barriers to access. Since communications skills are considered important to success in schools of management, limited verbal skills among newcomers remains a problem.

Access to medical school has become increasingly competitive, even for highly qualified Asian American applicants, because medicine was the career of choice for growing numbers of able Asian Americans in the 1970s, 1980s, and 1990s. Admission to medical school is highly competitive. Decisions are based not only on academic records and test scores, but upon letters of recommendation and interviews that use a subjective assessment of personal qualities and prediction of clinical or research performance.

In addition, the field of medicine is undergoing fundamental changes caused by changes in the U.S. health care delivery system. Primary care physicians, rather than specialists, will be increasingly in demand. The Association of American Medical Colleges (AAMC) changed the Medical College Admission Test (MCAT) format to meet these developing needs, since these scores are used by most medical schools as one criterion for admissions.

The number of Asian American medical school applicants doubled between 1985 and 1991. By 1990, 15 out of every 100 MCAT candidates were Asian American, higher than the Asian applicant ratio at other professional schools. Asian Americans scored higher than white MCAT applicants in four out of six areas: biology, chemistry, physics, and science problems. They typically scored lower than white and all other test applicants in reading and quantitative skills. Despite completing more than the prerequisite coursework and achieving higher-than-average GPAs and competitive MCAT scores, acceptance rate of Asian Americans remained low.

Overcoming Current and Future Obstacles to Access

By 1991, Asian Americans comprised 16.3 percent of all U.S. first-year medical students. Beginning in 1992, two essays were required in the MCAT. Asian Americans, whose first language is not English, found these more difficult than purely scientific questions. For the first time since 1985, the number of Asian American entrants to U.S. medical schools dropped slightly to 2,530 compared to 2,645 who entered in 1991. Entrants in 1993 increased to 2,680, but clearly the rapid rate of increase, which included the doubling of Asian first-year students from 1985 to 1990, was at an end.

Competition has also been growing. Total 1994 medical school applicants numbered over 43,000, almost twice as many as applicant numbers in 1988. This may have been caused by a trend toward a more regulated medical profession whereby physicians are employees of large service organizations, a shift that may have attracted a new group of applicants. For Asian Americans, other factors that may limit access to medical schools in the future include: greater competition with other ethnic group applicants, greater competition with other Asian Americans, less emphasis on scientific achievement, increased emphasis on writing ability, and ineligibility for affirmative-action slots. These factors may be especially significant for those from immigrant backgrounds.

Did the changes in MCAT yield test scores that predicted performance in medical school and later as physicians? A 1993 report of a longitudinal study of white and Asian American Jefferson Medical College students affirmed that compared to white classmates, Asian American students averaged higher SAT quantitative, MCAT chemistry, physics, and science problems scores; similar SAT verbal, MCAT biology and quantitative scores, and college-grade point averages; and lower reading skills. Asian Americans did as well as white peers during the two basic science years, but did not fare as well on their third clinical year, nor on parts I and II of the National Board of Medical Examiners (NBME) tests, which are used for initial licensure in many states. Asian Americans also scored lower on part III of NBME, offered after first year of residency, but received similar ratings in clinical work by their supervisors. Lower reading ability may have accounted for their performance on NBME tests.

For Asian Americans, the MCAT reading score was the most significant predictor of NBME parts I and II and medical class rank. For European Americans, the MCAT-science problem score was best predictor of NBME, while undergraduate GPA was the best predictor of class rank. The results of this longitudinal study suggest that for Asian Americans, reading ability is key to performance in medical school.

Summary

With growing demand from Asian American students, access to a limited number of slots in quantitative and engineering graduate studies, and to medical schools, may become increasingly difficult. Furthermore, access to highly selective undergraduate schools may also become tougher, because of recent changes in the SAT. Similar to the MCAT, in 1993 the SATs began to include writing samples. Validity studies have shown that SAT verbal scores overpredicted Asian American performance on essays, which was consistently lower than scores obtained by white and other minority students with similar SAT verbal scores. Although the holistic scoring systems used to assess writing samples focus on organization and expression rather than the mechanics of grammar, the essays, particularly by test applicants whose best language is not English, could well become the weakest link of otherwise strong profiles.

Communications skills are legitimate prerequisites for studying at academically demanding colleges and universities. The ability to speak, write, and read well is also essential for career success. For the future, Asian Americans who aspire to the most selective undergraduate and graduate institutions or to professional schools will need to hone their communications skills during their elementary and secondary school years. Students of college age with limited English proficiency (LEP) should enroll in English as a second language (ESL) courses before or while attending a higher education institution. ESL courses, though, are not always counted towards minimal English credits required in undergraduate programs.

Monitoring Admissions Practices

While blatant Asian quotas are not likely to be instituted without challenge, marginal applicants to selective programs and institutions may be subject to subtle bias. Continuous monitoring of admissions policies, practices, and patterns is needed to ensure that no documentable bias can occur without being noted and challenged.

Asian Americans must also help institutions and admissions systems better understand differences between the many subgroups that comprise the umbrella population segment known as Asian American, including the characteristics that profoundly affect experience and the ability to function within a competitive academic setting: native-born vs. newcomer, established immigrants vs. poorer newcomers, and heritage or ancestry traced to a highly educated Asian nation vs. a nonliterate society. To this end, California and Hawaii categorize their Asian student databases by ethnic groups. In addition, the research department of the Association of American Medical Colleges (AAMC) has also begun to record Asian ethnic data.

Suggested Actions

In scrutinizing access to higher education, Asian Americans need to keep in mind the complexity of issues. Institutions must serve many types of students, answer to many interest groups, and follow state and federal civil rights guidelines. Should a question arise with respect to access, there are published case studies providing models for the types of action taken. When an institution's admissions practices are suspected of bias, the relevant information must be collected and analyzed, and all administrative avenues to resolution must be explored before resorting to the courts. A 1989 "Note" in the *Yale Law Journal* outlines a legal framework for examining allegations of a quota in higher education admissions. It also describes the kinds of evidence needed to challenge the admission process and summarizes legal theories as basis for a complaint.

—Jayjia Hsia, Ph.D.

◆ FINANCING COLLEGE EDUCATION

A higher percentage of Asian American students aspires to a college education than students of other ethnic backgrounds. Among 1980 high school sophomores, for example, 73 percent planned to go to college right after high school, as compared to 48 percent of white, 52 percent of African American, 44 percent of Hispanic, and 33 percent of Native American students.

In 1990, Asian Americans still had the highest percentage of students planning to go on to college (78 percent), even though percentages of other ethnic groups planning to pursue a college education had increased to 60 percent for whites, 62 percent for African Americans, 53 percent for Hispanics, and 45 percent for Native Americans. Adding those who intended to enter college at a later date, a total of over 90 percent of Asian American students planned for higher education. These high aspirations generally became reality and Asian American students were indeed more likely than others to attain a college education.

This high attainment rate raises many interesting questions. For example, how do Asian American students finance their college education, particularly if they are from low-income families? What proportion of them receive financial aid? Do they differ from students of other ethnic backgrounds in their family support and financial aid participation?

Answers to these questions are important. They will give future Asian American students and parents information about financing college education and help

Table 29.22
Average cost of a higher education: 1992-93*

	Total	Tuition and Fees	Room Rate	Board
All institutions	$7,470	$3,532	$1,945	
Public				
University	6,449	2,610	1,858	1,981
Other 4-year	5,745	2,190	1,792	1,763
2-year	3,793	1,018	1,115	1,660
Private				
University	18,892	13,043	3,022	2,827
Other 4-year	13,997	9,636	2,157	2,204
2-year	9,972	6,101	1,946	1,925

Notes:
Tuition and fees for public institutions are in-state rates; room and board were based on full-time students. The in-state tuition and fees and room and board rates varied by state. In public four-year institutions, for example, tuition and fees ranged from $1,266 in North Carolina to $5,321 in Vermont; room and board rates ranged from $2,282 in Oklahoma to $6,762 in California.

Source: *Snyder, T. and C. M., Hoffman. Digest of Education Statistics, 1993. Washington, D.C.: U.S. Department of Education, 1993.*

them in their own planning. They will also help policy analysts and program developers identify areas for further study and pinpoint possible financial barriers for some Asian American students.

It is, therefore, the purpose of this section to present relevant data that begin to provide answers to these questions. Only a small number of national studies have probed student financial data, and their sample sizes do not allow detailed classifications of Asian American students who were lumped together as one group, despite their diverse backgrounds. Thus, the analysis may mask some groups' financial difficulties, such as Southeast Asians and Pacific Islanders, two groups with a large population of poor families.

Costs of Education

To understand how students finance their college education, one needs to know how much it costs to attend college. In 1992-1993, the national average was $7,470, including tuition, fees, and room and board—a 6-percent increase from the previous year. The cost varied by type of institution. The average cost for public four-year universities in the same year was $6,449 and $18,892 for private four-year universities. Details are shown in Table 29.22.

The total cost for attending college, however, also includes books, supplies, and other expenses. In 1989-90, for example, Asian American undergraduates attending public doctoral institutions had total expenses averaging $8,980. Students attending public nondoctoral institutions averaged $8,021. Because private institution costs are higher, Asian American

students at those schools reported average annual expenses of $17,931 to attend not-for-profit doctoral institutions and $13,869 to attend not-for-profit nondoctoral institutions (Table 29.23).

The total cost varied by the level of institution, although the pattern was not consistent. As shown in Table 29.23, two-to-three-year or less-than-two-year institutions do not always cost less than four-year institutions. Asian American and Hispanic students, in fact, reported a higher average total cost to attend two-to-three-year institutions than to attend four-year nondoctoral institutions.

Is Race/Ethnicity a Factor in College Cost?

Are there differences in the total cost of college attendance between Asian Americans and other ethnic groups? The pattern is quite mixed at the public institutions. In 1989-90, the total cost reported by Asian American students to attend public four-year doctoral institutions and two-to-three-year institutions ranked second, and the cost to attend public four-year nondoctoral institutions ranked the lowest among five ethnic groups (Table 29.23).

At private institutions, the pattern was clear. Asian American students reported a higher cost of attending private institutions than students of other ethnic backgrounds. These differences, however, do not mean that different charges are made by institutions to different students. The difference probably reflects the fact that Asian American students were more likely than others to attend highly selective private institutions that usually charge high tuition and fees. In addition, the

Table 29.23
Total Cost of College

Average student-reported total costs of attendance for undergraduates by the level and control of institution and study race ethnicity: 1989-90

Race/ethnicity	Public			PublicPrivate not-for-profit			Private for-profit
	two-to-three year	four-year non-doctoral	four-year doctoral	two-to-three year	four-year non-doctoral	four-year doctoral	two or more year
Asian American	$8,346	$8,021	$8,980	—	$13,869	$17,931	$13,765
Native American	9,601	9,454	9,665	—	12,848	15,149	—
African American	7,427	8,156	7,810	8,614	11,974	14,495	9,778
Hispanic	8,170	8,349	7,799	11,968	11,811	14,717	11,888
White	8,292	8,447	8,525	8,863	12,841	15,287	11,150

Notes:
— Sample size not sufficient for reliable estimates.

Source: *U.S. Department of Education, National Center for Education Statistics, National Postsecondary Student Aid Study, 1990, NPSAS:90.*

difference in total cost also reflects the variation in financial aid participation among different ethnic groups.

Sources of Financial Support

Students receive support from various sources to finance their college education, including the student's (and spouse's) finances, parents' contribution, and financial aid programs. How much did Asian American students rely on each of these sources? Did they differ from other students in the sources of financing for their college education? Answers to these questions differ by student backgrounds. Students that are more dependent, by the very definition of dependence, received financial support from their parents, but both independent and dependent students were equally likely to receive financial aid on the basis of financial need.

Table 29.24
Students Receiving Family Support
to Pay for College

Students receiving family support by dependence status and race/ethnicity, in percent.

	Dependent	Independent
Asian American	64.1	20.3
Native American	41.1	11.7
African American	46.9	9.2
Hispanic	48.6	10.6
White	66.3	16.3

Source: *U.S. Department of Education, National Center for Education Statistics, National Postsecondary Student Aid Study, 1990 NPSAS:90.*

Family Support

In the past, Asian American students were more likely than other students to be financially dependent on their parents. In 1989-90, for example, 55 percent of Asian American students were dependent. In contrast, only 45 percent of Native American, 39 percent of African American, 47 percent of Hispanic, and 49 percent of white students were classified as dependent students. This status was reflected in family support for college education. A high percentage of Asian American students—44 percent—who were attending college at least half time reported the receipt of family support.

Compared to other minority students in 1989-1990, dependent Asian American students were more likely (64 percent) to receive family support. In contrast, 41 percent of Native American, 47 percent of African American, 49 percent of Hispanic, and 66 percent of white dependent students reported receiving family support (Table 29.24). Among independent students, 20 percent of Asian American students received family support, as compared to about 10 percent of other minorities and 16 percent of white students.

Financial Aid Programs

Besides family support, students may receive financial aid from federal and state governments, as well as institutions and other private sources such as employers, organizations, unions, or foundations. Financial aid is awarded according to many different criteria. Some is awarded on the basis of financial need and some on merit. In general, financial-aid recipients were more likely than nonrecipients to come from lower-income families, to attend higher-cost institutions, and to live on campus.

Table 29.25
Who Gets What?

College students receiving aid by type of aid, by students' race/ethnicity, in percent: 1989-90.

Race/Ethnicity	Any Aid	Grants	Work	Loans	Other
Asian American	35.8	31.0	6.0	14.1	7.5
Native American	49.1	45.6	5.1	15.3	13.0
African American	60.2	53.1	7.5	29.0	7.7
Hispanic	49.9	46.9	5.4	19.0	7.2
White	40.1	33.3	4.3	17.7	8.1

Source: *U.S. Department of Education, National Center for Education Statistics. National Postsecondary Student Aid Study, 1990 NPSAS:90.*

Asian American students were least likely to receive financial aid among all ethnic groups. In 1989-90, only 36 percent received any financial aid, as compared to 49 percent of Native American, 60 percent of African American, 50 percent of Hispanic, and 40 percent of white students (Table 29.25). Of those Asian American students who received aid, 31 percent were awarded grants, 6 percent participated in work-study programs, 14 percent took out loans, and 8 percent received other aid.

It should be noted that more than one financial resource may be tapped to support college education. For example, a student may get loans and/or grants in addition to family support. Thus, the percentages by type of financial aid are not additive, nor does the total percentage of students receiving financial aid from all sources reflect the sum of the percentages of federal, state, and institutional aid.

Federal Financial Aid

Most financial aid comes from the federal government and is administered by the Department of Education. There are three types of aid: grants, work study, and loans. They are designed for financially needy students who attend college at least half-time and are either citizens or eligible non-citizens. To be eligible, students must prove their financial need. Some federal programs, such as the Pell grant program, use a mathematical formula to determine a student's eligibility for and amount of aid. Other financial-aid programs are administered by individual institutions. These programs vary considerably because aid is awarded at the discretion of the financial aid administrator, according to that particular institution's policies.

Based on 1989-90 national survey data (NPSAS:90), 26 percent of Asian American students received at

Table 29.26
Students Receiving Federal Aid

Students receiving federal aid by type of aid and by student race/ethnicity, in percent and by amount of aid, in dollars: 1989-90.

Race/ethnicity	All aid	Grants	Loans	Work	Other
Percentage receiving aid					
Asian American	25.7	20.1	13.3	6.0	1.5
Native American	34.8	29.7	14.8	5.1	4.8
African American	49.7	41.0	28.2	7.5	1.4
Hispanic	40.1	33.9	18.6	5.4	1.1
White	25.3	17.3	16.7	4.3	0.9
Average amount of aid, in dollars					
Asian American	3,283	1,724	2,835	1,489	—
Native American	3,302	1,644	3,100	1,179	—
African American	3,136	1,630	2,632	1,390	1,544
Hispanic	2,890	1,671	2,706	1,164	2,424
White	3,133	1,506	2,630	1,214	1,620

Notes:
— Sample not sufficient for reliable estimates. Average amount was based on recipients only.

Source: *U.S. Department of Education, National Center for Education Statistics, National Postsecondary Student Aid Study, 1990.*

Table 29.27
Profile of Students Receiving Federal Aid

Students receiving any federal aid by family income level, dependence status, and race/ethnicity, in percent: 1989-90

Aid	Asian	African	Hispanic	White
All students	25.7	49.7	40.1	25.3
Dependent students				
Less than $10,000	60.0	78.06	9.6	60.9
$10,000-29,999	36.9	60.1	43.8	39.2
$30,000-49,999	15.1	34.8	25.0	23.6
$50,000-69,999	12.4	23.6	13.0	13.7
$70,000+	6.6	10.4	4.1	5.7
Independent students				
Less than $5,000	42.0	72.4	62.6	52.1
$5,000-9,999	29.0	59.8	50.7	41.8
$10,000-19,999	21.0	35.3	36.5	25.5
$20,000-29,999	8.9	32.7	25.6	16.9
$30,000+	5.5	17.3	10.0	7.0

Notes:
Sample size of Native American was too small for this analysis.

Source: U.S. Department of Education, National Center for Education Statistics, National Postsecondary Student Aid Study, 1990.

least one type of federal aid (see Table 29.26): 20 percent were awarded grants; 13 percent took out loans; 6 percent participated in work study; and 2 percent found other types of aid. Asian American and white students were similar in their participation in these federal programs. However, Asian American students were less likely to get a grant or loan than other racial/ethnic minority students.

Based on students receiving aid, the average total amount of aid received by Asian Americans was $3,283 in the 1989-90 school year. The average grant was $1,724 and the average loan was $2,835. These were not significantly different from the amounts received by other racial/ethnic groups. This finding is not surprising since these aid programs were based on financial need determined by the same rule. The small variation in the average amount of aid most probably reflects the different institutions attended by these students.

As expected, participation in federal aid programs varied by students' family income level. As shown in Table 29.27, the percentage of Asian American dependent students receiving any federal aid in 1989-90 ranged from 60 percent of students with family income less than $10,000 to 6.63 percent of students with family income greater than $69,999. A similar pattern was also shown by different income categories for independent students, from 42 percent of students with income less than $5,000 to 5 percent of students with income greater than $29,999.

Except for a couple of income categories, Asian American students, both dependent and independent, received less federal aid than African and Hispanic American students. Independent Asian American students also had lower aid participation rates than white students in every income category. Reasons for these differences cannot be explained by data currently available. Future studies should examine whether Asian American students, particularly independent students, are less likely to apply for aid, receive other types of aid, or have other unknown reasons.

State and Institutional Aid Programs

State and institutional aid programs are major financial sources for supporting college education that have become increasingly important in recent years.

While there are state grants, work-study, and loan programs, not every state offers all of them. Every state, however, has some type of grant program, primarily because the federal government encouraged states to develop grant programs that qualified for the State Student Incentive Grant Program, a federal-state matching program. Many of these state grant programs are designed with specific goals—namely, targeting groups of students, specific types of institutions, particular fields, and those in financial need.

Similarly, institutions have both grant and loan programs and their own policies for awarding aid. It may

Table 29.28
Students Receiving Nonfederal Aid

Percentage of undergraduates receiving nonfederal aid by the type of aid and race/ethnicity: 1989-90

Racial/Ethnic Group	Any Aid	Grant	Loans	Work-Study	Other
State Aid					
Asian American	13.3	12.3	0.2	0.3	1.7
Native American	20.0	16.6	0.1	0.0	3.9
African American	15.8	13.9	0.4	0.2	2.2
Hispanic	16.2	13.8	0.6	0.3	2.5
White	11.9	10.1	0.8	0.2	1.7
Institutional Aid					
Asian American	13.9	12.9	0.8	—	2.5
Native American	13.2	12.4	0.3	—	0.7
African American	20.4	18.5	1.1	—	1.8
Hispanic	15.1	13.7	0.4	—	1.7
White	13.8	12.3	0.7	—	1.9

Notes:
—- No work-study programs.

Source: U.S. Department of Education, National Center for Education Statistics, National Postsecondary Student Aid Study, 1990.

or may not be based upon financial need, a parameter set at their discretion.

Based on 1989-90 data, about 13 percent of all Asian American undergraduates received some state aid, compared to 20 percent of Native American, 16 percent of African American, 16 percent of Hispanic, and 12 percent of white students (Table 29.28). Most state aid, as mentioned earlier, came from grant programs. About 12 percent of Asian American students received state grants.

The 1989-90 data also show that about 14 percent of Asian American undergraduates received institutional aid, as compared to 13 percent of Native American, 20 percent of African American, 15 percent of Hispanic, and 14 percent of white students. Like state aid, most institutional aid was in grant programs. For Asian American students, 13 percent were awarded grants, 0.8 percent were given institutional loans, and about 3 percent found other aid.

Summary and Discusson

In the early 1990s, about 90 percent of Asian American students aspired to college. The majority of them attended college at some point after high school. This trend is expected to continue.

How did they finance their college education? Fewer than half of them received family financial support, and about one-third received financial aid from both federal and nonfederal sources. In comparison with other racial/ethnic minority groups, Asian American students had lower participation rates in various aid programs, even among students from lower-income families. It is possible that some Asian American students were not comfortable applying for aid or were not aware of financial aid programs.

Future studies should investigate any possible barriers to Asian American student aid and examine whether this affects their ability to get a college education. Furthermore, researchers may want to study trends in higher-education financing for Asian American subgroups, such as Cambodian, Chinese, Filipino, Indian, Japanese, Korean, and Vietnamese. Current data only allow analyses of Asian Americans as a group, despite their economic and cultural diversity, allowing for serious misrepresentation of certain Asian groups.

Other intriguing research areas to be pursued include studies of Asian American students in inner cities as well as those from Pacific Islands and Southeast Asia, who tend to have lower educational attainment. A lack of financial resources may prevent them from achieving a college education.

—Samuel S. Peng and Tai A. Phan
National Center for Education Statistics
U.S. Department of Education

◆ TEACHING AND TEACHER EDUCATION

The increasing diversity and multiracial complexion of American society is particularly apparent in the nation's schools. Estimates predict that by the year

2020, 40 percent of school children will be nonwhite. Currently, at least 30 percent are children of color, according to the Center of Education Statistics, as are over 70 percent of total school enrollments in 20 of the largest school districts. Despite these statistics, the population of teacher educators, teachers, and administrators continues to be largely white.

This juxtaposition of a burgeoning minority school population against a far smaller number of minority teachers has received much scholarly attention in the past decade. Much of it, however, has either been in general terms or has concentrated on African American and Latino teachers. Very little is known about Asian Americans in teaching and teacher education. This section attempts to simultaneously desegregate and collate available data and focus specifically on Asian Americans and Pacific Islanders (API) in an effort to assess their presence in the teaching profession.

Asian American and Pacific Islander Teachers and Students: an Unequal Equation

In 1988, API teachers in public and private elementary and secondary schools numbered 25,294, or 0.9 percent of the teaching force. By 1990-91, the number of API elementary and secondary public teachers had reached 25,952, or 1 percent of the teaching force. However, this modest increase is not commensurate with the rapid growth in the API population.

Between 1970 and 1980, the API population grew by 143 percent and was estimated to have reached about 5 million by 1985. By 1990, according to the U.S. Bureau of Census, APIs numbered a little over 7 million, constituting over 3 percent of the U.S. population. Their numbers are expected to grow to 10 million by the year 2000 and 18 million by 2050, reaching 4 and 6.4 percent of the population, respectively.

Naturally, these increases are also reflected in demographic shifts in school enrollments. Between 1976 and 1988, the number of APIs enrolled in elementary and secondary schools rose from 535,000 to about 1.25 million. This represented a 137-percent increase, from 1.2 percent to 3.1 percent of the kindergarten through grade 12 population, according to the National Center for Education Statistics. By 1990, almost 1.4 million APIs were enrolled in elementary and secondary schools with Hawaii, New York, and California each boasting enrollments of over 100,000 API students. California topped the list with more than 600,000 API children enrolled. Four additional states—New Jersey, Illinois, Texas, and Washington—each included over 50,000 API students on their school rosters. Indeed, both the Western Interstate Commission for Higher Education and the College Board predict that API enrollees in public schools will reach 1.6 million by 1995, with the number of states educating significant numbers of API children certain to increase. Thus, APIs constitute a rapidly expanding portion of the U.S. school population, but are disproportionately represented among precollegiate teacher ranks.

Asian Americans in Teacher Education

College attendance among APIs has multiplied at rates that parallel the population expansion and the increase in school enrollments. Postsecondary enrollment of APIs rose from 1.8 percent in 1976 to 4 percent in 1990 and, therefore, are apparently attending college at a rate that is proportionate to their total population levels. However, APIs are still largely absent from undergraduate teacher preparation programs despite a 22-percent increase in participation rates between 1989 and 1991. In fact, mean API registration in schools and colleges of education hovers at about 1 percent, with teacher education programs preparing an average of eight API preservice teachers per year. However, this figure obscures the fact that in 39 states, API enrollment in schools and colleges of education is negligible (i.e., less than 1 percent) and that the largest percentages of API teacher-education students are clustered in only eight western states—Alaska, California, Hawaii, Idaho, Nevada, New Mexico, Oregon, and Washington.

In a study of teacher education sponsored by the American Association of Colleges for Teacher Education (AACTE) and Metropolitan Life, 472 students from 42 schools or colleges of education were surveyed. Of the total sample, only 18 respondents were APIs, a sample size too small to make any meaningful generalizations. However, the findings from this survey do provide detailed data that offer some insight into the experiences and thinking of API teacher-education students.

The results of the survey indicated that the API teacher-education students in this group were likely to have attended high schools with a majority API enrollment but were more likely than other minority students to attend mostly white colleges or universities. This phenomenon may explain the finding that APIs were more likely than African Americans or Latinos to assess their institutions as insensitive to minority concerns. Close to half of the API students reported attending colleges that were more than 2000 miles away from their homes, and most—73 percent—were attending the institution of their first choice. The survey also found that these APIs had attended two-year institutions before entering their current college of education at rates higher than their black or white counterparts. Only one-third of the API students in the sample considered English their native language. In terms of family income, 31.3 percent of APIs came from families earning less than $15,000 a year.

The survey also explored respondents' attitudes towards their teacher-education programs, as well as their future aspirations. Half of the APIs surveyed saw a baccalaureate as the highest degree they would attain, as compared to 17 percent of whites, 9 percent of blacks and 11 percent of Hispanics. Conversely, only one-third of API respondents aspired to master's degrees as compared to 41 percent of Hispanics, 54 percent of blacks, and 70 percent of whites.

Elementary education was selected by half the API respondents, early childhood education by 27.8 percent, secondary education by 11 percent, and special education by 5.6 percent. Interestingly, this survey found no API students who had chosen bilingual education as their education specialty.

These figures differ from those based on another AACTE survey of 685 schools and colleges of education (AACTE 1990b), which found that 1.4 percent of bilingual education majors were of API descent and that less than 1 percent of the remaining education majors—early childhood, elementary, secondary, special, vocational and other education, numbering about 300,000—were APIs.

Finally, API teacher education students in the AACTE/Metropolitan Life survey indicated (at the rate of 40 percent and above) that the availability of financial aid, personal/academic counseling, tutoring programs, and responsive faculty influenced their decision to attend their particular institution. Most API respondents also rated increased financial aid for minorities; minority-oriented cultural and social events; the presence of minority faculty/staff; special minority living accommodations; more remedial, tutorial or counseling help; greater attention paid to minority concerns; intensive recruiting by minority counselors, students, and faculty; and different admissions standards for minorities as helpful or very helpful in recruiting students of color to teacher education programs.

When considering API involvement in teacher education, it is important to consider faculty as well. In fall 1985, there were about 18,000 API college faculty at all ranks in the academy. Of these, just under 15,000 were men and 3,500 were women, giving a gender ratio of about 5 to 1. Since the overwhelming majority of teacher education professors are white and female, and given the low numbers of API women among faculty ranks, it is no surprise that APIs constitute only 1 percent of education faculty, even though APIs are well-represented in the doctoral pool. Compounding the shortage of API education faculty is the fact that API doctorates are concentrated in engineering and computer science and that API Ph.D.s enter academic employment at rates lower than the national average.

Apparently, the status of APIs in education during the mid-1990s, for both students in teacher preparation and faculty, was tenuous. While few APIs are in teaching and teacher education, they are increasingly filling precollegiate classrooms. An examination of the education pipeline may indicate that this trend will continue.

Asian Americans and Pacific Islanders in the Education Pipeline

Teaching as a professional pursuit ranks low among API undergraduates. In studies surveying the career choices of API college students, business/management and engineering are frequent first choices for the largest numbers of respondents, while education invariably ranks low. In fact, less than 4 percent of API college students prepare for teaching careers, unlike nearly 12 percent of all college students.

These data are confirmed by an examination of bachelor's degrees conferred on API graduates during the 1989-90 year. Of 29 fields of study, education ranked 13th, with APIs earning 931 bachelor's degrees in this field. This trend promised to continue according to the results of a 1992 survey of 10th graders' occupational expectations conducted by the National Center for Education Statistics. While more than half of the API 10th graders surveyed expected to be occupied in professional, business, or managerial fields by age 30, only 1.7 percent imagined themselves becoming teachers. In fact, out of 13 occupational choices, teaching ranked higher than only four—namely, farmer or farm manager, housewife/homemaker, laborer or farm worker, and service worker.

The estimates of the numbers of Asian and Pacific Islanders likely to join higher education faculty reflect similar participation rates. In 1989-90, the National Academy of Sciences reported that, while APIs accounted for 4.9 percent of all doctorates, they earned only 1.7 percent of education doctoral degrees. This number represents a loss of 0.2 percent when compared to the number of education doctorates earned by APIs in 1988-89, and a 0.7-percent loss when compared to 1987-88 figures, as reported by National Academy of Sciences. Thus, while 125 APIs received education doctoral degrees in 1988-89, only 95 education doctorates were earned by APIs in 1989-90. This situation is unlikely to change, as illustrated by the findings from an AACTE survey of teacher education students: only 16.8 percent of API respondents aspired to doctoral degrees as compared to 49 percent of Hispanics and 37 percent of blacks.

Where Are the API Teachers? Seeking an Explanation

Trying to understand why API high schoolers and college students seem not to rank teaching as a viable career demands a force field analysis of the motivations that draw individuals into the field and the impediments that deflect them.

Entering Teaching: Motivations and Impediments

A groundbreaking study of teachers in 1975 articulated the rewards of the profession as perceived by teachers. These included extrinsic rewards (such as salary) and psychic rewards (such as the opportunity to work with children). These findings were confirmed and expanded in a 1988 study of teacher beliefs, which found that in addition to the motivators listed above, individuals were also drawn to the profession by the promise of working autonomously and exerting an impact on society. Not surprisingly, low teacher salaries and status detracted from the profession.

In an effort to discover what motivates APIs to enter teaching, a survey of 22 Asian Americans was conducted during winter 1993. The research sample was almost entirely female (with only two males) and consisted of 13 newly certified teachers (less than two years experience), one experienced teacher and eight preservice teacher education students. Respondents were presented with seven reasons that are typically related to decisions to enter teaching and asked to rank as many of the seven as they chose. Respondents were also given the opportunity to offer additional reasons for entering teaching not covered by the seven items listed.

The three reasons selected by the majority of respondents as the most or second-most important reasons for choosing teaching were the desire to make a difference or engage in meaningful work (82 percent), a love for children/interactions with young people (56 percent), and a love of learning/being in schools (45 percent). The two motivators that received the lowest ranking by the largest percentage of respondents were teaching hours/school schedule (45 percent) and having a lot of autonomy in the classroom (41 percent). Six respondents each included an additional reason. Two were related to one of the responses already provided—enthusiasm for learning, love of learning/helping. Two reasons were related to diversity—supporting children of color and relating multicultural history. The last additional reasons seemed personal and perhaps unique to the respondents—the need to understand children and self, and the integrated nature of teaching.

The study also sought to ascertain the barriers that keep APIs away from teaching. Again, respondents were asked to rank six choices and invited to add their own thoughts. The responses to this item were more

Table 29.29
Scientists and Engineers by Racial Ethnic Group

Race/Ethnicity	Employed in science and engineering, in percent	Employed in total workforce, in percent
Asians and Asian Americans	5	2
Blacks	2.6	10
Hispanics	1.8	7.2

Source: *The 1990 Science Report Card: NAEP'S Assessment of Fourth, Eighth, and Twelfth Graders. Prepared by Educational Testing Service under contract with the National Center for Education Statistics, March 1992.*

mixed so that only one item was ranked either first or second by a majority of the group: 64 percent of the respondents felt that the perception of teaching as not intellectually challenging was a primary obstacle to entering the profession. Half of the respondents ranked two other barriers first or second—teachers' salaries (50 percent) and the perception of teaching as low status work (50 percent). The two barriers that received the lowest ranking by the largest percentage of respondents were negative publicity about the state of schools/education (41 percent) and the lack of support from parents, friends, or significant others (41 percent).

Conclusion

This chapter has detailed how grossly underrepresented APIs are among teaching ranks at both precollegiate and postsecondary levels. APIs are often not included in the recruitment projects, fellowships, and state programs designed to increase the number of teachers of color. APIs receive little encouragement to enter teaching, although it appears that recruitment strategies to attract other "minority"groups—African American or Latino—will also work for APIs.

This is not to imply that African American or Latino teachers are not in critical need, but rather that a racially and culturally diverse nation such as the United States needs a teaching force that is equally racially and culturally diverse. As long as Asian Americans and Pacific Islanders are underrepresented, the American teaching force will not reflect the diverse society it seeks to educate.

—A. Lin Goodwin
Teachers College, Columbia University

♦ ASIAN AMERICANS IN SCIENCE

Asian Americans in science and engineering fields exceed their representation in the U.S. workforce. In 1988, for example, Asians made up 5 percent of those

Table 29.30
Profile of Sample
Grade 4

	Asian Am	African Am	American Indian	Hispanic	White
Number of Students	199	1,075	15.7	1,161	3,715
% of Sample	1.9	15.2	1.6	11.0	70.2
Sex:					
Male	51.0	48.7	57.5	51.9	51.5
Female	49.0	51.3	42.5	48.1	48.5
Region:					
NE	8.4	21.7	14.8	19.0	22.5
SE	7.0	42.4	17.1	18.0	22.0
Central	10.7	21.5	32.1	15.4	29.6
West	74.0	14.4	36.0	47.6	25.9
Type of Community:					
Rural	1.7	3.8	13.8	6.3	13.2
Disadvantaged Urban	12.8	22.8	11.0	19.7	4.7
Advantaged Urban	25.9	4.7	7.2	7.8	12.8
Other	59.6	68.7	68.0	66.2	69.3
Parents' Education Level:					
Less than H.S.	4.1	4.3	5.8	7.7	5.0
Graduated H.S.	6.1	17.5	15.9	15.4	15.7
Some Postsecondary	6.7	6.3	6.7	7.3	9.5
Graduated College	37.1	38.9	30.9	27.6	35.9
Unknown	46.0	33.1	40.8	42.0	33.9
Type of School:					
Public	82.1	93.9	94.1	91.8	87.3
Private	8.5	2.3	2.0	2.3	5.2
Catholic	9.3	3.8	3.9	5.9	7.5

Source: The 1990 Science Report Card: NAEP'S Assessment of Fourth, Eighth, and Twelfth Graders. Prepared by Educational Testing Service under contract with the National Center for Education Statistics, March 1992.

employed in science and engineering fields in the United States, although they represented only 2 percent of the overall workforce and 3 percent of those employed in professional fields. In contrast, black and Hispanic professionals represented 2.6 percent and 1.8 percent, respectively, of the pool of employed scientists and engineers in 1988, percentages far below their representation in the workforce, which was 10 percent and 7.2 percent, respectively. Additionally, Asian scientists and engineers with doctoral degrees exceeded their representation among all scientists and engineers. In 1989, Asians made up 9.2 percent of employed doctoral scientists and engineers. These figures include non-citizens. Among doctoral-level scientists and engineers employed in 1989, roughly 68 percent of Asians were U.S. citizens.

Not all available databases distinguished between Asian U.S. citizens and noncitizens; others include noncitizens with U.S. permanent resident status. This presents a problem when making comparisons across databases and racial/ethnic groups. This is especially important for studies of Asian Americans in science and engineering, since so many Asian noncitizens are enrolled in these programs. In this paper, the term "Asian American" refers to U.S. citizens only; the designation "Asian" includes noncitizens as well as citizens.

Factors Contributing to Success in Science and Engineering

What are the antecedents of Asian American success in science and engineering fields? What are the home environments, attitudes, educational experiences, and achievements of Asian Americans as these factors relate to participation in science and engineering fields? This section will attempt to trace the process whereby Asian American students progress

Table 29.31
Profile of Sample
Grade 8

	Asian Am	African Am	American Indian	Hispanic	White
Number of Students	285	917	95	1,000	4,223
% of Sample	2.7	14.8	1.4	10.1	70.8
Sex:			!		
Male	52.9	45.1	**42.0**	51.9	50.9
Female	47.1	54.9	**58.0**	48.1	49.1
Region:			!		
NE	27.3	17.3	**11.4**	14.5	22.6
SE	5.2	42.4	**8.3**	9.3	23.7
Central	16.3	21.4	**17.5**	13.7	27.5
West	51.2	18.8	**62.8**	62.5	26.2
Type of Community:			!		
Rural	1.5	7.8	**44.8**	6.4	12.6
Disadvantaged Urban	16.8	19.8	**7.2**	20.7	5.0
Advantaged Urban	15.9	4.7	**2.9**	6.6	12.1
Other	65.8	67.7	**45.1**	66.3	70.3
Parents' Education Level:			!		
Less than H.S.	4.1	9.2	**8.2**	18.6	7.6
Graduated H.S.	12.4	26.3	**29.4**	24.0	25.0
Some Postsecondary	14.0	18.4	**23.1**	17.8	19.1
Graduated College	54.0	35.0	**28.4**	21.9	42.9
Unknown	15.5	11.2	**10.9**	17.8	5.4
Type of School:			!		
Public	75.1	93.2	**96.2**	85.9	88.4
Private	4.3	1.9	**0.8**	3.6	4.7
Catholic	20.7	4.8	**3.1**	10.4	7.0

Notes:
! Interpret with caution: Error cannot be estimated accurately since coefficient of variation of estimated number of students exceeds 20%.

Source: The 1990 Science Report Card: NAEP'S Assessment of Fourth, Eighth, and Twelfth Graders. Prepared by Educational Testing Service under contract with the National Center for Education Statistics, March 1992.

through the scientific pipeline to achieve success in scientific and engineering professions. Data from large-scale databases such as the National Assessment of Educational Progress (NAEP), the Student Descriptive Questionnaire (SDQ) of the Scholastic Aptitude Test (SAT), the National Research Council's Survey of Earned Doctorates, and others will be used.

Fourth, Eighth, and Twelfth Graders

Data was collected and published on students in the fourth, eighth, and 12th grades by the NAEP Science Assessment of 1990. These data reveal information on the demographic characteristics, educational experiences, background (including home environment and attitudes), and achievement in science of this group of students. Data collected at the elementary, middle school, and high school levels describe the experiences of students as they progress through the precollegiate portion of the educational pipeline.

Demographic Information

Tables 29.30, 29.31, and 29.32 give a profile of the NAEP samples for grades four, eight, and twelve, respectively.

The tables reveal that the sample is fairly evenly divided in terms of gender, with slightly more males in grades four and eight, and slightly more females in grade twelve for Asian Americans. For all grades, a

Table 29.32
Profile of Sample
Grade 12

	Asian Am	African Am	American Indian	Hispanic	White
Number of Students	263	872	51	700	4,443
% of Sample	3.6	14.2	0.7	8.2	73.2
Sex:			!		
Male	46.0	43.3	**56.9**	49.1	49.0
Female	54.0	56.7	**43.1**	50.9	51.0
Region:			!		
NE	21.3	19.0	**4.9**	13.9	26.2
SE	8.1	42.5	**17.1**	11.0	18.1
Central	8.8	18.6	**38.1**	9.8	30.6
West	61.8	19.9	**39.9**	65.3	25.1
Type of Community:			!		
Rural	3.2	8.3	**30.7**	5.0	12.3
Disadvantaged Urban	15.7	23.8	**8.5**	36.3	7.2
Advantaged Urban	13.4	9.7	**11.7**	8.2	10.4
Other	67.7	58.3	**49.0**	50.5	70.1
Parents' Education Level:			!		
Less than H.S.	5.5	8.8	**5.0**	25.0	5.4
Graduated H.S.	14.4	29.3	**26.0**	23.1	23.3
Some Postsecondary	18.6	27.1	**35.6**	22.1	26.7
Graduated College	59.2	30.5	**30.0**	23.2	43.5
Unknown	2.3	4.4	**3.4**	6.6	1.1
Type of School:			!		
Public	92.7	92.9	**93.5**	89.7	89.5
Private	3.3	3.0	**5.0**	2.8	4.9
Catholic	4.0	4.1	**1.5**	7.5	5.6

Notes:
! Interpret with caution: Error cannot be estimated accurately since coefficient of variation of estimated number of students exceeds 20%.

Source: The 1990 Science Report Card: NAEP'S Assessment of Fourth, Eighth, and Twelfth Graders. Prepared by Educational Testing Service under contract with the National Center for Education Statistics, March 1992.

majority of Asian American students in the sample reside in the western region of the nation. With the exception of fourth graders, the majority of Asian American students had parents who had graduated from college. (In the case of fourth graders, 46 percent did not know what was their parents' educational level, which is understandable given their young age.)

Overall, Asian American students' parents had higher educational levels than did any other racial/ethnic groups in the sample. In terms of types of school attended, Asian Americans in grades four and eight attended private or Catholic schools at a greater rate than did their counterparts from other racial/ethnic groups. By grade twelve, attendance at public schools

was roughly equivalent to that of other students. This sample of Asian American students, therefore, seems to have parents with higher educational levels and, during their elementary and middle school years, to attend private or Catholic schools at a greater rate than their peers from other racial/ethnic categories.

Educational Experiences and Background

Home Environment

The home environment also influences students' proficiency in science. In general, with access to more reading materials at home, students perform better than those with access to fewer materials. Students who watch six or more hours of television daily have lower

Table 29.33
Student Background/Home Environment
Grade 4

Question:	Asian Am %	African Am %	American Indian %	Hispanic %	White %
How often language other than English spoken in home?					
Never	25.0	69.3	64.8	33.1	72.6
Sometimes	53.1	24.0	29.2	46.3	24.4
Always	21.9	6.7	6.0	20.6	3.0
Missing	1.5	1.1	0.0	1.0	0.9
Does family get newspaper regularly?					
Yes	62.1	63.6	65.1	61.4	71.9
No	27.4	27.8	23.9	27.9	19.9
I don't know	10.5	8.6	11.0	10.7	8.3
Missing	0.7	0.8	0.0	0.8	0.7
Is there an encyclopedia in your home?					
Yes	59.8	65.1	59.1	56.5	70.1
No	32.5	29.3	30.5	35.3	22.8
I don't know	7.6	5.6	10.4	8.2	7.1
Missing	1.1	1.2	0.0	0.4	.7
Are there more than 25 books in your home?					
Yes	86.0	75.5	82.3	76.1	91.3
No	5.8	12.6	12.6	12.0	2.7
I don't know	8.2	11.9	5.0	11.8	6.0
Missing	0.4	0.8	0.0	0.7	0.8
Does your family get magazines regularly?					
Yes	56.6	53.3	59.9	50.2	62.4
No	28.6	33.2	26.2	33.5	22.9
I don't know	14.8	13.5	13.9	16.3	14.7
Missing	0.4	0.7	0.0	1.2	0.8

Source: The 1990 Science Report Card: NAEP'S Assessment of Fourth, Eighth, and Twelfth Graders. Prepared by Educational Testing Service under contract with the National Center for Education Statistics, March 1992.

proficiency than students who watch less television. Students from two-parent homes tend to have higher average proficiency than those in single-parent families or those who live apart from both parents. The following tables give student responses by grade and by race/ethnicity to questions concerning the home environment.

With the exception of Hispanic students, Asian American students at all three grade levels are much more likely to come from homes where a language other than English is spoken "sometimes" or "always." Surprisingly (given its impact on science ability), Asian American students have less access to newspapers, encyclopedias, books, and magazines than do their white counterparts. At the fourth grade level, they are, with the exception of white fourth graders, much less likely to watch more than six hours of television daily. By grade eight, they are less likely than their African American and Hispanic counter-

parts to watch more than six hours of television. They are the most likely of all groups to watch no television at all at the twelfth grade level, with 58 percent watching from zero to two hours a day, which represents less television watching than all others but white twelfth graders.

The presence of a mother or stepmother in the home is roughly the same across racial/ethnic categories for all grade levels. However, Asian American fourth, eighth, and twelfth graders are much more likely to report that a father or stepfather lives in the home than are their African American and Hispanic counterparts.

Study Habits

The amount of time students spend doing homework, the amount of help they receive with homework from someone in the home, and the number of pages

Table 29.34
Student Background/Home Environment
Grade 8

Question:	Asian Am %	African Am %	American Indian %	Hispanic %	White %
How often language other than English spoken in home?			**!**		
Never	18.6	72.7	**54.1**	17.4	76.2
Sometimes	52.2	24.2	**39.1**	50.1	20.7
Always	29.3	3.1	**6.8**	32.4	3.0
Missing	0.0	0.3	**0.0**	0.8	0.1
Does family get newspaper regularly?			**!**		
Yes	72.0	68.6	**70.5**	61.8	79.5
No	24.0	29.3	**25.9**	34.0	18.6
I don't know	4.1	2.1	**3.7**	4.2	1.9
Missing	0.0	0.4	**0.0**	0.4	0.1
Is there an encyclopedia in your home?			**!**		
Yes	67.8	76.5	**69.1**	65.7	81.6
No	28.9	20.7	**24.8**	30.9	16.7
I don't know	3.3	2.7	**6.1**	3.4	1.8
Missing	0.0	0.3	**0.0**	0.6	0.1
Are there more than 25 books in your home?			**!**		
Yes	91.5	86.4	**87.4**	81.5	93.3
No	4.5	7.9	**5.9**	11.9	3.3
I don't know	4.0	5.6	**6.7**	6.7	3.4
Missing	0.0	0.6	**0.0**	0.7	0.0
Does your family get magazines regularly?			**!**		
Yes	69.6	67.5	**75.1**	61.4	82.0
No	25.0	26.6	**20.1**	31.8	14.1
I don't know	5.4	5.9	**4.8**	6.8	3.9
Missing	0.4	2.2	**0.6**	1.4	0.5
Does mother or stepmother live at home with you?		**#**	**# - !**	**#**	
Yes	89.9	**88.7**	**87.2**	**91.5**	94.9
No	10.1	**11.3**	**12.8**	**8.5**	5.1
Does family or stepfather live at home with you?		**#**	**# - !**	**#**	
Yes	84.8	**54.8**	**75.5**	**76.1**	85.2
No	15.2	**45.2**	**24.5**	**23.9**	14.8

Notes:
Interpret with caution: Rate of nonresponse is high.
! Interpret with caution: Error cannot be estimated accurately since coefficient of variation of estimated number of students exceeds 20%.

Source: The 1990 Science Report Card: NAEP'S Assessment of Fourth, Eighth, and Twelfth Graders. Prepared by Educational Testing Service under contract with the National Center for Education Statistics, March 1992.

read in school and for homework are indicators of student achievement in school. Tables 29.36, 29.37, and 29.38 give students' responses to NAEP questions regarding general study habits for the different racial/ethnic groups in the sample.

Although at grade four Asian American students are less likely to spend more than one hour on homework than are African American and Hispanic students, by grades eight and twelve, Asian American students are much more likely to spend two or more hours daily on homework than are any of their counterparts.

Unexpectedly, Asian Americans are also the least likely of all groups to receive daily help with homework from someone in the home, as well as the most likely to report never receiving help with homework. In terms of pages read in school and for homework, a

Table 29.35
Student Background/Home Environment
Grade 12

Question:	Asian Am %	African Am %	American Indian %	Hispanic %	White %
How often language other than English spoken in home?			!		
Never	25.4	76.8	**69.6**	16.3	82.3
Sometimes	38.7	14.6	**27.2**	42.6	13.0
Always	35.8	8.6	**3.2**	41.2	4.7
Missing	0.0	0.8	**0.0**	0.6	0.2
Does family get newspaper regularly?			!		
Yes	69.7	74.6	**67.3**	61.5	83.5
No	29.1	23.3	**28.0**	35.8	15.4
I don't know	1.1	2.1	**4.7**	2.6	1.0
Missing	0.0	0.6	**0.0**	0.5	0.1
Is there an encyclopedia in your home?			!		
Yes	69.6	81.7	**76.3**	70.6	83.7
No	28.5	16.5	**21.8**	26.2	14.7
I don't know	1.9	1.8	**1.9**	3.1	1.5
Missing	0.0	0.6	**0.0**	0.4	0.0
Are there more than 25 books in your home?			!		
Yes	95.7	87.9	**87.1**	82.7	94.3
No	3.5	9.8	**2.5**	11.1	3.3
I don't know	0.9	2.3	**10.4**	6.2	2.4
Missing	0.0	0.4	**0.0**	1.0	0.1
Does your family get magazines regularly?			!		
Yes	74.9	75.0	**75.0**	71.1	88.2
No	22.7	24.1	**20.3**	25.6	10.5
I don't know	2.3	0.9	**4.7**	3.2	1.3
Missing	0.5	0.9	**0.0**	1.3	0.3
Does mother or stepmother live at home with you?		#	!	#	
Yes	88.1	**88.7**	90.9	**88.3**	92.4
No	11.9	**11.3**	9.1	**11.7**	7.6
Does family or stepfather live at home with you?		#	!	#	
Yes	80.4	**54.0**	83.8	**69.9**	83.0
No	19.6	**46.0**	16.2	**30.1**	17.0

Notes:
\# Interpret with caution: Rate of nonresponse is high.
! Interpret with caution: Error cannot be estimated accurately since coefficient of variation of estimated number of students exceeds 20%.

Source: The 1990 Science Report Card: NAEP'S Assessment of Fourth, Eighth, and Twelfth Graders. Prepared by Educational Testing Service under contract with the National Center for Education Statistics, March 1992.

smaller percentage of Asian Americans than any other group at the fourth grade level report reading five pages or fewer, but a larger percentage of African American and white fourth graders report reading more than ten pages. By grades eight and twelve, however, Asian Americans are much more likely to read more than ten pages daily in school and for homework than are any of the eighth and twelfth graders in the other racial/ethnic groups.

Students and Science

The science proficiency of students who report liking science is higher than the proficiency of those who do not like science. Furthermore, because meaningful

Table 29.36
Study Habits
Grade 4

Question:	Asian Am %	African Am %	American Indian %	Hispanic %	White %
How much TV do you usually watch each day?					
None	2.9	2.2	2.0	2.1	1.5
1 hour	22.6	12.4	14.7	18.0	17.4
2 hours	20.8	11.6	12.5	13.8	20.7
3 hours	14.3	11.5	14.8	15.1	17.5
4 hours	11.5	8.2	14.0	11.0	14.2
5 hours	7.2	7.4	9.1	7.5	8.9
6 + hours	20.6	46.8	32.9	32.4	19.8
How much time each day is spent on homework?					
Have none	16.7	15.3	21.4	14.5	23.8
Don't do	3.4	5.7	5.2	7.3	3.8
one-half hour	36.3	35.6	34.4	35.3	33.3
1 hour	25.2	20.7	22.3	23.6	24.4
1 + hours	18.4	22.7	16.7	19.2	14.8
How often does someone at home help with homework?					
Daily	17.9	44.6	34.7	34.4	29.8
Weekly	29.7	16.6	15.3	22.0	22.2
Monthly	8.4	2.8	4.3	5.3	8.5
Never	38.7	31.5	36.5	31.4	29.4
Have none	5.4	4.4	9.1	6.9	10.2
How many pages read in school and for homework?					
> 10 pages	50.6	52.5	50.3	49.5	53.5
6 - 10 pages	24.5	18.6	13.7	21.3	21.3
5 - fewer	24.9	29.0	36.1	29.2	25.2
Does mother or stepmother live at home with you?					
Yes	89.9	86.5	90.5	85.1	93.3
No	10.2	13.5	9.5	14.9	6.7
Does father or stepfather live at home with you?					
Yes	78.6	61.8	76.4	70.8	84.2
No	21.4	38.2	23.6	29.2	15.8

Source: The 1990 Science Report Card: NAEP'S Assessment of Fourth, Eighth, and Twelfth Graders. Prepared by Educational Testing Service under contract with the National Center for Education Statistics, March 1992.

experiences that involve science activities and projects facilitate students' learning of science, the NAEP student questionnaire assessed students' participation in selected science experiences. Tables 29.39, 29.40, and 29.41 report student responses to these questions by race/ethnicity and by grade.

When asked if they liked science, Asian Americans were more likely than African American and Hispanic students to reply "yes" at the fourth grade. By the eighth grade, however, their dislike of science was surpassed only by that of their white counterparts. At the twelfth grade level, however, only Native American

students surpass Asian Americans in liking science (and the Native American responses to this question are to be interpreted with caution, due to statistical sample error).

At grade four, a larger percentage of Native American and white students than Asian American students report having conducted five and six types of science experiments (involving plants or animals, electricity, chemicals, a telescope, a thermometer or barometer, and/or rocks or minerals). Furthermore, at this grade level, Asian American students are the least likely to have conducted between three and six types of science

Table 29.37
Study Habits
Grade 8

Question:	Asian Am %	African Am %	American Indian %	Hispanic %	White %
How much TV do you usually watch each day?			!		
None	1.7	1.1	**3.9**	2.0	1.7
1 hour	11.1	6.9	**11.3**	12.6	13.7
2 hours	24.8	11.9	**19.6**	21.3	24.2
3 hours	24.3	14.9	**27.1**	19.6	23.8
4 hours	17.3	20.0	**15.0**	16.5	17.1
5 hours	8.4	14.1	**11.0**	11.4	8.9
6 + hours	12.3	31.2	**12.1**	16.6	10.5
How much time each day is spent on homework?			!		
Have none	3.2	6.5	**9.2**	7.1	5.4
Don't do	3.6	6.0	**10.5**	8.1	7.5
one-half hour	12.7	19.1	**24.5**	17.7	20.6
1 hour	31.9	35.1	**29.4**	38.1	41.6
2 hours	28.4/20.2	22.8/10.5	**22.4**	21.3/7.7	18.1/6.9
2 hours +			4.0		
How often does someone at home help with homework?			!		
Daily	11.4	27.1	**25.2**	19.3	16.7
Weekly	21.4	25.2	**18.0**	24.1	25.7
Monthly	18.9	9.2	**15.3**	10.5	16.1
Never	42.7	34.2	**33.5**	41.4	36.6
Have none	2.8	4.3	**8.0**	4.8	4.8
How many pages read in school and for homework?			!		
> 10 pages	52.1	35.8	**33.7**	40.2	40.7
6 - 10 pages	29.2	27.6	**26.2**	27.2	28.3
5 - fewer	18.7	36.6	**40.1**	32.6	31.0
Does mother or stepmother live at home with you?		#	# - !	#	
Yes	89.9	**88.7**	87.2	**91.5**	94.9
No	10.1	**11.3**	12.8	**8.5**	5.1
Does father or stepfather live at home with you?		#	# - !	#	
Yes	84.8	**54.8**	75.5	**76.1**	85.2
No	15.2	**45.2**	24.5	**23.9**	14.8

Notes:
Interpret with caution: Rate of nonresponse is high.
! Interpret with caution: Error cannot be estimated accurately since coefficient of variation of estimated number of students exceeds 20%.

Source: *The 1990 Science Report Card: NAEP'S Assessment of Fourth, Eighth, and Twelfth Graders. Prepared by Educational Testing Service under contract with the National Center for Education Statistics, March 1992.*

experiments. By grade eight, a larger percentage of white and Native American students report having done five to six types of science experiments, and at grade twelve, only white students report having performed this number of science experiments at a greater rate than Asian Americans.

Asian American fourth and eighth graders are the least likely of all groups to report having science every day in school. By the twelfth grade, they are the most likely to report daily science classes and the least likely to report the lack of science study in school.

A majority of Asian American fourth graders reported spending between half an hour to one hour doing science homework each week, the largest percentage reporting this across racial/ethnic categories. Asian American and white students, however, were the

Table 29.38
Study Habits
Grade 12

Question:	Asian Am %	African Am %	American Indian %	Hispanic %	White %
How much TV do you usually watch each day?			!		
None	5.7	2.2	4.2	4.1	4.3
1 hour	27.3	15.8	19.9	26.2	33.1
2 hours	25.1	19.9	30.8	26.8	28.1
3 hours	23.6	21.4	24.9	19.4	18.5
4 hours	8.0	15.7	8.6	14.0	9.3
5 hours	4.6	11.5	4.0	4.9	3.4
6 + hours	5.8	13.5	7.6	4.5	3.3
How much time each day is spent on homework?			!		
Have none	2.8	10.7	27.3	10.8	12.3
Don't do	5.4	5.7	12.4	6.7	9.4
one-half hour	13.5	18.2	24.5	16.7	22.6
1 hour	23.4	31.6	21.8	31.0	32.2
2 hours	26.7	22.5	7.9	21.3	16.1
2 + hours	28.2	11.3	6.1	13.4	7.4
How often does someone at home help with homework?			!		
Daily	2.3	6.8	9.0	3.8	2.7
Weekly	7.7	14.0	13.8	11.9	8.7
Monthly	12.1	9.1	10.8	12.1	13.0
Never	76.3	63.3	45.7	65.9	67.4
Have none	1.5	6.6	20.7	6.3	8.3
How many pages read in school and for homework?			!		
> 10 pages	53.1	36.5	28.8	39.0	43.7
6 - 10 pages	22.4	28.1	22.7	27.0	23.6
5 - fewer pages	24.5	35.4	48.5	33.9	32.8
Does mother or stepmother live at home with you?		#	!	#	
Yes	88.1	88.7	90.9	88.3	92.4
No	11.9	11.3	9.1	11.7	7.6
Does father or stepfather live at home with you?		#	!	#	
Yes	80.4	54.0	83.8	69.9	83.0
No	19.6	46.0	16.2	30.1	17.0

Note:
Interpret with caution: Rate of nonresponse is high.
! Interpret with caution: Error cannot be estimated accurately since coefficient of variation of estimated number of students exceeds 20%.

Source: The 1990 Science Report Card: NAEP'S Assessment of Fourth, Eighth, and Twelfth Graders. Prepared by Educational Testing Service under contract with the National Center for Education Statistics, March 1992.

least likely to report spending between two and two-and-a-half hours weekly doing science homework. At the eighth grade level, Asian American students are the least likely to report spending no time doing science homework, and Asian Americans and whites are the most likely to report spending from two to two-and-a-half hours per week on science homework. By the twelfth grade, Asian American students are the most

likely to report spending more than two-and-a-half hours on science homework.

In terms of experiences in science classrooms, Asian American students in the fourth grade are less likely than students in any group, except African Americans, to have done a science project in school that took a week or longer. By the eighth grade, Native Americans are the only group to surpass Asian Americans in doing

Table 29.39
Science Experiences of Students
Grade 4

Question:	Asian Am %	African Am %	American Indian %	Hispanic %	White %
Do you like science?					
Yes	77.9	75.2	79.5	76.0	81.1
No	22.1	24.8	20.5	24.0	18.9
How often do you have science in school?					
Everyday	38.7	46.3	51.4	44.2	83.6
Several times a week	24.3	19.7	19.2	19.6	21.5
Once a week	20.8	16.8	13.2	17.6	12.2
Less than once a week	7.5	10.0	10.2	8.9	7.8
Never	8.6	7.2	6.1	9.7	4.9
When study science how often:					
Do science experiments?		#		#	
1 or > times a week	45.6	**46.8**	41.5	**45.2**	40.8
< once a week	27.3	**21.5**	25.2	**25.0**	36.4
Never	27.1	**31.7**	33.3	**29.8**	22.8
How much time spend doing science homework each week?					
None	28.2	26.4	33.2	27.8	34.2
1/2 - 1 hour	60.3	57.0	52.8	55.6	56.7
2/2 + hours	5.3	9.0	9.4	8.3	5.1
No science	6.2	7.7	4.6	8.3	4.0
Number of science experiments?					
None	4.2	7.8	5.4	5.8	7.5
1 - 2	39.4	33.1	21.7	31.0	32.3
3 - 4	41.1	48.5	55.6	51.2	44.4
5 - 6	15.3	10.6	17.3	11.9	15.7

Note:
\# Interpret with caution: Rate of nonresponse is high.

Source: The 1990 Science Report Card: NAEP'S Assessment of Fourth, Eighth, and Twelfth Graders. Prepared by Educational Testing Service under contract with the National Center for Education Statistics, March 1992.

week-long science projects. At the twelfth grade level, Asian Americans are much more likely than any other group to have done a science project lasting one week or longer. When asked how often they did a science experiment, among fourth and eighth graders, Asian American and white students were the smallest percentage groups to answer "never." By the twelfth grade, Asian Americans were by far the least likely of all groups to report that they "never" do science experiments.

Science Achievement

Average Science Proficiency

Although Asian Americans trail writers in grades four and eight in science achievement, Asians gradually close the gap until, the 12th grade level, when they score higher than whites in science. At the fourth

grade, white students score nine points higher than Asian American students; at the eighth grade, the gap with whites leading is two points; by the 12th grade, Asian American students outperform their white counterparts in science by five points.

Proficiency Levels

The four proficiency levels, as defined by NAEP, are: Level 200: understands simple scientific principles; Level 250: applies general scientific information; Level 300: analyzes scientific procedures and data; Level 350: integrates specialized scientific information.

Table 29.42 shows the percentage of students at or above each of the proficiency levels by grade and by race/ethnicity.

At grade four, a higher percentage of white and Asian/Pacific Islander students reached the first two

Table 29.40
Science Experiences of Students
Grade 8

Question:	Asian Am %	African Am %	American Indian %	Hispanic %	White %
Do you like science?			!		
Yes	69.5	699	**71.3**	70.9	67.0
No	30.5	301	**28.7**	29.1	33.0
How often do you have science in school?			!		
Everyday	70.6	820	**87.7**	78.8	86.2
Several times a week	16.8	87	**3.1**	11.5	9.2
Once a week	0.8	35	**4.3**	2.5	0.9
Less than once a week	0.5	08	**0.0**	0.6	0.5
Never	11.3	49	**5.0**	6.6	3.2
How much time spend doing science homework each week?			!		
None	16.5	219	**25.6**	19.7	19.7
1/2 - 1 hour	57.1	628	**58.5**	63.4	61.0
2/2 + hours	15.7	114	**11.6**	11.7	17.1
No science	10.7	39	**4.3**	5.3	2.2
Ever do science proj. in school that take week or more?			!		
Yes	64.0	562	**74.2**	55.3	59.6
No	36.0	438	**25.8**	44.7	40.4
When study science how often:					
Do science experiments?		# - !	!		
1 or > times a week	41.2	**363**	45.6	41.2	41.9
< once a week	37.2	**351**	30.4	33.1	39.6
Never	21.6	**285**	24.0	25.7	18.5
Number of type of science experiments?			!		
None	4.9	60	**10.6**	7.1	5.2
1 - 2	25.6	321	**20.3**	25.7	19.6
3 - 4	40.5	395	**34.8**	39.5	37.0
5 - 6	29.0	223	**34.3**	27.7	38.2

Note:
\#   Interpret with caution: Rate of nonresponse is high.
!   Interpret with caution: Error cannot be estimated accurately since coefficient of variation of estimated number of students exceeds 20%.

Source: The 1990 Science Report Card: NAEP'S Assessment of Fourth, Eighth, and Twelfth Graders. Prepared by Educational Testing Service under contract with the National Center for Education Statistics, March 1992.

levels (200 and 250) than did black and Hispanic fourth graders. Similar differences can be seen in data for eighth and 12th grades. Furthermore, by grade 12, it can be seen that Asian/Pacific Islander students overtake and surpass white students at the 300 and 350 levels of science proficiency.

Science Content

Table 29.43 shows the average proficiency in four content areas for the five different racial/ethnic groups by grade level. Here we see a similar pattern shown in previous tables. At grade four, in all content areas,

white students have higher average proficiency than students in the other racial/ethnic categories. By grade eight, the gap between white and Asian/Pacific Islander students is closing, so that by grade 12, the latter group shows a small gain in all four content areas.

Asian American Student Profile in Science

When we construct a profile of Asian American students in terms of demographic characteristics, educational experiences and background, home environment

Table 29.41
Science Experiences of Students
Grade 12

Question:	Asian Am %	African Am %	American Indian %	Hispanic %	White %
Do you like science?			!		
Yes	68.8	60.4	**70.9**	68.1	65.8
No	31.2	39.6	**29.1**	31.9	34.2
How often do you have science in school?			!		
Everyday	59.7	43.6	**28.1**	43.0	46.8
Several times a week	12.4	6.2	**6.8**	5.7	3.8
Once a week	2.5	2.0	**0.0**	1.9	1.1
Less than once a week	2.1	3.0	**4.9**	5.1	2.2
Never	23.3	45.2	**60.2**	44.3	46.0
How much time spend doing science homework each week?			!		
None	19.3	30.2	**55.2**	29.4	29.0
1/2 - 1 hour	33.6	28.3	**7.8**	26.6	23.0
2/2 + hours	34.8	11.1	**10.7**	13.8	18.6
No science	12.3	30.4	**26.3**	30.2	29.3
Ever do science proj. in school that take week or more?			!		
Yes	54.6	34.5	**23.7**	34.4	35.6
No	45.4	65.5	**76.3**	65.6	64.4
When study science how often:					
Do science experiments?			!		
1 or > times a week	58.7	42.8	**31.9**	45.2	45.9
< once a week	21.7	20.9	**13.9**	20.8	20.4
Never	19.6	36.3	**54.2**	34.0	33.7
Number of type of science experiments?			!		
None	2.5	5.9	**9.5**	4.0	4.1
1 - 2	15.1	14.6	**12.1**	15.8	10.3
3 - 4	27.0	34.0	**31.2**	34.0	27.7
5 - 6	55.4	45.5	**47.2**	46.2	57.8

Note:
! Interpret with caution: Error cannot be estimated accurately since coefficient of variation of estimated number of students exceeds 20%.

Source: The 1990 Science Report Card: NAEP'S Assessment of Fourth, Eighth, and Twelfth Graders. Prepared by Educational Testing Service under contract with the National Center for Education Statistics, March 1992.

and attitudes, and science achievement during the pre-college years, the result is puzzling. By the senior year in high school, this group of students is outperforming its racial/ethnic counterparts in science, even though earlier in the pipeline, it lagged slightly behind white students.

Furthermore, when we look at the home environment, attitudes toward science and educational experiences and background of Asian Americans, we find that some of the data contradicts our conventional notions of factors that contribute to science proficiency. For example, some of the Asian American home environments are not, according to research on the general population, favorable to high levels of achievement. Asian American students at the three grade levels are likely to come from homes where a language other than English is spoken and may have little access to reading materials at home, as well as be unlikely to receive daily help with homework. In terms of their study habits and experiences in science classrooms, an apparent progression of improvement culminates by grade 12 among Asian American students that work hard at their studies (both general and scientific).

More research on factors that contribute to the pre-eminence of Asian Americans in science is needed to resolve the contradictions suggested by these data. Such

Table 29.42
Percentages of Students at or above Four Proficiency Levels on the NAEP Science Scale
by Race/Ethnicity

	Percent of Students At or Above			
	Level 200	**Level 250**	**Level 300**	**Level 350**
Grade 4				
White	93 (0.8)	40 (1.6)	1 (0.3)	0 (0.0)
Black	58 (2.7)	5 (1.1)	0 (0.2)	0 (0.0)
Hispanic	66 (2.4)	10 (1.2)	0 (0.0)	0 (0.0)
Asian/Pacific Islander	88 (3.1)	29 (5.2)	2 (1.5)	0 (0.0)
American Indian	81 (5.3)	20 (4.8)	0 (0.0)	0 (0.0)
Grade 8				
White	97 (0.5)	74 (1.3)	23 (1.3)	1 (0.3)
Black	80 (2.5)	31 (2.5)	3 (0.8)	0 (0.1)
Hispanic	87 (1.7)	42 (2.8)	5 (0.9)	0 (0.1)
Asian/Pacific Islander	96 (1.9)	71 (4.8)	23 (4.1)	1 (0.6)
American Indian	92 (2.8)	54 (11.6)	8 (2.8)	0 (0.0)
Grade 12				
White	100 (0.1)	91 (0.8)	53 (1.4)	12 (0.9)
Black	94 (1.4)	57 (3.0)	12 (2.0)	1 (0.6)
Hispanic	98 (0.8)	70 (3.4)	23 (2.9)	3 (1.0)
Asian/Pacific Islander	99 (1.4)	90 (3.2)	60 (7.4)	17 (5.0)
American Indian	**100 (0.7)!**	**89 (5.6)!**	**33 (9.3)!**	**2 (0.0)!**

Notes:
The standard errors of the estimated percentages appear in parentheses. It can be said with 95 percent certainty that for each population of interest, the value for the whole population is within plus or minus two standard errors of the estimate for the sample. When the percentage of students is either 0 or 100, the standard error is inestimable. However, percentages 99.5 percent and greater were rounded to 100 percent and percentages less than 0.5 percent were rounded to 0 percent.
(!) Interpret with caution—the nature of the sample does not allow accurate determination of the variability of these estimated statistics.

Source: The 1990 Science Report Card: NAEP'S Assessment of Fourth, Eighth, and Twelfth Graders. Prepared by Educational Testing Service under contract with the National Center for Education Statistics, March 1992.

research might also help to shed light on these factors as they relate to students in other racial/ethnic groups.

Postsecondary Education in Science and Engineering

Few data on the achievement and participation of Asian American students as they progress through an undergraduate institution are available. However, profiles of college-bound students at the point of entry into undergraduate education are available for analysis. How prepared are Asian American students to study science or engineering at the undergraduate level? Information from databases such as the Student Descriptive Questionnaire (SDQ) of the Scholastic Achievement Test (SAT) collected from college-bound high school seniors show that Asian American students participate in higher-level mathematics and science courses in high school than the average U.S. student

and express higher degree aspirations. They also earn higher scores in the math section of the SAT.

SAT Test Takers

Table 29.44 compares selected characteristics of all college-bound SAT test takers in 1993. The data were collected from college-bound students who took the SAT and/or achievement tests in 1993. Of the Asian students, who made up 7.5 percent of the test-taking population, 57 percent were U.S. citizens and 28 percent were permanent residents. Because the data were disaggregated by gender within racial/ethnic group, it is possible to compare gender differences and similarities as well.

Both female and male Asian SAT takers scored a little below the national mean on the verbal portion of the SAT (as well as on the Test of Standard Written English [TSWE]), while performing well above the national mean on the math portion of the test. As with the national profile, males scored higher than females

Table 29.43
Distribution of Students and Average Proficiency in Science Content Areas by Race/Ethnicity

	Percent of Students	Life Sciences	Physical Sciences	Earth and Space Sciences	Nature of Science
Grade 4					
White	70 (05)	238 (1.0)	245 (1.2)	243 (1.1)	242 (1.1)
Black	15 (04)	204 (1.6)	207 (2.0)	204 (1.5)	212 (1.7)
Hispanic	11 (03)	209 (1.8)	213 (1.6)	215 (1.6)	212 (1.7)
Asian/Pacific Islander	2 (03)	227 (4.1)	238 (3.9)	233 (3.6)	238 (3.5)
American Indian	2 (03)	222 (3.8)	229 (4.0)	228 (3.6)	226 (3.8)
Grade 8					
White	71 (04)	273 (1.4)	271 (1.4)	276 (1.5)	270 (1.5)
Black	15 (04)	233 (2.3)	232 (2.3)	228 (2.6)	230 (2.7)
Hispanic	10 (03)	242 (2.4)	241 (2.2)	242 (2.3)	236 (2.4)
Asian/Pacific Islander	3 (04)	272 (4.0)	271 (3.9)	270 (4.3)	267 (5.2)
American Indian	1 (05)!	252 (9.7)!	250 (7.8)!	257 (7.3)!	24.4 (15.6)!
Grade 12					
White	73 (04)	305 (1.1)	300 (1.7)	301 (1.3)	307 (1.4)
Black	14 (05)	262 (2.0)	253 (3.1)	247 (2.8)	267 (3.0)
Hispanic	8 (03)	275 (2.7)	271 (3.2)	270 (2.9)	277 (3.9)
Asian/Pacific Islander	4 (02)	309 (7.1)	310 (8.3)	304 (6.6)	312 (6.9)
American Indian	1 (02)!	287 (4.5)!	283 (5.6)!	289 (6.1)!	283 (9.6)!

Notes:
The standard errors of the estimated percentages appear in parentheses. It can be said with 95 percent certainty that for each population of interest, the value for the whole population is within plus or minus two standard errors of the estimate for the sample. When the percentage of students is either 0 or 100, the standard error is inestimable. However, percentages 99.5 percent and greater were rounded to 100 percent and percentages less than 0.5 percent were rounded to 0 percent.
(!) Interpret with caution—the nature of the sample does not allow accurate determination of the variability of these estimated statistics.

Source: The 1990 Science Report Card: NAEP'S Assessment of Fourth, Eighth, and Twelfth Graders. Prepared by Educational Testing Service under contract with the National Center for Education Statistics, March 1992.

on both sections of the SAT, and females scored higher than males on the TSWE. When compared to their white counterparts, Asian SAT takers of both genders scored about 30 points lower on the verbal and 40 points higher on the math portions of the test. As might be expected, Asian college-bound seniors of both genders took more years of mathematics and natural science courses than did all other college-bound seniors. They also took more years of foreign and classical languages, and their total years of study overall were higher. Their years of English study were the same as the national average, but they lagged slightly behind the national average in hours of arts, music, social science, and history courses.

Table 29.45 gives the actual high school courses taken by all the SAT test takers and by the two subgroups in the natural sciences and mathematics, as well as by

intended science-related majors. The data indicate that more Asian students are well prepared academically for science-related majors than most other college-bound students. For example, while almost all students have taken biology courses, a somewhat larger portion of Asian students have taken chemistry and a much higher proportion have taken physics courses. A similar pattern emerges for coursework in mathematics. Large percentages of all students have taken algebra and geometry, but much larger proportions of Asians have taken trigonometry, precalculus, and calculus courses.

Gender differences for Asian college-bound students echo those of both the national and white profiles with the exception of chemistry, geology/earth/space science, trigonometry, precalculus, and honors courses in both mathematics and natural sciences. Nationally, females take trigonometry, precalculus,

Table 29.44
Profile of College Bound Seniors: 1993 Comparison of Profiles
of all SAT Test Takers, Asians and whites

	National (all test takers)		Asian		White	
	Male	**Female**	**Male**	**Female**	**Male**	**Female**
Total #	525,115	584,265	41,447	41,649	328,911	371,980
SAT Scores Verbal (Mean)	428	420	419	411	447	440
SAT Scores Math (Mean)	502	457	559	512	518	472
Test of Standard Written English (Mean)	41.2	42.6	39.0	40.2	43.3	44.9
Years of Study & GPA by Subject:						
Arts and Music	1.6 (3.56)	1.9 (3.72)	1.5 (3.62)	1.9 (3.76)	1.7 (3.60)	2.1 (3.76)
English	3.9 (3.00)	3.9 (3.24)	3.6 (3.15)	3.9 (3.36)	3.9 (3.04)	3.9 (3.28)
Foreign & Classical Languages	2.5 (2.96)	2.7 (3.22)	2.7 (3.21)	2.9 (3.45)	2.5 (2.96)	2.8 (3.24)
Mathematics	3.8 (2.96)	3.7 (2.94)	4.0 (3.27)	3.9 (3.20)	3.8 (2.99)	3.7 (2.99)
Natural Sciences	3.3 (3.05)	3.2 (3.06)	3.5 (3.25)	3.4 (3.23)	3.4 (3.09)	3.3 (3.11)
Social Sciences & History	3.4 (3.18)	3.4 (3.22)	3.3 (3.31)	3.3 (3.37)	3.4 (3.22)	3.4 (3.26)
Total of All Subjects	18.5 (3.06)	18.8 (3.20)	18.9 (3.27)	19.3 (3.37)	18.7 (3.10)	19.2 (3.25)

Source: *The 1990 Science Report Card: NAEP'S Assessment of Fourth, Eighth, and Twelfth Graders. Prepared by Educational Testing Service under contract with the National Center for Education Statistics, March 1992.*

chemistry, and honors courses in both areas at a higher rate than males; the same is true for white seniors. For Asian students, the opposite occurs, except for chemistry and honors courses in the sciences, where both genders are evenly distributed. Conversely, Asian females are less likely to take geology/earth/space science than their male counterparts while the opposite is true for other students.

College Major and Degree Aspirations

In terms of intended college majors and degree-level aspirations, Asian students are slightly more likely to opt for majors in biological sciences and somewhat more likely to choose engineering and health (and allied services) majors than the other two groups (see Table 29.45). White students are slightly more apt to major in the physical sciences than Asian or all other students. Gender differences for the national group and subgroups are similar, with females choosing biological sciences and health majors at a greater rate than males, and males opting for engineering, mathematics, and physical science majors at a greater rate than females. The gender difference for Asian students who opt for health and allied services majors is smaller than it is for the other two groups. It is interesting to note that for all three groups (national, white, and Asian American), a much greater percentage of males than females choose engineering and physical science majors.

Asian college-bound students are more likely to aspire to a doctorate than either white or all other

college-bound students (34 percent versus 20 and 23 percent, respectively). While a greater proportion of females than males in the white and national categories have doctoral degree level goals, an equal proportion of Asian males and females plan to earn a doctorate.

Bachelor's Degrees

Six percent of all science and engineering baccalaureate degrees went to Asian graduates in 1989, almost tripling the number for 1979. Approximately 35 percent of the undergraduate science and engineering degrees awarded to Asian graduates were in engineering, 20 percent were in the social sciences; 15 percent were in biological sciences; and 11 percent were in computer science.

Graduate Study

Asians made up three percent of all Graduate Record Examination (GRE) test takers in 1987, but represented four percent of those who had majored in science and engineering at the undergraduate level. Although they generally scored lower than whites on the verbal and analytical sections of the GRE, Asian American test takers scored higher on the quantitative section, where their average scores were 63 points higher than those of their white counterparts (604 versus 541) and 73 points higher than the total GRE test-taking population. On the verbal section, the overall score of Asian American test takers was 476, 40 points lower than that for whites and 29 points lower than all

Table 29.45
Profile of College Bound Seniors: Sciences and Math Coursework: 1993 Comparison of Courses
in Natural Sciences and Mathematics Taken by all SAT Test Takers, Asians and Whites

	National		Asian		White	
	Male	Female	Male	Female	Male	Female
Total #	525,115	584,265	41,447	41,649	328,911	371,980
Natural Sciences:						
Biology	46	54	49	51	47	53
Chemistry	47	53	50	50	47	53
Geology/Earth/Space Science	47	53	51	49	47	53
Physics	53	47	53	47	54	46
Other Sciences	43	57	50	50	44	56
Honors Courses Taken	47	53	50	50	47	53
Mathematics:						
Algebr (a)	46	54	50	50	47	53
Geometry	47	53	50	50	47	53
Trigonometry	48	52	51	49	49	51
Precalculus	49	51	52	48	50	50
Calculus	53	47	54	46	53	47
Computer Math	54	46	60	40	56	44
Other Math Courses	44	56	50	50	44	56
Honors Courses Taken	48	52	51	49	48	52
Intended College Major:						
Biological Sciences	42	58	45	55	42	58
Engineering	81	19	82	18	83	17
Health & Allied Services	32	68	41	59	32	68
Mathematics	54	46	53	47	55	45
Physical Sciences	65	35	62	38	67	33
Undecided	55	45	50	50	55	45
Degree-Level Goal:						
Certificate Program	49	51	54	46	48	52
Associate Degree	41	59	45	55	41	59
Bachelor's Degree	50	50	50	50	50	50
Master's Degree	47	53	52	48	47	53
Doctoral/Related Degree	43	57	50	50	45	55
Other	44	56	45	55	45	55
Undecided	46	54	47	53	46	54

Source: The 1990 Science Report Card: NAEP'S Assessment of Fourth, Eighth, and Twelfth Graders. Prepared by Educational Testing Service under contract with the National Center for Education Statistics, March 1992.

test takers. At 537 on the analytical portion of the test, Asian American test takers were 17 and 4 points lower than white and all test takers, respectively. Among science and engineering majors of both groups, these differences varied widely, however.

As can be seen in Table 29.46, the majority of Asian American GRE test takers were biological or physical sciences majors as undergraduates (64 percent), by far the highest percentage in these fields of any of the other racial/ethnic groups. In terms of intended major

of graduate study, 56 percent of Asian Americans responded that they intended to major in biological or physical sciences, again, by far, the largest racial/ethnic group pursuing these fields.

Graduate Enrollment in Science and Engineering Fields

Compared to their white counterparts, Asian science and engineering degree recipients (U.S. citizens and permanent residents) were much more likely to

Table 29.46
Characteristics of Students Taking the Graduate Record Examination, by Race/Ethnicity, 1988
Selected Characteristics of U.S.Citizens who took the GRE by Self-Reported Ethnic Group, in Percent

	American Indian	Black/ Afroamer	Mexican- American	Oriental or Asian	Puerto Rican	Oth Hisp Latin-Am	White	Other	No Response	Total
Number of Responses (a)	1,023	9,324	2,226	4,777	1,661	19,02	147,466	24.56	4,741	1,755.76
% Female	56.95	66.40	55.75	48.08	55.02	55.54	57.17	46.62	55.73	57.17
% English Best Language	96.38	98.39	94.42	8006	85.61	85.61	98.61	95.00	95.85	97.13
% Undergraduate Institution <20.000	74.78	82.64	72.37	58.79	68.87	68.87	72.00	68.39	73.13	72.15
% Public Undergraduate Institution	70.41	64.83	76.84	65.83	63.72	63.72	65.31	66.41	62.65	65.45
Mean Year of Receipt of B.A.	81.96	81.93	82.84	83.81	83.53	83.53	82.79	82.99	81.80	82.77
% in Each Undergraduate Major Field:										
Humanities	13.55	10.63	14.53	9.61	16.27	16.27	16.42	21.32	18.46	15.96
Social Sciences	52.68	53.94	52.19	25.07	44.32	44.32	42.57	40.44	44.03	42.86
Biological Sciences	18.40	17.44	15.30	20.17	16.37	16.37	20.30	15.75	18.33	19.97
Physical Sciences	11.93	14.91	15.35	43.98	21.33	21.33	18.46	19.29	16.72	18.94
Others and Undecided	3.44	3.08	2.64	1.17	1.71	1.71	2.24	3.21	2.45	2.28
Mean Age	30.06	28.34	28.26	25.51	26.76	26.76	27.56	28.08	28.84	27.59
% Degree Objective PhD or Beyond	41.65	37.85	34.89	40.19	41.95	41.95	37.84	49.13	40.62	38.23
% in Each Graduate Major Field:										
Humanities	11.56	6.87	9.71	7.89	12.36	12.36	12.31	16.83	13.41	11.93
Social Sciences	51.66	54.69	55.20	24.56	45.60	45.60	42.78	39.71	43.76	43.09
Biological Sciences	16.88	15.59	13.17	18.21	15.18	15.18	18.24	13.63	15.53	17.93
Physical Sciences	10.15	11.66	12.85	38.03	17.63	17.63	15.36	15.65	14.04	15.76
Other and Undecided	9.75	11.20	9.07	11.32	9.22	9.22	11.31	14.18	13.26	11.29
% in Each Region:										
Northeast	4.83	1.93	0.60	3.99	3.15	3.15	7.28	10.68	9.58	6.84
East	8.65	15.53	0.92	14.31	14.97	14.97	15.77	19.24	19.69	15.63
Midwest	19.62	14.50	6.18	11.94	8.12	8.12	24.10	12.52	18.18	22.53
South	35.41	59.23	46.31	18.64	45.97	45.97	34.18	21.92	29.48	35.17
West	31.49	8.82	45.99	51.12	27.79	27.79	18.67	35.63	23.07	19.82

Notes:
(a) These are the number of examinees in each category of ethnic group response. Examinees not responding to any of the other background questions in this table are omitted from the percent calculation for that variable.

Source: Educational Testing Service. (1988, June). A summary of data collected from Graduate Record Examinations Test Takers during 1986-1987. Data Summary Report #12, Graduate Record Examinations.

pursue graduate study. Approximately 28 percent of Asian baccalaureate degree holders who had received their degrees in 1988 or 1989 were in graduate school full time, and 10 percent attended on a part-time basis. Of their white counterparts, on the other hand, only 19 percent attended full time and 11 percent part time.

In 1990, Asian Americans represented 5.8 percent of total enrollment in graduate science and engineering programs, almost doubling their 1983 enrollment. Their representation in engineering programs was double that in science programs (9.5 versus 4.7 percent). Of all Asian Americans enrolled in science and engineering graduate programs in 1990, 30 percent were in engineering, 13 percent in biological science, and 16 percent in computer science programs.

Master's Recipients in Science and Engineering

In 1989, Asians (U.S. citizens and permanent residents) represented about 6 percent of science and engineering master's degree recipients. The increase in master's degrees in engineering awarded to Asians over a ten-year period—1979 to 1989—was 138 percent. In comparison, the number of engineering degrees earned by whites in the same period increased by 33 percent.

Doctorates Awarded in Science and Engineering

The number of science and engineering doctorates awarded to Asian Americans (U.S. citizens) in 1992 increased by 94 percent in a ten-year period, from 327 to 634. Asian Americans made up 2.5 percent and 4.4 percent of all science and engineering doctorates awarded to U.S. citizens in 1982 and 1992, respectively. In 1990, the largest percentage of these Asian American degree recipients were in engineering fields (34 percent); 22 percent earned Ph.D.s in agricultural/biological sciences and 17 percent in the physical sciences.

At this level, it is important that the distinction be made between Asian Americans (U.S. citizens and permanent residents) and non-citizens on temporary visas. In 1990, 80 percent of the total doctorates in science and engineering were awarded to non-citizens, up from 57 percent in 1980.

Postdoctoral Appointments

Asians (including both citizens and noncitizens) held 16 percent of all science and engineering postdoctoral appointments in 1989, while whites held 82 percent. The increase in these appointments for Asians between 1979 and 1989 was 104 percent, compared with a 40-percent increase for whites.

Summary

The pattern of Asian and Asian American participation in science and engineering is consistent at the postsecondary level from entry into the freshman year to graduation from a doctoral program. Asian American college-bound seniors show greater participation rates in higher level mathematics and science courses than the average U.S. student. They often score higher on the SAT and have higher degree aspirations. They are more likely to choose majors in biological sciences, engineering, and health than the average U.S. degree student. They are also more likely to aspire to earn a doctorate.

At the undergraduate level, Asian students obtaining science and engineering baccalaureate degrees are overrepresented, with the majority obtaining degrees in engineering. At the graduate level, Asian Americans are overrepresented among GRE test takers majoring in science and engineering at the undergraduate level. They obtain the highest scores of any racial/ethnic subgroup on the quantitative section of the GRE. Asian American GRE test takers also have the largest proportion of a subgroup intending to major in biological or physical sciences.

In terms of actual enrollment in graduate education, Asian baccalaureate degree recipients in science and engineering are much more likely to pursue graduate study, most of them in engineering. In 1989 and 1992, respectively, Asians accounted for 6 percent of all science and engineering master's degrees and 4.4 percent of all science and engineering doctorates awarded, with the numbers of awardees increasing rapidly over a ten-year span. The largest percentage of these degrees was in engineering.

At the postsecondary level, the data is unequivocal in supporting the preeminence and prevalence of Asians in science and engineering. Asian students are better prepared to succeed in a mathematics or science major upon entry into the freshman year. They tend to persist in the mathematics and science fields through attainment of a baccalaureate degree and to go on to graduate education in science and engineering, earning master's or doctoral degrees in science or engineering.

—*Beatriz C. Clewell*
The Urban Institute

◆ NOTABLE ASIAN AMERICANS IN EDUCATION

This section profiles the educational contributions of Asian Americans who have distinguished themselves within their fields of expertise. It recognizes Americans of Asian descent who are or were scholarly leaders in the education profession and who have contributed to the improvement of learning and understanding in kindergarten through postsecondary levels of education.

The scholars profiled are Kathryn Hu-Pei Au, a multicultural literacy expert of Chinese ancestry; Kenji Hakuta, a bilingual education expert of Japanese ancestry; Samuel Ichiye Hayakawa, the late university president, United States senator, and general semantics scholar of Japanese ancestry; Ronald Takaki, ethnic studies and multicultural scholar of Japanese ancestry; and Lily Wong Fillmore, a second-language and bilingual-education scholar of Chinese ancestry.

Kathryn Hu-Pei Au

Educator

Kathryn Au has devoted her professional life to the improvement of educational services at the Kamehameha Schools in Honolulu, a private institution designed to meet the unique educational needs of Native Hawaiian children. She developed and implemented the Kamehameha Elementary Education Program's (KEEP) language arts curriculum, which has earned national recognition for its innovative approaches toward multicultural literacy. Through KEEP, Native Hawaiian children are exposed to literature that connects their environment and history to their education.

Kathy Au received her A.B. in European history, cum laude, from Pembroke College at Brown University, then earned a professional diploma in elementary education and M.A. in psychology from the University of Hawaii. In 1978-79, after six years of teaching kindergarten through third grade at Kamehameha, Au took a leave of absence to pursue her Ph.D. at the University of Illinois, Urbana-Champaign. Receiving her doctoral degree in educational psychology in 1980, she returned to Kamehameha Schools and assumed responsibility as an educational psychologist and department head for KEEP. She also conducted educational research on the school literacy development of Native Hawaiian students.

As a scholar, Kathy Au has shared her expertise in the field of literacy instruction. Her publication record, filled with a number of thoughtful reflections on literacy development, is frequently cited as a reference by others writing in the field. Au has published over 60 articles and has edited volumes, reading programs, review columns, test reviews, and other technical reports. She has presented the results of her work at over 100 meetings, conferences, and seminars. In 1993, she published *Literacy Instruction in Multicultural Settings*, a resource for instructors concerned about literacy instruction in a culturally pluralistic environment. In 1994, Au published a number of articles pertaining to literacy instruction at the elementary level and a book she coauthored entitled *Literacy Instruction for Today*.

Besides her duties at Kamehameha Schools, Au has been highly active in several professional organizations. In 1993-94, she served as vice-president of the American Educational Research Association's (AERA) Division C which deals with learning and instruction. During her vice-presidency, Au made many program changes that were well received across the association. In particular, she developed more ways to include research on and by minorities in AERA's conference program.

Au next served AERA as a representative on Division C's Executive Committee, co-chaired the Outstanding Article Award Committee, became a member of the editorial advisory board for the *Review of Educational Research*, and reviewed proposals for Division C and several special interest groups.

Kathy Au's professional involvement extends well beyond AERA to include active roles in the National Reading Conference, International Reading Association, National Council of Teachers of English, and the Association for Supervision and Curriculum Development. In 1989, she was honored as a distinguished scholar by AERA's Standing Committee on the Role and Status of Minorities in Educational Research and Development. This award recognizes significant contributions to minority-related research. She was also presented with a National Scholar Award by the National Association for Asian and Pacific American Education in 1980.

For practitioners/researchers in literacy education, Kathy Au is a role model. The education profession, in general, and the children of Kamchamcha Schools, in particular, have benefitted from her leadership in providing direction for improvements in literacy instruction.

Kenji Hakuta

Bilingual-Education Scholar

A leading figure in the field of bilingual education, Kenji Hakuta contributed significantly to the field in the 1980s and 1990s. His extensive publications on bilingual education and second language acquisition are frequently cited in reference works.

Hakuta received both his B.A. (magna cum laude 1975) and Ph.D. (1979) at Harvard. He began his academic career at Yale, where he served as associate professor of psychology. In 1987, Hakuta moved to the University of California, Santa Cruz, where he assumed the dual role of professor of education and psychology, along with the directorship of the bilingual research group. In 1989, he left Santa Cruz to join Stanford University's School of Education faculty as professor of education.

During his academic career, Hakuta has received a number of awards for his contributions to bilingual education. In 1994, he received the Distinguished Scholar Award given by AERA's Standing Committee on the Role and Status of Minorities in Educational Research and Development, which recognizes significant contributions to minority-related research.

In addition to his academic responsibilities, Hakuta has served widely as board member, consultant, and advisor to numerous organizations and special groups focusing on bilingual education and minority education issues. He has been awarded a number of grants for his research work on bilingual education. As of 1993, Hakuta had received over $1.6 million to research bilingual education and second-language acquisition.

Hakuta has published extensively throughout his academic career; he has over 70 articles, books, and edited volumes as of October 1993. He has concentrated his research efforts on developing a clear rationale for providing language-minority children with the greatest opportunities for educational success, while maintaining a healthy appreciation for their culture. Through his work and publications, Hakuta has helped to frame the bilingual-education debate to the benefit of minority children across the country.

Born in 1952, Kenji Hakuta made great achievements relatively early in his career. Continuing to make great strides in 1994, he planned to publish a book entitled *Second Language*. His work provides a key framework for curriculum and policy development in bilingual education.

Samuel Ichiye Hayakawa

Semanticist, U.S. senator, and university president

S. I. Hayakawa was known to the world for his achievements as a general semanticist, United States senator, and former university president. However, his accomplishments exceed even further beyond these titles. Surrounded by controversy throughout his entire life, Hayakawa clung to his convictions. His critics often called him arrogant and egotistical, but appreciating his life fully requires an understanding of the era and environment in which he was reared. On July 18, 1906, in Vancouver, B.C., Ichiro and Tora Hayakawa, Japanese immigrants from Yamanashi and Kofu, Japan, had their first of four children, Samuel Ichiye Hayakawa (Ichiye meaning "first son" or "number one") in a rooming house.

Ichiro Hayakawa, an ambitious man, immigrated from Japan with his new bride to seek a better life in North America. Originally intending to settle in San Francisco, the Hayakawas ended up in Vancouver, as a result of abundant employment opportunities there. One of the few Japanese immigrants who could speak and write English, the elder Hayakawa voluntarily assisted others during his spare time with immigration paperwork and legal matters.

Struggling to support a family, Hayakawa's father moved the family wherever employment opportunities opened. The constant moving and readjustment to different environments were unsettling for the family, but necessary for survival.

For Hayakawa's mother, adapting to a new culture and lifestyle presented numerous challenges. Raised in an upper-class family in Japan, Tora Hayakawa had to learn how to dwell in humble surroundings. Many of the things that servants used to do for her as a child, she found herself doing in Canada. Despite her loneliness in a foreign country, she kept busy. One of her hobbies was reading sophisticated Japanese magazines—the equivalent to *Harper's* or *Atlantic Monthly* at the time. After her children were raised, Tora Hayakawa became involved with the Methodist church. Despite her inability to speak fluent English, she made a deep impression on people with whom she came into contact.

During this period, most Japanese immigrants were settling in California, Oregon, and Washington. In Vancouver, the Hayakawas were slightly acquainted with several other Japanese families, but contact between them was minimal. Samuel was raised in an environment where he never played or attended school with people of his own ancestry.

Since Hayakawa's mother could not speak English, conversations at home were strictly in Japanese. To educate her children on their heritage, Tora Hayakawa would tell fairy tales and stories about Japan. Having received a koto, a long wooden stringed musical instrument, from her parents in Japan, Tora would play for her children, giving them an appreciation of Japanese music and culture. In later years, Hayakawa became a skilled dancer and connoisseur of the performing arts.

As a young child, Hayakawa recalled living above a grocery store in Cranbrook, B.C. Later, the family moved to a farm outside of town. Times were tough for the Hayakawas, and the family was in constant transition. Moving to Raymond, AB, Ichiro Hayakawa took a job as a labor contractor on a sugar beet farm. When a premature freeze occurred, laborers were left with nothing.

The Hayakawas moved to Calgary at the beginning of World War I, where they opened a grocery store. Ichiro Hayakawa was a shrewd businessman, despite his nomadic lifestyle. Observing the war situation and a demand for imported products, he began an import-export business to supply the Canadian market with replacements from Japan. As the business grew, the Hayakawas moved to Winnipeg, the largest trade center in western Canada.

Throughout this period, Samuel and his siblings attended public elementary schools. He had the challenge of starting a new elementary school every year, which helped him to cultivate an abundance of internal strength. That served him well in later years.

Because he was raised in a traditional Japanese family, the importance of an education was stressed to him constantly. During his youth, Hayakawa's mother played a dominant role in his upbringing and education. Despite her inability to communicate in English, the children were able to converse with a mixture of Japanese and English. As Hayakawa grew older, communication with his mother became increasingly difficult, especially in areas related to schoolwork.

As the eldest child, Hayakawa was raised to be responsible at an early age. With the expansion of his import-export business, Ichiro Hayakawa was required to make numerous trips to Japan and throughout western Canada. This left a heavy burden on young Hayakawa. Attending high school during the day and acting as the man of the house forced him to mature rapidly. He did not, however, allow his responsibilities as eldest son to interfere with his performance as a student.

After graduating from a Winnipeg high school in 1923, Hayakawa entered the University of Manitoba, where he received his bachelor of arts degree in English four years later. During his senior year of college, his father decided to move the family—Hayakawa's parents and two sisters—back to Japan, while Samuel and his younger brother completed their education in Canada. Hayakawa did not see his parents again until 1935. Leaning toward a career in higher education, he enrolled at McGill University in Montreal and received his master of arts degree in 1928. Although his parents were gone, their influence and support were permanently imprinted on him. In his parents' minds, there was never a doubt about their eldest son's academic prowess.

After graduating from McGill, Hayakawa wanted to continue his education towards a doctor of philosophy degree in English, but financial constraints forced him to take a variety of jobs. In Montreal, he drove a taxi, worked in a department store, and served a short term as a stenographer for a tractor firm. In 1930, he was offered a fellowship in the United States at the University of Wisconsin-Madison. Hayakawa received his Ph.D. in 1935. His dissertation topic, the writings of Oliver Wendell Holmes, was published in 1939.

Immediately after graduating from Wisconsin, Hayakawa left for Japan to visit his family. His educational accomplishments were a dream come true of Ichira and Tora Hayakawa. Their import-export business had grown into a worldwide enterprise. Ichiro Hayakawa had hoped that one day his eldest son would take over the family business, but understood when Hayakawa decided to pursue an academic career in English. A highly literate man, Ichiro Hayakawa had a fond appreciation for writers and was visibly proud to see his son achieve something he had always wanted to do.

After visiting Japan, Samuel returned to North America. Hoping to gain a teaching position at a Canadian university, he encountered one roadblock after another. The somewhat naive Hayakawa was learning the harsh reality of racial discrimination. To complicate matters for the young scholar, he was denied U.S. citizenship. Although born and raised in Canada, U.S. immigration officials considered him Japanese, and thus, all the immigration restrictions resulting from the 1924 Exclusion Act were applicable to him. It was not until 1954 with the McCarran-Walter Immigration Act that Hayakawa gained naturalized U.S. citizenship.

In 1937, Hayakawa married Margedent Peters from Evansville, IN, a student and literary-magazine editor at the University of Wisconsin-Madison. As a result of this marriage, Hayakawa became related by marriage to the Soviet leader Joseph Stalin. His wife's brother, John Wesley Peters, was married to the daughter of Joseph Stalin; Hayakawa thus became the uncle to Joseph Stalin's grandchildren.

During the 1930s, the Hayakawas' interracial marriage was uncommon and raised a few eyebrows. Despite the racial tensions of the time, the Hayakawas endured the highs and lows to live a satisfying life together. They raised two sons and a daughter. Their middle child, Mark, was afflicted with Down's syndrome, but the Hayakawa family defied the mental health system and demonstrated that with a loving environment, a child with Down's Syndrome could lead a productive life.

Samuel Ichiye Hayakawa is known to the world for his academic and political achievements. Unfortunately, this underscored his greatest achievement—being a father. Of all his accomplishments, Hayakawa felt his parental responsibilities provided him with the most satisfaction.

Being of Japanese ancestry in the United States during World War II was a difficult experience. With the attack on Pearl Harbor, Americans reacted strongly against anyone appearing Japanese. For Hayakawa, it was a difficult and emotional time. While he supported the Americans and their allies, the fact remained that his parents and sisters lived in Japan.

Although he was never interned like other Japanese in the United States, Hayakawa suffered his own personal conflict, whose impact would be long lasting. Despite the stigma of being Japanese during World War II, Hayakawa was able to resolve the internal stress that consumed so many Japanese Americans by comparing his experiences to those of African Americans and other ethnic minorities that suffered discrimination.

During the war, Hayakawa advanced through the academic profession at the Armour Institute of Technology (now the Illinois Institute of Technology), where he taught from 1939 to 1947. Never one to limit himself to academic pursuits, he also wrote a column for the *Chicago Defender*, a black newspaper. Identifying with the African American, Hayakawa gained a greater appreciation for the racial inequalities he was experiencing by learning about what African Americans had experienced for over 200 years.

At the end of the war, a letter from his father reached Hayakawa by way of a U.S. soldier with the occupation forces. In the letter, the elder Hayakawa wrote of the relief that most Japanese people felt as a result of the surrender. Ichiro Hayakawa expressed his happiness that Japan had lost the war and shared his desire to see Americans help establish a democratic government, free of militarism and oppression. For the younger Hayakawa, World War II reshaped his philosophy and prompted him to actively work towards achieving equal opportunity for all.

Hayakawa, the Educator

As an assistant instructor and doctoral student at Wisconsin, Hayakawa was highly influenced by the work of Alfred Korzybski. When he later landed a position at Armour Institute of Technology, Hayakawa had numerous opportunities to interact with Korzybski, who was at the Institute for General Semantics in Chicago. Committed to the tenets of general semantics, Hayakawa began writing his major work, *Language in Action*, in 1938. (In later editions, the title of the book was changed to *Language in Thought and Action*.) As a result of the book's popularity and selling power, Hayakawa gained financial independence. The book was adopted by most U.S. universities and translated into nine foreign languages. Even in the 1990s, the book was still selling approximately 50,000 copies a year worldwide.

No longer dependent on teaching as his main source of income, Hayakawa began to concentrate on writing full-time. Leaving Armour in 1947, Hayakawa spent the next few years writing articles and supervising the International Society for General Semantics. From 1950 to 1955, Hayakawa lectured on semantics at the University of Chicago.

Maturing as a scholar during his tenure in Chicago, Hayakawa began to branch away from Korzybski. Criticized by many scholars of general semantics as theoretically subjective, Hayakawa split from Korzybski's school which claimed a more scientific interpretation of general semantics. This was the first of many professional conflicts Hayakawa experienced throughout his academic career.

During this time, Hayakawa began to teach summer classes at San Francisco State College. After receiving an offer to become a part of the faculty, Hayakawa accepted a lectureship position in the language arts department.

By now a well-known semanticist, Hayakawa's reputation preceded his arrival on campus. His charismatic, spontaneous personality attracted students like a magnet. Graduate students came from all over to learn about Hayakawa's perspectives on general semantics. A popular educator on campus, Hayakawa's time was in constant demand. With a large audience of students trying to gain access to him, some of his students became disenchanted with his inaccessibility. This discontent led to complaints about his effectiveness and teaching style.

During his teaching tenure, Hayakawa rarely stayed on campus except to teach classes. According to Hayakawa, the open campus environment at San Francisco State provided too many distractions for productive scholarly work. Outside campus, Hayakawa felt more at ease with himself and his students.

San Francisco State College

The 1960s were turbulent years. The United States was unpopularly involved in the war in Vietnam, and political unrest ran high at colleges and universities across the country.

At the time, San Francisco State College had an enrollment of approximately 18,000 students. Characterized as an open campus, San Francisco State was known for its innovative approaches to teaching and the development of courses in conjunction with students.

Political turmoil on campus began in 1968 when a Black Panther member, George Murray, was dismissed from school, and student militants called a strike. Using terrorist tactics, these groups intimidated and physically threatened students and professors if they crossed the picket line. Some of their demands included the formulation of an autonomous black studies department, promotion to full professor of a faculty member who had one year's experience, the firing of a white administrator, and the admission of all black students who applied for the next academic year.

While sympathetic to student needs, Hayakawa felt a strike was detrimental to their cause and to the process of education. He urged student leaders to reopen the campus, but his plea fell on deaf ears.

Hayakawa, one of the few faculty members willing to go back to work, felt it was his duty to cross the picket line and continue the education of the students who desired it. He believed the faculty had forgotten their primary mission—teaching, conducting research, and pursuing academic excellence.

On November 28, 1968, Hayakawa was named acting president of San Francisco State College by California Governor Ronald Reagan and the trustees of the California state college system. With no previous administrative or political experience, his selection was an unpopular choice among faculty members and students. Prior to his appointment, Hayakawa had served on a five-person presidential-selection committee whose members had reportedly agreed not to seek the office. Hayakawa denied any agreement had been made and accepted the job under extreme opprobrium from committee members. Hayakawa was viewed as eccentric in appearance and style. Wearing Hawaiian carnation leis and an Irish tam-o'-shanter, his personal appearance was indicative of his personality.

His first priority as acting president was to reopen the campus following Thanksgiving break ending the strike. To achieve this objective, he yielded on some student demands and rejected others. This, however, was unsatisfactory to student leaders, who employed 1,000 protesters to close the campus on the first day following Thanksgiving break. Taking a firm stance, Hayakawa countered by deploying police officers across the campus. Over 700 arrests were made, and campus casualties ran into the hundreds. Before a U.S. Senate Subcommittee in 1969, Hayakawa reiterated his stance, "Student protesters said they would destroy this campus, and I said they would not."

On the first day back, student protesters assembled around a truck with a loudspeaker on top. Hayakawa, at the age of 62, climbed atop the truck and ripped out the audio system. Captured on national television, Hayakawa was hailed by the public as a person who stood up to the extremists. A majority of students wanted to resume classes, but were reluctant to defy militant protesters for fear of retaliation. Following Hayakawa's confrontation with student protesters, 80 percent of the student body returned to classes. However, peace did not last long.

In January 1969, one month after order had been restored on campus, the American Federation of Teachers declared a strike and halted instruction. This re-ignited student unrest and, as a precautionary measure, Hayakawa once again called on the San Francisco police department to maintain peace.

In March 1969, after two months of negotiations, an agreement was reached with the teachers' union. Hayakawa again conceded some demands but held firm on others. At the same time, militant student leaders relinquished some of their original demands and worked out a settlement. The cooperation Hayakawa had sought was finally being realized.

With the media coverage of San Francisco State, Hayakawa launched himself into the public eye. A Gallup poll conducted during the student uprising found S. I. Hayakawa to be the most admired educator in the United States. Among civic clubs and the lay public, Hayakawa represented a no-nonsense position that people identified with. Invited to deliver speeches throughout the country, he used this opportunity to launch a political career that would eventually lead him to the U.S. Senate.

Educational Beliefs

Influenced by Alfred Korzybski, Hayakawa's educational philosophy became viewed as idealistic. Hayakawa advocated an educational system based on equal opportunity and rational decision making. Thoroughly disgusted by the focus on higher education for purposes of practical application, Hayakawa felt that education should cultivate and free the individual as a free thinker, from which true intellectual power develops.

In 1970, Hayakawa defined five basic goals of education. The first is to understand and take better care of the environment. According to Hayakawa, if future generations are to survive, education must instill a sense of scientific awareness of the interconnectedness of people, animals, climate, and natural resources.

Second, Hayakawa felt that education must foster harmony and cooperation among the human race. As a nation, Americans must learn to expand their thinking beyond the ethnocentric and help their children experience the richness of the world's various cultures. Without this, they will lack the necessary insight to make rational choices.

Third, each child must have a sense of aesthetics. Whether it be religious or not, children should be given the opportunity to create an inner peace. By doing this, we give children a way to cope with daily social problems.

Each person must also be allowed to earn a living and contribute to society. According to Hayakawa, before children have an opportunity to accomplish anything, we often lower their self-esteem by allowing them to take an easy way out. Instead of challenging them, we cradle them and, in the long run, society is weakened.

And finally, the most important aspect of education for Hayakawa was the development of an intellectual method. As the information age matures, the importance of making rational decisions will be based on our ability to separate truth from falsehood. By deriving a critical method with which to analyze and evaluate, people will be able to base their decisions on rational explanations and not false propaganda.

On February 27, 1992, S.I. Hayakawa died of a stroke near his home in Mill Valley, California, where he lived with his wife and second son, Mark; he was 85. In his last years, Hayakawa lectured on issues ranging from academic freedom to California's English Language Amendment, a piece of legislation whose passage he greatly influenced. Besides his professional endeavors, Hayakawa was a special advisor to the secretary of state.

The 1960s and the early 1970s will be remembered as an era of free expression and demonstration. As a man of conviction, S. I. Hayakawa stood up against adverse conditions and restored order to a campus filled with internal conflict. Whether or not one agrees with his positions on issues, S.I. Hayakawa was a man who made people think critically about their thoughts and actions.

Ronald Takaki

Professor

During the tumultuous 1960s, universities across the United States experienced a genesis in ethnic studies programs. One of the pioneers in the ethnic studies movement was Ronald Takaki. Born in 1939 on the Hawaiian island of Oahu, Takaki is a third-generation American of Japanese ancestry (sansei). Takaki's grandparents immigrated to Hawaii in the late 19th century and worked as plantation laborers. Their experience formed the basis of his book *Pau Hana: Plantation Life and Labor in Hawaii*, providing one of the most accurate portrayals of plantation experience ever written. For present and future generations, Takaki's *Pau Hana* provides linkage to the struggles of first generation Japanese immigrants (issei).

In the introduction to his 1993 book, *A Different Mirror: A History of Multicultural America*, Takaki tells of how he grew up with no past of his own in his schooling and how others mistook him for a foreigner, although he is a native-born American. Upon completing high school in Hawaii, Takaki attended and received his bachelor of arts from the College of Wooster, OH, in 1961. He subsequently entered the University of California, Berkeley and received his master of arts (1962) and Ph.D. (1967) in history. His first position was at San Mateo College as an assistant professor in American history. He later moved to the University of California, Los Angeles (UCLA), where in five years he established himself as a scholar and effective instructor.

Takaki was the first person to teach a black history course at UCLA, an intriguing concept for students. His presence in class made him an icon within the university community. As Takaki fondly remembers, "Students were going around saying, 'We have this bad Asian dude teaching black history.'" During this period, Takaki also was an architect in creating UCLA's centers for African American, Asian American, Latino, and American Indian studies programs.

In 1972, he returned to his alma mater, the University of California, Berkeley, where since he has been a professor of ethnic studies and history, a field in which few contemporary scholars have achieved as much recognition for their work.

Takaki has published a number of reference books pertaining to multiculturalism and ethnic studies; his research has addressed the social and intellectual history of race relations in the United States. Among his more noted books are: *Iron Cages: Race and Culture in 19th Century America; Strangers from a Different Shore: A History of Asian Americans; Raising Cane: The World of Plantation Hawaii;* and *A Pro-Slavery Crusade: The Agitation to Reopen the African Slave Trade.*

Takaki has received fellowships from the National Humanities Foundation (1970-71) and the Rockefeller Foundation (1981-82). He has also been honored with the Distinguished Teaching Award at the University of California, Berkeley, where his scholarly pursuits and writing have not deterred his effectiveness as a teacher. In fact, Takaki represents the ideal model, that of scholarship enhancing teaching ability.

Throughout his academic career, Takaki has advocated for multiculturalism. While addressing its integration into academia, Takaki said, " . . . in terms of race, people are not well educated. Students bring with them a whole terrain of ignorance. What the university leadership is trying to say is, we need more civility . . . . College campuses have in fact become the site of an experiment called integration . . . . We're on the threshold of something pretty exciting, but you have this backlash. Prejudices do get played out at the street level. When we talk about the need for understanding on campus, we're saying it's the lack of understanding that has consequences."

As the United States approaches the 21st century, issues pertaining to ethnic studies, multiculturalism, and diversity continue to be topics for heated discussion. While some people may choose to close their eyes

and ears (feeling multiculturalism does not affect them), Ronald Takaki issues the following warning, "We heard the rumblings [referring to the Los Angeles /Rodney King episode] . . . . For decades . . . race was defined as black and white . . . . We . . . only have to look at the faces of our students to understand how multicultural America had become." Takaki's challenge to educators is: help students understand that the United States was "forged in a crucible of diversity." The challenges will be great and there will be many setbacks as the United States strives to integrate multiculturalism, but as Takaki puts it, "We can never give up."

Lily Wong Fillmore

Scholar

For children whose first language is not English, public schooling in the United States can be a traumatic experience. Scholars such as Lily Wong Fillmore are continuing their struggle to explore ways in which public schools can be more accommodating for English as a second language (ESL) and bilingual children.

Lily Wong Fillmore received her Ph.D. at Stanford University in 1976. Her dissertation, "The Second Time Around: Cognitive and Social Strategies in Second Language Acquisition," launched her career into second-language learning and bilingual education. She is professor of education at the University of California, Berkeley.

Her publications in second-language learning have focused on the individual differences and the learner's social and cognitive strategies for acquisition of a second language. Two of her frequently cited works in second-language acquisition are "The Language Learner as an Individual" and "Individual Differences in Second Language Learning." Through her studies, Wong Fillmore has concluded that second-language learning and instruction require recognition of individual differences and awareness of social context.

Lily Wong Fillmore also specializes in bilingual-education research, in which she has examined the effects of instructional practices and language use on the learning process. Two of her noted works in this field include "Instructional Language as Linguistic Input: Second Language Learning in Classrooms" and a coauthored piece with Conception Valadez in the *Handbook of Research on Teaching* entitled, "Teaching Bilingual Learners."

Lily Wong Fillmore's work has not gone unrecognized within her profession. Like Kathy Au and Kenji Hakuta, she received the Distinguished Scholar Award from the American Educational Research Association in 1985. Within the fields of second-language acquisition and bilingual education, she has established herself as a leader among her peers.

For Lily Wong Fillmore, the social context of language learning cannot be separated or discounted from the learning process. Unless sociocultural considerations are examined and accounted for, students being taught English as a second language will continue to encounter widespread difficulty in U.S. public school settings. In the future, educators such as Lily Wong Fillmore will be needed to assist and direct educational programs that balance the needs of each child as they struggle to learn English while maintaining a healthy self-identity associated with their primary language.

Conclusion

In this section, five Asian Americans and their respective contributions to education are profiled. Common threads emerge from the achievements of these extraordinary individuals. For Hakuta, Hayakawa, and Wong Fillmore, the theme is language. For Au and Takaki, it is the integration of multiculturalism. Although their approaches toward dealing with minority-related issues are diverse and, in some instances, contradictory, there is little doubt that these scholars have significantly advanced the discussion in their fields of expertise.

In conclusion, these profiles represent more than scholarly achievements, awards, and honors; they illustrate what Asian Americans have contributed to the field of education. With the exception of S. I. Hayakawa, who died in 1992, Kathy Au, Kenji Hakuta, Ronald Takaki, and Lily Wong Fillmore continue to pursue their scholarship and will certainly continue to contribute to their chosen disciplines.

—Alan R. Shoho
University of Portland

References

American Association of Colleges for Teacher Education. *Metropolitan Life Survey of Teacher Education Students.* Washington, D.C.: American Association of Colleges for Teacher Education, 1990.

————. *Teacher Education Pipeline: Schools, Colleges, and Departments of Education Enrollments by Race and Ethnicity.* Washington, D.C.: American Association of Colleges for Teacher Education, 1988.

————. *Teacher Education Pipeline II: Schools, Colleges, and Departments of Education Enrollments by Race and Ethnicity.* Washington, D.C.: American Association of Colleges for Teacher Education, 1990.

————. *Teacher Education Pipeline III: Schools, Colleges, and Department of Education Enrollments by Race and Ethnicity.* Washington, D.C.: American Association of Colleges for Teacher Education, 1994.

Au, K. H. Curriculum vitae. Unpublished manuscript, 1994.

————. *Literacy Instruction in Multicultural Settings.* Fort Worth: Harcourt Brace Jovanovich College Publishers, 1993.

————. "Participation Structures in a Reading Lesson with Hawaiian Children: Analysis of a Culturally Appropriate Instructional Event." *Anthropology and Education Quarterly* 11, no. 2 (1980): 91-115.

————. "Portfolio Assessment: Experiences at the Kamehameha Elementary Education Program." In *Authentic Reading Assessment: Practices and Possibilities,* edited by S. Valencia, E. Hiebert, and P. Afflerbach, 103-126. Newark, Del.: International Reading Association, 1994.

————. "Social Organizational Factors in Learning to Read: The Balance of Rights Hypothesis." *Reading Research Quarterly* 17, no. 1 (1981): 115-152.

————. "Teaching Reading to Hawaiian Children: Finding a Culturally Appropriate Solution." In *Culture and the Bilingual Classroom: Studies in Classroom Ethnography,* edited by H. T. Trueba, G. P. Guthrie, and K. H. Au. Rowley, Mass.: Newbury House Publishers, 1981.

————. "Using the Experience-Text-Relationship Method with Minority Children." *The Reading Teacher* 32, no. 6 (1979): 677-679.

Au, K. H., and A. J. Kawakami. "Influence of the Social Organization of Instruction of Children's Text Comprehension Ability: A Vygotskian Perspective." In *Contexts of School-Based Literacy,* edited by T. E. Raphael, 63-76. New York: Random House, 1986.

————. "Vygotskian Perspectives on Discussion Processes in Small Group Reading Lessons." In *The Social Context of Instruction: Group Organization and Group Processes,* edited by P. L. Peterson, L. C. Wilkinson, and M. Hallinan. New York: Academic Press, 1984.

Banks, J. A. "Teaching Multicultural Literacy to Teachers." *Teaching Education* 4, no. 1 (1991): 135-144.

Baumrind, D. "Current Patterns of Parental Authority." In *Developmental Psychology Monographs,* no. 41, 1-103, 1971.

Bishop, K. "S. I. Hayakawa Dies at 85; Scholar and Former Senator. "*New York Times,* February 28, 1992, B6.

Byce, C., A. Khazzoom, and C. Schmitt. *Changes in Undergraduate Student Financial Aid: Fall 1986-Fall 1989.* Washington, D.C.: U.S. Department of Education, 1993.

Center for Education Statistics. *The Condition of Education.* Washington, D.C.: Government Printing Office, 1987.

Chinn, P. C., and G. Y. Wong. "Recruiting and Retaining Asian/Pacific American Teachers." In *Diversity in Teacher Education,* edited by M. E. Dilworth, 112-133. San Francisco: Jossey-Bass, 1992.

Coley, R. J., and M. E. Goertz. *Characteristics of Minority NTE Test-Takers.* Princeton, N.J.: ETS, 1991.

College Board. *Trends in Student Aid: 1983-1993.* Washington, D.C.: Washington Office of the College Board, 1993.

The Commission on Minority Participation in Education and American Life. *One-third of a Nation: A Report of the Commission on Minority Participation in Education and American Life.* Washington, D.C.: American Council on Education, 1988.

Commissioner's Task Force on Minorities. *A Curriculum of Inclusion.* Albany, NY: State Education Department, July 1989.

Contemporary Authors. Edited by S.M. Trosky and D. Oldendorf. Detroit: Gale Research, 1992.

Crew, L. *Children of the River.* New York: Dell, 1989.

Cummins, J. *The Empowerment of Minority Students.* Los Angeles: California Association for Bilingual Education, 1986.

Darling-Hammond, L. "Teacher and Teaching: Signs of a Changing Profession." In *Handbook of Research on Teacher Education,* edited by W. R. Houston, 267-290. New York: MacMillan, 1990.

Darling-Hammond, L. K. J. Pittman, and C. Ottinger. *Career Choices for Minorities: Who Will Teach?* Washington, D.C.: National Education Association and Council of Chief State School Officers Task Force on Minorities in Teaching, 1987.

Delatte, J. G. "Human Figure Drawings of Vietnamese Children." *Child Study Journal* 8 (1978): 227-234.

Derman-Sparks, L., and the ABC Task Force. *Anti-Bias Curriculum: Tools for Empowering Young Children.* Washington, D.C., National Association for the Education of Young Children, 1989.

Dilworth, M. E. "Reading between the Line: Teachers and their Racial/Ethnic Cultures." *Teacher Education Monograph* no. 11. Washington, D.C: ERIC Clearinghouse on Teacher Education and American Association of Colleges for Teacher Education, 1990.

Directory of American Scholars, 8th ed., s.v. "Takaki, R. T."

Dornbusch, S. M., P. L. Ritter, P. H. Leiderman, D. F. Roberts, and M. J. Fraleigh. "The Relation of Parenting Style to Adolescent School Performance." *Child Development* 58 (1987): 1244-1257.

Duff, O. B., and H. J. Tongchinsub. "Expanding the Secondary Literature Curriculum: Annotated Bibliographies of American Indian, Asian American, and Hispanic American Literature." *English Education* 22 (1990): 220-240.

Duncan, S. E., and E. A. De Avila. Bilingualism and Cognition: Educational Testing Service/Minority Graduate Education. *Increasing Minority Faculty: An Elusive Goal.* Princeton, N.J.: Educational Testing Service/Minority Graduate Education, 1988.

Fuller, M. L. "Teacher Education Programs and Increasing Minority School Populations: An Educational Mismatch?" In *The Education of African Americans,* edited by C. V. Willie, A. M. Garibaldi, and W. R. Reed, 148-158. New York: Auburn House, 1991.

Gall, S. B., and T. L. Gall., eds. *Statistical Record of Asian Americans.* Detroit: Gale Research, 1993.

Garibaldi, A. M. "Abating the Shortage of Black Teachers." In *The Education of African Americans,* edited by C. V. Willie, A. M. Garibaldi, and W. R. Reed, 148-158. New York: Auburn House, 1991.

Genishi, C. "Children's Language: Learning Words from Experience." *Young Children* 44, no. 1 (1988):16-23.

Gonzalez, R. D. "When Minority Becomes Majority: The Changing Face of English Classrooms." *English Journal* 79, no. 1(1990): 16-23.

Goodwin, A. L. "Problems, Process, and Promise: Reflections on a Collaborative Approach to the Minority Teacher Shortage." *Journal of Teacher Education* 42, no. 1 (1991): 28-36.

———. "Teaching Images: Unlocking Preservice Student Teaching Beliefs and Connecting Teaching Beliefs to Teaching Behavior." Ph.D. diss, Columbia University, 1987. In *Dissertation Abstracts* 48, 1741A.

Graham, P. A. "Black Teachers: A Drastically Scarce Resource." *Phi Delta Kappan* (1987): 598-605.

Hakuta, K. Curriculum vitae. Unpublished manuscript, 1993.

———. "Degree of Bilingualism and Cognitive Ability in Mainland Puerto Rican Children." *Child Development* 58 (1987): 1372-1388.

———. "English Language Acquisition by Speakers of Asian Languages." In *Comparative Research in Bilingual Education: Asian Pacific American Perspectives,* edited by M. Chu-Chung. New York: Teachers College Press, 1983.

———. "Language and Cognition in Bilingual Children." In *Bilingual Education: Issues and Strategies,* edited by A. Padilla, C. Valdez, and H. Fairchild. Newbury Park, Calif.: Sage Publications, 1990.

———. *Mirror of Language: The Debate on Bilingualism.* New York: Basic Books, 1986.

———. "Some Common Goals for First and Second Language Acquisition Research." In *New Dimensions in Research on the Acquisition and Use of a Second Language,* edited by R. Andersen. Rowley, Mass.: Newbury House Publishers, 1980.

Hakuta, K., and Cancino, H. "Trends in Second Language Acquisition Research." *Harvard Educational Review* 47, no. 3 (1977); 117-127.

Hakuta, K., and E. E. Garcia. "Bilingualism and Education." *American Psychologist* 44 (1989): 374-379.

Hakuta, K., and L. Gould. "Synthesis of Research on Bilingual Education." *Educational Leadership* 44 (1987): 39-45.

Hakuta, K., and L. Pease-Alvarez, eds. "Special Issue on Bilingual Education." *Educational Researcher* 21, no. 2 (1992).

Hamanaka, S. *The Journey: Japanese American, Racism, and Renewal.* New York: Orchard Books, 1990.

Harris, V. J., ed. *Teaching Multicultural Literature in Grades K-8.* Norwood, MA: Christopher-Gordon, 1992.

Hatton, B. R. "A Game Plan for Ending the Minority Teacher Shortage." *NEA Today* 6, no. 6 (1988): 66-69.

Hsia, J. "Cognitive Assessment of Asian Americans." In *Asian and Pacific American Perspectives in Bilingual Education,* edited by M. Chu-Chang, 123-152. New York: Teachers College Press, 1983.

———. *Asian Americans in Higher Education and at Work.* Hilldale, NJ: Lawrence Erlbaum Associates, 1988.

Huber, T., and C. Pewewardy. *Maximizing Learning for All Students: A Review of Literature of Learning Modalities, Cognitive Styles, and Approaches to Meeting the Needs of Diverse Learners.* Wichita, KS: Wichita State University, 1990. (ERIC Document Reproduction Service No. ED 324 289).

Hayakawa, S. I. "Academic Freedom: What It Means and What It Doesn't Mean." Paper presented at conference, Academic Freedom or Academic License, organized by Accuracy in Academia, Washington, D.C., June 1976.

————. "The Basic Goals of Education." *Register and Tribune Syndicate*, June 19-20, 1976.

————. Biographical data. Unpublished manuscript, 1987.

————. "Bringing up a Retarded Child." *Register and Tribune Syndicate*, May 1-2, 1976.

————. "Discovering New Ways with the Retarded." *Register and Tribune Syndicate*, May 8-9, 1976.

————. "Five Goals of Education." *Register and Tribune Syndicate*, February 7, 1970.

————. "Happy Birthday to a Great Lady." *Los Angeles Times Syndicate*, August 6-7, 1977.

————. *Language in Thought and Action.* 5th ed. San Diego: Harcourt Brace Jovanovich, Inc., 1990.

————. "A Letter from My Father." *Register and Tribune Syndicate*, August 15, 1970.

————. "Life with Father: Hayakawa Reminisces." *Vancouver Sun*, October 24, 1972.

————. "My Father, Ichiro Hayakwa (1884-1976)." *Register and Tribune Syndicate*, January 24, 1976.

————. "My Parents' Home in Yamanashi." *Register and Tribune Syndicate*, May 24-25, 1975.

————. "Prejudice of Higher Education." *Examiner Showcase*, January 9, 1971.

————. "A Retarded Adult and His Future." *Register and Tribune Syndicate*, May 29-30, 1976.

————. "A Retarded Child in the Family." *Register and Tribune Syndicate*, May 15-16, 1976.

————. *Symbol, Status, and Personality.* New York, Harcourt Brace and Jovanovich World, 1963.

————. *Through the Communication Barrier: On Speaking, Listening, and Understanding.* New York: Harper and Row, 1979.

————. *The Use and Misuse of Language.* Greenwich, Conn.: Fawcett Publications, Inc., 1962.

————. "What We Learned from Our Retarded Child." *Register and Tribune Syndicate*, May 22-23, 1976.

————. "Why the English Language Amendment?: An Autobiographical Statement." Paper presented at the national convention of Forty and Eight, Portland, Ore., September 1986.

Lee, Y. *Academic Success of East Asian American: An Ethnographic Comparative Study of East Asian American and Anglo American Academic Achievement.* Seoul: American Studies Institute, Seoul National University Press, 1987.

Lortie, D. *Schoolteacher.* Chicago: University of Chicago Press, 1975.

Mow, S. L., and M. T. Nettles. "Minority Student Access to, and Persistence and Performance in College: A Review of the Trends and Research Literature." In *Higher Education: Handbook of Theory and Research*, vol. vi. New York: Agathon Press, 1990.

National Academy of Sciences, National Research Council. *Summary Report 1990: Doctorate Recipients from United States Universities.* Washington, D.C.: National Academy of Sciences, National Research Council, 1990.

National Center for Education Statistics, United States Department of Education. *Digest of Education Statistics.* Washington, D.C.: U.S. Government Printing Office, 1992.

————. *Digest of Education Statistics.* Washington, D.C.: U.S. Government Printing Office, 1992.

————. *The Condition of Education.* Washington, D.C.: U.S. Government Printing Office, 1992.

Nozaki, Y. "An Ethnographic Study of Japanese Children in U.S. Schools: Rethinking Multiculturalist Pedagogy." Unpublished manuscript, University of Wisconsin-Madison, 1994.

O'Hare, W., and J. Felt. "Asian Americans: America's Fastest Growing Minority Group." *Population Trends and Public Policy* (19) Washington, D. C.: Population Reference Bureau, 1991.

Pallas, A., G. Natriello, and E. McDill. "The Changing Nature of the Disadvantaged Population." *Educational Researcher* 18, no. 5 (1989): 16-22.

Pang, V. O. "Asian American Children: A Diverse Population." *The Educational Forum* 55, no. 1 (1990): 49-66.

Pang, V. O., C. Colvin, M. L. Tran, and R. H. Barba. "Beyond Chopsticks and Dragons: Selecting Asian American Literature for Children." *The Reading Teacher* 46 (1992) 216-224.

Peng, S. S., and R. A. Korb. "Minority Participation in Higher Education: Access, Persistence, Completion, Choice." Paper presented at the annual forum of AIR, San Francisco, May 1991.

Peng, S. S., and R. Lee. "Diversity of Asian American Students and Its Implications for Education." Paper presented at the annual conference of the National Association of Bilingual Education, Washington, D.C., January 1991.

Reagan, R. "S. I. Hayakawa on Communicating." *Esquire*, April 1979, 16.

Research about Teacher Education Project. *RATE IV—Teaching Teachers: Facts and Figures.* Washington, D.C.: American Association of Colleges for Teacher Education, 1990.

Rumbaut, R. G., and K. Ima. *The Adaptation of Southeast Asian Refugee Youth: A Comparative Study.* Washington, D. C., U.S. Office of Refugee Resettlement, 1988.

Shoho, A. R. Interview with Dr. Robert Shafer, professor of English, Arizona State University, November 1987.

————. Interview with S. I. Hayakawa, November 1987.

————. "Samuel Ichiye Hayakawa." Paper presented at the meeting of the International Society for Educational Biography, Chicago, April 1988.

Shorris, E. "Dr. Hayakawa in Thought and Action." *Ramparts Magazine*, November 1969, 38-42.

Slaughter-Defoe, D. T., K. Nakagawa, R. Takanishi, and D. J. Johnson. "Toward Cultural-Ecological Perspectives on Schooling and Achievement in African and Asian American Children." *Child Development* 61 (1990): 363-383.

Smith, V., and P. van der Veen. "Trends in Medical School Applicants & Matriculants." 1991.

Snyder, T. D., and C. M. Hoffman. *Digest of Education Statistics.* Washington, D.C.: U.S. Department of Education, 1993.

Stevenson, H. W., and J. W. Stigler. *The Learning Gap: Why Our Schools Are Failing and What We Can Learn from Japanese and Chinese Education.* New York: Summit, 1992.

Stodolsky, S. S., and G. S. Lesser. *Learning Patterns in the Disadvantaged.* New York: Yeshiva University, 1967. (ERIC document reproduction service number ED 012 291).

Sue, S., and J. Abe. *Prediction of Academic Achievement among Asian American and White Students.* College Board Report no. 88-11. New York: The College Board.

Sung, B. L. *The Adjustment Experience of Chinese Immigrant Children in New York City.* New York: Center for Migration Studies, 1987.

Takaki, R. T. *A Different Mirror: A History of Multicultural America.* Boston: Little, Brown and Co., 1993.

———. *A Discontented Civilization: Race and Culture in 19th Century America.* New York: Knopf, 1979.

———. *Iron Cages: Race and Culture in 19th Century America.* New York: Knopf, 1979.

———. *Pau Hana: Plantation Life and Labor in Hawaii.* Honolulu: University of Hawaii Press, 1983.

———. *A Pro-Slavery Crusade: The Agitation to Reopen the African Slave Trade.* New York: Free Press, 1971.

———. *Raising Cane: The World of Plantation Hawaii.* New York: Chelsea House Publishers, 1993.

———. *Strangers from a Different Shore: A History of Asian Americans.* New York: Penguin Books, 1990.

———. *Violence in the Black Imagination.* New York: Putnam, 1972.

Tobin, J. J., D. Y. H. Wu, and D. H. Davidson. *Preschool in Three Cultures: Japan, China, and the United States.* New Haven, CT: Yale University Press, 1989.

"Today's Numbers, Tomorrow's Nation: Demographics Awesome Challenge for Schools." [no author given] *Education Week*, May 14, 1986, 14-37.

Trueba, H. T. *Raising Silent Voices: Educating the Linguistic Minorities for the 21st Century.* New York: Newbury House/Harper Collins, 1989.

Trueba, H. T., L. R. L Cheng, and K. Ima. *Myth of Reality: Adaptive Strategies of Asian Americans in California.* Washington, D.C.: Falmer, 1993.

Tsuang, G. W. "Assuring Equal Access of Asian Americans to Highly Selective Universities" *The Yale Law Journal* 98, no. 3 (January 1989): 659-678.

Uchida, Y. *The Bracelet.* New York: Philomel, 1993.

U.S. Bureau of the Census. *Census of Population: Asian and Pacific Islander by State.* Washington, D.C.: Government Printing Office, 1990.

Wasser, J. "Performance for Hayakawa." *Time*, July 18, 1969, 53.

Western Interstate Commission of Higher Education and the College Board. *The Road to College: Educational Progress by Race and Ethnicity.* Boulder: Western Interstate Commission of Higher Education and the College Board, 1991.

Who's Who in the West, 21st ed., s.v. "Takaki, R. T."

Williams, L. R. "Developmentally Appropriate Practice and Cultural Values: A Case in Point." In *Diversity and Developmentally Appropriate Practices*, edited by B. L. Mallory and R. S. New, 155-165. New York: Teachers College Press, 1994.

Wittrock, M. C., ed. *Handbook of Research on Teaching.* 3rd ed. New York: MacMillan, 1986.

Witty, E. P. "Increasing the Pool of Black Teachers: Plans and Strategies." In *Teacher Recruitment and Retention: With a Special Focus on Minority Teachers*, edited by A. M. Garibaldi. Washington, D.C.: National Education Association, 1989.

Wong Fillmore, L. "Individual Differences in Second Language Acquisition." In *Individual Differences in Language Ability and Language Behavior*, edited by C. J. Fillmore, W. S. Y. Wang, and D. K. Kempler. New York: Academic Press, 1979.

———. "Instructional Language as Linguistic Input: Second Language Learning in Classrooms." In *Communicating in the Classroom*, edited by L. C. Wilkinson. New York: Academic Press, 1982.

———. "Language and Cultural Issues in Early Education." In *The Care and Education of America's Young Children: Obstacles and Opportunities*, Part 1 of the 90th Yearbook of the National Society for the Study of Education, 30-49. Chicago: National Society for the Study of Education, 1991.

———. "The Language Learner as an Individual." In *On TESOL '82: Pacific Perspectives on Language Learning and Teaching*, edited by M. Clarke and J. Handscombe. Washington, D.C.: Teachers of English to Speakers of Other Languages, 1983.

Wong Fillmore, L., P. Ammon, M. S. Ammon, K. DeLucchi, J. Jensen, B. McLaughlin, and M. Strong. *Learning Language through Bilingual Instruction: Second Year Report* (Submitted to the National Institute of Education). Berkeley: University of California, 1983.

Xu, G., Veloski, J. J., M. Hojat, J. S. Connella, and B. Bachrach. "Longitudinal Comparison of the Academic Performances of Asian American and White Medical Students." *Academic Medicine* 68 (1993):82-86.

Yee, L. Y., and R. LaForge. "Relationship between Mental Abilities, Social Class, and Exposure to English in Chinese Fourth Graders." *Journal of Educational Psychology* 66 (1974): 826-834.

Yep, L. *The Star Fisher.* New York: Morrow, 1991.

Work Force

♦ The Professional Glass Ceiling

♦ THE PROFESSIONAL GLASS CEILING

The existence of a corporate "glass ceiling"—promotional barriers to upper-management positions for women and minorities—has been well documented by the United States Department of Labor. What has not been recognized, though, is a growing pool of Asian American professionals and the difficulties encountered in the quest for upward mobility, particularly among Asian American women.

In this chapter, we will discuss: (1) the glass-ceiling phenomenon; (2) the societal and sociopsychological factors associated with the glass ceiling; (3) the effect of these factors on the career development of Asian American women; and (4) strategies that can be implemented to effectively break through the glass ceiling.

Workplace Discrimination

Although Asian Americans have made significant strides in a variety of occupations, there are still salient barriers that impede their career development. Therefore, Asian American employees seeking to join management ranks have been stymied by a high level of discrimination.

In 1992, the U.S. Commission on Civil Rights, in its report entitled Civil Rights Issues Facing Asian Americans in the 1990s, found that Asian Americans are unfairly stereotyped as being "unaggressive, having poor communication skills and limited English proficiency, and being too technical to become managers, and . . . [are] excluded from networks necessary for promotions."

Moreover, according to the Commission, many Asian American professionals feel that racism, networking difficulties, a lack of mentors, insensitivity by non-Asian management, and a Western corporate culture that does not value Asian styles of communication and leadership impede their upward mobility.

Other studies indicate that the representation of Asian Americans in senior executive positions is merely one-tenth of their representation in the American population as a whole, despite their high level of educational achievement. A recent commission study indicated that U.S.-born Asian American men were less likely to be in managerial occupations than non-Hispanic white men with similar occupational characteristics.

At the state and local levels, Asian Americans had greater difficulty than their white counterparts in attaining managerial positions in a variety of occupations: business, engineering, aerospace industry, telecommunications, finance, insurance, protective services, skilled construction, health care, law, and government.

Discrimination Against Women

Employment discrimination against Asian American women was evident, in particular for immigrants, who by virtue of their small numbers in the workplace find it difficult to obtain support and advice from co-workers when encountering discrimination. They are also less informed of their rights, since many Asian American women, both Asian- and American-born have been culturally conditioned to avoid complaining about harassment and other forms of discrimination. This makes them more vulnerable—and less willing—to confront workplace mistreatment.

Societal Factors

One societal myth implies that Asian Americans are not victims of an organizational glass ceiling, but are, in fact, an advantaged group due to their status as a model minority. This stereotypical view, based on a generalized misreading of statistics, identifies Asian Americans as extremely successful in economic, educational, and occupational contexts. However, a more thorough examination of census demographic figures offers contrasting evidence. Asian Americans, especially recent immigrants, have larger families with more working members than their white counterparts; therefore, they generally report larger family incomes. Per capita statistics reveal that, in fact, the average income of Asian Americans is actually lower than that of whites. Persistently higher are the poverty and unemployment rates of Asian Americans.

According to U.S. Census data, over a third of Asian Americans age 25 and over have completed at least four years of college, almost double the rate for whites. Nevertheless, this comparatively high level of educational attainment has not been commensurate with earning power. U.S. government surveys have found that highly educated Asian Americans earned less than their white counterparts at similar educational levels. Furthermore, Asian Americans were much less likely to be found in upper-level management positions for longer periods than whites. Despite these statistical realities, the popular view of Asian Americans as enjoying societal success and for whom affirmative action is unnecessary and inappropriate still persists. This gross generalization has been fueled by other societal misconceptions about Asian Americans.

Sociopsychological Factors

The "glass ceiling" barrier is reinforced by workplace conflicts between Asian and Western mores. Depending on factors like birthplace and length of residence in the United States, Asian Americans retain traditional Asian values, merge Asian values with Western values, or adopt Western values.

In many organizations that have a Western management philosophy, behavior that reflects Western values is rewarded by appointments to management positions. Good technical work is also rewarded by upward mobility in a management track. Many Asian Americans (and other employees for that matter), although technically competent, may not reflect the Western behavioral patterns that are associated with leadership or management potential in the United States.

For example, an Asian American employee who values respect for authority, self-control, and harmonious relationships is unlikely to speak up at a meeting to question another's point of view or even to make a suggestion unless asked by others. This type of behavior has often been misinterpreted as indecisive or lacking initiative and confidence. Similar misconceptions have stereotyped Asian American women to an even greater degree.

Battling the "Suzy Wong" Syndrome

Just as stereotypes of successful Asian American men persist, so too do stereotypes of Asian American women, interpreting them as docile, submissive, and "Suzy Wong sexpots." These biased views most likely grew from a combination of the anti-Asian sentiment of the early 1900s, popular notions about the exotic characteristics of Asian women, and impressions brought back by American soldiers from World War II, Korea, and Vietnam. Fueling these stereotypes are Asian cultural norms that do not value achievement in women. For this reason, Asian American women have been less encouraged than their white counterparts to seek occupational advancement; instead, they encounter family and community pressure to marry and raise children. With each succeeding generation, however, more Asian American women have entered the work force and have sought and attained managerial positions.

Nonetheless, occupational statistics indicate that while only a small percentage of Asian American men occupy managerial positions, Asian American women fare even worse. They are commonly believed to be less assertive than their male counterparts, to lack leadership qualities, and to be more qualified to fill secretarial and support-staff roles.

It is apparent that the aspirations of both Asian American men and women to managerial positions have been thwarted by discrimination, cultural misunderstandings, and Western management criteria and expectations. Fortunately, the movement toward diversity in contemporary organizations and the expressed frustrations of Asian American employees have caused organizations to increase their understanding of subcultures in the United States.

Strategies and Programs

As an organization changes from a Western-dominated environment to a multicultural environment, several phases of personal identity and behavioral development are experienced by minority employees. Rita Hardiman and Gerald Jackson have identified several definitions of these stages: (1) naivete, in which new employees have little frame of reference about the organizational culture or rules; (2) acceptance, in which new employees accept all of the societal perceptions that managers and colleagues place upon them; (3) resistance, in which employees start to question and evaluate their own values and those of the organization; (4) redefinition, in which employees begin to carve out an identity and attempt to balance their cultural identity with the selected values of the organization; and (5) bridge-building, in which all employees reach out to interact, value diversity, and collaborate with others in the organization, enhancing cultural pluralism in an inclusive manner.

The stages of naivete, acceptance, and redefinition can be interpreted in an Asian-specific context of self-development. The redefinition stage can be related to another model of intercultural value management, namely, the Situational-Additive Model discussed by Jo Uehara and Joanne Yamauchi. This model, based on a situational or pluralistic perspective, identifies cultural adjustment patterns that depend on the specific intercultural context. For example, a person may send indirect verbal messages to someone from a Western cultural background.

Situational-Additive Model

The Situational-Additive Model includes a six-step learning process for successful intercultural value management. These steps include: (1) awareness, to identify values and communication behavior that are used by one's group; (2) assessment, to evaluate attitudes, communication methods, and styles of influential groups; (3) conflict management, to identify steps to change one's relationship with these other groups; (4) acquisition, to acquire the knowledge and skills necessary to communicate and work effectively with others of diverse cultural backgrounds; (5) application, to test the learned skills and acquired knowledge with the support of mentors, role models, and support groups; and (6) actualization, to incorporate new learning into one's daily routine, to achieve a comfort level acknowledging one's unique self, to balance personal and societal values, to resolve communication conflicts, and to concentrate efforts to facilitate cultural pluralism with members of all other cultural groups.

In addition to using communication strategies specific to the situation, a number of Asian American employees have formed official task forces at large corporations, such as AT&T, Proctor & Gamble, Avon Products, Pacific Gas and Electric Company, University of California, and the U.S. Public Health Service. These groups support other Asian Americans in career development, supply information that promotes cultural awareness, and train others in communication and assertiveness skills. The task force also advise corporate management seeking to understand Asian American concerns. Its members can become collaborative agents for interaction with other cultural groups and offer consultation on organizational change and cultural pluralism.

Asian Americans must reach out to and network with other groups (the bridge-building stage of multicultural identity development). Such collaborative alliances enhance mutual understanding and encourage contributions that can be made by all employees.

Management Strategies

Managers holding Western values should work to understand the stages of development that their Asian American employees experience. Individual Asian Americans may be at different stages of development at different points in their careers. Development depends on many factors, including birthplace. Asian Americans in the work force may be Asian-born immigrants, second-generation American-born, or fifth-generation, demonstrating more Western than Asian ways of thinking and behaving.

Leadership

Managers need to recognize that Asian Americans may have a different style of leadership, one that promotes less conflict, more harmonious relationships, and team cooperation. In recent years, this people-oriented style has been given increased attention in an effort to improve human resources management. Many companies have held seminars to help non-Asian managers understand contrasting Eastern and Western values coexisting in contemporary organizations and to learn more about Asian communication styles in order to relate more effectively to their Asian American employees. When corporate managers approve and support work force diversity, they convey to workers a concern to enhance cultural sensitivity, which can lead to increased productivity and an improved working environment.

Breaking the Glass Ceiling

Researcher Ann Morrison has identified five ways that organizations seeking to increase work force diversity can enhance opportunities for minority employees. These include: (1) encourage personal intervention from top management; (2) increase efforts to recruit minority employees; (3) include diversity enhancement as a category in performance evaluations; (4) hold diversity training classes; and (5) make diversity a factor in promotion decisions.

For Asian Americans who do not necessarily aspire to managerial ranks, some companies have a two-tiered system that also rewards technical competence. For those who demonstrate managerial aptitude, management training and positions are available. A parallel professional track allows technically competent employees to increase their earning potential without managerial responsibilities.

The formidable barriers encountered on the way to breaking through the glass ceiling stem from institutional, societal, and individual sources. As organizations evolve from a monoculture to a multicultural environment, it may become easier for Asian Americans and other minorities to achieve careers advancement. This fulfillment will depend on a sensitivity to and a respect for diversity by everyone from top management to the line staff. How well traditional organizations can integrate culture and balance different work styles, communication patterns, and leadership methods will determine the success of a pluralistic workplace, leading to increased opportunity for individuals of diverse cultural backgrounds.

References

Bennett, Claudine. *The Asian and Pacific Islander Population in the United States: March 1990 and 1991*. Washington, D.C.: U.S. Bureau of the Census, 1992.

Chun, Ki-Taek. "The Myth of Asian American Success and Its Educational Ramifications," *IRCD Bulletin*, 15, nos. 1-2, Winter/Spring, 1980, pp. 1-12.

Der, Henry. "Asian Pacific Islanders and the 'Glass Ceiling'— New Era of Civil Rights Activism?" In *Leadership Education for Asian Pacifics (LEAP) The State of Asian Pacific America: A Public Policy Report*. Los Angeles: LEAP and UCLA Asian American Studies Center, 1993.

Foster, Badig, Gerald Jackson, William E. Cross, and Rita Hardeman. "Workforce Diversity and Business." *Training and Development Journal*, April 1988, pp. 38-42.

Hurh, Won Moo and Kim, Kwang Chung. "The 'Success' Image of Asian Americans: Its Validity, and Its Practical and Theoretical Implications." *Ethnic and Racial Studies*, 12, no. 4, October 1989, pp. 512-538.

Leong, Frederick T. and Thomas J. Hayes. "Occupational Stereotyping of Asian Americans." *Career Development Quarterly*, 39, no. 2, December 1990, pp. 143-54.

Morrison, Ann. *The New Leaders: Guidelines on Leadership Diversity in America*. San Francisco: Jossey-Bass, 1992.

Nakayama, Thomas. "Dis/orienting Identities: Asian Americans, History, and Intercultural Communication." In *Our Voices: Essays in Culture, Ethnicity, and Communication*, edited by Alberto Gonzalez, Marsha Houston, and Victoria Chen. Los Angeles: Roxbury Publishing Company, 1994.

Uehara, Jo and Joanne S. Yamauchi. "Managing Intercultural Value Systems: An Asian/Pacific Perspective." *The Brown Papers*. Washington, D.C.: National Institute of Women of Color, 1985.

U.S. Commission on Civil Rights. *Civil Rights Facing Asian Americans in the 1990s*. Washington, D.C.: U.S. Commission on Civil Rights, 1992.

U.S. Department of Labor. *Glass Ceiling Initiative Report*. Washington, D.C.: U.S. Department of Labor, 1991.

U.S. Department of Labor. *Pipelines of Progress: A Status Report on the Glass Ceiling*. Washington, D.C.: U.S. Department of Labor, 1992.

U.S. Office of Personnel Management. *Thirteenth Annual Report to Congress on the Federal Equal Opportunity Recruitment Program*. Washington, D.C.: January, 1992.

Yamauchi, Joanne S. The Cultural Integration of Asian American Professional Women: Issues of Identity and Communication Behavior. Washington, D.C.: National Institute of Education, 1981.

—Joanne S. Yamauchi, Professor of Communication, The American University, Washington, D.C.

31

Entrepreneurship

♦ Immigration and Entrepreneurship ♦ Entrepreneurs and Ethnic Firms
♦ Consequences of Ethnic Entrepreneurship ♦ Conclusion

Korean American shopkeeper. (Jamie Lew.)

Asian-owned businesses make up one of the fastest-growing areas of the U.S. economy. In 1977, Asian and Pacific Islanders owned 105,158 firms, or 19 percent of all minority-owned businesses. Five years later, Asian Americans owned 187,691 firms. By 1987, the number of firms owned by these ethnic groups had risen to 355,331, representing 27 percent of all U.S. minority-owned enterprises. The gross receipts grew from $6.9 billion to

$34 billion between 1977 and 1987. From 1977 to 1987, Asian American businesses had grown by 238 percent.

Asian American growth in business ownership has been the largest of any ethnic category. Although the number of black-owned businesses in the United States grew by 83 percent and the number of Hispanic-owned businesses grew by 93 percent from 1977 to 1987, neither came close to matching the rapid expansion of Asian American businesses. Overall, there is one ethnic firm for every 18 Chinese, one for every 35 Filipinos, one for every 16 Japanese, one for every 16 Asian Indians, one for every 12 Koreans, and one for every 24 Vietnamese. Comparatively, there is only one ethnic firm for every 71 African Americans, and one for every 53 Hispanic Americans.

Some Asian American groups experienced greater economic growth than others. Table 31.1 shows the characteristics of Asian American-owned firms by national origin in 1987. Among the six major Asian American groups, Koreans and Asian Indians experienced the largest growth in business ownership between 1977 and 1987. Asian Indian, Korean, and Chinese firms were relatively larger and were more likely to hire employees than the other Asian American groups.

Immigrants were more likely than their U.S.-born counterparts to go into business. Table 31.2 shows different rates of self-employment among Asian American workers between the ages of 25 to 64 by ethnicity and national origin. With the exception of the Vietnamese Americans, the foreign-born Asian Americans showed higher rates of self-employment than their U.S.-born counterparts. The most extreme case is in the Korean American group: foreign-born Korean Americans were almost three times as likely as their U.S.-born counterparts to work for themselves.

Nearly all the national groups among Asian American workers show a self-employment rate that is higher than the national average. According to the 1990 Census,

Table 31.1
Characteristics of Asian American Owned Firms: 1987

National Origin	Number of Firms	Percent Increase since 1977 (1)	Sales and Receipts ($1,000,000)	Sales and Receipts per Firm ($1,000)	Percent Firms with Employees	Number of Employees
Chinese	89,717	285.5	9,610	107.1	29.6	126,763
Filipino	40,412	324.3	1,914	47.4	16.6	16,822
Japanese	53,372	94.9	3,837	63.5	19.1	38,389
Asian Indian	52,266	627.5	6,715	118.1	31.3	65,733
Korean	69,304	715.0	7,683	110.8	31.2	70,530
Vietnamese	25,671	414.6 (2)	1,361	53.0	22.7	13,357

Notes:
(1) Unadjusted estimates
(2) Since 1982. No estimate available for 1977.

Source: U.S. Bureau of Census, 1981 and 1991.

about 12 percent of all Asian American workers between the ages of 25 to 64 were self-employed. Koreans were most likely to be self-employed (27%), followed by Chinese (12%), Japanese (10%), Vietnamese (10%), and other Asians (9%). Filipinos had relatively fewer self-employed workers; however, their rate of self-employment (5%) was roughly similar to the rate of self-employment found among non-Asian, U.S.-born individuals.

These statistics raise a number of important questions: Why have Asian Americans gone into business in such disproportionate numbers? Why are immigrants more likely to be entrepreneurs than U.S.-born members of the same ethnic groups? Why do Asians from different national backgrounds have different rates of entrepreneurship?

Existing literature on Asian American entrepreneurship generally addresses the following issues: 1) why

entrepreneurship seems to offer Asian Americans greater advantages than other kinds of employment; 2) why Asian Americans may not have the opportunities that might lead other Americans away from self-employment; 3) why Asian immigrants are more likely to be business owners than their U.S.-born counterparts; and 4) are there cultural factors particular to specific Asian nations that encourage or discourage self-employment?

It is important to consider what attracts or deters Asian Americans from entrepreneurship and to know what types of businesses Asian Americans launch in general. In the following sections, the historical events that have led to Asian-owned businesses becoming such a fast-growing part of U.S. society are highlighted and a summary of the major theories explaining them follows. Second, the types of businesses that have been established by the different Asian American groups are described. Consideration is also given to why these businesses are concentrated in certain areas of activity and geographical locations. Third, the positive outcomes of entrepreneurship are presented. Fourth, some of the problems associated with business growth in Asian American communities are discussed. Finally, implications are drawn regarding such poignant issues as urban poverty, inter-ethnic relations, and immigrant adaptation to U.S. society.

Table 31.2
Percentage Distributions of Self-Employment among Asian American Workers: 1990 (1)

National Origin	Total	Foreign Born	U.S. Born
Chinese	12.2	12.7	9.6
Filipino	5.1	5.1	4.8
Japanese	9.9	10.5	9.5
Asian Indian	12.4	12.4	12.1
Korean	26.5	27.1	9.6
Vietnamese	9.6	9.5	12.4
Total	11.6	12.2	9.0

Notes:
(1) Including persons who were aged 25 to 64 and in the labor force.

Source: U.S. Bureau of Census, 1990 PUMS.

◆ IMMIGRATION AND ENTREPRENEURSHIP

Immigration and Settlement

Asian American business dates back to the nineteenth century, when policies of segregation were commonly practiced. The first significant wave of arrivals from Asia came from China, many of them from the coastal province of Guangdong (Kwangtung). Most were drawn to California in the late 1850s by the Gold Rush. In the 1860s, the Chinese entered into various types of manual employment, working as domestic servants, farm laborers, or factory workers. Their involvement in railroad construction, however, was their greatest source of employment and one of their greatest contributions to the westward expansion of the United States. About 12,000 Chinese workers contributed in the building of the Central Pacific Railroad, opening the western frontier to new settlers.

Despite the fact that by 1860 the Chinese made up 25 percent of the labor force of California, their distinct physical appearances, dress, and religious and cultural practices were perceived as unusual and served to ostracize them from the mainstream. In addition, as railroad construction slowed down and as the United States slipped into an economic depression in 1873, competition for jobs fueled more intense discrimination against the Chinese. Because the Chinese often worked for low wages, they were viewed as a threat to the growing U.S. labor movement, and workers began to adopt the slogan "Chinamen must go!" in rallying white workers and gaining political strength.

The 1870s and 1880s witnessed a period of anti-Chinese riots and massacres throughout the American West, especially in California where Chinese immigration was the most widespread. Chinese were barred from obtaining U.S. citizenship and in 1882, the U.S. Congress passed the Chinese Exclusion Act, barring the immigration of Chinese laborers. As anti-Chinese violence and discrimination intensified, the Chinese took refuge in their own communities in large towns, which emerged into Chinatowns. The Chinatowns of New York and other large, eastern cities grew as they absorbed Chinese fleeing persecution in the West.

These early Chinatowns were mainly male enclaves, consisting largely of workers that had immigrated to the U.S. to earn money for their families in China. Therefore, lacking the comfort of a nuclear family, they would seek fellowship in tea and coffee houses or restaurants after long hours of work. These meeting sites were the first Asian-owned businesses, formed to meet the fellowship needs of the Asian community. As these businesses grew, Asians who were locked out of jobs in the larger U.S economy were able to initiate other business enterprises in Chinatowns. The Chinese laundry, for example, emerged out of initial service to these Chinese communities. The Chinese went into the laundry business in large numbers in the twentieth century. By 1920, for example, well over a third of Chinese workers in New York (37.5%) were occupied in laundry work. Therefore, Chinatowns became environments of opportunity for Chinese Americans.

Business district in New York's Chinatown. (AP/Wide World.)

Many Chinese immigrated through family networks, which were retained as kinship ties in the United States. Bonds were also formed among those emigrating from the same geographical areas in China. Clan and district associations also made high levels of cooperation and networking possible. For example, a loan for starting a small laundry or restaurant could be sought through the assistance of rotating credit associations or other types of mutual aid societies among Chinese American communities.

Other Asian American groups also experienced discrimination, as well as cooperation and assistance within their particular communities. The Japanese, like the Chinese, originally came to the United States in response to the growing need for labor. In 1884, Japanese agricultural laborers began arriving in Hawaii to work the plantations of U.S. sugar planters. Between 1908 and 1924, the need for workers to produce and harvest specialty crops, such as grapes, brought more than 120,000 Japanese to the Pacific coast of North America.

The Japanese immigrants to the United States were usually rural people, dislocated from their native land by Japan's rapid modernization. The impoverished appearance of these immigrants served to cause further discrimination against them. This resulted in an anti-Japanese movement in the 1890s, which ultimately forced many immigrants to return to Japan. The opposition of U.S. workers to the competition of cheap Japanese labor led to physical attacks against Japanese laborers. While the Chinese started commercial enterprises in response to their difficulties in the mainstream labor market, the Japanese sought agricultural self-employment as tenant farmers, small landholders, and contract gardeners. In urban areas of the West Coast, however, Japanese businesses were concentrated in hotels and boarding houses, restaurants, barber shops, poolrooms, tailor and dye shops, supply stores, laundries, and shoe shops. These businesses not only provided services to the Japanese community but also created job opportunities for Japanese workers. Between 1900 and 1910, for every twenty-two Japanese workers, there was one Japanese business.

For both the Chinese and the Japanese, it appears that the difficulty in securing employment due to growing Anti-Asian sentiment in the workplace pushed them into entrepreneurship. Unfortunately, the agricultural focus of the Japanese fueled competition with other ethnic groups, leading farmers to organize in an attempt to force the Japanese out of agriculture. A series of alien land laws were passed to prohibit the ownership or leasing of land to Asians in California and in other states, thereby increasing the likelihood of Asians to dwell in urban communities. However, in spite of the pressures against them, many Japanese continued to work in gardening and farming until their properties were seized and they were sent to relocation camps during World War II. The experiences of the Chinese and Japanese were shared by other Asian American groups, such as Koreans and Filipinos, who were treated as "strangers from a different shore." Their businesses were founded in response to employment discrimination, ethnic community cooperation, and the demand for ethnic products.

Filipinos, Koreans, Asian Indians, and Vietnamese have had different immigration experiences than the Chinese and Japanese. Before 1965, most Filipinos arrived as seasonal agricultural workers or as spouses of U.S. service personnel stationed in the Philippines. Since 1965, however, Filipino immigrants have tended to be highly-educated professionals, such as physicians, nurses, educators, and engineers. Since Filipinos have been more widely dispersed and integrated in the United States, they have been less likely to take up self-employment than members of other Asian groups.

The largest waves of Korean and Asian Indian immigration to the United States have occurred since 1965. Like the post-1965 Filipinos, Asian Indians have generally been educated professionals immigrating to the United States for further education or to launch careers. While Koreans arriving in the United States have generally had high levels of education in Korea, for the most part, they have not had the more highly proficient English-language skills as that of Filipinos and Asian Indians, who come from countries in which English is an official language and is widely spoken. As a result, newly arrived Koreans may have the skills to manage businesses, but they have difficulty finding employment and sources of capital in the larger U.S. economy, and they must rely heavily on other members of their own ethnic group for financial assistance.

The Vietnamese immigrants are a special case among Asian Americans. Almost all Vietnamese Americans have arrived in the United States since 1975, as a result of the fall of U.S.-supported South Vietnam. Most arrived under U.S. government resettlement programs and were initially channeled into entry-level employment in existing U.S. businesses. As will be discussed below, the Vietnamese are only beginning to move into self-employment and to establish their own ethnic economies.

Modes of Immigrant Adaptation

Asian immigrants have not historically only been concentrated in small business activities; however, many recent Asian immigrants continue to seek their livelihoods in small business. Why are Asian Americans overrepresented in business? Is immigrant entrepreneurship a result of social conditions of the host society that are unfavorable to immigrant minorities or due to interaction between the charact·. istics of the host society and that of the immigrant groups? An explanation of the three major theories of immigrant entrepreneurship may provide insight.

The Middleman Minority

The term "middleman minority" has been used to describe ethnic groups that are in intermediate positions between ruling elites and those ruled. These middleman minorities are often business proprietors, as were the Asian Indians and Chinese that occupied positions between the European rulers of their countries and the general indigenous population. Sociologist Edna Bonacich has used the concept of the middleman minority to explain why immigrants in America, particularly Asian immigrants, are so heavily concentrated in small business. Bonacich has argued that some immigrants have a "sojourning" orientation toward their host country; that is, they emigrate only to raise money and return home afterward. Not seeking to establish roots, they tend to enter into businesses in which money can be raised relatively quickly and assets can be readily exchanged for cash. This inclines them

A street vendor in the Chinatown section of New York sells magnets for pain, tiger balm, and other items from his sidewalk stand. (AP/Wide World.)

toward small businesses that can be acquired relatively cheaply, often in poorer communities.

As sojourners profiting from sales in poorer communities, middleman minorities may experience resentment from members of these communities. This intensifies the sense of solidarity in the sojourning group, so that its members tend to band together and cooperate to defend one another against hostile forces, thereby increasing the business strength of the immigrant group.

Bonacich's middleman minority explanation depicts the experience of many Korean American small business owners that disproportionately serve minority communities in declining urban communities, with no intention to settle in those communities. As outsiders, they tend to distance themselves from the communities they serve. On the one hand, they serve as an effective buffer between absentee business owners and the residents living in poor, urban areas. On the other hand, they may be stereotyped by members of the mainstream society as a "model minority," denying that racism or racial discrimination adversely affect Asian American economic success. The tension born of Korean proprietorship in poor, urban communities has

on occasion escalated into intense interethnic conflicts. The riots in a black, impoverished area of Los Angeles in 1992 led to the loss of about 850 Korean-owned businesses—over half of all business losses—at a cost of $300 million. The conflict between middleman minorities and minority residents in urban ghettos, as Asian American specialist Darrell Y. Hamamoto argues, is not so much a cultural misunderstanding as it is "at bottom a displacement of the more fundamental problem: the profoundly disruptive effects of economic inequality."

The Market-Niche Approach

A second theoretical explanation of immigrant business concentrations applies the concept of "market niches" to account for immigrant entrepreneurial activity. Sociologists Howard E. Aldrich and Roger Waldinger are the primary proponents of the market-niche approach, which stresses three basic elements to an attempt to understand immigrant business from the point of view of market niches. These elements are: opportunity structures, group characteristics, and ethnic strategies.

Opportunity structures are the forms of opportunities presented to an ethnic group by the economy of the host country. Aldrich and Waldinger point out that there must be a demand for a business services in order for businesses to arise. An ethnic community provides a demand for products that immigrant businesses are qualified to provide. When the immigrant community offers sufficient, cheap labor, ethnic businesses may be able to grow and enter the mainstream market.

The ethnic market may be seen as a "niche," a position in the economic environment where immigrant businesses have an adaptive advantage. Another niche may be that of markets that are not adequately served by the large organizations of the host economy, such as inner cities that have been abandoned by large grocery stores. Still other niches may be in businesses where immigrants can take advantage of a willingness to put in longer hours, work more holidays, and accept lower profits on sales, or in unstable businesses that must meet continually changing demands that large, well-established mainstream firms cannot easily handle.

Finally, a host society's demand for "exotic" goods, such as ethnic clothes or goods, creates a niche similar to the ethnic market, but one that is larger, since such a demand provides an opportunity to sell goods to more numerous groups of customers. In order to fit into a niche, a group must have characteristics appropriate to it. Some immigrants may be predisposed to enter business because they possess the necessary business education and skills. Others may do well in entrepreneurial activities because their social networks and high levels of cooperation have enabled them to mobilize resources.

Ethnic strategies in the market-niche approach result from particular combinations of opportunity structures and group characteristics. For example, Korean Americans in Los Angeles have tended to pursue the strategy of opening small groceries in poor minority communities because other groups with access to capital have moved businesses out of these communities. Large chain groceries did not find it profitable to establish branches in inner city areas. Earlier middleman groups, such as Jewish Americans, have withdrawn from the inner city and have assimilated businesses into the mainstream economy over the course of several generations. As an adaptive strategy, Korean Americans have developed patterns of trust and cooperation with each other, which enabled them to raise the funds necessary to establish small businesses through loans and fill the vacant market niche.

The Enclave-Economy Theory

A third theoretical explanation is the enclave-economy approach developed by Alejandro Portes and associates. A key feature of the enclave economy is the co-ethnicity of entrepreneurs and workers. An enclave is a spatial concentration of ethnic firms with a wide variety of economic activities. The economic enclave provides co-ethnic members with privileged access to a particular supply of raw materials or finished goods, to jobs that require unusual skills, and to a low-wage, reliable co-ethnic workforce.

Economic activities in the enclave can include both productive industries and community-based goods and services. Sociologist Min Zhou identified an "enclave protected sector" and an "enclave export sector" in the Chinese American enclave economy in New York. The protected sector arises within the ethnic community itself. It represents a captive market, oriented toward ethnic specific goods and services that are not easily accessible outside the enclave and toward solutions to various adjustment and settlement problems relating to immigration. The enclave export sector contains a non-ethnic market characteristic of leftover niches of the larger secondary economy, such as the garment industry, but generates income to be circulated back into the ethnic markets and reinvested in both sectors. In sum, co-ethnicity of entrepreneurs and workers, spatial concentration, and economic diversity define an enclave economy.

In examining the spatial concentration of ethnic minority entrepreneurial activities, Sociologist John R. Logan and associates have identified visible Asian American enclaves, which include overrepresentations of both ethnic owners and workers in specific industrial sectors across metropolitan areas in the United States. Sizable Japanese American enclaves exist in Honolulu, Los Angeles, San Francisco, San Jose, and Anaheim; Chinese American enclaves are in New York, San Francisco, Los Angeles, Honolulu, and Chicago; Korean American enclaves are in Los Angeles, New York, Chicago, Washington, and Honolulu; Filipino American enclaves are in Los Angeles, Honolulu, San Francisco, San Diego, and Chicago; and Asian Indian American enclaves are in New York, Chicago, Los Angeles, Washington, and Houston.

The enclave-economy theory consists of both structural and cultural components. On the one hand, it conceptualizes the enclave as an ethnic labor market distinct from the larger labor market, where immigrants are provided with potential benefits, such as opportunities for self-employment and social advancement. On the other hand, it describes the enclave as an integrated cultural entity maintained by solidarity and enforceable trust—a form of social capital necessary for ethnic entrepreneurship. Within the enclave, immigrant entrepreneurs and workers are organized around the symbols of a common nationhood, familiar cultural norms and activities, and densely knit networks. The enclave-economy theory defines ethnic entrepreneurship as "an alternative mobility path compensating for lingering labor market disadvantage" that resembles

Table 31.3
Industry Sector Overrepresentations by Asian American Co-Ethnic
Employers and Employees: 1980 (1)

Metropolitan Area	Export Industries	Service/Trade Industries
Chinese		
New York	Apparel	Eating places
	Food products	Transportation
		Private household
		Personal services
		Hospitals
		Social services
San Francisco	Apparel	Food stores
		Eating places
		Personal services
		Auto/gas sales
Los Angeles-Long Beach	Apparel	Food stores
		Eating places
		Wholesale
		Retail
		FIRE (2)
		Personal services
		Social services
		Health services
Honolulu		Eating places
		Foot stores
		Transportation
		Wholesale
		FIRE (2)
		Education services
		Professional services
Chicago	Food products	Eating places
		Health services
		Social services
Japanese		
Honolulu	Apparel	Construction
	Agriculture	Food stores
	Food products	Auto/gas sales
		Repair services
		Health services
		Education services
		Personal services
		Eating places
Los Angeles-Long Beach	Agriculture	Food stores
	Printing	Eating places
	Apparel	Auto/gas sales
	Wood products	Retail
		Repair services
		Hospitals
		Education services
		Personal services
San Francisco	Agriculture	Transportation
		Eating places

**Table 31.3
Industry Sector Overrepresentations by Asian American Co-Ethnic
Employers and Employees: 1980 (1) (Continued)**

Metropolitan Area	Export Industries	Service/Trade Industries
		Personnel services
		Food stores
		Auto/gas sales
		Retail
San Jose	Agriculture	Health services
		Retail
		Eating places
		Repair services
		Personal services
Anaheim	Agriculture	Wholesale
	Machinery	Auto/gas sales
		Eating places
		Retail
		Health services
		Professional services
Korean		
Los Angeles-Long Beach	Agriculture	Food stores
	Apparel	Personal services
	Printing	Construction
	Fabricated metal	Transportation
	Manufacturing	Wholesale
		Merchandise stores
		Auto/gas sales
		Eating places
		Retail
		Repair services
		Hospitals
		Health services
		Social services
New York		Wholesale
		Food stores
		Hospitals
		Transportation
		Merchandise stores
		Eating places
		Retail
		FIRE (2)
		Personal services
Chicago	Manufacturing	Personal services
		Hospitals
		Wholesale
		Food stores
		Eating places
		Repair services
		Social services
Washington		Eating places
		Repair services
		Retail

Table 31.3
Industry Sector Overrepresentations by Asian American Co-Ethnic
Employers and Employees: 1980 (1) (Continued)

Metropolitan Area	Export Industries	Service/Trade Industries
Honolulu		Professional services
		Eating places
		Transportation
		Retail
Filipino		
Los Angeles-Long Beach		Health services
		Transportation
Honolulu		Auto/gas sales
San Francisco		Personal services
Chicago		Hospitals
		Health services
		Food stores
		Repair services
Asian Indian		
New York		Hospitals
		Health services
		Transportation
		Wholesale
		Retail
Chicago		Hospitals
		Transportation
		Eating places
		Health services
Los Angeles-Long Beach		Health services
		Eating places
Washington		Eating places
Houston	Mining	Food stores
		Retail
		Health services

Notes:
(1) Adapted from Logan et al., 1994.
(2) Including finance, insurance, and real estate.

Source: U.S. Bureau of the Census, 1980 PUMS.

many positive features of the larger economy, such as opportunities for self-employment.

Findings from Cuban American enclaves in Miami, as well as Chinese American and Korean American enclaves in New York and Los Angeles, have shown that immigrant businesses offer opportunities and advantages similar to those of the mainstream economy. For example, a recent study conducted by Min Zhou in New York City's Chinatown revealed evidence against the negative stereotype of Chinatown as an urban ghetto harboring exploited labor, poverty, crowded and deteriorating housing, and neighborhood gangs. The study concluded that the Chinatown community has worked to channel immigrant Chinese into U.S. society, rather than setting barriers to entry into that society.

Vietnamese Americans, who predominantly resettled in the United States as refugees after the Vietnamese War in the mid-1970s, have begun to rise socioeconomically with the building of their own communities and economies. They have begun to follow the route of ethnic entrepreneurship as a viable strategy for economic adaptation. The 1990 Census showed that their self-employment rate increased by more than half, from less than four percent of the labor force in 1980 to close to ten percent.

♦ ENTREPRENEURS AND ETHNIC FIRMS

Major Industry Groups of Asian-Owned Businesses

Asian American entrepreneurship in the United States is characterized by diversity as well as by rapid growth. Table 31.3 reports findings from the study conducted by Logan and his associates, which gives detailed information on industrial sectors that were overrepresented by co-ethnic entrepreneurs and workers in metropolitan areas with identifiable ethnic enclave economies in the 1980 Census.

There are several similarities and differences among these Asian American enclave economies worth mentioning. First, only Chinese and Japanese enclave economies had noticeable export industries. Chinese export industries were composed mainly of apparel or garment manufacturing while Japanese export industries involved agricultural activities. Second, in enclave service/trade industries for all Asian American groups, except for Filipinos, eating places seem to predominate. Other common industries were food stores, retail, repair, hospital and health services, and personnel, professional, and social services. Third, there was greater diversity of economic activities in Chinese, Japanese, and Korean economies than in Filipino and Asian Indian

Table 31.4
Asian American Owned Firms by Major Industry Groups: 1987

Industry Group	Asian American Firms Percent	All U.S. Firms Percent
Agriculture	2.7	2.6
Mining	.1	.9
Construction	3.8	12.1
Manufacturing	2.9	3.2
Transportation	3.4	4.3
Wholesale Trade	3.0	3.2
Retail Trade	25.0	16.4
Finance	7.7	9.0
Services	46.5	43.4
Industries not Classified	5.0	5.1
Total	100.0	100.0

Source: U.S. Bureau of the Census, 1991.

economies. The last two groups were highly concentrated in hospital and health services. This reflects the trend of Filipino and Asian Indian immigration in which a disproportionate number of health professionals have immigrated under the employment-based provisions of

Table 31.5
Percentage Distributions of Self-Employed Asian American Workers by Major Industry Groups: 1990 (1)

Industry Groups	Chinese	Filipino	Japanese	Asian Indian	Korean	Vietnamese
Agriculture	1.2	4.1	15.7	1.6	1.0	9.3
Mining	0.0	0.0	.1	.1	0.0	0.0
Construction	3.3	4.7	3.9	2.5	4.4	3.7
Manufacturing	6.5	4.7	4.9	5.0	6.4	9.6
Transportation	2.7	3.5	2.4	4.2	1.7	1.9
Wholesale Trade	7.0	3.1	4.6	3.6	5.3	2.7
Retail Trade	40.4	13.7	19.9	23.1	46.3	33.0
Eating places (2)	58.0	27.0	35.6	17.3	21.1	34.2
FIRE (3)	8.1	10.1	7.2	5.5	3.2	3.4
Business Services	5.1	7.6	10.2	4.1	5.4	7.7
Personal Services	6.6	5.9	6.1	10.5	15.3	17.3
Entertainment	1.1	1.5	1.7	.8	1.4	1.3
Professional Services	18.0	41.1	23.3	39.0	9.6	10.1
Health services (4)	55.3	70.0	47.8	77.3	63.6	50.5
Total	100.0	100.0	100.0	100.0	100.0	100.0

Notes:
(1) Including persons aged 25 to 64 and in the labor force.
(2) Limited to those who are in retail trade.
(3) Including finance, insurance, and real estate.
(4) Limited to those who are in professional services.

Source: U.S. Bureau of the Census, 1990 PUMS.

Table 31.6
Geographic Concentration of Asian American Owned Firms by States: 1987

State	Number of Firms	Chinese	Filipino	Japanese	Asian Indian	Korean	Vietnamese
California	147,633	42,828	18,471	24,711	10,248	28,158	11,855
New York	36,257	12,587	3,502	1,730	8,253	7,208	462
Hawaii	31,406	4,962	3,891	15,751	115	2,061	529
Texas	22,682	4,585	1,250	687	4,043	4,230	5,443
Illinois	14,872	2,380	1,891	1,054	3,766	4,278	272
New Jersey	12,665	2,880	2,059	453	3,937	2,480	237
Florida	8,902	1,673	1,482	484	2,520	952	629
Washington	8,241	1,728	927	1,676	485	1,723	467
Virginia	8,163	916	859	366	1,399	2,947	749
Maryland	7,953	1,437	744	336	1,607	3,067	212
Other States	77,937	13,741	6,195	6,760	15,893	12,200	4,816
Total	376,711	89,717	40,412	53,372	52,266	69,304	25,671

Source: U.S. Bureau of the Census, 1991.

Table 31.7
Percentage Distribution of Self-Employed Asian American Workers by States: 1990 (1)

State	Chinese	Filipino	Japanese	Asian Indian	Korean	Vietnamese
California	47.0	46.6	50.3	20.0	43.7	49.4
New York	13.1	6.8	3.9	15.4	12.2	1.9
Hawaii	4.4	7.8	26.3	.1	2.6	2.6
Texas	4.8	2.9	.8	8.6	3.2	15.7
Illinois	2.4	5.0	1.4	6.7	5.2	.9
New Jersey	3.7	5.3	1.2	8.0	6.2	.8
Florida	3.2	2.9	.9	6.6	1.6	2.5
Washington	2.4	2.5	3.4	.7	2.9	1.8
Virginia	1.1	2.2	.8	3.0	3.3	4.2
Maryland	1.6	1.8	.4	3.6	5.0	1.5
Other States	16.3	16.2	10.6	27.3	14.1	18.7
Total	100.0	100.0	100.0	100.0	100.0	100.0

Notes:
(1) Including persons aged 25 to 64 and in the labor force.

Source: U.S. Bureau of the Census, 1990 PUMS.

U.S. immigration policy for skilled foreign workers needed in the U.S. labor market. Table 31.4 shows the proportion of Asian American firms in each of the major industry groups in 1987. The largest concentrations were in retail trade and services, which together made up almost three quarters of all Asian American firms.

Table 31.5 further demonstrates the types of economic activities pursued by self-employed Asian Americans, based on 1990 Census information. Apparently, there are intergroup differences in industry concentration. Chinese and Korean entrepreneurs are more highly concentrated in retail trade than others, and Filipino and Asian Indian entrepreneurs are concentrated in professional services. Among those in retail trade, close to two-thirds of Chinese and about a third of Japanese-, and Vietnamese-operated businesses are restaurants or other eating establishments. Among those in professional services, Asian American entrepreneurs are

A market in San Francisco's Chinatown. (AP/Wide World.)

generally heavily concentrated in health-related services. The numbers of Filipinos and Asian Indians in those areas are particularly high.

These statistics suggest that, unlike traditional ethnic businesses, which are small in scale and "middleman" in nature, Asian entrepreneurship has undergone significant changes, from a lack of diversity to a wide range of economic activities. Ethnic economic enclaves such as Chinatown are not limited to small-scale retail or low-wage, labor-intensive garment manufacturing, but also include capital- and knowledge-intensive services such as banking, insurance, real estate, and medical/health and other professional services.

Geographic Concentration of Asian American Owned-Businesses

Table 31.6 displays the geographic concentration of Asian American firms in 1987. A large number are located in states fueled by rapid growth in the Asian American population. California ranks number one in the scale of Asian American entrepreneurship, followed by New York, Hawaii, Texas, Illinois, New Jersey, Florida, Washington, Virginia, and Maryland. These ten states contained 80 percent of all Asian American

firms in the country. California alone is home to 48 percent of Chinese firms, 46 percent of Filipino firms, 46 percent of Japanese firms, 20 percent of Asian Indian firms, 41 percent of Korean firms, and 46 percent of Vietnamese firms in the United States. Data presented in Table 31.7, offering the national distribution of self-employed Asian Americans, show the same general trends. The table reveals that approximately half of all Chinese, Filipino, Japanese, Korean, and Vietnamese entrepreneurs reside in California.

In general, Asian American entrepreneurs cluster around long-standing ethnic communities such as Chinatown, Koreatown, Little Tokyo, and Little Saigon, serving co-ethnic populations as well as the mainstream population. However, in recent years, many Asian American businesses have dispersed to other communities in urban and suburban areas. The pattern of Korean produce businesses is a prime example of the penetration into new markets. In large metropolitan areas such as Los Angeles and New York, Korean-run fruit and vegetable stores are seen on almost every street corner of residential neighborhoods, particularly of poor, minority neighborhoods where other entrepreneurs are unlikely to conduct business. The Chinese restaurant business is another example. Although the

Table 31.8
Socioeconomic Characteristics of Foreign-Born Asian Americans by Selected Place of Birth: 1980

Place of Birth	Percent Immigrated 1975-80	Percent High School Graduates (1)	Percent Completed 4 years or More of College (1)	Percent in Professional Specialty Occupations (2)	Median Household Income $
China	27.2	60.0	29.5	16.8	18,544
Hong Kong	34.9	80.3	42.7	19.1	18,094
Taiwan	54.6	89.1	59.8	30.4	18,271
Philippines	34.4	74.0	41.8	20.1	22,787
Japan	31.6	78.0	24.4	13.6	16,016
India	43.7	88.9	66.2	42.8	25,644
Korea	52.3	77.8	34.2	14.7	18,085
Vietnam	90.5	62.1	12.9	8.6	12,521
U.S. Average	—	66.5	16.2	12.3	16,841

Notes:
(1) Persons 25 years or over.
(2) Persons 16 years or over.

Source: U.S. Bureau of the Census, 1983, 1984.

best restaurants providing authentic Chinese cuisine are still more likely to be found in Chinatowns, Chinese-owned restaurants serving Chinese food have penetrated virtually every region of the United States and can even be found in rural towns.

Sources of Entrepreneurship

What enables Asian Americans to become successful entrepreneurs? Part of the answer to this question may be found in the advantages that Asian American immigrants have over other ethnic groups in establishing small enterprises. Among these advantages are: access to "human capital," that is, skills and education; financial capital, or the money needed to establish business enterprises; and "social capital," or patterns of cooperation among group members that provide resources. Asian American immigrants have either brought these major forms of capital with them or acquired them after arrival in the United States.

The first source of advantage is human capital, including education and work experience. Having group members with high-level education or specialized skills can help the group accumulate funds for investment. Unlike earlier immigrants that were poor and uneducated and hoping to return to their homelands, more recent immigrants from Asia are from a variety of socioeconomic backgrounds and often have clear intentions of settling in the United States to achieve success for themselves and their families. Many have come with strong educational and occupational credentials and with a life-long family savings to begin life in the United States. Table 31.8 shows the socioeconomic characteristics of foreign-born Asian Americans based on the 1980 Census data. For different reasons, including the preference for skilled labor in revised U.S. immigration law, recent immigration from Asia has been largely from the highly educated and professional segments of the population. Of the immigrants that have arrived in the last ten to fifteen years, more exhibit high levels of educational achievement than previous immigrants. Except for immigrants from Vietnam, college graduates were roughly twice as common among Asian immigrants than the rest of the U.S. population, and more than four times as common among immigrants from India alone. The number of professionals among Asian Americans is higher than in the rest of the U.S. labor force, except for Vietnamese immigrants. Taiwanese and Asian Indian immigrants include approximately three times as many professionals than the rest of the U.S. workforce.

Despite the high degree of professional skills and education among recent immigrants from Asia, many have chosen self-employment as a way to maintain their socioeconomic status, avoiding downward mobility. Using their education, experience, and ties to the ethnic community, they establish businesses.

A second source of ethnic entrepreneurship is financial capital, usually consisting of family savings and capital from overseas businesses. Many Asian immigrants, like some European immigrants, share the value of thrift and stress the importance of saving money for later purchases. They tend to perceive their present frugality as a means to fulfill future goals. Thus, it is not unusual for newer immigrants to spend money only on basic things, such as housing and food rather than leisure and luxury. Moreover, adult children often contribute their income towards the family savings. This way, even for some low-income immigrant families, starting up a small business becomes an attainable goal.

While a majority of ethnic entrepreneurs operate in small businesses that require low start-up capital and low operation costs and may be easily liquidated, many have established businesses such as banking, insurance, real estate, and larger businesses that depend not simply on pooled family savings but also on the influx of wealth from abroad. Start-up costs for small businesses, such as small garment factories and grocery stores, range from $2,000 to $30,000, which can possibly be pooled from family savings. For larger businesses, the greater amount of start-up capital often requires generating funds outside the family, and overseas financial capital is one important source.

Funds from fast-growing economies of Asia (Japan, Hong Kong, and Taiwan, in particular) have been invested in Asian American- launched enterprises in the United States. In New York, listed Chinese-owned banks, insurance, and real estate agencies grew by 8,000 percent from 1958 to 1988. In Honolulu, as well as in Los Angeles and New York, there was a large influx of funds from Japan to invest in real estate in the 1980s. Capital from Taiwan has turned Monterey Park, California, into "Little Taipei," where several modern shopping malls with bilingual signs offer testimony to the impact of Asians on the city. In other cities, that have experienced a rapid growth of Asian American population, such as Atlanta, Houston, and New Orleans, declining shopping malls have been bought and reopened by Chinese, Koreans, and Vietnamese. Many of these economic activities would not have been possible with family savings alone.

Newly established Asian American firms tend to be larger than firms owned by other minorities. For example, enterprises with employees in New York's Chinese business community average $308,638 in annual sales, exceeding sales of other minority-owned enterprises nationwide by more than $50,000. This appears to be due to the ties between investors in Asia and Asian American communities. Overseas investors have limited information and access to marketing networks in the United States; they need to know where they should invest for the best returns. They find that ethnic markets in the United States are readily accessible through their densely-knit kinship networks. In addition, they have at hand a familiar business environment and an easily manageable and ethnically loyal workforce, rendering them additional confidence in their investment decisions.

A third source of ethnic entrepreneurship is social capital. Asian American entrepreneurs raise capital and mobilize resources to establish businesses not simply through family savings or overseas investment, but also through close ties to the ethnic community, access to low-interest loans and funds made readily available within the group, and access to family labor and low-wage immigrant labor. Traditional ways of raising capital in China, Japan, and Korea are also practiced in the United States by Asian immigrants. One such tradition is the rotating credit association, which is organized through the church, alumni clubs, or kinship associations, and widely used for capital mobilization and social needs.

Sociologists Light and Bonacich give examples of how the *kye*—the Korean rotating credit association— works. There are different kinds of kyes: mutual aid kye, industry kye, money-making kye, and so on. Members usually do not have particular objectives in mind when joining a kye; they can borrow funds when in need or they can use the funds to extend private loans to other Koreans or invest in a business. According to Light and Bonacich, "when one sees a larger party in a Korean restaurant, . . . the group is usually a kye . . . Kyes typically included ten to fifteen persons, met in restaurants, and raised between $1,000 and $10,000 at every meeting." These credit associations frequently are the only source of financing for immigrant group members that do not have established credit to obtain loans through formal financial institutions.

Access to family labor and low-wage immigrant labor is also important to ethnic entrepreneurship. Many immigrant enterprises, especially labor-intensive grocery and food stores, restaurants, and garment factories, depend on unpaid family labor and low-wage immigrant labor, providing ethnic entrepreneurs a large savings in overhead and giving them a clear competitive edge.

From the point of view of ethnic workers, ethnic businesses offer material and symbolic compensations that cannot be accounted for simply in dollar terms. Although jobs in ethnic enterprises are characterized by low wages, long working hours, and sometimes poor working conditions, immigrant workers are provided with a familiar work environment in which they are effectively shielded from deficiencies in language and general knowledge of the larger culture. They can obtain first-hand information on employment and business opportunities through their kin and fellow Asian American entrepreneurs to avoid the cost of time and effort involved in finding "good jobs" in the larger market. They are able to work longer hours to quickly accumulate family savings for future plans. They can gain access to rotating credit, clan associations, and the family for financial support and resource mobilization. Finally, they can get job training and cultivate an entrepreneurial spirit at work and, possibly, be prepared for an eventual transition to self-employment.

For many new immigrants, low-wage menial work is a part of the time-honored path toward economic independence and the upward mobility of their families in the United States. It is the ethnic solidarity and mutual trust between workers and entrepreneurs, combined with human and financial capital, that facilitate ethnic entrepreneurship among Asian Americans.

♦ CONSEQUENCES OF ETHNIC ENTREPRENEURSHIP

Beneficial Consequences for Group Members

Without doubt, ethnic entrepreneurship can create job opportunities for immigrant group members that compensate for many of their disadvantages as newcomers to U.S. society. The disadvantages associated with immigrant status, such as English proficiency, transferable education and work skills, lack of access to employment networks in the larger society, and racial prejudice and discrimination, often block immigrant workers from entering the general U.S. labor market.

For immigrants with either sufficient human or financial capital, self-employment is their best strategy to adapt to the U.S. economy. By minimizing the possibility of downward social mobility, namely low-wage menial labor and depreciation of capital accumulated before immigration, this goal is achieved. Moreover, through ethnic entrepreneurship, Asian immigrants can effectively fight the loss of pride, self-value, and sense of achievement often experienced by immigrants and eventually enter the mainstream society with dignity, self-esteem, and a sense of identity. Furthermore, immigrant entrepreneurs can bypass the harmful psychological and social consequences of racial discrimination by creating conditions for their own economic mobility: the improvement of the economic status of families and family savings for purchasing homes or starting up businesses. Table 31.9 shows the median earnings, household incomes, and rates of home ownership of self-employed workers and salaried workers, based on 1990 Census data.

The data indicates that, except for the Japanese and Vietnamese, self-employed workers of all other Asian American groups show an absolute earnings advantage over their salaried group members. In terms of economic status of the family, self-employed workers have higher median household incomes than their salaried group members, except for Vietnamese. Without exception, self-employed workers are also much more likely than their salaried group members to own homes. These figures coincide with results reported a decade earlier based on the 1980 Census data. Among the foreign-born, the pattern is very similar.

Table 31.9
Incomes and Home Ownership of Asian American Workers: 1990 (1)

National Origin	Median Earnings (2) ($)		Median Household Income ($)		Home Ownership (%)	
	Self-employed Workers	Salaried Workers	Self-Employed Workers	Salaried Workers	Self-Employed Workers	Salaried Workers
Total						
Chinese	22,000	21,000	52,800	49,462	82.6	67.6
Filipino	25,000	21,000	65,560	54,846	80.6	66.5
Japanese	25,669	26,776	58,500	56,400	81.9	70.7
Asian Indian	35,000	24,988	68,600	53,125	80.3	63.7
Korean	25,000	18,000	49,080	39,991	68.4	53.4
Vietnamese	17,000	18,573	44,000	44,179	68.7	59.6
Foreign Born						
Chinese	20,000	19,012	50,800	46,653	82.6	65.4
Filipino	25,000	20,863	71,200	55,160	82.3	66.8
Japanese	22,250	24,000	48,000	49,283	75.8	55.0
Asian Indian	35,000	25,000	68,950	53,208	80.7	63.9
Korean	25,000	17,119	49,000	39,200	68.3	53.0
Vietnamese	17,000	18,575	44,000	44,184	68.6	59.6

Notes:
(1) Including persons who were aged 25 to 64 and in the labor force.
(2) Earnings for self-employed workers is the sum of salaried and self-employment incomes.

Source: U.S. Bureau of Census, 1990 PUMS.

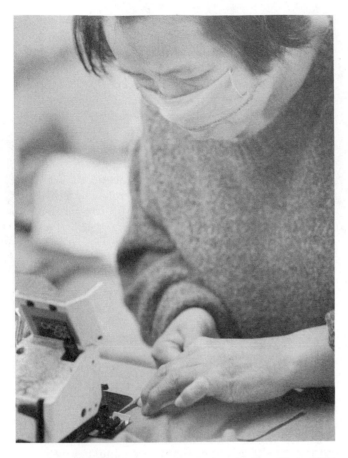

A seamstress works at a garment shop in New York. (AP/Wide World.)

Ethnic entrepreneurship benefits not only the self-employed, but also their immigrant workers, especially those lacking adequate English proficiency, transferable education, marketable skills, formal employment networks, and the necessary legal standing to compete in the larger labor market. A prime example is the role

Table 31.10
Unemployment rates of Asian American Workers: 1990 (1)

| National Origin | Total (2) | Foreign Born | |
		Self-Employed Workers	Salaried Workers
Chinese	4.0	1.3	4.7
Filipino	3.8	1.7	3.9
Japanese	2.1	.9	2.8
Asian Indian	4.7	2.3	5.2
Korean	4.1	0.0	5.3
Vietnamese	7.2	0.0	7.5

Notes:
(1) Including persons who were aged 25 to 64 and in the labor force.
(2) Including both foreign born and U.S. born workers.

Source: U.S. Bureau of the Census, 1990 PUMS.

of Chinatown's garment industry in creating job opportunities for immigrant Chinese women. In New York City, where the decline of the manufacturing sector has caused severe unemployment among minority workers, immigrant Chinese women that have low English proficiency, minimal education, and little work experience display exceptionally high rates of labor force participation; 74 percent are in the labor force as compared to only 22 percent of Puerto Rican women, who used to be largely garment and manufacturing workers. More than half of these Chinese women are employed in Chinatown's garment industry, which has grown rapidly over the last ten years. Without Chinatown's garment industry, many Chinese immigrants might be jobless.

Ethnic entrepreneurship accounts in part for the high labor force participation rate and particularly low unemployment rates among foreign-born Asian American workers. Table 31.10 shows that the Asian American unemployment rate matched that of the U.S. labor force, but was still lower than other minority groups such as African Americans and Puerto Rican Americans. Asian American immigrants had unemployment rates ranging from 2 to 5 percent, as compared to over 10 to 14 percent for other minority workers. Among the foreign-born, unemployment rates for self-employed workers were extremely low, and for salaried workers, the rates were still substantially lower than other U.S. minority workers.

In large cities where immigrants are disproportionately concentrated in relation to the non-immigrant population, the job situation is often paradoxical: while U.S.-born minority workers are hardest hit by declining manufacturing sectors and eroding employment opportunities, immigrant workers in the same cities have experienced growing economic opportunities. Some analysts argue that immigrants have taken jobs away from U.S.-born minorities. However, a more realistic picture reflects that immigrants simply respond to industrial downsizing by creating their own "match" between available opportunities and ethnic resources.

Finally, entrepreneurship contributes to the upward mobility of young Asian Americans by enabling families to accumulate funds for education, giving the younger generation a "jump-start" into the U.S. economy. In sum, both coethnic, immigrant workers and their employers benefit from a reciprocal relationship. They are both bound by sentiment, trust, and "face" (implying ethnic obligations) in pursuing each other's goals. It is true that workers in ethnic firms generally work for lower pay. However, this is an alternative to possible joblessness, and they have an opportunity to surmount structural obstacles and lift themselves and their families up socioeconomically.

The Downside of Ethnic Entrepreneurship

There are some negative aspects of Asian American immigrant entrepreneurship. The first problem of business growth in Asian American concentrations relates to costs that usually have to be incurred by the residents. The familiar growing pains in rapidly expanding Asian American communities include traffic congestion, skyrocketing real estate prices, overcrowding, and the displacement of the poor. Many long-time residents in new Asian American concentrated neighborhoods, such as Monterey Park, California, and Flushing, New York, fear that their neighborhoods are turning into microcosms of Hong Kong, Taipei, Seoul, or Saigon, which are among the most crowded and polluted cities in the world. Long-time residents also sometimes feel that they are being priced out of their homes and businesses by soaring rents and heavy influx of investment funds from Asia.

Relations with other U.S. racial groups pose another problem. Asian immigrants tend to penetrate into declining white working-class or lower middle-class communities. A sizable Asian American community is often accompanied by a concentration of ethnic businesses. Long-time residents, mostly whites, tend to view Asian Americans as outsiders interested in making money but not in contributing to the larger community. The high presence of entrepreneurship in a neighborhood paralleled by a low participation in local politics and community-based affairs by Asian Americans adds to inter-ethnic antagonism.

For Asian American businesses that are operated in poor, inner-city, minority neighborhoods, in which Asian Americans often avoid living, interethnic relations among businesses and communities are often fragile. Ethnic entrepreneurship in these neighborhoods can lead to friction between the "haves" and "have nots," which may be intensified by ethnic or racial allegiances. When Asian American business owners do not make special efforts to establish links with the communities of their customers, they may be viewed as invading strangers. Nationally, African American/Korean American conflicts have often escalated into violent incidents. Examples include: a sixteen-month long boycott of a Korean store in Brooklyn, New York, by African American residents because the store employees assaulted an African American accused of stealing; the neighborhood upheaval following a lenient five-year probation sentence given to a Korean store owner for shooting a black teenager to death in Los Angeles; and the 1992 Los Angeles riots, in which Korean businesses were targeted.

A third problem associated with Asian American entrepreneurship may be exclusion practices of Asian Americans. Until recently, Asian immigrants have been portrayed as indifferent to U.S. politics and uninterested in assimilation. This differs sharply from other immigrant groups. Most Asian immigrants have instead remained closely connected with events at home. The Korean "sponsored politics" is one such example, in which Korean immigrants and their emerging communities obtained resources from the Korean government to promote its own political and economic goals in foreign countries. This type of political isolation reinforces negative stereotypes of Asian Americans as clannish.

This political isolation can be accompanied by a social and psychological isolation. Asian American entrepreneurs frequently retain a sense of being "foreign," and may never bring themselves to become involved in the society of the host country, despite the fact that their lives and businesses become inseparable from the host economy.

♦ CONCLUSION

For all the difficulties of Asian American entrepreneurship, the trends and data indicate that ethnic businesses are not simply a marginal activity that Asians are forced into because of their status as newcomers and minorities. They are a crucial part of their path toward upward mobility in U.S. society.

Asian Americans have gone into small business in large numbers because entrepreneurship can provide the best economic opportunity for them. The theoretical explanations that we have examined may only differ in the emphasis of different reasons for which these opportunities exist. The middleman minority explanation draws attention to the fact that Asians have traditionally been outsiders in the United States. As outsiders, they often find positions between relatively privileged and relatively underprivileged groups of U.S. citizens, and they tend to develop high levels of cooperation that enable them to survive in a foreign and often hostile economic environment. The market niche explanation examines how the characteristics of immigrant groups may correspond to unmet demands in the economy of the host country. The ethnic enclave economy explanation looks at how shared ethnicity may be the basis for a small economy and how small ethnic economies may grow in size and power. Each of these theoretical perspectives provides some of the reasons that Asian American groups may be found in business, but to understand why these groups differ in rates of entrepreneurship and types of entrepreneurial activity, we need to consider the historical experiences of each group.

Although there is some basis to the stereotypical view of Asian American businesses as small, family-operated firms, in recent years these businesses have grown in size and diversity. The Chinese, for example, are no longer simply owners of laundries and restaurants. They have entered a wide variety of fields of endeavor. Restaurants do remain an important source of self-employment for most Asian American groups, but Asian American entrepreneurs may also be found in businesses more commonly associated with the majority U.S. population.

Asian American entrepreneurs have been spreading out across the United States, but their firms are still most often concentrated in areas with large and rapidly growing populations, especially in California. They are able to establish these firms because of their comparatively high level of skills and education, the influx of capital from the active economies of Asia, the cooperation with coethnic laborers resulting from shared cultural traditions and other factors.

Both workers and entrepreneurs may receive benefits from Asian American businesses. For employers, the relatively inexpensive labor of coethnics can provide a competitive advantage. Although the owners benefit more from this situation than employees, Asian American businesses provide newly arrived immigrants with a starting place in the U.S. economy. They also give new immigrants a familiar work environment in which they can amass savings, develop skills, and prepare children for upward socioeconomic mobility.

As the Asian American population of the United States grows, the number, size, diversity, and importance of Asian-owned businesses in the United States will also grow. While this growth will be greatest in California and other Asian American centers, Asian American entrepreneurs have put down roots in almost all parts of the United States, and entrepreneurship will continue to be a major source of employment and socioeconomic mobility for members of one of the United States' most rapidly growing ethnic categories.

References

Aldrich, Howard E. and Roger Waldinger. "Ethnicity and Entrepreneurship," *American Review of Sociology* 16: 111-35, 1990.

Bonacich, Edna. "A Theory of Middleman Minorities." *American Sociological Review* 37: 547-59 1973.

Chan, Sucheng. *Asian Americans: An Interpretive History.* Boston: Twayne Publishers, 1991.

Daniels, Roger. *Asian America: Chinese and Japanese in the United States since 1850.* Seattle: University of Washington Press, 1988.

Hamamoto, Darrell Y. "Black-Korean Conflict in Los Angeles," *Z Magazine.* July/August: 61-62 1992.

Hurh, Won Moo and Kwang Chung Kim. *Korean Immigrants in America: A Structural Analysis of Ethnic Confinement and Adhesive Adaption.* New Jersey: Associated University Presses, 1984.

Kelly, Gaily Paradise. *From Vietnam to America: A Chronicle of the Vietnamese Immigration to the United States.* Boulder, Colorado: Westview Press, 1984.

Kwong, Peter, *The New Chinatown.* New York: Hill and Wang, 1987.

Light, Ivan H. *Ethnic Enterprise in America: Business Welfare among Chinese, Japanese and Blacks.* Berkeley: University of California Press, 1987.

———, and Edna Bonacich. *Immigrant Entrepreneurs: Koreans in Los Angeles, 1965-1982.* Berkeley: University of California Press, 1972.

Logan, John, R., Richard Alba, and Tom McNulty. "Identifying Ethnic Enclave Economies in the United States," *Social Forces* 72: 3 (1994).

Mangiafico, Lusiano. *Contemporary American Immigration: Patterns of Filipino, Korean, and Chinese Settlement in the United States.* New York: Praeger, 1988.

Parillo, Vincent N. *Strangers to These Shores: Race and Ethnic Relations in the United States.* New York: MacMillan, 1990.

Portes, Alejandro and Robert L. Bach. *The Latin Journey: Cuban and Mexican Immigrants in the United States.* Berkeley: University of California Press, 1985.

Portes, Alejandro and Min Zhou. "Gaining the Upper Hand: Economic Mobility among Immigrant and Domestic Minorities," *Ethnic and Racial Studies* 15: 491-522 (1992).

Sassen, Saskia. *The Mobility of Labor and Capital.* New York: Cambridge University Press, 1988.

Saxton, Alexander. *The Indispensable Enemy: Labor and the Anti-Chinese Movement in California.* Berkeley: University of California Press, 1971.

Takaki, Ronald. 1989. *Strangers from a Different Shore: A History of Asian Americans.* New York: Penguin Books, 1989.

U.S. Bureau of the Census. *Census of Population and Housing, 1980: General Social and Economic Characteristics, U.S. Summary.* Washington, D.C.: U.S. Department of Commerce, 1981.

———. *Census of Population and Housing, 1990: Public Use Microdata Samples (A) [MRDF].* Washington, D.C.: U.S. Bureau of the Census [producer and distributor], 1990.

———. *Socioeconomic Characteristics of the U.S. Foreign-Born Population Detailed in Census Bureau Tabulations.* Washington, D.C.: U.S. Department of Commerce, 1984.

———. *Survey of Minority-Owned Business Enterprises, 1987, MB87.* Washington, D.C.: U.S. Department of Commerce.

Waldinger, Roger. "Structural Opportunity or Ethnic Advantage: Immigrant Business Development in New York. *International Migration Review* 23 (1):48-72 (1989).

Wong, Bernard. *Patronage, Brokerage, Entrepreneurship and the Chinese Community of New York City.* New York: AMS Press, 1984.

Zhou, Min. *Chinatown: The Socioeconomic Potential of an Urban Enclave.* Philadelphia: Temple University Press, 1992.

—Min Zhou and Carl L. Bankston III

Organizations

♦ Organization Profiles: Associations of Broad or National Scope
♦ Organization Profiles: Associations Dedicated to a Specific Issue
♦ Regional Asian American Organizations
♦ Organization Profiles: Associations Dedicated to a Specific Ethnic/Nationality

An old joke in Asian American circles is that if five Asian Americans are brought together, they will form seven organizations. Whether this perception reflects a tendency to bicker or a love of sociability is a matter of debate. What is clear, however, is that communities need different kinds of organizations as its members develop a variety of relationships with each other and with others in U.S. society.

For example, people who emigrated from Kagoshima, the southernmost prefecture (state) in Japan, would hold annual picnics or events and help each other get jobs. Even if they had different religions, economic stations in life, or political leanings, the anchor provided by a common dialect, common diet, and shared memories of local landscapes and events brought them together year after year.

That community is still composed mainly of their descendants, who face many of the transition issues addressed by immigrants of almost a century ago. Nevertheless, second, third, fourth, and fifth generations of Asian Americans face issues different from those of the first (immigrant) generation and, therefore, establish different types of organizations.

These later generation Asian Americans typically are English speakers who may or may not have knowledge of an Asian language. Unlike their immigrant predecessors, they may feel comfortable in Asian American social or church groups where English is spoken. They may pursue professional advancement in Asian American political or trade groups and join groups that are composed primarily of non-Asian Americans.

Although the various Asian American groups have many experiences in common, each Asian immigrant group has its unique history on these shores, and each has developed organizations to defend its people, language, culture, and religion. As a group forms into an ethnic enclave, a social group, church, or mutual aid organization is often established. Sometimes this is done with aid from federal or church-sponsored refugee relief agencies, as in the case of refugees from Southeast Asia in the 1970s and 1980s. More often, the group does this with its own initiative and resources.

Younger generations who realize their commonalities as Americans and are less tied to old-country antipathies and issues of their parents' generation, form pan-Asian organizations on local and regional levels. In recent years, local groups have formed statewide and national Asian American organizations in order to better participate in statewide and national policy debates.

A comprehensive review of Asian American organizations should examine the historical forces bringing Asian Americans to the United States and explore the economic and social organizations that have assisted them in surviving a frequently hostile environment. For example, according to historians such as Him Mark Lai, Rose Hum Lee, and Hyung-chan Kim, social organizations were formed in the 1850s among Chinese immigrants based on their districts of origin in the southern Kwangtung (Canton) province of China. Six major associations in San Francisco's Chinatown formed the Chinese Six Companies, also known as the Chinese Consolidated Benevolent Association (CCBA). This group helped immigrants find work, assisted with medical or funeral arrangements, interceded with government authorities, and kept peace within the ethnic community. Although invaluable to the immigrant community, the system often limited individual workers' abilities to protest unfair working conditions or to travel to other locations to find work. By the 1970s, the ascendancy of U.S.-educated Chinese Americans and other factors had diminished the influence of the CCBA, although it continues to be an important organization in many Chinatowns.

To establish more economic freedom, family or district associations in the late nineteenth century helped members to pool money to establish laundries or other small businesses. This practice continues today as a means of allowing recent Korean immigrants to open fruit stands or convenience stores. Eventually, factors such as hostility from competing non-Asian businesses led to the formation of trade organizations that brought together members across district or family lines. One example is the Chinese Hand Laundry Alliance, a trade organization formed in New York City in 1933 to protest onerous fees imposed only on Chinese laundries. The Korean American greengrocer associations were formed in similar circumstances and are found today in many large U.S. cities.

Moving beyond economic well-being, some early ethnic-specific Asian American organizations focused on political issues, such as freeing India or Korea from colonial domination, supporting Sun Yat Sen's efforts to overthrow the Ching Dynasty, or protesting the rise of militarism in Japan. During the 1960s and 1970s, these nascent political efforts led to the formation of broader Asian American organizations committed to social change. Meanwhile, on campuses from San Francisco to New York, Asian American students and their allies in Asian American community groups demanded the formation of Asian American studies programs. By the late 1980s, these successes led to modest but significant inroads into the power centers of this society. For example, Asian Americans became involved in local, state, and national politics, and therefore needed Asian American caucuses in the Democratic and Republican parties, as well as in the Rainbow Coalition and other political parties. Groups devoted to voter education and political participation were formed in many cities, and civil rights advocate centers for Asian Americans were established in Washington, D.C., and in many state capitals.

In the mid-1990s, organizations specific to one Asian nation of origin as well as pan-Asian American organizations exist in many parts of the United States and for many purposes. For example, Asian American chambers of commerce and associations of Asian American M.B.A. holders as well as organizations devoted to the arts and historical preservation; Asian American groups for undergraduates, medical students, and law students; single-issue groups focusing on providing health care to the indigent, eliminating lead paint and other environmental toxins, and developing a community economic base that is less dependent on tourism and the Chinatown restaurant trade; and professional organizations for teachers, journalists, lawyers, and librarians, members of labor unions, and employees of the federal government.

Although grouped with Asian Americans on U.S. census surveys since 1970, Pacific Islanders are distinct in terms of indigenous land claims and other issues, have set up their own support groups. As planning for the year 2000 Census has begun, some Pacific Islanders are demanding categorization with Native Americans.

Ironically, as new Asian American organizations proliferate, no one organization can recapture the lifetime loyalty and local rootedness seen in the prefectural organizations of old. One hundred years ago, there were not enough Asian American lawyers to consider forming an Asian American bar association; therefore, lawyers, farmers, and merchants came together as a group under social functions. Today, students searching for Asian American organizations near their local campuses can use the Internet to contact national Asian American advocacy groups in Washington, D.C. Asian Americans come together around issues, such as redress for interned Japanese Americans or annual Asian/Pacific American Heritage Month festivals in May.

In the end, Asian American organizations will continue to serve the needs of new arrivals as well as advocate for those affected by national policy. Houses of worship, Asian language schools, and small grassroots programs to assist elders or teens serve as community gathering places, as well as conference centers, meeting halls, and the corridors of Congress.

Groups may be formal, like the Asian Americans for Affirmative Action (4As) at AT&T, or informal, like the group of forty-something Asian American professionals who play basketball on Tuesday nights in the tiny fourth-floor gymnasium of the True Light Lutheran Church in New York's Chinatown. Some will keep a local focus, like Asian Americans United in Philadelphia, and others, like the Global Organization of People of Indian Origin (GOPIO), will operate internationally.

The list of national and prominent regional or local organizations that follows is intended as a starting place for the creation of a more comprehensive data base on Asian Americans. National or regional organizations as well as the editors of the more than two hundred Asian American publications can provide information about additional local organizations for specific groups and causes, as can many general purpose Asian American organizations on both national and local levels.

♦ ORGANIZATION PROFILES: ASSOCIATIONS OF BROAD OR NATIONAL SCOPE

Asian American Curriculum Project (AACP)

414 E. 3rd Ave.
PO Box 367
San Mateo, CA 94401-0367
(415) 343-9408

Founded in 1971 and formerly known as the Japanese American Curriculum Project (JACP), AACP develops, promotes, and disseminates Asian American studies and curriculum material to schools, libraries, and Asian Americans, and sponsors demonstrations when feasible. AACP publishes the annual *Japanese American Curriculum Project Catalogue*, which includes a listing of Asian American books, journals, posters, games, and dolls. It also includes an index of titles and book reviews.

Asian CineVision (ACV)

32 E. Broadway
New York, NY 10002
(212) 925-8685

Founded in 1976, Asian CineVision encourages the creation and presentation of Asian and Asian American media arts. Its objectives are to offer positive alternatives to Asian stereotypes in the mainstream media, to further public knowledge of Asian and American perspectives, and to lay the groundwork for deeper cultural understanding. ACV provides services in video documentation, screening, duplication and transfer, and post-production. ACV also maintains a video and print archive. Asian CineVision publishes *CineVue* five times per year and the *Asian American Media Reference Guide* annually.

Asian Pacific American Heritage Council (APAHC)

PO Box 23368
Washington, DC 20026-3368
(202) 659-2311

Asian/Pacific organizations united in 1978 to promote a better understanding of Asian/Pacific Americans. APAHC is responsible for the official recognition of Asian Pacific American Heritage Week held in May. A congressional reception, tennis and table tennis tournaments, festival, and poster competition are held in connection with Heritage Week. The APAHC bestows awards and maintains a speakers' bureau. It publishes *Heritage Week Booklet* annually.

Buddhist Council for Refugee Rescue and Resettlement (BCRRR)

800 Sacramento St.
San Francisco, CA 94108
(415) 421-6117

Founded in 1979, the Buddhist Council for Refugee Rescue and Resettlement is comprised of Buddhist congregations and mutual aid associations seeking to assist in the resettlement of refugees to the United States. BCRRR maintains refugee training centers for English language and acculturation assistance and offers employment training and placement services. BCRRR also provides child care services to refugee families receiving training and offers medical and other support services. BCRRR publishes the *Buddhist Council Newsletter*.

Church World Service Immigration and Refugee Program (CWSIRP)

475 Riverside Dr., Rm. 656
New York, NY 10115
(212) 870-3153

Founded in 1946, the Church World Service Immigration and Refugee Program is operated by the Church World Service. The program coordinates the resettlement of refugees from around the world through congregations and offices of participating denominations. CWSIRP works for the protection of refugees seeking safe haven in the United States and publishes the *Refugee Resettlement Appeal*.

Indochina Institute (II)

George Mason University
4400 University Dr.
Fairfax, VA 22030-4444
(703) 323-2690

The Indochina Institute collects and disseminates information on Southeast Asia and Southeast Asian refugees. The Institute conducts research into the Vietnam War and encourages the teaching of courses on that period in U.S. history. It sponsors lectures, seminars, musical performances, art exhibitions, poetry readings, and video and slide presentations, and maintains a library. Founded in 1979, its membership of 4000 is comprised of scholars, writers, journalists, businesspeople, clergy, and interested individuals. The Indochina Institute publishes a quarterly report and periodic directories, proceedings, reports, self-study packets, and occasional papers.

Indochina Resource Action Center (IRAC)
See Southeast Asian Resource Action Center (SEARAC).

National Association for the Education and Advancement of Cambodian, Laotian, and Vietnamese Americans

c/o Ms. Ngoan Le
7018 N. Ashland Ave.
Chicago, IL 60626

Founded in 1979, the association (formerly the National Association for Vietnamese American Education) seeks to provide equal educational opportunities for Indochinese Americans; to advance the rights of Indochinese Americans; to acknowledge and publicize contributions of Vietnamese and other Indochinese in U.S. schools, culture, and society; and to encourage appreciation of Indochinese cultures, peoples, education, and language. The association works toward meeting the legislative needs of Indochinese Americans in education, health, social services, and welfare. It encourages scholarly excellence and active participation of parents and community members in school and community activities. The association conducts networking activities and offers referrals for Indochinese professionals and others working with Indochinese in the fields of education and human services. It operates a speakers' bureau, sponsors scholarship contests, and conducts workshops. The association publishes the *Channel for Indochinese American Communication* quarterly. It also publishes a newsletter containing current information on the education and resettlement of Indochinese refugees and their communities; the newsletter also includes a calendar of events and a list of available resources. The association has also published the *Directory of Indochinese Personnel in Education and Social Services*.

National Institute for Women of Color (NIWC)

1301 20th St. NW, Ste. 702
Washington, DC 20036
(202) 296-2661

Founded in 1981, the NIWC aims to enhance the strengths of diversity and promote educational and economic equity for black, Hispanic, Asian American, Pacific-Islander, American Indian, and Alaskan Native women. The NIWC focuses on mutual concerns and needs, bringing together women who have traditionally been isolated. NIWC uses the phrase "women of color" to convey unity, self-esteem, and political status and to avoid using the term "minority," which the institute feels has a negative psychological and social impact. The NIWC serves as a networking vehicle for linking women of color on various issues or programs, promoting women of color for positions on boards and commissions; ensuring that women of color are visible as speakers at major women's conferences; supporting and initiating programs; educating women and the public about the status and culture of the various racial/ethnic groups they represent; and promoting cooperative efforts between general women's organizations and women of color. The NIWC sponsors seminars and workshops; it also provides technical assistance and conducts internship and leadership development programs. The NIWC bestows Outstanding Women of Color awards and compiles statistics. The NIWC has published *Brown Papers*, *NIWC Network News*, bibliographies, bulletins, fact sheets, and other related resources.

Organization of PanAsian American Women (PANASIA)

PO Box 39128
Washington, DC 20016

Founded in 1976 to provide a voice for the concerns of Asian Pacific American (APA) women and to encourage their full participation in all aspects of U.S. society, PANASIA seeks to promote an accurate and realistic image of APA women in the United States, develop leadership skills and increase occupational mobility, and maintain a national communications network. PANASIA produces legislative updates on national issues of concern to Asian Pacific Americans; sponsors workshops and lectures; and maintains a speakers' bureau. PANASIA publishes *Membership Directory* annually and *Pan Asia News*, a periodical; it has also published *Pan Asian Women: A Vital Force*.

Refugees International (RI)

220 1st St., NE, Ste. 240
Washington, DC 20002
(202) 547-3785

Founded in 1979, RI provides advocacy, information, public education, and community support to refugees and displaced persons worldwide. Through voluntary action, RI seeks alternative means of handling refugee migration and permanent resettlement. RI works to assist and support existing refugee relief and resettlement programs. It monitors and reports on events pertaining to refugees. RI fosters voluntary support in the form of funds, sponsorship of refugee families, letters urging government support, medical services, and relief for refugees around the world. RI maintains a 500-volume library and publishes the *RI Newsletter* quarterly. It also publishes occasional issue briefs.

Refugee Voices, A Ministry with Uprooted Peoples

c/o Fr. Frank Moan, SJ
713 Monroe St., NE
Washington, DC 20017
(202) 832-0020

Founded in 1987 for individuals with religious or humanitarian interests, Refugee Voices, A Ministry with Uprooted Peoples engages in a national campaign to educate Americans about the plight of refugees, displaced persons, undocumented aliens, and economic migrants. It hopes to eliminate myths concerning refugees by acknowledging their contributions to society, to inform U.S. religious groups about refugees, and to educate voters about legislation affecting uprooted peoples. Refugee Voices also acts as an information clearinghouse for groups aiding refugees. It produces "Refugee Voices," a four-minute radio program containing taped interviews with refugees and refugee workers, and produces quarterly public service announcements. Refugee Voices sponsors educational programs, bestows awards, and publishes *Refugee Voices*, a quarterly newsletter. It also publishes a brochure.

Southeast Asian Resource Action Center (SEARAC)

1628 16th St. NW, 3rd Fl.
Washington, DC 20009
(202) 667-4690

Formerly operating as the Indochina Resource Action Center, SEARAC was founded in 1979 to help refugee organizations initiate self-help programs in local communities. SEARAC maintains a library of international and domestic refugee documents and conducts research on the needs of refugees from Southeast Asia. It produces reports on refugee-related issues such as health, employment, vocational training, and social adjustment. It sponsors training workshops and offers one-on-one technical assistance to refugee community organizations throughout the country. SEARAC's publications include the quarterly, *The Bridge*, and the annual *Indochinese Business Directory in the Washington, D.C. Metropolitan Area*. It has developed a lettering system for Southeast Asian languages and has published *A Bibliography of Overseas Vietnamese Periodicals and Newspapers: 1975-1985*.

♦ ORGANIZATION PROFILES: ASSOCIATIONS DEDICATED TO A SPECIFIC ISSUE

Asian American Manufacturers Association (AAMA)

800 Menlo Ave., Ste. 115
Menlo Park, CA 94025
(415) 321-2262

Founded in 1980, the AAMA is an association of Asian American manufacturers of high technology products such as computers, microprocessors, semiconductors, and electronics equipment. The AAMA seeks to enhance members' business opportunities. It sponsors educational programs in management and business operations and bestows awards. Published monthly by the AAMA, the *AAMA Newsletter* contains the president's message, new member listings, a calendar of

events, and employment listings. The AAMA also annually publishes a brochure and a membership directory.

Asian American Psychological Association (AAPA)

c/o Dr. David S. Goh
Queens College/City University of New York
School of Education
Flushing, NY 11367
(718) 997-5236

Founded in 1972, the AAPA is an association of psychologists and graduate students in psychology to advance the welfare of Asian Americans and others through the use and development of psychology. The AAPA assists in and encourages research and services that affect Asian Americans. It makes known psychological issues facing Asian Americans; operates a placement service; and bestows an award for distinguished service. The AAPA publishes an annual journal.

Association of Asian/Pacific American Artists (AAPAA)

3518 Cahuenga Blvd. W., Ste. 302
Los Angeles, CA 90068
(213) 874-0786

Founded in 1976, the AAPAA is comprised of individuals in the entertainment industry, including performers, producers, designers, directors, technicians, and writers. Supporting members include students, individuals, and organizations. The AAPAA encourages equal employment opportunities in all aspects of the entertainment industry in order to promote realistic portrayals of Asian/Pacific peoples. The AAPAA sponsors business and professional seminars with industry leaders to expand members' knowledge of theatre, motion pictures, and television. The AAPAA maintains a speakers' bureau and library; offers specialized education; and bestows awards. AAPAA publications include: *Association of Asian/Pacific American Artists-Inside Moves*, published quarterly; a newsletter that lists business and professional seminars, lectures, and awards; and the *Directory of Asian/Pacific American Artists*, published annually. The AAPAA also publishes *Asian/Pacific American: A Handbook on How to Cover and Portray Our Nation's Fastest Growing Minority Group*.

Interracial-Intercultural Pride (I-PRIDE)

1060 Tennessee St.
San Francisco, CA 94107
(415) 399-9111

Founded in 1979, I-PRIDE includes members of interracial and intercultural families and other concerned individuals. I-PRIDE supports and encourages the well-being and development of children and adults of more than one ethnic or cultural heritage. I-PRIDE maintains a library and speakers' bureau. Membership is currently concentrated in the San Francisco, California area. *I-PRIDE's Newsletter* is published bimonthly.

National Asian American Telecommunications Association (NAATA)

346 9th St., 2nd Fl.
San Francisco, CA 94103
(415) 863-0814

Founded in 1980, NAATA is a group of individuals organized to promote the interests of Asian Americans in the media, including film, video, public television, and radio fields. NAATA offers fiscal/administrative and consultation services for independent film, video, and radio productions. NAATA acts as a public advocate for accurate portrayals of Asian Americans. It serves as a clearinghouse for information on Asian American and independent minority media. NAATA maintains the Cross Current audio facility to produce radio programs for public and community radio. NAATA sponsors film festivals, educational workshops, screenings, and exhibitions, and maintains a speakers' bureau. *Asian American Network*, published quarterly by NAATA, addresses developments and issues affecting Asian American audiences and media. *CrossCurrent Media*, a periodical published by NAATA, is an educational audiovisual catalog. NAATA also distributes videotapes and educational materials.

National Association for Asian and Pacific American Education (NAAPAE)

c/o ARC Associates
310 8th St., Ste. 220
Oakland, CA 94607
(415) 834-9455

Founded in 1977, NAAPAE includes Asian/Pacific Americans and others in bilingual/multicultural education. NAAPAE works to enhance awareness of the multicultural structure of the United States and to unify Asian/Pacific American communities through educational opportunities. It promotes inclusion of Asian/Pacific American culture and history in school curricula and advocates bilingual, multicultural, and other programs. NAAPAE encourages research on related educational topics and works to increase awareness of the educational needs, concerns, and contributions of Asian/Pacific Americans. It supports the increased participation of Asian/Pacific Americans in diverse educational roles, operates bilingual workshops and service projects, and bestows scholarship and distinguished

service awards. NAAPAE publishes a quarterly newsletter, a triennial directory, and monographs, a periodical.

National Association for Bilingual Education (NABE)

Union Center Plaza
810 1st St., NE, 3rd Fl.
Washington, DC 20002
(202) 898-1829

Founded in 1975, NABE includes educators, administrators, paraprofessionals, laypeople, and students. NABE's purposes are to recognize, promote, and publicize bilingual education. NABE seeks to increase public understanding of the importance of language and culture. NABE utilizes and develops student proficiency and ensures equal opportunities in bilingual education for language-minority students. NABE works to preserve and expand the nation's linguistic resources. It educates language-minority parents in public policy decisions.

NABE promotes research in language education, linguistics, and multicultural education. NABE coordinates development of professional standards; organizes conferences and workshops; supports state and local affiliates; and establishes contact with national organizations. NABE publishes a journal three times a year and a newsletter eight times a year.

National Association for Ethnic Studies (NAES)

Arizona State University
Dept. of English
Tempe, AZ 85287
(602) 965-3168

Founded in 1975, NAES was known as the National Association of Interdisciplinary Studies for Native American, Black, Chicano, Puerto Rican, and Asian Americans until 1976 and as the National Association of Interdisciplinary Ethnic Studies until 1985. Comprised of individuals, libraries, and institutions, NAES promotes research, study, and curriculum design in the field of ethnic studies. NAES annually bestows the Ernest M. Pon Award and publishes *The Ethnic Reporter* semiannually.

An NAES-published newsletter monitors developments in the field, discusses educational issues, and reports on activities of the association. NAES also publishes *Explorations in Ethnic Studies*, a refereed semiannual journal devoted to the study of ethnic groups, ethnicity, intergroup relations, and the cultural life of ethnic minorities. *Explorations in Sights and Sounds*, a supplement to *Explorations in Ethnic Studies* devoted to reviews of books and nonprint media about ethnicity, is published annually. NAES has also published proceedings and monographs.

National Federation of Asian American United Methodists (NFAAUM)

330 Ellis St., Rm. 508
San Francisco, CA 94102
(415) 776-7747

Founded in 1975, NFAAUM is comprised of Asian American members of the United Methodist church. NFAAUM's objectives are to form a national federation of Asian American caucuses of the five jurisdictions of the United Methodist church; articulate the concerns, interests, and needs of the Asian American constituencies in all jurisdictions of the church; and advocate the causes of Asian Americans before appropriate boards and agencies of the church. NFAAUM coordinates activities of the Asian American caucuses in relationship to boards and agencies of the church; promotes relevant and meaningful Asian American ministries at all levels; and encourages full participation of Asian Americans in all aspects of church life. NFAAUM provides cultural interpretation of religion in Chinese, Filipino, Indochinese, Japanese, Korean, Southern Asian, and Taiwanese. NFAAUM conducts a leadership training seminar, maintains a speakers' bureau, and publishes *Asian American News*, a quarterly newsletter that includes a calendar of events and federation news.

National Immigration, Refugee and Citizenship Forum (NIRCF)

220 1st St. NE, Ste. 220
Washington, DC 20002
(202) 544-0004

Founded in 1982, NIRCF includes churches, state and local governments, refugee and immigrant organizations, and labor and advocacy groups, and was formerly known as the National Forum on Immigration and Refugee Policy. NIRCF examines policies on immigration, refugee, and citizenship issues; coordinates policy-focused working relationships and information networks; and compiles statistics. Publications include the bimonthly newsletters; *Advisor, EPIC Events*, and *Forum; Information Bulletin*, published 12 to 15 times a year; and *Conference Proceedings*.

National Minority AIDS Council (NMAC)

300 1st St., NE, Ste. 400
Washington, DC 20002
(202) 544-1076

Founded in 1986 and comprised of public health departments and AIDS service organizations, NMAC serves as a clearinghouse of information on AIDS as it affects minority communities in the United States. NMAC facilitates discussion among national minority organizations about AIDS. NMAC maintains Project Health, Education, and AIDS Leadership, which provides computer usage, strategic planning, financial management, and volunteer program development assistance to AIDS service organizations; and Project Volunteer Information, Technical Assistance, and Leadership, which provides technical assistance in volunteer program development and maintenance. NMAC conducts training conferences; offers educational and research programs; compiles statistics; bestows awards; and maintains a speakers' bureau, biographical archives, and a library. NMAC publishes *Leadership Reprint Series* (quarterly), which includes information on strategies for addressing HIV/AIDS and scientific updates; *NMAC Healer* (bimonthly), which includes updates on projects, community needs and statistics; and *NMAC Update*, a bimonthly newsletter, which includes association information and coverage of HIV/AIDS issues. NMAC also publishes the *Technical Assistance Manual for Volunteer Program Development* and the *Computer Technical Assistance Manual*.

National Minority Business Council (NMBC)

235 E. 42nd St.
New York, NY 10017
(212) 573-2385

Founded in 1972, NMBC is a group of minority businesses in all areas of industry and commerce seeking to increase profitability by developing marketing, sales, and management skills among minority businesses. NMBC acts as an informational source for the national minority business community. NMBC programs include a legal services plan that provides free legal services to members in such areas as sales contracts, copyrights, estate planning, and investment; a business referral service that develops potential customer leads; an international trade program that provides technical assistance in developing foreign markets; an executive banking program that teaches members how to package a business loan for bank approval; and a procurement outreach program for minority and women business owners. NMBC conducts continuing management education and provides assistance in teaching youth the free enterprise system. NMBC also bestows awards. NMBC publishes *Better Business* semiannually; *Corporate Minority Vendor Director* annually; *NMBC Business Report* bimonthly; and the *NMBC Corporate Purchasing Directory*.

National Network of Minority Women in Science (MWIS)

c/o American Association for the Advancement of Science
Directorate for Education and Human Resource Programs
1333 H St., NW
Washington, DC 20005
(202) 326-6677

Founded in 1978, MWIS includes Asian, African and Hispanic American and Native American women, and other interested individuals involved in science-related professions. MWIS promotes the advancement of minority women in the science fields and the improvement of the science and mathematics education and career awareness among minorities. MWIS supports public policies and programs in science and technology that benefit minorities. It compiles statistics; serves as a clearinghouse for identifying minority women scientists; offers writing and conference presentations, seminars, and workshops on minority women in science; and sponsors local career conferences for students. MWIS local chapters maintain speakers' bureaus and placement services, offer children's services, sponsor competitions, and bestow awards. MWIS publishes a quarterly periodical and plans to publish a directory.

National Pacific/Asian Resource Center on Aging (NP/ARCA)

2033 6th Ave., Ste. 410
Seattle, WA 98121
(206) 448-0313

Founded in 1979, NP/ARCA's goals are to ensure and improve the delivery of health and social services to elderly Pacific/Asian Americans; to increase the capabilities of community-based services by expanding their information and technical base; and to include Pacific/Asian Americans in planning and organizational activities, thus maintaining a strong link between the center and the community. NP/ARCA compiles statistics and maintains a 500-volume library. Publications include the *National Community Service Directory: Pacific/Asian Elderly*, a biennial; *National Consultation Resource Roster*, a biennial; *Update*, a bimonthly newsletter; *Pacific/Asian Elderly: Bibliography*; *Proceedings of Pacific/Asians: The Wisdom of Age*; and the *Guide to the Utilization of Family and Community Support Systems*, a medical handbook.

U.S.-Asia Institute (USAI)

232 E. Capitol St., NE
Washington, DC 20003
(202) 544-3181

Founded in 1979, USAI includes Americans of Asian descent, individuals with an interest in U.S.-Asia relations, U.S. institutions and companies doing business with Asia, and Asian institutions and companies doing business with the United States. Its purpose is to strengthen ties between the East and the West and to foster cooperation, communication, and cultural exchange between the United States and Asia. USAI places special emphasis on the "unique capabilities" of

Asian Americans to assist in this process and on the contribution of Asian Americans to the cultural, social, and economic mainstream of U.S. life. USAI promotes a firm understanding in Asia of the issues important to the development of U.S. domestic and foreign policies through research, symposia, and special programs. They sponsor the Tom Chan Future Leader Award competition in which college students can earn an internship with the institute. USAI presents the USAI Achievement Awards, given annually to Asian Americans who have made outstanding contributions to the United States in their individual fields, and also bestows the Kay Sugahara Awards for the contributions of young Asian Americans. USAI sponsors the American Perspective Series of educational seminars on issues concerning U.S.-Asia relations for Asian leaders and groups and U.S. congressional aides planning visits to Indonesia, Japan, Malaysia, and the People's Republic of China. *US-Asia Institute-Policy Forum*, a newsletter published quarterly by USAI, covers economic, political, and strategic relations between the United States and Asia as well as institute activities and programs. *US-Asia National Leadership Conference Proceedings* is published annually by USAI. USAI has also published *U.S.-Asia Economic Relations: Policies and Prospects*; *An Asian/Pacific American Perspective: Future Directions of U.S.*; *The Communications Revolution: Key to U.S.-Asia Relations*; *U.S.-Asia Security: Economic and Political Dimensions*; *Immigration and Refugee Policy*; and booklets and brochures.

U.S. Catholic Conference Refugee Resettlement

810 18th Ave., No. 108
Seattle, WA 98122
(206) 323-9450

This group assists refugees and immigrants with services that include legal documentation, translation, counseling, English tutoring, cultural adjustment, and family reunification.

U.S. Pan Asian American Chamber of Commerce

1625 K St., NW, Ste. 380
Washington, DC 20006
(202) 638-1764

A group of businesspersons and professionals united to promote the interests of Asian American businesses, this organization conducts educational and networking activities, maintains a scholarship fund, and holds luncheons.

♦ REGIONAL ASIAN AMERICAN ORGANIZATIONS

Asian American Caucus for Disarmament (AACD)

48 Henry St.
New York, NY 10002

Founded in 1982, AACD includes Asian Americans and others advocating peace and total disarmament. AACD seeks to increase Asian American participation in disarmament campaigns and organize Hiroshima and Nagasaki memorials. AACD perceives civil rights, human needs, and peace as being closely related and hopes to increase awareness of what the caucus calls racist stereotypes about Asian Americans. AACD works to promote peace education among minorities, emphasizing community involvement. AACD compiles data on weapons tests in the Pacific and maintains a library and speakers' bureau. AACD publishes a quarterly newsletter and a brochure and also offers audiovisual materials.

Asian American Legal Defense and Education Fund (AALDEF)

99 Hudson St.
New York, NY 10013
(212) 966-5932

Founded in 1974, AALDEF is comprised of attorneys, legal workers, and members of the community who seek to employ legal and educational methods to attack critical problems in Asian American communities. AALDEF provides bilingual legal counseling and representation for people who cannot obtain access to legal assistance. Areas of concern include immigration, employment, housing, voting rights, and racially-motivated violence against Asian Americans. AALDEF litigates cases that have the potential for improving the quality of life in the Asian American community. It monitors and reports on incidents of racial discrimination against Asian Americans. AALDEF sponsors workshops, seminars, and training sessions to inform community workers and residents of their rights and benefits before legal problems arise. AALDEF conducts a law-student intern program to provide students with legal experience in a community setting. It also holds fundraising benefits. Publications include *Outlook*, a semiannual newsletter, and pamphlets in Chinese, Korean, Japanese, and English.

Asian American Voters Coalition (AAVC)

8837 Sleepy Hollow Ln.
Potomac, MD 20854
(301) 299-4859

Founded in 1983, AAVC is a coalition of organizations representing 6.5 million Asian Americans. AAVC seeks to enhance the political influence of Asian Americans; promotes equal treatment of Asian Americans in the U.S. political system; and lobbies the U.S. government on immigration legislation and other matters of interest to the Asian American community. AAVC attempts to influence party platforms and presidential candidates on issues pertinent to Asian Americans. It sponsors voter registration and education drives; encourages Asian Americans to run for public office; and maintains a speakers' bureau. AAVC publishes the *Annual Report* as well as brochures and press releases.

Asian and Pacific Americans for Nuclear Awareness (APANA)

2225 N. Beachwood, No. 201
Hollywood, CA 90068

Founded in 1980 to educate the public about nuclear war, disarmament, and especially the history of those who survived the atomic bombings of Hiroshima and Nagasaki, APANA presents a video/slide show to schools and church and community groups. APANA conducts research on a nuclear-free Korea and Philippines and strives for a nuclear-free Pacific. APANA compiles statistics, bestows awards, operates a speakers' bureau, and is developing a curriculum for children on peaceful resolution of interpersonal and global conflicts. APANA is working for the establishment of a memorial in Los Angeles, California, to house a flame, sent to the United States by Hioshima's mayor, that commemorates victims of atomic bombing. APANA publishes a newsletter and brochures.

Asian Pacific American Heritage Council (APAHC)

PO Box 23368
Washington, DC 20026-3368
(202) 659-2311

Asian/Pacific Islander organizations united in 1978 to promote a better understanding of Asian/Pacific Amerians. APAHC is responsible for the official recognition of Asian Pacific American Heritage Week, held in May. APAHC holds a congressional reception, tennis and table tennis tournaments, a festival, and a poster competition in connection with Heritage Week. APAHC bestows awards and maintains a speakers' bureau. The *Heritage Week Booklet* is published annually.

Center for Immigrant's Rights (CIR)

48 St. Marks Pl., 4th Fl.
New York, NY 10003
(212) 505-6890

Founded in 1981, CIR provides paralegal training and educational programs in immigration law for church, community, and labor organizations. CIR offers information to immigrants on their rights under law and strives to influence public policy. CIR provides documentation and intervenes in employer discrimination against immigrants. The organization offers advocacy and organizing training programs, clinics for immigrants, workshops, seminars, public benefits training, and labor rights; it also conducts a community outreach program. The *CIR Report*, a newsletter, is published quarterly. CIR also publishes fact sheets, briefing and policy papers, walletcards, and the *Guide to Immigration Counseling: A Step by Step Legal Handbook (2nd edition)*.

Committee Against Anti-Asian Violence (CAAAV)

PO Box 20756
Tompkins Square
New York, NY 10009
(718) 857-7419

An Asian American organization founded in 1977 to combat violence perpetrated against Asian Americans in the United States, CAAAV conducts forums for the discussion of the causes of and deterrents to racially-motivated violence in the United States.

Southeast Asia Center (SEAC)

1124-1128 W. Ainslie
Chicago, IL 60640
(312) 989-6927

Founded in 1979, SEAC was formerly known as the Association of Chinese from Indochina. Lao, Hmong, Cambodian, Vietnamese, and Chinese refugees from Indochina promote the independence and well-being of Indochinese refugees and immigrants and encourage cooperation and mutual understanding among all minorities. SEAC strives to sensitize people to the plight of refugees by serving as an advocate for Indochinese and other refugees who do not speak English. SEAC also maintains an interpretation network in Illinois for hospitals and government and private agencies. SEAC promotes equitable allocation of private and public funding without regard for language ability, educational background, or handicaps. SSEAC provides minority advocacy through national and international media, organizes legislative and administrative lobbying and legal action, and offers direct social services and English classes for new refugees. SEAC compiles statistics on the Indochinese population and maintains a 600-volume library. *New Life News*, a newsletter concerned with the relationships between various Indochinese ethnic groups in the United States, between Indochinese immigrants and Native Americans, and between Eastern and Western culture in general, is published quarterly. SEAC also publishes an Indochinese directory and the *Chicago Language Network*.

◆ ORGANIZATION PROFILES: ASSOCIATIONS DEDICATED TO A SPECIFIC ETHNIC/NATIONALITY

Asian Indian Americans

Association of Asian Indians in America (AAIA)

300 Clover St.
Rochester, NY 14610

Founded in 1967, AAIA members are U.S. citizens and residents of Asian Indian ancestry who seek to continue Indian cultural activities in the United States. AAIA is the oldest of the Pan Indian Organizations. Several subsidiary organizations based on common professional interests were created within AAIA to provide a forum for addressing issues of common interest. These include the Engineer's Council, the Council on Trade, and the Council on Medical Affairs. AAIA's major achievement was to obtain from the U.S. Census Bureau a separate category listing for identifying Asian Indians in the census of population beginning in 1980. Prior to 1980, Indians were classified with whites on the assumption that they belonged to the "Caucasian" race. By achieving a separate demographic classification, AAIA succeeded in obtaining a "minority" status for Asian Indians, making them eligible for government minority programs and funds. AAIA holds a yearly banquet, where Indians and Americans who have made significant scientific or artistic contributions to society are honored. AAIA has several regional chapters, each with its own program and agenda. The New York chapter is well known for its yearly festival of lights called "Deepavali," celebrated at the South Street Seaport in New York City and attended in large numbers by Americans of Indian and other ancestries.

National Federation of Indian American Associations (NFIA)

PO Box 462, Wakefield Station
Bronx, NY 10466
(718) 329-8010

The National Federation of Indian American Associations (NFIA) was formed in 1980 at the first convention of Asian Indians in North America (AIINA). This convention was organized by the Federation of Indian Associations (FIA). Indian American associations from all over the United States came together under NFIA to strengthen ties between the United States, India, and the Indian community through social, cultural, educational, economic, legislative and socio-political activities. NFIA was incorporated in 1983 as a non-profit tax-exempt organization in Denver, Colorado. It is an umbrella organization to which most of the non-religious Indian organizations belong. NFIA holds regional and national conventions biennially to identify projects, recruit new leadership, promote performing and fine arts, and evolve channels through which all member organizations can function in unison. NFIA publishes a bimonthly newsletter, *NFIA News*, and occasionally prepares position papers.

Indian American Forum for Political Education

Founded by former Equal Employment Opportunity Commissioner Joy Cherian in 1982, the Indian American Forum for Political Education seeks to enhance political awareness, involvement, and civic responsibility among Asian Indians through seminars and conferences on issues affecting them. It promotes voter registration, attempts to promote understanding and ongoing relationships between political officials and the Indian community, and educates U.S. politicians about Asian American issues.

Federation of Indian Associations (FIA)

The FIA was formed in 1971, but was renamed and reorganized in 1977 as a federated body of sixty associations. It has been mainly involved in social and cultural activities. It is principally associated with the celebration of Indian Independence Day in August, when it stages a parade of tableaus representing various facets of the community along Madison Avenue in New York. It also sponsors a yearly folk dance competition representing different parts of India. Some of its other activities have been organizing of voter registration drives, fund-raising for political campaigns, and more recently for restoration of the Statue of Liberty.

Cambodian Americans

Cambodian Americans Association of Cambodian Survivors of America (ACSA)

6616 Kerns Rd.
Falls Church, VA 22042
(703) 532-7931

Founded in 1981, ACSA consists of volunteer relief groups that provide assistance to Cambodian refugees in the United States and at the Kampuchean-Thai border. ACSA provides counseling services and information referrals.

Cambodian Buddhist Society (CBS)

13800 New Hampshire Ave.
Silver Spring, MD 20904
(301) 622-6544

Founded in 1978, CBS was formed in order to preserve the Cambodian Buddhist religion and the Cambodian tradition and culture. CBS counsels Cambodian refugees and organizes Cambodian religious and traditional ceremonies. It maintains the Cambodian

Buddhist Temple and a 400-volume library on Buddhism and Cambodian culture. CBS organizes classes on Khmer (Cambodian) language for children. The Khmer language newsletter of Buddhism and Cambodian tradition and culture, *Vatt Khmer*, is published quarterly.

Chinese Americans

Center for United States-China Arts Exchange

423 W. 118th St., No. 1E
New York, NY 10027
(212) 280-4648

Founded in 1978, the exchange promotes and facilitates exchanges of materials and specialists in the visual, literary, and performing arts between the United States and the People's Republic of China in an effort to stimulate public interest in the arts of both countries. It fosters collaborative projects among American and Chinese artists. The exchange arranges professional activities for exchange artists including lectures, conferences, performances and exhibitions, and research opportunities in their respective fields. The newsletter *U.S.-China Arts Exchange* is published annually.

China Information Center

169 Grove St.
Newton, MA 02166
(617) 332-0990

The center was founded in 1989 by Chinese students in the United States to offer support to students in Beijing, People's Republic of China and provide information to the Western public and media regarding the student demonstrations that took place at Tiananmen Square during May and June of 1989. The center received direct reports on the events as they transpired and initiated information campaigns to combat the Chinese government's efforts to cover up the killing of students. The China Information Center seeks to increase the awareness of the academic community and public of recent political, economic, and social changes in China as well as the potential impact of these changes. The center supports the efforts of Chinese students in the United States to develop programs that provide news of current developments in China. It plans to: create a human rights archive; provide a communications network for Chinese students who are unable to return to China; and conduct research on political, economic, military, legal, and business-related topics. It has provided financial and technical assistance to conduct nationwide teleconferences on topics of concern to Chinese students in the United States. The center sponsors educational programs; maintains a speakers' bureau; and compiles statistics. The newsletter *China Focus* is published bimonthly and contains in-depth analysis of current political, economic, and social conditions in China. It also issues reports.

China Institute in America (CI)

125 E. 65th St.
New York, NY 10021
(212) 744-8181

Founded in 1926 for individuals and corporations interested in the People's Republic of China and in furthering Chinese-U.S. understanding. CI works to promote better understanding between U.S. and Chinese citizens and to assist Chinese students and scholars in the United States. CI offers courses and lectures on art history, Chinese language (in both Mandarin and Cantonese dialects), contemporary China, folklore, geography, history, literature, religion, and Sino American relations. Studio courses include calligraphy, cooking, music, painting, and Tai Ji Quan. The China House Gallery presents exhibitions of unusual facets of Chinese classical and folk art. A weekly open house is held for visiting Chinese and U.S. students and scholars. CI produces educational materials on Chinese civilization and Chinese people in the United States and maintains a reference library of 2000 books. CI offers gallery talks, seminars, symposia, and workshops and organizes educational and recreational programs for exchange students from Chinese-speaking countries. CI conducts cultural and medical exchanges with China, presents annual Qingyun awards, and maintains a speakers' bureau. In addition to an annual report, CI publishes the *China Institute in America-Art Exhibition Catalogs*, which accompanies China House Gallery art exhibitions with object listings and scholarly essays, the *China Institute in America Bulletin*, a quarterly newsletter updating members on institute activities, and a semi-annual school catalog.

Chinese American Civic Association (CACA)

90 Tyler St.
Boston, MA 02111
(617) 426-9492

CACA provides assistance to the Chinese American community, including refugees and immigrants. CACA services include English classes, job counseling, and tax services.

Chinese American Civic Council (CACC)

2249 S. Wentworth, 2nd Fl.
Chicago, IL 60616
(312) 225-0234

CACC's members' goals are to become better U.S. citizens and to take an active part in the U.S. way of life. CACC works to provide a means for Chinese Americans to participate in and contribute to U.S. culture.

Founded in 1951, CACC seeks to improve housing, business, and educational standards and to develop parental responsibility and responsible behavior among youth. CACC provides youth career orientation programs and police department workshops. CACC also sponsors a girl scout troop; conducts lectures; and bestows awards to outgoing presidents. The booklet, *Chinese American Progress*, is published annually.

Chinese American Educational Foundation (CAEF)

c/o Albert Jen
8931 Shermer Rd.
Morton Grove, IL 60053
(708) 965-7097

Founded in 1965, CAEF is supported by individuals, churches, and corporations interested in aiding Chinese youth in higher education by granting scholarships to college students and youth awards to U.S. high school graduates of Chinese descent. CAEF publishes *Letter to Members*, a periodical, and published *A List of Doctoral Dissertations by Chinese Students in the U.S, 1964-94*.

Chinese American Food Society (CAFS)

c/o Dr. Daniel Y. C. Fung
Kansas State Univ.
207 Call Hall
Manhattan, KS 66506
(913) 532-5654

Founded in 1975 and formerly known as the Association of Chinese Food Scientists and Technologists in America (presently inactive), CAFS is comprised of Chinese American scientists, engineers, and managers involved in food and food-related industries; university students and professors; and research personnel of public and private research institutes. CAFS' goals are to advance food science and technology and to promote Chinese cultural and ethnic interests. CAFS conducts seminars and workshops; it also operates a placement service and a charitable program. The *Bulletin* and *CAFS Membership Directory* are both published annually. The *CAPS Science and Technology Monograph Series* is published as a periodical. The *Chinese American Food Society Newsletter* is published in English and Chinese four times a year.

Chinese American Forum (CAF)

606 Brantford Ave.
Silver Spring, MD 20904
(301) 622-3053

Founded in 1982, CAF includes individuals eighteen years of age or older with Chinese American bicultural heritage or interest. CAF cultivates understanding among U.S. citizens of the Chinese American cultural heritage; promotes the interest, active participation, and contribution of Chinese Americans in American society; and serves as a forum on issues of national, international, and general interest, as well as those related to China, from the standpoint of Chinese Americans. The *Chinese American Forum*, an association journal containing book reviews, is published quarterly.

Chinese American Librarians Association (CALA)

Auraria Library
Lawrence St. and 11th St.
Denver, CO 80204
(303) 556-2911

Founded in 1973, CALA's purposes are to promote better communication among Chinese American librarians in the United States, serve as a forum for the discussion of problems, and support the development and promotion of librarianship. Formerly known as the Mid-West Chinese American Librarians Association, CALA maintains placement referral service, offers scholarships for library school students, and bestows awards. CALA publishes the *CALA Membership Directory* annually and the *Chinese American Librarians Association-Newsletter*, which includes a calendar of events, list of employment opportunities, and new member news. The *Journal of Library and Information Science* (published semiannually in English and Chinese) covers problems common to librarians and information scientists; new concepts, systems and technology; leading events worldwide; and development of Chinese library and information services. CALA has also published the *Directory of Chinese American Libraries in the U.S.*

Chinese American Medical Society (CAMS)

c/o Dr. H. H. Wang
281 Edgewood Ave.
Teaneck, NJ 07666
(201) 833-1506

Founded in 1962, members include physicians of Chinese origin residing in the United States and Canada. CAMS seeks to advance medical knowledge, scientific research, and interchange of information among members; to establish scholarship and endowments in medical schools and hospitals of good standing; and to hold periodic meetings for professional purposes. Formerly known as the American Chinese Medical Society, CAMS conducts educational meetings; supports research; grants scholarships; bestows a scientific award annually to a member with the highest scholastic achievement; and maintains a placement service. CAMS also sponsors a limited charitable program. The *Chinese Medical Society-Bulletin* is published annually and includes scientific articles. The *Chinese Medical Society-Newsletter*, published three to four times a year, includes membership news, announcements, and a calendar of events. The *Membership Directory* is published as a biennial.

Chinese American Restaurant Association (CARA)

173 Canal St.
New York, NY 10013
(212) 966-5747

Founded in 1935, membership includes owners of Chinese restaurants who seek to resolve problems faced by restaurant owners. Membership is concentrated in New York City.

Chinese Consolidated Benevolent Association (CCBA)

62 Mott St.
New York, NY 10013
(212) 226-6280

Founded in 1890, CCBA is a community leadership institution that integrates traditional Chinese family, district, and business organizations. CCBA represents the interests of the Chinatown community; monitors business activities; and settles disputes. CCBA provides counseling and referrals to immigrants. CCBA maintains the New York Chinese School and adult English language classes; operates the Chinatown Day Care Center; and sponsors the New York City Summer Youth Employment Program as well as the Chinese New Year's Festival.

Chinese Culture Foundation of San Francisco (CCFSF)

750 Kearny St.
San Francisco, CA 94108
(415) 986-1822

Founded in 1965, CCFSF promotes the understanding and appreciation of Chinese and Chinese American art, culture, and history in the United States. CCFSF offers educational and cultural programs, including art exhibitions, lecture and film series, performances, workshops, classes, research projects, and Chinatown walks. CCFSF also sponsors events in conjunction with academic and cultural organizations in the San Francisco Bay area. CCFSF publishes a periodic newsletter and exhibition catalogs.

Chinese Development Council (CDC)

5 Division St.
New York, NY 10002
(212) 966-6340

Established by volunteers in 1968 to meet the pressing problems of immigrants in New York City's Chinatown, CDC conducts a Manpower Training and Referral Program to train the unemployed and refer the underemployed to better paying jobs. CDC, formerly known as the Chinese Youth Council, also offers sewing classes; educational counseling; a food stamp program; English language, typing, and bookkeeping classes; restaurant management classes; and recreational activities. CDC presents the annual Exxon Community Leadership Award.

Chinese for Affirmative Action (CAA)

17 Walter U. Lum Pl.
San Francisco, CA 94108
(415) 274-6750

Founded in 1969, CAA includes individuals and corporations seeking equal opportunities for and the protection of the civil rights of Asian Americans. CAA works with the larger community to help insure fair treatment under the law in employment matters. It has cooperated with state and local governmental agencies to help develop bilingual materials to aid Asian American job applicants; encourages the appointment and participation of Asian Americans on public boards and commissions; and works to secure a fair share of public resources for Asian Americans. CAA seeks to influence broadcasting stations to produce Asian American public affairs programming and to present accurate portrayals of Asian Americans. It provides counseling information on workers' rights, makes referrals to sources of additional assistance, and assists employers in meeting affirmative action goals. CAA trains Asian Americans to be public speakers and community spokespersons. CAA maintains a library of videotapes and sound recordings on Asian Americans and provides recommendations for speakers and guests for public and private institutions and radio/television talk shows; CAA has also produced a children's series. CAA publishes an annual report, and the *Chinese for Affirmative Action Newsletter*, published quarterly, informs readers of career counseling services and employment and apprenticeship opportunities and announces organization events. CAA also publishes *Practical English* and *Citizenship Made Easy* (books), brochures, and tapes.

Chinese Historical Society of America (CHSA)

650 Commercial St.
San Francisco, CA 94111
(415) 391-1188

Founded in 1963, CHSA is comprised of persons interested in studying and preserving manuscripts, books, and other artifacts that have a bearing on the history of Chinese Americans. CHSA promotes the knowledge of the contributions Chinese Americans have made to U.S. society. CHSA sponsors a monthly lecture series; it has also established a small museum, which contains artifacts, photographs, documents, and a collection of clippings. CHSA maintains a 500-volume library (which does not include newspapers and photographs housed at the University of California, Berkeley). CHSA publishes the periodical, *A History of the Chinese in California*, a compilation of Chinese American history that includes summaries of research. CHSA also publishes *Chinese America: History and Perspectives*, a journal including research reports, annually; the *Chinese Historical Society of America Bulletin*, a newsletter on Chinese American history that includes a calendar of events and an annual report, is published ten times a year. CHSA also publishes *The Chinese in America* catalog, books, and a historical syllabus.

Chinese Women's Benevolent Association (CWBA)

22 Pell St., No. 3
New York, NY 10013
(212) 267-4764

CWBA's members are Chinese women who volunteer in fundraising drives, aid students, and conduct other philanthropic activities. Founded in 1942, CWBA provides interpreting and translating services when needed. CWBA activities are centered in the New York City area.

June 4th Foundation

733 15th St., NW, Ste. 440
Washington, DC 2005
(202) 347-0017

Founded in 1989, the foundation is made up of Chinese students studying at more than forty U.S. universities and colleges. Their goal is to bear witness to and preserve the historic record of the June 4, 1989, assault by soldiers on students demonstrating for democracy in Tiananmen Square, Beijing, the People's Republic of China. The Chinese army's attack on students and others reportedly resulted in several hundred to several thousand dead and wounded. The foundation seeks to preserve "the terrible truth" of what occurred in Tiananmen Square before "the Chinese government's systematic campaign of intimidation and distortion succeeds in erasing forever the memories of what was done to Chinese men and women." The foundation works to compile a complete list of the names of the dead, injured, and missing Chinese in the Tiananmen Square assault through eyewitness accounts; to transmit radio broadcasts into China from Hong Kong, using technology that would make such broadcasts difficult to jam by the Chinese government; to maintain the flow of information into China through fax machines, telephones, telecommunication scramblers, and computers; and to create a permanent archive of film, videotape, still photographs, and radio records of the events in Tiananmen Square. The foundation works to secure a haven in the West for students and reformers fleeing China. They plan to erect a memorial statue in Washington, D.C., to honor the students who died and hope to raise a similar, larger memorial in Tiananmen Square "when Democracy comes to China." The June 4th Foundation publishes a periodic newsletter as well as press releases and monographs.

National Association of Chinese Americans

1186 Worcester Rd., No. 1031
Framingham, MA 01701
(508) 872-0008

The association offers numerous services to members, including cultural and economic exchanges between the United States and China, as well as economic and legal assistance.

North America Taiwanese Professors' Association (NATPA)

5632 S. Woodlawn St.
Chicago, IL 60637

NATPA's members include professors and senior researchers of Taiwanese origin or descent. Founded in 1980, NATPA encourages educational exchange and cultural understanding among the Taiwanese and other peoples worldwide. It promotes scientific and professional knowledge and seeks to further the welfare of Taiwanese communities in North America and Taiwan. NATPA sponsors research and lectures on topics related to Taiwan; holds symposia; bestows awards and scholarships; and maintains a speakers' bureau and biographical archives. The *Bulletin* is published semiannually; the *Directory*, annually; and the *Newsletter*, bimonthly.

Organization of Chinese Americans (OCA)

2025 Eye St., NW, Ste. 926
Washington, DC 20006
(203) 296-0540

OCA members are U.S. citizens and permanent residents over age eighteen, most of whom trace their ancestry to China. OCA's objectives are to foster public awareness of the needs and concerns of Chinese Americans in the United States; to promote participation through advancement of equal rights, responsibilities, and opportunities; and to promote cultural awareness. Activities include countering negative stereotypes and advocating for groups with special needs, such as refugees, and sponsoring cultural exhibitions and festivals. OCA conducts seminars and charitable programs, sponsors competitions, and bestows awards on distinguished Chinese Americans. OCA maintains a speakers' bureau and biographical archives, conducts research programs, and compiles statistics. There are two regional offices

and over forty local groups. OCA's publications include a textbook, *Chinese in America; Convention Proceedings* (biennial); *Image*, a bimonthly newsletter; and a semiannual membership directory.

Filipino Americans

Association of Philippine Physicians in America (APPA)

2717 W. Olive Ave., Ste. 200
Burbank, CA 91505
(818) 843-8616

Founded in 1972, APPA includes individuals from the Philippines who are licensed to practice medicine in the United States. The organization seeks to provide free medical care to indigent persons; establish a continuing medical education program for physicians; provide aid for the education of physicians; and support medical research. APPA was formerly known as the Association of Philippine Practicing Physicians in the United States. APPA sends medical missions to the Philippines and provides medical residency program placement services. It also bestows awards, maintains a speakers' bureau, and compiles statistics. APPA publishes the *Directory of Physicians*, a biennial; *Leadership Roster of Officers*, an annual; and the *Philippine Physician*, a periodic association and professional newsletter. APPA also publishes CME abstracts and plans to publish a journal of medicine.

Philippine American Chamber of Commerce

711 3rd Ave., 17th Fl.
New York, NY 10017
(212) 972-9326

Founded in 1920, the chamber of commerce operates a speakers' bureau, and publishes *Living in the Philippines*.

Philippine Association (PA)

425 Madison Ave.
New York, NY 10017
(212) 688-2755

Members of the Philippine Association include industrial, financial, and business firms in the Philippines and in the United States. Founded in 1951, PA promotes development of trade between the Philippines and the United States.

Philippine Statehood U.S.A. Movement (PSUSAM)

8876 Zeller Ave.
Arleta, CA 91331
(818) 892-9731

Founded in 1984, PSUSAM included Filipino Americans interested in the Philippines' becoming a member of the United States of America. PSUSAM conducted lobbying activities; compiled statistics; and cooperated with a similar group in the Philippines. It published the periodical *PSUSAM*. PSUSAM is presently inactive.

Filipinos for Affirmative Action

310 8th St.
Oakland, CA 94607
(415) 465-9876

This group provides a variety of services to Filipino immigrants, such as advocacy, counseling, vocational and social services, and community outreach programs.

Hmong Americans

Hmong National Council

4670 E. Butler
Fresno, CA 93702
(209) 456-1220

The council's goals include helping Hmong American children recognize their cultural heritage.

New National Hmong-Lao Foundation

332 S. St.
Fitchburg, MA 01420
(508) 342-8494

Services of the foundation include advocacy, referrals, crisis intervention, job training, and English as a Second Language (ESL) classes.

Southeast Asia Center (SEAC)

1124-1128 W. Ainslie
Chicago, IL 60640
(312) 989-6927

Founded in 1979 and formerly operating under the name Association of Chinese from Indochina, SEAC consists of Lao, Hmong, Cambodian, Vietnamese, and Chinese refugees from Indochina. SEAC promotes the independence and well-being of Indochinese refugees and immigrants and encourages cooperation and mutual understanding among all minorities. SEAC strives to sensitize people to the plight of refugees by serving as an advocate for Indochinese and other refugees who do not speak English. It also maintains an interpretation network in Illinois for hospitals and government and private agencies. It promotes equitable allocation of private and public funding without regard to language ability, educational background, or handicaps. Minority advocacy is provided through national and international media; SEAC organizes legislative and administrative lobbying and legal action and offers direct social services and English classes for new refugees. SEAC compiles statistics on the Indochinese population and maintains a 600-volume library. The newsletter, *New Life News*, published quarterly, is concerned with the relationships between various Indochinese ethnic groups in the United States, between Indochinese immigrants and Native Americans, and between the eastern and western cultures in general. SEAC also publishes a Indochinese directory and the *Chicago Language Network*.

Japanese Americans

Japanese American Citizens League (JACL)

1765 Sutter St.
San Francisco, CA 94115
(415) 921-5225

Founded in 1929, JACL has eight regional groups and 114 local groups. An educational, civil, and human rights organization, JACL works to defend the civil and human rights of all peoples, particularly Japanese Americans and seeks to preserve their cultural and ethnic heritage. It maintains a Japanese American Citizens League Legislative Education Committee, which conducts lobbying activities for legislation that will protect and benefit Japanese Americans. JACL sponsors athletic competitions; offers scholarships; and bestows awards; its resources include a library and audiovisual materials.

Japanese American Citizens League (JACL)

Central California Regional Office
912 F St.
Fresno, CA 93706-3309
(209) 237-4006

Japanese American Citizens League (JACL)

Pacific Southwest Regional Office
244 S. San Pedro St., Ste. 507
Los Angeles, CA 90012
(213) 626-4471

Japanese American Citizens League (JACL)

1730 Rhode Island Ave. NW, Ste. 204
Washington, DC 20036
(202) 223-1240

Japanese American Citizens League (JACL)

5415 N. Clark St.
Chicago, IL 60640
(312) 728-7171

Japanese American Citizens League (JACL)

2004 Juliet Ave.
St. Paul, MN 55105

Japanese American Citizens League (JACL)

9109 Rusticwood Trail
St. Louis, MO 63126
(314) 842-3138

Japanese American Citizens League (JACL)

120 S. 200 W., No. 201
Salt Lake City, UT 84101
(801) 359-2902

Japanese American Citizens League (JACL) Pacific Northwest District Council

671 S. Jackson, No. 206
Seattle, WA 98104
(206) 623-5088

Korean Americans

Korean American Coalition (KAC)

3921 Wilshire Blvd., Ste. LL100
Los Angeles, CA 90010
(213) 380-6175

Founded in 1983, KAC includes Korean Americans and other Americans working to educate, organize, and empower the Korean community in the United States. KAC seeks to acquaint non-Koreans with Korean culture. KAC collects and disseminates information and conducts educational programs on Korean community issues and leadership development. Other areas of interest to KAC include advocacy, community networking, and voter registration and information seminars. KAC maintains a 200-volume library on Korean and Korean American community-related issues. The *KAC Newsletter* is published monthly.

Korean Scientists and Engineers Association in America (KSEA)

6261 Executive Blvd.
Rockville, MD 20852
(301) 984-7048

Founded in 1971, KSEA consists of scientists and engineers holding single or advanced degrees. KSEA's goals are to promote friendship and mutuality among Korean and U.S. scientists and engineers; contribute to Korea's scientific, technological, industrial, and economic development; and strengthen the scientific, technological, and cultural bonds between Korea and the United States. KSEA sponsors a symposium in addition to maintaining a speakers' bureau, placement service, and biographical archives. KSEA also bestows awards, compiles statistics, and maintains a 100-volume library of scientific handbooks and yearbooks in Korean. The *Membership Directory* is published triennially and the *Newsletter* bimonthly.

Laotian Americans

National Association for the Education and Advancement of Cambodian, Laotian, and Vietnamese Americans

7018 N. Ashland Ave.
Chicago, IL 60626
(312) 793-6638

Founded in 1979, the association was formerly known as the National Association for Vietnamese American Education. It seeks to provide equal educational opportunities for Indochinese Americans; advance the rights of Indochinese Americans; acknowledge and publicize contributions of Vietnamese and other Indochinese in U.S. schools, culture, and society; and to encourage appreciation of Indochinese cultures, peoples, education, and language. The association facilitates the exchange of information and skills among Indochinese professionals and other professionals working with Indochinese Americans. It works toward meeting the legislative needs of Indochinese Americans in education, health, social services, and welfare. The association encourages scholarly excellence and active participation of parents and community members in school and community activities. It conducts networking activities and offers referrals for Indochinese professionals and others working with Indochinese in the fields of education and human services. The association operates a speakers' bureau, sponsors scholarship contests, and conducts workshops. The quarterly newsletter, *Channel for Indochinese American Communication*, contains current information on the education and resettlement of Indochinese refugees and their communities. It includes a calendar of events and a list of available resources. The association has also published a *Directory of Indochinese Personnel in Education and Social Services*.

New National Hmong-Lao Foundation

332 S. St.
Fitchburg, MA 01420
(508) 342-8494

The foundation's services include advocacy, referrals, crisis intervention, job training, and English as a Second Language classes (ESL).

Pacific Islanders

Congress of the Hawaiian People

98-1364 Akaaka St.
Aiea, HI 96701
(808) 488-6905

The congress in a coalition of Hawaiian organizations and individuals who seek to preserve the cultural heritage and improve the social, economic, and educational welfare of the Hawaiian people and their communities.

Daughters of Hawaii

2913 Pali Hwy.
Honolulu, HI 96817
(808) 595-6291

A nonprofit organization, the Daughters of Hawaii works to perpetuate the memory and spirit of old Hawaii and preserve the nomenclature and pronunciation of the Hawaiian language. The group holds meetings and conducts classes.

East-West Center

1777 East-West Rd.
Honolulu, HI 96848
(808) 944-7111

The center provides research conducted through the center's four institutes in the fields of population, economic and trade policies, resources and development, the environment, and culture and communication. Research is also conducted through Student Affairs and Open Grants (SAOG) and the Pacific Islands Development Program. The center was created to promote better relations and understanding between the United States and nations of Asia and the Pacific through cooperative study, training, and research. The center publishes *Asia-Pacific Report*, a periodic review of regional developments.

Center for Asians and Pacific Islanders

1304 E. Lake St.
Minneapolis, MN 55407
(612) 721-1229

State Council on Hawaiian Heritage

PO Box 3022
Honolulu, HI 96807
(808) 536-6540

The council conducts seminars in dance and presents the annual King Kamehameha Hula Competition. It also sponsors conferences and seminars on storytelling, legends, and related topics.

Embassy of New Zealand

37 Observatory Circle, NW
Washington, DC 20008
(202) 328-4800

Embassy of the Federated States of Micronesia

1725 North St., NW
Washington, DC 20036
(202) 223-4383

Embassy of the Republic of Fiji

2233 Wisconsin Ave., NW
Washington, DC 20007
(202) 337-8320

Embassy of the Republic of the Marshall Islands

2433 East-West Rd.
Honolulu, HI 96848
(808) 944-5414

Embassy of the Solomon Islands

c/o The Permanent Mission of the Solomon Islands
    to the U.N.
820 2nd Ave., Ste. 800
New York, NY 10017
(212) 599-6193

Embassy of Western Samoa

1155 15th St., NW, No. 510
Washington, DC 20005
(202) 833-1743

University of Hawaii at Manoa School of Hawaiian, Asian and Pacific Studies

Moore Hall 315
1890 East-West Rd.
Honolulu, HI 96822
(808) 956-8818

Formerly known as the Center for Asian and Pacific Studies, the University serves as the umbrella organization for centers and programs in Chinese studies, Hawaiian studies, Japanese studies, Korean studies, Pacific Island studies, Philippine studies, South Asian studies, Southeast Asian studies and Buddhist studies. Publications include: the *Journal of Contemporary Pacific* and the journals, *Asian Perspectives, Korean Studies,* and *Philosophy East and West.*

Pakistani Americans

U.S.-Pakistan Economic Council (USPAK)

500 5th Ave., Ste. 935
New York, NY 10110
(212) 221-7070

Founded in 1980, USPAK brings together companies interested in promoting U.S. trade with Pakistan and stimulating U.S. investment in Pakistan's economy. USPAK facilitates contact between U.S. and Pakistani government officials and business people, familiarizes the U.S. business community with opportunities for trade and investment, and keeps members informed on current economic conditions in Pakistan. USPAK sponsors conferences and seminars featuring government and business leaders, holds press conferences, and hosts receptions. USPAK publishes the monthly U.S.-Pakistan Bulletin; an annual *U.S. Pakistan Economic Council Membership Directory*, and provides periodic news bulletins on economic trends and business opportunities in Pakistan.

Vietnamese Americans

Indochina Project (IP)

2100 M St., NW, Ste. 607
Washington, DC 20036
(202) 955-0088

The Indochina Project, a project of the Vietnam Veterans of America founded in 1979, promotes peace and understanding by educating the public on current affairs in Southeast Asia. IP gathers and disseminates information on political, economic, and social issues in Laos, Cambodia, and Vietnam. IP maintains a library and archive and publishes the weekly *Indochina Digest* and *Indochina Issues*, ten times per year.

National Association for Vietnamese Education

1405 French St.
Santa Ana, CA 92701
(714) 558-5729

This association advocates for better education and social services for all Indochinese Americans.

Southeast Asia Center (SEAC) See listing under Regional Organizations.

Vietnam Refugee Fund (VRF)
6433 Nothana Dr.
Springfield, VA 22150
(703) 971-9178

Founded in 1971, VRF organizes community and professional volunteers to provide assistance and staff programs aimed at the smooth resettlement of Vietnamese refugees into the United States. It offers counseling, seminars, job information and placement services, and translation and interpretation assistance. VRF intervenes on behalf of Vietnamese refugees and residents in legal matters, assists in organizing citizenship classes, and operates a Vietnamese-language radio program in the Washington, D.C. area.

Religion

◆ Hinduism ◆ Buddhism ◆ Islam ◆ Confucianism ◆ Taoism ◆ Shintoism ◆ The Unification Church

Asian American religious practices are as diverse as those of any population segment. Many Asian Americans are Christians, and can be found in all denominations, from Catholic to Baptist. However, the majority of Asian Americans practice various Asian religions, each of which has specific tenets, teachings, and customs. The major Asian religions are described in the sections that follow.

◆ HINDUISM

Hinduism, or "the eternal religion," is the primary religion of the Indian people. Based upon ancient mythology, it has evolved over thousands of years. Unlike Christianity, Islam, and Buddhism, Hinduism has no founder and its exact history is not known. It has several books of sacred writings, although none of them are considered a definitive canon of beliefs common to all Hindus.

The oldest and most sacred of Hindu writings are the Vedas, a Sanskrit word meaning knowledge, or sacred teaching. These works, which Hindus consider divinely revealed, are vastly longer than the holy scriptures of Western religions—six times the length of the Old and New Testaments together—and predate them by centuries, with most estimates dating their origin no later than 1500 B.C. The Vedas are divided into four books: the Rigaveda, the Samaveda, the Yajurveda, and the Atharveda. Each of these books can in turn be divided into prayers and hymns (Samhitas), rituals (Brahmanas), mysticism (Aranyakas) and Philosophy (Upanishads). Of these sections, perhaps the most important are the Upanishads, which contain the philosophy and wisdom of the gurus ("Hindu spiritual leaders") often in the form of parables.

Over the centuries, Hinduism has produced several schools of thought, or darshanas. Of these belief systems, six are generally singled out as most important: nyaya, which emphasizes logic; vaisheshika, the oldest, which encourages a scientific exploration of nature; sankhya, which probes the evolution of the universe and the nature of consciousness; yoga, a broad term that in this context refers to a set of mental and physical exercises meant to free the spirit from the body; purva-mimamsa, which deals with the purifying nature of Hindu rituals; and Vedanta, which interprets the mystical teachings of the Upanishads.

One of the basic tenets of Hinduism is the immortality of the soul and its reincarnation after the death of the physical body. Hindus believe that the soul is on a timeless journey toward perfection, and that during each lifetime the soul is afforded the opportunity to live in accordance with spiritual principles or to reject them. Those who choose the latter are returned to life in an inferior life form after their death, while those who embrace Hindu principles and live a pure life, are reborn into a higher or improved, life form. These reincarnations continue until the soul achieves perfection and enters a new realm of existence called moksha, after which it is united with Brahman, the underlying force in the universe.

Hinduism also has a pantheon of hundreds of gods, which the faithful worship in a variety of ways. The three most important gods—referred to as the Hindu trinity—are Brahma, the creator of the universe, Shiva, the destroyer of the universe, and Vishnu, the preserver of the universe. Their relative importance varies throughout India. Hindus worship these and other gods in temples which often have several shrines devoted to various deities; the faithful worship as individuals at these shrines, rather than as a congregation. Many Hindus also have shrines in their homes devoted to a particular god at which the family will pray daily.

Hinduism at its heart is a religion and philosophy that teaches the existence of a grand, harmonic interdependence among all living things. It is a way of life in which human action takes on a higher meaning than can be known in the present, and promises greater

Chinese Americans pray in a Buddhist temple in Chinatown, New York, during Chinese New Year celebrations. (AP/Wide World.)

understanding of the nature of reality and ultimately, communion with Brahman.

Hinduism in America

In 1896 the Vedanta Society of New York was established by Swami Vivekanada, a disciple of the great Bengali spiritualist Ramakrishna. Vivekanada had come to the United States as an uninvited speaker at the World's Parliament of Religions held in Chicago in 1893. There, he made a spectacular speech on the oneness of all the world's great religions. Hinduism and the Vedanta Society became quite popular for a time among intellectuals and artists, attracting such turn-of-the-century luminaries as the actress Sarah Bernhardt and the scientist Nikola Tesla. Later Hindu converts included the writers Christopher Isherwood and Aldous Huxley.

Another school of Hinduism appeared in the United States early in the twentieth century with the arrival of Paramahansa Yogananda, a master of the Hindu philosophy known as yoga. He founded the Self-Realization Fellowship and authored the book *Autobiography of a Yogi*. His teachings emphasize exercise, stretching, and special breathing techniques intended to free the self from mind and body and to redirect energy invested in the outside world inward, toward one's spiritual center. Yoga became a very successful practice in the United States, and the Self-Realization Fellowship grew rapidly. Paramahansa (a title given to master yogis) Yogananda stayed in the United States for 30 years, becoming the longest-serving Hindu master in the West.

A more recent influx of Hindu thought occurred during the late 1960s and early 1970s with the Transcendental Meditation (TM) movement led by the Maharishi Mahesh Yogi. The Maharishi became an international celebrity in 1967 when members of the popular music group the Beatles became disciples during a trip to India. As a result, TM became a trendy, largely religionless movement emphasizing the physical, mental, and spiritual aspects of meditation, rather than the spiritual.

Other Hindu-associated movements have become popular in the United States, among them the Krishna Consciousness movement, whose members are known as the Hare Krishnas. Unfortunately, these popular usurpations of Hindu worship tend to attract celebrities such as the Beatles—whose largely ignorant adoption of Hinduism—a centuries-old religion, philosophy, and culture tends to trivialize it in the eyes of Americans. Many see it as exotic and trendy, cultist, or just plain lunatic, when in fact the vast majority of practicing Hindus in the United States are as devoted and serious about their faith as are Christians and Jews.

◆ BUDDHISM

Buddhism was founded in the sixth century B.C. by Siddharta Gautama, a prince in India who abandoned his life of wealth and prestige to seek enlightenment as a wandering monk. His faith in Hinduism had been shaken by his observation that life was full of meaningless suffering, and that if the Hindu doctrine of reincarnation were correct, this suffering would continue after death into the next life.

Gautama pondered this dilemma during his six years of itinerant poverty. In an instant of enlightenment, he is said to have discovered the solution, called the Four Noble Truths. These truths state that life is fraught with suffering brought about by ignorance and craving, and to remedy this existence one must follow the Eightfold Path, a series of laws geared toward living a more virtuous life. Gautama believed that by practicing the Eightfold Path enlightenment and salvation could be attained.

As Gautama began to teach his new insights, called the dharma, or "saving truth," he obtained a wide following and earned the name Buddha, meaning the "enlightened one." As his teachings began to take hold, the Buddha organized his followers into a community of monks and nuns, the Sangha, who were supported by a large lay following. Over time, Buddhism spread throughout India and then into other parts of southern Asia, especially Southeastern Asia, where today variations of Buddhism are the predominant religion. In India, where the religion was born, it is no longer a major force.

The major schools of Buddhist thought in existence today are Theravada, Mahayana, Mantrayana, and Zen. Theravada Buddhism, which is predominant in Sri Lanka, Thailand, Myanmar, and Cambodia, is based upon the Pali canon (sacred Buddhist texts) and supports a nontheistic universe in which salvation is reserved for a limited number of people. While it too is based upon the Pali canon, Mahayana Buddhism, which is practiced in China, Japan, Vietnam, and Korea, is more liberal than Theravada Buddhism, stressing universal salvation. Mantrayana Buddhism and Zen Buddhism, practiced in Tibet, Mongolia, and Japan, are closely related religious branches, which chiefly focus on meditation. It is difficult to estimate the number of Buddhists in the world because many adherents practice other religions as well.

Buddhist doctrine is contained in a collection of scriptures called the Tripitaka, or "Three Baskets" often referred to as the dharma. Its basic tenets, called samsara, are that existence is a cycle of life, death, and rebirth and that one's circumstances in the present life are largely a consequence of their behavior in a previous one. To attain higher and higher states of existence ultimately leading to nirvana—a condition of perfect peace and freedom from samsara—one must follow the Middle Way and the Noble Eightfold Path.

The Middle Way is a life void of extremes, not given entirely to satisfying human desires, nor to complete self-denial and self-torture. The Noble Eightfold Path is made up of (1) perfect view, which involves understanding the Four Noble Truths and the concept of collective existence; (2) perfect resolve, or resolving to do no harm to any being and to act with good will; (3) perfect speech, which decries lying, slander, and speaking in a way that would hurt others; (4) perfect conduct, or behaving in accordance with moral principle; (5) perfect livelihood, or avoiding professions that harm other beings; (6) perfect effort, or avoiding unwholesome behavior; (7) perfect mindfulness, or retaining mindfulness of one's body, feelings, and thoughts; and (8) perfect concentration.

Zen Buddhism

Zen Buddhism is Buddhist sect that is predominant in East Asia, particularly Japan, where it has had a deep cultural influence. Zen is also popular in the United States and is practiced by both Asian and non-Asian Americans. Like Buddhism itself, Zen has several schools of thought, two of which are most prominent. The Rinzai emphasizes meditation on koans, or unsolvable riddles, and the Soto relies upon emptying the mind through meditation. The ultimate goal of Zen Buddhism is the attainment of inner peace and spiritual enlightenment, called satori. Zen, more than any other form of Buddhism, teaches its followers to rely upon meditation when seeking enlightenment, while downplaying the importance of ritual and philosophical inquiry that mark other Buddhist schools.

In the history of Zen, many teachers have attained a sudden enlightenment, which is said to be transmitted from "heart-mind to heart-mind," a phrase that reflects the anti-intellectualism of the religion. A popular story illustrating this method tells of the master Buddha Shakyamuni, who gathered his disciples for a sermon in which he held up a single flower in silence. This gesture is said to have sparked a sudden enlightenment in one particular student, beginning the tradition of such enlightenment in Zen.

An artist paints lace designs on the hands of a Muslim bride in New York, using crushed henna leaves. (AP/Wide World.)

Buddhism in America

Of the major East Asian religions, Buddhism is perhaps the most prominent in the United States. Historically, it has been associated with counterculture figures like the poets of the Beat era and numerous intellectuals. The first Zen school in the United States was founded in 1930 by Shigetsu Sasaki. Following this school's decline after the Second World War, the practice and teachings of Zen were mainly transmitted in the writings of D. T. Suzuki and his American wife Beatrice Lane Suzuki. Suzuki lectured on Zen at Columbia University in the 1950s, influencing a generation of philosophers and writers, among them Christian Humphreys and Alan Watts, two of the most influential American writers on Zen. In the 1950s and 1960s the philosophy of Zen was popularized—some would say greatly simplified—by the writers of the Beat generation, most notably Jack Kerouac, who romanticized its charm and simplicity.

In more recent times Zen and Tibetan Buddhism have become popular among a new generation of intellectuals and artists. The Dalai Lama, the spiritual leader of Tibetan Buddhism who lives in exile in India,

has become something of a celebrity in the United States as he seeks to influence China's colonial grip on Tibet, which it has occupied for decades.

There are many Buddhist monasteries in the United States, and they have in recent times become favored celebrity retreats. As noted in the section on Hinduism, however, the vast majority of Buddhists in the United States are Asian Americans who practice their faith outside of the spotlight of popular culture.

♦ ISLAM

Islam is the fastest-growing religion in the world today, and its followers can be found on all inhabited continents. Founded by the prophet Mohammed in the seventh century, Islam has much in common with the Jewish and Christian religious traditions found in the Old and New Testaments. Like Judaism and Christianity, Islam is an Abrahamic faith, which means that its original followers are descendants of Abraham, a major figure found in the Old Testament and the Koran, the holy book of Islam. Followers of Islam consider Jesus a prophet, but, as followers of Judaism, deny the claim to his deity found in the New Testament—the cornerstone of Christianity. According to Islam, Mohammed is also a prophet, but his teachings are considered the final revelations of God, thus superseding all teaching that came before them. After Mohammed's death in 632, a series of caliphs, or religious leaders spread his teachings throughout the Middle East, southern Europe, northern Africa, and central and southern Asia.

Muslims (the name for adherents to Islam) believe that God revealed the Koran to Mohammed (believed to have been illiterate), who transcribed it. Muslims use the Koran as a guide for nearly every aspect of their lives, from relations within the family to, in some countries, the foundation of their laws. Islam teaches that God is just and merciful and that followers can attain paradise after death if they obey God's edicts in life. Islam, like Christianity and Judaism, commands a strict moral code on its adherents, emphasizing honesty, kindness, brotherly love, and obedience to God. Islam is a highly ritualized religion that imposes duties on its followers, which are called the Five Pillars of Faith. These pillars are: (1) belief in the unity of God and the prophethood of Mohammed; (2) prayer; (3) fasting; (4) almsgiving; and (5) pilgrimage. Worshippers gather in mosques for communal prayer, led by imams. Islam does not have an organized priesthood, so any suitably trained and educated person in a community can serve as an imam.

Many Americans associate Islam only with the Middle East, but it is the dominant religion in Pakistan, parts of India, Bangladesh, Indonesia, Malaysia, and parts of Africa. Immigrants from these areas, as well as those from the Middle East, combined with American converts, have contributed to the significant spread of Islam in the United States and throughout the world.

◆ CONFUCIANISM

Confucianism is not strictly a religion, but a set of moral beliefs taught by the Chinese philosopher Confucius (K'ung-tzu), who himself adapted them from ancient philosophers. The tenets of Confucianism center around the concepts of jen and li. Jen is a combination of the characters for "human being" and for "two"; it embodies the most important aspect of Confucianism, the empathetic humanity that should be at the foundation for human relations. Li is a combination of morality and etiquette, custom and ritual.

Confucianism does not have a clergy, nor does it address the metaphysical aspects of religion, such as the life of the soul or the meaning of death and suffering. Many people consider Confucianism an ethical, political, and civic philosophy—yet its impact on the history of China has been so profound that it defies such a limiting stricture.

Confucius was born into a noble family in 551 B.C. in what is now the Shantung province of China during a time of social upheaval. He spent his working life as a civil servant in various posts and studied China's ancient philosophers with a variety of teachers. He began to revive the teachings and ideas of the ancients in an attempt to restore the social and civil order in the country through philosophical enlightenment. While Confucius attracted a small group of followers who revered him and his teachings, he died in relative obscurity in about 479 B.C.

Scholars of Confucius have not been able to determine with any certainty if the philosopher wrote any books; however, several books have been attributed to him, and a collection of his teachings, the Analects, was compiled by his disciples. Aside from the concepts of jen and li, Confucianism teaches that successful individual human relations form the basis of society. To bring order to society, one must first bring order to the family, which will ultimately bring order to the community, which will bring order to the government. The process was also thought to work in reverse—that is, if a ruler is righteous, his subjects will be righteous as well.

Another Confucian belief is that roles have to be clearly articulated and fulfilled to avoid civic chaos. In other words a prince must be princely, a mother must be matronly, and a son must behave with filial reverence. Confucius taught that each name contains an essence, and that there is an assault on social order and harmony if this essence is done an injustice.

Confucianism heavily influenced Chinese, Korean, and Japanese life for more than two thousand years. Over time, many teachers added to the philosophical canon expanding its original ideas beyond the purely civic level. Its influence varied throughout Chinese history, but it fell into official disfavor with the Communist takeover of China in 1949. However, in deference to the people's continued reliance on its teachings, the communist government's lifted its official ban on Confucianism in 1977.

◆ TAOISM

While Taoism is often considered a religion, like Confucianism it is a philosophy as well. The word Tao means "the way," and was used by Lao-tzu, its founder, to describe the essence of reality that exists independent of human experience—the primordial essence of all things from which all appearances arise.

Taoism as a philosophy (called Tao-chia) originated in China and dates from the third century B.C. Its teachings are found in the writings of Lao-tzu, called the Tao-te Ching. Recent scholars of this text, however, believe that it may have been written by more than one person. In many ways Taoism was formed in reaction to Confucianism, then the dominant philosophy of China. Taoism, for example, encourages wu-wei, or spontaneous, non-premeditated action, which is an attribute of Taoist saints. Confucianism, on the other hand, prescribes strict rules of behavior and action. Like Buddhists, philosophical Taoists use meditation to achieve enlightenment, which they define as a mystical union with the Tao.

Religious Taoism, or Tao-chiao, dates from the first century B.C. its central tenet is the quest for spiritual immortality. There are many schools of religious Taoism, each with its own path to immortality. Among them are the Inner Deity Hygiene School, the Way of Right Unity, the School of the Magic Jewel, Five-Pecks-of-Rice Taoism, and the Way of Supreme Peace. All use meditation, breathing and physical exercises, alchemy, sexual practices, fasting, confession, and spiritual healing.

◆ SHINTOISM

Shintoism, or "the way of the gods," is the oldest religion still practiced in Japan. Adherents worship a large number of gods, called *kami*, several of which are believed to form the essence of nature and all of its parts, including mountains, trees, oceans, and rocks. For example, it is believed that the Japanese imperial family is descended from Amaterasu, the sun-goddess. Other kami include the divinities of great warriors, poets, scholars, and other historical figures, as well as the souls of family ancestors called uji. Kami are thought to determine human creativity, illness, and healing. Early shrines were probably rocks and trees, where kami were believed to live.

While Shintoism has no actual canon of scripture, elements of the religion can be traced back to ancient Japanese mythology and found in the kojiki and Nihonshoki texts. Shintoism places heavy emphasis on morality and rituals, as well as on matters of immediate concern. Unlike other religions, which tend to concentrate on the meaning of life or the nature of death, followers of Shintoism are far more likely to pray for good health, a bountiful harvest, or the end of a drought. Worshippers also pray during certain important stages of life, such as birth, marriage, and death. Many followers have one or more shrines, called inja, in their homes at which they make offerings to particular kami. Each shrine contains sacred objects, named go-shintai, significant to these kami. There are also public shrines throughout Japan. Shintoism has a strong link to Japanese society and even to the government. For many years, it was used to cultivate loyalty and devotion to the state.

The origin of Shintoism is not known, although many of its tenets and practices date back thousands of years to pre-agricultural Japan. No one person is credited with its founding and no human is venerated as a deity, although during the nineteenth century and through the end of World War II the emperor was considered a god.

Shinto priests often lead large ritual prayers such as the Great Purification Ceremony in which followers give a mass confession and plea for absolution. Historically, Shinto priests came from noble clans or families and served the local lord. They acted as a mediator between the people and the kami and directed the ritual offerings that were made to the spirits. In medieval Japan, these priests started schools that taught Shintoism in an effort to preserve the philosophy in the face of burgeoning Buddhist and confucianist influences. Today only large Shinto shrines have full-time priests; the smaller ones are served by part-time priests chosen from local families. After World War II and the subsequent occupation of Japan by the United States, many Shinto shrines were dismantled. Since that time, however, Shintoism has been revitalized and has come to be regarded as one of the most important religions in Japan.

◆ THE UNIFICATION CHURCH

Founded in 1954 after the Korean War, the Unification Church of Rev. Sun Myung Moon has become a worldwide ministry, noted as much for its fabled assets and behind-the-scenes power politicking as for its spiritual message.

According to church accounts, the beginnings can be traced to Easter 1936, when Jesus and other religious figures from world religions appeared to sixteen-year-old Moon, conferring on him a mission to establish the Kingdom of heaven on earth. After schooling in Seoul and a course of study in electrical engineering in Japan, Moon returned to Korea and, legend has it, was imprisoned in 1943 for subversive religious and political activities by the Japanese occupation forces. In 1946, after the end of the World War II, Moon established his first church in northern Korea at Pyeongyang. More torture and imprisonment in a Communist forced labor camp followed, until Moon's liberation by United Nations forces in 1950.

A refugee camp at Pusan became a base of operations for the teaching of Moon's message, referred to as "The Principle." He spread his message from a hut built of discarded ration boxes. The first major church was founded in 1954 in Seoul, and again Moon was imprisoned, this time by the civil government of South Korea for alleged ritual sexual activities. In 1955, the Church moved to Chungpadong, site of its world headquarters until 1971, when it was relocated to New York.

Since that time, Moon's movement has grown to include an immense following of at least 200,000 (Bob Larson's 1987 "Book of Cults" estimates 2 million) in some 100 countries. Reliable figures are not available, but the core of Unification Church membership in the United States is generally believed to number between 10,000 and 30,000.

Moon's theology reached expression in its present form in the 1957 publication, *The Divine Principle*, the 536-page basic text and bible of the Unification Church. Its complex teachings assert, among other things, that the Unification Church under the leadership of Reverend Moon has as its mandate from heaven the literal unification of all Christian sects, as well as all other faiths. The essence of the "Divine Principle's" message, and the foundation of the Unification Church is the unstated assumption that Moon is the Messiah, the actual Lord of the Second Coming. Much of the "Divine Principle" is devoted to demonstrations and scriptural "proofs" of the suitability of Korea as the birthplace of Moon and his movement, pinpointing the timeframe within which the final Messianic birth and action should take place.

In outline, the revelations of the "Principle" deny that the Crucifixion of Jesus was a part of God's plan, instead characterizing this central event of traditional Christianity as a sort of historical blunder, partly the fault of John the Baptist (who is believed to have failed to have recognized Jesus as the Messiah), and partly of the Jews as a nation.

The accomplishment of the true divine plan, according to Moon, was deferred until the present time, and must involve an acting out of the original scheme of redemption. Moon says that Eve had sexual relations with Lucifer in his serpent form, giving birth to Cain and polluting the bloodline of humanity. Had Jesus, considered by Moon to be the second Adam or incarnation of the "True Father," not been executed and his mission prematurely ended, he would have married his counterpart, the second Eve, and thus redeemed the first parents, saving and renewing mankind. This consummation, then, is part of Moon's task on earth, his role as the Third Adam. Moon's fourth marriage in the middle 1950s to Hak Ja Han seems to have marked his success in finding the Third Eve.

Unification theology also tells of the battle of good and evil, represented in our time by democratic and communist ideologies. It teaches that the final conflict or third world war is currently being fought, by relatively peaceful economic and spiritual means so far, thanks to Moon. Unification Church members have been best known as "moonies" in the United States during the 1980s and 1990s. They are unflappably serene proselytizers who roam the streets of U.S. cities seeking converts and selling roses. Whether some or any of these have in fact been victims of "brainwashing," as is frequently alleged in an alarmed press or by outraged parents, has been difficult to prove.

The scandal-provoking mass marriages of Church members conducted by Moon remain a typical feature of the religion. The September 14, 1992 edition of the *Japan Times* reported a ceremony in which 25,000 couples were married at Seoul's Olympic Stadium, rousing much antagonism in ecclesiastical and media circles. As single persons must wait seven years before the Church will hand-pick a mate for them, such ceremonies are scheduled at long intervals. Worth noting is the price tag—a fee of between $2400 and $8000 per head—is reported as the current rate for these mandatory Church marriages. As the movement has grown richer and more powerful, "Moonie" panhandlers and other "grassroots" aspects of the church's activity have become less visible. Moon's strategies in the 1990s, as gleaned from news reports, have typically involved the acquisition of major corporations and a gradual cultivation of political influence. This, in turn, is made possible through the patient nurturing of credibility in academic and journalistic spheres, through means both direct and oblique.

By the 1960s, estimates put the net worth of the Unification Church and its tea, titanium, and munitions conglomerates at around $20 million. Since then Moon, supported by key Korean and Japanese industrialists such as right wing shipping magnate Rioichi Sasakawa, has expanded his international holdings to include businesses and corporations as diverse as Christian Bernard (luxury jewelry), Bridgeport University in Connecticut, the New Yorker Hotel in Manhattan, *The Washington Times*, the *New York City Tribune*, *INSIGHT Magazine*, and fishing and restaurant interests like International Oceanic Enterprises and Uniworld Sea Enterprises. As of the mid-1990s, the net worth of all these is said to be in the billions, with at least $1 billion invested in the United States. Highlights of Moon's political moves include his 1975 defense of Richard Nixon during the Watergate scandal and a private 1990 meeting with Soviet leader Mikhail Gorbachev, during which Moon reportedly offered aid to the failing Soviet economy.

The Unification Church currently operates 55 large centers of worship in the United States, at least one in every state, plus 206 smaller churches. Moon's politically oriented operations and holdings include the American Freedom Coalition, Professors World Peace Academy, Washington Institute for Values in Public Policy, and CAUSA USA (Confederation of Associations for the Unification of American Societies), an organization specializing in anti-communist activities, from congressional lobbying to support of the Nicaraguan contras.

References

Barker, Eileen, *The Making of a Moonie*, Oxford: B. Blackwell, 1984.

Durst, Mose, *To Bigotry, No Sanction*, Chicago: Regnery Gateway 1984.

Encyclopedia Brittanica, Micropedia, *The Unification Church.*

Frahme, Robert A., and Katherine Farrish "UB Bailout," *Hartford Courant*, May 3, 1992 pg A1+.

Larson, Bob: *Larson's Book of Cults*, Wheaton, Ill.: Tyndale House, 1987.

Maxwell, Joe, "New Kingdoms for the Cults," *Christianity Today*, January 13, 1992, pg. 37-41.

Takahashi, Kazuko, "Media Madness Mirrors Mass Moonie Marriages," *Japan Times*, Sep. 14, 1992, pgs.6-7.

—*Jim Henry and Douglas Utter*

Literature

♦ Introduction ♦ Asian American Literary History ♦ Asian American Writers

♦ INTRODUCTION

What is "Asian American literature?" Is it literature written by people of Asian ancestry living in the United States? Does it include works written in Chinese or Korean, or only those written in English? Must it be written by Asian Americans, or can anyone write on Asian American themes and call it Asian American literature?

In the past two decades, Asian American writers have answered these and related questions more fully than can be done in this brief essay. They have produced a body of work that has revolutionized the way that Asian Americans are viewed by the mainstream culture, and the way that they view themselves. In describing the experiences of Asian Americans, they have swept away the stereotypical images of the "heathen Chinese," the "yellow peril," and the "Confucius-say Number One Son." In the process, meanwhile, they have started to define the contours of a field whose boundaries remain fluid.

Asian American literature remained relatively unpublished until the 1970s. The few hangouts for Asian American writers and artists were known only by word of mouth in the overlapping artistic and social change communities. They included the Kearney Street Workshop and Japantown Arts and Media in San Francisco, Visual Communications in Los Angeles, and the Basement Workshop in New York's Chinatown.

By the mid-1980s, the choice of literature had grown considerably. Reflecting the arrival of newer communities of South Asians and Southeast Asians to the established communities of Chinese, Japanese, Korean, and Filipino Americans, works by artists with names like Wong, Bulosan, and Yamamoto had been supplemented by those with names like Mukherjee and Tran. Asian American women's literature had begun to take shape, as well, and works in Asian languages were being added to the Asian American literary canon.

In the mid-1990s, literary works by Asian American authors are being published in record numbers. No firm sales figures are available because these books are often published by private and university presses as well as commercial ventures. Nevertheless, the commercial success of Maxine Hong Kingston, Amy Tan, and other best-selling authors proves not only that Asian Americans can write but that their work has mass-market appeal.

Following the advice of King-kok Cheung and Stan Yogi, who have compiled the most comprehensive bibliography of Asian American literature to date, this essay will assume a definition of Asian American literature that is as broad as possible. To paraphrase Cheung and Yogi, this definition includes every writer of full or partial Asian descent in the United States or Canada, regardless of where they were born, when they settled in North America, or how they interpret their experiences. Only writings in English will be discussed, although Asian American literature in Asian languages is an increasingly important field of inquiry since the immigrants' thoughts are expressed best in letters, poems, and diary entries in their native languages.

Professor Elaine Kim of the University of California at Berkeley wrote the first book-length treatment of Asian American literature in 1982, and noted two problems facing Asian American writers: Either their writing is interpreted as a sociological statement about the group, or their literary style is viewed as all-important while the content is virtually ignored. Following Kim's lead, this essay will place the writers and works in their socio-historical and cultural contexts, and, in so doing, show the limitations of both of these problematic approaches. Capsule biographies of selected Asian American writers will complete the chapter.

♦ ASIAN AMERICAN LITERARY HISTORY

Although Asian Americans have been in the United States in sizable numbers since the 1850s, passing down their stories as though oral narratives, the earliest surviving Asian American writing dates from almost 40 years later. Reasons for this include the fact that early immigrant laborers had neither time nor sufficient education to write down their experiences. In addition, the autobiographical writing style popular in European countries was too self-promotive to be popular in Chinese or other Asian literary traditions.

By the late 1800s, Asian Americans had already spent decades picking crops and hauling railroad ties, and many state and federal legislators had been busy passing laws to restrict immigrant lifestyles and business opportunities. Therefore, it was with some irony that the earliest surviving piece of Asian American literature deals not with the trials and tribulations of life in the United States, but with life in China. *When I Was a Boy in China*, published by Lee Phan Phou in 1887, is an autobiographical account of daily life in China, including food, ceremonies, and games. Two other early works written by sisters born of a Chinese mother and an English father were similarly removed from the experiences of the majority of their Chinese American brethren. Edith Maude Eaton, born in England and raised in Canada, wrote the short story "A Chinese Feud" in 1896 under the pseudonym Sui Sin Far. Younger sister Winnifred, using the pseudonym Onoto Watanna, wrote the novel *Miss Nume of Japan* in 1899.

Other early works included autobiographies such as Etsu Sugimoto's *A Daughter of the Samurai*, Younghill Kang's *East Goes West*, Pardee Lowe's *Father and Glorious Descendant*, and Jade Snow Wong's *Fifth Chinese Daughter*. Many of these early works were written by both immigrant and second-generation Asian Americans yearning for acceptance in white Christian society. The pen and ink in the authors parlors was a world apart from the hammers and chisels of their countrymen in the mining camps in Nevada. Seldom did these writers hear the voices of railroad workers being lowered in baskets down the sides of high mountains to insert dynamite charges into tiny crevasses of flint, or those of grape pickers sweating under a cloudless California sky. A notable exception is Carlos Bulosan, essayist, poet, and writer of the classic *America Is in the Heart*.

During World War II, the United States government unjustly uprooted and interned over 120,000 Japanese Americans, even though two-thirds were U.S. citizens by birth and not charged with any crime. Any illusion that Asian Americans were as American as their European American peers was shattered by three and a half years behind barbed wire in the windswept deserts of the American West. The brutal psychological and social impact of this experience was, for many internees, too painful to discuss openly, even with family. Paradoxically, this experience was eloquently described in an outpouring of notable stories, novels, plays, and poems. John Okada's novel *No No Boy*, Wakako Yamauchi's story and play *And the Soul Shall Dance*, Mine Okubo's pictorial essay *Citizen 13660*, Hisaye Yamamoto's "The Legend of Miss Sasagawara," and Toshio Mori's *Woman From Hiroshima*, are but a few of the works spawned by this tragic episode in U.S. history.

The social change movement of the early 1970s, seeking to redefine Asian American identity and empower Asian Americans while challenging many fundamental beliefs and practices of mainstream society, led several California-based Asian American writers to define a collective body of work known as Asian American literature. Notables in this regard include Bruce Iwasaki of UCLA's Asian American Studies Center and Ronald Tanaka of Sacramento State University, as well as the following authors and editors: Kai-yu Hsu and Helen Palubinskas, editors of *Asian American Authors*; Frank Chin, Jeffrey Paul Chan, Lawson Fusao Inada, and Shawn Wong, editors of *Aiiieeeee! An Anthology of Asian American Writers* as well as *The Big Aiiieeeee! An Anthology of Chinese American and Japanese American Literature*. (What was called Asian American in 1974 did not encompass the full breadth of Asian American writing published by 1991, so the editors narrowed the title's scope appropriately; the introductory essay of the 1991 edition discusses this and other provocative Asian American literature issues); Brenda Paik Sunoo, editor of *Korean American Writings*; the Basement Workshop artists who produced *Yellow Pearl*; and David Hsin-fu Wand, editor of *Asian American Heritage: An Anthology of Prose and Poetry*.

The emerging awareness that Asian Americans have a literature of their own, combined with growing numbers of post-1965 immigrants (Asian Indians, Southeast Asians, and others educated in U.S. schools), have resulted in even more Asian American writing. Authors such as Amy Tan and dramatists such as David Henry Hwang (see "Theatre"), have brought some aspects of the Asian American experience into the mainstream of U.S. culture. Lastly, with the publication of literary criticism of Asian American texts, a new stage has been reached in this burgeoning field.

From the anxious poetry inscribed in Chinese characters in 1910 on the walls of the detention center on Angel Island in San Francisco harbor, to the biting humor of Frank Chin's "Chicken-Coop Chinaman," to the feminist insight in Maxine Hong Kingston's best-selling novel *Woman Warrior*, Asian Americans have consistently sought to share their experiences with others. Nevertheless, despite their best efforts, European American authors who wrote stories about detective Charlie Chan, warlord Fu Manchu, and other mythical characters created stereotypes that continue to define the Asian American community for millions of U.S. readers.

Fortunately, in the more than two decades since the outpouring of Asian American literature that began in the 1970s, Asian American stories have appeared on television, movies, and on the stage. Asian Americans have appeared in anthologies as U.S. writers, whose poems and stories are of concern to all people. In short, the rivulet of Asian American writing that began in the late-nineteenth century has become a torrent that will mix with and help to define the flow of the U.S. literary stream for decades to come.

—*Philip Tajitsu Nash*

◆ ASIAN AMERICAN WRITERS

Adult Literature

Ai

Ai, a native of the American Southwest, has two poems included in *The Open Boat: Poems from Asian America*. Her first book, *Cruelty*, appeared in 1973. Her second work, *Killing Floor*, was the 1978 Lamont poetry selection of the Academy of American Poets. In 1986, her third book, *Sin*, was published and won an American Book Award from the Before Columbus Foundation. It was followed by her fourth book, *Fate*, published in 1991.

Agha Shahid Ali

Agha Shahid Ali is a poet from Kashmir. He has published two books of poetry, *The Half-Inch Himalayas* and *A Nostalgist's Map of America*. He has also published a book of literary criticism, *T. S. Eliot as Editor* and a translation of a book of poems by Faiz Ahmed Faiz, an Urdu poet, entitled *The Rebel's Silhouette*. He has won fellowships from the Pennsylvania Council on the Arts, Bread Loaf Writers' Conference, and the Ingram Merrill Foundation. Four of his poems were included in *The Open Boat: Poems from Asian American*.

Indran Amirthanayagam (1960-)

Born and raised in Sri Lanka, Amirthanayagam attended college in the United States, receiving his B.A. from Haverford College and M.A. in journalism from Columbia University. His first published collection of poems, *The Elephants of Reckoning* appeared in 1992. In addition, three of Amirthanayagam's poems were included in *The Open Boat: Poems from Asian America*; and other works have been published in *Grand Street*, *The Kenyon Review*, and *The Massachusetts Review*.

Lynda Barry.

Peter Bacho (1950-)

Peter Bacho is a novelist and short-story writer whose debut novel, *Cebu*, was published in 1991. He has also published short fiction in *Amerasia Journal*, *Zyzzyva* and the *Seattle Review*. Before becoming a writer, Bacho worked as an attorney, journalist, and professor of law and Philippine history at the University of Washington.

Lynda Barry (1956-)

Cartoonist Lynda Barry first recognized the value of her artistic talent in second grade when one day she drew an orange grove to illustrate the letter O. With her newfound recognition, she knew she had found her calling. It's a story, in short, that could have come straight out of her popular "Ernie Pook's Comeek," published weekly, in more than 60 alternative publications throughout the United States and Canada.

Barry was born in Seattle, and grew up in a working-class neighborhood. Her Filipino mother worked as a hospital janitor and her Irish-Norwegian father worked as a meatcutter at a supermarket. When Barry was 14, her father left her mother alone to raise her and her two brothers.

Barry studied fine arts at Evergreen State College in Washington, where she became friends with other cartoonists, including Matt Groening, the creator of "The Simpsons." Barry got her big break as a cartoonist a few years after graduation when the *Chicago Reader*, an alternative weekly, began running her strip. It soon caught the attention of other alternative weeklies, including New York's *Village Voice*, and eventually went in to syndication.

In 1977, the strip evolved into "Ernie Pook's Comeek," which she named after her little brother's turtles. The four-panel serial strip, drawn in a scratchy childlike style, follows the adventures of Arna, Arnold, Freddie, Maybonne, and Marlys, a group of children growing up in the 1960s.

Barry's works have been collected and published as books. Her earlier books often chronicled innocent rites of passage, like bad haircuts and a shared first smoke, but her later collections have tackled more serious subjects. Her 1992 collection, *My Perfect Life*, takes on issues like race, sex, alcoholism, and religion. In 1994 she released her eighth book, *It's So Magic*.

Barry has also tried other artistic media. In 1988, she published her first novel, *The Good Times Are Killing Me*, which later won the Washington State Governor Writer's Award. In 1990, she became a commentator for National Public Radio's "Morning Edition." Prior to that she wrote a strip on gender relations for *Esquire* magazine, and for several years she produced a fiction column for the progressive political magazine *Mother Jones*.

In 1994, Barry was living in Minneapolis, and had released a CD, *The Lynda Barry Experience*, featuring readings of her short stories. She also completed her first television special, *Grandma's Way-Out Party*, which aired on KCTS in Minneapolis. In addition, she was working on her second novel, *Crudd*. Despite her busy schedule, she has remained loyal to her first love, cartooning.

Mei-mei Berssenbrugge (1947-)

Born in Beijing in 1947, Mei-mei Berssenbrugge grew up in Massachusetts. She received her B.A. from Reed College and her M.F.A. from Columbia University. In 1989, Station Hill Press published her book, *Empathy*, which won the PEN/West Award in poetry. She has five poems included in *The Open Boat: Poems from Asian America*. Berssenbrugge lives in New Mexico.

Carlos Bulosan (1913-1956)

Bulosan, a Filipino American poet and author is one of America's most prolific writers. His autobiography *America Is in the Heart*, published in 1946, was hailed as one of the 50 most important U.S. books. In it, he told of his search for an ideal United States he had learned of in school, and the real, often harsh United States he found when he immigrated. The book captured the Filipino American experience during the 1930s and 1940s.

Born in the Luzon province of Pangasinan, he was 17 when he came to the United States at the beginning of the Great Depression, and often experienced the racism and violence other Filipinos suffered during the period.

Bulosan considered himself, above all, a poet and built his literary reputation on the genre. In the first year of the war, he published two thin volumes of poetry, *Letter from America* and *Chorus for America*. Later that year he was included in *Who's Who in America*.

In 1934 he published the historically significant long poem, "The Voice of Bataan," written in memory of soldiers killed there. The same year, he published *The New Tide*, a radical bimonthly literary magazine. In 1944, *The Laughter of My Father* was published. An instant wartime success, it was translated into several European languages and was transmitted worldwide over wartime radio.

Jeffrey Paul Chan

Chan is one of four coeditors of *Aiiieeeee! An Anthology of Asian American Writers*, and its sequel, *The Big Aiiieeeee!*.

Diana Chang

Diana Chang is a poet, novelist, and painter who teaches in both the English department and the Program in the Arts at Barnard College. Her novels are: *Frontiers of Love, A Woman of Thirty, A Passion for Life, The Only Game in Town, Eye to Eye, A Perfect Love*. Chang published a volume of poetry, *The Horizon Is Definitely Speaking*, in 1982. Her poems are also included in *Breaking Silence: An Anthology of Contemporary Asian American Poets*.

Edmond Yi-Teh Chang (1965-)

Edmond Yi-Teh Chang was born in Taiwan and lived both there and in Libya before coming to the United States in 1980 at the age of 15. He earned a B.A. with honors in history and international relations from Tufts University, and received an M.F.A. from the renowned Writer's Workshop at the University of Iowa in 1991. Three of Chang's poems are included in *The Open Boat: Poems from Asian America*.

Frank Chin (1940-)

Frank Chin is a playwright, critic, novelist, and short-story writer. He has published two novels, *Donald Duk* and *Gunga Din*; a collection of short stories, *The*

Chinaman Pacific and Frisco R.R. Co.; and several plays and essays. He is also an editor and a highly quotable activist in the field of Asian American literature.

In 1974, he coedited *Aiiieeeee!: An Anthology of Asian American Writers*, and in 1991 coedited *The Big Aiiieeeee!: An Anthology of Chinese American and Japanese American Literature*. Both works take rigid stands in defining Asian American literature that the editors consider worthy of note and true to the cultural heritage of Asian Americans. Chin faults many mainstream writers with pandering to what he considers white America's delusions about the nature of Asian American culture, and as such has created considerable public controversy with writers such as Maxine Hong Kingston and Amy Tan.

Chin has received many awards for his work, including a grant from the National Endowment for the Arts, the 1992 Lannan Literary Fellowship for fiction, the Joseph Henry Jackson Award, the 1971 East-West Players Playwrighting Award and a Rockefeller Playwright's grant in 1974.

Marilyn Chin

Marilyn Chin was born in Hong Kong and raised in Portland, Oregon. She received her undergraduate degree in ancient Chinese literature from the University of Massachusetts at Amherst, and her M.F.A. in poetry from the renowned Writer's Workshop at the University of Iowa in 1981. Chin is a highly regarded poet whose work is frequently anthologized. She is included in *The Norton Introduction to Poetry* and *The Open Boat: Poems from Asian America*. Her first collection of poetry, *Dwarf Bamboo*, was nominated for a Bay Area Book Reviewers Award in 1987. Her poems have appeared in such publications as *The Iowa Review*, *Ploughshares*, *The Kenyon Review*, and *Parnassus*. She is the recipient of a Stegner Fellowship, a National Endowment for the Arts writing fellowship, and a Mary Roberts Reinhart Award. Chin has held residency grants from Yaddo, the MacDowell Colony, Centrum, Virginia Center for the Creative Arts, and the Djerassi Foundation.

Eric Chock (1950-)

Eric Chock received his B.A. from the University of Pennsylvania and his M.A. from the University of Hawaii. He is poet and program coordinator for the Hawaii Poets in the Schools Program in Honolulu. His first book, *Last Days Here*, was published in 1990; three of his poems are included in *The Open Boat: Poems from Asian America*.

Chitra Banerjee Divakaruni (1956-)

Chitra Banerjee Divakaruni, originally from India, teaches at Foothill College in California and directs the annual national creative writing conference. She has published three books of poetry, *Dark Like the River*, *The Reason for Nasturtiums*, and *Black Cnalde*. She is also editor of *Multitude*, an anthology of multicultural writing. Her poems are included in *The Open Boat: Poems from Asian America*.

Indira Ganesan (1960-)

Indira Ganesan's short fiction has appeared in *Poughkeepsie Review*, *Mississippi Review*, and *Shankpainter*. Her first novel is *The Journey*.

N.V.M. Gonzales (1915-)

Nestor V. M. Gonzales, born 1915, has won all the major Philippine literary awards: the Commonwealth Literary Award, the Republic Award of Merit, the Republic Cultural Heritage Award, and the Rizal Pro Patria Award. These honors may not seem lavish, though, when considering the quantity and quality of his works: *The Winds of April*, *Seven Hills Away*, *Children of the Ash-Covered Loam*, *A Season of Grace*, *The Bamboo Dancers*, *Look*, *Stranger*, *On This Island Now*, *The Bread of Salt and Other Stories*, and others.

The best of Gonzalez's stories present the rhythm and pulse of the Filipinos' lives, particularly of those in the villages and frontiers freshly wrested from wild nature. The indomitable, stoic spirit of a pioneer farmer, the indestructible desire of an uneducated maidservant for her share of life and happiness, the tearless sorrow of a young mother who has just lost her infant, the feeling of loss and awe of a rustic settler suddenly plunged into an urban center—all are persuasively portrayed without any frills or fanfare of rhetoric.

The son of a teacher in Romblon province, Gonzalez studied law and journalism before turning to creative writing. He has received several Rockefeller grants to travel and write on three continents. He was on the faculty of the University of the Philippines, and he divides his time between fiction writing and magazine editing.

Vince Gotera (1952-)

Vince Gotera was born in San Francisco, but lived part of his childhood in the Philippines. He received both his M.F.A. and Ph.D. from Indiana University, and is currently on the faculty at Humboldt State University. Gotera has won the Academy of American Poets Prize, the Felix Pollak Poetry Prize at the University of Wisconsin, and the Mary Roberts Rinehart Award in poetry. In addition to having his work included in *The Open Boat: Poems from Asian America*, Gotera is poetry editor of *Asian America*, a journal of arts and culture published by the University of California at Santa Barbara.

Jessica Hagedorn (1949-)

Born in the Philippines in 1949, Jessica Hagedorn's work has appeared in *Four Young Women, Third World Women, Time to Greez, The Third Woman* and *Yardbird Reader*. Her first novel, *Dogeaters*, was nominated for a National Book Award when it was published in 1990. Hagedorn is hailed as one of a handful of minority women in the United States today who have not only created and pursued a literary tradition of their own, but have created works that represent some of the most exciting innovations in contemporary literature.

Prior to publication of *Dogeaters*, she was a well-known poet and playwright, having produced two collections of short works and poems, one of which, *Pet Food and Tropical Apparitions* (1983) received an American Book Award. She has also produced a collection of poetry and short stories called *Danger and Beauty* (1993) and edited and wrote the introduction for *Charlie Chan is Dead: An Anthology of Contemporary AsianAmerican Fiction* (1993). In addition, her work was included in *The Open Boat: Poems from Asian America. See also* "Who Are the Filipino Americans?" and "Theatre"

Garrett Hongo (1951-)

Garrett Hongo edited *Open Boat, Poems from Asian America*, published in 1993 by Doubleday. Hongo was born in Volcano, Hawaii, and grew up on Oahu and in Los Angeles. He attended Pomona College and the University of Michigan, and he earned an M.F.A. from the University of California at Irvine. Included in his published works are *Yellow Light*, and *The River of Heaven*, which was the Lamont poetry selection of the Academy of American Poets and a finalist for the 1989 Pulitzer Prize in poetry. Hongo has been given residency grants from the MacDowell Colony and the Bellagio Study Center, and has received two National Endowment for the Arts fellowships. In 1990-91, he was awarded a Guggenheim fellowship. He is professor of English and director of creative writing at the University of Oregon.

Lawson Fusao Inada (1940-)

Lawson Inada was born in 1940, a third-generation Japanese American. He is the author of *Before the Way*, and the recipient of two fellowships from the National Endowment for the Arts. Inada has served on the literature panel for the endowment and on the commission of racism and bias in education for the National Council of Teachers of English.

He is one of four coeditors of *Aiiieeeee! An Anthology of Asian American Writers*, and its sequel, *The*

Cynthia Kadohata. (Joyce Ravid.)

Big Aiiieeeee!. In 1978, with Garrett Hongo and Alan Chong Lau, he wrote *The Buddha Bandits Down Highway 99*.

Inada is a professor and poet who describes his poetry as structured and musical. Much of his work deals with his experiences in an internment camp during World War II and with his life as a Japanese American. His work is included in *The Open Boat: Poems from Asian America*.

Since 1966, he has taught multicultural literature and creative writing classes at Southern Oregon State College. The state of Oregon awarded him the Excellence in Teaching Award in 1985. Inada also writes a column each month for the *International Examiner*, a Seattle-based Asian American community newspaper, and also writes longer prose, including children's stories.

Gish Jen (1955-)

Born in New York in 1955, Gish Jen has published stories in *The Atlantic Monthly, The New Yorker*, and in numerous quarterlies. Her work is included in anthologies and textbooks, including Norton's *World of Literature, The Heath Anthology of American Literature*, and *Best American Short Stories 1988*. Her first novel, *Typical American*, was a finalist for a National Book Critics' Circle Award. Jen has an undergraduate degree from Harvard University and an M.F.A. from the Iowa Writers' Workshop. Before becoming a writer, Jen attended Stanford Business School. She lives in Cambridge, Massachusetts.

Cynthia Kadohata (1956-)

Cynthia Kadohata is a short-story writer and novelist whose work has been published in *The New Yorker, Grand Street,* and *The Pennsylvania Review.* She has published two novels, *The Floating World* and *In the Heart of the Valley of Love.* She has received a grant from the National Endowment for the Arts and a 1991 Whiting Writers' Award.

Maxine Hong Kingston (1940-)

Maxine Hong Kingston, a highly acclaimed writer of fiction and nonfiction, was one of the first Asian Americans to make it to the top of the U.S. literary world. Her first book, a memoir published in 1976 called *The Woman Warrior: Memoirs of a Girlhood among Ghosts,* won the National Book Critic's Circle Award and made her a literary celebrity at the age of 36. Kingston has since written two other critically acclaimed books: *China Men,* a sequel to *The Woman Warrior* published in 1980 that also earned the National Book Critic's Circle Award, andher first novel, *Tripmaster Monkey: His Fake Book.*

Kingston attended University of California at Berkeley, at first intending to study engineering, but eventually changed her major to English literature.

Joy Kogawa (1935-)

Japanese-Canadian Joy Kogawa was born Joy Nozomi Nakayama in Vancouver, British Columbia, Canada, on June 6, 1935. Her three published volumes of poetry, no longer in print, are *The Splintered Moon, A Choice of Dreams,* and *Jericho Road.* Her novel, *Obasan,* won the Books in Canada First Novel Award, Canadian Authors Association Book of the Year Award, and the Before Columbus Foundation American Book Award. *Obasan* was also chosen as a notable book by the American Library Association, and was selected by both the Book of the Month Club and the Literary Guild.

Alan Chong Lau (1948-)

Alan Chong Lau received his B.A. in art from the University of California at Santa Cruz in 1976. With Lawson Fusao Inada and Garrett Hongo, he wrote *The Buddha Bandits Down Highway 99.* His solo book, *Songs for Jadina,* won an American Book Award from the Before Columbus Foundation. In 1983, Lau

received a Japan-U.S. Creative Artists Fellowship under the joint sponsorship of the Japan-U.S. Friendship Commission, National Endowment for the Arts, and the Agency for Cultural Affairs of the Japanese Government. His work is included in *The Open Boat: Poems from Asian America.*

Gus Lee (1946-)

Gus Lee is a novelist and attorney. His first novel, the semi-autobiographical *China Boy,* was published in 1991, when he was 45 years old. It was begun as a personal memoir and became a best-seller. His second novel, *Honor and Duty,* was published in 1994 and also became a best seller, in addition to being selected by the Book of the Month Club and recorded as a Random House AudioBook.

Lee was born in San Francisco August 8, 1946, to a once-wealthy and aristocratic couple who had fled China in 1945. After graduating from law school and a three-year stint in the military, Lee worked for the state of California in a progression of positions ranging from deputy district attorney in Sacramento to senior executive for the State Bar of California. In 1993, following the success of *China Boy,* Lee left the law to become a full-time writer.

Russell Leong (1950-)

Russell Leong was born in San Francisco in 1950, and received his B.A. from San Francisco State College and his M.F.A. from University of California at Los Angeles School of Film and Television. His work has been included in *Asian American Authors, Aiiieeeee! An Anthology of Asian American Writers,* and *The Open Boat: Poems from Asian America.* Since 1977, he has been the editor of UCLA's *Amerasia Journal.* In 1991, he called *Moving the Image: Independent Asian Pacific American Media Arts.* Leong has also produced video documentaries, including *Morning Begins Here* (1985) and *Why is Preparing Fish a Political Act? The Poetry of Janice Mirikitani* (1990).

Genny Lim

Genny Lim is a writer and playwright, author of the award-winning play *Paper Angels* and coauthor of *Island: Poetry and History of Chinese Immigrants on Angel Island, 1910-1940.* Lim has also published a children's book, *Wings for Lai Ho.* She teaches creative writing in the University of California at Berkeley Asian American Studies Department.

David Wong Louie (1954-)

David Wong Louie is the author of the critically acclaimed short-story collection *Pangs of Love, and Other Stories.* Published in 1991, *Pangs of Love* was

David Wong Louie. (Amy Cheng.)

reviewed in the *New York Times*, the *Voice* literary supplement, and the *Los Angeles Times*, among others—a considerable amount of attention for a first collection of short fiction.

David Wong Louie was born in the suburban community of Rockville Center, New York, in 1954. He attended Vassar College, graduating in 1977 with a degree in English. He then moved to New York City where he worked at a small advertising agency before deciding to pursue graduate studies at the University of Iowa, home of the country's best graduate writing program. He graduated from the University of Iowa in 1981.

In 1982, he married and moved with his wife to the Los Angeles area, where he taught composition part time, devoting the rest of his time to writing. He taught at various schools in southern California including California State University and San Bernadino.

During this time, Louie's short stories were being published by some of the most prominent literary journals in the country. In 1989, his story "Displacement" was included in *Best American Short Stories, 1989*, published by Houghton Mifflin. In 1990, he found a publisher for his collected short stories and *Pangs of Love*, which was published the following year.

Darrell H. Y. Lum (1950-)

In 1978, Darrell Lum cofounded Bamboo Ridge Press, a nonprofit venture dedicated to publishing the works of Hawaiian writers. He is a short-story writer who has been published in the *Seattle Review*, *Chaminade Literary Review*, *Hawaii Herald*, and *Hawaii Review*. He has published two collections of short fiction, *Sun* and *Pass On, No Pass Back!*

Diane Mei Lin Mark

Born in Hawaii, Diane Mark received her B.A. in English and Asian studies from Mills College in Oakland, California, and her M.A. in American studies from the University of Hawaii. She studied filmmaking at New York University, and traveled and lived in Asia on a scholarship from the East-West Center Communication Institute. Her work, both prose and poetry, has appeared in publications such as *Bulletin for Concerned Asian Scholars*, *Sino American Relations*, *Asian Women*, *Third World Women*, *Impulse*, and *Asian Americans in Hawaii*. Mark was project director and writer of *A Place Called Chinese America: A History of Chinese in the U.S.*

Ruthanne Lum McCunn (1946-)

Born February 21, 1946 is San Francisco's Chinatown to a Scottish American father and a Chinese mother, McCunn grew up in Hong Kong surrounded by her mother's extended family. She was known as Roxey Drysdale as a child, but took her mother's maiden name of Lum when she started writing to reflect her Asian American identity. She was educated through high school in Hong Kong, but traveled to the United States for college, where she has lived ever since. While attending the University of California at Berkeley, she met and married Donald McCunn. She completed her undergraduate degree in English at the University of Texas at Austin in 1968.

Her first book, *An Illustrated History of the Chinese in America*, was published in 1979, and has been used as a college text. Her second book, *Thousand Pieces of Gold*, was published in 1981, and became the basis for an American Playhouse film. It tells the story of Lalu Nathoy, a Chinese woman who was shipped to the United States as a slave and became Polly Bemis, a well-loved pioneer woman in Idaho. McCunn's next book was a children's story, *Pie-Biter*, an Chinese American folktale. In 1985, Sole Survivor told the stody of Poon Lim, a Chinese sailor who miraculously survived 133 days adrift in the Atlantic Ocean.

In 1988, McCunn published *Chinese American Portraits: Personal Histories 1828–1988*. *Chinese Proverbs*, a collection of bits of Chinese wisdom, followed in 1991. And in 1995, *Wooden Fish Songs*, based on an

Ruthanne Lum McCunn.

actual story, is slated for publication by Dutton. It is the story of one Chinese American man, told by three different women: his mother in China, his European American mentor in Massachusetts, and the mentor's cook in Florida.

Ved Mehta (1934-)

In 1957, Ved Mehta published the critically and commercially successful autobiographical work *Face to Face*. His novels, books of nonfiction, screenplays, and autobiographical studies reflect his sense of himself as an Indian expatriate.

Ved Prakash Mehta was born on March 21, 1934, in Lahore, a town in present-day Pakistan, which was part of British colonial India at the time. He was the fifth of Dr. Amolek Ram Mehta and Shanti (Mehra) Mehta's seven children. Permanently blinded by spinal meningitis at the age of three, Mehta's early life was spent in boarding schools, hospitals, and institutions. His 1982 book *Vedi* chronicles the four years he spent in the Dadar School for the Blind in Bombay, where he endured poor medical treatment and instruction.

After 12 years of schooling in India, Mehta went to the Arkansas State School for the Blind in Little Rock, then earned a B.A. in 1956 at Pomona College in Pomona, California, while attending Harvard and the University of California at Berkeley during the summer. He then went to England to study modern history at Oxford, earning a second B.A. degree in 1959. After returning to the United States, he received a fellowship to attend Harvard, earning his M.A. and planning for an academic career. In 1960, he published *Walking the Indian Streets*, which recounts his trip to India and Nepal with a friend.

In 1961, *New Yorker* editor William Shawn, who had encouraged Mehta in his writing, invited him to join the magazine staff, a post he still holds. Mehta continued his autobiographical, critical, and fiction writing, publishing works such as: *Fly and the Fly-Bottle: Encounters with British Intellectuals*, *The New Theologian*, and the novel *Delinquent Chacha*, which was made into a 1980 British film for which Mehta wrote the screenplay. Works that followed include: *Portrait of India*, *John is Easy to Please*, *Daddyji*, *Mahatma Ghandi and His Apostles*, *New India*, *Mammaji*, *The Photographs of Chachaji*, *A Family Affair: India under Three Prime Ministers*, *Vedi*, *The Ledge between the Streams*, *Sound-Shadows of the New World*, *Three Stories of the Raj*, *The Stolen Light*, and *Up at Oxford*.

Anchee Min. (Joan Chen.)

Janice Mirikitani. (George T. Kruse.)

Anchee Min (1957-)

Anchee Min, the author of the critically acclimed 1994 memoir *Red Azalea*, was born in Shanghai, China, in 1957. The book details her life in China during the Cultural Revolution. At the age of 17, Min was sent to a labor camp, where she endured brutal living conditions. In 1984, the actress Joan Chen intervened in her case and helped her to get permission to come to the United States. She settled in Chicago, met and married Quigu Jiang, and began writing about her experiences in China. Published by Pantheon Books, the work received generally favorable reviews.

Janice Mirikitani

Janice Mirikitani, a second-generation Japanese American, has become a leading poet on the Asian American literary scene. She has published two collections of poetry and prose— *Awake in the River* and *Shedding Silence*—and edited others. She is also well known as a community activist in the San Francisco area, serving as president of the nonprofit Glide Corporation and as program director of the Glide Church/ Urban Center.

Mirikitani has edited such anthologies as *Making Waves*, an anthology sponsored by Asian Women United, and *Watch Out! We're Talking: Speaking out about Incest and Abuse.*

James Masao Mitsui (1940-)

James Masao Mitsui was born in 1940 in Skykomish, Washington. He received a B.A. in education from Eastern Washington State University in 1963. He continued his education at the University of Washington, earning an B.A. in English in 1973 and a Ph.D. in 1975. In 1976, he received a National Endowment for the Arts Fellowship. His published works include *Journal of the Sun, Crossing the Phantom River* and *After the Long Train.* Seven of Mitsui's poems are included in *The Open Boat: Poems from Asian America.* Mitsui teaches high school English.

Bharati Mukherjee (1940-)

Bharati Mukheree's writings hold a mirror up to the South Asian community in North America. A professor of English at the Unviersity of California at Berkeley, she is the author of more than a dozen novels and severl short stories. In 1994, Mukherjee published *The*

Holder of the World (Knopf). In 1988, her collection of short stories, *The Middleman and Other Stories* won the National Book Critics Circle Award for best fiction. In 1981, her essay "An Invisible Woman," won the National Magazine Award.

Born July 27, 1940, to upperclass Bengali Brahmin parents, Bharati Mukherjee is the second of three daughters. She earned her bachelor's degree from the University of Calcutta in 1959 and a master's degree from the University of Baroda in 1961. That same hyear Mukherjee moved to the United States to study creative writing at the University of Iowa.

While at Iowa, she met and married Clark Blaise, a Canadian student. She received her Ph.D. in 1968 and moved to Canada with her husband. The couple has two sons, Bart Anand and Bernard Sudhir.

Her first book, *The Tiger's Daughter*, was published in 1972 by Houghton Mifflin. It is the story of an Indian woman who returns to India after having lived for many years in the West. In 1985, Mukherjee published a collection of short stories, Darkness, exploring Canadian prejudice against South Asians. Her works depict her own experiences as an immigrant—the clash of cultures, the longing for security of home, and the dilemmas these conflicts present.

David Mura (1952-)

David Mura is a *sansei*, or second-generation Japanese American. Both his parents were interned during World War II, when people of Japanese descent on the West Coast were forcibly moved from their homes and imprisoned in camps.

Mura earned his B.A. from Grinnell College and his M.F.A. from Vermont College. He is a poet, playwright, and essayist who has distinguished himself in all three fields. His collection of poetry, *After We Lost Our Way*, won the National Poetry Series competition in 1989. His memoir *Turning Japanese: Memoirs of a Sansei* chronicled his childhood in the United States and the year he spent in Japan. It won the 1991 Josephine Miles Book Award from the Oakland PEN and has been translated into Japanese and Dutch. In 1987, he published *A Male Grief: Notes on Pornography and Addiction*. He also wrote and performed a theater piece entitled *Relocations: Images from a Sansei*, and in 1993 his play *Invasion* premiered at Pillsbury House Theater in Minneapolis. His work is included in *The Open Boat: Poems from Asian America*.

He has received many awards including two literature fellowships from the National Endowment for the Arts, several grants from the Minnesota State Arts Board, two Bush Foundation fellowships and a Discovery/*The Nation* poetry prize. His poems and essays have been published widely in national journals and

Bharati Mukherjee. (Jerry Bauer.)

magazines including *The Nation, The Utne Reader*, the *New York Times, Mother Jones*, and *The American Poetry Review*.

Kirin Narayan

Kirin Narayan is the author of *Love, Stars, and All That*, published by Pocket Books Hardcover in 1994. An Asian Indian American, Kirin Narayan's work has enjoyed acclaim and popularity.

Fae Myenne Ng (1956-)

Fae Myenne Ng published her highly acclaimed Bone in 1993. It tells the story of a Chinese American family of three daughters, considered unlucky in the Chinatown community where they grew up.

Kim Ronyoung (1926-1987)

Kim Ronyoung was born in Los Angeles and married at age of 19. Kim came to writing late in life, after returning to college in her 50s. After her children (three daughters and one son) graduated from college, she earned a degree in Far Eastern art and culture. Her first novel, *Clay Walls*, published in 1986, was nominated for the Pulitzer Prize.

Vikram Seth. (Aradhana Seth.)

Bienvenido N. Santos (1911-)

A native of the Philippines, Ben Santos spent World War II in the United States, acquiring advancededucation first at the University of Illinois, then at Columbia and Harvard. Later, he traveled under U.S. government sponsorship to give talks on Philippine culture and to meet Filipinos in the United States. Those years saw a great change in him: a popular storyteller describing charming, unaffected, simple folk in his tales before he left the islands, he returned to his homeland sad and disheartened, more matured as a writer, but full of stories about lonely and lost fellow exiles in the United States.

Among his publications are a collection of stories, *You Lovely People, What the Hell for You Left Your Heart in San Francisco, The Man Who (Thought He) Looked Like Robert Taylor, The Volcano, Villa Magdalena, The Praying Man,* and volumes of verses including *The Wounded Stag and Other Poems.* His latest book is a personal history entitled *Memory's Fiction.*

Santos's early education was through the public schools and the University of the Philippines in his hometown of Manila. He was president of the Legaspi

Colleges before accepting a Rockefeller grant and a Guggenheim Award in 1957 that allowed him to devote all his time to fiction writing. In 1965 he was honored with the Philippine Republic Cultural Heritage Award.

R.A. Sasaki (1952-)

R.A. Sasaki is a short-story writer whose work has been published in *Short Story Review, Pushcart Prize XVII,* and *Story.* In 1983 she won the American Japanese National Literary Award for her short story, "The Loom." In 1991 she published a collection of short fiction entitled *The Loom and Other Stories.*

Cathy-Lynn Song (1955-)

Cathy Song was born and raised in Honolulu. She holds degrees from Wellesley College and Boston University. In 1983, her *Picture Bride* won the Yale Series of Younger Poets Award and was nominated for the National Book Critics Circle Award. Her second book, *Frameless Windows, Squares of Light,* was published by W.W. Norton in 1991. Song's poetry has been included in a number of anthologies, such as *The Morrow Anthology of Younger American Poets, The Heath Anthology of American Literature, The Norton Anthology of Modern Poetry,* and *The Open Boat: Poems from Asian America.*

Vikram Seth (1952-)

In 1993, after six years of self-imposed exile, Vikram Seth offered the draft of his novel of epic proportions, *A Suitable Boy,* to publishers. Seth's story was one of the longest English-language novels to be published in the twentieth century, and Harper Collins eventually won the right to publish by offering Seth a $600,000 advance.

Vikram Seth was born in 1952 in Calcutta, India, but spent most of his early childhood in London. While in Londond, Seth's mother, Leila, studied law. She eventually became India's first female high court justice. When Vikram was six, his family moved back to India, where he was educated at the expensive and exclusive Doon School. He went on to Oxford University in England, where he studied philosophy, politics, and economics. He entered graduate school at Stanford University in California in 1975 to study economics. He published his first book of poems, Mappings, in 1980, while he was doing research for his dissertation at the University of China in Nanjing. In 1981, he hitchhiked to Delhi via Tibet, keeping a journal which was later published as *From Heaven Lake.* In 1986, he became a literary sensation when he published *The Golden Gate,* a story of five friends and lovers. Because of the intensity of the attention brought by its publication, Seth decided to leave his job as an editor at Stanford University Press to return to India to write. The resulting work, *A Suitable Boy*, is a bestseller, and Seth has now turned his energies toward writing plays.

Arthur Sze (1950-)

Arthur Sze was born in 1950 in New York City. His published works include: *The Willow Wind, Two Ravens, Dazzled, River River*. His work was also included in *The Open Boat: Poems from Asian America*. Sze has won three National Endowment for the Arts Writer-in-Residence grants, three Witter Bynner Foundation for Poetry grants, a creative writing fellowship from the National Endowment for the Arts, and a fellowship from the George A. and Eliza Gardner Howard Foundation. Sze is director of the creative writing program at the Institute of American Indian Arts in Santa Fe, New Mexico.

Amy Tan (1952-)

Amy Tan is one of the most successful new writers of serious fiction to emerge in the last decade. Her first novel, *The Joy Luck Club*, remained on the *New York Times* best-seller list from April to November of 1989 and was the basis for major feature film. Her second novel, *The Kitchen God's Wife*, was a commercial and critical success as well. Tan was born in Oakland, California, to first-generation Chinese Americans. In 1992, Tan published a children's book, *The Moon Lady*.

Amy Uyematsu

Amy Uyematsu is a third-generation Japanese American. A member of Pacific Asian American Women Writers West, she has served as coeditor of *ROOTS: An Asian American Reader*. Uyematsu's poems have been published in journals and anthologies including *Amerasia Journal, Poetry/LA,* and *The Open Boat: Poems from Asian America*.

Jose Garcia Villa (1914-)

Jose Garcia Villa was born in the Philippines. His book *Have Come, Am Here* was published in 1942 to immediate critical praise.

Villa has edited many magazines, won numerous literary prizes, and has a long list of publications, including *Footnote to Youth, Many Voices, Poems, Volume II, Selected Stories,* and *The Essential Villa*.

Jade Snow Wong (1922-)

Jade Snow Wong came to national prominence in 1950 with the publication of *Fifth Chinese Daughter*, a memoir of her childhood in San Francisco's Chinatown. In 1951, it was awarded the Commonwealth Club's Silver Medal for non-Fiction and was made into

an award-winning special for public broadcasting in 1976. Her second book, *No Chinese Stranger*, was published in 1975. In addition to being regarded as a pioneer Asian American writer, Wong is also an accomplished ceramist with works at the Chicago Art Institute and the Metropolitan Museum of Art.

Nellie Wong (1934-)

Nellie Wong has published *Dreams in Harrison Railroad Park* and *The Death of Long Steam Lady*. In 1981, she was featured in Allie Light's documentary film, *Mitsuye & Nellie, Asian American Poets*. Wong's work has appeared in *This Bridge Called My Back: Writing by Radical Women of Color, Breaking Silence, 13th Moon: A Chinese American Poetry Anthology,* and *The Open Boat: Poems from Asian America*.

Shawn Wong (1949-)

Shawn Wong's first novel, *Homebase*, won both the Pacific Northwest Booksellers Award and the Washington State Governor's Writers Day Award when it was published in 1979. He is one of four coeditors of *Aiiieeeee! An Anthology of Asian American Writers*, and its sequel, *The Big Aiiieeeee!*. Wong was born in Oakland, California in 1949, and grew up in Berkeley, California. He is a graduate of San Francisco State University and the University of California at Berkeley. Wong is a long-time advocate of Asian American literature and is the director of the University of Washington's Asian American studies program.

David Woo (1959-)

David Woo was born in Phoenix, Arizona, and studied English at Stanford and Harvard, and Chinese at Yale before teaching English for four years in China. From 1990-1992, he was a Wallace Stegner fellow in poetry at Stanford. His poems have appeared in *The New Yorker, ZYZZYVA,* and in *The Open Boat: Poems from Asian America*.

Hisaye Yamamoto (1921-)

Hisaye Yamamoto is one of the pioneering writers in Asian American history. Her short stories were first published in the 1930s in such publications as *Kenyon Review, Harper's Bazaar, Fuioso,* and *Asian America*. In 1949 her short story "Seventeen Syllables" was published in the *Partisan Review*. Her work is still held in high esteem today and is frequently anthologized. Yamamoto worked for several years as a journalist and even wrote for the camp newspaper when she was imprisoned at the Poston Internment Camp during World War II. In 1950 she received the John Hay Whitney Foundation Opportunity Fellowship, and earned the American Book Award for Lifetime Achievement from the Before Columbus Foundation in 1986. In 1989 she was presented with the literature award from the Association of Asian American Studies.

Wakako Yamauchi (1924-)

Wakako Yamauchi is a playwright and writer of short fiction whose work has been published in such journals as *Amerasia Journal, Southwest, Bamboo Ridge: The Hawaii Writers Quarterly,* and the *Christian Science Monitor.* Her most famous work, *And the Soul Shall Dance,* was first published in 1966. It has been repinted inseveral anthologies as both a drama and as fiction. It won the American Theatre Critics Regional Award for Outstanding Play in 1977 and has been produced for broadcast on public television. She has received several awards for her work, including a grant from the Rockefeller Foundation. In the mid-1990s, she worked primarily in drama. Her plays have been produced by such prestigious theater companies as the New York Public Theater and the Yale Repertory Theatre.

John Yau (1950-)

John Yau is an art critic, curator, and poet who has received many awards. His three published collections of poetry are *Corpse and Mirror, Radiant Silhouette: New and Selected Work 1974-1988,* and *Edificio Sayonara.* He has received fellowships from the National Endowment for the Arts, the Ingram Merrill Foundation, the New York Foundation for the Arts, and the General Electric Foundation for Younger Writers. He was also honored with the Lavan Award for Younger Poets from the Academy of American Poets.

Children's Literature

Jose Aruego (1932-)

Jose Aruego was born August 9, 1932, in Manila. He holds a B.A. and a law degree from University of the Philippines, but practiced law for only three months—just long enough to lose one case. He left the country and moved to New York, where he enrolled in the Parsons School of Design. After graduating in 1959, he worked for six years at various magazines and advertising agencies. Upon selling several cartoons to the *Saturday Evening Post,* he became a full-time freelance cartoonist.

In the 1970s, he turned his talents to children's book illustration. His list of published works is extensive. In 1970, he illustrated *Whose Mouse Are You?* by Robert Kraus, and it was named an ALA Notable Book. He won the Outstanding Picture Book of the Year Award from the *New York Times* three times for his self-illustrated works in *Juan and the Asuangs* (1970), *The Day*

They Parachuted Cats on Borneo (1971), and *Look What I Can Do* (1972). In 1972 and 1973, three of Aruego's works were chosen as Children's Book Council Showcase Titles: *Look What I Can Do, The Chick and The Duckling,* and *A Crocodile's Tale.*

Aruego has traveled extensively in the U.S. and around the world, but his favorite city, New York, is his home. His mural of New York City may be viewed at the International House on Riverside Drive in that city.

Steven Chin

Steven Chin, a reporter for the *San Francisco Chronicle,* is also an author of works for young people. His writings include fiction—*Dragon Parade*—and nonfiction—*When Justice Failed, The Fred Korematsu Story.*

Cynthia Chin-Lee

Cynthia Chin-Lee is an author of young people's fiction including *Almond Cookies and Dragon Well Tea.*

Marie G. Lee

Marie G. Lee is an award-winning writer of novels for children. In 1992 she published *Finding My Voice,* which won the Friends of American Writers Award. In 1993 she published *If It Hadn't Been for Yoon Jun.* Lee is a native of Hibbing, Minnesota, and of Korean descent. Her first essay was published in *Seventeen* when she was 16 years old. She has also been published in *YM* and in the *New York Times.* She holds a bachelor's degree from Brown University and lives in New York City where she belongs to an Asian American writers' group.

Wendy Lee

Author Wendy Lee writes fiction for young people. Her works include *One Small Girl.*

Dhan Gopal Mukerji

Dhan Gopal Mukerji is best remembered for his children's books. He wrote about animal life, frequently including Hindu folklore and philosophy in his work. His family, members of India's Brahmin priest, managed the temple in his native jungle village near Calcutta. In 1910, Mukerji immigrated to the United States and earned a graduate degree from Stanford University. In 1922, he published *Kari, the Elephant,* which was followed in 1923 by *Jungle Beasts and Men,* a collection of stories. Next came *Hari, the Jungle Lad,* followed by *Gay-Neck: The Story of a Pigeon,* his most acclaimed work. *Gay-Neck* was selected by the American Institute of Graphic Arts as one of the 50 best books of the year in 1927; it also won the American Library Association's

Marie Lee.

Allen Say's *Tree of Cranes*.

Newbery Medal in 1928. In the same year Mukerji's work *Ghond, the Hunter* was named to the American Institute of Graphic Arts list of 50 best books. Mukerji died in 1936 at the age of 46.

Allen Say (1937-)

Allen Say was born August 28, 1937, in Yokohama, Japan, to a Korean father and a Japanese American mother. His award-winning books for children often explore the experience of being an immigrant in the United States.

He illustrated his first children's book, *A Canticle of Waterbirds*, written by Brother Antonius in 1968. Four years later he wrote and illustrated, *Dr. Smith's Safari*. In 1979, *The Inn-Keeper's Apprentice*, which he also wrote and illustrated, received the American Library Association's Notable Book Award and Best Book for Young Adults. The book tells the story of a young Japanese man who apprentices himself to a great comic-strip artist.

In 1989 Say wrote *The Lost Lake* and in the same year won the Caldecott Honor Medal for his illustrations in *The Boy of the Three-Year Nap*, written by Diane Snyder. This success brought enough recognition for Say to write and illustrate full time.

In 1990 he published the critically acclaimed *El Chino*, followed by *The Tree of Cranes* in 1991. In 1993 Say produced *Grandfather's Journey*, which tells the story of his grandfather's, life in Japan, and the United States; the book won the Caldecott Medal for most distinguished picture book the following year.

In describing his status in the United States as a non-European immigrant, Say told *Booklist* "I know that I am categorized as an ethnic, as a multicultural artist, but that's not really where I'm coming from. All I'm trying to do is art. I consider myself a uniquely American artist and author because I certainly would have done this kind of work had I stayed in Japan, or had I been born here."

Marlene Shigekawa

Marlene Shigekawa writes for young people. Her *Blue Jay in the Desert* is a novel for young adults.

Yoshiko Uchida

Between 1948 and 1991, Yoshiko Uchida wrote 29 books, all but two of them for children. She is generally credited with creating a body of literature for children about the Japanese American experience. During her senior year of college in 1941, Japan bombed Pearl Harbor, triggering the United States' entry into World War II. Wartime hysteria on the West Coast resulted in the issuing by President Roosevelt of Executive Order 9066, authorizing the forced relocation of Japanese Americans from the West Coast states. Uchida experienced personally the trauma of this relocation and internment. Her college diploma was delivered to her in a cardboard tube addressed to Stall Number 40 at Tanforan, a San Mateo, California, race track used as an "assembly center." She was awarded government clearance to leave Topaz, the internment camp where her family had been imprisoned, to pursue graduate study at Smith College. In 1944, she received her master's degree. In 1991, she published her last work, *The Invisible Thread*, an autobiography for teens. She died in 1992.

Laurence Yep (1948-)

Laurence Yep was born June 14, 1948, in San Francisco. He is best-known as an author of children's books, although he has written works of historical fiction and mythology, short stories, and novels and has produced picture books. His two best-known books, *Dragonwings* and *Dragon's Gate*, both were named Newbery Honor books, the highest distinction awarded to children's books in this country.

While a student at Marquette University in Milwaukee, Wisconsin, Yep had his first story published by the now-defunct science fiction magazine, *Worlds of If*. In 1969, the story was included in an anthology, *The World's Best Science Fiction of 1969*. Yep eventually returned to the University of California at Santa Cruz in 1970 to earn a master's degree in literature.

In 1973, his first novel, *Sweetwater*, was published; Yep earned his Ph.D. from the University of New York at Buffalo in 1975. That same year saw the publication of Yep's *Dragonwings*, a young adult novel that tells the true story of a Chinese American aviator who built and flew a flying machine in 1909. In addition to being chosen a 1976 Newbery Honor Book, *Dragonwings* earned other awards, including the 1976 IRA Children's

Book Award, Notable Children's Book of 1971-75, the Best of Children's Books for 1966-78, and the 1976 Carter G. Woodson Award.

In the mid-1980s, Yep began writing plays. One of his most successful productions was a stage adaptation of *Dragonwings* produced at such noteworthy venues as the Lincoln Center in New York and the Kennedy Center in Washington, D.C.

In 1989 he published *The Rainbow People*, a retelling of 20 Chinese folk tales, followed two years later by a second collection, *Tongues of Jade*. In 1991 he published *The Star Fisher*, which tells the remarkable story of his maternal grandmother's life in rural West Virginia.

In 1994, Yep was working on two children's books, *Dream Soul* and *Thief of Hearts*, both sequels to *The Star Fisher* and *Child of the Owl*.

Ed Young

Ed Young writes and illustrates picture books for children. In 1992 his book *Seven Blind Mice* was a Caldecott Honor Book.

References

Asian American Literature: An Annotated Bibliography. New York: The Modern Language Association, 1988.

Chin, Frank, et al., eds. *The Big Aiiieeeee!: An Anthology of Chinese American and Japanese American Literature.* New York: Meridian Books, 1991.

Chin, Frank et al., eds. *Aiiieeeee! An Anthology of Asian American Writers.* Washington: Howard University Press, 1983.

Kim, Elaine. *Asian American Literature: An Introduction to the Writings and Their Social Context.* Philadelphia: Temple University Press, 1982.

Lim, Shirley Geok-lin and Amy Ling, eds. *Reading the Literatures of Asian America.* Philadelphia: Temple University Press, 1992.

Wong, Sau-ling Cynthia. *Reading Asian American Literature: From Necessity to Extravagance.* Princeton: Princeton University Press, 1993.

—*Jim Henry*

Theatre

◆ Theatres—The Original Five ◆ New Generation of Venues ◆ Playwright Pioneers
◆ Second Generation of Playwrights ◆ Theatrical Innovators ◆ Emerging Artists
◆ Behind the Scenes ◆ Future of Asian American Theatre ◆ Asian American Theatres

In Philip Kan Gotanda's 1991 play, *Yankee Dawg You Die*, two actors from different generations confront, accuse, and finally learn from each other. The older, Vincent Chang, is an old-time survivor who "never turned down a role" no matter how demeaning. The younger, Bradley Yamashita, is the idealist whose "sense of social responsibility" would not allow him to accept stereotypical roles even "if they paid [him] a million dollars." By the play's end, Vincent turns down the part of "Yang, the Evil One" to take a "wonderful" role without pay as the father of a Japanese American family living in Sacramento before World War II. Bradley, on the other hand, takes the role as "Yang, the Evil One's number one son," explaining to Vincent, "I figure once I get there I can change it." Ultimately, the survivor realizes that better roles exist while the idealist must accept that those better roles are often too few and rarely available.

Throughout the history of American film, television, and theatre, portrayals of Asians and Asian Americans have long suffered under the overbearing weight of stereotypes: the silent servant, the exotic geisha, the evil prison camp commandant, the prostitute with a heart of gold, or the sexless geek, to cite just few of the degrading caricatures of Asians on public display.

Not only were Asians denied accurate depictions, but for decades they were not allowed even to play the few Asian roles available. In 1902, the musical *Chinese Honeymoon* imported from London to Broadway featured Caucasian chorus girls in exaggerated slant-eyed makeup. The truly chic among the idle rich as depicted in the drawing-room comedies of the 1920s and 1930s had comic Chinese servants. At the same time that white minstrels were finding fame impersonating African Americans, a number of vaudeville performers prospered as "Chinese impersonators."

Sab Shimono (right) and Kelvin Han Yee in a performance of Philip Kan Gotanda's "Yankee Dawg You Die" at the Berkeley Repertory Theatre, Berkeley, California. (Courtesy of Berkeley Repertory Theatre.)

Major New York stages flourished after World War II with shows that focused on Asian characters created by non-Asian writers, such as *The King and I* with Yul Brynner and *The Tea House of August Moon* with

573

Asian American actor and theatre pioneer, Mako. (Courtesy of Mako.)

David Wayne. In such depictions, Asians always remained foreigners—the exotic King, the Japanese peasant—always in foreign settings.

Not until 1958 with *Flower Drum Song*, a Rodgers and Hammerstein musical based on a novel by Yale Drama School-educated Asian American, C.Y. Lee, did the public witness a major production that was about Asian Americans, performed by Asian Americans. The play, however, was not much of an improvement from its predecessors written by non-Asians. The stereotypes were as strong as ever with the wise Confucian father, the China-doll vamp, and the submissive bride, while the setting in a postcard-perfect Chinatown was devoid of any realistic economic or racial problems.

Although the play provided an opportunity for Asian Americans to work, it did little to counter rampant stereotypes. Not surprisingly, non-Asian casting continued, as evidenced, for example, by the choice of Colleen Dewhurst for the title role in the 1970 revival of *The Good Woman of Szechwan* at the Repertory Theater of Lincoln Center. Even more discouraging was that as late as 1989, Jonathan Pryce could be seen in exaggerated "yellow-face" makeup as the supposedly Eurasian "Engineer" in both the London and New

York productions of the controversial musical extravaganza, *Miss Saigon*.

In spite of a history that dates back to the 1920s when Gladys Li wrote what is believed to be the first play ever written in the United States by an Asian American—*The Submission of Rose Moy* which tells about a Chinese American girl's reaction to an arranged marriage—it was not until the mid-1960s and early 1970s with the founding of East West Players, Kumu Kahua Theatre, Asian American Theater Company, Northwest Asian American Theatre, and Pan Asian Repertory Theatre that Asian American theatre finally began to gain national recognition as an important, viable, expanding form of artistic expression. That struggle continues into the 1990s.

◆ THEATRES—THE ORIGINAL FIVE

East West Players
Los Angeles, California

When veteran Asian American actor, Mako, returned from New York to Los Angeles in 1960, he spent five years doing "small features and next-to-nothing-parts." He got to know many Asian American actors with whom he would meet informally. "All we talked about," remembers Mako, "was just like with that young Bradley Yamashita character in *Yankee Dawg You Die*; we talked about the lack of decent roles for Asian Americans. Even actors who were more established than I was were talking about the same thing. So one thing led to another and eventually it came down to a group of seven of us who were totally committed to forming an organization." (Mako. Telephone interview with author. March 7, 1994).

In 1965, Mako together with James Hong, June Kim, Guy Lee, Pat Li, Yet Lock, and Beulah Quo founded East West Players, the first Asian American theatre in the United States. Staged in a small church basement in 1966, *Rashomon*, a play based on the short story by Japanese writer Akutagawa Ryunosuke, was East West Players' inaugural production. By 1968, East West Players found a permanent home on Santa Monica Boulevard in Los Angeles' Silverlake area. For the first time in theatre history, Asian Americans had a venue in which to perform rewarding roles in a realistic setting.

Under the artistic direction of Mako, East West Players initially focused on play adaptations by Asian novelists such as Yukio Mishima. At the same time, the group staged Western classics by such writers as Lorca and Goldoni, providing Asian American actors with the opportunity to try roles that had been previously inaccessible to them due to their skin color. Soon after, the company began to concentrate on plays written by Asian Americans, premiering at least one original work almost every season. During Mako's more

Nobu McCarthy.

than two-decade reign, he not only directed and performed in plays, he even wrote an original production, *There's No Place for a Tired Ghost*, about Japanese Americans who died in internment camps during World War II. Since 1977, when East West Players won three Los Angeles Drama Critics awards for the debut production of Wakako Yamuchi's *And the Soul Shall Dance*, thecitations and awards have continued almost every year, including numerous Drama-Logue and Los Angeles Weekly Theatre awards.

In 1989, Mako resigned from East West Players after disagreements with the Board of Directors that could not be reconciled. In retrospect, he considers two elements outstanding regarding his experience: "One, being able to teach acting, to share my experiences with aspiring actors, which meant sharing an understanding of the craft of theatre as well as exposing them to the racist-oriented conditions of the theatre; and two, being able to develop a short story writer or novelist into a playwright and making them aware of the collaboration that goes on in theatre." Although he is no longer involved with the group he helped found, Mako remains a seminal figure in Asian American theatre, producing plays on his own" the right pieces for which [he] personally sees potential."

Mako was succeeded by actress Nobu McCarthy, his co-star in the 1987 film version of Philip Kan Gotanda's Japanese American family drama, *The Wash*. While balancing a busy acting career with her East West responsibilities, McCarthy was artistic director for almost five years. During that time she diversified the theatre, opening it up to new artists, especially actors and directors who had never worked before at East West Players. In addition, according to current East West Artistic Director Tim Dang, "Nobu had a gift for talking with corporate funders and private donors. She really put the theatre financially back on its feet again"

As film and stage offers outside of Los Angeles grew in number, McCarthy felt she could no longer refuse the opportunities. Actor/director/producer Tim Dang, who had been involved with East West since 1980 under both Mako and McCarthy's leadership, was a natural choice to succeed McCarthy in 1993.

"We hope to become a total arts organization," explains Dang. "We would like to add dance concerts, classical music performances, poetry readings, a visual arts gallery in the lobby, a bookstore focusing on Asian American literature, and a performing conservatory of classes throughout the year." Dang also hopes to move East West Players to a larger venue in the next two or three years. The current Silverlake location is a single 99-seat theatre while the proposed location in Los Angeles' "Little Tokyo" would be a multivenue location with two theatres. "It's a matter of funding now," adds Dang.

After almost 30 years of history, the country's oldest Asian American theatre remains a vital part of the arts community. "We do more than just present theatre," explains Dang. "We're truly a part of the Asian American community with classes and community events; we go into schools and teach kids about ethnic identity, perform at Chinese New Year's festivals, donate the proceeds from certain shows to community organizations." In his expanding vision for the future, Dang talks about "a whole, bigger picture, a picture that's bigger than East West, that's bigger than all Asian American theatres put together. In past years, Asian American companies were in competition with each other because there were so few Asian American writers, actors, directors. Now is a time when there has to be a coalition of Asian American theatres. If one dies, then weall die. We must work together in a time when we finally have a full generation of Asian American voices. That's what we need to look at. That's the bigger picture."

Kumu Kahua Theatre
Honolulu, Hawaii

Founded in 1971, the Kumu Kahua Theatre, whose name means "original platform or stage," is the second-oldest Asian American theatre in the United States. Self-described as "home-grown theatre," Kumu Kahua

Frank Chin. (Corky Lee.)

is dedicated to staging "plays about life in Hawaii, past and present; plays by Hawaii's playwrights; [and] plays for Hawaii's people."

Started by a group of University of Hawaii students and University of Hawaii professor Dennis Carroll, Kumu Kahua has established itself as a five-production-per-season group, solidly entrenched in the Hawaiian arts community. In the more than 20 years since its founding, Kumu Kahua has offered well over 100 productions reflecting Hawaii's multiethnic community. The company's performances are not limited to Honolulu, but travel to neighboring islands. Each year in May or June, Kumu Kahua sends out a new staging of the production that was the most successful during the previous season. The show then travels to the other islands of Kauai, Maui, and Hawaii.

In addition to a statewide reach, Kumu Kahua productions also tour the mainland and abroad. In 1990, the company traveled to the Edinburgh International Festival, Washington, D.C., and the Los Angeles Festival of the Arts. That year, Kumu Kahua became the first group to present plays abroad that had been written in whole or in part by people of Hawaiian ancestry. In the summer of 1993, the company had the unique experience of traveling to Micronesia for a pioneering

collaborative work—creating, staging, and locally casting a theatre piece based on the Micronesian legend, *Taimuan the Demon*. The company plans eventually to bring the work to Kumu Kahua's Honolulu stage.

Besides touring and mounting five productions a season, Kumu Kahua also helps to develop local writers through an annual playwriting contest (co-sponsored with the University of Hawaii Department of Theatre and Dance) and workshop productions of three new plays a year. The contest offers cash prizes for both full-length and one-act plays. The workshop program for new plays provides writers the opportunity to work with a dramaturge, director, and actors during an intense week of development and rewriting that culminates in a public reading of the play.

Twenty-two years after its inception, Kumu Kahua finally acquired a permanent home in time for its 1993-94 season. The new 100-seat theatre is housed on the lower floor of the historic Kamehameha V Post Office in downtown Honolulu, with headquarters for the State Foundation on Culture and the Arts on the upper level. With a new home and full-time administrative staff for the first time ever, Kumu Kahua looks forward to continuing to serve the community as Hawaii's local theatre company.

Asian American Theater Company
San Francisco, California

While East West Players was initially founded to give Asian American actors greater opportunities to perform, the Asian American Theater Company (AATC) was originally established as the Asian American Theater Workshop (AATW), devoted to developing Asian American writers. Sponsored by the American Conservatory Theatre (ACT), the San Francisco Bay Area's oldest and largest regional repertory theatre, AATW began in 1973 as a personal vision of writer Frank Chin: "I founded the Workshop as the only Asian American theatre that was conceived as a playwright's lab and not a showcase for yellows yearning to sell out to Hollywood. I failed. I was director of the workshop until 1977." (Chin, Frank. Autobiographical article sent to author. 1994).

While Chin might be quick to dismiss his involvement with AATW, his achievement is undeniably long lasting. According to Frank Abe, one of the original workshop members who is currently communications director for Seattle politician Gary Locke, AATW provided "both a theatrical and cultural experience." Abe explains, "Many of us did not have an Asian American consciousness at the time. Mine was strictly suburban Californian. Through the workshop, I came to understand and embrace the fact that Asian American was a unique sensibility with a unique history. Through the written word, the goal was to recover our history, that which had been lost, falsified, and suppressed." (Abe, Frank. Telephone interview with author. March 13, 1994).

As AATW grew and evolved, the focus shifted from the writers to the actors until, as Abe described it, "the inmates took over the asylum." In frustration and disgust, Chin left AATW in mid-1977. After his departure, AATW continued as a theatre group, renaming itself a "Company." As an expanded group, AATC flourished, attracting numerous Asian American writers, actors, directors, and designers with little or no previous experience. Throughout its more than 20-year history, AATC has been a testing ground for playwrights such as Philip Kan Gotanda and David Henry Hwang, and a training facility for actors including Dennis Dun, Kelvin Han Yee, Amy Hill, Brenda Wong Aoki, and others who have moved on to star in films, on television, and in other venues. "These people cut their first teeth here," explains former Artistic Director Lane Nishikawa. (Nishikawa, Lane and Wu, Pamela. Interview with author. March 16, 1994).

Until 1983, AATC remained stable, producing at least three shows a season. However, by 1984, severe financial difficulty led to the loss of AATC's 99-seat theatre and the company was forced into operating and producing in rented spaces. Productions were cut back and the company concentrated on developing new scripts through workshops and readings. By 1989, AATC secured a new home and resumed producing full seasons. The Asian American Theater Center now has a 135-seat main stage, a 60-seat second stage, dance and rehearsal studios, and offices.

In 1993, Eric Hayashi, a 20-year veteran with AATC, resigned as artistic director to become the assistant director of the Theater Program at the National Endowment for the Arts in Washington, D.C. Since then, AATC has been under the leadership of Executive Director Pamela Wu and Artistic Director Emiko Takei. According to Wu, writers are once again the focus at AATC: "We develop Asian American actors, producers, technicians, etc., but the playwrights always come first." In addition, AATC differs from other Asian American theatre companies in that it does not produce Western classics. "I'm not saying that we'll never do them," explains Wu, "but we tend to leave the Western classics for mainstream stages. Other companies give Asian Americans a chance to work on dead playwrights. They're not doing world premieres, works that are changing and developing every day. Classics tend to be easier, too, especially for the directors and actors." (Wu, Pamela. Interview with author. January 13, 1994).

Like East West Players, in the future AATC would like "to become a real Asian American community center . . . theatre that branches out to different areas of entertainment, whether it be film, video . . . dance . . . a children's theatre," adds Wu.

Currently burdened with heavy financial problems, AATC remains hopeful, concentrating energies on fundraising and grant-writing. "And we're looking for our angels. They are out there," say both Wu and Nishikawa.

Northwest Asian American Theatre
Seattle, Washington

Although the Northwest Asian American Theatre (NWAAT) is more than 20 years old, its name is just over ten. NWAAT began as two separate arts groups, both founded in 1973 and both dedicated to serving the Asian American arts community in Seattle.

The Asian Multi Media Center (AMMC) began as an acting group which expanded into a multimedia production center which included photography, graphic arts, and journalism with a training program that encouraged inner city youth to enter the mass-communication field. Initially funded by a local grant of $14,500, AMMC opened its doors to the public in late January 1973.

Simultaneously, a group of students from the University of Washington who were particularly concerned about the negative stereotyping of Asian Americans in mass media, the use of non-Asian actors to portray Asian characters, and the lack of local performance opportunities for Seattle's Asian American actors, directors, and playwrights formed the Theatrical Ensemble of Asians (TEA). The group produced their first play, Carlos Bulosan's *Philippine Legends, Folklore, and American Impressions*, in 1974.

The next year, TEA moved from the University of Washington campus and became affiliated with AMMC. Under AAMC's sponsorship, TEA produced and developed an original work, *Nisei Bar and Grill* by Garret K. Hongo. Together, TEA and AAMC began to provide a showcase for such notable Asian American playwrights as Frank Chin and Wakako Yamauchi.

In 1978, the two groups merged and became the Asian Exclusion Act (AEA). Through the efforts of an unpaid, all-volunteer staff led by Bea Kiyohara who would remain as artistic director for the next 15 years, AEA tried to maintain its visibility in the community by mounting at least one production a year. By 1981, AEA evolved into Northwest Asian American Theatre, a name that reflected both its regional and ethnic identities. Soon NWAAT was able to produce two or three major shows a year, including such works as David Henry Hwang's *FOB*, Philip Kan Gotanda's *Song For a Nisei Fisherman*, and Rick Shiomi's *Yellow Fever*.

NWAAT opened the doors of its permanent home, Theatre Off Jackson, in 1987, after several years of fundraising and renovation of what had been a vacant parking garage in the International District of Seattle's downtown. The opening was marked by the world premiere of *Miss Minidoka 1943*, about a beauty pageant held in a Japanese American internment camp. This musical comedy, written by Gary Iwamoto, became NWAAT's most popular show to date.

With its own theatre space, NWAAT finally had the ability and capacity to produce a full season, expanding to three or four shows a year. While developing new works through staged readings and numerous workshops, NWAAT continues to showcase the best of Asian American plays such as *The Wash* by Philip Gotanda.

As NWAAT developed and ingrained itself into the Seattle community, it continued to grow, adding a children's segment to its season, as well as the annual Winterfest, which offers a wide spectrum of Asian American entertainers from all over the United States, including jazz musicians, improvisational comedy groups, and solo performers.

In 1993, actor/director/writer and NWAAT founding member Judith Nihei was appointed the company's first full-time artistic director. Nihei's position differed from that of her predecessor, Kiyohara, in that Nihei holds a full-time, paid staff position. According to Nihei, "nonprofit theatre, however, is much more than a full-time job, although you're barely compensated for a full-time job. You have to really enjoy it unless you're a masochist because it means 12-hour days, even on Saturdays" (Nihei. Telephone interview with author. January 10, 1994).

Regardless of the long hours and low wages, Nihei is more than content in her position at NWAAT: "If one were to go to a major theatre, you would see great sets, great actors, minks in the audience, etc. That means that these theatres have a level of support, a level of talent that few of us have access to. Asian American theatres have never had that kind of support on the one hand, but on the other, everyone involved in Asian American theatre is doing it because they want to be there, their hearts are really there."

Pan Asian Repertory Theatre
New York, New York

"My earnings on Broadway literally made it possible to fund my first production," says Tisa Chang, founder and artistic director of Pan Asian Repertory Theatre in New York City. In May 1977, while Chang was playing Al Pacino's Vietnamese girlfriend on Broadway in *The Basic Training of Pavlo Hummel*, Pan Asian mounted their inaugural production, *The Legend of Wu Chang*. "It was more important to do my own show," explains Chang, which meant that she opened at LaMama E.T.C. downtown at 7:30 p.m., and rushed up toBroadway to do the second act of *Hummel* after her understudy filled in during the first act. "It just proves the symbiosis of commercial and nonprofit theatre," Chang adds.

Such tenacity and dedication is the reason for Chang's unwavering success as the leader of the East

Coast's foremost Asian American theatre, which celebrates the talents of Asian American Theater artists. "The founding of Pan Asian wasn't something whimsical. It was a culmination of skills and dreams. I had experience as a working professional in the field, so by the time I founded Pan Asian, I was very focused and purposeful, and ready for new challenges as a director and producer," says Chang. She remains at the helm of her "hand-carved institution" (Chang, Tisa. Interviews with author. March 10, 1994).

With the assistance of LaMama E.T.C., a leading New York venue for nontraditional, ground-breaking theatre, and its founder Ellen Stewart, who donated theatre, rehearsal, and office spaces, Pan Asian continued to mount distinctive, innovative productions that ranged from adaptations of Chinese classics to original works by new Asian American voices. Throughout its history, Pan Asian's focus has been on the actor, maintaining a resident ensemble of senior artists.

In 1981, Pan Asian moved from LaMama into the 28th Street Theater. During its four years there, highlights included a trilogy of plays on the Japanese internment experience written by new Asian American writers. "Although the works were perhaps not entirely finished, the important statement was that audiences were made to remember the 40th anniversary of the incarceration of thousands of Japanese Americans," explains Chang. In addition, Pan Asian produced Rick Shiomi's detective-story spoof, *Yellow Fever*, which was so successful that it transferred off-Broadway where it remained for six months.

Pan Asian moved into their current space, Playhouse 46, in time for the 1985-86 season. In 1986 when the company presented *Shogun Macbeth*, an original adaptation of the Shakespeare classic, Mel Gussow of *New York Times* described it as "a dynamic variation on the original . . . a Kurosawa film on stage." Nineteen ninety-two saw the world premiere of Pan Asian's most ambitious work to date, *Cambodia Agonistes*, a "musical theatre epic" by actor/director/writer Ernest Abuba, which tells the story of Cambodian refugee women who have gone blind, not because of any medical reason, but because they were witnesses to the horrors of Cambodia's killing fields in the 1970s.

Chang describes Pan Asian's history in "phases." During the first phase (or the beginning five years), Chang remarks, "by hook or by crook, I did the artistic work to make Pan Asian happen." She continues, "In the second phase, we were able to pay our artists more, to implement a 'senior artist wage' and become more mainstream. The third phase is financial stabilization." With a $100,000 grant in the early 1990s from the Ford Foundation and a multiyear grant from the Lila Wallace-*Reader's Digest* Foundation Theater for New Audiences Program (in addition to grants from the

National Endowment for the Arts, New York State Council on the Arts, and New York City's Cultural Affairs, as well as contributions from foundations, corporations, and individuals), Pan Asian is settling comfortably into financial stability.

Currently poised to move into a fourth phase, Chang is ready to take Pan Asian into the twenty-first century. "We're looking for a permanent facility, a building of our own. We'll be 25 years old and I have this dream of a marble building with a fish pond and Japanese gardens." Chang predicts that in the next four to five years, the company will outgrow its current space. "This dream facility—I will not compromise on it. I have never compromised on any important issues. That's why if it cannot be said that Pan Asian is flourishing, then it is doing very well," insists Chang.

◆ NEW GENERATION OF VENUES

National Asian American Theatre Company
New York, New York

Executive Director Richard Eng and Artistic Director Mia Katigbak together founded the National Asian American Theatre Company, Inc. (NATCO) in 1988 with the goal "to provide performance and production opportunities for skilled Asian American actors, directors, technicians, and designers . . . The company performs European and American classics."

"As Asian American actors, it's nearly impossible to get cast in classical productions," explains Katigbak. "At the same time, we didn't want to force a cultural association between the original classic and Asia in order to justify Asian American faces in productions of Western classics. This is what has been happening—for example, *Lear* with a Chinatown accent. We felt that was doing a great disservice to the text" (Katigbak, Mia. Telephone interview with author. January 13, 1994). The answer was to mount productions of such classics by Shakespeare, Chekhov, and Strindberg with cast members who just happened to be Asian American. For the most part, the text remained unchanged—no accents, no setting changes, just pure nontraditional casting.

Limited by budget constraints, NATCO attempts to mount one major production a year. The 1990 production of three Chekhov one-act plays was hailed by New York press as a "superb effort," while NATCO was praised as "a serious contributor to off-off-Broadway theatre." The group's 1992 production of Shakespeare's *A Midsummer Night's Dream* was received as "a solid, energetic mounting . . . by a company of young and imaginative performers."

Katigbak notes that it has been more difficult for NATCO to gain access to American plays while European works have been readily available. "It's just so

ironic that it's so hard to get American works in America, but we feel it's very important to show American plays to Asian American audiences," Katigbak says.

Both Katigbak and Eng envision NATCO as "a stepping stone to truly nontraditional, color-blind casting where an actor is assessed purely by his or her talent. The reason we have productions with all-Asian American casts is to prove that Asian American actors are capable of doing the classics."

Angel Island Theatre Company
Chicago, Illinois

In spite of a markedly sizable population of Asian Americans outside of the West Coast, Chicago did not have an Asian American theatre company until 1989 when eight local Asian American community leaders and theatre artists banded together to form Angel Island Theatre Company (AITC). Their goal was "to present high-quality professional theatre which accurately depicts the Asian American experience, creates positive Asian role models, shatters narrow and negative stereotypes, preserves our cultural heritage, and enhances understanding between East and West through the arts." AITC's first production in the fall of 1989 was David Henry Hwang's *FOB*. According to AITC cofounder and president Christina Adachi, "The play was so well received by the Asian American community. They made it absolutely clear that they were happy to have a theatre with Asian American actors who were playing something besides soldier number four" (Adachi, Christina. Telephone interview with author. January 13, 1994).

Due to funding restrictions, AITC has not yet established a regular season plan. Adachi estimates that productions have averaged approximately one per year. Her goal is to do two productions a year, eventually growing into an annual three- or four-production season.

What makes AITC different from other Asian American theatre companies, Adachi feels, is that in spite of Chicago's sizable Asian American population, the city does not have a history of Asian American activism or even the same level of political organization or movement that is present on the West and East coasts. "We're a little bit of an island here in the Midwest," says Adachi. "We tend to be isolated, which has made it difficult developing AITC."

Amidst the Chicago isolation, Adachi feels that Chicago Asian Americans "have a unique story to tell." In that vein, AITC's 1993 world premiere of *The Salad Bowl Dance*, written by local playwright and poet Dwight Okita, was an important breakthrough production. For the first time, a Chicago author was presenting an original Chicago story. *Salad* told the comic/dramatic tale of Grace, a young *nisei* (second-generation

Christina Adachi. (Courtesy of Angel Island Theatre Company.)

Japanese American) who moves to Chicago after being interned for three years in Manzanar, and her attempts to assimilate into American life.

While Adachi recognizes the importance of establishing Asian American identity by performing works created by Asian authors with an Asian theme, she does not want to limit AITC to only that. Following the example of other Asian American theatres, Adachi hopes to do plays that are not specifically Asian American. "I like to kid myself that one day we're going to do a Kabuki version of *Cat on a Hot Tin Roof* or a Kabuki *I Love Lucy*."

For now, Adachi recognizes that there are many important stories to be told, especially by the new Asian American groups—the Vietnamese, Laotians, and Cambodians. "We're hoping to be able to identify and support some writers and performers from newer Asian American communities and to help them to develop and present their work," says Adachi. "Above all else, every time we do a show, it's magic. There's such electricity in the audience and on the stage." That sort of supportive outburst is what will keep AITC going and growing into the next century.

Theater Mu
Minneapolis, Minnesota

The youngest of the Asian American theatres was founded by a core group of four individuals—Rick Shiomi, Dong-il Lee, Diane Espaldon, and Martha Johnson—who first met in May 1992 "to share ideas and dream aloud about creating a theatre company that would build community among Asian Americans in the Twin Cities (Minneapolis and St. Paul, Minnesota)." In a state that has the largest population of adopted Koreans in the United States, as well as the fastest-growing Asian American minority group (with the population almost quadrupling in the past decade), Theater Mu committed itself to "giving voice to Asian Americans . . . to share our personal experiences, distinct cultures, and Asian American vision, creating and producing theatre works that can draw on both Asian and Western traditions."

The name of the young group comes for the Korean pronunciation of the Chinese character that symbolizes "shamanistic theatre." The actual ideogram of *mu* represents the shaman/warrior/artist who connects the heaven and earth through the tree of life. Theater Mu believes that "performance is a ritual in which the shaman/warrior/artist takes the audience on a spiritual journey of transformation. This act of transformation changes the audience's perception of time, space, and reality, transforming their awareness of themselves and society."

Managing Director Diane Espaldon stresses the group-oriented nature of the Theater Mu founders. "We have an unusual leadership structure in that we develop the administrative and creative aspects of the company together . . . We don't have the typical hierarchical structure like other Asian American companies might have. That works better for us. It makes us grow faster" (Espaldon, Diane. Telephone interview with author. March 11, 1993).

"We focus almost exclusively on new works by newer Asian American groups," explains Espaldon, "not so much Japanese and Chinese Americans, but the newer communities of Korean, Vietnamese, and Cambodian Americans. We're also trying to explore traditional art forms by integrating them into the new works we're creating. It's a synthesis, because that's what our lives as Asian Americans is like, the mix of Asian American and Asian Asian. We want to reflect that in our art, so our performances are not necessarily straight theatre; there's a lot of dance, movement, traditional music, etc., interwoven into the work."

In keeping with their focus on developing new works, Theater Mu offers an aggressive series of labs and workshops. In 1993, the group established an annual playwriting festival called *New Eyes* that showcases short new works by Asian American writers. The

Diane Espaldon. (Courtesy of Theatre Mu.)

first festival was a "critic's choice" and hailed as "more than promising," earning favorable reviews throughout the Twin Cities. In its second season, Theater Mu continues a full schedule of workshops and readings, an original production of *Mask Dance*, a play about the experiences of adopted Koreans in Minnesota, the second annual *New Eyes* festival, and a revival of Rick Shiomi's comic detective thriller, *Yellow Fever*.

Through its constant development of new voices, "Theater Mu" wants to push the boundaries . . . to expand the definition of Asian American theatre, especially to include other Asian groups who have been less visible in the past." Says Espaldon, "I feel a rumbling lately among Korean American artists. Their visibility is really growing especially in New York and Los Angeles. There's a national consciousness that arose recently among Korean Americans, and artists are really starting to tap into that. I think artists from the Vietnamese American community will come later. We're just starting to see a few of them now."

In the meantime, Espaldon says Theater Mu will continue to stabilize structurally and grow artistically, "developing our artists, drawing more theatre professionals to the area, and helping actors and writers to mature."

For further research, other Asian American theatre/performance groups include The Ark Ensemble, Great Leap, Inc., Ma-Yi Theatre Ensemble, Ping Chong & Company, Silkroad Playhouse, Wise Fool Productions, and Theatre of Yugen.

◆ PLAYWRIGHT PIONEERS

Wakako Yamauchi

Undeniably one of the classic Asian American plays, Wakako Yamauchi's *And the Soul Shall Dance*, began as a short story, one of the first stories that Yamauchi ever wrote. "I couldn't sell it to white magazines," she remembers, "but in 1974 four young men up in San Francisco put together an anthology of Asian American writers [the seminal *Aiiieeee! An Anthology of Asian American Writers*]. They selected *Soul* for the book, and when it came out, Mako, the artistic director of East West Players, contacted me. He wanted me to turn it into a play."

In 1977, *Soul* received its first professional production at East West under the codirection of Mako and Alberto Isaac. The play tells the story of two Japanese American families, the Muratas and the Okas, trying to survive as farmers in Southern California's Imperial Valley in the early 1930s. The sharp contrast between the two daughters in the story—Masako Murata, an 11-year-old *nisei* (second generation) and Kiyoko Oka, a 14-year-old who has just arrived in the United States from Japan—is especially effective in the way the two girls laugh. Masako opens her mouth and lets a loud, joyous noise come forth while Kiyoko can only giggle behind a hand that hides her merriment.

In the years that followed, *Soul* became one of the most produced Asian American plays, seen at Pan Asian Repertory, Asian American Theater Company, Northwest Asian American Theatre, the University of Hawaii at Manoa, Kauai Community Theater, and Cal State Asian American Theatre. In 1978, a 90-minute filmed version was aired on the Public Broadcasting System. Almost two decades later, *Soul* remains an actively produced work.

Yamauchi continues to write successfully for the stage. Some of the more than dozen works she has authored include *The Music Lessons*, (1980 New York Shakespeare Festival Public Theater premiere), *12-1-A* (1982 East West Players premiere), *A Memento* (1984 Pan Asian Repertory premiere), and *The Chairman's Wife* (1990 East West Players premiere).

Momoko Iko

Although Momoko Iko began writing in college, it was not until years later when she read a notice about a playwriting contest sponsored by East West Players that she first tried writing plays. "That was the catalyst;

I saw that there was a theatre that was looking for my plays." Two of Iko's plays, *Gold Watch* and *Old Man* won East West's contest in 1970 and 1971.

Of Iko's repertoire of plays, *Gold Watch* has been her most-produced work. Premiered in 1970 at the Inner City Cultural Center in Los Angeles, the play portrays a Japanese American family caught in the midst of racist fervor on the eve of the evacuation order of Japanese Americans to relocation camps. Caught between the Japan they left behind and the crumbling promise of a new life in America, the Murakami family is forced to reevaluate their position in their adopted, unfamiliar, changing society. In 1975, *Gold Watch* was produced for television by PBS.

Iko's other works include *When We Were Young* (1974 East West premiere), *Flowers and Household Gods* (1981 Pan Asian premiere), and *Boutique Living and Disposable Icons* (1988 Pan Asian premiere).

Frank Chin

After fifth-generation Chinese American Frank Chin left the Asian American Theater Workshop in mid-1977, he eventually abandoned all of the theatre world. Today, he insists, "I am out of theatre. I will not work with any theatre, producer, writer, director, or actor who plays and lives the stereotype. So I write fiction, essays, and articles."

Although Chin is no longer active in Asian American theatre, he will forever be an important part of its history, billed as the first Asian American playwright to have work produced in New York. In 1972, *The Chickencoop Chinaman* was mounted off-Broadway at The American Place Theatre. In this irreverent work, Chin introduces three unpredictable, often comic characters that defy generalizations of any kind, who challenge and satirize existing media stereotypes of Asian Americans. A hip and raunchy piece, a new generation of questioning Asian Americans found in Tam Lum an unlikely hero "with a gift of gab and an open mouth, [a] multi-tongued word magician losing his way to the spell who trips to Pittsburgh to conjure with his childhood friend and research a figure in his documentary."

After the play's opening to glowing reviews from such publications as *The New Yorker* and *Newsweek*, Chin wrote: "That this play is the first play by an Asian American to, in any sense, make it, that people should be surprised at our existence, is proof of the great success white racism has had with us. America might love us. But America's love is not good. It's racist love. I don't want it."

Chin,s next play, *The Year of the Dragon*, was also mounted at The American Place Theatre, in 1974. The play's theme was the disintegration of the Chinese American family: Pa Eng, the respected "Mayor" of Chinatown, is dying; Ma Eng sings about Chinese "slave girl"; first son Fred Eng, head of Eng's Chinatown Tour 'n Travel, hates himself for having built a business whose success demands that he assume a demeaning persona not unlike the humble, passive Charlie Chan; daughter Mattie chooses Boston and escapes Chinatown with a white husband; and young Johnny is little more than a hoodlum. On the whole, the play received generally good notices and went on to be filmed as a PBS production in 1975.

In spite of Chin's stated unwillingness to work in theatre, he continues to write plays. Other works include *Gee, Pop!*, *Chinatown Mortuary*, and *Oofty Goofty*.

♦ SECOND GENERATION OF PLAYWRIGHTS

Genny Lim

San Francisco native Genny Lim is best known for her groundbreaking one-act play, *Paper Angels*, which premiered at Asian American Theater Company in 1980. The work focuses on the experiences of Chinese immigrants detained on Angel Island in the San Francisco Bay. The unjust Chinese Exclusion Act of 1882 drastically curtailed Chinese immigration into the United States, granting entry only to merchants, students, and tourists. Would-be immigrants who did not fit into the designated categories attempted to enter the United States with falsified papers linking them to Chinese American "relatives" already living here. Lim, herself a descendent of an Angel Island detainee, became interested in the plight of the detainees after reading an article in the Asian American newspaper *East West* about the discovery of Chinese characters inscribed on the walls of the detention center. In the fear, anger, and frustration of waiting, detainees scratched poems onto the very walls that kept them from entering the land of Gold Mountain, the term used by Chinese to describe the United States. Lim, together with historians Him Mark Lai and Judy Yung, eventually collaborated on the book, *Island: Poetry and History of Chinese Immigrants 1910-1940.*

Lim's detainees in *Paper Angels*, who are of different generations and various backgrounds and who experience a spectrum of emotions from hope to despair, rashness to timidity, and acceptance to fury, are a cross-representation of the approximately 175,000 Chinese immigrants who entered the United States between 1910 and 1940 through Angel Island. In 1985, *Paper Angels* was produced by American Playhouse for PBS.

Since writing *Paper Angels*, Lim has produced other historically based, realistic works such as *Bitter Cane* which focuses on the virtual imprisonment of laborers

Genny Lim.

by Hawaiian sugar cane plantations, told through the story of a young Chinese son who follows in the laboring footsteps of his missing father. More recently, however, Lim has moved toward multimedia performances that integrate music, movement, voice, poetry, and visual art,preferring to work collaboratively with other artists.

Valena Hasu Houston

Born in Japan to an American G.I. father and Japanese mother, Valena Houston's ethnic background is half-Asian, a quarter Native American, and a quarter African American. Her multicultural, multiethnic identity has been pivotal to her works. Best known among them are the first and final plays in a trilogy based on her family, which includes *Asa Ga Kimashita* (Morning Has Broken), *American Dreams*, and *Tea*.

The first of the trilogy, *Asa Ga Kimashita*, is a work based on Houston's mother's decision to marry an American soldier. It premiered in 1981 at the Studio Theater, University of California at Los Angeles. Set in Japan during the beginning of the U.S. occupation after World War II, *Asa* tells the story of the patriarch of an old, wealthy landed family who, in the face of American "democratization," longs to return somehow to the

glories of old Japan. The play focuses on the precious quality of life in the midst of uncontrollable currents of change, best characterized by the depiction of a dying mother, who represents the prewar traditional woman trapped in silence, and her postwar daughter [based on Houston's mother] to whom the mother wills the life of freedom she denied herself. In spite of the countless adversities the mother has faced and continues to face, she instills in her daughter an unbending sense of survival: "There is never anything but the present moment, the one we can grasp in our fists and feel."

Houston refers to *Tea*, the final play of the family trilogy, as "a poem to my mother." Often considered Houston's signature work, *Tea* received its world premiere at the Manhattan Theatre Club in 1987. In the play, Houston draws on her own experience of growing up on an obscure Kansas army base, surrounded by war brides married to American servicemen. *Tea* reveals the lives of five Japanese-born wives of U.S. servicemen who are brought together after one of them commits violent suicide. Through the ritual of sharing tea, the one common denominator that links these five women of diverse backgrounds, the remaining four come to understand the desperate struggles and quiet strength of the woman who could not bear to continue her isolated life any longer.

Houston, who wrote her first play at age 13, remains one of today's most prolific playwrights.

Philip Kan Gotanda

Having first tried careers in law and songwriting, Philip Gotanda found himself "writing for the theatre—by accident" when his first theatrical endeavor, a musical called *The Avocado Kid*, was accepted and then staged at East West Players in 1980 (Gotanda, Phillip Kan. Telephone interviews with author. Octover 10, 1993, and January 25, 1994). Gradually, he moved from musicals to plays. "I became more interested in the spoken word, in hearing characters talk," he explains.

The following year, Gotanda wrote *Song for a Nisei Fisherman*,a Japanese American family saga with autobiographical underpinnings, which was first produced at Asian American Theater Company. In 1984, a fantastical fairy-tale-like work set in ancient Japan, *The Dream of Kitamura*, premiered also at AATC.

Gotanda's next play, *The Wash*, a poignant depiction of the troubled marriage of an older Japanese American couple, brought him national acclaim and moved him into the mainstream. First staged at San Francisco's Eureka Theatre in 1987, the play was made into a 1988 PBS American Playhouse film (which starred East West founder, Mako, and second artistic director, Nobu McCarthy), then staged by the Manhattan Theater Club in coproduction with Los Angeles' Mark Taper Forum in 1990.

Philip Kan Gotanda.

David Henry Hwang.

The Wash was followed by the acclaimed *Yankee Dawg You Die*, which began at the Berkeley Repertory Theater in 1988, went on to New York's Playwrights Horizon in 1990. The play, in which two actors face off—the elder who has survived in the industry by doing character parts and the younger who, in the thralls of idealism, still believes he will find substantial roles—has become a representative mouthpiece for the plight of Asian Americans working in the media.

In 1992, Gotanda garnered "some of the best notices [he has] ever gotten" with *Fish Head Soup* which also premiered at Berkeley Repertory. His latest work, *Day Standing on Its Head*, about law professor Harry Kitamura who, on the verge of middle age, embarks on a dreamscape/nightmare journey toward his true self, premiered at Manhattan Theatre Club in early 1994 and made its West Coast debut at the AATC in late spring of the same year.

Gotanda is currently working on a new play, *The Ballad of Yachiyo*, "something [he's] been trying to write for years." Set on the Hawaiian island of Kauai, the play is based on the life of an older aunt who died tragically in the early 1900s.

Guggenheim, Rockefeller, National Endowment of the Arts, and McNight fellowships interspersed throughout Gotanda's "accidental" career confirm his immense talent. His latest accolade comes from the prestigious Lila Wallace-*Reader's Digest* Fund in the form of a three-year grant that began in 1993 and will support his projects at East West Players.

David Henry Hwang

As a senior at Stanford University, in the second week of an introductory playwriting tutorial, David Henry Hwang turned in a play called *FOB*. [The term *FOB* refers to a new immigrant, someone who is "fresh off the boat."] Based on a night out Hwang had with a Chinese American cousin who was dating a boy from Hong Kong, *FOB* tells the story of the culture clash between the new immigrant and the westernized Asian American. From a first production in 1979 in a Stanford dormitory to a staging at New York's Public Theater in 1981 to an Obie for Best New Play barely two years after he graduated from college, Hwang's first play propelled him toward stardom at an age when most young adults have not even decided on a career.

The plays and accolades followed. Hwang's second work, *Dance and the Railroad*, inspired by the experiences of Chinese railroad workers in the

Kevin Han Yee as Victor and Stan Egi as his long-lost brother Mat meet in the San Joaquin Valley home of their parents in the world premiere of Philip Kan Gotanda's Fish Head Soup in March 1992 at Berkeley Repertory Theatre, Berkeley, California. (Ken Friedman.)

United States in 1867, was nominated for a Drama Desk Award. His next play, *Family Devotions*, was a semiautobiographical work in which Hwang questioned the Christian tradition that obstructed his journey into his cultural past. In 1983, the Public Theater produced a pair of one-act plays: *The House of Sleeping Beauties*, inspired by the short story of the same name by Japanese novelist Yasunari Kawabata, and *The Sound of a Voice*, about a samurai who intends to kill an old witch but instead falls in love with her as she rejuvenates into a beautiful woman.

After such sudden success, Hwang found himself unable to write for the next two years. When he finally started writing again, he created his first non-Asian play, *Rich Relations*. The play was his first flop, and he said it was the most liberating thing that happened to him since the first phenomenal success of *FOB*. "I realized, it's okay. I'm still alive. It's not the end of the world" (Hwang, David Henry. Telephone interview with author. February 9, 1994).

Shortly after the closing of *Rich Relations*, Hwang heard the story of a French diplomat who was involved in a 20-year affair with a male Chinese spy whom he

believed to be a woman. His interest evolved into the 1988 Tony Award-winning gender-bender, *M. Butterfly*, which became one of the most successful nonmusical works in Broadway history, grossing over $35 million. In addition to the Tony Award, the play also garnered the Drama Desk, Outer Critics Circle, and John Gassner awards in 1988, followed by a 1991 Los Angeles Drama Critics Circle Award. The show was eventually produced in three dozen countries, making Hwang at age 32 the first U.S. playwright to become an international phenomenon since the days of Edward Albee. In 1989, *Time* magazine referred to Hwang as "potential[ly] . . . the first important dramatist of American public life since Arthur Miller, and maybe the best of them all."

With the worldwide success of *M. Butterfly* came new opportunities and venues for creative expression. A few months after the opening of *M. Butterfly*, Hwang and avant-garde composer Philip Glass produced *1000 Airplanes on the Roof*, a multimedia extravaganza about a close encounter with aliens.

In 1992, Hwang premiered another one-act, *Bondage*, at the Humana Festival of New American Plays at

Ping Chong.

Jessica Hagedorn. (Karen Dacker.)

the Actors Theatre of Louisville. The play is a gender-bending, race-changing, label-challenging work that confronts the inherent racism and sexism rampant in society.

Hwang's next production was a second Broadway opening. *Face Value*, a racially and sexually ambiguous farce inspired by the controversy over the casting of a white man in the lead role of the Eurasian pimp in the blockbuster *Miss Saigon*, was extremely short-lived. Although it closed after less than a week of troubled performances, Hwang's writing career has continued to flourish, especially in writing for the film industry.

In spite of a long list of screenplay credits to his name, Hwang "prefer[s] writing for the theatre because of the practical issue of control. A play can't be changed without the playwright's involvement, but with movies, it's very common that changes get made in the filming or editing process that the writer just isn't aware of." Hwang plans to pursue opportunities to direct in the future.

For further research, other pioneering, ground-breaking playwrights include Ernest Abuba, Rosanna Yamagiwa Alfaro, Jeannie Barroga, Mel Escueta, Dom Magwili, Edward Sakamoto, Rick Shiomi, Jon Shirota, Elizabeth Wong, and Laurence Yep.

◆ THEATRICAL INNOVATORS

Ping Chong

Ping Chong refers to what he does as "making works" (Chong, Ping. Telephone interview with author. March 10, 1994). The work he makes is found at the intersection of text, choreography, music, sounds, slides, and other visual designs—what he calls "interdisciplinary" or "contemporary" theatre. Since the late 1960s, Chong has been stretching the limits of theatre, originating more than 20 interdisciplinary performances and installations throughout the United States, Europe, and Asia. "What I'm doing is the exploration of a new syntax in theatre which reflects the changes in the contemporary world . . . I chose not to do traditional eurocentric theatre and so had to create my own syntax. In that way, I'm very American, perhaps American in a truer sense because I'm influenced by everything this country is. I don't stop at just Europe."

Chong began his theatrical career as a member of Meredith Monk's The House Foundation, eventually collaborating with Monk on such major pieces as *The Travelogue Series* and *The Games*. He branched out on his own, gathering a group of artists to create *Lazarus*, his first independent theatre work in 1972. The group began

A scene from Ping Chong's *Deshima.*

as The Fiji Theatre Company, evolving into Ping Chong & Company. Since then, his "contemporary theatre" includes *Humboldt's Current* (1977 Obie Award), *Nuit Blanche, A.M./A.M.—The Articulated Man* (1982 Villager Award), *Nosferatu, Angels of Swedenborg, Kind Ness* (1988 USA Playwrights' Award), *Brightness* (two 1990 Bessie awards), *Deshima,* and *Undesirable Elements.*

Always unpredictable, Chong is currently making *Chinoiserie,* an exploration of the relationship between China and the West, and *A Feather on the Breath of God,* a work with puppets slotted to premiere at the 1996 Olympics in Atlanta.

Jessica Hagedorn

"I knew I didn't want to write mainstream plays. I wanted to write for performance and eventually for film, so I just started doing it," says musician/poet/screenwriter/novelist/multimedia artist Jessica Hagedorn. The result is eclectic—part narrative, part music, part dance, part poetry, and wholly experiential and experimental. She cites Ping Chong as one of her important influences: "Ping Chong's *Nuit Blanche* had a lot of impact on me. It was so visually pristine, so clean, and yet Ping was playing with so many ideas. That taught me a lot."

Hagedorn's multimedia theatre pieces have been presented at New York's Public Theater, The Kitchen, and Dance Theater Workshop; works include *Tenement Lover: no palm trees in new york City, A Nun's Story, Alive From Off Center, Holy Food, Teenytown,* and *Mango Tango.* In spite of her experimental approaches and her changes in expressive medium, Hagedorn's themes have remained surprisingly consistent throughout her artistic endeavors: "In all my writing, there are always these characters who have a sense of displacement, a sense of being in self-exile, belonging nowhere—or anywhere. I think these themes are the human story. When it comes down to it, it's all about finding shelter, finding your identity. I don't care whether you're an immigrant or nativeborn, you're discovering who and what and where you are all the time.

Nobuko Miyamoto

With a career that spans over three decades, Nobuko Miyamoto is one performer who has experienced numerous incarnations as a Broadway dancer, choreographer, singer, composer, teacher, and actress, to name but few of Miyamoto's accomplishments. In 1978, she founded Great Leap, Inc., an Asian American arts organization that produces works in music, dance, and multimedia for the stage, as well as video, film, and recordings. "We don't have a stable home," explains Miyamoto. "Instead we have offices from which to reach out to different communities and areas. We bring our work to those communities rather than having a geographical center that forces people to come to us. We're really about reaching out to various communities, and not just to Asian American groups" (Miyamoto, Nobuko. Telephone interview with author. March 16, 1994).

In her latest work, Miyamoto draws on her various talents to create *A Grain of Sand*, a full-length, one-person performance piece. "The overriding theme," explains Miyamoto, "is the issue of finding a voice." Some of the voices Miyamoto expresses range from those of her parents and ancestors—"the voices that were quieted and suppressed"—to her own voice as both "a puppet voice for the entertainment world, the American cultural scene that I was a part of" and as "a voice that was part of the Asian American movement which happened for me about 1968 and '69." She includes not only the experiences of the Asian American community, but those of the Latino American, African American, and Native American communities as well. Fifteen years after the hopeful times of the Asian American movement, Miyamoto is convinced that "the world today is even more divided that ever before." In *Grains of Sand*, Miyamoto echoes, "once the world was changing, but now life is reduced to a one-woman show in search of meaning."

The show—which combines music, movement, poetic, and dramatic narratives with a dramatic backdrop of archival footage from the internment camp at Manzanar and the civil rights movements—debuted in December of 1992. Constantly in development, it reappeared in a second version at East West Players in January 1994 and is currently being toured. "It's a piece designed for touring," adds Miyamoto.

For further research, other notable multimedia and solo-performance artists include Brenda Wong Aoki, Charlie Chin, Amy Hill, Shishir Kurup, Dan Kwong, Sachiko Nakamura, Jude Narita, Lane Nishikawa, Dwight Okita, Nicky Paraiso, Dawn Saito, and DeniseUyehara.

◆ EMERGING ARTISTS

Han Ong

Han Ong, a very young artist currently in the state of moving, is not quite sure where he is going. "I do know that I'm quitting L.A.," he says with certainty (Ong, Han. Telephone interview with author. March 15, 1994). For the time being, he will follow his productions around the country.

At just 26 years of age, Ong's works already has an impressive production history. The year 1993 proved to be a fruitful one with *The L.A. Plays*, an autobiographical work comprised of two short works, *In a Lonely Country* and *A Short List of Alternate Places*, which premiered in April at the American Repertory Theatre in Cambridge, Massachusetts, and traveled in November to one of the most important fringe theatres of London, the Almeida. *The London Observer* said of the production, "You hear the unmistakable sound of new talent. Personal, stark, alienated." Also in 1993, Circle Repertory Company Theatre Lab staged a reading of *Wide Screen Version of the World*, a work Ong describes as "not representative of my body of work." In spite of his uncertainty toward the piece, it was nevertheless well received.

In 1994, Ong collaborated with Jessica Hagedorn to present *Airport Music* at New York's Public Theater in May. "It's about immigration," Ong begins. "Jessica and I are both from the Philippines. So it's about coming to the States when the Philippines was considered home. This work questions the idea of home, what home means. It's about the idea of home recreating itself in a new country." The play transferred to Berkeley Repertory Theater in June.

Sung Rno

With an undergraduate degree in physics from Harvard University and a masters of fine arts in poetry from Brown, Sung Rno [pronounced "no"] writes plays about floating Volkswagons, Connie Chung, and Christopher Columbus. His one full-length play to date is *Cleveland Raining*, about Ohio, Koreans, alienation, and global flooding. An inventive, unique, enchanting, humor-filled piece, it is slotted for a full production in spring 1995 at East West Players. *Cleveland* has already received numerous workshop productions and staged readings. Venues include the Mark Taper Forum in Los Angeles and New Dramatists in New York, as well as two full college productions at Brown and Grinnel. In the fall of 1992, Rno was commissioned by the New York Shakespeare Festival to write a new full-length play.

Over the last few years, Rno has been steadily building his repertoire, which thus far includes a varied body of one-act plays. A trilogy based on stories by Korean author Hwang Sun-Wun—*In a Small Island Village, Drizzle*, and *Masks*—was presented as a workshop production at Circle Repertory and as a staged reading at Northwest Asian American Theatre. In addition, *Konishiki, Mon Amour*, a play about media, Twinkies, and Connie Chung, was presented at New York's Public Theater as part of the Asian American Playwrights' Workshop and *New World*, which deconstructs the

Diana Son.

legends surrounding Christopher Columbus, was presented at Circle Repertory Lab.

The recipient of a 1993 Van Lier Playwrighting Fellowship at New Dramatists, Rno is working in a mentor program with the playwright Eduardo Machado. Rno's latest project was his involvement with *Out of the Shadows*, a multicultural festival created by six artists, which opened the 30th anniversary of Dance Theater Workshop in New York in fall 1994. Rno's piece, titled *Gravity Falls from Trees*, is "an expressionistic meditation" about a young Korean American girl who, after losing her grandmother in the downing of Korea Airlines flight 007 over Soviet airspace, tries to find the remnants of the plane with the help of Isaac Newton, a bereaved pilot, and local villagers.

Imaginative and irreverent, chimerical and questioning, Rno's young voice as it matures will certainly be heard loudly and clearly.

Diana Son

"Writing is a gift," says Diana Son. "I didn't earn it or cultivate it. Right now, I'm trying to deserve it. I'm trying to do something with it." Son's goal as a playwright is to be "highly entertaining" (Son, Diana. Telephone

interview with author. March 12, 1994). So far, she's successful. From her 1990s take on the classic tale of the two Greek sisters Procne and Philomela in *Stealing Fire*, which premiered at New York's Soho Rep in 1992, to the young, angry, sexy Asian American women of a new decade in *The R.A.W.* [R.A.W., for Raunchy Asian Woman] *Plays: R.A.W. ('Cause I'm a Woman)* and *The Joyless Bad Luck Club*, which has played various venues in New York, Son entertains with the comedy of a stand-up show, the poignancy of a tragedy, and the understanding of a seasoned performer.

She explains, "you really have to win over an audience first. Because then you can take them anywhere, even drag them through the stinkiest mud puddle. As long as you make the process of getting there as easy as possible, they [the audience] will endure with you, and you can deliver them somewhere, even new, risky, dangerous places, as long as you deliver them somewhere."

In her own writing, Son promises "to land you back on the ground, but [she] will definitely take you through some turbulence, some loopdy loops and tailspins before [she] return[s] you to solid ground."

Son's current work, *Boy*, a gender-challenging full-length play, will definitely take the audience on a ride to remember. The protagonist, named Boy, is actually a girl. Born the fourth daughter in family praying for a son, Boy is brought up from birth by everyone around her believing that she is just as her name states, a boy. At 11, Boy inevitably learns the shocking truth that she's a girl. She can no longer be Momma's Boy, the only son, and one of the boys. Instead, she must forge an entirely different identity for which she is completely unprepared. But little by little, she eventually learns that away from everyone else's expectations for defining her identity, she can just be a woman named Boy.

Other writers to watch for include Eugenie Chan, Susan Kim, Lesli-Jo Morizono, Dawn Saito, Alice Tuan, and Cary Wong.

♦ BEHIND THE SCENES

Phyllis S.K. Look
Director

Yale Drama School-trained with years of experience as an actress, Phyllis S.K. Look has spent the last seven years directing at Berkeley Repertory. She does some of her best work while dreaming, she says. "Creativity happens best when you're not working at it. As a director, I find that some of my best work comes intuitively and from the unconscious. I have the clearest connections with a play first thing in the morning or walking down the street when I'm not thinking" (Look, Phyllis. Telephone interview with author. March 16, 1994).

Chiori Miyagawa.

While she is one of the few Asian American directors working today in a major mainstream regional theatre, Look still finds "something very special about directing Asian American plays." She remembers Laurence Yep's *Dragonwings* as the play that originally propelled her career forward and gained her national recognition. More than that, the play "helped distill for [Look] what [her] voice is as a theatre director." She continues, "There are few opportunities in one's lifetime where a piece *really* uses all of you. That's how I felt about this work. I felt so connected emotionally, aesthetically, and politically to it."

Another play with special significance for Look is *FOB*, which she directed during her final year at Yale: "Going back to that piece brought back my own identity as a Chinese American. It was with that production that I began to use the initials of my middle name as part of my professional name. I didn't want to be mistaken for a white director, and I thought that the double initials would definitely suggest a Chinese name. I realized with *FOB* that my Chinese identity is very much at the center of who I am. Up to then, so much of my training had been through Eurocentric classics, especially at a place like Yale."

At the end of the 1994 season, Look will leave Berkeley Rep to embark on a freelance directing career. In addition to her responsibilities at Berkeley Repertory, she is co-artistic director of the Bay Area Playwrights Festival, wading through piles of scripts to find the six that will be developed in summer 1994. She is talking to yet another theatre about yet another production of *Dragonwings*, which is testimony to her vision as its conceiving director. And she is talking with two local universities about teaching and directing.

Look finds herself currently engrossed in the work of three up-and-coming Asian American women playwrights—Eugenie Chan, Alice Tuan, and Diana Son. So convinced is Look of their talents, she says she "would be happy to spend the rest of [her] career with them." She adds, "Working with these playwrights gave me a feeling of homecoming, maybe even stronger than I felt with *Dragonwings*." For the time being, Look is "placing [her] bets on these women."

"There seem to be waves of talent coming from many fronts," Look remarks. "Hopefully, I can be some place to help bring them together."

For further research, other directors include Ernest Abuba, Tisa Chang, Tim Dang, Philip Kan Gotanda, Shizuko Hoshi, Alberto Isaac, Mako, Ron Nakahara, Judith Nihei, Lane Nishikawa, and Roberta Uno.

Chiori Miyagawa
Dramaturge

Probably the only full-time Asian American dramaturge in the theatre world today, Chiori Miyagawa is on a mission "to work with mainstream systems, to change things from within." Her motto is multicultural, multidisciplinary, multiethnic; her battle is "to place enough artists of color out there so that the mainstream is no longer owned by mainstream people" (Miyagawa, Chiori. Telephone interviews with author. September 22, 1993 and March 10, 1994).

Miyagawa's career has deposited her in several major regional mainstream theatres, including Actors Theatre of Louisville in Kentucky, and Arena Stage in Washington, D.C. In 1992, Miyagawa returned to New York to join New York's Public Theater as one of 21 artistic associates.

At the Public Theater, Miyagawa developed a playwriting workshop to which she invited six young emerging Asian American playwrights: Eugenie Chan, Lesli-Jo Morizono, Sung Rno, Dawn Saito, Diana Son, and Cary Wong. Over an eight-week period, each wrote a one-act play on the theme of "intercultural experience." Miyagawa then brought in two nontraditional directors and produced a staged reading. The overfilled theatre in February 1993 confirmed for Miyagawa that "there are definitely people out there who are interested in young Asian American writers."

In fall 1993, Miyagawa became involved with HERE, the new multidisciplinary arts center in New York's Soho district. She curated a multiethnic performance series called "EVERYWHERE" that featured various solo performances, including *Reckless Angels* by Nicky Paraiso and *The R.A.W. Plays* by Diana Son. Miyagawa's latest project, which she co-curated with performance artist George Emilio Sanchez, was *Out of the Shadows*, a theatre/performance festival comprised of works by six emerging artists of color which opened Dance Theater Workshop's 30th anniversary in fall of 1994.

Miyagawa's goals are clear: cultures, ethnicities, genders, and mediums without boundaries. "In the future, all of us need to work together to create new

Ming Cho Lee.

forms of art so that we don't get caught up in recycled Broadway plays."

Ming Cho Lee
Set Designer

If you've seen pipes and scaffolding, if you've noticed collage on the stage, you've seen the work of Ming Cho Lee. He's been called the dean of American design and described as the most influential figure in the history of set design. For that matter, any reference to Lee is usually flowered with countless mosts and bests, with a few other superlatives thrown in. After almost 30 years of teaching, more than half of the set designers working in the 1990s have either been trained by him or have worked as his assistant. The others wouldn't hesitate to admit that they've been influenced by his style and method in some way.

In spite of a career that spans generations, Lee readily admits to a "terrible Broadway career." He adds, almost jovially, "I've had more Broadway flops than anyone in the history of theatre." He is bluntly honest. "It's very difficult to work on a theatre project where the ultimate goal is everyone's greed," he states. "In every show, there must be a victim," he explains. "The trick is not to be that victim. How can you do real

work in an environment like that?" Another hazard Lee points out on Broadway is that "whole lives' works are based on *one* reviewer. You always have to be guessing whether or not [New York Times theatre critic] Frank Rich—now David Richard—will like something or not. It's like Russian roulette." He adds in all seriousness, "I didn't go into theatre to gamble."

Broadway record aside, Lee has spent 11 years designing for The New York Shakespeare Festival, 14 years with New York City Opera, and 20 years at the Metropolitan Opera. He has designed productions in probably every major regional theatre in the United States and in many international venues as well.

Lee balances his design career with teaching. Now in his 25th year at Yale, he currently chairs the design department at the Drama School. "I love teaching," he states.

He comments that he has had very few Asian American students who have graduated in design. "It's very frustrating that after more than 25 years of teaching, I've only had one lighting designer," he cites as an example. The set designer Wing Lee is also one of his few graduates. "I think a career in the arts is not really totally acceptable to Asian families, especially for male offspring. In a way, there seems to be a distrust of the arts. Earning a living at it is very difficult. Asian Americans, especially first-generation Asian Americans, tend to be pragmatic people and it's very hard for them to imagine a life of insecurity for their children. The arts and theatre somehow don't always have tangible results. A career in arts can be enormously meaningful and have nothing to do with success." Referring to his own decision to enter set design, Lee remembers "it was a tremendous crisis in my family."

But after countless awards (including a Tony, Drama Desk, and Outer Critics Circle), fellowships (including Guggenheim and National Endowment for the Arts), and at least two honorary doctorates, the only crisis Lee might have to deal with is where he'll find the time to finish all his projects.

Willa Kim
Costume Designer

Willa Kim must be one of the most decorated artists working in theatre. She has won Tony awards for Duke Ellington's *Sophisticated Ladies* (1981) and *The Will Rogers Follies* (1991). She has received Tony nominations for Peter Allen's *Legs Diamond* (1988), Andrew Lloyd Webber's *Song and Dance* (1985), Bob Fosse's *Dancin'* (1978), and Joel Grey's *Goodtime Charley* (1975). She won an Emmy for San Francisco Ballet's production of *The Tempest* (choreographed by Michael Smuin, 1981), Drama Desk awards for Maria Irene Fornes's *Promenade* (1969), Sam Shepherd's *Operation Sidewinder* (1988), and Jean Genet's *The*

Screens (1971); and an Obie for Robert Lowell's *The Old Glory* (1976).

Kim, who studied fashion illustration at the Chouinard Institute of Art in her hometown of Los Angeles, fell into costume design straight out of art school: "One of my art instructors insisted that I take my portfolio around to art studios and department stores. I was so delighted when Western Costume asked me to leave it. It was as big as I was and it was so heavy to carry around. The next thing I knew, I was working in the studios." Her first New York production was Arnold Weinstein's 1961 off-Broadway play *Red Eye of Love*. "I had to create 50 costumes with a budget of $250. I used to fall asleep on the floor in the theatre and get up and sew at the strangest hours," recalls Kim. In spite of this difficult beginning, she was hooked. Just five years later, she was designing on Broadway for Edward Albee's *Malcolm*. By the time she was working on *Will Rogers Follies*, Kim's budget had escalated to $1 million with costumes each costing in the thousands.

During her more than three-decade career which shows no signs of slowing down, Kim has been a pioneer in her field. Credited with being the first designer to use thin stretch fabric for dancer's tights as well as painting designs onto fabrics, Kim continues to design for dance, opera, and theatre. She voices a special preference for musicals.

Willa Kim designed the costumes for the revival of *Grease* that opened on Broadway in late spring 1994. The projects that followed *Grease* are two new musicals: Blake Edward's stage version of *Victor/Victoria* starring Julie Andrews and *Busker*, a musical from Tommy Tune.

Victor En Yu Tan
Lighting Designer

"I'm a college dropout from Columbia University," says Victor Tan. "I was first an assistant to various lighting designers and that's how I learned to design and I've been designing ever since" (Tan, Victor. Telephone interview with author. March 16, 1994). Today, Tan shares his more than 20 years of experience with graduate students at the University of Michigan at Ann Arbor's Theatre and Drama department where he is associate professor. Since he entered academia, he has had to cut back on his yearly schedule of 20 to 25 shows, but he still manages to get in about eight to 12 productions.

Tan's first design opportunity in New York turned out to be the 1974 production of Frank Chin's *The Year of the Dragon* at The American Place Theatre. "I came about it in a strange, roundabout way," recalls Tan. "Up until then, I had been an assistant to other designers. On a certain project, there had been problems between

the director and the [lighting] designer and as the assistant, I ended up mediating for both sides. Afterwards, the director told me that I had saved the show and that he wanted me to do his next show, which turned out to be Chin's *Year of the Dragon*."

The play was a lucky charm for Tan. One night during *Dragon*'s run, a friend approached Tan, unaware that Tan had done the lighting. That friend turned out to be Oz Scott who offered Tan his second design job—Ntozake Shange's *For Colored Girls . . .* —and a four-play collaboration between Tan, Scott, and Ntozake Shange began.

Since 1979, Tan has been a freelance lighting designer and has completed over 400 productions in the United States and abroad, including over 25 productions at New York's Public Theater. Notable among these are: David Henry Hwang's *FOB* and *Dance and the Railroad*, and George Wolfe's *The Colored Museum*. Tan's regional theatre credits include designs for the Actors Theatre of Louisville's annual Humana Festival of New American Plays, the Mark Taper Forum, American Repertory Theater, and Pasadena Playhouse.

Since 1980, Tan has been the resident lighting designer for Pan Asian Repertory, where he recently designed the revival of *FOB*, directed by David Henry Hwang. He won an Obie in 1985 for Sustained Excellence in Lighting and most recently a Dramalogue for *The Colored Museum*.

As both a professional and teacher in the field, Tan has noticed the lack of Asian Americans in design fields. "There are not too many Asian Americans in theatre, anyway," he adds. "When I meet an Asian American with designing interest, I encourage them to come and study . . . and I'm always trying to get people interested in design."

Other important designers include Loy Arcenas and Wing Lee (sets), Lydia Tanji, Susan Tsu, Susan Watanabe (costumes), and Dawn Chiang (lighting).

◆ FUTURE OF ASIAN AMERICAN THEATRE

Judi Nihei at Northwest Asian American Theatre (NWAAT) said that 20 years ago she thought Asian American theatres would not still exist today because there would not be a need for them. From her perspective in the early 1970s, Nihei believed that by the 1990s, Asian American playwrights would be welcomed and nurtured by mainstream theatres, while color-blind casting would be the norm rather than the exception and that theatre would be just theatre, without boundaries resulting from labels and definitions. Nihei's thoughts were certainly hopeful and perhaps a reality the theatre world is still heading toward. The pace, however, is noticeably slow—more Asian American writers than not are still unable to get work produced in larger, mainstream venues while the stereotype of the passive Asian woman who sacrifices her life for the great white man is still one of the largest and most dependable box-officedraws on Broadway and beyond.

Perhaps playwright Philip Gotanda expressed it best when he said, "It's the best of times, and the worst of times . . . we as Asian American artists and writers are marginalized now as much as we ever were. While *The New York Times* will run an article about me acknowledging my work as a known writer, I still walk down the street and someone will yell out [a racist epithet]. I'm still a one-dimensional stereotype. In some ways, nothing has been resolved and that's something we as Asian Americans must all live with."

In spite of the success of pioneers like Gotanda, David Hwang, Ming Cho Lee, and Willa Kim, on many levels, each Asian American is still perceived as the foreigner, the other, and outside of the mainstream. Based on Gotanda's experience, even those Asian Americans who by some arbitrary definition have "made it" continue to be stereotyped.

How do the stereotypes affect the institution of Asian American theatre? As observed by Judi Nihei, the very existence of Asian American theatres means that Asian Americans have not been embraced by the mainstream. However, to preserve Asian American identities and to educate this new global village about the unique Asian American sensibility, history, and experiences, there will always be a need for Asian American theatres, writers, performers, actors, directors, and designers as beacons to challenge the established patterns of the so-called mainstream and to continue to lead the theatre world in new directions.

♦ ASIAN AMERICAN THEATRES

Asian American Theater Co.

403 Arguello Blvd.
San Francisco, CA 94118
(415) 751-2600

East West Players

4424 Santa Monica Blvd.
Los Angeles, CA 90029
(213) 660-0366

Great Leap, Inc.

244 S. San Pedro St., Ste. 408
Los Angeles, CA 90012
(213) 687-3948

Ma-Yi Theatre Ensemble, Inc.

P.O. Box 661
New York, NY 10159-0661
(212) 662-0079

Northwest Asian American Theatre

409 7th Ave.
Seattle, WA 98104
(206) 340-1445

National Asian American Theatre Co.

200 W. 20th St. Ste. 211
New York, NY 10011
(212) 675-0767

Pan Asian Rep

47 Great Jones St.
New York, NY 10012
(212) 505-5655

Ping Chong and Co.

47 Great Jones St.
New York, NY 10012
(212) 529-1557

Theater Mu

1201 Yale Place, Ste. 911
Minneapolis, MN 55403
(612) 332-5763

Theatre of Yugen

Noh Space
2840 Mariposa St.
San Francisco, CA 94110
(415) 621-0507

Wise Fool Productions

125 Seaman Ave., Ste. 6G
New York, NY 10034
(212) 569-1836

References

Books

Aronson, Arnold. " "Ming Cho Lee." *American Set Design*, 86-103, New York: Theatre Communications Group, 1985.

Berson, Misha. *Between Worlds: Contemporary Asian American Plays.* New York: Theatre Communications Group, Inc., 1990.

Chin, Frank. "The Chickencoop Chinaman" and "The Year of the Dragon." *Two Plays by Frank Chin.* Seattle: University of Washington Press, 1981.

Chin, Frank et al. *Aiiieeeee! An Anthology of Asian American Writers.* New York: Mentor, 1974.

———. *The Big Aiiieeee! An Anthology of Chinese American and Japanese American Literature*. New York: Meridian, 1991.

Gotanda, Philip Kan. Manuscripts of *Day Standing on Its Head, The Dream of Kitamura, Fish Head Soup, In the Dominion of Night,* and *A Song for a Nisei Fisherman.* [no other bibliographical information available].

———. *Yankee Dawg You Die.* New York: Dramatists Play Service, 1991.

Hagedorn, Jessica. *Charlie Chan is Dead: An Anthology of Contemporary Asian American Fiction.* New York: Penguin Books, 1993.

Houston, Valena Hasu. *The Politics of Life: Four Plays by Asian American Women.* Philadelphia: Temple University Press, 1993.

Hwang, David Henry. *"FOB" and Other Plays.* New York: Plume, 1990.

Lai, Him Mark, Genny Lim, and Judy Yung. *Island: Poetry and History of Chinese Immigrants on Angel Island, 1910-1940.* Seattle: University of Washington Press, 1980.

Lee, Ming Cho. "Designing Opera." *Contemporary Stage Design U.S.A.* Middletown, Connecticut: Wesleyan University Press, 1975.

———. "Introduction." *American Set Design 2.* New York: Theatre Communications Group, 1991.

Pecktal, Lynn. *Costume Design: Techniques of Modern Masters.* New York: Backstage Books, 1993.

Prince, Harold. "Foreword." *American Set Design.* New York: Theatre Communications Group, 1985.

Smith, Ron. "Loy Arcenas." *American Set Design* 2. New York: Theatre Communications Group, 1991.

Uno, Roberta. *Unbroken Thread: An Anthology of Plays by Asian American Women.* Amherst: University of Massachusetts Press, 1993.

Newspapers and Periodicals

Chin, Frank. "Backtalk." *News of The American Place Theatre* 4, no. 4, May 1972.

Chin, Frank. "Don't Pent Us Up in Chinatown." *New York Times,* October 8, 1972.

Chung, L. A. "Chinese American Literary War." *San Francisco Chronicle,* August 26, 1991, People Section, D4.

Coveney, Michael. "Tales of the City." *London Observer,* November 14, 1993, Review Section, 17.

Duka, John. "She Made 'Ladies' Look Sophisticated." *New York Times,* September 20, 1981, D3.

Fields, Sidney. "Only Human: Oriental Overture to Broadway." *New York Daily News,* January 9, 1978, 81.

Gardella, Kay. "Star of 'Manzanar' Film Gives Japanese View of Us." *New York Daily News,* March 5, 1986, 98.

Gussow, Mel. "Critic's Notebook: Striding Past Dragon Lady and No. 1 Son." *New York Times.* September 3, 1990, sec. 1, 11.

———. "Stage: 'Shogun Macbeth,' *New York Times,* November 21, 1986.

Haru, Sumi. "and Sumi Haru." *AsianWeek,* February 18, 1994, A12.

Henry, William A. III. "When East and West Collide." *Time.* August 14, 1989, 62.

Howard, Beth. "Designers on Designing: Willa Kim." *Theater Craft,* (March 1989): 29-33.

Keyishian, Harry. "A Midsummer Night's Dream." *Shakespeare Bulletin,* 10, no. 3, (Summer 1993).

Kroll, Jack. *Newsweek,* June 19, 1972.

M., E. "Three Plays Beckon Local Theatergoers." *New York Nichibei* [no other bibliographical information available].

MacKay, Patricia. "Designers on Designing: Ming Cho Lee." *Theater Craft,* (February 1984), 15-21.

Pacheco, Patrick. "When Worlds Collide." *Los Angeles Times,* April 19, 1992, Calendar Section, 3.

Pais, Arthur J. "Willa Kim's Fashion 'Follies'." *USAir Magazine,* (October 1993), 64-67.

Smith, Roberta. "Behind the Painted World of 'Once On This Island'." *New York Times,* October 14, 1990, Section 2, 5.

Steele, Mike. "Critics Choice / Theater." *Star Tribune,* April 16, 1993, Calendar Section.

Talbot, Margaret. *Image,* January 13, 1991: 11-17.

Wong, Wayman. "Willa-Mania!" *TheaterWeek,* July 8-14, 1991: 24-7.

—Terry Hong

Media

♦ Portrayal in Mainstream Media ♦ Newspapers ♦ Television and Radio Broadcasting
♦ Magazines ♦ Films ♦ Advertising

♦ PORTRAYAL IN MAINSTREAM MEDIA

Asian Americans are the nation's fastest growing ethnic minority, although they comprise only 2.9 percent of the total population. They are also the most diverse group, with immigrants from China, Japan, Korea, Cambodia, Vietnam, the Pacific Islands, and other East Asian nations, as well as South Asians from India, Pakistan, Bangladesh, Sri Lanka, Maldives, Nepal, and Bhutan. There is no single language, religion, or racial characteristic common among Asian Americans except that they all come from different parts of Asia where cultures and civilizations have been interactive for thousands of years. Asian Americans share a history of Buddhism, trade along the silk route, the spread of Islam, and colonialism. They also share a legacy of socially conservative cultures, hierarchical societies, and ancient philosophies.

Of Asian Americans in the United States, South Asians are the more recent immigrants, fewer in number and rarely covered by the mainstream media. On those occasions when they are covered, the film industry usually portrays them as exotic turbaned Indian Maharajas or New York City taxi drivers with strong accents. Moreover, Asian Indians, Sikhs, and Pakistanis are increasingly portrayed in films as naive new immigrants. They often form the backdrop of the urban metropolis: a hospital doctor, a hotel owner, or street vendor. The larger segment of this ethnic group—namely Asian/Pacific Americans—has been given the most significant attention by the mainstream American media. The treatment of an ethnic group in the media is often influenced by economic, political, and cultural factors. Movies like *Rising Sun* (a murder mystery interwoven with the theme of the dismantling of American industry by Japan) sometimes portray Japan bashing as result of American anxiety about economic hardship. Such movies serve to demonstrate anti-Asian

sentiment and antagonism increase whenever there is an economic crisis or conflict between Japan and the United States.

Asian Americans are frequently stereotyped in the media as being "model minorities," or as being submissive and obedient. Chinese Americans are often associated with laundries whereas Korean Americans are usually depicted as grocery store owners. These images reflect a lack of knowledge on the part of writers who resort to stereotypes to present their ideas. Other words used to describe Asians are "sinister" or "inscrutable," both with connotations of hidden danger. Furthermore, the flippant and insensitive use of ethnic slurs such as Japs to refer to the Japanese can dehumanize entire communities. Often when prominent Asian Americans are profiled by the media they are identified by their country of origin even though they are born and brought up in the U.S. and have never seen their parents' or grandparents' country. These references portray Asian Americans as outsiders in their own homeland. Military metaphors such as "Asian invasion" also imply that Asian Americans are part of a massive force overrunning the country. Such detrimental images are the focus of *Project Zinger*, a media watchdog publication of the Asian American Journalists Association and the Center for Integration and Improvement of Journalism at San Francisco State University. Any periodical or broadcast report that perpetuates an ethnic stereotype is examined by a research team and discussed in an effort to sensitize journalists. Founded in 1991, *Project Zinger* also highlights examples of good reporting on Asian American people and issues.

In public opinion polls the Asian American perspective is often ignored by the mainstream media, who focus only on such sensational community happenings, as crimes or major social events. Since the news shapes public policy, an absence of a minority voice is a serious issue. This omission was apparent in the initial coverage of the Los Angeles riots in 1992. Although more than 11 percent of the area population is Asian American, their perspective was grossly overlooked, a direct result of nonintegrated newsrooms that are unaware of different cultures and attitudes.

♦ NEWSPAPERS

There have been numerous Asian American-oriented newpapers in the United States. Founded in 1854, the *Golden Hill News* in San Francisco was one of the earliest, and it featured reports from China. This periodical was followed by the Japanese *Hawaii Hochi*, the 55-year-old *Sing Tao Daily*, and *Asian Week*, an established San Francisco newspaper that covers Asian American activity in California. Many such publications were—and still are—bilingual. Although ethnic papers continue to flourish, it is the way Asian Americans are represented in the mainstream media that influences public opinion. Unfortunately, such representation can lead to stereotyping that is difficult to erase. During World War II, the *San Francisco Examiner* published an editorial cartoon showing Japanese Americans in concentration camps. The paper justified the imprisonment with the caption "It is entirely too difficult to tell a good Jap from a bad Jap." All the cartoon figures looked alike with overbites, slanted eyes, and glasses. They were also drawn crossing their fingers as they pledged allegiance to the U.S. flag. In a 1992 editorial, the *Examiner* finally apologized for its "wrong judgment."

However, it is not that easy to correct the damage that these images have had on the mainstream perception of Asian Americans. Cultural biases continue to permeate newsrooms which lack adequate diversity. In a 1993 survey by the American Society of Newspaper Editors (ASNE), newsroom minorities had risen to slightly over 10 percent of total employees for the first time. This fact is far from the goal set by the ASNE of achieving minority employment that matches the true proportions minority populations by the year 2000. Such an accomplishment would amount to the employment of minorities in approximately 27 percent of newsroom staff positions. The survey also showed that 55 percent of U.S. dailies employ minority professionals and that the percentage of minority supervisors has increased to 7.1 percent. The remaining 45 percent have no minority employees and are mainly smaller papers representing 31 percent of the country's daily circulation. Critics suggest there is a "glass ceiling" that discourages minority promotion. At present approximately 1,025 Asian American journalists work at newspapers, forming 1.91 percent of the newsroom workforce. A survey by the Asian American Journalist's Association shows that Asian American journalists are likely to leave the profession at higher rates than whites because they find that they cannot advance after a certain point in their careers.

In cities like Atlanta, Los Angeles, Washington, D.C., and New York where 40 percent of the population is made up of minority groups, minority employment newsrooms is nevertheless lower and therefore unrepresentative of the areas they cover. This imbalance leads to inadequate news coverage of ethnic communities; instead, the possibility exists that minorities will be written about as curiosities or outsiders, setting the stage for sensationalism. One example of such coverage occured in a 1992 *Torrance Daily Breeze* story about the increase in the Asian Pacific population entitled "Asian Invasion."

For newspapers to report on all communities in the United States both accurately and impartially, they must diversify their staffs in an effort to offer their readership news that is relevant to all constituents. In recent years numerous news organizations have funded programs and job fairs in an attempt to recruit minorities, including Asian Americans, although statistics show that a more sustained endeavor is needed.

In an effort to promote fairness and accuracy in the media coverage of Asian American issues, the Asian American Journalists Association was formed in 1981. The association encourages Asian American students to pursue careers in journalism and provides mentor programs and job hotlines to help recent graduates secure professional positions. Each year the AAJA hosts a convention where there are job fairs, exhibitions, and workshops. In 1994, the AAJA hosted its convention in Atlanta along with the National Association of Black Journalists, the National Association of Hispanic Journalists, and the Native American Journalists Association. The event, called Unity 94, marked the first time that journalists from all four minority groups met to share views on the status of minorities in the media.

♦ TELEVISION AND RADIO BROADCASTING

Broadcasting, particularly television, is the most visible medium of mainstream communication, and a number of Asian American figures have made it to the screen in the last decade. Celebrity news anchors are often named as proof of Asian American participation in this medium. These personalities include Connie Chung, Tritia Toyota, Wendy Tokuda, and Kaity Tong. In radio, the voice of Chitra Raghavan on National Public Radio is a reflection of increasing diversity at the national level. However, real influence in broadcasting generally exists far from the screen or microphone. Decisions on production, direction, budgets, and time are made by producers, managers, and news directors. Therefore, the presence of a high profile Asian American anchor does not necessarily imply an integrated newsroom.

It is true that Asian Americans have joined the broadcasting industry in record numbers since the 1970s. Records indicate that about 800 Asian American journalists were working at TV and radio stations in 1992, 11 of which were news directors at commercial TV stations. Broadcast media are ahead of newspapers in terms of minority employment since 11.3 percent of radio personnel come from minority groups, as do 18.5 percent of TV professionals. African Americans comprise over half of these numbers, followed by Hispanics, Asian Americans, and Native Americans.

Increasingly, Asian Americans are not only reporters and anchors, but also managers, writers, and videographers. In San Francisco, ten percent of TV news professionals are Asian Americans. Few of these professionals have attained management positions, however, and an overwhelming majority of them are women, who seem to have found a niche as coanchors. The pairing of a white male with an Asian female seems to have become a more common screen image on TV news. The dearth of Asian males on-screen is troublesome to critics who argue that it implies that Asian males are not authoritative. Sam Chu Lin, anchor and news reporter for KTLA says, "Women are accepted more than men for several reasons. Asian American women are nonthreatening and perceived as more attractive than Asian American men. Asian American men are generalized as being first of all—the Asian businessman . . . a competitor in business against Americans. It has always been portrayed in television series, unfortunately, that Asian men have been fighting against the Americans."

The other reason cited for the preponderance of Asian women reporters is the networks' desire to fulfill quotas. Asian women fill two—they are minorities and women. An absence of role models has also resulted in fewer Asian men pursuing a career as TV reporters. Dan Woo, a network news associate producer, describes the standard formula for a newscast as having a "male anchor who's either a macho-looking `Ken doll' or an older, distinguished-looking guy, and a pretty minority woman, usually black or Asian, for the other anchor, a jock for sports and a funny man for weather." Given this practice, it is unlikely that Asian American men will get a chance to be anchors any time soon.

Like most television professionals, Asian Americans start at the bottom of the ladder as news assistants or secretaries at TV stations. Diane Fukami, the assistant news director at KPIX in San Francisco, is the first Asian to hold that position in a major market. She started out as secretary to the station's news director. Overall, there are very few Asian Americans who have made it up to managerial levels. This absence cannot be made up by a growing number of on-screen professionals.

The coverage of Asian American issues on network news reflects a lack of depth due to limited awareness. David Liu, an Emmy award-winning producer who is also a founding member of the National Asian American Telecommunications Association says, "There's always coverage of a Chinatown gang murder or of a Chinese New Year's celebration . . . there should be more coverage in a case like Vincent Chin's (racially motivated murder) in the Detroit area, there's not nearly the proportion of coverage that there should be."

Recently WNYE, a PBS affiliate in New York, started a weekly 30-minute prime-time program in English that covers social, political, economic, and cultural topics concerning Asian Americans. The program, called *Asian America*, consists of panel discussions, interviews, and personality profiles. Its mission is to provide information on Asia and Asian Americans and to educate not only the Asian American community but the general public as well. The first person interviewed on the show was Nora Chang Wang, New York Mayor Rudolph Guiliani's employment commissioner; this conversation was followed by a discussion on the lifting of the Vietnam trade embargo. The show is produced by Morning Calm Productions and is underwritten by AT&T. It reflects a new trend in the news media—targeting the growing number of English-speaking Asian Americans who no longer wish to be limited by ethnic stereotypes and who are tired of being ignored or misrepresented by the mainstream media.

♦ MAGAZINES

An increased awareness of an English-speaking Asian American identity is evident in the magazine industry as well. Earlier publications generally focused on a single national origin or region and many were bilingual. The most recent venture, *A. Magazine*, is aimed at the entire English-speaking Asian American audience and addresses issues and concerns that neither ethnic nor mainstream media fulfill. Founded in 1993 by Jeff Yang and Phoebe Eng in New York, the quarterly has a circulation of about 60,000 (subscribers), and focuses on young Asian Americans, combining news with commentary and fashion. About 44 percent of the target audience is between 25 and 35 years of age and 33 percent is between 18 and 25. College degrees are held by 88 percent of its readership, and the median household income of subscribers is $57,000. Some of the topics covered by the magazine are interracial romances, problems in the workplace stemming from bias, cosmetic surgery, and Asian American stereotyping in the media.

Another magazine called *Face* is published by Transpacific Media. It is a bimonthly beauty magazine for Asian American women in the tradition of *Vogue* and *Glamour*. The contents focus on makeup tips, fashion, food, entertainment, and interviews with prominent women. Only Asian American models are used. The magazine has approximately 20,000 subscribers with a median household income of $90,000 to $100,000. Its publisher Tom Kagy asserts that *Face* examines "the technology of Asian beauty." One of the magazine's articles discussed the plastic surgery most commonly sought by Asian/Pacific Americans, including the creation of "double eyelids." Kagy also publishes *Transpacific Magazine*, which has been in existence for seven years and has a circulation of 59,000. He plans to start a magazine for Asian American men called *XO*.

With regard to academic periodicals, University of California law students in both Los Angeles and Berkeley have begun to publish English-language law journals focusing on Asian American issues. These publications serve to provide information to a growing numbers of Asian American lawyers and students, many of whom feel that their ethnic concerns are neglected by existing publications. In 1991, 5,028 Asian Americans were enrolled in law school, according to the American Bar Association. The UCLA journal plans to use student writers and focus on issues concerning Asian American activity in Southern California. The Berkeley journal will tackle issues like international trade by involving scholars from around the world in an attempt to create a global forum.

♦ FILMS

In 1981 an independent movie called *Chan is Missing*, made by Wayne Wang, caught the imagination of moviegoers. Unlike the stereotypical "dragon lady" and "kung fu" movies, this low-budget ($25,000) film had humor and vision. It won acclaim from film critics and heralded a new era for Asian filmmakers. A young director from Hong Kong, Wang went on to produce *Dim Sum, Slamdance, Eat a Bowl of Tea,* and *Life Is Cheap.* His latest feature was *The Joy Luck Club,* which he made with the help of producers Janet Yang and Oliver Stone. This film grossed over $22 million and played at 600 theaters nationwide. It has been argued that the movie's appeal lay in the universality of its central theme: the relationship of mothers and daughters. Such a technique has become the trend for successful commercial ventures by Asian American filmmakers in that they depict a part of their culture in a way that touches everyone.

Over the past few decades, a number of Asian American filmmakers have surfaced. At the 1994 Los Angeles Asian Pacific Film and Video Festival more than 40 entries were screened. In 1991 Berkeley filmmaker Steve Okazaki won an Oscar for *Days in Waiting.* Since then a number of Asian filmmakers have had their works nominated for an Academy Award. These movies include Mira Nair for *Mississippi Masala* and *Salaam Bombay,* Okazaki for *Unfinished Business,* Renee Tajima and Christine Choy for *Who Killed Vincent Chin?,* Arthur Dong for *Sewing Women,* Michael Uno for *The Silence,* and Lise Yasui for *Family Gathering.* New directors like Srinivas Krishna (*Masala*) and Greg Araki (*The Living End*) have been praised by critics and art film patrons alike. International filmmakers such as Ismail Merchant, Satyajit Ray, Shyam Benegal, Akira Kurusawa, and numerous others have received worldwide acclaim and serve as role models for young Asian American filmmakers.

In Hollywood no more than 40 or 50 Asian Americans hold junior positions in studios and production companies, and very few make it to high-level management. To address this problem the Coalition of Asian/Pacifics in Entertainment—a group of 200 Asian Americans—was formed to improve the status of Asian Americans in show business by overcoming the cultural biases of white media executives.

♦ ADVERTISING

Asian Americans are the fastest growing immigrant community in the United States and they have the highest annual median income of any group at $42,245, followed by whites at $36,915. Perhaps it is not surprising then that advertisers are begining to recognize this segment of society. Despite the potential for tapping the Asian American market, little research has been done to indicate how profitable it is to advertise in English for Asian Americans. Asian American magazines in English have not been around long enough to determine success rates. One particular issue of *A. Magazine* had 23-full-page advertisements and an issue of *Face* had approximately 10. Advertisers are also unsure if there is a unified Asian American market. A small New York advertising agency that specializes in Asian marketing launched a Chinese-language magazine called *Megachine* in 1991. The publisher believed that there was no cohesion in the Asian American population and therefore elected to tackle the majority segment which is Chinese American. It remains to be seen whether a pan-Asian approach or a specific language approach is more successful. Some companies use both avenues, advertising in native-language and English-speaking publications.

References

American Society of Newspaper Editors. "Newsroom Minorities top 10 Percent, ASNE 1993 Survey Shows." Press release, ASNE, Baltimore, March 30, 1993.

Cocoran, Katherine. "Reaching for Diversity." *Washington Journalism Review.*

"Dot's all. . .," *Daily News*, March 1, 1994.

Duignan-Cabrera, Anthony. "Asian American Reporters Conference Focuses on Jobs." *Los Angeles Times*, August 20, 1993.

Eng, Alvin, "New York: In the Picture but Not in Focus." *Rice*, March 1988, 41.

Galbraith, Jane. "Group Takes *Rising Sun* Protest Public." *Los Angeles Times*, April 7, 1993.

Hinge, John B. "Agency to Launch Magazine Aimed at Asian Americans." *Wall Street Journal*, August 23, 1991.

Iwata, Edward. "Asian Movies Take Flight; Filmmakers Make Move into the Mainstream." *Los Angeles Times*, May 13, 1993.

Kannellos, Nicolas. *Hispanic American Almanac*, Detroit: Gale Research Inc., 1993, 621-74.

Lai, Ivan. "Asian Americans in Broadcasting," *Rice*, March 1988, 37.

———. "Fifteen Minutes to Air Time: A Day with Executive Producer Janice Gin." *Rice*, March 1988, 45.

Lee, Bill J. ed. *Asian American Media Reference Guide*, 2nd ed., New York: Asian CineVision, 1990.

Lee, Felicia R. "Phoebe Eng; Publisher Sees Asian-American Identity as a Work-in-Progress." *New York Times*, October 10, 1993.

Marshall, Brenda. "Los Angeles: Window of Opportunity or Closed Door?" *Rice*, March 1988, 43.

Morning Calm Productions, Inc. "Asian America." Press release, New York, 1994.

"Asian View for WYNE." *New York Post*, March 1, 1994.

"American Identity as a Work-in-Progress." *New York Times*, October 10, 1993.

"The Media Business: A Window on the Fast-Growing Audience of Asian Americans." *New York Times*, March 22, 1993.

"Two New Law Journals Plan to Focus on Asian Americans." *New York Times*, January 29, 1993.

"Newspapers, Diversity and You 1993-94," The Dow Jones Newspaper Fund, Inc. 1993.

Project Zinger, A critical look at news media coverage of Asian Pacific Americans, Center for Integration and Improvement of Journalism, Asian American Journalists Association, August 29, 1992, Washington D.C. and August 20, 1993, Los Angeles.

Seay, Elizabeth. "Two English Speaking Magazines Target Affluent Asian Americans." *Wall Street Journal.*

Stone, Vernon A. "Good News, Bad News." *Communicator*, August, 1993.

———. "Little Change for Minorities and Women." *Communicator*, August, 1992.

Tan, Alexis S. "Why Asian American Journalists Leave Journalism and Why They Stay." Paper presented to the national convention of the Asian American Journalists Association, New York, August 23, 1990.

—Natasha Rafi

Sports and Athletics

◆ Baseball ◆ Fencing ◆ Figure Skating ◆ Football ◆ Ice Hockey ◆ Martial Arts ◆ Sumo Wrestling
◆ Tennis ◆ World Rugby ◆ Asian American Olympians

◆ BASEBALL

Ron Darling (1960-)
Pitcher

Ron Darling is an award winning pitcher who played in one World Series—with the victorious New York Mets in 1986—and three championship series—two with the Mets and one with the Oakland A's.

Darling was born on August 19, 1960, in Honolulu, Hawaii. He went to high school at St. John's Academy in Worcester, Massachusetts, and college at Yale. He was selected by the Texas Rangers in the first round of the free agent draft in 1981, and played one season with the Rangers' farm team in Tulsa, Oklahoma. Prior to the 1982 season, he was traded to the New York Mets organization. He played that season (1982) and part of the next on the Mets' farm team at Tidewater. In mid-1993, he was called up to the majors and finished up that year with a record of one win and three losses.

In the next few seasons Ron Darling became one of the better known pitchers in baseball. In 1985, his record was sixteen wins and six losses, and he was selected to the National League All-Star Team, though he did not play in the game. The next year the Mets went to the World Series. In the World Series, Darling won one game and lost another, pitching a total of 17 and 2/3 innings with an ERA of 1.53. He threw twelve strike outs and walked ten. He finished the 1986 season with a record of fifteen wins and six losses. The next year his record was twelve wins and eight losses, followed in 1988 with a record of seventeen wins and nine losses. In 1988, the Mets played in the championship series and Darling pitched one game, which he lost. In 1989, Darling won the National League Golden Glove Award for his position.

In the middle of the 1991 season, Darling was traded to the Montreal Expos, who traded him to the Oakland Athletics two weeks later. In 1992, the A's went to the championship series, and Darling pitched one game, which he lost. He finished the 1992 season with a record of fifteen wins and ten losses.

Sid Fernandez (1962-)
Pitcher

Sid Fernandez is a pitcher with the New York Mets who came to national prominence as part of the 1986 world championship team. Born on October 12, 1962, in Honolulu, Hawaii, Fernandez went to high school at Kaiser High in Honolulu. He was drafted by the Los Angeles Dodgers in the third round of the free agent draft in 1981. He played in the Dodgers' farm system for two years and then briefly with the Dodgers in 1983. Following the 1983 season, Fernandez was traded to the Mets and, in 1984, pitched twelve games in the majors, winning six and losing six. In the 1985 season, Fernandez again played in both the minors and the majors, and in 1986, he played his first full season in the majors—the year the Mets won the World Series. In the National League Championship Series, Fernandez pitched six innings of one game, taking a loss. In the World Series, he did not pitch a complete game. He was selected to the National League All-Star team in both 1986 and 1987. Fernandez' best season was 1989, when he won fourteen games to five losses and had a .737 winning percentage.

Wendell Kim (1950-)
Coach

Wendell Kim is the first and only Korean American to wear a major league uniform. From 1989 to 1991, he served as the Giants' first base coach, moving the next year to coach at third base. As a player, he spent seven seasons with the San Francisco Giants' farm teams as an infielder, never making it to the major leagues. He began at Decatur, an A team, in 1973, and subsequently

Wendell Kim. (Courtesy of San Francisco Giants.)

Chan Ho Park. (Courtesy of Los Angeles Dodgers.)

played at Fresno, California, and Lafayette, Texas, (AA teams) where he led the Texas League in hits (164) and at-bats (537) and topped all Texas League second basemen in fielding (.983). He played two seasons at Phoenix, hitting a career-high of .313 in 1979. Kim was born March 9, 1950, in Honolulu, Hawaii, and currently resides in Mesa, Arizona, with his wife Natasha and three children, Shannon, Donald, and Patrick. In his spare time, he enjoys his hobby of magic.

Masanori Murakami
Pitcher

Masanori Murakami was the first Japanese baseball player to play major league baseball in the United States. Murakami was a pitcher in 1964-65 for the San Francisco Giants.

Chan Ho Park (1973-)
Pitcher

In the spring of 1994, Chan Ho Park became the first Korean national to play on a major league baseball team when the Los Angeles Dodgers signed the right-handed pitcher to a six-year contract with a signing bonus of $1.2 million, the second highest bonus given

to a rookie in Los Angeles Dodger history. The twenty-one-year-old first caught the attention of the Dodgers in 1991 when he pitched in Los Angeles during the Annual Friendship Series, a tournament between the United States, Japan, and South Korea. He pitched again in the United States as the starting pitcher on the Korean National Team at the World University Games in Buffalo, New York, in 1993.

Chan Ho Park was born in Kong Ju City, South Korea, on June 30, 1973. As a young boy, he began participating in track and field events at the Jung Dong elementary school in Kong Ju. In high school, however, he switched to baseball because of his unusually large hands and feet. Kong Ju High School, where Chan went to school, won the Korean National Championships during the National Sports Festival in 1992, and came in second in the Blue Dragon Flag Tournament, where Chan recorded two saves. He graduated from Kong Ju High in 1992.

The first team to recruit Mr. Park was the Atlanta Braves, who offered him $200,000 on the condition that he join the team immediately after serving his military service in Korea, which is mandatory for all males except university students. Officials of the Dodger organization visited high government officials in Seoul to persuade them to let Chan out of this obligation.

In spring training of 1994, Chan showed excellent promise. His fastball had been clocked in Korea at 99 miles-per-hour. In his first start against a major league team on April 7, 1994, Mr. Park threw three scoreless innings against the New York Mets, giving up one hit and walking one. Of the eleven batters he faced, he retired six in order and at one point threw thirteen consecutive strikes.

Chan Ho Park is a favorite with the crowds, who see in his demure and humble attitude an innocence and reverence for the game of baseball. This young Korean shows great potential to become a significant factor in major league baseball.

Len Sakata (1954-)
Utility infielder

Len Sakata is native of Honolulu, Hawaii, who played for ten years in the major leagues, with the Milwaukee Brewers, Baltimore Orioles, Oakland Athletics, and the New York Yankees. He was a utility infielder on the 1983 world champion Baltimore Orioles. His best performance as a batter came in 1982 when he hit .259 in 136 games.

Makoto "Mac" Suzuki
Pitcher

"Mac" Suzuki is a baseball whiz kid from Japan who, at the age of 18, became a member of the Seattle Mariners in September 1993. The pitcher's first season in the United States was spent with the California League's San Bernardino Spirit team, where he had control problems early on, and was used initially in middle relief, a purgatorial level in baseball.

Even with all of the international media attention showered upon him, Mac remained focused on baseball. The baseball phenom's natural ability and his work discipline helped him work his way into star status on the team by the end of the season—by which time he had an earned run average of 3.68 and a 4-4 record. Suzuki's statistics for the 1993 season were strong, including surrendering only 59 hits while striking out 87 batters in 80 2/3 innings pitched. His pitches have been measured at 96 mph; in most games he averages 92 to 93 mph.

Don Wakamatsu (1963-)
Catcher

Don Wakamatsu was born in Hood River, Oregon, on February 22, 1963. He was drafted by the Cincinnati Reds in 1985, in the eleventh round of that season's free agent draft. He played with the Reds organization for the next four years, primarily in the minor leagues. In 1989, he was signed by the Chicago White Sox's Birmingham farm team, and was granted free agency status at the close of the 1991 season. He was then signed by the Los Angeles Dodgers. He led the Pioneer League with 416 total chances in 1985 and the Southern League catchers with a .990 fielding percentage in 1989. His best batting season was 1992, when he hit .323 for Albuquerque in the Pacific Coast League.

◆ FENCING

Within the Asian American sporting community there are several fencers of note.

Mark Oshima (1968-)
Fencer

Mark Oshima was a finalist at the 1990 and 1992 Division I National Championships, and placed 9th in 1993. He was the 1991 NCAA National Champion and Outstanding Fencer of the Year. He was born July 17, 1968 in Minneapolis, Minnesota, and lives in New York City. He earned a bachelor's degree from Columbia University in 1991 in East Asian Studies.

Jennifer Yu (1964-)
Fencer

Jennifer Yu was the 1990 U.S. Fencing Association Division I National Champion in women's foil. She was a member of the 1987 and 1991 World University Games team, and was a gold medalist at the 1987 and 1990 United States Olympic Festivals. She was born September 21, 1964 in New York City, and earned a bachelor's degree in biology from Stanford University in 1987. While at Stanford, she was All-American in fencing. Her brother Marty and her sister Jessica are nationally prominent fencers as well. Her mother is Connie Young Yu (*See* Prominent Asian Americans).

Marty Yu (1968-)
Fencer

Marty Yu was a member of the 1990 U.S. World Championship team. In college, he was a three-time All-American and took sixth place in the 1990 NCAA Championships. He was born September 27, 1968. His sisters, Jennifer and Jessica, are also nationally prominent fencers. His mother is Connie Young Yu (*See* Prominent Asian Americans).

Felicia Zimmerman (1975-)
Fencer

Felicia Zimmerman was the first alternate to the women's Olympic team in 1992. She was a member of the 1993 World Championship and World Under-20 Championship Teams. She finished 20th at the 1993 World University Games, and was the youngest finalist in the women's foil final at the 1992 Division I National

Championships/Final Oympic Trials, where she finished fourth. She was born on August 16, 1975, in Rochester, New York. In addition to fencing, she is an accomplished pianist, and her younger sister, Iris, won a bronze medal in the Uner-19 women's foil at the 1993 National Championships.

♦ FIGURE SKATING

1992 U.S. Figure Skating Championships

Kristi Yamaguchi (Japanese American) is the first Asian American to win this championship in figure skating.

1991 and 1992 World Figure Skating Championships

Kristi Yamaguchi (Japanese American) of the United States wins consecutive world figure skating titles.

♦ FOOTBALL

Walter Aichu
Running back/punter

The first Asian American to play professional football, Walter Aichu was a 150-pound running back/punter for the Dayton Triangles in the 1927 and 1928 seasons. His ethnicity was listed as "Hawaiian-American-Caucasian."

Eugene Chung
Offensive Tackle

In physical appearance—6 feet 5 inches and 295 pounds—Korean American Eugene Chung breaks the stereotype citing Asians as small in stature. He began his football career at Oakton High School in Oakton, Virginia (suburban Washington, DC), and was selected All-District and All-Region after recording 86 tackles, eight sacks, and six fumble recoveries.

Chung also competed in judo, winning the Virginia State Judo Championship in 1990. His football career continued at Virginia Polytechnic Institute in Blacksburg, where he broke into the starting lineup seven games into his freshman season. He testifies to not having experienced anti-Asian sentiment in college. "I faced more prejudice being an athlete. There's that stereotype of a football player. . . People think athletes get everything paid for, get grades given to them . . . None of that's true." Chung reports.

In 1992, Chung became the first Asian American drafted in the first round to play football in the National Football League, and only the third Asian American ever to play in the NFL. Chung headed for the New England Patriots with the hope that his presence in the NFL would give visibility to the Korean

Eugene Chung. (Courtesy of New England Patriots.)

American community. "I think by having a chance to play in the NFL . . . it will let people know back in Korea and in the United States to be aware that we are able to do this. We're not a meek people." In 1992, Chung was presented with the Sports Award of the Mainstream American Award for Excellence by the Asian-Pacific Coalition.

Leo Goeas (1966-)
Offensive lineman

Los Angeles Rams offensive lineman Leo Douglas Goeas was born in Hawaii on August 15, 1966. Goeas played college football at the University of Hawaii where he started every game at left tackle and was named a second team All-American and a first team All-Conference player in the Western Athletic Conference his senior year.

Goeas was a third-round choice (60th overall) by the San Diego Chargers in the 1990 National Football League draft. While playing for the Chargers he received the Ed Block Memorial Award and also earned All-Rookie honors from various sport magazines. The 1991 season was marked by the death of his father. In the 1992 season he started five games in place

Alfred Pupunu. (Courtesy of San Diego Chargers.)

Ron Rivera. (Courtesy of Chicago Bears.)

of injurued started Broderic Thompson and at the end of the season was traded to the Los Angeles Rams.

Goeas has done a little acting, appearing in episodes on television series such as *Jake and the Fat Man* and *Magnum P.I.* He raises German Shepherd with his wife Kathy and has two children.

John Lee
Placekicker

Once a placekicker for the St. Louis Cardinals and Los Angeles Raiders, John Lee is a Korean American who was drafted by the Cardinals in the second round of the 1986 National Football League draft. He received a four-year, $900,000 contract and was released after one season. He was picked up by the Los Angeles Raiders, but finally left professional football after only two seasons. He was one of the most prolific kickers in National Collegiate Athletic Association (NCAA) history, setting a collegiate record for consistency in field goal attempts.

Alfred Pupunu (1969-)
Tight end/halfback

Born in Tonga, Alfred Sione Pupunu is a tight end/halfback for the San Diego Chargers, who lost the

Super Bowl to the San Francisco 49ers in 1995. During the 1992-93 season, Pupunu caught 13 passes for a total of 142 yards gained, or an average of 10.9 yards per reception. He resides in Salt Lake City, Utah.

Ron Rivera (1962-)
Linebacker

Ron Rivera joined the Chicago Bears in 1984. By 1989, he was the fourth leading tackler with 96 stops during the searson. That year he was nominated for the Traveler's Man of the Year Award.

During his college career, he was a consensus first-team All-American, a finalist for the Lombardi Award, and Pac Ten co-Defensive Player of the Year at California.

Rivera's father made his career in the military, taking the family to Germany, Panama, Washington, DC, and Maryland before settling in California. In 1987, Ron Rivera received the Frito-Lay "Unsung Hero" award. In 1988, he toured Chicago high schools with the "Say No to Drugs" campaign. He has been a spokesman for the Chicago Fire Department, doing radio public service announcements in Spanish promoting fire alarms. His wife, Stephanie, played college basketball.

Jesse Sapolu. (Courtesy of San Francisco 49ers.)

Jesse Sapolu (1961-)
Offensive lineman

Manase Jesse Sapolu was born in Apia, Western Samoa on March 10, 1961. He began his collegiate career at the University of Hawaii where he started his first three years as guard and then moved to center as a senior. Sapolu was a freshman All-American in 1979, and was distinguished as the only sophomore to be selected to the All-Conference team of the Western Athletic Conference. He was an honorable mention to the All-American team in 1980, was again named to the All-Conference team in 1981, and was once again an honorable mention to the All-Conference team in 1982. Sapolu ended his college career as co-most valuable player and played in the Hula and Japan Bowls.

Sapolu was drafted in the 11th round (28th overall) by the San Francisco 49ers in the 1983 college draft. Sapolu completed his first full injury-free season in 1987 after playing only sporadically due to several injuries, primarily to his right foot. Since then, he has emerged as a prominent fixture in the San Francisco offensive line. He started on the Super Bowl-winning team in the 1989-90 season.

Jesse Sapolu now lives in Moreno Valley, California during the off-season with his wife Melanie Ann and their three children.

Tiaina "Junior" Seau (1969-)
Linebacker

Born in San Diego to American Samoan parents, Junior Seau spent his preschool years in American Samoa before returning to San Diego to enter school. Seau is a linebacker with the San Diego Chargers, and played a key role in the 1995 season, culminating in the Chargers appearance in the Super Bowl where they lost to the San Francisco 49ers. In 1993, Seau won many awards, including being voted co-Most Valuable Player by his teammates. He was selected NFL Players Association Linebacker of the Year and voted All-Pro by the Associated Press, *Football Digest*, *Pro Football Writers Association*, *Sporting News*, *College & Pro Football Newsweekly*, and *Sports Illustrated*. Seau resides with his wife and daughter, Sydney (born August 27, 1993) in La Jolla, California.

♦ ICE HOCKEY

Jim Paek (1967-)
Defenseman

Jim Paek was born in Seoul, Korea, on April 7, 1967. As a member of the Pittsburgh Penguins, he made professional hockey history by becoming the first Korean American to play for a Stanley Cup championship team. In the seventh and deciding game of the 1991 Finals, Paek scored a third-period goal, helping to clinch an 8-0 rout and giving Pittsburgh its first Stanley Cup. Defenseman Paek and the Pens duplicated the feat the following year with a four-game sweep of their opponent in the Finals. During the 1993-94 season, Jim Paek was traded to the Ottawa Senators, a promising NHL expansion team.

♦ MARTIAL ARTS

See also Martial Arts

Jhoon Rhee
Grand Master in Tae Kwon Do

Jhoon Rhee, known as the father of U.S. Tae Kwon Do, introduced this martial art form in 1957. That year, he taught unaccredited courses in Tae Kwon Do, and in 1958 he established the first Tae Kwon Do school in San Marcos, Texas.

During his tenure in office, U.S. President George Bush named Jhoon Rhee the 721st "Daily Point of Light," an honor given to Americans who successfully address a pressing social problem through acts of community service.

Junior Seau. (Courtesy of San Diego Chargers.)

Jim Paek. (Courtesy of Pittsburgh Penguins.)

♦ SUMO WRESTLING

Salevaa Atisanoe, known as Konishiki

A Samoan American who goes by the name "Konishiki," this 578-lb. sumo wrestler has achieved the highest rank of yokozuna in sumo wrestling in Japan.

♦ TENNIS

Michael Chang (1972-)

Michael Chang's defining moment occurred in June 1989, when he became the youngest male tennis player in the world to win a Grand Slam tournament and the first U.S. male in thirty-four years to win the French Open. Only seventeen years of age, Chang went into the tournament ranked nineteenth in the world; by the end of 1989, he was ranked in the top five.

Chang remains a solid, well-established player on the U.S. professional circuit. He achieved his career-high world ranking of fourth in 1992, and was ranked seventh as of early 1994. Though his 1989 French Open probably will always be considered the tournament of his career, he generally takes at least one singles title every year. His winnings have paid him nearly $4.5 million since he turned pro at age seventeen.

♦ WORLD RUGBY

Pacific Islanders

Two prominent players on the world rugby scene are both of Pacific Islander descent. They are Brian Williams and Michael Jones.

♦ ASIAN AMERICAN OLYMPIANS

V Olympiad (Summer), Stockholm, Sweden, 1912

Swimming, Men

Duke Kahanamoku (1890-1968), Gold Medal, 100 Meter Free Style, Time: 1:03.4.

See also Prominent Asian Americans

VII Olympiad (Summer), Antwerp, Belgium, 1920

Swimming, Men

Duke Kahanamoku (1890-1968), Gold Medal, 100 Meter Free Style, Time: 1:01.4, Olympic record.

P. Kealoha, Silver Medal, 100 Meter Free Style.

Warren Kealoha, Gold Medal, 100 Meter Backstroke, Time: 1:15.2.

Korean American diver Sammy Lee. (Courtesy, Sammy Lee.)

Victoria Manolo Draves, whose mother was English and father was Filipino. (International Swimming Hall of Fame.)

D. Kahanamoku, P. Kealoha, P. McGillivray, N. Ross, Gold Medal, 800 Meter Relay, Time: 10:04.4, Olympic record.

VIII Olympiad (Summer), Paris, France, 1924

Swimming, Men

Duke Kahanamoku (1890-1968), Silver Medal, 100 Meter Free Style.

Sam Kahanamoku, Bronze Medal, 100 Meter Backstroke.

Warren Kealoha, Gold Medal, Time: 1:13.2, Olympic record.

IV Olympiad (Summer), London, 1948

Diving, Men

Sammy Lee, Bronze Medal, Men's Springboard, 145.52 points. *See also* Prominent Asian Americans

Sammy Lee, Gold Medal, Men's Platform, 130.05 points.

Diving, Women

Victoria Manoloo Draves, Gold Medal, Women's Springboard, 108.74 points

Victoria Manolo Draves, Gold Medal, Women's Platform, 68.87 points

XV Olympiad (Summer), Helsinki, Finland, 1952

Diving, Men

Sammy Lee, Gold Medal, Men's Platform, 156.28 points. In addition, Lee was the first person of Asian descent to win the Sullivan Award. The Sullivan Award, given by the Amateur Athletic Union (AAU), is a trophy presented to the "amateur athlete who, by performance, example, and good influence, did the most to advance the cause of good sportsmanship."

Weightlifting

Tommy Kono, Gold Medal, Lightweight Division. *See also* Prominent Asian Americans

XXI Olympiad (Summer), Montreal, 1976

Diving, Men

Greg Louganis (1960-), Silver Medal, 576.99 points. *See also* Prominent Asian Americans.

Weighlifter Tommy Kono . (AP/Wide World.)

XIV Olympiad (Winter), Sarajevo, Yugoslavia, 1984

Figure Skating, Women

Tiffany Chin (1967-), Chinese American, Fourth Place.

XXIII Olympiad (Summer), Los Angeles, California, USA, 1984

Greg Louganis (1960-) became the first diver in 56 years to win both men's springboard and platform diving events at this Olympiad. He also became the first diver in history to score over 700 points in an Olympic competition. In 1985, Louganis was awarded the Sullivan Award by the Amateur Athletic Union (AAU), a trophy given to the "amateur athlete who, by performance, example, and good influence, did the most to advance the cause of good sportsmanship."

Louganis is of American Samoan and European descent and overcame a severe stutter, dyslexia, and racism (Classmates in California taunted him about his brown skin.) to become one of greatest divers ever to participate in the Olympic games. When Dr. Sammy Lee, Olympic gold medalist in diving in 1948 and 1952, first saw Greg dive, he recalls thinking, "That's the greatest talent I've ever seen!" When he took dancing lessons as child, Louganis learned the power of visualization, a technique which he used to full advantage in perfecting his dives. Coached from 1978 through 1988 by Ron O'Brien, Louganis built his repertoire of dives to include the jewel, the reverse 3-1/2 somersault tuck. The first time he attempted it, Louganis stood on the platform for thirty minutes, only to climb back down. O'Brien would not allow him to give up, and the next day Louganis successfully accomplished the dive on the first try.

XXII Olympiad (Summer), Seoul, Korea, 1988

Diving, Men

At this Summer Olympiad, Greg Louganis became the first diver to win two medals in two successive Olympics. He was also presented with the 1988 Olympic Spirit Award, awarded to the most inspiring athlete (of 9,600 assembled in Seoul).

Fencing

Jennifer Yu, Stanford All-American and the 1990 National Women's Foil Champion, was an alternate to 1988 Olympics.

XVI Olympiad (Winter), Albertville, France, 1992

Figure Skating, Women

Kristi Yamaguchi, Japanese American, becomes the first Asian American to win a Gold Medal in figure skating in the Olympic games. *See also* Prominent Asian Americans

XXIII Olympiad (Summer), Barcelona, Spain, 1992

Pistol Shooting Team

Roger Mar was the youngest U.S. pistol shooter at the 1992 Olympics. He specializes in rapid-fire pistol, though he also competes with an air pistol. Mar grew up in Seattle, Washington, graduating from Evergreen High School in 1986. His father, a Scoutmaster, taught him to shoot a rifle at the age of seven. Roger decided to exercise his independence from his three brothers who all shot rifles, by taking up the pistol at the age of 12. He won his first national pistol match that year and has been competing ever since. He competed in the 1990 and 1991 U.S. Olympic Festivals, placed fifth at the 1991 World Cup USA, and took a bronze the same year at the USISC. He earned a team gold at the 1991 Pan American Games, placed fourth at the 1992 Milan World Cup, and took an individual bronze and team gold medal at the 1992 Mexico World Cup. Roger married Colleen Walker in 1992. They live in Colorado Springs, Colorado; his hobbies include hunting, fishing, hiking and photography.

Volleyball

Liane Sato, women's volleyball.
Erik Sato, men's volleyball player.

XVII Olympiad (Winter), Lillehamer, Norway, 1994

Figure Skating, Women

Michelle Kwan (1980-)

An alternate for the 1994 Olympic Games in Norway at only age 13, Michelle Kwan who is less than five feet tall and weighs less than eighty pounds, is one of the few women skaters who can complete triple jumps in competition.

Roger Mar, Chinese American, Olympic Marksman. (United States Shooting Team.)

Born July 7, 1980, in Torrance, California, she is the daughter of Daniel and Estella Kwan. At age seven, Kwan watched Brian Boitano on television and was instantly taken with the sport. Kwan's competitiveness, while making her a world-class skater, has sometimes dismayed her coaches. When she was only 12, Kwan took a test without her coach's knowledge, allowing her to skate with Olympic caliber athletes.

Instead of faltering, Kwan did well. Title wins in the 1993 Southwest Pacific and Pacific Coast Senior as well as the Gardena Spring Trophy, 1993 Olympic Festival, and 1994 World Junior Championship were proof Kwan was on her way to achieving her goal, a trip to the Olympics.

Martial Arts

♦ History ♦ Martial Arts in the United States

The martial arts encompass a number of systems of self-defense and self-discipline that grew out of early Asian fighting methods. These techniques are used today for fitness and sport as well as self-defense; police officers have also discovered their effectiveness in law enforcement.

Although in their broadest definition the martial arts include armed methods, such as archery and swordsmanship, this chapter focuses exclusively on the unarmed branches, which use techniques such as hand and foot blows, throws, and holds that immobilize or unbalance the opponent. Prominent among these systems are aikido, judo, karate, kung fu, and tae kwan do, along with many others too numerous to mention here.

Each discipline emphasizes certain aspects over others. Some, for example, promote power and strength; these are known as the "hard" schools. Others, the "soft" schools, develop speed and precision instead. Some methods stress the importance of kicks; still others train their adherents to deliver devastating hand blows. Each type ranks its participants' skill levels by designated belt colors, which vary with each sport. Local, regional, and national competitions allow individuals to progress through the ranks, usually by sparring and/or performing *kata*, a series of prescribed movements.

All branches of the martial arts emphasize the harmony of the physical and the spiritual and promote a state (called *mushin,* or "no mind," in Japanese) in which logic and reason are arrested, freeing the body and mind to respond as one. This harmonious state reflects much of classical Eastern religion and philosophy, particularly Taoism and Zen Buddhism. Even today, aside from their usefulness as a means of self-defense, martial arts are often practiced for the spiritual growth and enlightenment they produce.

♦ HISTORY

Scholars disagree on the exact genesis of the martial arts, since unarmed methods of combat were known in many early civilizations, some dating from 2000 B.C. The Asian styles, however, almost certainly came to China from India and Tibet, where they were used during centuries of lawlessness and upheaval by unarmed monks, who were a prime target of bandits flourishing in those lands. These fighting styles, which eventually spread to all of Asia, began, according to legend, with an Asian Indian Buddhist monk named Bodhidharma (A.D. 470-543).

In the year 527, the story goes, Bodhidharma traveled to China as a Zen Buddhist missionary and later founded the Shaolin temple in Honan province. Finding his disciples unable to withstand the intensity of Zen's asceticism, he is said to have developed a series of exercises to toughen them both mentally and physically. With or without Bodhidharma's influence, the Shaolin monks eventually transformed these techniques into a martial way called *kempo* that became known throughout China.

Unarmed combat in Korea has been documented in tombs and paintings that date from A.D. 37. By the period of the Koro Dynasty (953-1392), a system of martial arts called *soo bahk* was taught to members of the Korean military. During the Japanese occupation of Korea (1907-1945), the Korean arts were suppressed—until the Japanese found that conscripted Korean troops fought much better when the national style was given expression. During this time, many Japanese styles, such as judo, aikido, and karate, were adapted to Korean techniques.

Isolated and far to the east, Japan was the last Asian nation to develop martial arts. As early as A.D. 220 a collection of primitive fighting skills called *chikara kurabe* was used in battle, and an ancient warrior's training included both armed and unarmed combat. The invention of armor was a temporary stumbling block, but combatants soon discovered that it was far more effective to tumble an armored opponent to the ground than it was to hit him, and fighting styles were quickly adapted. By the seventeenth century these early martial arts, known as *ju-jitsu* in Japan, were so effective that knowledge of them was limited by law to feudal warriors. The tradition continued through World War II, when Japanese soldiers were trained in these methods. Although their instruction was banned after the war, by the mid-1950s they were again legalized.

♦ MARTIAL ARTS IN THE UNITED STATES

The history of the martial arts in the United States can be traced to the presidency of Ulysses S. Grant, who attended a demonstration of judo techniques by a young master while on a state visit to Japan in the late 1800s. Later, a professor from Yale traveled to Japan to study judo; by the early 1900s, there were judo clubs in the United States, and the sport had attracted a moderate following.

It was not until the World War II, however, that the martial arts became more widely known and practiced in this country. U.S. service personnel in occupied Japan were fascinated by the arts and began studying them in large numbers. Upon returning to the states, a few of them set up schools and invited Japanese masters to come and teach. Some *dojos*, or practice halls, did exist before this time, but they were little known and hard to find; both teachers and students were almost exclusively Asian. After the war, however, a wave of popularity made the martial arts a part of mainstream U.S. society. Similarly, the Korean War led to the importation of the Korean art of tae kwan do.

Judo

Judo was founded in 1882 in Japan by Jigoro Kano, a master of several *ju-jitsu* methods, who synthesized the techniques of different schools to create a new martial art form that eliminated much of the risk of injury to its practitioners. Roughly translated as "gentle way," judo is a system of barehanded fighting that combines throws and holds, along with hand and foot blows, to unbalance or immobilize opponents, using their own weaknesses and the bulk of their bodies against them. Learning to fall safely is an important part of judo training, allowing participants to be thrown without serious injury.

Judo matches are based on strict rules of performance and ritual. The combatants are either *tori*, the thrower or aggressor, or *uke*, the one who falls. Tori earns points for his throwing technique, for pinning or immobilizing uke, or for a combination of throws and holds. Although sport and competition were important, Kano believed they were only a portion of judo's aim, which he called *kyushin-do*, a complete integration of mind, body, and spirit.

Today, judo is one of the most widely practiced of the martial arts in the United States. It received Olympic recognition in 1964 and is governed by the International Judo Federation, based in Japan. Students of the art are called *judoka*.

Judo first came to the United States around the turn of the century when Yoshiaki Yamashita was invited to this country by Graham Hill, a wealthy railroad owner. Through one of Yamashita's first students, President Theodore Roosevelt became interested in the sport. A demonstration was arranged at the White House in which Yamashita fought the wrestling coach of the U.S. Naval Academy, pinning him easily several times. President Roosevelt was very impressed by this display and began to study the sport himself, earning a brown belt after leaving the presidency,. At the same time, judo was also being taught in areas that had been heavily settled by Japanese immigrants, mainly the West Coast and Hawaii.

The first recorded judo competition in U.S. collegiate athletics was in the early 1930s, when students from the University of California at Berkeley fought exhibition matches in San Francisco. In 1937, judo was introduced as a sport at San Jose State College; later that year, a group from the school took on a team from the University of Southern California.

After World War II, a weight system was introduced, and in 1953 the first collegiate judo championships were held at U.C. Berkeley. San Jose State hosted the first national amateur Athletic Union Judo Championships in that same year and sponsored the first international amateur judo competition in the United States two years later. In 1962, the National Collegiate Judo Association was formed and the first National Collegiate Judo Championships were held. Today, the NCJA hosts tournaments at colleges throughout the United States; amateurs from these schools also compete internationally.

Aikido

Aikido, meaning "way of harmony" or "way of the spirit" is another *ju-jitsu*-based art founded in 1943 by Morehei Ueshiba in Japan. A sophisticated, precise martial art employing wrist, elbow, and shoulder twists, aikido is an effective defense against one or even several attackers. Practitioners of this art strive to develop themselves in four areas: strengthening themselves physically; adopting and practicing a disciplined, nonviolent attitude; increasing suppleness in their joints through rigorous twisting and stretching exercises; and cultivating a more refined posture, thereby improving total body health and increasing coordination.

Beginning-level aikido students concentrate on its physical aspects. As they become more expert in the art, further dimensions of mind and spirit are added to their training. At higher levels, students study not only the art of aikido but the philosophy behind it as well. This philosophy, closely allied with Zen Buddhism, emphasizes a person's harmonious relations with the physical world around him. Students of both aikido and Zen Buddhism are taught that the center of the body's strength and source of mental energy, called the *ki*, is located in the abdomen, approximately 1-1/2 inches above the navel. Aikido is an essentially nonviolent martial art that emphasizes principles of meditation and cultivation of the ki.

Rankings within aikido are similar to those of other Japanese martial arts and are divided into two categories. *Kyu* are student grades ranging from a low of fifth or sixth to first, which are differentiated by a series of colored belts. *Dan* rankings, beginning with black belt, start from an initial grade of first dan to a high of eighth. It is possible, although extremely rare, to transcend the eighth *dan*.

There are dozens of different sects of aikido today, some emphasizing the mental aspects of the art, with others more combative. Perhaps the most popular form in the United States is *yoshin* aikido, the type taught in U.S. universities and represented by the Aikido Yoshinkai Association of North America, founded in the mid 1970s. Worldwide aikido is overseen by the International Aikido Federation in Tokyo.

Karate

Karate, literally meaning "empty hand," is the most popular martial art worldwide. It has more than 100 styles, with varying degrees of emphasis on the sporting and artistic aspects. The origins of karate can be traced to ancient India, China, and Japan. It is thought that a Buddhist monk, perhaps Bodhidharma, brought a primitive form of Asian Indian fist-fighting to China where it proliferated, eventually making the jump to the island of Okinawa, in present day Japan, during the fifteenth century. Modern karate was developed in Okinawa around the turn of the century by Gichin Funakoshi. After World War II, it spread around the world. In the 1970s, in an attempt to provide a unified management of the sport among its many different schools, two organizations were established that largely control amateur karate today: the World Union of Karate-Do Organizations and the International Amateur Karate Federation.

Students of karate are ranked by means similar to the other martial arts in two categories, kyu and dan. Kyu are the student grades and dan are the varying degrees of expertise among those who have achieved black-belt status. There are up to ten degrees of dan.

Karate techniques, whether offensive or defensive, are made up of hand and foot moves. Defensive moves, known collectively as *uke-waza*, block or deflect an opponent's weapon. Some karate styles emphasize circular, or "soft," blocks, while others emphasize linear, or "hard," blocks, although most styles use both methods to varying degrees. Offensive techniques are divided into striking and punching. Punches are usually delivered in a straight line and are generally a closed fist thrown from the attacker's hip to the target, although practitioners also use the heel of the palm, fingers, or the fore knuckles as points of contact. Strikes usually follow a circular path and are what people generally think of as a "karate chop."

Karate also incorporates many different kinds of kicks—from snap kicks to flying kicks to stomping kicks. A critical feature is the stance, which allows combatants to stay balanced while delivering and receiving the wide variety of blows allowable in a match. Some styles of karate advocate high stances, which allow for more mobility, while others advocate a low stance, which permits greater defensiveness.

Karate first came to the United States in the 1920s, when it was practiced among Japanese immigrants in Hawaii. They did not seek to spread the art, as the founder of judo did, and karate remained a largely secretive, ethnic practice until after World War II, when U.S. service personnel who had studied karate in occupied Japan brought it back to the United States with them.

In 1946, the first karate school in the mainland United States was established in Phoenix, Arizona, by Robert Trias, who had served in the Navy. In 1948, Trias established the United States Karate Association, the first such organization in the country. In 1952, a prominent Japanese student of karate, Mas Oyama, undertook a widely publicized tour of the United States during which he fought professional boxers and wrestlers, demonstrating his strength and concentration by using blows to break boards, bricks, and stones.

The 1950s saw a wide proliferation of karate schools around the country after the art was popularized on television and in the movies, especially its more sensational aspects, such as breaking bricks and stones. In 1961, Hidetaka Nishiyama established the All American Karate Federation, a branch of the powerful Japan Karate Association. In 1963, the first World Karate Tournament was held at the University of Chicago. Contestants came from around the country but the event was in no way a "world" championship. Other organizers held similarly misnamed tournaments in the ensuing years in a competitive bid to form an official national championship. In 1965, ABC television's "Wide World of Sports" broadcast parts of the U.S. National Karate Championships.

In the late sixties and early seventies, full-contact karate, or American kick-boxing as it is sometimes known, emerged in this country. A point system was introduced to full-contact karate in 1970 that eliminated much of the sport's violence and allowed for longer matches. In the same year, the World Union of Karate-Do Organizations hosted its first World Karate Championships, in which 32 countries participated. The tournament was not well administered, however, which led to the establishment of a rival international karate organization, the International Amateur Karate Federation. These two organizations remain the chief regulators of amateur karate around the world.

Tae Kwon Do

Tae kwan do, meaning the "art of kicking and punching," is a martial art native to Korea that is closely related to Japanese karate. Its history can be traced back to the first century B.C., when images of men fighting in a style like tae kwon do were painted on the ceiling of a royal tomb. Additional evidence is found from the Silla dynasty of the seventh through tenth centuries A.D. Later influences of Chinese kung fu altered the art, although it retained a distinct Korean flavor.

The study of karate was brought to Korea during Japanese occupation of Korea, which ended after World War II. After Korea's liberation, thousands of exiles and refugees returned to their homeland, bringing with them martial arts training in a variety of practices. All of these influences produced a newly synthesized art, which was named tae kwon do in 1955 by Korean martial arts masters.

Tae kwon do's emphasis is on the kick, which is elevated to an art form. With this emphasis, the student of tae kwon do devotes substantial work to developing his legs, hips, and back. Tae kwon do kicking techniques are divided into the circular and the linear. The latter, as the name suggests, travels in a straight line to the target, while the former travels in a variety of directions before making contact. Tae kwon do is famous for its flying kicks, which when performed with all their grace and strength by a master can be devastating to an opponent and breathtaking to observe.

Tae kwon do was introduced in the United States by Jhoon Rhee, who is known as the father of U.S. tae kwon do. In 1956, he came to the United States as a student at San Marcos Southwest Texas State College. The following year he taught unaccredited courses in tae kwon do, and, in 1958, he established the country's first tae kwon do school in San Marcos.

Tae kwon do did not become popular until the early 1960s, however, when a demonstration was held at the United Nations in New York City. In November 1967, the United States Tae Kwon Do Association was formed. In 1974, the Amateur Athletic Union accepted it as an official sport and established as its governing body the AAU National Tae Kwon Do Committee.

Kung Fu

Kung fu is a generic term applied to several hundred loosely allied forms of unarmed Chinese martial arts. Literally translated, the term refers only to skill or ability and can just as easily be applied to a potter or chef as it can a practitioner of a martial art. Over time, however, the term has come to encompass a wide array of martial arts that emphasize everything from fierce hand-to-hand combat to subtle exercises stressing methodically slow, ritualized movement more like dance than battle. Among the many varieties of kung fu are the *hop-gar* style, used for fighting; the *chang-chuan* style, used as gymnastics and theater; and the *tai chi chuan* style, used to promote physical and mental well-being.

The systems of kung fu that developed in primarily Buddhist northern China relied on strength and speed in combat, utilizing short-arm striking tactics. In Taoist southern China more circular systems of combat developed, using both short- and long-arm strikes and elaborate, stylized footwork. Both these systems apply style varieties developed for fighting, physical fitness, theater, and mental fitness.

Kung fu has been practiced in the United States since the beginning of Chinese immigration in the mid-nineteenth century. It was an integral part of the mining towns and labor camps of the old West. Kung fu grew as immigration increased in the early part of the twentieth century and Chinese communities grew. It remained, however, a hidden practice and very few people were schooled in the art.

In 1957, the first known school of kung fu opened in Honolulu, Hawaii, taught by Tinn Chan Lee, who emphasized only tai chi. In 1964, Ark-Yueh Wong opened a school in Los Angeles, California, that was the first to offer kung fu training to non-Asians. During the 1970s, prompted by media glamorization of the art, kung fu instruction became more widespread. However, despite this popularization, most aspects of the various arts of kung fu remain parochial secrets of the Chinese American community and are largely unknown outside of Chinatowns.

Kali

Aside from the major martial arts listed above, there are hundreds more lesser-known varieties with subvarieties within these. The martial arts proliferated throughout most of Asia and many of them have been imported, albeit in small ways, into the United States.

Kali is an ancient martial art from the Philippines dating back to the ninth century. It is a complete self-defense system that can be employed by both the unarmed and by those wielding traditional kali weapons: swords, sticks, clubs, lances, long knives, and projectile weapons. A kali master named Angel Caballes established the first kali school in the United States in 1964. The conditioning coach of the Dallas Cowboys football team once invited a kali instructor to the Cowboys training camp to help improve team members' hand-eye coordination.

Bando

Bando is a martial art native to Myanmar, formerly known as Burma. It is similar to karate in its techniques of striking and kicking and has aspects of judo in its throwing, but also incorporates weapons such as swords, knives, spears, and sticks. Bando was introduced to the United States in 1960 by Dr. Maung Gyi, a college professor. In 1968, Dr. Gyi established the American Bando Association at Ohio University in Athens, Ohio.

Kalari Payat

Kalari payat is an ancient art practiced in southern India that originated as a form of combat. The introduction of firearms rendered it obsolete and is now practiced as a highly stylized form of physical fitness.

Ninjutsu

Ninjutsu is a highly specialized Japanese discipline encompassing espionage, belief in occult powers, commando-like tactics, and a high degree of secrecy. The art was developed between the thirteenth and seventeenth centuries by mystics living in Japan's mountains as a means of defending themselves and their isolated way of life from increasingly intrusive warlords. Practitioners of this art are called *ninjas* and have been glamorized by Western media in recent years, sparking a vigorous interest in this ancient, bafflingly secretive art.

Pentjak-Silat

Pentjak-silat is the national defense sport of Indonesia. It is a very intricate martial art with hundreds of varieties and a long history of development. Pentjak-silat systems of all varieties use movements similar to the unarmed arts, usually while wielding a weapon, such as a knife, sword, stick, or rope.

—Jim Henry

39

Prominent Asian Americans

As the fastest-growing segment of the U.S. population, Americans who trace their ancestry to Asia and the Pacific Islands are becoming more visible in positions of prominence and power. The individuals profiled here are recognized by their peers for their achievements. Although some may be well known by the general public, most have contributed to their chosen profession or community without gaining celebrity status. It would be impossible for this section to be all-inclusive; rather, it is designed to illustrate the range and variety of contributions being made by Asian Americans.

Daniel K. Akaka (1924-)
Politician, educator

Senator Daniel K. Akaka is a quiet presence in Congress. As the U.S. Senate's first native Hawaiian ever to serve and the only currently sitting native Hawaiian and Chinese American member of Congress, he has been successful with a sharp focus: to preserve and bolster Hawaii's interests. So intensely devoted is he to his native land that in 1990 he delayed accepting an appointment to the U.S. Senate after serving in the U.S. House of Representatives for fourteen years, until he could ensure that several projects in Hawaii would advance by the House Appropriation's Committee.

Born in Honolulu on September 11, 1924, Daniel K. Akaka was the youngest of eight children in a deeply religious family that managed to live in a cramped, two-bedroom house. At his parents' urging, Akaka sought an education by enrolling in the Hamehameha School for Boys, a private school from which he graduated in 1942. He began looking for work to earn money for college. He became a welder with the Hawaiian Electric Company before joining the U.S. Army Corps of Engineers as a welder-mechanic. By 1945, the nation was at war and he was stationed with the Army Corps in Saipan and Tinian. After the war, he enrolled at the

Daniel K. Akaka.

University of Hawaii to fulfill his dream of becoming a teacher. He obtained a bachelor's degree in education in 1953, a certificate to teach secondary education the following year, and a master's in education in 1966.

It wasn't long before Akaka became known as a rising star on the state's education front. At an education convention in 1963, Akaka got his first taste of politics. It was his first year as a school principal and he had

617

Toshiko Akiyoshi.

been chosen as a delegate to the National Convention of the Department of Elementary School Principals, which was held in Hawaii that year. Before the national convention had adjourned, he was approached to run for the National Board of Directors.

In 1968, Akaka was named program specialist for the state Department of Education. Six years later, Democratic gubernatorial candidate George R. Ariyoshi tapped him as his choice for lieutenant governor. Although Akaka lost in the Democratic primary, Ariyoshi won his bid for governor and appointed Akaka as his special assistant for human resources.

In 1976, Akaka decided to run for U.S. representative. He took eighty percent of the vote and has won by substantial margins in every election since. Akaka served nearly seven terms in the U.S. House of Representatives before he was appointed in 1990 to fill the senate seat left vacant after the death of Senator Spark M. Matsunaga. In both his House and Senate positions, Akaka earned a reputation for being a liberal Democrat. In 1984, the House Democratic leadership was one vote shy on a crucial roll call to block President Ronald Reagan's request for production of the MX missile, a controversial weapons system. Akaka's last-minute

vote was critical for the anti-MX forces victory, several observers say. And later in the Senate, Akaka vigorously spoke out and voted against the confirmation of Clarence Thomas, who was viewed as a conservative candidate for Supreme Court Justice.

Akaka worked to get a congressional joint resolution signed in 1993 that formally apologized to Hawaiians for the 1893 overthrow of the islands' native government. He also got bills signed into law to commend civilians who acted heroically in the aftermath of Pearl Harbor.

Overcoming the barriers of racial discrimination and his impoverished roots are the things that Akaka most likes to reflect on. He has been married to Mary Mildred Chong since 1948, and the couple has four children and fourteen grandchildren.

Toshiko Akiyoshi (1929-)
Jazz pianist, band leader, composer, arranger

When jazz legend Oscar Peterson first heard Toshiko Akiyoshi play in 1953, he referred to her as the greatest female jazz pianist he had ever heard. Akiyoshi lived up to Peterson's praise. Twenty years later, her band formed the 17-piece Toshiko Akiyoshi Jazz Orchestra. The group eventually garnered 12 Grammy nominations and earned its founder the Best Arranger and Best Big Jazz Band awards in the 1978 *Down Beat* readers' poll. Winning these awards made Akiyoshi the first woman in jazz history to be so honored. Akiyoshi and the band held these titles for four consecutive years. In 1992, they celebrated Akiyoshi's 35th year in the United States, recording Toshiko Akiyoshi Live at Carnegie Hall, their first album for Columbia Records.

Born in Manchuria, China, on December 18, 1929, Toshiko Akiyoshi was the youngest of four daughters. Growing up in China, she first considered a career in medicine. "My father always wanted me to go to medical school. . . I suppose he was disappointed he never had a son, and for some reason he thought I would be the one to accomplish something," she said in a 1992 press release.

Feeling restless in her small town, Akiyoshi moved to Tokyo, Japan, where there was an active jazz scene, and by 1952, she had her own group. In 1956, Akiyoshi came to the United States to study at the prestigious Berkeley College of Music in Boston. After graduating in 1959, she played in numerous clubs across the country, where she encountered both racial and sexual prejudice.

In 1973, Akiyoshi moved to Los Angeles. With her husband, saxophone player Lew Tabackin, she formed a band which evolved into the Toshiko Akiyoshi Jazz Orchestra. Its first recording, *Kogun*, is one of the best-selling big band jazz albums in history.

Susan Au Allen.

Later Akiyoshi moved from Los Angeles to New York, and in 1982, her career was depicted in *Jazz is My Native Language*, a documentary portrait of her move. The band adjusted to the relocation quickly, and made their Carnegie Hall debut as part of the Kool Jazz Festival one year later in 1983.

Akiyoshi continues to perform all over the world with her band, as well as in a quintet or trio. Her career, spanning more than 30 years, is testament to her tenacity and talent.

Susan Au Allen (1946-)
Executive

Susan Au Allen is president of the United States Pan Asian Chamber of Commerce, a nonprofit organization representing the interests of Asian/Pacific American businessmen and women.

Allen grew up in Hong Kong. She came from a poor background, sharing an apartment with a number of relatives, all of whom were refugees from China. She was educated at a convent school where she worked with opium addicts and the disabled.

Her work at the convent school was noticed by American officials, and she was invited to Washington, D.C., to join President Richard Nixon's Commission on

Employment of the Handicapped. Allen had not planned to stay in the United States permanently, but while serving in Washington she met Paul Sherman Allen, a tax lawyer, whom she married in 1975. After Allen graduated from law school, she and Paul opened Paul Sherman Allen & Associates, a successful immigration-law practice with offices in Washington and Hong Kong.

In 1985, Allen founded the U.S. Pan Asian Chamber of Commerce (USPACC), an organization that represents approximately 1800 Asian business professionals. With over 1,000 members and supporters nationwide, it sponsors various events, operates a job bank, and once a year hosts "Excellence 2000," a program that recognizes prominent Asian Americans who have made outstanding contributions to the United States.

Brenda Wong Aoki (1953-)
Performance artist

Brenda Wong Aoki is a storyteller and performance artist who uses her ethnic heritage as the basis of her art. Aoki performs her show, "The Queen's Garden," in which she tells of her youth as a Los Angeles gang member. The story's power and passion is enhanced by a performed musical score.

Hiroaki "Rocky" Aoki (1938-)
Restaurateur, entrepreneur

Hiroaki "Rocky" Aoki is the founder of Benihana restaurants, a chain of Japanese-style eateries in the United States, Canada, Mexico, England, South Korea, Japan, Australia, and Thailand. He is also well known as a world-class sportsman, a noted philanthropist, and a fund-raiser for international art exchanges and environmental causes.

Aoki was born on October 9, 1938, in Tokyo, Japan, the first child of Yunosuke and Katsu Aoki. He was a gifted athlete, competing in track and field, karate, and, most successfully, wrestling. He became the captain of the Keio team and one of Japan's top wrestlers at the age of 19. In 1959 he toured America as an alternate on Japan's Olympic Team and was undefeated in his weight class.

For some time, Aoki wanted to open a restaurant and had set aside $10,000 from part-time jobs to meet this goal. In 1963, after graduating from New York City Community College, he was offered prime restaurant space in midtown Manhattan. Aoki's parents helped him secure a loan, and in May 1964 the first Benihana's American restaurant opened. What made the restaurant unique and propelled it to success was the way food was prepared. Guests were seated around a teppanyaki grill where they could watch their food being prepared by chefs known for their dramatic flair.

Hiroaki "Rocky" Aoki.

George Aratani.

When the food critic for the New York Herald Tribune gave Benihana a glowing review, Aoki's business took off. Soon there were Benihana restaurants all over the United States, and shortly thereafter Benihana expanded worldwide.

George Aratani (1917-)
Business leader

George Aratani is the founder and chairman emeritus of Mikasa Corporation, one of the largest privately owned international firms. He was born in Gardena, California, south of Los Angeles, on May 22, 1917. His family settled in Guadalupe, a small town ten miles west of Santa Maria, California. Aratani graduated from Santa Maria High School in 1935. Because his parents felt, that as a Japanese American, Aratani should know about Japanese culture, language, and traditions, they sent him to Japan to study. Before he could graduate from Keio University in Tokyo his father became ill, forcing his return to the United States. Although Stanford University accepted Aratani's transcript from Keio University, and he was not able to complete his schooling; after his first term at

Stanford, his father died, and Aratani quit school to take care of his father's business empire.

In 1941, World War II broke out, and President Franklin D. Roosevelt issued Executive Order 9066, allowing the U.S. military to forcibly relocate from the West Coast 120,000 people of Japanese descent, even native-born U. S. citizens. Because of the size of Aratani's company, it was very difficult to dispose of it on short notice, so the whole business was put into a trust. When the Aratani's were interned in Arizona, the trustees, facing rising anti-Japanese sentiments, sold the company. Whe the war ended in 1945, with his business gone, Aratani decided to try foreign trade with Japan. It took a few years of study and development, but by 1950, Aratani began to grow into what would become Mikasa Corporation, importing dinnerware from Japan and marketing it in America. By 1960, Mikasa was well established, and the business-wise Aratani latched on to the idea of high-fidelity to launch a second company to manufacture equipment in Japan under the Kenwood name. Kenwood was a wholly-owned subsidiary of Mikasa.

Aratani married Sakaye Inouye in 1944. They have two daughters, Donna and Linda.

George Ariyoshi (1926-)
Politician

In 1974, George Ariyoshi became the first American of Japanese descent to be elected governor of a state when he was elected to that post in Hawaii. It was the first of three consecutive terms that Ariyoshi served.

Born in Honolulu to Japanese immigrant parents on March 12, 1926, Ariyoshi went on to distinguish himself in academics and politics. He won his first election in 1954 to Hawaii's territorial house of representatives. From there he went to the territorial senate (which became the state senate in 1959 when Hawaii became the 50th state), and then on to become the lieutenant governor. He won the governorship in elections in 1974, 1978, and 1982, finishing his last allowable term. (The Hawaiian constitution limited governors to three terms in 1986). Since leaving office he has returned to the occupation he held before becoming a politician, practicing law. In addition, Ariyoshi sits on many important cultural and civic boards, runs several international trade consulting services, and manages lucrative real estate ventures in Hawaii.

Salevaa Fuauli Atisanoe "Konishiki"
Sumo wrestler

Sale (pronounced Sally) Atisanoe is a famous and enormously popular sumo wrestler in Japan. He is the eighth of nine children born to Lautoa, a Samoan navy rigger, and his wife Talafaaiva. The family settled in Oahu, Hawaii, in 1959, where it encountered financial hardship. Everyone slept on mats in a communal room and showered outside. Atisanoe's unusual build was apparent when, at age 11, he already weighed 180 pounds; by high school age, he could bench-press 550 pounds. He was too big to play college football, and decided to try undercover police work, when he was discovered by the scout of a famous sumo wrestler. His meeting with the master Kukualua convinced him to pursue wrestling.

Atisanoe joined a sumo stable in 1982 and began the brutal traditional training. His perseverance enabled him to set the record of reaching the highest of the sport's six divisions after only six tournaments. When he reached the rank of "ozeki" at the Emperor's cup in 1989, the first foreigner to do so, he upset conservatives in Japan who wanted to keep the sport strictly Japanese. He later went on to become the first American yokuzuna (grand champion), one of only 62 inducted since the creation of modern sumo in the 1750s.

At 579 pounds, Atisanoe is the weight of an entire average Japanese family. Having reached the top in the sport of sumo wrestling, fans touch him for good luck, and tickets to his wrestling matches sometimes sell for more than $4,000. His success was evident when the Japanese telecast of his wedding to Sumika Shioda, a

George Ariyoshi.

former model, put the 1992 Olympics off the air for two hours.

Kavelle R. Bajaj (1950-)
Entrepreneur

Having immigrated to the United States from India in 1974 Kavelle R. Bajaj raised two sons, started her own computer company, and within a decade, built it into a flourishing enterprise.

She was born Kavelle Maker in India on June 15, 1950. Her mother, Agya Kaur, was a homemaker. Her father, Daljit Singh, was an entrepreneur who owned a construction business. Bajaj was educated in Bihar and New Delhi, and received her bachelor of science degree from Delhi University. In 1973, her marriage was arranged with Ken Bajaj. Soon after the wedding, the couple immigrated to the United States.

In 1985, Bajaj wanted to do something useful outside the home. She borrowed $5,000 from her husband, Ken, to start a computer business, although she had no experience in establishing an organization and knew nothing about computers. With this limited amount of money she launched I-Net, a computer firm that provides all services for computer-based networking. Bajaj started I-Net as a minority-owned business

Kavelle R. Bajaj.

Maniya Barredo.

receiving contracts from government programs, and it quickly grew. In 1988, her husband joined I-Net as executive vice-president.

In 1993, Bajaj was one of six women selected to receive the prestigious Women of Enterprise award from the Avon Company and the U.S. Small Business Administration. Bajaj also won the coveted Entrepreneur of the Year award, given jointly by Ernst & Young, Inc. magazine, and Merrill Lynch, in the woman-owned business category. In the same year, I-Net was also recognized by Government Computer News as one of the top ten minority businesses.

By 1994, I-Net's revenues exceeded $200 million, and it had grown into a company with 2000 employees working in 38 locations in 22 states. Also that same year, Federal Computer Week ranked it among the country's top ten small businesses in the information technology industry.

Bajaj has begun to organize a national resource center for East-Indian women to provide relevant information at governmental, industrial, and political levels. She believes that such a center would help improve images of East-Indian women by disseminating accurate information about them.

Maniya Barredo (1951-)
Dancer

On November 19, 1951, Josephine Carmen Barredo was born in Manila, the Philippines, the fourth child of Eugenio and Grizelda Barredo. She began dancing when she was four, and later took ballet lessons with her aunt, Julie Borromeo, one of Manila's best-known ballet teachers. By the time she was nine, she had her own children's TV show and was contributing money toward her siblings' educations.

When she was 14, Barredo joined Hariraya Dance Company, and quickly became the darling of the troupe. Later, she was chosen by a teacher for the famed Bolshoi Ballet Company to train for the La Fille Mal Garde, a ballet the instructor was mounting for the company.

When Barredo was 18, however, she announced that she intended to get married. Her teacher and her mother pleaded with her to return to dancing, but she was unswayed. Her mother then talked to former first lady Imelda Marcos, who convinced Barredo that she owed it to herself and to her country to be a great ballerina.

Julia Chang Bloch.

Barredo left the Philippines and flew to New York City, where she received a scholarship to the American Ballet Center, the official school of the Joffrey Ballet. Robert Joffrey took a keen interest in her and renamed her Maniya Barredo. (Being given a new name by Joffrey was an honor bestowed only on a few dancers). For two years she trained daily from nine in the morning to seven at night.

When auditions for the National Ballet of Washington were announced, Joffrey sent six of his students, but not Barredo. She went to the auditions anyway and found 60 other girls in competition—all tall, long-limbed, and white. Barredo, who counted pirouettes among her strengths, completed 32 fouettés, a quick whipping movement of the raised leg often accompanied by continuous turning on the supporting leg. She was accepted at once, but eventually turned down the National Ballet contract in favor of a J.D. Rockefeller Fund Fellowship in ballet, which she was awarded that same month.

In May 1972, Barredo gave a solo dance concert at Carnegie Hall, the first ever given by a Filipina in the United States. In the fall of 1973, she joined Montreal's Les Grand Ballets Canadiens, one of three major ballet companies in Canada, becoming its youngest principal dancer. It was at Les Grands Ballet that she met Mannie Rowe, a principal dancer, whom she married. In September 1975, the couple traveled to the Philippines to dance Time Out of Mind and Romeo and Juliet, a piece that Les Grand Ballets Canadiens' choreographer, Brian Macdonald, presented them as a wedding gift.

In 1976, Barredo left Les Grand Ballets Canadiens, and took a large pay cut to join the Atlanta Ballet, then a civic ballet company with a small $800,000 budget. She did this because, as she explained, she had fallen in love with the city of Atlanta and was eager to escape the Canadian winters. She also wanted to do more classical roles. In the next decade, the Atlanta Ballet blossomed into a fully professional company and increased its budget to more than $3 million.

In 1979, Dame Margot Fonteyn invited Barredo to join the "Stars of the World Ballet" tour, where she was the only dancer not aligned with a New York or European company. Aside from serving as prima ballerina for the Atlanta Ballet, Barredo also became its coach in 1983. In early 1986, she was divorced from Mannie Rowe, then ballet master of the Atlanta Ballet, but their friendship and professional relationships continued.

She is most widely known for her classical repertoire, including the title roles in Gisèle, Sleeping Beauty, Romeo and Juliet, Swan Lake, La Sylphide, and Coppelia. Her interpretations of the Sugar Plum Fairy in the Nutcracker Suite and the new roles she has taken on, including Karen in Thor Sutowski's The Red Shoes and Titania in Dennis Nahat's A Midsummer Night's Dream, were widely praised.

In January 1994, Barredo danced her farewell performance in Manila, performing Gisèle at the Cultural Center of the Philippines. When she finished, she received a 15-minute standing ovation. In May 1994, she announced her decision to dance for the Atlanta Ballet another year, and then concentrate on coaching, lecturing, and writing an autobiography. Barredo, who now lives in suburban Atlanta with her second husband, L. Patterson Thompson III and their five dogs, eventually plans to open her own ballet school.

Lynda Barry
See Literature

Julia Chang Bloch (1942-)
Businesswoman, political appointee

Julia Chang Bloch was born in China on March 2, 1942. She came to the United States at age nine and earned a bachelor's degree in communications and public policy from the University of California at Berkeley in 1964. After serving two years in the Peace Corps in Malaysia, she went on to Harvard University, where she earned a master's degree in government and

Phyllis Jean Takisaki Campbell.

East Asia regional studies in 1967. Later that same year, she went to work for the Peace Corps administration.

In 1971, Chang Bloch moved from administrative to legislative work upon becoming a congressional staffer for the Senate Select Committee on Minority Affairs. In 1976, she became the committee's chief minority counsel. In 1977, Chang Bloch was named deputy director of the Office of African Affairs of the International Communication Agency, and in 1980, she was awarded a one-semester fellowship to the Institute of Politics at the Kennedy School of Government at Harvard.

In 1981, she became assistant administrator of the Food for Peace and Voluntary Assistance Bureau, an organization within the Agency for International Development (AID). In 1987, Chang Bloch served one year as assistant administrator of the Asia and Near East Bureau of AID before returning to an academic setting as an associate in the U.S.-Japan Relations Program at Harvard's Center for International Affairs.

In 1989, she came to national prominence when President George Bush named her ambassador to Nepal, making her the first Asian American ambassador in the history of the U.S. diplomatic corps. During her tenure there, Nepal experienced a popular uprising that brought about the first democratically elected

government in the country's history. Chang Bloch was responsible for asserting the United States' position during this tumultuous time and lending diplomatic assistance to the tenuous process of democratization.

In 1993, Chang Bloch left public service to become a group executive vice-president for corporate relations at BankAmerica Corporation, were she was responsible for the corporation's government, media, and internal and external communications programs.

Julia Chang Bloch has received many awards during her career. Chief among them are the International Award of Honor from the Narcotic Enforcement Officers Association (1992), the Woman of the Year Award from the Organization of Chinese American Woman (1987), an honorary doctorate of Human Letters from Northeastern University (1986), and the Hubert H. Humphrey Award for International Science (1979).

Irene Bueno
Political appointee

Irene Bueno is the special assistant/counsel to the assistant secretary for legislation at the Department of Health and Human Services, and has also served as a health-care surrogate (an expert on the Health Security Act of 1993) in the Clinton administration.

Bueno attended the University of California at Berkeley and graduated from the University's Hastings College of Law. At the federal level, she has worked for Representative Edward Roybal (Democrat of California) and Senator Alan Cranston (Democrat of California), and has also held numerous leadership positions in the Asian American community. She chaired the Conference on Asian Pacific American Leadership (CAPAL), and belongs to the Asian Pacific American Bar Association (APABA) and the Filipino American Women's Network (FAWN). She has also served as Asian American coordinator on the Clinton inaugural committee, and as an assistant for "Asian Americans for Clinton/Gore" during the 1992 presidential campaign.

Phyllis Jean Takisaki Campbell (1951-)
Banker

Over the span of 20 years, Phyllis Campbell has enjoyed an impressive rise through the ranks of banking. Starting as a management trainee fresh out of college, she has gone on to become the president and chief executive officer of the U.S. Bank of Washington in Spokane, one of the state's leading financial institutions.

In 1987, after the U.S. Bank of Washington acquired Old National Bank, Campbell was promoted to senior vice-president and area manager for eastern Washington. In 1989, she became executive vice-president and manager of the Distribution Group for U.S. Bank of Washington, and in 1992, she was chosen to lead the Seattle-King County area. In 1994, as president and chief executive officer, Campbell was responsible for the leadership and management of all U.S. Bank of Washington retail and business banking done in the state, including three area banks representing over 160 branches.

Born in Spokane on July 25, 1951, Phyllis Jean Takasaki was the oldest of five children born to Marion Takisaki, a medical technologist, and Raymond J. Takisaki, a merchant who owned and operated a dry cleaning business. Campbell's grandfather, who immigrated from Japan and settled in Seattle, owned a grocery store. His ethics of hard work and community service were instilled into the whole family.

While growing up, Campbell always had a talent for business management and leadership. Working in the family business in high school, she enjoyed accounting and dealing with people. Working her way through Washington State University, she received a bachelor's degree in business administration and later a master's in the executive marketing program. She is also a graduate of the University of Washington's Pacific Coast Banking School and Stanford University's marketing management program.

Today Campbell lives with her husband, a civil engineer and construction works manager, in the Seattle suburb of Issaquah, where she serves as vice-chair of the Greater Seattle Chamber of Commerce, vice-president of the Board of Regents at Washington State University, and chair of the Association of Washington Business. She is also a board member of the Washington Roundtable and Puget Power and Light. In 1992, Campbell received the Puget Sound Matrix Table's Woman of Achievement Award for her civic service. One of her favorite charitable causes is Success by Six, a program that emphasizes the need of helping young children learn.

Tia Carrere (1969-)
Actress

In 1992, Tia Carrere scored major roles in the Hollywood productions of *Wayne's World* and *Rising Sun*. In the box-office success *Wayne's World*, she played Cassandra, a heavy-metal rock-and-roller and girlfriend of the main character, Wayne, played by Mike Myers. In *Rising Sun*, a thriller based on the best-selling novel by Michael Crichton, she played a computer hacker and love interest of star Sean Connery. Some of Carrere's other roles were in *Quick*, in which she portrayed a police officer on the trail of drug smugglers, and in *Wayne's World II*, in which she reprised her role as Cassandra.

In spite of her blossoming acting career, Carrere's real interest is singing. By late 1993, she was promoting her career as a singer with the release of her solo album. Ironically, she happened to be at the office of a record company executive, Mo Ostin, when word came that Paramount Pictures was looking for an Asian rock-n-roller, which led to her star-making role in *Wayne's World*. Although she contributed two cuts to the *Wayne's World* platinum sound track album, the heavy-metal sound she created for the film is not her solo style.

Carrere was born Althea Janairo in 1969 in Hawaii, but has always used her childhood nickname, Tia. Of primarily Filipino descent, she is the oldest in a family that includes sisters Alesaundra and Audra Lee. She changed her last name to Carrere.

Carrere received several lucky breaks in her career. After she graduated at 17 from a Catholic girls' school in Hawaii, she was spotted at a Honolulu grocery store by the mother of a movie producer, which led to a major role in the beach movie *Aloha Summer*. Following this release, she moved to Los Angeles where she continued to perform in films, including *Harley Davidson and the Marlboro Man* and *Showdown in Little Tokyo*. Carrere also appeared on the television soap opera "General Hospital," as Jade, a nursing student.

Benjamin J. Cayetano (1939-)
Politician

Benjamin J. Cayetano is Hawaii's lieutenant governor and the nation's highest elected Filipino American. He's often listed as one of Hawaii's most effective legislators. With Governor John D. Waihee set to retire in 1994, Cayetano will seek the state's top elected position.

Benjamin Cayetano was born November 14, 1939, in the Honolulu neighborhood of Kalihi, a tough industrial area not known for the lush greenery or peaceful waterfalls typically associated with Hawaii. His parents divorced when he was six, after which he and his younger brother, Kenneth, stayed with their father, a Filipino immigrant who worked as a waiter and often left the task of child-rearing to others.

As a teenager, Cayetano sought community in the rough-and-tumble world of pool halls, fistfights, and fast cars. He once spent a night in jail, and he barely graduated from high school. Although he dreamed of becoming a lawyer, he was told to consider a profession more suited to his circumstances, but ignored the advice.

As the product of a tough blue-collar Honolulu district, Cayetano was forced to become an adult much too soon. In the eighth grade, Cayetano wrote a book report about Clarence Darrow, the attorney who defended the theories of scientific evolution during the Scopes trial. Darrow's own troubled background and his persuasive arguments inspired Cayetano to consider a career in law. In 1958 he became married, and the prospect of supporting a wife, and soon, three children, seemed to instill more responsibility in him. He held

Benjamin J. Cayetano. (C.W. Monaghan.)

Maryles V. Casto.

various jobs—including a junkyard metal packer and state highway crew member. Feeling that he could not get ahead in Hawaii, he packed up the family and moved to Los Angeles.

There, for the first time, he saw whites—doing manual labor. It helped him realize that hard work and education could make a difference. So he decided to enroll in a junior college. In the afternoons he worked, and in the evenings he took his wife to Los Angeles Airport where she worked as a waitress. Later he was admitted to UCLA, and eventually to law school at the Loyola University School of Law.

When Cayetano earned his law degree in 1971, he decided that it was time to return to Hawaii, where he joined a multiethnic law firm. In 1972, an influential politician, governor John A. Burns, appointed Cayetano to the Hawaii Housing Authority, an appointment based on creating diversity. When Cayetano thanked Burns for the appointment, Burns told Cayetano that there were not many Filipinos from the rough Kalihi area who go on to become attorneys. However, Burns's remark did not annoy Cayetano as it might have a few years earlier. Instead, he appreciated Burns's effort to give all ethnic groups opportunity within Hawaii's state administration.

The appointment plunged Cayetano into politics. He ran for the state house of representatives in 1974, defeating a popular Japanese American incumbent, which unburdened him of the feeling that he would unfairly be passed over for jobs. He served two terms in the state house and two terms in the state senate before running successfully for lieutenant governor in 1986. He was reelected to a second term in 1990.

Cayetano is widely known for defending Japanese investments in Hawaii and for promoting equal opportunities for minorities in the private sector. He has led a fight for education reform and helped put into effect an After-School Plus (A+) Program, the nation's first state-funded after-school program for working families.

Maryles V. Casto
Businessperson

Maryles Casto is founder, owner, and manager of Casto Travel, the largest privately owned corporate travel agency in northern California. She established Casto Travel in 1973, drawing from her experience as a flight attendant, manager of in-flight service for Philippine Airlines, and manager of a major travel agency in the San Jose area.

Born in San Carlos City in the Philippines, Maryles Casto grew up in a close, caring Catholic family of seven children. She followed the professional path of her older sister, also a flight attendant. In 1964, Casto moved to the United States with her husband. Although the couple divorced in 1989, she maintains friendships with both her ex-husband and her son, Marc.

Maintaining an ethic of service to others, Casto is committed to a variety of community causes. In recognition of her achievement in the travel industry, Casto was named Woman of the Year in 1985 by the San Francisco Chamber of Commerce. In the same year, Casto Travel joined the "Savvy 60" list of top businesses owned by women. She was the first woman to receive the Asian Pacific American Heritage award from former President George Bush in 1992 and the second woman to be inducted into the Santa Clara County Junior Achievement Business Hall of Fame in 1993. That same year, Casto was appointed by Governor Pete Wilson to the California Council to promote business ownership by women.

In 1994, the U.S. Pan Asian Chamber of Commerce (USPACC), an organization representing approximately 1800 Asian professionals, awarded Casto and five others its "Excellence 2000" Award.

June Chan (1956-)
Community activist

June Chan is the cofounder of Asian Lesbians of the East Coast (ALOEC), a personal and cultural support group headquartered in New York City. She was born on June 6, 1956, in New York's lower Manhattan, and was educated in the New York City public school system. She later enrolled in the City College of New York, from which she graduated in 1977.

After graduate school Chan began working in women's political organizations, specifically in the areas of reproductive rights. She began looking for other ethnic lesbians, and in 1983 joined with Katherine Hall, of mixed Asian descent, to form Asian Lesbians of the East Coast, the first such organization of its kind. The idea behind the group was primarily to provide support and education for other Asian lesbians, although the group does involve itself in political activism.

ALOEC helped organize the Asian American presence at the 1989 march on Washington, in which gay and lesbian groups from around the country descended on the nation's capital to demand civil rights and equal protection under the law. While working on the march, Chan discovered a network of similar groups around the country and together they formed the Asian Pacific Lesbian Network (now known as the Asian Pacific Bi-Sexual Lesbian Network).

In addition to her organizational activities, Chan also works as a laboratory technician at Cornell Medical

June Chan. (Mariana Romo-Carmona.)

College in Manhattan where she conducts research in neurobiology. She lives in New York with her companion Mariana Romo-Carmona, a writer and activist, and her son.

Subrahmanyan Chandrasekhar (1910-)
Astrophysicist, Nobel Prize winner

A winner of the Nobel Prize in 1983, "Chandra" as he is known in scientific circles, is most famous for his studies of the structure of white dwarf stars, studies he completed at only 30 years of age.

Chandrasekhar was born October 10, 1910, in what is now Pakistan. His uncle was a Nobel Prize winning physicist, and Chandrasekhar followed his uncle's path publishing his first research paper at age 18. As a student of physics at Presidency College, Mandra University, he began studying works on the life cycle of stars. He received his bachelor of arts degree in 1930 and continued his education at Trinity College, Cambridge University, on an Indian research scholarship. Chandrasekhar found flaws in long-held theories regarding stars, and by 1934, he had developed a complete theory on white dwarf stars. However, it was decades before these theories were accepted.

Subrahmanyan Chandrasekhar.

Elaine Chao.

Chandrasekhar is also well known for his work involving radiative energy transfer, the general theory of relativity, and the mathematical theory of black holes.

Elaine L. Chao (1952-)
Association executive

Elaine Chao, who on November 16, 1993, assumed the office of president of the United Way of America, is one of the most visible of Asian American women. Her previous positions as head of the Peace Corps, White House Fellow, BankAmerica vice-president, Federal Maritime Commission deputy administrator, Federal Maritime Commission chair, U.S. Department of Transportation deputy secretary, and Harvard Business School class marshal make Chao one of the highest-ranking Asian Americans ever. As the new United Way president, Chao must manage a budget that has been decreased to $21 million from $30 million, and must efficiently manage a staff that was cut to 185 from 300. She also must deal with an expanded board of directors. Chao's key concerns are the reinstatement of local agencies' service levels and the management of the budget.

Stephen Chao (1956-)
Television executive

Stephen Chao is the producer of "Q2," an upscale at-home shopping network. Prior to assuming this position, Mr. Chao made a name for himself by creating shows such as "America's Most Wanted," "Cops," and "Studs."

Stephen Chao was born in Ann Arbor, Michigan, in 1956 to a middle-class family. He was educated at Exeter Academy and Harvard, where he graduated cum laude in classics in 1977.

After graduation Chao worked for two years as a reporter with the *National Enquirer*. He then returned to Harvard to study for a master's degree in business administration. He later landed a management position with Fox Television, and eventually helped contribute to network programming.

His first successful show was "America's Most Wanted," which reenacts violent crimes and then enlists viewers' help in capturing the criminals. Chao's next show, "Cops," followed police officers in the line of duty. After "Cops" was "Studs," a late-night talk/dating show.

Chao left Fox Television amidst the controversy surrounding his hiring a male stripper to perform during a

Tony Yao-Tung Chen.

Joy Cherian.

conference of television executives. After leaving Fox, Chao travelled and developed ideas for Fox's movie division. In 1993, he was hired by his old boss at Fox Television for the newly developed television shopping network, "Q2."

Tony Yao-Tung Chen
Businessman, political appointee

Tony Yao-Tung Chen gained national prominence in 1989 when he was named Asian Affairs director of the Republican National Committee (RNC). In this position, Chen built an outreach network to attract Asians to the Republican party. He also worked to increase voter registration within the Asian American community, recruited Asian Americans to run for political office, promoted the Republican platform in the ethnic press, and organized fund-raising activities on behalf of Republican candidates nationwide. In anticipation of the 1992 general election, Chen organized a project called Asian Victory '92, a combination voter registration/fundraising drive that netted $250,000 for the GOP. He left the RNC in 1993 to pursue a career in private industry.

Chen has a bachelor's degree in western language and literature from Tunghai University in Taiwan, and a master's degree in political science from the University of Nebraska.

Joy Cherian (1942-)
Political appointee, community activist

Dr. Joy Cherian came into the national spotlight during the period of 1987 to 1993 when he served as a commissioner on the federal government's Equal Employment Opportunity Commission. After leaving the commission, Dr. Cherian founded J. Cherian Consultants, Inc., a Washington-based government-relations firm that represents international corporations and conducts seminars on equal employment opportunity issues.

Joy Cherian was born in India in the city of Cochin on May 18, 1942. In 1963, he earned a bachelor of science degree from the University of Kerala, and went on to earn a law degree in 1965 from the same institution.

Dr. Cherian practiced law in India before coming to the United States in 1967 to study at the Catholic University of America in Washington, D.C. In 1970, he earned a master's degree in international law, followed by a Ph.D. in international law in 1974. In 1975, Dr. Cherian reworked his doctoral dissertation and published it as *Investment Contracts and Arbitration*, a reference book that is still widely used today. In 1978, he received his fifth university degree, a master of comparative law (American practice) from George Washington University's National Law Center.

In 1973, while working on his Ph.D., Dr. Cherian joined the legal department of the American Council of Life Insurance, the largest trade association of American life insurance companies. In that position, he traveled to Asia, Europe, and North America promoting international trade in services. In 1982, he was promoted to director of International Insurance Law.

While working as a private citizen, Dr. Cherian was politically active. In 1982, he founded the Indian American Forum for Political Education, a national nonprofit organization that works with the federal government to increase political awareness and participation among East Indian Americans. In 1986, Dr. Cherian was elected national chairman of the Asian American Voters Coalition, an umbrella group representing more than a dozen national ethnic organizations.

In 1987, President Ronald Reagan appointed Cherian to the Equal Employment Opportunity Commission (EEOC). During his tenure with the commission, Dr. Cherian championed many causes and was published widely in law journals on the topic of equal opportunity. He was especially active in the area of national origin-based discrimination. In 1987, the year Dr. Cherian joined the EEOC, there were 9,653 complaints of ethnic discrimination filed with the commission—or 8.8 percent of the agency's caseload. In 1990 there were 11,688—or 11.1 percent.

In 1993, Dr. Cherian's term on the EEOC ended and he left government service to found J. Cherian Consultants, Inc. Dr. Cherian has become especially successful as a consultant to business and government in the area of fostering ethnic diversity within organizations. He holds seminars on topics including diversity training, success with respect, the factual basis for assertions about workforce diversity, and harassment on the basis of race, color, and national origin, among many other related topics.

In addition to his book, *Investment Contracts and Arbitration*, Dr. Cherian has compiled and edited a law reference manual and authored several dozen articles for a variety of professional journals and popular magazines. He has also presented papers and spoken before many organizations around the world, including the Kennedy School of Government at Harvard and the Center for Management Development and Organizational Research at the City University of New York.

Doug Chiang.

Doug Chiang (1962-)
Art director, Academy Award winner

Doug Chiang is the art director and associate creative director at Industrial Light and Magic (ILM), the renowned special-effects company. He is responsible for the creation and design of a great number of special effects and movie sets, including the Oscar-winning *Death Becomes Her* in 1992.

Born in Taiwan in 1962, Doug Chiang was five years old when he and his family moved to the United States. As a 15- year-old high school student, Chiang filmed his first short feature in his backyard. A year later, he made a second short film called *Gladiator*, using clay animation. This animated short landed him the grand prize in a statewide film festival for students. *Gladiator* caught the eye of John Prusak, a media production teacher at the William D. Ford Vocational/Technical center. Prusak encouraged Chiang to enroll in the school, and offered him a job as a teaching assistant. The course gave Chiang hands-on instruction in still photography and film and video production, which included lighting, editing, sound, animation, and special effects.

Chiang transferred to UCLA and graduated in 1986 with a bachelor's degree in fine arts. He soon involved himself in numerous freelance projects, mostly commercials. Eventually, he landed a job with Digital Productions. While working for Digital, he contributed design direction to such productions as "Oprah Winfrey" and "Good Morning America." In 1987, he worked as a designer and key animator for CBS TV's innovative children's show "Pee Wee's Playhouse."

Since joining ILM in 1988 Chiang has received both American and British Academy awards for his work. Some of his more notable recent projects included developing the special effects for *Forrest Gump* and *The Mask*.

Leroy Chiao (1960-)
Astronaut

In July of 1994, less than a month before his 34th birthday, Leroy Chiao fulfilled a lifelong ambition to travel in space when he took off on the space shuttle Columbia as a mission specialist. It was a goal he had dreamed of achieving from the time he was a seven year-old child watching the Gemini and Apollo missions.

Leroy Chiao was born on August 28, 1960, in Milwaukee, Wisconsin, to Tsu Tao and Cherry Chiao, but considers his home to be Danville, California, where his family moved when he was quite young. His father has a master's degree in chemical engineering and his mother holds a Ph.D. in material sciences and engineering. His parents continually stressed to their children the importance of education to achieve what one wants in life. Young Chiao took the advice to heart, and received a bachelor of science degree in chemical engineering from the University of California at Berkeley in 1983. He later earned a master of science degree from the University of California at Santa Barbara, as well as his doctorate in 1987.

Chiao's first job was with Hexcel, a supplier to the aerospace industry. There he worked with NASA and the CalTech Jet Propulsion Laboratory developing materials for future space telescopes. This position brought him a step closer to fulfilling his dream of becoming an astronaut. Chiao then moved to the Lawrence Livermore Laboratory, a government-funded research institution administered by the University of California on the Berkeley campus. He continued working in materials science and applied to the astronaut training program at NASA.

Chiao was selected for the astronaut training program in 1990, and became an astronaut in 1991. As a mission specialist on the July 1994 Columbia launch, Chiao conducted life and material sciences experiments in the International Microgravity Laboratory II—commonly called the Space Lab—a pressurized module within the shuttle cargo bay that offers the astronauts extra room in which to conduct their experiments. He is also being trained as one of two mission specialists

Leroy Chiao.

who will go on space walks outside the shuttle if minor problems should develop.

Margaret Cho (1968-)
Comedian

A second-generation comedian as well as a second-generation Korean American, Margaret Cho was barely into her twenties when she became known as the reigning Asian American funny woman. A child of the 1980s, she has broken barriers and stereotypes by performing on such television shows as the "Bob Hope Special," "Evening at the Improv," "Arsenio Hall," and "Star Search." In 1994, Cho was the first Asian American to star in her own television show, "All-American Girl," a sitcom about a Korean American family.

Margaret Cho was born on December 5, 1968, and raised in San Francisco. She derives much of her material from her upbringing in a liberal, yet religious Korean American home. As a child, her parents encouraged her to learn voice, dance, and piano, but stopped short of endorsing her venture into acting. Undaunted, Cho pursued her dream, gaining admission to San Francisco's prestigious High School of the Performing Arts and later enrolling in San Francisco State University's

Margaret Cho.

Rachelle Chong.

theater department. She had hoped to continue her acting studies at Juilliard or Yale, but became frustrated by the limited roles available to Asian women. It was then that, at the suggestion of a friend, she began stand-up comedy.

Since 1991, when she became the West Coast division champion of the U.S. College Comedy competition that led to a billing with comic Jerry Seinfeld, Cho has accumulated numerous credits. She has appeared on MTV's "Half-Hour Comedy Hour," Lifetime's "Six Comics in Search of a Generation," and Fox's "Comic Strip Live." Cho portrayed a Brooklyn nurse in *Angie*, starring Geena Davis, and has also starred in the film *The Doomed Generation* with Dusting Nguyen. She has also been admitted to the Friar's Club, an exclusive comedy fraternity.

Rachelle Chong (1959-)
Political appointee, attorney

Rachelle Chong is one of five commissioners on the Federal Communications Commission (FCC), a post to which she was nominated by President Bill Clinton in April 1994. Rachelle Blossom Chong was born on June 22, 1959, in Stockton, California to second-generation

Chinese Americans. She was educated at the University of California at Berkeley where she majored in political science and journalism, graduating in 1981 as a Phi Beta Kappa member. She went on to Berkeley's prestigious Hastings College of Law, where she served as editor in chief of *COMM/ENT*, the school's communications and entertainment law journal. She earned her J.D. in 1984.

Chong then moved to Washington, D.C., where she went to work for the law firm of Kadison, Pfaelzer, Woodward, Quinn & Rossi. In 1987 she left the nation's capital to work at Graham and James in San Francisco. Her first position was with the public utilities group, where she focused on issues related to the wireless communication industry.

Chong was chosen for the FCC spot after winning praise from Republican lawmakers in 1993. She had served from 1992 through 1994 as commissioner of the Republican Party's legal services trust fund commission in San Francisco, and was contacted by an administration official in September of 1993 who told her that the White House was looking for a female minority candidate with 15 to 20 years experience in communications. Chong's ten years professional experience proved adequate to serve on the commission. Her position is

Christine Choy.

Connie Chung. (Tony Esparza.)

certain to become more important as the communications industry spawns a huge new subset involving information, telephone, and entertainment delivery and production.

Christine Choy (1954-)
Filmmaker

Christine Choy is a pioneer filmmaker, producer, director, and cinematographer. She has completed 36 films, including the Academy Award-nominated *Who is Vincent Chin* and *Fortune Cookie* for the Public Broadcasting System. Founder of Third World Newsreel and executive director of Film News Now Foundation, she is currently serving as chair of the New York University School of Film.

Paul C. W. Chu (1941-)
Astrophysicist, academician

Paul C. W. Chu is a University of Houston physicist who develops superconductors. Time magazine called him "science's version of a champion pole vaulter," whose continuing research may be used for advancement of life. He was named best researcher in the United States in 1990 by *U.S. News and World Report*. He is the director of the Texas Center for Superconductivity.

Connie Chung (1946-)
Television journalist

Connie Chung has become one of the most recognizable personalities in U.S. culture, and one of the most sought-after and highly-paid broadcasters in contemporary media.

Constance Yu-hwa Chung was born on August 20, 1946, in suburban Washington, D.C., to Margaret Ma and William Ling Ching Chung. Her father had been an intelligence officer in China's Nationalist Army who fled his war-torn homeland for the United States in 1944.

Chung earned a degree in journalism from the University of Maryland in 1969. Her first job was with WTTG-TV, an independent television station in the nation's capital. Later she secured a job at CBS' Washington bureau, aided in part by the Federal Communications Commission's timely mandate for stations to hire more minorities. In her early years with CBS, Chung covered stories such as the 1972 presidential campaign of George McGovern, anti-Vietnam War protests, and the presidency of Richard M. Nixon.

In 1976, Chung moved to Los Angeles to become an anchor at the local CBS affiliate, KNXT (now KCBS).

Lilia C. Clemente.

She began hosting three news broadcasts a day, and the station went from third to second place in ratings. In 1983, she took a drastic pay cut and moved to NBC where she worked as a correspondent and anchored several shows and prime-time news specials. She also served as political analysis correspondent for the network.

In 1989, Chung announced that she would leave NBC for CBS when her current contract expired. Her contract with CBS was reported to be worth $1.5 million annually. Her initial duties at CBS included hosting "West 57th," "The CBS Sunday Night News," and serving as the principal replacement for Dan Rather on "The CBS Evening News."

On June 1, 1993, Connie Chung became the co-anchor of the "CBS Evening News." She became the first Asian and only the second woman ever to be named to the coveted post of nightly news anchor at a major network, traditionally thought of as the pinnacle of broadcast journalism. In addition to her role as co-anchor, Chung hosts "Eye to Eye with Connie Chung," a popular prime-time television news magazine that highlights interviews with controversial newsmakers, a specialty of Chung's.

Chung has received numerous accolades for her work, including three National Emmy Awards, a Peabody, a 1991 Ohio State Award, a 1991 National Headliner Award, two American Women in Radio and Television National Commendations, a 1991 Clarion Award, and in 1990 she was chosen as favorite interviewer by *U.S. News and World Report* in their annual "Best of America" survey.

On December 2, 1984, Chung married television journalist Maury Povich, currently the host of "The Maury Povich Show," a syndicated day-time television talk show.

Eugene Chung
See Sports and Athletics

Lilia C. Clemente
Investment manager

As chairman, CEO, and founder of Clemente Capital, Lilia Clemente leads a fast-paced life in global investments. Her father, Jose Calderon, was a prominent, politically active businessman in the Philippines who sat on the boards of several mining companies. Her mother, Belen Farbos Calderon, was a university teacher and provincial governor who also held a seat on the stock exchange and raised seven children.

At the age of 19, Clemente came to the United States to study at the University of Chicago. She graduated with a master's of business administration in 1969, and was hired by the Ford Foundation. Seven years later she rented a modest office on Park Avenue and with $25,000 in capital, began playing the stock market. Her firm has since launched many global funds, investing in firms in the United States, Japan, Germany, the Philippines, Thailand and Mexico. Clemente married her husband Leopoldo, a fellow Filipino and recipient of an MBA from Northwestern. Together they run their successful financial management firm.

Robert D'Araujo
See Asian Americans in the Military

Victoria Manolo Draves (1924-)
Olympic diver

Victoria Manolo Draves is a former national champion diver and the winner of two Olympic gold medals. In the 1948 Olympic Games she became the first woman to win gold medals in both the ten-meter platform and three-meter springboard diving events. After her Olympic victory, she toured Europe in a swimming exhibition with the Olympic swimmer and Hollywood film star, Buster Crabbe. *See also* Sports and Athletics.

Dinesh D'Souza.

Phoebe Eng.

Dinesh D'Souza (1961-)
Writer, political analyst

In 1991, Dinesh D'Souza published *Illiberal Education: The Politics of Race and Sex on Campus*, a critique of the academically stifling atmosphere permeating life on some American university campuses. The fame he achieved with the success of this book made him a much-demanded lecturer and contributor to the nation's prestigious op-ed pages. He has written extensively for the Wall Street Journal, the New York Times, the Los Angeles Times, the Boston Globe, and the Washington Post.

Dinesh D'Souza was born in Bombay, April 25, 1961, into a family practicing Catholicism, a minority religion in India. He was educated in private Jesuit schools that stressed a traditional, Western, mostly British curriculum. In 1978, Dinesh came to the United States for his final year of high school, and then enrolled at Dartmouth College, where he began writing for the campus newspaper. In his junior year, he became an editor of the *Dartmouth Review* (a newspaper not affiliated with the college), which opposed what its editors viewed as the mindless liberalism exhibited in nearly all campus affairs, classrooms, and publications. The

newspaper gained national attention for its controversial editorials and inferred insensitivity to minorities.

D'Souza graduated from Dartmouth in 1983, and moved to Princeton, New Jersey, to become editor of *Prospect*, a magazine published by Princeton alumni. The next year, he published his first book, *Falwell: Before the Millennium*, a critical biography of Jerry Falwell, evangelist, conservative political activist, and founder of the Moral Majority. Two books followed in the next three years, during which time he also moved to Washington, D.C., to work as an editor with the Heritage Foundation's journal, *Policy Review*. In 1986 he published *The Catholic Classics*, a two-volume series of interpretive essays, and in 1987 collaborated with Gregory Fossedal on the novel *My Dear Alex: Letters from the KGB*. In the same year D'Souza took a job in the Reagan administration as assistant to domestic policy chief Gary Bauer.

Phoebe Eng (1961-)
Publisher

Phoebe Eng is the confounder and former publisher of *A. Magazine*, a nationally distributed consumer magazine directed at Asian American professionals. Since

March Fong Eu.

Hiram Fong.

its founding in 1990, the magazine has grown rapidly and today has a circulation of 80,000.

Eng was born in 1961 in Philadelphia to professional second-generation Chinese Americans. Her father is an architect who traces his ancestry to Hong Kong, and her mother is a nursing supervisor whose family came to the United States from Taiwan. Eng earned a bachelor's degree in finance from the University of California at Berkeley in 1983 and a law degree from New York University Law School in 1989. She worked briefly in corporate law for the international firm of Coudert Brothers before going into the publishing business in 1992. She lives in New York City with her husband, British photographer Zubin Schroff.

March Fong Eu (1922-)
Politician

In 1993, when March Fong Eu was two years into her fifth term as California Secretary of State, President Bill Clinton appointed her ambassador to Micronesia. Since beginning her career in health education, she has used her determination and empathy to meet a series of challenges which, in 1974, led her to become California's first female Secretary of State. Eu

was also named by *Ladies' Home Journal* as one of America's 100 most important women.

A third-generation Californian, her ancestors originated in Guangton, China. As a young child, Eu moved to the small community of Richmond, California. After attending high school there, she attended Salinas Junior College for one year, then completed a Bachelor of Science degree at the University of California at Berkeley. Eu received her master of education degree from Mills College in Oakland, and her doctoral degree in education at Stanford University. An interest in science led her to a career as a dental hygienist and later as a professional health educator.

In 1966 when she won election to the California state legislature, she became the first Asian American Assemblywoman in California.

Theo-Dric Feng
Radio producer

Theo-dric Feng is the producer of the Gold Mountain Radio Show, broadcast from WPFW-FM in Washington, D.C. The program deals with subjects of interest to Asian Americans in the Greater Washington, D.C., area.

Hiram Fong (1907-)
Politician, attorney

Hiram Leong Fong was born in the Kalihi district of Honolulu, on October 1, 1907, the seventh of eleven children. Both his parents were immigrants from Kwangtung Province, China. His father, Lum, was a sugar plantation worker.

Fong was the first American of Asian descent to be elected to the U.S. Senate when he was chosen as Hawaii's first senator in 1959. A Republican, he served Hawaii for three terms until retiring in 1977. Prior to becoming a senator, Fong had served in Hawaii's territorial legislature from 1938 to 1954, including four years as vice-speaker of the house of representatives and six years as speaker. He was vice-president of the Hawaii state constitutional convention held in 1950, and was a longtime, ardent supporter of Hawaiian statehood.

Matthew K. Fong (1953-)
Politician

Matthew K. Fong is vice-chairman of California's State Board of Equalization, a state-wide administrative entity that sets tax policy and manages a variety of tax programs—such as sales, gasoline, hazardous waste, and alcohol taxes—involving over $36 billion annually.

Matt Fong is a fourth-generation Californian of Chinese descent. His mother is March Fong Eu, a perennial California politician and activist, who for many years served as that state's secretary of state until her 1993 appointment as ambassador to Micronesia. His father is a colonel in the United States Air Force. Matthew was educated at the United States Air Force Academy, where he received a bachelor of science degree in 1975, and after which he served in active duty in the air force for five years.

Upon returning to civilian life Fong managed his mother's third successful reelection campaign, then served on her staff while continuing his education. After earning a law degree from Southwestern Law School and a master's of business administration from Pepperdine University in 1982, he went to work for the Los Angeles-based international law firm of Sheppard, Mullin, Richter & Hampton, where he specialized in transactional law.

In 1990 Fong ran for state controller, an election he lost. In 1991, however, Governor Pete Wilson appointed Fong to the State Board of Equalization. In this position Fong has supported lowering taxes on manufacturing and lessening the government regulations to let businesses prosper in California. He has been active in Republican circles, having served as cochairman of both the Bush/Quayle 1988 California campaign committee, and the Pete Wilson for Senate committee.

Matthew K. Fong.

Haijing Fu (1957-)
Opera singer

Haijing Fu is a rising star in the world of opera, an award-winning baritone who has performed with the Metropolitan Opera in New York, the Boston Symphony Orchestra, the Cleveland Orchestra, and Opera de Nice.

Haijing Fu was born on September 12, 1957, in the northeastern Chinese resort city of Dalian. He is a popular performer in China, appearing in television and radio concerts. In early 1986, he earned a scholarship to study at the Boston University School of Arts. In 1988, he won the Metropolitan Opera National Council Competition.

Fu began his career with the Boston Symphony Orchestra. In 1989 he performed his first big roles with the Opera Company of Philadelphia in Luisa Miller and Lucia with Luciano Pavoratti. In 1990, Fu made his debut at the Metropolitan Opera in La Traviata, where he was the first Chinese to sing a major role.

As of mid-1994, Mr. Fu was rehearsing a Met production of Lucia, in which he will sing the part of Enrico. Mr. Fu is married to Jin Chuan Wang, a former folk dancer. The couple has one child, a daughter, Xiao.

Haijing Fu.

John Liu Fugh
See Asian Americans in the Military

Roman Gabriel
See Sports and Athletics

Jorge M. Garcia (1941-)
Surgeon

Jorge Garcia is one of the premier heart surgeons in the United States. The former chief of the cardiac surgery division at the Washington Hospital Center in Washington, D.C., he was named in a poll of his colleagues to be the surgeon they would most want to operate on their hearts. He has worked to bring modern cardiovascular surgery to underdeveloped countries, spending much of each year in Egypt, China, and the Philippines, teaching local doctors to perform heart surgery.

Jorge Garcia was born in the city of Binan in Laguna Province, the Philippines. He earned his bachelor's degree in biology from University of Santo Tomas in Manila in 1959 and entered medical school that year. In 1967 Dr. Garcia came to the United States to intern at Washington Hospital Center in Washington, D.C., where he trained for five years to become a general surgeon, and an additional two years to become a certified thoracic and cardiovascular surgeon. In 1978 he was named as chief of the hospitals cardiac surgery division.

In 1988 Dr. Garcia began to teach and perform heart surgery in underdeveloped countries. He started the Makati Heart Foundation in the Philippines to upgrade the quality of cardiac care in his homeland, an ambition dating back to his medical school days. In 1991, he gave up his position as chief of cardiac surgery at Washington Hospital and now travels nearly year-round. He goes to the Philippines with special frequency, and on May 28, 1994, he performed the country's first heart transplant.

Yun Gee (1906-1963)
Artist

Yun Gee (1906-1963) was an immigrant from Canton, China, who joined the modernist art scene in the 1920s in the United States. He suffered the stigma of being a refugee from Chinatown in a white world. Married to a white woman, he was physically attacked several times while walking down the street with her. His dramatic surreal painting, "Where is my mother" reveals an immigrant's loneliness in the tearful face of the artist and a ship which brought him to America in the background. His works were shown in many prominent museums and galleries. In 1945 he suffered a mental breakdown and never resumed his brilliant career.

Lillian Gonzalez-Pardo, M.D. (1939-)
Physician

Born on February 5, 1939, in Manila, Philippines, Lillian Gonzalez-Pardo was the first Asian American woman to serve as president of the American Medical Women's Association. A clinical professor of pediatrics and neurology at the University of Kansas Medical Center in Kansas City, Kansas, she has worked to promote better health care for women and children, both nationally and internationally.

Following her father's advice, Lillian enrolled in the University of the Philippines in Quezon City. She graduated with an associate of arts in premed in 1957 and a doctorate of medicine in 1962. In 1961 she served an internship at Philippines General Hospital in Manila, after which she received her certification from the Phillipines Medical Board in May 1962.

She then traveled to the United States to begin her post-graduate training at the University of Kansas Medical Center (UKMC) in Kansas City, Kansas. In 1967, she was a fellow in pediatric neurology at Children's Mercy Hospital in Kansas City, Missouri. She subsequently returned to UKMC, where she was a fellow in developmental pediatrics from 1972 until 1973 and a resident in pediatrics in 1974.

Returning to the Philippines, Gonzalez-Pardo became an instructor in medicine at the University of the Philippines College of Medicine in Manila from July 1969 to April 1971. She also was a consultant in neurology at three Manila hospitals, Phillipines General Hospital, Metropolitan General Hospital, and Quezon Institute. She continued her teaching in 1975, when she became an assistant professor of pediatrics and neurology at the University of Kansas School of Medicine. From 1979 until 1981, she also worked as the medical director of the Children's Rehabilitation Unit/University Affiliated Facility at UKMC. In 1980 she was granted her U.S. citizenship. She became a full clinical professor at UKMC in 1992. While continuing this position, she began work in 1994 on a master's degree in health services administration at the University of Kansas.

Apart from her teaching duties, Gonzalez-Pardo has also been active in many medical associations and community service projects. She has been a member of the Asian Council of Greater Kansas City, the Filipino Association of Greater Kansas City, the Advisory Group of the Kaw Valley Arts and Humanities Council, and the International Women's Forum, among many other organizations.

For her dedication as a physician and a citizen, Gonzalez-Pardo has received several awards. She was named the Outstanding Alumnus of the University of the Philippines College of Medicine in 1991. And in May 1993, she was given the Excellence 2000 Award as Outstanding Asian American by the U.S. Pan Asian American Pacific Chamber of Commerce in Washington, D.C.

Gonzalez-Pardo and her husband, Manuel P. Pardo (faculty and staff psychiatrist at UKMC) have three children, Manuel, Jr., who is also a doctor, Lillie, and Patrick. They reside in Mission Hills, Kansas.

Philip Kan Gotanda (1951-)
Playwright, filmmaker

Philip Kan Gotanda, the acclaimed playwright whose works include *The Wash* and *Yankee Dawg You Die*, is one of the few Asian Americans who have made a mark in the cultural mainstream.

Born in Stockton, California, on December 17, 1951, Philip Kan Gotanda was the youngest of three sons. A third generation Japanese American on both sides, his ancestors came from Hiroshima. Growing up, his role model was Elvis Presley.

From Stockton, Gotanda went to the University of California at Santa Cruz, stayed for a couple of years, and left. He traveled to Japan, then returned to California, this time to University of California at Berkeley and later moved on to University of California at Santa

Barbara, where he earned a degree in Japanese art. He went to law school and eventually found work as a legal aide in San Francisco.

At the same time, Gotanda began to compose music, and eventually wrote his first musical, *The Avocado Kid*. He sent the script to East West Players in Los Angeles, the first Asian American theater in the United States. Gradually, he moved from writing musicals to plays.

In the following years, Gotanda wrote *Song for a Nisei Fisherman*, a Japanese American family saga with autobiographical underpinnings, and *The Dream of Kitamura*, which premiered in 1984.

Shortly after the premiere of *Fish Head Soup*, Gotanda stopped writing plays altogether. In the meantime, he wrote, directed, and starred in a short film, *The Kiss*. When Gotanda picked up his pen again, he wrote *Day Standing on Its Head* in just two-and-a-half weeks.

Wendy Lee Gramm (1945-)
Economist, political appointee

Wendy Lee Gramm has achieved much in the areas of academics, government, and private industry. A former college professor, she is a member of the Chicago Mercantile Exchange's governing board and a board member of the Enron Corporation. Prior to that she served as chairperson of the United States government's Commodity Futures Trading Commission, where she was responsible for regulating the trade of commodities such as wheat, cattle and precious metals. As such she oversaw the activities of some 55,000 commodities traders, and presided over the turbulent days in the wake of the Wall Street market breaks in 1987 and 1989.

Wendy Lee was born on January 10, 1945, in the city of Wailaua, Hawaii, on the island of Oahu. Her grandparents had come from Korea at the turn of the century to work in the Hawaiian sugar fields. Her father, Joshua Lee, had left the islands during the Great Depression to attend Tri-State College in Angola, Indiana. After earning an engineering degree from Tri-State College, he returned to Hawaii and got a job with the sugar company harvesting sugar. He worked his way up through the company and became a vice president. Gramm's mother, Angeline, was a librarian.

In 1957, the then-Soviet Union made history when it launched an artificial satellite, Sputnik, into space and initiated a fierce competition with the United States to be first in space exploration. Along with the rest of America's students, these events led Gramm to become interested in math and science. When she earned a scholarship to Wellesley College, she decided to major in math, but later changed to economics because in that field she could use both her business and math skills. In 1966 she graduated from Wellesley with a bachelor's degree in economics.

Emil Guillermo. (Max Hirshfeld.)

Gramm started her career as an assistant professor of economics at Texas A&M University shortly after receiving her Ph.D. in economics from Northwestern University in 1971. For her dissertation at Northwestern Gramm studied women as part of the labor force. She met and married a fellow faculty member, Phil Gramm, while on the faculty at Texas A & M.

In 1976 Phil Gramm ran for the Senate as a Democrat and lost in the primaries to Lloyd Bentsen, who later became Secretary of State in the administration of President Bill Clinton. In 1978 he ran for the House of Representatives and won. Gramm followed her husband to Washington and found a job at the Institute for Defense Analysis. In 1982 she began working for the Federal Trade Commission.

Her husband was reelected to the House of Representatives in 1980 and 1982 as a Democrat, but he changed his party affiliation from Democrat to Republican in 1983, Gramm also changed her party affiliation. She began working for the Office of Management and Budget in 1984, where she worked on limiting the amount and scope of regulations issued by the government. That same year her husband was elected to the Senate.

Gramm was appointed to the Commodity Futures Trading Commission in February of 1988 by then-president George Bush. On January 20, 1993, the day President Clinton was inaugurated, she resigned from her post and became a board member of the Chicago Mercantile Exchange shortly thereafter.

In early 1995, Phil Gramm declared his candidacy for the U.S. presidency. The Gramms have two sons: Marshall Kenneth, who was born in 1973, and Jefferson Philip, who was born in 1975.

Emil Guillermo (1955-)
Humorist, broadcast journalist

Emil Guillermo is a radio and television journalist who came to national prominence as the weekend anchor of National Public Radio's news program "All Things Considered," which he hosted from 1989 until 1991. His commentaries and humorous essays became very popular with the show's audience and led to his column "Amok," which is published monthly in *Filipinas* magazine.

Guillermo was born on October 9, 1955, in San Francisco, California, to first-generation Filipino immigrants. His father was a fry cook who had immigrated to the United States in the 1920s. Guillermo was an excellent student, and after graduating high school in 1973 he won a scholarship to Harvard where he graduated in 1977 after only three years of study. After graduation, Guillermo returned to San Francisco, uncertain of what he wanted to do. He had often been encouraged to try his hand at stand-up comedy, and for a while, he considered it. Ultimately, though, the idea just didn't appeal to him.

His first on-air job in television news was in 1979 at KOLO in Reno, Nevada, where he was a reporter, sportscaster, and backup anchor. In 1980 he went to KXAS in Dallas where he worked in his first major news-market. He stayed in Dallas for about fourteen months and then was offered a job back in San Francisco at KRON. Eventually, he started his own radio show called "Bay Area Filipino with Emil Guillermo." The show was a half-hour news and entertainment program which featured Guillermo's personal essays and had a wide listening audience. He ended the show in 1989 when he was offered a position with National Public Radio (NPR).

In 1991, Guillermo left NPR and began hosting a talk show on a local Washington, D.C. radio station. He called the show "Amok in Washington: the Emil Guillermo Show" and described as "a sort of anti-Rush Limbaugh." In 1992, he published his first column on the editorial page of *USA Today* and wrote in a number of other publications.

Guillermo decided he wanted to experience politics firsthand, so from 1993 until spring of 1994, he served

Rajat Gupta. (Joe Berger.)

Maria Luisa Mabilangan Haley.

as press secretary to Norman Y. Mineta, California's fifteenth district representative in the U.S. Congress and the highest-ranking Asian American in the House. He enjoyed working in politics but ultimately missed the freedom he had had as a writer and journalist.

Rajat Gupta (1948-)
Business leader

Born on December 12, 1948, in Calcutta, India, Rajat Gupta was the second of four children. When he was five years old, his family moved to New Delhi, where his father was an editor and active in India's independence movement and his mother was a Montessori teacher. Tragedy struck early as Gupta lost both his parents by the time he was eighteen.

Gupta earned an undergraduate degree in mechanical engineering at the Indian Institute of Technology. In 1971, he won a scholarship to attend the Harvard Business School. Harvard classmates remember Gupta as being exceptionally gifted and smart. In 1973, Gupta graduated from Harvard with a master's degree in business administration. He applied for a position at the prestigious management consulting firm, McKinsey and Company, but was rejected due to a lack of work

experience. A professor intervened and urged McKinsey to reconsider its decision. The company changed its mind.

Gupta joined McKinsey and in 1980 was made junior partner. One year later, he was sent overseas to manage McKinsey's foothold in Scandinavia. In three years, the Scandinavian operations grew to one hundred consultants from the original twenty-five. He was head of McKinsey's Chicago office before being named managing director in March of 1994, the first non-Westerner to lead the giant firm.

Maria Luisa Mabilangan Haley (1940-)
Political appointee, entrepreneur

In 1993, when Maria Haley entered the Oval Office as special assistant to President Bill Clinton and associate director of presidential personnel for economics, commerce, and trade, she felt her life had come full circle. The highest-ranking Filipino American in the Clinton administration, she is the daughter of Felipe Mabilangan, who as a Filipino political science student at Syracuse University, had testified before Congress appealing to them to grant his homeland independence 65 years ago.

Ross Masao Harano.

Born in Manila on November 14, 1940, three weeks before the bombing of Pearl Harbor, Maria Mabilangan, along with her brother and parents, spent the next five years hiding from the Japanese in the mountains of Batangas. In 1950 her father became the first Philippine Consul General in New Delhi, India. Her family traveled widely, living in Pakistan, France, and Spain, with a short stay Laos.

In 1964, Mabilangan pooled her resources with a friend to open the Karilagan Finishing School, the first of its kind in Southeast Asia. A year later, she joined a managerial training program at the Hilton International in Manila. In just two years, she became the second female sales manager in an international hotel chain.

In 1971, after marriage to John Haley, an American lawyer from Little Rock, Arkansas, Haley worked first as a travel agent and then, in 1974, as general manager of a division of a retirement community firm. From 1979 to 1990, she served as International Marketing Consultant and Director of Marketing for the Arkansas Industrial Development Commission (AIDC), a state cabinet agency. She advised then-governor Bill Clinton on foreign relations, trade, and investment activities; took charge of the state's national and international marketing, export development, and foreign programs;

supervised the establishment and expansion of the state's overseas offices in Brussels, Tokyo, and Taipei; and coordinated all of the governor's international business missions.

When Clinton decided to run for president in 1991, Haley was quick to volunteer for his campaign. After Clinton's election in November 1992, she was named deputy director of personnel in the transition team, a completely new job that required her to move on 24-hours notice, leaving her home of 22 years, her friends, and family. In 1993, she was named special assistant to the president and associate director of presidential personnel for economics, commerce, and trade. In 1994, Haley accepted an appointment by President Bill Clinton and became Board Director for the Export Import Bank based in Washington, D.C.

Ross Masao Harano (1942-)

Businessman, political activist

Ross Harano remembers the time in elementary school when he first realized he was Japanese, a realization that motivated him to learn more about his ethnicity and take an active role in the Japanese American community. By 1994, he had become president of the World Trade Center Chicago Association as well as chairperson of the Chicago chapter of the Japanese American Citizens League.

Born September 17, 1942, in an assembly center for Japanese Americans interned during World War II, Ross Masao Harano was relocated with his family to an internment camp in Jerome, Arkansas. In 1960, Harano entered the University of Illinois where he earned a bachelor's degree in finance. He earned a graduate degree in sociology from DePaul University.

Harano began his professional career in insurance and moved on to banking, eventually assuming the position of vice-president at the Bank of Chicago and later of the Community Bank of Edgewater. In 1988, he joined the Office of the attorney general of Illinois, serving as equal opportunity officer, director of advisory councils and finally, the chief of the crime-victims division before leaving in 1993 to assume the presidency of the Illinois World Trade Center.

Harano has been recognized by the Japanese Americans Citizens League, and in 1992, became the first Asian American to be appointed as an elector for the electoral college in Illinois.

Sumi Sevilla Haru (1939-)

Producer, actor, journalist, writer, poet

Sumi Sevilla Haru wears many hats. She is a performing arts program coordinator for the City of Los Angeles, a newspaper columnist, radio commentator, and actress; in 1994, she was elected first national vice-president of the Screen Actors Guild (SAG).

Conceived in Manila, Sumi Sevilla Haru was born on August 25, 1939, in Orange, New Jersey. She spent her childhood in the Midwest, and enrolled in the University of Colorado, where she studied music with a concentration in piano and flute. In 1964, Haru moved to Los Angeles to pursue an acting career, and in 1967, became involved with East West Players, the first Asian American theater company in the United States.

In 1971, Haru came to national attention when she helped found SAG's Ethnic Employment Opportunities Committee, which launched the first concerted efforts toward establishing affirmative action in the hiring of actors. In 1976, she helped draft and negotiate the affirmative-action clauses of national theatrical and commercial contracts. The phrase, "American scene," which requires realistic film depictions of all aspects of American life, especially the portrayals of minorities, has through her efforts, become a necessary clause in all SAG and American Federation of Television and Radio Artists (AFTRA) contracts.

In addition to her involvement with SAG, Haru has served on AFTRA's local and national boards since 1976. She is copresident of the County of Los Angeles Media Image Coalition, which seeks balanced media images and career opportunities for underrepresented groups in the television and film industry; and is cofounder and president of the association of Asian/Pacific Artists. She is a member of the national executive board of the Asian Pacific Labor Alliance, an affiliate of the AFL-CIO, and is the executive vice-president of the organization's Los Angeles chapter. As first vice-chair of the National Conference of Christian and Jews, Asian/Pacific American Focus Program and member of the Media Image Task Force, Haru helped publish *Asian Pacific Americans: A Handbook on How to Cover and Portray Our Nation's Fastest Growing Minority Group*, in cooperation with the Asian American Journalists Association and the Association of Asian/Pacific American Artists.

The credits of Haru's production company, Iron Lotus Productions, include Women Pioneer videos for Los Angeles' telecommunications department and television programs for Pacific Asian Alcohol Program and Asian/Pacific American Legal Center.

Lon S. Hatamiya (1959-)

Businessman, attorney, government administrator

Lon Hatamiya has parlayed two of his family's strongest values—hard work and community commitment—into a successful career in both private business and public service. His appointment by President

Sumi Sevilla Haru.

Bill Clinton in September 1993 as administrator of the Agricultural Marketing Service (AMS) of the United States Department of Agriculture (USDA) has been the crowning achievement in a lifetime of diverse interests and accomplishments.

Lon Hatamiya was born on January 26, 1959, in Marysville, California, to George and Kashiwa Hatamiya. His grandfather, Sennichi Hatamiya, had come to Marysville from Hiroshima in the early 1900s and had purchased a farm after working for a number of years as a farmhand and railroad worker. Today the family farm, H.B. Orchards Company, comprises 1200 acres of plum, peach, walnut, and almond trees. Hatamiya helped on the farm during his childhood, along with his parents, two sisters (Kim and Jil), and two uncles and their families. He was also active in the Boy Scouts, becoming an Eagle Scout at the age of 14.

When Americans of Japanese ancestry were forcibly removed from areas of the West Coast, his father's family was interned first at Tule Lake, California, and then at Amache, Colorado. His mother's family was interned at Topaz, Utah, and then at Crystal City, Texas. During these years the family's farm was tended by neighbors.

Hatamiya left Marysville for the first time in 1977 to attend Harvard, where he graduated in 1981 with a

Lon S. Hatamiya.

bachelor's degree in economics, with honors. His first job after college was as a purchasing manager for the Proctor and Gamble Company in Cincinnati. He later returned to California, earning a master's of business administration in entrepreneurial studies and international business from the Anderson Graduate School of Management at the University of California, Los Angeles (UCLA) and a law degree from the UCLA School of Law in 1987. While in graduate school, he worked in Japan as a consultant for the Sony Corporation, where he developed a marketing strategy for broadcast equipment in Western Europe; he also served as a consultant to the Port of Long Beach, California, in 1985 and 1986. After completing his education, Hatamiya practiced public finance, corporate, and political law with the national law firm of Orrick, Herrington, and Sutcliffe in Sacramento, California, from 1987 to 1989, when he returned to Marysville and his family's farm.

Agricultural expertise, community involvement, business and political savvy, and experience combined to make Hatamiya a logical choice for AMS administrator in 1993. His responsibilities there include managing and directing a variety of marketing programs: commodity grading, classing and quality inspection, commodity procurement, market news and development,

commodity research and promotion, and commodity standardization. Hatamiya also oversees the agency's traditional regulatory programs such as marketing agreements and orders, and enforces laws designed to ensure fair trading in the produce and seed industries.

Kayo Hatta
Filmmaker

Kayo Hatta is a Japanese American filmmaker whose first major motion picture is *Picture Bride*, an epic period film. Hatta, the film's director and cowriter, became interested in Japanese Americans in Hawaii when she heard recordings of worksongs sung by Japanese female plantation workers. The spirit and pathos they embodied inspired Hatta to learn more about the picture brides who left Japan in the early 1900s to marry plantation contract laborers—who they knew only through letters and photographs—in Hawaii.

Based on the experiences of women Hatta read about and talked with, *Picture Bride*, a $1-million movie, tells the story of Riyo, an 18 year-old Japanese woman whose personality was inspired by Hatta's own grandmother's determination and strength. Riyo leaves her homeland in 1915 to marry a man she has never seen who works as a plantation contract laborer in Hawaii. She soon discovers that Hawaii's difficult plantation life is not what she expected, and neither is her husband-to-be. In their new land, the picture brides often felt a keen sense of alienation and loneliness, and the cane fields became a place where they would go to be alone and cry.

Hatta, a graduate of Stanford University, was involved in writing, art, and photography before she tried filmmaking. Most of her projects are related to her experience as an Asian American woman. In describing her reasons for making *Picture Bride*, Hatta says she felt responsible for telling the picture brides' stories out of respect and honor for them.

James Hattori
Journalist

Hattori was born and raised in Los Angeles, the youngest of three children. He lived with his parents and his older brother and sister in the inner-city Crenshaw neighborhood where there was a community of Japanese American families. When Hattori was in junior high school, his family moved to a community near Torrance, a Los Angeles suburb. After finishing high school in Torrance, Hattori entered the University of Southern California School of Journalism. It was in college, at about the age of twenty, that Hattori decided to pursue a reporting career.

Hattori graduated cum laude from the University of Southern California in 1977.

His first job as was a weekend assignment editor and writer at KGTV-TV in San Diego. Shortly afterward, he joined KFMB-TV in Spokane, Washington, as a reporter and midday anchor. Hattori spent the following four years at KREM-TV, his longest time at a station to date. In 1982, he joined KING-TV in Seattle as a reporter, legislative correspondent, and weekend anchor. After five years in Seattle, Hattori joined KPRC-TV in Houston as a reporter in the special projects unit. CBS News soon offered him the post of Dallas correspondent.

As a correspondent of CBS News, Hattori reported on a wide range of stories for the "CBS Evening News," "Sunday Morning," "48 Hours," "CBS Morning News," and "CBS This Morning." During the 1992 presidential campaign, Hattori covered the beginning of Ross Perot's bid as an independent candidate for the presidency, as well as the Republican National Convention in Houston. Since 1992, he has been serving as CBS News correspondent from Tokyo.

Samuel Ichye Hayakawa (1906-1992)
United States Senator, educator, writer

S.I. Hayakawa was born in Canada to parents of Japanese descent. A staunch conservative senator from California, it was his behavior as well as his legislative record that made him famous. His eccentricities, modest stature, and habit of dozing off were frequent topics of conversation. Less well known was that the senator suffered from narcolepsy, a disorder that would, without warning, sends him involuntarily into a deep sleep.

He was an esteemed scholar, college administrator, and author of *Language in Action*, a semantics text book now in its fifth edition (as *Language in Thought and Action*). He was also cofounder of the International Society for General Semantics (ISGS) and *ETC.: A Review of General Semantics*, a scholarly language journal. In addition, from 1983 until 1990 he served as Special Adviser to the Secretary of State for East Asian and Pacific Affairs.

Hayakawa was born in Vancouver, British Columbia. His Canadian citizenship kept him from being placed in internment camps during World War II, although he had been a U.S. resident since. He was barred from becoming a permanent U.S. citizen until the 1950s on the basis of his race, and his marriage to a European American woman was not recognized as legal in many states. Yet he not only defended the United States government internment order, but voted against the reparations payment bill.

Hayakawa was elected to the Senate in 1976. Although he was not reelected in 1982, he remained active in politics. He continued to write books and articles until his death from a stroke on February 27, 1992.

James Hattori.

Dennis Hayashi (1952-)
Lawyer, civil rights activist, political appointee

Dennis Hayashi, a third-generation Japanese American, is committed to preserving the rights of Japanese Americans. He was born in Los Angeles on May 31, 1952, to parents who, along with thousands of other Japanese Americans, were interned in camps during World War II because, due to their Japanese ancestry, they were deemed threats to U.S. national security.

Hayashi earned his bachelor's degree in philosophy cum laude from Occidental College in 1974, and earned his law degree from Hastings College in 1978. As a student, he spent one year as a law clerk to Robert Takasugi of the U.S. District Court. He worked for the Asian Law Caucus in San Francisco from 1979 to 1991, specializing in employment and racial discrimination cases. In 1991 he became national director of the Japanese American Citizens League, the country's oldest Asian/Pacific Islander civil rights organization. He is also cofounder of the National Network against Asian American Violence, which monitors and investigates cases of anti-Asian violence.

When Bill Clinton was elected president in 1992, Hayashi was selected as a member of the Clinton/Gore

Irene Y. Hirano.

civil rights transition cluster. In May 1993, Clinton announced Hayashi as his choice for director of the Office for Civil Rights, an appointment made official by Health and Human Services Secretary Donna E. Shalala in June the same year. His responsibilities include ensuring that any program or group that receives funds from Health and Human Services complies with all civil rights laws. He also oversees the activities of the organizations ten regional offices.

Hayashi has also published articles in the *Washington Post*, *Los Angeles Times*, the *Yale Law Review*, and the Kennedy School of Government's *Asian American Policy Review*, and has taught at the New College of California Law School in San Francisco.

Le Ly Hayslip
See Literature

Irene Y. Hirano (1932-)
Executive, community activist

Irene Y. Hirano serves as executive director and president of the Japanese American National Museum, and is responsible for its overall administration, development, and programs. Prior to accepting that position,

she served for over 13 years as executive director for T.H.E. Clinic, an innovative nonprofit community health facility. She has chaired the California Commission on the Status of Women, the President's Community Advisory Committee of the University of Southern California, and the National Asian Pacific Women's Coalition.

Alex Kitman Ho (1950-)
Film producer

Alex Kitman Ho is an Academy Award-winning producer of feature films. He has produced such highly regarded films as *Platoon*, *Wall Street*, and *JFK* for filmmaker Oliver Stone, as well as all of Stone's other directorial projects.

Alex Kitman Ho was born in Hong Kong on January 15, 1950; his family moved to the United States when he was four years old. He was educated at Goddard College in Plainfield, Vermont, where he earned a bachelor's degree in cinema studies in 1972. Following his graduation he enrolled in the Tisch School of the Arts at New York University, where he earned a master's degree in fine arts in 1974.

His first major assignment was as a unit manager for *To Kill a Cop* in 1978. In the next two years he worked on *One-Trick Pony*, *Heartland*, *Fame*, and *First Deadly Sin*. In 1981 he supervised domestic production for Warren Beatty's epic *Reds*.

Ho's work established him as a producer who could assemble quality casts in well-written productions. In 1984, while working on *Year of the Dragon*, Ho met Oliver Stone, who was struggling to become a mainstream director, having made such critically successful but commercially overlooked films as *Salvador*. The two joined forces to produce *Platoon* in 1986, which earned both critical praise and big box office receipts.

In 1987 Ho and Stone released *Wall Street*, a cynical portrayal of greed in U.S. financial markets followed by an adaptation of a play by the off-Broadway playwright Eric Bogosian called *Talk Radio* in 1988. The next year the pair released the film that would earn Ho his first Academy Award: *Born on the Fourth of July*, the story of a disabled Vietnam Veteran who returns to the United States and becomes a national spokesman for the anti-war movement. Two years later Ho and Stone produced *JFK*, a controversial speculation that President Kennedy was killed by a secret group within the government. The film, which created a huge debate when released, earned Ho his second Oscar.

David D. Ho (1952-)
Medical doctor, AIDS researcher

In 1981, before the disease even had a name, Dr. David Ho was already treating AIDS patients as the chief resident at Cedars-Sinai Medical Center at the

University of California at Los Angeles (UCLA) School of Medicine. In 1984, Ho and his co-workers at Massachusetts General Hospital first isolated HIV in semen. Their report also documented the "healthy carrier state" of HIV infection that identified individuals who tested positive for the virus but did not show any physical signs of the disease. One year later, Ho's studies on the saliva of infected patients established the infrequency of HIV in this fluid and helped assure the public that AIDS cannot be casually transmitted.

Having devoted most of his research career to the problems of AIDS and human retroviruses, Ho is recognized as a pioneer in the field. In 1990, he was named head of New York City's Aaron Diamond AIDS Research Center, one of the largest AIDS research facilities in the world. Under Ho's leadership, the center has earned an international reputation for excellence, attracting top scientists from around the world and serving as a central resource for the latest updates and discoveries that may someday control one of the most potentially devastating epidemics in history.

Born in Taiwan on November 3, 1952, David Ho immigrated with his family to Los Angeles when he was 12 years old. After completing junior high and high school in Los Angeles, Ho received a bachelor's degree from the California Institute of Technology in 1974, summa cum laude, and went on to Harvard Medical School, where he was one of four Asian Americans in a class of 140. Ho returned to Los Angeles for his internship and residency in the UCLA hospital system. During the last of his three years there, Ho met two of the first five patients with what would be identified in mid-1982 as AIDS. That year, Ho returned to Harvard and Massachusetts General Hospital prepared to focus on virus research.

By 1990, the Aaron Diamond Aids Research Center was being formed in New York City, and Ho was hired to create a world-class laboratory. With a team of 40 scientists, Ho has made ground-breaking progress, and is convinced that the AIDS vaccine is about five to ten years away. In 1994, Ho was a member of President Bill Clinton's Task Force on AIDS and a member of the national HIV Vaccine Working Group, In spite of his preeminent position in the medical world it was only as basketball star Magic Johnson's doctor that he became a celebrity.

Reginald C.S. Ho (1932-)
Physician

Reginald C.S. Ho, a respected oncologist, was the first Hawaiian to head the American Cancer Society. Since his appointment in 1992, he has worked to raise national awareness about prostate cancer, a disease that is the second-leading cause of cancer death in men

David D. Ho.

and one that has touched Ho personally—a close friend died of the disease in 1989. Ho believes that early detection could improve a patient's prognosis and has worked to institute a public-education program that promotes early screening. Ho has also been head of the department of oncology and hematology at Honolulu's Straub Clinic and Hospital since 1978.

Ho was born March 20, 1932, in Hong Kong. His great-grandfather had emigrated from China to Hawaii in 1876, but when Ho's father went to Hong Kong to study, he married and stayed. Ho's parents gave birth to five children—four sons and one daughter—and returned to Honolulu, where Ho's father managed a bakery.

Ho studied philosophy at St. Louis University in Missouri, and entered the university's medical school in 1956. He completed his residency in internal medicine at the University of Cincinnati Hospitals, and won a fellowship in hematology and oncology at Barnes Hospital in St. Louis. He joined the Straub Clinic and Hospital in 1973 as an attending physician. There, Ho met his wife, Sharilyn, a former nurse. They were married November 14, 1964, and have four children—three sons and a daughter.

Reginald C.S. Ho.

Florence Makita Hongo.

Florence Makita Hongo (1928-)

Educator, publisher, community activist

In 1969, Florence Hongo brought a dozen educators together to discuss how to teach public schoolchildren about the internment of Japanese Americans during World War II. Twenty-five years later, she has transformed that group (originally known as the Japanese American Curriculum Project) into the nation's largest nonprofit clearinghouse for Asian American books and educational materials—the Asian American Curriculum Project (AACP). Hongo built AACP working as a full-time volunteer, striving to strengthen the image of Asian Americans through her teaching, lecturing, curriculum development, and consultations with writers and publishers.

Born Florence Makita on November 21, 1928, she grew up in Cressey, California, a small rural town in north Merced county. She was the fifth of seven children of immigrant parents who were brought together through an arranged marriage. Hongo never experienced discrimination in Cressey until World War II began. She remembered crying when her family was forced, under the internment order, into a Merced assembly center and later sent to the Amache Detention

Center in Colorado. When the family finally returned to Cressey in 1946, vines had overtaken the house and the family's belongings had vanished.

From 1950 to 1970, Hongo married and raised three girls and two boys. In 1969, the San Mateo School District brought her in as a community specialist to help the district adjust to its newly integrated classes. Soon after, she read *America's Concentration Camps* by Alan Bosworth, a book that changed her life. For the first time, she understood why her family and 120,000 other Americans Japanese descent had been forced to live behind barbed wire for three-and-a-half years.

Before 1970, few Japanese Americans would talk to their children about their camp experiences, let alone discuss them in public. That year, Hongo's group produced *Japanese Americans, The Untold Story*. Although the book was submitted to the state for adoption as a supplemental textbook, strong community outcry led to its rejection. The event proved pivotal, however, cementing JACP teachers as a united group. The group later created several internment-camp filmstrips, including *The Inside Look for Elementary Schools* and *Prejudice in America* for high schools and colleges. In the mid-1970s, JACP broadened its scope to include materials about all Americans of Asian descent, and launched a mail-order operation from Hongo's garage.

From 1978 to 1992, Hongo was an instructor at the College of San Mateo. In May 1994, during Asian/Pacific American Heritage Month commemorations in San Francisco, Hongo was honored by the Public Broadcasting affiliate, KQED-TV. The citation read "In recognition of your outstanding service to the Bay Area Asian Community [by] providing schools and the community with resources that enhance understanding of the Asian American experience."

Velina Hasu Houston
Playwright, screenwriter

Velina Hasu Houston, award-winning playwright and screenwriter, is the author of the critically acclaimed *Tea*. She Also edited the first anthology of plays by Asian American women, *The Politics of Life: Four Plays by Asian American Women*. She is head of the playwriting program at the University of Southern California, a member of Writers Guild/West and cofounder of the Amerasian League, a Santa Monica—based organization for multicultural and multiethnic Asian/Pacific Americans.

James Wong Howe (1899-1976)
Cinematographer

James Wong Howe was one of the finest cinematographers of Hollywood's golden age. In 1933 he was the highest paid cinematographer in the world, although he had no formal education in the art, and was a high-school dropout whose first job in the movies was as a janitor. In a career that spanned over 50 years, James Wong Howe photographed 125 films, and earned ten Academy Award nominations, winning two. His Notable films include *Peter Pan* (1924), *The Thin Man* (1934), *The Rose Tattoo* (1953), *The Old Man and the Sea* (1957), *Hud* (1963), and *The Heart is a Lonely Hunter*.

Wong Tung Jim (James Wong Howe) was born on August 28, 1899, in Kwantung, China. In 1904 he came to the United States to live with his father, who had emigrated a few years earlier. His father died in 1914, and Howe left home shortly thereafter, drifting up and down the West Coast for several years. Through luck and determination he became an assistant cameraman in some of film mogul Cecil B. DeMille's early productions. In 1938 he received his first Academy Award nomination for his work on *Algiers*. From 1938 to 1947, Howe shot 26 films for Warner Brothers and four others for different studios. In 1953 Howe won an Academy Award for his photography of *The Rose Tattoo*, and the award helped revive his career with the major studios. Later in the 1950s he filmed *Picnic* and *The Old Man and the Sea*.

In 1963 he won a second Academy Award for *Hud*. After this, Howe became ill and did not complete a film again until 1974, when he took over the financially troubled *Funny Lady*. Howe earned another Academy Award nomination for his work on this film, which was to be his last. He died on July 12, 1976.

Tom Hsieh
Politician

Tom Hsieh was the first Chinese American elected to the Board of Supervisors in San Francisco, home of America's oldest Chinatown.

Josephine S. Huang
Government administrator

Josephine Huang is assistant deputy undersecretary for environmental security at the Environmental Protection Agency. Formerly, she served as toxicologist and program manager of the EPA's multidisciplinary and multimedia regulatory programs in health effects, risk assessment, environmental monitoring, technology development, and hazardous waste.

David Henry Hwang (1957-)
Playwright, screenwriter

David Henry Hwang's 1988 Tony Award-winning gender-bender play, *M. Butterfly*, is one of the most successful nonmusical works in Broadway history.

Born August 11, 1957, David Henry Hwang was the only son of a Shanghai-born banker who founded the first Asian American-owned national bank in the United States and a Chinese pianist raised in the Philippines.

At Stanford University, Hwang first tried journalism and instrumental music before he attempted playwriting. After he found a teacher who was willing to work with him on his writing he completed *FOB*, which tells the story of the cultural clash between a new immigrant and a westernized Asian American. Hwang's second success, *Dance and the Railroad*, inspired by the experiences of Chinese railroad workers in 1867, was nominated for a Drama Desk Award. These were followed by another acclaimed work, *Family Devotions* (See also Asian American Theatre.)

Paul M. Igasaki
Lawyer, civil rights advocate

In 1994, Paul Igasaki, a well-known civil rights attorney and executive director of the Asian Law Caucus (a San Francisco-based civil rights and legal advocacy organization for the Asian American community), was appointed to the Equal Employment Opportunity Commission.

Igasaki received his bachelor's degree from Northwestern University and his J.D. from the University of

Daniel Ken Inouye.

Daniel Ken Inouye (1924-)
Politician, war hero

Daniel Ken Inouye was the first American of Japanese descent elected to the United States Congress, where he has served continuously since 1958. He is a highly decorated war hero, earning the Distinguished Service Cross for his heroics in the World War II, and was a member of the famed 442nd Regimental Combat Team, the most decorated Army unit in U.S. history.

Inouye was born on September 7, 1924, in Honolulu, to Japanese immigrant parents. He attended both Japanese-language school and Honolulu public schools graduating from Honolulu's McKinley High School in 1942. He enrolled in the University of Hawaii's premedical program, but dropped out to join the Army, when Japanese Americans were allowed to serve.

He was sent to the European theater with the 442nd, an all-Japanese unit, as a sergeant. He fought in several campaigns, including the famous "Lost Battalion" campaign. In another battle in Italy, Lt. Inouye was shot twice and hit in the arm with a grenade, but still managed to take out a machine gunner that had his men pinned down.

After the war, Inouye earned a bachelor's degree from the University of Hawaii and a law degree from the George Washington University Law School. He entered politics in 1954 when he won election to Hawaii's legislature. When Hawaii was granted statehood, Inouye became its first congressional representative. After serving two terms in Congress, he won a Senate seat in 1962, which he has held continuously since.

During his Senate career, Inouye has sat on the Senate Watergate Committee and has chaired several others, including Select Committee on Intelligence, the Democratic Central America Study Group, and the Iran-Contra hearings. In 1994, he chaired the Select Committee on Indian Affairs, the Appropriations Subcommittee of Defense, and the Commerce, Science, and Transportation Subcommittee on Communications.

Paul Isaki (1944-)
Executive, Seattle Mariners

Paul Isaki is the Seattle Mariner's vice-president for business development. A third-generation Japanese American (or *sansei*), Isaki was born June 6, 1944, in Topaz, Utah, where his family was interned with other West Coast Japanese Americans imprisoned by the U.S. government after the Japanese attack on Pearl Harbor. In 1945, the family moved back to the San Francisco Bay area. Isaki grew up in Oakland, attending public schools and graduating from the University of California at Berkeley in 1965.

His career began in public service, working in agencies involved with President Lyndon Johnson's War on Poverty. Isaki's success in merging private enterprise

California at Davis. He is licensed to practice law in both Illinois and California. In Chicago, Igasaki was the city's Asian American liaison for Mayor Harold Washington, providing legal and management counsel to the city's civil rights agency, and working with all city departments to make government more responsive to Asian and immigrant Chicagoans. He served on the mayor's affirmative-action council and was the first director of the city's commission on Asian American affairs.

Before joining the Asian Law Caucus, Igasaki was the Asian funding director for Robert Matsui's Senate campaign. He was also the Washington, D.C., representative for the Japanese American Citizens League, where he worked on such issues as the Civil Rights Act of 1989-91, immigration reform, access to higher education, confronting and eliminating media stereotypes, and funding for the Japanese American redress program.

Igasaki also co-chairs the civil rights committee of the American Bar Association and the legislative committee for the National Asian/Pacific American Bar Association, serves on the executive committee of the State Bar of California legal services section, and is a founder and former vice-president of the Asian American Bar Association of Chicago.

Paul Isaki.

and the public sector led him to his next job, heading Washington state's department of economic development. In 1992, during his tenure in that department, Hiroshi Uamauchi, president of Nintendo, the Japanese conglomerate, became a major shareholder in the Seattle Mariners.

When Isaki joined the team in 1993, he filled a post created especially for him, vice-president of business development, to target the development of the Mariners business interests both in the Pacific Northwest and in Japan. Although the players' strike in the summer of 1994 has delayed development plans, Isaki has begun arrangements for the Mariners to play a regular season game against another American League team in Japan, along with possible exhibition games against Japanese teams in 1996.

Isaki lives in Seattle with his wife, Lucy, an attorney.

Eiko Ishioka
Graphic designer, art director

Having won prestigious awards for her design in both Japan and the United States, Eiko Ishioka is one of the most gifted costume, set, and graphic designers in the world.

In 1965, Ishioka she was the first woman to win the most coveted award in the Japanese advertising industry, the JAAC Price (Japan Advertising Artists Club) for a series of nine posters entitled *Symposium: Discovery Today.* By the 1970s, Eiko (as she prefers to be called) had begun to do film art direction, fabric design for the fashion designer Issey Miyake, and corporate logotypes. She designed posters for Japanese and American films, including Francis Ford Coppola's *Apocalypse Now.*

In 1980, Eiko closed her Tokyo studio and went to New York for an extended vacation that lasted until February 1982. During this visit, Eiko met Eleanor Coppola, the film director's wife. Almost a decade later, Francis Ford Coppola drafted Eiko as costume designer for his production of *Bram Stroker's Dracula.* Her distinctive designs won the 1993 Academy Award for best costume design.

Lance Ito
Judge

Judge Lance A. Ito is assistant presiding judge in Los Angeles Superior Court in California. He came to national attention in the summer of 1994 when he was named to preside over the sensational double-murder trial of sports hero O.J. Simpson.

Judge Ito, whose parents were both schoolteachers, graduated from the University of California at Los Angeles with honors in political science in 1972, and from the University of California at Berkeley law school in 1975. He worked for a decade as a prosecutor, becoming a municipal court judge in 1987. He was named to the superior court in 1989, and presided over the securities fraud prosecution of Charles Keating in 1991. The Los Angeles County Bar Association named him trial judge of the year in 1992. Ito's wife, Margaret Ann York, is a captain and a former homicide detective in the Los Angeles Police Department.

Duke Kahanamoku (1890-1968)
Olympic athlete, surfer, actor

A full-blooded Hawaiian, Duke Paoa Kahinu Mokoe Hulikohola Kahanamoku was born on August 24, 1890, in the palace of Princess Ruth in Honolulu. A descendent of the 19th century King Kamehameha, Kahanamoku could trace his name to the Duke of Edinburgh.

The ocean always had a powerful pull on him, and he left school in 11th grade to pursue a life in the water. Shortly before the Olympic trials in August 1911, the first AAU (Amateur Athletic Union) swimming meet was held in Hawaii. When young Duke Kahanamoku broke the world record for the 100-yard freestyle by an astonishing 4.6 seconds and tied the 50-yard-freestyle world record, mainland officials refused to believe the times were accurate. The young swimmer not only

Duke Kahanamoku .

went to the 1912 Olympics, but went on to compete in four more Olympiads, winning three gold and two silver medals.

Eager to prove to officials and the public that Kahanamoku's performance and time were authentic, Hawaiian locals raised funds to send him to the mainland. In Chicago, Kahanamoku, swimming in a pool for the first time, dominated the 50- and 100-yard freestyle events. At the Olympic qualifying trials in Philadelphia, Kahanamoku won the 100-meter freestyle and was the top qualifier for the 4-x-200-meter relay team.

At the 1912 Olympic Games in Stockholm, Kahanamoku tied the world record in a qualifying heat for the 100-meter freestyle. At the time of the final, officials found him asleep under a bridge, snoring. He got up, got in the water and won the race. He performed so well that he took time to look back and survey the pool. The Stockholm Games made Kahanamoku an international sensation. In the 1920 Olympics held in Antwerp, Kahanamoku broke his own world record for the 100-meter freestyle just in time for his 30th birthday. He also anchored the world-record-setting 800-meter relay team. Kahanamoku's first defeat came in 1924 at the Paris Games, where he finished second in the 100-meter event behind 19-year-old Johnny Weissmuller, who later starred in Tarzan films.

In 1925, Kahanamoku and a group of friends saw a boat capsize during a fierce storm off the coast of southern California. Without hesitation, Kahanamoku grabbed his surfboard and made three trips through the violent waves, saving eight people in a disaster that claimed 17 out of 29 lives.

Although Kahanamoku died at age 77, Hawaii commemorated the 100th anniversary of his birth by dedicating a nine-foot bronze statue on Waikiki Beach.

Ken Kashiwahara (1940-)
Journalist

Ken Kashiwahara is a correspondent for ABC News and was one of the first Asian American journalists to work in network television. He has been a correspondent for ABC News since 1974, and has served as San Francisco bureau chief since 1978.

Kashiwahara was born on July 18, 1940, in Waimea, Hawaii, on the island of Kaui. Both his parents were schoolteachers. He describes himself as an average student in high school, from which he graduated in 1958. He then enrolled in Washington and Jefferson College, in Washington, Pennsylvania. He studied there for two years, but was confronted so frequently with racism that he transferred to the University of Hawaii. He completed his education at San Francisco State College, where he earned a bachelor's degree in broadcasting in 1963.

After college, Kashiwahara served as an information officer in the Air Force, providing military information to both civilian and government media while touring both Europe and Vietnam. He left the service in 1969, and began his career in broadcast journalism with KGMB-TV in Honolulu, first as a political reporter and eventually as an anchor.

In 1972, Kashiwahara moved to KABC in Los Angeles, where he was an on-air reporter and co-anchor of weekend news broadcasts. In 1974, he became a network correspondent with ABC. In this capacity, he covered several stories in Southeast Asia, where U.S. military involvement was drawing to a close. He was one of the last American journalists airlifted out of Saigon in 1975, as that city fell to the North Vietnamese.

In 1975, Kashiwahara was named the ABC News bureau chief in Hong Kong. He served at that post for three years, covering regional events, and, in 1977, the civil war in Beirut. In the 1980s, he covered national stories, including one entitled "In the Fire's Path," for which he won an Emmy. He was honored with a second Emmy in 1988 for the documentary "Burning Question—The Poisoning of America." In 1988 and 1989, Kashiwahara accompanied Vietnam veterans on a return trip to Vietnam, where three of them were reunited with children they had fathered during the war. He also contributed to an hour-long Nightline special focusing on eight veterans suffering from post-traumatic-stress disorder and who were coming to terms with their experiences during the war.

Kashiwahara broke the ground for many of today's Asian American journalists, and in 1993, the Asian American Journalists Association awarded him a lifetime achievement award.

Le Xuan Khoa (1931-)
Executive, community activist

Le Xuan Khoa is the president and executive director of the Southeast Asia Resource Action Center (SEARAC), a Washington, D.C.-based national organization that works to assist Southeast Asians in the often-difficult transition from refugee to productive citizen. Since its founding in 1979, SEARAC has been a leading advocate for refugee protection and human rights both in the United States and in refugee camps abroad, and has served as a clearinghouse for information on Cambodia, Laos, and Vietnam. In addition, the center offers technical assistance for the empowerment of the Southeast Asian American community.

A native of South Vietnam, Dr. Khoa earned a Ph.D. at the Sorbonne in Paris in 1960. He became deputy minister of culture and education for the South Vietnamese government before going to the University of Saigon, where he taught Oriental philosophy and served as vice-president of the University. He fled Vietnam when the government fell to the invading armies of the North in 1975.

Dr. Khoa spent his first three years in the United States as a researcher with a Washington, D.C., consulting firm analyzing refugee resettlement patterns across the country. In 1978, he became the associate director of the Indochinese Mental Health Program at the Eastern Pennsylvania Psychiatric Institute in Philadelphia. When the program ended in 1980, he returned to Washington to join the Center for Applied Linguistics, where he developed a set of orientation materials to be used by refugees and their U.S. sponsors to help

Ken Kashiwahara.

smooth the refugees' adjustment process to U.S. culture. In 1981, he was hired by the Indochina Refugee Action Center as deputy director and became chief executive in 1982. Under Dr. Khoa's leadership the organization changed its name twice, finally settling on the Southeast Asian Resource Action Center, as it took a more active role in refugee advocacy, leadership, and community development.

As SEARAC's executive director, Dr. Khoa has earned a distinguished reputation as an authority on refugee policy and issues. He has testified before both houses of Congress on numerous occasions and is a regular participant in international meetings addressing refugee issues. Recently, Dr. Khoa visited Hong Kong to meet with the colony's refugee coordinator and discuss its repatriation policy for Indochinese boat people. He was able to persuade Hong Kong officials to postpone their next scheduled repatriation.

He also works with both government and private agencies to help Indochinese people alleviate poverty in their native countries, reducing their need to flee. In one such program, SEARAC received partial funding for a two-year pilot program to provide medical treatment and preventive health care to two tribal populations living in Vietnam's Binh Thuan province that were

Andrew Byongsoo Kim.

enduring extremely high rates of mortality and morbidity from malaria and related illnesses.

Dr. Khoa has received many awards and honors in recognition of his service. In 1984, he was honored by the Citizens' Committee for Immigration Reform as one of several prominent refugees and immigrants who have made significant contributions to the United States. In 1988, he was selected by the Board of the Asian and Pacific American Civil Rights Alliance to receive its annual civil rights award. He is currently vice-president of the Asian/Pacific American Chamber of Commerce and serves on several other civic and cultural boards.

Andrew Byongsoo Kim (1936-)
Investor, financial analyst

Andrew Kim is the president of Sit/Kim International Investment Associates, Inc., a joint venture with Sit Investment Associates and the Fremont Group, formerly Bechtel Investment.

Andrew Byongsoo Kim was born on September 12, 1936, in Seoul, Korea, then under Japanese domination. He spent his childhood living under Japanese occupation and then, as a teenager, experienced the horror of the Korean War, which ended in an uneasy armistice in

1953. In 1955, Andrew graduated from high school and began three years of study at Seoul National University. Because of the instability in Korea at that time, however, he came to the United States to study at Adelphi University, where he earned a bachelor's of arts degree in 1960. From there he went to Columbia, where he studied for a year before transferring to Cornell, where he earned an MBA degree in 1963.

Kim was very interested in finance and went immediately to work on Wall Street. His first position was with Francis I. duPont, then the second-largest brokerage firm in the country. In 1965, he was hired as a research analyst for the asset management, investment banking, and institutional brokerage firm of F. Eberstadt & Co, where he dealt primarily with the air transportation and aerospace industries. In 1977, he was named director of research and was subsequently appointed executive vice-president, a post he held until 1985. From that point until he established Sit/Kim in 1989, Kim worked in a variety of positions on Wall Street.

When Kim began his career, there were virtually no Asians in financial analysis. However, he encountered almost no racism or bigotry in those days and adds that his career was most likely neither helped nor hindered by his ethnicity. He feels differently about the environment today. In the 1960s and 1970s, he and the few other Asians on Wall Street were widely regarded as anomalies, not as a threat. Today, 10 to 20 percent of the traders on Wall Street are Asian, in Kim's opinion, and there is increased resentment towards them as a group. Contrary to the commonly held perception that a pioneer makes it easier for those that follow, Kim believes being successful on Wall Street today is more difficult for an Asian than it was 25 years ago.

Andrew Kim is married to Wan Kyun Kim, a painter and collector of Asian art; the couple has two children. Kim is involved in several community and civic organizations including The Asia Society and the Council on Foreign Relations.

Elaine Kim (1942-)
Academician

Elaine H. Kim is a professor of Asian American studies at the University of California at Berkeley, perhaps the foremost university in the country in the promotion of ethnic studies. She is a leading national activist and a prolific contributor to mainstream, ethnic, and academic newspapers, magazines, and journals; she also produces educational videos and documentaries.

Elaine Kim was born in Tacoma Park and grew up in Silver Spring, Maryland. In grade school, she was confronted with repeated instances of racism in her nearly all-white community. She graduated from high school in 1959, and went on to earn a bachelor's degree in English from the University of Pennsylvania in 1963,

Elaine Kim.

and a master's degree in English in 1965 from Columbia University. In 1966, Kim took a position as a lecturer in the English department of Ewha University in Seoul, South Korea.

In 1968, she moved back to the United States and enrolled in the University of California at Berkeley as a Ph.D. candidate in English. She switched to the education program, however, when her interests in non-European literature ran contrary to the accepted canon of the time.

In 1969, Berkeley students organized a strike to protest low minority representation on the faculty and among students and demand the establishment of ethnic-studies programs. Kim was an active participant and was also instrumental in the development of English courses teaching non-European literature—a commonplace today, but something that was groundbreaking in 1970.

Kim has worked extensively as an advocate for the Asian community in the Bay area. In 1981 and 1982, she served as project director of Asian Women United of California Project on Asian women's employment and education. Under her direction, the project produced four books and four 30-minute television programs designed to increase awareness of job options for young Asian American women. She also served for many years as president of the board of directors of the Korean Community Center of the East Bay. In her tenure there, she has helped to raise more than $650,000 for a variety of programs serving the community.

Kim has written and published extensively on issues of concern among the Asian community. In 1992, she produced a documentary called *Sa-I-Gu: From Korean Women's Perspective.* The film was shot three months after the 1992 Los Angeles riots.

As of spring 1994, Kim was at work on two publications: *Korean American Life Stories: Portrait of a Los Angeles Community* and *Fierce Dreams: Lives and Work of Asian American Visual Artists.* In addition to her writing and other projects, Kim is a much-sought-after speaker and academic panelist.

Jay C. Kim (1939-)
Politician, civil engineer

As the nation's first Korean American congressman, Jay C. Kim hopes to be a model for all Asian Americans. He told AAA, "They can look at me and say, 'He made it as an immigrant with a strong accent. Why can't I?'" In a surprise landslide, Kim, a Republican, was elected to Congress in November 1992 to represent California's newly created 41st district. Following the election, Kim was selected to serve on the Public Works and Transportation and Small Business Committees. Convinced there is too much waste, Kim joined Public Works determined to trim budgets and curtail spending.

Born in Seoul, on March 27, 1939, Kim arrived in California in 1961 at the age of 22, recently discharged from the South Korean Army. After a series of menial jobs, he earned both bachelor's and master's degrees in civil engineering at the University of Southern California. Kim then marked his adoption of the United States as his home by legally changing his name from Chang Joon to Jay.

In 1976, Kim founded Jaykim Engineers, a highly successful engineering design firm specializing in road building and water-reclamation projects. It was one of five minority-owned companies hired to demolish buildings damaged by the 1992 Los Angeles riots. Following his election to Congress, however, Kim sold the firm to avoid any possible conflict of interest.

Kim's political career began in 1990, when he won a seat on the city council of Diamond Bar, a town in eastern Los Angeles County. He later served the town as mayor from 1991 to 1993. Kim decided to run for Congress in January 1992, when he was facing laying off more than 20 employees while Congress was voting itself a 40-percent pay raise. Kim's campaign touted him as an alternative to the polished politician. His heavy accent—despite more than 30 years in the United

Jay C. Kim.

Ki Ho Kim.

States—combined with his tendency for blunt honesty worked to his advantage, as did his entrepreneurial success in a predominantly white-collar, conservative, and affluent district.

Ki Ho Kim (1929-)
Physician

Ki Ho Kim is one of the country's most renowned specialists in physical medicine, rehabilitation, and the treatment and management of chronic pain.

Ki Ho Kim was born in Seoul, on April 9, 1929, the oldest of four children in a family of wealthy land-owners and textile factory operators. In 1946, he enrolled in the premedical program at Severance Medical College in Seoul, from which he graduated two years later. He went on to medical school, but in 1950, when the North Korean Army invaded the South and occupied Seoul, where Kim was studying, the entire college was evacuated to Pusan, at the southern tip of the Korean peninsula. In 1952, Kim graduated from Kwang Ju Medical College of Chon Nam University in Kwang Ju City.

In 1955, after a tour of duty in the air force, Kim was named by presidential appointment to the post of medical director of the Korean National Rehabilitation Center, where he served until 1957. That year, he left his country for what was intended to be a short stay in the United States, serving a residency in physical medicine and rehabilitation at the Bellevue Medical Center of New York University. In 1959, he became the chief resident at the Kessler Institute for Rehabilitation, a pain-management facility in New Jersey.

In 1969, Kim left the Kessler Institute to found the Kim Institute of Rehabilitation Medicine, a 162-bed hospital specializing in inpatient physical rehabilitation and pain management. Kim founded his institute because he was dissatisfied with the medical establishment's treatment and rehabilitation of spinal cord- and brain-injured patients. He wanted to introduce new ideas, such as acupuncture into their treatments, which met with a great deal of resistance. Supporting Kim's beliefs that patients should not be treated like "sick" people, there was no hospital clothing at the institute. He also built an apartment in the hospital for the spouse of a patient to occupy prior to the patient's release, so the couple could practice living together again, often an extremely difficult process in cases of severe paralysis. Kim counseled the couple in everything from the manner in which their sexual relations would change to how to get around a kitchen in a wheel chair.

In 1982, he opened the Kim Rehabilitation Institute in West Orange, New Jersey, which unlike the old institute offered only outpatient treatment for brain and spinal cord injuries and pain management. Kim is a widely respected expert in this field and serves as a consultant to both the insurance industry and the legal community, evaluating the severity of spinal cord and brain injuries and establishing the prognosis and the degree to which patients can expect to recover.

Miky Kim
Fashion model

Miky Kim is an Asian American fashion model with Ford Models of New York.

Wendel Kim
See Sports and Athletics

Lillian Chiyeko Kimura (1929-)
Community leader

In 1993, the government of Japan held a special ceremony to honor three Japanese Americans long recognized as leaders in promoting U.S.-Japan relations. Among them was Lillian Kimura, who received the prestigious Order of the Precious Crown, Wisteria Award. During the ceremony, the Consul General of Japan referred to Kimura as a "person who personifies the spirit of the words 'public service'. . . someone who cares very much about people and the society in which they live."

Trained as a social worker, Kimura has spent the majority of her life working for the good of others. When she retired in 1992, she left a legacy of commitment and dedication at the Young Women's Christian Association (YWCA), where she served as the associate national executive director for five years. Lillian Chiyeko Kimura was born in Glendale, California, on April 7, 1929, the second of three daughters born to Hisaichi Homer and Hisa Muraki Kimura, both from Japan. The family remained in Glendale until 1942, when they were evacuated to Manzanar in Lone Pine, California, one of the ten internment camps for Japanese Americans during World War II. When the war was over, the family moved to Chicago.

Kimura received her B.A. degree in psychology and a master's degree in social work from the University of Illinois. Following graduation, Kimura joined Chicago's Olivet Community Center, eventually becoming its director. During 16 years with that facility, she supervised the center's community activities, helping local public schools and other community agencies in efforts to prevent gang activities. Kimura left Olivet in 1971 to join the YWCA as a program consultant.

When the YWCA reorganized in 1978, the Chicago office closed and Kimura was transferred to St. Louis

Lillian Chiyeko Kimura.

as director of the mid-states office. Two years later, she was promoted to executive of the field services unit and moved to New York, where she gave technical assistance and management training to the staff and board members of 400 YWCAs throughout the country. In 1983, she became the assistant national executive director, and in 1987, was promoted to associate national executive director. As such, she supervised the agency's work with all member YWCAs.

Kimura also remained actively involved with the Japanese American community. From 1973 to 1979, she served as the first and only woman president of the Japanese American Service Committee (JASC). During her tenure, JASC services expanded, especially in aiding older, first-generation Japanese Americans by providing meals, day care, and housekeeping services.

In 1992, Kimura retired from the YWCA to devote more time to the Japanese American Citizens League, becoming the first woman national president of the 25,000-member, 113-chapter organization. Kimura has served the JACL for more than two decades in a number of capacities and played a primary role in the redress issue, in which the government compensated internment camp survivors and their descendants.

Dong Kingman (1911-)
Artist

Dong Kingman is one of foremost watercolorists of the United States. His paintings hang in some of the country's most prominent museums, including the Museum of Modern Art, the Metropolitan Museum of Art, and the Art Institute of Chicago. He was born in Oakland, California, in 1911, the second of eight children to first-generation Chinese immigrants from Hong Kong.

In 1936, after working various jobs in and around San Francisco, he was hired as an artist by the federal government through the Works Progress Administration, a Depression-era New Deal program. Kingman had his first solo show that year at the San Francisco Art Center, receiving generally good reviews. In 1940, the Metropolitan Museum of Art in New York bought its first Kingman watercolor—the first painting in its collection by an Asian American artist. In 1941, Kingman's stature as an artist was furthered when he received a two-year Guggenheim Fellowship.

Throughout the remainder of the 1940s and the early 1950s, Kingman continued to show and sell his paintings. He taught painting at Columbia University, and in 1948, became a full-time instructor at Hunter College. In 1957, he began to hold annual painting workshops in different countries around the world. He continues to paint and show, particularly his favorite subject, the urban landscape, especially that of New York, his home for more than 50 years.

Harry Kitano (1927-)
Academician, author

Harry Kitano, professor of Social Welfare and Sociology at UCLA, has crystallized for many Americans the identity crisis and trauma suffered by Japanese Americans as a result of their internment in U.S. camps during World War II. His book, *Japanese Americans*, provided the first coherent account of the experiences of Japanese Americans after the war. Published in 1969 and translated into Japanese, the book was a success and led to Kitano lecturing throughout the United States as well as in Japan, where he enjoyed near celebrity status.

Following the release of *Japanese Americans*, Kitano wrote dozens of other articles and books on Asian Americans and race relations, including *Asian Americans: A Success Story?*; *Generations and Identity: The Japanese American*; and *Applied Research on Health and Ethnicity: Asian and Asian American Elderly.*

The youngest of seven children, Kitano grew up in San Francisco's Chinatown. His questions about identity and his Japanese American heritage began early in

Harry Kitano.

childhood, coming as a result of barbs and taunts from other children who called him "Jap." Kitano recalls several incidents of prejudice and discrimination, but those experiences with racism were minor until the Japanese attack on Pearl Harbor in 1941. Then a high school freshman, Kitano recalled feeling confused and even guilty that Japan had attacked the United States, but he thought that it wouldn't drastically affect his life. He was wrong. Soon afterward the FBI came to his home and removed his father as a prisoner of war.

Thus began the nightmare for 120,000 Japanese Americans incarcerated during World War II. Considered potential traitors and dangerous to the war effort, they were ordered by the U.S. government to close their businesses and homes, sell their belongings and property, and assemble at designated sites. There they were herded into railroad cars and transported to temporary camps. Kitano and his family, along with 20,000 other Japanese Americans, were detained in Santa Anita, California, until more permanent inland camps were developed. The experience intensified Kitano's silent struggle for an identity. He felt like an American. "I belonged to the ROTC band at Galileo, and played 'The Stars and Stripes Forever,' marched behind the flag, and had little identification with Japan," he wrote in *A*

History of Race Relations Research. Yet he was treated like an outcast by the very people he identified with.

Kitano later moved to Topaz, a permanent camp set up in the middle of the desert in Utah where he lived from 1942 to 1945. Unlike the camp in Santa Anita, where he could see cars driving by and detainees could even wave to acquaintances on the street, this camp was guarded by armed soldiers and its perimeters sealed with barbed-wire fences..

After his release from Topaz, Kitano traveled to Milwaukee and worked briefly as a farm hand. Although the war was over, lingering racial hostility toward Japanese Americans worried Kitano, so he changed his name to Harry Lee. He played trombone with several bands in Minnesota, where he had the opportunity to work with black musicians. It was an eye-opening experience for Kitano, for here was an ethnic group that suffered even more hostility and discrimination than his own.

In 1946 Kitano returned to California to attend the University of California in Berkeley where he earned a bachelor's degree in 1948, a master's in social work in 1951, and in 1958 a doctorate.

Kitano has spent the better part of his career trying to make sense out of what happened to Japanese Americans and to determine whether such action could take place again in a democratic society. He believes that the lessons learned from such studies can help other minority groups who feel despair, frustration, and alienation much like the Japanese Americans once did.

Kitano now makes his home in Bel Air, California, where he lives with his wife Lynn and his daughter Christine.

Key Kobayashi (d. 1993)
Community activist

Key Kobayashi of Falls Church, Virginia, died November 15, 1993. The long-time Japanese American leader and activist was buried with military honors on November 21, 1993, at Arlington National Cemetery. Most of his 34 years of government service was spent as assistant Japanese section head at the Library of Congress. He had also been president of the Japanese American Citizens Alliance's Washington, D.C., chapter for three terms.

Yuri Kochiyama (d. 1994)
Civil Rights Activist

Yuri Kochiyama, a well-known civil rights activist who lived in New York, died in 1994. She had been pictured in Life magazine cradling the head of the slain Malcolm X.

Ronald A. Kong
Educator, academician

Ronald A. Kong, a Chinese American, became chancellor of the San Jose Evergreen Community College District in 1991, the first Asian American to do so. The district includes San Jose City College (enrollment approximately 12,000) and Evergreen Community College (enrollment of 11,000).

Kong began his career in Hawaii in 1959 as an instructor in biology, science, and math. After graduate work at Oregon State University, he held faculty positions at American River College in Sacramento for 19 years, and served as president of Irvine Valley College in Irvine, California, for two years. Prior to assuming his post as chancellor, he served as president of the College of Alameda.

K. V. Kumar (1945-)
Businessman, community activist

K. V. (Krishnamurthy Vyas) Kumar is the president and chief executive officer of American Systems International, Inc., a Maryland-based software development and professional services company. He is also the founder and a former president of the National Indian American Chamber of Commerce, as well as a powerful Republican Party activist. He also volunteers in a number of social-service organizations, most notably the National Head Injury Foundation, whose services he himself has needed after suffering multiple head injuries in two separate accidents in 1992.

Krishnamurthy Vyas Kumar was born in Bangalore, India, on April 14, 1945. He went to college at the Bangalore Polytechnic University, earning a bachelor's degree in business administration in 1967. He came to the United States in 1968 as a student, attending school at the University of the District of Columbia, and later finishing his graduate studies at Saidi University in Manila, the Philippines. He began working at the World Bank, where he would eventually become an operations analyst.

In 1987, Kumar left the World Bank and founded the First Liberty National Bank in Washington, D.C. The following year he served as a strategic planner for the Bush-Quayle presidential campaign, primarily working to get the campaign's message out to minority voters. After Bush was elected, Kumar worked as a deputy chief to the director of systems management in the telecommunications center at the White House. In 1991, Kumar founded the National Indian American Chamber of Commerce, Inc., an organization representing many of the more than 100,000 Asian Indian business owners throughout the United States.

In addition to his business success and his political activism, Kumar is a strongly active charitable works.

K. V. Kumar.

Paul Kuroda.

He is especially interested in helping the elderly, the homeless, and impoverished. He worked as a volunteer leader for the Washington, D.C.-based group "Help the Senior Citizens." He has also become involved with the National Head Injury Foundation, working as a volunteer since June 1994. Kumar counsels family members of patients, many of whom never completely recover. Kumar became involved in this organization after suffering head injuries of his own in two falls in 1992 that left him nearly dead. This experience had a profound impact on changing his perspective on the meaning of status and accomplishment.

Paul Kuroda (1954-)
Photojournalist

Through his haunting pictures of the silent, the forgotten, and the downtrodden, Kuroda has gained distinguished recognition as one of the most effective photojournalists working today. In 1991, Kuroda was named Newspaper Photographer of the Year by the National Press Photographers Association and the University of Missouri School of Journalism. The competition, for which 1,750 entrants submitted 35,000 photographs in thirty-five categories, is considered among the most prestigious in the world. The title is

the most coveted recognition in newspaper photojournalism. The bulk of Kuroda's portfolio was comprised of two subjects: desperate Mexicans attempting to illegally cross the border into California, driven by the promise of earning wages to send back to waiting families; and young, lost Vietnamese gang members trying to survive day-to-day in Orange Country, California, caught between an unaccepting new country and the unbending cultural expectations of the faraway motherland. Kuroda was lauded for his ability to get close to his subjects, to develop a certain rapport that translated onto his vivid, startling images. In 1992, those same images of the illegal immigrants made Kuroda a Pulitzer Prize finalist in photojournalism.

Born on February 13, 1954, in Fresno, California, Paul Kuroda was one of three children of a Japanese mother and a second-generation Japanese American. Kuroda grew up on the twenty-acre family farm on the edge of Fresno. Kuroda's father had been interned, along with thousands of loyal Japanese Americans, during World War II and, as a result, had lost a successful trucking business. Farm life was extremely difficult for the family and Kuroda spent his childhood in poverty.

Kuroda's interest in photography began in childhood and continued into college, when he was a reporter for the student newspaper. He also did photo-related work at the school's audio-visual center.

The highlight of Kuroda's academic career was the creation of two 16-mm films. One depicted the plight of elderly immigrant Filipino men living in what was San Francisco's International Hotel, which served as a form of low-income housing. Kuroda's other film captured the relationship between Japanese American farmers' organizations and the United Farm Workers Union, exploring the possible racism of the Japanese American farmers toward their predominantly Mexican labor forces.

In 1976, Kuroda joined the staff of the *Clovis Independent and Tribune*, a small community newspaper, where he worked for two years. Kuroda quickly moved from the *Independent* to the *Fresno Bee*. In 1984, the *Fresno Bee* was a finalist for a Pulitzer Prize for its coverage of the Coalinga, California earthquake. At the forefront of the coverage were images Kuroda captured so soon after the first shake that even the police had not yet begun to cordon off potentially dangerous streets.

After some eleven years, Kuroda joined the *Orange County Register*, where, after six years, Kuroda left a solid legacy: Two projects brought Kuroda considerable acclaim—one on Vietnamese gang violence in southern California's Little Saigon and the other documenting illegal aliens crossing the Mexican border into southern California.

Kuroda left the *Register* in 1993, and early in 1994, became a photo editor for Associated Press. In this position, he is responsible for a staff of photographers based from Sacramento to San Francisco, covering the area from Fresno, California, to northern Nevada.

Cheryl Lau (1944-)
Politician

Even as a student at Hilo High in Hawaii, Cheryl Lau was fascinated with politics. But the woman who is Nevada's secretary of state, the state's first Asian American to hold elected office at the executive level, and the woman who made an unsuccessful bid to become the first Asian American woman to be elected a state governor, never dreamed of making politics a career.

Lau was born December 7, 1944. Although her father, Ralph K.Y. Lau, has only a high school education, he taught his daughters the importance of balancing a good education with a strong work ethic and respect for other people. Lau, who worked at her family's dry goods store as a teenager, believes that experience shaped many of her political views.

Lau studied piano and flute and entered Indiana University's highly-reputed School of Music intending to go into performance. After earning a master's from Smith College, and doctorate from the University of

Cheryl Lau.

Oregon, she became a professor of music at California State University in Sacramento, eventually becoming director of the graduate division of the university's music department. In the 1980s, she took a leave to attend law school at the University of San Francisco. Shortly after passing the bar exam in 1986, she was offered a position as a deputy attorney general in Nevada. The attorney general, her supervisor, decided not to run for re-election in 1990. Instead, the secretary of state decided to make a bid for the attorney general post, which left the secretary of state position open. So, at age forty-five, Lau—an underdog and a political novice—entered the race for Nevada's secretary of state as a Republican—and won. Her victory was remarkable, considering that the eventual winners of the gubernatorial, attorney general, and majority of general assembly seats in Nevada were Democrats.

Lau's affiliation with the Republican party often produces lively debate when she gets together with her father, mother, and two sisters. Lau's younger sister campaigned for Bill Clinton in his 1992 bid for president, and served on Clinton's transition team.

During her term as secretary of state, Lau has made it easier for businesses to obtain licenses in Nevada. After considering her options and the record she has

Ang Lee.

built on such issues, Lau decided to try to climb the next step on the political ladder. On April 28, 1994, she announced she would run for governor, but lost in the November elections.

Ang Lee
Filmmaker

Ang Lee is a filmmaker whose three films, *Pushing Hands*, *The Wedding Banquet*, and *Eat Drink Man Woman* have received considerable critical and commercial success in the United States, his native Taiwan, and Europe.

Lee was born in Taiwan, the son of a high school principal. When he did not qualify for the Taiwanese higher education system he came to the United States, where he studied theater at the University of Illinois and film at New York University's graduate film school, where he was a classmate of Spike Lee, the renowned African American filmmaker. Ang Lee's thesis film, made at NYU, was a comedy called *Fine Line*. It was about an Italian trying to escape the Mafia and a Chinese trying to escape the Immigration and Naturalization Service. The film was voted the best student film award in 1984, the year he graduated.

For the next six years, Lee worked on two screenplays, polishing them and trying to get them produced, while his wife Jane [Lin], a microbiologist, worked to support them and their two children. In 1990, he entered the screenplays in the Taiwanese government's annual screenplay competition, and, remarkably, took both first and second prize. *Pushing Hands* came in first, giving Lee nearly half a million dollars to produce it. Although the film was shot in the United States, it has never been released here. In Taiwan, the film did remarkably well, earning nine Chinese Academy Award nominations.

Based on the success of that film, Lee was given $750,000 to produce his next, *The Wedding Banquet*, which tells the story of a gay Chinese American who marries a woman to disguise the true nature of his sexuality from his parents. The film took top prizes at both the Berlin and Seattle film festivals and had been highly praised all over the world. It achieved remarkable success in Taiwan as well earning $4 million, making it the most lucrative film in that country's history.

C.Y. (Chin-Yang) Lee (1917-)
Writer

Lee is a pioneering Asian American author whose best-selling 1957 novel *Flower Drum Song*—his first—was turned into both a Rogers and Hammerstein Broadway musical and a movie. He is often cited as an inspiration by many young Asian American writers of today.

Chin Yang Lee was born on December 23, 1917, in the Hunan province of China. He earned his bachelor's degree from the Southwest Associated University in Kumming in 1942, after which he sold his few possessions and came to the United States and enrolled in the graduate comparative literature program at Columbia University in New York City.

He went on to study writing at Yale, graduating in 1947. Lee made plans to return to China, but while in Los Angeles got word from his family that the communist government takeover was imminent. He found a job as a daily columnist at a Chinese-English newspaper published in San Francisco's Chinatown called *Chinese World*. His column, called "So I Say," became very popular. In 1949, a short story he had sent to his agent in New York—"Forbidden Dollar"—won $750 in a contest sponsored by Writer's Digest; it was eventually anthologized in *Best Original Short Stories* in 1949.

Lee began working on *Flower Drum Song* in earnest after becoming a citizen and completed it in mid-1955. After many rejections, it was finally published by Farrar, Strauss, and Culhady, an eminent literary publishing house. The book exceeded everyone's expectations, including the publisher's. It became something of a sensation, earning a spot on the New York Times bestseller list and creating a bidding war among Hollywood studios for the film rights. Lee become a celebrity; in 1959, the mayor of San Francisco presented him with a key to the city, and the governor sent him a letter of congratulations.

In 1958, Lee published *Lover's Point*, followed by *The Sabwa and His Secretary: My Burmese Reminiscences* in 1959, *Madame Goldenflower* in 1960, *Cripple Mah and the New Order* in 1961, *The Virgin Market* in 1964, and *The Land of the Golden Mountain* in 1967. This marked the end of an incredibly prolific period in Lee's career: five novels and two memoirs in a decade.

Lee did not publish again until the historical novel *China Saga* in 1987. In 1990, he published *The Second Son of Heaven*. Lee was also deeply affected by the pro-democracy movement in his homeland and the Tienanmen Square massacre that ensued. In response to this horrific event, he wrote a novel called *Gate of Rage: A Novel of One Family Trapped by the Events of Tienanmen*. It was published in 1991.

Christopher Lee (1956-)
Entertainment executive

Christopher Lee, senior vice president of motion picture production for TriStar Pictures, is one of Hollywood's top executives. He was supervising production executive for the 1994 film, *Philadelphia*, and Tom Hanks won the 1994 Best Actor Oscar for his portrayal of a young homosexual lawyer with AIDS in the film. Lee considers the film to be his greatest professional achievement.

Born on October 30, 1956, in New Haven, Connecticut, to a Chinese American father and Scottish American mother, Christopher Lee is fifth-generation Asian American, with ancestors who first arrived in the United States to work on the transcontinental railroad. When he was very young, the family moved to Hawaii, which he considers home. Lee later returned to New Haven to follow in his father's footsteps by attending Yale University. He graduated in 1980 with a degree in political science.

Lee began his entertainment career in television in New York, working on ABC's *Good Morning America* as an entertainment segment producer. In 1983, he worked as first assistant director and assistant editor with Wayne Wang (possibly Asian America's preeminent director) on Wang's second feature film, *Dim Sum*. After *Dim Sum*, Lee decided to seek opportunities in project development as a studio executive. Toward that goal, in 1985, Lee walked into the offices of TriStar Pictures as a free-lance script analyst. After two weeks, he was hired as assistant story editor, beginning his ascent through the TriStar ranks, to senior vice-president of motion picture production, a position he assumed in 1989.

Christopher Lee.

Lee's fast-track career is crowded with credits. He has recruited new and innovative filmmakers to TriStar, including Gus Van Sant (*Drugstore Cowboy*), John Woo (*The Killer*) and Cameron Crowe (*Singles*), while developing successful new projects with established talents, such as Paul Verhoeven (*Basic Instinct*); Jean Jacques Annaud (*The Lover*); Anthony Hopkins (*Legends of the Fall*, also starring Brad Pitt and Aidan Quinn); Norman Jewison (*Just in Time*, with Marisa Tomei and Robert Downey, Jr.).

While Lee has earned one of the top seats in Hollywood, he has also established himself in the Asian American. He is a member of the Board of Governors of the Los Angeles Festival, a founding member of the Coalition of Asian Pacifics in Entertainment, and served as executive producer of the 1991 Association of Asian Pacific American Artists Media Awards. In 1992, he was cited as Asian Business Person of the Year by the Asian Business League of Southern California.

Corky Lee (1947-)
Photojournalist

For Corky Lee, the political and the artistic are inseparable. A community activist turned self-taught photographer, Lee uses black-and-white photography to make social and political commentaries on Asian American life. He describes himself as the "undisputed, unofficial Asian American photographer laureate," and he states that his goal is "to show that Asian Americans are part and parcel of the American experience."

Lee was born in New York City in 1947, the son of Chinese immigrants. His mother and father—who was by trade a welder—ran a laundry business. He attended Queens College, City University of New York, where he studied U.S. history. During his college years, he explored the relationship between Chinese and U.S. history and began to question anti-Asian bias in the United States. At the same time, he became involved with other Asian American activists in New York's Chinatown.

After college, he became a tenant organizer with the Two Bridges Neighborhood Council, photographing tenement buildings before and after rehabilitation to document improvements in housing conditions. This experience sparked his interest in photography. Meanwhile, Lee continued to work for social change in the Chinese American community, contributing to the 1969 *Chinatown Report*, the first comprehensive study of the area. He also helped plan a Chinatown street fair in 1969 that led to the establishment of the Chinatown Health Clinic, the first clinic to offer free health services to local residents.

Throughout the 1970s, he continued to photograph Chinatown and turned his camera toward other Asian American communities as well. His pictures documented demonstrations for workers' and tenants' rights, the Japanese American redress and reparations movement, and scenes from everyday life. One picture that holds special significance for Lee was taken in 1972, at Promontory Point near Salt Lake City, Utah, where he photographed the meeting point of the two halves of the Transcontinental Railroad, which was built largely by Chinese immigrant workers. Describing the experience as deeply moving, he expressed, "This place is one of the great monuments of Chinese American history, but almost no one has ever heard of it."

Lee's work shows the connections between Asian and U.S. cultures. His photographs include portrayals of a Chinese American woman taxi driver, the Korean proprietors of a kosher Jewish deli, an Indian man in traditional dress carrying a boom box on his shoulder during an Indian Independence Day parade, and a young boy waving U.S. flag and wearing a T-shirt commemorating the 1986 Philippine revolution.

Lee has had relative success in bringing his images of Asian America to the mainstream press. During the 1970s, his work found its way into various publications, including several New York daily newspapers. In addition, 1979 marked his first gallery exhibit at the Floating Foundation of Photography in a group show that focused on Chinatown. Since then, his work has appeared in *Time*, the *New York Times*, and the *New York Post*.

In 1993, Lee was awarded the National Annual Special Recognition Award for leadership and activism by the Asian American Journalists Association. He was also honored in the same year by the City of New York at the "All-Star Salute to Chinese American Cultural Pioneers," when May 7 was declared as "Corky Lee Day." Finally, in 1993, Lee received the Photographer-Artist in Residence Award from Syracuse University.

The ethnic press has been very supportive of his work over the years, and Lee believes that he owes much of his success to these publications, as mainstream news outlets have demonstrated only benign interest. Magazines and newspapers exhibiting Lee's photographs include the *Asian New Yorker, NY Nichibei, Rafu Shimpo, Hawaii Herald, Filipinas Magazine, A. Magazine*, and *Transpacific Magazine*.

Lee reflects that he has no real role models because few before him have done the same type of work. Therefore, he hopes to be a role model for other Asian Americans interested in photography. He plans to publish several books of his photographs, focusing on Chinese American life, Asian American life, the Asian American civil rights movement, and the Pan-Asian Repertory Theatre, a New York-based group that he has documented for 12 years.

Lee's motivations stem from his personal commitment to Asian American activism and social change. He has commented, "It is important for people to see Asians in positive roles, to document the lives of their families and communities. I don't mind that I won't lead a caviar-and-champagne lifestyle doing what I do. I do this because I feel it is the right thing to do." With his dedication to political and social commentary through photography, Corky Lee has played a pivotal role as both an advocate and an artist, communicating to his audiences the juxtaposition and melding of cultures found in Asian American life.

Sammy Lee

See Sports and Athletics

Tsung Dao Lee (1926-)
Physicist

Co-recipient of the Nobel Prize for physics in 1957, Lee is best known for his work with Dr. Chen Ning Yang on parity laws in physics. Lee is also noted for his work on statistical mechanics, hydrodynamics, turbulence, and astrophysics.

Born November 25, 1926, in Shanghai, Lee's father was a businessman. Lee met Yang at the National Southwest Associated University, where Lee earned his degree in 1946. After several months as a research associate at the Yerekes Astronomical Observatory at Lake Geneva, Wisconsin, during 1950, Lee found a similar position next year at the University of California at Berkeley. He then joined the Institute for Advanced Study at Princeton and was reunited there with Yang.

In 1956, at the age of 29, Lee was named a full professor at Columbia University, the youngest ever at Columbia. In 1957, Lee was presented with the Albert Einstein Commorative Award and earned an honorary degree from Princeton in the same year. Lee is also a fellow with the American Physical Society.

Yuan T. Lee (1936-)
Chemist

Yuan T. Lee, one of three chemists who shared the 1986 Nobel Prize in chemistry, is famed for his work in combustion chemistry, which combines laser technology and molecular beam chemistry.

Born in Taiwan in 1936 to Tse Fan Lee, an artist and art teacher, and Pei Tsai, an elementary school teacher, his education was interrupted by World War II, when the Japanese controlled the island. His family was relocated from the city of Hsinchu, having had to hide in the mountains to avoid Allied bombers.

Lee completed school, and his strong grades got him acceptance into National Taiwan University without even taking an entrance exam. In 1959, he received his bachelor's of science degree from the school. After earning his master's degree at the National Tsinhua University, he continued graduate studies at the University of California at Berkeley, where he received his Ph.D. in 1965. Lee left California in 1968, but returned in 1974 as professor and principal investigator at the University of California's Lawrence Berkeley laboratory.

Lee's research has led him to receive several prestigious awards and honors. While at Berkeley, he worked with Dudley R. Herschbach, with whom he and John C. Polanyi shared the 1986 Nobel Prize in chemistry. Lee also developed the first successful universal crossed-molecular beam device. Lee has also won the Ernest Orlando Lawrence Memorial Award for Physics given by the United States Energy Research and Development Agency, the Harrison E. Howe Lectureship, the Peter Debye Award in Physical Chemistry, and the National Medal of Science from the National Science Foundation. He was also granted an honorary degree from the University of Waterloo, Canada.

Ginger Lew
Political appointee

Appointed by President Bill Clinton in 1992, Ginger Lew is one of several Asian American women to serve in the Clinton administration.

Choh Hao Li
Scientist

Dr. Choh Hao Li is one of the leading authorities on the pituitary gland and winner of the 1962 Albert Lasker Medical Research Award.

Channing Liem (1909-)
Diplomat, scholar, minister

Channing Liem is a long-time Korean expatriate living in the United States. He is a fervent, lifelong supporter of Korean democracy and independence who served briefly as the Republic of Korea's ambassador to the United Nations and as emmisary to several southwest African states.

Channing Liem was born on October 30, 1909, in Ul Yul, a rural village just north of the 38th parallel, the line that has divided the Korean peninsula since World War II. In 1930, he graduated from Sung Sill College in Pyongyang, in modern-day North Korea. With the help from the school's president, Liem emigrated to the United States. He enrolled in Lafayette College in Easton, Pennsylvania, and earned a bachelor's of science degree there in 1934.

In 1936, Liem moved to New York, where he entered the New York Theological Seminary. He studied sociology and religion, becoming a pastor at the Korean Church and Institute, the only Korean church in the United States at the time. He worked in the church for six years, helping the immigrant Korean community in New York, which was made up mostly of single men living in or near poverty.

In 1942, Liem was offered a full scholarship to continue his studies at Princeton. While working toward his master's degree, he served the U.S. government in the Office of Censorship, where he helped translate sensitive documents seized from the Japanese and embassy consulates in the United States. Liem received his master's degree in 1943 and earned his Ph.D. in 1945. He then took a post-doctoral fellowship, which he retained for two years. During the 1950s, Liem taught government and political theory at various colleges, including Chatham College and the State University of New York at New Paltz.

Meanwhile, in Korea, the post-World War II government established by Syngman Rhee was deposed in 1959, and Rhee's vice-president, John Myung Chang was elevated to the presidency. Chang and Liem had met in the United States when Chang was the Korean ambassador, and the two had become friends. When Chang became president, he asked Liem to return to Seoul to help form the new South Korean delegation to the United Nations; Liem only briefly served in this position. He was a strong advocate of Korean neutrality in the superpowers' Cold War and worked hard to

Channing Liem.

persuade the Korean assembly to adopt a neutral position. When a coup, led by Park Chung Hee, overthrew Chang's government, Liem resigned his post in protest.

Since leaving the government of Korea, Liem has been an international activist in support of democracy, independence, and neutrality in his homeland. Since 1976, he has made four trips to North Korea to promote peace and reconciliation, and in 1977, he founded Han Min Yun, the United Democratic Movement of Overseas Koreans, to foster peace and democracy.

Jeff K. Lin
Entrepreneur

Jeff K. Lin, Asante Technologies Inc.'s chairman of the board, received the Minority Manufacturer of the Year award from the Minority Business Development Agency in San Francisco on September 30, 1993. Since its founding in 1988, Asante has grown an astounding 9,400 percent.

Maya Lin (1959-)
Architect, sculptor

At the age of 21, Maya Lin became one of the best known sculptor/architects in the United States when her design for the Vietnam Veteran's Memorial was chosen in a national competition. Her design, a black granite wall inscribed with the names of each of the nearly 58,000 service personnel who died in the Vietnam War, has become one of the most visited sites in Washington, D.C. Other works of Lin's include the Civil Rights Memorial (1989) in Atlanta, the new lower-Manhattan home of the Museum of African Art, and the Women's Table at Yale University, a visual documentation of women's history at that university.

Maya Lin was born in Athens, Ohio, on October, 5, 1959. Her father is an accomplished ceramicist and the director of fine arts at Ohio State University; her mother taught literature at Ohio University in Athens. Lin was an accomplished student and, after high school, went to Yale University to study architecture. In her senior year, she took a class in funerary design, which required students to submit a design to the national competition for the planned Vietnam Veteran's Memorial.

Lin's entry was chosen from 1,420 others in May 1981. Her design was criticized by veterans' groups, who were accustomed to memorials with realistic military depictions. In 1982, a petition drive was initiated to have a more traditional monument added to Lin's memorial. She vehemently opposed these efforts, and a compromise was eventually reached whereby a statue of men in battle was installed near, but not on, the memorial site.

After the memorial was dedicated, Lin returned to graduate school at Harvard, where she had gone for her master's degree in architecture. The pressure of the national spotlight and the intensity of the criticism she had encountered proved distracting, and in 1983, she took a year off to work at an architectural firm in Boston. She returned and continued her studies at Yale, from which she graduated in 1986.

In 1988, Lin was offered the opportunity to work on another large outdoor memorial by the Southern Poverty Law Center in Montgomery, Alabama. The memorial was meant as a commemoration of all the men, women, and children who had given their lives in the civil rights struggle. In recent years, Lin has made the transition from sculpture to architecture, having designed two houses, one in Santa Monica, California, overlooking the Pacific, and one in Williamstown, Massachusetts. The latter has a Japanese influence, as does much of Lin's art and designs. She acknowledges the Eastern influence in her work and feels that Western art and architecture can be overly cerebral, whereas Eastern design offers simpler and more emotional images.

Maya Lin lives in New York City with her long-time boyfriend, Peter Boynton, a sculptor. Aside from her architectural work, she is an accomplished sculptor of small pieces, which she exhibits in several New York galleries.

Jahja Ling (1951-)
Conductor/Pianist

Jahja Ling is recognized as one of the most talented young conductors in the music world today. He has earned a reputation for insightful and highly expressive interpretations as both conductor and pianist, and has already amassed an impressive list of guest conducting engagements with some of the most renowned orchestras in the world. As of 1995, he held two posts: resident conductor of The Cleveland Orchestra and music director of the Florida Orchestra.

Jahja Ling was born in Jakarta, Indonesia, to a family of Chinese descent. His Dutch-educated father enjoyed many aspects of Western culture, especially classical music. His grandmother had once been a violinist and provided the Ling household with the piano that young Jahja first began to play. At age six, he began formal piano instruction and by age twelve had taught himself Tchaikovsky's *Piano Concerto No. 1*. At age seventeen, he won the first of two Jakarta Piano competitions, and when he graduated from the Jakarta Music School, he travelled to the United States as the recipient of a Rockefeller grant to study at the Juilliard School of Music in New York under the tutelage of famed teacher Mieczyslaw Munz.

While a Juilliard student, Ling got his first taste of conducting as the director of his church choir. He became interested enough to sign up for a conducting course at Juilliard where his teacher, John Nelson, recognized his talent and encouraged him to pursue conducting seriously.

After graduating from Juilliard in 1975 with a master's degree in music, Ling was accepted into the highly competitive conducting program at the Yale University School of Music, where he received his doctor of musical arts degree in 1985. As a student of Otto-Werner Mueller, Ling's career as a conductor was launched, although Ling also maintained his position as a pianist. He won the bronze medal at the 1977 Artur Rubinstein International Piano Master Competition in Israel and a certificate of honor at the 1978 Tchaikovsky International Piano Competition in Moscow. In 1979, Ling was accepted as a scholarship student into the noted conducting program at the Berkshire Music Festival at Tanglewood, and was awarded a Leonard Bernstein Conducting Fellowship the following summer. In 1981, Ling joined the conducting staff of the San Francisco Symphony through the Exxon/Arts Endowment program, where he served until 1984 when Christoph von Dohnanyi, music director of The Cleveland Orchestra, offered Ling a job as associate conductor. The following season, Ling was appointed as The Cleveland Orchestra's resident conductor, becoming only the fourth person in history to hold the title.

Jahja Ling. (Herbert Ascherman, Jr.)

The year 1988 provided Ling with two distinctive honors. He was one of three conductors to receive the Seaver/National Endowment for the Arts Conductor's Award, a career development grant made to American conductors judged to be of extraordinary promise. That same year, Ling was appointed music director of the Florida Orchestra, which serves the Tampa Bay area. The doubling of subscriptions since his arrival as music director at the Florida Orchestra has been attributed to his dynamic leadership and commitment to the community.

Ling's plan is to continue to seek quality conducting opportunities while reserving time to spend with his wife Jane, and sons, Gabriel and Daniel. "He'll always be busy and always working," ventured Michael Steinberg, part-time annotator for the San Francisco Symphony, and longtime colleague of Ling's. "He has a sort of magical personality. He'll bring people joy for years to come."

Juanita Tamayo Lott
Social scientist, statistician

Juanita Tamayo Lott is president of Tamayo Lott Associates, a public policy consulting firm in Silver

Spring, MD. She is also research associate with the National Academy of Sciences, Washington, D.C., investigating requirements for future censuses and federal racial/ethnic standards.

Lott advises a variety of federal agencies, nonprofit agencies, and school systems nationally. She writes and lectures on the implications of demographic change, racial classification, Asian American communities, multicultural curricula, and the status of women.

Her 1994 publications include *Reflections on Women, Power, and the Nonprofit Sector* published by Jossey-Bass, and a chapter on the relationship of blacks and Latinos for a forthcoming reader by Greenwood Publications, *Blacks, Latinos, and Asians in Urban America: Status and Prospect for Politics and Activism*. Her seminal article, "Policy Purposes of Race and Ethnicity: A Reassessment of Federal and Ethnic Categories" was published in the summer 1993 issue of the *Journal of Ethnicity and Disease*. She also wrote *Knowledge and Access: A Study of Asian and Pacific Islanders Communities in the Washington, D.C., Metropolitan Area*, commissioned by the Smithsonian Institution.

Lott is a trustee of the Population Reference Bureau and a director for the Organization of Pan Asian American Women, Inc. She also chaired the Census Bureau Advisory Committee on Asian and Pacific Islander Populations for the 1990 Census.

She was employed at the U.S. Commission on Civil Rights as director, Program Analysis Division, Office of Program Planning and Evaluation, and deputy director, Women's Rights Program Unit. She served as social science analyst, Office of the Assistance Secretary for Planning and Evaluation, U.S. Department of Health, Education and Welfare, where she directed the first Asian American Affairs Division of the federal government. From 1969 to 1971, she served on the planning committee for the School of Ethnic Studies at San Francisco State University, co-chaired the Filipino Studies Program, and was a special assistant to the dean.

In 1992, Lott was featured in an exhibit, *Maryland Women's History, A Patchwork of Many Lives*, that was displayed in all Maryland public schools.

Gary Locke (1950-)
Politician

As executive of King County, encompassing the greater Seattle, Washington area, Gary Locke is the first Chinese American to head a county government in North America. Prior to becoming King County executive, Lock spent eleven years as a state legislator in Washington State, earning a reputation for brilliance in budget-writing, for working sixteen-hour days, and for his obsession with detail.

Gary Locke.

Gary Locke was born January 21, 1950, in one of Seattle's poorest neighborhoods, the son of a Chinese immigrant mother and a World War II army combat officer. His father, James, owned a restaurant in the Pike Place Market and later a grocery. Locke grew up speaking Chinese at home, learning English only after starting kindergarten. A straight-A student and a Boy Scout, Locke studied political science at Yale University, graduating in 1972. He went on to earn a law degree from Boston University in 1975, and then returned to Seattle to take a job as a King County deputy. His involvement in government and politics led to his own successful run for the state house of representatives in 1982. In 1994, he won the King County executive post.

John Lone (1952?-)
Actor, director, choreographer, composer

With a growing list of theatre and film acting credits to his name, John Lone is fast distinguishing himself as one of Hollywood's most versatile actors. He has won numerous awards, including two Obies for his work collaborating with David Henry Hwang. In 1981, Hwang's play, *FOB*, and Lone won Obie Awards. Lone and Hwang worked together on additional projects, including Hwang's *The Dance and the Railroad*, for which Lone won his second Obie, and *M. Butterfly*, the 1993 film adaptation of Hwang's Broadway blockbuster.

John Lone's actual date of birth, although set in 1952, remains unknown. As an orphan, proper records weren't available on the details of his birth. As he grew older and needed travel documents, a birth date and name were chosen for him. At the age of about ten, Lone was taken by his guardian from his impoverished home in Hong Kong to join the Beijing Opera, a company that had fled China during the Revolution, which took in and trained children who did not have money but had the promise of talent.

He left the Beijing Opera, and, although he had other opportunities in Hong Kong and Europe, Lone decided to go to the United States.

In 1984, Lone made his film debut in the feature film, *Iceman*, about a prehistoric man found frozen in the Arctic ice and brought back to life by an anthropologist played by Timothy Hutton. His next role was the leader of the Chinese Mafia in Michael Cimino's *(The Deer Hunter)* controversial *Year of the Dragon*. In 1987, he spent six months in China filming the title role in Bernardo Bertolucci's *Last Emperor* which won the Oscar for Best Picture. Almost immediately following his return, he appeared in Alan Rudolph's *The Moderns* as an enigmatic businessman/art collector living among the expatriates in Paris of the 1920s. He then portrayed a Hong Kong businessman in a political thriller, *Shadow of China*, and an underworld crime lord in a gangster epic, *Shanghai 1920*. Both were Asian-produced and Asian-directed English-language films with an international cast. In 1993 Lone starred in David Cronenberg's film adaptation of Hwang's Broadway hit, *M. Butterfly*. In 1994, Lone appeared opposite Alec Baldwin in the film *The Shadow* as Shiwan Khan, the last warrior descendant of thirteenth-century Mongol conqueror Genghis Khan. In 1995, Universal Pictures will release *The Hunter* starring Christopher Lambert and John Lone with director Jonathan Lawton.

Greg Louganis (1960-)
Olympic diver, actor

As Greg Louganis prepared mentally for his last dive at the 1984 summer Olympic games in Los Angeles, he quietly sang "Believe in Yourself" from the musical *The Wiz*. Standing on the platform ready to launch into a reverse 3-1/2 somersault tuck, a dive so difficult it killed a man a year earlier, Louganis thought: "No matter what happens, my mother still loves me." When he emerged from the water, his final score was 710.91. Not only had Louganis won the gold medal, but he became the first diver in history to break the 700-point mark. Born in 1960 of Samoan and northern European ancestry,

John Lone. (Robert McEwan.)

Gregory Efthimios Louganis was adopted shortly after birth by Peter and Frances Louganis. Raised in El Cajon, a San Diego suburb, he was just 18 months old when he began taking dance lessons with his older sister, Despina. To help students memorize new dance combinations, the teacher asked them to visualize the routine from beginning to end, a technique Louganis would apply to diving years later.

The stage gave Louganis an outlet from the frustrations he felt in his day-to-day life. In a school full of fair-skinned children, Louganis fell out of place. His brown skin, inherited from his biological Samoan father, made him the target of racial slurs. Already uncomfortable among his peers, Louganis' childhood was made more difficult by asthma, a stutter so serious it could only be corrected with speech therapy, and dyslexia, which was mistaken by teachers as a mental impairment until he entered college.

Louganis compensated for the ridicule and health problems by concentrating on dance and later gymnastics, which he took up on the advice of a doctor who believed exercise might help cure Louganis's asthma. When he began practicing acrobatic routines off the diving board into the family's backyard pool, his mother decided to enroll him in diving classes.

Greg Louganis.

Louganis scored a perfect 10 in the 1971 AAU Junior Olympics. Among the spectators was Dr. Sammy Lee, a physician and former gold medalist at the 1948 and 1952 Olympic games. Four years later, Peter Louganis enlisted Lee's help in coaching his son for the 1976 Olympics in Montreal. The 16-year old Louganis finished sixth in the springboard and second in the platform event. By 1978, Louganis had a new coach, Ron O'Brien. That year, Louganis garnered four national diving titles, a world championship, and a scholarship to the University of Miami. Louganis spent two years in Miami, where his dyslexia was finally diagnosed. He then transferred to the University of California at Irvine to be closer to O'Brien, who was coaching at the world-famous Mission Viejo Club near San Diego. Louganis graduated with a degree in theatre and dance.

With the U.S. boycott of the 1980 games, Louganis had to wait until 1984 to compete for Olympic gold. In 1985, he received the Sullivan Award as the nation's outstanding amateur athlete. By the time Louganis went to Seoul for the 1988 Olympics, he had garnered 47 national diving titles, six Pan American gold medals, five world championships and two Olympic golds.

Louganis arrived in Seoul with an injured wrist and low-grade fever. He also contracted the same sore throat symptoms that hampered many other competitors. He also sustained the famous three-inch head gash in a preliminary round. Yet, Louganis won the gold for the springboard event by just over 20 points and won gold again for the platform event. In the final dive of the day, he needed a hefty 85.57 points to take the lead. The last dive of his Olympic career brought him 86.70 points. He became the only athlete in the world to win two diving medals in successive Olympics. During the games, Louganis was also awarded the Olympic Spirit Award, an honor given the most inspiring athlete among the participants.

Post-Olympics life has kept Louganis in the limelight. He has performed with Dance Kaleidoscope, starred in *Cinderella* at the Los Angeles Civic Light Opera, had a part in *The Boyfriend* at the Sacramento Music Circus, and sang and danced with the Cincinnati Pops Orchestra. Most recently, he appeared off-Broadway in the comedy, *Jeffrey*, portraying Darius, a dancer in the chorus of the musical Cats who succumbs to AIDS by the play's end. Louganis is currently at work on his autobiography.

In 1994, Louganis received the Robert J. Kane Award, which honors athletes who achieved success at the United States Olympic Festival and continue to give back to their sports. In 1995, Louganis revealed that he has Acquired Immune Deficiency Syndrome (AIDS).

David Wong Louie
See Literature

Yo-Yo Ma (1955-)
Cellist

Yo-Yo Ma is indisputably the most extraordinary cellist alive. He began playing a child-sized version of the cello at age four, and gave his first public recital at age five at the University of Paris, playing both the cello and the piano. At nine, Ma began studying with the legendary cellist Leonard Rose at the Juilliard School in New York City, an arrangement orchestrated by the noted violinist Isaac Stern. Ma was hailed unequivocally not only for his technical superiority, but for his astoundingly mature powers of interpretation.

Yo-Yo Ma was born on October 7, 1955, the second of two children of musical expatriates living in Paris, France. Ma's father, Hiao-Tsiun Ma, a violinist and former professor from Nanjing University in mainland China, had arrived in 1936 to further his musical studies. Ma's mother, Marina, gifted with a beautiful voice, was Hiao-Tsiun's former student at Nanjing and moved to Paris in 1949. The two were soon married and in 1951, had a daughter, Yeou-Cheng, and four years later, a son, Yo-Yo.

After high school, while continuing his lessons with Rose, Ma entered Columbia University. Still living at

Yo-Yo Ma. (J. Henry Fair.)

Two major events finally convinced Ma to reevaluate what was most important in his life. In 1980, Ma had an operation for scoliosis, a curvature of the spine, and faced the very real possibility that he might never play the cello again. Fortunately, the operation proved a total success and even after six months in a body cast, Ma's cello playing was unimpaired. The second event that dramatically changed Ma's life was the birth of his first child, Nicholas, in 1983. With his family as first priority, Ma has learned well how to balance both the professional and personal aspects of his fast-paced, ever-changing life.

While he is lauded for his interpretations of Bach, as well as Mozart and Beethoven, Ma constantly challenges his own abilities by determinedly expanding his repertoire. Ma plays a considerable amount of twentieth century music, including Samuel Barber, Benjamin Britten, William Walton, Penderecki, Lutoslawski, Kirchner, Carter, Henze, Dutilleux, as well as new American works. Ma has taken on new projects that push the boundaries of traditional music. In 1992, he performed with jazz vocal artist Bobby McFerrin to create *Hush*, a collection of duets that paired Ma's cello and McFerrin's chameleon voice.

With over fifty recordings and eight Grammy awards, Ma's genius has already proven itself.

Tess Manalo-Ventresca
Community activist

Tess Manalo-Ventresca is a longtime community activist, who works in San Francisco's Tenderloin district, a poor, predominantly minority neighborhood. She is the project coordinator of the Tenderloin Improvement Project and the Western Addition Deaf Awareness Program. Among the many awards she has received for her deep commitment to community service are the KRON-TV Award for Those Who Care and the Asian Business League's Distinguished Leadership Award in community service.

Tess Manalo (formerly Medina) was born in the Philippines into a middle-class family. Her father was a mining engineer, and her grandfather a judge and agriculturist. The mood of the family home was of intellectualism, and Tess grew up a curious child, more interested in study than play, something for which she is grateful.

In 1964, she earned a bachelor's degree in agriculture from the University of the Philippines, and a year later a master's degree in agronomy. She left the Philippines in 1965 to study plant sciences at the University of Hawaii. She returned to the Philippines in 1971 to earn a second bachelor's degree in secondary education. In 1978, she went back to the United States, settling in San Francisco.

home, Ma quickly realized that taking college classes was little different from going to high school. Without telling his parents, he eventually dropped out and began hanging around Juilliard. At the age of seventeen, following the advice of Isaac Stern among others, Ma entered Harvard University. In four years, Ma finished a full course of study while continuing to give regular cello performances. For Ma, college was a period of maturation and growth, both personally and professionally. At the same time, his musical knowledge grew vastly.

Ma made his London debut during his years at Harvard. As concert requests began to come more frequently, Ma realized it would be possible for him to support himself as a musician. At his father's suggestion, he remained at Harvard, limiting his performances to one a month. Not only did Ma survive college, but his long-term, long-distance relationship with Jill Horner, whom he had met at age sixteen, blossomed and the two were married in 1977.

After graduation, the Mas spent three more years at Harvard with Yo-Yo as artist-in-residence at Leverett House and Jill teaching German. They eventually settled in Cambridge, Massachusetts, and figured out ways to survive Ma's demanding concert schedule.

Tess Manalo-Ventresca.

Since moving to the United States, Manalo-Ventresca has worked a variety of jobs in labor relations, management, and teaching. She has also spent time in native communities, such as the Tlingit of the Pacific Northwest and the Navajos and Hopis of the Southwest desert, where she was impressed with the peoples' sense.

In 1988, she started the Tenderloin Improvement Project, which employs local students, aged 11 to 14, ten hours a week sweeping sidewalks, picking up garbage, and collecting recyclables. The workers are paid minimum wage and are required to maintain passing grades in school and perform monthly volunteer community service. In citing her achievements upon bestowing its 1992 award to her, the Asian Business League of San Francisco remarked, "Most noteworthy of her projects is the direct effect upon teenage youths, whereby their lives have been greatly enriched. Her projects have created opportunities for these teenagers to develop their leadership skills and thus earn scholarships, find permanent employment, and also gain public recognition for their own contribution to the Bay Area." And indeed, several of the young participants in the Tenderloin Improvement Project have gone on to college with scholarships supported by the project.

In addition to her part-time paid position with the San Francisco Culinary, Bartenders, and Service Employees Trust Funds, where she manages health, welfare, legal, and pension programs for members of local unions, Manalo-Ventresca volunteers in many other organizations. She is the project coordinator and resource adviser for the Western Addition Deaf Awareness Project for the Bay Area Women's Resource Center, a Sunday school teacher for the hearing impaired at St. Benedict's Parish, and an advisory board member at the *Tenderloin Times*.

Manalo-Ventresca is married to Joe Ventresca, a budget and policy analyst for the San Francisco Airport Commission. She has three children.

Pablo Manlapit
Labor activist

Pablo Manlapit, a Filipino American labor leader, founded the Filipino Federation of Labor in Hawaii in 1911, Hawaii's first Filipino ethnic union. He continued to push for the rights of sugar cane workers by organizing the Filipino Unemployed Association in 1913.

Tom Matano (1947-)
Automobile designer

Tom Matano is the executive vice-president of the design division of Mazda Research and Development of North America. His studio has produced the designs for such popular cars and trucks as the Navajo, MX-3, 929, MX-6, 626, and the new B-series trucks. He was also a contributor to the design of the Miata, one of the most successful cars in recent history.

Tom Matano was born on October 7, 1947, in Nagasaki, Japan. His family lived on the other side of a mountain from ground zero, and so survived the city's nuclear destruction in 1945. Tom was exposed to cars at a young age, at a time when few people in Japan owned automobiles. He was fascinated by them and would leave school to haunt auto shops.

In high school, Tom was an above-average student. After graduation, he entered Seiki University in Tokyo, where he studied analysis engineering. He wanted to study design, but the structure of the Japanese education system would have required him to take an additional two years of classes before being considered for admittance into a design school.

After three years at Seiki University, Matano left Japan for the United States to study at the Art Center College of Design in Los Angeles, California. In 1974, he earned a bachelor's of science degree in transportation design.

After graduation, Matano was hired by General Motors to work on its design staff in Michigan. He had trouble renewing his visa to continue working in the United States, however, and after just 18 months left the country. He landed a General Motors position in Australia for six and a half years and then, looking for a change, took a job with BMW in Munich, Germany.

Matano joined the Mazda design studio in the winter of 1993. Two of his first jobs were the MPV, Mazda's entry in the lucrative minivan market, and the Miata, a classic roadster that became so popular when it was introduced that Mazda had difficulty filing orders for it.

Matano was made vice-president of the design division in 1991. He distills the work of several designers into a finished design, which is then sent to Japan to be reviewed. Along with the drawings and computer-imaging techniques used to express the designers' concept of a car, a full-scale, hand-crafted clay model is sent along as well. Even as vice-president of design, Matano still likes to work on these clay models, molding them into his ideal design.

Doris Matsui
Community activist, political appointee

Doris Matsui is a recognized community leader with over 20 years of public service to her credit. She currently serves as the White House deputy director of public liaison. Prior to that, she was a member of President Clinton's transition team.

She was born in the remote farming community of Dinuba, California, and was educated at the University of California at Berkeley. After moving to Sacramento, Ms. Matsui became almost immediately involved in community-service organizations such as the Sacramento Symphony League and the board of directors of KVIE, the local public television station; she served as president of both organizations.

Matsui moved to Washington, D.C., in 1979, when her husband, Robert, was elected to Congress, where he has served continuously since. In Washington, she was active in Peace Links, an international cultural-exchange organization. In 1990, she led a delegation of Congressional spouses to the Soviet Union and has also long been involved with Congressional Wives for Soviet Jewry, attending a conference in Vienna to discuss the Soviet Union's compliance with the Helsinki accords.

Doris Matsui is a former president of the Congressional Club, a bipartisan civic, social, and philanthropic organization of spouses of members of the House, Senate, Cabinet, and Supreme Court. In her position as president, she served as a chief sponsor of a 1991 program called Project Awareness, a breast cancer awareness and educational initiative. In this capacity, Matsui helped establish pilot projects throughout the country, promoting early detection of breast cancer and, in association with the YWCA and private corporations and donors across the country, providing mammogram screening for low-income women.

Tom Matano.

Robert Matsui (1941-)
Politician, attorney

Congressman Robert Matsui has represented California's fifth district in the House of Representatives since 1978. In time, he has become a senior member of the House Ways and Means Committee, perhaps the most powerful committee in Washington, and has taken the lead on many public policy issues dealing with tax policy, social issues, health care, and welfare reform. In late 1993, he was entrusted by the Clinton administration with marshaling congressional support for the North American Free Trade Agreement (NAFTA), a hotly debated free trade agreement among the United States, Canada, and Mexico. Matsui's leadership on the issue put him in the national spotlight, and the treaty's ultimate approval—considered a remarkable political achievement for the presiding administration—was due in no small part to Matsui's efforts.

Robert Takeo Matsui was born in Sacramento, California, in 1941, to second generation Japanese American parents. In April 1942, Matsui—then less than a year old—and his family were sent to an internment camp where the young boy spent the next three years of his life. After their release at the end of the war, the

Robert Matsui.

Midori.

Matsuis turned to Sacramento and attempted to rebuild their lives.

After high school, Matsui enrolled in the University of California at Berkeley, where as a sophomore he recalls being inspired by President John F. Kennedy's now famous call to public service. After graduation, he enrolled in Hastings College of Law where he earned his J.D. in 1966. In 1967, the young lawyer returned to his hometown of Sacramento with his new wife, Doris (Okada), to begin a private practice.

In 1971, Matsui saw his opportunity to run for public office when Sacramento's city council districts were redrawn, leaving the incumbent Republican in his district vulnerable. Matsui won the race and served on the Sacramento City Council until 1978 when he ran for the U.S. Congress. He has served as treasurer of the Democratic National Committee since 1991.

Matsui has received many honors for his years of public service. In 1993, the Children's Defense Fund honored him for his work on behalf of children. He has also been honored with Lifetime Achievement Award from the Anti-Defamation League.

Ved Mehta

See Literature

Midori (1971-)
Violinist

Even before she celebrated her twentieth birthday, Midori—who uses only her first name—was considered one of the world's most celebrated violinists. Born October 25, 1971, in Osaka, Japan and considered a child prodigy, she trained at Juilliard School of Music and performed at Carnegie Music Hall by the age of eighteen. She won the respect of even the most cynical critics at age fourteen, when a series of broken strings forced her to complete a difficult concerto on two borrowed violins. Now in her twenties, she commands performances with world-famous ensembles: the Philadelphia Orchestra under Wolfgang Sawallisch; the Maggio Musicale in Florence, Italy; the NDR Symphony in Hamburg, Germany; La Scala Philharmonic; Orchestre de Paris; and the Frankfurt Radio Symphony, among others.

In 1992, she founded the Midori Foundation, which seeks to expose children to the arts. She devotes her time to the foundation by giving special concerts in schools, hospitals, and institutions where children often don't have the opportunity to come into direct contact with the arts.

Norman Mineta.

Patsy Takemoto Mink.

Norman Mineta (1931-)
Politician

Representative Norman Mineta (D-Calif.) has become the first Asian/Pacific American to lead a major United States Congressional committee. Elected the House Public Works and Transportation Committee chair, Mineta received the most votes of any committee chair, 242-7. Mineta, who was interned during World War II, asserted the United States' greatest strengths—its commitment to fairness and its diversity—were demonstrated by his election.

Patsy Takemoto Mink (1927-)
Legislator, lawyer

In her thirty-year career as a legislator at the state and federal levels, Patsy Takemoto Mink has championed legislative reforms in health care, education, women's rights, environmental affairs, cancer research, and employment. Mink is one of the first Japanese American woman attorneys in Hawaii, and has worked to maintain her independence and integrity during her eight terms as Hawaii's representative in the U.S. House.

Born in 1927 on the island of Maui, Hawaii, Patsy Takemoto Mink enjoyed a comfortable life in her family's cottage on two acres of land. Mink's penchant for

challenging established traditions was borne out early in her life when she insisted on starting school at age four, a year earlier than the normal practice. Reading about leaders like Mahatma Gandhi led her to dream about being a medical doctor, a career she had entertained since undergoing surgery for appendicitis at the age of four. Her experiences at school became more unpleasant when the Japanese attacked Pearl Harbor and Japanese Americans throughout the United States—except for Hawaii—were interned in concentration camps. Despite being spared internment, Mink and other Asians in Hawaii were not spared the indignity of frequently being reminded that they were the enemy of the United States. After later transferring to Maui High School, her career interests began to turn to politics when she was elected student body president. After graduating from high school as class valedictorian, she enrolled at the University of Hawaii. Following her sophomore year, she spent her remaining college years transferring to two different colleges before finally graduating from the University of Nebraska. Heeding the suggestion of a mentor that she pursue a law career proved to be a major turning point in Mink's life. She was soon admitted to law school at the University of Chicago, where she met and married John Mink,

Noriyuki "Pat" Morita. (Courtesy of the Academy of Motion Picture Arts and Science.)

a graduate student in geophysics. Their first and only child, Gwendolyn Rachel was born a year later.

The couple moved back to Hawaii following their daughter's birth, and Mink had difficulty finding work—even after she passed the Hawaii Bar Exam. So, with the assistance of her father, she started her own law practice and taught business classes at the University of Hawaii.

In 1954, Mink was elected president of the Young Democrats, signaling the beginning of her active participation in politics. Between 1957 and 1964, Mink held elected positions as a representative and a senator in the legislature of Hawaii, which at the time was a U.S. Territory. In January 1965, she took the oath of office for the first of six consecutive terms as Hawaii's—and the nation's—first Asian American woman elected to Congress. During her tenure as a congresswoman, she supported the regulation of strip mining, sponsored the Women's Educational Equity Act, was outspoken in her opposition to the U.S. role in the Vietnam War when it was considered politically risky to do so, and successfully sued the federal government in a Freedom of Information Act case that was later cited as legal precedent for obtaining the tapes in the Watergate scandal

which led to Richard Nixon's forced resignation as president. Following unsuccessful campaigns for president (as the first Asian American to run) the U.S. Senate, Mink served for three years in the Carter administration as Assistant Secretary of State for Ocean and International, Environmental and Scientific Affairs until she resigned in 1980 to serve for three straight terms as national president of the Americans for Democratic Action. In 1983 she was elected to the Honolulu City Council where she served for four years.

Though she was defeated in subsequent races for state governor in 1986 and mayor of Honolulu mayor in 1988, Mink won an election in 1990 to serve the remainder of Representative Daniel Akaka's unexpired term in the U.S. House; Akaka had been appointed to the Senate seat left vacant after the sudden death of Senator Spark Matsunaga that same year.

Noriyuki "Pat" Morita (1933-)
Actor

Pat Morita is a star of television and film who is probably best known for his role as the karate master in the film *The Karate Kid,* for which he received an Academy Award nomination. He also appeared in the film's two sequels, *The Karate Kid: Part II* and *The Karate Kid III,* and has been a regular in several television shows, including *Sanford and Son* and *Happy Days.*

Noriyuki Morita was born on June 28, 1933, in Isleton, California. His father was a migrant farmer in the fruit orchards of California. Noriyuki was a very sickly child; he suffered from spinal tuberculosis—at that time a usually fatal disease—and spent nine years, from age two to eleven, in a hospital.

Right around the time Morita was released from the hospital, the war between the United States and Japan broke out and Americans of Japanese descent, both citizens and resident aliens, in the Western states were being imprisoned in internment camps in clear violation of the Constitution. The Moritas were sent to a camp in Arizona. When the family was released they moved to Fairfield, California, and his father opened a Chinese restaurant in a black neighborhood of the nearby city of Sacramento. Morita attended public schools and tried college briefly before giving it up to work with his father at the family restaurant. When the family restaurant closed, Morita found a job at Aerojet-General Corporation near Sacramento.

In 1964, Morita was working as the emcee of a Japanese nightclub in San Francisco when he got his first break. Singer Sam Cooke had been shot and the owner of the famed Copacabana in Los Angeles needed someone to fill the bill. Morita's agent Sally Marr (comedian Lenny Bruce's mother) got Morita , who billed himself as the "Hip Nip" the show that night. He continued performing for many years under that name, which at the time set Morita in with a crowd of many minority comedians (like Dick Gregory and Mort Sahl) who drew attention to their ethnic heritage, using at times slanderous nicknames in an attempt to diffuse the power those names had over people.

In the late sixties and early seventies, Morita was a popular opening act for comedians and singers. In 1973, Morita was offered the role of Al, the local hamburger shop owner, on the television show *Happy Days*. This was the first role that brought him national recognition. The next several years were very difficult for Morita, both personally and professionally. From 1980 to 1982, Morita lived alone in Hawaii, separated from his family. They were reunited in Los Angeles in 1982. In 1984 Morita was hired to play the role of Miyagi, the master in the movie *The Karate Kid*, earning Morita an Academy Award nomination. In 1986, *The Karate Kid: Part II* was released, and in 1989, *The Karate Kid III*.

Morita lives with his second wife, Yuki, a community organizer, in Los Angeles.

William Mow (1936-)
Entrepreneur, engineer

As an entrepreneur, William Mow has achieved phenomenal success in two dramatically different industries: electronics and clothing. A twist of fate propelled Mow to preside over one of the leading U.S. clothing companies for middle America: Bugle Boy Industries. Mow is the founder, chairman, and chief executive of the private company he launched in 1977. Bugle Boy boasts annual sales of $500 million, providing the clothing collections coveted by families all over the country.

Mow was born in Hangchow, China, in 1936. Mow's father was chief of the military committee for Chiang Kai-shek's Nationalistic government at the United Nations in New York when Mao Tse-tung's revolution swept China. Mow's father remained in the United States and the whole family, including Mow and his four brothers, emigrated to the United States when Mow was thirteen years old.

Mow grew up in Great Neck, New York, and worked his way through Rensselaer Polytechnic Institute in New York where he studied electrical engineering. In 1967, he earned his Ph.D. in electrical engineering from Purdue University. After graduating, Mow took a job at Litton Industries and two years later, in 1969, founded a computer-controlled instrumentation firm. The firm, Macrodata, developed new techniques to test large scale integrated computer chips. In five years, Macrodata posted sales of twelve million collars annually.

In the mid-1970s, Mow sold control of Macrodata to a Milwaukee-based conglomerate, Cutler-Hammer, but stayed on as chairman and chief executive officer.

William Mow.

Within the first year under the new management, the conglomerate accused Mow of concealing $2 million in Macrodata losses. In 1988 Mow was exonerated when a California appeals court found Cutler-Hammer executives engineered the accounting fraud. The loss of his job at Macrodata pushed Mow into finding a new line of business, which turned out to be wholesale and retail clothing. Mow met his partner Vincent Nesi in 1976 when Nesi was working at A. Smile, a boutique jeans resource. Mow started Buckaroo International Inc. a year later and signed Nesi on as a merchandise manager. In September of 1980, Mow reorganized Buckaroo, and the partners decided to focus on one product: jeans and casual pants. The company's name was officially changed to Bugle Boy Industries, a name chosen by Mow to reflect his interest in the Civil War era, after the young men who played bugles during battle.

As of 1994, Mow and Nesi are the sole shareholders of Bugle Boy. Mow is based at Bugle Boy's Simi Valley, California, headquarters, which handles administration, operations, advertising, and the distribution of Bugle Boy products. Mow and his wife have two small children. He also has two grown children from his first marriage.

Kent Nagano. (Christian Steiner.)

Mira Nair.

Kent Nagano (1948-)
Orchestra conductor

Since the 1980s, Kent Nagano has been a rising star in the classical music world. Nagano is the music director of the Berkeley Symphony Orchestra, director of the Opera de Lyon and the Halle Orchestra in Manchester, England, and the associate principal guest conductor of the London Symphony Orchestra. He has also moved into the international music recording scene, signing in 1993 a contract with Erato Records to deliver fifteen compact discs over a five-year period.

Kent Nagano was born in 1948, a third-generation Japanese American. Raised on a farm in Morro Bay, California, Nagano came from a Japanese-speaking household. His mother, an amateur cellist, introduced the family to music. Nagano studied at Oxford University in England and graduated from the University of California at Santa Cruz with a sociology/pre-law degree. A multi-talented musician who plays the piano, viola, clarinet and koto, Nagano studied for his master's degree in music at San Francisco State University, while serving as assistant to conductor Laszlo Varga and working for the San Francisco Opera.

In 1978, the young maestro took over the then-financially flagging Berkeley Symphony Orchestra. A passionate advocate for the work of living composers and a master of complex contemporary scores, Nagano is credited with transforming the Berkeley Symphony into a group much respected for its performance of twentieth-century music.

Aside from leading the Berkeley Symphony, Nagano has conducted orchestras at home and abroad. He has chosen a path of broad experiences, including tackling such unusual projects as recording Frank Zappa's orchestral works with the London Symphony for Zappa's label, Barking Pumpkin Records.

In 1985, Nagano won a Seaver Conducting Award, a $75,000 prize intended to foster the development of "American conductors on the threshold of major international careers." Nagano lives in San Francisco with his wife, renowned pianist Yvonne Loriod.

Mira Nair (1957-)
Filmmaker

Filmmaker Mira Nair has translated her passion for her native culture onto film, sharing with worldwide audiences the beauty and hardships both of life in India and as an Asian American in the United States. Her first feature film, *Salaam Bombay!*, won the top awards in 1988 at the prestigious Cannes film festival. *Salaam Bombay!* was also nominated for an Academy Award that year. Her first English-language film, *Mississippi Masala*, starring Denzel Washington, tackled the thorny problem of racism in a southern rural town.

Born in 1957, she grew up in comfortable surroundings in Bhubaneswar, a small town in the delta region of eastern India. Her first passion was theater. After graduating from an Irish Catholic missionary school in Simia, she attended Delhi University for one year where she was an actress with an amateur theater group that performed Shakespeare. In 1976, when Harvard University offered her a full scholarship, Nair grabbed the opportunity to travel to the U.S. It was at Harvard where she discovered her love for film, especially documentaries.

In *India Cabaret*, made in 1985, Nair told the story of the hard lives of women dancers working in a Bombay nightclub. The film won best documentary prizes at the American Film Festival and the Global Village Film Festival. After completing four documentaries, Nair wanted more control over the filmmaking process and decided to branch out to feature films. Her first attempt was *Salaam Bombay!* about homeless children living on the streets of Bombay. Made on a $900,000 budget, the film was a commercial and critical success.

In 1992 came *Mississippi Masala*. (The word *masala* refers to the colorful mix of spices used in Indian cooking.) The 1992 film was a humorous yet thought-provoking look at the lives of Indians who were forced to leave their native land of Uganda when dictator Idi Amin expelled Asians from the country in 1972. Many moved to the U.S., settling in Mississippi and buying motels. Nair got the idea for the movie from a *New Yorker* magazine article about the subject. Nair had trouble financing this film because of its mostly non-white cast. Even her casting of a big star like Washington and her successful track record would not convince financial backers. Eventually she collected the $7 million she needed.

While in Uganda filming *Mississippi Masala*, she met and fell in love with Mahmood Mamdani, a political scientist who was born in India but grew up in Uganda and earned his Ph.D from Harvard. Mamdani moved to Tanzania after Amin's expulsion order, and returned to Uganda in 1979 when the restrictions against Asians were lifted. The couple eventually married and bought the Kampala, Uganda, home Nair used in *Mississippi Masala*. In 1992, Nair gave birth to a son, Zohran.

Don T. Nakanishi.

Don T. Nakanishi (1949-)
Academician, community activist

Don Toshiaki Nakanishi, director of the Asian American Studies Center at the University of California at Los Angeles, is one of the country's foremost authorities on American race relations and the politics of diversity. He is a prolific writer who has published widely in academic journals on issues of education and ethnic diversity. He is also the cofounder and editor of *Amerasia Journal*, a highly regarded academic journal dealing with Asian American studies. In addition, Mr. Nakanishi is a frequent guest speaker and panelist at symposia all over the country.

Born on August 14, 1949, in East Los Angeles, California, into a Japanese American working class family. Nakanishi was an excellent student who planned to become a doctor. He graduated from Theodore Roosevelt High School in 1967 and attended Yale University on an academic scholarship. In his senior year, he was awarded the Frank M. Patterson Prize in political science for the outstanding senior essay on American government. He graduated cum laude in 1971 and was granted the Saybrook College Fellows Prize as the outstanding graduating senior at Yale.

After Yale, Nakanishi won a fellowship for graduate study at Harvard and won another in 1973. In 1978, he graduated from Harvard's Center for International Affairs with a Ph.D. in political science and was hired that same year by the University of California at Los Angeles as an associate professor in the Asian American studies program. He continued to publish widely in the field of race relations and diversity and, in 1982, became the program's director.

In 1986, Nakanishi was denied tenure by the UCLA tenure review board in what he considered a race-biased decision and decided to challenge the administration. The ensuing battle lasted three years and drew national attention. He was eventually granted tenure in a rare reversal of the university's decision. As of mid-1994 Don Nakanishi was finishing a book on the political history of Asians in the United States.

Philip Tajitsu Nash (1956-)
Activist, lawyer, teacher, writer

Philip Tajitsu Nash is a civil rights activist, lawyer, teacher, and writer. From 1992 to 1994, he was executive director of the National Asian Pacific American Legal Consortium, a not-for-profit, nonpartisan organization which was formed by Asian American Legal Defense and Education Fund (AALDEF), the Asian Law Caucus, and the Asian Pacific American Legal Center of Southern California. The Consortium's mission is to advance the legal and civil rights of the nation's Asian Pacific Americans through litigation, advocacy, public education, and public policy development. Nash has served on the board of the Japanese American Citizens League (JACL) in New York as a legal advocate for Japanese American redress. He helped found the Coalition of Asian Pacific American Association which has been responsible since 1979 for the annual Asian Pacific American Heritage Week Festival in New York City. In addition to activism, Nash also has taught Asian American studies at Yale University, law at Georgetown University and City University of New York law schools, urban legal studies at City College of New York, and metropolitan studies at New York University. Born December 3, 1956, in New York City, Philip Tajitsu Nash was the first child born to a Japanese American mother and a European American father. At the end of 1994, Nash left the Consortium to pursue his interest in writing.

Irene Natividad (1948-)
Political activist, feminist, educator

For Irene Natividad, the world is truly a global village. Through Natividad and Associates, she develops and leads political training workshops from Toronto to Taipei. She is a director of the Global Forum of Women,

Irene Natividad.

a biannual gathering of women leaders from around the world. In 1994, she developed a program on political empowerment that focused on "nuts and bolts" techniques of running for public office and skills-building workshops for policymakers for the Forum held in Taiwan. She chairs the National Commission on Working Women, an organization working to improve the economic status of working women in the United States, and serves as executive director of the Philippine American Foundation, dedicated to alleviating poverty in the Philippines by fostering grass-roots rural development. In 1985, she was the first Asian American to be elected to head the National Women's Political Caucus, and in 1988, *Ladies' Home Journal* named her to the list of "100 Most Powerful Women in America." She is a regular panelist on the Public Broadcasting Service's news commentary program, *To the Contrary* hosted by Bonnie Erbe.

Born in Manila, the Philippines on September 14, 1948, Natividad lived with her family in Okinawa, Iran, Greece, and India. Her ability to master languages and her sensitivity to cultures and customs explains why her expertise is sought by savvy politial leaders (and aspiring leaders) around the world.

Josie Natori (1947-)

Entrepreneur, fashion designer

Josie Natori left a lucrative career as an investment banker in the late 1970s with the intention of starting a business importing products such as furniture and baskets from the Philippines. But when Natori lengthened a traditional hand-embroidered blouse into a nightshirt, her phenomenally successful lingerie line was launched. As of the mid-1990s, The Natori Company, which Josie runs with her husband Kenneth, employs about 900 local craftsman at their own factory in the Philippines. This factory, where Natori fashions are sewn, allows Natori to utilize the unique designs and craftsmanship of the Philippines. Her soft, body-hugging designs are distinguished by their embellishment—delicate golden embroidery, silver beads, and brilliant jeweled appliques.

The Natori Company is a thriving empire. In 1991, they launched Josie Natori Couture, featuring elegant evening wear and dresses. In 1993, Natori introduced a fashion jewelry collection, and in 1994, a daytime and evening shoe line. In spring 1995, Avon Products will introduce a collection of Natori fragrance and bath products.

Josie Natori credits her family for her self-confidence and business savvy, and she is proud of her Filipino heritage. She is driven to contribute to the development of the Philippines, even beyond her accomplishments in trade and job creation. In 1988, Natori was honored with the Galleon Award by then-president of the Philippines, Corazon Aquino, in recognition of The Natori Company's rank as a prime exporter.

Born Josefina Cruz on May 9, 194 in Manila, Philippines, Natori is the eldest daughter in a family of six children. She married Kenneth Natori in 1972; the couple has one son, Kenneth, Jr., born in 1976.

Haing Ngor (1947-)

Physician, actor

Haing Ngor is a physician who survived the murderous reign of the Khmer Rouge in his native Cambodia, fleeing to the United States in 1980. He came to national prominence for his portrayal of Cambodian journalist Dith Pran in the 1985 film *The Killing Fields*. Ngor had never acted before, but his work was so powerful he earned an Academy Award. Since winning the award, Ngor has used his high profile to publicize the holocaust perpetrated on his people by the Khmer Rouge, and devoted considerable time to organizations serving the refugee population in the United States.

Haing Ngor was born in 1947 in the farming village of Samrong Yong, south of the Cambodian capital of Phnom Penh. By the time Ngor was a small boy, a civil

Haing Ngor.

war had already started. Ngor decided on a medical career, and specialized in gynecology and obstetrics. When the communist forces, the Khmer Rouge, overran the capital in 1975 and began their genocidal regime, Ngor could only work in utmost secrecy. The Khmer Rouge exterminated as many as two million people, including Ngor's mother, father, and brothers and their wives. In May 1979, Ngor escaped to Thailand. He worked as a doctor in refugee camps until October 1, 1980, when he left for Los Angeles.

In March 1982, he auditioned for a part in the film *The Killing Fields*—he realized it was an opportunity to tell the story of the Cambodian people. Despite this being his first attempt at acting, Ngor played the role of Dith Pran with such depth that in 1985 it earned him an Oscar for best supporting actor. Ngor has been the subject of two documentaries, *A Man Without a Country* and *Beyond the Killing Fields*. In 1987 his autobiography, *Haing Ngor: A Cambodian Odyssey*, co-written with journalist Roger Warner, was published to critical acclaim.

Since winning the Oscar and a number of other awards for his role in *The Killing Fields*, Ngor has interspersed occasional acting roles with his life's work, heading six organizations devoted to caring for

Southeast Asian refugees and resettling them in the West. Ngor currently lives alone in Los Angeles, California. Of his three sisters and five brothers, only two brothers are still living, one in the United States and one in Cambodia.

Isamu Noguchi (1904-1988)
Sculptor, architect

At his death in 1988 at the age of 84, the sculptor and architect, Isamu Noguchi, had achieved worldwide renown few artists of this century have known. His career spanned five decades during which he worked with such seminal 20th-century figures as George Balanchine, Igor Stravinsky, William Butler Yeats, Ezra Pound, and Martha Graham. His major works include Red Cube (1968), which stands on the plaza of the Marine Midland Building in New York City, the Billy Rose Sculpture Garden in Jerusalem, 2 Peace Bridges in Hiroshima, and the sculpture garden that he created for the Yale Beinecke Rare Book and Manuscript Library in New Haven, Connecticut. Aside from sculpture and architecture, Noguchi also designed theater sets and masks most notably for the Balanchine/Stravinsky ballet *Orpheus* and John Gielgud's *King Lear*.

Isamu Noguchi was born in 1904 in Los Angeles to an American mother and a Japanese father. In describing his childhood in the United States, he told the *Journal of Modern Literature* that it "had nothing to do with art, it had to do with the Middle West and the American idealism that flourished in the twenties and thirties."

After high school, the young Noguchi had already decided to be a sculptor. A family friend arranged an apprenticeship for him with Gutzon Borglum, who at the time was sculpting the presidential monument on Mount Rushmore. "So I really grew up in the Midwest," Noguchi emphasizes, "though I am a mixture of extreme differences in heritage. Please do not forget I am a real product of the Midwest."

Borglum told Noguchi that he would never make it as a sculptor, so in the mid-1920s Noguchi moved to New York and enrolled as a pre-medical student in Columbia University. Not wanting to give up on his dream, however, he also enrolled in the Leonardo da Vinci Art School on the Lower East Side, where he continued to study sculpture. Noguchi described his experiences at the da Vinci school as pivotal, and the encouragement he received there prompted him to drop out of Columbia and pursue sculpture full time.

Noguchi exhibited in a show called the Roman Bronze Exhibit, where Harry Guggenheim saw his work and suggested that he apply for one of the newly established Guggenheim Fellowships. Noguchi did so, with the help and encouragement of others, including Alfred Stieglitz, the photographer. Noguchi won the award and spent the money traveling through Europe, where, in Paris, he spent time under the tutelage of the sculptor Constantin Brancusi.

Noguchi returned to New York in 1929 and began a successful career making portrait busts. It was in 1936 in Mexico, however, that Noguchi completed what is considered his first major work: a high-relief mural in colored cement called History Mexico (1936) for the Rodriguez market.

Following the outbreak of World War II, Noguchi founded an organization called the Nisei Writers and Artists for Democracy in an attempt to counter the anti-Japanese hysteria that gripped the United States after the attack on Pearl Harbor. Noguchi was outraged when Japanese Americans were imprisoned during the war, and although he was a resident of the East Coast and therefore not subject to detention, he voluntarily entered an internment camp in Arizona, where he was held for seven months.

In 1982, Noguchi received the prestigious Edward MacDowell Medal for outstanding lifetime contribution to the arts. Two years later, his sculpture Bolt of Lightning, a 102-foot-tall stainless steel structure designed as a memorial to Benjamin Franklin, was installed near the Benjamin Franklin Bridge in Philadelphia, 50 years after Noguchi conceived it. In 1987, President Ronald Reagan awarded him the National Medal of Arts, and in 1988, the Japanese government gave him the Order of the Sacred Treasure.

Isamu Noguchi died on December 30, 1988, from complications of a virus he contracted while working in Italy. He was survived by a sister, Ailes Spindem, and two half-brothers, Michio and Tomiji Noguchi.

Gyo Obata (1923-)
Architect

Architect Gyo Obata's long and remarkable career encompasses projects as diverse as the National Air and Space Museum in Washington, D.C. (the world's most-visited museum) to the King Khalid International Airport in Saudi Arabia (the world's largest airport). The St. Louis firm he cofounded is one of the largest architecture firms in the world, with offices on four continents.

Obata was born in San Francisco on February 28, 1923, to Chiura and Haruko Obata. His father, grandfather, and great-grandfather were all painters from Japan, and his mother taught flower arrangement. When he was five years old, the family moved to Sendai, Japan, the family's ancestral home, returning to San Francisco the following year to settle in Berkeley, California.

Obata enrolled at the University of California architecture school, quickly distinguishing himself. But his

first semester coincided with the Japanese attack on Pearl Harbor in December 1941, which spawned anti-Japanese hysteria and drew the United States into World War II. Just months after the attack, those of Japanese descent living on the West Coast were forced to enter internment camps because they were perceived as a national security threat. Because the War Department allowed those accepted to a Midwestern college to leave, Obata's father urged him to continue his education at Washington University in St. Louis. Obata left for his new school the night before his parents, brother, and sister were bussed to a camp in Utah. But the relative normalcy he found in the Midwest only heightened the outrage he felt over the treatment of his family and other Japanese. After the war his family joined him in St. Louis.

Obata's move to St. Louis had been a turning point in many ways. It was in the Midwest that he met many of the people who would later play important roles in his life, including the man he considers his mentor and greatest architectural influence, Eero Saarinen. After graduating from Washington University in 1945, Obata received a scholarship to study with Saarinen at Cranbrook Academy, outside Detroit. It was from Saarinen, the famed designer of the Gateway Arch in St. Louis, that Obata learned about urban planning and project design. After a year and a half at Cranbrook, Obata went to Chicago, but he was soon drafted, sent to Fort Lewis near Tacoma, Washington, then to the Aleutian Islands with the Corps of Engineers to study arctic warfare. In 1947, he returned to Chicago for a year before joining architect Minoru Yamasaki in Michigan, where he was assigned to the design of a new airport terminal in St. Louis. For several years, he spent most of his time commuting from Detroit to St. Louis.

In 1955, three members of the Yamasaki office in St. Louis—George Hellmuth, George Kassabaum, and Obata—split from the Detroit office after Yamasaki became ill. The move marked the birth of Hellmuth, Obata and Kassabaum, or HOK. The fledgling company benefited from postwar prosperity and the baby boom, which ensured a steady flow of work—mostly elementary and secondary schools and colleges. Today, HOK is one of the largest architecture firms in the world, with eight U.S. offices and four overseas, and more than 900 architects, designers, engineers, and planners on the payroll. HOK's specialties have expanded to include everything from commercial buildings to shopping centers to hospitals. The firm's credits already include three baseball stadiums: Jacobs Field in Cleveland, Oriole Park at Camden Yards in Baltimore, and the new Comiskey Park in Chicago. Obata, who now serves as cochairman of HOK, is the only remaining partner; Kassabaum died in 1982 and Hellmuth retired in 1986. Obata still spends the bulk of his time designing, with

Gyo Obata.

projects such as the Priory School and Chapel in St. Louis, the campus of Southern Illinois University, and the Smithsonian Institution's National Air and Space Museum. Other high-profile projects Obata has done include the headquarters for Mobil Oil, the 1980 Winter Olympics facilities at Lake Placid, New York, Taiwan's Taipei World Trade Center, which dominates that city's skyline, and the acclaimed renovation of the St. Louis Union Station.

In recent years Obata has become a strong advocate for environmental issues, pushing his fellow architects to play more of a role in the environmental debate. Obata is a member of the Presidio Council, a citizens group established by the Golden Gate National Park Association to formulate the transfer of the San Francisco Presidio from the military to the National Park Service. Obata and his wife, Courtney Bean Obata, a ceramist and sculptor, have four children.

Angela Oh (1955-)
Lawyer, community activist

Angela Oh came to national prominence as a spokesperson for Korean Americans in Los Angeles in the aftermath of the 1992 riots, in which more than

2000 Korean businesses were damaged or destroyed. In recognition of this work, Oh was appointed by California State Assembly Speaker Willie Brown to co-chair a special committee on the Los Angeles crisis. She also chairs Senator Barbara Boxer's judiciary advisory committee, where she recommends candidates for judgeships in the central district of California.

Angela Eunjin Oh was born in Los Angeles to first-generation Korean immigrants on September 8, 1955. Her mother was a schoolteacher and her father a laboratory technician. After graduation from high school in 1973, she enrolled in the University of California at Los Angeles, where she earned a bachelor's degree in psychology. While in college, she worked as tutor in the Chicano Youth East Barrio Project, which provided general tutoring for public school students in one of Los Angeles' poorer neighborhoods.

In 1979, she enrolled in UCLA's public health doctoral program. Her studies on occupational health led to a concern with labor-related issues. In 1980, she founded LACOSH, the Los Angeles Committee of Occupational Safety and Health, part of a network of loosely affiliated nationally active worker-safety and health-advocacy organizations. In 1981, Oh left the doctoral program with a master's degree and began working with LACOSH full time, lobbying on local, state, and national levels for issues related to all aspects of worker health and safety. In 1983, she became the health and safety director of the Federated Firefighters of California, a statewide union representing firemen.

In 1985, Oh entered the law school at the University of California at Davis, and in June 1986, earned her J.D. Her first job after law school was as a political consultant for an organization called "No On Proposition 63," where she worked unsuccessfully to defeat the statewide initiative to make English the official language of California.

After the passage of Proposition 63, Oh went to work for private law firms where she specialized in labor-management relations as a union advocate. She then went into trial law with the firm of Beck, De Corso, Barrera & Oh, where she remains today.

In the wake of the 1992 Los Angeles riots, she emerged as a national spokesperson for many of those whose businesses were destroyed in the rampage, especially those in the Koreatown section of the city, the largest expatriate Korean community in the world. Oh also made television appearances, wrote several articles for national newspapers like the *New York Times* and the *Los Angeles Times*, and became a sought-after panelist and speaker at academic conferences. In these venues, Oh draws attention to the concerns of the Korean community. Her *New York Times* article stated that a year after the riot, only one in four destroyed Korean businesses had reopened. She also

tries to heal the rift between Korean American and African American communities, which she sees as vital to the rebuilding of downtown L.A.

Angela Oh has been involved for years in a variety of civic and community affairs organizations, including the American Civil Liberties Union (ACLU), where she was a board member; the Korean American Bar Association, where she served as president in 1992; the California Women's Law Center; and the Women's Organization Reaching Koreans, where she served a term as president. In recognition of her expertise in community development and the problems of urban conflict, Oh was appointed a fellow of the British America Project, a privately funded annual symposium that brings together academicians, artists, politicians, and professionals from several fields to discuss the problems of urban conflict in both Great Britain and the United States.

Yoichi R. Okamoto (1915-1985)
Photojournalist

Yoichi R. Okamoto was head of the White House Photo Office and served as the principal presidential photographer from 1964 through 1968, during the presidency of Lyndon Baines Johnson. In a long career as a distinguished photojournalist Okamoto's subjects have included J. Edgar Hoover, head of the Federal Bureau of Investigation; Warren Burger, chief justice of the U. S. Supreme Court; and Lyndon Baines Johnson, president of the United States. His work has been featured on the covers of the *Smithsonian* and *Time* magazines. As head of the White House Photo Office, Okamoto made significant contributions to the body of photographic work documenting government in operation.

Okamoto was born on July 3, 1915, the oldest of two boys. His parents, both nisei (first generation Japanese American), divorced when Okamoto was young, and he was raised by his mother in Yonkers, New York. After graduation from Colgate University, Okamoto enlisted in the army. He served with the 442nd Regimental Combat Team, a legendary all-Japanese infantry regiment that accrued one of the most distinguished records of service and bravery in the history of the U.S. Army while fighting in the European theater from 1942 until 1945. After the war, Okamoto transferred to the foreign service and was stationed in Vienna with the United States Information Agency (USIA) until 1954. While in Vienna, he worked for General Mark Clark as a photographer. In September of 1947, he married Paula Schmuck-Wachter. In 1954, Okamoto was transferred back to the United States to USIA headquarters, where he continued his work as photographer. An auspicious meeting occurred when Lyndon Johnson, then vice-president, made a trip to West Germany. Okamoto

Yoichi R. Okamoto. (LBJ Library Collection.)

was given the assignment to accompany him on the trip, and the two got along so well that Johnson requested that Okamoto accompany him on subsequent foreign trips.

In 1964, Okamoto became head of the White House Photo Office for President Johnson. In addition to managing a team of five photographers, he also served as the primary White House photographer. In that capacity, his main responsibility was to photograph President Johnson's activities on a daily basis. In previous administrations, most photography consisted of ceremonial setups and other planned photographs.

Upon his retirement from the White House in 1968, Okamoto and two others founded Image, a professional photo lab in Washington, D.C. Okamoto continued his work as a freelance photographer, assembling a long list of photo credits, including all the stage bills for the Kennedy Center of the Performing Arts in Washington, D.C., for a twelve-year period beginning in 1968. Many Okamoto photographs have been published in the *Smithsonian* magazine, including the first informal photos of Justice Warren Burger of the U. S. Supreme Court. Okamoto, on another assignment from Smithsonian, photographed all the judges of the Supreme Court, both at the court and at home. Another Okamoto

photograph of note was the last formal portrait and photograph of J. Edgar Hoover for the cover of *Time*.

One hundred twenty of Okamoto's dramatic photographs of Johnson and the White House years are included in a book edited by Harry Middleton, the former Johnson speechwriter who directs the LBJ Library and Museum. The book, *LBJ: The White House Years* was published in 1990 to coincide with the silver anniversary of Johnson's inauguration as the thirty-sixth president in 1965. For seven years prior to his death in 1985, Okamoto had been working on a book of photographs of Vienna and the surrounding Austrian countryside, making one or two trips to Austria each year and shooting over 500 rolls of film in the process. In 1987, Okamoto's widow, Paula, completed and published *Okamoto Sieht Wien: Die Stadt Seit Den Funfziger Jahren [Okamoto's Vienna]*, (Tafel Spitz Wien, 1987) featuring Okamoto's photographs. (The book was published in two versions, English and German.)

Major Ellison S. Onizuka (1946-1986)
Astronaut

Onizuka was a mission specialist on the space shuttle's first Department of Defense mission, launched from Kennedy Space Center, Florida, January 24, 1985.

On January 28, 1986, Onizuka was one of seven persons killed when the space shuttle Challenger exploded. The U.S. Air Force named a base in California in his honor.

Onizuka was born June 24, 1946, in Kealakekua, Kona, Hawaii. He graduated from Konawaena High School in 1964 and received bachelor and master of science degrees in aerospace engineering in June and December 1969, respectively, from the University of Colorado.

Onizuka began active duty with the U.S. Air Force (USAF) in January, 1970, after receiving his commission through the University of Colorado's four-year Reserve Officer Training Corps (ROTC) program. He was selected as an astronaut candidate by NASA in January 1978 and, in August 1979, completed a one-year training and evaluation period.

Yoko Ono (1933-)
Artist, filmmaker, musician

Born in Tokyo, Japan, on February 18, 1933, into one of Japan's most prominent and wealthy families, Yoko Ono is an avant-garde artist and filmmaker who became popular in New York's underground art scene in the early 1960s and then became internationally famous in 1968, first as the girlfriend and then as the wife of the late John Lennon, the former Beatle.

As a member of the loosely banded group of artists known as Fluxus, Ono made several films, contributed art and sculpture to shows, and worked on many staged productions. With Lennon, she orchestrated much of the couple's peace activist performances and the famous "bed-in" of 1969. She and Lennon also formed and recorded with the Plastic Ono Band, and she collaborated on many of his compositions, including "Imagine."

In the financially and legally stormy years following the breakup of the Beatles, Ono managed Lennon's finances and parlayed them into one of the largest personal fortunes in the country. Since Lennon's murder in 1980, Ono has recorded two albums, had a retrospective of her art and films at the Whitney Museum in New York, and has written and produced a rock opera for an off-Broadway theatre in New York.

Steven Okazaki
Film Producer, 1991 Academy Award Winner for "Days of Waiting"

In response to the popular and controversial 1993 film *Rising Sun*, Steven Okazaki has produced *Rising Sons*, a movie that uses dramatic and documentary elements to examine the increase in racism against Asian Americans in the 1980s and 1990s. Interviews with Asian Americans from across the United States are

Steven Okazaki.

reenacted by a cast of six actors, including Lane Nishikawa and Kelvin Han Yee. Okazaki states that the film examines the deep pain and anger that racism causes in the lives of minorities.

Ayub Khan Ommaya (1930-)
Neurosurgeon

Dr. Ayub Khan Ommaya is an accomplished neurosurgeon and a scientist.

Ayub Khan Ommaya was born April 14, 1930, in Mian Channu, a small rural town in Pakistan, to a French mother and a Pakistani father. He grew up speaking French, English, Urdu, Pashto, and Panjabi. At age fifteen Ommaya read a magazine article about the work of pioneer neurosurgeon Dr. Wilder Penfield that set the path for his profession. He also read about the work of Sir Hugh Cairns, professor of neurosurgery at Oxford University, and was determined to study under his direction after completing his medical training in Pakistan in 1954. For his academic excellence and versatility, Ommaya was selected as a Rhodes scholar to Oxford where he studied physiology, biochemistry, psychology, and philosophy. His doctorate focused on the mechanisms of traumatic unconsciousness.

Ommaya's path from Oxford to the United States was accidental. He had planned to go back and open the first neurosurgery department at King Edward Medical College in Lahore, Pakistan. A fellow Rhodes scholar, Dr. Barry Bloomberg, who later won the Nobel Prize for discovering the hepatitus-B virus, had started working at the National Institutes of Health (NIH) in Maryland. He suggested to Ommaya that he come and work at NIH for awhile, where he eventually became chief or neurosurgery. His many appointments in the United States have included Chief of Applied Neuroscience Research, NIH; Chief Medical Adviser, Department of Transportation; Chairman of Committee on Head Injury, North Atlantic Treaty Organization (NATO); Advisory Panels at the U.S. House of Representatives, Bureau of Disease Prevention and Environmental Control. In addition, he continues to serve as consultant and adviser on many international bodies such as the International Red Cross and the International Brain Research Organization, among others.

Ommaya, while successful in his chosen profession in the United States, remains steeped in his culture and maintains strong ties to Pakistan. He was one of the founding presidents of the Association of Pakistani Physicians of North America. He is a member of the Resident Associate Program at the Smithsonian where he lectures on Reform, Science and Politics in the World of Islam. He is also working to establish a Brain Institute in Pakistan. The government of Pakistan awarded him the Sitari-i-Imtiaz (Star of Achievement) in 1982. He is currently, among his other appointments, director of the Center for Interdisciplinary Brain Research, where he is testing a new invention, a spinal fluid flow-driven artificial organ for treating type–I diabetes which may also be used to deliver useful substances to the brain in other nervous system disorders such as Parkinson's and Alzheimer's. In addition to his professional duties, he immerses himself with equal vigor into his hobbies—Italian and French opera singing and, in his words, "good conversation with my family and friends."

Alfonso Ossorio (1916-1990)
Artist

Alfonso Ossorio was an important artist of the New York School, a mid-20th-century group of legendary abstract expressionists that included artists such as Jackson Pollack, Lee Krasner, and Clyford Still. Ossorio's work hangs in some of America's premiere museums, including the Metropolitan Museum of Art, the Whitney Museum of American Art, the Museum of Modern Art, and the Guggenheim. Later in life, Ossorio dedicated himself to the creation of a large arboretum and sculpture garden called The Creeks.

Ayub Khan Ommaya.

Alfonso Ossorio was born on August 2, 1916, in Manila, Philippines, the fourth of six sons in a wealthy and racially mixed family. At the age of eight, Ossorio was sent to a Catholic prep school in England called St. Richard's, and at 14, he came to the United States to study at the Portsmouth Priory, a school run by Benedictine monks in Rhode Island.

He entered Harvard in 1934, where he studied fine arts, working mainly in wood engravings and watercolors. Ossorio graduated from Harvard in 1938 and enrolled in the Rhode Island School of Design (RISD), where he continued his pursuit of graphic design. In 1939, he left RISD for an extended vacation in the West, later renting a studio in Boston.

Two years later, he held his first one man show in New York at the Wakefield Gallery. He was inducted into the U.S. army in 1943, and was stationed in Illinois. While in the service, Ossorio nearly died during an operation and spent his recovery in the Mayo General Hospital, where he did medical drawings until his discharge. Twenty-two of these ink and watercolor drawings were exhibited in 1945 at the Moritimer Brandt Gallery in New York.

In 1949, Ossorio met and became friends with the American painter Jackson Pollack and his wife, Lee

Seiji Ozawa. (Christian Steiner.)

Krasner. Through the Pollacks, he also met the French painter Jean Dubuffet and became immersed in what was becoming the East Hampton, Long Island art scene.

In 1951, Ossorio embarked on a hectic exhibition schedule. He began in Paris at the Studio Paul Facchetti with a large series of abstract watercolors he had done while in the Philippines and some new experimental paintings in oil and enamel on canvas that was mounted on shaped plywood. These three-dimensional works were the precursors of the "assemblages" that would distinguish Ossorio in later years. The show received mixed reviews in the French press, but it sold well.

In the 1950s, Ossorio began taking his art in a new direction. While the purists of the New York School of abstract expressionism were paring down their paintings, achieving a cool, detached, and minimalist effect, Ossorio was experimenting with the older tenets of cubism. In 1960, he began producing works in three dimensions called collages or montages—both of which had been done by the cubists—that Ossorio would later called assemblages.

He continued working and showing in this new style, and his reputation as a serious artist—albeit one difficult to label—grew. His shows were widely reviewed by

the nation's top art critics, and his works were being acquired by top museums.

In the 1970s, Ossorio worked mainly at The Creeks, his Long Island estate. He had collected exotic trees for the arboretum through the 1960s, and by the mid-1970s, some 600 varieties grew on the 80-acre grounds. He began adding large outdoor sculptures that were made, in classic assemblage style, of objects inlaid in poured concrete.

In the year before his death, there was a highly successful retrospective of his work at the Benton Gallery in Southampton, Long Island, where interest in the artist grew. Mr. Ossorio died in New York City at the New York University Medical Center on December 6, 1990. He was 74 years old.

Seiji Ozawa (1935-)
Conductor

Seiji Ozawa became the first Asian music director of a major American symphony in 1973, when he took over the directorship of the Boston Symphony Orchestra, a position he retains to this day. He was born in Shenyang in the Manchurian province of China in 1935—the third of four sons. His father was an expatriate Japanese dentist. The family returned to Japan when World War II broke out, marked by Japan's invasion and occupation of Manchuria.

The young Ozawa studied conducting in Tokyo under the legendary teacher Hideo Saito at the Toho Gakuen School of Music. In 1959, he left Japan for Europe where he won a series of prestigious conducting awards that brought him to the attention of two of the major conductors of the United States, Charles Munch of the Boston Symphony Orchestra and Leonard Bernstein of the New York Philharmonic. In 1961, Bernstein invited him to be assistant conductor of the New York Philharmonic. From that one-year post he went on to positions with the Chicago, Toronto, San Francisco, and Boston Symphonies.

Ozawa has received worldwide acclaim for his work with the BSO and other world class orchestras in the United States, Europe, and Asia. He has toured all over the world, recorded extensively, received several honorary doctorates, and has won an Emmy. In 1992, he cofounded the Saito Kinen Festival in Matsumoto, Japan, in honor of his old teacher at the Toho Gakuen School. His tenure at the Boston Symphony is the longest of any major orchestra in the country.

I. M. Pei (1917-)
Architect

I.M. Pei is one of the most respected architects alive; more than half of his 50 projects have won major awards, including the Arnold Bruner Award of the

National Institute of Arts and Letters, The Medal of Honor of the New York Chapter of the American Institute of Architects, the Excellence 2000 Award, and the Colbert Foundation's First Award for Excellence. He was also presented the Medal of Freedom for his contributions to world peace and service to the United States Government.

Born in 1917 to a prominent banker and economist in Shanghai, China, Pei came to the United States to study architecture at Massachusetts Institute of Technology. In 1940, he received his bachelor's degree and was awarded the Alpha Rho Chi Medal, the MIT Traveling Fellowship, and the AIA Gold Medal at graduation. While enrolled at Harvard in 1942, he volunteered his services to the National Defense Research Committee at Princeton, New Jersey. He returned to Harvard in 1944 and completed his master's degree while teaching as an assistant professor.

In 1948, after traveling on a fellowship given him by Harvard, Pei became the director of architecture with Webb & Knapp, Inc. In 1955, he formed the partnership, I.M. Pei and Associates, which became I.M. Pei & Partners in 1966, and finally Pei Cobb Freed & Partners in 1989.

Pei gained national attention with his designs for the East Building of the National Gallery of Art in Washington D.C. and the John F. Kennedy Library in Boston. Pei has completed over 30 institutional projects and has also designed a number of corporate buildings including the Bank of China in Hong Kong, Asia's tallest building.

A patron of the arts and education, Pei has numerous memberships on visiting committees at Harvard, MIT, and the Metropolitan Museum of Art. He also served on the National Council on the Humanities and the National Council on the Arts. He also holds many honorary degrees and has established a scholarship for Chinese students who wish to study architecture.

Arati Prabhakar (1959-)
Scientist, government administrator

In 1993, President Bill Clinton offered the leadership of the National Institute of Standards and Technology (NIST) to a young India-born engineer-scientist, Arati Prabhakar. NIST's mandate is to develop and apply technology, measurements, and standards in collaboration with industry to stimulate economic development. With her appointment, Prabhakar became the tenth director of the organization and the first Asian to hold the post.

Arati Prabhakar was born in New Delhi, India, on February 2, 1959. When she was two years old her mother, Raj, immigrated to the United States to pursue an education in the field of social work. Within a year, Arati and her father, Jagdish, followed her. From an

Arati Prabhakar.

early age, Prabhakar was exposed to the fields of science and technology, directing her academic and career choices. Prabakhar pursued her bachelor's and master's degrees in electrical engineering and completed a doctorate in applied physics from the California Institute of Technology (Cal Tech), earning the first Ph.D. in applied physics awarded to a woman at that institution.

Prabhakar's first job was as a congressional fellow at the U.S. Office of Technology Assessment (OTA), which led to the directorship of the Microelectronics Technology Office in the Defense Department's Advanced Research Projects Agency (ARPA). It is from this position that she was selected by the administration in 1993 to take over the helm of NIST.

Beulah Quo (19??-)
Actress

Beulah Quo has acted in films as well known as *Chinatown*, *Love Is a Many Splendored Thing*, and *Girls, Girls, Girls*. Her television credits include parts in "Starsky and Hutch," "Hawaii Five-O," "Magnum P.I.," and "Trapper John, M.D." On the stage, she was seen in *The World of Suzie Wong* and *Martyrs Can't Go*

Beulah Quo.

Home. She was nominated for an Emmy for her role in "Chinese Chess Piece," a feature of the 1990 Los Angeles Film Festival. But unless you have been a longtime member of her "General Hospital" fan club, you probably wouldn't recognize her walking down the street.

An actress for four decades and now a community activist, Quo has dedicated her life in recent years to trying to change these casting policies—not for herself, but for future generations of Asian American artists to follow. From 1985 to 1991, Quo played Olin, a fast-talking, hip housekeeper on the television soap opera, "General Hospital." She was the only Asian American actor whose story line reccurred over several years.

Beulah Quo was born in Stockton, California, a quiet, central California community. Quo graduated with honors from Stockton High School, graduated Phi Beta Kappa from the University of California at Berkeley, and earned a master's degree from the University of Chicago. She was trained to be a teacher and taught college in both the United States and China. She and her husband, Edwin, were teaching at Ginling College in Nanjin, China in the 1940s when the Communist Revolution engulfed the country. Quo and her husband fled with a two-month-old baby. Her acting career began by accident. In 1954, she applied for a job as a dialect

coach for Jennifer Jones in the movie, *Love is a Many Splendored Thing.* Quo auditioned for the job, and director Henry King told her that her accent was too "California." But he wondered whether she'd be interested in playing the part of Jones' aunt. One role led to another, and soon Quo was working full time as an actress. Throughout the 1960s and 1970s, Quo acted in films and dozens of popular weekly television dramas. Her film roles included parts in *Flower Drum Song, The Sand Pebbles,* and *Chinatown.* One of her favorite roles came in *The Sand Pebbles,* when her petite, five-foot three-inch frame was built up with stuffing so she could play a "fat mama." Quo played the role of empress of Kublai Khan in the NBC production of *Marco Polo,* one of the first major American film projects to be made in China. Firm in her belief that the media is an important vehicle for reaching out to people, Quo began working in public affairs programming, and began producing documentaries of well-known Asian Americans, including the Oscar-winning cinematographer James Wong Howe. This documentary, *James Wong Howe: The Man and His Movies,* aired shortly before Howe died, and won a Hollywood-area Emmy Award.

Safi U. Qureshey (1951-)
Entrepreneur, engineer

Safi Qureshey and his two friends, Thomas Yuen and Albert Wong came to the United States as engineering students and established a multi-million dollar manufacturing company. The three Asian immigrants pooled their resources, which amounted to $2,000 in 1980, and started a small electronic design consulting firm, using their initials to name the firm AST Research. Fourteen years from its conception, AST Research, a half-billion dollar manufacturing company is headed by Qureshey, the only remaining founder. AST is based in Irvine, California and ranks 431 on the Fortune 500 list of leading U.S. companies, and is the nation's fourth largest computer maker behind IBM, Apple, and Compaq.

Qureshey was born in 1951 in Karachi, Pakistan, and spent his childhood there. He graduated from the University of Karachi with a bachelor's degree in physics in 1970. He came to the United States shortly thereafter, and received an electrical engineering degree at the University of Texas-Austin in 1975. He became a U.S. citizen in 1984. Qureshey is a soft-spoken man, the father of three children, and a devout Muslim whose humility is surprising in comparison with other company CEOs.

Besides his success as an entrepreneur, Qureshey is also a prominent citizen in southern California. He is a member of the Southern California Technology Executives Network and holds a position on its board of directors. In 1992, he accompanied Congressman

Christopher Cox on his visit to see Mexico's President Carlos Salinas de Gortari regarding the North American Free Trade Agreement. Qureshey is a well-known Orange County Republican, who in 1993 welcomed a visit from Democrat Vice-President Al Gore.

Attipat K. Ramanujan (1929-1993)
Academician

Attipat K. Ramanujan, who liked to say he was "the hyphen in Indo American," served on the University of Chicago faculty for 32 years and was a former chairman of its department of South Asian languages and civilizations. He was considered a leading scholar of Tamil, the oldest-living Indian language. He wrote poetry in both English and Kannada, another Indian language, and translated Kannada and Tamil poems into English. His translation "Speaking of Siva" was nominated for a National Book Award and was the basis for an opera produced by the British Broadcasting Company.

Syngman Rhee (1875-1965)
Political activist

Syngman Rhee was the founder and the first president of the Republic of Korea, the first democratic government to rule on the Korean peninsula in 4,000 years. The government was formed in exile during the Japanese occupation and ruled from Hawaii, where Rhee lived for many years.

Syngman Rhee was born in Whanghai Province, Korea, on March 26, 1875. He was the only son of Lee Kyung Sun and Lee Kim Hai and was a descendant of the rulers of the Yi Dynasty, which ruled Korea from 1392 until the Japanese invasion and occupation in 1910. Rhee was educated by Methodist missionaries in Korea. As a young man, he joined the Independence Club, which demanded democratic reform of the monarchy and an end to Japanese influence within the country. In 1895, when the leader of the group fled the country, Dr. Rhee became its leader. In that same year, he founded Korea's first daily newspaper, *Independence*. His continued insistence on reform made him a threat to the monarchy, and he was consequently jailed and tortured for seven months. While in prison, he converted to Christianity and became a missionary within the jail.

In 1904, the monarchy issued a general amnesty and Dr. Rhee was released and left Korea for the United States, where he earned a bachelor's degree from George Washington University, a master's degree from Harvard, and a doctorate in international law from Princeton, where he was greatly influenced by the teachings of Woodrow Wilson.

Safi Qureshey.

In 1911, he returned briefly to Korea, which in his absence had been annexed by Japan. He was again forced to flee, going this time to Hawaii, where he founded the Korean Methodist Church and the Korean Christian Institute. In 1919, in a secret meeting in Seoul, Dr. Rhee was elected president of the Korean Provisional Government in Exile. In this post, he helped organize the guerrilla fighters in Korea who fought for the next 25 years to destabilize the Japanese colonial government, a notoriously brutal regime.

Independence proved difficult, however, and did not come until the Japanese were defeated by the United States in World War II. Elections were held in 1948, after three years of vicious political infighting and superpower posturing over the division of the Korean peninsula. Rhee was elected to a four-year term as president, but political turbulence continued during his tenure with the Soviet-backed North assuming an increasingly threatening posture. On June 25, 1950, the North invaded the South, beginning three years of warfare between the North and their backers in Moscow and the South and their backers in Washington. The war was finally resolved with an armistice that resulted in the partition of the peninsula along the heavily fortified 38th parallel.

Rhee won reelection as president of the Republic of Korea in 1952, 1956, and 1960. The 1960 elections, however, were widely regarded as fraudulent and a student-protest movement swept the country, prompting Rhee's resignation and exile to the United States. He settled in Hawaii at the oceanside home of a wealthy Korean nurseryman along with his wife, Francesca [Donner], the daughter of a Viennese merchant he had met and married in Geneva in 1932.

In 1963, the Korean government announced that Rhee—until then unwelcome in his country—would be allowed to return. His health, however, was such that the trip was impossible. He died from complications of a stroke at the age of 90 on July 19, 1965, in Honolulu.

Shirley Sagawa
Political appointee

Appointed by President Bill Clinton, Shirley Sagawa is one of several Asian American women to serve in the executive branch of government.

Patricia Saiki (1930-)
Politician

Patricia Saiki has lived a life of public service. She was the first Republican to represent Hawaii, from 1987-1991, in the U.S. House of Representatives after it attained statehood in 1959. She was appointed in 1991 by President George Bush to head the U.S. Small Business Administration, an agency with 4,000 employees and a budget of $382 million. Saiki has taught at the Kennedy School of Government at Harvard University, and was an unsuccessful candidate for governor of Hawaii in 1994.

Patricia Fukuda Saiki was born May 28, 1930, in Hilo, Hawaii, the oldest of three girls born to Kazuo and Shizue (Inoue) Fukuda. Saiki's paternal grandfather had come to Hawaii from Japan and labored in the sugar cane fields, earning a dollar a day. Saiki's father worked as a clerk and her mother worked at home as a seamstress. Saiki was the first of her family to attend college, graduating with a double major in education and history from the University of Hawaii in 1952.

On June 19, 1954, Saiki married Stanley Mitsuo Saiki, a doctor twelve years her senior. Shortly after their marriage, the couple left Hawaii for the mainland when Saiki was pregnant with their first child, Stanley, Jr. The growing family then moved to Toledo, Ohio, for Stanley's residency and the birth of two more Saiki children, Sandra and Margaret. With three young children and her husband's meager pay as a resident, Saiki decided to return to teaching.

The Saikis returned to Hawaii in the late 1950s, just in time for statehood in 1959. There they welcomed

Patricia Saiki.

their fourth and fifth children, Stuart and Laura. Saiki entered the political arena as a precinct officer in St. Louis Heights. In the 1960s, while teaching at Kaimuki Intermediate School, Saiki helped to organize a teachers' union. She became increasingly active in politics, serving in a number of different capacities for the Republican party in Hawaii. In 1968, at the urging of her fellow teachers, Saiki ran for public office and was elected a delegate to the Hawaii State Constitutional Convention. The following year President Richard Nixon appointed Saiki to the Presidential Advisory Council on the Status of Women. She served on the committee for eight years and was reappointed by Nixon's successor President Gerald Ford. During that time, Saiki oversaw the funding of the Hawaii State Commission on the Status of Women and served as a watchdog for women's rights. She was elected to the Hawaii House of Representatives where she served from 1968 to 1974, and the Hawaii State Senate where she served from 1974 to 1982. She authored twenty-five bills dealing with equal rights for women, including the Equal Rights Amendment. In 1987, she was elected to the U. S. Congress and had the opportunity to work on a national level to address her concerns about women's and children's issues.

After a successful term as congresswoman, Saiki decided to run for the U. S. Senate. After losing lost her election bid, she accepted an appointment by president George Bush to head the U.S. Small Business Administration. Two weeks after being sworn in as the administrator of the SBA, Saiki's husband died. She continued in her capacity at the SBA until November 1992, when she decided to return to Hawaii to be near family. She wasn't home long, however, before she was offered a teaching post for spring 1993 by the Kennedy School of Government at Harvard University. The following year, she began an unsuccessful campaign for governor of Hawaii. The lifelong encouragement and support Saiki has received from family has served to make her an energetic supporter of issues concerning children and families.

Richard Sakakida (1920-)
Counterintelligence agent

Retired Lieutenant Colonel Richard M. Sakakida of the United States Air Force is a career military officer and a decorated undercover agent who worked as a counterintelligence agent in the Philippines from April 22, 1941, to September 20, 1945. During this time Sakakida was held as a prisoner by the Japanese, who repeatedly tortured him to find out his position with the U.S. military. He was eventually released by the Japanese, but continued to work among them, and used an underground network of Filipino guerrilla fighters to transmit intelligence to General Douglas MacArthur's command in Australia.

Richard M. Sakakida was born November 19, 1920, in Maui, Hawaii. His parents, both of Japanese descent, raised their three children—two sons and one daughter—in Honolulu. Sakakida graduated from Honolulu's McKinley High School in 1939, two years before the American involvement in the World War II. In 1941, nine months before the Japanese bombing of Pearl Harbor, Sakakida was sworn in as a sergeant in the Corps of Intelligence Police.

Sakakida was sent along with another Japanese American, Arthur Komori, to the Philippines on April 7, 1941. Sakakida moved into the Nishikawa Hotel in downtown Manila, where he posed as a representative of the Marsman Trading Company, Sears and Roebuck's outlet in the Philippines. On December 8, 1941, the Japanese air force bombed Manila, beginning their invasion of the islands. In the aftermath of the bombing, Japanese nationals were rounded up for detention by the American officials. Sakakida, whose mission was secret even to American officials in Manila, was arrested on suspicion of being a spy for Japan. He spent a few days in prison with his fellow agent Komori before being released by his superiors. After his

Richard M. Sakakida.

release, he began working in uniform translating military prison interrogations.

On May 6, 1942, the U.S. forces in the Philippines surrendered to Japan. Sakakida was arrested and spent six months in jail being interrogated by the Japanese who doubted his cover story of being an American deserter. They considered him a traitor and tortured him cruelly throughout his imprisonment, but they finally gave up and released him from prison. He was sent to work in the office of Colonel Nishiharu, the chief judge advocate of the Fourteenth Army Headquarters which allowed him privileged access to regulated documents. He began issuing visitor's passes to the families of Filipino guerrillas being held by the Japanese, thereby gaining access to the guerrillas themselves. Sakakida arranged a daring prison break that freed nearly five hundred guerrilla fighters.

In December of 1944 the United States launched its invasion of the Philippines. Sakakida joined up with a band of guerrillas in the jungle and was wounded in a battle and separated from the guerrillas. He wandered upon an American unit. The Americans were of course suspicious of Sakakida's story, but the major in charge checked it out and within hours a jeep from the counterintelligence corps was sent for him.

Scott M. Sassa.

Sakakida continued to work for the U.S. military from 1946 to 1948 in helping the intelligence community round up persons suspected of committing war crimes. Sakakida was awarded the Bronze Star Medal for his distinguished, selfless, and crucial service to the American military. From 1948 to 1975, Sakakida served the air force in its Office of Special Investigations (AFOSI) until his retirement on April 1, 1975. At the time of his retirement, he was commander of AFOSI in Japan.

In 1994, Sakakida was honored by the government of the Philippines with the Legion of Honor (Degree of Legionnaire) presidential award in recognition of his exceptionally meritorious service to the Filipino American Freedom Fighters and as a U.S. Army undercover agent.

Scott M. Sassa (1959-)
Broadcasting

Scott Sassa is one of the youngest executives in the television business. In less than ten years, he went from being a low-level employee at a public relations firm to president of Turner Entertainment Group with the start-up of two programming networks to his credit. The most successful of these was Turner Network Television (TNT), the largest launch in cable television history. TNT started with 17 million subscribers and in a short time has grown to its more than 57 million subscribers as of the mid-1990s. Sassa serves on the Turner Broadcasting System (TBS) board of directors, on the TBS executive committee and as TBS corporate vice-president of the Entertainment Group. He is responsible for all operations and programming for Turner Entertainment Networks, which includes TBS Superstation, TNT, the Cartoon Network, TNT Latin America, the Cartoon Network in Latin America, TNT and Cartoon Network in Europe, and Turner Home Entertainment. He also oversees Hanna-Barbera Productions, Turner Entertainment Company, and Turner Pictures Worldwide.

Scott Sassa was born on February 2, 1959, in Los Angeles and grew up in Hollywood. He attended University of Southern California but never completed his business degree since he did not get credit for a television internship he took during the 1980 election. Rather than contest the university's decision and officially get a diploma, Sassa decided to enter the workforce. A year later at a fraternity dinner in Los Angeles Sassa met a colleague who was leaving Turner and offered him his job. Sassa, at only age twenty-three, joined Turner in 1982 as assistant to Gerry Hogan, a Turner executive now with Whittle Communications. After some interim job changes, Sassa took the helm at TNT, creating a phenomenal success.

Sassa married Ellen Griffin on September 22, 1990. Sassa is now preparing for the hundreds of channels that will be competing for viewers in the future. According to Sassa there is not enough quality programming for the number of possible channels.

Bright Sheng (1954-)
Composer

In 1982, Bright Sheng made a decision that would alter the course of his life. He decided to leave the Shanghai Conservatory of Music, where he already had proven himself to be the school's most talented student, to try making it in music as an unknown in New York. He decided to give himself a test: if, after five years, he could get enough work as a composer to live in one room with a piano, he'd stay in the United States. Otherwise, he'd go back to China.

He was born Liang Sheng, December 6, 1954, in a suburb of Shanghai, to a relatively wealthy family. (*Liang* is a literal translation for Bright, which is how he began to identify himself after emigrating to the United States.) His grandfather owned nearly five thousand acres of rice fields, and at a time when many Chinese immigrants to the United States worked as laborers, he studied engineering at a U.S. university.

Bright Sheng. (Wah Lui.)

Pitambar Somani.

Sheng's father worked as a medical radiologist. The family's education and wealth made Western culture and arts a fixture around the household. Sheng began taking piano lessons at age four, first from his mother, then from a tutor. But in 1966, when he was eleven, the cultural revolution started, and his family's wealth and Western education suddenly came under suspicion. Members of the Communist party came to their apartment, took away the piano, and took over many rooms. In 1982, he joined his parents, who had left China in 1980, in the United States. He earned his master's of music at Queens College, and completed his doctorate in musical arts at Columbia University. While studying, Sheng also began writing and trying to find work as a composer. He could see he was very Chinese, with a deep understanding of the time-free joy of listening to an Asian musical piece slowly evolve. At the same time, all of his training was Western. Sheng is best known for his orchestral work *H'un*, which tells the story of how Mao Zedong systematically destroyed all free thought and creativity in China during the ten-year cultural revolution that began in 1966. The work was named as the first runner-up for a Pulitzer Prize in 1989. He came up with the theme—social tragedy and the cost a country must pay—and then tried to write a

melody, but a melodic line seemd too beautiful for such a sad theme. He eventually decided to leave out the melody and the piece was a thunderous success.

Sheng, whom some critics consider a Chinese Bartok, has served as composer-in-residence for the Lyric Opera of Chicago, where he composed his opera *The Song of Majnun*; the Santa Fe Chamber Music Festival, and La Jolla Chamber Music Summerfest. Sheng also was artistic director for the highly acclaimed "We Ink 93" festival in San Francisco, and composer-in-residence for two years with the Seattle Symphony Orchestra.

Pitambar "Peter" Somani (1937-)
Physician

Pitambar Somani is director of health at the Ohio Department of Health, making him the highest-ranking American of Asian Indian descent to serve in state government in the United States and the first to serve in a cabinet-level position. As director of health, Somani oversees an agency of 1500 employees and is responsible for the agency's mission of protecting and maintaining the health of all of Ohio's people. He is also a noted author and researcher and holds four U.S. patents.

Anna Sui. (Kevin Leong.)

Somani was born on October 31, 1937, in Chirawah, India, the youngest of four children. His father, Shri Narendra Kumar Somani, was a well-regarded headmaster of the local high school. When Somani was one year old, his family moved to Gwalior, in central India, where Somani grew up. As a senior in high school, Somani surprised his family by scoring the second highest marks in the state on a college entrance exam. In 1955, he enrolled in the G.R. Medical College of Vikram University in Gwalior, India, and five years later received his M.D. He graduated at the top of his class, earning honors in six subjects in the medical curriculum. He also continued to participate in organized athletics, playing on the university's field hockey team, and winning the G.R. Medical College table tennis championships five years in a row.

After medical school, Somani enrolled in the All India Institute of Medical Sciences, where he completed his medical training in 1962. In that year he immigrated to the United States with his wife and newborn daughter as a postdoctoral fellow of the Wisconsin Heart Association at Marquette University in Milwaukee, Wisconsin. In 1965, Somani earned a Ph.D. in pharmacology from Marquette.

In 1980, Somani was appointed director of the division of clinical pharmacology and professor of medicine and pharmacology at the Medical College of Ohio at Toledo. His clinical research concentrated on beta blockers, and other groundbreaking drugs, such as calcium channel blockers, anti-arrhythmic drugs, cholesterol lowering agents, and drugs for congestive heart failure.

In 1989, Somani took a sabbatical from the Medical College of Ohio to serve as a United Nation's technical adviser to the government of Thailand to help establish cardiovascular research laboratories that would be used to test traditional Thai medicines for their usefulness in treating high blood pressure and heart failure.

In 1991, Somani was appointed by Ohio's governor, George Voinovich, to be the assistant director of health. And, in 1992, when the director stepped down, Somani was given that position. Some of Somani's initiatives include providing funding for families of hemophiliacs to help them purchase and maintain adequate private insurance coverage; funding a program to immunize poor and indigent infants against hepatitis-B; creating the Women's Health Initiatives, one of the first offices of its kind in the United States; and establishing the Medicare Balance Billing Program, which protects Medicare patients from being overbilled.

Somani is married to Kamlesh, also a native of Gwalior, India. The couple has three children.

Anna Sui (1955-)
Fashion designer

Anna Sui made a name for herself in the highly competitive world of fashion design in an almost word-of-mouth way. Her eccentric, kitschy designs attained a cult-like following among pop-culture icons such as Madonna, Lady Miss Kier of Dee-Lite, and internationally famous models like Naomi Campbell and Linda Evangelista. Sui runs a $1.75-million business selling fashion in over 200 department stores in the United States, Canada, Japan, and Europe, as well as her own retail outlet in Manhattan's Soho district.

Anna Sui was born in Dearborn, Michigan, to first-generation Chinese American parents. Her father, Paul Sui, is a structural engineer and her mother, Grace Sui, is a homemaker who once studied painting in Paris. She became interested in fashion early in life and would create elaborate tissue-paper dresses for her brothers' toy soldiers, pretending they were on their way to her imaginary version of the Academy Awards. Sui herself became a flamboyant dresser while still young, gaining a reputation as an eccentric in her junior high school, developing what would later become a Sui trademark: outfits with matching shoes, hats, and handbags. She was voted the best-dressed student in her ninth-grade class.

In 1980, after studying at Parsons School of Design and working with fashion photographers as a stylist, she showed six original Lycra garments and received an order from Macy's, the giant New York retailer. The store eventually used one of these designs in an advertisement in the *New York Times*. This early success encouraged Sui's ambitions and in that same year she launched a design business, out of her apartment. "There were boxes piled up to the ceiling, and we were shipping clothes out of here," she told *Vogue* in 1992.

In 1991 she reached a landmark in the fashion-design business: her first runway show, due in part, to the encouragement of her old friends, photographer Steven Meisel and public relations executive Paul Cavaco. Writing about the show in the *New York Times*, Woody Hochswender said of Ms. Sui's designs that, "There was a fashion collision Wednesday evening. It looked as if Sly and the Family Stone crashed into Coco Chanel and then got rear-ended by Christian Lacroix. The show, the first by Anna Sui, was a riot." In February of 1993, she was awarded the coveted Perry Ellis Award for New Fashion Talent.

Today, Anna Sui continues to create some of the liveliest, most engagingly original designs in current fashion. She has steadfastly refused to allow her prices to skyrocket along with her fame—an Anna Sui jacket sells for about half the price of those of comparably prominent designers.

Betty Lee Sung (1924-)
Academician

Betty Lee Sung is a highly regarded scholar of Asian American studies. Her 1967 book, *Mountain of Gold*, detailing the Chinese immigrant experience in America, was a landmark in the field of ethnic studies, having received excellent reviews and selling surprisingly well for an essentially academic book. Dr. Sung has written eight other books and contributes extensively to magazines, journals, and anthologies. Until her retirement in 1992, she chaired the department of Asian American studies at the City College of New York.

Betty Lee Sung was born in Baltimore, Maryland, on October 3, 1924 to Chinese parents. She spent her early childhood living in both China and the United States. While living in China, her mother died and the family was forced to flee the country. They settled in the Washington, D.C., area where Betty's father worked as a laundryman.

Ms. Sung earned a bachelor's degree in both economics and sociology from the University of Illinois in 1948. She worked as a scriptwriter for the Voice of America after college, writing about the Chinese immigrant experience in the United States—a topic about which she could find little reliable, scholarly, objective information. She worked at the Voice of America until

Betty Lee Sung. (Corky Lee.)

1954 when she left the workforce to devote herself to raising her children, which she considers to be, by far, the most important of her life achievements.

In 1964, Ms. Sung returned to work outside the home, taking various jobs in the publishing industry. In 1967, she wrote *Mountain of Gold* in response to the frustration she had encountered while doing research for the Voice of America and as an attempt to establish an accurate historical record of Chinese contributions to the building of the United States, especially in the West.

In 1970, Ms. Sung was hired as an assistant professor of Asian American studies at the City College of New York. Her 1976 book, *Survey of Chinese American Manpower and Employment*, won recognition as the Outstanding Book of the Year by *Choice* magazine, the foremost reviewing magazine for academic libraries. Other books she has written include *Album of Chinese Americans* (1977), *Adjustment Experience of Chinese Immigrant Children In New York City* (1987), and *Chinese Intermarriage* (1990).

Ms. Sung earned a master's degree in library sciences from Queens College in 1968, and a Ph.D. in 1983 from City College. In 1992, she retired as chair of the department of Asian American studies at City College

Bob Suzuki.

and is currently working with a National Endowment for the Humanities grant to convert 581 boxes of Chinese immigration records to computer databases which, she uncovered while doing research on the history of New York's Chinatown.

Bob Suzuki (1936-)
University administrator

Bob Suzuki was named president of California State Polytechnic University at Pomona in September 1991. He came to the post with impressive credentials: bachelor's and master's degrees in mechanical engineering; a Ph.D. in aeronautics; a solid background in administration, teaching and community service; and a lengthy list of published materials. And, like many distinguished Japanese Americans, Suzuki's resume includes a strong background in political and civil rights work. This stems, in many ways, from some of his earliest and most painful childhood memories: World War II and years spent in relocation camps.

Bob Suzuki was born January 2, 1936, in Portland, Oregon, to Japanese immigrants. When World War II started, he and his family were forced under armed guards to board a train bound for a relocation camp in

southern Idaho. Suzuki was only six years old. For three years, the family lived in the Idaho desert behind a fence of barbed wire and guard towers. Some of the time was spent living in stalls used to exhibit farm animals. Suzuki received his first three years of schooling in the internment camps. After World War II ended, Suzuki's family left the relocation camps and settled in Spokane, Washington, where they raised cucumbers, lettuce, and strawberries. When the crops failed, the family didn't eat. Although Suzuki's mother had only an eighth grade education she taught Suzuki the value of a good education. He was student body president in high school and graduated as class valedictorian. He then went on to the University of California at Berkeley where he received a bachelor of science degree in 1960 in mechanical engineering, and a master's degree in 1962. He worked for two years as a research engineer for Boeing Aircraft in Seattle before returning to graduate school at the California Institute of Technology in Pasadena, where he completed his doctorate in aeronautics. He then went on to teach aerospace engineering at the University of Southern California (USC).

Suzuki served as chair of the national education commission of the Japanese American Citizens League (JACL), and as vice-governor of the Pacific Southwest Division of the JACL. In this position, he initiated action that eventually led to the inclusion of Asian Americans as a protected group in federally-mandated affirmative action and equal opportunity programs.

In 1971, Suzuki decided to devote himself full time to work that would directly address societal problems. He took a job in the School of Education at the University of Massachusetts in Amherst teaching science/math education, Asian American studies, and urban education. Two months after his arrival, he was appointed assistant dean for administration in the School of Education, a position he held for over three years before he decided to return full-time to teaching and research.

Since the early 1980s, Suzuki has become a nationally recognized expert on multicultural education. He was, for instance, among the first scholars to break down the "model minority" myth, which portrayed Asian Americans as ideal immigrants, often pitting their ability to blend into mainstream culture, against African Americans, who for centuries have been unable to do so. His knowledge makes him a frequent keynote speaker at conferences and symposiums, as well as a seminar leader and multicultural consultant to numerous school and community groups throughout the United States.

Suzuki remained at the University of Massachusetts at Amherst until January 1981, when he returned to academic administration, serving as dean of graduate studies and research at California State University in

Los Angeles from 1981 to July 1985. He then became vice-president for academic affairs at California State University in Northridge. Before joining California Polytechnic University, Suzuki spent months reading about campus issues and formulating ideas, and pledged to step up programs to recruit and retain minority students and to help organize workshops and seminars on multicultural issues. "I'm not the type of administrator who's satisfied with the *status quo*," he told the *Los Angeles Times* in 1991. "I will push the campus toward change."

Shirin R. Tahir-Kheli (1944-)
Ambassador, academician

In 1995, Dr. Shirin Tahir-Kheli was working on her autobiography *Ambassador from Where?*—a question she was often asked when serving as an ambassador at the United States Mission to the United Nations. Tahir-Kheli's career is marked by many "firsts"—the first Asian ambassador to represent the United States at the United Nations; the first Muslim ambassador to represent the United States at the United Nations; the first Muslim senior government official appointed by the President and confirmed by the Senate, to name a few. She is also one of the few women in the field of national security, which is usually dominated by men with a military background.

Shirin Tahir-Kheli was born in Hyderabad, India, in 1944. Her grandfather was the premier minister to the nizam of Hyderabad. The family moved to Pakistan when Hyderabad lost its independence during the partition of India. Her father, who had always encouraged Tahir-Kheli to pursue her interests, became the vice-chancellor of Peshawar University—one of Pakistan's premier academic institutions.

Tahir-Kheli's initial career choice was textile design. Since cotton textiles were the upcoming industry in Pakistan, she initially completed a bachelor of arts in textile design at Ohio Wesleyan University in 1961 at the age of seventeen. The dire predictions of family and friends that sending a young girl to study in the United States would lead to disaster turned out to be untrue when Tahir-Kheli returned to Pakistan and married Dr. Reza Tahir-Kheli, a nuclear physicist. Following her husband back to the United States, Tahir-Kheli switched careers to study international relations at the University of Pennsylvania where her husband taught.

The first phase of Tahir-Kheli's career was in academics. She taught at Temple University as an assistant and then associate professor from 1973 to 1985. She resign from tenure when she took up the second phase of her career—in government. She has published extensively on Pakistan's foreign policy, U.S. policy in South and Southwest Asia, and the former Soviet Union's policy in Afghanistan. In 1982 she was asked to

Shirin Tahir-Khel.

join the Office of the Secretary of State as a member of the policy planning staff. She was later made director of political-military affairs (1984 to 1986) and subsequently director of Near East and South Asian affairs (1986 to 1989). Her tenure in government culminated in her appointment as ambassador and alternate U.S. representative for special political affairs to the United Nations (1990 to 1993). Tahir-Kheli also felt pressure from people in both Pakistan and India on her role as representing the interests and goals of the United States. Tahir-Kheli definitely sees her experience as a role model for other Asian Americans, particularly women. She became a U.S. citizen as soon as she was eligible in 1971 and credits her clarity of purpose as the key to her success in government.

When George Bush lost the 1992 presidential election to Bill Clinton, Tahir-Kheli returned to academia and policy analysis. She is currently a fellow at the Center of International Studies at Princeton University, and she cochairs a study group on "The Future of United States Policy in India and Pakistan." She is also working on an initiative on technical cooperation between India and Pakistan on energy/environment issues, while working on her autobiography.

Ronald Takaki. (Carol Takaki.)

Ronald Takaki (1939-)
Academician, historian, writer

Ronald Takaki is a well-regarded professor and scholar in the area of multicultural studies and history. Takaki's first professorial post took him to the University of California at Los Angeles where he taught the school's first African American history course. During his five years at UCLA, he helped found its centers for African American, Asian American, Chicano and Native American studies. In 1972, Takaki returned to Berkeley where had earned his Ph.D. to serve as chairperson of the ethnic studies department and to help found the first Ph.D. program in ethnic studies in the United States.

In 1979, Takaki published the critically acclaimed study, *Iron Cages: Race and Culture in Nineteenth Century America*. His fifth book, *Strangers from a Different Shore: A History of Asian Americans*, received numerous awards, including a 1989 Pulitzer Prize nomination for nonfiction, the Gold Medal for nonfiction by the Commonwealth Club of California, and Notable Book of 1989 by the *New York Times Book Review*. In 1993, his publication of *A Different Mirror: A History of Multicultural America*, covering the years from the founding of Jamestown in 1607 to the end of the Cold War in the 1990s, received similar praise.

Born on April 12, 1939, Ronald Takaki grew up in a working class, multiethnic neighborhood in Honolulu, Hawaii. His mother was second-generation Japanese American and his father was first-generation. At the age of five, Takaki failed the entry exam to the local English standard school, a school system he would need to attend for future college entry. In the fifth grade, Takaki's parents transferred him to a private school. Takaki recalled that as a teenager, he wasn't too interested in academics. His parents owned a restaurant on Waikiki Beach, and when he finished his tasks of cutting onions and peeling shrimp, he would go surfing. During his senior year in high school, a teacher recommended that Takaki go to a small liberal arts college on the mainland, and he wrote on Takaki's behalf to the dean of the College of Wooster in Ohio, where Takaki was accepted as one of only two Asian Americans in a student body of approximately one thousand. At Wooster, Takaki studied history and went on to graduate school at the University of California, Berkeley in the 1960s, where he got swept up in the civil rights movement. In the fall of 1967, Takaki joined the faculty at UCLA where he offered the school's first

African American history course, and became involved in organizing the Black Students Union, acting as the group's faculty adviser. He was also actively involved with the Chicano and Asian American students. After two years of teaching African American history, Takaki developed another ground-breaking course, "The History of Racial Inequality," a comparative study of inequality across various minority groups.

Although Berkeley is home base, Takaki has also been invited to lecture at universities throughout the United States, including Cornell University. In 1988, he was awarded the Goldwin Smith University Lectureship at Cornell and, in 1993, he was the Distinguished Messenger Lecturer, which is Cornell's most prestigious lecturer appointment. In addition, Takaki has made numerous television appearances, including NBC's "Today Show," ABC's "Good Morning America," CNN's "International Hour," PBS's "McNeil/Lehrer Report" and many others.

Jokichi Takamine (1854-1922)
Chemist

Jokichi Takamine was the chemist responsible for the isolation of adrenalin—the first of the gland hormones to be discovered in pure form—from the suprarenal gland in 1901. Takamine's discovery has benefitted the advancement of medicine and surgery in incalculable ways.

Takamine was born in Takakao, Japan, in 1854. His father was a physician, as were many of his ancestors. In 1884, he first visited the United States as one of Japan's commissioners to the International Cotton Centennial Exposition in New Orleans. It was here that Mr. Takamine met his future wife, Caroline Field Hitch, the daughter of an American colonel. In 1890, he moved to the United States to attempt to find commercial applications for his discovery, Takadiastase, a powerful starch-digesting enzyme. He first tried the distilling industry, but found little success. In 1894, the production of his enzyme was taken over by the pharmaceutical manufacturer Parke Davis, and Co. of Detroit, which used it for medicinal purposes.

Around 1900, Takamine focused on furthering relations between Japan and the United States. He became cofounder and president of the Japanese Association of New York and the Nippon Club. He was honored by the Imperial University of Japan in 1899, 1906, and 1912; became a member of the Royal Academy of Science in 1913; received the Fourth Order of the Rising Sun in 1915 and the Senior Degree of the Fourth Rank (Sho Shii) and the Third Merit (Kum Santo) in 1922. He was also influential in the creation of the Imperial Research Institute in Japan in 1913. At his death in 1922, he was survived by his wife and their two sons.

George Takei.

George Takei (1940-)
Actor

George Takei is a television, theater, and film actor who is best known for his portrayal of Sulu in the *Star Trek* television series of the late 1960s and the *Star Trek* films of the 1970s and 1980s.

George Hosato Takei was born on April 20, 1940, in Los Angeles to second-generation Japanese Americans. When he was one year old the Takeis were sent to a prison camp in Arkansas for most of World War II. After graduation from high school, Takei enrolled in the University of California at Berkeley, where he intended to study architecture, in deference to his parents who persuaded him against pursuing acting.

However, after his second year of college, Takei transferred to the University of California at Los Angeles (UCLA) and switched his major to acting. Shortly thereafter he was contacted by an agent who landed him a role in a Playhouse 90 episode called "Made in Japan." He was soon cast in small parts in television shows like *Hawaiian Eye* and *77 Sunset Strip*.

After graduation from UCLA, Takei lived briefly in New York, where he starred in a small production of the play *Fly Blackbird*. After touring Europe, he enrolled in the master's program in theater arts at UCLA. It was then that his agent called him to say that the producer Gene Rodenberry wanted to interview him for the role of the astrophysicist Sulu in a potential series called *Star Trek*.

The interview went well, and Takei was offered the part. Early into the first *Star Trek* season his role was changed, however, from that of an astrophysicist to helmsman to get Takei's character, whom the producers found intriguing, into the thick of the action on the bridge with the other main characters. The show lasted only three seasons but inspired a tremendous cult following. Conventions of "trekkies," as they came to be known, were held around the country for years after the show was cancelled and continue to be held today.

After the show's demise, Takei became involved in civic and community affairs in a more visible way. He began hosting a local talk show on the Los Angeles Public Broadcasting Service station called "Expressions: East/West." He also became active in local Democratic politics and served as a delegate to the 1972 Democratic National Convention in Miami Beach. In 1973, he ran unsuccessfully for the Los Angeles city council seat vacated by Tom Bradley when he was elected mayor. For the remainder of the 1970s, Takei worked in a variety of television shows including Kung Fu, Ironside, The Six Million Dollar Man, Chico and the Man, Hallmark Hall of Fame, and The Blacksheep Squadron.

With a huge body of dedicated fans, it was only a matter of time before another *Star Trek* project was put together. In 1979, Paramount released *Star Trek—The Motion Picture*, in which Takei revived his role of Sulu. Takei also wrote a book entitled *Mirror Friend, Mirror Foe* in collaboration with the science-fiction writer Robert Asprin. It was published by Playboy Press in 1980 and did remarkably well. Despite unfavorable reviews, *Star Trek: The Motion Picture* also did well at the box office and spawned a series of sequels: *Star Trek II: The Wrath of Khan* in 1982, *Star Trek III: The Search for Spock* in 1984, and *Star Trek IV: The Voyage Home* in 1986, all by Paramount.

In addition to his role as Sulu in the *Star Trek* films, George Takei has played in several foreign-film productions and in the theater in New York. In 1991, he starred in *The Wash*, a play written by Philip Kan Gotanda, a prominent Asian American playwright.

Amy Tan
See Literature

Thomas Tang (1922-)
Judge

Thomas Tang is an appellate court judge serving the Ninth Circuit Court of Appeals, a position he has held since 1977. The nation's highest-ranking Chinese American federal judge, Tang is currently fourth in seniority among the 28 active judges on the Ninth Circuit, the jurisdiction of which covers nine western states.

Tang was born on January 11, 1922, in Phoenix, Arizona, to second-generation Chinese immigrants. When the Korean War broke out, Tang, who had remained in the military reserves, was recalled into action. He served mostly in Tokyo as a military intelligence officer, but also served time on the Korean peninsula interrogating prisoners in Pusan, among other duties. Upon his discharge in 1953, Tang was appointed the deputy county attorney for Maricopa County (Arizona). In this position, he prosecuted criminal cases on behalf of the state. Tang served in this position until 1957 when he was appointed assistant attorney general of the state of Arizona, where he represented the state in appeals. In 1960, Tang left the attorney general's office to go into private practice. He entered politics and was elected to the Phoenix city council, where he served two terms. In his second term, he was elected by his fellow councilmen to the position of vice-mayor, which he held until 1963 when he was elected to the superior court of Arizona for Maricopa County. There he heard both civil and criminal cases on the state level. He served on the trial bench for eight years, leaving in 1970 to return to private practice. Also at this time, he sat on the Arizona State Bar Board of Governors and in 1977 was elected that organization's president.

Tang was appointed to the U.S. Court of Appeals for the Ninth Circuit in October of 1977. He was nominated under President Jimmy Carter's new merit-selection system. Other presidents had allowed senators to recommend appointees, which often resulted in cronyism. The merit system allowed the local legal community—lawyers, judges, and law professors—to nominate persons they recognized as the most qualified for judicial appointments. Tang was one of five persons recommended for the Ninth Circuit appointment, and then chosen as judge by the President.

Doan Van Toai (1946-)
Writer

Doan Van Toai is a Vietnamese exile who came to national prominence in the mid-1980s as the author of three books chronicling the oppression of the communist regime in Vietnam that took power after the United States left Vietnam. His books, *Portrait of the Enemy*, *A Vietcong Memoir*, and *The Vietnamese Gulag*, had a major impact on international recognition of human rights abuses in the postwar Vietnam.

Doan Van Toai was born in a small village in the Mekong Delta called Cai Von on September 14, 1946. As a young man Toai became politicized by the warring and violence rampant in his homeland, and he began to work intermittently with the Vietnam underground in the south, a loose confederation of groups that sought

Doan Van Toai. (Trung Doan.)

In 1975, Toai took a job with the provisional government set up in the South after the final victory of the North that year. Later in the year, he was arrested by the government and held in "reeducation" camps for over two years, although he was never charged with any crime. Then one day—November 1, 1977—without explanation, he was released and told to go to France, where his wife and children had already gone.

In 1979, Toai moved permanently to the United States, where he enrolled in the Fletcher School of Law and Diplomacy at Tufts University outside of Boston. Toai remained at Tufts for three years. In 1983, he became a research associate for the Institute of East Asian Affairs at the University of California at Berkeley. In 1987, he served for one year as the program analyst at the Institute for Foreign Policy Analysis in Cambridge, Massachusetts. That year, he also became executive director of the Institute for Democracy in Vietnam, a post he holds still. As of mid-1994, Mr. Toai was director of the International Program at the Southern California University for Professional Studies.

Toai has written extensively on both his experiences in Vietnam and the field of international relations. He has coauthored three books, all in collaboration with David Chanoff: *A Vietcong Memoir* (1986), *The Vietnamese Gulag* (1986), and *Portrait of the Enemy* (1987). He is also the editor and publisher of *Vietnam Update*, an English-language journal covering events in Vietnam.

to undermine the South Vietnamese regime of Ngo Dinh Diem. After the 1963 coup that deposed Diem, Toai spoke at a rally in celebration of the event at his high school.

Toai began studies at Saigon University in 1964, studying in the school of pharmacy. While a student he formed a newspaper for pharmacy students called *Hoa Sung*. In 1966, he worked for an aide of Senator Edward Kennedy interviewing war refugees in central Vietnam. In 1969, Toai founded an opposition magazine called *Tu Quyet*, *(Self-Determination)*. The magazine became a leading voice of the opposition parties who were allied under an umbrella organization called the National Liberation Front, or more simply, "the Front." Toai himself resisted joining the group, but he continued work as a student activist and contributed to each issue of *Tu Quyet*.

In 1971, Toai got married and took a job with the Nam Do bank as a manager. He worked in various branches around the country, using his position to discreetly aid the Front in subverting the government. Other than these small forays into politics, Toai's involvement in the war and the antigovernment forces was minimal over the next few years.

Tamlyn Tomita (1966-)
Actress

Tamlyn Tomita is one of the most recognized Asian American faces on the big screen. She played Ralph Macchio's love interest in *The Karate Kid, Part II* (1986), Dennis Quaid's wife in *Come See the Paradise* (1990), and the adult Waverly, the chess prodigy, in the film adaptation of *The Joy Luck Club* (1993).

Born in 1966 in Okinawa, Japan, to a second-generation Japanese American father and a Japanese Filipino mother, Tamlyn Tomita arrived in the United States at age three months with her parents. Growing up in the San Fernando Valley in southern California, Tomita went to the University of California at Los Angeles (UCLA) to study history. While a student at UCLA, Tomita attended a Japanese American festival in Los Angeles where she met, Helen Funai who would later become her manager. Funai suggested that Tomita audition for a role in the upcoming *The Karate Kid, Part II*, and Tomita won the role. After this first role, Tomita began taking acting lessons, practicing her craft in television roles, including *Santa Barbara, Quantum Leap, The Trials of Rosie O'Neill, Raven*, and *Tour of Duty*. Tomita also had starring roles in *Vietnam, Texas* with

Eugene Huu-Chau Trinh.

Dr. Haing Ngor and *Hawaiian Dream*, the first Japanese-produced film shot entirely in the United States.

In 1990, Tomita starred opposite Dennis Quaid in Alan Parker's *Come See the Paradise*, the story a Japanese American family interned during World War II. Filming *Come See the Paradise* was a personal journey for Tomita. Her father and his family were interned at Manzanar, California, during the war years,

In 1993, Tomita portrayed the adult Waverly, a child chess prodigy, in the adaptation of Amy Tan's blockbuster bestseller, *The Joy Luck Club*. The film, directed by veteran Chinese American Wayne Wang and produced by Oliver Stone and Janet Yang, was the first mainstream Hollywood film with a virtually all-Asian cast.

When Tomita is not in front of the camera, she continues to learn new roles for the theatre. In January 1994, she played in the world premiere of Philip Kan Gotanda's *Day Standing on Its Head* at the Manhattan Theatre Club in New York. Other theatre credits include the world premiere of *Nagasaki Dust* for the Philadelphia Theatre Company, *Don Juan: A Meditation* for the Mark Taper Forum's Taper Too and the title role in *Winter Crane* at the Fountain Theatre, for which Tomita received a Drama-Logue Award. Tomita is a charter member of the Antaeus Project, an actor-run classical

repertory company assisted by the Mark Taper Forum/ Center Theatre Group.

Eugene Huu-Chau Trinh (1950-)
Physicist, astronaut

Eugene Trinh is a physicist and astronaut who flew as a payload specialist aboard the space shuttle as a member of STS-50, the first microgravity laboratory mission. In addition to his work for NASA, Dr. Trinh is a highly regarded physicist working in the field of fluid dynamics. He holds three patents and has been widely published.

Eugene Huu-Chau Trinh was born in Saigon on September 14, 1950. At the age of two, Trinh's father sent his family to live in Paris. Trinh was educated in the French public school system and came to the United States in 1968 to attend Columbia University, to which he had won a full academic scholarship.

Trinh graduated from Columbia in 1972 with a bachelor's of science degree in mechanical engineering and applied physics. In 1974, he earned a master's of science degree applied physics, a master's of philosophy in 1975, and a Ph.D., also in applied physics, in 1977, all from Yale University. After completing his doctoral dissertation, Trinh remained at Yale where he worked as a postdoctoral fellow for one year. He then moved to the Jet Propulsion Laboratory (JPL) at Cal-Tech, where he conducted laboratory based experimental research in fluid mechanics.

Dr. Trinh first applied to work aboard the space shuttle in 1983 as part of a group of physicists headed by Taylor Wang that was preparing the Drop Dynamics Module experiment for Spacelab 3. Wang was selected as the payload specialist for the 1985 flight, with Dr. Trinh as his backup. The next NASA mission that Dr. Trinh was involved in was the U.S. Microgravity Laboratory 1 (USML-1), scheduled to be launched in June of 1992.

The experiments Dr. Trinh performed in space concerned the surface tension of liquids in low gravity. They allowed scientists to probe the magnitude of surface tension, to test the strength of this bond in a condition that does not occur on earth, and to observe the dynamics of oscillating liquid globes or bubbles. Dr. Trinh's space experiments can help scientists understand the ocean's movement and how it transfers gases to the atmosphere, and vice versa.

Yoshiko Uchida
See Literature

Huynh Cong Ut (1951-)
News photographer

Huynh Cong "Nick" Ut is an award-winning photojournalist, known best for his work with the Associated

Huynh Cong Ut.

David M. Valderrama.

Press during the Vietnam War. In 1972, he took a photograph of a nine-year-old Vietnamese girl, Kim Phuc, running down a dirt road near Trang Bang, Vietnam, after her family home had been hit and burned by Napalm—the chemical used to destroy the thick jungle foliage that hid the North Vietnamese so effectively in guerrilla warfare. The photo, which clearly documented the indiscriminate horror of war was widely reproduced around the world, won nearly every major photojournalism award, including the Pulitzer Prize and the George Polk Memorial Award, and fueled the anti-war movement.

Huynh Cong Ut was born on March 29, 1951, to a family of rice farmers in rural Long An Province, southwest of Saigon in the Mekong Delta. Huynh covered the Vietnam War for the Associated Press until the fall of Saigon in 1975. In 1977, he was transferred to Los Angeles, again as a general assignment photographer, where he continues to work today.

David Valderrama (1933-)
Politician, lawyer

David M. Valderrama, a naturalized American, was the first probate judge in the United States of Filipino ancestry. As a Delegate to the Assembly of Maryland,

he is also the first high ranking Filipino elected official in mainland United States.

Born in Manila, Philippines, David Valderrama was 27 when he came to the United States to study for a masters degree in law. Valderrama received his Bachelor of Laws degree from Far Eastern University, Manila, Philippines and his Master of Comparative Law degree from George Washington University, Washington, D.C. When the Japanese invaded the Philippines, which was then under American rule, David Valderrama's father refused to serve the Japanese government. So his hands and legs were cut off and he was brutally executed.

After practicing law in the Philippines, Valderrama emigrated to the United States in 1961. His first political task was to manage the campaigns for Maryland Democratic candidates running for United States Congress. In 1985, Governor Harry Hughes of Maryland appointed Valderrama to serve the remainder of an unexpired term as Judge of the Orphans' Court, an elected position. In 1986, he stood for election and won overwhelmingly in a field of 11 candidates. Following his election, Valderrama became the Maryland State representative to the National College of Probate Judges and the Orphans' Court Liaison Judge from Prince George's County to the Maryland General Assembly.

Three and a half years into his second term, Valderrama resigned as judge to run for the Delegate to the Maryland General Assembly. When he won, he became the first and highest ranking Filipino Americn elected official in the United States.

Valderrama serves on a number of boards, including the Board of Directors of the Southern Christian Leadership Conference (Prince George's Chapter). He is a member of the NAACP, Common Cause, MD Network Against Domestic Violence, and a number of Asian cultural, business, and professional organizations. His legislative committees include, Constitutional and Administrative Law, Environmental Matters, and Law Enforcement. He was also a part of the 1992 Presidential campaign as a National Surrogate Speaker for President Bill Clinton.

David Valderrama is married to Nellie and has two daughters: Kriselda, born in 1971, who is studying respiratory therapy in Salisbury, Maryland, and Vida, born in 1973, a graduate of American University (with high honors) where she majored in economics and political science.

Phillip Villamin Vera Cruz (1904-1994)
Labor leader

Phillip Villamin Vera Cruz was a longtime leader of the farmworkers union movement, which began in the 1960s to unite the immigrant, itinerant workers, who do much of the backbreaking low-wage work on a majority of large nongrain farms in the United States. Vera Cruz led the successful sit-down strike in the vineyards of Coachella, California, in 1965—one of the first organized work stoppages among agricultural laborers in the United States. The galvanizing event led to the creation of the United Farmworkers of America.

Phillip Villamin Vera Cruz was born on December 25, 1904, in Ilacos Sur province in the Philippines. He emigrated to the United States in 1926, in the wave of Filipino immigration that followed the government's ban on Chinese and Japanese workers. From the time of his arrival in the United States until the mid-1960s when Vera Cruz began organizing farmworkers, he worked on these farms throughout California and the country.

In 1965, Vera Cruz began his work as a labor activist when he joined the Agricultural Workers Organizing Committee (AWOC) of the AFL-CIO. He was very active in this union and later that year helped organize the aforementioned strike against Coachella vineyard owners. The strike was successful and the tactic spread with the union organizing a similar action later that year in Delano, California. This strike brought together labor leaders from various organizations, and with its successful resolution the United Farmworkers of America (UFW) was born.

In the 1970s, Vera Cruz helped build a retirement village for single, farmworkers who, like himself, had been unable to marry due to anti-miscegenation laws and found themselves alone after a lifetime of backbreaking field work. The site Vera Cruz chose for the facility was the grounds of the United Farmworkers' headquarters in Delano. The complex, built almost entirely by volunteer labor, opened in 1975 and was called Agabayani Village, after Paul Agabayani, a farmworker who was shot to death during the strike.

Vera Cruz resigned from the UFW in 1977 and moved to Bakersfield, California, two years later, where he stayed until his death in 1994. In 1989, the government of the Philippines awarded Vera Cruz the first Ninoy M. Aquino award for lifelong service to the Filipino community in America.

John D. Waihee (1946-)
Governor

John D. Waihee was Hawaii's fourth elected governor, the first of Hawaiian ancestry. His second term as governor ended in 1994, and state term limit laws prohibited him from running for re-election. When Waihee was first elected in 1986, after edging out a favored Democrat in the state's primary, he was widely regarded as a rising political star.

Waihee was born May 19, 1946, in Honokaa, on the island of Hawaii. His father worked as a telephone company line worker. His mother, born Mary Parker Purdy, was a descendant of a Massachusetts sailor who eventually became an adviser to King Kamehameha I. After earning his bachelor's degree in history and business from Andrews University in Michigan, Waihee returned to Hawaii to become a member of the first graduating class of the William S. Richardson School of Law. He practiced law at a Hawaiian firm for four years, before starting his own law practice in 1979.

In 1972, at age twenty-six, he joined a renegade political force called "Coalition 72" which attempted to challenge the Democratic party leadership at the party's state convention. The challenge failed and placed Waihee firmly outside the political establishment. Six years later, at the state's 1978 Constitutional Convention, he shrewdly brought together the old-time political establishment with young activists and emerged from the convention as a clear leader.

Waihee was elected to the state House of Representatives in 1980, and two years later, jumped into a race for lieutenant governor, challenging a front-runner, then-state senator Dennis O'Connor. Four years later, he entered the gubernatorial race and won the race, narrowly defeating a political favorite. In his eight years as governor, Waihee takes credit for promoting a tax-reduction program that resulted in the return of $700 million to taxpayers. He also has worked to reform education so that schools are managed at the local level. A $200 million program championed by Waihee resulted in increased levels of affordable housing. And during Waihee's tenure, Hawaii grew rapidly and boasted one of the lowest unemployment rates in the nation.

Waihee and his wife, Lynne Kobashigawa Waihee have two children, Jennifer and John.

An Wang (1920–1990)
Inventor, entrepreneur, philanthropist

From an initial investment of $600, An Wang, inventor of the magnetic core memory (an instrumental component of early computers), built a one-person electrical fixtures store into one of the most successful businesses in U.S. history. From its inception in 1951 through the late 1980s, Wang Laboratories grew at an astonishing annual rate of 42 percent, becoming one of the giants in the computer business. In 1984, Wang and his family owned approximately 55 percent of the company stock. His personal wealth was estimated to be $1.6 billion by *Forbes* magazine, making him at the time the fifth-richest person in the United States. Wang was of Chinese descent.

Charles Pei Wang (1940-)
Social worker, political appointee

As head of the Chinese American Planning Council (CPC) in New York City for more than twenty years, Charles Pei Wang was instrumental in making the CPC one of the largest and most prominent social service agencies for the Chinese American community. He has worked tirelessly on behalf of Chinese Americans on the local, state, and national level, and in 1990 was appointed by former President George Bush to a five-year term as vice-chairman of the U.S. Commission on Civil Rights.

Charles Pei Wang was born in 1940, during World War II, in the small town of Baipei in China. His father added the middle name "Pei" to his name because he wanted his son to remember where he was born. Wang's family traveled from place to place until the war was over and eventually settled in Taiwan.

As the ninth in a family of eleven children—five boys and six girls—Wang received a lot of help from his siblings. Following Asian traditions, his older brothers and sisters, who were all educated and working, supported him both emotionally and financially throughout his schooling.

Wang studied Chinese language and literature at Cheng Chi University in Taiwan, receiving his bachelor's degree in 1964. He left for the United States one year later to attend graduate school at St. Johns University in New York, where he got his masters in Asian history. It

John D. Waihee.

was after finishing graduate school, however, that he firmly decided on his career, responding to the recruitment efforts of New York City's social service agencies, eventually landing a job in a private children's organization. The job opened his eyes and got him interested in social work. Next, he responded to a newspaper advertisement for a job with the Chinese American Planning Council. Wang remained at the CPC from 1968 until 1989, holding various positions including managing director and executive director. During his tenure the CPC grew to be an important social service agency for the Chinese American Community. Some of Wang's most notable accomplishments include arranging the first public hearing on New York–Asian American affairs sponsored by the U.S. Commission on Civil Rights in 1974, the opening of a social security administration branch office in Chinatown in 1976, and a Chinatown post office in 1978. He has also served on the Asian American panel of the President's Commission on Mental Health and on the New York State Crime Prevention Task Force on Bias Related Violence. In the 1970s, he was a member of the New York State Advisory Committee to the U.S. Commission on Civil Rights. He was also chairman of the Pacific Asian Coalition-Mid Atlantic Region, co-chairman of the Asian American Council

Taylor G. Wang.

of Greater New York, vice-chairman of New York City Health System Agency, secretary of the Private Industry Council and chairman of the U.S. Bureau of the Census 1990 Asian and Pacific Islanders Committee. In 1994, Wang was secretary on the board of directors of United Way of New York City, co-chairman of the New York City Human Services, treasurer of the Federation of Asian American Social Service organization, and a member of the New York City Partnership.

Taylor G. Wang (1940-)
Astronaut, scientist

Taylor G. Wang is the Centennial Professor of Applied Physics and the director of the Center for Microgravity Research and Applications at Vanderbilt University. He is also an astronaut with NASA who flew aboard the space shuttle *Challenger* as a payload specialist during the STS-51 mission from April 29 to May 5, 1985.

Taylor Gangjung Wang was born on June 16, 1940, in Shanghai, China. The family fled their homeland for Taiwan, however, in the civil war that led to the Communist victory in 1949. At the age of twelve, Wang decided to become a physicist rather take over his father's successful business.

After high school all students in Taiwan must take a college entrance exam before being admitted to a university. Wang had always done well in school, and assumed he would do well on the entrance examination. When he failed the exam, however, he realized that he would have to devote himself seriously to achieving what he wanted to accomplish in life. He came to America for his education and in 1971 he finished work for his Ph.D. at the University of California at Los Angeles. In 1972 Wang accepted a position at the Jet Propulsion Laboratory (JLP) at the California Institute of Technology in Pasadena, California, where he worked in applied physics. In 1974 NASA accepted a proposal he had made for an experiment to be conducted in space at some point in the future. Wang's particular field of interest—fluid dynamics and containerless experiments—was one that was especially suited to the zero gravity conditions of outer space. NASA announced an open selection for astronauts and, from a huge pool of applicants, Wang was chosen. Wang was trained in all aspects of space flight before being fully accepted as a payload specialist.

Wang holds more than twenty U.S. patents and is the author of approximately 160 articles published in scientific journals. He is the recipient of many awards, including the NASA Exceptional Scientific Achievement Medal (1987), the NASA Space Flight Medal (1985), and the Chinese Institute of Engineering Outstanding Accomplishment Award. He was honored by the government of the United States with "Taylor G. Wang Recognition Day" in Washington, D.C., celebrated on October 11, 1985. Another of Wang's experiments was chosen to be conducted aboard a space shuttle mission, this one during the summer of 1993.

Wang and his wife, Beverly, were married in 1965. The couple has two children, Kenneth and Eric. Wang's philosophy is that to succeed in life it is necessary to "do your best, but never accept failure as a conclusion."

Vera Wang (1948-)
Fashion designer

Vera Wang is perhaps the most prominent designer of bridal wear in the United States today. She also runs a separate couture business called Vera Wang Made to Order that designs both bridal and evening wear. Her designs are sold in her own shops and the New York-based Barney's department store. In 1994, she added a line of evening clothes to be sold through upscale retailers, such as Saks Fifth Avenue, I. Magnin, and Neiman Marcus.

Vera Wang was born in 1948 in Manhattan. She was educated in private schools and went to college at the Sorbonne in Paris for one year, and then at Sarah Lawrence in New York, where she earned a bachelor's degree in art history. Wang stayed at her first job after

Vera Wang.

college as senior editor at *Vogue* (where, at 23, she was one of the youngest editors in the magazine's history) for 16 years before taking a job with Ralph Lauren in fashion design.

She opened her bridal-gown design shop Vera Wang Bridal House, Ltd., on New York City's Madison Avenue in 1990, after finding it very difficult to find a gown of her liking for her wedding in 1989. The new business was financed by her father, who remains her major investor. Although Wang's businesses have yet to show a profit (she expected 1994 to be her turn-around year), she does a brisk and high-profile business. She is also well respected among celebrities for her couture designs, which have been worn by actresses Sharon Stone, Marisa Tomei, and Holly Hunter. She also designed costumes for Olympic ice skater Nancy Kerrigan.

Wayne Wang (1949-)
Filmmaker

The success of the film adaptation of Amy Tan's *The Joy Luck Club* has made Wang the most powerful Asian American director in Hollywood. Made under the auspices of Walt Disney Studios for a relatively low budget of $10.5 million with a screenplay written by author Tan and Ronald Bass (*Black Widow, Rain Man, Sleeping with the Enemy*) and executive-produced by Oliver Stone and Janet Yang, *The Joy Luck Club* proved to be a bonafide blockbuster hit, grossing some $32 million before its release on home video.

Wang's career is founded on critically acclaimed, low-budget features dealing with Chinese American life, including *Chan is Missing*, about two Chinatown taxi drivers in search of a shady entrepreneur to whom they entrusted money, *Dim Sum*, about the relationship between a Chinese mother and her American-born daughter, *Eat a Bowl of Tea*, about newlyweds in 1949, and *Life Is Cheap . . . but Toilet Paper Is Expensive*, about a Japanese/Chinese American cowboy getting into trouble in Hong Kong.

Wayne Wang was born in 1949 in Hong Kong, six days after his family arrived in the city, fleeing the Communist Revolution in their homeland of China. Wang's father, an engineer and businessman fluent in English, was so enthralled with American movies that he named his second son after the Hollywood star, Joyh Wayne. Growing up in Hong Kong, Wang was educated by Jesuits while attending Roman Catholic schools and learned English as a child. At age eighteen, he arrived in the United States, and enrolled at Foothill College near Palo Alto, California, to study painting. After two years at Foothill, Wang attended the California College of Arts and Crafts in Oakland, eventually earning an MFA in film and television.

With his new degree, Wang returned to his native Hong Kong, but the work he found—directing segments on small films and television series—left him creatively frustrated. He returned to the United States, settling in San Francisco's Chinatown where he immersed himself in making films for community activism. *Chan is Missing*, completed in 1982, was Wang's first feature and his first success. Made for just $22,000, which Wang received in grants from the American Film Institute and the National Endowment for the Arts, the black-and-white film was a surprise hit, quickly earning some fifty times its initial investment.

In 1984, Wang completed the acclaimed *Dim Sum* with a budget twenty times that of *Chan*. Three years later, Wang directed *Slamdance*, his first film with a non-Asian cast. Starring Tom Hulce and Mary Elizabeth Mastrantonio, *Slamdance* was well received at the Cannes Film Festival, but it was not a commercial success. Wang returned to the world of Chinese America in his 1989 film, *Eat a Bowl of Tea*, based on the novel of the same name by Louis Chu, about a newly wed couple in 1949. He cast as the young bride from China his own wife, Cora Miao, a popular Hong Kong actress he had met in 1983. Leading man Russell Wong played the American-born groom who was one of the first Chinese American men after World War II to bring his bride to New York's Chinatown. While filming in Hong Kong, Wang was inspired to create *Life Is Cheap . . . but Toilet Paper Is Expensive*, in which he explored for the first time the cultural clash he himself had been experiencing. Released in 1990, the black, almost hallucinatory thriller/comedy follows the adventures of a half-Japanese, half-Chinese American cowboy sent to Hong Kong handcuffed to a briefcase that is to be delivered to the The Big Boss. The film captures the jarring, sometimes violent cultural clash that occurs when the two worlds of an Asian American collide.

In 1994, Wang next project was a film adaptation of stories by Paul Auster entitled *Smoke*.

Michiko Nishiura Weglyn (1929-)
Costume designer, writer, activist

Michi Nishiura Weglyn has achieved acclaim in two careers: as a noted writer and activist for civil rights of Japanese Americans and other, and as a costume designer. At the age of twenty-one, she was the first nationally prominent Japanese American costume designer in the United States. From 1956 to 1965, Weglyn was best known for her flattering, successful costume creations for *The Perry Como Show*, a weekly musical variety hour. Weglyn's designing career, which lasted nearly two decades, took her onto the sets of many of the most popular television musical variety series of the late 1950s and 1960s, including *The Jackie Gleason Show*, *The Patti Page Show*, *The Tony Bennett Show*, and *The Dinah Shore Show*. She eventually established her own manufacturing and design studio.

Born in Stockton, California, on November 29, 1926, Michiko Nishiura was one of the two daughters of Tomojiro and Misao (Yuasa) Nishiura. The family lived on a 500-acre farm approximately fifty miles east of San Francisco. Growing up, Weglyn fed the chickens and horses before she went to school to prove to her father that she was just as valuable as the son he never had.

The day after Japanese bombers attacked Pearl Harbor on December 7, 1941, Weglyn felt very anxious about going to school. On February 19, 1942, President Franklin Roosevelt signed Executive Order 9066, calling for the evacuation of all persons of Japanese descent (two-thirds of whom were American citizens) on the West Coast to ten "relocation camps." Families were given six to ten days to dispose of their property and businesses. When the evacuation order reached the Nishiuras, they were in the midst of packing. Weglyn recalled that people wanted to buy their chickens for a quarter apiece so the family tried to kill and eat as many chickens as they could before they left. When Michi and her sister recall that period, the hurried killing and eating of their pet chickens was one of the most traumatic aspects of the evacuation. On May 12, 1942, the Nishiuras were loaded on buses to begin a journey eventually ending in the internment camp at Gila River, Arizona. Young Michi was not yet sixteen years old, and she ironically recalls feeling a sense of relief and liberation in her new home, because she was suddenly with her peers, with no reason to feel inferior. She emerged as a true leader and achiever among her peers, becoming president of her Girl Scout and organizing a day-long Girls League Convention that brought 500 high school girls from various Arizona cities to the camp, where they participated in a talent show, were given a tour of the camp, ate together in the mess halls, and discussed timely issues.

In 1944, Weglyn took and the entrance examinations for Mount Holyoke College in Massachusetts, traveling from Gila River to Phoenix for the test. At Mount Holyoke, she won a campuswide design contest—for costumes, sets, and scenery for a college production. In 1945, Weglyn was forced to leave Mount Holyoke to receive treatment for tuberculosis which she had contracted at Gila. In 1947, she returned to school, this time to Barnard College in New York City, but again was forced to leave for health reasons. Weglyn later studied costume design at New York's Fashion Academy between 1948 and 1949. One year later, on March 5, 1950, she married Walter Matthys Weglyn, a perfume chemist, a Holocaust survivor who had come to the United States in 1947.

In 1967, Weglyn metamorphosed from glamorous designer into an acclaimed historical writer. Then-U.S. attorney general Ramsey Clark appeared on a television show and stated that there had never been, and never would be, concentration camps in America. Having spent more than two years of her life at the camp in Gila (pronounced HEEL-AH) River, Arizona, Weglyn recalled to *Rafu Shimpo* in 1993, "I decided they were not going to get away with that. That was the catalyst for my book." In 1976, the result of her passionate labors, *Years of Infamy: The Untold Story of America's Concentration Camps*, was published by William Morrow and Company. For the first time in history, Weglyn was able to break the paralyzing guilt that had bound Japanese Americans in silence. With careful research and documentation, Weglyn shed light on the abuses of power in the highest reaches of the U.S. government that failed to protect the basic rights of Americans of Japanese descent. Her work helped release a new social activism among Japanese Americans, to become more involved in promoting civil and human rights, which eventually led to the redress movement of the late 1980s and early 1990s. Both the book and Weglyn have been lauded for changing the face of Asian American history.

Since 1976, Weglyn has remained actively involved in the Asian American community and beyond. She has been an adviser and consultant on countless projects,

Anna May Wong. (Courtesy of the Academy of Motion Picture Arts and Sciences.)

B. D. Wong.

including the Japanese American National Museum in Los Angeles (1988–1990), The Japanese American Library in San Francisco (1987–present), Loni Ding's award-winning film, *Color of Honor* (1987), the Congressional Study on the Commission on Wartime Relocation and Internment of Civilians (1981–1982), and the Smithsonian Institution's exhibit, "A More Perfect Union: The Japanese Americans and the U.S. Constitution" (1975–1976).

Weglyn has become a laudable example for all those who seek truth and justice with unwavering dedication and compassion.

Anna May Wong (1907-1961)
Actress

Anna May Wong was the first Chinese American woman to succeed in Hollywood, starring in silent films during the 1920s.

B. D. Wong (1962-)
Actor

Only twenty-something when he won theater's highest accolade—a Tony Award as best featured actor in 1988 for his performance in *M. Butterfly*—B. D. Wong

could have rested on his many laurels. He is the first Asian American actor to receive awards from Actors' Equity, Theatre World, Outer Critics Circle, and Drama Desk—in addition to his Tony. B.D. Wong has become a well-known name among Asian Americans for his dedication to fair portrayals of Asians as much as for his famed acting ability.

Born in San Francisco on October 24, 1962, Bradley Darryl Wong is the second of Roberta and Bill Wong's three sons. Second-generation Chinese Americans, his parents lived in San Francisco's North Beach area bordering Chinatown when B.D. was born. When he was a toddler, they moved to the city's Sunset district, now a popular area for Chinese families, but in the 1960s, they were isolated.

As a child he loved drawing and art and considered becoming an architect, but he was terrible at math and technical design. At Lincoln High School, Wong performed in a number of school productions, each succeeding role feeding his passion for acting. His parents supported his efforts at community theatre, but were uncertain about his future. In high school, Wong felt he could play any role, in part because he didn't think of himself as *Asian* American. But when he auditioned for the role of a sailor in *Anything Goes* in a community

Flossie Wong-Staal.

theatre production and instead was selected to play a coolie, he found he couldn't bring himself to play the part. After graduating from high school, Wong attended San Francisco State University for a year, but spent so much time in the drama department he received "Incompletes" in all his courses. Once he had saved enough money, he moved to New York in 1981. After a role in the chorus with national touring company of *La Cage Aux Folles* took him to Los Angeles in 1985, he decided to stay and study with Donald Hotton, a student of Lee Grant and Mira Rastova. While in Los Angeles, he was asked to audition for *M. Butterfly*, written by David Henry Hwang.

Ever since his acclaimed performance as Song Lingling, a man who fooled a French diplomat into believing he was a woman while maintaining an intimate relationship for several years, Wong has acted in many challenging roles. He has played the lead in *Peter Pan*, a student in *Crash Course*, a Chinese gang lord in *Mystery Date*, an assistant wedding coordinator in *Father of the Bride*, a gay artist in *And the Band Played On*, the nerdy geneticist in Steven Spielberg's *Jurassic Park*, and the brother of comedian Margaret Cho in *All American Girl*, the first television sitcom featuring an Asian American family.

Wong took a very public stand on his principles when the play *Miss Saigon* first opened on Broadway—featuring a white actor in "yellow face" playing the role of the Eurasian Engineer. No Asian male actors had been auditioned for the part, and Asian American actor and activists were outraged. In spite of possible recriminations for his own career, Wong spoke up against the casting for the play. He has received numerous awards from Asian American community groups for his courageous stand.

Wong lives in New York City with his manager Richard Jackson, and is committed to seeing roles for Asian Americans continue to evolve.

Herb Wong
Music promoter

Herb Wong, a well-known, jazz promoter is president of the Association of Jazz Educators and has been a disc jockey on a San Francisco-area jazz radio station for over 30 years. Wong enjoys counseling young Asian musicians, encouraging them to be creative and improvise in music and in life, because, as he says, "I am an antagonist to stereotypes."

Flossie Wong-Staal (1947-)
Medical Researcher

Flossie Wong-Staal is considered one of the top AIDS researchers in the United States. She was the first researcher to clone an AIDS (Acquired Immune Deficiency Syndrome) virus and work out its anatomy in 1984. An internationally recognized leader in virology, Wong-Staal is a professor of medicine and biology and Florence Seeley Riford Chair in AIDS Research at the University of California, San Diego (UCSD). In the May 28, 1990, issue of the *Scientist*, she was named "one of the ten superstars of science."

She was born Yee Ching Wong in China in 1947. At age five in 1952 her father took her and her brothers and sisters to Hong Kong to escape Communist China. At the Catholic school where she was enrolled, she was given an English name, chosen by her father from a newspaper report about a typhoon named "Flossie" which had hit Hong Kong the previous week. In high school she excelled in her studies and her teachers insisted she become a scientist. Wong-Staal attended graduate school at UCLA, becoming a research assistant in bacteriology. Along the way she married a physician, whom she later divorced, though she has kept her married name. In 1972 she became a postdoctoral researcher at UCSD, and in 1974, she joined Robert Gallo's team in the laboratory of the National Cancer Institute.

Wong-Staal worked at the institute for more than a decade, during which time her reputation as an AIDS researcher grew. In 1990, she became chair of AIDS

S.B. Woo.

research at the UCSD, where she is focusing her efforts on the development of an AIDS vaccine and therapy. In the mid-1990s, she embarked on the exciting project of using gene therapy for treating AIDS.

Wong-Staal lives in San Diego and is the single parent of two daughters: Stephanie, who was born in 1972, and Caroline, who was born in 1983.

S.B. Woo (1937-)
Physicist, politician

For most of his adult life, S.B. Woo has devoted his efforts to research and teaching in physics. In 1984, however, he was elected lieutenant governor of Delaware, becoming the highest ranking Asian American in elected office at the state level in the continental United States. He has also been involved at the local and national levels in efforts to help Asian Americans, specifically Chinese Americans, to understand and appreciate their heritage while living in and contributing to American society.

Shien-Biau (S.B.) Woo was born in Shanghai, China, on August 13, 1937, to Koo-ing Chang Woo, a homemaker, and C. K. Woo, a wool merchant. The family, including a brother and two sisters, moved to Taiwan in 1949, then to Hong Kong a few months later. At eighteen,

Woo traveled to the United States to study physics and math, earning his bachelor of science, summa cum laude, in mathematics and physics from Georgetown College in Kentucky. He continued his studies at Washington University in St. Louis, earning his Ph.D. in physics in 1964. He then did postdoctoral study at the Joint Institute for Laboratory Astrophysics (JILA) in Boulder, Colorado from 1964 to 1966.

For the next twenty years, Woo taught physics at the University of Delaware. During this time, he observed that the United States was lagging behind other countries in technology and education, especially in the sciences. With this as his motivation, and after becoming a U.S. citizen at the age of thirty-five, Woo chose a new career path and sought public office.

In 1984, Woo was elected to the office of lieutenant governor of Delaware, serving under a Republican governor. During his term, he was responsible for a report to the state on developing high tech industry. He stepped down from office in order to run for the U.S. Senate, winning the primary but losing the general election. He later ran for a seat in the U.S. House of Representatives, with the same results.

Woo did not limit his public involvement to elected office, but served his community in many other areas.

He founded both the Chinese School of St. Louis in 1963 and the Chinese School of Delaware in 1967. Children of Chinese American families attended classes on weekends to learn about their culture. The schools never asked for federal aid, but were completely funded by the parents. He was an Institute Fellow at the Kennedy School of Government at Harvard University in 1989, and president of the Organization of Chinese Americans (OCA) from 1990 to 1991. At OCA, he was guided by a simple vision—to help make the Asian American an equal partner in the making of the American dream.

Woo married Katy K.N. in 1963. They have a son, Chih-I, and a daughter, Chih-lan. They live in Newark, Delaware, where Woo is currently professor of physics at the University of Delaware.

Chien-Shiung Wu (1912-)
Physicist

Chien-Shiung Wu was born on May 31, 1912, in Liuhe, a small town near Shanghai, China. Her father, Wu Zhongyi, a participant in the revolution of 1911 that toppled the Manchu dynasty, was the founder and principal of a private girls school—one of very few in China, where educating girls has never been a high priority. Wu attended this school until the age of nine at which time she was sent to the Soochow Girls School, where she received an excellent education, and in 1930, graduated at the top of her class.

Wu studied physics at Nanjing University, graduating in 1934. While doing research in the field of X-ray crystallography at the National Academy of Sciences in Shanghai, she met a woman scientist who encouraged her to continue her studies in the United States. With the encouragement of her family, Wu sailed for America in 1936.

Wu studied at the University of California at Berkeley, an exciting place to be in the 1930s for a student of physics. Wu began her work at Berkeley in the area of nuclear physics, which at the time was headed by the renowned particle physicist Ernest Livermore. She worked as an assistant to Emilio Segre, a future Noble laureate. She received her Ph.D. in 1940, staying on at Berkeley for two years as a research assistant. In 1942, she married Luke Yuan and the couple moved to the East Coast, where Yuan found a job working at the RCA Laboratories in Princeton, New Jersey, and Wu took a position teaching at Smith College in Northampton, Massachusetts. She soon left Smith for a position at Princeton, allowing her to live with her husband.

In 1944, Wu was recruited by the Division of War Research at Columbia University. She worked at a secret facility in New York in the development of sensitive radiation detectors for the atomic bomb project. In the late 1940s and early 1950s, Wu studied problems in the area of beta decay as theorized by the eminent physicist Enrico Fermi. This work was widely regarded as monumental within the scientific community. After her work with beta decay, Wu began work with Tsung Dao Lee of Columbia University and Chen Ning Yang of the Institute for Advanced Study at Princeton. Wu began working independently of Lee and Yang, but her experiments were based on their observations. Her laboratory was underfunded and much of the equipment was below standard. Nevertheless, in January of 1957, Wu's team had sufficient experimental corroboration to publicize their findings, which took the scientific world by storm. Wu, Yang, and Lee became national celebrities, their findings reported on the front page of the *New York Times* and in *Time* and *Newsweek*. Later that year, Yang and Lee won the Nobel prize for physics. Wu was not included for her work because the idea behind her experimental research was not original to her.

Wu continued her research in other areas of physics. In 1963 she experimentally confirmed a difficult hypothesis involving beta decay hypothesized by Richard Feynman and Murray Gell-Mann, two world-renowned American theoretical physicists. Their theory had been widely tested for years by scientists around the world, but none had been able to confirm or disprove it. In confirming this theory, Wu contributed to the unified theory of fundamental forces.

Wu was given an endowed professorship by Columbia University in 1972. She was the first woman to receive the Comstock Award from the National Academy of Sciences, the first woman to receive the Research Corporation Award, the first woman to serve as president of the American Physical Society, and the seventh woman selected into the National Academy of Science. Wu has received honorary degrees from more than a dozen universities, including Harvard, Yale, and Princeton, where she was the first woman ever to receive an honorary doctorate of science degree. She is also the first living scientist with an asteroid named after her.

Wu retired in 1981 and has since traveled and lectured extensively. Wu has been an outspoken critic of the dismissive attitude institutional science has toward women, encouraging girls to break the imposed barriers and study science.

Kristi Yamaguchi (1971-)
Figure skater

See also Sports and Athletics

Carrying the title of reigning world figure skating champion into the 1992 Winter Olympics in Albertville, France, Kristi Yamaguchi received the highest scores from all nine judges for her short program. Although she fell on a triple loop—her easiest jump—during the long program, she made fewer errors than her rivals and captured the gold. Midori Ito of Japan took the silver, with Nancy Kerrigan of the United States winning the bronze medal.

Born on July 12, 1971 in Hayward, California, and raised predominantly in nearby Fremont (both cities in the San Francisco Bay area), Kristi Tsuya Yamaguchi is one of three children of Jim Yamaguchi, a dentist, and Carole Yamaguchi, a medical secretary. The infant Kristi, who would become renowned for her elegant footwork on ice, was clubfooted at birth, a problem treated with corrective shoes, and from which she did not suffer any long-term damage.

Although Yamaguchi's parents and grandparents were interned during World War II, along with other Americans of Japanese descent, they rarely discussed that period of their lives with Yamaguchi and her two siblings. In 1976, when Dorothy Hamill captured gold at the Winter Games, Yamaguchi's desire to someday compete in the Olympics was born. At age five, she began skating lessons and quickly showed natural talent. She entered her first competition at age eight, and by age nine she was getting up at four o'clock in the morning to practice at the local skating rink for several hours before going to school.

Yamaguchi embarked on pairs skating in 1983 with partner Rudi Galindo. Under the direction of their coach, Jim Hulick, the two young athletes won the National Junior Championships in 1986. Yamaguchi was also developing into a strong singles skater, becoming the Central Pacific junior champion and placing fourth in the national junior medal event. In 1988, she took gold in both the singles and pairs categories at the World Junior Championships, prompting the Women's Sports Foundation to name her the Up-and-Coming Artistic Athlete of the Year.

In 1989, Yamaguchi won her first senior title—the gold medal in the pairs competition at the National Championships in Baltimore, Maryland. She also placed second in the singles division and became the first woman in thirty-five years to win two medals at the nationals.

In March of 1989, Yamaguchi competed for the first time in the World Championships, held in Paris placing sixth in singles, and fifth with Galindo in pairs. The next three years leading up to Yamaguchi's dream of entering the 1992 Olympics proved personally difficult and professionally challenging. In the spring of 1989, her singles coach married a Canadian and moved to Edmonton, Alberta. Yamaguchi left California for Edmonton the day after her high school graduation, and her partner, Galindo, relocated too. The pair commuted between Canada and San Francisco to continue training with their pairs coach until his death in December of 1989 of colon cancer. About the same time, Yamaguchi's maternal grandfather passed away.

Yamaguchi and Galindo could not find a pairs coach to succeed Hulick. That loss, together with their inability to better their fifth-place finish during the 1990 World Championships, led Yamaguchi to withdraw from pairs competition in May 1990 and devote herself fully to singles. At the 1990 national and world competitions finished second and fourth, respectively. At the 1991 nationals, Yamaguchi placed second to a new challenger, Tonya Harding. At the world competition in Munich, Yamaguchi garnered eight 5.9s (out of a possible 6.0) for technical merit, and seven 5.9s and one 6.0 for artistic impression to win first place. The following year, Yamaguchi captured gold again at the World Championships.

One months after winning the gold medal at the Olympic Games in Albertville, France, Yamaguchi successfully defended her world championship, becoming the first American skater to defend the world title since Peggy Fleming did so in 1968.

In September 1992, Yamaguchi became a professional, which meant she could no longer compete in amateur competitions such as the World Championships and the Olympic Games.

Since her Olympic victory, Yamaguchi has been busy, not only with professional skating performances throughout the country, but also with her numerous endorsement contracts. Hours after her gold medal win in Albertville, the cereal giant Kellogg began printing her picture on "Special K" cereal boxes becoming the only athlete to grace a Special K box. Yamaguchi signed lucrative contracts with Hoechst Celanese Corporation, makers of acetate fabrics for fabric designers, Dura-Soft contact lenses and Wendy's restaurants. Yamaguchi is currently appearing in major cities throughout North America as part of the Discover Card Stars on Ice tour, joined by fellow Olympic medalists Paul Wylie and Scott Hamilton.

Minoru Yamasaki (1912-1987)
Architect

Minoru Yamasaki was a self-made architect who distinguished himself in the 1950s with a series of graceful textile-like buildings, and then gained worldwide fame as the architect of the twin towers of New York's World Trade Center. The two identical 110-story buildings standing side-by-side at the southern tip of Manhattan are arguably the world's most recognizable modern skyscrapers.

Minoru Yamasaki was born in Seattle, Washington, on December 1, 1912, to first-generation Japanese immigrant parents. His father had been a land-owner in Japan, but in America the family lived in near poverty. In high school, Yamasaki did very well. It was during his high school years that he had an experience that altered

Minoru Yamasaki. (Taro Yamasaki.)

the course of his life. As he recalled in his autobiography, *A Life in Architecture,* "My Uncle Koken had just graduated in architecture from the University of California. After graduation he had been promised a job in Chicago, and he stopped to visit us on the way there. He unrolled the drawings he had made at the university and I almost exploded with excitement when I saw them. Right then and there I decided to become an architect."

After graduation Yamasaki enrolled in the University of Washington to study architecture. Yamasaki supported himself through college working in the canneries of Alaska. It was grueling work with long hours and poor pay, about fifty dollars a month, plus twenty-five cents for overtime.

Yamasaki graduated from college in 1934 and headed for New York with very little money and a few letters of reference. There was almost no work in New York for architects, so he was forced to take a job wrapping dishes for a Japanese company that distributed Noritake china in the United States. His first architectural job in New York came in 1935 when he was hired by Githens and Keally. One year later he went to Shreve, Lamb and Harmon, architects of the Empire State Building. He stayed there until 1943, working primarily in the production and checking of shop drawings. His next move was to Harrison, Fouilhoux and Abramowitz, architects of Rockefeller Center. From there he went to Raymond Loewy Associates, a firm that specialized in industrial design, which Yamasaki hated.

In 1945 Yamasaki went to Detroit to become the head of design at Smith, Hynchman and Grylls. Four years later he began his own firm of Yamasaki, Hellmuth and Leinweber. The firm's first major job was the St. Louis Airport, built in 1953. Major works of Yamasaki's in the 1950s include three buildings in Detroit—the American Concrete Institute, the Reynolds Metals Company offices, and McGregor Memorial Building for Wayne State University—and one in Japan, the American consulate in Kobe. In the 1960s, as his international reputation grew, Yamasaki designed the Dharhan Air Terminal in Dharhan, Saudi Arabia; the United States Pavilion at the World Agricultural Fair in New Delhi, India; and the Queen Emma Gardens in Honolulu, Hawaii. He also designed the Woodrow Wilson School of International Affairs at Princeton, New Jersey.

In 1962, the Port Authority of New York and New Jersey asked Yamasaki Associates, as the firm was then called, if they would be interested in the architectural development of a project with an estimated cost of $280 million—the World Trade Center. There were more than forty architectural firms considered, but Yamasaki Associates was chosen for the job.

Notable works Yamasaki designed after the World Trade Center include the Century Plaza Towers in Century City, California; the Ranier Bank Tower in his home town of Seattle, Washington; and the Eastern Province International Airport in Saudi Arabia.

Minoru Yamasaki died of cancer on February 6, 1987, at the age of seventy-three. He married Teruko Hereshiki in 1941, and they had three children: two sons, Taro (who won a Pulitzer Prize for photography while with the *Detroit Free Press*) and Kim, and a daughter, Carol Yamasaki Chakrin.

Janet Yang (1956-)
Producer/filmmaker

Janet Yang is president of Ixtlan, the film production company of Academy Award-winning director Oliver Stone. Yang, one of the most influential Asian American film executives in Hollywood, was recognized for her work as executive producer of *The Joy Luck Club*, a film based on Amy Tan's best-selling novel.

Yang was born July 13, 1956, in New York City to mainland Chinese parents who had fled their country in 1945 after the Communist takeover. Her mother, Anna, came to the United States from Hunan to study and eventually established a career at the United Nations. Her father, T.Y., an engineer from Shanghai, emigrated in 1947. Yang was raised on Long Island in the only Chinese family in a predominantly Jewish community. As an American-born Chinese or second-generation immigrant, Yang had difficulty as a child reconciling family values of modesty, duty, and familial piety with those of others around her, but at the time it never occurred to her to explore her heritage or question the differences between herself and her peers.

In a trip to China in 1972 when Yang was fifteen she and her mother returned to Hunan, China. Upon her return to the United States, Yang submerged herself in the study of the Chinese language for a summer term at Middlebury College. After graduating from Phillips Exeter Academy, Yang pursued Chinese studies for two years each at Brown and Harvard, where she learned of a position available in Beijing with the Foreign Language Press (FLP). She took the job and spent a year and a half in China. When not polishing the English in books and magazines designed for export by the FLP, Yang plunged into the underground culture of the prolific Chinese film industry. Inspired by a desire to market Chinese films in the United States, Yang returned to

Janet Yang.

New York and earned a master's in business administration at Columbia University. She then moved to San Francisco where she took a job with World Entertainment, running the company and traveling regularly to China to develop and buy films by Chinese filmmakers for American audiences. A few years later, her talent and unique background evident, she was lured by MCA/Universal Studios to be their Far Eastern director. Before leaving Universal, Yang persuaded the studio to produce *Dragon: The Bruce Lee Story*, a movie biography about the Asian movie star.

Fluent in Mandarin and competent in both Shanghaineze and Cantonese, Yang was asked by Steven Spielberg's Amblin Entertainment to serve as a consultant on the film *Empire of the Sun*. Subsequently, she joined Oliver Stone's production company, Ixtlan.

Yang, now president of Ixtlan, works with Stone in a complementary relationship—he is the artist and she is the managers. Pouring through hundreds of scripts, ideas, books, and magazines each month, Yang and her staff select ideas and, together with Stone, select those that warrant development. Among the films co-produced by Yang and Stone are *The Joy Luck Club*, *The Doors*, *JFK*, *South Central*, *Zebrahead*, *The Mayor of Castro Street*, and *Johnny Spain*.

Shirley Young.

Jeff Yang (1968-)

Writer, publisher

Jeff Yang is the publisher and editor-in-chief of *A. Magazine: Inside Asian America*, the nation's premier publication for English-speaking Asian Pacific Americans. He founded the magazine with three friends in 1989, shortly after Yang graduated from Harvard University. Since that time, the magazine has grown from a small regional publication to an international bimonthly with a circulation of over 100,000 in North America and the countries of the Pacific Rim. Yang is also a the first Asian American columnist to write features writer and cultural criticism for the New York weekly, the *Village Voice.*

Yang was born in the Park Slope neighborhood of Brooklyn while his father, a medical doctor in his native Taiwan, served the residency required to get his U.S. medical credentials. Yang's mother was a social worker. When Yang was six, the family moved to Staten Island, at that time was a predominantly white suburb.

Yang was educated at St. Ann's High School in Brooklyn Heights, a private high school that emphasized the arts, while giving its students a free hand to study math and science as their abilities allowed. Yang went along with his family's assumption that he would become a doctor until his second year at Harvard University, when he realized that he was interested in English and switched his major to psychology and English. He became involved in Asian American activist groups in the Boston area and on Harvard's campus, and started a publication called *Eastwind*, a biannual undergraduate publication. After graduation in 1989, Yang and a group of friends from *Eastwind* and the *Harvard Lampoon* decided to start a new publication that expressed and celebrated issues of emerging identity and concern to Asian Americans. Yang and his friends put together a premier issue in the summer of 1990 and sold out all 5,000 copies in a matter of weeks. In June of 1992, Phoebe Eng became the magazine's full-time publisher. Since then, *A. Magazine* has attracted a lot of attention. When Eng retired as publisher in 1994, and Yang assumed the role of publisher in addition to his responsibilities as editor-in-chief.

Laurence Yep

See Literature

Ying Quartet

Musicians

The Ying Quartet was formed in 1988 when the four siblings, born in Winetka, Illinois, were together at the Eastman School of Music in Rochester, New York. The quartet is made up of: David Ying, cellist (1965-); Timothy Ying, first violinist (1966-); Phillip Ying, violist (1968-); and Janet Ying, second violinist (1970-). In 1989, they won the International Cleveland Quartet Competition and, in 1991, made a successful New York debut at Lincoln Center's Alice Tulley Hall.

During its first professional season, the Ying Quartet won the Naumberg Chamber Music Award and came in second at the 1992 Banff International String Competition. They have been featured on National Public Radio's *St. Paul Sunday Morning* and TV's *CBS Sunday Morning*. In addition to the Yings' busy performing schedule, they were participants in the 1993 National Endowment for the Arts Rural Residency Initiative, spending a year of residency in Jessup, Iowa. This program places artists in rural communities in Iowa, Kansas, and Georgia.

Shirley Young (1935-)

Business executive

Shirley Young is the vice-president for consumer market development with General Motors Corporation, a post she has held since June 1, 1988. Prior to her work at GM, Young worked for more than 25 years at the New York-based Grey Advertising.

Ying Quartet. (Peter Schaaf.)

Shirley Young was born in Shanghai, China, on May 25, 1935. She was educated at Wellesley College in Wellesley, Massachusetts, from which she graduated in 1955 with a bachelor's degree in economics. After graduation, her first job was with the Alfred Politz Research Organization, working as a project director. She held this job for three years and then went to the Hudson Paper Corporation as a market research manager. In 1959, she was hired by Grey Advertising.

Her first position with the prestigious Madison Avenue agency was as a researcher, where she helped pioneer what are now known as attitudinal studies. Young continued her market research at Grey, taking various marketing positions, and was eventually named executive vice-president. In 1983, she became president of Grey strategic marketing and was elevated to chairman in 1988.

Shirley Young first began working with General Motors in 1983 as a consultant. She was hired full-time by General Motors' chairman Roger Smith in 1988 to help the foundering automaker regain some of the market share it had lost over the years. To this end, she began a campaign with the tagline "Putting Quality on the Road." She also worked to establish distinctions among the automaker's five divisions, creating brand recognition and customer loyalty, Young's specialty. The marketing images she developed for each division attempts to link them to specific images or ideas in the consumer's mind. In addition to her work at General Motors, Young sits on the board of directors of Bell Atlantic and the Promus Companies. For 12 years, she was a consultant director for the Dayton Hudson Corporation and, in 1980, served as a vice-chairman of the nominating committee for the New York Stock Exchange.

Young is also involved in several community-service and cultural organizations. She is chairman of the Committee of 100, a national Chinese American leadership resource and is a founding member of the Committee of 200, an international organization of leading businesswomen. She also serves on the national board of directors of Junior Achievement, Inc. and is a trustee of Wellesley College, as well as a member of the board of directors of the associates of the Harvard Business School, Wellesley's sister school. She was awarded an honorary doctorate of letters from Russell Sage College, and in 1986, was given the Wellesley College Alumna Achievement Award.

Connie Young Yu. (David Weintraub.)

Connie Young Yu (1941-)
Writer

Connie Young Yu is the author of countless articles—including a chapter for *Asian American Almanac.* (*See* "Who Are the Chinese Americans?")—and two books (*Profiles in Excellence: Peninsula Chinese Americans* and *Chinatown San Jose, U.S.A.*) that focus predominantly on Chinese Americans. Yu has established herself as a writer with a historical cause. Through articles, essays, lectures, and community

activities, Yu has devoted her energies for more than a quarter of a century in rediscovering a history of Chinese and Asian America that has, for the most part, been forgotten, overlooked, and even hidden.

Born on June 19, 1941, in Los Angeles, California, Connie Young Yu lived in nearby Whittier for the first six years of her life. In 1947, Yu's family moved to San Francisco's Chinatown where her father became a soy sauce manufacturer. The family later moved to the Richmond district of San Francisco, becoming one of the first Chinese American families there. She grew up surrounded by Chinese Americans of various generations. In addition to grandparents who lived with the family for many years, the Young house also provided a home base for many older Chinese American bachelors. Both her grandparents and parents were active in the Chinatown community's reform movements of the 1940s and 1950s.

Yu attended public schools in San Francisco, then enrolled at Mills College in 1959. After graduating with a degree in English, Yu married Dr. John Kou-Ping Yu (currently chief of oncology at Kaiser Permanente in Santa Clara, California) and spent three years in New York City. The Yus three children were born in the early 1960s. When Yu returned in 1967 to the San Francisco Bay area with her growing family, she became more involved in researching Chinese American history, writing short articles for Asian American publications. She received local recognition when her full-page article, "The Unsung Heroes of the Golden Spikes," appeared in the May 10, 1969 Sunday edition of the *San Francisco Examiner.* The focus of the article was about the Chinese railroad workers, a subject familiar to Yu because her own great-grandfather had worked on the Transcontinental Railroad.

During the 1960s and 1970s, Yu became heavily involved with the anti-war movement, the social change movement and the ethnic studies movement. In 1973, Yu helped found Asian Americans for Community Involvement (AACI), an organization whose purpose was "to make social changes and social justices for Asian Pacific Americans a reality." From a group of twelve community leaders, AACI today has a staff of more than fifty professionals, a budget of almost $5 million and a 100,000-square foot facility in San Jose. In October 1993, in celebration of AACI's Twentieth anniversary, the group honored Yu, together with Congressman Norman Mineta (a Democrat from California), with the Freedom Award.

In 1986, the Stanford Area Chinese Club published Yu's *Profiles in Excellence: Peninsula Chinese Americans,* a collection of biographies of thirty-seven notable Chinese Americans. Her second book, *Chinatown San Jose, U.S.A.,* published in 1991, was commissioned by the San Jose Historical Museum Association to tell the

Diane C. Yu.

Teddy Zee. (Danny Feld.)

story of a Chinatown that was once located in San Jose, California.

Yu is also recognized as a teacher, not only of Chinese American history, but of the art of fencing. Yu teaches fencing in San Jose and Palo Alto and manages The Fencing Center at San Jose as a volunteer.

Diane C. Yu (1951-)
Lawyer

Diane Yu should be used to "firsts" by now. In 1983, at the age of thirty-one, Yu was the first minority, woman, and youngest person ever to be appointed superior court commissioner for the Alameda County Superior Court in Oakland, California. Three years later, she was the first White House fellow ever appointed from the judicial branch of government to serve as special assistant to the U.S. trade representative. And in 1987, at age thirty-six, she was the first minority, woman, and youngest person ever appointed as general counsel of the State Bar of California. In addition to being named one of Ten Outstanding Young Women of America in 1985 for professional achievement and community service, Yu was also featured as one of Twenty Young Lawyers Whose Work Makes a

Difference by *Barrister*, a publication of the American Bar Association's Young Lawyers Division in 1986. Her name and career are cited in *Who's Who in American Law*, *Who's Who of American Women*, *Who's Who in the West*, *Who's Who in California*, and the *International Directory of Distinguished Leadership*. She also argued and won a case in the U. S. Supreme Court in 1989.

Yu was born December 25, 1951, and grew up in Rochester, New York, where she lived until she left for college. Her father was a cardiologist and the first minority and foreign-born person to ever serve as president of the American Heart Association. Her mother was also a pioneer—a woman pediatrician in the 1950s, a time when two career families and women professionals were the exception rather than the rule.

Since high school, she has given much time to volunteerism, serving on the board of directors of University YWCA, the advisory committee of the University of San Francisco Center for the Pacific Rim, the board of directors of the Chinese Cultural Foundation of San Francisco, the Commonwealth Club of California, the Ad Hoc Study Committee for Professional Education in Law at the University of California, the California Consortium to Prevent Child Abuse, the Attorney General's

Asian/Pacific Advisory Committee and Commission on Racial, Ethnic, Religious and Minority Violence, and the San Francisco Regional Panel of the President's Commission on White House Fellowships.

Since becoming a lawyer, Yu has continuously devoted a significant portion of her time toward efforts to eradicate bias and discrimination in the legal profession and judiciary, and to promote better relationships between different racial and cultural groups. As a member of the American Bar Association (ABA), she has served on numerous commissions and committees. Yu is the first Asian American woman to serve on the ABA commission on minorities, commission on women, and its accreditation committee.

Teddy Zee (1957-)
Entertainment executive

Born May 15, 1957, in Liberty, New York, Teddy Zee is among the power elite in Hollywood, combining business acumen and creative instinct to produce winning entertainment products. In 1994, he was executive vice-president of movie production at Columbia Pictures, with projects such as *First Knight* starring Sean Connery and Richard Gere, and *Blankman* starring Damon Wayans and David Alan Grier underway. With major successes such as *Indecent Proposal* starring Robert Redford, Demi Moore, and Woody Harrelson and *My Girl* starring Macauley Culkin and Anna Chumsky, Zee has proven his ability to combine a keen business sense with a strong instinct for finding and shaping an idea that will capture the imagination (and admission dollars) of the movie-going public.

Zee is as devoted to his family as he is passionate about his work. His wife, Elizabeth, was a classmate at the Harvard Business School, where he completed a master' degree in business administration. They were married in 1986, and have two daughters.

40

Historic Landmarks of Asian America

◆ Arizona ◆ Arkansas ◆ California ◆ Colorado ◆ Florida ◆ Hawaii ◆ Idaho ◆ Illinois
◆ Massachusetts ◆ Nevada ◆ New York ◆ Oregon ◆ Pennsylvania ◆ Utah ◆ Washington
◆ Washington, D.C. ◆ Wyoming

The traces of Asians and Pacific Islanders can be found throughout the United States in Chinatowns, temples, vineyards, and railroads. In these places, early Chinese immigrants worked and lived, often on the fringes of society and in relative obscurity. Their mark, though often faint, remains visible nonetheless. Darker memories are stirred at other places—massacre sites and incarceration camps. Though painful to revisit, they remind all Americans of the perils of intolerance. For good or ill, they are part of the fabric of U.S. history.

Although the first Asian Americans arrived about 150 years ago, most events of historical significance occurred during the last 100 years; the development of ethnic communities, the enactment and eventual repeal of exclusionary immigration and property laws, the establishment of internment camps during World War II, and the flood of Asian immigration since 1965.

Given the diversity and relative youth of the Asian American population, an historic site is not determined by its age or culture, but by the events that occurred there. Thus cities and farms, ghost towns and fishing villages are all included here, in what can be only a partial listing of the landmarks and monuments that permeate the history of Asians in the United States.

◆ ARIZONA

Gila River Relocation Center

The Gila River Relocation Center was one of ten internment camps in which Japanese Americans, most of them U.S. citizens, were incarcerated during World War II. Constructed on Native American reservation land, the facility was in operation from July 20, 1942, to November 10, 1945; its peak population reached 13,348. Most of the detainees were Californians relocated from the Sacramento River Delta, Fresno County, and the Los Angeles area. The center contained two camps, Canal Camp 1 and Butte Camp 2; both sites are difficult to discern today. One of the few visible remnants is the Gila River Honor Roll Monument, currently in ruins and covered with graffiti.

See also entries for Poston Relocation Center (Arizona), Jerome and Rohwer Relocation Centers (Arkansas), Manzanar and Tule Lake Relocation Centers (California), Amache Relocation Center (Colorado), Minidoka Relocation Center (Idaho), Topaz Relocation Center (Utah), and Heart Mountain (Wyoming).

Poston Relocation Center (Parker)

The larger Arizona's two internment sites, the Poston relocation center was one of ten camps in which Japanese Americans were incarcerated during World War II. Like the Gila River site, Poston was also established on Native American land. The camp opened May 8, 1942, and closed November 28, 1945; peak population reached 17,814. Most internees had been relocated from California, especially Fresno, the Monterey Bay Area, Sacramento and Kern counties; others came from southern Arizona. Of the ten camps, the Poston complex has the most buildings still standing, including an adobe auditorium and classroom buildings erected by the internees in sweltering desert heat. The Poston climate was so severe that choking dust storms would sometimes tear away roofs. Today, a 30-foot-high single concrete column marks the site. Six memorial plaques around the bottom portion give a short history of the evacuation, the establishment of the Poston complex, its administration, the resettlement of the internees, and a tribute to Poston's 24 internees who perished in World War II.

See also entries for Gila River Relocation Center (Arizona), Jerome and Rohwer Relocation Centers (Arkansas), Manzanar and Tule Lake Relocation Centers (California), Amache Relocation Center (Colorado), Minidoka Relocation Center (Idaho), Topaz Relocation Center (Utah), and Heart Mountain (Wyoming).

♦ ARKANSAS

Jerome Relocation Center

Jerome and the Rohwer Relocation centers were the eastern most of the ten relocation camps where Japanese Americans, mostly U.S. citizens, were incarcerated during World War II. Jerome opened October 6, 1942, and closed June 30, 1944; peak population at the camp reached 8,497. Most of the internees were relocated from the central San Joaquin Valley and the San Pedro Bay area in California. Today, a 10-foot-tall granite monument commemorates the site.

See also entries for Gila River and Poston Relocation Centers (Arizona), Rohwer Relocation Center (Arkansas), Manzanar and Tule Lake Relocation Centers (California), Amache Relocation Center (Colorado), Minidoka Relocation Center (Idaho), Topaz Relocation Center (Utah), and Heart Mountain (Wyoming).

Rohwer Relocation Center

One of ten Japanese American relocation camps, Rohwer opened September 18, 1942, and closed November 30, 1945; its peak population reached 8,475. Most of the internees were relocated from Los Angeles and Stockton. Today, the Rohwer Memorial Cemetery contains three monuments and twenty-four gravestones. The tallest monument, inscribed with a poem written in Japanese, was erected by Rohwer internees in 1944. The second, a replica of a tank, was erected during the war to honor the Rohwer internees who died serving their country. The third and newest monument was dedicated in 1982 to commemorate the site.

See also entries for Gila River and Poston Relocation Centers (Arizona), Jerome Relocation Center (Arkansas), Manzanar and Tule Lake Relocation Centers (California), Amache Relocation Center (Colorado), Minidoka Relocation Center (Idaho), Topaz Relocation Center (Utah), and Heart Mountain (Wyoming).

♦ CALIFORNIA

Ah Louis Store, San Luis Obispo

Founded in 1874 by On Wong, popularly known as "Ah Louis," this two-story, brick building was the first Chinese American store in San Luis Obispo County. Ah Louis, who was born in China and came to the United States as a young man, was a labor contractor who also sold dry goods, tea, sugar, rice, and Chinese merchandise. He also set up one of the area's first brick-making kilns; his bricks were used for the roundhouse, the old courthouse, and the east wing of the San Luis Obispo Mission. In his later years, Ah Louis became a pioneer in the flower and vegetable seed industry.

Angel Island Immigration Station, San Francisco Bay

Angel Island was the entry point for most of the 175,000 Chinese immigrants who came to the United States between 1910 and 1940. Chinese immigration had been severely restricted by the Chinese Exclusion Act of 1882, which allowed only government officials, merchants, students, teachers, visitors, and those claiming U.S. citizenship to enter. All potential immigrants, both new arrivals and returning U.S. residents, if admitted, were subjected to medical scrutiny and an elaborate questioning process before being released. The process could take as little as two days or as long as two years. At any given time, between 200 and 300 males and 30 to 50 females were detained on Angel Island. Evidence of the immigrants' ordeal is recorded in the form of poetry that was carved into the barrack walls. These poems expressed the immigrants' impressions of their voyage to the United States, their longing for families back home, and the outrage and humiliation they felt at the often unjust treatment they endured. In 1940, when a fire destroyed the administration building, the government abandoned the immigration station. By 1970, the remaining two-story detention barrack had been marked for destruction until a park ranger noticed characters inscribed on the walls. The discovery sparked the local Asian American community to lobby for the building's preservation, and in 1976, the state legislature appropriated $250,000 for the purpose. Today, the detention center is the site of a picturesque state park in the middle of San Francisco Bay.

Bodie's Chinese American Community, Bodie

Chinese miners came to Bodie in the 1860s and 1870s in search of gold, but soon found themselves excluded from the mines and relegated to service occupations. The 1880 Census lists several hundred Chinese Americans in Bodie who worked as laundry workers, cooks, peddlers, servants, storekeepers,

Chinese American poet Him Mark Lai reads poetry carved by Chinese immigrants into the walls of the U.S. Immigration Station at Angel Island during their detention. Him Mark Lai's father was among those detained in 1910. (AP/Wide World.)

wood haulers, teamsters, dishwashers, a waiter, a druggist, a restaurant owner, a lodging house owner, and miners. Today, only three badly deteriorated buildings remain from Bodie's Chinese American community, all located on the outskirts of town on King Street, once the center of Bodie's Chinatown.

Bowles

Japanese Americans claim that there are two towns called Bowles: one on the Santa Fe Railroad south of Fresno, and the "Japanese Bowles," a farming community of Japanese Americans, a few miles further west. During the early 1900s, mail for these farms was delivered to the Bowles train station; farmers had to go there to pick it up. The community is now legally part of Fresno, but the Japanese still refer to it as Bowles. Bordered by Chestnut Avenue to the east, Raisin City to the west, Central Avenue to the north, and Dinuba Avenue to the south, it remains predominantly farmland for grapes and tree fruit.

The first Japanese man in Bowles came to work on the Santa Fe Railroad. Because land around the tracks was already settled, he bought property east of Highway 41 in 1902-03. By 1910, 28 Japanese American families owned some 1,450 acres; ten years later, there mere nearly 100 families who owned 3,500 acres. In the 1930s, the farmers were plagued with economic difficulties and 95 percent of them lost their land to the banks. Ironically, many of them were able to buy their farms back for less than half their worth, because the banks found holding the land unprofitable. During the internment years of World War II, many Japanese leased their farms to non-Japanese friends. In 1979, Japanese farmers owned almost 4,000 acres of land. Today, Bowles remains an active farming community.

Buddhist Church of Bakersfield, Bakersfield

This one-story, light gray clapboard structure is the country's oldest Japanese Buddhist church building constructed by its congregation that is still used for religious services. Completed in June 1911, it cost $3,314.50. The church altar, which was shipped in pieces to Bakersfield from Japan and reassembled upon arrival, is the oldest altar in the United States. The Buddhist Church and St. Andrews Methodist Church are the remains of a once bustling Japanese community of more than 400.

China Camp State Park, San Rafael

This lush 1,600-acre park on San Pablo Bay is home to a Chinese fishing village that dates from the 1860s, when Chinese fishermen began shrimping in California. As their enterprise grew in the decades that followed, other "shrimp camps" were founded along the shores of both the San Francisco and San Pablo bays. China Camp was one of the largest and longest lived. Its peak population was 469 inhabitants, 368 of them directly associated with shrimp fishery, according to the 1880 Census. Records indicate that the village also had three general stores, one marine supply store, and a barber shop. Ironically, shrimp was not yet a part of the average U.S. diet, and most of the shrimp caught were dried and sent to China.

Today, China Camp is a near ghost town of tumble-down buildings. Remaining historic structures include a shrimp drying shed, a pier, a shrimp grinding shed, two floating houses (now beached), and several other residences. Frank Quan, a descendent of an early Chinese American shrimp fisherman, maintains the last standing pier and buildings. The camp is now surrounded by a wilderness park.

Chinatown, Los Angeles

Los Angeles's current Chinatown is actually its third, created by developers after the first and second Chinatowns were moved to make way for large construction projects. Compared to San Francisco's Chinatown, Los Angeles's is small both in area and population. About 15,000 Chinese and Southeast Asians (mostly Vietnamese) live in the area, although many times that number frequent the area's shops, markets, and restaurants. Located in downtown Los Angeles near the intersection of the Pasadena Freeway and Highway 101, Chinatown's main street is North Broadway, where elaborate Chinese New Year celebrations are held each year. The neighborhood is bordered by Yale, Bernard, and Ord Streets, and Alameda Avenue.

Chinatown, Oakland

Smaller compared to San Francisco's crowded community, Oakland's Chinatown across the bay is filled with markets and restaurants. The area, defined by Eighth and Ninth Streets between Harrison and Franklin, is located just south of Old Oakland and east of the Produce District.

Chinatown, San Francisco

Home to some 100,000, San Francisco's Chinatown is second only to New York City's. San Francisco's original Chinatown burned down in the fire that followed the 1906 earthquake. Today, this bustling, vital downtown area comprises approximately 24 blocks—a city within a city. Set on an incline, where San Francisco's famously steep streets begin their sharp ascent, Chinatown is located just south of North Beach, and defined approximately as Bay Street south to California Street and Sansome Street west to Van Ness Avenue. The green-tiled, dragon-crowned Chinatown Gate, at Bush Street and Grant Avenue, is the most obvious and most popular entrance. Highlights include Old St. Mary's Church (Grant and California streets), built with granite quarried in China; Portsmouth Square, a favorite hang-out for local *t'ai chi* artists by morning and chess players by day; the Chinese Cultural Center (Kearny Street), which frequently displays both Chinese American art exhibits and traveling exhibits of Chinese culture; the Old Chinese Telephone Exchange (Washington Street near Kearny Street), a three-tiered pagoda built in 1909; Buddha's Universal Church (720 Washington Street), a five-story, hand-built temple decorated with murals and tile mosaics; Tien Hou Temple (125 Waverly Place), an ornate temple dedicated to the Queen of the Heavens and Goddess of the Seven Seas by Day Ju, one of the first three Chinese to arrive in San Francisco in 1852; and the Chinese Six Companies building (843 Stockton Street), an example of Chinese architecture with its curved roof tiles and elaborate cornices.

Chinatown, San Jose

During the 1850s, when San Jose was the gateway to the southern mines for Chinese immigrants, a Chinese American community gradually developed around Market and San Fernando Streets. As the city grew, officials fretted over the valuable land in the central business district that was inhabited by the Chinese. On March 18, 1887, the city council requested its lawyers to devise a legal means of moving the Chinese to the edge of the city. On May 4 of the same year, Chinatown was razed by a suspicious fire. According to a local newspaper, "a well-known fireman says that he was one of the first men at the fire and when he arrived flames were issuing from three different points in wooden Chinatown, as if an incendiary had been at work." Incredibly, the 10,000-gallon water tank from which Chinatown received its water was almost empty when the fire began. The loss to Chinese Americans was immeasurable.

When the flames died down, the city refused to allow Chinatown's residents to rebuild in the same location. Laws that prevented Chinese from owning land in California made relocation for Chinatown's homeless residents even more difficult. Eventually, land at Sixth and Taylor Streets, leased from its owner John Heinlen, grew to become the new Chinatown, also known as Heinlenville. Although it flourished at the turn of the century, nearby residents protested its growth and formed home protective associations to drive out the Chinese. By 1931, many of the brick buildings in the 44-year-old Chinatown were pulled down to expand of the Department of Public Works.

Today, San Jose has no Chinatown. Its only remnants are the Ken Ying Low Restaurant and two vacant buildings.

Chinese Historical Society of America, San Francisco

Located at 650 Commercial Street in San Francisco's Chinatown, the society is the first of its kind in North America. Conceived in the fall of 1962, it became a reality on January 5, 1963. The society provides information about the history of Chinese immigrants and their contributions to California's rail, mining, and fishing industries. Exhibits trace the Chinese American experience from the 1850s to the present. The present headquarters, near Sacramento and Montgomery, contains a small museum, which claims to house the largest collection of Chinese American artifacts in the country.

Fiddletown's Chinese American Community

During the 1850s and 1860s, Chinese immigrants first came to Fiddletown looking for gold. The area was then the trading center for mining areas in Amador County, and oral history claims that its Chinese population was once between 3,000 and 12,000—second only to San Francisco's Chinatown. The U.S. Census records, however, do not corroborate this. By 1900, as mines shut down and racism grew, only 11 Chinese Americans were reported to be living in Fiddletown. Three historic buildings remain as evidence of the Chinese American population, including a one-story herb shop (Chew Kee Store), which is currently a museum, a one-story gambling hall, and a two-story general store. The owner of the herb shop, Chew Kee, and his wife returned to China in 1911, leaving their extensive property holdings to their adopted son, Chow-You Fong (also known as Jimmie Chow). When Chow died in 1965, he was the last Chinese American resident of Fiddletown.

Harada House, Riverside

The Harada case *(The People of the State of California v. Jukichi Harada, et al.)* was the first to confront the unconstitutionality of California's Alien Land Law of 1913 which prohibited Asian immigrants from owning property. (It was not abolished until 1952.) In December 1915, Jukichi Harada purchased a one-story saltbox cottage in a middle-class neighborhood in the name of his three U.S.-born children. Neighbors sued Harada, charging that he was an alien ineligible for U.S. citizenship and therefore not allowed to possess, acquire, transfer, or enjoy any real property in the state of California. The trial, which began December 14, 1916, was not resolved

until September 17, 1918, when Judge Hugh H. Crain of the Riverside County Superior Court reached a favorable verdict for the Harada family. He ruled that although aliens who were ineligible for citizenship could not own land, their U.S.-born children had rights equal to those of any other U.S. citizen. Generations of Haradas lived in the famous home.

Haraszthy Buena Vista Winery, Sonoma

In 1857, Agoston Haraszthy, owner of the Buena Vista Vineyards and father of the California wine industry, employed Chinese workers to tunnel into a hillside, creating a cellar for 5,000 gallons of wine. They built a second tunnel in 1858, and a third in 1862. They also plowed the soil, pruned the vines, filled and corked bottles, and performed other duties as needed to ensure the smooth operation of the winery. Historians agree that viticulture in California would have been set back 30 to 50 years without their labors.

Hercules Powder Plant, Hercules

Most employees at the California Powder Works, a dynamite plant that opened in 1881, were Chinese Americans. They worked sixty-hour, six-day work weeks in the very dangerous nitroglycerine lines. This was back-breaking, life-threatening work, for which the Chinese earned only $1.25 per hour—far lower than the wages of white workers with less hazardous jobs. Moreover, the Chinese were isolated in two long, narrow, box-like dormitories, in which nearly 400 men slept in three tiers of bunks along the length of the walls. White workers lived in family cottages. During 1881 and 1919, 59 workers were killed in explosions, most of them in the nitroglycerine house and the dynamite production buildings.

Japanese American National Museum, Los Angeles

The Japanese American National Museum, which opened in 1992, is the first museum in the United States dedicated to sharing the experiences of Americans of Japanese ancestry. The museum is located in Little Tokyo and is housed in the recently restored sanctuary of the former Nishi Hongwanji Buddhist Temple, which was built in 1925. The planned Phase II expansion will triple its size, increaseexhibit and collection space more than five-fold, and offer a state-of-the-art database system, a National Resource Center, and a long-term core exhibit that will focus on the history of Japanese American life over the past 130 years.

Japantown, San Francisco

Japanese Americans had settled in the neighborhood known as the Western Addition before the 1906 earthquake. After the quake and its subsequent fire destroyed much of San Francisco, many Japanese Americans relocated to the Western Addition. By the 1930s, these pioneering residents had opened shops, markets, meeting halls, restaurants, and temples. During World War II, when many of the area's residents were unjustly incarcerated, the area was virtually deserted.

Today's Japantown, or Nihonmachi, is centered on the slopes of Pacific Heights, north of Geary Boulevard, between Fillmore and Laguna streets. One of the community's signature events is the Cherry Blossom Festival, which is celebrated over two weekends every April. At the heart of Japantown is the three-block long, five-acre Japan Center, a multimillion-dollar development created by Japanese American architect Minoru Yamasaki, which opened to the public in 1968 with a three-day festival. The center is dominated by the Peace Plaza and a five-tiered pagoda, both designed by Yoshiro Taniguchi of Tokyo, an authority on ancient Japanese buildings. A *yagura*, "wooden drum tower," spans the plaza entrance, and the copper-roofed *heiwa dori*, "peace walkway," connects the East and Kintetsu buildings.

Koreatown, Los Angeles

Koreans are one of the newest and largest ethnic groups to settle in Los Angeles, where they constitute the single-largest Korean community in the United States. Located south of Wilshire Boulevard, along Olympic Boulevard between Vermont and Western avenues, it has become a cohesive neighborhood with an infrastructure of active community groups and newspapers. The many signs written in Korean is strong evidence of the presence of recent immigrants. Koreantown was the scene of the infamous riots of April 1992. Thanks to dedicated residents and merchants, the area has been largely rebuilt and restored.

Lang Station Site, Saugus

Charles Crocker, president of the Southern Pacific Railroad Company, drove a golden spike into the ground here on September 5, 1876. The act marked the completion of the San Joaquin Valley Line, which connected Los Angeles and San Francisco by rail for the first time. Most of the railroad workers who made this achievement possible were Chinese Americans. Although the station building no longer exists, railroad tracks, crossing signals, and equipment still mark the site.

Little Tokyo, Los Angeles

Located in downtown Los Angeles, Little Tokyo was the Japanese community's original ethnic neighborhood in Los Angeles. Defined by First, San Pedro, Third, and Los Angeles streets, the area today is less residential since many Japanese Americans have relocated to the suburbs of Gardena and West Los Angeles; Little Tokyo, however, remains a cultural focal point for the community. Nisei Week is celebrated every August with traditional drums, O-Bon dancing, and a huge parade.

Locke

The village of Locke in the Sacramento-San Joaquin Delta region is the only rural community in the United States to have been built solely by and for Chinese Americans. The population remains largely unchanged today. The town's original isolation resulted from alien land laws that barred early Chinese immigrants from owning land in California and prevented them from establishing permanent communities. They could only live in areas no one else wanted to be, and if the landowner wanted the property for other uses, the immigrants were forced to vacate.

Chinese Americans were allowed to establish communities in the Sacramento-San Joaquin Delta region because their labor was needed to drain swamps, build levees, and grow crops. Founded in 1915, the village of Locke gave Chinese farm laborers and their families a social and recreational infrastructure, including schools, churches, temples, stores, community organizations, tea houses, restaurants, and a Chinese-run movie theater.

Today, many of Locke's fewer than 100 residents can trace their ancestry to the immigrants who mined the gold fields, built the transcontinental railroad, and constructed the delta's intricate levee system. The town is reminiscent of an outdoor museum. One can still stroll along wooden sidewalks, see the tumbledown two-story buildings along the block-long Main Street and wander through the orchards and communal gardens that residents have tended for generations. Along the ridgetops of the false-front buildings, one can still discern the outlines of hand-lettered signs for the Chinese Bakery and Lunch Parlor, the Star Theatre, or Waih and Co. Groceries & Dry Goods.

Los Angeles Massacre Site, Los Angeles

The Los Angeles Massacre, which occurred on October 24, 1871, left 19 Chinese Americans dead. Part of the massacre area is now within the boundaries of El Pueblo de Los Angeles State Historic Park, although New High and Los Angeles streets still exist.

The event that sparked the riot happened on October 23, 1871, when a quarrel between two Chinese Americans led to a shooting and subsequent arrest. The dispute continued the next day, and when a police officer tried to step in more gunshots were fired, and a bystander accidentally shot and killed. Spectators began attacking the Chinese residents who sought refuge in a nearby adobe building. A mob began to build and random shooting followed. The crowd forced its way into the building, torturing, hanging, and shooting the innocent Chinese inside. In addition, every Chinese building on the block was ransacked and robbed. The estimated loss in money was $30,000 to $70,000. Among the murderers, a few were imprisoned for a short period at San Quentin, but the mob leaders escaped punishment.

Manzanar Relocation Center

One of ten relocation camps where Japanese Americans, mostly U.S. citizens, were incarcerated during World War II, Manzanar opened March 21, 1942, and closed November 21, 1945. The peak population at the camp reached 10,046. The majority of the internees were Californians relocated from Los Angeles, San Fernando Valley, and San Joaquin County, although others came from Bainbridge Island, Washington. Located between Independence and Lone Pine, Manzanar was originally established as one of 13 temporary detention centers in California; three months later, the War Relocation Authority took over the site, and Manzanar became the first of ten permanent centers. Today, two stone entrance stations, a high school auditorium, and a 15-foot-high cemetery monument, interspersed with concrete barracks foundations, tea garden ruins, grave sites, and mess hall debris are all that remain of the camp.

See also entries for Gila River and Poston Relocation Centers (Arizona), Jerome and Rohwer Relocation Centers (Arkansas), Tule Lake Relocation Center (California), Amache Relocation Center (Colorado), Minidoka Relocation Center (Idaho), Topaz Relocation Center (Utah), and Heart Mountain (Wyoming).

Mo Dai Miu or Temple of Kuan Kung, Mendocino

This temple is the last remaining Chinese house of worship on the northern coast of California. The building dates from at least 1883, although oral history suggests that it may have been built as early as 1854. The temple is an important reminder of the contributions of early Chinese pioneers, especially since written records make little mention of them. The 1880 Census recorded 346 Chinese in the county, although many more are said to have gone uncounted. The simple rectangular building is still maintained for continuous worship by the great-grandchildren of one of the temple's founders, Joe Lee (or Chong Sung), one of the county's earliest settlers.

National Japanese American Historical Society, San Francisco

Founded in 1980 and located at 1855 Folsom Street, Suite 161, the mission of the National Japanese American Historical Society is to ensure that stories of the Japanese American experience are remembered. Through traveling exhibitions, publications, and educational programs, the society is a vital national and international resource for institutions and individuals.

Nippon Hospital, Stockton

The Nippon hospital, completed in 1919 at a cost of $20,000, was built by Stockton's Japanese community in reaction to the belief that it did not receive adequate medical care during the flu epidemic of 1918. The hospital was in operation until 1930, when financial difficulties forced it to close. The building was later used as a hotel and then as housing for senior citizens.

Quick Ranch Stone Wall, Mariposa

Often referred to as a miniature Great Wall of China, this rock boundary wall is four miles long and four feet high. Quick Ranch records show that it was constructed in 1862 by Chinese builders, under the direction of a Chinese boss. Each worker had to complete a rod and a half (24-3/4 feet) every day to earn the $0.25 daily wage. The ranch's founder, Morgan Quick, provided food for the workers from a herd of hogs he had bought at about a cent and a half a pound. The Chinese overseer, who sat under an umbrella and kept count of each foot of wall on his abacus, was paid $1.75 per rod (16-1/2 feet). Most of the original wall, constructed for a total cost of $6,000, is still standing. It is a prime example of Chinese stone masonry technique and has been used to help identify other Chinese stone walls throughout the state.

Terminal Island, East San Pedro

Before World War II, Terminal Island was a fishing village where approximately 3,000 Japanese Americans lived and worked. It began as an all-male community, and by the summer of 1907, when canning companies began production on the island, was home to several hundred Japanese fishermen. The number of women and children soon increased, especially when women were hired to work in the canneries. The island's main language was Japanese and many cultural activities reflected Japanese influences. Fisherman Hall, the island's community center, was built in 1916.

In February 1942, however, the island's inhabitants were forcibly relocated to internment camps, the first of the more than 120,000 Japanese Americans to be imprisoned during the war. Many of the men had already been imprisoned by the FBI in December 1941, months before Executive Order 9066, which mandated the Japanese incarceration, was issued. When the war ended, the residents of Terminal Island did not return to their homes.

Today there is no trace of the Japanese community—the fishermen's houses and shops have been destroyed. The only remaining structure is the Terminal School, once attended by Japanese schoolchildren, and is now used by the Marine Corps.

Truckee

The town of Truckee was the site of several riots and periods of racial unrest in which the local Chinatown was repeatedly burned and Chinese Americans driven from their homes. After the first fire, a new community was built behind Front Street near the old jail. On May 29, 1875, fire again destroyed the entire Chinese American community—a $50,000 loss to its residents. The Chinese rebuilt, but on November 18, 1878, a mob of 400 to 500 whites set fire to all thebuildings in the Chinese quarter. In spite of these attacks, a fourth Chinatown appeared on the south side of the Truckee River outside the city limits. Its last remaining structure, the Old Chinese Herb Shop, still stands. Built in 1878, the small, one-story rectangular brick building is surrounded by various modern homes to the south and a trailer park to the north and east.

Tule Lake Relocation Center, Newell

One of ten relocation camps where Japanese Americans, mostly U.S. citizens, were incarcerated during World War II, Tule Lake opened May 27, 1942, and was the last camp to close on March 20, 1946. Its peak population reached 18,789, making it the single-largest camp. The majority of its internees were initially relocated from the Sacramento area, southwestern Oregon, and western Washington.

Located six miles south of the California-Oregon border, the camp encompassed 7,400 acres, most of it for agricultural activities. Approximately 1-1/4 square miles made up the residential area, which was surrounded by barbed-wire fence and guard towers. The enclosure held 64 blocks, each divided into 14 20-by-100-foot-long barracks designed to accommodate 250 people. The blocks were further subdivided into four or six apartment units.

In July 1943, Tule Lake was designated as the segregation center for internees who wished to be repatriated to Japan or who had replied in the negative to Questions 27 and 28 of the U.S. Government's Loyalty Questionnaire. Internees who arrived after this time came from all West Coast states and Hawaii. Due to its program of segregation, more than any of the other relocation camps, Tule Lake's history is most heavily

marked by human tragedy and inner disturbance. The Tule Lake Historic Monument marker, a large semicircular, red stone, is located on California Highway 139 in Newell.

See also entries for Gila River and Poston Relocation Centers (Arizona), Jerome and Rohwer Relocation Centers (Arkansas), Manzanar Relocation Center (California), Amache Relocation Center (Colorado), Minidoka Relocation Center (Idaho), Topaz Relocation Center (Utah), and Heart Mountain (Wyoming).

White Point, San Pedro

During the 1890s, Japanese immigrants pioneered an abalone fishing industry in White Point. The venture proved profitable for about a decade until racist propaganda alleged that a group of Japanese were spying on the southern California coastline for the Japanese government. By 1905, California barred Japanese Americans from continuing the abalone enterprise. Ten years later, the area was developed by Ramon Sepulveda and Tamiji Tagami into a seashore spa around the nearby sulfur springs. The White Point Health Resort, consisting of sulphur water baths, an Olympic-sized swimming pool, and a sulfur hole, was one of the few recreational venues open to Japanese at the time. Unfortunately, the 1933 Long Beach earthquake reduced the resort to ruins. Today, only the remains of a crumbling fountain are left.

Won Lim Temple, Weaverville

The facade of this Taoist temple is painted to resemble the blue tiles and stone of traditional Chinese temples. Originally built in the early 1850s, it burned down on June 28, 1873, but was rebuilt and dedicated the following year. The temple, located in an area of scattered residential dwellings, is close to the former Chinese section of Weaverville, where ruins of three Chinese stores still remain. Chinese Americans, who first arrived in Trinity County looking for gold, numbered 1,951 (mostly miners) by 1880. At least three known Taoist temples were built, two in Weaverville and one in nearby Lewiston. Only the Won Lim Temple exists today.

Yamato Colony, Livingston

In 1904, Kyutaro Abiko purchased 3,000 acres in Livingston and divided them into 40-acre units. He planned to establish Yamato Colony, an agricultural Japanese community in the Central Valley, confident that the future of Japanese in California was in farming. In November 1906, the first Japanese purchased land in Yamato, and by 1908, 30 individuals had bought into the venture. From 1910 to 1915, the new farmers toiled at converting open land to productive fields.

The initial crops included eggplant, sweet potatoes, asparagus, tomatoes, and melons. A food-buying cooperative began in 1910; a marketing cooperative was established in 1914; and a packing shed was built in 1917. Yamato residents understood that only in the agricultural sector would they avoid any competition with non-Japanese, thereby decreasing the chances of racial tension developing. To that end, residents of Yamato never developed commercial enterprises, such as grocery stores, laundries, or other businesses.

Prior to World War II, 69 Japanese American families were reported to be farming more than 3,700 acres in Yamato. During the war and the internment years, 54 families from Livingston and the neighboring town of Cortex hired a land manager to oversee their property. Upon return, many of the first-generation farmers passed management of the farms to the next generation. In recent years, the Livingston Farmer's Association listed 65 members of which 57 were second-generation Japanese Americans.

◆ COLORADO

Amache Relocation Center, Granada

One of ten relocation camps where Japanese Americans, mostly U.S. citizens, were incarcerated during World War II, Amache opened August 24, 1942, and closed October 15, 1945. The peak population at the camp reached 7,318. The majority of the internees were relocated from the northern California Coast, west Sacramento Valley, northern San Joaquin Valley, and Los Angeles. Today, the site of the camp is marked by "Amache Remembered," a monument that commemorates the 31 patriotic internees who lost their lives in World War II as well as the approximately 7,000 stateside internees, 120 of whom died while incarcerated. In the cemetery stands a ten-foot *I-Tei-To* monument, ten graves, and a small building housing another, smaller *I-Tei-To* monument.

See also entries for Gila River and Poston Relocation Centers (Arizona), Jerome and Rohwer Relocation Centers (Arkansas), Manzanar and Tule Lake Relocation Centers (California), Minidoka Relocation Center (Idaho), Topaz Relocation Center (Utah), and Heart Mountain (Wyoming).

◆ FLORIDA

The Morikami Museum and Japanese Gardens, Delray Beach

The Morikami Museum and Japanese Gardens, founded in 1977, in Delray Beach in Palm Beach County, Florida, is the only museum in the United States dedicated exclusively to the living culture of Japan. The idea of the museum was born through an act of generosity by George Sukeji Morikami (1886-1975), a Japanese farmer who came to the U.S. in 1906 as a penniless 19-year old indentured worker in the Yamato Colony, the experimental cooperative community settled by Japanese farmers in Boca Raton in the early 1900s. Morikami went on to build a million-dollar land empire from the sandy soil of southern Florida. Out of gratitude for the people of his adopted homeland, this last living pioneer of the Yamato Colony donated 35 acres of his land to Palm Beach County in 1974. Additional gifts in 1974 and 1975 increased the park to nearly its present size of 200 acres.

The park's and the museum's initial development grew out of a friendship between George Morikami and Seishiro Tomioka, a young Japanese landscape architect on the staff of Palm Beach County. Together with support from the County Parks and Recreation Department and, ultimately, the Board of County Commissioners, the Morikami was designed and created as both a monument to the Japanese settlers of Yamato, Florida, and a place where Americans could learn about and gain appreciation for the culture of Japan. Financial support was secured through a private arm, Morikami, Inc., which initiated a bi-national fund raising effort in Japan and the U.S.

The original Morikami Museum building, "Yamato-kan," is situated amid pine forests, nature trails, lakes teeming with golden *koi*, waterfalls, and formal Japanese gardens. Modeled after a Japanese imperial villa and opened in 1977, it houses a permanent exhibition detailing the history of Yamato Colony In 1993, the Morikami was expanded by the addition of a new 32,000 square-foot museum building designed in the Japanese style, which houses an array of exhibitions, special events and cultural activities.

Focusing on folk art, crafts, and ethnographic materials, most of which date from 1868 to the present, exhibits range from an extensive collection of Japanese folk toys and everyday items made from clay, wood, paper, or bamboo, to traditional *kimono* textiles, exquisite lacquerware, and modern comic book art. Demonstrations and classes illuminate the living arts of Japan such as dance and musical performances by guest artists. The museum also houses an authentic tea room with regularly scheduled demonstrations of the traditional Japanese tea ceremony. The new Morikami includes a 225-seat theatre for Japanese film festivals, a library and audio-visual resource center, classrooms, a Museum Store offering authentic Japanese gifts, a Japanese cafe and surrounding terraces planted with *bonsai* miniature tropical trees, and picnic pavilions and gardens. An added attraction for visitors to the Museum are the seasonal Japanese festivals celebrated on site such as the *Hatsume Fair*'s taiko drums, arts, crafts, and plants, the summer *Bon Festival*'s fireworks and lantern-floating, and *Oshogatsu*, the Japanese New Year family games and crafts.

Educational programs offered at the Morikami are designed for all ages to develop a deeper appreciation and understanding of Japanese art and culture. Ongoing programs include gallery talks, lecture series, hands-on activities, and family workshops, docent tours, *bonsai* and orchid-growing classes, *origami*, *Kakizome* (New Year's calligraphy), *Hina shikishi* (Hina doll collage), Japanese language, *Sumi-e* (ink painting), martial arts, and the Zen-inspired ritual art of preparing and serving tea.

The 200-acre Morikami Park is a picturesque and tranquil reserve of pine forests surrounded by modern Palm Beach and suburban communities. An untamed nature trail winds through the forest of slash pines while ferns and giant palmettos punctuate picnic pavilions along the way. In a novel blending of East and West, traditional Japanese gardening techniques and vegetation indigenous to Florida come together in the gardens which host a wide range of native species of flora and fauna. Even integral elements like stones are hand-picked locally from Okeeheelee Park in West Palm Beach.

A future development phase in the museum will introduce a replica of a Japanese farming village, complete with resident artisans, rice paddies, bamboo and pineapple groves, and a country store, which will be the actual Delray Beach historic Sundy Feed Store from the Yamato Colony built in 1912 beside the Florida East Coast Railroad tracks, and relocated and restored on this site.

♦ HAWAII

The Alexander & Baldwin Sugar Museum, Puunene, Maui

Puunene is a working plantation village surrounded by sugarcane fields. The town's museum tells the story of sugar in Hawaii, beginning with Samuel Alexander and Henry Baldwin who bought massive chunks of Hawaiian land. Also on display is a turn-of-the-century labor contract from the Japanese Emigration Company that set wages at $15 a month for ten hours per day of field work, 26 days a month (less $2.50, which was deducted for return passage to Japan). Such conditions were typical of those endured by immigrant laborers who came to work in Hawaii's vast plantation fields, many of whom were imported from China and Japan, and later from the Philippines and Korea.

Aliiolani Hale, Honolulu, Oahu

The first major government building constructed by the Hawaiian monarchy, Aliiolani Hale (House of Heavenly Kings) housed the Hawaiian legislature until it became the home of Hawaii's Supreme Court in 1874. Almost 20 years later, in January 1893, Sanford Dole, the son of a pioneer missionary, proclaimed the establishment of a provisional government and the overthrow of the Hawaiian monarchy on the steps of Aliiolani Hale.

Byodoin, Kaneohe, Oahu

The Byodoin, or Temple of Equality, is the main attraction in the Valley of the Temples, an interdenominational cemetery. The temple was dedicated in 1968 to commemorate the 100th anniversary of Japanese immigration to Hawaii. It is a replica of a 900-year-old temple of the same name in Uji, Japan.

Chinatown, Honolulu, Oahu

Located west of downtown Honolulu, Chinatown is bordered by Honolulu Harbor, Nuuanu Avenue, and River Street. It became a Chinese enclave around 1860, when Chinese sugar-plantation workers who had worked off their labor contracts settled in the area and opened small businesses there. In December 1899, when the bubonic plague ravaged Chinatown, the entire area was cordoned off, and its 7,000 Chinese, Japanese, and Hawaiian residents were forbidden to leave their homes. As plague cases increased, the Board of Health attempted to control the disease by burning infected houses. On January 20, 1900, the building on the corner of Beretania Street and Nuuanu Avenue was set on fire; however, a strong wind spread the blaze uncontrollably and eventually 40 acres of Chinatown burned to the ground. Police guards even tried to prevent quarantined residents from fleeing during the blaze. Some argue that the accidental fire was actually a deliberate act to drive the Chinese out what had become prime real estate on the edge of a growing downtown district. Moreover, when the United States annexed Hawaii in 1898, the Chinese Exclusion Laws were applied to the islands, which stopped Chinese immigration. Despite this adverse climate, the Chinese refused to be driven out and quickly rebuilt a new Chinatown. Today, Chinatown is home to a diverse group of Asian immigrants, with recent Vietnamese, Thai, and Filipino influences. Highlights of the area include Oahu Market (corner of Kekaulike and King Streets), which is the heart of Chinatown and a local institution since 1904; Wo Fat (corner of Hotel and Maunakea Streets), which was built in 1900 just after the fire and is the oldest restaurant in Honolulu; the Izumo Taisha Shrine (Kukui Street), a small wooden Shinto shrine built in 1923; and the Taoist Temple (corner of River and Kukui Streets), which is the temple for the Lum Sai Ho Tong Society, first organized in 1889.

Foster Botanic Garden, Honolulu, Oahu

This 20-acre garden near the northern end of Chinatown contains the site of the first Japanese language school in Oahu. During the bombing of Pearl Harbor, a stray artillery shell exploded into a room filled with young Japanese American students. A memorial marks the site, which today is the garden's herb section. The entrance is on Vineyard Boulevard, opposite the end of River Street.

Hongwanji Mission, Lahaina, Maui

Built in 1927, the Hongwanji is a Buddhist temple still in use today.

Honokaa, Hamakua Coast, Hawaii Island

The sugar mill in the town of Honokaa opened in 1873 and has been the town's chief industry ever since. Most of Honokaa's residents are descendants of the immigrants contracted to work on the town's sugarcane plantations, many of them Chinese and Japanese laborers.

Iolani Palace, Honolulu, Oahu

The Iolani Palace is the only royal palace in the United States. From 1882 to 1891, it served as the official residence of Hawaii's last king, King Kalakaua, and his consort Queen Kapiolani. Kalakaua's sister, Queen Liliuokalani, took residence in 1891 upon her ascension to the throne as Hawaii's last monarch. When the monarchy was overthrown in 1893, the palace became the capitol, first for the Republic of Hawaii, then for the U.S. territory, and later for the state of Hawaii.

Kamehameha's Birthplace, North Kohala, Hawaii Island

Located one-third of a mile from Mookini Heiau, near one of the oldest and most historically significant *heiaus*, "ancient stone temples," in Hawaii, lies a stone enclosure that marks the birth site of King Kamehameha I. The great king is said to have been born here in 1758 on a stormy winter night. According to local legend, the king's mother was told that her son would become a destroyer of chiefs and a powerful ruler. In fear, the high chief of the island ordered the newborn killed. However, the infant was taken to Mookini Heiau for his birth rituals and then sent into hiding in the Kohala Mountains. The prophecy was fulfilled when Kamehameha united all the Hawaiian islands under his rule in 1810.

Kamakahonu, Kona, Hawaii Island

The beach at the north end of Kailua Bay, named Kamakahonu (which means "eye of the turtle"), was the site of the royal residence of King Kamehameha I.

Also known as King Kamehameha the Great, he eventually united all of the Hawaiian Islands under his rule and called them Hawaii after his home island. The King died here in 1819. Today, the ancient sites have been incorporated into the grounds of the Hotel King Kamehameha. A few thatched structures and carved wooden statues that stand erect (called kii gods) have been reconstructed above the old stone temple. Nearby is the Ahuena Heiau, an ancient site of human sacrifice.

Lahaina Jodo Mission, Lahaina, Maui

A bronze Buddha, which overlooks the Lahaina Jodo Mission compound, was erected in 1968 to commemorate the 100th anniversary of Japanese immigration to Hawaii. The statue has been placed with its back toward the mountains, looking out over the Pacific toward Japan.

Pearl Harbor, Oahu

On December 7, 1941, a wave of more than 350 Japanese planes attacked Pearl Harbor, home of the U.S. Pacific Fleet. Approximately 2,335 soldiers died in the two-hour attack, 1,177 of them on the battleship *U.S.S. Arizona*, which suffered a direct hit and sank in nine minutes. The attack served as the catalyst for the United States entrance into World War II. Three months later, on February 19, 1942, claiming that Americans of Japanese ancestry posed a potential threat to national security, President Franklin D. Roosevelt signed Executive Order 9066, which unjustly incarcerated over 120,000 Japanese Americans in ten relocation centers throughout the West for the duration of the war. Over 1.5 million people "remember Pearl Harbor" each year by visiting the U.S.S. *Arizona* memorial run by the National Park Service, making it Hawaii's most visited site.

Puuhonua O Honaunau National Historical Park, Honaunau, Hawaii Island

Commonly called the Place of Refuge, the park encompasses ancient temples, royal grounds, and a *puuhonua*, a "place of refuge" or "sanctuary." The temple on the point of the cove, called Hale O Keawe Heiau, was built around 1650. The bones of 23 royal chiefs are purported to be buried there.

Royal Mausoleum State Monument, Honolulu, Oahu

In the Royal Mausoleum, located at 2262 Nuuanu Avenue, lie the remains of Kings Kamehameha II, III, IV, and V, as well as King David Kalakaua and Queen Liliuokalani, Hawaii's last two reigning monarchs. The only monarch missing is King Kamehameha I, the mighty ruler who united the Hawaiian islands. He was the last king to be buried in secret, in accordance with Hawaii's old religion.

St. Andrew's Cathedral, Honolulu, Oahu

Attracted by the royal trappings of the Church of England, King Kamehameha IV and his consort Queen Emma founded the Anglican Church of Hawaii in 1858. The King decided to build his own cathedral, but died on St. Andrew's Day—hence the name—four years before the cornerstone was finally laid in 1867 by King Kamehameha V. The French Gothic church, shipped in pieces from England, is at the corner of Alakea and Beretania Streets.

Shinmachi/Little Tokyo, Hilo, Hawaii Island

Before the fatal tsunami (tidal wave) of 1946 that inundated Hilo Bay and much of the Big Island, Hilo's bayfront community was known as Little Tokyo, for its Japanese American contingency. The tsunami levelled the enclave, killing 96 people in Hilo alone, but the surviving residents of Little Tokyo quickly rebuilt on the same spot and named it Shinmachi, which literally means "new city." Fourteen years later, another tsunami leveled Shinmachi, but this time, the surviving residents relocated to higher ground. Today, the remains of curbs and partial driveways to businesses that once made up Shinmachi stretch along Kamehameha Avenue.

Wo Hing Temple, Front Street, Lahaina, Maui

The Wo Hing Temple was built in 1912 by the once-flourishing Chinese community of Lahaina. The two-story building has also been used as a meeting hall and served as a home for elderly Chinese men after World War II. Today, the temple is a museum featuring cultural artifacts, a historic photography collection, and a Taoist shrine.

♦ IDAHO

Minidoka Relocation Center

One of ten relocation camps where Americans of Japaneseancestry were incarcerated during World War II, Minidoka opened August 10, 1942, and closed October 28, 1945. The peak population at the camp reached 9,397. The majority of the internees were relocated from the Seattle and Pierce Counties in Washington and from Portland and northwestern Oregon. Located between Jerome and Eden, the site of the camp is marked by a wooden sign that bears the following inscription:

> This is the site of the Minidoka Relocation Center, one of ten American concentration camps established in World War II to incarcerate the 110,000 Americans of Japanese descent living in coastal regions of our Pacific states. Victims of war time hysteria, these people,

two-thirds of whom were United States citizens, lived a bleak humiliating life in tar paper barracks behind barbed wire and under armed guard. May these camps serve to remind us what can happen when other factors supersede the Constitutional right guaranteed to all citizens and aliens living in this country.

Four additional memorial plaques, installed as part of the Idaho State Centennial Project in 1990, also commemorate the site.

See also entries for Gila River and Poston Relocation Centers (Arizona), Jerome and Rohwer Relocation Centers (Arkansas), Manzanar and Tule Lake Relocation Centers (California), Amache Relocation Center (Colorado), Topaz Relocation Center (Utah), and Heart Mountain (Wyoming).

♦ ILLINOIS

Chinatown, Chicago

During the 1880s, at the height of the anti-Chinese campaigns on the West Coast, more and more Chinese workers began heading east. A small group of Chinese congregated in Chicago in a one-block Chinatown at Clark and Van Buren streets, south of the downtown area. Until the mid-1990s, most of these Chinatown residents worked in laundries, restaurants, and grocery stores. In 1910, due to rising rents, the need for expansion, and conflict between two rival organizations, a second Chinatown was formed five miles away in the ten-block area centered on Cermak and Wentworth streets known today as Chinatown. While the new area prospered, the old Chinatown was eventually razed for new construction. A third small Chinatown was eventually established uptown on Argyle and Broadway streets where a number of Chinese already lived. Located 12 miles from the second Chinatown, this area is growing with the latest influx of ethnic Chinese-Vietnamese refugees.

♦ MASSACHUSETTS

Chinatown, Boston

In 1875, 75 Chinese workers from San Francisco were contracted to work in a shoe factory in North Adams, Massachusetts. They were hired under a three-year contract as strikebreakers. A number of these workers later settled in Boston near the South Railway Station. They were soon joined by another group of West Coast workers who were under contract to build the Pearl Street telephone exchange. This was the beginning of what, in the 1970s, would become the fourth-largest Chinatown in the United States. Centered on Beech Street, Boston's Chinatown was originally a middle-class enclave that was abandoned by its white residents, then quickly taken over by Chinese immigrants, most of whom were poor. This segregated, tightly clustered community remained a bachelor society for many years due to the anti-Chinese immigration laws that began with the Chinese Exclusion Act of 1882.

With the advent of World War II and the repeal of the exclusion acts in 1943, immigration increased and the Chinatown population grew quickly. Families were finally reunited, women were allowed to immigrate, new families were formed, and a fresh generation of U.S.-born Chinese Americans grew up. The 1950s through the 1970s saw an increase of immigrants from Hong Kong and other cosmopolitan Asian cities. Today, although only about 10 percent of Boston's Chinese American population lives in Chinatown, the area remains a focal point for social and business activities in the community. Chinatown provides the diverse Chinese American community with language schools, movie theaters, bookstores, a newspaper, community center, and arts center.

◆ NEVADA

Dayton

One of the oldest settlements in Nevada, the town of Dayton went through a series of names before it was finally named after surveyor John Day in 1861. For six years prior, much to the chagrin of the white settlers in the area, the settlement was called Chinatown, a direct result of the presence of approximately 200 Chinese laborers who were hired in 1855 to dig a ditch from Carson River to Gold Canyon. A century later, Dayton found new fame, this time as the location for the film *The Misfits*, starring Clark Gable and Marilyn Monroe.

◆ NEW YORK

Chinatown, New York City

According to the 1980 Census, New York's Chinatown has the largest Chinese American settlement in the United States. On July 10, 1847, the *New York Herald* reported that 35 Chinese had arrived in New York; they were the crew of the ship *Keying*. The first permanent Chinese resident in Manhattan was Quimpo Appo, a tea merchant who arrived in the late 1840s or early 1850s. Not until the 1870s, however, spurred by growing anti-Chinese violence in the West, did significant numbers of Chinese immigrants begin arriving in New York.

In 1878, the same year that the U.S. government denied Chinese immigrants the right to become citizens, the first Chinese grocery store, Wo Kee, opened on Mott Street. Immigrants who had been forced out of a variety of occupations entered low-status service work, finding jobs especially in hand laundries. These workers frequented Wo Kee, cementing the New York Chinese community. Unfortunately, the Chinese Exclusion Act of 1882 and subsequent anti-Chinese immigration laws made it nearly impossible for Chinese women and children to enter the United States. This created an artificial "bachelor society" in New York and other Chinatowns across the country. These ethnic communities served as a social, cultural, and recreation center for immigrants and were a link to families and villages in China. As with other immigrant groups, such neighborhoods helped immigrants integrate into their new society. Unlike European immigrants, however, Chinese men were hindered from having families and denied the possibility of citizenship.

Despite these restrictions, Chinatown's male population grew. More businesses opened to cater to them, including the Wyong Yen Shing general store at 32 Mott, which has remained intact since the 1890s. With their limited career options, the Chinese began to encourage tourism in their district. If they could only get laundry jobs outside Chinatown, then they would bring outsiders into the community and create other opportunities. The ploy was successful, and the area quickly became a tourist attraction.

Old Chinatown, clustered in the lower Mott Street area, remains at the neighborhood's heart. In 1965, however, when immigration restrictions were lifted, an influx of Chinese and other Asian immigrants flooded the community. Today, with more than 150,000 residents, the area has grown from below Canal Street into SoHo and the Lower East Side, with another 150,000 living in satellite communities in Brooklyn and Queens. Today's Chinatown has become the city's manufacturing center, as well as an important jewelry district. Points of interest include the Kim Lau Memorial Arch (Chatham Square), which was erected in memory of Chinese Americans who died in World War II; the Church of the Transfiguration (25 Mott Street), which was built in 1801 as the English Lutheran Church and through its long history has been a religious center for many of the city's ethnic groups, including the Chinese; and the Rear Tenements (between Mulberry and Mott streets), which are examples of the now-illegal rear tenements.

Chinatown History Museum, New York City

The Chinatown History Museum's mission is to reclaim, preserve, and share Chinese American history and culture with a broad audience. Originally established as the New York Chinatown History Project in 1980, the museum's immediate focus is the New York area. Its core exhibit is an interactive, interpretive look at the Chinese-immigrant experience in the United

States. Public programs include lectures, readings, symposia, and family events. The museum, located at 70 Mulberry Street, also houses a library whose extensive archives contain oral histories, photographs, documents, and artifacts. The museum's Asian American bookstore offers the East Coast's most comprehensive source of publications by or about Asian Americans.

Koreatown, New York City

Centered around 32nd Street between Broadway and Fifth Avenue, Koreatown is less a residential area than a commercial district filled predominantly with wholesale shops and restaurants, many identified by signs written only in the Korean language. Koreatown developed gradually during the early 1970s when an influx of Korean immigrants came to New York. Originally clustered on Broadway between 23rd and 31st Streets, Koreatown has helped renovate an once-decaying area. In the last decade, the area has moved slightly uptown, pushing slowly toward the East Side.

♦ OREGON

Chinatown, Portland

Just west of the Old Town area of Portland is a small Chinatown, no larger than a few blocks. The main serpent-adorned entrance is on 4th Avenue, and fiery red and yellow lampposts decorate its streets. In 1989, the area north of Burnside between 3rd and 6th avenues was designated as a national historic district, making the area the oldest and the largest historic district in Oregon.

Gin Lin Trail, Applegate Valley

One of the most diligent Chinese-immigrant miners was Gin Lin, whose mining site is still visible south of Ruch, on the Gin Lin Trail in southern Oregon's Applegate Valley. Gin Lin began mining here in 1881, and throughout the decade, deposited over a million dollars worth of gold dust in a neighboring Jacksonville bank before he returned to China. According to one source, as he got off the return ship in China, he was robbed and fatally beaten.

Kam Wah Chung Museum, John Day

In the 1880s, Chinese outnumbered other groups two to one in the mining town of John Day. The museum, which was once a store, an herbalist's office, and a Chinese social center, offers an informative introduction to the gold mining industry in northeastern Oregon during the late-nineteenth century.

♦ PENNSYLVANIA

Chinatown, Philadelphia

The Chinese make up one of Philadelphia's oldest ethnic communities. Since their arrival in the late 1800s, they have made Chinatown the residential and commercial hub of the Chinese American community. Located just two blocks north of Market Street, centered on 10th and Race Streets, Chinatown is a self-supporting community of grocery stores, gift shops, martial arts studios, restaurants, and other businesses. Chinatown highlights include the Chinese Friendship Gate (10th and Arch Streets), an intricate and colorful 40-foot-tall arch which is the largest authentic Chinese gate outside China, and the Chinese Cultural Center (125 North 10th Street), which occupies a building constructed in 1831 in the Beijing Mandarin palace style.

Philip Jaisohn Memorial House, Media

In 1888, Philip Jaisohn (1864-1951) became the first Korean to become a naturalized U.S. citizen. Four years later, he became the first Korean American to receive a medical degree in the United States. A physician, businessman, civil servant, and newspaper publisher, Jaisohn played an important role in building a bridge between Korea and the United States. The Philip Jaisohn Memorial Foundation, established in 1975, founded the Philip Jaisohn Memorial House in 1987 to preserve some of Jaisohn's possessions, including his books and writing. The home, located at 100 E. Lincoln Street, is a research center that offers a collection of documents pertaining to Korean immigration; in the near future, it will house the oral histories of Korean immigrants on audio-cassettes.

♦ UTAH

Corinne

Just weeks after the May 10, 1869, ceremony in Promontory Point (See Golden Spike National Historic Site entry.) celebrating the completion of the first transcontinental railway, some 5,000 Chinese railroad workers settled in the nearby town of Corinne, comprising two-thirds of the population of this instant city. In 1872, a diphtheria epidemic swept through the town killing hundreds. Many others deserted the area. Today, the once thriving district is a near ghost town.

Golden Spike National Historic Site, Promontory Point

On May 10, 1869, the Great Plains were linked by rail when spikes of Nevada silver and California gold were driven into a railroad tie made of California laurel. The hammer that drove the spike was connected to telegraph wires so that the sound would be carried across the country. The Union Pacific and Central Pacific Railroads had finally come together, creating the country's first transcontinental railway. The western portion of the venture, the Central Pacific line, snaked its way eastward from San Francisco to meet the Union Pacific line, built westward from Omaha. The Central Pacific line through the Sierra Nevadas, was built predominantly by Chinese laborers, who worked for extremely low wages under life-threatening conditions.

Topaz Relocation Center, Sutherland

One of ten relocation camps where Japanese Americans, mostly U.S. citizens, were incarcerated during World War II, Topaz opened September 11, 1942, and closed October 31, 1945. The peak population at the camp reached 8,130. The majority of the internees were relocated from the San Francisco Bay area. Sixteen miles away in the city of Delta, the Topaz Monument stands in a park on the city's main street; the town's Great Basin Museum also houses an internment exhibit. At the camp itself, a five-and-a-half-foot monument is surrounded by dry, desolate, sagebrush land.

See also entries for Gila River and Poston Relocation Centers (Arizona), Jerome and Rohwer Relocation Centers (Arkansas), Manzanar and Tule Lake Relocation Centers (California), Amache Relocation Center (Colorado), Minidoka Relocation Center (Idaho), and Heart Mountain (Wyoming).

◆ WASHINGTON

International District, Seattle

The area that comprises the International District, or "I.D." as locals call it, was also the site of two Chinatowns and a Japanese area called Nihonmachi. Its boundaries are South Weller Street to South Washington Street between 2nd Avenue South and 12th Avenue South.

In the 1880s, Seattle's first Chinatown was centered in a much smaller area around 2nd Avenue and Washington Street. The inhabitants had come to the area to work on railroads and in lumber mills or mines. White laborers, who resented the Chinese and their cheap labor, invaded Chinatown in February 1886 and herded almost all of the city's 350 to 400 Chinese toward ships bound for San Francisco. The expulsion was stopped, but many of Seattle's Chinese left anyway. Not until after the Great Fire of 1889, when they were needed to provide the labor to rebuild the city, did they begin to return.

In the early 1900s, a second Chinatown sprang up, clustered around King and Jackson streets. At the same time, large groups of Japanese laborers settled just north of the second Chinatown area. This community, which developed into Nihonmachi, had more than

6,000 residents by 1910. World War II took a drastic toll on both ethnic communities, especially because of the displacement of its Japanese residents to concentration camps throughout the West. Fortunately, during the 1970s, a concerted effort to revitalize the area encompassed Chinatown and Nihonmachi into the integrated International District. Families returned to the area; more businesses began to open; and I.D. became a pan-Asian melting pot filled with a rich mix of Chinese, Japanese, Filipino, Korean, and most recently, Southeast Asian influences.

Within the I.D. is the Nippon Kan Theatre (628 South Washington Street), a historic reminder of Nihonmachi that originally opened as the Astor Hotel in 1909, and later became a performance hall for Kabuki theater. It is best known for its Japanese performing arts series. Also in the district is the Wing Luke Museum (407 Seventh Avenue), which was named after Seattle's first Chinese American city council member who was also the first Asian American elected to public office in the continental United States. The museum offers rotating exhibits and permanent displays of photographs which chronicle the experience of early Asian immigrants on the West Coast.

◆ WASHINGTON, D.C.

Chinatown, Northwest Washington

Primarily a commercial center, the current Chinatown was established in the early 1930s. Bordered by G Street to the south, I Street to the north, 5th Street to the east, and 7th Street to the west, this is one of the smallest Chinatowns in the United States. The original site off the eastern end of Pennsylvania Avenue was forced to move when the city's municipal center was constructed. The Chinese Friendship Archway (7th and H Streets), which marks the entrance into Chinatown, was built by the District government in coordination with the Municipality of Beijing as part of a sister-city exchange program. Part of Chinatown lies within the boundaries of the Downtown Historic Preservation District, which boasts an eclectic architectural mix of Victorian buildings and renovated Chinese-style buildings. The Washington Convention Center, which is one block west of Chinatown, hosts more than a million people a year, and has had a positive impact on Chinatown. The area is growing and its borders are slowly expanding.

◆ WYOMING

Heart Mountain Relocation Center

One of ten relocation camps where Americans of Japanese ancestry were incarcerated during World War II, Heart Mountain opened August 12, 1942, and closed

November 10, 1945. The peak population at the camp reached 10,767. The majority of the internees were relocated from Santa Clara County and Los Angeles, California, as well as central Washington. Today, the campsite is listed on the National Register of Historic Places as Wyoming #226. Located between Cody and Powell, it is marked by four memorial plaques and a visitor registering post that also provides information about the internment.

See also entries for Gila River and Poston Relocation Centers (Arizona), Jerome and Rohwer Relocation Centers (Arkansas), Manzanar and Tule Lake Relocation Centers (California), Amache Relocation Center (Colorado), Minidoka Relocation Center (Idaho), and Topaz Relocation Center (Utah).

Rock Springs Massacre Site, Rock Springs

Rock Springs, located along the Overland Trail, was founded around 1862. The town was an important point on the Union Pacific Railroad and a coal mining center. Until 1875, only white laborers worked in the coal mines run by the Union Pacific. That year, however, the miners went on strike. The company fired them and hired 150 Chinese and 50 white strikebreakers.

By 1885, 331 Chinese and 150 whites worked in the mines, with racial tension building during the decade. On September 2, 1885, violence erupted when a group of whites went into Rock Springs' Chinatown and killed 28 Chinese, wounded another 15, and drove hundreds out of town. Property damage was estimated at almost $150,000.

One week later troops from nearby Camp Murray were called in to escort the fleeing Chinese back to Rock Springs. The Union Pacific put them back to work immediately. Sixteen men were eventually arrested and jailed for the attack. However, no indictments were brought against the men, and they were soon released. The surviving Chinese were never compensated for losses to their property. Eventually, most of them left Wyomingg.

References

Chen, Jack. *The Chinese of America.* San Francisco: Harper & Row, Publishers, 1980.

Daws, Gavan. *Shoals of Time: A History of the Hawaiian Islands.* New York: The MacMillan Company, 1968.

Drinnon, Richard. *Keeper of Concentration Camps: Dillon S. Myer and American Racism.* Berkeley: University of California Press, 1987.

Iritani, Frank and Joanne Irilani. *Ten Visits: Accounts of Visits to All the Japanese American Relocation Centers.* San Mateo: Japanese American Curriculum Project, Inc., 1994.

Kim, Illsoo. *New Urban Immigrants: The Korean Community of New York.* Princeton: Princeton University Press, 1981.

Kinkead, Gwen. *Chinatown: A Portrait of a Closed Society.* New York: Harper Collins Publishers, 1992.

Lai, Him Mark, Genny Lim, and Judy Yung. *Island: Poetry and History of Chinese Immigrants on Angel Island, 1910-1940.* Seattle: University of Washington Press, 1980.

Leung, Peter C.Y., and L. Eve Armentrout Ma. "Chinese Farming Activities in the Sacramento-San Jaoaquin Delta," *Amerasia Journal.* 14, no. 2, (1988): 1-18.

Liem, Channing. *Phillip Jaisohn.* Kyujang Publishing Company, 1984.

Lillard, Richard G. *Desert Challenge: An Interpretation of Nevada.* Lincoln: University of Nebraska Press, 1942.

Nee, Victor G., and Brett De Bary. *Longtime Californ': A Documentary Study of an American Chinatown.* Boston: Houghton Mifflin Company, 1974.

O'Brien, David J. and Stephen S. Fugita. *The Japanese American Experience.* Bloomington: Indiana University Press, 1991.

Waugh, Isami Arifuku, A. Yamato, and R. Y. Okamura. "A History of Japanese Americans in California." In *Five Views: An Ethnic Historic Site Survey for California.* pp. 159-203, Sacramento: Office of Historic Preservation, 1988.

Weglyn, Michi Nishiura. *Years of Infamy: The Untold Story of America's Concentration Camps.* New York: William Morrow & Company, 1976.

Wey, Nancy. "A History of Chinese Americans in California." In *Five Views: An Ethnic Historic Site Survey for California*, pp. 103-158. Sacramento: Office of Historic Preservation, 1988.

Tour Guides

Bendure, Glenda, and Ned Friary. *Hawaii—A Travel Survival Kit.* Victoria, Australia: Lonely Planet, 1993.

Brewster, David, and Stephanie Irving. *Seattle Best Places.* Seattle: Sasquatch Books, 1991.

Castleman, Deke. *Nevada Handbook.* Chico, CA: Moon Publications Inc., 1990.

Chinatown History Museum. Chinatown Guide and Map.

Duffield, Judy, William Kramer, and Cynthia Sheppard. *Washington, D.C.: The Complete Guide.* New York: Vintage Books, 1994.

Irving, Stephanie, ed. *Portland Best Places.* Seattle: Sasquatch Books, 1990.

Jewell, Judy. *Oregon.* New York: Fodor's Travel Publications, Seattle: Sasquatch Books, 1994.

Magalaner, Jillian, ed. *Fodor's Philadelphia and the Pennsylvania Dutch Country 91.* New York: Fodor's Travel Publications, 1991.

Mullen, Michael, ed. *On the Loose in California.* New York: Fodor's Travel Publications, 1992.

Peterson, Larry, ed. *Fodor's California 93.* New York: Fodor's Travel Publications, Inc., 1992.

Pierce, J. K. *Seattle Access.* New York: Access Press, 1993.

Riegert, Ray. *Hidden San Francisco and Northern California.* Berkeley: Ulysses Press, 1994.

Wharton, Tom, and Gayen Wharton. *Utah.* Discover America series. New York: Fodor's Travel Publications, 1993.

Wilson, D. Ray. *Wyoming Historical Tour Guide.* Carpentersville, IL: Crossroads Communications, 1984.

—Terey Hong

Speeches

♦ RECOLLECTIONS ON THE DECEMBER 7, 1941 BOMBING OF PEARL HARBOR

Personal recollections of Senator Daniel K. Akaka of Hawaii on the events which took place in Hawaii on December 7, 1941 when the Japanese bombed Pearl Harbor.

On December 7, 1941, I was a junior at The Kamehameha School for Boys. That morning, in our dormitory, my classmates and I were preparing to go to church when faint explosions intruded upon our Sunday morning routine. From Kapalama Heights, we looked out our windows toward Honolulu. Our attention was drawn toward Pearl Harbor. Plumes of black smoke rose from that area. None of us realized what was transpiring, except that there seemed to be furious activity going on at the naval base.

To gain a better view, some of us climbed onto the dormitory roof. It was approximately 8:00 a.m. I could now see more explosions at Hickam, while the billows of oily smoke from Pearl continued to increase in numbers and size. Suddenly, we noticed a swarm of aircraft coming toward us. In an instant, they roared over our heads. It was then that we saw the rising suns emblazoned on their wings. I later learned that the group we had observed was headed toward their next target, Kaneohe Air Station.

Someone in the dormitory turned on the radio. It was confirmed; we were under attack by Japan.

As youngsters, though we found ourselves in the midst of that awesome assault, we did not truly and immediately sense the gravity of what was happening. Even as the warplanes streaked past us, there was more an automatic, childish rush of excitement than a logical analysis of what it all meant.

Soon after the onslaught ended, however, so did that overwhelming excitement. In the eerie aftermath, instinctive reactions gave way to more orderly thoughts, and we were suddenly anxious: "Gee, what's going to happen to us now?"

It was a question quickly answered. Orders came for all military units to marshal themselves, and The Kamehameha School's ROTC members were assembled into a battalion. We were given the mission of guarding Kapalama Heights. It was a task that I know must seem as peculiar to anyone hearing of it now as it did to us when we were first given those orders 50 years ago. To our consternation, we soon discovered that it was not the eccentric but "soft" duty it appeared to be.

By that evening, we were satisfactorily organized and began to establish our headquarters in the area behind the girls' school, which was further up the mountain.

Then we received the information that polished off the last vestiges of our exhilaration over "playing soldier." The military command was concerned about the possibility that Japanese paratroopers would be dropped into the hills, infiltrating the high ground overlooking the entire city of Honolulu. We were charged with detecting their landings and sending word of the incursions to the proper authorities. I suppose we were also expected to attempt to hold them at bay because we were all issued rifles.

That was really the beginning of the war for me. During the night, we took up one-man guard positions along the mountainside. Over the course of a month, we had several reports of parachute sightings. Of course, they were unfounded. Still, we were so young, and alone in those hills, every new rumor played heavily on our fears.

We stood our posts for hours on end. Even being relieved was a cause for apprehension. You could never simply assume that the approaching footsteps belonged to your comrade, and everyone's voice quavered when calling out to ask for the password.

There was nothing to do in the dark but think—actually, wonder and speculate are closer to describing it. All of your senses were straining for input. So much so that you began to see, hear, and feel things that were never there.

Even on the actual school grounds, of course, we were required to ensure that there was no light visible from the outside. In the brightness of day, though, unexploded shells were often found on campus. We later learned that, in fact, they were from our own anti-aircraft guns firing at the invaders.

Needless to say, our well-ordered activities as students of The Kamehameha Schools were totally disrupted. The forces of war had taken control of our lives, the Territory of Hawaii, our country, and the world. Uncertainty was the only certainty.

Hawaii took on a whole new meaning to the military; and the military took on a whole new meaning for Hawaii—especially her young people. Nearly all of us entered into service.

In my case, the vagaries of circumstance were to impose a great irony upon my life.

On that tragic day in 1941, I bore witness to the opening act of our war with Japan.

In 1945, while stationed on Saipan with the Army Corps of Engineers, I saw the curtain descend as I stood beside a runway and watched the Enola Gay take off on its fateful journey to Hiroshima.

◆ SPECIALIZING IN THE IMPOSSIBLE: WOMEN AND SOCIAL REFORM IN AMERICA, 1890-1990

A keynote address presented by Irene Natividad at the symposium of the National Museum of American History Smithsonian Institution in Washington, D.C. In 1985, and again in 1987, she was elected President of the National Women's Political Caucus—the first Asian American to head a national political organization. She currently runs her own consulting firm in Washington, D.C. and was a Director of the 1992 Global Summit of Women.

When the scribes of history sit down to write a chapter on the past three decades, they ought to call it the Wonder Years. . . . From the first shaky steps out of our kitchens in the late fifties, to the fortifying sessions of consciousness-raising groups formed in our own parlors during the sixties, and the growing pains of entering the work world in the seventies and eighties, women in the nineties have indeed come of age. Unquestionably, we are now enjoying the largest measure of personal and political freedom in this country's history. There are those among you in this audience who will agree that the path to progress has been a bumpy one, but no one doubts that indeed we have moved forward.

As we have come of age, from the very basic and revolutionary struggles of our early foremothers who are celebrated by this exhibit, through the seasoning experience of our more recent fights for equality, we have all learned that the personal is indeed the political. You might say we have gone public over the years, and the world has not been the same. The result today is that we are in the fortunate position of having power, serious power, within our reach: power to win our rights, to fulfill our dreams, and to assume full partnership in the public business of this nation.

Today we are fortunate to have Ann Richards serving as the governor of the third-largest state in this country—Texas. The nation's capital is governed by a woman, Sharon Pratt Dixon. And she is joined by many other women mayors: in Houston, for instance, with Kathy Whitmire; in Dallas with Annette Strauss; in Charlotte, North Carolina, with Sue Myrick. Kansas distinguishes itself by being the only state that has a woman governor, Joan Finney, a woman senator, Nancy Kassebaum, and a woman congressional representative, Jan Meyers, all serving at the same time. Equally important, women of color have broken through the dual barriers of race and gender, so that for the first time, there are four African American women serving in Congress—Cardiss Collins, Eleanor Holmes Norton, Barbara Rose Collins, and Maxine Waters—as well as one Asian American, Patsy Mink, who was there long before, and one Hispanic American, Ileana Ros-Lehtinen.

The leadership breakthroughs in business and the professions are legion. Mickey Siebert's history-making feat in the early seventies, being the first woman to buy a seat in the New York Stock Exchange, no longer confounds us, as a series of firsts have happened in rapid succession: the first woman on the Supreme Court, Sandra Day O'Connor; the first woman astronaut, Sally Ride; most recently, the first woman surgeon general, Antonia Novello, and so on.

We have come to accept that certain notoriety that comes with being the first woman to enter the rooms of power—be they economic, political or social. Men have entered those rooms in the past, assuming their rightful place as if they had been expected. Well, we are not yet expected in large numbers, for the time being, but as more women enter the room the spotlight will dim and not focus exclusively on the newest member of the club. Instead, the focus will shift to our numbers. Women are now the majority of students in colleges and graduate schools all across this nation. Large numbers of women are studying in medical schools, law schools, and business schools. Women are projected to be the majority of workers in the next century, and the majority of new small businesses are now started by women.

But the most important numerical fact, which underscores our power to shape the forces of 21st century America, is that women are the majority of voters in every state of the United States. That means that no one can get elected without our votes: not to the House, not to the Senate, not to the presidency, let alone to school boards. The gender gap, or the women's vote as I prefer to call it, provided the margin of victory for Ann Richards in the last election, for Governor Doug Wilder in Virginia, and for Mayor David Dinkins in New York city in the 1989 elections.

Equally important, the threat of the women's vote propelled the issue of child care into the 1988 presidential campaign. And we saw candidates for the first time tripping over themselves at child care centers. It's not that they had discovered children lately. It's just that the mediagenic politics of the last decade dictates that you go to a child care center because it resonates among women voters. Lastly, the large female electorate has encouraged officeholders interested in re-election to make record numbers of women's appointments at both the state and the federal levels. Right now, President Bush's record stands at 22 percent of all senior-level positions held by women, beating all prior presidents' records. I don't think it's an accident that President Bush suffered a gender gap, against him, prior to being elected.

The successes of the past three decades that I've been recounting to you were the result of efforts from the early suffrage movement to the modern women's movement. These extraordinary gains challenge us to reach yet another plateau in history—to top our gains, so to speak.

But I didn't come here tonight merely to sing the praises of women's achievements of these past thirty years. I came to provide, if I can, a frank assessment.

The organized women's movement is far from being a small band of feminists doing consciousness-raising, or "hell-raising," as some would have said a few decades ago. Over the years the movement has acquired sophisticated, grass-roots organizing, coalition-building, political skills that have helped to win many a victory. The quest for equality in employment, education, in all areas of public life, has been embraced by this nation. The pioneers of women's freedom of the late sixties have been transformed into the largest mainstream movement of the late eighties. Yet the test that confronts this movement is one of durability. It is, in effect, a dare—a dare to continue to thrive when powerful vehicles, such as the presidency and the courts, are no longer available to support basic rights won earlier in the struggle for social reform along gender lines. All successful movements must face the fact that with successes come failures. To live beyond the moment of ascendancy, to live to get the whole job done, great movements must reinvest themselves. To sustain themselves, movements must not only grow, they must change. That great feminist theorist, Simone de Beauvoir, phrased it well when she titled one of her last essays "Feminism: Alive, Well, and in Constant Danger." The fact of the matter is that, ironically, women have created enough change to be significant, but too little change to be sufficient. This uncomfortable dichotomy makes it difficult to chart a future course as definitive as that pursued during the seventies, when equal rights, embodied in the fight for the equal rights amendment, made the mission so clear and seemingly so simple.

The contradictions to women's successes have proved most frustrating. The public consensus we had for women's equality has had little effect on the wage gap. Today women still earn only two-thirds of what men earn, no matter what area or level of employment. As Jesse Jackson said so well, the loaf of bread does not cost the woman any less, so why pay her less? It seems so clear, but no one is listening. The consensus for women's equality has not produced a coherent and caring system of child care for families and for the women that society has encouraged to work. The equal rights majority has not been able to gain recognition and protection for the rights of women in the nation's most basic legal document, the Constitution of the

United States. Reproductive choice has been won and now is threatened state by state.

These mixed results confuse and confound. So while women are buoyed by their successes, they are simultaneously bedeviled by the inability to sustain the fast pace they had set for themselves in the sixties and seventies. The result is frustration. Frustration is inevitable for a country in which we still must reargue the basics of reproductive choice, affirmative action, and civil rights as a whole. Frustration is justified when a group that is 53 percent of the population numbers as its representatives only 2 percent of the Senate, only 6 percent of the House, only 16 percent of the state legislatures, and only 9 percent of the federal district court judges. Frustration is justified when there seems to be an inverse relationship between the number of women in public life and the degree of power that they exercise. The higher you go, the less accessible it seems. Frustration is justified when a majority of the poor are still women and children and women workers are still clustered, for the most part, in low-paying clerical, sales, and service jobs. Frustration is justified when the largest industrialized nation in the world is unable to pass a family and medical leave bill at a time when two-earner families are the norm in this country.

These frustrations make the organized women's movements' efforts seem sisyphean at times. For every step up the hill, we roll back a few times. But women are resilient and persistent, and so are our organizations. Women's groups didn't fold up their tents and go home when the ERA (Equal Rights Amendment) failed or when the Supreme Court handed down the Webster decision almost two years ago. Instead they learned to coalesce, not just among themselves, but with civil rights groups, labor groups, and, in some instances, even business groups to fight for issues demanding their attention. The results are palpable: the passage of a child care bill—many of us do not deem it to be sufficient but, at least, a significant first step; the passage of the Civil Rights Restoration Act, which restored institution-wide coverage of civil rights bills for minorities, women, the aging, and the handicapped; the defeat of judicial nominations deemed to be contrary to the interests of the disadvantaged in this society. In addition, women have become experts in using the media to reach the majority of Americans, so that more than any one piece of legislation, the women's movements best achievement of late is the creation of a growing constituency for a family support system in a society where women's disproportionate responsibilities for work at home and work at work often make time more valuable than money.

The threat to women's reproductive rights actually proved to be a boon to a movement that had not been able to attract young adherents in large numbers prior to the Supreme Court's Webster decision. For the first time, women leaders were able to make a direct connection for young women—as they had never been able to do before—between politics and their daily lives, between the act of voting and preserving a right. Young women understood, all of a sudden, that indeed the personal is the political. The challenge, of course, is how to maintain the commitment of these young women, energized and politicized by an issue that is no longer on the front pages of the nation's newspapers, and, equally important, how to extent that commitment to choice to the other issues affecting women.

The women's vote remains the most powerful tool for social change in the coming decades. Not always voting as a bloc, except recently on the issue of choice, women have increasingly come to view their vote as the expression of their hopes and dreams for a better world. The candidate who makes direct appeals to this vote wins, as Governor Doug Wilder discovered. Women are also much more likely to cross party lines to vote their interests.

The enlightened, self-interest dimension of the women's vote is, to a large extent, a product that we might call an economic gender gap. Focus groups of infrequent women voters were asked in 1988 what the issues were that propelled them to vote. The results were not surprising. "Not earning as much as a man" was the number one answer—not pay equity, not comparable worth, but "not earning as much as a man." Crime—or personal vulnerability as a whole—was the second most important issue. Employment. Environment. And the prism through which women saw all of these issues—children.

It is important to note that there is a strong correlation between the increasing number of women in the workplace and the increasing number of women voters. The more women become charged with their economic destiny, the more likely they are to vote. Shirley Chisholm phrased it well when she said that women vote according to their pocketbooks. The truly liberating issue for women is economic security.

The task that remains, however, is how to mobilize that vote. Like most Americans, women are still voting only half their strength—a fact which I find personally frustrating. I have told women all across this country that if they do not vote, then they have not earned the right to complain about crime, about education, about discrimination, about the environment. I remind them that in other countries—in Latin America, for instance—people get shot for exercising their right to vote. But in this country, we take that right for granted. On election day, many of us go shopping, which is all right as long as we shop as well for a candidate who represents our interests. I tell them the story of my friend who lost a state legislative race in South Dakota by one vote, even after a recount. And most recently, in that same state, an anti-choice bill was defeated in the senate, again by one vote.

There is no substitute, however, for promoting social reform through our own leaders, our own representatives. The impact of one Pat Schroeder, who pushes for a child care bill; the impact of one Claudine Schneider, who sponsors an environmental bill; one Connie Morella, who pushes for legislation for the aging; one Marge Roukema, who fights for family and medical leave, would be even more dramatic if there were 290 of them in Congress, out of 435, instead of 29 out of 435. Clearly, token numbers of us on the inside cannot speak for the millions of us who are out here. And it remains the most challenging task of the women's movement to make those numbers grow bigger. It is not an easy task. It is an effort that's a little bit like carving a woman's face on Mt. Rushmore. It will take years to chip away at stubborn rock before a woman's face begins to emerge. But trust me, emerge it will.

A 1987 survey of voters' attitudes towards women candidates, commissioned by the National Women's Political Caucus, revealed that the future of women candidates is positive. From school board to Congress to the presidency, the poll showed that the bias against women candidates is eroding. In part, this is due to the public's becoming more accustomed to the notion of women holding office. Madeleine Kunin so eloquently articulated this when she said, "I couldn't have been elected governor of the State of Vermont. . . without Dixie Lee Ray, without Martha Layne Collins. In a very real way we create public confidence through one another."

Given the changing demographics of the United States, which project a next century when minorities will be the majority, the Madeleine Kunins of the future will come from various ethnic groups. The next plateau for the women's movement, which so far has been largely white and middle class, is how to embrace pluralism in its maturity. How to arrive at consensus in the future—given the possibility of emerging political tensions between the ethnic groups that will come into ascendance—will pose a difficult challenge for many of us.

Where the women's movement will be in the new political mosaic of the coming decades will be interesting to see, as Hispanics conflict with Asian or African Americans, or vice versa, in carving out new districts. How do you coalesce the interests of the young with the interests of the old? Will it be child care versus Medicare at a time when 25 percent of the American population will be older Americans, the majority of whom will vote, when children can't?

Clearly the task before us is enormous. But we women are more than up to it. Like Wonder Woman,

we are smart, we are patient, we are persevering. There are more of us and we live longer. The hurdles that we face are real. But we cannot move forward if we spend our time bemoaning our fate and the foibles and arrogance of the other gender.

Nancy Astor, the first woman to sit in the British House of Commons, said it best when she said, "Mercifully, women have no political past. We have all the mistakes of one-sex legislation with its appalling failures to guide us. We should know what to avoid. It is no use blaming the men. We made them and now it's up to us, the makers of men, to be a little more responsible."

Thank you very much.

Audience question:

"An obvious question: What are some of the factors that you have observed that make women reluctant to run for office?"

Ms. Natividad's response:

What are the factors that make women reluctant to run for political office? It's called money, money, and money. It is very, very expensive to run a race. The first question I ask women who say, "I'm thinking about running for office," is "How much have you raised? How much do you plan to raise, and where do you think you're going to get it from?" Those who come up with the good answers are the ones who understand that indeed it will require a lot of money to run for any seat, whether it's a city council seat, mayoral seat, or congressional seat.

The other barriers have to do with what Madeleine Kunin calls that instinctive pause between imagining change and imagining yourself as the agent of change. For a lot of women, it takes a lot of training before they decide to run for office. I know because we conduct a lot of training around the country. There's a point when you want to say to a woman who's thinking about running, "Go! Risk losing." And then you think of all the examples of the people who lost and came back—several times—and then won. Jill Long is a good example—three times and then she won. We'd all like not to lose that first time, but it's one of the ways in which women learn. Women gain name identification by running and losing.

Audience question:

"Could you tell us a little bit about the upcoming Global Summit for Women?"

Ms. Natividad's response:

Thank you. The Global Summit for Women that's planned for 1992 intends to bring together women leaders who are considered visionaries, theorists, and thinkers with those who are practitioners—women members of Parliament, ministers of government agencies in various countries around the world—to talk about possible new paradigms or structures. There is the sense among a lot of women around the world that perhaps the reason why we are moving so slowly is because we're trying to make progress within existing structures that were set up by men and without us in mind. This conference, this summit, will take place in Reykjavik, Iceland, upon the invitation of Icelandic women members of Parliament; in Iceland because they have a woman president, 22 percent of their Parliament is made up of women, and they are still complaining that the issues they care about won't move. So what's wrong? That's what we want to talk about. And here we look at Iceland and say we'd love to be where you are, with a woman president. In the Philippines, where I was born, we have a woman president. And we can only dream about that here. There is something wrong.

Audience question:

What words of wisdom do you have to offer about the strategies that we should be using to have a more multiracial, multiethnic women's movement?

Ms. Natividad's response:

I think there have been ongoing attempts over the years to bring pluralism into the women's movement. I think it will be forced upon us much more rapidly in the next few years precisely because of the changing numbers. I think we ought to anticipate that change by taking the lead in what I call cross-cultural dialogues. For instance, Asian Americans and African Americans are pitted against each other in certain neighborhoods because of the Korean stores that are there. I think it's incumbent upon us to bring the groups together—not the men, the women—to talk about our similarities, our differences, to talk about each other. . . so what we try to get at is what is common to all of us no matter what ethnic group we belong to. And I think we should be doing more of that in the future.

Audience question:

What qualities do women need to exhibit as political winners?

Ms. Natividad's response:

Political winners? I like that. Let me start with this: The Caucus did a survey of voters' attitudes towards women candidates in 1987, and the stereotypes that emerged were that women candidates were seen as good managers, good administrators; as seeing the human side of issues; as able to come up with new ideas. And the last thing, that surprised us, was that they were seen as best able to curb government spending—which is not a surprise, because guess who handles the family budget? Women do. So I think the formula for a woman candidate is to underscore those very same qualities, as opposed to trying to cut against the grain. I think the best thing to do is to be yourself, to stand for those things that you care about; to stress the experience that you bring to that race; to stress the fact that you will work hard. For a woman candidate to be qualified means she is overqualified.

♦ POLITICAL AND CULTURAL DIVERSITY: AMERICA'S HOPE AND AMERICA'S CHALLENGE

Irene Natividad is President of the Philippine American Foundation. In 1985, and again in 1987, she was elected President of the National Women's Political Caucus—the first Asian American to head a national political organization. She currently runs her own consulting firm in Washington, D.C. She was a Director of the 1992 Global Summit of Women. This speech was given on February 19, 1991 at the ARCO Forum, John F. Kennedy School of Government, as the keynote address for Actively Working Against Racism and Ethnocentrism (AWARE) week. This event was sponsored by the Office of Race Relations and Minority Affairs, Harvard University.

The United States is now in the midst of a great wave of immigration. Since 1980, immigrants have made up one-third of our nation's population growth. Were it not for the foreign newcomers, California would gain only two congressional seats, not seven. These are but two of the many indices of the growing diversity in the American population—a diversity which will bring about profound changes in American culture. We must prepare ourselves for such changes.

As many of you can see, I'm an Asian American. I would like to open a window into our awareness of cultural diversity by talking about the group of Americans to which I belong, to share with you how others see us, and how we see ourselves. In so doing, I hope to convey to you the challenge of multicultural sensitivity that will be required of each of us in the next century.

A few years ago, there was a great deal of press attention paid to a Vietnamese girl graduating as valedictorian of her class, who only four years earlier had been one of the boat people. It seemed to me the feat was indeed remarkable, but the attention was out of proportion. I soon realized the fascination with this young woman's story had to do with the fact that for most Americans this young woman was the latest version of the American Dream.

Most Asian Americans, in fact, are viewed as Horatio Alger's stories replicated a thousandfold in miniature. We are known as the people who pull ourselves by our bootstraps. I'm referring, of course, to the model minority image that has been heaped on us, of late, by every media outfit you can think of— *60 Minutes*, *U.S. News & World Report*, *Newsweek*, *Parade Magazine*, and so on. And based on the numbers alone, it would seem as if we Asian Americans, as a group, are doing well. For instance, according to the Population Reference Bureau, the median family income for Asian Americans is $23,000, as opposed to $20,800 for white families. Not evident in that figure, however, is that more members of Asian American families work, thereby increasing the overall family income. It's not just the father, it's the mother, it's the uncle, it's the cousin, etcetera. Therefore, it looks like we make a lot of money from one family.

Our academic prowess has become a matter of lore. The high school and college completion rate for Asian Americans is greater than any other population group in this country. We are so overrepresented in the so-called "good schools" that informal quotas have been put into place to limit our admissions. For instance, many of you may have heard that the [former] chancellor at U.C. Berkeley acknowledged that such quotas were indeed in place, apologized for their existence, and announced plans to change that policy direction. Unsurprisingly, the unemployment rate for this highly educated, hard-working group is very low.

Now let me share with you a Garry Trudeau cartoon strip which underscores what I have just said. And this is important because I think Garry manages to catch the pulse of our general American culture. In this strip, we have two female students—one white and one Asian American. Jennifer, the white student, says "National Merit Scholar! How do you do it, Kim?"

And Kim says, "I don't know. I guess I just study."

"No way, I tried that once. You've got some edge," replies Jennifer.

"Edge? Like what, Jennifer?"

"You know. Some genetic edge. Getting good grades is a racial characteristic, isn't it? An Asian thing?"

"You won't tell everyone, will you?" asked Kim.

"I knew it!" Jennifer exclaims, "You guys are some sort of super race aren't you?"

"We mean you no harm. We only seek computers for our young."

I laughed and then called Garry and said, "You know it really hits closer to home than I would like because this is indeed what people think we are—these super technicians." This cartoon and the success stories hyped in the press promote the perception that we are highly-educated, hard-working, over-achieving automatons who do not make waves. It is an image which fills me with a great deal of ambivalence. It both angers me and instills pride.

I'd be less than honest if I didn't say how proud I am when I hear that a majority of the finalists at the Westinghouse Science contest are Asian American students—year after year after year. Or, when I read in an academic journal that if America is to regain its premier position in science and engineering, it will be because of Asian Americans majoring and doing research in those very disciplines. I'd be a liar if I did not admit my wonder at how a minority group, which now only makes up 2% of the U.S. population, comprises 30% of the student body at U.C. Berkeley, and other major segments at Harvard and the other Ivies.

I am pleasantly astounded when I discover that the premier cellists and violinists of this country are Asian Americans and that, in general, Asian Americans are reshaping the culture of this country for the better— according to many—by adding a little complexity here, a little simplicity there. It does seem as if we have achieved much as a group, but I am angered because while we're carted out and shown off as models, we are also treated differently for the way we look. The question, "Where do you come from?," will often refer to another country as opposed to another state, even if we have been here for four generations. Other people may never believe that this, too, is our country. I suspect, as well, that our uniqueness as models has more to do with our small numbers, and that should we mushroom to become a significant population group, there would be fear among many of our doing too well.

The model minority stereotype tends to gloss over the fact that we, too, are discriminated against. I am angered because while the Wall Street Journal chronicles the corporate world's effort to tap the Asian American market because supposedly we're so rich, the San Francisco Chronicle reports a surge in anti-Asian racism supported by Department of Justice figures. The Chronicle attributes this violence against Asian Americans to our increased visibility, to an unstable economy, and a trade imbalance between the U.S. and Japan.

I am angered because the term, "Model Minority," invites resentment, not only from other minority groups, but from white Americans as well. Such stereotypes generate the kind of climate that created the Vincent Chin tragedy in Michigan, where a Chinese man was clubbed to death by unemployed auto workers who thought he was Japanese, or the recent boycotts of Korean-owned grocery stores by African Americans in New York and Washington D.C. I am angered because this term does not include the entire truth about the Asian American experience. The high personal cost of our so-called success, for instance, or the fact that Harvard and Berkeley statistics do not include the Hmongs or the Vietnamese who are having a difficult time adjusting to or simply living in the U.S. Not all of us become valedictorians. Instead, there are far too many of us with college degrees who will never reach the higher echelons of management in American institutions because we are perceived as technicians, not as managers, executives, or administrators. Moreover, we are, for the most part, underpaid given our high educational attainment.

The stereotypes that I have described for you not only limit how other people see us, but also have great impact on public policy. Because Asian Americans are perceived as able to take care of themselves, they have to fight to be included in government programs designed for minorities, including bilingual education, business setasides, and affirmative action. In fact, in Washington D.C., there was a point where Asian Americans considered filing a suit against the local government because they were not included as a minority group.

Language does make a difference, and the blame is partially ours. Asian Americans have achieved excellence in academia, art, and business, but not in politics and governance. The majority of us are not even involved in the most elementary form of political involvement—voting. So, I run around all over the country exhorting my fellow Asian Americans to make a difference by increasing their presence in the voting booth. I tell them that if we do not vote, then we haven't earned the right to complain about the streets, about crime, about education, about discrimination against our own people. People in my home country of the Philippines wrap their arms around ballot boxes in order to protect the right to vote, but once they get here they take that right for granted. The result is our political invisibility, our lack of presence in the policy-making bodies of this country.

As corny as it may sound, I personally believe that with citizenship comes responsibility. This is true for Asian Americans as well, and therefore, ought to have a say in the way it is run. It sounds very simple and rational, but it is difficult to actually convince people to vote. Asian Americans have yet to see the direct relationship between politics and their daily lives, between the act of voting and the ability to right a wrong.

This problem also exists for Hispanic Americans—the fastest growing minority group in this nation [sic]—for whom I have had the same message since many of them do not vote either. The actual political power of this group has yet to be felt. We have much to learn from our African American brothers and sisters who discovered long ago the power of political action, whether it is lobbying, voting, or holding elected or appointed office in order to have their concerns addressed. Civil rights have not been fully secured, but think of where minorities would be, were it not for the African American leaders of the Sixties who broke ground and led the fight for equality.

The century of diversity is upon us: it's not around the corner. On the radio the other day, I heard that in the greater Washington metropolitan area, only 29% of the labor force is white male and native-born, the rest are women, minorities, part-time workers, or immigrants. In fact, the surge in immigration will speed up what is called the "browning of America." Would you believe that even in Indiana, a state whose population is 90% white, the population growth this year was purely attributable to the 36,000 immigrants who went there. If it were not for the 36,000 immigrants, the state of Indiana would be witnessing a loss in population. There are many who fear this change, who think "Oh, my god, more people to compete in what is already a very tight labor market, more people for whom we have to provide social services, more people than this country can withstand."

But let me remind those who may have those fears that just as the first wave of immigration at the turn of the century provided America with new talents, skills, and ideas, the current wave of immigration will also bring a new vitality. This new vitality will result in increased economic growth. Already decaying areas of major cities have been revitalized by the arrival of new residents. There are also those who believe that America's preeminent position in science and engineering will be sustained by the talents represented by this wave of newcomers.

America, as we now know it, will never be the same. But until these immigrants are successfully absorbed, their arrival will cause additional strains, especially in major cities which now face diminished resources. New York City, for instance, has 178 identifiable ethnic groups, many of whom cannot speak English and make very big demands of medical and social services. So, in the short run, there will indeed be some problems. In addition, as they become more a part of the existing minority groups, political tensions are also bound to develop. Juan Williams in the Washington Post offered what I consider one of the better analyses of what this new political mosaic. According to Mr. Williams, there are four major shifts, shifts which will define the new terms of political confrontation.

First of all, because of the rapid growth of the Hispanic population, this group will become major political players for the first time. Race relations in the United States will not just be a matter between blacks and whites, but browns as well. By the end of this decade, Hispanics will be the largest minority in this nation. Second, the baby boomers will age and the over 55 population will comprise 25% of this country's population, with the ability to exert a major political influence. What is important is that the social security benefits for these baby boomers who are predominately white will be supported by a smaller group of workers who will be disproportionately Asian, Hispanic and African American.

Third, political power in congressional and presidential elections will shift to the South and the West. Hispanics will be a major segment of the population in Florida, Texas, and California. According to Mr. Williams, since Hispanics are predominantly Catholic, they will keep those states politically and culturally conservative. Lastly, the underclass of poor people in the cities, the majority of them black, will continue to grow. As other minorities, including blacks, move into middle-class neighborhoods, this underclass will become increasingly isolated. Given this scenario, no doubt increased tensions between competing interests will emerge—one minority group versus another, the rich versus the poor, the young versus the old, child care versus Medicare, the Northeast versus the Southwest. Some of this is already beginning to happen.

On the positive side, a shrinking labor force will mean more opportunity for women and minority workers. The 1990s, in short, will offer the best chance for these groups to gain an economic foothold in this society. More blacks and other minorities will move into the middle class as well. In addition to this potential economic clout, commensurate political clout will emerge as more and more members of these groups become participants in the political arena. Sheer numbers alone will push both major parties to develop strategies to lure these constituencies in order to win.

Take, for instance, the Republican Party's latest effort to attract African Americans, Latino Americans, and Asian Americans. The appointments of minorities to some senior level positions in the Bush Administration reflect that commitment. It is, therefore, a desire of that party which has traditionally been seen as predominantly white, conservative, and representing the establishment, to somehow broaden itself for sheer survival. Unfortunately, political strategy has run counter to public policy. The President, as you know, has recently vetoed the Civil Rights Act because he disapproves of quotas. There is a sense among minority communities that perhaps his commitment is not as deep as they thought it was before.

Many of you have heard about the controversial Jesse Helms campaign ad against Harvey Gantt. A pair of white hands crumple a piece of paper, ostensibly a notice that this person has not gotten a job. The spokesman denounces racial quotas and he links them to the other candidate, Harvey Gantt, who is black. Such Republican Party appeals to people's fears of blacks taking jobs, scholarships, or promotions away from white Americans enabled them to portray the Democratic Party as only caring for a narrower segment of people, the poor and the disadvantaged.

When asked about the issue of affirmative action, Harvey Gantt wisely responded that it is not a question of what racial remedy you employ to bring equality into the work place, but whether you want America to be truly competitive in the future. If, indeed, America's future workforce will be browns, blacks, and women, then it's incumbent upon our society to provide the best training and the best education for this labor pool to be most productive for our nation. This is a sound argument which I support, but it will not stop Republican Party strategies from using quotas as a tool in the upcoming presidential election.

The Democratic Party, traditionally supported by a multi-racial coalition and generally perceived to be more progressive on issues of concern to women and minorities, is not entirely blameless either. While women and minorities continue to be the most dedicated segments of this party, there is a great sense among these voters that somehow many of the issues that are most important to them are not always fully addressed. With each presidential election, the same platform fight emerges, where we try to maintain the same statement in every election cycle. The challenge facing the Democratic Party is how to maintain its base of women and minorities, and at the same time appeal to the American middle class.

However these two parties decide to attract or retain the emerging constituencies which will determine America's future, it is still incumbent upon those very constituencies to make their own grab for power. Seats at the decision-making table are not going to be given away. Consequently, it is important for new Hispanic districts to be carved out as in Los Angeles, where Gloria Molina and Art Torres are running for supervisor. In New York's Chinatown, possible new seats will enable an Asian American to be a member of the City Council for the first time in well over a century since Asian Americans first got there.

With these new districts, of course, we have new leaders, and therein lies America's hope. No one race and no one gender has a special corner on good ideas. So, the promise of a diversified decision-making body, whether in the state legislature or in Washington D.C., may be a wealth of new expertise and hopefully new solutions to age-old problems. But until such time as we, peoples of color, have representatives in sufficient numbers to articulate our concerns, we must vote as if our lives depended on it. Because frankly, they do.

For too long, women and minorities have suffered whisker-burns from the lip service both parties have paid to the sharing of power. And it is time that we remind both the Democratic and the Republican Party that it is our votes that have loaned them this power, and that it is not an interest-free loan. The interest on our loan demands fairness and equality in every segment of our society. But to collect on that loan, we must not only march, we must not only write letters— we must vote. In other words, the responsibility is ours, to gain a political foothold in this country. And it is the responsibility of society as a whole to support our claims for equal representation because that is the premise on which this country was built.

The successful leaders of the future will not only try to manage diversity, but also to celebrate it. That is the painful challenge facing whites, Asians, blacks, Latinos, and Native Americans. The myth of the American melting pot must give way to the American tossed salad with each ingredient retaining its own integrity, while forming a delicious whole. Our hope is embedded in the first paragraph of the Constitution, and it remains our task, even today, to form that more perfect Union. It is difficult even to define that perfect Union, but surely it must be a place where women are the equals of men, where African, Hispanic, Asian, and Native Americans are the equals of white Americans.

♦ ON CHANGING THE FACE OF POWER

Delivered by U.S. Senator Daniel K. Akaka of Hawaii at the National Asian Pacific American Bar Association's fourth annual convention on September 26, 1992.

I would like to express my gratitude to the National Asian Pacific American Bar Association for inviting me to speak this evening. To Bill Hou, Peggy Nagae Lum, Judge Thomas Tang, Pam Chen, Mary Kennedy, Francey Youngberg, Alan Webster, Susan Lee—my good friend from the Senate Governmental Affairs Committee, John Nakahata—and all of you members and supporters of NAPABA—ALOHA!

As pleased and honored as I am to be here with you tonight, I must say that I was somewhat intimidated, at first. I plod along every day in a working environment where somewhere in the area of 60 percent of my colleagues are attorneys. That is a trial in itself!

However, this group certainly far eclipses even that ratio. Moreover, when I read your convention brochure, I quickly noted the opening line: Lawyers hold the keys to power!

It made me wonder. What is it that I should share with you? What advice do I have to offer? What rousing battle cry could I shout to spur you onward toward Changing the Face of Power?

Well, I'll be truly candid with you. Dramatics are not my style. In my 68 years, I have not broken down castle gates. I have not toppled the columns of prejudice. I have not indignantly seized the scepter of authority from the jealous hands of those who thought "our kind of people" could not capably hold them.

However, I did become the first Native Hawaiian member of the U.S. House in more than half a century. I *am* only the second Hawaiian ever to serve in the United States Senate.

So, I am not here to grab the reins of the revolution and urge the storming of the ramparts. I am here, I suppose, more as your proud and caring uncle, sitting with you by the fireside, sharing some stories and, maybe, providing you with some useful advice. And for those of you who are saying to yourselves that "grandfather" would be more like it—just hold that thought.

With your indulgence, I would like for you to follow me through some reflections and experiences. Note where they might coincide with yours. Note also where they don't, because a significant part of my point is that we must all be open to consider and to prepare to accept a multitude of different paths.

This is how the glorious tale begins. I had a grand dream about what I wanted to do with my life from the time I was very young. And at the risk of being immodest, whenever I look back, I think: Gee, I was pretty doggone realistically mature for that age. You see, by the time I entered elementary school, I had my professional ideals already firmly set. When I grew up, I would get a government job at Pearl Harbor, and man, I would be on top of the world! To this day, I never believe the revisionist memories of those who say: I knew from my earliest childhood years that this was what I was going to do. Of course, there are many who would say that sticking to my original plan would have been more contributory to society than doing what I am now.

I got my first experiences in elective office when I was chosen for the Student Council in the 7th grade and voted Student Body President in the 9th. It was not especially exhilarating. Basically, no one else wanted to do it. However, once I got beyond what I thought was the initial lesson to be derived from that—Learn how to say no—I discovered some things far more valuable. I developed a fascinating awareness of group dynamics and a fulfilling sense of contribution and satisfaction. Never underestimate the potential of serendipity—or getting stuck with a job that no one else wants.

When I graduated from the University of Hawaii and entered practice teaching, I formulated the second career plan of my life. Someday, I would be Superintendent of the Hawaii Department of Education. I would devote two years each to gaining experience in every school environment there was: Elementary, intermediate, high school, rural, urban, military and private. At the same time, I would get my School Administration Certificate and my Master's Degree. I would move on to Vice Principal and then, Principal.

And do you know what? It worked perfectly, and I walked directly into the second significant political lesson of my life. In my first year as a principal, I was chosen to be a delegate to the National Convention of the Department of Elementary School Principals. Being sort of the new kid on the block, I was honored but overwhelmed. I was so concerned about adequately representing my State and the Aloha Spirit, I took with me what must have been a truckload of flower leis, macadamia nuts and the like. I was determined not to be found lacking in spreading goodwill on Hawaii's behalf. Somewhere along the way, there was even a need for some impromptu entertainment to keep atmosphere moving, and I agreed to help. I ended up singing Blue Hawaii before 6,000 delegates.

All the time—well, I'm certain you've guessed it by now—exposure and recognition were building. Before the convention adjourned, I was approached to run for the National Board of Directors. Seven months later, I had won the first election of my professional life.

Now, there is no question that the exposure and recognition aspects of this anecdote are as fundamental as any in political pursuits. However, consider this lesson a two-parter, with the second as precious as any you will come across.

I do not have a single doubt that, in the minds of many of you out there, a particular reaction is really grating at your sensibilities. Flower leis, you say!? Macadamia nuts!? My goodness, singing Blue Hawaii? Is this the stuff of Uncle Koma—the Hawaiian translation of Tom?

Never confuse being gracious with bootlicking. Never lose sight of the reality that what may be trivial to you may be of consequence to another. If you are sincere in your own intent and intelligent and perceptive enough to see when there is sincerity in the intent of others, you are never demeaned—only enhanced.

In any event, I went on to serve three years on the National Board. As my term ended, I was encouraged to enter the contest for National Vice President.

Before the election, however, I withdrew. The Superintendent of Education asked me to move from the schools to the State Office to implement his ideas about a new program for Compensatory Education. I agonized about leaving the kids, but entering the realm of statewide policymaking offered the chance to do more for more youngsters.

Eventually, because I also served as education liaison to the Model Cities Program, working with the Mayor's and Governor's offices, I was asked by Governor Jack Burns to join his staff as Director of the Office of Economic Opportunity.

As time went by, I would occasionally be called to have breakfast with Governor Burns, during which we would discuss the widest range of topics. One day, out of nowhere, he said: You know, Danny, the Hawaiians really need leaders. I wholeheartedly agreed. Then he said: Well, what about you? I have never been so taken aback, honored, humbled, anxious, or dumbfounded in my life. Calmly, he went on with his pitch. He made it all seem so reasonable and necessary and right. He had me convinced.

Then, as breakfast drew to a close, he added one more bit of advice. In this usual down-home, plain-talking way, he threw in a time-worn aphorism. He said: Danny, remember one more thing. Even monkeys fall out of trees. Lesson Number Three . . . and a good one it was!

With determination, zeal, and the profoundest sense of obligation to The Old Man, as we called him, I ran for Lieutenant Governor in 1974. I lost.

I climbed back up that tree, though. And in 1976, I became the first Native Hawaiian in the U.S. House since Prince Jonah Kuhio Kalanianaole—and the first of Chinese ancestry, period.

Have I been lucky? You bet. I consider myself a truly lucky individual indeed. I make no excuses for it. Sometimes, good fortune is a major function of opportunity. Just never depend on it. Opportunity has a much larger component to it, though, it's most critical—the human component. A brilliant mind, innate talent, top notch education—none of these can guarantee success. No one is going to win recognition or advancement just because he or she thinks it's deserved, even if it totally and undeniably is. Someone else has to think so too. And even when opportunities seem defiled by prejudice, believe me, there are always "Other Someone Elses" out there.

Even in a society where exclusion may be all-too-common, while it is your obligation to watch each other's flanks, don't circle the wagons. You can defend yourself without becoming defensive. I don't care whether you're networking with other attorneys, going to the PTA, partying in a karaoke bar—*or passing out macadamia nuts at a convention.* Always be open to what might be out there. The great philosopher Wayne Gretzky once said: You miss 100% of the shots you never take. If you start losing faith in your fellow human beings, you stop reaching out. . . and people stop reaching back. You become a barrier to yourself.

No, I will not fill you with old fuddy-duddy sayings about keeping your nose to the grindstone, your shoulder to the wheel, your eye on the ball and your ear to the ground. In fact, someone said trying to maintain all those positions makes it tough to climb the ladder of success at the same time. What I WILL tell you, however, is that no one can convince me that this is not still THE land of opportunity.

Now, let me make it clear that, just because my remarks have been sparse in their mention of discrimination or indignation or hardship, it does not mean that I have skimmed the gentle path.

The largest part of my 68 years spanned a period of our nation's history when there was racial and ethnic prejudice of a degree most of you could not imagine.

And, while I have lived my life in a place called the Melting Pot of the Pacific, where the perception of that ideal is based on the fact that no group is a majority, the harshest of realities is that Native Hawaiians have been at the very absolute bottom of the socio-economic ladder from before I was born until today.

With thoughts of my wife and children churning in my mind, I have resigned from a position of great comfort and security in professional and philosophical outrage—because it was right.

I have gone into debt and mortgaged my family home, because that is what it took to pursue my goal of public service.

I joined the redress battle the moment I stepped foot on Capitol Hill; I spoke twice in opposition to and voted against the confirmation of Clarence Thomas; and I am an original cosponsor of the measure to eliminate the Wards Cover Packing Company exemption from the Civil Rights Act of 1991.

In other words, I am neither an Anointed Fortunate Son nor am I someone who feels he has now earned his claim to comfort and the privilege of watching others fight the fight.

What I am is a steadfast believer in the inherent goodness of humankind, the fundamental soundness of our country—despite its shortcomings—and the dignity and worth of every individual.

You may think me utterly naive. But here I am—brown, yellow, and beautiful—and as you can see, I possess no magic wand.

Yes, I do have faith. And because of fine people like you and wonderfully dedicated groups such as this, it has been proven time and again that when I do place that faith in someone or something, I have seldom been in error.

You are our strength. You are our hope. Your skills and commitment provide the tools we need to change what is wrong today and build what is right for tomorrow. You do indeed hold the keys to power. . . the power to help. All I ask is that you never let anger and fear and hurt displace the pureness of your hearts as the force that drives your search for it or your use of it.

Mahalo! Thank You! ALOHA!

♦ TO BE SUCCESSFUL YOU HAVE TO DEAL WITH REALITY: AN OPPORTUNITY FOR MINORITY BUSINESSES

A speech by Susan Au Allen, President of the U.S. Pan Asian American Chamber of Commerce delivered to the National Minority Supplier Development Council, Cleveland, Ohio, October 20, 1992.

Ladies and gentlemen, my first priority today is to salute every important ally. Twenty years ago, the National Minority Supplier [Development] Council was little more than an acorn—few people and few dollars.

But as the song goes, you had high hopes. You more than made up for your small numbers with a great deal of enthusiasm. Now, look what has happened to you in twenty years. A magnificent exhibition hall populated by some of America's leading firms.

Just one week ago today, *The Wall Street Journal* carried a page one article on the growing political might of the black middle class. Since 1967, according to the United States Census Bureau, the number of affluent black middle-class families has nearly quadrupled. With race barriers removed by laws, millions of black Americans achieved the American dream.

[The National Minority Supplier Development Council] was in no small way responsible for this achievement, because it helped to remove the barriers and proved through its efforts that quality did not depend upon one's color or ethnic origin. The acorn has changed into a magnificent tree with branches all over this nation. And its strength grows daily.

The United States Pan Asian American Chamber of Commerce represents a diverse group of Asian Americans. We are Japanese, Filipinos, Chinese, Asian Indians, Koreans, Vietnamese, Laos, Thais, Cambodians, Hmong, Pakistanis, and Indonesians. Each has a distinct beautiful ethnic cultural heritage but our goals are the same as [other minorities]. We want to remove racial barriers, we want equal opportunity for our members, and we want to create greater horizons for those who follow. And that is what I want to talk about—about how those great horizons can be obtained by removing racial barriers and increasing business opportunities.

My first premise is one as business people you know thoroughly: that to be successful you have to deal with reality, not the way things should be, appear to be, but as they are. Known reality gives us the wherewithal to create opportunity.

Let's go back to *The Wall Street Journal* article to make a point. Millions of affluent black American families. Think for a minute—on commercial television, where is that successful black American? For the most part, he or she isn't there. The successful black businessman or woman is invisible. The image we have is of the failure of blacks to begin businesses in the inner city, of blacks bashing Asian Americans. You have given lie to that image, and a *Business Week*/Lou Harris poll shows another lie: black Americans above all others are less prejudiced against Asian Americans. The point is that through invisibility, an image was born which in turn created a stereotype which distorts reality. We must move past that distortion.

The problem of reality, the problem of false images and stereotypes occurs with Asian Americans, and as you can tell, I happen to be one. I was born in China and raised in Hong Kong. I am a naturalized American citizen, proud of my oriental heritage, and proud to be an American. I say that even though I have experienced many personal painful moments from ignorant Americans. Even though my country—our country—has committed atrocious acts against loyal Asian Americans. So just as I know what black and Hispanic stereotypes are, I am only painfully aware of what are unjust, unethical, and even immoral views towards Asian Americans.

Let me give you some examples:

We have been stereotyped. We have been depicted in cartoons as the menacing "yellow peril." Hollywood has cast us as sinister, exotic and inscrutable. Women are perceived as "dragon ladies." We have been slurred by such notables as columnist Jimmy Breslin, who called a female Korean colleague a "yellow cur." John Silber, the Democratic candidate for governor in Massachusetts in 1990 said the town of Lowell, heavily populated by Cambodian refugees, was a welfare magnet that "has become popular for people…accustomed to living in a tropical climate."

Allow me a relevant tangent. In 1930, President Herbert Hoover reacted against jibes from Fiorello LaGuardia, the Italian mayor of New York by saying "Go back to where you belong…Like a lot of other foreign spawn you do not appreciate the country that supports and tolerates you."

We have been brutalized. It's called Asian bashing. Asian businessmen and Asian businesswomen have been attacked by black mobs and by white mobs. In Los Angeles, Yasue Kato, a 49-year-old developer, was stabbed to death last February. His son said two white motorcyclists had approached his father and demanded money because Kato was Japanese and Japan was responsible for American's recession. This type of incident—thugs brutalizing Asian Americans because of Japan's economic success—happens all the time.

In Detroit, it's almost commonplace. You drive a Japanese-made car at great risk. But let's be candid. Ignorance, fear, anger, hate are not the sole properties of any one class, color, race or nation. They belong to us all. By no means are Asian Americans all virtuous. We have our mobs and our gangs too.

We have been the victims of job discrimination. We are denied jobs and promotions. The 1990 Census shows that Asian Americans with four years of high school make a median income of $19,290 annually, compared to $22,050 for whites with similar educational backgrounds. As professionals, Asian Americans earn on average $1,600 less per year than whites. College-educated Asian Americans are rarely found in executive suites. A bamboo ceiling exists between the executive suites and management row.

The American Engineering Association, a trade group representing U.S.-born engineers, complains that Asian immigrants are stealing their jobs and driving down wages. But a study by the highly respected National Research Council shows just the opposite— that many U.S. industries and workers benefited from Asian brainpower and talents. That's reality.

We have been the victims of college admission policies. The *Washington Post* had an article on Harvard's admission policies, which are copied by other schools. The article said, in essence, that admission was based to some extent on the evaluation of a student's leadership potential—manliness, self-pride, initiative, political savvy. The standards for evaluation did not include such noble Asian characteristics as humility, deference to elders, and respect for others. So we Asians do not do well on Harvard's leadership exams.

Well, with all this prejudice, with all these racial injustices, why am I proud to be an American? Why do I love this country? The simple answer is despite its many imperfections, drawbacks, and racial bigotry, America remains a great nation, and a land of unlimited opportunity for Asian Americans.

As a class, we Asian Americans have benefited enormously from the opportunities America has to offer. The Statue of Liberty still means something to Asians. It is the primary reason why the number of Asian immigrants more than doubled from 1980 to 1990, and why by the end of this century the Asian population could grow by as much as 40 percent.

On the college level, the percent of Asian Americans who have completed college is almost 40 percent, compared to 22 percent for whites. Our median household income at $35,900 is higher than whites' and our unemployment rate is below whites and other Americans.

The cartoonist Gary Trudeau in a recent Doonesbury cartoon perhaps best explained why American is so attractive to Asian Americans. He sent a white character to interview an Asian American to find out why Asian Americans are so successful. In a touch of perhaps great irony, the character found that the Asian American had a strong belief in American values, a belief in a caring family with father and mother nourishing the children with commands to study, work hard, save, and invest.

Asian Americans not only save and invest, we buy, and we buy quality products and services. We spend about $38 billion on retail each year; we gave just one insurance company—MetLife—$100 million in premiums in 1990. We buy 15 percent of the 2,500 Steinway pianos Steinway makes each year in North America.

We have returned American's investment in us. We have made major contributions to America's growth. We have supplied America's high-tech industry with scientists, engineers, and entrepreneurs, and Asian Americans have helped our industries capitalize on the emerging global market. We help sell what we make here to our former homelands, and we are very, very good at it.

So though we have been victimized by racial hatred, the much larger truth is that America has given us much. And we want, as do all minority citizens, to continue our progress. That means we need two basic strategies—one to knock down racial barriers where they exist, and the second to increase business. When we do that, we will create those grand horizons.

You remember the *Wall Street Journal* article I told you about that was published just last week? There's a marvelous quote by William L. Thompson, owner of a group of Boston-based businesses called the Summit Group. Here is what he has to say, and I quote: "While civil rights is still a major item on my agency, at the same time I think there's the realization on my part and other professional people like me that, OK, the law is on the books, you are always going to have this subtle, covert racism that exists. So let's get beyond that and talk about ways we can make money."

So let us talk about making money. But let us be up front with the obvious: that the more we are able to knock down racial barriers, the greater the opportunity we are going to have. We know that at least in principle, those who man the executive suites want to obey the laws and open up opportunities for minority firms. We know this doesn't always happen in the corporate purchasing department. We are often not taken seriously or patronized. They put us through the motions of filling out forms without any intention of giving us business. They have a quota of forms to fill, and we are the way to do it.

In addition to the problem of race, we have the problem associated with any small business. Some of us don't have the resources to go unpaid for finished work for any extended period. So when a buyer is months late, we hurt. And some of the forms and procedures we have to cope with would have made it big in Dante's Inferno.

So we need a strategy to deal with all the above, just as we need a strategy to capitalize on the future, on the growing global market.

Let's take a look at that.

You have probably hear about the North American Free Trade Agreement. It will bring about 360 million consumers in one gigantic market and generate a yearly output of $6 trillion—that's $6 trillion in goods and services.

You have heard about EC-92. Before the year is out, the 12 countries of the European Community will be united in one large trading block. And Russia and other Eastern bloc nations have expressed a desire to join that bloc. That means more competition for U.S. businesses, but it can mean more business. Right now, about 30 percent of all our exports go to the EC.

And if you haven't heard about business with the Pacific Rim, let me tell you about that. It consists of 14 Asian and Pacific countries, most of whom are represented in our membership. *It is the largest single regional market for U.S. exports, and the largest source of goods we import.* In 1990, U.S. exports were worth $112 billion, 28 percent of all exports. And we expect and hope for those numbers to increase.

In my view, the development of the world economy represents a unique opportunity for minority businesses. We are now a pluralistic society and by the time this century ends, our plurality will be even greater. For an American firm to prosper and grow, it must of necessity use a diverse employment base to capitalize on an overseas market that in itself is very diverse. Let me repeat that: Our diversity of culture offers businesses something they need to compete globally.

But if the global market of today and tomorrow offers a great opportunity, it also offers a challenge. According to a number of experts, American firms that intend to compete in the global economy are looking for long-term dependable partners, firms that have been around for awhile, and firms that intend to stay around to learn and grow in the global market of tomorrow.

In my view, that means to compete, we have to offer more value. Forget about quotas, forget about affirmative action, just concentrate on making your products or services better than anyone else's. In a very large sense, that's the American way, and by being better we will help knock down many of the remaining racial barriers. We needed Civil Rights laws to overcome past injustices, and we needed new immigration laws to eradicate past wrongs. We have all needed helping hands to grow, and those of us who have reached tall oak status can now play by better ground rules. By competing on diversity and value, we can help build this nation into a land that is dominated by people who view color and ethnic diversity as both powerful and beautiful.

This is what occurred with the Irish, with the Italians, and with other immigrants. It is happening now to us, to all of us. We are making America's melting pot bigger and better. We are continuing this heritage.

Thank you.

◆ 50 YEARS: INTERNMENT, REDRESS, AND BEYOND

Delivered on February 15, 1992 by Rep. Norman Y. Mineta (California) at the 1992 Day of Remembrance in San Francisco.

I am proud to join you here today. Very proud. And as I stand before you—my friends and neighbors here in San Francisco—I feel a great sadness, but I also feel an even greater hope.

I know my sadness is shared throughout this center, throughout this city, and throughout the Japanese American community here in the United States. Our sadness is not for ourselves, but for our parents and grandparents who did not live to see this day. These pioneers and survivors would have been proud of this moment, and proud of us. Proud of us all.

There would have been a time, not all that many years ago, when I would have wondered if anyone other than Americans of Japanese ancestry would—or could—feel the power of this anniversary, as we do. Some would say that no one could truly know the tragedy of our internment by the United States Government as we know it. And this is true. But today, the difference is that people from all across the country—and indeed, from around the world—want to know.

Earlier this year, my Washington office got a call from representatives of Czechoslovak President Vaclav Havel, requesting information about redress so that they might try to redress injustices done to that nation's Hungarian minority. This is our legacy to the world.

The fact that our nation—the United States of America—has now apologized to us for our internment 50 years ago tells me how much this nation has changed, and that the changes have been for the better. With those changes have come understanding, reflection, and the recognition that basic human rights either apply to us all—or they belong to no one. However, there is no escaping another truth: that the specter of racism is lurking in us all.

In times of acute economic hardship or jingoistic pressures, this evil can surface all too easily. We've seen that when Vincent Chin was beaten to death in Detroit by unemployed auto workers. We've seen that during the war in the Middle East, when Arab Americans were the target of bigotry and suspicion. And we see it today as a result of Japan-bashing.

Why should an American, who by accident of birth happens to be of Asian ancestry, have to face the prospect of being beaten with a baseball bat, or have his car spray painted with the words "Die Nip?" The answer is, there is no answer. No one should have to face such crimes of hate. So, too, was it in 1942.

It was here in California and the West Coast 50 years ago that this standard was put to the test. Our life as a community was forever transformed by an attack that struck at the heart of the U.S. Constitution. This was an attack not of our making. But 3,000 miles away in Washington, D.C., the Government of the United States—our government—decided that Americans of Japanese ancestry were a categorical threat to the United States.

No matter that these threats were unproven, or that we were either American citizens or permanent resident aliens. All were tarred with the same indiscriminate brush of racial hatred and fear.

We were all scared, those of us who were alive at the time. The entire world was at war. The United States had been brought into this war—The Second World War—after the Empire of Japan had attacked Pearl Harbor, Hawaii on December 7, 1941. One of the first casualties of that attack was faith and trust within our American nation. . .

America quickly saw little value in distinguishing between the attackers that Sunday morning and loyal Japanese Americans who were every bit as much the target of that dawn air raid in Hawaii. All too much effort was invested, instead, in expedience. And the search was on for scapegoats.

Headlines told this story. And by February of 1942, those headlines had reached a fevered pitch.

Wednesday, February 18th. The San Francisco Chronicle. Headline: Enemy Aliens: Demand for State Martial Law Sent to General DeWitt by Impatient Congressmen.

Thursday, February 19th. Headline: Enemy Aliens: Congressmen Demand All American-Born Japs be Moved from Coastal Areas.

Friday, February 20th. Headline: Enemy Aliens: Second Generation Japs to be Evacuated from Coast, War Department Predicts. Civil Liberties May Go By the Boards.

And finally, on Saturday, February 21st. Headline: Drive Against Enemy Aliens: FDR Orders Army Rule for All Strategic Areas. Even Citizen Japs May be Cleared from Coast.

And the story in the Chronicle read, in part: "Bringing California only a step short of martial law, the President slashed through a web of legal entanglements directed military commanders to mark whatever zones they need, and to oust immediately any unwanted aliens and citizens."

And the story continued: "His orders smashed directly at 60,000 American-born Japanese on the West Coast, all hitherto protected under a cloak of U.S. citizenship."

Think about that for a moment. "A cloak of U.S. citizenship." When you came down to it in 1942, that was all the illusory protection we had: a cloak.

When the signs went up telling us, as Americans of Japanese ancestry, that we would have to leave our homes, the signs said, "ATTENTION: ALIENS AND NONALIENS." Our own government wouldn't even acknowledge us as citizens.

In a way, that was not surprising. Our parents and grandparents had not even that much, since they were forbidden by racial exclusion laws from becoming American citizens. So, with the stroke of a pen at the White House, even that illusory cloak—which my father thought would protect his children—was stripped away.

One by one, Japanese American communities along the West Coast disappeared: removed into stark, barren camps scattered throughout some of the most inhospitable regions of the United States. The myth that this forced relocation was being done for our protection was a lie exposed by the first sight of camp guard towers with their machine guns pointed in at us, instead of out.

Tens of thousands of us spent up to four long years in these camps. The vast majority of us cooperated with our government, determined to prove our loyalty in the long run by sacrificing peacefully in the short run our most basic rights as Americans. And we served this country well. Far above and beyond the call of duty.

The all-nisei 442nd Regimental Combat Team and its 100th Battalion were volunteers from the camps, enlistees fighting Nazi Germany and Fascist Italy while their families remained behind barbed wire. These men became the most-decorated Army fighting force in all of American history. They gave of themselves, they gave of their blood, and they gave of their lives to protect America even though America did not see fit to protect their rights.

In the Pacific, a top-secret war was fought by Japanese Americans in the Military Intelligence Service—a story untold for decades. But it was they, these volunteers, who cracked code after code—saving countless American lives. And yet, after the war, the stigma of shame born of the internment lived on in all of us.

Internment drained and crippled many Japanese American families. Homes, farms, and businesses were lost. Lives were ruined. The hot brand of disloyalty hung over our heads like a thundercloud ready to burst at the mention of our subjugation as second-class citizens.

The result was that once the war had ended and the camps were closed, we tried to forget the internment.

Parents never spoke of it to their children. But here there was an inescapable contradiction: How can you prove your loyalty once and for all, as we had tried to do, if you allow personal justice denied to stand silently in a specter of shame? The answer is, you can't.

And the lesson I learned was that wronged individuals must stand up and fight for their rights if our nation is to be true to its principles, without exception. That's what our successful effort to redress the internment was meant to do.

For me, that 10-year struggle in Congress won back for us our dignity. In the Civil Liberties Act of 1988, there is a passage that is more everlasting a testament than any I know to our national ethic. I am proud that this legislation was written in my office, put together by a brilliant legislative director I had at the time, Glenn Roberts. It says, and I quote:

"The Congress recognizes that, as described by the Commission on Wartime Relocation and Internment of Civilians, a grave injustice was done to both citizens and permanent resident aliens of Japanese ancestry by the evacuation, relocation, and internment of civilians during World War II."

"As the Commission documents, these actions were carried out without adequate security reasons and without any acts of espionage or sabotage documented by the Commission, and were motivated largely by racial prejudice, wartime hysteria, and a failure of political leadership."

"The excluded individuals of Japanese ancestry suffered enormous damages, both material and intangible, all of which resulted in significant human suffering for which appropriate compensation has been made."

"For these fundamental violations of the basic civil liberties and constitutional rights of these individuals of Japanese ancestry, the Congress apologizes on behalf of the Nation."

That last sentence means more to me than perhaps any other in law, for it represents everything that our government is designed to do when it works at its best. And today, 50 years after Executive Order 9066 was signed, the successful effort to redress that wrong stands as a reminder of what ultimate accountability can and should mean in the United States.

It should mean truth. It should mean justice. And it should mean universality of the rights guaranteed by the U.S. Constitution.

But today, we must remain vigilant to ensure that these truths hold true for our children and grandchildren. The most recent wave of Japan-bashing and America-bashing holds for us a special danger. Those who prefer not to learn from the mistakes of the past, those who prefer a jingoism of hate, those who prefer to seek scapegoats continue to pose a threat.

We have seen these latest headlines, and experienced these latest hate crimes. And the specter of tragedy remains all too real. But today, unlike 50 years ago, we have the political strength to bear witness—and to protect ourselves and our neighbors from more senseless tragedies.

The war in the Middle East last year demonstrated how genuine a concern this is for every minority community. In

1942, Japanese Americans were threatened, there were voices within government and without to bear witness. We helped stop history from repeating itself.

None of us can predict who might next fall target to hysteria, racism, and weak political leadership. But with our strength of conviction, and witness to history, I do believe that we can ensure that such a tragedy as our internment never befalls anyone ever again here in the United States.

♦ ASIAN PACIFIC AMERICAN HERITAGE MONTH 1992: ENTERING INTO THE PACIFIC CENTURY

Remarks by the Honorable Eni F. H. Faleomavaega, delegate to the U.S. Congress, American Samoa, delivered during Asian Pacific American Heritage Month to the United States House of Representatives in Washington, D.C. on May 26, 1992.

Mr. Speaker, I rise today, along with my esteemed colleagues from Hawaii, The Honorable Patsy Mink, and The Honorable Neil Abercrombie, to commemorate the deep and rich legacy of Americans who have come from Asia and the Pacific Islands. Due to prior commitments in their districts, our distinguished colleague from Guam, The Honorable Ben Blaz, and the respected delegation from California, The Honorable Robert Matsui and The Honorable Norman Mineta, were not able to be present. Their thoughts and hearts are with us today, however, and I submit their statements for the record.

This month, as many of you know, is a special month. President Bush has honored and recognized the contributions of our people by proclaiming May as Asian Pacific American heritage month. The president's action is welcome, overdue, and only fitting, as our nation prepares for the twenty-first century, the dawning of the Pacific Century.

It has always bothered me that our presidents visit Europe so often that they qualify for "Frequent Flier" status, yet they have rarely traveled to the Asia-Pacific region. I believe this has sent the wrong message to the countries of the Pacific, that our friends there continue to take a backseat to Europe and the Middle East when it comes to U.S. foreign policy.

It was thus noteworthy to see President Bush make his first trip abroad to our part of the world. As the President declared early after taking office—America, too, is a Pacific nation and we must renew our determination to strengthen ties and relationships with our allies and partners in the Pacific. Since then, the President and Vice-President have attempted to make good on this commitment by coming to the Pacific on four separate occasions.

It's a beginning, yet, still, not enough attention is being paid by our government to the Asia-Pacific region. The evolving events of the world make it imperative that this change.

In this decade and into the next century, the countries of the Pacific shall play a more crucial role in the economic, political, strategic and security needs of the United States and the world. As has been often-stated, the twenty-first century—the Pacific Century—shall truly be an era marked with miraculous economic advancement by this the world's most dynamic and rapidly developing region.

As many of you know, I was born and raised in the Pacific and my love and interest lie in this part of the world. Although I do not claim to be an expert, my years of travel throughout the Pacific, followed by years of service as a member of the house foreign affairs committee and subcommittee on Asian and Pacific affairs, have given me a perspective which I would like to share with you.

The economy of the Asia-Pacific region today is staggering in size and breathtaking in growth.

Last year, according to the U.S. Department of Commerce, our nation did just shy of $325 billion worth of total trade with the region—easily matching U.S. trade with Europe, and throwing in another $135 billion in excess of our trade relationship with Europe.

Since 1981, U.S. trade with the Asia-Pacific region has expanded by 148%, and is expected to increase to $400 billion by the end of this decade.

Almost two-thirds of the world's population resides in Asia and the Pacific, which perhaps accounts for the Pacific basin's production of two-thirds of the world's gross national product.

Japan and America—key trading partners—alone, accounted for 40% of the world's GNP last year.

Also, in 1991, according to Commerce Department figures, the Asia-Pacific countries purchased close to $125 billion worth of U.S. products. It is significant to note that American exports to the region have increased by 130% since 1981.

South Korea, Taiwan, Hong Kong and Singapore—known in Asia as the "Four Tigers" for their astoundingly rapid economic growth, have been joined by a new wave of "Little Dragons," Indonesia, Malaysia and Thailand, as the economic miracle has spread in the Asia-Pacific region. All of these countries have vigorously expanding economies, some up to 11% annually, placing them among the fastest growing in the world.

These facts paint a picture that has many experts in international finance and economics predicting that the Asia-Pacific region will shortly replace the North Atlantic as the center of world trade. My feeling is that this has already occurred. Yes, my friends, the Pacific Century has indeed begun.

And during this month for celebration, it is only fitting that we honor our fellow Americans of Asian Pacific descent—both from the past and the present—that have blessed and enriched our nation. I submit that Asian Pacific Americans have certainly been an asset to our country's development, and it is most appropriate that our President and Congress have proclaimed May as Asian Pacific heritage month.

The people of the Pacific have contributed much to America's development in the sciences and medicine. For example, in 1899 a Japanese immigrant arrived on the shores of this nation. After years of study and work, this man, Dr. Hideyo Noguchi, isolated the syphilis germ, leading to a cure for this deadly, wide spread disease. For decades, Dr. Makio Murayama conducted vital research in the U.S. that laid the groundwork for combating sickle-cell anemia. In 1973, Dr. Leo Esaki, an Asian immigrant to our country, was awarded the Nobel prize in physics for his electron tunneling theories. And, in engineering, few have matched the several architectural masterpieces created by the genius of Chinese American, I. M. Pei.

Major contributions to U.S. business and industry have also been made by Asian Pacific Americans. Wang laboratories, the innovative business enterprise in computer research and development, was founded in 1955 by Chinese American, An Wang. This nation's largest Tungsten refinery was built in 1953 by industrialist K. C. Li and his company, The Wah Chang Corporation. And, in 1964, an immigrant from Shanghai, China, Gerald Tsai, started from scratch an investment firm, The Manhattan Fund, which today has well over $270 million in assets.

In the entertainment and sports fields, Chinese American martial arts expert Bruce Lee entertained the movie audiences of this nation, while destroying the stereotype of the passive, quiet Asian male. World-class conductor Seiji Ozawa has led the San Francisco and Boston symphonies through many brilliant performances over the years.

A native Hawaiian named Duke Kahanamoku shocked the world by winning the Olympic gold medal in swimming seven decades ago followed by Dr. Sammy Lee, a Korean American who won the Olympic gold medal in high diving. Then there was Tommy Kono of Hawaii, also an Olympic gold medalist in weightlifting. And, yes, perhaps the greatest Olympic diver ever known to the world, a Samoan American by the name of Greg Louganis—whose record in gold medals and national championships will be in the books for a long time. This year, Japanese American Kristi Yamaguichi's enthralling gold medal ice-skating performance at the winter Olympics continues the legacy of milestone achievements by Asian Pacific Americans.

In professional sports, of course, we have Michael Chang blazing new paths in tennis, Pacific-Islanders Brian Williams and Michael Jones of world rugby, and the tens of dozens of Asian Pacific Americans who have made their mark as professional football players in the national football league.

We also have an Asian Pacific American who is making his mark on history, not in our country, but in Japan. Samoan American Salevaa Atisanoe is a 578-pound sumo wrestler in Japan who goes by the name of Konishiki. Salevaa, or Konishiki, incidentally, also happens to be a relative of mine.

Konishiki is the first foreigner in this centuries-old sport to reach the rarified air of sumo's second-highest rank. More importantly, though, he is on the verge of attaining the exalted status of grand champion or Yokozuna. No foreigner has ever been permitted to fill this position, as the Japanese associate the Yukozuna with the essence of Shinto's guardian spirits. The ascendance to grand champion status goes to the heart of the Japanese religion and culture.

Although Konishiki has defeated the only existing Yokozuna and has an excellent tournament record, a controversy has erupted as to whether he has the necessary "character" to become a grand champion. By merit and skill, it is uncontested that Konishiki qualifies as a Yokozuna. Many commentators speculate it is because he is not Japanese that he is being denied promotion. For the benefit of my cousin and relations between the U.S. and Japan, I hope that this situation does not escalate into a burning issue of racism.

In honoring Asian Pacific Americans that have served to enrich our country, I would be remiss, as a Viet-Nam veteran, if I did not honor the memory of the Asian Pacific Americans who served in the U.S. Army's 100th Battalion and 442nd Infantry Combat Group. History speaks for itself in documenting that none have shed their blood more valiantly for America than the Japanese Americans that served in these units while fighting enemy forces in Europe during World War II.

The records of the 100th Battalion and 442nd Infantry are without equal. These Asian Pacific American units suffered an unprecedented casualty rate, and received over 18,000 individual decorations, many posthumous, for valor in battle. With so much blood spilled warranting the high number of medals given, it is disturbing and unusual that only one medal of honor, 24 distinguished service crosses and 60 silver stars were awarded. The great number of Asian Pacific American lives lost decreed that more of these ultimate symbols of sacrifice should have been awarded. Even so, the 442nd combat group emerged as the most decorated combat unit of its size in the United States Army.

I am proud to say that we can count The Honorable Daniel K. Inouye a recipient of the distinguished service cross, and the late, highly-respected Senator Spark Matsunaga, both from Hawaii, as members from Congress that distinguished themselves in battle as soldiers of The 100th Battalion and 442nd Infantry.

These Japanese Americans paid their dues in blood to protect our nation from its enemies. It is a shameful black mark on the history of our country that when the patriotic survivors of The 100th Battalion and 442nd Infantry returned to the U.S., many were reunited with families that were locked up behind barbed-wire fences, living in concentration camps. You might be interested to know, my colleagues on The Hill, Congressmen Robert Matsui and Norman Mineta, were children of the concentration camps.

The wholesale and arbitrary abolishment of the constitutional rights of these brave Americans will forever serve as a reminder and testament that this must never be allowed to occur again. It was outright racism and bigotry in its ugliest form. I pray that this will never happen again in America.

Which brings me to the increasingly volatile and complicated subject of our country's state of relations with the nation of Japan.

With Japan leading the way amongst democratic countries of the Asia-Pacific Region—being the world's greatest creditor nation, the world's largest donor of foreign aid, and America's strongest financial partner and ally in the defense of our strategically important sea lanes of the Pacific basin—I am concerned with the hostility mounting in the U.S. against our longtime friend and ally.

Many have said that with the recent collapse of the Soviet Union and the end of the cold war, Americans just have to find someone or something to worry about. Numerous polls verify that Japan is the new public enemy number one.

The myth of the voracious Japanese economic machine that plays by unfair rules, consumes anything in its path and gives nothing back in return, has been set upon by certain politicians needing a quick public relations fix, corporate America facing sagging sales, and workers running out of unemployment checks. Jumping on the Japan-bashing wagon is fashionable and easy, and a good way to absolve responsibility for the state of our nation's ills. Unfortunately, it does little to improve our situation but sets loose a Pandora's box of hysteria, nonsense, and outright bigotry, compounding the already difficult period of development our country faces.

When you look at the facts—the statistics of our own Department of Commerce—Japan is actually one of America's best customers, buying over $48 billion of U.S. goods in 1991. The Japanese buy more U.S. goods than any nation in the world, except for our neighbor, Canada. Since 1987, Japan has increased imports from

our country by 70%, and in the same period reduced its trade surplus with the U.S. by 30%.

Taking a longer look back over the last decade, Commerce Department figures reveal that U.S. exports to Japan rose by 117%, which is more rapid growth than our exports to the rest of the world over the past ten years.

It is significant to note, also, that the latest figures on Japanese investment in the U.S. show that $130 billion was added to our economy in 1990. The Department of Commerce estimates for 1990 that Japanese investment produced 897,000 jobs for America's labor force. I would be interested to know how many Americans lost their jobs that year as a result of U.S. corporations and companies deciding, for cheaper labor costs, to set up factories and operations in foreign countries.

Rather than mindlessly point the finger of blame at Japan, perhaps we in this country should look inward for the cause of America's economic malaise. Many experts in the field suggest that Americans must address fundamental problems with our society that lead to problems with the economy. In short, we must put our house in order.

The first job is to rigorously renovate our educational system, from kindergarten on up. America's present system is not producing enough skilled workers, managers, and leaders that can compete effectively in the international marketplace.

We must also concentrate on producing engineers and specialists in math and the sciences, vocations that produce actual products and technology. Too many of our brightest minds are diverted to professions that deal with non-productive paper shuffling for profit. As an attorney, I know a little about this.

The second major task is to rid the public and private sectors of the tremendous debt incurred in the 1980s. In the span of one decade, the U.S. went from the world's greatest creditor nation to one of its worst debtors. The American people, on the federal, state, local and personal levels, must resolve to rid ourselves of this heavy anchor, and start saving. Only then can we hope to compete freely and unburdened, with sufficient capital, as a creditor nation.

Returning to the phenomenon of Japan-bashing, this mindless behavior has precipitated all over the U.S. increasingly ugly and sometimes violent action against Americans—our Americans of Asian Pacific descent. Distinction as to ethnicity, let alone nationality, seems not to be evident. Asian features alone have provoked attacks and beatings against Japanese Americans, Chinese Americans, Thai Americans and Korean Americans, where the assailants thought the victims were Japanese nationals.

As the U.S. economy has remained stagnant, documented incidents of racist graffiti, name-calling, verbal threats, fire-bombings and physical assaults have spread like wildfire from California to Colorado to Michigan to North Carolina and to New York. The pattern of Asian American killings, such as Jim Loo's beating death last year in Raleigh, Vincent Chin's clubbing murder in Detroit in 1982, the machine gun massacre of five Indochinese kids in 1989 at Stockton, and the unexplained murder of a Japanese businessman in Ventura county a few months ago, underscore that these are not isolated incidents.

Taken as a whole, this is clearly a crisis of national dimension brewing for our Asian Pacific American communities. Even survivors of the Japanese American concentration camps and WWII hysteria have commented—it is happening all over again.

So, how do we stop the wholesale destruction of our birthrights as U.S. citizens that occurred in the 1940s from becoming the same nightmare for us today?

I believe Stewart Kwoh of The Asian Pacific American Legal Center of Southern California has some good ideas.

He recommends that we not remain complacent about Japan-bashing but that we should take a very active stance. Our Asian Pacific communities must come together for protection, and not remain isolated, fragmented and thus vulnerable.

Our communities must also aggressively articulate a position against scapegoating, and monitor and hold responsible those elements that make inflammatory anti-Asian statements.

Furthermore, the Asian Pacific communities must reach out and establish ties with other ethnic groups. With the shocking experience of the burning of Koreatown during the L. A. riots fresh in our minds, it is clear that we must work harder to further understanding, compassion, and mutual respect between people of the Asia-Pacific and all other races. Another lesson to be learned from the L. A. riots is that during hard economic times, all people of color and low income are in the same predicament. Let us learn not to feed on each other. As Rodney King said, "Can we get along?"

We must also learn to trust and work with law enforcement authorities. Even in the wake of the King beating and legal travesty, and the recent manslaughter mistrial of a Compton, California, police officer who shot down in cold blood two unarmed Samoan Americans, shooting them 19 times with 13 bullets in their backs—the vast majority of our men and women in blue are good, honest people, professionals that ensure the peace and stability of our communities. We must use this resource to protect us by religiously and quickly reporting all incidents of hate crime.

Finally, our Asia-Pacific communities must be prepared to network with other associations in the nation to provide a unified response to combating racial violence and hostility against anyone, regardless of race, color or creed.

In concluding, let me say that although Mr. Kwoh's points for protection of our communities are well-taken, I believe that the repulsive Japan-bashing America has witnessed is a temporary affliction.

Ladies and gentlemen, our nation has the strength of character, the resilience of ingenuity and the depth of resources necessary to resolve any problem before her, including our present economic woes. When you see young, upstart entrepreneurs like Bill Gates create a computer software giant like Microsoft—which, incidentally, is worth more on the market than Honda and Sony combined—you know that the United States has the right stuff. So do Motorola, Intel, Merck, Emerson Electric, IBM, Corning and many other U.S. companies that are thriving in the international marketplace. America has done it before and we will do it again.

Meanwhile, recent events have shown the world that Japan is, as the Wall Street Journal put it, not the invincible economic terminator of our imaginings. In the past several weeks, Japan's stock market has crashed by 50% from its peak two years ago, and her real estate values in financial centers like Tokyo and Osaka have plummeted drastically. With this unprecedented economic instability, a tremendous amount of Japan's wealth—tens of billions of dollars—has amazingly vanished overnight, and she may be facing for the first time—a recession.

With the dismantling of the evil empire, the birth of numerous new democracies from Communist ruins, a victory over a dictator in the Gulf War and a vibrant stock market that portends a strong economic recovery, indeed, the United States is still strong, and remains the most powerful country on the face of this planet.

Against this backdrop, our fellow American citizens of Asian Pacific decent can take pride, especially this month, in being Americans.

As our nation enters into the Pacific Century, Asian Pacific Americans can hold their heads high, knowing the contributions of our people have ensured America is, despite her problems, the greatest democracy in the world.

♦ ADDRESS TO THE JAPANESE AMERICAN CITIZENS LEAGUE

Presented by Senator Daniel K. Inouye of Hawaii to the Japanese American Citizens League on August 8, 1992 in Denver, Colorado.

Most Asian Americans would find it difficult, if not impossible, to differentiate between an Irish American and a German American, or for that matter, between an

Italian American or a Spanish American. Why? Because they all look alike. And, in the same way, an Irish American may find it difficult, if not impossible, to differentiate between a Chinese American and a Japanese American or Korean American and a Vietnamese American. Why? Because we all look alike. The above may sound humorous and facetious, but it does described a major problem that exists in our community.

We don't take the time to acquaint ourselves with each other—our neighbors—[to get to know] each other's cultural heritage, each other's contributions to our national history. So we rely on stereotypes: stereotypes generated by prejudice, hatred, and lack of respect; stereotypes generated by exaggerated ware stories; or stereotypes generated by a false sense of superiority.

Needless to say, productive and friendly relationships between diverse peoples cannot be based upon a foundation of negative stereotypes. And this seems to describe the present-day situation.

Our nation is fast approaching that moment in our history when the European Americans will no longer constitute the majority of our nation's people. We will soon be a nation of diverse ethnic and racial minorities—minorities viewing each other with unease, distrust, and in some cases, outright hatred. This nation cannot long survive as a viable democracy under these conditions.

So what should we do?

1. Recognize and acknowledge the existence of this problem—racism—up front. Let's attack racism—as an evil disease.

2. Improve our educational system. This situation [of failure in our educational system] cannot be tolerated. Equal opportunity is not possible with unequal education.

3. Convene a summit conference of national leaders to openly and candidly discuss this matter. A national dialogue must be started.

4. Begin a national educational program utilizing our school systems, business leaders, and their communities, national ethnic leaders, together with expert guidance, to simply acquaint ourselves with each other.

Today, for example, we are confronted with a problem brought about by misunderstanding and the lack of open dialogue.

Those who know anything about global trade will agree that today's world marketplace is in the Pacific. This is where the opportunities exist for growth, development, and creativity. Yet, in listening to the American debate, one would get the impression that that is still Europe and the Atlantic.

The two most important powers in the Pacific are Japan and the United States. For this reason, it would seem obvious that good relations be maintained between these two nations, because any deterioration would result in economic, political, and social havoc for the United States and Japan, as well as the other Pacific Rim nations.

On the other side of America, Europeans have realized that, as separate nations, it would be very difficult to compete against such economic powers as the United States and Japan. Accordingly, they constitute a formidable economic force, and are calling for open competition with both the United States and Japan, and may also consider playing one against the other.

In closing, I believe it is well that we remind ourselves that bashing—whether it be Japan-bashing, China-bashing, Philippine-bashing, Vietnam-bashing—that all bashing begins with eloquent words. [It begins with the] words of diplomacy. This diplomatic rhetorical bashing is then taken up by those who are accustomed to harsher words—words of hate, words of racism, and words of anger. Rhetorical bashing can then easily deteriorate into violent bashing. It was not too long ago when two unemployed auto workers in Detroit beat a Chinese person to death. Their explanation of innocence was their belief that they were beating a Japanese. Somehow they felt justified in beating a Japanese.

On December 7, 1991, our nation paused to observe the 50th anniversary of the bombing of Pearl Harbor. I hope that Americans, after 50 years, will begin to put behind us the pain and hatred that December 7th represents. We should not continue to look back to the past by keeping this pain and hatred in the forefront of our memories—it can only hamper and narrow our path into the 21st century. We, as Americans, must look forward, closing the dark chapter of December 7, 1941, and each nation accepting the other's hand of friendship. Hand-in-hand—let us move forward for the next 50 years.

♦ KEYNOTE ADDRESS TO THE ASIAN AMERICAN JOURNALISTS ASSOCIATION (AAJA)

Delivered by Helen Zia at the Asian American Journalists Association's annual convention on August 27, 1992.

Welcome to AAJA's annual national convention. I've been given the task of saying something meaningful (and hopefully rousing) on our role as Asian American journalists today. You know, something about whether we are Asian Americans who happen to be journalists, or journalists who happen to be Asian Americans. I have only a short time to address this complete question—and this will be a challenge. It's been an amazing year in the news for Asian Americans; news events that involve and directly impact the Asian American community have figured prominently in the national headlines:

• We've been on the front pages as crime victims—who can forget the sweet, youthful face of Konerak Sinthasimphone, the Laotian boy who was raped, murdered and cannibalized by serial killer Jeffrey Dahmer—while police said they thought the 14-year-old was an adult.

• And what about front page/front cover/top of the news image of the smiling, charming, victorious face of Olympic gold medal figure skater Kristi Yamaguchi, the fourth-generation Japanese American who defeated Midori Ito of Japan?

• Then there was the media event of this half century—that is, of course, the 50th anniversary of the bombing of Pearl Harbor. Virtually *every* media outlet in the country played some special Pearl Harbor angle.

• This was followed by very cursory coverage, if there was any coverage at all, of the 50th anniversary of the racist incarceration of 120,313 Japanese Americans in U.S. concentration camps.

• We witnessed [in George Bush's infamous trip to Japan] the spectacle of a U.S. president going overseas to ask for economic relief, which, following the hype over Pearl Harbor, resulted in even greater anti-Asian fervor.

• Two major reports on Asian Americans were released nationally—one by the U.S. civil rights commission on the rise of anti-Asian prejudice, and one by AAJA—our media resource handbook on covering the Asian American community. Both reports were ridiculed by some national media (such as *US News and World Report*, *New Republic*, and *Readers Digest*) because they dared to discuss issues of sensitivity to Asian Americans.

• But the most dramatic news involving Asian Americans this year took place during the L.A. rebellion—which, to Asian Americans, represents the selective targeting of an entire Asian nationality—and it implicates all other look-alike Asians. The riot coverage *also* represents the overall failure of our business to go beyond the surface in reporting on the Asian community. Not only was there inadequate reporting, but considerable mischaracterization and disinformation about Korean Americans disseminated in the name of news.

Those are just some of the Asian American news highlights since our last convention. Pretty big visibility for a community that's used to being invisible in the national news—and I think this change reflects the dynamic period of history that we're in. We are on the verge of the next millennium—tagged the century of Asia and the Pacific Rim.

As Asian Americans, we find ourselves at the crossroads of two major trends: First, there is the decline of U.S. economic might, while the nations of Asia are on the ascendancy. This trend involves major shifts in global power relationships. Does anyone here doubt that there will be fundamental repercussions of all kinds for Asian Americans?

Secondly, Asian America is changing. Our numbers have doubled every 10 years for each of the last four census reports, making us the fastest growing minority in the U.S. It wasn't so long ago, that being Asian American meant being either Chinese or Japanese. But now, we are so diverse that even many Asian Pacific Americans know little about their fellow Asian brothers and sisters.

And we, as Asian American journalists, have a very big role to play during this historic period—precisely because we are at the crossroads and in a position to give shape to who this Asian American community is to a nation that really doesn't have a clue.

I, like most of you, remember what it was like never to see people who looked like me in the world beyond my immediate circle. When I was growing up in the 1950s, Asians were nowhere to be found in the media, except occasionally in the movies. There, at the Saturday matinee, my brothers and I would sit with all the other kids in town watching old World War II movies—you know, where the evil zero pilots would be heading for their unsuspecting prey, only to be thwarted by the all-American heroes—who were, of course, always white. These movies would have their defining moment, that crescendo of emotion when the entire theater would rise up, screaming "Kill them, kill them, kill them!" ("them" being the Japanese). When the movie was over and the lights came on, I wanted to be invisible so that my neighbors wouldn't direct their red-*white*-and blue fervor toward me.

When I was a little older, I was inspired by the civil rights movements of the 1960s. In my high school, the social unrest often took the form of bomb scares and other disruptions. One afternoon, as my classmates and I stood in the schoolyard talking about racism while waiting for the bomb squad, one of my black girlfriends turned to me and said somberly, "Helen, you've got to decide whether you're black or white."

These incidents took place many years ago—and I wish I could say things have changed a lot since, but I can't. In spite of the news coverage this year and the relative visibility of Asian Americans, a closer look at the coverage shows that we're still rendered invisible:

• Take the front page coverage of Konerak Sinthasimphone. How much, or perhaps I should ask how little, consideration was given to the fact that he was Laotian? What was the response of the Laotian community, which is a sizable and impoverished minority group in the Midwest? Does anybody know? Did any reporters bother to try to find out? Was there any mention made of the anti-Asian racism that was exhibited by the Milwaukee police, in addition to their homophobic and anti-black attitude?

• What about the very interesting social/political implications of Kristi Yamaguchi's ancestry at this particular point in history, especially following all the Pearl Harbor type? Not too many news organizations wanted to touch that one—or maybe it never occurred to them how. *Newsweek's* long essay by Frank Deford described her physique down to the two "cute" little moles on her face—but not a bit of analysis about how her Japanese heritage might be playing in Peoria.

• Speaking of Pearl Harbor, what news value is there really to have so many polls—in just about every media market—asking how much more do Americans hate the Japanese today than they did yesterday? [Of course, these "Americans" are presumed to be non-Asian.] And don't you agree that this is a strange question? Would we ever see such widespread polling on how much more we hate the Germans today than yesterday, or the Russians, or the Cubans? Somehow it is assumed to be accepted behavior to hate Japanese people—and this is biased, non-objective journalism coming from our news directors at some of our most esteemed news organizations. The *New York Times* runs this poll every few years, and both the *Wall Street Journal* and the *Los Angeles Times* asked: Was America right in dropping the atom bomb on Hiroshima and Nagasaki? (The surprise answer—a high proportion of respondents said yes), or their question, "Was America right to intern 120,313 Japanese Americans?" (Surprise again, a significant proportion said yes.) I mean, we might imagine a poll that asked, "Do you think Germany was right to try to exterminate the Jews?" and we might even get a considerable response that said yes—but what journalistic purpose would this question serve? And what assumptions are being made in even asking the question?

• Many of you may be involved in the coverage of Soon-Yi Farrow, adopted daughter of Mia Farrow, who was raised as a daughter of Woody Allen. Some of our colleagues (or even some of us) call it a love triangle—but would we be more likely to call it incest if she looked more like she could be his biological daughter—instead of an Asian female, with all those sexual connotations? What does this so-called affair mean for an entire generation of adopted Korean children? Soon-Yi's Asian face is all over the news, but her Asianness is ignored and invisible.

This kind of invisibility was never so apparent than in the national coverage of Los Angeles, the story in which the nation's news media discovered Korean Americans—but then could only fixate on the image of Korean men with guns. A demonstration involving thousands of Korean Americans calling for justice for Rodney King was barely covered. *Nightline* let only one Korean spokesperson—Angela Oh—appear for an abbreviated broadcast, after days of prolonged interviews with African American gang members who made grossly incorrect statements about Korean people that largely went unchallenged. (And only then after community protests.) As John Lee and Dean Takahashi wrote in the AAJA newsletter, a *Los Angeles Times* post-riot survey reported only the responses of whites, blacks, and Latinos—and "other." As explanation, they said that Asians are not statistically significant enough to count, even though they comprise 11 percent of L.A.'s population—and even when Asians were so strongly impacted by the rebellion.

At some points, the insurrection seemed to be portrayed as a black-Korean issue (forget about police brutality and economic injustice). There was virtually no news analysis on the potential impact on other Asian Americans, or the fact that several hundred stores owned by Cambodians, Chinese, Japanese, and South Asians were also looted and burned.

This stuff is simply poor journalism. It wouldn't get out of Reporting 101—you know, the section on how to ask the right questions. But when it comes to Asian Americans, some people just don't seem to know what questions to ask to get beyond the superficial stereotypes.

I know I'm making this sound a lot like "us vs. them," even though as journalists, many of us are the "them." But the fact is that many of us—perhaps *most* of us—are still outsiders in our own newsrooms. Jimmy Breslin almost got away with calling Mary Ji-Yeon Yuh a "little yellow dog," and a "slant-eyed cunt"—and when he didn't get away with it, many of his colleagues (*our* colleagues) rushed to his defense. We're just not in the newsrooms in sufficient numbers yet or in enough positions of authority to be taken seriously. How many Asian American journalists were sent to cover L.A.? Shockingly few. I've heard several accounts of experienced Asian American journalists who requested to go and cover the riots—and were turned down even if the organization had no other Asian reporters. Yet if she or he pushed too hard or criticized too loudly, the consequences could be harsh, including the ultimate insult—being labeled as "not objective."

Now I'd like to deal with this objectivity issue for a moment: somewhere, somehow we ourselves have started to buy into this backlash mythology that to be a professional journalist means we can have no point of view—and if that were possible, that it would be a virtue. This is a fiction and an hypocrisy that only serves to keep us doubting ourselves.

Last year at the Seattle convention, I sat in a workshop and listened to a young woman in her first journalism job as an education reporter, questioning her own ability to cover issues like bilingual education simply because she is Asian and *that* might be a conflict in and of itself. Obviously *every* story has implicit assumptions that steer the reader or viewer to some kind of impression. The issue is who determines those assumptions? Who decides what questions to ask, or not to ask?

For example, so much media hype is made on the point of Japanese investment—yet in the news media itself several of the largest companies are owned by British, German, Australian, Canadian and French interests. Imagine how differently the news coverage would play if the late Robert Maxwell had been Japanese. Can you imagine the headlines? "Maxwell-san Says Sayonara After Kamikaze Strike on Tribune Company." "Maxwell's Sons Make Sneak Attack on US Workers' Pensions." But Maxwell was British, not Japanese, and instead we see very staid, very respectful coverage. Is this not an inherent bias?

Personally I think the whole issue of objectivity is a smokescreen to make us and others think that *we* are somehow deficient for not fitting the mold that the traditional white male standard created in its own image. We of all groups should never forget that we work in an industry that was singularly responsible for the systematic vilification and exclusion of Asian immigrants. Some venerable newspapers played a key role in the incarceration of Japanese Americans. Radio helped spearhead the Red scares of the McCarthy era that led to the persecution of many Chinese Americans. More recently, the Kerner Commission in 1968 outlined how the news media and its lack of diversity contributed to the civil disorders of the 1960s—and sadly, progress has been at a glacial pace.

So when *we* get accused of not being objective, we need to be able to stand our ground and point out the double standard that is being applied to us at the expense of good journalism.

I should also note that I do not believe these editors and news directors and colleagues of ours are necessarily being deliberately racist. I think they're just doing what they've been taught, acting out some of their own biases. Don't you know that some of them were sitting near me, or near you, shouting "*Kill them! Kill them! Kill them!*" Or perhaps they were explaining to another kid in another schoolyard, how you have to decide whether you're black or white.

It's a vicious cycle: news gets shaped by people who are not even aware of their own prejudices. Journalists produce news that often reinforces their own beliefs, thereby steering public opinion in a way that perpetuates the same crap. And so on and so on. That's what we saw in L.A.—*some* black people using their prejudices toward Asians in general Koreans in particular to justify their actions; and *some* Korean people using their prejudices toward blacks to justify their actions—and where did each group learn these prejudices? Mostly through news and entertainment media.

Indeed, this is our historic role at this historic time with the confluence of these trends. *We* can interrupt this crazy feedback loop of misinformation about our communities and cultural heritage. We are in a very powerful position to outline the public perception of who Asian Americans are—not only within our newsrooms but to build bridges with other communities through the various minority journalists' organizations.

This is not an easy task. Look around in this room. What you see are pioneers in this effort—every one of us is a pioneer. As you go through this convention picking up skills for professional development, and networking for career advancement, remember that our collective development includes being role models for each other as part of this historic position we hold.

There will be times when an issue of fairness stands out so blatantly that you will be moved to act—and you will find strength in knowing that you don't have to act alone because there is an entire organization that stands with you. There's nothing radical about this—it's simply about trying to create the newsroom environment in which the Asian American journalists can reach their fullest potential—without having to explain why they speak English so well, or having to deal with colleagues who try to second guess if the color of their skin or the shape of their eyes had anything to do with a job, a promotion, or a story assignment.

As you look around this room and think how comfortable it is not to have a worry about such things—imagine being able to feel this way at a meeting of the Society of Professional Journalists, the American Society of Magazine Editors, the American Society of Newspaper Editors, and so on, or even your own newsroom. One day it will be that way for all of us, because of our pioneering efforts in AAJA. So enjoy the convention, be good role models to each other, and remember that history is on our side.

♦ PRESIDENT BILL CLINTON'S ADDRESS AT THE PROCLAMATION SIGNING FOR ASIAN PACIFIC HERITAGE MONTH

These remarks were made by President Clinton at the White House during the proclamation signing for Asian Pacific Heritage Month on May 3, 1993.

Let me begin by extending a warm welcome to all of you, especially those who have traveled very great distances, as many of you have, to help celebrate Asian Pacific American Heritage Month. I'm pleased to be joined on the state by Senator Dan Akaka, with whom I played golf last weekend—(laughter)—less well than he did, I might add; and Rep. Bob Matsui, Norm Mineta, Robert Underwood, Patsy Mink, Eni Faleomavaega . . . and Jay Kim. And let us also honor the memory of the late Senator Spark Matsunaga, who left such a wonderful legacy as the true friend of the Asian Pacific community.

My campaign and my administration have gained so much from the talents of Asian Pacific Americans, and I'd like to recognize just a few of them: Barbara Chow, my special assistant for legislative affairs; Neil Dhillon, at the Department of Transportation; Atul Gawande, who has been working on the Health Care Task Force; Maria Haley on our personal staff; Goody Marshall with the Vice President's staff; Doris Matsui in public liaison who did such a wonderful job with this event; Shirley Sagawa in legislative affairs; Debra Shon at the United States Trade Representatives Office; Melinda Yee at the Department of Commerce; and many others who are an essential part of our efforts every day.

Fifteen years ago, Rep. Frank Horton introduced the first resolution proclaiming Asian Pacific American Heritage Week, honoring the significant contributions of Asian Pacific Americans in all walks of life. In 1990, Congress designated and President Bush proclaimed the month of May as Asian Pacific Heritage Month. And last year with the help of Rep. Horton and 106 of his colleagues, the designation of May as Asian Pacific Heritage Month each year became the law of the land.

The month of May was chosen because of its significance to Asian Pacific American history. In the first week of May in 1843, the first Japanese arrived in America. And on May 10, 1969, Golden Spike Day, the transcontinental railroad, built partly with Chinese labor, was completed. Today, 150 years after these historic events, nearly eight million Asian Pacific Americans can trace their roots to Asia and the islands of the Pacific.

It is astonishing to realize the breadth of diversity among Americans of Asian Pacific heritage. The Asian Pacific community stretches across thousands of miles and encompasses millions of diverse people. In our country the Asian Pacific American community can trace its roots to at least 25 different nationalities, more than 75 different languages, and literally hundreds of different ethnic groups. Now, that's diversity.

And still Asian Pacific Americans have something in common and something to emulate—a commitment to strong families, to community, and to instilling in each new generation a respect for educational opportunity and hard work. These values have been an essential part of success in achieving the American Dream, as so many Asian Pacific Americans know.

And while we realize all the rich opportunities America has given to all our people, we are aware also of how much Asian Pacific Americans have given back to this country. Immigrants from Asia and the Pacific helped build our country. Today their descendants are making us even better. They are prominent among our scientists, artists, doctors, teachers and other professionals who have enriched the lives of all of us in America.

I want to talk for a moment about the importance of education. The Asian Pacific community has demonstrated that a commitment to education is truly key to bettering our lives. Among Asian Pacific Americans 25 years old and over, 82 percent have had four years of high school or more; 39 percent have completed four years of college or more. For individuals, education is the key to economic parity and social mobility. But for America, it is the key to our strength and our competitiveness in the global economy.

I want to thank you all again for coming here today to recognize all the achievements and the contributions that Asian Pacific Americans have made to this great nation. I hope that we can continue to come together as we have today to rejoice in our diversity as we renew the bonds of community that bring all Americans together. I believe that if we embrace those things which we share, if we embrace our common values and our common goals, we strengthen ourselves, our community and our democracy and we make ourselves free to celebrate the richness of our diversity.

Therefore, it is with great pride and admiration that I take this opportunity, my first one, to sign the proclamation proclaiming this Asian Pacific American Heritage Month. Thank you very much.

♦ THE UNITED STATES AND THE ASIA-PACIFIC: A PARTNERSHIP FOR THE PACIFIC CENTURY

Remarks by Eni F. H. Faleomavaega, member of the U.S. Congress, delivered in honor of Asian Pacific Heritage Month to the United States House of Representatives in May of 1993.

Mr. Speaker, I rise today to honor the deep and enduring legacy of those Americans whose roots extend from the soil of the nations of Asia and the Pacific Islands. Due to prior commitments that could not be rescheduled, our Asia-Pacific colleagues, The Honorable Patsy Mink and The Honorable Neil Abercrombie of Hawaii, and The Honorable Robert Matsui and The Honorable Norman Mineta of California, and the distinguished gentleman from Guam, The Honorable Robert Underwood, are unable to be with us. Nonetheless, their hearts and thoughts are with us today and I submit their statements for the record.

A few weeks ago, I was privileged, along with my Asia-Pacific colleagues, to attend a special White House ceremony, at which President Clinton signed an official proclamation declaring this month—the month of May—as "National Asian Pacific American Heritage Month."

I am very appreciative of the fact that federal agencies and local governments throughout the United States, as well as our armed services around the world, are making preparations for recognition of the Asian Pacific American community. Certainly, the contributions of Asian Pacific Americans have immeasurably enriched our great nation, which has been blessed with a mosaic of cultural and ethnic diversity representing just about every country on this planet.

In order to truly appreciate the eight million Asian Pacific Americans living today in the United States, however, I believe it is helpful to attain a perspective on the Asia-Pacific region and its importance to America. Asian Pacific Americans are amongst the newest wave of immigrants coming to the United States in recent years.

Let me share with you some of the highlights of our current relationship with the Asia-Pacific region, and why it is in our national interest to maintain strong economic, social, and political ties with this area of the world.

As America and the countries of the Asia-Pacific region prepare to leave the 20th century, the world has changed at a frantic pace. Of particular importance has been the cessation of the cold war. It is imperative that the United States dramatically reassess her foreign policy not only towards Europe but just as importantly towards the Asia-Pacific region.

As the United States and the nations of the Asia-Pacific region enter the 21st century—what many have called the dawning of the "Pacific Century"—it is evident that many of our interests are the same in this increasingly important part of the globe.

In this decade and into the next century, the Asia-Pacific region shall play an increasingly pivotal role in the economic, political, strategic and security needs of the world. As has been often stated, the 21st century—the Pacific Century—shall truly be an era marked with miraculous advancement by this the world's most dynamic and rapidly developing region.

Having served as a member of the House Foreign Affairs Committee for the past four years, I have argued that the U.S. has an unhealthy fixation with the affairs of Europe and the Middle East. This is unfortunate, as it has resulted in America's indifference—some might even call it failure—to address the serious issues affecting our nation's relationship with the countries of the Asia-Pacific region.

I. U.S. Economic Interests in The Asia-Pacific Region:

The economy of the Asia-Pacific region today is staggering in size and breathtaking in growth. The United States has a substantial stake in the region's economy.

Today, according to recent U.S. Department of Commerce figures, America conducts over $328 billion worth of total trade with the countries of the Asia-Pacific—easily matching, and nearly doubling, the trade we conduct with Western Europe.

Since 1981, U.S. trade with the Asia-Pacific region has expanded by 150% and is expected to increase to $400 billion by the end of this decade.

Almost two-thirds of the world's population resides in Asia and the Pacific, which perhaps accounts for the Pacific basin's production of two-thirds of the world's Gross National Product.

Despite recent economic slowdowns, Japan and America, key trading partners—alone—accounted for 40% of the world's GNP in 1991.

Also that year, according to Commerce Department figures, the Asia-Pacific countries purchased $130 billion worth of U.S. products. It is significant to note that American exports to the region have increased by well-over 130% since 1981. Last year, almost one-third of America's exports to the world were bought by nations of the Asia-Pacific.

Today, over 2.6 million American jobs are dependent on trade with the region, and U.S. firms have over $62 billion invested there. These trade ties are rapidly escalating.

South Korea, Taiwan, Hong Kong, and Singapore—known in Asia, as well as in America, as the "Four Tigers" for their astoundingly rapid economic growth—have been joined by a new wave of "Little Dragons," led by Indonesia, Malaysia, and Thailand, as the economic miracle has spread in the Asia-Pacific region. All of these countries have vigorously expanding economies, some up to 11% annually, placing them among the fastest growing in the world.

Joining this tidal wave of economic development has come the sleeping giant of Asia, The People's Republic of China (PRC). By cultivating economic growth recently estimated as high as 13%—the highest rate of economic expansion in the world in 1992—China may be the first example of a communist system that will succeed in meeting the economic needs of her people. Feeding China's 1.3 billion hungry people has, alone, been a monumental accomplishment.

Establishing numerous financial links with Taiwan and Hong Kong, with cross-border investments exceeding $36.5 billion over the past 12 years, the PRC has emerged as a new economic entity termed "Greater China." The combined gross domestic product of greater China last year totaled over $626 billion. Due to the rapid blossoming of greater China's integrated economy, it is foreseen that this will increasingly act as a counterbalance to Japan's considerable economic clout in the region.

These facts paint a picture that has many experts in international finance predicting that the Asia-Pacific region will shortly replace the North Atlantic as the center of world trade. My feeling is that this has already occurred.

Due to this explosive economic boom in Asia and the Pacific, the United States can no longer expect to have unchallenged economic supremacy in the region—a former pillar of U.S. policy in the Asia-Pacific. Moreover, as America's balance of trade deficit has grown, relations with countries of the region have the potential to become increasingly volatile. Our nation's rocky relationship with our most important partner and ally in the Pacific, Japan, is illustrative.

Although trade restrictions are partly responsible, rather than solely point the finger of blame at Japan and other Asia-Pacific nations, perhaps we in the U.S. should look inward for the cause of America's economic malaise. Many experts in the field suggest that Americans must address fundamental problems with our society that lead to problems with the economy. In short, we must put our house in order.

The first job is to rigorously renovate our education and training systems. America's present system is not producing enough skilled workers, managers, and leaders that can compete effectively in the international marketplace.

America must also concentrate on producing engineers and specialists in math and the sciences, vocations that produce actual products and technology. Too many of our brightest minds are diverted to professions that deal with non-productive paper shuffling for profit.

Another major task is to rid America's public and private sectors of the tremendous debt incurred in the 1980s. In the span of one decade, the U.S. went from the world's greatest creditor nation to one of its worst debtors. The American people—on the federal, state, local and personal levels—must resolve to rid ourselves of this heavy anchor, and start saving. Only then can we hope to compete freely and unburdened, with sufficient capital, as a creditor nation.

Hand in hand with reduction of the national deficit is the tremendous challenge for America to make massive investments in her public infrastructure, private-sector plants, equipment, and technology. The lack of investment is responsible for much of America's declining competitiveness in the international marketplace. Last year, for example, Japan out-invested the U.S. by $440 billion.

It is also imperative that our government coordinate to play a more aggressive role in promoting American products overseas, along with assisting the growth of U.S. industries developing new vital technologies. Of primary importance is the conversion of America's talent-laden defense industry to the pursuit of cutting-edge technology for peaceful purposes. Our government's efforts in these areas have been scattered and disjointed in the past, and we may need the creation of a single agency to focus on this crucial economic mission.

With respect to international competition, the United States cannot afford a trade policy of "protectionism, America-First" towards the Asia-Pacific region. We cannot allow ourselves to become outsiders looking in at the unprecedented pace of economic development in a part of the world that is fast becoming the center for world trade. By erecting trade barriers, increasing tariffs, and imposing more product quotas, as some have called for in Congress, this will do little to revitalize and rebuild America's economy. I strongly oppose such protectionist efforts.

Last, hand in hand with these measures, is the need for the United States to reassess her policy priorities, especially towards Japan and China, the two engines driving the economic future of the region.

I join others in advocating that the first priority should be stopping the deterioration of the U.S.–Japan relationship. A solid and stable partnership between America and Japan is the only foundation upon which peace and economic prosperity in the region can be ensured. New U.S. policy must be forged that will allow common ground to be reached on economic and political concerns with our longtime ally.

It is my belief that America's trade conflicts with Japan have been emphasized too much, to the point where many in the U.S. have lost sight of the big picture. Although certainly the U.S. trade deficit with Japan is important, this issue should not be permitted to dominate—poisoning the trust, the confidence and the mutual respect that have bound our two nations in friendship for decades.

If America is to increasingly view and treat Japan as an equal partner, however, Japan must also demonstrate willingness to shoulder greater responsibility for global affairs. With a surplus of over $130 billion from global trade, Japan has profited handsomely from free trade. To signal her good faith in assuming a position of world leadership, Japan could start by removing the country's multiple barriers to free trade, such as those protecting her rice markets. There is also the necessity for Japan to play a more prominent role in supporting GATT and the current round of negotiations in Uruguay.

I am confident these trade disputes will be transcended. The U.S. and Japan can then turn to the broad range of interests that our two nations share not only in the Asia-Pacific region but in addressing the needs of the global economy.

Another crucial priority for America involves the stabilization of relations with the People's Republic of China. Some members in Congress have pointed accusing fingers at China, criticizing her for the lack of individual freedoms and democracy that we in the West take as God-given rights. Some have moved for economic punishment of China for human rights violations and other shortfalls by withdrawing her most-favored-nation (MFN) trading status.

I join those members of Congress that question the wisdom of such action, however. It is imperative that China's awe-inspiring progress toward a free market economy be supported by the United States. History has proven time and time again that economic success is a precursor to the growth of democratic reform and political pluralism. For proof, we need only look to the vibrant democracies flourishing today in South Korea and Taiwan; the wave of economic prosperity in those nations devoured the repressive regimes in power only yesterday.

The lesson to be learned is that America must be patient.

Threats to revoke China's MFN can often be counter-productive. More importantly, if America chooses to unilaterally apply economic sanctions against China with the goal of isolating her, we are only deluding ourselves. Increasingly, events have shown that such action will not gain the multilateral support of the nations of the Asia-Pacific nor the world. The net result is that America is the one isolated.

In the months after the Tiananmen square tragedy, while Washington justifiably took the high moral ground, our European and Asian allies flocked to fill the vacuum of business interest, laying the ground for innumerable business ventures in the future. While America was right in expressing shock and apprehension over the tragic events of Tiananmen, the years since have revealed a China that has changed in important ways, as economic freedoms have subtly laid the foundation for future growth of increased political freedom. Given the changing picture, at a time of financial crisis and economic weakness in the United States, I ask can we afford to continue handcuffing America's access to the largest and most rapidly developing market on the planet?

While I certainly do not condone the infringement of human rights that has been and perhaps is being perpetrated by Beijing this must be balanced against recognition of China's sovereign right to control her domestic matters in nurturing the transition from a poor agrarian state to a diversified free market economy—all the while providing for the welfare of a population that numbers almost five times that of America. Some have said that the right to subsistence—to have adequate food and shelter—is the most fundamental of human rights, and I certainly cannot argue against that in observing China's struggle to feed, clothe, and shelter her masses.

In recognizing that China's task is a difficult one, the U.S. must demonstrate restraint and patience. And we must also show vision by not limiting our focus to humanitarian concerns to the detriment of the vast, broad range of interests that America has in common with China. In addition to our sizable economic incentive, we must also form strong ties to China to address pressing environmental concerns, escalating arms sales, and the uncontrolled spread of nuclear proliferation.

It is only when fundamental interests of the United States are at stake that we should consider the use of the ultimate economic sanction—the withdrawal of MFN. In my opinion, the time for that has not come for China, and President Clinton should be given the flexibility and time to forge through diplomacy and alternative sanctions a closer relationship with China for our mutual benefit.

The Asia-Pacific region is immersed in a renaissance of economic prosperity and relative peace. For America to become a greater participant in and beneficiary of that dynamic process, we must adopt new approaches demonstrating flexibility and sensitivity to the needs and concerns of countries of the Asia-Pacific. In so doing, America and nations of the region will achieve greater harmony through a true Trans-Pacific partnership.

II. United States Security Interests in the Asia-Pacific Region:

Despite the tremendous transformations taking place around the world, one thing that has remained unchanged is that the United States has key security interests in the Asia-Pacific region that demand America remain a predominant military power there.

Before and since World War II, the U.S. has played and continues to play a paramount role in maintaining stability and peace in Asia and the Pacific. Our participation in the affairs of the region has greatly laid the foundation upon which the Asia-Pacific's present prosperity has been built.

I strongly support the U.S. Department of Defense's strategic framework for the Asian Pacific rim in the 21st century, and have drawn liberally from their recent report to Congress. I also agree with the Pentagon that our Nation's security policy in the Asia-Pacific region must be flexible yet premised on six basic principles.

First, there exists the absolute assurance that America will continue to engage herself in the affairs of Asia and the Pacific;

Second, there is the understanding that America will continue to foster a strong system of bilateral security arrangements with nations in the region;

Third, it is agreed that the U.S. will continue to maintain a reserve of forward-deployed forces, although reduced in number, in the region;

Fourth, our nation is committed to maintaining overseas bases and equipment necessary to support those U.S. forces;

Fifth, it is understood that our friends and allies in the Asia-Pacific must continue to bear greater responsibility for their self-defense;

Last, our defense cooperation with our allies shall be complementary in nature and not duplicative.

In applying this broad security policy to the Asia-Pacific, the United States seeks to ensure that key security interests are protected.

Foremost among these is the protection of the U.S. and her allies from attack. In addition to defending Alaska, Hawaii, the U.S. territories, and their lines of communication and navigation to the Continental United States, America has pledged to assist in the defense of her allies and their vital sealanes.

By so doing, another key security interest in the Asia-Pacific is achieved: preservation of regional peace and stability.

Other vital U.S. interests focus on preserving political and economic access to the countries of the region, while fostering the growth of democratic government and the protection of human rights.

A final major security interest pertains to averting the proliferation of nuclear, chemical, and biological weapons in the Asia-Pacific region, while contributing to nuclear deterrence where necessary.

There exist many sources for potential instability and flashpoints in the Asia-Pacific region that concern the United States.

One of the most urgent threats is posed by Communist North Korea and her desperate quest for nuclear weapons. Acquisition of nuclear warheads, combined with a ballistic missile program and an intimidating military force numbering over a million soldiers, could lead to a major conflict on the Korean peninsula. Needless to say, such a conflict would hold ramifications for the entire world.

With North Korea's stated intent to withdraw from the nuclear non-proliferation treaty (NPT) after disputes with the international atomic energy agency (IAEA), a major escalation of that threat has occurred. The move has sent shock waves through Asia and the global community. Nuclear weapons in the hands of North Korea potentially threaten not only South Korea, but Japan, Taiwan, and even China.

Some in the Congress have called for surgical strikes to destroy suspected nuclear weapons facilities in North Korea before their nuclear capacity becomes more deadly. Such a move, however, would be tantamount to a declaration of war. No doubt, South Korea's populous capital, Seoul, within artillery range of the DMZ, would be sacrificed. Also, a war with North Korea would be the ultimate litmus test of our alliance treaties with South Korea and Japan. In such a scenario, it is unclear just how committed our allies are to engaging their troops alongside American soldiers on the frontline. Undeniably, the cost in human life from a full-blown conflict on the Korean peninsula would be unthinkable.

Cooler heads have prevailed, however, and I join them in urging that President Clinton use all diplomatic measures necessary to bring Pyongyang back to the negotiating table and into compliance with the NPT. With recent reports, I am hopeful that negotiations between Pyongyang and the IAEA will allow this matter to be resolved peacefully.

If necessary, however, the U.N. Security Council may have to move for economic sanctions and related measures to convince North Korea to fulfill her obligations under the NPT. The world community cannot permit North Korea to blatantly violate the NPT without punishment. To acquiesce here would set a terrible precedent, encouraging other countries to make similar maverick attempts to join the "nuclear club."

The ominous incident with North Korea exemplifies why a high priority for U.S. policy in the Asia-Pacific must be the halting of nuclear and missile proliferation. Effective nuclear and missile arms control regimes must be pursued that will bring North Korea and China into the fold.

The People's Republic of China, as noted earlier, has recently enjoyed great economic success. With her cash reserves, China has raised concern in the Asia-Pacific region by investing massive sums in high-tech military hardware. While the Soviet Union has collapsed and Japan remains pacifist, China has increased her military budget by over 50% since 1989.

In so doing, China has purchased a number of advanced Soviet jet fighters and bombers, and seeks to procure an aircraft carrier—the foundation for a Blue Water Fleet in the South China sea. China is also obtaining advanced missile guidance systems, which, seen in light of her largest-ever nuclear detonation last year, is particularly worth noting.

At a time when relative peace is at hand, many in the region and the U.S. question China's heavy military buildup. With China's aggressive assertion of claims to the Spratly Islands and Taiwan, and her conducting of well-publicized military offensive exercises, it is feared that Chinese expansionism in the Asia-Pacific region may result.

On the other hand, China's military investment has been perceived in some quarters as being a reasonable modernization of their aging, outmoded weaponry systems for self-defense. After witnessing America's state-of-the-art lightning-like devastation of Iraq in the Gulf War, China has understandably felt inadequate and behind the times. With military hardware being offered at fire sale prices by Russia and the Ukraine, China has capitalized on the opportunity. Seen in light of America's military budget of over $250 billion per year and Japan's annual defense expenditure of $30 billion, China's military spending of $7 billion last year appears relatively modest.

With the withdrawal of U.S. forces and closure of bases in the Philippines, the developments in that nation bear watching. Widespread poverty, a weak economy, and a long-existing Communist and Muslim insurgency present a volatile combination that could spell problems for President Ramos's administration. Most Asian nations, as well as the U.S., acknowledge that security of the Philippines and the sealanes surrounding her are essential to the stability of all of Asia.

A measure that is vitally needed in the Asia-Pacific and holds great promise for increased regional stability, in my opinion, is the creation of a multilateral security framework. This month, Assistant Secretary for East Asian and Pacific Affairs, Winston Lord, will travel to Singapore to meet with senior officials from Asia-Pacific countries. A primary subject of discussion shall be regional security.

I would strongly urge the Clinton Administration to support the formation of an Asia-Pacific Regional Security Regime, whether or not it is shaped after NATO or the Conference on Security and Cooperation in Europe. (CSCE). The lack of such a forum facilitating dialogue on security concerns has resulted in an escalating arms race in the region, as many of the smaller Asia-Pacific countries fear the defense buildup by China as well as the potential for Japan to unilaterally remilitarize.

A new post-cold war defense arrangement in the Asia-Pacific would go a long way towards defusing regional security anxieties and the powder keg of arms procurements. In a time of reduced U.S. military spending in the Asia-Pacific, such an arrangement could be a cost-effective supplement and complement to existing U.S. bilateral security treaties. The initiative could realize significant financial savings for the U.S. by spreading burdensharing with the numerous nations of the Asia-Pacific.

For the multilateral security regime to work, I feel it is fundamentally important that both China and Japan participate as key players, in addition to the ASEAN countries, the remaining countries of northeast Asia, the nations of the South Pacific, and perhaps later Russia and Viet-Nam. In pursuing this initiative, the United States could further the exchange, sharing the flow of information between nations of the Asia-Pacific, easing much of the uncertainty and paranoia in the region about hidden agendas of fellow nations. In addition to reducing regional tensions, a major benefit would be the freeing of capital in many Asia-Pacific countries, allowing the diversion of funds from costly arms procurements to much needed programs fostering economic growth and societal improvements.

In the Asia-Pacific region, unlike Europe where the end of the cold war has fundamentally transformed the security equation, there exist numerous security interests that mandate the United States remain militarily engaged. Our forward deployed presence in Japan and South Korea, in conjunction with our bilateral security alliances with those countries, Thailand, Australia, the Philippines, and Singapore, among others, ensures that the United States will continue to provide stability in the Asia-Pacific region.

With the dynamic economic growth of the region, it is increasingly vital to the welfare of our nation as well as the world that America continue to play a major role in the bilateral and multilateral security affairs of Asia and the Pacific.

As we prepare to depart the 20th century, the countries of the Asia-Pacific should take comfort in the knowledge that America—their friend and ally—is determined more than ever to maintain a deep and enduring partnership that will last throughout the Pacific Century. Thank you.

◆ KEYNOTE ADDRESS AT THE GOLDEN ANNIVERSARY OF THE 442ND REGIMENTAL COMBAT TEAM

Presented by Senator Daniel K. Inouye at the 50th reunion of the 442nd Regimental Combat Team, an all-Japanese American regiment that fought in World War II, on Wednesday, March 24, 1993 in Hawaii.

This gathering is an important one—it will be a gathering of nostalgia. . . a gathering of sad memories. . . a gathering of laughter and fun. . . a gathering of good-byes for this may be our last roll call of the Regiment.

We have travelled vast distances—from every state and from many foreign lands to be together in Honolulu. We have travelled a lifetime together for this meeting in Honolulu. When did this journey to Honolulu begin?

Although this is our 50th reunion, our journey began before that date. Our fate was decided 52 years, 3 months and 2 weeks ago on that tragic Sunday in December. Our journey began on December 7, 1941.

Soon after that tragic Sunday morning, we, who were of Japanese ancestry, were considered by our nation to be citizens without a country. I am certain all of us remember that the Selective Service system of our country designated us to be unfit for military service because we were "enemy aliens." Soon after that, on February 19, 1942, the White House issued an extraordinary Executive Order—Executive Order 9066. This dreaded Executive Order forcibly uprooted our mainland brothers and their families and their loved ones from their homes with only those possessions that they were able to carry themselves and they were granted 48 hours to carry out this Order.

Our mainland brothers were not charged or indicted or convicted for the commission of any crime—

because no crime was committed. Their only crime, if any, was that they were born of Japanese parents and for that crime, they were incarcerated in internment camps surrounded by barbed wire fences, guarded by machine gun towers. They were sent to strange places with strange names—Manzanar, Tule Lake, Rohwer, Gila, Topaz. Although a few members of Hawaii's Japanese community were interned in Honouliuli (a rather well-kept secret), very few, if any of us in Hawaii, were aware of the mass internment of our mainland brothers and their families.

Although we were separated by a vast ocean and mountain ranges, we from the mainland and Hawaii shared one deep-seated desire—to rid ourselves of that insulting and degrading designation, "enemy alien." We wanted to serve our country. We wanted to demonstrate our love for our country.

After many months of petitions and letters, another Executive Order was issued with the declaration that ". . . Americanism is a matter of mind and heart; Americanism is not, and never was, a matter of race of ancestry." By this Executive Order, the formation of the special combat team made up of Japanese Americans was authorized.

More than the anticipated numbers volunteered, in fact in Hawaii, about 85% of the eligible men of Japanese Americans volunteered. Those who were selected assembled in Schofield Barracks to prepare for our departure from Hawaii. That was 50 years ago. In early April, we boarded railway flatbeds in Wahiawa and rode to Iwilei. There we got off the trains with our heavy duffel bags to march to Pier 7. But keep in mind that most of us had less than two weeks of military training and many of us were yet to be toughened and hardened. And so we found ourselves struggling with those heavy bags on a march of over a mile. This was the farewell parade of the 442nd. For many parents this was the last sight of their sons. I cannot understand why the Army did not place those duffel bags in trucks and permit us to march heads up and tall as we said good-bye to Hawaii. For many, the last look of their sons must have been a rather sad one because we looked like a ragtag formation of prisoners of war. I will never forget our sad departure from Hawaii.

But after several weeks, we from Hawaii and the mainland gathered in Camp Shelby in Hattiesburg, Mississippi, the home of chiggers and ticks, sweat and dirt.

All of us were of the same ancestry, but somehow our first encounter was an unhappy one. In a few days, violent arguments and fights erupted within our area and these fights became commonplace. The men of the Regiment found themselves segregated into two camps, one from Hawaii and the other from the mainland. This relationship was so bad that senior army officers seriously considered disbanding the Regiment.

Many projects were initiated and many lectures were delivered to bring about unity, but all failed except the Rohwer experiment. Our Regimental records will not disclose the name of the author of this experiment, but history will show that we owe much to him.

Whoever he was, he suggested that the internees of Rohwer send an invitation to the Regiment inviting young enlisted men from Hawaii to join them for a weekend of fund and festivities in the Camp. As I recall, each company selected ten enlisted men. I was fortunate to be one of those selected by E Company. On the appointed day, these men from Hawaii, all cleanly showered, smelling of "after shave" lotion, with their guitars and ukuleles, boarded trucks for this journey to Rohwer. Rohwer was an internment camp in Arkansas.

From the time we left Shelby in the early morning hours, this special convoy was a convoy of laughter and music. All were anticipating happy times with the young ladies of Rohwer. Suddenly, this fantasy was shattered. We came in sight of the Rohwer internment camp. In the distance, we could see rows of barracks surrounded by high barbed wire fences with machine gun towers. The music stopped and there was no laughter. Keep in mind that very few, if any of us, were aware of these camps. Our mainland brothers never spoke of them, never complained, and so we did not know. When we finally came to the gate, we were ordered to get off the trucks. We were in uniform and were confronted by men in similar uniforms but they had rifles with bayonets. For a moment, I thought that there would be a tragic encounter, but fortunately nothing happened as we were escorted through the gate. There we were greeted by the people of Rohwer who were all persons of Japanese ancestry—grandparents, parents, children, grandchildren. Although a dance was held that evening, I doubt if any of us really enjoyed ourselves. but it was an unforgettable evening. When we left Rohwer the following morning, the singing and the laughter and music that filled our trucks when we left Camp Shelby was replaced by grim silence. The atmosphere was grim and quiet and I believe that all of us, as we reflected upon that strange visit, asked ourselves the question, "Would I have volunteered from a camp like Rohwer?" To this day, I cannot give an answer because I really do not know if I would have volunteered to serve our nation if I had been interned in one of those camps.

So suddenly, our respect, admiration, and love for our Kotonk brothers rose to phenomenal heights. They suddenly became our blood brothers and overnight a new, tough, tightly united military fighting machine was formed. It was a Regiment made up of blood brothers and we were ready to live up to our motto, "Go for

Broke." And thus, the 442nd Infantry Regimental Combat Team was formed.

There are too many battles to recall—from Belvedere to Bruyeres, from Hill 140 to the Po Valley. But there is one we will never forget and one hopefully that our nation will always remember—the battle of the "Lost Battalion."

This battle began during the last week of October 1944. The members of the First Battalion of the 141st Infantry Regiment of the 36th Texas Division found themselves surrounded by a large number of enemy troops. This "Lost Battalion" was ordered to fight its way back, but could not do so. The Second and Third Battalions of the Texas Regiment were ordered to break through but they were thrown back and so on October 26th, the 442nd was ordered to go into the lines to rescue the "Lost Battalion." On November 15th, the rescue was successfully concluded.

Two days later, we were ordered to assemble in formal retreat parade formation to personally receive the commendation of the 36th Division from the Commanding General of the Texas unit. The men of the Regiment assembled in a vast field of a French farm. I can still hear the Company Commanders making their reports—A Company, all present and accounted for; B Company, all present and accounted for; E Company, all present and accounted for. It was an eerie scene. It has been reported that General Dahlquist who had ordered this formation was at first angered by the small attendance and reprimanded our Commander, who in reply is reported to have said, "Sir, this is the Regiment." As a result of the Battle of the "Lost Battalion," 2,000 men were in hospitals and over 300 had died. The price was heavy. Although we did not whimper or complain, we were sensitive to the fact that the rescuers of the Texas Battalion were not members of the Texas Division. They were Japanese Americans from Hawaii and from mainland internment camps. They were "enemy aliens."

I can still hear the proud and defiant voices of the Company Commanders as they made their reports. I can still see the Company Commander of E Company making his report. E Company had 42 men and though we were less than a quarter of the authorized company strength, E Company was the largest Company at that retreat parade. K Company was led by a Staff Sergeant. K Company was made up of 12 men. When I heard the last Commander shout out his report, "all present and accounted for," like many of you, I could almost feel the insulting and degrading designation that was placed on our shoulders long ago in December 1941— the designation of "enemy alien"—fall crashing to the ground in that far away French farm. And we knew that from that moment on, no one could ever, ever, question

our loyalty and our love for our country. The insulting stigma was finally taken away.

Years later, the United States Army called upon a special commission of military historians, analysts and strategists to select the ten most important battles of the U.S. Army Infantry from the Revolutionary War to the Korean War. The Battle of the Lost Battalion was selected as one of the honored ten. Our battle is listed together with our nation's most glorious and historic battles, such as the Battle of Vicksburg during the Civil War, the Battle at Meuse-Argonne in France during World War I, and the Battle of Leyte in the Philippines during World War II. Today, specially commissioned paintings of these ten most important battles are proudly displayed in the Pentagon.

Over the years, many have asked us—"Why?" "Why did you fight and serve so well?" My son, like your sons and daughters, has asked the same question—"Why?" "Why were you willing and ready to give your life?" We have tried to provide answers to these questions and I hope that my answer to my son made sense.

I told my son it was a matter of honor. I told him about my father's farewell message when I left home to put on the uniform of my country. My father was not a man of eloquence but he said, "Whatever you do, do not dishonor the family and do not dishonor the country." I told my son that for many of us, to have done any less than what we had done in battle would have dishonored our families and our country.

Second, I told my son that there is an often used Japanese phrase—"Kodomo no tame ni." Though most of us who went into battle were young and single, we wanted to leave a legacy of honor and pride and the promise of a good life for our yet-to-be-born children and their children.

My brothers, I believe we can assure ourselves that we did succeed in upholding our honor and that of our families and our nation. And I respectfully and humbly believe that our service and the sacrifices of those who gave their all on the battle field assure a better life for our children and their children.

Yes, I believe we can stand tall this evening in knowing that our journey together, a journey that began on that tragic Sunday morning, was not in vain. And so tonight, let us embrace with our hearts and minds the memory of those brothers who are not with us this evening and let us do so with all of our affection and gratitude. Let us embrace with deep love our loved ones for having stood with us and walked with us on our journey. Let us embrace with everlasting gratitude and Aloha the many friends and neighbors who supported us throughout our journey. Let us embrace with everlasting love our great nation.

And finally, let us embrace our sons and daughters with full pride and with the restful assurance that the story of our journey of honor will live on for generations to come.

And so, my brothers, let us this evening, in the spirit of our Regiment, stand tall with pride, have fun, and let's "Go for Broke."

♦ RACISM, HATE CRIMES, AND PORNOGRAPHY

Presented by Helen Zia at the "Equality and Harm Conference" in Chicago, Illinois, on March 6, 1993.

My remarks focus on a very specific intersecting area of racism, hate crimes, and pornography—that is, where race and gender overlap and where current civil rights law *can* but *fails to* address racially motivated, gender-based crimes against women of color. I'm talking about the area of bias-motivated sexual assault against women of color, which has also been called ethno-rape and which I sometimes refer to as hate rape.

Before I begin, I want to acknowledge a fact that is well known within the battered women's movement and the sexual assault movement: that most sexual assaults, probably some 80 percent, are perpetrated by men of the same race as the victim and most of whom were known by the victim. But a probe into the area of bias-motivated rape can offer some insight into the separate but sometimes parallel legal remedies for race- and gender-based crimes.

I started looking into this issue after years of organizing around hate killings of Asian Americans. After a while, I noticed that all the cases I could name involved male victims—and I wondered why. Maybe it was because Asian American men came into contact with perpetrator types more often. Maybe it's because Asian American men are more hated and therefore attacked by racists. But a feminist analysis of the subordination and vulnerability of Asian American women whose dominant stereotype is to be sexually exotic and subservient and passive conflicted with that argument. So where were the Asian American women victims of hate crimes?

Once I began looking, I found them, through random news clippings, footnotes in books, word of mouth. Let me share with you some of what I consider to be examples of bias-motivated attacks and sexual assaults:

• In February 1984, Ly Yung Cheung, a 19-year-old Chinese woman who was 7 months pregnant was pushed in front of a New York City subway train and decapitated. Her attacker, a white male high school teacher, claimed he suffered from "a phobia of Asian people" and he was overcome with the urge to kill this woman. He successfully pleaded insanity. If this case had been investigated as a hate crime, there might have been more information about his so-called phobia and whether there was a pattern of racism. But because she was Asian and because she was a woman, it was not investigated as a hate crime.

• On December 7, 1984, 52-year-old Japanese American Helen Fukui disappeared in Denver, Colorado; her decomposed body was found weeks later. The fact that she disappeared on Pearl Harbor day, when anti-Asian speech and incidents increased dramatically, was considered significant in the community. But the case was not investigated as a hate crime and no suspects were ever apprehended.

• In 1985 an 8-year-old Chinese girl named Jean Har-Kaw Fewel was found raped and lynched in Chapel Hill North Carolina—two months after *Penthouse* featured pictures in various poses of bondage and torture, including hanging bound from trees, in death-like poses. Were epithets or pornography used? No one knows—her rape and killing wasn't investigated as a possible hate crime.

• Last year [1992] a serial rapist was convicted of kidnapping and raping a Japanese exchange student in Oregon, where he was also a student. He had also assaulted a Japanese woman in Arizona, and another in San Francisco. He was sentenced to jail time for these crimes, which were not pursued as hate crimes, even though California has a hate statute. Was hate speech or race-specific pornography used? Who knows, since it wasn't investigated as a hate crime.

• At Ohio State University, two Asian women were gang raped by fraternity "brothers" in two separate incidents. One of the rapes was part of a racially targeted "game" called the "Ethnic Challenge" in which the fraternity men followed an ethnic checklist indicating what kind of women to gang rape—in this case, Asian women. Because the women feared humiliation and ostracism by their communities, neither woman reported the rapes. However, the attacks were known to a few campus officials, who did not take them up as hate crimes or anything else.

All of these incidents could have been investigated and prosecuted as state hate crimes and/or federal criminal civil rights cases. However, to do so would have required awareness and interest on the part of police investigators and the prosecutors, and we know they have a lousy track record on race and gender issues; and failing that, it would have helped to have awareness and support for civil rights charges by the Asian American community—which is also generally lacking when it comes to issues like women, gender, sex and sexual assault. The result is a double-silencing effect in the assaults and deaths of these women, silencing and invisibility because of their gender and their race.

I would like to point out that although my empirical research centers on hate crimes toward Asian women, this silencing and what amounts to the failure to provide equal protection has its parallels in all of the other classes protected by federal civil rights and hate statutes. That is, all other communities of color, to my knowledge, also have a similar hate crimes prosecution rate for the women in their communities—in other words—zero, zilch. This dismal record is almost as bad in the lesbian and gay anti-violence projects—the vast preponderance of hate crimes reported, tracked and prosecuted involve gay men—very few lesbians. *So where are all these women?*

The answer to this question lies in what was said yesterday in many different ways—that this system of justice was not designed for women. In yet another way, we are mere shadows in the existing civil rights framework. But in spite of all this, I still think federal civil rights and state hate crimes law offers a legal avenue for women to be heard.

Federal civil rights prosecutions, for example, are excellent platforms for high visibility community education on the harmful impact of hate speech and behavior. When two white autoworkers in Detroit called Chinese American Vincent Chin racial slurs and said, "It's because of you motherfuckers that we're out of work," the national civil rights campaign that followed launched a new social movement and raised the level of national discourse on what constitutes racism toward Asian Americans. When we began that campaign, constitutional law professors and members of the ACLU and NLG told us that we were wasting our time—that Asian Americans are not covered by civil rights law. We dealt with that misconception.

Hate crimes remedies can be used to force the racist, sexist criminal justice bureaucracy to take on new attitudes. When Patrick Purdy went to an elementary school in Stockton, California, that was 85 percent Southeast Asian students, and when he selectively aimed his automatic weapon and killed five 8-year-olds and wounded 30 others—the first response by the police and the media was that this couldn't possibly be a bias-motivated crime. (Kind of reminiscent of the denial response by the Montreal officials in the femicide of 14 women students.) But an outraged Asian American community forced a state investigation into the incident and uncovered hate literature in the killer's effects. As a result, the sense of the community was validated and empowered, and there was a new level of understanding of the community as a whole—including the criminal justice system and the media.

Imagine if a federal criminal civil rights investigation were launched in the rape of the St. John's University student—the African American student who was raped and sodomized by white members of the school lacrosse team, who were later acquitted. Issues could be raised about those white men's attitudes toward the victim as a black woman, to see whether hate speech or race-specific pornography was involved, to investigate the overall racial climate on campus, and to bring all of the silenced issues to the public eye. Perhaps it would lead to a guilty verdict this time, for deprivation of her civil rights; but even if not, at a minimum the community discourse could be raised to a higher level, paving the way for other legislation, like the Dworkin-MacKinnon civil rights law, or the Violence against Women Act.

This will not be an easy road. Hate crimes efforts go for blatant cases, with high community consensus, not cases that bring up hard issues like gender-based violence. But these are the very issues we must give voice to.

There are a few serious issues in pushing for use of federal and state hate remedies. First and foremost is that some state statutes have already been used against men of color: specifically, on behalf of white rape victims against African American men. We know that the system, if left unchecked, will try to use anti-hate laws to enforce unequal justice.

At the same time, the state hate statutes could be used to prosecute men of color who are believed to have assaulted women of color of another race. Interminority assaults are increasing. Also, if violence against women were made into a general hate crime, Asian women could seek prosecutions against Asian men for their gender-based violence. This would make it even harder to win the support of men in communities of color, as well as women in those communities who would not want to be accused of dividing the community.

But at least within the Asian American anti-violence community, this discourse is taking place now. Asian American feminists in San Francisco have prepared a critique of the Asian anti-hate crimes movement and the men of that movement are listening. I hope what's happened in the Asian American community can be used by other communities to examine the nexus between race and gender for women of color, and by extension, all women.

This has been a very abbreviated, non-legal summary of a longer, more complex analysis. Please understand this strategy is not seen as a panacea. We know that civil rights cases can be lost: after five years in federal court, the Vincent Chin campaign for justice was ultimately lost, and as we all know, the outcome of the federal civil rights trial of Rodney King's attackers is far from certain. This is, however, another way to give voice to the experience of women—especially women of color who have been so silenced in our society.

I would like to challenge attorneys and theorists to push the boundaries of existing law and to include the most invisible women. There are hundreds and hundreds of cases involving women of color that are waiting to be taken on. I also challenge the activists in the violence against women movement to reexamine current views on gender-based violence, and not to view all sexual assaults as the same. They are not. Racism used in a sexual assault adds another complex wrinkle to the pain and harm that are inflicted on women.

By taking women of color out of the shadows of legal invisibility and moving toward personhood, all women gain status toward full human dignity and human rights.

♦ BANQUET SPEECH FROM THE 6TH ANNUAL GAY ASIAN PACIFIC ALLIANCE (GAPA)

Presented by Helen Zia in San Francisco on January 29, 1994.

I'm truly honored and proud to be a part of GAPA's celebration of the diversity of Gay and Bisexual Asian Pacific Islander Men. Even before I moved to San Francisco a year and a half ago, I had heard of this magazine called *Lavender Godzilla*, published by a really right-on group called GAPA that was doing incredible work to increase visibility of gay and bisexual men of Asian Pacific ancestry, to provide support around issues of coming out, community and family, HIV/AIDS, and to build powerful role models.

Building role models for visibility and empowerment is no small task. When you look in this wide world around us, where can you find us, the Asian Pacific Islander gay/lesbian/bisexual/transgender people?

• Will you find us in media portrayals and popular images of the gay and lesbian community? No—you won't find us there. The quintessential standard for who is queer is white and male.

• Will you find us in the leadership of the national gay and lesbian organizations and institutions? With a few exceptions that you can count on one hand, you won't find us there either.

• If you go home, to the diverse Asian American communities across the United States where many of our parents and families are, you won't find us there. After all, our aunties and uncles and cousins watch TV too—and have concluded that "homosexuality is white man's problem."

• And this shouldn't come as a surprise either, because if we were each to trace our roots across the Pacific and visit one of our many sexually repressive ancestral homelands in search of gays, lesbians and bisexuals, we'd again be very hard put to find our gay sisters and brothers—except perhaps in mental wards, prisons, or living as outcasts who are infected with the dreaded Western disease of homosexuality.

• Speaking of sexual repression, when we think about the popular concept of Asian sexuality, what do we find? Asian men in general are viewed as asexual, so being "gay" and "Asian" is an impossible construct. Meanwhile, Asian women are viewed as supersexual exotic creatures who are hot for white men, so it's similarly not possible to think of us as lesbians.

All this negation makes it incredibly tough to be a queer API. When there isn't a group like GAPA around, where in the world can we find validation of ourselves (let alone find positive images that build our sense of self esteem and self-respect)?

I know the damage this can do from my own personal experience, as I suspect most of you do. When I first became aware of my attraction to the same sex as a kid, I didn't have a place for it in my consciousness. And coming from an immigrant Chinese family, we never spoke of sex—ever. I got my sex education from reading the *Encyclopedia Britannica*. Having read the entry on "Reproduction" several times, I can assure you that there was no mention of "Homosexuality."

When I finally got the courage to go to lesbian bars, it was great to be around women loving women, but I didn't exactly feel like I had found my home, either. All the dykes I met were white and I didn't know of any Asian lesbians. That situation made me feel like I couldn't be a real lesbian. And because I didn't think I could be a real lesbian, I also didn't feel I could be attractive to real lesbians.

But the worst part was how my fellow Asian American community activists reacted when they realized I was hanging out with a lot of white lesbians. This was back in the early 70s, before "gay" was an accepted word yet, and it was at the height of the Asian American movement and the radical Third World liberation movements, the days when the revolution was right around the corner.

I was one of those Asian American movement activists, and my strongest sense of myself at that time was as an Asian American. But my Asian American comrades—my Asian community/family—had determined that homosexuality was "counterrevolutionary" and a "petty bourgeois degenerate deviation." They called a special meeting to investigate my sexual proclivities. I remember sitting through that difficult meeting in rolled-up T-shirt sleeves and a leather bomber jacket that was too big for me, already confused and anxious about my sexuality. As you can imagine, this didn't help my coming-out process.

Luckily for me, I finally found my way to those Sapphic pleasures, and over time have struggled through many issues like being out in the straight Asian Pacific Islander community. Coming out to Asian community groups has its lighter moments. A few years ago, I was delivering a speech to the Asian American Journalists Association national convention in Washington, D.C., and the speech was going to be carried on C-SPAN. I tried hard to write something into the speech about being a lesbian, but it just wasn't going to fit the topic of my speech. So I asked the person who was going to introduce me to be sure to include the fact that I was a lesbian in the introduction—you know, just to blend it in with the other stuff and not to make it a big deal. She said, "Fine, no problem." But when it came time for her to stand in front of AAJA and the C-SPAN cameras to introduce me, here's what she said: "Helen Zia is a long-time feminist and Asian community activist and she's a L-L-L lesbian. . . " and then she sort of coughed, fiddled with the microphone and said, "Is the microphone working? Did you all hear that, she's a L-L-L Lesbian. . ."

I just thought, "well, so much for subtlety." But if the alternative was invisibility, I'm glad she went the other way. Because the price we end up paying for this invisibility is far too high. We have all experienced our own forms of personal hell as a result of being invisible. But there are other costs too.

We all know how bias-motivated crimes against gay men and lesbians have been increasing at frightening rates; in areas like Oregon and Colorado, where the anti-gay initiatives have been organized, it's open season against us. We also know that anti-Asian hate crimes have been increasing, especially as racist hysteria against Asian imports and Asian immigrants has heated up. Well, we—Asian Pacific queers—are directly in the fire for both hate trends.

Yet how can we effectively respond to and counter attacks when they happen? The unfortunate answer is that we can't when we're invisible to a community that is unable—or unwilling—to see us.

I'm sad to say that there have been several incidents of hate violence against Asian American gays and lesbians as well as an ambivalent response by our Asian communities. Only last year we witnessed the near fatal beating of Loc Minh Truong by a group of teenage boys near a local gay bar in Laguna Beach, California. Truong, a Vietnamese refugee who was 55 years old at the time of the attack, was so badly beaten that authorities could not initially determine his race. His left eye was out of his socket and a rock was impaled nearly an inch into his skull. Troung was in critical condition for several days; police described the attack as one blow short of murder.

Truong's attackers were apprehended and two pleaded guilty to attempted murder, felonious aggravated assault, and committing a hate crime against Loc Minh Truong. The attackers admitted to saying to Truong, "You fucking faggot. . . we're going to get you!" and "If a fag approached me, I'd beat him on the spot." They denied that Truong's race was a factor in the beating. Asian community Anti-Asian violence activists monitored the case, but *Truong's family and the local Vietnamese community denied that he is gay and did not want to associate him with being gay.* Much Asian community energy went into speculating whether Truong was gay and to try to establish a race-biased motive instead. In point of fact, Truong's actual sexual orientation is irrelevant, since his attackers perceived him to be gay, and since sexual orientation and race are both protected under the California hate crimes law.

Does this mean that our Asian Pacific Islander community would be less likely to support a hate crime victim because of his or her sexual orientation? Well, as long as we remain invisible to our API communities, we make it easy for homophobia to rule their reactions.

Homophobia may have been the reason that there was little community response to the 1988 murder of Paul Him Chow, a gay Chinese American who was killed in New York City's Greenwich Village. Homophobia and racism may explain the subsequent lack of aggressive police investigation.

And both anti-gay prejudice in the API community and racism came into play in the 1991 murder of Konerak Sinthasimphone, a 14-year-old Laotian boy, by serial killer Jeffrey Dahmer. Then, the racist and homophobic police were all too willing to return a naked, bleeding 14-year-old to Dahmer, accepting the word of a white man that this Asian child was his adult lover. And after the atrocities were exposed, our Asian communities were, again, silent.

Actually, the only time I recall hearing of a grass-roots community discussion of "homosexuals" was in the context of a community-wide alert against child sexual molesters of Asian boys—and the public posters suggesting that homosexuals were lying in wait to molest their sons. Not only was this homophobic, but also a complete heterosexual fantasy, since it's a well-established fact that the vast majority of child sexual abuse is committed by heterosexual men, and mostly toward girls.

As we all know, this silence, coupled with ignorance, can only mean death when it comes to a community-based response to HIV/AIDS. At a time when API men and women of all sexual orientations are at extremely high risk of HIV infection—largely because of community denial—we cannot afford to live with this invisibility.

That's why GAPA and the handful of other Asian gay, lesbian, bi, and transgender organizations are playing such a critical historic role today. Fighting for a spot in the Chinatown Lunar New Year parade, for example, is exactly the kind of VISIBILITY that we need to take on the challenges of today and tomorrow.

Looking forward to the future, what do we see? In six short years, we will be entering a new century, already dubbed "Century of Asia and the Pacific." There will be a tremendous transfer of economic and political might to the nations of Asia and the Pacific Rim, with incredible ramifications for APIs in the U.S.

To the extent that national visibility and power gets transferred to a sense of individual esteem, think of all the Asian gay men and lesbians who will potentially become more empowered. How many more will find the courage to be true to themselves and come out?

Let's do the math. In the U.S. today, there are 3.4 million Asian Pacific Islanders. Within a decade, that should more than double to 8-10 million—or 800,000 to 1 million gay, lesbian, bi, transgender Asian Americans. Next, I challenge you to think globally. Looking across the Pacific, there's 1+ billion people in China; 1 billion in India, plus several hundreds of millions more in other Asian nations. At least 3 billion Asian people in the world, and if 10 percent are gay, lesbian, and bi: That's 300 million Asian Pacific Islander queers! It's more than the entire population of the United States—that's a lot of invisible queer power looking to come out!

And where will all these 300 million Asian gays, lesbians, and bisexuals be turning to for role models on what their lives can be and how they can be recognized for who they are?

I believe they'll be looking right here at GAPA and other courageous Asian queers, at all of you to learn who they are, to get reassurance that they have a right to live and love in dignity and respect and that as proud Asian queers they have an important contribution to make to their communities. That is the historic role and responsibility we have to play *today*.

So while you go about your daily lives and do all the important programs that you do for GAPA, think about how we must each strive to be good role models for each other and all those many other APIs who are desperately seeking some affirmation of who they are so they can be out and proud too. And get ready for the day that you'll have to crank out 100+ million membership cards. Now that's Lavender Godzilla power!

Bibliography

♦ Asian Americans and Asian Canadians—General ♦ Chinese ♦ Filipino ♦ Asian Indian ♦ Japanese ♦ Korean ♦ Pacific Islanders ♦ Vietnamese, Cambodian, Laotian, and Hmong

♦ ASIAN AMERICANS AND ASIAN CANADIANS—GENERAL

A

Asians in America: A Selected Annotated Bibliography—Expansion and Revision. Davis: University of California, Asian American Studies, 1983. Annotated bibliography on historical and sociological writings.

C

Chan, Sucheng. *Asian Americans: An Interpretive History.* Boston: Twayne Publishers, 1991. Comprehensive history of Asian Americans in the United States. Includes list of films about the Asian American experience, a chronology of Asian American history from 1600 to 1989, and a bibliographic essay describing available works for those interested in further research.

F

Fawcett, James T. and Benjamin V. Carino. *Pacific Bridges: The New Immigration from Asia and the Pacific Islands.* New York: Center for Migration Studies, 1987.

Furtaw, Julia C., ed. *Asian American Information Directory.* Detroit: Gale Research, 1990.

H

Hsia, Jayjia. *Asian American in Higher Education and at Work.* Hillsdale, NJ: Lawrence Erlbaum Assoc., Publishers, 1988. A 218-page book reporting on education and employment trends in the 1980s. 83 tables, 11 pages of references.

Hune, Shirley. *Pacific Migration to the United States: Trends and Themes in Historical and Sociological Literature.* Washington, DC: Research Institute on Immigration and Ethnic Studies, 1977.

K

Kim, Hyung-chan, ed. *Dictionary of Asian American History.* Westport, CN: Greenwood Press, 1986. Entries by various authors on a range of topics.

Kim, Hyung-chan, ed. *Asian American Studies: An Annotated Bibliography and Research Guide.* Westport, CN: Greenwood Press, 1989. Bibliography on historical and sociological writings, especially for Asian American studies programs.

Kitano, Harry H. L. and Roger Daniels. *Asian Americans: Emerging Minorities.* Englewood Cliffs, NJ: Prentice Hall, 1988. 195-page book covering Chinese, Japanese, Korean, Filipino, Asian Indians, Southeast Asians, and Pacific Islanders, with appendix of tables of 1980 U.S. census data, and suggestions for further reading.

Knoll, Tricia. *Becoming Americans: Asian Sojourners, Immigrants, and Refugees in the Western United States.* Portland, OR: Coast to Coast Books, 1982.

L

Lee, Joann Faung Jean. *Asian American Experiences in the United States: Oral Histories of First to Fourth Generation Americans from China, the Philippines, Japan, India, the Pacific Islands, Vietnam, and Cambodia.* Jefferson, NC: McFarland and Co., Inc., Publishers, 1991.

Lieberson, Stanley and Mary C. Waters. *From Many Strands: Ethnic and Racial Groups in Contemporary America*. New York: Russell Sage Foundation, 1988. From *The Population of the United States in the 1980s: A Census Monograph Series*. A 268-page book examining trends in ethnic and racial composition in the U.S., based on data from the 1980 Census. 51 tables, bibliography.

P

Poon, Wei-Chi. *A Guide for Establishing Asian American Core Collections*. Berkeley: University of California Asian American Studies, 1988.

R

Roy, Patricia E. "'White Canada Forever': Two Generations of Studies." *Canadian Ethnic Studies* XI, no. 2 (1979).

T

Takaki, Ronald. *Strangers from a Different Shore: A History of Asians Americans*. Boston: Little, Brown and Company, 1989. A 570. book recounting history of Chinese, Japanese, Koreans, Asian Indians, Filipinos, and Southeast Asians, with extensive reference notes and index.

W

Ward, W. Peter. *White Canada Forever: Popular Attitudes and Public Policy towards Orientals in British Columbia*. Montreal, 1978. Introduction to white response to Asians in Canada through 1941.

◆ CHINESE

C

Chan, Anthony B. *Gold Mountain: The Chinese in the New World*. Vancouver, BC: New Star, 1982. Reports the author's own family experience and focuses on the 1970s.

Chan, Sucheng. *This Bittersweet Soil: The Chinese in California Agriculture, 1860-1910*. Berkeley and Los Angeles: University of California Press, 1986.

Chinn, Thomas W. *Bridging the Pacific: San Francisco's Chinatown and Its People*. San Francisco: Chinese Historical Society of America, 1989.

Con, Harry and Ronald J. Con, et al. *From China to Canada: A History of the Chinese Communities in Canada*. Toronto, 1982.

D

Daniels, Roger. *Asian America: Chinese and Japanese in the U.S. since 1850*. Seattle: University of Washington Press, 1988.

G

Glick, Clarence E. *Sojourners and Settlers: Chinese Immigrants in Hawaii*. Honolulu: University of Hawaii Press, 1980.

Great Basin Foundation, ed. *Wong Ho Leun: An American Chinatown*. San Diego: Great Basin Foundation, 1988. This study deals with the Chinese settlement in Riverside, California.

L

Lai, Him Mark. *A History Reclaimed: An Annotated Bibliography of Chinese Language Materials on the Chinese of America*. Los Angeles, 1986.

Lydon, Sandy. *Chinese Gold: The Chinese in the Monterey Bay Area*. Capitola, CA: Capitola Book Company, 1985.

Lyman, Stanford M. *Chinese Americans*. New York: Random House, 1974.

M

Mark, Diane Mei Lin. *A Place Called Chinese America*. Dubuque, IA: Kendall/Hunt. A history of Chinese in America prepared under the sponsorship of Organization of Chinese Americans.

Minnick, Sylvia Sun. *Samfow: The San Joaquin Chinese Legacy*. Fresno: Panorama West, 1988.

P

Posner, Gerald L. *Warlords of Crime: Chinese Secret Societies—The New Mafia*. New York: McGraw-Hill Book Co., 1988. 261-pages. book on Triads, the Chinese secret societies, with 14 pages. bibliography.

T

Tan, Jin and Patricia E. Roy. *The Chinese in Canada*. Ottawa: Canadian Historial Society, 1985. A 24-page booklet describing the Chinese population segment in Canada.

Tsai, Shih-san Henry. *The Chinese Experience in America*. Bloomington, IN: Indiana University Press, 1986.

W

Wong, Bernard. *Patronage, Brokerage, Entrepreneurship and The Chinese Community of New York*. New York: AMS Press, 1988.

Y

Yee, Paul. *Salt Water* City. History of Chinese in Vancouver.

Yung, Judy. *Chinese Women of America: A Pictorial History*. Seattle: University of Washington Press, 1986.

◆ FILIPINO

A

Alcantara, Ruben R. *Sakada: Filipino Adaptation in Hawaii*. Washington, DC: University Press of America, 1981.

B

Bulosan, Carlos. *America Is in the Heart*. Seattle: University of Washington Press, 1973.

M

Mangiafico, Luciano. *Contemporary American Immigrants: Patterns of Filipino, Korean, and Chinese Settlement in the United States*. New York: Praeger, 1988.

T

Teodoro, Luis V., Jr., ed.. *Out of This Struggle: The Filipinos in Hawaii*. Honolulu: University of Hawaii Press, 1981.

◆ ASIAN INDIAN

C

Chandrasekhar, S., ed. *From India to America*. La Jolla, CA: Population Institute, 1984.

G

Gibson, Margaret. *Accommodation without Assimilation: Sikh Immigrants in an American High School*, 1988.

J

Jensen, Joan M. *Passage from India: Asian Indian Immigrants in North America*. New Haven and London: Yale University Press, 1988. A 350-page. book with extensive notes, selected bibliography, and listing of unpublished sources and court cases.

L

La Brack, Bruce. *The Sikhs of Northern California, 1904-1975*. New York: AMS Press, 1988.

Leonard, Karen. *Ethnic Choices: California's Punjabi-Mexican Americans, 1910-1980*. Philadelphia: Temple University Press, 1991.

S

Saran, Parmata. *The Asian Indian Experience in the United States*. Cambridge, MA: Schenkman, 1985.

Singh, Jane. *South Asians in North America: An Annotated and Selected Bibliography*. Berkeley: Center for South and South Asian Studies, 1988.

◆ JAPANESE

A

Adachi, Ken. *The Enemy that Never Was: A History of the Japanese Canadians*. Toronto, 1976. Emphasis on the 1940s.

C

Conroy, Hilary and T. Scott Miyakawa, eds. *East across the Pacific: Historical and Sociological Studies of Japanese Immigration and Assimilation*. Santa Barbara, CA: ABC-Clio Press, 1972.

D

Daniels, Roger. *Asian America: Chinese and Japanese in the Unites States Since 1850*. Seattle: University of Washington Press, 1988.

Daniels, Roger. *Concentration Camps, North America: Japanese in the United States and Canada During World War II*. Melbourne, FL: Krieger, 1981.

I

Ichioka, Yuji. *The Issei: The World of the First Generation Japanese Immigrants, 1885-1924*. New York: Free Press, 1989.

K

Kitano, Harry H. L. *Japanese Americans: The Evolution of a Subculture.* Englewood Cliffs, NJ: Prentice-Hall, 1969.

Kimura, Yukiko. *Issei: Japanese Immigrants in Hawaii.* Honolulu: University of Hawaii Press, 1988.

L

LaViolette, F.E. *The Canadian Japanese and World War II: A Social and Psychological Account.* Toronto, 1948. Examines the wartime crisis in the Japanese Canadian community.

Lukes, Timothy J. and Gary Y. Okihiro. *Japanese Legacy: Farming and Community Life in California's Santa Clara Valley.* Cupertino: California History Center, 1985.

N

Niiya, Brian, ed. *Japanese American History: An A-to-Z Reference from 1868 to the Present.* New York: Facts On File, 1993.

Noda, Kesa. *Yamato Colony, 1906-1960: Livingston, California.* Livingston: Japanese American Citizens League, 1981.

P

Petersen, William. *Japanese Americans: Oppression and Success.* New York: Random House, 1971.

W

Walls, Thomas K. *The Japanese Texans.* San Antonio: Institute of Texas Cultures, University of Texas, 1987.

Ward, W. Peter. *The Japanese in Canada.* Ottawa: Canada Historical Association, Booklet No. 3, 1982. A 21-page booklet describing the Japanese population in Canada.

♦ KOREAN

C

Choy, Bong-youn. *Koreans in America.* Chicago: Nelson-Hall, 1979.

H

Hurh, Won Moo, et al. *Assimilation Patterns of Immigrants in the United States: A Case Study of Korean Immigrants in the Chicago Area.* Washington, DC: University Press of America, 1978.

K

Kim, Hyung-chan, ed. *The Korean Diaspora.* Santa Barbara, CA: ABC–Clio Press, 1977.

Kim, Illsoo. *New Urban Immigrants: The Korean Community in New York.* Princeton, NJ: Princeton University Press, 1981.

Y

Yoo, Jay Kun. *The Koreans in Seattle.* Elkins Park, PA: Philip Jaisohn Memorial Foundation, 1979.

♦ PACIFIC ISLANDERS

M

Macpherson, Cluny, Bradd Shore, and Robert Franco, eds. *New Neighbors: Islanders in Adaptation.* Santa Cruz, CA: University of California, 1978.

♦ VIETNAMESE, CAMBODIAN, LAOTIAN, AND HMONG

C

Caplan, Nathan, et al. *The Boat People and Achievement in America: A Study of Family Life, Hard Work, and Cultural Values.* Ann Arbor: University of Michigan Press, 1989.

Criddle, Joan and Teeda Butt Mam. *To Destroy You Is No Loss: The Odyssey of a Cambodian Family.* New York: Atlantic Monthly Press, 1987.

D

Downing, Bruce T. and Douglas P. Olney, eds. *The Hmong in the West: Observations and Reports.* Minneapolis: University of Minnesota Center for Urban and Regional Affairs, 1982.

E

Espiritu, Yen Le. *Vietnamese in America: An Annotated Bibliography of Materials in Los Angeles and Orange County Libraries.* Los Angeles: Asian American Studies Center, 1988.

F

Freeman, James A. *Hearts of Sorrow: Vietnamese-American Lives.* Stanford, CA: Stanford University Press, 1989.

G

Gim, W. and T. Litwin. *Indochinese Refugees in American: Profiles of Five Communities*. Washington, DC: U.S. State Department, 1980.

H

Haines, David W. *Refugees as Immigrants: Cambodians, Laotians and Vietnamese in America*. Totowa, NJ: Rowman and Littlefield, 1989.

Hayslip, Le Ly (with Jay Wurts). *When Heaven and Earth Changed Places: A Vietnamese Woman's Journey from War to Peace*. New York: Doubleday, 1989.

Hendricks, Glenn, ed. *The Hmong in Transition*. Staten Island, NY: Center for Migration Studies, 1985.

K

Kelly, Gail. *From Vietnam to American: A Chronicle of the Vietnamese Immigrants to the United States*. Boulder, CO: Westview Press, 1978.

L

Loescher, Gil and John A. Scanlan. *Calculated Kindness: Refugees and America's Half-Open Door, 1945 to the Present*. New York: Free Press, 1986.

Liu, William T. *Transition to Nowhere: Vietnamese Refugees in America*. Nashville, TN: Charter House, 1979.

M

May, Someth. *Cambodian Witness: The Autobiography of Someth May*. New York: Random House, 1986.

Montero, Darrel. *Vietnamese Americans: Patterns of Resettlement and Socioeconomic Adaptation in the Unites States*. Boulder, CO: Westview Press, 1977.

Muir, Karen L. *The Strongest Part of the Family: A Study of Lao Refugee Women in Columbus, Ohio*. New York: AMS Press, 1988.

N

Ngor, Haing (with Roger Warner). *Haing Ngor: A Cambodian Odyssey*. New York: MacMillan, 1987.

Q

Quincy, Keith H. *Hmong: History of a People*. Cheney: Eastern Washington University Press, 1988.

S

Strand, Paul J. and Woodrow Jones, Jr. *Indochinese Refugees in America*. Durham, NC: Duke University Press, 1985.

Szymusial, Molyda. *The Stones Cry Out: A Cambodian Childhood, 1975-1980*. New York: Hill & Wang, 1986.

T

Tepper, Elliot L., ed. *Southeast Asia Exodus: From Transition to Resettlement*. Ottawa, 1980. Provides insights into the refugee crisis and problems of resettlement in Canada.

W

Wain, Barry. *The Refused: The Agony of the Indochina Refugees*. New York: Simon and Schuster, 1982.

Y

Yathay, Pin. *Stay Alive, My Son*. New York: Free Press, 1987.

Index

I